INTERNATIONAL COPYRIGHT AND NEIGHBOURING RIGHTS

VOLUME I

INTERNATIONAL COPYRIGHT AND NEIGHBOURING RIGHTS

The Berne Convention and Beyond

SECOND EDITION

SAM RICKETSON AND JANE C GINSBURG

VOLUME I

OXFORD
UNIVERSITY PRESS

OXFORD
UNIVERSITY PRESS

Great Clarendon Street, Oxford OX2 6DP

Oxford University Press is a department of the University of Oxford.
It furthers the University's objective of excellence in research, scholarship,
and education by publishing worldwide in

Oxford New York

Auckland Cape Town Dar es Salaam Hong Kong Karachi
Kuala Lumpur Madrid Melbourne Mexico City Nairobi
New Delhi Shanghai Taipei Toronto

With offices in

Argentina Austria Brazil Chile Czech Republic France Greece
Guatemala Hungary Italy Japan Poland Portugal Singapore
South Korea Switzerland Thailand Turkey Ukraine Vietnam

Oxford is a registered trade mark of Oxford University Press
in the UK and in certain other countries

Published in the United States
by Oxford University Press Inc., New York

First published 1987
Second edition 2006

British Library Cataloguing in Publication Data
Data available

Library of Congress Cataloging in Publication Data
Data available

Typeset by RefineCatch Limited, Bungay, Suffolk
Printed in Great Britain
on acid-free paper by
Biddles Ltd, King's Lynn

ISBN 0-19-825946-8 978-0-19-825946-6

1 3 5 7 9 10 8 6 4 2

FOREWORD

The first edition of Sam Ricketson's history of the Berne Convention for the Protection of Literary and Artistic Works was written for the centenary of that Convention. It was a work of very considerable scholarship and it rapidly established itself as a major source for information and analysis of the Convention's content. With Jane Ginsburg joining Sam for this second edition, the two authors have produced what is well-nigh a new book, given the range of developments that have affected authors' copyright at the international level in the intervening eighteen years. It shows the same careful attention to the sources reviewed and the same sensible appreciation of the political pressures which have been at work in those developments. In rather greater measure than before, it seeks also to predict the future of the rights involved—rights that are now enveloped in swirls of ideological and practical uncertainty.

1986 is difficult accurately to recall, for it was an analogue age ago. The centenary of Berne did not fall at a time of much hope for copyright's future, threatened as it then was by copying technologies now almost forgotten and subject to considerable suspicion from developing countries. The Convention had last been revised in 1967 in Stockholm under the magisterial guidance of Professor Eugen Ulmer. But even that New Deal required four years before the concerns of newly emergent nations could be met in the Paris arrangements. That was just a beginning of friction. By the 1980s it was doubtful whether further revision could even be contemplated, and indeed so it has proved to be in a direct sense.

What was still scarcely foreseeable in 1986 was the allure of freer global trading under a revised GATT. It proved strong enough for the round of negotiations that would create the WTO and require its member states, developing as well as developed, to accept the TRIPs Agreement as part of the parcel. So it was that 'Berne-plus' conditions became obligations across most of the world—obligations backed by dispute-settlement mechanisms between governments and ultimately the deployment of retaliatory trade measures. Before that Berne may have been little more that a code of polite behaviour. Suddenly it acquired the voice of positive command. That this should have happened exactly in time with the greatest revolution in information and entertainment since the invention of printing is perhaps no coincidence, though the legal developments designed to impose copyright order on an anarchic Internet came only afterwards—with the self-advertising 'WIPO' Treaties and then a spate of regional and national enactments under grandiloquent titles.

The technologies of information and the commerce they breed have become so much more complex that their legal organization appears to have acquired a wholly new dimension. The new media hold a vital place in spreading access around the world to knowledge, entertainment, and many perquisites of the good life and the bad. The international dimension of copyright is accordingly of far greater significance than seemed to be the case even in 1986. Accordingly this new edition could not be more timely. It will be seized upon by all who take the subject seriously, whether their background is in a civil law or a common law system. The authors will be not allowed to keep their silence for the next eighteen years before providing a third edition.

William R Cornish
Faculty of Law
University of Cambridge
April 2005

PREFACE TO THE NEW EDITION

It is almost eighteen years since the first edition of this work appeared, and it seems that a revolution, both technological and legal, has occurred in this time.

The technological revolution comes first, and is usefully illustrated by the experiences of the authors in writing this work. When Sam Ricketson began research on the first edition in 1984, it was still a hard-copy world: electronic typewriters were still commonly used and the most significant office advance was the dedicated word processor that allowed draft manuscripts to be more readily corrected and manipulated. The personal computer was only becoming an everyday reality towards the end of 1986, at least in the UK where the bulk of this work was done, and footnoting capabilities really only became user-friendly in the following year. When Sam returned to Australia at the end of 1986, he was fortunate enough to have electronic files of all the draft chapters that he had completed, but there was no ready means of transmitting these files back to publishers on the other side of the world. The most helpful technology available at the time was the facsimile machine, then still in its infancy, and the transmission of hundreds of pages of hard-copy text was a time consuming and daunting process (although relatively instantaneous in comparison to airmail, still the most common form of swift communication at that time, the latter in itself being a vast improvement over the sending of packages by ship and overland carrier).

The present edition, by contrast, has been done with all the advantages of modern computing and Internet communications, and between two authors, Sam Ricketson and Jane Ginsburg, who, for the most part, have been situated on two different continents with a publisher located on a third. Such has been the blessing of new technology that it has almost seemed that we have been sitting in adjoining offices, or at least just down the passage from each other!

The technological revolution has had another dimension with respect to the carrying out of research and the gathering of materials. When Sam began his research in 1984, access to many of the original documents meant trips to the WIPO library in Geneva or the Max Planck Institute library in Munich. Holdings in London were dispersed and often difficult to track down; photocopying of original documents was often impossible because of conservation concerns and long hours of tedious transcription were often required. Since 1984, access to many of these materials has become much easier, beginning with the publication by WIPO in 1986 of most of the original Berne Conference documents in its centenary celebration volume. Since the mid-1990s, WIPO documentation has become available online and research into current developments in the international conventions can be done at the click of a mouse (with the necessary Internet access). These developments have certainly made the writing of the second edition easier, but with some regrets for the rigours (and delights) of earlier times when dusty volumes and documents had to be tracked down and studied in places far from the normal comforts and conveniences of one's desk and office (one should not overstate here the difficulties involved in being 'required' to spend time in such places as Geneva and Munich in the pursuit of scholarship!).

The technological revolution feeds into the legal revolution that has also occurred in this area. In 1986, in its centenary year, Berne appeared to be a static institution; to be sure, it had an interesting and illuminating past, but its future prospects were less than exciting. It was a good time to write a history of this important convention, with a reasonable expectation that updating would not really be necessary, at least for a long time. But fact is always stranger than fiction, and, almost as the first edition was published, a series of events began that have made this second edition almost indecently overdue. These events are discussed at some length in Chapter 4, but three, in particular (and not in any order of importance) can be given here: first, the beginning of the Uruguay Round of GATT and the implementation of the negotiations on trade-related intellectual property rights based on the standards of Berne gave the latter a much greater prominence than had hitherto been the case; secondly, the entry of the United States into Berne in 1989, followed soon thereafter by China and the Russian Federation, gave the membership of Berne a universality that it had previously lacked; and thirdly, the technological and communications revolutions discussed above gave the impetus to the creation of new international instruments related to Berne. While all these developments—and a number of others—took place outside Berne in the strict sense, they took Berne as their starting or reference point. Hence, the second edition is concerned as much with these 'beyond Berne' developments as it is with a reappraisal of the ancient texts in the light of these new developments.

In terms of substance, some of the original text, particularly that dealing with the history of the Convention (Chapters 1–3), has been retained, but much of the original text has also been reworked or repositioned, with a fresh arrangement of topics and chapters (from Chapters 4–13). Some material, such as that in Chapters 14 (developing countries) and 18 (the Universal Copyright Convention) no longer retains the currency of interest that it had in 1987, but has been retained as containing useful insights into matters that have been of particular importance in the development of the present Berne Convention. Considerable amendments were required to the material dealing with the administrative, financial, and final clauses of the Berne Convention (Chapters 16 and 17), although this may be of only limited interest to some readers. Treatment of new international obligations with respect to technological protection measures and copyright management information is given in Chapter 15; there is an enlarged discussion of related rights in Chapter 19 (taking particular account of the adoption of the WPPT in 1996); and private international law issues are dealt with in Chapter 20. Finally, throughout the text, we have sought to deal sequentially, first, with Berne and, then 'beyond Berne', the latter heading encompassing the relevant requirements of the TRIPs Agreement and the WCT/WPPT. In this way, we hope that the historical emphasis of the first edition is blended appropriately with our discussion of the present texts and possible future developments.

It is trite, perhaps, to remark again that the world has changed greatly since 1986, the year of Berne's centenary. But while Berne itself has remained unrevised (apart from some minor administrative amendments), its stature and importance have changed beyond recognition. In 1986, it was still a Eurocentric instrument, with a number of hangers-on (including Australia). In 2005, it is now a truly universal instrument that, in reach and effect, must far outstrip the expectations of those early pioneers of the *Association Littéraire et Artistique Internationale* (ALAI) who set about drafting a modest instrument for multilateral adoption in 1883, beginning with an informal lunch meeting in a Roman trattoria at the Rome Congress of ALAI in 1882 (see Chapter 2). Other challenges, of course, remain, but it is still worth celebrating the centrepiece position that Berne now occupies as the foundation stone of the contemporary international copyright system.

Authorial responsibility for the whole edition is both joint and several, but primary responsibility for individual chapters has been as follows: Sam Ricketson—Chapters 1–5, 13–14, and 16–19; Jane Ginsburg—Chapters 6–12, 15, and 20.

ACKNOWLEDGEMENTS

In the first edition, many people were thanked whose contributions added greatly to the achievement of the final work. These thanks must be expressed again because the intellectual debt owed continues: particular mention must be made here of Adi Dietz, Jim Lahore, Bill Cornish, the late Stephen Stewart, and Mihaly Ficsor.

Work on the new edition began nearly a decade ago when Sam Ricketson posed the idea to Jane Ginsburg and was delighted that she was happy to undertake the task. Since this time, the project has been pursued fitfully by both of us, as other responsibilities have intervened and drawn our attention elsewhere. Nonetheless, the work has always been resumed with enthusiasm, involving virtual and actual meetings in and across most parts of the globe, from New York to Melbourne and even in an orchard in a monastery outside Montreal.

Many students and colleagues have provided advice and research support over the years of the writing of the new edition. We thank in particular, at the University of Melbourne, Associate Professor Richard Garnett, Dr David Brennan, David Lindsay, and Kim Weatherall; at the University of Cambridge, Professors William R Cornish and Lionel Bently; and at Columbia University School of Law, June Besek, Executive Director of the Kernochan Center for Law, Media and the Arts. Columbia Law School students enrolled in the Seminar on International and Comparative Intellectual Property Law offered research assistance and thoughtful criticism; in particular we thank Toby Headdon, Florian Schuhmacher, Yu Cao, Sébastien Evrard, and Maria Gonzalez Ordoñez, all LL M Class of 2003. Emma Barrett Prete and Tom Paskowitz, both Columbia JD Class of 2005, and Vigdis Bronder, Columbia JD Class of 2007, supplied much appreciated help with cite-checking.

Many thanks as well for administrative support to Gabriel Soto, of Columbia Law School, and to Sarah Ross, of the University of Cambridge Law Faculty, for assistance in assembling the final manuscript.

Sam Ricketson dedicates the book to his wife Rosemary Ayton, and to his children Philip, Jon, and Elizabeth, and notes with pleasure the way in which the culinary and cultural experiences of the Ricketson family have been immeasurably enhanced by the regular visitations of his co-author to this sunny land! With gratitude for the quality-of-life compliments, and acknowledging her co-author's climatic advantages, Jane Ginsburg observes that the gastronomic and intellectual esteem are amply returned. She dedicates the book to her husband George Spera, and to her children Paul, and especially to Clara, who will no longer be able to justify her own tardy completion of tasks by reference to her mother's.

Sam Ricketson
Melbourne
Jane Ginsburg
Cambridge
19 April 2005

CONTENTS—SUMMARY

VOLUME I

CONTENTS

VOLUME I

VOLUME II

14. Developing Countries

All of the Appendices are available as documents to download from the companion website for the book. The following documents (listed in italics) are only available on the companion website of the book, which is freely available to readers at: **http://www.oup.com/uk/booksites/content/9780198259466/**

NOTE ON SOURCES

A note on sources used for the book is also relevant at this stage. Throughout its lifetime, the Berne Convention has generated an ever-increasing body of records, both from its periodic conferences of revision and from its continuing administration. Although there is little problem for most readers to gain access to the records of the last thirty years, those of earlier years are more difficult to locate, particularly outside continental Europe. Yet these records, from the original conferences of 1884–6 onwards, throw important light on the background and meaning of many of the articles of the present Convention, and provide at least partial explanations for the compromises and concessions that lie behind them. Such records are by no means complete accounts of these matters, but they nonetheless constitute an indispensable first tool for any comprehensive study of the Convention. We have therefore sought to deal with them as fully as possible throughout the book, in the hope that this will be of assistance to readers who lack the time and the resources to locate and read the originals.

A further vital source for a study of the Convention is to be found in the monthly record of its operations which was published, from its inception, by the International Office of the Convention which is now administered by the World Intellectual Property Organization ('WIPO') in Geneva. This record, *Le Droit d'Auteur/Copyright*, which was only discontinued in 1998, contains all the official information relating to the Convention (accessions, ratifications, denunciations, and the like), as well as reports of national legislation and jurisprudence relevant to the Convention, and accounts of the activities of national and international bodies concerned with copyright matters. It has also carried, from its first year, scholarly commentaries on the Convention, and these form a most important corpus of learning on its interpretation and scope. As with the early records of the Convention, the early volumes of *Le Droit d'Auteur* are not easy to obtain, but WIPO has recently made them available in microfiche. There is, of course, a wide range of other, modern periodical literature dealing with various aspects of the Convention, but this is all readily available to any investigator (for further details, see the Bibliography).

It should also be stressed, at the outset, that the first edition of the present book was by no means the first study of the Berne Convention; nor was it the first in the English language. At each stage of its existence, the Convention has attracted a considerable body of sustained, critical writing. As with the early records and issues of *Le Droit d'Auteur*, some of these commentaries are no longer readily available, but it is worthwhile making brief mention here of the more important of them.

A number of short commentaries were written during and immediately after the original Berne Conferences of 1884–6, including those of the French scholars Clunet[1] and Rivière,[2] and the Swiss writers Soldan[3] and Droz.[4] However, the first major work dealing with the background and events leading up to the foundation of the Convention was that of Darras which was published just as the Convention was coming into force.[5] Another excellent study was published by Bastide in 1890,[6] and in 1906 the first account in English by Briggs[7] was published. This was followed in the next year by an extremely thorough commentary in German by Ernst Röthlisberger[8] who later became Director of the International Office of the Berne Union. After the revision of the Convention in Berlin in 1908, several shorter studies were published by the Belgian writer Wauwermans[9] and the French writer Potu.[10] Following the revision in Rome in 1928, further important commentaries were written by Raestad (a Norwegian),[11] Ruffini (an Italian),[12] and Hoffmann (a German).[13] However, the most significant work was that written by the distinguished American lawyer,

[1] E Clunet, *Étude sur la Convention d'Union internationale pour la protection des oeuvres littéraires et artistiques* (1887).

[2] L Rivière, *La Protection Internationale des Oeuvres Littéraires et Artistiques: Étude de législation comparé* (1897).

[3] C Soldan, *L'Union internationale pour la protection des oeuvres littéraires et artistiques: Commentaire de la Convention de Berne du 9 Septembre 1886* (1888).

[4] N Droz, articles in *Journal du droit international privé et de la jurisprudence comparée (Clunet)*, (1884) vol 11, 441, (1885) vol 12, 163 and 481.

[5] A Darras, *Du Droit des auteurs et des artistes dans les rapports internationaux* (1887).

[6] L Bastide, *L'Union de Berne de 1886, et la Protection internationale des droits des auteurs et des artistes* (1890).

[7] W Briggs, *The Law of International Copyright* (1906).

[8] E Röthlisberger, *Die Berner-Uebereinkunft zum Schutze von Werken der Literatur und Kunst und die Zusatzabkommen: Geschichtlich und rechtlich beleuchtet und kommentiert* (1906).

[9] P Wauwermans, *La Convention de Berne (Revisée à Berlin) pour la Protection des Oeuvres Littéraires* (1910).

[10] E Potu, *La Convention de Berne pour la protection des oeuvres littéraires et artistiques . . .* (1914). This appears to have been prepared on the basis of studies which had earlier appeared in *Le Droit d'Auteur.* See also A Petit, *Étude sur la Conférence de Berlin . . .* (1911).

[11] A Raestad, *La Convention de Berne révisée à Rome . . .* (1931).

[12] F Ruffini, *De la protection internationale des droits sur les oeuvres littéraires et artistiques* (1927).

[13] W Hoffmann, *Die Berner Uebereinkunft zum Schutze von Werken der Literatur und Kunst vom 9. September 1886 revidiert in Berlin am 13 November 1908 und in rom am 2 June 1928* (1935). See also W Goldbaum, *Berner Übereinkunft zum Schutze von Werken der Literatur und Kunst, vom 2 juni 1928* (1928); B Marwitz, *Die Berner Uebereinkunft und die Römische Konferenz* (1928).

Stephen P Ladas in 1938.[14] In its account of the origins and development of the Convention up to this time, this last work was previously the most comprehensive text, but as it was printed in a relatively limited edition, it is now very difficult to obtain. Another useful book, which appeared several years before that of Ladas was a concise and well-written memoir of the first half-century of the Convention published by the International Office,[15] and this was supplemented fifty years later by the WIPO publication of a collection of commentary and primary documents on the centenary of the Convention.[16] Several other commentaries (in German) were published following the Brussels Revision Conference,[17] and the decade preceding the publication of the first edition of this book saw the appearance of three authoritative works. The first, published by WIPO, was written by the late Claude Masouyé;[18] the others were a study in French by Desbois, Françon, and Kéréver,[19] and another in German by Nordemann, Vinck, and Hertin.[20] These last two books also dealt with the other multilateral conventions concerning copyright and neighbouring rights. With respect to the important new international instruments that have emerged in the 'beyond Berne' period since the first publication of this book in 1986, there are now a number of English-language commentaries. While it may be invidious to single out only a few of the most significant of these commentaries, mention should be made of the work of Daniel Gervais;[21] Jörg Reinbothe and Silke von Lewinski;[22] and Mihály Ficsor.[23]

The above list only takes account of the major works written in the French, English, and German languages; there have, of course, been further studies written in these and other languages. Furthermore, the vast majority of texts on

[14] S P Ladas, *The International Protection of Literary and Artistic Property* (1938).

[15] *L'Union internationale pour la protection des oeuvres littéraires et artistiques: Sa fondation et son développement, 1886–1936, Mémoire.*

[16] WIPO, *1886–Berne Convention Centenary–1986* (1986).

[17] A Baum, *The Brussels Conference for the Revision of the Berne Convention* (1949) (translated by the US Copyright Office, published originally in [1949] *GRUR* 1); W Bappert and E Wagner, *Internationales Urheberrecht: Kontmentar* (1956); W Goldbaum, *Verfall und Auflösung der sogenannten Berner Union und Uebereinkunft zum Schutz von Werken der Literatur und Kunst* (1959).

[18] C Masouyé, *Guide to the Berne Convention for the Protection of Literary and Artistic Works* (1978) (also published in French and Spanish).

[19] H Desbois, A Françon, and A Kéréver, *Les Conventions internationales du droit d'auteur et des droits voisins* (1976).

[20] W Nordemann, K Vinck, and P W Hertin, *Internationales Urheberrecht und Leistungsschutzrecht der deutschsprachigen Länder unter Berücksichtigung auch der Staaten der Europäischen Gemeinschaft, Kommentar,* Werner, Düsseldorf (1977). Also published in French under the title of *Droit d'auteur international et droits voisins: Commentaire* (1983) and in English in 1990.

[21] D Gervais, *The TRIPS Agreement: Drafting History and Analysis,* 2nd edn (2004).

[22] J Reinbothe and S von Lewinski, *The WIPO Treaties 1996* (2002).

[23] M Ficsor, *The Law of Copyright and the Internet* (2001).

national copyright laws deal inevitably, at lesser or greater length, with the Berne Convention and related copyright and neighbouring rights agreements, at least insofar as they affect these laws. The problem, then, for any student of this area is not the paucity of material, but the sheer bulk of it. Our hope therefore is that this book, being concerned solely with the conventions themselves, will draw this material together and present it in a coherent way.

NOTE ON TERMINOLOGY

A problem of terminology arises before we begin, namely is copyright the correct name by which to describe the rights covered by the Convention? In its literal sense, which was that accorded it in the early cases under the first British copyright statute, it is far more limited than the equivalent expression 'author's right' which is used in France, Germany, Italy, and Spain ('*droit d'auteur*', '*Urheberrecht*', '*diritto di autore*', and '*derecho de autor*'). Nonetheless, in its general legal usage in English-speaking countries today, 'copyright' comprehends all those rights (apart, perhaps, from moral rights) included within the continental concept of 'author's rights'. Indeed, in some respects, it goes further than this, being used to describe legal rights conferred on corporate persons, which are usually only covered in European jurisdictions under the rubric of 'neighbouring rights' ('*droits voisins*', '*Leistungsschutzrecht*', etc).

Although the latter are not at the centre of the present study (they do receive separate treatment in Chapter 19), there can be nothing misleading in using the word 'copyright' as an equivalent for the expression 'author's rights' as long as this usage is clearly understood. While the term 'literary and artistic property' might be more appropriate to describe these rights, its use was rejected in the present context at the very beginning of the Convention's existence.[1] From this time on, 'copyright', '*droit d'auteur*', and '*Urheberrecht*' have been used interchangeably as the terms denoting the subject matter dealt with by the Berne Convention.

Another terminological problem concerns the use of the term 'performing right' or 'performance' in relation to dramatic and musical works. In French, the word '*représentation*' is usually adopted in relation to the first (including dramatico-musical works), while the word '*éxécution*' is used in relation to musical works. While these terms can be directly, and appositely, translated into 'representation' and 'execution' in English, for the sake of brevity it seems easier to use the term 'performance' to cover both kinds of act. This is in accordance with long-established English practice, and imports no difference from the sense in which the words 'representation' and 'execution' are used in French.

---

[1] *Actes* 1885, 20 (mainly due to objections from the German delegation).

A further point of explanation, mainly for English-speaking readers, concerns the word 'Act' which is used throughout the book to refer to the different texts of the Convention which have been adopted by successive conferences of revision. Thus, the expression 'Berne Act' is used to refer to the text adopted by the original conferences held at Berne in 1884–6, 'Berlin Act' to refer to the text settled at the revision conference held at Berlin in 1908, and so on.[2] To English-speaking lawyers, this usage may appear unusual, as the term 'Act' generally refers to the highest form of instrument enacted by a sovereign legislative body. In French, however, the term '*acte*' has a broader meaning. referring to any kind of formal deed or instrument, and it has been used in this sense to refer to the final text which has been agreed to by the member nations of the Berne Union at each successive conference at which the Convention has been revised. We have therefore followed this usage in the present text, substituting the English word 'Act' for '*acte*'. It should also be noted that there is another sense in which *acte* is used, and this is to refer to records of proceedings. We have therefore adopted the abbreviation '*Actes* 1884–6' to refer to the records of the 1884 to 1886 Conferences at Berne, '*Actes* 1908' to refer to the records of the Berlin Revision Conference of 1908, and so on. Where later conferences' proceedings were published in English, they are referred to as '*Records*'.

Another terminological problem is how to refer to the different kinds of legal systems that are to be found in the various countries of the Berne Union. Broad descriptive labels, though useful as a form of shorthand, are often inaccurate and misleading unless their meaning and scope are made clear in advance. Where appropriate, we have used geographical or regional adjectives to designate particular groups of countries, for instance 'Western European', 'Eastern European', 'Asian', 'African', and so on. In a more general sense, we have used the expressions 'civil law' and 'common law' to refer to the main categories of legal system that are found in most countries of the world. The first term is very loose, and covers all countries of continental Europe, with the exception of the UK and Ireland, and those countries whose legal systems are derived from those of continental Europe, such as Japan, the South American states and African

[2] The full fist of expressions used are as follows: Berne Act—text adopted by Berne Conference 1886; Paris Additional Act—text adopted by Paris Conference 1896; Berlin Act—text adopted by Berlin Conference 1908; Rome Act—text adopted by Rome Conference 1928; Brussels Act—text adopted by Brussels Conference 1948; Stockholm Act—text adopted by Stockholm Conference 1967; Stockholm Protocol—Protocol adopted by Stockholm Conference; Paris Act—text adopted by Paris Conference 1971; Paris Appendix—Appendix adopted by Paris Conference 1971; Stockholm, Paris Acts—this composite phrase refers to the substantive articles (arts 1–20) of both the Stockholm and Paris Acts, which are identical. Note, however, that as the Paris Act is an entirely separate Act, it would be wrong to refer to the two Acts as the Stockholm–Paris Act. See further para 14.37 below.

states that were formerly French colonies. The expression 'common law', on the other hand, refers to those countries whose legal systems are derived from British law, including the United States of America. The adjective 'Anglo-Saxon' is used by some authors for this purpose, but this hardly seems appropriate in view of the fact that most of the peoples of these countries are not Anglo-Saxon in origin; indeed, the UK itself has component parts that are Celtic in origin rather than Anglo-Saxon. Similar objections could be made to the use of the term 'Anglo-American', while the adjective 'Commonwealth' would leave out the USA as well as several other important Berne member countries that are no longer part of the British Commonwealth. 'Common law' therefore seems the most appropriate description to cover all these diverse nations whose legal systems ultimately derive from that of the UK. A third category, no longer relevant for this edition, was that of 'socialist countries', which was used in the first edition to refer to the USSR and the socialist regimes of Eastern Europe. A final category which cuts across each of those already mentioned is that of 'developing countries'. This term involves some difficulties of interpretation, and these are discussed further in Chapter 14 (para 14.51ff).

The last matter of terminology concerns the use of the expression 'International Office' to refer to the body which undertook the administrative tasks of the Berne Union prior to the Stockholm Act. This is in accordance with the usage adopted by WIPO in its English translations of the earlier Acts of the Convention. In these, the French title '*Bureau del'Union internationale pour la protection des oeuvres littéraires et artistiques*' was rendered as 'Office of the International Union for the Protection of Literary and Artistic Works', and the abbreviated titles 'Bureau international' and 'International Office' were used. However, these were not 'official' translations of the authentic French text,[3] and, in new translations published by WIPO as part of the centenary celebrations of the Berne Convention in September 1986,[4] the expression 'Bureau' is used instead of 'Office'. As these texts are not binding, we have maintained the earlier translation, and therefore refer only to the 'International Office' when discussing the body that administered the Berne Union prior to the Stockholm Act.[5] This has the slight advantage that it serves to distinguish this body more clearly from the 'International Bureau' of WIPO which now administers the

[3] In this regard, however, it should be noted that in art 31 of the Brussels Act, English was established for the first time as an 'equivalent text', and this was done by a committee of English-speaking delegates who adopted the word 'Office': *Documents de la Conférence réunie à Bruxelles du 5 au 26 juin 1948*, 89, 531.

[4] WIPO, *The Berne Convention for the Protection of Literary and Artistic Works from 1886 to 1986* (1986), 228–36.

[5] The terms 'Berne Office', 'Berne Bureau', 'Office of Union' and the 'Secretariat' are also to be found in various writings.

Union. In this regard, it should also be noted that, from its inception, the International Office was combined with the 'International Bureau for the Union for the Protection of Industrial Property', and these were later known, unofficially, as the '*Bureaux Internationaux Reunie pour la Protection de la Propriete Intellectuelle*' or 'BIRPI'.[6] As for the terms 'Berne Union' and 'Union', the meaning of these is discussed in detail in Chapter 5.

[6] See further Chapter 16 below.

NOTE AS TO TRANSLATIONS

As the original language used in the records of conferences and publications concerning the Berne Convention was French, we have supplied English translations of any quotation that has been used in the text. Except where the contrary is indicated, these translations are our own and, where it seems necessary, we have included the French original in the accompanying text or in a footnote. In the case of proper and place names, we have used English translations throughout, except in the case of several well-known and generally used abbreviations of the original French names, such as ALAI and BIRPI. All titles of books, monographs, and periodical articles appear in the language of the original text.

FOREWORD TO THE FIRST EDITION

It is a pleasure to welcome this magisterial work by Mr Sam Ricketson, of the Melbourne Law School, on the Berne Convention for the Protection of Literary and Artistic Works.

We were privileged to have Sam Ricketson with us for over two years as the Herchel Smith Senior Fellow in Intellectual Property Law, and his new work is the product of his prodigious labours during that period. It is the most comprehensive work to have been published on the Berne Convention, the centenary of which was celebrated last year. The author's treatment of this complex subject is both wide and penetrating, a skilful blend of history, policy discussion, examination of relevant issues of treaty law and a rigorous analysis of the text of the Convention and its effect on national laws. Those who have a serious interest in copyright will find this handsome volume an indispensable guide through this important and complex branch of intellectual property law.

R M Goode
Centre for Commercial Law Studies
Queen Mary College
April 1987

PREFACE TO THE FIRST EDITION

Background to the present study

In September 1986, the Berne Convention for the Protection of Literary and Artistic Works was a century old. From an original membership of nine nations, chiefly concentrated in Europe, it now covers all continents, and, as of January 1986, had seventy-six member states. These include nations at all stages of economic and social development, and embrace all kinds of political ideologies. At the same time, significant imbalances and gaps remain in the membership of the Convention, or the Berne Union (as it is often called). It is still largely Eurocentric in character, and three of the most important countries in the world have not yet become members—the USA, the USSR, and the Peoples' Republic of China. Indeed, the area to which the Convention now applies in 1986 is not much larger than was the case in 1886, when it was extended to the vast colonial empires of several of its original members.

In this period, the problems to which the Convention was originally directed have also radically changed. From an initial, and laudable, concern with the rights of authors and the encouragement and reward of intellectual creativity, the present century has witnessed major technological developments which have had the contradictory effects of undermining and extending those rights. Furthermore, the pressure from users of copyright material, always strong, has intensified, with demands for readier access to this material from developing nations. An international convention, conceived at a time when Western European culture and civilization were in their most dominant and crusading phase, has had to adapt to changing times and circumstances, and, despite its periodic revisions, this process of adjustment has not always been an easy or even adequate one. Problems of relevance have become more pronounced, and, as with other major multilateral international agreements the differences between member states have become more marked. Moreover, it no longer remains the only major world copyright convention: since 1952, the Universal Copyright Convention (the UCC) has come to embrace a wider membership than the Berne Convention, and includes both the USA and the USSR. In recent years, there have come into existence several other important conventions dealing with subject matter and rights that are closely related to those dealt with in the Berne Convention (often referred to as 'neighbouring rights'): these include the Rome Convention for the Protection of Performers, Producers of Phonograms and Broadcasting Organizations 1961 (the 'Rome Convention') and the Convention for the Protection of Producers of Phonograms against Unauthorized Duplication of their Phonograms, 1971 (the 'Phonograms Convention').

None of the above comments should be taken as meaning that the Berne Convention is presently in crisis. The opposite is the case: the Convention embodies an impressive and uncompromising level of protection for authors and their works, and its geographical reach is still very considerable. In addition, the UCC and the neighbouring rights conventions are complementary, and not in contradiction, to the Berne Convention system, and have their origins in it. Nevertheless, it is true to say that the development of the Convention has now reached a plateau, and the questions of where to proceed and how to do this appear more intractable than in the past.

In the light of what has been said, it will be clear that there is a need to take stock of this century of development, to evaluate what it means, and to consider what the future may hold in store for the Berne Convention.[1] In the belief that the past informs both the present and future, I have attempted to undertake these tasks in this study, which falls into the following parts. The first examines the history and development of the Convention to the present time. This leads naturally to the second part, which is a consideration of the present scope and operation of the Convention. The concluding part seeks, albeit tentatively and briefly, to give a *tour d'horizon* of the future problems and challenges facing the Convention.

By its very nature, Part II is the largest section of the book. Unlike some earlier commentaries I have not attempted to provide a chronological account of the separate articles of the Convention, but have arranged the study under subject headings, such as the conditions necessary for protection, the works protected, the rights protected, and so on. The focus throughout is on the provisions of the Convention itself, and no systematic effort is made to examine the way in which a member country gives effect to its Convention obligations. In view of the large size of the present membership of the Berne Union, such an undertaking would require a study far longer than this one. Accordingly, where readers require detailed information on the laws of particular countries, they are referred, in the first instance, to the relevant publications of WIPO and UNESCO, and then to any of the specialist texts dealing with these countries. To assist readers in this task, a suitable bibliography is provided at the end of this text. Where national laws are referred to in the present study, this is done only by way of background explanation or illustration, and nothing more. On the

[1] Note that the description of the structure of the first edition that follows is significantly different from that which has now been adopted in the new edition.

other hand, in order to ensure that my treatment of the substantive provisions of the Convention is as full as possible, I have treated each in a historical way, beginning with a consideration of the origins of each provision and examining the changes which have been made to it in each successive revision of the Convention. To a limited extent, this approach means that there is an overlap with the broader historical survey in Part I. However, I would justify this overlap on the following grounds. First, Part I is intended to set the overall context against which the Convention has developed; it therefore contains a great deal of subject matter that is not directly related to particular provisions of the Convention. Secondly, it is only possible to understand the meaning and scope to be accorded to many of the present provisions of the Convention by detailed reference to what has preceded them. Thirdly, many Union countries are still bound by earlier versions of the Convention, and an understanding of these earlier texts therefore remains of immediate practical importance.

ACKNOWLEDGEMENTS IN THE FIRST EDITION

Although I accept full responsibility for everything that appears in this book, I must give my thanks to all those who helped me with its writing and final production.

At the institutional level, I must express my gratitude to the University of Melbourne for the extended leave which I was granted for this purpose. In the same way, I must thank the Centre for Commercial Law Studies of Queen Mary College, London, for providing me with the necessary facilities and support.

On a personal level, my debts are far greater. I am particularly grateful to the following persons: Cohn Howard, the former Dean of the Law School at the University of Melbourne, for his assistance in arranging my leave; Roy Goode, the Director of the Centre for Commercial Law Studies, who unflinchingly took on the burden of publication; and Jim Lahore, the former Herchel Smith Professor of Intellectual Property Law in the University of London, who was a constant source of advice and support throughout. Above all, I must give my warmest thanks to Dr Herchel Smith for funding my position, and thus enabling me to undertake and complete this project without interruption.

I must also thank the following persons for the time that they have taken to read draft chapters and to discuss knotty problems of substance and style: Stephen Stewart, Jeremy Phillips, Bill Cornish, Denis Galligan, Alan Boyle, and Paul Katzenberger. Mihály Ficsor of WIPO gave me great help in relation to the administrative and financial provisions of the Convention, providing me with a great deal of necessary information, while Hamish Sandison of Washington performed a similar service in keeping me informed of developments in the USA concerning the movement in that country in favour of accession to the Berne Convention. In particular, I must thank Adolf Dietz of the Max-Planck Institute in Munich for the time and guidance which he so generously afforded me. I benefited greatly from my discussions with him, and these did much to clarify my overall perspective of the subject of authors' rights.

On a more practical level, I must also express my appreciation to Hilaire Omokolo and the library staff at WIPO for their unflagging and courteous assistance during my visits to Geneva, and to the administrative and secretarial staff at the Centre for Commercial Law Studies here in London for all the help they have given. In particular, I must mention Suzanne Emmery, Nicola Jones,

Michelle Balgobin, and Janet Bush. Louise Herron, a postgraduate student at the Centre, rendered a most important (and necessary) service in verifying my translations, and Toks Williams and John Herbert undertook the onerous task of editing and preparing the final text for printing. The index was skilfully compiled by Robert Spicer and the bibliography by Rosemary and John Ayton. I must also pay tribute to the work of Hilary Norman in the design of the book, in particular the cover. In the same way, I must thank Alan Hawkins of The Eastern Press for his advice and assistance throughout the production process.

Finally, my warmest thanks are due to my wife, Rosemary, and my brother-in-law, John, for their help and support throughout the writing of the book. Living with an author while he is in the throes of writing is never easy, and I am sure they will be as pleased as I am that the task is finally completed!

Sam Ricketson
London
December 1986

TABLE OF CASES

TABLE OF NATIONAL LEGISLATION

Germany

Germany, Federal Republic

Greece

Guatemala

Haiti

Hungary

Peru

Poland

Portugal

Romania

Russia

Rwanda

Senegal

South Africa

Spain

Venezuela

LIST OF ABBREVIATIONS

ALAI	*Association Littéraire et Artistique Internationale*
ABU	Asian Broadcasting Union
ACC	Authors' Consultative Committee
AID	International Alliance for Diffusion by Wire
AIPO	African Intellectual Property Organization
AJIL	American Journal of International Law
Am Jo Int Law	American Journal of International Law
ASBU	Arab States Broadcasting Union
ASCAP	American Society of Composers, Authors and Publishers
AUFFT	Archiv fur Urheber-, Film-, Funk- und Theaterrecht
BBC	British Broadcasting Corporation
Berkeley Tech LJ	Berkeley Technology Law Journal
BFSP	British and Foreign State Papers 1812/13–1939
BIRPI	*Bureaux Internationaux Reunie pour la Protection de la Propriete Intellectuelle* (unofficial name for the International Office (the body which undertook the administrative tasks of the Berne Union prior to the Stockholm Act) and the International Bureau for the Union for the Protection of Industrial Property, with which from its inception it was combined
Bull Cop Soc USA	Bulletin of the Copyright Society of the USA
BUPC	Berne Union Permanent Committee
Burr	Burrow's King's Bench Reports 1757–1771
BYIL	British Year Book of International Law
Cardozo Arts & Ent LJ	Cardozo Arts and Entertainment Law Journal
Cd	Command Paper
CISAC	International Conference of Authors and Composers
CGE	Committee of Governmental Experts
CO	country of origin
Colum L Rev	Columbia Law Review
Colum-VLA J L & Arts	Columbia-VLA Journal of Law and the Arts
COMECON	Council for Mutual Economic Assistance
Copyright	Copyright: Monthly Review of the World Intellectual Property Organization

DA	*Le Droit d'Auteur*
DBS	Direct Broadcast Satellites
de Paul L Rev	de Paul Law Review
DMCA	Digital Millennium Copyright Act 1998 (USA)
DSB	Dispute Settlement Body
EBU	European Broadcasting Union
EC	European Commission
ECJ	Court of Justice of the European Communities
EEC	European Economic Community
EIPR	European Intellectual Property Review
ER	English reports
ESC	European Convention Relating to Questions on Copyright Law and Neighbouring Rights in the Framework of Transfrontier Broadcasting by Satellite (May 1994)
EU	European Union
EYB	Europa Year Book
FIAD	International Federation of Film Distributors' Association
FIAPF	International Federation of Film Producers' Associations
FIEJ	International Federation of Newspaper Publishers
FIM	International Federation of Musicians
FRG	Federal Republic of Germany (1949–90)
FSS	Fixed Satellite Service
FTA	Free trade agreement
GATS	General Agreement on Trade in Services
GATT	General Agreement on Tariffs and Trade
GDR	German Democratic Republic
GRUR	Deutsche Vereinigung fur Gewerblichen Rechtsschutz und Urheberrecht
Harv L Rev	Harvard Law Review
Hastings Comm & Ent LJ	Hastings Communication and Entertainment Law Journal
ICJ	International Court of Justice
ICLQ	International and Comparative Law Quarterly
IFA	International Federation of Actors
IFPI	International Federation of the Phonographic Industry
IGC	Intergovernmental Committee
IIC	International Institute for Intellectual Co-operation
ILO	International Labour Organization
INTEGRU	International Copyright Society
IPA	International Publishers' Association
IPRs	intellectual property rights
ITU	International Telecommunications Union
JBL	Journal of Business Law

J Copyr Soc USA	Journal of the Copyright Society of the USA (Formerly Bulletin)
JDIPJC (Clunet)	Journal du droit international prive et de la jurisprudence compare (Clunet)
JPOS	Journal of the Patent Office Society
LQR	Law Quarterly Review
Mich J Int'l L	Michigan Journal of International Law
NGOs	Non-governmental organizations
OED	Oxford English Dictionary
OJ	Official Journal of the European Communities
PCT	Patent Cooperation Treaty
PRC	Peoples' Republic of China
RIDA	Revue internationale du droit d'auteur
Rome Convention	Rome Convention for the Protection of Performers, Producers of Phonograms and Broadcasting Organizations 1961
SACEM	Societe des Auteurs, Compositeurs et Editeurs de Musique
SCCR	Standing Committee on Copyright and Related Rights
So Cal LR	Southern California Law Review
SOED	Shorter Oxford English Dictionary
TRIPs Agreement	Agreement on Trade-Related Aspects of Intellectual Property Rights 1994
UCC	Universal Copyright Convention
UCLA Law Rev	University of California Los Angeles Law Review
UK	United Kingdom of Great Britain and Northern Ireland
UN	United Nations
UNESCO	United Nations Educational and Scientific Organization
UNIDO	United Nations Industrial Development Organization
UNIDROIT	International Institute for the Unification of Private Law
URTNA	Union of National Radio and Television Organizations of Africa
USC	United States Code
Va J Int'l L	Virginia Journal of International Law
Vienna Convention	Vienna Convention on the Law of Treaties 1969
WCT	WIPO Copyright Treaty
WG Guidelines	Advisory Notes on the implementation of the System of Translation and Reproduction Licences for Developing Countries under the Copyright Convention (1982)
WHO	World Health Organization
WIPO	World Intellectual Property Organization
WPPT	WIPO Performances and Phonograms Treaty
WTO	World Trade Organization
Yale LJ	Yale Law Journal

LIST OF ABBREVIATIONS OF WORKS TO WHICH REFERENCE IS COMMONLY MADE IN THIS BOOK

Actes (1884)	Actes de la Conference internationale pour la protection des droits d'auteur reunie a Berne du 8 au 19 septembre 1884
Actes (1885)	Actes de la 2me Conference internationale pour la protection des oeuvres litteraires et artistiques reunie a Berne du 7 au 9 septembre 1885
Actes (1886)	Actes de la 3me Conference internationale pour la protection des oeuvres litteraires et artistiques reunie a Berne du 6 au 9 septembre 1886
Actes (1896)	Actes de la Conference de Paris de 1896
Actes (1908)	Actes de la Conference de Berlin 1908
Actes (1928)	Actes de la Conference reunie a Rome du 7 mai au 2 juin 1928
Annales (1858)	*Annales de la Propriété Industrielle, Artistique et Littéraire* (1858)
Bastide (1890)	L Bastide, *L'Union de Berne de 1886 et la Protection internationale des droits des auteurs et des artistes* (1890)
Baum (1949)	A Baum, *The Brussels Conference for the Revision of the Berne Convention* (1949)
BFSP	*British and Foreign State Papers*
Bogsch (1986)	A Bogsch, 'The First Hundred Years of the Berne Convention for the Protection of Literary and Artistic Works' [1986] *Copyright* 330
Bowett (1982)	D W Bowett, *The Law of International Institutions*, 4th edn (1982)
Briggs (1906)	W Briggs, *The Law of International Copyright* (1906)
Correspondence (1908)	*Correspondence Respecting the Revised Convention of Berne for the Protection of Literary and Artistic Works, signed at Berlin, November 13, 1908*
Correspondence No 1 (1886)	*Switzerland No 1 (1886), Correspondence Respecting the Formation of an International Copyright Union*, C-4606 (1886), Papers presented to Parliament in Jan 1886
Correspondence No 2 (1886)	*Switzerland No 2 (1886), Further Correspondence Respecting the Formation of an International Copyright Union*, Papers presented to Parliament in Aug 1886
Correspondence No 3 (1886)	*Switzerland No 3 (1886), Further Correspondence Respecting the Formation of an International Copyright Union*, Papers presented to Parliament in Sept 1886

Darras (1887)	A Darras, *Du Droit des auteurs et des artistes dans les rapports internationaux* (1887)
J Delalain (1866)	J Delalain, *Recueil des Conventions conclues par la France pour la Reconnaissance de la Properiété Littéraire et Artistique* (1866)
Desbois (1978)	H Desbois, *Le Droit D'Auteur en France*, 3rd edn (1978)
Desbois et al (1976)	H Desbois, A Françon, and A Kéréver, *Les Conventions internationales du droit d'auteur et des droits voisins* (1976)
Dietz (1978)	A Dietz, *Copyright Law in the European Community* (1978)
Dock (1963)	M-C Dock, *Étude sur le droit d'auteur* (1963)
Documents 1948 (1951)	*Documents de la Conférence réunie à Bruxelles du 5 au 26 juin 1948* (1951)
Duchemin (1948)	J-L Duchemin, *Le Droit de Suite des Artistes* (1948)
Ficsor (2003)	Mihály Ficsor, *The Law of Copyright and the Internet: The 1996 WIPO Treaties, Their Interpretation and Implementation* (2003)
Gervais (2003)	D Gervais, *The TRIPS Agreement: Drafting History and Analysis*, 2nd edn (2003)
Histoire (1889)	*Association Littéraire et Artistique Internationale: Son Histoire, Ses Travaux (1878–1889)* (1879)
Holdsworth (1939)	W Holdsworth, *A History of English Law*, 2nd edn, vol VI (1939, reprinted 1966)
Johnson (1970)	C F Johnson, 'The Origins of the Stockholm Protocol' (1970) 18 *Bull Cop Soc USA* 91
Ladas (1938)	S P Ladas, *The International Protection of Literary and Artistic Property* (1938)
Laddie et al (2000)	Hugh Laddie, Peter Prescott, and Mary Vitoria, *The Modern Law of Copyright and Designs*, 3rd edn (2000)
Lavollée (1887)	R Lavollée, *Propriété Littéraire et la Convention de Berne* (1887)
LCD (1889)	C Lyon-Caen and P Delalain, *Lois françaises et étrangères sur la Propriété littéraire et artistique . . .* (1889)
McNair (1961)	Lord McNair, *The Law of Treaties* (1961)
Maillard (1928)	G Maillard, 'Conférence de Rome', *ALAI Bulletin*, Oct 1928
Masouyé (1978)	C Masouyé, *Guide to the Berne Convention for the Protection of Literary and Artistic Works* (1978)
Mémoire (1936)	*L'Union internationale pour la protection des oeuvres littéraires et artistiques: son fondation et son développement—Mémoire 1886–1936* (1936)
Nordemann et al (1977)	W Nordemann, K Vinck, and P W Hertin, *Internationales Urheberrecht und Leistungsschutzrecht der deut-*

	schsprachigen Länder unter Berücksichtigung auch der Staaten der Europäischen Gemeinschaft, Kommentar (1977)
Nordemann et al (1990)	W Nordemann, K Vinck, P W Hertin, and G Meyer, *International Copyright and Neighbouring Rights Law* (1990)
Pataille and Huget (1855)	Pataille and Huget, *Code internationale,* 1st edn (1855)
Plaisant and Pichot (1934)	M Plaisant and O Pichot, *La Conférence de Rome: Commentaire pratique de la nouvelle Convention pour la protection internationale de la propriété littéraire et artistique* (1934)
Records (1967)	Records of the Intellectual Property Conference of Stockholm, June 11 to July 14, 1967
Recueil (1904)	International Copyright Office, *Recueil des conventions et traités concernant la propriété littéraire et artistique, publiés en français et dans les langues des pays contractants avec une introduction et des notices* (1904)
Reinbothe and von Lewinski (2002)	J Reinbothe and S von Lewinski, *The WIPO Treaties 1996* (2002)
Rivière (1897)	L Rivière, *La Protection Internationale des Oeuvres Littéraires et Artistiques: Étude de législation comparé* (1897)
Schrader (1970)	D M Schrader, 'Analysis of the Protocol Regarding Developing Countries' (1970) 17 *Bull Cop Soc USA* 166
Spoor et al (1980)	J H Spoor, W R Cornish, and P F Nolan, *Copies in Copyright* (1980)
Stewart (1989)	S Stewart, *International Copyright and Neighbouring Rights,* 2nd edn (1989)
Wildhaber (1971)	L Wildhaber, *Treaty-Making Power and Constitution: An International and Comparative Study* (1971)

PART I

THE HISTORY AND DEVELOPMENT OF INTERNATIONAL COPYRIGHT AND NEIGHBOURING RIGHTS CONVENTIONS

1

THE DEVELOPMENT OF INTERNATIONAL COPYRIGHT RELATIONS

A. National Copyright Laws Prior to the Berne Convention

(1) The system of privileges and early copyright laws

Although the legal theories underlying copyright protection differ greatly from country to country, the origins of this form of protection in Europe are strikingly similar: the grant of exclusive printing rights or privileges which were made to printers and publishers by national authorities soon after the introduction of **1.01** printing in Europe in the late fifteenth and early sixteenth centuries.[1] In each country, the reasons for such grants of protection were also much the same, springing from governmental concern with the need to control a new means of disseminating information which was at once full of promise and danger to the established order, the need to encourage a new kind of industry, and the self-centred concern of printers and publishers to secure the practice (and fruits) of their craft against the ravages of unfettered competition.[2] In all of this, the role and status of the 'author' was minimal. One reason, perhaps, for this state of affairs was that, in this early period, most of the books which were printed were old or classical texts.[3] Another may have been that this was still the 'Age of Patronage' in which authors received their chief remuneration and recognition from wealthy and aristocratic patrons rather than through the sales of their works.[4] Nevertheless, with the rapid social and economic changes of the following two centuries the position of authors gradually altered, and the notion of the author's right came to be accepted, in differing degrees, in most European countries.

1.02 The first to do so was the UK which, in an Act of 1709 (the 'Act of Anne'),[5] granted to authors and their assigns a short period of statutory protection for their books. The main proponent of this Act was the London Company of Stationers (or publishers) which was concerned to revive the protection which its members had received previously for their 'copies' under the old Star Chamber ordinances and Licensing Acts of the Restoration period. It therefore used the claims of authors for recognition as a vehicle for advancing their own

---

[1] The first recorded grant appears to have been that made by the Venetian Senate to Gio in 1469: A Darras, *Du Droit des auteurs et des artistes dans les rapports internationaux* (1887), 170 ('Darras (1887)'). As for the possibility that authors' rights were recognized in classical times, see M-C Dock, *Etude sur le droit d'auteur* (1963), Book One ('Dock (1963)').

[2] For further readings on this history, see Darras (1887), ch 2; S M Stewart, *International Copyright and Neighbouring Rights* (1983), ch 2; L Rivière, *La Protection Internationale des Oeuvres Littéraires et Artistiques: Étude de législation comparé* (1897), ch 11 ('Rivière (1897)'); W Holdsworth, *A History of English Law,* 2nd edn, vol VI (1939, reprinted 1966), 360–79 ('Holdsworth (1939)'); M-C Dock, 'Genèse et evolution de la notion de propriété littéraire' [1974] *RIDA* 127; Dock (1963); C Lyon-Caen and P Delalain, *Lois françaises et étrangères sur la Propriété littéraire et artistique* . . ., vol I (1889), Introduction ('LCD (1889)'); W Bappert, T Maunz, and G Schricker, *Verlagsrecht: Kommentar zum Gesetz über das Verlagsrecht vom 19.6.1901,* 2nd edn (1984), 18ff (and references noted on that page); L Gieseke, *Die geschichtliche Entwicklung des deutschen Urheberrechts* (1957); M Vogel, *Deutsche Urherber und Verlagsrechtsgeschichte zwischen 1450 and 1850: Archiv für Geschichte des Buchwesens* (1978), 1ff.

[3] Darras (1887), 169–70.

[4] B Ringer, 'Copyright and the Future of Authorship' [1976] *Copyright* 155.

[5] 8 Anne, c 19 (1709). For further background to the Act of Anne, see L R Patterson, *Copyright in Historical Perspective* (1968); H Ransom, *The First Copyright Statute* (1956); Holdsworth (1939), 360–79; B Kaplan, *An Unhurried View of Copyright* (1967); V Bonham-Carter, *Authors By Profession,* vol I (1978); H B Abrams, 'The Historic Foundations of American Copyright Law: Exploding the Myth of Common Law Copyright' (1983) 29 *Wayne Law Review* 1119.

interests.[6] Nevertheless, the adoption of this device indicates something of the way in which the status of authors had changed in the preceding century. During the following century, their position was more firmly established as the bonds of patronage were further loosened and they became independent figures in British cultural life. At the same time, this early identification of the publishers' interests with those of authors gave British copyright law, and laws derived from it, a decidedly economic or pecuniary bias which persists even today. In keeping with this approach, the early British laws required registration as a precondition for the grant of protection, and accorded this for a short term only, subject to a right of renewal.

Similar social and cultural developments were also occurring in continental **1.03**
Europe at this time, although there was to be some delay before copyright was recognized as a legal right to be protected by positive law, rather than as a mere concession granted to an author, publisher, or bookseller under a system of privileges. The first continental country to grant protection appears to have been Denmark which, in 1741, promulgated an ordinance providing:

> That no one shall be allowed to reprint, pirate or introduce or offer for sale a reprint of any book or manuscript to which another person in this town [Copenhagen] is lawfully entitled, be it a spontaneous gift or donation, through purchase or by virtue of a translation or amendment already made and by which he has incurred a considerable expense . . .[7]

This ordinance was scarcely a recognition of the author's natural or inalienable right in his work, but was rather a measure to protect the investment made by a person, whether an author or not, in the production of a printed book. Furthermore, in the public interest, the ordinance excluded certain categories of works from protection, such as church hymn books, Luther's catechism and alphabet books, as well as books which had not been reprinted within a certain time of the exhaustion of their edition, these times varying from three to twelve months 'according to the extent and value of the script'. The thrust of the ordinance was therefore similar to that of the Act of Anne and the other British copyright enactments of the eighteenth century.

(2) The development of national copyright laws

The system of privileges, however, continued in other European countries until **1.04**
the last decade of the eighteenth century, when the revolution in France began

[6] See the preamble to the Act: 'An Act for the Encouragement of Learning, by vesting the Copies of printed books in the Authors or Purchasers of such Copies, during the Times therein mentioned . . .'.

[7] The English translation of this ordinance is to be found in S P Ladas, *The International Protection of Literary and Artistic Property* (1938), vol I, 18 ('Ladas (1938)').

to spread its influence to its neighbours.[8] The French revolutionary laws of 13 to 19 January 1791 and of 19 July 1793 represent the first, explicit recognition in Europe of the rights of authors, dramatists, composers, and artists. The first law accorded an exclusive performing right to authors of dramatic and musical works for a period lasting until five years after their death.[9] The second dealt with what we would now call the 'exclusive reproduction right', providing:

> Art. 1. Authors of writings of all kinds, composers of music, painters and designers who make engravings or drawings, shall enjoy during their entire life the exclusive right to sell, prepare for sale, and distribute their works in the territory of the Republic, and to assign the property therein in whole or in part.[10]

Article 2 provided that the beneficiaries and assigns of the author were to enjoy the same right for a period of ten years after the author's death. The remaining articles dealt with penalties for infringement, formalities, and procedures for enforcement of the new right.

The revolutionary French legislators sought to reconcile divergent bases for literary and artistic property. As in England, anticorporatist motivations underlay the recognition of authors' individual claims: the exclusive performing right, for example, followed the dissolution of the monopoly of the *Comédie Française.* French lawmakers also saw in authors' rights a means to advance the progress of learning; indeed, jurisdiction over copyright laws, originally vested in the Committees on the Constitution and on Agriculture and Commerce, had been transferred by 1793 to the Committee on Public Instruction. Much of the revolutionary rhetoric emphasized the public benefits that would flow from recognizing and enforcing authors' rights. At the same time, however, French advocates of authors' rights urged an additional justification, rooted in Enlightenment concepts of property. The 1789 Declaration of the Rights of Man had pronounced property rights 'inviolate and sacred'. The 1793 law clearly evoked that conception when its Reporter trumpeted as the 'Declaration of the Rights of Genius' the law's enunciation of an exclusive right of reproduction—a right the law's first article labelled 'property'.[11]

---

[8] For succinct accounts of the system of privileges in different European countries, see the introductory notes to each of the national sections in LCD (1889), vol I, 5–9 (France), 51–5 (Germany), 123 (Austria), 141 (Hungary), 167–70 (Belgium), 187 (Denmark), 205–7 (Spain), 377–9 (Italy), 457 (Netherlands), 467 (Portugal). See further, in relation to France, Dock (1963); Darras (1887); Rivière (1897).

[9] For the text, see LCD (1889), vol I, 11. See also the further laws of 19 July 1791 and 30 Aug 1792: LCD (1889), vol I, 12–13.

[10] For the text, see LCD (1889), vol I, 15–17.

[11] See generally Jane C Ginsburg, 'A Tale of Two Copyrights: Literary Property in Revolutionary France and America', in Brad Sherman and Alain Strowel (eds), *Of Authors And Origins: Essays On Copyright* (1994), and sources cited therein.

This new conception of authors' rights had a great effect on the law of France's neighbours, particularly during the period of French military and diplomatic ascendancy over the next two decades. Belgium came directly under French jurisdiction from 1795 following its joinder with France in that year, and, shortly afterwards the Netherlands, under the Batavian Republic, adopted similar laws.[12] The dissolution of the Holy Roman Empire in 1806 led to the end of imperial privileges in Germany, and to great confusion as authors and publishers then had to seek privileges from upwards of forty different petty sovereigns.[13] This led to pleas from publishers for a wider form of protection, and in article 18 of the Federal Act of Vienna of 8 June 1815 it was provided that, at its first meeting, the Diet of the new Germanic Confederation should consider the adoption of uniform measures to guarantee protection to authors and publishers against infringements of their works.[14] This project was slow in getting under way and, when it did, there were many delays. By the mid-nineteenth century however, most of the German states had some kind of copyright law. In general, these laws were based on a series of broad principles enunciated in resolutions made by the Federal Diet in 1837, but there were many differences in matters of detail. Uniform laws for the whole of Germany (excepting Austria) had to await the eve of the proclamation of the Second German Empire. In 1870, under the auspices of the short-lived North German Confederation, a law relating to the rights of authors in their writings, drawings, musical compositions, and dramatic works was passed.[15] This was extended to the whole of the Empire from 1 January 1871, and was supplemented by two further laws relating to the figurative arts and photographs in 1876.[16] A similar process occurred in Italy. After the Napoleonic period, most of the Italian states adopted some form of protection for the rights of authors, but following the proclamation of the new Kingdom of Italy in 1861 a common law on the subject was passed in 1865 and within five years this had been extended to the whole of the peninsula.[17] By the 1830s Spain had also adopted laws protecting authors.[18] Austria,[19] Portugal,[20] and the Scandinavian countries[21] followed suit over the next two decades, while the UK, in its inimitable fashion, continued throughout the century to extend the scope of its copyright protection through a series of enactments.[22] In the **1.05**

[12] LCD (1889), vol I, 458. [13] ibid, 52. [14] ibid.

[15] Law of 11 June 1870.

[16] Laws of 9 and 10 Jan 1876; see also LCD (1889), vol I, 53–4.

[17] LCD (1889), vol I, 378–9.

[18] Decree of 4 Jan 1834 and 5 May 1837; see also LCD (1889), vol I, 206.

[19] Law of 19 Oct 1846. [20] Civil Code, 1 July 1867.

[21] Law of 29 Dec 1857 (Denmark); Law of 8 Nov 1876 (Norway); and Law of 3 May 1867 (Sweden).

[22] eg the Sculpture Copyright Act 1814; the Dramatic Copyright Act 1833; the Lecture Copyright Act 1835; the Literary Copyright Act 1842; the Fine Arts Copyright Act 1862.

Americas, the United States had had a copyright law since 1790, a year before the initial French decrees. By 1886 (the year of the Berne Union's formation), the following European countries had general laws on copyright (many of which were revisions of earlier laws on the subject): Austria,[23] Belgium,[24] Denmark,[25] France,[26] Germany,[27] the UK,[28] Hungary,[29] Italy,[30] Luxembourg,[31] the Netherlands,[32] Norway,[33] Portugal,[34] Russia,[35] Spain,[36] Sweden,[37] and Switzerland.[38] This was also true of eight American states: Bolivia,[39] Chile,[40] Columbia,[41] Guatemala,[42] Haiti,[43] Mexico,[44] Peru,[45] and the United States.[46] A number of other countries protected authors' rights in a partial or incidental fashion through provisions in their civil, criminal, and press laws.[47]

---

[23] Law of 19 Oct 1846 (text in LCD (1889), vol I, 123–8).

[24] Law of 22 Mar 1886 (text in LCD (1889), vol I, 167–83).

[25] Laws of 29 Dec 1857, 31 Mar 1864, 24 Mar 1865 and Amending Laws of 10 Apr 1865, 23 Feb 1866, 21 Feb 1868, 24 May 1879, and 12 Apr 1889 (texts in LCD (1889), vol I, 181–203).

[26] Laws of 13–19 Jan 1791, 19 July–6 Aug 1791, 30 Aug 1792, 19 July 1793, 1 Sept 1793, 13 June 1795; Decrees of 22 Mar 1805, 29 Mar 1805, 8 June 1806, 20 Feb 1809, 5 Feb 1810; Penal Code 1810; Decrees of 6 July 1810, 15 Oct 1812; Ordinance of 6 June 1814; Law of 6 May 1841; Ordinance of 13 Dec 1842; Law of 3 Aug 1844; Decree-Law of 28 Mar 1852; Law of 8–18 Apr 1854; Decrees of 9 Dec 1857 and 6 Jan 1864; Laws of 16 May 1866, 14 July 1866, 29 July 1881, and 29 Oct 1887 (texts in LCD (1889), vol I, 11–50).

[27] Laws of 11 June 1870, 9 Jan 1876, and 10 Jan 1876 (texts in LCD (1889), vol I, 55–93).

[28] See n 22 above.

[29] Law of 26 Apr–4 May 1884 (text in LCD (1889), vol I, 142–62).

[30] Laws of 10 Aug 1875 and 18 May 1882, and Decree of 19 Sept 1882 (texts in LCD (1889), vol I, 379–99).

[31] Law of 25 Jan 1817 (text of this, and Amending Laws in LCD (1889), vol I, 407–22).

[32] Law of 28 June 1881 (text in LCD (1889), vol I, 459–66).

[33] Laws of 8 June 1876, 12 May 1877, and 20 June 1882 (texts in LCD (1889), vol I, 437–56).

[34] Provisions of the Civil Code of 1 July 1867 and the Penal Code 1886 (texts in LCD (1889), vol I, 467–76).

[35] Regulations of 1857 relating to Censorship of the Press (revised edition 1886) (text in LCD (1889), vol I, 485–504) and, in Finland, the Law of 15 Mar 1880 (text in LCD (1889), vol I, 505–16).

[36] Law of 10 Jan 1879 (text in LCD (1889), vol I, 207–27).

[37] Laws of 3 May 1867, 10 Aug 1877, and 10 Jan 1883 (texts in LCD (1889), vol I, 521–30).

[38] Law of 23 Apr 1883 (text in LCD (1889), vol I, 532–3).

[39] Law of 13 Aug 1879 (text in LCD (1889), vol II, 47–56).

[40] Law of 24 July 1834 (text in LCD (1889), vol II, 60–2).

[41] Law of 26 Oct 1879 (text in LCD (1889), vol II, 66–84).

[42] Decree of 29 Oct 1879 (text in LCD (1889), vol II, 117–24).

[43] Law of 8 Oct 1885 (text in LCD (1889), vol II, 125–6).

[44] Relevant provisions of the Civil Code 1871 (texts in LCD (1889), vol II, 131–52).

[45] Law of 3 Nov 1849 (text in LCD (1889), vol II, 157–8).

[46] Laws of 8 July 1870 and 18 June 1874 (text in LCD (1889), vol II, 106–16).

[47] eg Argentina, Brazil, Egypt, Greece, Costa Rica, Honduras, Paraguay, Romania, Turkey, Uruguay, Venezuela, and Salvador. See generally LCD (1889), vols I and II. Venezuela and Ecuador adopted general copyright laws in the following year, as did Japan: 12 May 1887 (Venezuela), 3 Aug 1887 (Ecuador), and 28 Dec 1887 (Japan).

Some of these statutory provisions, in particular the later ones, were more comprehensive than the French ones.[48] During the nineteenth century, French copyright law was developed as much through the jurisprudence as through legislative enactments, although, as we shall see, in the middle part of the century there were several very significant enactments which kept the French law on copyright the most generous to authors in Europe.[49] The influence of France was also to be seen, in varying degrees, in the other continental European laws, whereas in the case of the United States and the British colonies and possessions the models were to be found in the numerous Copyright Acts of the UK. Closer similarities were also to be seen where one country had consciously followed or adopted the law of another, as in the case of the Belgian law of 1886 which was really a codification of the French law. Again, in Germany, the resolutions of the Diet of the German Confederation led to a considerable uniformity between the laws of the different German-speaking states. Likewise, the laws of the Scandinavian countries were very similar, while the Spanish law was found reflected in the laws of the Spanish-speaking South American countries. **1.06**

(3) The principal provisions of national copyright laws

Despite these broad similarities, great differences still remained between the provisions of the various national copyright laws: while the problems addressed might be the same, the solutions adopted were often extremely varied. For our present purposes, a brief comparative survey[50] of these national measures is of considerable value in illuminating the efforts that began to be made from 1840 onwards towards achieving some kind of international copyright law. They are best dealt with under the following heads: (a) the kinds of works protected, (b) duration of protection, (c) rights recognized, (d) restrictions on the exercise of these rights, and (e) formalities required for protection. A consideration of these matters leads naturally to a consideration of the extent to which these national laws protected foreign works and authors, and will help explain why these countries began to enter into international copyright agreements with each other. **1.07**

(a) Works protected

In general, protection was extended to all intellectual productions having a literary or artistic character, as well as to works intended for performance, that **1.08**

[48] eg those of Italy, Spain, Belgium, and Germany.

[49] Notably the Decree-Law of 28 Mar 1852 (concerning the protection in France of foreign authors) and the Decree of 14 July 1866 (concerning the duration of protection).

[50] For a more detailed survey of these matters, see LCD (1889), vol I, Introduction, and Ladas (1938), 30–44.

is, musical, dramatic, and dramatico-musical works.[51] Many of these laws included, among the works protected, oral works which had not been fixed in any material form, such as sermons, speeches, lectures, and the like.[52] Some countries, principally the UK,[53] accorded protection to different kinds of works in a series of separate enactments, while others did so within a single legislative instrument.[54]

1.09 However, while there were fundamental points of identity between the works protected by each country, there were marked divergences in relation to particular categories. As will be seen below, these differences were to give rise to considerable debate in the early years of the Berne Convention. One instance, noted in the preceding paragraph, was in relation to oral works. Another concerned architectural works. Most countries protected architectural plans, but allowed the reproduction of the structures or edifices built from those plans.[55] Under Russian law, however, both plans and structures were protected,[56] and while there was no special law on the matter in France, the balance of opinion in that country was in favour of protecting both.[57] A further point of difference arose concerning photographs. The laws of some countries, in particular those of France, Italy, and Austria, did not deal with them expressly, and there was accordingly some controversy in those countries as to whether photographs should be protected as works of art.[58] A number of other countries expressly accorded photographs the same length of protection as for other artistic works,[59] while another group of countries gave protection but only for a shorter

---

[51] Except, however, in the Netherlands where artistic works were not protected under art 1 of the 1881 Law and in Guatemala where only literary property was protected: Guatemalan Decree on Literary Property of 29 Oct 1879.

[52] eg the Netherlands Law of 1881, art 1; Austrian Law of 1846, art 4(b); Mexican Civil Code, art 1249.

[53] See para 1.05, n 22 above. See also the separate German Laws of 1870 and 1876, those of France and those of the Scandinavian countries.

[54] These were usually the later laws, eg the Hungarian Law of 26 Apr–4 May 1884, the Belgian Law of 22 Mar 1886, the Spanish Law of 10 Jan 1879, and the Netherlands Law of 28 June 1881.

[55] See eg the German Law of 11 June 1870, art 43, and Law of 9 Jan 1876, art 3; Danish Law of 31 Mar 1864, art 4; Hungarian Law of 4 May 1884, arts 66–7; Swedish Law of 10 Aug 1877, art 1. See also Swiss Law of 1883, art 6 which gave the purchaser of architectural plans the right to reproduce them, unless the contrary was stipulated.

[56] Russian Regulations of 1857 relating to Censorship of the Press (revised edition 1886) (text in LCD (1889), vol I, 485–504), art 41(4)(a).

[57] LCD (1889), vol I, xlii.

[58] LCD (1889), vol I, xliii, 15 (n 2) (re France) and 381 (n 1) (re Italy). See also [1889] DA 25, 35, and 47 (Mar, Apr, and May), and *Juristisches Blätter* [1885] nos 28 and 29, [1889] nos 32 and 33.

[59] Spanish Regulation of 10 Jan 1879, art 1; US Copyright Act 1870, s 4952; UK Fine Arts Copyright Act 1862, s 1; Mexican Civil Code, art 1306; Russian Regulations of 1857 relating to Censorship of the Press (revised edition 1886) (text in LCD (1889), vol I, 485–504), art 53.

term, usually five years.[60] Yet another category of work which was later to be protected under the Berne Convention was that of choreographic works.[61] Prior to 1886, these appear only to have been given express legislative protection in Italy.[62]

(b) Duration of protection

There was great diversity here. Only two countries, both in Latin America, gave protection in perpetuity: Guatemala[63] and Mexico.[64] In other countries, the formula that was generally adopted was a term comprising the life of the author together with a certain period after his death (so as to give the possibility of some benefit to his beneficiaries or assignees). However, there were considerable differences in this post-mortem period. Many countries, following the example set by France in its 1866 Law,[65] adopted a fifty-year period,[66] but several had periods of eighty years[67] while a number had lesser terms, ranging between five and ten years and thirty years.[68] Despite these differing post-mortem periods, one contemporary French commentator, Charles Lyon-Caen, characterized the laws of these countries as having three features in common: **1.10**

1. they accorded the author an exclusive right throughout the remainder of his life;

---

[60] eg the German Law of 10 Jan 1876, art 6; Danish Law of 24 Mar 1865, art 1; Finnish Law of 1880, art 17; Hungarian Law of 1884, art 70; Swiss Law of 1883, art 9(b).

[61] These were not expressly included within the expression 'literary and artistic works' in art 2 of the Convention until the 1908 Revision: see para 3.11 below.

[62] Law of 18 May 1882, art 1(a).

[63] Guatemalan Decree of 29 Oct 1879, art 5.

[64] Mexican Civil Code 1871, art 1253. Note, however, that in the case of performing rights in relation to musical and dramatic works, protection was limited to a period of the life of the author plus thirty years: art 1284. In its Law of 12 May 1887, art 6, Venezuela also opted for perpetuity of protection.

[65] Law of 14 July 1866, art 1.

[66] Belgian Law of 1886, art 2; Danish Law of 21 Feb 1868, art 1 (extending the thirty-year period fixed by the earlier laws of 29 Dec 1857 and 23 Feb 1866); Hungarian Law of 1884, art 11; Monégasque Ordinance of 27 Feb 1889, arts 1 and 8; Norwegian Law of 8 June 1876, art 7; Portuguese Civil Code 1867, arts 576 and 579; Russian Regulations of 1857 relating to Censorship of the Press (revised edition 1886) (text in LCD (1889), vol I, 485–504), art 7; Bolivian Decree of 13 Aug 1879, arts 7 and 10. In Sweden, the exclusive reproduction right lasted for fifty years *post mortem auctoris*, but only for five years in the case of performing rights: Law of 10 Aug 1877, arts 7, 13, and 14.

[67] Spanish Law of 1879, art 6 (but only for the life of the author plus twenty-eight years if assigned before death and then for another twenty-eight years in favour of his beneficiaries): art 6; Columbian Law of 29 Oct 1886, art 10.

[68] Swedish Law of 10 Aug 1879, arts 13 and 14 (five years *post mortem auctoris* for performing rights); Austrian Law of 1846, art 13 (thirty years for publication and reproduction rights) and art 22 (ten years for performing rights); Peruvian Law of 3 Nov 1849, art 3 (twenty years); Brazilian Criminal Code, art 261 (ten years); Chilean Law of 24 July, arts 1 and 2 (five years); German Law of 11 June 1870, art 8; and Swiss Law of 1883, art 2 (thirty years).

2. they accorded a further period of protection following the author's death before the work fell into the public domain; the total length of protection therefore depended upon the length of the author's life; and
3. they gave the same rights after the author's death to his beneficiaries or legal representatives.[69]

There were a number of notable exceptions to this general system. In the Netherlands, the period was fifty years from the date of deposit following first publication, or the life of the author if still alive at the end of this time.[70] In the case of unpublished works, the period was the life of the author plus thirty years.[71] However, the performing right in relation to published dramatic and dramatico-musical works was severely limited, being ten years from the date of deposit.[72] In the United States the period was twenty-eight years from the date of registration of the work, but this could be extended to forty-two years by the author if he were still living at the end of this time, or by his spouse or children.[73] In Greece, which only accorded protection to the reproduction right, the period was fifteen years from first publication.[74] In the UK, the period of protection depended upon the kind of work: in the case of literary, dramatic and musical works, it was the life of the author plus seven years, or forty-two years, whichever was the longer.[75] For prints and engravings, it was twenty-eight years after first publication,[76] while paintings, drawings, lithographs, and photographs received protection for the life of the artist plus seven years.[77] In the case of sculptures, however, the period of protection was only fourteen years, with the possibility of a further fourteen years if the artist were still alive at the end of this time.[78] Finally, in Italy a special system obtained. There, an author enjoyed an exclusive reproduction right during his life; if he died before the passage of forty years from first publication, his successors enjoyed this right until the end of that period.[79] However, after this a second period of forty years began when third parties might, if they wished, reproduce the work, subject to paying the author's beneficiaries a fee fixed by the law.[80] This attempt to strike a balance between the rights of the author and the interests of the public was known in French as *le système du domaine public payant*, which means literally 'paying public domain'. In the UK, analogous provision was made, through the device of a compulsory licence which could be granted by the Privy Council where, after the author's death, the person entitled to the reproduction right had refused

---

69 LCD (1889), vol I, xxxiv.
70 Law of 28 June 1881, art 13.
71 ibid, arts 14 and 15(1) (performing rights).
72 ibid, art 15(2).
73 Copyright Act 1870, ss 4953 and 4954.
74 Penal Code 1833, art 432.
75 Literary Copyright Act 1842, s 3.
76 Prints and Engravings Act 1766, s 7.
77 Fine Arts Copyright Act 1862, s 1.
78 Sculpture Copyright Act 1814, s 1.
79 Decree of 19 Sept 1882, art 9.
80 ibid.

to republish or authorize the republication of a book.[81] In both Italy and the UK, these regimes only applied in the case of the reproduction right. Under Italian law, performing rights were protected for eighty years from the time of first performance, and after this time performance of dramatic and musical works was in the public domain.[82] In the UK, the duration of performing rights was the same as for reproduction rights in relation to literary, dramatic, and musical works.[83]

(c) *Rights recognized*

The basic rights recognized were the exclusive rights of reproduction and public performance. These rights were enforceable by civil and criminal proceedings in most countries, and were capable of being assigned or otherwise dealt with by the authors upon whom they were conferred. However, as might be expected, there were a number of different national approaches to these matters. **1.11**

In relation to reproduction there were significant differences as to the detail with which this right was defined in the legislation and in the jurisprudence, as well as in its scope.[84] An important question arose concerning the right to translate literary and dramatic works, and the length of time for which this was to be protected. Although it can be argued that translation is simply one of the ways in which works of these kinds may be reproduced, only a few countries took this approach and assimilated translation rights completely to that of reproduction. This seems to have been the case in France, in the absence of any legislative enactment,[85] and was expressly provided for in those countries which derived their copyright laws directly from France, such as Belgium[86] and Haiti.[87] It was also allowed in Spain,[88] Portugal,[89] and several Spanish American countries.[90] However, in a number of other countries, it was required that the author should have expressly reserved his translation right at the time of first publication of his work (usually on the title page or in some other prominent place), and that he should have made or authorized the making of a translation within a given time **1.12**

[81] Copyright Act 1842, s 5.
[82] Decree of 19 Sept 1882, art 10.
[83] Copyright Act 1842, s 20.
[84] Compare eg the detail of arts 4 and 5 of the Austrian Law of 1846, or art 5 of the German Law of 11 June 1870, with the broad formulation of art 1 of the Belgian Law of 1886. As to the jurisprudence, compare that of France and the UK: T E Scrutton, *The Laws of Copyright* (1883), ch VII, and E Pouillet, *Traité théorique et pratique de la propriété littéraire et artistique et du droit de representation*, 2nd edn (1894), 451ff.
[85] LCD (1889), vol I, li.
[86] Law of 1886, art 12.
[87] Law of 8 Oct 1885, art 5. Similar laws were adopted in 1889 by Monaco (Law of 27 Feb 1889, art 4) and Tunisia (Law of 15 June 1889, art 4).
[88] Law of 19 Jan 1879, arts 1, 2, 10, and 13.
[89] Civil Code 1867, art 577.
[90] Bolivian Law of 15 Aug 1879, art 8; Columbian Law of 26 Oct 1886, art 39.

after this date.[91] Even where these conditions were complied with, the translation right was often of a far shorter duration than the reproduction right,[92] and usually covered only the making of translations into the language or languages for which the reservation had been made or into which the translation had actually been made. There was a range of variations to these general rules. For example, in Germany translation rights in works in 'dead languages' were protected for the whole copyright term without any need for reservation, as were translations from one language into another where the work was originally published in both languages.[93] Again, in the Scandinavian countries, only rights as regards translations from one dialect to another of the same language were reserved (Danish, Norwegian, and Swedish being regarded as 'dialects of the same language' for this purpose).[94] In addition, in many countries special restrictions applied in the case of foreign works and authors.[95] This last problem is considered below in more detail.[96] For the moment, it suffices to note that the question of translation rights is obviously of more importance to foreign, rather than national, authors, at least as far as most monoglot countries are concerned. This was something which was to attract a lot of attention as the century progressed, and was to become the subject of an increasing number of bilateral agreements between states. These agreements often had the result that one regime governing translations would apply to national authors under national law, another regime to foreign authors who were covered by the bilateral agreement, and yet another to foreign authors who were not covered by the agreement (and were usually denied any protection at all).

1.13 Although at this time the reproduction of musical works by mechanical means, such as piano rolls, musical boxes, phonographs, and the like, was in its infancy, several countries had laws dealing expressly with this problem. Under the French Law of 10 March 1886, it was provided that the manufacture and sale of

---

[91] See eg the German Law of 1870, art 6 (a year in the case of literary works, six months in the case of dramatic works); Hungarian Law of 1884, art 7 (translation to be commenced within one year and finished within three years; only six months in the case of dramatic works); the Netherlands Law 1881, art 5 (three years); UK International Copyright Act 1852, ss 1–5 (ten years); Austrian Law of 1846, art 5 (six months).

[92] eg in Italy, where there was no need to make any express reservation of translation rights, the latter only lasted for ten years: Italian Law of 1882, art 12. See also the Swiss Law of 1883, art 2 (five years). Compare these laws with that in the UK where the translation had to appear within ten years, but was then protected for the whole of the duration of the reproduction right. Likewise in the United States, the same regime applied so long as a reservation was made: Copyright Act 1870, s 4953.

[93] German Law of 1870, art 6. See also the Hungarian Law of 1884, art 7, and the Norwegian Law of 8 June 1876, art 15.

[94] Norwegian Law of 8 June 1876, art 15; Danish Law of 24 May 1879, art 1; Swedish Law of 10 Aug 1877, art 2.

[95] See eg the Spanish Law of 1879, arts 12–15; Portuguese Civil Code 1867, art 577.

[96] See paras 1.25–1.28 below.

instruments serving to reproduce musical works mechanically was not an infringement of the copyright in those works; this immunity, however, did not extend to the making of public performances by these instruments. The Swiss Law of 1883 also had similar provisions (the Swiss being the leading manufacturers of musical boxes at that time).[97] With the advent of commercially viable phonographic sound recording in the last decade of the century, the scope for mechanical reproduction of musical works expanded enormously, and this was a problem which was to become of the greatest concern to copyright owners, not to mention national legislators and the early revision conferences of the Berne Convention after 1886.[98]

In the case of artistic works, there were important national differences concerning the scope of the reproduction right. For example, in some countries the copyright in an artistic work in one dimension could be infringed by the reproduction of that work in another dimension, for instance, by the making of a sculpture of a painting.[99] However, in other countries such reproductions were not considered as infringements.[100] Again, where artistic works were applied industrially, some countries, such as France, simply regarded this as one of the ways in which the exclusive reproduction right could be exercised.[101] Other countries, on the contrary, limited the artist's rights in such cases,[102] denied them altogether,[103] or, as in the case of the UK, denied them while providing a shorter-term, alternative mode of protection through a registered designs system.[104] **1.14**

There were further national differences with respect to performing rights in published musical and dramatic works. Several countries required the author to **1.15**

[97] Law of 1883, art 11; see also LCD (1889), vol I, 547, n 547.

[98] See para 3.17 below.

[99] Austrian Law of 1846, art 3; Hungarian Law of 1884, art 6(1); Belgian Law of 1886, art 1; Spanish Law of 1879, art 3(3). In France, where there was no express legislative provision to this effect, it seemed to be allowed in the jurisprudence: LCD (1889), vol I, xlvi, and Pouillet (n 84 above), nos 574–6, 551–7. In Italy, the reproduction of an artistic work in another dimension was regarded as a translation and was therefore subject to similar limitations: Italian Law of 1882, art 12(1).

[100] See eg the German Law of 9 Jan 1876, art 6(2); Finnish Law of 1880, art 16; Norwegian Law of 12 May 1877, art 11; Russian Regulations of 1857 relating to Censorship of the Press (revised edition 1886) (text in LCD (1889), vol I, 485–504), art 43. This also seemed to be the position in the UK: see *Hanfstaengl* v *Empire Palace* [1894] 2 Ch 1.

[101] France: LCD (1889), vol I, xlvii; Belgian Law of 1886, art 21; Spanish Law of 1879, art 3(4) (by implication).

[102] eg the Danish Law of 31 Mar 1864, art 6 (if reservation was made, ten years' protection).

[103] See eg the Finnish Law of 1880, art 18(3); Mexican Civil Code 1871, art 1322(17); Norwegian Law of 12 May 1877, art 11b; Russian Regulations of 1857 relating to Censorship of the Press (revised edition 1886) (text in LCD (1889), vol I, 485–504), art 43 (formerly art 336).

[104] UK Patents, Trade Marks and Registered Designs Act 1883.

reserve these rights expressly in advance on each copy of the published work,[105] and in Switzerland they were subject to a kind of compulsory licence which allowed other parties to perform the work if a minimum payment were made to the author.[106] A number of countries also forbade the unauthorized making of arrangements, transcriptions, and variations of musical works,[107] but some permitted the incorporation of a motif from one work into another where the latter constituted a new work.[108] However, in the last instance, distinctions of this kind were frequently difficult to make, and led to uncertainty in these countries as to what constituted infringement of a musical work.[109]

(d) Restrictions on exercise of rights

1.16 The exercise of the rights outlined above, particularly the reproduction right in relation to literary works, was subject to a number of significant restrictions in favour of members of the public. These varied from country to country. In relation to literary works, the taking of selected extracts without the author's consent was generally allowed when this was done for teaching purposes or for inclusion in a chrestomathy,[110] and, in some instances, for use in religious services and other ceremonial purposes.[111] Some laws, such as those of the Germans, Austrians, and Danes, were quite detailed, covering a wide range of related uses of a 'public nature'. At the other extreme was the Belgian provision which said simply:

> 13. The right of the author does not exclude the right to make citations when these are made for the purposes of criticism, polemical discussion or instruction.

Nevertheless, whatever their detail, these provisions were often difficult to apply, and accordingly certain laws sought to apply quantitative limits on the extracts which could be taken[112] or prohibited such borrowings before the passage of a

---

105 UK Musical Copyright Act 1882, s 1 (for musical works); Netherlands Law of 1881, art 12 (for dramatico-musical and dramatic works); Finnish law of 1880, art 12 (dramatic works).

106 Swiss Law of 1883, art 7.

107 Spanish Law of 1879, art 7; Belgian Law of 1886, art 17. This was also the position in French jurisprudence: LCD (1889), vol I, xlv–xlvi.

108 German Law of 11 June 1870, art 46; Austrian Law of 1846, art 6; Italian Law of 1882, art 3; Norwegian Law of 8 June 1876, art 13.

109 LCD (1889), vol I, xlvi.

110 See eg the German Law of 11 June 1870, art 7(a); Austrian Law of 1846, art 5(b); Hungarian Law of 1884, art 9(1); Belgian Law of 1886, art 13; Danish Law of 29 Dec 1857, art 13(5); Finnish Law of 1880, art 9; Norwegian Law, art 16(b); Russian Regulations of 1857 relating to Censorship of the Press (revised edition 1886) (text in LCD (1889), vol I, 485–504), art 16; Swiss Law of 1883, art 11(1).

111 Austrian Law, art 5(b); Hungarian Law, art 9(1); Norwegian Law, art 16(b).

112 Austrian Law, art 5(b) (for periodical articles, no more than two instalments in a year); Russian Regulations, art 17 (formerly art 299) (citations not to be more than a third of the length of the work borrowed from, and the new work to be at least twice as long).

given period from the date of first publication of the work.[113] Under most laws it was necessary to indicate the name of the author of the work from which the extract was taken.[114]

Another problem in relation to literary works concerned the reproduction of newspaper articles. Here, in general, a regime unfavourable to the interests of authors prevailed. Most laws permitted articles from newspapers and reviews to be freely reproduced, unless this had been expressly prohibited in advance by the author.[115] In the case of 'political articles', however, such a reservation was frequently not possible, and these works were, in effect, in the public domain.[116] Some laws required the source of the article taken and the author's name to be indicated,[117] and some laws also made distinctions between different categories of articles.[118] However, there were many differences, both of substance and detail, in these laws, and these differences in national approach were to give rise to lengthy discussions in the early conferences on the Berne Convention when it was sought to reach agreement on a uniform set of rules to govern such borrowings.[119] These differences may also, in part at least, have arisen from conflicting views of the purpose of such provisions. On the one hand, it was theoretically possible to argue that the articles excluded did not fall within the ambit of literary works, at least where they were simple news reports or factual accounts. This was on the basis that copyright laws should protect only the form in which works were expressed, not their ideas or factual foundations. Such an approach therefore made it difficult to allow borrowings from articles of a more 'literary' nature. On the other hand, there was a strong public-interest argument that, even in the case of articles of this second kind, borrowings should be allowed where this had beneficial effects as far as education, research, or general information were concerned. **1.17**

A further public-interest limitation on copyright in literary or artistic works was to be found in a number of laws which provided for either the grant of compulsory licences or the expropriation of the work to the public domain where it had not been republished after a certain period of time. An example of the first kind **1.18**

---

113 Danish Law, art 13(5) (a year); Norwegian Law, art 16(b) (a year).

114 See n 110 above.

115 See eg the German Law of 11 June 1870, art 7(b); Hungarian Law, art 9(b) (this applied only to isolated communications extracted from newspapers); Italian Law, art 26; Swiss Law, art 11(4); Netherlands Law, art 7; Norwegian Law of 8 June 1876, art 17; Spanish Law, art 31 (*écrits et télegrammes*).

116 See eg the Swiss Law, art 11(4).

117 See eg the Italian Law, art 26; Netherlands Law, art 7; Spanish Law, art 31; UK International Copyright Act 1852, s 57.

118 See eg the Hungarian Law, art (2) (excluding literary and scientific articles from its scope); Norwegian Law, art 17 (excluding poetry and scientific articles).

119 See paras 3.06 and 3.15 below.

of provision occurred in the UK where the Judicial Committee of the Privy Council was empowered to grant a licence to republish a book which was out of print if the copyright owner had refused to do so after receiving the appropriate notice.[120] Examples of the second kind of provision were to be found in Spain,[121] Denmark,[122] and Norway[123] where works would fall into the public domain if they had not been available for given periods of time, and in Italy,[124] Mexico,[125] Guatemala,[126] and Portugal[127] where expropriation by public authorities for public purposes was provided for, subject to particular conditions.

(e) Formalities

1.19 By 1886, most national copyright laws required an author to comply with some kind of formality before he gained protection. There were considerable differences in the nature of these requirements. Under some laws, the deposit of copies of the work was necessary,[128] while other laws required registration of the work[129] or the making of a declaration (often together with some kind of deposit). In some countries, these requirements differed according to the nature of the work, the most notorious example of this being found in the various British Copyright Acts.[130] Failure to comply with formalities within the prescribed times also had differing effects. In some countries, it meant that the work fell into the public domain.[131] On the other hand, in a number of other countries, including France,[132] it meant simply that the copyright owner could not enforce his rights until such time as his omission was rectified. This second approach was consistent with the theoretical basis of French *droit d'auteur*, according to which formalities were only declaratory of the pre-existing natural right of property in a work and had nothing to do with its creation.[133] Following this through to its logical conclusion, some countries (though not France

120 Literary Copyright Act 1842, s 5.
121 Spanish Law of 1879, art 40.
122 Danish Law of 29 Dec 1857, art 12.
123 Norwegian Law of 8 June 1876, art 19.
124 Italian Law of 1882, art 20.
125 Mexican Civil Code 1871, art 1381.
126 Guatemalan Decree of 29 Oct 1879, art 21.
127 Portuguese Civil Code 1867, art 587.
128 See eg the French Law of 29 July 1881, arts 3 and 4.
129 See eg the Spanish Law of 1879, arts 33–4; Austrian Law of 1846, arts 42–4; Norwegian Law of 20 June 1882, arts 1–12; Italian Law of 1882, arts 21–31; Portuguese Civil Code, arts 603–6; Netherlands Law, arts 10–11; Russian Regulations of 1857 relating to Censorship of the Press (revised edition 1886) (text in LCD (1889), vol I, 485–504), arts 10, 44, and 52; US Copyright Act 1870, ss 4948ff. For a summary of these different requirements, see Ladas (1938), 35–8.
130 Compare the Literary Copyright Act 1842, ss 11–14, the Fine Arts Copyright Act 1862, s 4, and the Sculpture Copyright Act 1814, s 1.
131 See eg the Spanish Law, arts 38 and 39; Italian Law, art 28.
132 French Law of 29 July 1881, art 4. See also the British laws referred to in n 130 above.
133 See Ladas (1938), 5–10.

herself) had abolished these kinds of formalities,[134] except in certain special circumstances, such as in the case of pseudonymous or anonymous works, where questions of proof in such matters as time of publication might be of importance.[135] In those countries where it was still necessary to comply with formalities, this often involved considerable expense and trouble for both national and foreign authors, and the only useful end that was served was evidentiary.

B. The Problem of International Piracy of Works

Thus far, we have only discussed the protection given to literary and artistic works under national laws in the nineteenth century. There is, however, an equally, if not more, important international dimension to be considered. The printed word, the musical composition, and the artistic creation know no national boundaries. They may just as readily be appreciated by the citizens of one country as by those of another, even where translation into another language from the original, in the case of a book or a play, is necessary for this potential to be fully realized. As a consequence, unauthorized reproduction and use of foreign works were, for a long time, established features of European cultural and social life, and continued to be so for a considerable period after the adoption of national copyright laws by most countries.[136] 'Counterfeiting' or 'piracy' were the words most often used to describe this form of 'reaping without sowing'.[137] Nevertheless, the attitudes of most countries to this practice were highly anomalous: while protecting the works of their national authors, they did not regard the unauthorized exploitation of foreign works as either unfair or immoral. Indeed, in some countries, it was considered an honourable practice, contributing to the spread of learning and enlightenment to the local populace, and enabling this to be done at considerably less cost than would have been the case had copies of the original work been obtained from their source.[138] The **1.20**

[134] eg Germany, Belgium, the Netherlands, and Switzerland.

[135] See eg German Law of 11 June 1870, art 6 and Law of 9 Jan 1876, art 9 (anonymous works); Belgian Law of 1886, arts 4 and 11 (posthumous works and governmental publications).

[136] For two interesting accounts of this history, see W Briggs, *The Law of International Copyright* (1906), ch II ('Briggs (1906)'), and Darras (1887), Part I, ch 1. See further B Sherman and L Bently, *The Making of Modern Intellectual Property Law: The British Experience, 1760–1911* (1999), 112–14, in particular the material in nn 55–9.

[137] 'Piracy' is the term generally used by Briggs (1906), and '*contrefaçon*' by Darras (1887).

[138] See eg the comments made by a Committee of the French Chamber of Peers in 1833 on a proposed new copyright bill to establish a system of reciprocal protection between France and England: 'The only English books reprinted at Paris, and sold at a very moderate price compared with English editions, give buyers and French booksellers a real advantage. In England, where the cost of manufacture is greater than in France, no French work is reprinted. Reciprocity between the two countries will be most favourable to Great Britain; and will deprive us, without any

circulation of pirate copies, moreover, was not necessarily confined to the pirate's own country; as these were more cheaply produced, it was often profitable to export them back to the work's country of origin where they could undercut the price of copies of the original work.

1.21 The history of international piracy of works goes back nearly as far as that of the system of privileges; and, at times, this activity even received official support and patronage.[139] Countries with high levels of literary and artistic output were clearly most at risk, particularly where the pirate printers and publishers were resident in a country which was geographically proximate or which shared a common tongue. Thus, English authors suffered from the activities of Irish pirates until the Act of Union with Ireland in 1800, and from those of United States' publishing houses throughout the nineteenth century. Significant piracies of English works were also carried on in France, the Netherlands, and Germany until the middle of the century.[140] French authors, in turn, suffered from the depredations of pirates in Switzerland, Germany, the Netherlands, and Belgium. These injuries were perhaps even more severe than those suffered by English authors, as the long land frontier of France made it easier for pirate copies to pass into the French market. The worst of these offenders were the Belgians, which is an ironic circumstance in the light of their country's adoption, later in the nineteenth century, of a highly progressive law on domestic and international copyright. Nevertheless, it took the French Government a long time before it was able to secure protection for its authors from Belgian infringements.[141] Piracy was also rampant in the German-speaking states, and only diminished when the process of political unification began.[142] Similar piracies also occurred in the Italian states until their unification.[143]

1.22 The prevention of this international piracy was the principal reason for the gradual development of international copyright relations during the nineteenth century. The arguments for and against the protection of foreign authors at this time were analogous to those which are made today in the context of developing

compensation, of the means of procuring at a reasonable price English books of which the price is excessive when it is necessary to import them from beyond the seas.' (Translated by Briggs (1906), 38. For the original French text, see Darras (1887), 214.)

139 Dr Briggs cites two examples of such official support: in France, in the sixteenth century, the King's Printer had the sole right to reprint foreign works, while in the Netherlands, nearly three centuries later, King William directly subsidized such activities: Briggs (1906), 36.

140 Darras (1887), 145ff; Briggs (1906), 49ff.

141 Not until the French-Belgian Convention of 22 Aug 1852; see para 1.29 below.

142 Briggs (1906), 54ff.

143 See also International Copyright Office, *Recueil des conventions et traités concernant la propriété littéraire et artistique, publiés en français et dans les langues des pays contractants avec une introduction et des notices* (1904), 345ff ('*Recueil* (1904)').

countries.[144] On the one hand, it could be said that the activities of the pirate printers resulted in cheaper copies and greater availability of the work in question. In countries hungry for knowledge and new sources of entertainment and enlightenment, this could be postulated as an overriding necessity, and this argument, in fact, formed the basis of the United States' persistent refusal to protect foreign works throughout the nineteenth century.[145] It could also be argued that the public in the work's country of origin would benefit if cheaper, albeit pirate, copies became available there. On the other hand, there was, of course, a strong moral argument that the author or his assignee was being robbed of the fruits of the author's creativity, labour, and investment, and that this was unfair. Furthermore, a more pragmatic argument could be mounted to the effect that, if an author was deprived of his reward in this way, this would diminish the incentive for him to engage in creative activity, with the result that both his own, and other, countries would soon be the poorer.

These various arguments can be, and often are, couched in more absolute terms—indeed the widespread use of the term 'piracy' in this context conveys with it some kind of moral condemnation of the practice at the very outset. Nevertheless, things were never quite as bad as may first appear from the above description. Thus, in the early years when the system of privileges was still prevalent in most countries and the notion of authors' rights had scarcely emerged, the widescale reproduction of works from abroad could hardly be regarded as a contravention of either these inchoate rights or of any privilege as the latter could have only a national or local significance. Again, in later years it appears that authors quite often reached arrangements with foreign publishers and received remuneration for these foreign editions, even though they were entitled to no legal protection in those countries. This was particularly true in the United States where a system of 'courtesy copyright' operated for some time during the nineteenth century.[146] Under this, American publishers would refrain from publishing editions of works (usually of English origin) in respect of which one of their number had reached a publishing agreement with the author. This system of mutual self-restraint had a number of advantages: it meant that an American publisher could lay out the capital necessary for the publication of a new work without having to fear the appearance of rival editions; it also secured **1.23**

[144] See generally Chapter 14 below.

[145] On the early background to the position adopted by the USA, see J J Barnes, *Authors, Publishers and Politicians: The Quest for an Anglo-American Copyright Agreement 1815–1854* (1974).

[146] Briggs (1906), 111ff. See also G H Putnam, *International Copyright: Considered in Some of its Relations to Ethics and Political Economy* (1879), 45ff; J H Harper, *The House of Harper: A Century of Publishing* (1912), 107ff; Darras (1887), 162ff; Copyright Commission, *Report* (1878), paras 241–2.

the author some return (often quite substantial), and gave him a degree of control over the quality of the final product. Although there is evidence that English (and other European) authors suffered large losses as a result of the activities of United States publishers, at the same time a significant number of these authors still earned large sums from the North American market in the absence of formal legal protection.[147] A similar system seems also to have obtained in the Netherlands and certain of the German states.[148]

1.24 'Courtesy copyright', however, was only a very partial substitute, so far as authors were concerned, for the proper legal protection of their rights in other countries. The half-century preceding the formation of the Berne Union therefore saw a gradual move towards the elimination of international piracy and the consequential recognition of the rights of foreign authors in most European countries (the United States, however, remained aloof from this process). The reasons for this are complex and merit closer examination than is possible in the present book. Nevertheless, it seems correct to point to the operation of two important factors. The first was the strong and pervasive influence of the French doctrine of *droit d'auteur*, with the emphasis that this placed on the natural right of property of an author in his intellectual creation. French law led the way in relation to such issues as the subject matter protected, the scope of rights recognized, and the duration of those rights. More importantly, in a decree of 1852,[149] France extended the protection of its laws unilaterally to all works published abroad, without any requirement of reciprocity in relation to the protection of French works in those countries. The philosophical basis for this act of national altruism was that authors' rights, being natural rights of property, should not be restricted by artificial restraints such as nationality or geographical boundaries. These rights, therefore, were of a universal character, and the French decree was simply giving formal effect to what was already the case. At the same time, a practical motivation also lay behind the decree, and this leads us directly to the second important factor in the growth of international copyright relations during this period. France was eager to secure protection for her authors abroad, but had found that other nations, prior to 1852, were reluctant to enter agreements to this effect.[150] It was therefore hoped that the unilateral

[147] Note, however, the strong comments about his poor earnings from American publishers by Anthony Trollope in *An Autobiography* (1883; 3rd edn, 1946), 272–4.

[148] Briggs (1906), 111.

[149] Decree-Law of 28 Mar 1852.

[150] eg in Belgium, this did occur until the new law of 22 Mar 1886 was drafted: see the discussion of these preparatory drafts in LCD (1889), vol I, 169–70. Note the argument of Bastide that foreign authors were entitled to protection in France prior to this as a result of the revolutionary decrees: L Bastide, *L'Union de Berne de 1886 et la Protection internationale des droits des auteurs et des artistes* (1890), 14–25 ('Bastide (1890)'). Note further that France has now reintroduced the principle of reciprocity in relation to the protection of foreign works by Law No 64–689 of 8 July 1964, now codified at Code de la propriété intellectuelle, art L 111–4.

grant of protection in France to the works of foreign authors would encourage their countries to make agreements with France for the protection of French authors.[151] France's policy might be described as one of 'pragmatic altruism', that is, using its generosity towards foreigners as a means of 'shaming' countries to which those persons belonged into taking action. But France was not alone in her desire to gain protection for her authors abroad. The UK also sought, from the 1830s on, to enter into conventions with other countries to secure such protection. The French and British concern seems hardly surprising, given the pre-eminent position occupied by both Britain and France in the areas of literature and the arts; but their attitude was increasingly shared by most other European countries. Each had some kind of cultural product which it wished to protect abroad, and this included those countries, such as Belgium and the German states, which had long been the centres of international piracy. While 'free riding' has its advantages, there comes a point at which these are outweighed by its disadvantages. In the present context, this occurs when the productions of indigenous authors and artists begin to assume some significance, and there are real monetary gains as well as enhanced international prestige to be made from their export. While the point at which this happens is hardly susceptible of precise determination, it is difficult to envisage that many countries, in the absence of international coercion, would be tempted to be altruistic where there are clear economic benefits to be reaped from piracy. On the other hand, there is obviously a broad middle area where appeals to higher principle (whether or not coupled with pressure from outside sources) may be crucial in tipping the balance in favour of protecting foreign works in return for the protection of one's own authors. This point was clearly passed by most European countries by the middle of the nineteenth century. The steps by which this was achieved require consideration at two levels: first, the provisions of national laws concerning foreign authors, and secondly, the international agreements about these matters which were reached by various countries during this period.

C. The Protection of Foreign Works by National Laws

The only country which, by 1886, had followed France's example of unilateral protection of works published abroad was Belgium, which did so in its new law of that year.[152] However, so far as France was concerned, this extension of **1.25**

[151] Briggs (1906), 106 and 135, Darras (1887), 221ff. Such states would find themselves 'morally obliged' to accord reciprocal protection: Pataille and Huget, *Code international de la propriété littéraire et artistique*, 1st edn (1855), 56 ('Pataille and Huget (1855)').

[152] Belgian Law of 1886, art 38.

protection was not perhaps as generous as appeared at first sight. According to Darras and other leading authorities of the period, the effect of the 1852 French decree was simply to allow a foreign author to enjoy in France the rights given to him under the laws of his own country.[153] They were therefore not assimilated to French nationals, that is, were not accorded national treatment, and were entitled to no further rights under French law than they had under their own. As a consequence, if another country desired national treatment for its authors in France, it was still necessary for some further measure to be taken, perhaps pursuant to a specific treaty with that country.[154] The later Belgian law, however, did accord complete assimilation to foreign authors, except that the length of protection accorded to their works in Belgium could not exceed that granted to national authors; furthermore, if the foreign work ceased to be protected in its country of origin, its protection in Belgium came simultaneously to an end.[155]

1.26 The laws of other countries were considerably more restrictive than those of France or Belgium, limiting the availability of protection for foreign works by reference to a criterion of nationality (of the author) or place of publication (of the work). Germany was an example of the first: its laws applied to all works of German nationals, whether unpublished or published (the place of publication being irrelevant).[156] Foreign authors whose works were published in Germany were also protected, but this publication had to be by a German publisher.[157] A similar position existed in Norway,[158] Switzerland,[159] and Hungary,[160] except that, in the last two countries, domicile, rather than nationality, was the criterion of protection. Nationality alone, however, was the criterion of protection in Greece,[161] Portugal,[162] Spain,[163] Sweden,[164] Finland,[165] and the United States,[166] and in none of these countries were the works of foreigners protected, even if published locally. By contrast, in a number of other states, the criterion of territoriality (or place of publication) was applied, and all works published within the territory of the state in question were protected, regardless of the

[153] Darras (1887), 221ff; LCD (1889), vol I, 37, n 3; L Renault, *De la propriété littéraire et artistique au point de vue international* (1879), 21–2; Bastide (1890), 90. Cf the doubts expressed in Pouillet (n 84 above), 780–4. See further C Fliniaux, *Essai sur les droits des auteurs étrangers en France et des auteurs françaises en pays étrangers* (1879), 7ff.

[154] See further Briggs (1906), 135–6.

[155] Belgian Law, art 38.

[156] German Law of 11 June 1870, art 61; Law of 9 Jan 1876, art 20.

[157] ibid.

[158] Norwegian Law of 8 June 1876, art 451; Law of 12 May 1877 (artistic property), art 15.

[159] Swiss Law of 1883, art 10.

[160] Hungarian Law of 1884, art 79.

[161] Greek Penal Code 1833, art 433.

[162] Portuguese Civil Code 1867, art 576.

[163] Spanish Law of 1879, art 50.

[164] Swedish Law of 10 May 1877, art 19; Law of 8 May 1867, art 8.

[165] Finnish Law of 1880, art 32 (residents were also assimilated to Finnish authors and artists).

[166] US Copyright Act of 1870, ss 4952 and 4971 (residents were also assimilated to US citizens).

author or publisher's nationality. This, then, gave foreign authors some limited opportunity to gain protection for their works abroad. The states adopting this regime included the UK,[167] Austria,[168] the Netherlands,[169] Italy,[170] Mexico,[171] and Chile.[172] In the remaining states, there was no effective protection of foreign works.

(1) Protection on condition of reciprocity

1.27 Most states, however, were prepared to grant protection to foreign works on condition of reciprocity, that is, on condition that their own works received protection in the country of origin of the foreign work. The provisions dealing with reciprocity varied considerably from country to country, but the two main approaches adopted were by no means peculiar to international copyright, and remain relevant today. They were as follows:

(a) Material reciprocity

Under which country A accorded protection to works from country B, if the latter gave substantially equivalent protection to works from country A. In the pre-Berne period, an example of this approach was to be found in the law of Austria, which protected works appearing abroad in the measure in which the same rights were accorded to Austrian works by the law of the foreign country in question.[173]

(b) Formal reciprocity

Under which country A accorded protection to works from country B on condition that the latter protected works from country A in the same way as it protected the works of its own authors. In other words, the consideration for granting reciprocity was that the other country assimilated the works of country A to those of its own authors. In such a case, substantial equivalence in the level of protection accorded by each state was not necessarily present, but the attraction of such an approach to country A was that its works received some protection at

---

[167] UK Literary Copyright Act 1842, s 1; see also *Routledge* v *Low* (1868) LR 3 HL 100.

[168] Austrian Law of 1846, art 36.

[169] Netherlands Law of 1881, art 27.

[170] Italian Law of 1882, art 42.

[171] Mexican Civil Code 1871, art 1383. Mexicans and foreigners resident in Mexico who published works outside Mexico could gain protection provided they complied with the registration requirements of arts 1349–52.

[172] Chilean Law of 24 July 1834, art 6.

[173] Austrian Law of 1846, art 39 (note that art 38 provided specially for the protection of works that had appeared in the territory of the German Confederation, provided that the formalities of the state in question had been complied with). According to Pataille and Huget (1855), the Danish law of 1744 was the first to offer material reciprocity: 50–1.

least in country B where previously there had been none. It will be seen below that this approach, known also as that of 'national treatment', is fundamental to the operation of the present Berne Convention, although the provisions of that Convention also contain a large number of substantive requirements as to the level of protection which each country must assure to the works of other Union countries. The result is that a very significant degree of equivalence is now to be found in the protection which each country accords to the works of the others. In the pre-Berne period, formal reciprocity was adopted by many European countries, and a good example was provided by article 10 of the Swiss Law of 1883:

> The author of a work appearing or published abroad, who is not domiciled in Switzerland, enjoys the same rights as the author of a work appearing in Switzerland, if the latter is treated, in the foreign country, on the same footing as the author of a work appearing in that country.[174]

Under either approach, reciprocity could be awarded automatically in relation to the works of authors from countries which satisfied the respective criteria of material or formal reciprocity. This was the case in a number of national laws, including those of Italy,[175] Spain,[176] Portugal,[177] and Greece,[178] but this often led to uncertainty in particular instances. Thus, an author from country B might be unsure whether he enjoyed protection in country A until a tribunal in that country had determined that the conditions of material or formal reciprocity were, in fact, fulfilled as far as country B was concerned. This was cumbersome and time-consuming, as it is always difficult for a tribunal in one country to inform itself of the state of the law in another country. In consequence, some national laws sought to avoid this problem by making protection available for works from another country only where some formal declaration to this effect, such as a royal or governmental decree or ordinance, had been made specifically in relation to works from that country.[179] It was usually provided that this protection could be restricted in scope so as to avoid obvious inequalities of treatment where the foreign country did not protect particular categories of works or rights at all.[180] However, the question of whether (and to what extent) the foreign country accorded material or formal reciprocity was settled clearly in

[174] Swiss Law of 1883, art 10.
[175] Italian Law of 1882, art 46.
[176] Spanish Law of 1879, art 50.
[177] Portuguese Civil Code 1867, art 578.
[178] Greek Penal Code 1833, art 433. See also the Mexican Civil Code 1871, art 1386.
[179] See eg the UK International Copyright Act 1844, s 2; Danish Law of 29 Dec 1857, art 23; Law of 31 Mar 1864, art 9 (and amending Laws); Norwegian Law of 8 June 1876, art 46; Law of 12 May 1877, art 16; Law of 12 May 1877, art 8; Swedish Law of 10 Aug 1877, art 19; Law of 8 May 1867, art 8; Finnish Law of 1880, art 32.
[180] See eg the UK Act (n 179 above).

advance, and authors from that country knew what protection was available to them in the country which had made the declaration.

In the preceding paragraph, we have discussed reciprocity of protection in isolation, as though this were purely a matter for unilateral decision by the country concerned, with each extending protection to works from a foreign country where the latter happened to have satisfied the necessary condition of material or formal reciprocity. However, while this sometimes occurred, it was obviously a more haphazard method of securing international copyright protection. A surer way of doing this was for countries to make agreements between themselves under which the terms and conditions of the reciprocity to be accorded were more precisely determined. Such agreements were most readily achieved at a bilateral level, and they began to be made almost as soon as countries acknowledged the need to obtain international protection for their authors. Some knowledge of this development is necessary for a proper understanding of the next stage of international co-operation which succeeded it—that of the multilateral agreement, to which a number of states adhered. As the principal subject of this book—the Berne Convention—remains the foremost example of such a multilateral agreement, it is appropriate to consider briefly the form and content of these earlier bilateral agreements. The latter are therefore the subject of the next section. **1.28**

D. Bilateral Agreements Concerning Copyright

(1) The early agreements

The first bilateral agreements were entered into by Prussia with the other German states between the years 1827 and 1829. It will be recalled that a project for a uniform law of copyright throughout the German states had been the subject of an Act of the Federal Diet in 1815, but that progress on this had been very slow. Accordingly, in 1827 the Prussian Cabinet decided not to await the completion of the federal project, but to enter into separate negotiations with each of the German states so as to gain provisional agreement on the basis of formal reciprocity, that is, on the basis that, in the application of existing laws, any distinction between national and foreign authors (meaning here Prussian and other German authors) would be reciprocally abolished with respect to the subjects of the contracting states so that foreigners would enjoy the same protection as nationals.[181] Following this decision, Prussia signed conventions to this **1.29**

[181] Darras (1887), 193–4.

effect during the next two years with thirty-two German states.[182] In the succeeding decades, the need for these conventions was to disappear as the various German states began to adopt similar laws in accordance with the resolutions of the Federal Diet.[183] In this context, however, it should be noted that formal reciprocity, or national treatment, can have its drawbacks. An instance of this is provided by the case of Würtemberg which at this time did not protect its nationals against infringement of their works. Accordingly, assimilation of Prussian authors to native Würtembergers provided nothing by way of protection to the former (although it was undoubtedly very helpful to the latter).[184] This is an extreme example of a problem that frequently arises in the context of agreements to grant national treatment in the area of copyright: if one country has a higher level of protection than another, this will be to the disadvantage of its own authors and a boon to the authors of the other. In later treaties, to minimize this imbalance, it therefore became standard practice to insert provisions containing common rules that each country would undertake to apply in protecting the works of the other's authors, for example, in relation to such matters as translation and performing rights, duration of protection, reproduction of newspaper articles, the making of musical arrangements, and so on. The first example of such a convention seems to have been that between Austria and Sardinia which was made on 22 May 1840.[185] This convention also had the distinction of being the first multilateral copyright convention, albeit one of a very special kind. Thus, under article 27 it was provided that both governments were free to invite the other governments of Italy (of which there were a number at this time) as well as the Swiss canton of Ticino to accede to the Convention. This was duly done by five Italian states (Lucca, Modena, Parma, Rome, and Tuscany) in the same year.[186] A similar kind of multilateral agreement in relation to the German states was to be found in the Anglo-Prussian Convention of 13 May 1846, to which twelve other German states had acceded by 1853.[187] A limited multilateral agreement was also entered into by a number of the Swiss cantons in the years 1856 and 1857.[188] The multilateral character of each of

[182] These were Anhalt-Bernberg, Anhalt-Dessau, Anhalt-Koethen, Baden, Bayern, Brunswick, Bremen, Denmark (as regards the Duchies of Holstein, Lauenberg, and Schleswig), Hamburg, Hanover, Hesse, Hesse-Hohenzollern-Helchwegen, Hohenzollern-Siegmaringen, Lübeck, Mecklenberg-Schwerin, Mecklenberg-Strelitz, Nassau, Oldenberg, the principalities of Reuss, Sachsen, Saxe-Coburg, Saxe Gotha, Saxe-Meiningen, Saxe-Weimar, Schaumberg-Lippe, Schwartzberg-Rudolfstadt, Schwartzberg-Sonderhausen, Waldeck, Würtemberg: Darras (1887), 194.

[183] Darras (1887), 194ff. See also *Recueil* (1904), xix and Briggs (1906), 66.

[184] Briggs (1906), 66.

[185] 31 *British and Foreign State Papers* 1117 ('*BFSP*'); see also the summary of the provisions of the Convention in J Delalain, *Recueil des Conventions conclues par la France pour la Reconnaissance de la Properiété Littéraire et Artistique* (1866), xxvixff ('J Delalain (1866)').

[186] J Delalain (1866), xxvixff.

[187] 34 *BFSP* 4; see also J Delalain (1866), xxvixff.

[188] *Recueil* (1904), 425.

these early agreements was clearly the product of the geopolitical circumstances of the countries concerned—Italy and Germany, as national units, did not exist until 1861 and 1871 respectively[189] while Switzerland did not adopt a federal copyright law until 1883.[190] Thus, it was not to be until 1886 that the first truly multilateral copyright agreement open to all states—the Berne Convention—was established; until this time the great majority of international copyright agreements were of a purely bilateral character.

(2) The spread of bilateral agreements on copyright

The main actors in these early agreements were the UK and France. Apart from its convention with Prussia in 1846, the UK entered into important conventions with Hanover,[191] France,[192] Belgium,[193] Spain,[194] and Sardinia-Italy.[195] However, with respect to the country whose publishers were inflicting the greatest degree of injury on British authors—the United States—the UK failed to reach any agreement, although there were movements in favour of such a treaty on both sides of the Atlantic.[196] France also sought to limit the effect of international piracy on its authors by entering conventions with the countries that were centres of such activities. With this aim, she made an agreement with Sardinia in 1843,[197] but thereafter found difficulty in inducing other states to do so. Three further agreements were reached in 1851 with Portugal,[198] Hanover,[199] and the UK.[200] However, after her famous decree of 1852 concerning the protection of foreign works in France,[201] the blockages were cleared, and by the end of 1865 France had made agreements with the majority of European states. These were Belgium (the main source of pirated editions of French works),[202] Spain,[203] the Netherlands,[204] Luxembourg,[205] the Russian Empire,[206] Prussia[207] (to which agreement some thirteen other German states belonging to the **1.30**

[189] See D Thompson, *Europe since Napoleon* (revised edn, 1966), 300ff.
[190] Law of 23 Apr 1883.
[191] 4 Aug 1847. [192] 3 Nov 1851 (40 *BFSP* 27).
[193] 12 Aug 1854 (44 *BFSP* 30). [194] 7 July 1857.
[195] 30 Nov 1861 (34 *BFSP* 1025).
[196] See J J Barnes, *Authors, Publishers and Politicians: The Quest for an Anglo-American Copyright Agreement 1815–1854* (1974).
[197] 28 Aug 1843. [198] 12 Aug 1851 (J Delalain (1866), 15).
[199] 20 Oct 1851 (J Delalain (1866), 23).
[200] 3 Nov 1851 (J Delalain (1866), 27 and 40 *BFSP* 27).
[201] Decree-Law of 28 Mar 1852.
[202] 22 Aug 1852 (J Delalain (1866), 42).
[203] 15 Nov 1853 (J Delalain (1866), 99).
[204] 29 Mar 1855 (J Delalain (1866), 130 and 178).
[205] 4 July 1856 (J Delalain (1866), 154).
[206] 6 Apr 1861 (J Delalain (1866), 181).
[207] 2 Aug 1862 (J Delalain (1866), 206).

Zollverein acceded[208]), the newly constituted state of Italy,[209] the Swiss Confederation,[210] some twelve other German states,[211] Portugal,[212] and Austria-Hungary.[213] After this time, France's diplomatic activities in relation to copyright virtually ceased for fifteen years, until the early 1880s when she revised her conventions with Belgium,[214] Switzerland,[215] Germany,[216] and Italy,[217] as well as making an 'arrangement' with Sweden and Norway.[218] The new German Empire also entered a number of major conventions during this latter period with: Switzerland,[219] France,[220] Belgium,[221] Italy,[222] and the UK.[223] After 1852, copyright conventions were also made by a number of other important European states, notably Belgium,[224] Spain,[225] and Italy.[226] Many of

[208] Hesse-Cassel (8 Feb 1865) (J Delalain (1866), 232); Reuss-Gera (11 Mar 1865) (J Delalain (1866), 243); Saxe-Altenburg (18 Mar 1865) (J Delalain (1866), 298); Brunswick (29 Mar 1865) (J Delalain (1866), 256); Saxe-Meiningen (6 Apr 1865) (J Delalain (1866), 258); Oldenberg (20 Apr 1865) (J Delalain (1866), 267); Hesse-Hamburg (21 Apr 1865) (J Delalain (1866), 269); Waldeck and Pyrmont (26 Apr 1865) (J Delalain (1866), 282); Saxe-Weimar-Eisenbach (26 Apr 1865) (J Delalain (1866), 279); Schwartzberg-Sondershausen (28 Apr 1865) (J Delalain (1866), 284); Schwartzberg-Rudolstadt (5 May 1865) (J Delalain (1866), 286); Reuss-Greitz (6 May 1865) (J Delalain (1866), 289).

[209] 29 June 1862 (J Delalain (1866), 198 and 57 *BFSP* 766).

[210] 30 June 1864 (J Delalain (1866), 215).

[211] Hamburg (4 Mar 1865) (J Delalain (1866), 234); Lübeck (4 Mar 1865) (J Delalain (1866), 234); Bremen (4 Mar 1865) (J Delalain (1866), 234); Bavaria (24 Mar 1865) (J Delalain (1866), 248); Frankfurt (18 Apr 1865) (J Delalain (1866), 260); Würtemberg (24 Apr 1865) (J Delalain (1866), 272); Saxony (26 May 1865) (J Delalain (1866), 301); Mecklenberg-Schwerin (9 June 1865) (J Delalain (1866), 309); Baden (12 May 1865) (J Delalain (1866), 291); Hesse-Darmstadt (14 June 1865) (J Delalain (1866), 318); Nassau (5 July 1865) (J Delalain (1866), 326); Mecklenberg-Strelitz (24 Aug 1865) (J Delalain (1866), 334).

[212] 11 July 1866 (replacing that of 12 Apr 1851).

[213] 11 Dec 1866 (LCD (1889), vol II, 269 and *Recueil* (1904), 90).

[214] 31 Oct 1881 (LCD (1889), vol II, 278).

[215] 23 Feb 1882 (LCD (1889), vol II, 363).

[216] 19 Apr 1883 (LCD (1889), vol II, 251 and *Recueil* (1904), 70).

[217] 9 July 1884 (LCD (1889), vol II, 303 and *Recueil* (1904), 282).

[218] 15 Feb 1884 (LCD (1889), vol II, 361 and *Recueil* (1904), 311).

[219] 23 May 1883.

[220] 19 Apr 1883 (LCD (1889), vol II, 251 and *Recueil* (1904), 70).

[221] 12 Dec 1883 (*Recueil* (1904), 61).

[222] 20 June 1884 (*Recueil* (1904), 74).

[223] 2 June 1885 (77 *BFSP* 64).

[224] Belgium and the Netherlands, 30 Aug 1858 (*Recueil* (1904), 125); Belgium and Spain, 30 Apr 1859 (*Recueil* (1904), 117) replaced by Convention of 26 June 1880 (*Recueil* (1904), 121); Belgium and Sardinia, 24 Nov 1859 (57 *BFSP* 761); Belgium and Russia, 18 July 1862 (*Recueil* (1904), 118); Belgium and Prussia, 28 Mar 1863 (*Recueil* (1904), 117); Belgium and Portugal, 11 Oct 1866 (*Recueil* (1904), 130); Belgium and Switzerland, 25 Apr 1867 (*Recueil* (1904), 118); Belgium and the UK, 12 Aug 1854 (44 *BFSP* 30). See generally *Recueil* (1904), 115–19.

[225] Spain and Italy (Sardinia), 9 Feb 1860 (*Recueil* (1904), 211) replaced by a new Convention, 28 June 1880 (*Recueil* (1904), 231); Spain and Portugal, 5 Aug 1860 (*Recueil* (1904), 211); replaced by a new Convention, 9 Aug 1880 (*Recueil* (1904), 235); Spain and the UK (54 *BFSP* 1025) replaced by new Convention, 11 Aug 1880 (71 *BFSP* 74); Spain and Netherlands, 31 Dec 1862 (*Recueil* (1904), 211); Spain and France, 16 June 1880 (*Recueil* (1904), 220).

[226] Italy (Sardinia) and the UK, 30 Nov 1860 (54 *BFSP* 1025); Italy and Switzerland, 22 July 1868 (*Archives Diplomatiques* IV, 1346); Italy and the *Zollverein*, 12 May 1869; Italy (Sardinia) and Belgium, 24 Nov 1850 (57 *BFSP* 761); Italy and Spain, 28 June 1880 (*Recueil* (1904), 231). See generally *Recueil* (1904), 345–52.

these were made as part of, or in conjunction with, broader trading and commerce treaties entered into by these countries, and this had some undesirable side effects which are referred to below.[227] The net result was that, by 1886, there was an intricate network of conventions, declarations, and arrangements in place between the majority of European states, as well as between several Latin American states.[228]

By and large, the format of each convention was fairly standard: their basis was national treatment, supplemented by specific obligations undertaken by each state to accord a particular level of treatment to authors of works from the other state in relation to such matters as translation and performance rights, restrictions on rights, subject matter protected, and so on. By 1886, a number of the older conventions had been revised or replaced, either to take account of such geopolitical changes as the unifications of Germany and Italy, or to refine or enlarge the level of protection granted (or both). A summary of the bilateral conventions in force in 1886 is given at the end of this chapter.[229] This shows that France had the most international agreements on copyright (thirteen), and was followed closely by Belgium (nine), Italy, and Spain (eight apiece). Although the UK had been one of the first countries to initiate such agreements in the 1840s, by 1886 it was only party to five. However, with the exception of its convention with Belgium, all these agreements were with the largest European states. The same was true of the German conventions, which were also probably the most 'advanced' in terms of the level of protection offered, and which, with those of France, were to be frequently cited as useful precedents in the drafting sessions that led up to the Berne Convention. The international copyright relations of the smaller European countries were less developed. The Scandinavian countries, for instance, still felt themselves to be more in the position of users of copyright material than creators of it.[230] the Netherlands, too, was still of the 'free rider' persuasion, at least so far as German works were concerned; although she signed a convention with the German Empire in 1884, she failed to ratify it, and unauthorized reproductions of German works in the Netherlands continued to be made until after the turn of the century.[231] However, two European states which can hardly be regarded as small remained relatively aloof from this intense pre-1886 period of bilateral convention-making. These were the Russian and Austro-Hungarian Empires. Both had **1.31**

[227] See paras 1.32–1.33 below. [228] See Figure after para 1.42 below.

[229] See also Ladas (1938), 44–50; and the introductory notes to each national section in *Recueil* (1904), in particular, 45 (Germany), 79 (Austria), 115 (Belgium), 189 (Denmark), 209 (Spain), 243 (USA), 259 (France), 313 (UK), 339 (Hungary), 345 (Italy), 379 (Norway), 389 (Netherlands), 395 (Portugal), 401 (Russia), 415 (Sweden), 423 (Switzerland).

[230] See *Recueil* (1904), 379–80 and 416–17.

[231] Ladas (1938), 49. See also *Recueil* (1904), 391–2.

large populations and flourishing cultural lives, but were not as advanced industrially as the other major Western European nations. Russia had entered into two conventions with France in 1861 and Belgium in 1862, but apparently felt that these had been imposed upon her. Accordingly, she denounced both conventions in 1885, and refrained from entering into agreements with other states on copyright matters.[232] In the case of Austria-Hungary, the reason seems to have been more to do with the chaotic arrangement of the internal laws of its component parts, and the difficulty of entering international agreements on matters which would require changes to those laws.[233] The only countries in Europe without any international arrangements by 1886 were Greece, Monaco, Serbia, Romania, Bulgaria, and Montenegro. The same was true of Turkey, Siam, China, and Japan, while in the Americas the only states that were parties to such arrangements (and then only with Spain) were Salvador and Columbia. The major country that stood out completely from any international copyright arrangements was the USA. Throughout the nineteenth century, this country was a major centre for book piracy, particularly for books from the UK. Although it had a vigorous literary and artistic life, the vested interests of publishers and printers, on the one hand, and the strong public pressure for plentiful supplies of cheap books, on the other, militated against any moves for the United States to enter into international copyright relations.[234]

(3) Contents of bilateral agreements

1.32 There were great variations in the contents of these pre-1886 conventions; nevertheless, particular provisions tended to recur.

(a) Persons protected

1.33 Various approaches were evident here. Some conventions, for example, limited protection to authors who were nationals of the contracting states;[235] others gave protection, on the basis of territoriality, to authors of works published in the respective territory of each contracting state, regardless of nationality.[236] Several conventions, while adopting the criterion of nationality, also protected the publishers of works published in the territory of either contracting state where the

[232] See *Recueil* (1904), 402–3. See further M F de Martens, *Traité du droit international*, vol II (1884–7), 229, 233; 'La Russie et la Convention de Berne' [1888] *DA* 122.

[233] *Recueil* (1904), 83ff.

[234] This situation began to change slowly after 1886: see *Recueil* (1904), 243ff.

[235] eg the Convention between Belgium and Spain of 26 June 1880, art 1; Convention between Spain and Salvador, 23 June 1884, art 1; Arrangement between France, Sweden, and Norway, 15 Feb 1884, art 1; Arrangement between Italy, Sweden, and Norway, 9 Oct 1884, art 1.

[236] See eg the Convention between Belgium and Portugal, 11 Oct 1866, art 1; France and Portugal, 11 July 1866, art 1.

authors of these works were nationals of other states.[237] Finally, there were a number of conventions which adopted neither the criterion of nationality nor territoriality, but simply required each state to accord protection to authors to the extent to which they were protected in the other state. Thus, if country A limited its protection to those authors who were nationals, only these would be entitled to protection in country B. But if the latter country gave protection to all works published within its territory, these works would be entitled to protection in country A.[238] Under most conventions, the assignees and legal representatives of authors were given the same rights and protection as authors. It should also be noted that there were significant differences in the case of several conventions with Switzerland. This country did not have a federal copyright law until 1883; accordingly, any promise to accord national treatment prior to this time would have been meaningless. Thus, in the first convention between Switzerland and France in 1864, the convention itself supplied the provisions to be applied to French authors in Switzerland, that is, by self-executing provisions. This approach was followed in several other conventions made with Switzerland prior to 1883.[239]

(b) Works protected

There were a number of differences in the terminology used here. Many of the early conventions required protection to be given to authors of 'works of the intellect and of art', to which dramatic and musical works were often added.[240] Later conventions spoke more commonly of 'literary and artistic works', to which the adjective 'scientific' was sometimes added. This was usually followed by an extensive definition, such as that in the Franco-German and Franco-Italian Conventions of 1883 and 1884: **1.34**

> The expression 'literary or artistic works' includes books, pamphlets or other writings; dramatic works, musical compositions, dramatico-musical works; drawings, paintings, sculptures, engravings; lithographs, illustrations, maps; plans, sketches and plastic works relating to geography, topography, architecture or natural science, and, in general, to any other production in the literary, scientific or artistic domain.[241]

[237] See eg Conventions between Belgium and Germany, 12 Dec 1883, art 2, France and Germany, 19 Apr 1883, art 2; Germany and Italy, 20 June 1884, art 2.

[238] See eg the Conventions between France and Spain, 16 June 1880, art 1; Spain and Italy, 28 June 1880, art 1. Ladas (1938), 52, points out that in the case of France, such a provision would need to be subject to some implied limitation so as to apply either only to French authors or to works published in France, as France protected all works wherever published.

[239] Ladas (1938), 51; *Recueil* (1904), 423–5.

[240] See eg the Conventions between Spain and Belgium, 30 Apr 1859, art 1; France and Hanover, 20 Oct 1851, art 1; France and England, 3 Nov 1851, art 1.

[241] Convention between France and Germany, 19 Apr 1883, art 1. See also the Conventions between Germany and Belgium, 12 Dec 1883, art 1; France and Italy, 2 July 1884, art 1.

These enumerations often differed from convention to convention; some also omitted or expressly excluded particular categories of works,[242] while others protected unpublished as well as published works.[243] In addition, they merely set the limits or boundaries of the protection potentially available under the convention. This did not necessarily mean that such works were to be accorded protection in each country, as the principle of national treatment meant only that each country was required to give the same level of protection as that accorded nationals under its own law.[244] Thus, if one country did not protect a particular kind of work, protection for it could not be claimed by virtue of the convention by authors belonging to the other contracting country, even if such protection was available in the latter country. On the other hand, it was often required that persons claiming protection under a convention should be able to prove that they were entitled to that protection in their own country.[245]

(c) *The principle of national treatment*

1.35 This was the general rule adopted in the conventions, and meant that authors from country A were entitled to receive, in country B, the same rights and remedies accorded to its own authors by country B. This requirement was differently expressed, but to the same effect, in the various conventions, but was usually subject to the limitation, either expressly or impliedly made, that protection claimed under a convention should not exceed the level of protection accorded to the author in his own country.[246] The basic rights in respect of which national treatment was accorded were those of reproduction and public performance (in the case of dramatic and musical works). Translation rights, however, were generally subject to special limitations, and were dealt with in separate provisions (see para 1.36 below). There were, almost invariably, a number of restrictions that were placed on the reproduction right, for example, in relation to newspaper articles and use for teaching purposes (see para 1.37 below), and sometimes restrictions were placed on the exercise of public performing rights. Most conventions also contained provisions which expressly prohibited (in addition to their reproduction) the importation, exportation, sale, and circulation in each country of infringing copies of works, wherever those copies originated.

[242] eg the Convention between France and the Netherlands, 29 Mar 1855, did not include musical and artistic works.

[243] See eg the Conventions between France and Italy, 9 July 1884, art 1; Belgium and Germany, 12 Dec 1883, art 1.

[244] In the case of Swiss conventions prior to 1883, the enumerations of works were differently worded, and were intended to secure protection for those works in Switzerland, as well as in the other country, in the absence of an adequate Swiss copyright law: Ladas (1938), 54–5.

[245] Ladas (1938), 54.

[246] See the detailed discussion of these provisions in Ladas (1938), 55–8.

(d) Translation rights

Although these were the most important rights for authors seeking protection for their works in foreign countries, the majority of conventions placed significant restrictions on the way in which such rights were to be exercised. This may have been due to a lingering distrust, on the part of various governments, of the willingness or capacity of authors to supply translations of their works in different languages, or to do so within reasonable periods of time. Allied to this may have been the fear that, unless there was some means by which this gap could be closed by the making of other translations, their respective publics would suffer. Again, there may have been a residual desire to continue the protection of vested interests that had profited, for a long time, from the making of unauthorized translations of foreign works. But whatever the reason, by 1886 there were still only a few conventions that protected translation rights unreservedly, assimilating them wholly to reproduction rights.[247] The other conventions generally contained some kind of limitation on the exercise of translation rights, requiring the translation to be made within a particular time of first publication of the original work, and then only according rights for a relatively short period, such as between five and ten years.[248] A number of conventions, notably those made by the UK, required registration of the work within a given time after publication in its country of origin, and also that the author reserve his translation rights at the time of original publication.[249] Several older conventions still in force in 1886 had no provisions concerning translation rights, with the result that these rights were not protected at all under those conventions.[250] **1.36**

(e) Restrictions on reproduction rights

As a consequence of the general adoption in these conventions of the principle of national treatment, authors claiming protection for their reproduction rights in another country by virtue of a convention were accorded the same level of protection as were national authors or works first published in that country. Such national treatment was also subject to the limitations on those rights that were imposed by the law of that country. In addition, there were restrictions to be found in most conventions. The most frequent were those dealing with the copying of works for inclusion in chrestomathies or anthologies, or of parts of works for educational or scientific purposes. Such copying was usually allowed, **1.37**

---

[247] eg the Conventions of Spain and Belgium, 26 June 1880, art 35; France and Spain, 16 June 1880, art 3; Spain and Portugal, 9 Aug 1880, art 3.

[248] eg the Conventions of France and Italy, 9 July 1884, art 8; Germany and Belgium, 12 Dec 1883, art 10; Germany and Italy, 20 June 1884, art 10.

[249] See eg the Conventions between the UK and Belgium, 12 Aug 1854, art 5; the UK and Spain, 7 July 1857, art 5.

[250] See eg the Conventions between France and the Netherlands, 29 Mar 1855, and France and Russia, 6 Apr 1861.

but subject to various conditions.[251] More liberal were the provisions dealing with the making of reproductions of newspaper and periodical articles. Such borrowings were also usually permitted, but some conventions had restrictions in relation to particular categories of articles,[252] and most forbade reproduction (except in the case of articles of political discussion) where the author had expressly reserved his rights in advance. Both kinds of provision raised difficult issues concerning the appropriate balance to be struck between the rights of authors and those of the public, and these issues continued to be hotly debated in the context of the Berne Convention for the first forty years of its existence.[253] In this regard, however, the provisions of the pre-1886 bilateral conventions were of little assistance, in the sense of providing a common or uniform approach to the permissible limits for such borrowings.

(f) Duration of protection

1.38 Since the provisions of the various national copyright laws revealed little uniformity on this question, uniformity at an international level was hardly to be expected. The general approach taken was a further gloss on the principle of national treatment: protection was only accorded under the conventions to authors as long as their rights in their country of origin subsisted, and, in any event, the duration of their protection in the other country was not to exceed that accorded to nationals by the law of the country in which protection was claimed.[254] There were exceptions to this general rule: in a number of conventions, the period of protection was determined by the law of the country in which protection was claimed,[255] while some others actually fixed the period of copyright protection for authors claiming under them.[256] As with the provisions of national laws, however, it is difficult to discern any uniform approach in these last-mentioned conventions to the question of duration.

[251] eg requirements that the name of the author and the work be included, as in art 4 of the German Conventions with Belgium (12 Dec 1883), France (19 Apr 1883), and Italy (20 June 1884), or requirements that extracts reproduced in works for teaching purposes be accompanied by explanatory notes in a language other than that in which the original work was published, as in art 9 of the Convention between Portugal and France, 11 July 1866 and art 4 of the Convention between Spain and France, 16 June 1880.

[252] eg the exclusion of serial stories and articles on science or art, as in art 5 of the Convention between France and Italy, 9 July 1884, and art 5 of the Convention between Germany and Belgium, 12 Dec 1883.

[253] See paras 2.30–2.31 and 2.45 below and see further Chapter 3 below.

[254] See eg the Conventions between Germany and Belgium, 12 Dec 1883; France, 19 Apr 1883; and Italy, 20 June 1884 (art 1 in each case).

[255] As in several Belgian conventions: see art 1 of the Convention between Belgium and Spain, 26 June 1880, and art 1 of the Convention between Belgium and the Netherlands, 30 June 1858.

[256] As in art 1 of the Convention between Spain and France, 16 June 1880 (life of the author plus fifty years) and art 1 of the Convention between Spain and Portugal, 9 Aug 1880.

(g) Internal policing powers

In the earliest conventions, there appeared an article which was repeated, in almost identical form, in virtually every subsequent convention, and which still finds a place in the present Berne text. This concerned the right of states to regulate or prohibit the circulation of works pursuant to their domestic laws, for example, by powers of censorship or laws on such matters as defamation or national security. The conventions left these powers intact (for obvious reasons), a good example being provided by article 9 of the Franco-Sardinian Convention of 28 August 1843: **1.39**

> The depositions of the present Convention do not in any way carry any prejudice to the right reserved expressly to each of the two states to permit, supervise or prohibit, by legislative or internal police measures, the circulation, performance or exhibition of such works or productions in respect of which it is thought appropriate or necessary to exercise that right.[257]

In a period where most countries were still subject to some form of strict internal censorship or police control, copyright was therefore not seen, in any way, as a vehicle for the promotion of freedom of expression. In the 160-odd years since the Franco-Sardinian Convention, this position does not seem to have changed.

(h) Formalities

The conventional requirements as to these differed markedly, and were the cause of much cost and confusion to authors seeking protection for their works abroad. Only a few conventions dispensed entirely with the need to comply with formalities such as registration or deposit in order to gain protection under them. For example, several conventions made by Germany required only that the author's name be indicated at the beginning of the work,[258] and the Franco-Spanish Convention of 1880 required no formalities as long as the author could prove his 'right of property' under the law of the country of origin.[259] A number of other conventions were satisfied if proof of compliance with the formalities of **1.40**

[257] For the text of this, see J Delalain (1866), 1.

[258] Article 7 of the Convention between Germany and Belgium, 12 Dec 1883; art 7 of the Convention between Germany and France, 19 Apr 1883; and art 7 of the Convention between Germany and Italy, 20 June 1884.

[259] Article 1, Convention of 16 June 1880 ('*qui justifieront de leur droit de propriété . . .*'). To similar effect, see art 1 of the Convention between Spain and Portugal, 9 Aug 1886. Note also that under art 1 of the Convention between Spain and Belgium, 26 June 1880, no formalities were required of Spanish authors seeking protection in Belgium, but Belgians seeking protection in Spain were required to show that they had complied with the formalities prescribed by Belgian law.

the country of origin was shown.[260] On the other hand, there were a significant number of conventions, most notably those made by the UK, under which registration and deposit in the country where protection was claimed was necessary, at least in relation to some categories of works.[261]

(i) General comments

1.41 From the above, it will be seen that there were many differences between the various bilateral copyright conventions in force immediately prior to the entry into force of the Berne Convention. Of these, the most liberal in terms of scope of rights recognized, duration of protection, minimum of formalities and the like, were those made by France, Germany, and Spain in the years 1880 to 1886. By contrast, the most limited in each of these respects were probably those made by the UK. The lack of uniformity therefore made the task of ascertaining an author's entitlement to protection in a country other than his own a difficult and laborious one.[262] This undertaking was complicated by two other factors: the uncertain duration of many conventions and the prevalence of 'most favoured nation' clauses. As to the first, most conventions were linked to some broader treaty of trade or commerce which had been negotiated at the same time.[263] In many other cases, this was indirectly so, these conventions containing a clause providing that they should remain in force for a fixed period of time, for example, six years, and thereafter indefinitely, subject to denunciation by either side by a year's notice.[264] As such denunciations would often occur at the time of renegotiation of a new treaty of commerce, this might mean a sudden loss of their rights for authors, and was therefore a continual source of uncertainty.

1.42 'Most favoured nation' clauses were also an 'unhappy borrowing'[265] from general commercial treaties. Under such clauses, usually made as part of a tariff

[260] See eg art 2 of the Convention between Belgium and the Netherlands, 30 June 1858 and art 2 of the Convention between France and the Netherlands, 29 Mar 1855, under which a certificate from a competent authority in the other country was required. Note that in some conventions, such as that between Italy and Spain, 28 June 1880, each country undertook to communicate to the other, every three months, a list of the books registered under its law (see art 5).

[261] See further Ladas (1938), 55–7.

[262] Ladas (1938), 66.

[263] See eg art 15 of the Convention between Austria and France, 11 Dec 1866 and art 11 of the Convention between France and the Netherlands, 29 Mar 1859. This has become a feature of international copyright agreements in the twenty-first century, as intellectual property rights generally are linked to trade in such agreements as the TRIPs Agreement and bilateral free-trade agreements, such as those being pursued at the time of writing by the USA in respect of countries such as Australia, Singapore, and Chile: see further paras 4.54ff below.

[264] See eg the German Conventions with Belgium, 12 Dec 1883 (art 17) and Italy, 20 June 1884 (art 17), and the Belgian Conventions with Spain, 20 June 1880 (art 8), and Portugal, 11 Oct 1866 (art 18).

[265] Darras (1887), 555. See also Ladas (1938), 66–7, and '*La clause de la nation la plus favorisée dans les traités et accords concernant la protection du droit d'auteur*' [1908] *DA* 2, 17.

agreement, the contracting states promised to admit each other to the benefits that might be accorded to a third state under another treaty made by one of them with that state. In the context of a copyright convention between states A and B, the effect of such a clause was that if state A subsequently entered a convention with state C and this convention offered a higher level of protection to C's authors than was provided under the earlier convention to authors of B, the latter could then claim for themselves in state A the more favourable treatment accorded to the authors of C. The effect of these clauses differed, as they might be operative generally, or be limited to particular rights or categories of subject matter. Nevertheless, as a practical matter, they made the operation of bilateral copyright conventions uncertain, as these might be abrogated, in whole or in part, by the terms of another convention to which one state was party. In the words of Alcide Darras:

> . . . each day new conventions are signed; authors and artists should always be aware of any progress made; by the operation of this clause, their treatment may, in effect, be modified without their government being party to the arrangement.[266]

Such clauses were to be found in a number of important conventions made by Germany, Belgium, France, Spain, and Italy.[267] As a matter of principle, however, they were open to the objection that they were inappropriate in the sphere of copyright: literary and artistic works do not have to fear the same kind of competition that arises in the context of tariffs where one country favours another country to the prejudice of a third. On the other hand, it is difficult to agree with Darras's argument that, if Spanish authors were more completely protected in France than English authors, this certainly resulted in a situation of inequality but it was not one that caused any prejudice to the Englishman.[268] In such a case, a French publisher would be more inclined to deal with a Spanish author than an English author, so some detriment to the latter would be inevitable. Nevertheless, the fact remains that 'most favoured nation' clauses in copyright conventions added greatly to the complications of international copyright protection in the pre-Berne period.

---

[266] Darras (1887), 556.

[267] See eg art 16 of each of the Conventions between Germany and Belgium, 12 Dec 1883; France, 19 Apr 1883; and Italy, 20 June 1884; art 6 of the Convention between Belgium and Spain, 26 June 1880; and art 12 of the Convention between Belgium and the Netherlands, 30 June 1858; art 6 of the Convention between Spain and France, 16 June 1880; art 10 of the Convention between France and Italy, 9 July 1884.

[268] Darras (1887), 555–6.

BILATERAL CONVENTIONS IN FORCE IN 1886

(The numeral after each country is the total number of conventions to which that country is party.)

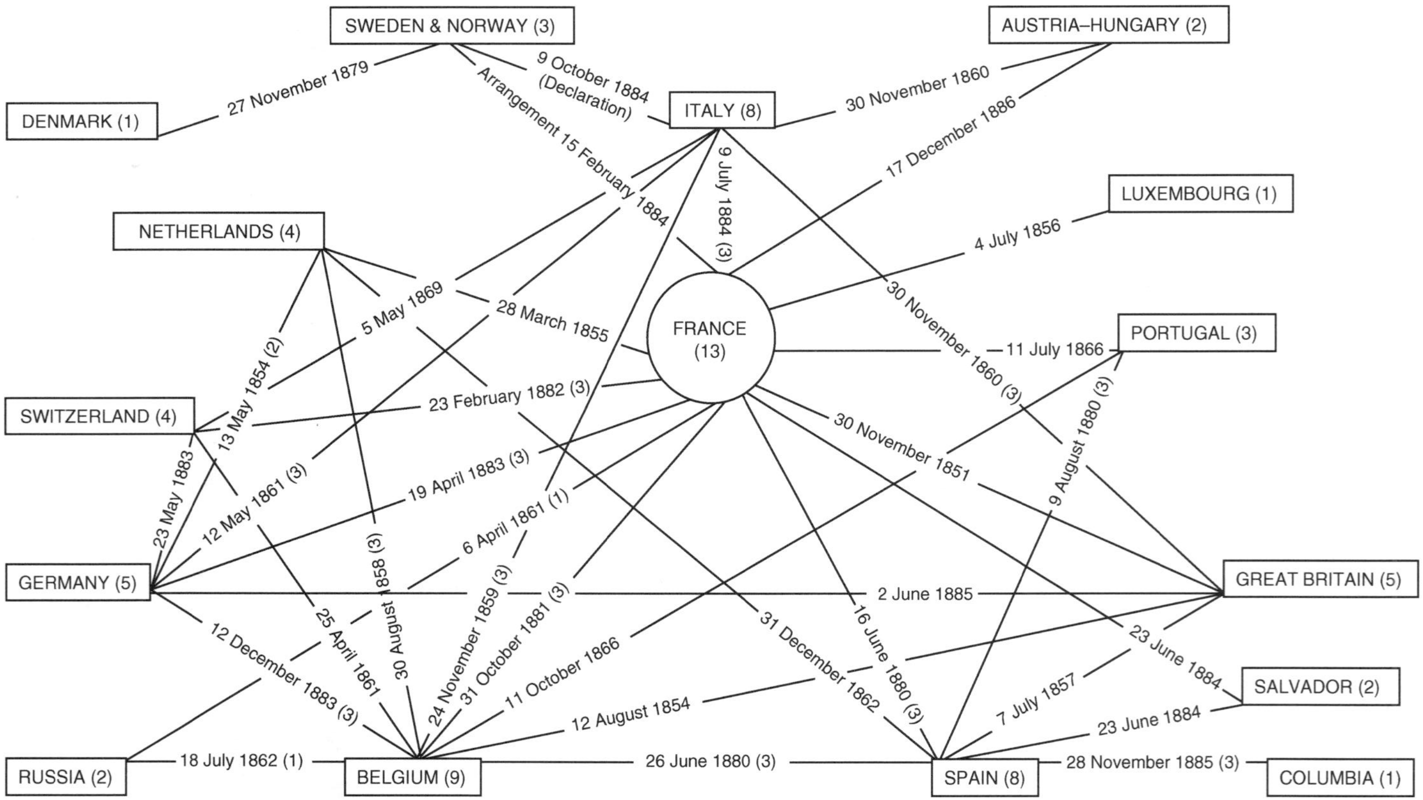

(1) Both denounced by Russia in 1885 to have effect from 14 July 1887 re France & 14 January 1887 re Belgium.
(2) Not ratified by Netherlands.
(3) Treaties with most favoured nation clauses.

2

ORIGINS OF THE BERNE CONVENTION

'Not only international, but universal'

F O Adams[1]

A. Introduction

2.01 Although the network of bilateral copyright arrangements in force prior to 1886 was extensive, the protection which this offered to authors in countries other than their own was far from comprehensive or systematic. Apart from the early treaties with the German and Italian states, multilateral copyright agreements in the true sense took time to emerge. Of these, the Berne Convention was to be the first, and the most important. However, the need for a more uniform and broader-based kind of international protection had been recognized some time before this by authors and artists. The present chapter deals with this development, and the different stages by which this early recognition was eventually transformed into the Berne Convention.

B. The Proper Basis for International Copyright Protection

(1) A universal law of copyright

2.02 A multilateral convention containing similar provisions to those found in the usual kind of bilateral convention is only one way in which uniformity in international copyright relations can be achieved. In theory, if such a convention was based only on national treatment, it might be thought that this would be the least desirable way of doing this, as the uniformity achieved would be only very limited, with many differences of substance and nuance still remaining in the national laws which would become applicable to foreign authors under the principle of national treatment. A more comprehensive solution would obviously be for each country to adopt uniform, general laws applicable to both foreigners and nationals alike. If this could be done, there would, in truth, be a universal law of copyright. It would also accord directly with the conception of the author's natural right of property in his work, existing independently of, and prior to, the formal rules and sanctions of positive law, and admitting no artificial restrictions such as a limited term of protection or national boundaries. As a purely practical matter, the contents of this law might necessitate some prior agreement (formal or otherwise) between all states to bring it into being,

[1] British delegate to all three Berne Conferences, 1884–6: *Actes* 1886, 15. For further background on Adam's diplomatic career, see B Sherman and L Bently, 'Great Britain and the Signing of the Berne Convention in 1886' (2000) 47 *Journal of the Copyright Society of the USA* 311.

but in principle (so the argument would go) this should not cause difficulty as these provisions would be easy to deduce, once the fundamental and universal character of the author's right had been recognized.

(2) The pragmatic view

The universalist conception outlined in the preceding paragraph can readily be criticized as utopian and unrealistic. It depends, ultimately, upon all states acknowledging, in equal degree, the compelling claim of authors and artists to protection, and then according this claim both formal and substantive recognition. But would each state do so? Would there even be consensus on the *Grundnorm* of this protection, namely the author's natural right of property in his works? There are differing approaches to this question, even among the major civil law systems,[2] while it is an unfamiliar notion to the common law jurisdictions where authors' rights are usually viewed in predominantly economic terms.[3] Furthermore, many countries' approach to copyright today ranks the public's interest equal, if not superior, to the author's.[4] Finally, even if agreement were to be reached on a certain number of uniform measures, is it likely that countries with higher levels of protection would be ready to abandon these, at least in relation to their own nationals? True universality in the absence of agreement on the fundamental nature of authors' rights would therefore seem unlikely, if not impossible. These realities indicate the need for compromise—for acceptance of some kind of minimal or restricted universality to which all, or at least the largest number possible, can agree. **2.03**

The history of the Berne Convention, and of international copyright relations in general, has been characterized by conflict between these differing viewpoints (although it must be pointed out that the battleground has shifted considerably in the past three decades or so). From an early stage, there was a strong school of thought in favour of a universal codification of copyright law, based on the **2.04**

[2] cf eg the different approaches taken by the French and German jurists: A Darras, *Du Droit des auteurs et des artistes dans les rapports internationaux* (1887) ('Darras (1887)'), Part I; E Pouillet, *Traité théorique et pratique de la propriété littéraire et artistique et du droit de représentation*, 2nd edn (1894); J Kohler, *Urheberrecht an Schriftwerken und Verlagsrecht* (1906–7). See also S P Ladas, *The International Protection of Literary and Artistic Property* (1938) ('Ladas (1938)'), ch 1.

[3] This is a grand generalization, as natural-rights views are to be found expressed in some of the judgments in the famous eighteenth-century English cases on the 'Question of Literary Property': see, in particular, *Millar* v *Taylor* (1769) 4 Burr 2303; 98 ER 201 and see further M Rose, *Authors and Owners: The Invention of Copyright* (1995). As for the USA, see Jane C Ginsburg, 'A Tale of Two Copyrights: Literary Property in Revolutionary France and America', in Brad Sherman and Alain Strowel (eds), *Of Authors and Origins: Essays on Copyright* (1994) (discussing expressions of natural-rights rationales for early US copyright law).

[4] See eg the decision of the US Supreme Court in *Sony Corp of America* v *Universal City Studios, Inc*, 464 US 417 (1984).

concept of the author's immutable right of property in his works. The proponents of this view have often been uncompromising in their advocacy, invariably convinced of their correctness, and, at times, apparently prepared to sacrifice all for the integrity of their beliefs. On the other hand, there has always been a strong countervailing influence provided by those who might be termed the 'pragmatists', that is, those who have been prepared to sacrifice high principle in order to gain the widest possible adherence to a particular proposition. As a broad generalization, France and the French-speaking countries have usually been found in the first camp, with the UK and the common law countries in the second. Naturally, there are good and bad things to be said for both sides, and there has always been a range of intermediate viewpoints expressed as well. Nevertheless, the universalists have been responsible for the steady increase in measures on which general agreement has been reached, so much so that the Berne Convention can now be regarded as a limited kind of international copyright code. At the same time, the modifying influence of the pragmatists has ensured that these changes have generally enjoyed the widest possible support, an approach which (to the universalists' dismay) has often meant the dilution or even emasculation of such measures. On the other hand, the uncompromising attitude of the universalists has often led to the defeat of proposals which could sensibly have been modified without much damage to their essential content. Sufficient instances of these differing approaches will be given throughout the remainder of this Part and in the second Part to demonstrate the truth of these generalizations. While it is true that both attitudes have now been overtaken, if not replaced, by new concerns during recent years, for the moment the tension between universalists and pragmatists serves to elucidate the following discussion of the origins of the Berne Convention.

C. The 1858 Brussels Congress on Literary and Artistic Property

2.05 Support for a universal law of copyright is to be found at a relatively early period. Thus, Rivière quotes Viscount Siméon speaking to this effect in the French Chamber of Peers in 1839, and Lamartine in the Chamber of Deputies two years later.[5] However, the first organized expression of opinion from groups directly affected is to be found in the resolutions of a Congress on Literary and Artistic Property which was held in Brussels in September 1858.[6] In this regard,

[5] L Rivière, *La Protection Internationale des Oeuvres Littéraires et Artistiques: Étude de législation comparé* (1897) ('Rivière (1897)'), 141.

[6] Rivière (1897), 142ff; Darras (1887), 519–22. For a summary of the proceedings of the Congress, see *Annales de la Propriété Industrielle, Artistique et Littéraire* (1858), 401–63 ('*Annales* (1858)'). For the full proceedings and records of the Congress, see E Romberg, *Compte rendu des Travaux du Congrès de la Propriété Littéraire et Artistique* (1859).

it is worth noting that the nineteenth century was, among other things, the age of the international congress, beginning with the great diplomatic Congress of Vienna in 1815 which settled the boundaries of post-Napoleonic Europe. The precedent was soon followed in other areas, and by the mid-nineteenth century the calling of international meetings to deal with particular problems had become quite common.[7] The irony of the 1858 Brussels Congress was that it was held in the city which had been, until quite recently, the principal international centre for piracies of French works.[8] Its Committee of Organization comprised a number of Belgian authors, artists, civil servants, and representatives of cultural organizations, and was presided over by Charles Faider, a lawyer and former Belgian Minister of Justice.[9] It lasted for four days, and was attended by nearly 300 persons, including fifty-four delegates from learned societies, forty-seven from universities, twenty-one economists, sixty-two men of letters, twenty-four artists, sixteen journalists, twenty-nine lawyers, twenty-nine publishers and printers, and some forty other persons (officials, politicians, judges and the like).[10] Some states, such as Saxony, Denmark, the Netherlands, Sardinia, Parma, and Portugal sent official delegates, and there were unofficial representatives from each major European country, as well as the United States.[11] The agenda for the Congress was set by a series of leading questions prepared by the Committee of Organization. These were arranged into five distinct categories, entitled 'international questions', 'property in literary and artistic works in general', 'dramatic and musical works', 'artistic works', and 'economic questions' (chiefly those concerning customs duties imposed on copyright works).[12] The debates of the Congress displayed fairly general consensus on the need for international copyright protection, but one of the chief points of difference arose in relation to the question of the length of protection. A strong body of opinion favoured perpetuity, but this was ultimately rejected in favour of a definite time limit, although the period preferred was longer than that then accorded under most national laws.[13] The view of the majority on this issue was determined to some extent by pragmatic considerations, but also by a concern for the interests of the general public.[14] The resolutions which were finally passed by the Congress on this and other matters took the form of

[7] See generally I L Claude, *Swords into Ploughshares: The Problems and Progress of International Organization*, 4th edn (1982), ch 2; D W Bowett, *The Law of International Institutions*, 4th edn (1982), ch 1 ('Bowett (1982)').

[8] Darras (1887), Part II; Alfred Villefort, *De la propriété littéraire et artistique au point de vue internationale: Aperçu sur les législations étrangères* (1851), 11–12 (detailing Belgian piracy of French books in 1847).

[9] *Annales* (1858), 401.

[10] ibid, 417.

[11] ibid, 416–17. See also Darras (1887), 521.

[12] *Annales* (1858), 404–5, 419.

[13] See the report of the second section (by Victor Fouchet): *Annales* (1858), 432–9.

[14] ibid, 436–7.

positive answers to the questions formulated by the Committee of Organization.[15] As such, they constituted a rudimentary outline of a programme for a universal copyright law. The most important of them were as follows:

I. International law

1. The Congress is of the opinion that the principle of international recognition of the property of authors in their literary and artistic works should be enshrined in the legislation of all civilised peoples.
2. This principle should be adopted in every country, even in the absence of reciprocity.
3. The assimilation of foreign and national authors should be absolute and complete.
4. There should be no restrictions placed on foreign authors as to particular formalities to be complied with in order for them to invoke and enforce their right of property. Compliance with the formalities required by the law of the country where original publication has taken place should be sufficient for them to be entitled to this right.
5. It is desirable that the laws in all countries relating to literary and artistic property should have a common basis.

II. Literary and artistic property in general

1. Authors of literary and artistic property should enjoy, during their lifetime, the exclusive right to publish and to reproduce their works, to sell them, to have them sold or distributed, and to assign, in whole or in part, their property or the right of reproduction. The surviving spouse should enjoy the same rights also during his or her life, and the beneficiaries or legal representatives of the author should enjoy the same fifty years from either the death of the author or from the extinction of the rights of the surviving spouse.
2. In the application of these rights, there should be no distinction between the different categories of literary and artistic works, musical compositions, productions of artistic design.—There should be no distinction made between pseudonymous works and works signed by the author.—There should be no longer any distinction made, in relation to the duration of rights, between legal representatives, infants, beneficiaries, volunteers or assignees.
3. The duration of the right of the first publisher of an anonymous work should be thirty years from the date of publication.—If the author makes himself known before the expiry of this legal term, he should be entitled to the same rights as would have belonged to him had the work originally appeared under his name.
4. As far as posthumous works are concerned, if the rights of the author's spouse and those of the beneficiaries or legal representatives have not expired, the posthumous work shall belong to them for a period equal to that granted to them by law.—If these rights have expired, the proprietor

[15] ibid, 452–4.

of a posthumous work shall have an exclusive right for thirty years from the date of publication.

5. The author's exclusive right should be guaranteed in respect of the publication of court proceedings, sermons and other speeches which may be published singly or as part of a larger work, without the consent of their authors or their representatives.—In the case of speeches delivered in court or in political assemblies, this consent should only be necessary for their publication as part of a collection of the author's works.
6. The author's right of reproduction of his original work should include the right of translation, subject to the following restriction:
   For ten years from the publication of the translation, the author shall have the exclusive right to translate, have translated, his work into all languages, provided that this right be exercised before the end of the third year following the publication of the original work.—If, at the end of the third year, the author has not exercised this right, any person may exercise it concurrently, except in the country of origin.—If the author has not made use of his right, after the expiry of ten years any person may translate the original work and sell translations of it in all countries, except in the country of origin.
7. There should be no restrictions as to formalities placed on the authors of literary or artistic works as a condition for recognition of those rights.—If certain formalities are necessary, this shall be either as an administrative or official requirement, or as a means of establishing and proving the right of property; if it is agreed to assure the accomplishment of these formalities by any kind of sanction, failure to comply with them should not entail the loss of the right.—It is important to render these formalities as simple as possible; the registration and deposit of one or several copies of a work, at the office of a public authority constituted for this purpose, would appear to be the most advantageous method of doing this.

III. Dramatic and musical works

1. The right of performance of dramatic and musical works should be independent of the exclusive right of reproduction.
2. No distinction should be made between the two rights as regards their duration.
3. The right of property in musical compositions shall prevent the public performance by any person of the musical work without the author's consent, regardless of the importance of the work and the mode of performance.—The author's right, however, should not be invoked to prevent private or public musical sessions, where there is a theoretical aim which does not interfere with the interests of art.
4. The right of property in musical compositions shall include the right to make arrangements of the motifs of the original work.

IV. Works of art

1. The author of a drawing, painting, work of sculpture or of architecture or of any other kind of artistic work should alone have the right to reproduce or to authorise the reproduction of it by a similar or distinct art, and in the same or a different scale.

2. . . .
3. The right of property in artistic productions should also include any industrial application which may be made of these works.
4. Special formalities should not be required for works of art, any more than in the case of literary productions, as a prerequisite to the acquisition and maintenance of this right . . .

V. Economic questions

The Congress requests:

1. The abolition of customs duties on books and works of art, or at least the reduction of these duties to more modest levels, and their simplification where different rates of tariffs apply to different categories of literary and fine arts productions . . .

2.06 The effect of these resolutions on national governments is difficult to gauge. In a general sense, they foreshadowed many of the provisions that came to be incorporated in national laws and in bilateral conventions over the next three decades, and finally, of course, in the Berne Convention itself. So far as Belgium was concerned, there was a more immediate effect: the organizing committee of the Congress was constituted a legislative drafting commission, and prepared a draft law based on the resolutions.[16] This draft law was not enacted, but it served as the basis for discussion at an artistic congress which was held at Antwerp three years later. This 1861 Congress gave its support to the 1858 resolutions, and called for efforts by governments to negotiate between themselves for the protection of artistic property.[17] The following decade and a half saw a number of important international conferences and agreements on other matters, including the formation of the International Committee of the Red Cross, the first Geneva Convention on Warfare in 1864, and the founding of the International Telegraph Union in 1865 and the Universal Postal Union in 1874,[18] but there were no further international meetings on copyright. There were some important national meetings, notably in France and Germany,[19] but it was not until 1877 that the question of copyright was raised in an international forum. This was at another artistic congress in Antwerp which was held to commemorate the third centenary of the birth of Rubens.[20] Its resolutions, in substance, were the same as those of the 1858 Congress. Of particular interest, however, was a unanimously adopted motion requesting the recently established

[16] Darras (1887), 522.

[17] Rivière (1897), 143. The Congress met from 19–21 Aug 1861 and was attended by well over 1,000 practising artists. The records of its proceedings are to be found in E Gressin, *Compte Rendu des Travaux du Congrès Artistique d'Anvers* (1862).

[18] See generally Bowett (1982), 6–7; G A Codding, *The International Telecommunications Union* (1952), 20–23; G A Codding, *The Universal Postal Union* (1964), ch 2.

[19] E Röthlisberger, *Die Berner-Uebereinkunft zum Schutze von Werken der Literatur und Kunst und die Zusatzabkommen: Geschichtlich und rechtlich beleuchtet und kommentiert* (1906), 4–5.

[20] ibid.

Institute of International Law to prepare a draft universal law on artistic works.[21] This request was agreed to by the Institute at a meeting later in the same year in Zurich, and a study group was appointed, consisting of legal and artistic representatives from five countries (Belgium, the UK, Italy, the Netherlands, and France). Nonetheless, despite the initial, enthusiastic response from the Institute, and a proposal to extend its terms of reference to include literary works, the working party was not formally constituted until 1882. Thereafter, it appeared to do nothing, and writing in 1887 Alcide Darras said, 'at the present moment, the project must be considered as tacitly abandoned'.[22] By this time, however, the role of the Institute had become irrelevant, in view of the formation of the International Literary Association in 1878 and the consequences that flowed from this. This development is considered in the next section.

D. The Foundation of the International Literary Association and the First Moves Towards the Berne Convention

In 1878, the French Government held a 'Universal Exhibition' in Paris, and it was against this background that the French *Société des gens de lettres* organized an international literary congress in that city. The Congress opened on 17 June under the presidency of no less a figure than Victor Hugo, and further sessions were held over the next 12 days. Apart from Hugo, other distinguished authors, publishers, and prominent public figures from three continents were present, including Turgenev from Russia, Bancroft from the United States, Löwenthal from Germany, and Jerrold from the UK.[23] The Congress concerned itself first with fundamental questions of principle, and after lengthy and somewhat unstructured debates[24] passed a number of resolutions. The most important of these were as follows: **2.07**

> (i) The right of the author in his work constitutes, not a concession by the law, but one of the forms of property which the legislature must protect.
> (ii) The right of the author, his beneficiaries and legal representatives is perpetual.
> (iii) . . .
> (iv) All literary, scientific and artistic works will be treated, in all countries other than their country of origin, according to the same laws as those

[21] '. . . un projet de loi universelle, relatif aux oeuvres artistiques': Darras (1887), 523.
[22] ibid.
[23] For a general account of this meeting (and subsequently early meetings of ALAI), see *Association Littéraire et Artistique Internationale: Son Histoire, Ses Travaux (1878–1889)* (1889), 1–12 ('*Histoire* (1889)').
[24] See the comments by Darras (1887) on this at 524–5. See further V C H Carmichael, *The Paris International Literary Congress* (1878).

applicable to works of national origin. The same system will apply to the performance of dramatic and musical works.
(v) For this protection to be assured, the author need only comply with the formalities of the country in which the work was first published.[25]

2.08 While the last two resolutions calling for national treatment and simplification of formalities were the same as those passed by the 1858 Congress, the first two reflected a more absolutist approach than had been taken at the earlier meeting (although the Paris Congress also passed a motion recommending the adoption, in present national laws, of a transitional system of *domaine public payant*). A more militant spirit was abroad, and this was further displayed at another international artistic congress held in Paris later in 1878.[26] This second congress also called for the constitution between the different states of Europe, and elsewhere, of 'a general Union which would adopt a uniform law in relation to artistic property'.[27] The literary congress made a similar call, requesting the French Government to undertake the initiative of summoning an international conference to formulate 'a uniform convention for the regulation of the use of international property'.[28] However, this request was not taken up by the French Government which therefore lost, to Switzerland, the honour of being the first government to take the international lead in this direction. This Swiss initiative, which gave rise directly to the birth of the Berne Union, was not to occur for another six years, and is dealt with below. In the meantime, a more immediate and practical development that flowed from the 1878 literary congress was the decision, in its session on 27 June, to establish the International Literary Association.[29] This was to be open to literary societies and writers from all countries, and was given the following objects:

1. The protection of the principles of literary property.
2. The organization of regular relations between the literary societies and writers of all countries.
3. The initiation of all enterprises possessing an international literary character.

2.09 Commencing its life under the presidency of Victor Hugo, the new association had a committee of honour comprising notable literary figures from ten countries in both the New and Old Worlds and a larger executive committee with members from nearly twice as many countries.[30] Since that time, it has

[25] *Histoire* (1889), 2. [26] Rivière (1897), 143.
[27] See *L'Union internationale pour la protection des oeuvres littéraires et artistiques: son fondation et son développement—Mémoire 1886–1936* (1936), 26 ('*Mémoire* (1936)').
[28] *Histoire* (1889), 12ff. [29] ibid.
[30] The Committee of Honour appointed at the first congress of the Association in London in 1879 was even more distinguished, containing such heavyweights as Longfellow, Emerson, Tennyson, Trollope, Disraeli, Gladstone, the Emperor of Brazil, de Lesseps, Dostoyevski, Tolstoy, Auerbach, the Prince of Wales, the King of Portugal, and the President of France: *Histoire* (1889), 29.

played a significant, and frequently catalytic, role in international copyright developments. Although there has always been a strong French influence in the Association (with its headquarters in Paris, and a sizeable French-speaking membership), it has held regular congresses in many different cities since this time, beginning with London in 1879. Five years later, its membership was expanded to include artists, and its name was changed to its present title, the 'International Literary and Artistic Association' (*l'Association littéraire et artistique internationale*, or 'ALAI' as it is commonly known).[31] Although concerned with all matters relating to the interests of authors and artists, legal questions have also occupied a central place on the agenda of every congress.[32] This was particularly so in the early congresses, where the Association soon became the leading advocate for fuller international copyright relations. At its 1880 Congress in Lisbon and that of 1881 in Vienna, strong universalist views in favour of uniform national copyright laws were expressed, and at least one model law was privately prepared and listed for discussion at the 1882 Congress in Rome.[33] At the last-mentioned congress, however, a more practical suggestion for a multilateral convention was adopted, based on a cannily conceived proposal put forward by Dr Paul Schmidt of the German Publishers' Guild.[34] This began by postulating that the necessity of protection for 'intellectual property' was the same in each country, and that this need would only be fully satisfied by the constitution, between states, of a union of literary property (*une Union de la propriété littéraire*) similar to that which had been created in the case of the Postal Union.[35] It went on to say that this proposed union should be based on the ideas and views of all interested parties: not only authors, but also publishers, booksellers, composers, and music houses. Acknowledging that the present Congress was not the place in which this process of consultation should occur, it proposed:

[31] *Histoire* (1889), 214. The first meeting under the present name was held in Brussels in Sept 1884.

[32] eg at the London Congress in 1879, Jules Lermina (the first Secretary General of the Association) presented a long report on translation rights in different countries, and there was a further report on adaptations by Jules Claretie (from *la Société des auteurs dramatiques de France*), following which the Congress passed resolutions on both subjects: *Histoire* (1889), 16–27. Again, in Lisbon in 1880 and Vienna in 1881, there were lengthy reports (and consequential resolutions) on various bilateral conventions and aspects of national laws: *Histoire* (1889), 41–66 and 94–107. A similar pattern of reports and resolutions is to be found in each of the annual congresses held throughout the following decades. See further C Masouyé, 'The Role of *ALAI* in the Development of International Copyright Law' [1978] *Copyright* 120.

[33] *Histoire* (1889), 120.

[34] According to Jules Lermina, the form of this proposal was determined by an informal meeting of himself, Schmidt, and Baetzmann (a Norwegian delegate) in a Roman trattoria during the Congress: *La Nation*, 18 July 1910, quoted in *Mémoire* (1936), 28.

[35] *Histoire* (1889), 122.

> . . . that the office of the International Association should be responsible for taking the steps necessary to initiate in the press of all countries as extensive and profound a discussion as possible as to the possible formation of a Union of literary property and the proposal that, at a place and date to be fixed subsequently, a conference composed of the organs and representatives of interested groups should meet to discuss and settle a scheme for the creation of a Union of literary property.[36]

This proposition was unanimously adopted by the Congress, which also (on the motion of Baetzmann, a Norwegian delegate) fixed Berne as the meeting place for the proposed conference.[37] This was appropriate as Berne, in neutral Switzerland, had already been the venue for a number of important international meetings, and served as the headquarters of several international organizations, such as the offices of the Postal and Telegraph Unions, and the International Red Cross.[38]

E. The 1883 ALAI Conference at Berne

(1) Background to the Conference

2.10 Following the adoption of the Schmidt proposal by the 1882 Rome Congress, the president of ALAI, M Torres Caicedo, the Salvadorian Minister to Paris, sought the support of the Swiss Government for the proposed conference. In particular, he requested that government to undertake the diplomatic initiatives necessary to call a conference of states, should the occasion arise.[39] Unlike the French Government in 1878, the Swiss Government readily agreed to this request, and it nominated Numa Droz, a distinguished Swiss legal figure, member of the Federal Council, and head of the Department of Agriculture and Commerce, to act as its representative in the projected proceedings.[40] Droz was an admirable choice for this role from the point of view of authors, as he had a strong interest in copyright matters, and had, in an article published shortly after the Rome Congress, declared himself in favour of an international convention on literary and artistic property.[41] In the same article, he had also argued that this should be easier to attain than had been the recently concluded multilateral convention on patents of invention (the Paris Convention of 1883), and he had minimized the points of difference between the various national copyright laws. During the next three years and four international conferences (over each of which he presided), he was to play a crucial role in the realization of the final convention.

36 *Histoire* (1889), 122–3. 37 ibid.
38 See generally Bowett (1982), 4.
39 *Histoire* (1889), 129–30. 40 ibid.
41 Published in the *Revue Universelle de Lausanne*, and extracted in *Histoire* (1889), 130–2.

The meeting of the conference in Berne, which was fixed for 10 to 17 September 1883, was preceded by the work of three national commissions (one French, one German, and one English) which considered the questions to be put to the conference. A series of five draft propositions, deriving, it seems, from the work of the French commission,[42] were circulated by ALAI before the conference to serve as the bases of discussion. Headed 'Universal Literary Convention, Scheme of Proposals',[43] they were limited in their scope, and were to be supplemented by the work of another commission which was appointed when the conference first met. The first proposal was for national treatment without formality for the authors of literary or artistic works appearing or performed in one of the contracting states in all other contracting states. This was accompanied by a wide definition of the expression 'literary and artistic works' which, after enumerating different kinds of eligible subject matter (in similar terms to many of the later bilateral conventions), concluded with the residual category of 'any production whatsoever in the literary or artistic domain which may be published by any method of printing or reproduction whatever'. The second proposal was the most radical, calling for complete assimilation of translation rights to those of reproduction. The next two dealt with enforcement proceedings by foreign authors in national courts, and with the distinction which was to be drawn between the right of reproduction and the right of property in the object in the case of artistic works. The fifth proposed the establishment of a central, International Office to act as a depository for copies of all copyright laws (present and future) of the contracting states, and to publish a regular review in French containing all relevant documentation and information. From the point of view of the development of international co-operation and co-ordination on copyright matters, this last proposal was perhaps the most significant. **2.11**

(2) The work of the Conference

The Conference held its opening session on 10 September 1883, and was attended by a small but representative number of authors, publishers, lawyers, and officials of literary and publishers' societies. Droz was appointed as president of the Conference, and Louis Ullbach, the French president of ALAI, and Blanchard Jerrold, the British writer, as co-presidents. A drafting commission was also appointed by ALAI before the Conference began, to examine and refine the proposals already circulated for discussion.[44] The most prominent members of this commission were the French jurists Eugene Pouillet (who acted **2.12**

[42] *Mémoire* (1936), 30–1. [43] For the text, see *Histoire* (1889), 135–6.

[44] *Histoire* (1889), 142–3. See also *Bulletin de l'Association Littéraire Internationale*, No 18, Nov 1883, for the full records of the Conference.

as president) and Edouard Clunet (who acted as secretary).[45] Both men were to provide much of the creative tension that prevailed throughout the Conference sessions, as they could usually be relied upon to take opposite sides on most issues. Clunet acted as a kind of *rapporteur général*, opening up discussion and introducing the commission's draft proposals, while Pouillet often provided a more radical perspective. The result, after three days' intense discussion and debate, was a compact draft convention of ten articles, most of which were to survive the deliberations of the three diplomatic conferences which followed over the next three years, and were to provide the basis for the Berne Convention.

(3) The draft convention

(a) Persons and works protected

2.13 The aim of the draft convention was stated as being 'to constitute a general Union for the protection of the rights of authors in their literary works and manuscripts'.[46] Article 1 then embodied the basic principle of national treatment or assimilation, doing so on the basis of place of publication or performance, rather than the author's nationality. Thus, it was provided that the authors of literary and artistic works appearing or performed in one of the contracting states would enjoy in other contracting states of the Union, irrespective of their nationality, the same rights as nationals. This was subject to the condition that these authors had complied with the formalities required by the laws of the country where such publication or performance had taken place. Although this approach gave protection to nationals of non-contracting states (if they published or performed their works in a contracting state), it left a gap covered by the nationality approach which afforded protection to works published in non-contracting states by nationals of contracting states. The merits of the two approaches, in fact, provoked considerable discussion in the conference sessions, and proposals to combine them, as in the Franco-German Convention of 1883, were considered.[47] Nonetheless, the version above (drafted by Pouillet) prevailed.[48] It was supplemented by two further articles which extended protection to manuscripts and unpublished works (article 3), and accorded the same rights to their beneficiaries and legal representatives as were given to authors (article

[45] The other members were Carl Baetz (Germany), Aloys d'Orelli (Switzerland), Laurent de Rille and de Bailly (France), and Teichmann (Switzerland). Schmidt, whose proposal had initiated the calling of the Conference, did not attend: as the Franco-German Convention of 1883 had been concluded since the Rome Congress, he felt that the interests of German publishers had been adequately safeguarded, and therefore withdrew from the organization of the Conference: *Histoire* (1889), 143 (opening speech to Conference by Jules Lermina).

[46] *Histoire* (1889), 182.

[47] ibid, 156ff.

[48] ibid, 161.

4). The expression 'literary and artistic works' was defined in article 2 as including:

> . . . books, brochures and all other writings; dramatic and dramatico-musical works, musical compositions with or without words, and musical arrangements; works of design, painting, sculpture, engraving, lithographs, maps, plans, scientific sketches and in general any literary, scientific and artistic work whatsoever, which may be published by any method of printing or reproduction.

(b) Translation rights

Thanks largely, it seems, to the efforts of Pouillet,[49] the Conference supported the complete assimilation of translation rights, and article 5 of the draft provided: **2.14**

> Authors belonging to one of the contracting states will enjoy, in all the other states of the Union, the exclusive right of translation throughout the duration of their right in their original works.

In clarification of the expression 'their right', there was a rider to article 5: 'This right comprehends the rights of publication of performance . . .'. A further article (article 6) provided that an authorized translation was protected in the same way as the original work, and that, in the case of a translation of a work that had fallen into the public domain, the translator could not prevent the making of further translations of the same work by other writers.

(c) Infringement proceedings

Article 8 dealt further with the question of national treatment, providing that in infringement proceedings to enforce their rights under the Convention foreign authors were entitled to seek and obtain the same civil relief that was available to nationals under national laws. A significant addendum to this article stipulated that adaptation was to be considered as infringement and was to be proceeded against in the same way. This was approved without much discussion by the Conference, and no consideration was given to the question of defining or clarifying the term 'adaptation'.[50] This was to become an important issue at subsequent international meetings.[51] **2.15**

(d) Other provisions

The retroactivity of the Convention (another vexed issue for future conferences) was dealt with in article 8, which provided simply that the Convention would apply to all works which had not yet fallen into the public domain, in the country of origin of the work, at the moment of the Convention's entry into **2.16**

[49] ibid, 169. [50] ibid, 172–3.
[51] See paras 3.05 and 3.17 below.

force.[52] A further significant provision was found in article 9, which reserved to states of the Union the right to enter separately into particular arrangements between themselves for the protection of literary and artistic works, so long as these arrangements did not contravene the dispositions of the proposed convention. A similar provision had been included in the recently concluded Paris Convention on Industrial Property,[53] and was an implicit acknowledgement that the projected literary convention was far from being a universal copyright codification. This was, of course, inevitable, given that the Convention's basic principle was that of national treatment, supplemented by some fundamental requirements in relation to such matters as translation rights. It was therefore clear that the draft convention established only a minimum level of protection which each state was obliged to apply to persons claiming under the Convention, and which each state was entitled to augment through bilateral or other multilateral arrangements; this has remained true of the subsequent Berne Convention, in all its revised forms. Finally, article 10 of the draft convention dealt with the establishment of an International Office of the proposed Union to act as a clearing house for information relating to the copyright laws of the member states.

(e) Appraisal of the draft convention

2.17 In comparison with the provisions of many of the bilateral conventions already in force, the ALAI draft convention was a relatively limited document. Apart from its commitment to complete assimilation of translation rights, and its treatment of adaptations as infringements, it was silent on several important matters. One of these was the duration of rights, an omission which would confer windfall gains on authors from contracting states with shorter terms of protection who sought protection in contracting states with longer terms, and corresponding disadvantages to authors from the second category of states seeking protection for their works in states of the first category. Another omission was the Convention's failure to clarify the precise classes of rights that were to be recognized by each country, a particular problem in the cases of adaptations and reproductions of artistic works in different dimensions. A further lacuna was the failure to include any provisions dealing with restrictions on reproduction rights, although there were many precedents for such provisions in existing bilateral conventions. There was also no reference to moral rights, although this was understandable as these were only beginning to gain protection under national laws, and their scope and content was not yet adequately defined.

52 *Histoire* (1889), 183.
53 Article 15.

(4) Developments following the 1883 Conference

Despite these defects, the ALAI text was to form the basis for formal negotiations on a governmental level for a multilateral copyright agreement. These came shortly after the conclusion of the ALAI Conference, following on the initiative of the Swiss Government. In December 1883, the latter, acting at the request of ALAI, addressed a circular note to the governments of 'all civilised nations'. This began with the following homily: **2.18**

> The protection of the rights of authors in their literary and artistic works (literary and artistic property) is becoming more and more the object of International Conventions. It is, in fact, in the nature of things that the work of man's genius, once it has seen the light, can no longer be restricted to one country and to one nationality. If it possesses any value, it is not long in spreading itself in all countries, under forms which may vary more or less, but which, however, leave in its essence and its principal manifestations the creative idea. This is why, after all civilized States have recognised and guaranteed by their domestic legislation the right of writer and of artist over his work, the imperative necessity has been shown of protecting this right in international relations, which multiply and grow daily. This need has been responded to by the numerous conventions entered into between the principal States during the last few years.
>
> But regardless of the advantages presented by these conventions it must first be recognized that they are far from protecting the author's rights in a uniform, efficacious, and complete manner. This insufficiency results, without doubt, from the diversity of national laws, which the conventional regimes must necessarily take into account.
>
> The inequalities, and even the grave omissions, in the present international law cannot fail to affect deeply those concerned, authors, publishers, and other interested parties. We therefore see great efforts on their part to secure, on the one hand, universal recognition of the rights of authors without distinction of nationality, and on the other, the desirable uniformity in the principles which govern this matter.[54]

The circular note then went on to relate the founding of ALAI in 1878, and the work of the recent Berne Conference, the *procès-verbaux* of which was enclosed, together with the draft convention. It then stated:

> The Federal Council has not hid from the initiators of this project that it sees difficulties in its immediate realization in its entirety. In fact, the conventions recently concluded, or in force for the last few years, are more or less in contradiction with some or some part of the dispositions of this project, and it is not to be expected that these conventions can be easily modified before they lapse.
>
> But, on the other hand, it would certainly be a great gain to agree at present to a general understanding by which the higher principle, and, as it were, the natural

[54] For the text of this letter (in French), see *Actes* 1884, 8–9. For another English translation, see *Switzerland No 1 (1886), Correspondence Respecting the Formation of an International Copyright Union*, C-4606 (1886), Papers presented to Parliament in Jan 1886 ('*Correspondence No 1* (1886)').

> right should be proclaimed, that the author of a literary or artistic work, no matter what may be his nationality, or the place of reproduction, ought to be protected everywhere equally with the natives of each state. This fundamental principle, which does not interfere with any existing convention, once admitted, and with a general Union constituted on this basis, it is beyond doubt that, under the influence of the exchange of views which would be established between the states of the Union, the most objectionable differences which exist in international law would be, by degrees, removed, to give place to a more uniform regime which is more certain for authors and their legal representatives.[55]

It was in this sense, then, that the Swiss Federal Council lent its support to the ALAI initiative. It went on to say that if this was favourably received, it would hold a diplomatic conference, in the course of the following year, which would examine the common dispositions which each state, either in their internal laws, or in international law, could currently adopt.

F. The Diplomatic Conference of 1884[56]

(1) The background to the Conference

2.19 The Swiss Government circular received an immediate, favourable response from eleven countries which declared themselves ready to be represented at a diplomatic conference. These were Germany, Argentina, Colombia, France, the UK, Guatemala, Italy, Luxembourg, Salvador, Sweden, and Norway.[57] Six other states which did not respond to the circular—Austria-Hungary, Belgium, Costa Rica, Haiti, Paraguay, and the Netherlands—were nonetheless to send delegates to the conference when it was held.[58] Another five states—Greece, Denmark, Saint Dominica, Nicaragua, and Mexico—gave negative responses, citing as

[55] *Actes* 1884, 9.

[56] For general accounts of the work of the 1884 Conference and its successors in 1885 and 1886, see: Rivière (1897), ch IV; Darras (1887), 518ff; C Soldan, *L'Union Internationale pour la protection des oeuvres littéraires et artistiques. Commentaire de la Convention de Berne du 9 Septembre 1886* (1888); R Lavollée, *Propriété Littéraire et la Convention de Berne* (1887) ('Lavollée (1887)'); N Droz, 'Conférence diplomatique de Berne dans le but de constituter Une Union pour la protection des droits d'auteur' (1884) 11 *Journal du droit international privé et de la jurisprudence comparée* (*Clunet*) 441, and 'Deuxième conférence diplomatique de Berne dans le but de constituer une Union pour la protection des oeuvres littéraires et artistiques' (1885) 12 *JDIPJC* (*Clunet*) 481; A D'Orelli, *La Conférence internationale pour la protection des droits d'auteur réunie à Berne du 8 au 19 Septembre 1884* (1884), from *Revue de Droit International*, Dec 1884; A D'Orelli 'Les dispositions impératives et normatives de la Convention internationale de 9 Septembre 1886' [1889] *DA* 1, 13; 'Le Vingt-Cinquième Anniversaire de la Convention de Berne du 9 Septembre 1886' [1911] *DA* 116, 129; A D'Orelli, *La Conférence Internationale pour la protection des droits d'auteur réunie à Berne du 8 au 19 Septembre 1884* (1884); E Clunet, *Étude sur la Convention d'Union internationale pour la protection . . .* (1887); E Bricon, *Des Droits d'auteur dans les rapports internationaux* (1888).

[57] *Actes* 1884, 9.

[58] ibid.

their reason either the current state of their copyright laws or their lack of literary development.[59] Bulgaria and the USA gave no commitment as to their participation in the conference.[60] However, the latter country made a general declaration to the effect that while it was, in principle, prepared to accept the proposition of the Federal Council in favour of international protection, it saw immense practical obstacles in the way of bringing all states into one convention.

> Differences in tariffs, and the fact that, apart from the author or artist, several industries have an interest in the production or the reproduction of a book or a work of art should be taken into account when considering whether to accord to the author of a work the right to have it reproduced or to prevent its reproduction in all countries. There is a distinction between the painter or the sculptor, whose work is saleable as made by his hands, and the literary author, to whose work the paper manufacturer, the type-setter, the printer, the bookbinder and many other persons in commerce contribute.[61]

This statement is of some significance, as it reflects the basic attitude which the USA was to take to international copyright agreements, an attitude that has remained essentially unchanged until quite recently. As a consequence, while the United States Government was to be represented at each of the early Berne Conferences, economic considerations caused it to remain aloof from these present negotiations, and were to keep it outside the Union that was ultimately formed.

(2) The Federal Council programme

Following these favourable responses to its circular, on 28 June 1884 the Swiss Federal Council sent out a formal invitation to other governments to send delegates to a diplomatic conference to begin in Berne on 8 September 1886.[62] Adopting a pragmatic approach, the Council stated that it did not **2.20**

> . . . think that the proposed Conference should take resolutions of a kind that would bind the different states, but rather it should be of a preliminary nature and should not have any object other than determining the general principles which would have the greatest chance of being realized in current circumstances. The provisional results thus obtained should then be submitted for examination by the sovereign governments, and it would then be apparent whether or not there is any way of constituting the projected general Union.[63]

On 22 August 1884, the Federal Council circulated a programme for the conference. This comprised a draft convention of 18 articles, a transitional disposition, and a closing protocol. These were based closely on the ALAI text, but contained a number of significant drafting changes and additions of

[59] ibid. [60] ibid. [61] ibid. [62] *Actes* 1884, 10. [63] ibid.

an organizational or machinery kind. Thus, the constitution of the proposed Union was dealt with in a separate article (article 1), rather than appearing in the preamble as in the ALAI draft. Adaptation was also made the subject of a separate article (article 10), rather than being part of the general article on infringement as in article 7 of the ALAI text. Another article (article 3), which no doubt drew its inspiration from the recent Swiss federal law of 1883,[64] assimilated to subjects or citizens of contracting states those subjects or citizens of non-contracting states who were domiciled or had published their works in the territory of one of the states of the Union. The last five articles (articles 14–18) dealt with a number of practical matters, such as new accessions to the Union (article 15), its duration (to be indefinite), denunciations (article 17), and ratifications (article 18). Another significant provision stipulated that there would be regular revisions of the Convention (article 14). The models for these last provisions were to be found in the recently concluded Paris Convention on Industrial Property.[65] The transitional disposition dealt with the relationship of other bilateral conventions to the proposed convention, and the Closing Protocol contained a number of provisions elaborating on the role and finances of the proposed International Office of the Union. The Protocol also had several provisions dealing with the interpretation of certain expressions used in the body of the Convention, namely 'adaptation' and 'musical arrangement'.[66]

(3) The work of the Conference

(a) Countries represented

2.21 Twenty delegates from thirteen countries were nominated to attend the Conference, which opened in the Hall of the Council of States in Berne on 8 September 1884. Of these, the delegates from Paraguay and Salvador were unable to attend, nor were those of Italy, although the Italian Government made known its support for the idea of the proposed Union and reserved the right to give its adhesion to the decisions of the Conference after examining the *procès-verbaux*. Thus, delegates from ten countries actually attended the Conference: Germany, Austria-Hungary (with separate representation for both Austria and Hungary), Belgium, Costa Rica, France, the UK, Haiti, the Netherlands, Sweden and Norway (both separately represented though at that time under one monarchy), and Switzerland.[67] During the course of the Conference, further apologies for absence and expressions of interest in its outcome were received from the governments of Brazil, Argentina, Spain, and Portugal.[68]

[64] Swiss Law of 1883, art 10.
[65] Paris Convention 1883, arts 14–19.
[66] Paras 3 and 4.
[67] *Actes* 1884, 15–20.
[68] ibid, 39–40 (17 Sept 1884).

(b) The delegates

The delegates themselves were a varied group. In the main, they were either diplomats already accredited to Switzerland by their respective governments (in the case of France, Belgium, the UK, and the Netherlands), or high officials from their countries' foreign, justice, or commerce ministries (in the case of Germany, Austria-Hungary, Sweden, and Switzerland).[69] Costa Rica and Haiti were represented by academics, and Norway by the Norwegian vice-president of ALAI (F Baetzmann).[70] The president of ALAI (L Ullbach) was also present in the capacity of an adviser to the French delegation; in addition, there were several distinguished academic lawyers attached to the German and Swiss delegations (Dambach and D'Orelli respectively).[71] The Conference, in contrast to those that were to follow was a small-scale affair, perhaps not much larger than many of WIPO's present day working groups or committees of experts. Furthermore, despite the presence of so many diplomatic and governmental officials, there was still a high general awareness of, and familiarity with, the issues involved in international copyright protection. Three particular exemplars of this interest were Adams (the British minister to Berne), Arago (the French ambassador to Switzerland), and Reichardt (the senior counsellor at the German legation). **2.22**

(4) The preliminary character of the Conference

At the opening session, Numa Droz was again appointed as president of the Conference, and the chief French delegate (Arago) was made vice-president.[72] A set of procedural rules for the conduct of the Conference was also adopted, the most important of which were provisions to use the Federal Council's draft programme as the basis for discussion, and to appoint a drafting commission in which each state would be represented to consider these proposals before submitting them to the consideration of the full Conference.[73] In addition, separate votes were accorded to Austria, Hungary, Sweden, and Norway in recognition of their separate *de facto* legal systems.[74] The preliminary or provisional character of the Conference's work was also underlined at the opening session by the declarations of the British and Netherlands representatives that they were charged by their governments only to attend in a consultative capacity, and not to vote or bind their governments as to the acceptance of any conclusions which might be reached by the Conference.[75] The Swedish and Norwegian delegates made similar declarations, the latter stressing that the present state of **2.23**

---

[69] See generally ibid, 15–20. [70] ibid.

[71] Louis Renault, the leading French academic lawyer of his day, had also been appointed by the French Government to assist its delegation, but was unable to attend at the last moment, and his place was taken by René Lavollée, the French Consul General.

[72] *Actes* 1884, 22, 289.

[73] ibid, 22–3. [74] ibid, 23. [75] ibid.

Norwegian law would not allow this.[76] Declarations to the same effect were also made by the Austrian and Hungarian delegates.[77]

(5) The German initiative

(a) The resolution

2.24 The discussions at the first session of the Conference were largely directed by the German delegation which took the initiative in two ways. First, at the opening session, it declared itself as a strong supporter of universal codification by proposing the following question to the Conference:

> Instead of concluding a convention based on the principle of national treatment, would it not be preferable to aim for a codification, in the framework of a convention, regulating in a uniform manner for the whole projected Union, and in the framework of a convention, the totality of dispositions relating to the protection of copyright?[78]

This raised negative responses from the French, Swedish, and Swiss delegations, chiefly as regarded the appropriateness of such a proposal in the light of the many differences in national copyright laws which still existed.[79] It is safe to assume that a similar view was shared by other delegations, in particular the British, although there is no report of any opinion which they may have expressed on this question. The result, however, was a compromise motion proposed by the Swiss Government which stated the chief objection to universal codification in the following terms:

> Whereas, desirable as may be a universal codification of the principles which regulate the protection of the rights of the author, in view of the differences in existing laws and conventions, it is to be feared that such a project would postpone for a long time the conclusion of a general understanding;
>
> Whereas the essential aim to be attained, for the present, is the constitution of a Union, the successive development of which will lead to the desired uniformity,
>
> The Conference decides that:
>
> (i) It is necessary to formulate the bases of an international convention that will command immediate acceptance by the largest number of States.
> (ii) It is equally necessary to formulate resolutions under which uniformity between laws and conventions will be recommended to States.[80]

At the request of the chief German delegate, no vote was taken on this resolution at this stage of the proceedings. Nevertheless, it was clear that the German proposal had had a salutary effect, as it had made delegates consider the overall objectives they were seeking to attain. As will be seen below, this question was returned to at the end of the Conference.

76 *Actes* 1884, 23–4. 77 ibid, 24. 78 ibid. 79 ibid, 28–9. 80 ibid, 29.

(b) The questionnaire

Discussion then ensued on the second part of the German initiative. This comprised a series of detailed questions which sought to clarify or challenge the provisions of both the Federal Council and ALAI drafts; it also pointed to a number of gaps in the two documents.[81] It queried whether it would not be better to accord conventional protection only on the basis of nationality and, in relation to the formalities and conditions required for protection, asked whether these should be those of the country to which the author belonged, those of the country where publication of the work took place, or those of the country where protection was claimed. It also questioned why musical arrangements were included in the list of works protected, but not works of the plastic arts relating to geography, topography, architecture, or the natural sciences. As to omissions in the draft texts, it raised the issue of duration of protection, strongly urging the adoption of some uniform term by all the countries of the proposed Union. In the event that there was not agreement on this, it advocated the application of the principle found in many of the earlier bilateral conventions, under which protection accorded reciprocally to authors of two contracting countries was only assured to them during the existence of their rights in their country of origin and, in the other country, was not to exceed the period fixed by law for its national authors. It also asked whether similar restrictions on the reproduction right to those appearing in other conventions should be included, for example, in relation to scientific or instructional uses, inclusion of extracts in chrestomathies, and reproduction of newspaper articles. It further suggested the adoption of a uniform term of protection throughout the Union for translation rights, if these were not given the same protection as reproduction rights. It also raised the question of whether there was a need for a uniform conventional regime in relation to performing rights in musical, dramatic, and dramatico-musical works, and whether the definition of the term 'adaptation' would be better left to the discretion of national courts. Other issues referred to in the questionnaire included the scope for separate arrangements between contracting states, the retroactivity of the proposed convention, and the status of current bilateral conventions. The final matter was formalities: as such things as registration or deposit were not required in some countries (including Germany), it was asked if it might be desirable for the proposed convention to relieve parties, in legal proceedings, from the requirement of formally justifying their copyright. 2.25

(c) Responses to the questionnaire

The German questionnaire has been described in some detail in the preceding paragraph because of the important focus for discussion and expression of views 2.26

[81] ibid, 25–6.

which it provided before the drafting commission began its work. These discussions lasted two days (9 and 10 September). During these sessions, the attitudes of the different delegations on various issues were ventilated, and certain decisions in principle were taken. Thus, it emerged that opinion was sharply divided on the appropriate criterion for conventional protection. The Germans opposed protecting non-nationals, while the French and Scandinavians argued that to do so would encourage the accession of non-contracting states to the Union.[82] On the other hand, it was agreed to include works of the plastic arts in the definition of literary and artistic works,[83] but to delete musical arrangements which should be dealt with in the context of adaptations.[84] Discussion on duration of protection, however, was inconclusive. There was little support for the adoption of a uniform term, and there was division between the delegates as to whether the period should be determined by the law of the country of origin (as suggested by Germany), or by the law of the country in which protection was claimed (preferred by France and Switzerland).[85] The question of restrictions on reproduction rights was referred to the commission, with clear warnings by the French that these should be kept to a minimum.[86] On the matter of translation rights marked differences also emerged. The French, Germans, and Swiss favoured complete assimilation, but the Swedes stated that they would only be prepared to accept a much shorter term of protection, and that the solution of this question would be decisive so far as their participation in the Union was concerned,[87] The matter of performing rights was referred to the commission,[88] as was that of adaptation, but not before there had been marked disagreement between the French and Germans as to the possibility of arriving at an acceptable definition of the term 'adaptation'.[89] After discussion, the remaining questions were also referred to the commission.[90]

(d) The work of the commission

2.27 Following these discussions, the commission began its work. There were, in fact, two commissions: a drafting commission of five members (from Germany, France, Austria-Hungary, Sweden, and Switzerland),[91] and a special commission, again of five members (from Germany, France, Belgium, Norway, and

[82] *Actes* 1884, 29. [83] ibid, 30. [84] ibid. [85] ibid, 30–1. [86] ibid, 31.
[87] ibid, 31–2. [88] ibid, 34. [89] ibid.
[90] ibid, 36. On the matter of formalities and legal proceedings, however, while there was support from the French for the German view that these could be dispensed with, the British delegate (Adams) made it clear that his country still required registration and deposit, and that this had recently prevented the UK from entering a convention with Switzerland, a country which had no such requirements.
[91] Reichardt (Germany), Steinbach (Austria-Hungary), Ullbach (France), Lagerheim (Sweden), Droz (Switzerland): *Actes* 1884, 40.

Switzerland),[92] which was charged with considering the organization of the proposed International Office. After six days, on 17 September these commissions brought back five documents to the Conference for adoption: a draft convention concerning the creation of a general Union for the protection of the rights of the author, an additional article to that Convention, a closing protocol, a set of principles for an 'ulterior unification', and the final *procès-verbal* of the Conference.[93] After a further day's debate, these documents were adopted, with some changes, by the Conference on 18 September. Although only of a provisional character, these documents contain the first formal proposals, at a governmental level, for a full multilateral copyright convention. In brief, they contained the following proposals.

(6) The draft convention (and additional article)[94]

(a) Persons and works protected

This was longer than either the ALAI or Federal Council drafts, and comprised **2.28** twenty-one articles. As in the ALAI draft, it provided that the contracting states were establishing a 'Union for the protection of the rights of authors in their literary and artistic works' (article 1). The principle of national treatment was applied in substantially the same way as in the ALAI draft (article 2), but the matter of duration of protection was also taken into account. Thus, it was stipulated that national authors of each contracting state were to enjoy, in all other countries of the Union, in respect of their works, whether in manuscript form, unpublished or published, the advantages currently accorded or to be accorded in the future to nationals. The same treatment was also accorded to the legal representatives and successors in title of such authors (article 5). However, in all cases, this was subject to the temporal limitation that this treatment was only to be reciprocally assured during the subsistence of the authors' rights in their own country (or 'country of origin').[95] This last provision was essentially a compromise between, on the one hand, the adoption by all contracting states of a uniform term of protection,[96] and, on the other hand, the application of national treatment 'pure and simple' (with the consequence that a work which had fallen into the public domain in its country of origin might continue to receive protection in other contracting states with longer terms).[97] A further limitation dealt with formalities, providing that national treatment was to be

[92] Dambach (Germany), De Dudzeele (Belgium), Lavollée (France), Baetzmann (Norway), Orelli (Switzerland): *Actes* 1884, 40.

[93] *Actes* 1884, 40.

[94] *Actes* 1884, 77–82. See also Appendix 2(d) below.

[95] The commission thought that to provide that this protection should last no longer than that of nationals (as stipulated in many bilateral conventions) was superfluous: *Actes* 1884, 42.

[96] *Actes* 1884, 42.

[97] ibid. Note the particular objections made to this by the Swedish delegates.

subordinated to compliance with the formalities and conditions prescribed by the law of the country of origin of the work, or in the case of unpublished works, by the law of the country of which the author was a national. In addition, the Federal Council's proposal for assimilation of foreign residents to nationals was rejected (principally because of German objections),[98] and was replaced by a separate article (article 3) that accorded national treatment to the publishers of literary and artistic works published in one of the countries of the Union, and of which the author was a national of a non-Union country. In adopting this provision, the Conference accepted the opinion of the commission that the word 'publisher' (*éditeur*) was to be understood in the widest possible sense, so as to apply, for example, to the producer of a dramatic performance.[99] Furthermore, the Conference accepted the clarification sought by the French delegate that it was implicit in the general requirement of national treatment under article 2 that authors claiming protection under the Convention would have the same protection and recourse to law against infringement as were enjoyed by nationals (a matter expressly provided for in the discarded Federal Council draft).[100] As for the definition of the expression 'literary and artistic works', the Federal Council (and ALAI) draft was in substance retained (article 4), with the removal of 'musical arrangements' to a separate clause dealing with adaptations, the inclusion of 'illustrations',[101] and the replacement of the words 'natural sciences' by the words 'in general'.[102] Photographs, however, were not included, as these were not protected as copyright works under German law.[103]

(b) Translation rights

2.29 The proposal in the draft convention concerning these (article 6) was considerably more cautious than the proposals for complete assimilation contained in the ALAI and Federal Council drafts. Several different formulations had been considered by the commission, but the one which it put forward was based on proposals by the German and Swedish delegations. This provided for a limited period of protection, on condition that the translation was done within a certain period following publication of the original work.[104] This approach was strongly

[98] *Actes* 1884, 43–4 (apparently the Germans feared that this would not encourage non-contracting states to join the Union).

[99] ibid, 44. This formulation still met with disapproval from the French delegate (Lavollée) who gave the example of Rossini, an Italian subject living in France, who would not have protection for any of his works published for the first time in Italy, if that country did not become a member of the proposed Union.

[100] ibid, 43. [101] ibid, 44. [102] ibid.

[103] ibid, 44–5. It was nonetheless accepted that this did not exclude photographs of works that were themselves protected. In Germany, photographs were protected as a kind of 'neighbouring right' under the law of 10 Jan 1876.

[104] *Actes* 1884, 78–9.

opposed by the French delegate who made eloquent pleas for complete assimilation.[105] The more restrictive view finally prevailed in the Conference, largely because of the Swedish arguments that readily available translations were of great important to the Scandinavian countries in view of their small, dispersed populations and educational needs.[106] The regime adopted was quite detailed but basically required each Union country to accord to national authors of other Union countries an exclusive translation right in their works of ten years' duration following first publication of the work in any Union country. To enjoy the benefits of this disposition, it was necessary that an authorized translation appeared, in full, within three years of the original date of publication; furthermore, the exclusive right thereby conferred was limited to the language (or languages) of the authorized translation. A series of special provisions also covered the cases of works published in instalments or in several volumes,[107] while a separate article stipulated that translated works were to be protected as original works in their own right (article 7). These proposals were hardly a step forward from the provisions of many of the bilateral conventions then in force. Nevertheless, they demonstrate very clearly that, even at this early stage, there were considerable gulfs between what may be called the 'producing' nations—that is, those nations, such as the French, that were net exporters of literary and artistic products—and those nations, such as the Scandinavians, which were 'users'—that is, net importers—of these products. As a result, however distasteful the present compromise was from the point of view of authors' rights, pragmatically it had the best chance of commanding agreement from those 'user' nations present at the Conference, to say nothing of those not present but whose later adherence might be desired. At the same time, once the principle of translation rights (however attenuated) was accepted, this opened the way to further extensions to these rights in the future.

(c) Restrictions on reproduction rights

A further series of compromises between authors' rights and user demands were to be found in articles 8 and 9, which contained a number of restrictions on the reproduction right. The first of these articles provided that each contracting state was to permit, reciprocally, the publication of 'extracts, fragments and whole parts' (*d'extraits, de fragments ou de morceaux entiers d'un ouvrage*) of a literary or artistic work that had first appeared in another Union country, 'provided that this publication was specially made and adapted for educational purposes or had a scientific character'.[108] Equally to be protected was the reciprocal publication of chrestomathies comprised of pieces of works of different authors, as well as the insertion, in a chrestomathy or in an original work **2.30**

105 ibid, 47–8 (speech by Lavollée).
106 ibid, 48.
107 Article 6, paras 3–5.
108 Article 8, para 1.

published in one of the countries of the Union, of a whole work of small compass published in another Union country.[109] These borrowings were subject to the requirement that the name of the author of the work borrowed, or its source, was to be indicated;[110] furthermore, the benefit of these exemptions was not to be applicable to the inclusion of musical compositions intended for use in schools of music.[111] The form of article 8 was based on a German draft, which had been adopted by the commission.[112] However, similar kinds of provisions were to be found in earlier bilateral conventions, including the Franco-German Convention of 1883.[113] Nevertheless, while these restrictions were accepted—and adopted—by the majority of conference delegates, they were trenchantly criticized by the French delegates who thought that this kind of clause did not belong in a general convention but should be confined to special conventions (such as the Franco-German one).[114]

2.31 The limitations proposed in article 9 concerned the reproduction of newspaper and periodical articles. These again were based on a German draft, but there were precedents for such provisions in a number of bilateral conventions.[115] The main part of this article provided that articles extracted from newspapers or periodical collections published in any Union country might be reproduced, either in the original or in translation, in other Union countries.[116] The rationale for this considerable restriction on authors' rights was the public interest in the dissemination of information and news on an international level. Nevertheless, the licence conferred was curtailed in a number of significant ways. It did not apply to serial novels (*romans feuilletons*) or to articles on science or art.[117] Nor did it apply to 'other articles of some length' extracted from newspapers or periodicals in relation to which the authors or publishers had expressly declared, in the issues in which the articles appeared, that reproduction was prohibited.[118] These exclusions from the general licence granted by the article pointed to the informatory rationale suggested above, and this was underlined by a further provision to the effect that in no case were these exclusions to apply to articles of 'political discussion' (*articles de discussion politique*).[119] Nevertheless, there was an obvious lack of precision in the expressions used in the article, for example, 'articles on science or art', 'other articles of some length', and 'articles of political discussion'. No clarification of these questions was attempted in the article itself, but a final paragraph provided that difficulties arising with regard to the application of the article were to be decided by national courts 'conformably to

[109] Article 8, para 2. [110] Article 8, para 3. [111] Article 8, para 4.
[112] *Actes* 1884, 50–1.
[113] Convention between France and Germany, 19 Apr 1883, art 4.
[114] *Actes* 1884, 51–2. [115] See para 1.37 above. [116] Article 9, para 1.
[117] Article 9, para 2. [118] ibid. [119] Article 9, para 3.

the domestic law of each country'.[120] In the Conference the main criticism of this article came from a 'user', rather than a 'producer', nation. The Haitian delegate made a forceful speech, urging the deletion of articles on science from the category of prohibited articles, and pointed to the contradiction that this would otherwise create with respect to article 8 under which such copying was permitted in the case of books.[121] He also maintained that to permit the copying of scientific articles would encourage the spread of scientific learning, particularly in more backward countries, such as the one he represented.[122] These arguments, however, were rejected by the Conference, which adopted the article without any change.[123]

(d) Arrangements and performance

Articles 10 and 11 dealt with musical and dramatic works. Under the first **2.32**
(which stemmed again from a German proposal), it was provided that the right of protection in musical works entailed the prohibition of musical arrangements, as well as of other pieces which, without the author's consent, were composed on themes taken from these works, or which were reproductions of an original work with modifications, reductions, or additions.[124] It was left to national courts to determine, in accordance with the laws of their respective countries, the way in which this provision was to be applied.[125] This was the only article of the draft convention to deal directly with the question of adaptations, and then only in this limited fashion. Article 10 of the Federal Council draft had included a simple provision to the effect that adaptations of works were to be considered as infringements, but this provision had given rise to extensive debate, both in the commission and the Conference. Thus, the French delegation advocated a lengthy definition of the concept which contained guidelines as to what acts came within it.[126] A simpler, and perhaps more restrictive, definition was put forward by the Swedish delegation to the effect that an adaptation was a reproduction of an original work with non-essential changes, additions, or deletions which could not be considered as a new and original work in its own right.[127] Finally, the commission concluded that it was difficult to arrive at any satisfactory definition, and that it was best to omit any reference to the matter in the body of the Convention. At the same time, it acknowledged that there was a need for guidelines to assist national courts, and it therefore decided to refer to this in the Closing Protocol (see further para 2.35 below).[128] As for article 11, this dealt with performing rights, providing that the stipulations of article 2 were to apply to the public representation of published or unpublished dramatic or dramatico-musical works,[129] and further that the

120 Article 9, para 4. 121 *Actes* 1884, 52–4. 122 ibid. 123 ibid.
124 Article 10, para 1. 125 Article 10, para 2. 126 *Actes* 1884, 57.
127 ibid. 128 ibid, 58. 129 Article 11, para 1.

authors of these works, during the period of their exclusive translation rights, were to be reciprocally protected against the unauthorized public representation of translations of these works.[130] A similar provision was made in the case of musical works, but this was only to apply where the author had expressly indicated on the works that he prohibited their public performance.[131] The precedent for this last provision was to be found in a number of recent national laws where it had been adopted to prevent vexatious claims by musical copyright owners.[132]

(e) Enforcement of rights under the Convention

2.33 With respect to the rights secured to them under article 2, and in particular the right to institute legal proceedings to enforce these rights before national courts, article 12 provided that it was sufficient evidence of their entitlement for authors of works to indicate their names on the title pages of their works, at the bottom of the dedication or preface, or at the end of the work.[133] This was another article which had its basis in a German proposal.[134] In the case of anonymous or pseudonymous works, it was further provided that the publisher whose name was indicated on the work was entitled to protect the rights belonging to the author, and was, without further proof, to be deemed the representative of the anonymous or pseudonymous author.[135] These, then, were the only requirements which authors belonging to one Union country would have to comply with in order to gain protection for their works in another Union country (although it will be recalled that article 2 still made this protection subject to compliance with the conditions and formalities required by the law of the author's country of origin). This protection was supplemented by article 13 which provided for the seizure of imported pirated works.[136] It was left to the domestic legislation of each country to determine whether this seizure should take place at the request of the relevant public authority or that of the interested party.[137] Another borrowing from bilateral conventions was to be found in article 14, which reserved to the governments of Union countries the right to control the circulation, performance, or exhibition of works within their territories (the 'police power').[138]

(f) Final provisions

2.34 The remaining articles of the draft convention were substantially similar to those in the Federal Council programme, although some changes and additions were made. The retroactive effect of the Convention was made subject to the

130 Article 11, para 2.
131 Article 11, para 3.
132 eg the UK Copyright (Musical Compositions) Act 1882, s 1.
133 Article 12, para 1.
134 *Actes* 1884, 55–6.
135 Article 12, para 2.
136 Article 13, para 1.
137 Article 13, para 2.
138 See para 1.39 above.

'reserves and conditions to be settled by mutual consent'; it was also expanded to include manuscripts and unpublished works (article 15). The right of contracting states to make separate (but non-conflicting or more extensive) agreements between themselves was retained (article 16), and the article dealing with revisions of the Conference was softened, leaving this as a possibility but not as a positive requirement (article 18). It was also made clear that, in the case of countries wishing to accede to the Convention, their internal laws should be in compliance with the requirements of the Convention (article 19). The articles dealing with entry into force of the Convention, denunciations, and ratifications remained essentially unchanged (articles 20 and 21). This was also true of the provisions dealing with the establishment, functions, and finances of the International Office (article 17 and the Closing Protocol). An additional article dealt with existing bilateral conventions. This was more strongly worded than the draft provision included in the Federal Council programme, which had maintained the pre-existing conventions until their expiry, even if they departed from the proposed Convention on one point or another.[139] Under the new draft, it was provided that nothing in the Convention was to affect the maintenance of the conventions currently in force between contracting states, insofar as these conventions conferred upon authors or their representatives more extensive rights than those accorded by the Union, or included other stipulations which were not opposed to the Convention. This change was consistent with article 16, which took a similar approach to agreements subsequently made between contracting states.[140]

(7) The Closing Protocol

This contained a number of points of clarification or interpretation arising out of the principal provisions of the Convention. The most detailed were concerned with the organization and finances of the proposed International Office,[141] and require no further discussion at this point.[142] As for the rest, paragraph 1 dealt further with the question of retroactivity, and the way in which this was to be settled between Union members. This was an important matter, and was to give rise to dispute in the early years of the Convention.[143] Paragraph 2 was also concerned with an important matter—the manufacture **2.35**

[139] This draft had also provided that, in the case of conventions with such provisions, the subjects and citizens of Union countries which were not bound by these conventions were to be admitted to the benefit of most favoured nation treatment in the respective countries: *Actes* 1884, 62.

[140] This was the view of the commission: *Actes* 1884, 62.

[141] See further para 2.48 below.

[142] See further Chapter 16 below for an extended treatment of the administrative and financial arrangements of the Berne Union today.

[143] See paras 3.05 and 6.112ff below.

and sale of instruments by means of which musical works might be mechanically reproduced—and contained a declaration that these acts were not to be considered as acts of piracy. A similar provision was to be found in the laws of several countries, including France and Switzerland.[144] At this time, the leading examples of such instruments were pianola rolls and musical boxes, and the dangers posed to authors of musical works did not appear great. However, this position was to change radically with the development of the phonogram over the next few years.[145] Paragraph 3 dealt with adaptations, but hardly took matters any further. While it evidenced a general agreement by the delegates that piracy comprised all kinds of illegal attempts against authors' rights, it went on to state that they were of the opinion that 'in place of enumerating and defining them it is preferable to entrust to the [national] tribunals the responsibility of determining, in each particular case, the prejudice resulting from any particular form of piracy'. Finally, paragraph 4 dealt with photographic works. These had not been included among the list of works to which the Convention was to apply, because they were not protected by the copyright laws of several countries represented at the Conference.[146] All paragraph 4 did, therefore, was to reserve to governments of Union countries the power to make subsequent agreements between themselves to secure the reciprocal protection of photographic works within those Union countries.

(8) Principles recommended for an ulterior unification and the *procès-verbal final*

2.36 The origin of the first of these was to be found in the far-reaching German proposal calling for international codification of copyright law which had been presented at the first session of the Conference.[147] After consideration of this, and also of the compromise Swiss proposal,[148] the commission prepared a further set of proposals under the above title which incorporated features from both earlier ones. It read as follows:

> The International Conference for the protection of authors' rights,
>
> Having seen the diversity of the stipulations in force in different countries regarding several important aspects of the protection of the authors' rights;
>
> and
>
> Considering that, desirable as the unification of the principles which govern the subject may be, at the present time a Convention regulating these points in a uniform manner would not perhaps obtain the adhesion of a certain number of countries;
>
> and

[144] French Law of 10 Mar 1866; Swiss Law of 1883, art 11.
[145] See further para 3.17 below. [146] See n 103 above. [147] See para 2.24 above.
[148] ibid.

Considering, moreover, that an international codification is in the nature of things, and will be effected sooner or later, and that the way for it should be paved by indicating the way in which it is desirable that this codification should be made;

Thinks it right to submit to the Governments of all countries the following views:—

(i) The protection accorded to authors of literary or artistic works should last for their entire lifetime, and after their death for a period of years which should not be less than thirty.

(ii) It is right to favour as much as possible the tendency towards the complete assimilation of the right of translation to the right of reproduction in general.[149]

These principles were not accepted without hesitation by some members of the Conference. The French delegates would have preferred a period of fifty, rather than thirty, years, as well as some explicit reference to the need to accord justice to authors.[150] In addition, the Austrians and Hungarians declared that they were unable, in the light of their domestic laws, to associate themselves with the second resolution concerning translations.[151] These qualifications aside, the principles were adopted by the Conference without a vote. The *procès-verbal final*, which was signed at the same time by all the delegates, recorded their agreement to submit the draft convention for the examination of their respective governments, the Convention being described as 'embodying the minimum of rights which, in the opinion of the Conference, the Contracting Governments would be able reciprocally to guarantee to the authors of literary or artistic works'.[152]

(9) Evaluation of the work of the 1884 Conference

This Conference went further and was more permeated with universalist views **2.37**
than could reasonably have been expected at the outset. There was predictable disappointment among authors' and artists' societies that universal codification was still a long way off, and that the justice of their claims had not been fully recognized,[153] but this obscures the important advances that had been made. In large part, the achievements of the Conference were due to the efforts of the German delegation, and their carefully prepared series of questions, which provided a clear focus for the delegates' debates. As the British delegate, F O Adams, put it, the Germans 'succeeded in transforming a moderate programme into a draft Convention of considerable dimensions'.[154] In this regard, it is

[149] *Actes* 1884, 65. [150] ibid, 65–6. [151] ibid, 65. [152] ibid, 66.

[153] See eg the criticisms of the French *Syndicat des sociétés littéraires et artistiques* in (1885) 12 *JDIPJC* (*Clunet*) 55 and the response made to these by Numa Droz in (1885), 12 *JDIPJC* (*Clunet*) 163.

[154] *Correspondence No 1* (1886), 29 (despatch to Earl Granville, 26 Sept 1884).

interesting that the French, usually the leaders in this field, had been overshadowed by the Germans,[155] and that a number of French proposals, such as those regarding assimilation of translation rights, had not been accepted by the Conference. On the other hand, this was only a preliminary, or exploratory, meeting, and it was notable for the number of delegates who had been given only a watching brief by their respective governments. Referring again to the view of the British delegate, at this stage only four nations looked certain to join the proposed Union—France, Germany, Switzerland, and Sweden[156] (and Adams was to be proved wrong with respect to the last country). As far as several other countries were concerned, changes in their domestic laws would be required for them to be in a position to join. This applied particularly to Austria-Hungary but also to Switzerland. Accordingly, another diplomatic conference was necessary before the final form of the Convention could be settled.

G. The Diplomatic Conference of 1885

(1) Preparations for the Conference

2.38 Following the conclusion of the work of the 1884 Conference, the Swiss Government wasted no time in informing all interested governments of the details of its work, and seeking their views on the further steps which might be taken to assure the constitution of the proposed Union. The Government also foreshadowed its intention to hold a further conference in September 1885 to conclude this project.[157] In the light of the favourable responses received, including a number from countries which had not sent delegates to the earlier conference, formal invitations to the new conference were issued in April 1885.[158] This began its deliberations on 9 September, once again in Berne.

(2) The delegates

2.39 This time, twenty-six delegates from sixteen countries attended: from Germany, the USA, Argentina, Belgium, Spain, France, the UK, Haiti, Honduras, Italy, Paraguay, the Netherlands, Sweden and Norway (again separately represented), Switzerland, and Tunisia.[159] Notable additions were, of course, the USA, Italy, and Spain; equally noticeable, however, was the absence of Austria-Hungary and the continued aloofness of the Russian Empire. It also appears likely that the UK would not have been represented at the Conference, but for the strong representations in favour of this that had been made by British authors' groups

[155] For a contrary view of the proceedings, however, see Lavollée (1887), 9–10.

[156] *Correspondence No 1* (1886), 29.

[157] *Correspondence No 1* (1886), 33.

[158] ibid, 35.

[159] *Actes* 1885, 7. Costa Rica announced its intention to attend, but sent no delegates.

and the announcement by the USA that it was attending.[160] Mainly because of this the British contribution to the Conference proceedings was to be quite significant, and provided a considerable boost to the ranks of the pragmatists.[161] As for the delegates themselves, there was considerable continuity here as many of the delegates had also attended the Conference of the previous year.[162] Once again, they were chiefly diplomats or high-ranking officials from relevant government ministries, but there was a sprinkling of expert advisers, either from the universities[163] or the literary and artistic societies.[164] Continuity was also assured by the re-elections of Numa Droz and Emmanuel Arago as the president and vice-president of the Conference respectively.[165]

(3) The work of the Conference

The Conference was conducted along similar lines to that of 1884. The bases **2.40** for discussion were the draft convention and accompanying documents prepared by the previous conference, and time was allowed in the opening sessions for the presentation of amendments and statements of position by the various delegates, before more detailed work was done by a smaller drafting commission. In particular, the French delegation resumed its prominent role as an advocate of fuller copyright protection, putting forward a number of proposals to strengthen the Convention. These included fresh proposals for complete assimilation of translation rights,[166] the addition of photographs to the list of works protected,[167] and the reduction of restrictions on reproduction rights.[168] The British delegates also stepped out decisively from their role of silent observer at the first conference to become the most persuasive advocates of the principle of national treatment 'pure and simple'. Thus, wherever there was disagreement over the adoption of a uniform rule on a particular matter, they would urge that this was best left to be regulated by national legislation.[169] As for the other delegations, the Scandinavians again represented the views of 'user' nations in relation to translation rights,[170] while the Haitian delegate repeated

[160] *Correspondence No 1* (1886), 36. See further the interesting study of UK involvement in the Berne drafting conferences by Sherman and Bently (n 1 above) and see also B Sherman and L Bently, *The Making of Modern Intellectual Property Law: The British Experience, 1760–1911* (1999), 111–28.

[161] F O Adams, the British minister to Berne, and H G Bergne, the superintendent of the treaty department in the Foreign Office. Note the interesting biographical details of both men given by Sherman and Bently (n 1 above).

[162] Adams (the UK); Reichardt, Meyer, and Dambach (Germany); Arago, Ulbach, and Lavollée (France); Verwey (the Netherlands); Ruchonnet, Droz, and D'Orelli (Switzerland); Lagerheim (Sweden); and Baetzmann (Norway).

[163] eg D'Orelli (Switzerland), Renault (France and Tunisia), and Dambach (Germany).

[164] eg Tamayo y Baus (Spain), Ulbach (France), Rosmini (Italy), and Baetzmann (Norway).

[165] *Actes* 1885, 14. [166] ibid, 26 [167] ibid, 21. [168] ibid, 29.

[169] ibid, 27, 32. [170] ibid, 26–8, 30.

his forthright criticism of the exclusion of scientific articles from the free usage permitted by article 10.[171] The Germans also continued to play an active part,[172] while the Italians and Spanish, in general, provided further support for the French position.[173] Of the other states represented, the delegates from the USA, Argentina, and Paraguay made it clear early on that they were attending only as observers.[174]

2.41 After two days, the Conference was adjourned, and the work of the drafting commission began. As in 1884, this was a small body and comprised only seven members: Reichardt (Germany), Tamayo (Spain), Renault (France and Tunisia), Bergne (the UK), Rosmini (Italy), Lagerheim (Sweden), and Droz (Switzerland).[175] Its conclusions were embodied in three draft documents which it submitted to a full session of the Conference on 17 September, together with a lengthy formal report which detailed the various drafts that had been considered.[176] The three documents were a draft convention, an additional article, and a closing protocol.

(4) The draft convention

(a) General comments

2.42 If the 1884 draft was like a tree that had had an unexpected spurt of spring growth, the work of the 1885 Conference was similar to that of the gardener who does the pruning before the next spring. This is not to say that efforts were not made, particularly by the French delegation, to preserve, and even extend, the earlier year's growth; nor were such efforts wholly unsuccessful. However, the basic sentiment of the Conference is to be found summed up in the opening paragraphs of the commission's report where it referred to the two choices before the delegates: to have a convention embodying a considerable degree of uniformity from which countries not so advanced in copyright would be excluded, or to have a less rigorous convention to which as many countries as possible would be able to adhere.[177] The commission, and subsequently the Conference, adopted the second approach, although not without some expressions of dissent by several delegations.[178] The substance of the earlier text was retained, but a number of areas were cut back or simplified. However, several extensions of the text were also made. Leaving aside a number of drafting amendments, the principal changes of substance concerned the principle of national treatment (article 2 of the new draft), translations (article 5),

[171] *Actes* 1885, 30–2. [172] See eg ibid, 20–3, 26–7, 29–30, 34.
[173] See generally ibid, 20–37.
[174] ibid, 7. A similar treatment was also made by the Dutch delegate at 34.
[175] ibid, 59. [176] ibid, 39–57. [177] *Actes* 1885, 39.
[178] Lavollée (1887), 9–10.

reproductions of newspaper and periodical articles (article 7), adaptations and musical arrangements (article 10), and enforcement proceedings under the Convention (article 11). A new article (article 19)[179] dealt with the application of the Convention to the colonies and other possessions of signatory countries, and the closing protocol also contained a number of changes, particularly in relation to the financing of the International Office.

(b) National treatment

2.43 The commission was concerned that the wording of the 1884 draft left it open to national tribunals to apply the law of an author's country of origin where this was less favourable to him than that of the country in which he was claiming protection in matters other than duration of protection.[180] While this was a questionable interpretation of article 2 of the 1884 draft, the commission was nonetheless concerned to remove any ambiguity. It therefore proposed a rewording of the article which made it clear that the law of an author's country of origin was only relevant in two respects: as regards compliance with formalities and duration of protection.[181] Further provisions dealt with the determination of the country of origin of a work where it was published[182] and unpublished.[183] These changes were duly accepted by the Conference, and incorporated into the final text.

(c) Translation rights

2.44 These again attracted considerable controversy, both in the commission and in the Conference. The French delegates sought a return to the principle of complete assimilation, but this was strongly opposed by user nations such as the Scandinavians, and was narrowly defeated on the ground that its adoption would prevent a number of important nations from joining the proposed Union.[184] A number of other amendments were also discussed, including changes to the periods fixed in the 1884 draft. In this regard, a British proposal to leave the fixing of these periods to national laws was also rejected,[185] and the final compromise approved by the Conference was the deletion of the three-year period.[186] This left authors with an absolute right of translation for ten years after publication, and was clearly simpler. On the other hand, it was stated that this was a minimum period, and that there was nothing to prevent contracting states agreeing among themselves to accord longer periods of protection.[187]

[179] *Actes* 1885, 35–6. [180] ibid, 41–2. [181] Article 2, para 2.
[182] Article 2, para 3. [183] Article 2, para 4.
[184] *Actes* 1885, 26–8 and 43–5. The vote was six to five, with Belgium, Spain, France, Haiti, and Tunisia voting for complete assimilation.
[185] ibid, 44. The vote in the commission was eight to four.
[186] ibid, 62–3 (declaration by Lavollée, for France), and 63 (declaration by Lagerheim, for Sweden and Norway).
[187] ibid, 45 (the report of the commission).

(d) Restrictions on reproduction rights

2.45 Both articles 8 and 9 of the 1884 draft received considerable amendment (becoming, in the process, articles 7 and 8 of the new draft). In the case of reproductions of newspaper and periodical articles, there was a British proposal to delete this article altogether, as it contradicted the requirement of their law that the sources of such borrowings should be indicated. This was decisively lost, and, drawing on a Norwegian proposal, the commission proposed a new draft which deleted any reference to indications of source, and continued the limitation contained in the 1884 draft concerning the author's right to prevent the reproduction of articles of political discussion, while adding a new limitation relating to reproduction of 'news of the day or current topics' ('*la reproduction des nouvelles du jour et des faits divers*').[188] At the request of the British delegates, the Conference agreed that, under this formulation, those countries whose laws required that the source of newspaper articles which were reproduced within their territories should be indicated were free to continue to impose this requirement, but that there was no reciprocal obligation to do so on the part of those countries whose laws did not contain such a requirement.[189] The Conference further confirmed (at the request of the German delegation) that the expression 'articles of political discussion' only applied to writings on current politics, and not to essays or studies on economic or political questions.[190] It was finally declared that the reproduction licence conferred by the article did not extend to the reproduction of a series of articles appearing in the same newspaper.[191] The new article 8 dealing with borrowings of extracts of works was also discussed extensively before its final form was settled. Several delegations, including the French and British, favoured the complete deletion of the 1884 draft, while other delegations were opposed to particular parts of it.[192] By way of compromise, it was severely modified so as to leave the regulation of lawful borrowings for educational and scientific purposes, and for inclusion in chrestomathies, as a matter for the domestic legislation of contracting states or for particular arrangements between two or more of those states.

(e) Adaptations

2.46 Further changes were also made in relation to indirect appropriations of works. Article 10 of the 1884 draft had been solely concerned with musical arrangements, while the closing protocol had made more general reference to the overall question of indirect appropriations. In the 1885 Conference, the French delegation again sought to have included an article which listed particular kinds of acts which should be forbidden, rather than leaving this question of

---

188 *Actes* 1885, 46. The difficulty in drawing this distinction hardly requires any comment.
189 ibid. 190 ibid. 191 ibid. 192 ibid, 47.

definition to national tribunals.[193] Once again, however, there was strong opposition to this proposal, and it was decisively defeated.[194] Nevertheless, there was general recognition by the delegates that reproductions which were not essentially different from the original work or which lacked the character of a new work should not be allowed. The result of these debates was the adoption of a new article (article 10), based on a Swedish proposal which, without defining the term 'adaptation', declared that non-essential changes to a work which did not give it the character of a new and original work should be regarded as unauthorized indirect appropriations. Musical arrangements were given as an instance of these unauthorized appropriations, but the article also declared that the application of this article was to be left to national tribunals acting in accordance with the laws of their respective countries.[195] It was also accepted by the Conference that dramatizations were to be considered as unlawful indirect appropriations.[196]

(f) Other changes

Only minor changes were made to the remaining articles of the 1884 draft convention, except for a new article 19 dealing with accessions to the Convention by metropolitan governments on behalf of their colonies and other possessions, and the addition of a new paragraph to article 17, which required that changes to the Convention should only be made with the unanimous consent of all Union countries. The latter stemmed from the concern expressed by the British delegates that countries which needed to change their domestic copyright laws in order to adhere to the Convention would be reluctant to do so if the Convention could be readily changed at a later time.[197] As will be seen below, this requirement of unanimity has not prevented the emergence, over time, of different Convention texts which enjoy the adherence of some, but not all, Union countries. This development is discussed in detail below.[198] It should also be noted in this regard that article 15 of the 1885 text retained the facility provided in the 1884 draft for individual member states to make agreements between themselves, provided that these agreements did not run contrary to the stipulations of the Convention. **2.47**

As for the closing protocol, this received considerable revision. The paragraph dealing with adaptations was deleted, and now appeared in article 10. More explicit provision was also made in relation to photographs, it being provided that those countries which treated photographs as artistic works would admit them to the benefits of the Convention. In addition, authorized photographs of protected works of art were to be accorded the same protection as the principal **2.48**

193 ibid 48. 194 ibid, 49. 195 ibid. 196 ibid, 50.
197 ibid, 53. 198 See further paras 3.06 and 3.19 below.

work.[199] A new paragraph also dealt with choreographic works of art,[200] under which those countries of the Union that implicitly included choreographic works amongst dramatico-musical works agreed to admit them to the benefits of the Convention, although national courts were to decide any questions which arose concerning the application of this paragraph.[201] As for the manufacture and sale of instruments for the mechanical reproduction of musical works, the paragraph exempting these acts from the taint of infringement was carried over from the 1884 draft.[202] Finally, a new system of financing the activities of the proposed International Office was outlined, under which the contributions of member states were to be determined according to which one of six classifications a country placed itself upon its accession to the Union.[203] This system, which remains largely unchanged today, is dealt with in detail in Chapter 16 below. As for the 'Principles recommended for an ulterior unification' in the 1884 draft, these were deleted altogether at the recommendation of the commission: while agreeing with the principles, the latter thought that there was little point including them in the Convention which was to be a statement of binding obligations between Union countries.[204]

(5) Evaluation of the 1885 draft

2.49 This was more of a compromise document than its predecessors. In large part, this was due to the influence of the British delegates, but there had also been a general desire among most delegates that the Convention should not be couched in terms so absolute as to discourage countries with lesser levels of copyright protection from acceding to the proposed Union. Nevertheless, although the 1885 text was to remain essentially unchanged, there were still reservations among the delegates as to whether or not their governments would approve it. In the case of the UK, for example, legislative changes were necessary before it could accede to the Convention, and the Scandinavian countries were in a similar position.[205] Belgium was also in a state of flux, as its domestic law was still undergoing a complete revision.[206] France, on the other hand, made it clear that she felt that the Convention did not go far enough in relation to such matters as assimilation of translation rights, and that her support for the present text was simply to ensure the adherence of states such as the UK. In other words—and in keeping with article 17 which provided for regular revisions of

---

[199] Closing Protocol, para 1. [200] *Actes* 1885, 21. [201] Closing Protocol, para 2.

[202] Closing Protocol, para 3. But note that, on the recommendation of the commission, the Conference left open the question of whether the use of these devices in public to perform a musical work would constitute an infringement of the copyright in that work: *Actes* 1885, 55.

[203] Closing Protocol, para 5.

[204] *Actes* 1885, 57. [205] ibid, 61 and 62 (declarations by respective delegates).

[206] ibid, 60 (declaration by delegate). Note also the positions of the Dutch and Spanish delegates: ibid, 60 and 62.

the Convention—the 1885 text was only the first step along the path to full and uniform international protection for authors.[207] Of the sixteen delegations represented at the Conference, twelve[208] signed the final *procès-verbal* which requested the Swiss Federal Council to take such steps as would be necessary to convoke a further diplomatic conference of the states represented at the present Conference, to be held within a year's time, to transform the draft text into a formal diplomatic instrument.[209] The birth of the Berne Union was therefore only a year away.

H. The Diplomatic Conference of 1886

This was essentially a formal proceeding, and there was no intention that the **2.50** text settled by the 1885 Conference should be subject to any significant amendment. The Swiss Federal Council sent out invitations to the new conference on 6 November 1885, fixing September 1886 as the date for its meeting. However, there was considerable domestic activity in this intervening period, as governments considered the question of accession, particularly in the UK where considerable changes to its copyright laws were required to enable this to occur.[210] There was, in fact, in that country a move for a complete revision of its archaic and chaotic Copyright Acts, but considerations of time prevented this from occurring. The subsequent legislative changes were therefore limited to those necessary to enable the UK to sign the Convention.[211] The progress of affairs in that country was of considerable importance to the territorial scope of the proposed Convention: as Numa Droz pointed out at the opening session of the 1886 Conference, the accession of the UK and its colonies and other possessions brought some 300 million people within the Union, more than doubling the combined populations of all the remaining original members.[212] Difficulties with their domestic laws, however, proved too much for Sweden and Norway to sign the Convention, although their governments indicated their

[207] ibid, 62 (declaration by delegate).

[208] Germany, Spain, France, the UK, Haiti, Honduras, Italy, the Netherlands, Sweden, Norway, Switzerland, and Tunisia. The four which did not sign were the USA (see the further declaration by Boyd Winchester, the United States delegate, in *Actes* 1885, 60–1), Argentina, Paraguay, and Belgium. However, in the case of the last, her reason for not signing was the pending changes in her laws, and she reserved her right to sign at a later stage (which she duly did): *Actes* 1885, 60.

[209] *Actes* 1885, 81.

[210] See generally *Correspondence No 1* (1886) and *Switzerland Nos 2 and 3 (1886), Further Correspondence Respecting the Formation of an International Copyright Union*, Papers presented to Parliament in Jan, Aug, and Sept 1886 respectively. See also H G Bergne, 'The International Copyright Union' (1887) 3 *Law Quarterly Review* 14.

[211] ibid. [212] *Actes* 1886, 13–14.

desire to do so as soon as possible.[213] Their domestic laws also prevented the Netherlands and Austria-Hungary from acceding.[214] The same was true of the USA, but that country still expressed its general support for the aims of the Convention, and hinted that it might accede in the future.[215]

2.51 When the Conference met on 6 September 1886, twelve countries were represented: Germany, Belgium, Spain, the USA, France, Haiti, Italy, Japan, Liberia, Switzerland, the UK, and Tunisia.[216] Both the USA and Japan attended only as observers, but this first official indication of its interest by the latter is of some significance. Thus, unlike the USA, which only acceded to the Convention in 1989, Japan was to do so in just over a decade's time, as part of its overall policy of industrial modernization.[217] The other states represented signed the Convention and its annexes (the additional article and closing protocol) on the last day of the Conference, 9 September 1886.[218] These documents were, with some minor drafting amendments, the same as those settled by the 1885 Conference. In the *procès-verbal de signature*, the French and British Governments declared further that their accession covered all their colonies and foreign possessions, while the Spanish Government reserved the right to make known its determination as regarded its own colonies at the time of exchange of ratifications.[219]

2.52 The new Convention came into force on 5 December 1887, this being three months after the exchange of ratifications which took place in Berne in September of that year.[220] All but one of the states which had signed the *procès-verbal de signature* at the 1886 Conference ratified it, the exception being Liberia, which acceded nearly twenty years later.[221] Despite this relatively limited membership, the geographical sweep of the new Union was considerable when account is taken of the colonial possessions of France, Germany, Italy, Belgium, Spain, and the UK. In addition, the last-mentioned state had acceded to the Convention on behalf of her principal self-governing dominions, namely the Australian colonies, New Zealand, Canada and Nova Scotia, the Cape Colony and Natal, and India. However, the new Union was very far from being universal, even in the limited nineteenth-century conception of that term. A number of important European states remained outside it, most notably Austria-Hungary, Portugal, the Netherlands, the Scandinavian countries (although these

213 *Actes* 1886, 14 (opening speech by Droz). 214 ibid.
215 ibid, 19 (declaration by Winchester, United States delegate, to the Conference).
216 ibid, 7 and 8.
217 Japan adhered to the Berne Union on 15 July 1899: see [1899] *DA* 49.
218 *Actes* 1886, 26–41.
219 ibid, 42–4. See further para 17.49 below.
220 See arts 20 and 21.
221 On 16 Oct 1908: [1908] *DA* 145.

were soon to come in),[222] and the vast Russian Empire. Although this was the age of colonialism and it is therefore inappropriate to bemoan the lack of involvement by those African, Middle Eastern, and Asian countries that were still independent powers, such concern was justified in the case of the USA and the Spanish and Portuguese-speaking American republics.[223] While the USA and several of the latter had been represented at some of the Berne conferences, it was obvious that the concept of a universal copyright union did not yet appear to be of direct relevance to them or to their authors. Even a century later, following the entry of a wide variety of countries into the Berne Union after World War II, it still lacked real universality, retaining unmistakeable signs of its Old World origins and orientations. This state of affairs, of course, changed as the Union entered its second century, and this development is examined in Chapter 4. It remains to survey the development of the Union since its inception in 1886, and then to examine the scope and effect of its present operation. The first of these matters is addressed in the following two chapters, and the second in Part III.

[222] Sweden on 1 Aug 1904: [1904] *DA* 89; Norway on 13 Apr 1896: [1896] *DA* 65; Denmark on 1 July 1903: [1903] *DA* 73.

[223] Nonetheless, the example of the Berne Convention did have an effect as far as South American countries were concerned. In 1889, the Montevideo Convention, which was modelled closely on the Berne Convention, was formed, and comprised a number of South American countries. See further Chapter 18 below and Ladas (1938), chs XXII and XXIII.

3

THE SUBSEQUENT DEVELOPMENT OF THE BERNE CONVENTION, 1886–1971

A. Introduction

The present chapter deals with the changes which have been made to the Berne Convention from its inception in 1886 until the adoption of its last revised text in Paris in 1971. Article 17 of the 1886 Act provided for periodic revisions, and these (apart from the first and last) have occurred at roughly twenty-year intervals during this period: in 1896, 1908, 1928, 1948, 1967, and then, finally, 1971. There was also one minor addition made in 1914. The purpose of this chapter is to outline the main changes that were made in these revisions, so as to give an overall picture of the development of the Convention. These changes will be referred to in more detail in the chapters of Part II which deal with the individual articles of the current Convention text, and appropriate cross-references are made where necessary. **3.01**

Since 1971, developments concerning the Berne Convention have largely happened 'off stage', or in different arenas, such as the new World Trade Organization. Nonetheless, in this post-1971 period, the Convention has continued to be the centrepiece of the international copyright system and, in many ways, has become even more critical than it was in the pre-1971 period. These post-1971 developments are the subject of the following chapter.

B. The 1896 Paris Revision Conference[1]

(1) Background to the Conference

3.02 Paragraph 6 of the Closing Protocol of the 1886 Act provided that the first conference of revision of the Convention should be held in Paris within six years of the entry into force of the Convention. The reason for this comparatively short period stemmed from the belief of several delegations, notably the French and Swiss,[2] that, if the dynamic character of the Convention were to be preserved, an early date for its revision should be set so as to maintain momentum and to stimulate countries to adhere to the Convention. Although this evoked some opposition from the British delegates, who were anxious to avoid the necessity of making too frequent changes to their domestic laws so as to conform with changes in the Convention,[3] in the event the Paris Revision Conference did not take place until nine years after the date of entry into force of the Convention. During this time, the membership of the Union had risen to thirteen, with the accessions of Luxembourg,[4] Monaco,[5] Montenegro,[6] and Norway.[7] In addition, the International Office of the Union had been established in Berne, and since January 1888 had published a monthly record of information relating to the affairs of the Union and to national copyright laws in general in its journal *Le Droit d'Auteur*.

The programme for the Paris Conference, prepared jointly by the French Government and the International Office, consisted of a series of changes to

[1] For further background on the 1896 Revision Conference, see A Huard, 'La prochaine Conférence de Paris' [1893] *DA* 81, and the extensive series of studies published in *DA* between the years 1898 and 1905: [1898] *DA* 32 (Pt I—General), 53 (Pt II—Posthumous Works), [1899] *DA* 1 (Pt III—Architectural Works), 13 (Pt IV—Choreographic Works), 62 (Pt V—Photographs), [1901] *DA* 138 (Pt VI—Photographs), [1902] *DA* 2 (Pt VII—Photographs), 14 (Pt VIII—Non-Unionist Authors), 26 (Pt IX—Definition of 'publication'), 73 (Pt X—Reproduction in newspapers and periodicals) [1903] *DA* 18 and 26 (Pt XI—Translation Rights), 62 and 74 (Pt XII—Adaptations), [1904] *DA* 14 and 25 (Pt XIII—Seizure of infringing copies) [1905] *DA* 81, 93, and 106 (Pt XIX—Retroactive effect of Convention). See also L Rivière, *La Protection internationale des Oeuvres littéraires et artistiques: Étude de Législation Comparée* (1897), ch V, and the work done by ALAI at another conference held in Berne in 1889 and reported on by A Darras in *Rapport sur la deuxième conférence réunie à Berne par l'Association littéraire et artistique internationale* (1890). See also the work done by the *Institut de Droit International* in its fifth commission held in Cambridge in 1895: *Révision de la Convention de Berne du 9 septembre 1886 créant une Union internationale pour la protection des oeuvres littéraires et artistiques: Conclusions présentées au nom de la Commission par Mm Roguin rapporteur et Renault co-rapporteur.* See also G Huard, *Étude sur les modifications apportées à la Convention de Berne par la Conférence réunie à Paris, du 15 avril au 1er mai 1896*, extract from *Bulletin de la Société de législation comparée* (1897).

[2] *Actes* 1886, 18.

[3] ibid, 17.

[4] 20 June 1888: [1888] *DA* 64.

[5] 30 May 1889: [1889] *DA* 94.

[6] 1 July 1893: [1893] *DA* 33.

[7] 13 Apr 1896: [1896] *DA* 65.

provisions of the principal text and Closing Protocol. At the same time, the International Office published a number of supporting papers relating to the subject matter of the proposed amendments.[8] In general, these amendments were cautiously framed, with a view to closing gaps left by the 1886 Act, while providing for limited advances on selected fronts. Nevertheless, as several countries made clear at the outset of the Conference their reluctance to accept any major changes to the Convention,[9] those finally made were even more limited in their scope. Furthermore, unanimity was not reached on several questions, with the consequence that some Union countries did not accept either some or any of the new amendments. While the general aim of the Conference was consolidation and clarification of the 1886 Act, one of its major consequences was to be the replacement of one single Union by several restricted Unions as various countries became bound by slightly differently worded texts. This process of fragmentation is described further below.

(2) States represented at the Conference

The Conference met from 15 April to 4 May 1896 in the Hall of Clocks at the French Ministry of Foreign Affairs. All Union countries, with the exception of Haiti, were represented, the largest delegations being those of the French, Germans, British, and Belgians.[10] A number of delegates had also been present at the earlier Berne Conferences from 1884 to 1886, notably Reichardt and Dambach from Germany, Borchgrave from Belgium, Pouillet and Renault from France, Bergne from the UK and Baetzmann from Norway.[11] As before, the delegates were principally diplomats or civil servants, but an important part in the Conference proceedings was played by two distinguished French lawyers: Eugène Pouillet, the veteran protagonist of the ALAI Conference of 1883, who gave an extended historical exegesis on the background to the Convention at the opening session of the Conference,[12] and Louis Renault, the eminent academic international lawyer (also the delegate for Tunisia), who prepared the final report of the commission and drafting committee. However, the most significant feature of the Conference was the large number of delegations from non-Union countries which attended in the capacity of observers. These totalled fourteen and, apart from the perennial United States delegate, comprised representatives from the majority of European states which were still outside the **3.03**

[8] *Actes* 1896, 35–50 (the programme); Union international pour la protection des oeuvres littéraires et artistiques, *Études sur diverses questions relative à la revision de Convention de Berne (Droit de traduction. Instruments de musique mécaniques. Oeuvres d'architecture. Oeuvres photographiques. Principe fondamental de la Convention. Reproduction des articles de journaux. Protection des auteurs non-unionistes)* (1896).

[9] Notably the UK and Norway: ibid, 35–6.

[10] *Actes* 1896, 85–6.

[11] ibid.

[12] ibid, 104–9.

Union (with the notable exceptions of the Austro-Hungarian and Russian Empires), and a significant number of Central and South American states.[13] Under the Conference rules, which were similar to those adopted at the earlier conferences, these non-Union delegates were given the right to take part in the proceedings of both the Conference and the commission.[14]

(3) The work of the Conference

3.04 The amendments arrived at by the Conference were of a relatively limited nature, and affected only a small number of articles. Article 2 was amended so as to make it explicit that the expression 'published' meant 'published for the first time', and a new paragraph was added, including posthumous works amongst protected works. The anomaly in article 3 under which only the publishers of works of non-Union authors published for the first time in a Union country were protected was also removed, and this article henceforth applied to the authors themselves, on the ground that 'the gates of the Union should be open to all'.[15] No changes were made to article 4, although proposals by Belgium and France to include architectural and photographic works in the list of works protected were fully debated, as was a proposal by Italy to include choreographic works.[16] Extensive debate also occurred over the vexed question of translation rights, '*la question internationale par excellence*'.[17] Although there was a strong majority in favour of complete assimilation of these rights, agreement could still not be achieved, largely because of British and Norwegian opposition.[18] However, a considerable advance was made, on the basis of a Belgian proposal for complete assimilation which was subject to the qualification that the translation right would be lost if it had not been exercised within ten years from first publication of the original work by publication in one of the countries of the Union of a translation in the language for which protection was claimed. Accordingly, any unauthorized translation made within the ten-year period would be prohibited, but after this time the right to do so would fall into the public domain for all languages, except for those in which an authorized translation had appeared.[19] This was viewed as a transitional measure by the majority of Union delegates, and it was drafted in such a way that the ten-year limitation could be simply deleted at a later conference in order to attain complete assimilation.[20] While it secured British support, the Norwegian delegate was unable to agree to it, since his country had recently changed its copyright law so as to

[13] These countries were Argentina, Bolivia, Brazil, Bulgaria, Colombia, Denmark, the USA, Greece, Guatemala, Mexico, Peru, Portugal, Romania, and Sweden: *Actes* 1896, 87–8.

[14] ibid, 99, 100 (art 6 of the *Règlement*).

[15] ibid, 165 (report of Renault).

[16] ibid, 122 (text of amendments), 166 (Renault).

[17] ibid, 168.

[18] ibid, 114–15, 168–9.

[19] ibid, 169.

[20] ibid.

adhere to the 1886 text, and there would have been difficulties in making further changes to that law so as to conform with the new text.[21]

A number of different amendments seeking either to narrow or extend the range of lawful borrowings from newspaper and review articles which could be made under article 7 were also considered.[22] However, the final draft approved by the Conference simply provided that this did not include the reproduction of serial novels (*romans-feuilletons*),[23] and the article was left essentially unchanged. There was also a French proposal to delete the requirement of reservation in respect of performing rights under article 9, but this was opposed by both the German and British delegations which cited public opinion in their countries as being hostile to the notion that an author should be able to prevent performances of his work where he had not previously reserved his rights.[24] Accordingly, this matter was deferred to the next revision conference for consideration. There was also British opposition to another French proposal to amend article 10 so as to include dramatizations of novels, and the making of a novel from a play, as forms of illicit reproduction. This was not proceeded with, and was dealt with in an interpretative declaration (see para 3.06 below).[25] The only other changes made to the principal text were minor amendments to articles 12 and 20.[26] As for the Closing Protocol, paragraph 1 was amended so as to admit architectural works to the benefit of the provisions of the Convention in those countries of the Union where such works were protected.[27] Likewise, paragraph 4 (dealing with retroactivity) was amended so as to make it clear that its stipulations, together with those of article 14, applied equally to the extended right of translation now conferred under article 5, and to make these provisions applicable in the case of new accessions to the Union.[28] **3.05**

(a) The form of the 1896 Revision

This also requires special mention. There were two ways of proceeding: making a new Convention, embodying the above amendments, to replace the 1886 Act, or embodying these amendments in an Additional Act separate from the 1886 Act. The first course had the advantage of simplicity: there would only be one text to consult. However, this gave rise to a practical problem with respect to those countries which needed parliamentary approval before they could agree to **3.06**

[21] ibid, 134–5 (declaration by Baetzmann, Norwegian delegate).
[22] ibid, 123–4. [23] ibid, 171. [24] ibid, 172 (Renault).
[25] ibid, 173 (Renault). The status of both dramatizations and 'novelizations' was uncertain under English law at this time: see further *Warne* v *Seebohm* (1888) 39 Ch D 73 and W Briggs, *The Law of International Copyright* (1906), 393 ('Briggs (1906)'). See also H Rosmini [1895] *DA* 21.
[26] *Actes* 1896, 220–1. [27] ibid, 166 (Renault). [28] ibid, 174–5 (Renault).

the revised text. If this approval was not forthcoming, the Convention would be limited to those who were able to sign it, and would either result in a much more restricted Union, or in nothing at all. On the other hand, with a separate Additional Act, it would be possible for these states to refuse to sign it, but for the old Convention to continue to subsist.[29] There were precedents for such a method of proceeding,[30] and this was accepted by the Conference. Furthermore, it was left open to Union members which did not accede to the Additional Act within the time specified for the exchange of ratifications to do so at any time after this, and a similar latitude was allowed to other countries which acceded in the future to the 1886 Act.[31] On the other hand, it was not possible for a country to accede to the Additional Act in part only: it had to be accepted or rejected *in toto*.[32] Although clearly motivated by the desire to ensure the continuity of the Union, and to ensure that its membership remained as wide as possible, it will be clear that these provisions contained within them the seeds of fragmentation. If only some states acceded to the Additional Act, this would mean in effect that two Unions would exist side by side: the first, a restricted Union consisting of those states which had accepted the revised text; the other, a wider Union comprising those which accepted only the original Act of 1886, plus those in the first group (which continued to be signatories to the original Act as well). Matters were complicated further by the preparation of another document, an Interpretative Declaration which could be signed separately by each country, either at the time of signing of the Additional Act, or at any later time. This Declaration sought to interpret certain provisions of both the 1886 Act and the Additional Act, relating to compliance with formalities,[33] the meaning of the expression 'published works',[34] and the scope of article 10 (which dealt with illicit reproductions of works).[35] These points received almost unanimous approval by the Conference, except for the UK which found its domestic and colonial views at variance, to a greater or lesser degree, with each of the interpretations contained in the Declaration.[36] It was mainly because of this difficulty with the UK that these matters were dealt with in a supplementary Declaration which could be assented to separately, rather than being incorporated in the Additional Act. As a result, further kinds of restricted Unions were possible: one between those states which accepted both the Declaration and Additional Act, another between those states which accepted only the Additional Act, and yet another between those states which accepted

[29] *Actes* 1896, 179–80 (Renault).

[30] eg recent amendments made to the Postal Convention in Lisbon in 1885 and the Railways Convention in Paris in 1890: ibid, 179 (Renault).

[31] Additional Act 1896, art 3. [32] *Actes* 1896, 180 (Renault).

[33] Interpretative Declaration, para 1. [34] ibid, para 2. [35] ibid, para 3.

[36] *Actes* 1896, 142 (Sir Henry Bergne, the UK delegate).

the Declaration but not the Additional Act. In the end, eleven member states[37] ratified the Additional Act, while ten of these, with the exception of the UK,[38] ratified the Declaration. On the other hand, Norway felt unable to accept the Additional Act, in the light of its domestic law, but nonetheless ratified the Declaration insofar as this related to the Berne Act.[39] For the benefit of some modest advances in the provisions of the Convention, an element of complexity had been introduced into the relations of signatory states. Furthermore, the device of adopting separate instruments which could be individually accepted or refused, as the case may be, circumvented the original principle of unanimity contained in article 17. 'Unanimity' under the 1896 regime meant merely that only those states which wished to be so were bound by the new changes.

(b) Resolutions of the Conference

The 1896 Conference also passed unanimously a series of resolutions, inspired mainly by the French delegation, which were concerned with future objectives to be pursued at the next conference of revision. While these were non-binding statements of opinion, they are nonetheless of considerable interest as they foreshadowed the future lines of development to be taken by the Union.[40] Thus, it was declared 'desirable' that all Union countries should protect photographic works for at least fifteen years, that the need for the making of reservations in respect of performing rights should be abolished, and that national laws should adopt penal sanctions against the usurpation of an author's name or signature on a literary or artistic work.[41] Procedural and machinery matters were also addressed. The hope was expressed that each Union country would examine the special conventions in force between it and other Union countries with a view to determining whether these were in conformity with the revised Berne text, so that unnecessary or inconsistent arrangements could be denounced before the next Berne revision conference.[42] It was also resolved that the deliberations of that conference should result in a single instrument. Finally, although this was not embodied in a formal resolution, the commission reiterated, in its report, the view taken by the 1884 Conference that it would be useful for Union countries to arrive at a common accord as to the duration of authors' rights in **3.07**

[37] Belgium, France, Germany, Italy, Luxembourg, Monaco, Montenegro, Spain, Switzerland, Tunisia, and the UK: [1897] *DA* 109. The UK also ratified the Additional Act on behalf of the Australian colonies, New Zealand, Canada, Natal and Cape Colony, and India: [1897] *DA* 109.

[38] The UK's refusal to sign the Declaration was likewise made on behalf of the countries referred to in n 37 above: ibid.

[39] See [1897] *DA* 109.

[40] For the text of these, see *Actes* 1896, 229.

[41] Resolutions I, II, and IV. See also ibid, 179 (Renault).

[42] Resolution III: ibid. This was based on a German proposal. It is also worth noting that a number of other resolutions concerning the collection of information relating to such matters as national registration and deposit requirements and national bibliographies were discussed by the Commission but were not proceeded with: ibid, 177–8 (Renault).

their literary and artistic works.[43] The same report also noted the view of the 'great majority' of delegates that there should be complete assimilation of translation to reproduction rights.[44]

C. The 1908 Berlin Revision Conference[45]

(1) Preparations for the Conference

3.08 In its penultimate session, the 1896 Conference fixed Berlin as the venue for the next revision conference, to be held within six to ten years time.[46] This did not take place until 1908, but it was a far more substantive revision than its predecessor. In the period between the two conferences, there were some significant revisions of their domestic copyright laws by several Union members, most notably Germany.[47] In the same period, the membership of the Union slowly increased to sixteen, with the accession of the two remaining Scandinavian states, Denmark[48] and Sweden,[49] and the most important independent Asian power, Japan.[50] There was also continued pressure for reform and extension of the conventional regime from a number of non-governmental organizations.[51] The most active of these was ALAI which, in 1900, began the preparation of a model law for the unification of national laws on literary and artistic property.[52] On a more practical level, successive ALAI congresses proposed a series of reforms to the Berne Convention for consideration at the proposed Berlin Revision Conference, culminating in the formulation of a draft revision of the

[43] *Actes* 1896, 179. [44] ibid.

[45] For general background studies and commentaries on the 1908 Revision Conference, see H Desbois, A Françon, and A Kéréver, *Les Conventions internationales du droit d'auteur et des droits voisins* (1976) ('Desbois et al (1976)'), 2ff; J Lermina, *Convention de Berne: Unification des Législations—Historique de l'Association littéraire et artistique internationale* (1906); J Borchgrave, *Les Résultats de la Convention de Berlin et la Rapport de M Taillefer au Syndicat pour la Protection de la Properiété Intellectualle* (1909); A Vaunois, *Protection des oeuvres littéraires et artistique d'après la Convention d'Union de Berne signée à Berlin le 13 novembre 1908* (1909); 'La Conférence de Berlin, ses travaux et ses résultats' [1909] *DA* 1, 19; 'La Convention de Berne revisée, du 13 novembre 1908', 'Classification des dispositions adoptées. Combinaison du droit interne et du droit conventionnel; source de droit des auteurs Unionists. Portée des engagements réciproques; le minimum de protection légale' [1909] *DA* 34, 45; 'Les oeuvres protégees: Commentaire des articles 4 et 15' [1910] *DA* 2; 'Commentaire de l'article 7: durée de la protection' [1910] *DA* 18, 29; 'Commentaire des articles 4, 5 et 6: personnes protégées; publication, pays d'origine' [1910] *DA* 59, 76, 93.

[46] *Actes* 1896, 146–7. [47] Acts of 1901 and 1907.

[48] 1 July 1903: [1904] *DA* 73 (only to the 1886 text and Interpretative Declaration).

[49] 1 Aug 1904: [1904] *DA* 89 (only to the 1886 text and Interpretative Declaration).

[50] 15 July 1899: [1899] *DA* 49.

[51] For a collection of the most important votes and resolutions of these organizations, both at an international and national level, see *Actes* 1908.

[52] [1900] *DA* 55. See also Borchgrave (n 45 above), 19ff.

Convention.[53] Throughout this period, the International Office also continued to perform its important role as the clearing house for information relating to international and national copyright laws. This material was mostly contained in its monthly organ, *Le Droit d'Auteur*, but another valuable publication prepared by the Office was a collection of the texts of international conventions currently in force between member states of the Union, together with useful commentaries on these texts.[54] As in 1896, the Office also undertook, in conjunction with the host German Government, the preparation of all the documentation necessary for the Berlin Conference, which met in that city between 14 October and 14 November 1908.[55]

(a) States represented at the Conference

All member states of the Union, except for Haiti, were represented at the Conference. Most delegations were larger than at previous conferences, particularly those of France, Germany, and Italy, and much of the intimacy of the earlier conferences was therefore missing.[56] Time was also beginning to take its toll, and only a few of the delegates had been present at the earlier meetings.[57] Furthermore, the size of the Conference was nearly doubled with the attendance of observer delegations from twenty-one non-Union nations, including China, Siam, Persia, Russia, the USA, and most of the Latin American states.[58] The presence of a sizeable Russian delegation was of particular note, although nothing was eventually to come of this show of interest. Nevertheless, in recent years there had been a marked increase in support within the Russian Empire for an upgrading of that country's international copyright relations, and in particular there had been discussion of the desirability of joining the Berne Union.[59] This **3.09**

[53] This was at the Congress at Neuchatel in 1907: [1907] *DA* 110, 118. See also the proceedings of the Weimar Congress of 1903: [1903] *DA* 110, 115–16.

[54] International Copyright Office, *Recueil des conventions et traités concernant la propriété littéraire et artistique, publiés en français et dans les langues des pays contractants avec une introduction et des notices* (1904).

[55] For the records of the Conference, see *Actes* 1908.

[56] See *Actes* 1908, 139–44 for the full list of delegates.

[57] ibid. Two veterans of earlier conferences were Renault and Kohler.

[58] There were observer delegations from Argentina, Chile, Colombia, China, Ecuador, Greece, Guatemala, Liberia, Mexico, the Netherlands, Nicaragua, Paraguay, Persia, Peru, Portugal, Romania, Russia, Siam, the USA, Uruguay, and Venezuela: see *Actes* 1908, 139–44.

[59] eg in April 1906, the Tsar had convened a special conference of interested parties to consider these matters: *Annexe au journal de la conférence spéciale convoquée sur l'ordre de sa majesté l'empereur pour étudier la question des Conventions littéraires* (1907). For a note about the meeting, see [1906] *DA* 62. See also 'La Russie et la Convention de Berne' [1888] *DA* 122; 'Les droits des auteurs étrangers en Russie' [1894] *DA* 21; 'La propriété intellectuelle en Russie' [1897] *DA* 99, 112; 'Le droit d'auteur en Russie' [1899] *DA* 40; 'La Russie et la protection internationale des auteurs (Opinions et idées récente)' [1904] *DA* 46; 'Russie: État de la réforme législative en matière de droit d'auteur; la Russie et la Convention de Berne' [1907] *DA* 94.

was reflected in the following declaration which was made to the opening session of the Conference by the first Russian delegate:

> I am instructed by my Government to thank the Imperial German Government for their invitation. Russia is greatly increasing her exchange with foreign countries of literary, musical and artistic productions, and my Government considers that the time has come when this exchange should be regulated by international Agreements. Among such Agreements, those brought about by the labours of the international Union undoubtedly occupy the first place. The Imperial Government has appointed us to take part in the Conference with a view to facilitating the adhesion of Russia to the International Union for the Protection of Literary and Artistic Property.[60]

The United States delegate made a similar declaration of interest, expressing his general sympathy with the objects of the Union, but stating that the United States Government was not at present in a position to adhere to the Convention.[61] Similar expressions of sympathetic interest were made by a number of other non-Union delegates.[62]

(2) **Work of the Conference**

3.10 The Conference adopted a similar method of proceeding to that of its predecessors, taking the proposals prepared by the German Government and the International Office as the basis for its deliberations.[63] However, numerous other amendments were proposed by other countries, both before the commencement of the Conference and during its first plenary sessions.[64] Following these, the Conference moved into commission under the chairmanship of Louis Renault for more detailed discussions. There were some ten sessions in commission, and a final report and draft convention were then settled by a smaller drafting commission.[65] Two further sub-commissions were appointed to consider the question of mechanical reproduction and musical works and the

[60] *Actes* 1908, 149. For the English translation, see *Correspondence Respecting the Revised Convention of Berne for the Protection of Literary and Artistic Works, signed at Berlin, November 13, 1908; Miscellaneous No 2 (1909)*, 4–5 ('*Correspondence* (1908)').

[61] *Actes* 1908, 174.

[62] ibid, 150–3 (statements by the Argentinian, Greek, and Dutch delegates).

[63] ibid, 35.

[64] For the records of these sessions, see ibid, 139ff. For the text of amendments, see ibid, 77 (French), 78 (Japanese), 184 (for a table of propositions, counter-propositions, and amendments submitted to the Conference). See also ibid, 80 for a table of resolutions passed by different congresses and assemblies, such as ALAI since the 1896 Conference (a useful compilation made by the International Office which has been a feature of every set of conference records since the 1896 Conference).

[65] This consisted of Goebel (Germany), de Borchgrave (Belgium), Leconte and Renault (France), Bergne with Askwith (UK), Ferrari (Italy), de Ugglas (Sweden): *Actes* 1908, 225 (note).

practical matter of superannuation for the staff of the International Office.[66] The Conference then went back into full plenary session, and the text of the revised convention was approved.[67] From a drafting point of view, its most significant feature was that it was now contained within a single consolidated text (giving effect to the wish expressed by the 1896 Conference). From the point of view of substance, it contained a significant number of major changes and additions which, in retrospect, make it the most extensive revision of the Convention to date. The most important of these amendments are described below.

(a) Works protected

These were dealt with in article 2, which was more clearly drafted than in the 1886 Act. Each state was expressly obliged to protect the works listed in the first two paragraphs: these were the same as in the 1886 Act, but architectural works, choreographic works, and pantomimes were now included. It was further provided that translations, adaptations, arrangements of music, and other reproductions in an altered form of a literary or artistic work, as well as collections of different works, were to be protected as original works without prejudice to the rights of the author of the original work. A final paragraph provided that works of art applied to industrial purposes were to be protected as far as the domestic law of each country allowed. Although there had been strong support for according such works the same protection as other works of art, particularly from the French, German, Belgian, and Italian delegations,[68] this formulation left it open to countries such as the UK, which only accorded a more limited form of protection through a registered designs system, to continue to do so. As for photographic works, these again had been the subject of considerable discussion, as some countries still did not protect these as works of art.[69] The final compromise was contained in a separate article (article 4) under which states were bound to protect 'photographic works and . . . works produced by a process analogous to photography'. The effect of this requirement, however, was modified by article 7 which provided that a shorter term of duration could be accorded to such works (see para 3.13 below). **3.11**

(b) Persons protected; independence of protection and absence of formalities

Article 4 was the main article dealing with the questions of who was protected by the Convention and the scope and effect of this protection. It embodied and refined several important principles towards which national and international thinking had been moving for some time: those of national treatment, absence **3.12**

[66] ibid. [67] ibid, 209ff.
[68] ibid, 233 (report of the commission). [69] ibid, 234–5.

of formalities, and independence of protection. Under this article, authors who were subjects or citizens ('*ressortissants*') of a Union country were entitled, in countries other than the country of origin of the work, in respect of their works, whether unpublished or first published in a Union country, to the same rights which the respective laws of those countries accorded, or might subsequently accord, to their own authors, as well as to the rights specially granted by the present Convention. This was the basic principle of national treatment, but the reference to those rights 'specially granted by the present Convention' also reflected the extensions that had been made to the substantive protection offered by the Convention. The principle of absence of formalities was to be found in the stipulation that the enjoyment and exercise of rights under the Convention were not to be subject to any formality. This was the logical conclusion of a long process of development in which the need for compliance with formalities, both at a national and international level, had been steadily reduced. Even though there were still a number of Union countries, such as the UK, which required formalities such as registration and deposit, they were prepared to accept this change. Finally, independence of protection was effected by the provision that this enjoyment and exercise of rights, as well as their enforcement, was to be exclusively governed by the laws of the country in which protection was claimed. Both absence of formalities and independence of protection were major advances, although their adoption and application occasioned considerable debate among the delegations. The Germans, in particular, were strong advocates of independence of protection, but this was criticized by the French in the absence of some common rule being established as to duration of protection.[70] On the other hand, some delegations, such as the Swedes, still thought that the enjoyment of rights in a Union country should be subordinated to compliance with the conditions and formalities laid down for protection in the work's country of origin.[71] While the German position concerning independence of protection was adopted in article 4, this was made subject to qualification so far as the question of duration was concerned (see para 3.13 below). The concept of 'country of origin' was also refined,[72] and an extended definition of the term 'published works' was included in article 4.[73] Finally, the protection of non-Union authors was continued from the Additional Act as regarded the works of such authors which were first published in a Union country.[74]

[70] *Actes* 1908, 238–40 (report of the commission). [71] ibid, 239ff.

[72] This article was described by the commission as being 'simply explanatory': *Actes* 1908, 242.

[73] Article 4, para 4. [74] *Actes* 1908, 243.

(c) Duration of protection

A major achievement of the 1908 Conference was that it took the first step towards establishing a common period for the duration of rights in works. The earlier texts had remained silent on this point, but it had long been advocated by the French who favoured a minimum term of the life of the author plus fifty years.[75] This was already the position in a number of Union countries, and it was made the yardstick under article 7 of the Berlin text. This period was accepted in principle, even by countries such as the UK (and Germany itself) which only accorded shorter periods of protection at that time.[76] However, in recognition of the existence of these differences, article 7 was not made mandatory. It was further provided that in case the life-plus-fifty-year period was not uniformly accepted by all Union countries, the term of protection of works was to be regulated by the law of the country where protection was claimed, and was not to exceed the term fixed in the country of origin of the work. While the attainment of a mandatory common rule on duration was to take another forty years (in the Brussels Act of 1948), this 1908 solution was a considerable step forward, as it established agreement on the principle of the life-plus-fifty-year term. However, until this period was uniformly adopted by all Union countries, it meant that there would be varying periods of protection for works for which protection was claimed under the Convention. It was also a derogation from the principles of national treatment and independence of protection, since the duration of a work's protection in another Union country was determined by the law of that work's country of origin. On the other hand, article 7 fulfilled its normative role admirably over the next few years, as the vast majority of Union countries soon incorporated the life-plus-fifty-year rule into their laws.[77] So far as photographic, posthumous, anonymous, and pseudonymous works were concerned, article 7 treated these separately, providing simply that their term of protection was to be regulated by the law of the country in which the protection was claimed, but was not to exceed the term fixed in the work's country of origin. 3.13

(d) Translation rights

The Berlin Conference saw the final triumph of the principle of complete assimilation of translation rights to reproduction rights. This was now embodied in article 8, and former opponents of the principle, such as the Norwegians, were now reconciled to it.[78] Nevertheless, although article 8 has remained 3.14

75 ibid, 244.

76 eg the UK adopted it as the general term of protection for works in the Copyright Act 1911, s 3.

77 See paras 9.18ff below.

78 *Actes* 1908, 245.

virtually unchanged to the present time, it should not be thought that the Berlin Conference settled the question of translation rights completely. Even during that conference, doubts about the principle were expressed by two countries whose membership of the Union was much desired, the Netherlands and the Russian Empire.[79] Furthermore, a quite contrary proposal was advanced by the Japanese, to the effect that translations into the Japanese language should be free.[80] Although this last amendment was rejected, the Japanese desire, as a rapidly developing country, to gain ready access to European technical and other literature was obvious, and many European countries had only recently been in that position themselves. Nevertheless, the attitude of the Japanese at the Berlin Conference foreshadowed later, and more radical, opinions on the question of translations that were to be expressed by developing countries nearly sixty years later at the Stockholm Conference.[81]

(e) Newspaper and periodical articles

3.15 The question of which articles (if any) should be lawfully reproduced provoked extensive discussion, and a great many amendments were considered.[82] While the draft finally adopted by the Conference (article 9) reflected the compromises which had necessarily been made, it was an advance on the 1896 Act, as it drew a clear distinction between articles in periodicals and articles in newspapers. Reproduction of the former without the author's consent was not to be permitted, but newspaper articles could be freely reproduced by other newspapers unless this had been expressly forbidden. This licence did not extend to serial stories and 'tales' ('*des romans-feuilletons et des nouvelles*'),[83] and a proposal to include drawings within its scope was rejected as being too restrictive of the rights of authors.[84] On the other hand, 'news of the day' and 'miscellaneous information . . . simply of the nature of items of news' continued to be in the public domain.[85]

(f) Public performance rights

3.16 These were dealt with in article 11, and the principal change made was the abolition of the requirement for authors to reserve their rights in advance of

---

[79] *Actes* 1908, 247 and 201 (Japanese memorandum outlining their reasons).

[80] ibid, 247–8.

[81] See further para 3.64 and Chapter 14 below.

[82] *Actes* 1908, 249–59 (report of the commission).

[83] The commission made it clear in its report that the word '*nouvelles*' did not refer here to '*nouvelles du jour*' ('news of the day'), but to short stories—'works of fiction' (in English) and '*Novellen*' (in German). It would also include '*de petits dialogues, de petits recits historiques etc*': ibid, 250. 'Tales', the rather inadequate English translation which is used above, derives from the translation made by His Majesty's Government in its *Correspondence* (1908), 28.

[84] *Actes* 1908, 251.

[85] As a matter of principle, this might simply be regarded as a statement of the obvious, such subject matter not being 'works' and therefore not capable of protection in any case.

the performance of their works. The only opposition to this change came from the Swiss and Swedes, who withdrew their objections 'in a spirit of conciliation'.[86]

(g) Indirect appropriations and mechanical reproduction rights

The earlier opposition to the listing of different kinds of indirect appropriation **3.17**
in the Convention itself had by now disappeared. Article 12 of the new Act therefore contained quite a comprehensive list, including musical arrangements, novelizations, dramatizations, and abridgements. However, there was extensive discussion on one particular form of adaptation. This was the mechanical reproduction of musical works by such devices as phonograph recordings, piano rolls, and the like. The Closing Protocol of the 1886 Act had declared that this should not be an infringement of copyright, as such devices were not at that time very widespread. This position was left unchanged by the 1896 Conference. However, even before that date, and certainly after it, a large industry which specialized in the manufacture of these instruments had come into existence. One of the factors contributing to this rapid growth was the lack of enforceable rights by copyright owners. In consequence, the latter had mounted campaigns, at both a national and international level, for recognition of these rights, arguing that this was simply another form of reproduction. These arguments had been met by assertions from the recording interests that recognition would mean the ruin of their industries, which had been built up, in good faith, in the absence of legal restriction. Caught between these conflicting views, the Berlin Conference settled finally for a compromise solution.[87] Article 13 expressly recognized the exclusive rights of musical copyright owners in relation to the adaptation of their works to instruments capable of reproducing them mechanically, as well as the public performance of those works by means of these instruments. On the other hand, it left the application of this article to such 'reservations and conditions' as might be determined by the domestic legislation of each country. This general formula was wide enough to comprehend a system of compulsory licensing (in favour of the recording interests) of the kind that had been already proposed in countries such as Germany.[88] At the same time, however, there was nothing in the formula which compelled member countries to adopt such a system.[89]

[86] *Actes* 1908, 256. [87] ibid, 258–64 (discussion of this matter by the commission).

[88] Briggs (1906), 421; [1899] *DA* 128. A law imposing such a system, following the first making or licensing of the mechanical reproduction of his musical work by an author, was introduced in Germany by the Law of 22 May 1910, arts 22–22c: [1910] *DA* 88–9.

[89] Such a requirement was, in fact, proposed by the German delegation: *Actes* 1908, 293.

(h) Cinematographic works

3.18 Another major technical advance since 1886 in the means of disseminating works had been the cinematographic film. From being an interesting novelty in the period before the turn of the century, by 1908 it was becoming the foundation of a formidable mass entertainment industry. As this was clearly another means by which works could be reproduced and performed, a French proposal to bring these acts within the purview of the Convention was considered and approved by the Conference.[90] The result was embodied in article 14, which also provided that cinematographic works should be protected as literary or artistic works in their own right if they possessed an original character by reason of the 'arrangement of the acting form or the combination of the incidents represented'.[91]

(i) Other changes

3.19 The changes made to the other articles of the 1886 Act and the provisions of the 1896 Act were mainly of a consequential and drafting nature. However, one new article worthy of note from a doctrinal point of view was article 19, which underlined the basic proposition that the Convention embodied only a 'minimum of protection', rather than being an all-embracing code. Thus, it provided that the provisions of the Convention were not to prevent the making of a claim for the application of any wider provisions which might be made by the laws of a Union country in favour of foreigners in general. This answered a Belgian concern that an author from another Union country should not, by reason of his country's membership of the Union, be precluded from obtaining in Belgium the more liberal treatment provided under Belgian law in favour of foreigners generally.[92] Another difficult question which was dealt with in the new text was the relations between member states of the Union, and the status of the different Convention texts. There was an understandable desire on the part of delegates that, in advancing the level of protection offered under the Convention, the Union should not lose existing members who might feel unable to accede to the new Act because of the state of their domestic copyright laws or because they disagreed with particular provisions.[93] It was certainly true that in the past the provisions of the Convention had exercised a beneficial effect in that they had led both member and non-member states to modify their domestic laws. However, as a number of reservations of position in relation to particular articles of the proposed text had been made by different delegations

[90] *Actes* 1908, 264–5. [91] Article 14, para 2.

[92] *Actes* 1908, 269–70 (report of the commission) and 197–200 (Belgian memorandum on the subject).

[93] '*. . . si nous avons l'Union, nous n'avons pas l'unité*': ibid, 297 (commission).

during the course of the Berlin Conference,[94] there was a clear risk that an 'all or nothing' approach might lead to a smaller Union when the new Act came into force. Accordingly, article 27 provided that, although the new text was to replace the earlier Acts of 1886 and 1896, the latter instruments should remain in force with regard to relations with states which did not ratify the Berlin Act. Thus, if country A signed the new text, but country B did not, the relations between the two countries would continue to be governed by the earlier Acts which both had signed. As an inducement to states to adhere to the new text, it was further provided that those states which signed it should be able, at the time of exchange of ratifications, to declare that they desired to remain bound, as regarded any specific point, by the provisions of the texts which they had previously signed. For the sake of preserving the Union, this provision was to have the effect of perpetuating the system of restricted Unions which had been inaugurated by the 1896 Conference, with differing texts governing the relations between individual Union members. New signatories were also granted a similar facility: under article 25, they were permitted to indicate, at the time of their accession, the provisions of the earlier texts which they judged necessary, at least provisionally, to substitute for the corresponding provisions of the Berlin text.

(3) Assessment of the Berlin Revision

Apart from its achievement of a single text, the Berlin Act must be regarded as **3.20** a significant advance towards an international copyright codification. While it remained essentially neutral on the difficult question of the nature of authors' rights, it now contained many more substantive requirements as to the protection to be accorded to authors claiming under the Convention. This had been achieved with a reasonable degree of unanimity between countries whose copyright traditions were very different, and despite the fact that some of these countries would have to make extensive revisions of their laws before they could ratify or accede to the new Act. On the other hand, the facility allowed to states to continue to adhere to earlier texts on particular points meant that some time would elapse before all members adhered to a single text.[95] Furthermore, the outlines of future problems had become apparent during the Conference, even if those had not precipitated any major crisis on this occasion. The most notable was the threat posed to authors' rights by the emergence of new technological means of reproducing and disseminating their works, and the growth of powerful interest groups engaged in the exploitation of these new technologies. In this

[94] ibid, 213–18 (declarations by Spain *re* art 4, the UK *re* art 7, Japan and Spain *re* art 8, Belgium and Italy *re* art 13).

[95] The commission, however, did not regard this as likely: ibid, 277.

regard, the gramophone recording and the cinematographic film were the harbingers of other more startling developments which were already in train, such as sound and visual broadcasting. A second problem for the future was that of developing countries which were in the position of 'users' rather than 'producers' of copyright material. Although their time was still to come, their concerns had been clearly anticipated, even at this early stage, in the Japanese proposal on translation rights.

D. The Berne Additional Protocol 1914[96]

3.21 The 1896 Act had admitted to the benefits of the Convention authors from non-Union countries who first published their works in a Union country. This generosity was usually justified as reflecting the international character of authors' rights, but a more practical reason was that it provided some inducement for the countries to which these authors belonged to join the Union, so as to gain the full benefits of membership, for example, in relation to unpublished works. On the other hand, it was often the case that authors from Union countries did not receive adequate protection for their works in these non-Union countries. In practice, this imbalance in protection did not appear to give rise to great concern among Union countries, but Canada was a major exception to this. This country shared a long common border with the USA, as well as a common language, and first publication of their works in Canada became a common gateway to the benefits of the Berne Convention for United States authors. However, the restrictive United States copyright laws made it difficult for authors of Union countries to gain protection in that country. This remained a problem even after the passing of a new US copyright law in 1909,[97] because its notorious 'manufacturing clause' still applied to works written in English.[98] When the UK Government convened an Imperial Copyright Conference of its self-governing Dominions in 1910 to discuss the question of Imperial ratification of the Berlin text, the following resolution was passed:

> The conference is of opinion that, if possible, it should be made clear on ratification that the obligations imposed by the Convention on the British Empire should relate solely to works the authors of which are subjects or citizens of a country of the Union or *bona fide* residents therein; and that in any case it is essential that the

[96] On the background to this, see 'Le nouveau protocole additional à la Convention revisée de 1908' [1914] *DA* 79, 93.

[97] Copyright Act 1909, USC Title 17 (Copyright). [98] ibid, s 16.

above reservation should be made in regard to any self-governing Dominion which so desires.[99]

In the event, the UK Government did not make any reservations of the kind outlined in the resolution when it ratified the Berlin text on its own behalf and on behalf of its self-governing Dominions.[100] However, Canada refused to allow ratification so far as it was concerned, and at Canada's request the UK Government drafted a protocol permitting the government of a Union country to restrict protection in the case of authors from non-Union countries which failed to protect the authors from the Union country 'in an adequate manner'.[101] This was submitted to the International Office which prepared an Additional Protocol which was signed in Berne in March 1914.[102] The only country which subsequently made use of this facility was Canada.[103]

E. The 1928 Rome Conference

(1) Preparations for the Conference[104]

At the closing session of the Berlin Conference, Rome was chosen as the venue for the next conference of revision, the expectation being that this should occur within six to ten years.[105] The new text came into force on 9 September 1910 following the exchange of ratifications by twelve states.[106] Within two years, 3.22

[99] *Imperial Copyright Conference, 1910 Memorandum of Proceedings*, Cd 5272 (1910), Resolution 4(b).

[100] [1912] *DA* 90.

[101] As to why this was a preferable method of proceeding rather than formulating a reservation on Canada's behalf to art 6, see [1914] *DA* 80.

[102] [1914] *DA* 45. See further *L'Union internationale pour la protection des oeuvres littéraires et artistiques: son fondation et son développement—Mémoire 1886–1936* (1936) ('*Mémoire* (1936)'), 86–7 and [1914] *DA* 79, 93.

[103] Canada subsequently restricted protection in respect of US works in accordance with ss 13, 14, and 27 of the Canadian Copyright Act 1921: [1924] *DA* 13.

[104] See generally on the Rome Revision Conference, Desbois et al (1976), 43ff; *Mémoire* (1936), 88ff; M Plaisant and O Pichot, *La Conférence de Rome: Commentaire pratique de la nouvelle Convention pour la protection internationale de la propriété littéraire et artistique* (1934) ('Plaisant and Pichot (1934)'); A Raestad, *Convention de Berne revisée à Rome 1928 . . .* (1931); 'L'article 7 de la Conference de Berne revisée et la future Conference de Rome' [1926] *DA* 49; 'Les propositions arrêtés en vue de la Conference de Rome pour les Gouvernements allemand, autrichien, brittanique, français et suisse' [1927] *DA* 116, 126, 137; 'La Conférence de Rome—Études' [1928] *DA* 80, 90; G Maillard, 'Conférence de Rome', *ALAI Bulletin*, Oct 1928 ('Maillard (1928)'); B Marwitz, *Die Berner Übereinkunft und die Römische Konferenz* (1928); W Goldbaum, *Berner Übereinkunft zum Schutze von Werken der Literatur und Kunst, vom 2 juni 1928* (1928).

[105] *Actes* 1908, 219–20.

[106] Belgium, France, Germany, Haiti, Japan, Liberia, Luxembourg, Monaco, Norway, Spain, Switzerland, and Tunisia: [1910] *DA* 85, 86, 113, 115, and 129.

there were accessions by another four states,[107] including the UK which also acceded on behalf of India and the new Commonwealth of Australia.[108] However, further progress was halted by the outbreak of World War I, in which a number of member states were involved as belligerents.[109] The effect of war on the relations between member states is considered in Chapter 17 (para 17.92) below, but for the moment all that needs to be said is that, although it delayed the calling of a further revision conference, it did not affect the continuance of the Union. Another consequence of the War was the major reordering of the European state system that followed it, and the subsequent emergence of a number of new states following the disintegration of the Hapsburg, Hohenzollern, and Romanov empires. Most of these states moved rapidly to engage themselves within the international order, and for the majority of them this included adherence to the Berne Union.[110] They were joined by those European states which had remained outside the Union prior to World War I, so that by 1928 almost the entire European continent, except for the Soviet Union, was within the Union.[111] Other accessions were made at the same time by the self-governing British Dominions, which now did so in their own right,[112] and by several countries subject to French influence.[113] Representation from the South American continent, however, was confined to Brazil which acceded in 1922.[114] On the other hand, while membership from Africa and Asia was similarly restricted, the prevailing colonial situation on both continents meant that the Convention was in operation in most places there.[115] By the Rome Conference (7 May 1928), the Union had thirty-seven members, all but three of which had also ratified the Protocol of 1914.[116]

[107] Denmark, 1 July 1912: [1912] *DA* 91; the Netherlands, 1 Nov 1912: [1912] *DA* 146; Portugal, 29 Mar 1911: [1911] *DA* 45; UK, 1 July 1912: [1912] *DA* 90. Note that Italy, an original signatory to the 1886 text, acceded to the 1908 text on 23 Dec 1914: [1914] *DA* 129.

[108] The UK subsequently gave notice for New Zealand on 1 Apr 1914: [1914] *DA* 46; for South Africa on 1 May 1920: [1920] *DA* 49; and for Canada on 1 Jan 1924: [1924] *DA* 13.

[109] Namely Belgium, France, Germany, Italy, Japan, and the UK.

[110] Austria, 1 Oct 1920: [1920] *DA* 109; Czechoslovakia, 22 Feb 1921: [1921] *DA* 25; Danzig, 24 June 1922: [1922] *DA* 77; Estonia, 9 June 1927: [1927] *DA* 89; Finland, 1 Apr 1928: [1928] *DA* 45; Hungary, 14 Feb 1922: [1922] *DA* 25; Poland, 28 Jan 1920: [1920] *DA* 25.

[111] Bulgaria, 5 Dec 1921: [1921] *DA* 2; Romania, 1 Jan 1927: [1926] *DA* 121. Except for Yugoslavia which acceded to the Berlin text on 17 June 1930: [1930] *DA* 85.

[112] Australia, 14 Apr 1928: [1928] *DA* 57; Canada, 10 Apr 1928: [1924] *DA* 57; India, 1 Apr 1928: [1928] *DA* 58; Ireland, 5 Oct 1927: [1927] *DA* 125; New Zealand, 24 Apr 1928: [1928] *DA* 78; Union of South Africa, 3 Oct 1928: [1928] *DA* 133.

[113] Lebanon, 1 Aug 1924: [1924] *DA* 85; Morocco, 16 June 1917: [1917] *DA* 73; Syria, 1 Aug 1924: [1924] *DA* 85.

[114] 9 Feb 1922: [1922] *DA* 25.

[115] See further paras 17.35ff below.

[116] These states were Haiti, Italy, and Portugal.

(a) The problem of reservations

One legacy of the Berlin Act which had become apparent by 1928 was the number of reservations which states had made upon their ratification. In all, some eighteen states had availed themselves of this facility, the majority of reservations relating to translation rights,[117] the reproduction of newspaper articles,[118] the protection of works of art applied to industrial purposes[119] and the retroactive effect of the Convention.[120] This obviously gave rise to considerable complexity and confusion in determining the exact relationships between different states of the Union. To quote two distinguished French commentators, Marcel Plaisant and Oliver Pichot, the system of reservations '. . . had resulted in the rupture of unity. The Convention was no longer a tablet of the law; it was a mosaic pavement.'[121] Although the provisions of the Convention sought to assure a minimum of protection to authors claiming under the Convention, the result was that the 'rhythm of this unitary law had been paralysed by these reservations'.[122] The elimination of the latter therefore became of prime concern to the new revision conference. Other subjects for consideration were radio-diffusion, the recognition of moral rights, and the perfection of the Convention in relation to such matters as the range of works protected, duration of protection, mechanical reproduction rights, and restrictions on rights. Each of these had been the subject of resolutions and votes by various non-governmental organizations, in particular ALAI, during the preceding decade.[123] Each, furthermore, was a potent source of controversy, and the achieving of unanimity across the larger and more diverse membership of the Union was now far less likely than at the previous conferences. The organization of the Rome Conference was undertaken jointly by the Italian Government and the International Office, which issued lengthy preparatory documents, including a proposed programme, some time before the Conference started.[124] These documents also included numerous amendments proposed by various member states.[125] When the Conference finally assembled in Rome on 7 May 1928 (its original meeting had been proposed for October 1927), it had before it a wide array of proposals. **3.23**

[117] Estonia, Greece, Ireland, Italy, Japan, and the Netherlands: see *Actes* 1928, 11–12 (full summary of the reservations made).

[118] Denmark, Finland, Greece, Norway, the Netherlands, Romania, and Sweden: ibid.

[119] France, Tunisia: ibid.

[120] Australia, the UK, India, New Zealand, and South Africa: ibid.

[121] Plaisant and Pichot (1934), 34. [122] ibid, 35.

[123] Most notably at the ALAI Congress of Lugano in June 1927: see further Maillard (1928), 5 and [1927] *DA* 77–83. For a collection of the most important resolutions passed by various congresses and assemblies from 1909–28 see *Actes* 1928, 29–60.

[124] See *Actes* 1928, 24–85.

[125] ibid, 87–129. Propositions were advanced by eleven states: Germany, Austria, the UK, France, Hungary, Italy, the Netherlands, Norway, Poland, Sweden, and Switzerland.

However, while the Conference made several notable advances in relation to the protection of authors' rights, its overall achievements were disappointing.

(b) States represented at the Conference

3.24 All member states, except for Haiti and Liberia, were represented.[126] As with previous conferences, most of the delegates were diplomats and government officials, but a number of the larger states, such as France, Italy, and Germany, had expert advisers from various copyright interest groups attached to their delegations.[127] In addition, there were observer delegations from twenty-one other states, including the USA, most of the Central and South American states, Egypt, Turkey, and Siam.[128] There were also representatives of the League of Nations, the International Institute for Intellectual Co-operation, and the International Office (which provided the secretariat of the Conference).[129] The procedure adopted by the Conference was essentially the same as that adopted by earlier conferences.[130] The programme of the Italian Government and the International Office, together with the amendments submitted by other member states, was taken as the basis of discussion. After several plenary sessions, at which delegations made general declarations as to position,[131] the Conference moved into commission. These meetings occupied the rest of the month of May,[132] but in addition five sub-commissions were appointed to report on matters of particular difficulty: moral rights,[133] radiodiffusion,[134] mechanical reproduction rights, and compulsory licences,[135] cinematography and photography,[136] and works of art applied to industrial purposes.[137] Finally, a small drafting commission of five members[138] was appointed to prepare a final text. This was adopted, together with five resolutions, at the final plenary session on 1 June 1928.[139]

(2) The work of the Conference

3.25 As stated above, the progress made by the Rome Conference was disappointing, at least from the point of view of those advocates of a further unification of

[126] *Actes* 1928, 131ff. [127] ibid.

[128] In full, these were Bolivia, Chile, Columbia, Cuba, Egypt, Ecuador, the USA, Guatemala, Latvia, Lithuania, Mexico, Nicaragua, Peru, Persia, San Marino, Salvador, Yugoslavia, Siam, Turkey, Uruguay, and Venezuela: ibid, 137ff.

[129] ibid, 139. [130] For the text of the rules of procedure, see ibid, 155.

[131] ibid, 160ff.

[132] No minutes for these meetings were kept; the only minutes were those of the plenary sessions: see reg 6 of the Conference rules of procedure: ibid, 156.

[133] See report at ibid, 181. [134] ibid, 183. [135] ibid, 187.

[136] ibid, 185. [137] ibid, 190.

[138] The members were Caselli (Italy), Maillard (France), Beckett (UK), Zoll (Poland), and Colman di Alker (Hungary): ibid, 158.

[139] ibid, 285ff.

international copyright law. There was controversy over most major points, with the views of user interests, particularly in relation to mechanical reproduction, being well to the fore.[140] In some instances, maintenance of the status quo was, in itself, an achievement. Two important additions, however, were made to the Convention. These were the recognition of moral rights and rights over radio-diffusion. In more detail, the principal matters considered by the Convention were as follows.

(a) Reservations

This was one of the main issues addressed by the Conference. It was generally recognized that the facility to make reservations should be restricted, if not eliminated, so as to enhance the integrity of the Union.[141] To this end, a number of delegations announced during the Conference that, as a token of their commitment to this objective, their governments were abandoning reservations which they had previously made.[142] However, there was opposition to abolishing the reservations system altogether,[143] and the compromise worked out in the redrafted article 27 provided for the new text to replace the previous instruments, but the latter remained in force with respect to those states which did not ratify that text.[144] It was further provided that those countries signing the new text would be allowed to retain the benefit of reservations previously formulated, on condition that they made a declaration to this effect at the time they deposited their ratifications.[145] The same facility was extended to countries which were members of the Union, but did not sign the present text, and adhered to it at a later time.[146] In the case of new members, their capacity to make reservations was limited to translation rights: under the new article 25 all they could now do was to indicate, provisionally at least, that they wished to substitute for article 8 of the present text (providing for complete assimilation), the provisions of article 5 of the 1886 Act, as revised at Paris in 1896.[147] These changes did not mean the end of the reservations system, but they at least restricted its growth and meant that it would slowly wither with time. **3.26**

(b) Inclusion of oral works

A proposal to include these in the list of works protected was made in the joint Italian Government/International Office programme.[148] There were some **3.27**

[140] See eg the submission made to the British Government by the mechanical music industry of the UK: G S Wood, *Preliminary Observations upon . . . the amendments to the Berne Convention . . . proposed by the Italian Government* . . . (1929).
[141] *Actes* 1928, 214–16 (report of the commission).
[142] ibid, 163 (Japan); 167 (Norway); 295 (the Netherlands).
[143] ibid, 214–16 (report of the commission).
[144] Article 27(1).
[145] Article 27(2).
[146] Article 27(3).
[147] ibid.
[148] *Actes* 1928, 64ff.

objections to this from a number of countries,[149] and the additions made to article 2 were therefore limited to 'lectures, addresses, sermons, and other works of the same nature'. A new article, article 2*bis* reserved to the domestic laws of member states the right to regulate the conditions of protection in the case of political speeches and speeches delivered in legal proceedings, as well as the conditions under which lectures, and the like, might be reproduced by the press.

(c) Moral rights

3.28 The recognition and protection of these rights, which were steadily establishing a foothold in many national laws, were proposed by several countries, and a number of different drafts were put forward.[150] There was some opposition to the general proposal from the common law countries, whose copyright laws did not directly protect such rights, but did so indirectly through other legal remedies such as the law of defamation.[151] In the event, a compromise article (article 6*bis*) was agreed to. This required the protection of the two basic moral rights recognized in many European legal systems, namely the right to claim authorship of a work (*droit à la paternité*) and the right to claim respect for its integrity (*droit au respect de l'oeuvre*). However, the determination of the conditions under which these rights were to be exercised and enforced was left to the domestic laws of each Union country. This allowed member states flexibility in the way in which they protected these rights, and the article did not make it mandatory that this be done through their copyright laws. The article was also silent on the question of the continuance of these rights after the author's death, but a resolution in favour of this was passed by the Conference.[152] There was no decision by the latter on whether there could be contractual renunciation of moral rights.[153]

(d) Radiodiffusion rights

3.29 A new article 11*bis*, deriving from the programme,[154] recognized the exclusive right of authors to authorize the communication of their works to the public by means of radiodiffusion. This was another instance of a new technological development which had profound implications for authors' rights. However, it was left to member states to regulate the conditions under which this new right was to be exercised within their territory. The latter clearly comprehended such

[149] Notably Germany, Australia, Brazil, the UK, Japan and Norway: ibid, 195 (report of the commission).

[150] *Actes* 1928, 236–7 (report of the commission, describing the different proposals put forward by the French, Italian, Polish, Romanian, Czech, and Belgian delegations). See further Plaisant and Pichot (1934), 26ff.

[151] *Actes* 1928, 201.

[152] For text, see ibid, 349, and see further para 3.31 below.

[153] *Mémoire* (1936), 93.

[154] *Actes* 1928, 76.

restrictions as compulsory licences, but it was provided that these conditions should not in any way prejudice the author's moral right, nor his right to obtain equitable remuneration. A proposal in the programme[155] to grant performers a similar exclusive right in relation to the radiodiffusion of their performances was not proceeded with, as the commission thought that there was not yet enough uniformity in national approaches to justify attempting an international solution.[156] The question of protecting the rights of performers was therefore left to a resolution on the subject.[157]

(e) Other changes

A new article 7*bis* dealt with the duration of protection in works of joint authorship; some modifications were made to the regime governing borrowings from periodicals under article 9; there was a more precise and extensive regulation of cinematographic rights under article 14, with the inclusion of adaptations; and the substance of the Berne Additional Protocol of 1914 was incorporated in article 6. On the negative side, there was renewed discussion and controversy over the general question of duration of protection, and the failure of some member states to implement the life-plus-fifty-year term fully.[158] There was also debate over the protection on works of art applied to industrial purposes,[159] and mechanical reproduction and performance rights,[160] but on each issue there was lack of agreement and the status quo established by the Berlin text was maintained. Another novel proposal, put forward by Sweden and Norway[161] with the support of a number of other smaller nations,[162] concerned the recognition of the competence of the Permanent Court of International Justice to determine disputes concerning the interpretation of the Convention. There was opposition to this from some of the larger states, such as Italy and France,[163] and the matter was left for consideration at the next revision conference.[164] As a point of drafting, it should be noted that there was no renumbering of articles to include new articles: the latter were simply appended to the relevant article of the Berlin text as article—, article—*bis*, article—*ter*, and so on. This practice has been followed in subsequent revisions of the Convention text. **3.30**

155 ibid, 76–7. 156 ibid, 210–11. 157 For text, see ibid, 350.

158 ibid, 204ff (report of the commission), 292ff (final plenary session).

159 ibid, 287ff (final plenary session). See further Plaisant and Pichot (1934), 21ff and Maillard (1928), 10.

160 *Actes* 1928, 187ff (report of sub-commission). 161 ibid, 113, 278.

162 Finland, Czechoslovakia, Switzerland, the Netherlands, Denmark, and the International Institute for Intellectual Co-operation: ibid, 278.

163 ibid, 279–80. 164 ibid, 280.

(f) Resolutions of the Conference

3.31 A large number of resolutions were also passed by the Conference concerning matters on which international consensus still seemed unattainable, but which it drew to the attention of national legislators.[165] These included the further protection of moral rights after the death of the author, limitations in relation to the lawful borrowings from works, the recognition of performers' rights and the system of *droit de suite*, and the means of proving the date of creation of works (the preferred method being by the use of the *enveloppe Soleau*[166]). A final resolution called for world unification of authors' rights through reaching a reconciliation between the member countries of the Berne and Buenos Aires Conventions. The second of these conventions covered most countries in the Americas, although the level of protection offered under it was generally of a lower level than that offered by the Berne Convention. The move for reconciliation of the two conventions was to become a continuing quest over the next twenty-five years, and the need for this will be immediately apparent: up to this time, very few of the American states had acceded to the Berne Union, although they had usually been well represented by observers at its various conferences. In the event, this quest culminated in the creation of a third multilateral copyright convention, the Universal Copyright Convention, in 1952. The Buenos Aires Convention is dealt with in more detail at para 18.09 below, as is the Universal Copyright Convention (and its relationship to the Berne Convention).

(3) Assessment of the Rome Revision

3.32 Although the largest so far held, this Conference achieved relatively little as far as advancement of the rights of authors was concerned. In part, at least, this was due to its size, as the range of national interests represented was more diverse than at earlier conferences and the scope for disagreement was obviously much increased. On the other hand, the official fifty-year commentary on the Convention describes the Conference as having achieved a 'defensive victory'.[167] This seems an accurate description inasmuch as it contained attempts to limit authors' rights in relation to such matters as compulsory licences and the increasing demands of user interests.

---

165 For the text of these resolutions, see *Actes*, 1928, 282–3.

166 This was a method used for proof of the date of creation of works, particularly with respect to industrial property rights, such as designs. It involved the deposit of copies in a special envelope: see further [1925] *DA* 83 and see also the resolutions in favour of the method made by the ALAI Congress in Warsaw in 1926, noted in [1926] *DA* 127, 131–2.

167 *Mémoire* (1936) 95. See also the less enthusiastic comments of Plaisant and Pichot (1934), 3, and Maillard (1928), 7.

F. The 1948 Brussels Revision Conference[168]

(1) Preparations for the Conference

At the final plenary session of the Rome Conference, Brussels was proposed as the venue for the next conference of revision, and after some discussion it was fixed for 1935.[169] Once again, this deadline was not reached, and then World War II intervened to delay matters further. Nevertheless, the Belgian Government and International Office began their preparatory work for the Conference at an early stage, circulating the first set of preliminary documents on 20 July 1935.[170] Two factors, however, led to the Conference being postponed, first to 1936, and then to a later date. The first was the slowness with which member states ratified the Rome Act: by 1 August 1931 (the date on which this text came into force pursuant to article 28 of the Rome text), only thirteen had done so.[171] By the end of 1934, this number had risen slowly to twenty-five,[172] and twelve states still remained bound by the Berlin text,[173] although the majority of these last-mentioned states ratified the Rome text fairly soon after this date.[174] The difficulties involved in trying to revise a text which has not been fully ratified are obvious. The second reason for delay was to be found in the desire, expressed in one of the resolutions adopted by the Rome Conference, that some accommodation should be reached between the Berne and Buenos Aires/Havana **3.33**

[168] On the general background to the Conference, see Desbois et al (1976), 57ff; A Baum, *The Brussels Conference for the Revision of the Berne Convention* (1949); *Report of the US Observer Delegation to the International Conference for the Revision of the Berne Convention . . . held in Brussels* . . . (1949); 'Les Travaux préparatoires de la Conférence de Bruxelles' [1933] *DA* 73, 90, 97, 112, 121; [1934] *DA* 7, 13; M Boutet and R Plaisant, *Régime International de droit d'auteur: La Convention de Berne, révisée à Bruxelles* (1950).

[169] *Actes* 1928, 314–15.

[170] See generally *Documents de la Conférence réunie à Bruxelles du 5 au 26 juin 1948* (1951), 35ff (circulars from the Belgian Office), 44ff (circulars from the International Office) ('*Documents 1948* (1951)'). See also 'Les Travaux préparatoires' (n 168 above).

[171] Namely Bulgaria, Canada, Danzig, Finland, Hungary, India, Italy, Japan, the Netherlands, the UK, Sweden, Switzerland, and Yugoslavia: see [1930] *DA* 85; [1931] *DA* 73, 96; [1932] *DA* 38.

[172] Germany, 21 Oct 1933: [1933] *DA* 109; Belgium, 7 Oct 1934: [1934] *DA* 109; Brazil, 1 June 1933: [1933] *DA* 49; Denmark, 16 Sept 1933: [1933] *DA* 97; Spain, 23 Apr 1933: [1933] *DA* 37; France, 22 Dec 1933: [1933] *DA* 133; Greece, 25 Feb 1932: [1932] *DA* 13; Luxembourg, 4 Feb 1932: [1932] *DA* 14; Morocco, 25 Nov 1934: [1934] *DA* 121; Monaco, 9 June 1933: [1933] *DA* 61; Syria, 24 Dec 1933: [1933] *DA* 133; Tunisia, 2 Dec 1933: [1933] *DA* 133.

[173] [1935] *DA* 2–3.

[174] Australia, 18 Jan 1935: [1935] *DA* 3; Austria, 1 July 1936: [1936] *DA* 73; Ireland, 11 June 1935: [1935] *DA* 61; Poland, 21 Nov 1935: [1935] *DA* 121; Portugal, 29 July 1937: [1937] *DA* 73; Romania, 6 Aug 1936: [1936] *DA* 73; Czechoslovakia, 30 Nov 1936: [1936] *DA* 121; South Africa, 17 May 1935: [1935] *DA* 49. Saint-Siège acceded on 12 Sept 1935: [1935] *DA* 97.

Conventions.[175] This desire was crystallized further in a resolution of the General Assembly of the League of Nations which, on 18 September 1935, charged the International Institute for Intellectual Co-operation and the International Institute of Rome for the Unification of Private Law with the tasks of 'preparing, by the reconciliation of the Conventions of Berne and Havana, a general accord sufficient to assure in both continents the efficacious protection of intellectual works'.[176] Following this resolution, a committee of experts began work, and asked the Belgian Government to postpone the Brussels Revision Conference until it would be possible to call a conference at the same time in Brussels at which the international accord proposed in the League of Nations resolution could be discussed. The committee did not anticipate that this work would take more than several years, but by 1938 the international situation was already quite threatening, and the outbreak of war in 1939 precluded any international meetings until after its conclusion.[177] When this happened, the Belgian Government acted quickly to revive its proposals for a revision conference. These preparations were based largely on the preliminary documentation which had been prepared for the postponed conferences of 1935 to 1936,[178] but they were no longer tied to the proposal for holding a second international meeting at the same time to discuss the formation of a more general international accord in copyright. Work on this matter was taken over by the United Nations Educational and Scientific Organization (UNESCO), and this led to the creation of the Universal Copyright Convention which was signed in Paris in 1952. As for the Brussels Revision Conference, this was held four years earlier, in June 1948. This was a considerable feat of organization by the Belgian Government, given that its country had recently suffered the ravages of war and occupation.

(a) Membership of the Union

3.34 By 1948, there were forty members of the Berne Union, the most notable new additions being Yugoslavia, Siam (Thailand), and the Holy See.[179] Representation from Asia, Africa, and Central and South America was still meagre, and the USA continued to remain aloof. On the other hand, as the process of post-war decolonization had not yet fully commenced, the Convention was still in operation in a large number of places on these continents which were British,

---

175 *Actes* 1928, 350.

176 Set out in the 'Brief Historial Note' at the beginning of the *Documents 1948* (1951), 13.

177 *Actes* 1928, 350. Note though that some studies on this question were carried out prior to World War II: 'Le Rapprochement des Conventions de Berne et de la Havane' [1935] *DA* 100, 109; [1936] *DA* 13, 25; [1937] *DA* 67, and 'La Convention universelle sur le droit d'auteur' [1939] *DA* 13, 25. See further Chapter 18 below.

178 *Documents 1948* (1951), 48ff.

179 ibid, 14–15.

French, Belgian, Spanish, or Portuguese territories or colonies to which the Convention had been applied by their metropolitan power. In addition, two populous, newly independent states had remained in the Union and were therefore separately represented at the Conference: these were India and Pakistan.[180] On the other hand, the Union had also suffered an actual loss of members, as several states (Haiti[181] and Liberia[182]) had denounced the Convention since 1928, and several others (Estonia and Latvia) had ceased to exist as independent national entities after World War II. By 1948, the Rome Act bound all members and their territories, except for Siam and the League of Nations mandated territory of South West Africa in which the Berlin Act remained in force.[183] As for reservations, these were retained by only seven states.[184]

(b) States represented at the Conference

Thirty-five member states were represented at the Conference.[185] The largest **3.35**
delegations, complete with batteries of expert advisers, were from Belgium, France, and Italy.[186] Three member states—Romania, Siam, and Japan—were not represented, while Bulgaria and Germany were given only observer status.[187] Observers were also sent by eighteen other states, as well as by UNESCO and the International Office (which provided the secretariat for the Conference).[188] However, proposals to give observer status to non-governmental organizations, such as the International Confederation of Societies of Authors and Composers, were rejected by the Conference, on the basis that this was a meeting between governments only.[189] On the other hand, it is worth noting that, among the expert advisers attached to a number of delegations, there were representatives

---

[180] See further paras 14.03ff below.

[181] 26 Mar 1943: [1943] *DA* 1 and 4.

[182] 22 Feb 1930: [1930] *DA* 1.

[183] *Documents 1948* (1951), 20.

[184] Namely Iceland, France, Greece, Ireland, Japan, Tunisia, and Yugoslavia: ibid, 20–1.

[185] Austria, Australia, Belgium, Brazil, Canada, Denmark, Spain, Finland, France, the UK, Greece, Hungary, India, Ireland, Iceland, Italy, Lebanon, Liechtenstein (represented by Switzerland), Luxembourg, Monaco, Morocco (French Zone), Norway, New Zealand (represented by the UK), Pakistan, the Netherlands, Poland, Portugal, Sweden, Switzerland, Syria, Czechoslovakia, Tunisia (represented by France), South Africa, Vatican City, and Yugoslavia: ibid, 14–15.

[186] There were some fourteen members of the Belgian delegation, twenty-one in the French and ten in the Italian. These included some of the most prominent figures in the international copyright world, from government, the universities, and authors' societies, eg Guislain and Recht from Belgium, Plaisant, Boutet, and Tournier from France, and Pilotti and de Sanctis from Italy. The British, on the other hand, took the view that in smallness lies efficiency, and their delegation numbered only five. See generally ibid, 54ff.

[187] Germany was represented by members of the British Control Commission: ibid, 60.

[188] The other states which sent observers were: Argentina, Bolivia, Chile, China, Cuba, Dominican Republic, Egypt, Ecuador, the USA, Haiti, Iraq, Iran, Liberia, Mexico, Peru, San Salvador, Turkey, and Uruguay: ibid, 60–1.

[189] ibid, 69 (French proposal to this effect rejected, sixteen noes, twelve in favour, and seven abstentions).

of authors', composers', and artists' societies.[190] Of more significance, with respect to the future development of the Convention, was the presence of representatives of some of the emerging interests that were based on the exploitation of copyright works, in particular the broadcasting industry.[191]

(2) The work of the Conference

3.36 In a sense, the Brussels Conference was to be the last meeting of the 'old Union', that is, the last occasion where the strong, traditional Eurocentric orientation of the Convention was to be clearly in the ascendancy. As noted above, the commitment in terms of expert representation at the Conference was very great on the part of three of the original founders of the Union (Germany being absent on this occasion because of the recent war). Furthermore, these delegations put forward numerous amendments for the purpose of 'perfecting' the Convention in accordance with their conception of an ideal international copyright law based firmly on the rights of authors.[192] Nonetheless, the challenges posed by new technological developments and the arguments of user interests now proved to be more difficult to overcome. These factors, together with the size and increasing diversity of the membership of the Union, put the advocates of extensions of authors' rights in a more defensive position: considerable strengthening of these rights was necessary simply to maintain the status quo. Changing the Convention therefore, even in quite small respects, was a far more formidable process than before. Some indication of this fundamental shift in orientation is to be seen in the fact that French, long the language of international diplomacy, was no longer the language most readily used by the majority of delegates. It was now being steadily replaced by English. One reason for this was undoubtedly the recent and sudden rise to world eminence of the USA, even

[190] Thus, the Austrian delegation was headed by the President of the Society of Authors and Dramatic Composers of Vienna (Friesenburger). On the Belgian delegation, there were at least two members identified with authors' interests (Coppieters de Gibson and Vanderhaegen), two on the Spanish delegation (Forns and Duran), six on the French delegation (Boutet, Bedel, Willemetz, Duchemin, Ferdinand, and Vilbois), one on the Greek delegation (Renieris), one on the Hungarian delegation (Palagyi), four on the Italian delegation (de Sanctis, Sorrentino, Ciampi, and Pasquera), one from the Polish delegation (Dobrowolski), one on the Swedish delegation (von Konow), and two on the Czech delegation (Scheinpflug and Valenta): ibid, 54ff. This is not to take account of other delegates who may have had close links with these groups, but were present in other capacities, eg as government officials, or simply as 'expert advisers'. Nor, does it take account of other delegates who represented publishers' associations.

[191] Representatives of broadcasting interests were to be found on the following delegations: Belgium (van Imschoot), Denmark (Jensen), France (Lenoble), Luxembourg (La Chartre), Monaco (La Panouse, Straschnov), Norway (Lid), the Netherlands (de Vries), Poland (Waskiewicz), and Sweden (Mattson): ibid. There were also other delegates representing film and publishing interests.

[192] See the preparatory documents for the Conference: ibid, 133ff, and the collection of resolutions passed by different congresses and assemblies between 1927 and 1948 at 433ff.

though that country still remained outside the Berne Union. Nevertheless, as the British Empire had been a member of the Berne Union from its very inception, English had always been, in fact, the largest language group within the Union. By 1948, this was the language used by many of the newly independent states, even if it was not their native tongue, and the long linguistic and cultural ascendancy of the French language in the affairs of the Union therefore came under direct attack. In a real sense, therefore, the 1948 Conference can be seen as the end of an era in the history of the Berne Union.

In terms of practical results, the Brussels Conference's principal achievement **3.37** was the refinement and consolidation of the changes made by the Berlin and Rome Conferences. While some new additions were made, these were only of a limited nature. As at the earlier conferences, the main work was done in commission, and a number of sub-committees were also appointed to report on particular matters, including photographs and cinematographic works, radio-diffusion and mechanical reproduction, moral rights and works of applied art.[193] The chief changes made were as follows.

(a) Works protected

Cinematographic works, without qualification, were included in the primary **3.38** list of works protected under article 2, as were photographic works (article 3 of the previous text being deleted). 'Works of applied art', previously described as 'works of art applied to industrial purposes', were also promoted to this list, representing a triumphant conclusion to the strenuous efforts which had been made in this regard by the French and other delegations at the Berlin and Rome Conferences.[194] The effect of this victory, however, was somewhat blunted by the inclusion of a provision which left it to national legislation to determine the extent of the application of their laws to such works and industrial designs and models, as well as the conditions under which they would be protected. This accommodated countries such as the UK, but a further provision made it clear that works protected in their country of origin solely as designs and models were only entitled in other countries of the Union to such protection as the laws of those countries accorded to designs and models. Finally, a French proposal to extend the provisions of article 2 dealing with oral works was rejected.[195]

(b) Persons protected

No substantive changes were made here, but there was some clarification of **3.39** certain expressions used in article 4. These included 'simultaneously published

[193] ibid, 72.
[194] ibid, 94 (general report of the commission, prepared by Marcel Plaisant).
[195] ibid, 95.

in several countries',[196] 'published works',[197] 'publication',[198] and 'country of origin'.[199]

(c) Moral rights

3.40 There was a French proposal to extend these rights, in particular to make them inalienable.[200] This inevitably encountered resistance from some delegates who were concerned that further obstacles should not be placed in the way of new countries wishing to accede to the Convention.[201] The final compromise was an amendment to article 6*bis* under which it was declared that the moral rights granted to the author in that article should be maintained after his death until at least the expiry of the copyright (economic rights), but that national laws should regulate the person or persons who were to control and exercise those rights. This extended the Rome Act, but still left the way in which these enhanced rights were to be maintained to each member state to determine for itself.

(d) Duration

3.41 Article 7 was made more absolute in its requirements, with the deletion of the transitional arrangement made in paragraph (2) of the Berlin and Paris Acts.[202] Accordingly, paragraph (2) of article 7 was now changed so as to make comparison of periods of protection necessary only where Union countries accorded longer periods of protection than fifty years *post mortem auctoris*.[203] The remaining paragraphs of article 7 dealt with duration of protection in relation to particular kinds of work, including cinematographic works.[204]

(e) Lawful uses of copyright works

3.42 There was a French proposal to place article 9 on a more systematic basis, particularly in relation to press usage.[205] However, there was strong opposition to this from several countries who were concerned that these changes might restrict the free flow of information.[206] Accordingly, the earlier text was

---

196 Article 4(3). 197 Article 4(4). 198 ibid. 199 Article 4(5).

200 *Documents 1948* (1951), 187ff. Note also the different amendments proposed by Austria, Poland, the Netherlands, Spain, and Switzerland.

201 eg Finland: ibid, 98.

202 The reason this became possible was the making of declarations by several member countries which had shorter or qualified terms of protection that they would now make these terms unqualified and absolute: see *Documents 1948* (1951), 98, 201–2 in relation to the UK, and 98 in relation to Sweden and Switzerland.

203 Brussels Act, art 7(2).

204 Article 7(3) (cinematographic and photographic works, works of applied art), (4) (anonymous and pseudonymous works), (5) (posthumous works).

205 *Documents 1948* (1951), 231ff.

206 Notably the Scandinavian countries, the Poles, Dutch, and Czechs: ibid, 232ff and 99 (report by Plaisant, *rapporteur général*).

maintained without change. There was a further French proposal to systematize the regime of lawful borrowings allowed under article 10,[207] and this resulted in some modifications to article 3. The basic position in relation to the inclusion of excerpts from literary or artistic works in educational and scientific publications or chrestomathies was maintained,[208] but the making of short quotations from newspaper articles and periodicals, as well as their inclusion in press summaries, was made permissible.[209] It was further provided that quotations and excerpts should be accompanied by an acknowledgement of their source, and by the author's name, if that appeared on the work.[210] A new article (article 10*bis*) dealt with the increasing problems posed by the use of new technology in the reporting of current events, leaving it to each country to determine the conditions under which the recording, reproduction, and public communication of short extracts of literary or artistic works might be made for the purpose of reporting current events by means of photography, cinematography, and broadcasting.[211]

(f) Public performance, radiodiffusion, and public recitations

Article 11, which dealt with the first of these rights was strengthened, in that it **3.43** was made explicit that this was a right protected by the Convention, not simply a right that was only protected to the extent that it was recognized under national law (this having been the case under the earlier texts).[212] A significant declaration in relation to this article was made by the UK, which reserved its freedom to promulgate legislation where necessary in the public interest to oppose or remedy the abuse of this right by copyright owners within the UK.[213] A number of other countries associated themselves with this declaration.[214] As for article 11*bis*, this was extended in several important ways from the 1928 text, embracing television broadcasts, retransmissions, public communication of transmissions by such means as loudspeakers,[215] and the fixation of works after transmission.[216] The scope for member states to determine the conditions under which these extended rights were to be exercised within their territories was retained from the Rome Act, leaving open, presumably, the possibility of compulsory licence schemes under which the interests of authors and users might be more fairly balanced.[217] Finally, a new article 11*ter*, amplified article 11 by conferring on authors of literary works the exclusive right of authorizing public recitations of their works.

207 ibid, 246ff. 208 Article 10(2). 209 Article 10(1). 210 Article 10(3).
211 *Documents 1948* (1951), 100 (Plaisant's report), 250ff.
212 ibid, 252ff. 213 ibid, 82.
214 Namely New Zealand, South Africa, Switzerland, Canada, Ireland, the Netherlands, Australia, India, Pakistan, Norway, Sweden, Denmark, and Finland: ibid.
215 Article 11*bis*(1).
216 Article 11*bis*(3) (subject to limitations concerning ephemeral fixations of works broadcast).
217 Article 11*bis*(2).

(g) Indirect appropriations, mechanical reproductions, and cinematographic adaptations

3.44 After extensive discussion,[218] article 12 was considerably simplified. Rather than listing a series of different indirect appropriations that were to be regarded as illicit reproductions, the article now expressly recognized the exclusive right of authors of literary, scientific, and artistic works to authorize 'adaptations, arrangements and other alterations of their works'. The position in relation to mechanical reproduction rights (article 13) and cinematographic adaptations (article 14) were left essentially unchanged, except that the latter article was altered so as to make it clear that cinematographic works per se were now protected as original works (see article 2).

(h) Droit de suite

3.45 Article 14bis, following resolution 3 of the Rome Conference, brought the system of *droit de suite* into the Convention. The 'inalienable right' conferred under the article extended to both works of art and the original manuscripts of writers and composers. However, it was not mandatory for member states to accord this protection, as it was further provided that it could be claimed in a country of the Union only if the legislation of the country to which the author belonged permitted this, and then only to the degree granted by the law of the country where such protection was claimed. As many member states did not recognize *droit de suite*, and some did not even regard it as part of copyright law,[219] the effect of this article was to create a sub-Union between those states which did recognize *droit de suite.*

(i) Other changes

3.46 Only minor changes were made to the remaining articles of the Rome Act, which were retained in substantially the same form. However, two fresh articles dealing with disputes resolution and the languages of the Convention were added. The first, article 27bis, recognized, without imposing, the jurisdiction of the International Court of Justice to determine disputes between member states concerning the interpretation or application of the Convention. As at the Rome Conference, this stemmed from a Scandinavian proposal, and was the culmination of a long campaign to secure international jurisdiction for the settlement of disputes between states.[220] The second new article, article 31, provided for the establishment of an 'equivalent text' of the Convention in the English language. While French remained the language of the 'official text', and was to prevail in

218 *Documents 1948* (1951), 314ff.
219 See declaration by the Australian delegate to this effect: ibid, 82.
220 ibid, 107 (Plaisant's report).

cases of conflict over the interpretation of the two texts, even this modest change brought forth strong resistance from the French delegates,[221] and was deeply symbolic of the general changes occurring in the composition and orientation of the Union. Provision was also made in article 31 for the translation of the Convention into other languages, and, following the conclusion of the Conference, texts in Spanish[222] and Portuguese[223] were published with the official records of the Conference.

(j) Resolutions and votes of the Conference

In keeping with the practice of other conferences, the Brussels Conference passed one 'resolution' and a series of '*voeux*' or motions on various matters relating to the Berne Union and its organization. The 'resolution' created an advisory committee of twelve representative member states to assist the International Office in its functions. The membership was to rotate, with three members retiring every three years.[224] As for the '*voeux*' passed by the Conference, these covered a wide spectrum of issues, including the need for wider dissemination of knowledge relating to copyright, the desirability of achieving universal protection, the extension of moral rights so as to include the destruction of literary and artistic works within their scope, the advantages of the system of paying public domain, and the need for relief against double taxation of authors' incomes.[225] At a more immediate level, there were calls for protection (without prejudice to the rights of authors) of sound recordings and radio emissions ('neighbouring rights'), and of performers.[226] Finally, there was a vote calling for the International Office and its employees to be treated in the same way as in the other international organizations based in Switzerland.[227] Of these votes, those dealing with 'neighbouring rights' were to receive the most attention during the next ten years, although this was not to occur within the framework of the Berne Union.[228] **3.47**

(3) Assessment of the Brussels Revision

While it is true that the Brussels Conference made many changes to the Rome text, these did not embody fundamental extensions to authors' rights. The reality is that the Conference was very much a 'holding operation': the rights of authors were maintained, rather than advanced, by the changes made to the text in relation to such matters as broadcasting, cinematography, and recording. Even more than in 1928, these rights were in danger of being outflanked by the **3.48**

[221] ibid, 69–70, 107–8. [222] ibid, 557ff. [223] ibid, 571ff. [224] ibid, 585.
[225] ibid, 585–6 (votes I, II, III, IV, and V). [226] ibid, 587 (votes VI, VII, VIII).
[227] ibid (vote IX). [228] See further Chapter 19 below.

rapid and revolutionary changes in technology that were occurring.[229] While none of the passion displayed by the advocates of these rights at the early Berne Conferences was lacking in their successors at Brussels, their task was more difficult, being rather like that of a person running the wrong way on a moving conveyor belt. Furthermore, the new technological developments had spawned, or were spawning, a number of powerful interests concerned with their exploitation, and the aims of these groups were generally antithetical to those of authors. There was also a greater concern on the part of most, if not all, Union governments that the general public interest with respect to access to copyright material should be more adequately recognized. Finally, the following twenty years were to see the particular demands of developing countries come to the fore. These diverse pressures meant that henceforth cries for justice on the part of authors were no longer to be seen as possessing any intrinsic merit that set them apart from the pleas for fairness being mounted from other quarters, for example, from the broadcasting interests, educationalists, or developing countries. The idealistic arguments which had inspired the founding of ALAI and the constitution of the Berne Union would therefore begin to look outmoded in the years before the next revision of the Berne Convention, in Stockholm in 1967.

G. The 1967 Stockholm Revision Conference[230]

(1) Preparations for the Stockholm Conference

3.49 In its closing plenary session, the Brussels Conference chose Stockholm as the venue for the next conference of revision, but no date was fixed.[231] The new text came into force on 1 August 1951, with ratifications by ten states.[232] After this, ratifications from other member states followed slowly, but there were a significant number of new accessions. By June 1967, the date of the Stockholm

[229] See also the remarks of the *rapporteur*, Plaisant: *Documents 1948* (1951), 107.

[230] See generally Desbois et al (1976), 69ff; W Nordemann, K Vinck, and P W Hertin, *Internationales Urheberrecht und Leistungsschutzrecht der deutschsprachigen Länder unter Berücksichtigung auch der Staaten der Europäischen Gemeinschaft, Kommentar* (1977), 25ff; E Schulze, *The Forthcoming Stockholm Revision Conference 1967* (1964); T Hesser, 'Quelques questions concernant la future révision de la Convention de Berne' [1961] *DA* 238; [1962] *Copyright* 11 (in English); C Masouyé, 'La prochaine conférence de Stockholm' (1962) 34 *RIDA* 3; collection of articles in (1967–8) 54–5 *RIDA*; B Mentha, 'A Glance at the Principal Substantive Clauses of the Berne Convention Adopted at Stockholm on July 14, 1967' [1967] *Copyright* 321; I Henneberg, 'Scope of Protection According to the Stockholm Act of the Berne Convention' [1968] *Copyright* 167; E Schulze, *Intellectual Property Conference of Stockholm 1967* (1967).

[231] *Documents 1948* (1951), 83, 87.

[232] South Africa: [1950] *DA* 61; Belgium: [1951] *DA* 85; Spain: [1951] *DA* 97; France: [1951] *DA* 61; Liechtenstein: [1950] *DA* 133; Luxembourg: [1950] *DA* 62; Monaco: [1951] *DA* 85; Portugal: [1951] *DA* 109; Saint-Siege: [1951] *DA* 85; and Yugoslavia: [1951] *DA* 98, 110.

Revision Conference, there had been some seventeen of the latter, including Israel,[233] Argentina,[234] Mexico,[235] Turkey,[236] the Philippines,[237] and a large group of African nations which were former French territories.[238] By June 1967, there were fifty-eight member states of the Union, but only forty-two of these were bound by the Brussels text.[239] More significant, however, from the point of view of the Union's development was the fact that over a third of its membership was now in the category of 'developing country'.[240]

Preparation for the Stockholm Conference did not begin properly until the early 1960s. However, several important developments which occurred before this time should be noted. The first was the conclusion of the long projected Universal Copyright Convention, which was signed, under that name, in Paris in 1952. It was joined by the majority of Berne Union members, but as the level of protection which it provided was somewhat lower than that of the Berne Union, a significant number of non-Berne countries, including the USA, also acceded to it. The relationship between the Universal Copyright Convention and the Berne Convention is discussed in detail in Chapter 18 below. The second important development was the conclusion of a convention relating to neighbouring rights, that is, the rights of makers of phonographic recordings, broadcasting organizations, and performers. This Convention was signed in Rome in 1961, following a considerable amount of preparatory work carried out under the auspices of BIRPI, UNESCO, and the ILO, and had the effect of removing these rights from the potential umbrella of the Berne Union. Once again, the relationship between the Rome Convention and the Berne Convention is considered in detail in Chapter 19 below. **3.50**

(a) The Swedish Government/BIRPI programme

In 1963, the Swedish Government decided that the Stockholm Conference should take place in 1967.[241] This Conference, in fact, was not to be limited to copyright matters, as it was decided to undertake, at the same time, a limited revision of the Paris Convention for the Protection of Industrial Property, as well as a revision of the structural and administrative provisions of both the Berne and Paris Unions and of the other agreements concluded in connection with the Paris Convention. A further proposal to be considered at this general 'Intellectual Property Conference' was the adoption of a new convention **3.51**

[233] 24 Mar 1950: [1950] *DA* 25. [234] 10 June 1967: [1967] *DA* 95.
[235] 11 June 1967: [1967] *DA* 95, 119. [236] 1 Jan 1952: [1951] *DA* 133.
[237] 1 Aug 1951: [1950] *DA* 97.
[238] Cameroon, Congo, Dahomey, Gabon, Ivory Coast, Madagascar, Mali, Niger, Senegal, Upper Volta: see [1967] *DA* 132–3.
[239] ibid. [240] See further Chapter 14 below.
[241] [1963] *DA* 68. See also *Records* 1967, 71.

establishing an international intellectual property organization.[242] As far as the copyright aspects of the Conference were concerned, a small study group comprising representatives of the Swedish Government[243] and BIRPI[244] began work on a preliminary draft programme for the Conference in 1963. The study group was able to draw upon a number of earlier studies and investigations that had been carried out in the preceding decade by various experts at the request of the Advisory Committee of the Union (now called the 'Permanent Committee') in relation to such matters as the protection of cinematographic works,[245] the protection of news and other items of information,[246] and the question of duration of protection.[247] This study group made its first report, together with draft texts, on 1 June 1963.[248] This was submitted to an international committee of experts[249] which met in Geneva from 18 to 23 November 1963. These experts acted in their own capacity, and did not represent their respective governments.[250] Following their deliberations, the study group drew up a second report, complete with draft texts, on 1 July 1964,[251] and these were then examined by a Committee of Governmental Experts which met in Geneva just over a

242 ibid.

243 These were Torwald Hesser, Justice of the Supreme Court, and Professor Svante Bergström of the University of Uppsala: ibid.

244 'BIRPI' was the French acronym for the 'United International Bureaux for the Protection of Intellectual Property', and consisted of the International Offices of the Berne and Paris Unions. The BIRPI representatives on the study group were Professor G H C Bodenhausen, Director, and C Masouyé, Head of the Copyright Divisions: ibid.

245 The Permanent Committee discussed this at its fourth session in Neuchâtel in July 1952: [1952] *DA* 100ff. Research was carried out in this field under instruction from the Committee in 1953 by Eugen Ulmer (see [1953] *DA* 97ff) and G Lyon-Caen (see [1959] *DA* 217ff). Following a Resolution of the Permanent Committee at its ninth session held in London in Oct and Nov 1960 ([1960] *DA* 335), an international Committee of Film Experts under the chairmanship of Ulmer, with Henri Desbois as *rapporteur*, presented a report in 1962 ([1962] *DA* 24ff).

246 This was discussed by the Permanent Committee at Geneva in Aug 1958 and was suggested as an item for discussion at the Stockholm Conference: [1959] *DA* 188ff.

247 This was discussed by the Permanent Committee at each of its sessions from 1959–61: [1959] *DA* 206ff; [1960] *DA* 324ff; [1961] *DA* 318ff. These deliberations led to the appointment of two Committees of Experts which met at Geneva in Jan 1961: [1961] *DA* 56ff and Rome in May 1962: [1962] *DA* 113ff.

248 BIRPI, *General Report of the Swedish/BIRPI Study Group Established at 1 June 1963*, Document DA/20/2. See further *Records* 1967, 77.

249 See BIRPI, *Stockholm Conference, Committee of Experts (November 1963), Report of the Debates*, Document DA/20/29rev. This met under the chairmanship of Eugen Ulmer, and was composed of experts from Belgium, Czechoslovakia, France, the FRG, India, Italy, Poland, Spain, Sweden, Switzerland, Tunisia, and the UK. There were also observers from the USA and from a number of interested inter-governmental and non-governmental organisations: Document DA/20/15 (list of participants) and [1964] *DA* 21ff.

250 *Records* 1967, 77.

251 BIRPI, *General Report of the Swedish/BIRPI Study Group Established at 1 July 1964*, Document DA/22/2.

year later (5–14 July 1965).[252] This time, these experts did represent their governments, but nothing decided at this stage was finally binding. This second committee asked the study group to consider some matters which had not been settled, and following this request the latter suggested some further changes to its proposals. In addition, in the early stage of these preparations, there had been consultation with authors' societies, through the constitution of an Authors' Consultative Committee which had offered comments on the report of the 1963 Study Group.[253] These proposals, as amended, then constituted the official programme for the Conference that was adopted by the Swedish Government.[254]

The authors of the Conference programme described their aims as follows: **3.52**

> . . . the Programme of the Conference is based on the conception that improvements of this nature should include not only the enlargement of the protection granted to authors by the creation of new rights or by the extension of rights which are already recognised, but also the general development of copyright by reforms intended to make the rules relating to it easier to apply and to adapt them to the social, technical and economic conditions of contemporary society.
>
> It should be stressed, within its context, that care must be taken to prevent the proposed rules from creating, for no valid reason, difficulties that might hinder access to the Union by countries at present outside it.[255]

One further objective was the accommodation, within the framework of the Convention, of the needs of the developing countries which now formed so significant a proportion of the membership of the Union, and which were concerned to gain readier access to the copyright works of the developed nations. Pressure for concessions in favour of developing countries had begun in the early 1960s, and had crystallized at the African Study Meeting on Copyright which was held at Brazzaville in August 1963.[256] This Meeting had recommended, among other things, reductions in the term of protection, free use of protected works for educational and scholastic purposes, and the protection of folklore (a particularly vulnerable subject matter from the point of view of developing countries). The Stockholm Conference study group and the subsequent committees of experts sought to take account of these demands in their

[252] BIRPI, *Diplomatic Conference of Stockholm, 1967, Committee of Governmental Experts (1965), Report of the Debates*, Document DA/22/33. The chairman of this committee was Hans Morf (Switzerland). Its members were from Austria, Belgium, Brazil, Bulgaria, Congo (Léopoldville), Czechoslovakia, Denmark, Finland, France, the FRG, Greece, Hungary, India, Ireland, Israel, Italy, Japan, Lebanon, Luxembourg, Monaco, Morocco, the Netherlands, Norway, Poland, Portugal, Senegal, South Africa, Spain, Sweden, Switzerland, Thailand, Tunisia, Turkey, the UK, and Yugoslavia. There were also US observers and observers from other intergovernmental and non-governmental organizations. See further [1965] *DA* 194.

[253] BIRPI, *Report of the Authors' Consultative Commission, 1963*, Document DA 20/4.

[254] *Records* 1967, 77.

[255] ibid, 80.

[256] ibid, 137. For a report of this meeting, see [1963] *DA* 250.

deliberations, and a proposal concerning developing countries was included in the Conference programme.

3.53 While it did not embody any radical departures from, or extensions to the Brussels Act, the proposals in the programme contained a large number of amendments which were directed at the refinement and clarification of the substantive provisions of the Convention. The most important of these were: deletion of the requirement of fixation in the case of choreographic works and entertainments in dumb show; extensions to the term 'cinematographic work'; enlargement of the principle of national treatment as a criterion of eligibility for protection of authors; new criteria of secondary eligibility for some categories of works, such as cinematographic and architectural works; the strengthening of moral rights; minor changes to clarify and systematize the rules in relation to duration of protection, as well as proposals for a fifty-year minimum term from first publication or broadcast for cinematographic works, and a twenty-five-year minimum term from the time of making for photographic works; the express recognition, in article 9, of the right of reproduction *jure conventionis*, reserving the right of national laws to make exceptions to this in particular instances, such as for private use or for judicial and administrative purposes; a more general drafting of article 10 relating to the right of quotation, and clarification of article 10*bis* relating to reports of current events; and new rules of interpretation relating to the exploitation of cinematographic works.[257] In relation to developing countries, a draft protocol was proposed under which such countries would be permitted to make certain reservations, for specified periods of time, with respect to translation and radiodiffusion rights, duration of protection, reproduction by the press of articles on current topics, and educational, scientific, and scholastic use of literary and artistic works.[258] Two other additional protocols dealt with the protection of the works of stateless persons and certain international organizations.[259] Finally, a separate document dealt with proposed changes to the Convention of a structural and administrative nature (articles 21–31); these were linked to the changes proposed for the Paris Union, as well as to the general proposal for a new international intellectual property organization.[260]

---

257 *Records* 1967, 80–2, 83ff (Preparatory Document S/1).

258 ibid, 137ff. 259 ibid, 145–6.

260 ibid, 419ff (Preparatory Document S/9). See also 187ff (Preparatory Document S/3—relating to the Paris Union) and 489 (Preparatory Document S/10—relating to the International Intellectual Property Organization).

(b) Parties represented at the Conference

Fifty members of the Berne Union were represented at the Stockholm Conference,[261] and there were observers from a number of other nations, including the USA, and from various intergovernmental organizations, including the United Nations, UNESCO, and the EEC.[262] Observers from a large number of non-governmental international organizations interested in copyright also attended. Some of the latter, such as ALAI, CISAC, and the International Writers' Guild, represented authors,[263] but a larger number was representative of interests concerned with the use of copyright material, such as the European Broadcasting Union and the International Federation of the Phonographic Industry.[264] The presence of these observers gives some idea of the importance which was attached to the deliberations of the Conference by a wide spectrum of interested parties. In addition, the delegations of a number of member states, namely Belgium, Canada, Denmark, France, Greece, Italy, Luxembourg, Monaco, Spain, and Sweden, included as advisers persons who were connected with authors' or users' organizations.[265] As at previous conferences, some of the delegates were diplomats, but a larger proportion were officials from relevant government departments, such as justice, education, economics, and trade.[266] **3.54**

(2) The work of the Conference

The Union met four times in plenary session at Stockholm, but the principal work of revision was undertaken in committee. Consideration of the proposals for revising the substantive provisions of the Convention was done by Main Committee I which met twenty-eight times between 13 June and 11 July.[267] **3.55**

[261] Those countries which did not attend were Ceylon, Cyprus, Dahomey, Lebanon, Mali, New Zealand, Pakistan, and Upper Volta: ibid, 17 and 585–93.

[262] ibid, 594. Other important organizations which were represented by observers and whose activities were relevant to copyright included the United Nations Industrial Development Organization (UNIDO), the International Institute for the Unification of Private Law (UNIDROIT) and the Council for Mutual Economic Assistance (COMECON).

[263] ibid, 594–5.

[264] ibid. Others were the Asian Broadcasting Union (ABU), the International Alliance for Diffusion by Wire (AID), the International Federation of Film Distributors' Association (FIAD), the International Federation of Film Producers' Associations (FIAPF), the International Federation of Newspaper Publishers (FIEJ), the International Publishers' Association (IPA) and the Union of National Radio and Television Organizations of Africa (URTNA). There were also observers from several organizations concerned with the interests of persons involved in the performing arts, such as the International Federation of Actors (IFA), the International Federation of Musicians (FIM) and the International Secretariat of Entertainment Trade Unions.

[265] ibid, 585–93. [266] ibid.

[267] For summary minutes of the meetings of Main Committee I, see *Records* 1967, 837ff, and for the Committee's report, see 1131ff.

This was presided over by Professor Eugen Ulmer, the distinguished German academic intellectual property lawyer, and the *rapporteur* was Svante Bergström of Sweden, who had also served on the Swedish Government/BIRPI study group which had prepared the programme for the Conference. This committee, in turn, elected a drafting committee, consisting of representatives from Australia, Czechoslovakia, France, India, Mexico, the Netherlands, Romania, Senegal, and Sweden.[268] In addition, in the course of discussions, four working groups were set up to consider particular problems of special importance, namely exceptions to the right of reproduction proposed in the new article 9, cinematographic works, protection of folklore, and the conditions mentioned in article 2*bis*.[269] The proposals concerning developing countries were considered by Main Committee II, which also appointed two working groups to consider matters of substance and the definition of the criteria of countries that would be entitled to avail themselves of the new provisions.[270] Finally, the proposals concerning the administrative provisions and final clauses of the Berne Convention, as well as those of the Paris Convention and the other Special Agreements, were considered by Main Committee IV.[271] The basis of discussion in each committee was the preparatory documents drawn up by the Swedish Government and BIRPI, but before and during the Conference these were supplemented by numerous other proposals and counter-proposals put forward by other delegations.[272]

3.56 The changes to the substantive provisions of the Convention that were finally adopted by the Conference were of a fairly limited nature. As stated above, the basic extensions of rights had been made at the earlier conferences, in particular that of Berlin. Rome, and Brussels had seen some further additions, but these had been confined in scope and had been mainly designed to prevent the rights secured by the earlier revisions from being outflanked by subsequent technological developments. Apart from its structural and administrative reforms (which were major) and its provisions concerning developing countries (which were a clear derogation from authors' rights), the substantive changes made by the Stockholm Conference were restricted in scope, although their significance from the point of view of clarification and systematization should not be minimized. The most important were as follows.

(a) Eligibility criteria and country of origin

3.57 The nationality of the author was made the general criterion for protection under the Convention: protection was henceforth accorded to authors who were

[268] *Records*, 1967, 1131–2 (report of Main Committee I). [269] ibid, 1132.
[270] ibid, 941 and 947 (minutes) and 1193 (report of Main Committee II).
[271] ibid, 1009 (minutes) and 1207 (report of Main Committee IV).
[272] These are to be found at ibid, 603–783.

nationals of one of the countries of the Union, not only for their unpublished works and works first published in a Union country (as under the Brussels text), but for their works wherever published.[273] In addition, authors having 'their habitual residence' in a Union country were assimilated to nationals of that country, a formula which was wide enough to make the proposed additional protocol concerning the works of stateless persons unnecessary.[274] Some modifications were also made to the definitions of the expressions 'country of origin'[275] and 'published works'.[276] Finally, new criteria of eligibility in the cases of cinematographic and architectural works were added, to take account of the peculiar nature of those kinds of works.[277]

(b) Right of reproduction and exceptions

Under earlier Acts, the right of reproduction, the most basic author's right, had not been expressly recognized, although the articles dealing with lawful borrowings and adaptations were clearly premised on the existence of such a right. The programme therefore proposed that this should now be formally acknowledged in article 9, and this was approved by the Conference, although a proposal for a right of circulation or distribution was rejected,[278] and a further proposal to provide for the possibility of compulsory licences met with considerable opposition.[279] As a corollary to the general right of reproduction recognized in article 9(2), article 13(1) which dealt with the right of recording musical works was now superfluous, and was therefore deleted.[280] However, the scope for national legislation to provide for compulsory licences in respect of recordings was retained,[281] and was extended to cover words accompanying music.[282] Further exceptions to the reproduction right were to be found in a new article 9(2), and in articles 10 and 10*bis*. **3.58**

(c) Works protected

A number of changes, mostly of a drafting and ordering nature, were made to the provisions of articles 2 and 2*bis*. The most significant of these were the deletion of the requirement of fixation in respect of choreographic works and entertainments in dumb show, and the insertion of a new paragraph (2) which left it to member countries to prescribe for themselves whether fixation in some material form was necessary for the protection of works in general or of any specified categories of works.[283] **3.59**

273 Article 3(1)(a) of the Stockholm Act. 274 Article 3(2). 275 Article 54(4)(c).
276 Article 3(3). 277 Article 4.
278 *Records* 1967, 1143 (report of Main Committee I).
279 ibid. 280 ibid, 1169. 281 Article 31(1). 282 ibid.
283 *Records* 1967, 1153.

(d) Moral rights

3.60 With the deletion of any reference to the author's lifetime, article 6bis was transformed into a general provision on moral rights that was no longer subject to any express temporal limitation. Article $6^{bis}(2)$ which dealt with the protection of moral rights after the death of the author was also strengthened, although this was done in such a way as to accommodate those countries whose legal systems did not protect moral rights within the framework of copyright,[284] and which therefore had considerable difficulty in providing complete protection for them after the author's death.[285]

(e) Duration of protection

3.61 The main changes made here were the fixation of terms of protection for cinematographic and photographic works and works of applied art. In the Brussels Act, these had been left as matters for national legislation, but the Stockholm Act now stipulated a fifty-year term for the first[286] and a minimum twenty-five-year term for the second two.[287]

(f) Cinematographic works

3.62 The inclusion of cinematographic works under the umbrella of the Berne Convention had long been the cause of considerable difficulty, both from a doctrinal and a practical point of view, as these works were closer in character to subject matter such as sound recordings and radio broadcasts which fell outside the Convention. Accordingly, there were many national differences in the treatment of cinematographic works, particularly in relation to the questions of authorship and ownership. There had been a series of studies on these matters conducted on behalf of the Permanent Committee in the fifteen years preceding the Stockholm Conference,[288] and they had also been given considerable attention in the preparatory work for the Conference.[289] The result was the adoption of a new conventional regime governing cinematographic works. This was embodied in article 14, which dealt with the rights of authors with respect to cinematographic reproductions and adaptations of their works, and a new article 14bis, which dealt with rights in the cinematographic works themselves and the exploitation of these rights. There were also other consequential amendments in relation to such matters as definitions, criteria of eligibility for protection, and duration of protection. These provisions are discussed in detail in paras 7.24ff and 8.31ff, and 9.47 below.

---

284 eg Australia, the UK, Finland, Ireland, Norway, and Sweden: ibid, 1158.
285 ibid, 1159. 286 Article 7(1). 287 Article 7(4). 288 See para 3.51 above.
289 See *Records* 1967, 55ff (programme), 1175ff (report of Main Committee I).

(g) Other changes

The right of public recitation in article 11*ter* was made more explicit so as to include recitation by any means or process, and any communication to the public of such recitation.[290] Provision was also made in article 15 for the protection of anonymous works of folklore by national 'competent authorities', although the word 'folklore' was not actually mentioned.[291] Apart from these, there were no major changes to the remaining substantive provisions of the Convention, although there was discussion on the interpretation of several of them in Main Committee I.[292] As stated above, the proposed additional protocol on the protection of works of stateless persons was withdrawn as being superfluous, and a similar view was taken with respect to the proposed additional protocol on works of international organizations.[293] **3.63**

(h) The Protocol Regarding Developing Countries

One of the most significant developments in the years immediately preceding the meeting of the Stockholm Conference was the growing pressure from developing countries for some kind of special concessions in relation to their use of copyright works, most of which originated from the developed nations. These claims were chiefly concerned with reproduction and translation rights, as many developing countries argued that large publishing houses located in the developed nations charged high prices for the works they controlled, and had little or no interest in supplying proper translations to developing nations.[294] The Stockholm Conference therefore provided a ready forum for these demands to be considered in the context of the Berne Convention system. Many of the developed countries at the Conference favoured the making of some concessions at least, on the ground that, if these were not made, there would be a drop in membership of the Berne Union as the developing countries withdrew from it. To adopt a metaphor, it could be said that if the Convention were to leap forward in the future, it might be necessary at this stage to take a few steps backwards. As a result, the Protocol adopted by the Stockholm Conference went a considerable way towards accommodating the demands of the developing countries. Nonetheless, these concessions were only grudgingly made by the developed countries,[295] and it soon became apparent that they were not prepared to be bound by the new Protocol. This dispute between developed and developing country members of Berne in the period 1967 to 1971 almost led to the **3.64**

[290] *Records* 1967, 1168–9. [291] ibid, 1172–3.
[292] eg on art 11*bis* (ibid, 1167–8) and art 17 (ibid, 1173–5). [293] ibid, 1190–1.
[294] See further N Kumar, 'Cultural Imperialism and Third World Publishing' [1983] *Copyright* 17.
[295] *Records* 1967, 808ff (Plenary Meeting of the Berne Union).

collapse of the Berne system and many of the issues that were then hotly contested remain relevant today. These matters are reviewed in detail in Chapter 14. For the purposes of the present overview, however, it suffices to note that the provisions of the Protocol permitted developing countries, for a given period of time, to accord shortened terms of protection to works protected under the Convention, to grant non-exclusive translation and reproduction licences under certain conditions, to allow the broadcasting of works where this was done for non-profitmaking purposes, and to provide for compulsory licences in respect of uses that were 'exclusively for teaching, study and research in all fields of education'. These generous provisions in favour of developing countries were destined never to come into force and led directly to the formulation of a further revision of the Convention in Paris in 1971 (see paras 3.66–3.67 below).

(i) Reforms to the administrative and final clauses[296]

3.65 These were the most significant changes made to the Convention text by the Stockholm Revision Conference. They were made in concert with the revisions made to the equivalent provisions of the Paris Convention and the other Special Agreements connected with that Convention, and were closely linked to the new Convention establishing the World Intellectual Property Organization. An Assembly of the Union consisting of all member countries was set up; this was to meet triennially and was to have overall responsibility for the direction of the affairs of the Union (article 22). It was assisted by a smaller Executive Committee of rotating membership, which was to meet on a more regular basis (usually once a year), and which had the oversight of matters between meetings of the Assembly (article 23). Finally, an International Bureau was established to take over all the administrative tasks concerning the Union (article 24). The latter was a continuation of the International Office which had been constituted under the original Berne Act and which had been combined administratively with the International Office of the Paris Union (BIRPI). Its functions were, in fact, to be carried out by the new World Intellectual Property Organization (WIPO),[297] which was henceforth to act as the secretariat of all the major international intellectual property conventions, with the exception of the UCC which continued to be administered by UNESCO. Extensive changes were also made to the budgetary arrangements of the Union (article 25), and the final clauses, dealing with such matters as ratifications, accessions, reservations, revisions and the like, were significantly restructured (articles 26–38). A full discussion of these matters is to be found in Chapters 16 and 17.

---

[296] See generally Desbois et al (1976), 70–1, 186ff; C Joubert, 'Les clauses administratives et les clauses finales' [1967–8] *RIDA* 472.

[297] WIPO Convention, art 4(ii).

(3) Consequences of the Stockholm Revision: the 1971 Paris Conference[298]

As the work of the Stockholm Conference, and its immediate successor, the Paris Conference of 1971, occupy so much of the remaining part of this book, it is unnecessary at this stage to give anything more than the barest outline of the events that occurred after the conclusion of the Stockholm Conference. However, it is essential to understand the following matters. **3.66**

Ratification of, or accession to, the Stockholm Act could be done either as to the whole of it, or as to part: any country could declare in its instrument of ratification or accession that this ratification or accession was not to apply to either the substantive provisions of the text (articles 1–21 and the Protocol Regarding Developing Countries), or to the administrative provisions (articles 22–26).[299] The result was that the achievements of the Stockholm Conference in relation to the problems of developing countries were to be stillborn, unless a sufficient number of developed nations were prepared to be bound by the Protocol. This did not happen. Although thirty-nine nations signed the Stockholm text within the prescribed time, by January 1971, the required number of ratifications had only been given in respect of articles 22 to 38 of the Stockholm text, which duly entered into force in early 1970. The substantive provisions (including the Protocol), however, had not come into force, and there were clear signs that this would not occur, as the developed nations were becoming increasingly reluctant to commit themselves to the special regime proposed for developing countries.[300]

The result was a series of international meetings, at both a governmental and non-governmental level, at which the need for an immediate revision of the Protocol Regarding Developing Countries became obvious.[301] Calls for such a revision did not only come from the developed nations, although the latter were strongly influenced by their own authors' and publishing interests; they also came from many of the developing countries which were aware that they might gain nothing at all if a solution more acceptable to the developed nations could not be found. The prospect of a more restricted Union comprised principally of the developed nations seemed very real, and accordingly both sides accepted the **3.67**

[298] For general background on the Conference, see Desbois et al (1976) 255ff; E Ulmer, 'International Copyright after the Paris Revisions' (1972) 19 *Bull Cop Soc USA* 263; A Françon, 'Actes de Paris portant révision des Conventions internationales sur la propriété littéraire et artistique' (1976) 103 *Journal du droit international* 29; V de Sanctis, 'Paris Revisions (July 1971) of the UCC and the Berne Convention' [1972] *Copyright* 241–7.

[299] Stockholm Act, art 28(1)(b).

[300] *Records* 1971, 33 (report of Professor Bodenhausen, Director General of WIPO). See also 'Historical Outline of the Preparations of the Revision of the UCC and the Berne Convention' [1971] *Copyright* 19.

[301] *Records* 1971, 34ff.

need for some kind of salvage operation. With a speed unusual in international relations, a new conference of revision was held in Paris in July 1971. This was done in conjunction with the revision conference of the UCC which was also held in the same place at the same time. The Berne revision was essentially concerned with the Protocol Regarding Developing Countries, and with consequential changes to the final and administrative clauses of the Stockholm Act; the substantive provisions of the latter, however, were left untouched. The ultimate solution adopted by the Conference (and embodied in an Appendix to the Paris Act) closely paralleled the less rigorous regime relating to developing countries under the UCC. The details of this Conference, and the merits and defects of its work, are discussed in Chapter 14. For our present purposes, however, it suffices to say that an accommodation was reached which still acknowledged the special claims of the developing nations, although it also substantially shifted the balance back in favour of the developed nations. Nevertheless, the integrity of the Union was preserved, and the membership of the Union has increased steadily since that date. By 1 January 1986 (the date of the first edition of this work), there was a total of seventy-six member states, of which forty-eight were bound by the Paris Act, and a further ten were bound by articles 22 to 38 of that Act (these being essentially the same as those of the Stockholm Act).[302] By 17 January 2005, the membership had increased to 159:[303] all of these are bound by the Paris Act, with the exceptions of three countries that remain bound by Brussels and Stockholm (articles 22–48),[304] two by Brussels and Paris (articles 22–38),[305] one by Brussels alone,[306] two by Rome,[307] one by Rome and Stockholm (articles 22–38),[308] and two by Rome and Paris (articles 22–38).[309] The developments in international copyright arrangements, both within and outside the Berne Union, since 1971 are treated in more detail in the following chapter.

H. A Perspective on the Growth of the Berne Union, 1886–1971

3.68 This chapter has sought to provide an overall perspective on the development of the Berne Union during its first eighty-five years of existence. Inevitably, this treatment has become somewhat abbreviated in relation to the Convention's history immediately prior to 1971, as this material belongs more properly to the discussion of the present operation of the Convention which follows in Part III.

302 [1986] *Copyright* 6–8.

303 The list is to be found, regularly updated, at www.wipo.int/treaties/en/ip/berne/index.html.

304 Chad, Fiji, Ireland.

305 Bahamas, South Africa.

306 Madagascar.

307 Lebanon, New Zealand.

308 Pakistan.

309 Sri Lanka, Zimbabwe.

As the next chapter will demonstrate, there is another broader dimension to Berne that has developed outside and since the 1967 to 1971 texts, through the formulation of further instruments such as the WCT, the TRIPS Agreement and new agreements on neighbouring rights. However, so far as the period 1886–1971 is concerned, three principal stages in the Union's development can be identified: an initial period where the Eurocentric doctrine of authors' rights advanced by leaps and bounds (Berne to Berlin); a middle period where this advance was impeded, if not checked, by technological changes and the emergence of new interest groups (Rome to Brussels); and a later period where the interests of users, particularly those from developing countries, radically changed the terms of debate about international copyright protection (Stockholm and Paris). As the next chapter will show, there have been further and more far-reaching changes in the period following 1971.

4

COPYRIGHT AND NEIGHBOURING RIGHTS COME OF AGE: DIGITIZATION AND INTERNATIONAL TRADE

A. Introduction

In the first edition of this book (written in 1986), the following comment appeared concerning the position following the 1967 to 1971 Revisions of the Berne Convention: **4.01**

> At present, a state of rough equilibrium appears to have been reached, and there are no current plans in train for another revision of the Convention. Nevertheless, as with most human institutions, changes are still occurring and new pressures emerging. It would be futile, therefore, to think that the second century of the Berne Convention will not be as eventful, in one way or another, as its first.[1]

As this chapter will show, this 'state of rough equilibrium' changed radically in the period immediately after these words were written.

A number of influences are to be seen at play here, but two in particular have been crucial. First, there has been the effect of technological change, in particular the advent of digital technologies and the subsequent development of networked communications and the Internet. Second, there has been the linking of protection of intellectual property rights with trade issues, culminating in the adoption of the Agreement on Trade-Related Aspects of Intellectual Property Rights in 1994 ('TRIPs Agreement') as one of the annexed agreements of the newly established World Trade Organization ('WTO'). Underlying the adoption of the TRIPs Agreement, in turn, was widespread dissatisfaction with the way that existing intellectual property rights agreements such as Berne dealt with questions of enforcement and the absence therein of any effective dispute-resolution mechanism between states. **4.02**

[1] S Ricketson, *The Berne Convention for the Protection of Literary and Artistic Works: 1886–1986* (1987), 125.

4.03 Both these issues are closely connected, but for the purposes of exposition it is helpful to deal with the way they were resolved in the different fora of the World Intellectual Property Organization ('WIPO') and Berne, and then of the General Agreement on Tariffs and Trade ('GATT') and the WTO. As the centre point of this commentary is the Berne Convention, we shall begin by considering that agreement and the possibility of its revision post-1971, leading to the adoption of the two WIPO treaties in 1996; we shall then move to a short description of the adoption of the TRIPs Agreement and the implications of this development. Inevitably, this style of treatment will mean that chronologies will overlap, but this is an inevitable consequence of the double helix that is now formed between Berne and its associated agreements, on the one hand, and TRIPs, on the other. A further twist in the helix is to be found in the adoption of separate international agreements concerning 'neighbouring rights', but consideration of these is left for separate treatment in Chapter 19 below.

B. Revising Berne Again

(1) The period 1971–86: a period of reflection and regrouping

4.04 Enough has been said in the preceding chapter to indicate that, following the last two revision conferences in Stockholm (1967) and Paris (1971), it looked unlikely that the Berne Convention would be further revised in the foreseeable future. This was because these last two conferences had almost seen the complete breakdown of the international copyright system, as a huge gulf emerged between developed and developing countries, particularly on the issues of compulsory translation and educational copying licences. While these divisions were finally painted over at the Paris Conference of 1971, the prevailing opinion of experts was that it would be too dangerous to institute a new revision process in case these divisions were reopened. Subsequent developments, most of them external to the Berne Convention, began to alter this position from the mid-1980s on, and a new process of revision did, in fact, begin in 1991. Although this did not result in a revision of the Convention itself, within the comparatively short period of five years, a separate new treaty on copyright (the WIPO Copyright Treaty) was adopted in Geneva in December 1996—an outcome that looked unlikely even at the beginning of that year. This treaty, and its companion on performers and phonograms, came into force in early 2002. In this same period, of course, the TRIPs Agreement had also been formulated, adopted, and come into operation.

4.05 In recounting this most recent chapter in the history of international copyright relations, it is worth beginning with a reprise of the views that were expressed in the final chapter of the first edition of this commentary which was published in

1987—at a midpoint, as it transpired, between the period of cautious reflection and development that followed the adoption of the 1971 Paris Act of Berne and the period of frenetic norm-making that occurred in the years from 1987 to 1996.

In 1986, it was possible to view the Berne Convention through the prism of the following metaphor: a reasonably sized river craft that had just survived passage through some particularly steep and turbulent rapids and that was now entering a long stretch of shallow, sluggish water, which the paddlers hoped would continue, at least for the time needed to regain their strength and energy. But while all appeared smooth on the surface of the water, there was a much stronger underlying current: indeed, there were several such currents, with one in particular that was flowing in another adjoining riverbed that was shortly to add its force to the main stream. Viewed in less aquatic terms, it can be said that the Berne Convention, even as modified in Paris in 1971, was a reasonably impressive instrument so far as its embodiment of substantive copyright norms was concerned, for example, its prohibition on formalities, its mandatory term of protection, and its list of exclusive rights to be protected: in this regard, it compared favourably with its companion convention in the industrial property sphere, the Paris Convention for the Protection of Industrial Property. On the other hand, Berne was still a 'work in progress', with many significant gaps, so far as its objective of providing protection, in as 'effective and uniform a manner as possible', for the rights of authors in their literary and artistic works was concerned. As noted in the first edition of this commentary, two particular areas of concern were left relatively untouched by the 1971 Paris text: those dealing with questions of ownership and exploitation of the rights protected under the Convention, and those dealing with the means of enforcing those rights. The first of these matters is dealt with at some length in Chapter 7 below where it will be seen that, to date, attempts to deal with ownership and exploitation issues, even in the limited area of cinematographic works, have been very limited in their effect. This is an area of concern, moreover, that involves difficult issues of private international law, and these questions are addressed further in Chapter 20 below. **4.06**

As for the second matter—enforcement—this was a significant lacuna in the Convention umbrella that became more evident as the Convention neared its centenary celebrations. **4.07**

(a) Enforcement and compliance

In this regard, the Convention relied on the application of the principles of national treatment and independence of protection, under which the extent of protection and the means of redress afforded to the author are governed exclusively by the laws of the protecting country. This was qualified in two **4.08** respects: first, as regards the requirement that the exercise of rights under the Convention should not be subject to any formality, such as registration or the need for the lodging of security,[2] and secondly, with respect to the seizure of infringing copies.[3] Otherwise, the Convention left the question of enforcement of rights to the law of the protecting country. Historically, this may be seen as a reflection of the late nineteenth-century conditions in which the Convention was born: its purpose was to secure recognition of the entitlement of authors to protection and, once this was accorded, it was left to the individual claimants to pursue the enforcement of their rights according to the laws of the country where protection was sought. A century on, however, the assumption that protecting countries would provide the necessary enforcement of rights could no longer be so confidently made, particularly in the absence of effective mechanisms at the international level to ensure that member countries would comply with their Berne obligations. As will be seen below, enforcement and compliance issues were the driving forces behind the adoption of the TRIPs Agreement in the early 1990s. Beyond this, there were also concerns about the efficacy of many national court and administrative procedures: for many rights owners, it was of little comfort to receive formal protection of their rights in a country where it might take years and great expense to have a case finally determined.

(b) Gaps in substantive protection: the continuing debate

4.09 As Chapters 1 to 3 above demonstrate, the history of Berne up to 1971 had been the gradual development of a body of uniform substantive rules of protection to be applied by an increasing number of countries constituted as a 'Union for the Protection of the Rights of Authors'. But even this apparently simple ideal can raise questions of definition: which rights are to be protected in the first place, and what properly pertains to authors and their successors? At the Berne Conferences of 1884 to 1886, a number of delegates saw the instrument that was finally achieved only as a first step towards an ultimate universal codification of copyright.[4] While a considerable number of rights were added to the Convention in its successive revisions, the 1971 text was still some way from embodying a uniform set of rights to be protected. Even at that time, it was clear there were significant and obvious gaps in substantive protection, for example, in the case of a right of distribution, while the formulation of some of the rights that were protected left considerable scope for the adoption of conflicting interpretations by member countries, for example, those of reproduction, broadcasting, and cable distribution (these matters are analysed in depth in Chapters 11 and 12 below). Furthermore, considerable variations were to be found with respect to

---

[2] Paris Act, art 5(2). See further paras 6.101ff below. [3] Paris Act, art 16.

[4] *Actes* 1884, 28–9 (debate on the German motion in favour of a universal codification).

the protection of such subject matter as cinematographic works, while it was quite unclear whether new kinds of subject matter, such as computer software and databases, came within the scope of the Convention and, if so, how these matters were to be dealt with. In addition, the Convention left a wide discretion to member countries in relation to the important matter of exceptions to protection. Much therefore was subject to the application of the principle of national treatment, meaning that the protection accorded to authors claiming under the Convention still varied considerably from country to country. As the first edition of this commentary, written in 1986, stated, 'uniformity of protection, under the present [1971] Act, therefore is still only partial'.

Complete and absolute uniformity of protection, in the sense of an international codification of copyright applicable everywhere, is undoubtedly a utopian and unattainable goal, and may not even be ultimately desirable if states are to maintain some differences in their cultural and other copyright-related policies. However, the advantages of increased uniformity are clear, particularly the greater certainty that this gives authors in protecting and exploiting their rights in different countries of the Union. At the regional level, notably in the European Union, it has been possible to see a strong movement towards the harmonization of copyright in a number of key areas, such as rental rights, computer software, duration of protection, cable and satellite transmissions, and databases. In the larger context of the Berne Convention, there would be great scope for a new revision covering such matters if this were politically and practically possible. Somewhat hopefully, the first edition of this commentary suggested that a possible 'shopping list' for such a revision would include the following matters: **4.10**

1. The exclusion of software from article 2(1) and a more precise definition of the meaning of 'literary and artistic'.
2. A proper definition of the term 'author'.
3. Recognition of a right of distribution, including rights of rental and lending.
4. Reformulation of the rights of broadcasting and performance to take account of the present uncertainties posed by satellites and cable distribution.
5. The proper regulation of the minor exceptions to performing rights implicitly allowed at present within the framework of the Convention, as well as the exceptions presently implied with respect to translations.
6. Some clearer definition of the meaning of 'private' in the context of copying and dissemination in a non-material form.
7. Regulation of the situations where compulsory licences and levies may be permitted.
8. Provision for criminal sanctions and similar remedies against pirates.

9. Regulation of the basic conditions under which collective administration of rights may occur.
10. Provision of general principles to govern: (a) employee authors, (b) contracts between authors and publishers, and (c) contracts between authors and other disseminators of works.
11. Residual rules governing the application of laws in the case of the ownership and exploitation of rights under the Convention.

4.11 Even more hopefully, the first edition went on to state that this list contained 'only a minimum number of changes that might be made to the Convention in order to attain a greater degree of uniformity', but acknowledged that it was 'still highly ambitious and, to an experienced eye, . . . [would] appear unrealistic'. Nonetheless, it was a programme for action, and led to consideration of the possible routes by which some, at least, of these objectives might be reached. In view of subsequent events, these possibilities are worth recounting briefly.

(c) A conference of revision in the near or medium future

4.12 In 1986, the first edition described this as the 'ten-year option'—the holding of a revision conference some time before 1996. As noted above, this seemed an unlikely, even undesirable, prospect when viewed against the near collapse of the Berne system at the time of the 1967 to 1971 conferences.[5] Having reached a settlement that all could live with, there was a general reluctance on all sides to reopen debates that might lead to a similar impasse. On the other hand, it could be said that the problems facing the Convention in 1986 were different in kind from those that were at the forefront in 1967. While the difficulties of developing countries had hardly disappeared, the threats to copyright protection were now coming from other quarters, mainly the new modes of exploitation made possible by technological development, while the possibilities of networked communications were already being dimly perceived. However, it was also likely that these very developments would make it even more difficult to achieve agreement than was the case in 1967 and 1971, particularly given the increasing membership of the Berne Union. The reality is that the hothouse atmosphere of a revision conference, held within a relatively confined period of time, can readily lead to stalemate, unless a fair degree of consensus between states on the matters to be discussed has emerged beforehand. This was so at each of the earlier successful revision conferences, notably those of Berlin and Brussels. But as far as the issues listed in the preceding paragraph were concerned, it could not have been said in 1986 that any significant level of agreement on any of them had yet been reached between Union countries. Accordingly, a full-scale revision

[5] See eg the discussion in S M Stewart, *International Copyright and Neighbouring Rights*, 2nd edn (1989), 296ff.

conference, even within a ten-year timeframe, would most likely have been a pointless exercise and it does not seem that there was ever any serious consideration of this possibility.

(d) The 'guided development' of international practice with a view to its ultimate confirmation by a revision conference

An alternative, and perhaps more appealing, strategy was to delay preparations for a revision conference indefinitely so as to allow the necessary consensus referred to above to emerge. The growth of this consensus could be assisted by a number of measures: the convening of international groups of experts, the holding of forums, the carrying out of national and comparative studies and the formulation of model principles or provisions. The process would be slow and incremental, and might aptly be described as a policy of 'guided development',[6] or, perhaps more accurately, 'seeding the ground'. Nevertheless, over time it could lead Union members to identify far more clearly their points of agreement. If these points were adopted, or at least accepted, in national laws, this would finally lay the basis for a conference of revision that could amend the provisions of the Convention accordingly. **4.13**

(2) 'Guided development': activities leading up to the Berne Protocol process, 1991

In essence, 'guided development' appears to have been the policy of WIPO from the late 1970s, with initiatives occurring in the following areas: reprography;[7] storage of protected works in computers and computer-created works;[8] computer software;[9] cable television;[10] expressions of **4.14**

[6] This expression has been utilized by Dr Ficsor to designate this period of development in his detailed commentary on the 'Internet Treaties': M Ficsor, *The Law of Copyright and the Internet* (2001), 5, n 7 ('Ficsor (2001)').

[7] Committee of Experts on the Photographic Reproduction of Protected Works (Paris, 1–5 July 1968): [1968] *Copyright* 201; Working Group on Reproduction of Works Protected by Copyright (Paris, 2–6 May 1973): [1973] *Copyright* 172; Subcommittees of Executive Committee of the Berne Union and the IGC on Reprographic Reproduction: (Washington, 16–21 June 1975) [1975] *Copyright* 159.

[8] In particular, the reports of the Committee of Government Experts on Copyright Problems Arising from the Use of Computers for Access to or the Creation of Works (Paris, 15–19 Dec 1980): [1981] *Copyright* 73; (Paris, 7–11 June 1982): [1982] *Copyright* 239.

[9] See the reports of the Expert Group on the Protection of Software (Geneva, 27–30 Nov 1979): [1979] *Copyright* 36; and the Committee of Experts on the same subject matter (Geneva, 13–17 June 1983): [1983] *Copyright* 271; Group of Experts on the Copyright Aspects of the Protection of Computer Software (Geneva, 25 Feb–1 Mar 1985): [1985] *Copyright* 146.

[10] In particular, see the report and statement of the Group of Independent Experts on the Impact of Cable Television in the Sphere of Copyright (Geneva, 10–13 Mar 1980): [1980] *Copyright* 154; see also [1981] *Copyright* 218; Annotated Principles of Protection of Authors, Performers, Producers of Phonograms and Broadcasting Organizations in Connection with Distribution of Programs by Cable (Geneva, 5–7 Dec 1983): [1983] *Copyright* 131.

folklore;[11] rental and lending of phonograms and videograms;[12] private copying;[13] direct broadcasting satellites;[14] employed authors;[15] publishing contracts;[16] piracy;[17] paying public domain;[18] model statutes for authors' organizations in developing countries;[19] and the problems of handicapped readers.[20] Furthermore, in the year of the Berne centenary (which was attended by celebrations in many Berne member states), WIPO announced that it was undertaking a systematic examination of new modes of exploitation in relation to each principal category of protected works, namely the printed word, audiovisual works, phonograms, works of visual art, works of architecture, works of applied art, dramatic and choreographic works, and musical works.[21] Work on these

---

[11] The work in this area was extensive, but the most important meetings were those of the Working Group on the Intellectual Property Aspects of Folklore Creation which led to the preparation of a model law: [1980] *Copyright* 110 and [1982] *Copyright* 282. Work was also done on a draft multilateral treaty by the Group of Experts on the International Protection on Expressions of Folklore (Paris, 10–14 Dec 1984): [1985] *Copyright* 40. For further studies, see A Bogsch, 'The First Hundred Years of the Berne Convention for the Protection of Literary and Artistic Works' [1986] *Copyright* 291, 295 ('Bogsch (1986)').

[12] In particular, the WIPO/UNESCO Group of Experts on the Rental of Phonograms and Videograms (Paris, 26–30 Nov 1984): [1985] *Copyright* 16.

[13] Report of the Group of Experts on Unauthorized Private Copying of Recordings, Broadcasts and Printed Matter (Geneva, 4–8 June 1984): [1984] *Copyright* 280. See further Bogsch (1986) 331.

[14] In particular, the WIPO/UNESCO Group of Experts on the Copyright Aspects of Direct Broadcasting by Satellite: [1985] *Copyright* 180.

[15] Report of the Committee of Governmental Experts on Model Provisions for National Laws on Employed Authors (Geneva, 27–31 Jan 1981): [1982] *Copyright* 72; report of the WIPO/UNESCO Committee of Governmental Experts on Model Provisions for National Laws on Employed Authors (Geneva, 21–31 Jan 1986): [1986] *Copyright* 72.

[16] Report of the Working Group on Model Provisions for National Laws on Publishing Contracts for Literary Works (Geneva, 18–22 June 1984): [1984] *Copyright* 307; Working Group on Model Contracts Concerning Co-Publishing and Commissioned Works (Paris, 2–6 Apr 1984): [1984] *Copyright* 250; report of the WIPO/UNESCO Committee of Governmental Experts on Model Provisions for National Laws on Publishing Contracts for Literary Works (Paris, 2–6 Dec 1985): [1986] *Copyright* 40.

[17] See n 13 above.

[18] Report of the Committee of Non-Governmental Experts on the 'Domaine Public Payant' (Geneva, 26–9 Apr 1982): [1982] *Copyright* 179.

[19] Report of the WIPO/UNESCO Committee of Governmental Experts on the Drafting of Model Statutes for Institutions Administering Authors' Rights in Developing Countries (Geneva, 17–21 Oct 1983): [1983] *Copyright* 348.

[20] Report of the Working Group on Access by the Visually and Auditory Handicapped to Material Reproducing Works Protected by Copyright (Paris, 25–7 Oct 1982): [1982] *Copyright* 354.

[21] A Bogsch, 'The Berne Convention: Towards the Future', in Börsenverein des Deutschen Buchhandels and International Publishers Association, *International Copyright Symposium, Heidelberg, 24–25 April 1986* (1986), 49. Eight such categories were established for this purpose as follows: printed works, audiovisual works (see further the preparatory document and report of the WIPO/UNESCO Committee of Governmental Experts on Audiovisual Works and Phonograms (Paris, 2–6 June 1986): [1986] *Copyright* 218), phonograms, works of visual art, works of architecture, works of applied art, dramatic and choreographic works and musical works.

categories was subsequently focused on seven committees of governmental experts that met and reported during 1986 to 1988,[22] followed by a more general 'synthesizing' committee in 1988.[23] These committees formulated non-binding 'principles' to guide solutions at the national level, the most influential being in the areas of audiovisual works and phonograms and the printed word where issues concerning private copying, satellite and cable distribution, reprography, and electronic uses were exposed for consideration.[24] Further work during 1989 to 1991 was directed towards the production of a Model Law on Copyright which was 'supposed to include all the results of the "guided development period" '.[25] This document, produced by a further committee of experts, was never formally published, as by this time preparations for the Berne Protocol/WIPO Copyright Treaty (the 'WCT') had begun (see below) and it was not thought to be 'appropriate to publish [it] before the possible adoption of new binding norms'.[26]

The advisory and training activities of WIPO with respect to development co-operation in developing countries during this period were also extensive, leading to a large number of accessions to the Convention by such countries.[27] Much of this work 'in progress' still continues today, but, as will be seen below, it formed an important backdrop to the developments that occurred from 1991 with respect to the formulation of a separate new treaty, the WCT.

(3) Beginning the process of revision: 1991 and beyond

(a) Initial proposals for a 'Berne Protocol'

While the period of guided development was incremental and fragmented in character, these activities were important in setting the scene for the process that was initiated in 1991 by WIPO for the preparation of a 'possible protocol' to the Berne Convention. Also extremely influential here were events occurring outside the arenas of Berne and WIPO, in particular the inclusion of 'trade-related' intellectual property rights in the agenda for the Uruguay Round of the GATT that had begun in late 1986 (see paras 4.31ff below). Finally, it should be noted that, from 1989, Berne had a vigorous new member, the USA, which was **4.15**

[22] The preparatory papers and reports of these various committees of governmental experts are to be found in [1986] *Copyright* 208–9 (audiovisual works and phonograms), [1986] *Copyright* 403–11 (works of architecture), [1987] *Copyright* 70–82 (works of visual art), [1987] *Copyright* 185–215 (dramatic, choreographic, and musical works), [1987] *Copyright* 356–73 (works of applied art), [1988] *Copyright* 42–97 (printed word), [1988] *Copyright* 262–80 (photographic works).

[23] Committee of Governmental Experts on Evaluation and Synthesis of Principles and Various Categories of Works, Geneva, June–July 1988: [1988] *Copyright* 364–98, 445–76, and 506–27.

[24] See further the discussion of this work by Ficsor (2001), 10–11.

[25] ibid, 12. [26] ibid. [27] For a general survey, see Bogsch (1986) 333ff.

now taking a close and continuing interest in developments in this particular arena for the first time (see further paras 4.43ff below).

(b) A note about Additional Acts and/or special protocols and agreements

4.16 By way of introduction to what has subsequently occurred, it is worth noting other devices that have been used in the past to introduce changes to the Berne Convention, but in a more limited fashion than occurs through a full revision of the existing text: an Additional Act, special protocols and special agreements. As seen in Chapter 2 above, an Additional Act was adopted in 1896 and was proposed, though not adopted, in 1971.[28] The principal advantage of such an instrument is that it can provide for limited changes to the Convention that may then be accepted by all or part of the existing membership without disturbing the status and operation of the current Act. In other words, it is only a partial revision and can therefore provide a framework for limited changes to take account of more pressing matters (as in 1896). The problem with this approach, however, is that it creates yet another layer of conventional obligations where a number of member countries prefer to remain bound by the current Act only or by earlier Acts.

As for special protocols, the chief examples in the history of the Berne Convention are those of 1914 and 1967. Like an Additional Act, they may leave member states with the option of adherence, but are usually devoted to one particular matter and need not be directly incorporated into or appended to the Convention.

More generally, there is provision in article 20 of the Convention for parties to enter 'special agreements' between themselves, so far as such agreements 'grant to authors more extensive rights than those granted by the Convention, or contain other provisions not contrary to this Convention' (see further paras 6.132ff below). It is therefore possible to conceive of the development of a series of special agreements associated with the Convention that deal with particular matters of concern but are not otherwise embodied in, or incorporated into, it. In the first edition of this work, it was suggested that this might be an appropriate method for dealing with such issues as software or expressions of folklore, as well as the ownership and exploitation of rights, extensions of terms, and paying public domain. Until the adoption of the WCT, this procedure had not proved successful in the context of the Berne Union, with the failure of two attempts to develop treaties on software[29] and folklore.[30]

[28] *Records* 1971, 53 (Document B/DC/5).

[29] See n 9 above.

[30] See n 11 above.

(c) Beginning the process of revision

As might be expected, the first steps taken here were modest, compared with the preparations that had attended earlier revisions. According to one of the key participants, the 'vague idea' for a more systematic norm-setting exercise arose out of the deliberations of the meetings of the WIPO governing bodies, including the Berne Union Assembly held in September to October 1989.[31] One of the items in the 1990–1 programme for WIPO that was adopted at this session was a proposal for the International Bureau to convene meetings of a committee of government experts to draw up a protocol to the Convention that would be concerned with matters of clarification of the existing text or the establishment of new international norms where there were doubts under the present text of the Convention as to the extent to which it applied. The nature of the instrument to be drawn up was a little unclear at this stage, ie whether it would take the form of a protocol *strictu sensu* or that of a special agreement under article 20. The formal starting point was the convening of a 'committee of government experts' that met in late 1991. Although this is only the recent past, it is salutary to recall that there were still only ninety members of Berne at this time, although, as noted above, one important new member, the USA, was now present. A committee of governmental experts is, in one sense, an exploratory kind of process, as, at a meeting of this kind, representatives cannot bind their governments officially. On the other hand, contributions at this stage are of great importance in reflecting the present or probable views of their countries on particular issues. As with other WIPO meetings, observers from a large number of non-governmental organizations with interests in copyright issues also attended this first (and subsequent) meetings, including representatives of computer manufacturers, software producers, film producers, publishers, and the like. The representatives of these organizations were given the right to contribute to the discussions of the committee, and there was considerable lobbying that took place, both in the formal submissions made to these sessions and behind closed doors. **4.17**

Unlike previous Berne revisions, there was no 'host government' overseeing the proceedings, and it was the WIPO secretariat alone that prepared a programme of proposals for consideration by the committee. This drew heavily on the work that it had undertaken in the period of 'guided development' over the preceding decade or so. Although the proposals covered a wide range of topics, they were somewhat vaguely formulated as a 'possible protocol' to the Convention, rather than as a full revision of the principal text. The strategic and pragmatic considerations operating here are readily apparent, in that there is usually less

[31] Ficsor (2001), 18.

difficulty in getting states to agree to a protocol or separate special agreement, if it is not necessary for them then to become a party to it in order to retain their membership of the principal convention. On the other hand, there is the possibility that states that do not adhere to the new instrument may still obtain the benefits of any enhanced level of protection that is accorded by it in those states that do join it. This is because there is often a requirement in such agreements that parties should apply the provisions of the new instrument to non-signatory states that are still members of the parent convention, and there was, indeed, a provision to this effect in the original WIPO proposals. One may suppose that underlying this enforced benevolence was the view that the recipients of this higher level of protection would ultimately feel morally obliged to adhere to the protocol themselves.

4.18 The initial programme of proposals advanced by WIPO at the first meeting of the committee in November 1991 included proposals relating to both new and old subject matter (the protection of databases, artificial intelligence and computer-produced works, recognition of the status of computer programs as literary works, and separate protection for sound recordings) and new rights (including distribution, rental, and public display rights and clarification of the rights of reproduction and satellite broadcasting). There were also proposals for lengthening the term of copyright protection to the life of the author plus seventy years, abolition of the exception in favour of the mechanical recording licence, and for regulation of the collective administration of rights.[32] Nothing at this stage, however, was directed to the rapidly emerging phenomenon of the Internet and the specific challenges that this posed to the protection and exploitation of authors' rights. The discussion at this first meeting was inconclusive on many of the issues that had been raised by WIPO, with the 'most passionate debates'[33] centring on the question of whether sound recordings might properly be dealt with in any proposed protocol. Following a second meeting of the committee in February 1992, governments were asked to reflect on their views and to submit further proposals to WIPO for presentation at a third session of the committee to be held in November 1992. Very few national submissions were forthcoming and WIPO then proposed to defer further meetings of the committee indefinitely.[34] At this stage, it might have been thought that efforts at revision were premature, although it should be noted that, in the

[32] For the texts of these proposals and reports of the first two meetings in Nov 1991 and Feb 1992, see [1992] *Copyright* 30–49, 66–82, and 93–110. See further the descriptions of these sessions in Ficsor (2001), 19–22.

[33] Ficsor (2001), 21.

[34] [1992] *Copyright* 182–7. In his commentary, Dr Ficsor takes a rather more positive view of this request to member states for their views, remarking that this reflected a concern by the delegates to get more actively involved in the process and to take over the running from the International Bureau: Ficsor (2001), 22–3.

other negotiating arena of GATT, discussion of a new agreement dealing with trade-related intellectual property rights was in full swing (see further paras 4.31ff below). It is also possible, at this stage, that there was some uncertainty about the respective roles of WIPO and GATT (soon to become the WTO) with respect to 'norm creation' in the intellectual property field, and this matter was not to be clarified for a little while yet. From a longer-term perspective, it can be seen that the TRIPs Agreement negotiators' principal concerns with matters of enforcement and compliance did not really pre-empt the task of WIPO and the 'traditional' intellectual property conventions, such as Berne, from investigating and developing new substantive norms, but it was also true that, in the period from 1986 to 1993, the 'main game' was taking place in the TRIPs forum and that was where most of the time and energies of Berne members were focused. Nonetheless, it was significant that, in September 1992, a meeting of the Assembly of the Berne Union (the governing body of the Union) voted to continue the revision process, and, in fact, to bifurcate it with the creation of another committee of experts to prepare a possible new instrument on the protection of the rights of producers of phonograms, which were coupled to proposals on the rights of performers. Thereafter both committees met on five further occasions, holding their sessions one after the other (June to July 1993, December 1994, September 1995, February and May 1996). At its December 1992 meeting, the Assembly also decided to add two items to the agenda for the possible Berne Protocol—enforcement of rights and national treatment, the first of these reflecting the emphasis given to enforcement issues in the concurrent TRIPs Agreement negotiations.[35]

(d) The shift to the 'digital agenda'

Inevitably, things began to move more quickly after the completion of the GATT Uruguay Round and the adoption of the TRIPs Agreement. The most significant development to occur here was the move away from a 'possible protocol' to Berne that dealt with a number of disparate topics to proposals for a separate new instrument, albeit a 'special agreement' within the meaning of article 20 of Berne, that dealt specifically with issues arising from the challenges of the networked environment, or the 'digital agenda' as it was called. The reasons for this shift and its timing are not easy to pin down in precise terms, but it was a prescient response to developments that were occurring at the national and regional levels where policymakers and legislators were beginning to grapple with the challenges of the new phenomenon known as the Internet.[36] **4.19**

[35] 'Report of the Twenty-Third Series of Meetings of the Governing Bodies of WIPO' [1992] *Copyright* 236 and 237.

[36] See in particular the work of President Clinton's Information Infrastructure Task Force that produced both a Green and White Paper on intellectual property: *Green Paper—*

Digital technologies and networking now posed challenges to the proper protection and exploitation of works that had not been so apparent, even at the start of the Berne Protocol process. It is difficult now for us to appreciate how swift the advent of the Internet was in this area, given that it appears always to have been with us. But in 1994 and 1995, its dimensions and challenges were only beginning to be properly appreciated, and it was something of a shrewd strategic move for WIPO and its members to incorporate these matters into the protocol revision process. Indeed, the shift to the 'digital agenda' enlivened a process that, up to this stage, had been somewhat faltering and reactive (to the changes occurring in the TRIPs arena). It now became proactive, with a theme and coherence that had previously been missing. In this regard, WIPO appears to have played an important catalysing role, sponsoring a series of impressively titled 'worldwide' or 'global' symposia[37] dealing with digital issues, beginning with one in Harvard in 1993,[38] then in Paris in 1994,[39] Mexico City in May 1995,[40] and Naples in the same year.[41] The centrepiece of the proposals was now a new right of communication to the public which extended to the making available of works online. This was coupled with proposals for technological protection measures and the protection of rights management information, while other proposals were modified to take more specific account of digital and network issues. As part of this refinement of the programme, the original proposals relating to collective management and duration were quietly jettisoned (although a more limited proposal affecting the length of the term of protection for photographic works remained); it was also thought to be premature and/or unnecessary to deal with issues relating to artificial

Intellectual Property and the National Information Infrastructure: A Preliminary Draft of the Report of the Working Group on Intellectual Property Rights, July 1994, and *White Paper—Intellectual Property and the National Information Infrastructure: The Report of the Working Group on Intellectual Property Rights*, Sept 1995; in the EC, note the following reports: Commission of the European Community, *Green Paper—Copyright and Related Rights in the Information Society*, Document COM(95) 385, 19 July 1995; Commission of the European Community, *Communication from the Commission—Follow-up to the Green Paper—Copyright and Related Rights in the Information Society*, Document COM(96) 568, 20 Nov 1996; and, in Japan, see the Agency of Cultural Affairs, Japan, *A Report on Discussions by the Working Group of the Subcommittee on Multimedia Copyright, Copyright Council: Study of Institutional Issues regarding Multimedia*, Feb 1995.

[37] Descriptions of the symposia and the casts of players are provided by Ficsor (2001) at 29–32.

[38] *WIPO Worldwide Symposium on the Impact of Digital Technology on Copyright and Neighbouring Rights*, Harvard University, Mar–Apr 1993, WIPO publication No 723(E), 1993.

[39] *WIPO Worldwide Symposium on the Future of Copyright and Neighbouring Rights*, Louvre, Paris, June 1994, WIPO publication no 731(E), 1994.

[40] *WIPO Worldwide Symposium on Copyright in the Global Information Infrastructure*, Mexico City, May 1995, WIPO publication no 746(E/S), 1995.

[41] *WIPO World Forum on the Protection of Intellectual Creations in the Information Society*, Naples, Oct 1995, WIPO publication no 751(E), 1996.

intelligence and computer-generated works, and it was decided to deal with the subject of databases in a separate instrument. Within a relatively brief time, at least by international standards, two draft treaties were ready for consideration and adoption by a formal diplomatic conference—these were the WCT and the Performances and Phonograms Treaty ('WPPT'), to which was added a draft treaty on databases. At the meeting of the diplomatic conference in Geneva in December 1996, the first two of these, with necessary amendments and revisions, were adopted and laid open for signature. Both are now in force, with the WCT becoming so on 6 March 2002 and the WPPT on 20 May 2002. Consideration of the proposed databases treaty, however, was deferred for the time being and had not been proceeded with at the time of writing. For sake of completeness, it should also be noted that, in the post-1996 period, a further diplomatic conference was held in 2000 in relation to the protection of audio-visual performers, but failed to adopt a final text (see further paras 19.83ff below), while a proposal for the protection of the rights of broadcasting organizations was under consideration by WIPO at the time of writing (see further paras 19.87ff below). The WIPO agenda for formulation and extension of international copyright and related rights norms has continued apace in the post-1996 period, with the establishment of a Standing Committee on Copyright and Related Rights that replaces the former system of committees of experts and which meets on a regular basis.[42]

C. The WIPO Copyright Treaty

(1) The diplomatic conference

This was held in Geneva from 2 to 20 December 1996 and, as noted above, dealt with the two treaties that were finally adopted (the WCT and WPPT) in back-to-back sessions. From the perspective of the Berne Union, this was the largest diplomatic conference that had ever been held on copyright and related rights issues, with representatives from 127 countries attending.[43] These included delegates from a number of notable 'new' Berne members, including Russia, China, the Republic of Korea, Indonesia, and, of course, the United States of America, as well as a number of new states that had only come into **4.20**

[42] In Mar 1998, the system of committees of experts was replaced by standing committees, with the relevant one here being the Standing Committee on Copyright and Related Rights ('the SCCR'): WIPO Document A/32/INF/2, available at www.wipo.int/documents. See further the discussion of the role of this committee in Chapter 16 below.

[43] For full details, see WIPO, *Records of the Diplomatic Conference on Certain Copyright and Neighboring Rights Questions, Geneva 1996*, vol II (1999), 119ff. See also J Reinbothe and S von Lewinski, *The WIPO Treaties 1996* (2002), 8–14.

existence after the centenary of Berne in 1986, for instance, Slovenia, Belarus, Slovakia, and Georgia. There was also a sizeable delegation from a major regional grouping, the European Community, with observers from a further three states (Ethiopia, Iran, and Dominican Republic), and seven intergovernmental organizations. Some national delegations were very well supported, such as those of the USA with nearly thirty members and the EC with fifteen, but a number of others had more than ten members, including Indonesia, Thailand, and Japan. Observers from a large number of non-governmental organizations representing every sector of copyright owners and users were also present, as well as representatives of several independent research institutions, such as the Max-Planck Institute in Munich. By comparison with the intimate nature of the early Berne conferences, this was a huge gathering, attended with all the colour and movement of any modern international meeting, with hurried corridor conferences, hectic lobbying, and frantic mobile telephone and e-mail communications between delegates, interest groups, and home bases. For WIPO as an organization, it could also be seen as a considerable achievement, following the apparent relegation of that organization to the background during the TRIPs Agreement negotiations. Two completed agreements within the space of three weeks is something of a record for any international gathering, particularly in view of the large number of states involved. The provisions of the WCT are analysed in detail, and in their relationship to the Berne Convention, at the relevant points of this commentary. For present purposes, the following summary will simply indicate the overall structure and principal features of the new treaty.

(a) Relationship to Berne

4.21 While not an Additional Act, protocol or appendix to Berne, the WCT is nonetheless a 'special agreement' within the meaning of article 20 of Berne: WCT, article 1(1). It is further provided that nothing in the WCT is to derogate from obligations that member countries might have between themselves as Berne members: article 1(2). Finally, although Berne membership is not a requirement for membership of the WCT, compliance with articles 1 to 21 and the Appendix of Berne is expressly required: article 1(4). In particular, protection is required of the categories of works protected under article 2 and 2*bis* of Berne (see further Chapter 8 below), while the points of attachment required for protection under articles 3 to 6 of Berne (see further Chapter 6 below) are to be applied *mutatis mutandis* to protection under the WCT: article 3.

(b) Points of clarification

4.22 A number of articles of the WCT 'clarify' matters previously thought to have been unsettled or unclear under Berne. Thus, article 2 embodies the well-known principle that '[C]opyright protection extends to expressions and not to ideas, procedures, methods of operation or mathematical concepts as such.' The status of computer programs as literary works within the meaning of article 2 of Berne 'whatever may be the mode or form of their expression' is also declared: WCT, article 4. In addition, the status of compilations of data as literary works under Berne is clarified under article 5 of the WCT so as to apply to '[C]ompilations of data or other material, in any form, which by reason of the selection or arrangement of their contents constitute intellectual creations.'

(c) 'Agreed statements'

Clarification, both of existing Berne provisions and of new provisions embodied **4.23** in the WCT itself, is also provided in the form of a series of 'agreed statements' adopted by the 1996 Diplomatic Conference at the time of adoption of the final text of the WCT. The legal status and effect of these 'agreed statements' is dealt with at length in the next chapter (in particular at para 5.19), as well as at the appropriate points in the following commentary. For present purposes, however, it suffices to state that their purpose is to provide guidance in the interpretation of particular treaty provisions, both past (in the case of Berne) and future (in the case of the WCT). Significant, so far as Berne is concerned, are the following agreed statements:

- on the scope of the reproduction right and exceptions to article 9 of Berne (agreed statement to WCT, article 1(4));
- the scope of protection for computer programs under article 2 of Berne, and the TRIPs Agreement (agreed statement to WCT, article 4);
- on compilations of data under article 2 of Berne and the TRIPs Agreement (agreed statement to WCT, article 5);
- the scope of permissible limitations and exceptions in the digital environment (agreed statement to WCT, article 10).

Other agreed statements relate more specifically to the new provisions of the WCT, but are also concerned to maintain compliance with relevant provisions of Berne:

- the rights of distribution and rental under articles 6 and 7 of the WCT (agreed statements to articles 6 and 7 as well as to article 7 on its own);
- the provision of physical facilities for the making of communications (agreed statement to article 8 of the WCT);
- obligations with respect to 'copyright management information' (agreed statement to article 12 of the WCT).

(d) New exclusive rights in relation to physical copies

4.24 Articles 6 and 7 of the WCT contain new exclusive rights with respect to the subsequent exploitation of physical or tangible copies of protected works: the distribution of copies of literary and artistic works generally, at least up to and including first sale (WCT, article 6), and the rental of computer programs, cinematographic works, and works embodied in phonograms (WCT, article 7). These requirements are amplified in accompanying agreed statements.

(e) Right of communication to the public

4.25 The centrepiece of the WCT, so far as the advent of the networked environment is concerned, is to be found in article 8 which confers on authors the exclusive right of authorizing the 'communication of their works to the public by wire or wireless means, including the making available to the public of their works in such a way that members of the public may access these works from a place and at a time individually chosen by them'. This covers both 'push' and 'pull' communications technologies, and fills in gaps in the exclusive right of broadcasting and other transmissions under article 11*bis* of Berne, as well as expanding the scope of those rights. (These matters are analysed at length in Chapter 12 below, notably paras 12.55ff.)

(f) Exceptions and limitations

4.26 These are dealt with in article 10, which adapts the three-step test contained in article 9(2) of Berne and applies it to the new rights contained in the WCT, as well as more generally to uses in the digital environment. As noted above, there is an important agreed statement attaching to this article. (These matters are dealt with in detail in Chapter 13 below at paras 13.03ff.)

(g) Collateral protections

4.27 Articles 11 and 12 contain provisions that, for the first time, provide protection for copyright owners outside the usual framework of a law of authors' rights with its traditional classifications of conditions for protection, protected subject matter, exclusive rights, and allowable limitations and exceptions. Both articles are responses to the perceived threats to works that arise in the digital context where technology can be readily and effortlessly used to undermine or bypass authors' exclusive rights. Thus, article 11 states that member states are to provide 'adequate legal protection and effective legal remedies against the circumvention of effective technological measures that are used by authors in connection with the exercise of their rights under this Treaty or the Berne Convention and that restrict acts, in respect of their works, which are not authorized by the authors concerned or permitted by law'. There is a similar, although rather more detailed, provision in article 12 with respect to protection against the removal of 'right management information'. (Both these articles are analysed at length in Chapter 15 below, and, as noted above, there is an agreed statement with respect to article 12.)

(h) Other matters

Although the original WIPO programme proposal for a general extension of protection to life-plus-seventy years was not proceeded with, article 9 of the WCT has an important provision with respect to the term for photographic works, assimilating these to other works (see further para 9.64 below). On the matter of the application of the WCT 'in time', that is, the extent to which its provisions are to be retrospectively applied, article 13 of the WCT applies the rules contained in article 18 of Berne (and see further paras 6.112ff below). Finally, in the area of enforcement, there is a general obligation in article 14 of the WCT that 'Contracting Parties shall ensure that enforcement procedures are available under their law so as to permit effective action against any act of infringement of rights covered by this Treaty, including expeditious remedies to prevent infringements and remedies which constitute a deterrent to further infringements.' **4.28**

In other matters of a procedural character, the WCT follows closely the model provided by the Berne Convention, with the establishment of an Assembly of Contracting Parties (article 15) and the delegation of administrative tasks associated with the treaty to WIPO (article 16). Membership of the WCT is open to any WIPO member (article 17(1)), but is also extended to any 'intergovernmental organization . . . which declares that it is competent in respect of, and has its own legislation binding on all its Member States on, matters covered by this Treaty and that it has been duly authorized, in accordance with its internal procedures, to become party to this Treaty' (article 17(2)). The latter provision is expressly extended to the European Community, 'having made the declaration' referred to there (article 17(3)). At the time of writing, the European Community had not availed itself of this facility, although its 2001 Directive on the Information Society covers almost all of the matters dealt with in the WCT. **4.29**

D. The WIPO Performances and Phonograms Treaty, Geneva 1996

As noted above, this instrument grew out of the work of the initial committee of experts on a possible protocol to the Berne Convention (see above), where there had originally been a proposal to deal with phonograms within the context of the proposed Berne Protocol. This proposal was rejected, consistently with the historic attitude of Berne members to the inclusion of such subject matter within the scope of a convention concerned with authors' rights (see further **4.30** para 8.112 below). Nonetheless, phonograms, together with performers' protection, were now given to a second committee of experts, which, in tandem with the first committee developed a draft text for a separate agreement that would supplement and amplify the protection already given to these subject matters under the Rome Convention for the Protection of Performers, Producers of Phonograms and Broadcasting Organizations. (The background and history of the Rome Convention and its relation to Berne are set out in more detail at paras 19.05ff below.) The provisions of the WPPT are also considered in that chapter, so for present purposes it suffices to note that these go considerably further than those contained in the Rome Convention, and 'track' the provisions of the WCT so far as the 'digital agenda' is concerned, that is, with respect to the recognition of an exclusive right of communication to the public, protection against technological circumvention, and the removal of rights management information. A notable aspect of the provisions with respect to performers is the requirement to protect their moral rights (see further paras 19.52ff below). On the other hand, audiovisual performances are excluded from the scope of the WPPT, and there have been faltering and, as yet unsuccessful, attempts within the WIPO framework to formulate a further treaty on this question (see further paras 19.82ff below).

E. Uruguay Round of the GATT and the Influence of Trade Concerns

(1) In general

4.31 As we have already noted, the pressure for a revision of the Berne Convention in the late 1980s not only came from the activities and efforts of WIPO. There were several other very significant external factors that were relevant here. The first and most notable of these was the Uruguay Round of GATT trade negotiations that began in 1986 and concluded in 1994 with the constitution of the World Trade Organization (WTO) with the TRIPs Agreement as one of its annexed agreements. The latter seeks to eliminate the barriers to trade that may be caused by insufficient protection of intellectual property rights in different countries. So far as copyright materials are concerned, the standards of protection contained in the TRIPs Agreement are based on those contained in the Berne Convention, but, to a limited extent, they also build upon and clarify those standards. A curious situation has thus arisen where the impetus for countries to adhere to Berne standards of protection has not emanated so much from WIPO, as from a different international forum that is concerned with trade, namely the WTO, the international organization that now has responsibility for the agreements that were negotiated in the Uruguay Round. Countries that wish to join the WTO must accept the requirements of the TRIPs Agreement, along with all the other trade agreements that are administered by that body.

(2) The background to the TRIPs Agreement

It is unnecessary, for the purposes of the present work to trace in detail the developments that led to the negotiation and adoption of the TRIPs Agreement: this material has been well traversed by a number of other commentators.[44] However, a brief description of the pre-Uruguay Round position and the steps leading up to the adoption of the TRIPs Agreement is useful in setting the background for a proper understanding. **4.32**

(a) The pre-Uruguay Round position

The idea of an international trade organization was originally envisaged as a complement to the International Monetary Fund that was established at Bretton Woods in July 1944.[45] After some negotiations, a charter for an International Trade Organization (the 'Havana Charter') was adopted by the United Nations Conference on Trade and Employment in March 1948, but this never came into **4.33**

[44] The principal of these is D Gervais, *The TRIPS Agreement: Drafting History and Analysis*, 2nd edn (2004) ('Gervais (2003)'). See also F Beier and G Schricker (eds), *GATT or WIPO? New Ways in the International Protection of Intellectual Property* (1989) (in particular the papers by Katzenberger, von Lewinski, Dreier, Kretschmer, and Ullrich); M Blakeney, *Trade Related Aspects of Intellectual Property Rights* (1996); C M Correa and A A Ysef (eds), *Intellectual Property and Trade: The TRIPS Agreement* (1998); T R Stewart (ed), *The GATT Uruguay Round: A Negotiating History (1986–1992)* (1993). For further readings on the background and development of the TRIPS Agreement, see C J Arup, 'The Prospective GATT Agreement for Intellectual Property Protection' (1993) 4 *Australian Intellectual Property Journal* 181; P Drahos, 'Global Property Rights in Information: The Story of Trips and GATT' (1995) 13 *Prometheus* 6–19; E Simon, 'US Trade Policy and Intellectual Property Rights' (1986) 50 *Albany Law Review* 501; P E Geller, 'Intellectual Property in the Global Marketplace: Impact of TRIPS Dispute Settlements?' (1995) 29 *The International Lawyer* 99; S Ricketson, 'The Future of the Traditional Intellectual Property Conventions in the Brave New World of Trade-Related Intellectual Property Rights' (1995) 25 *IIC* 872; K J Burchfiel, 'The Effect of United States Trade Legislation on Intellectual Property Rights' (1988) 19 *IIC* 295; J H Reichman, 'The TRIPS Component of the GATT's Uruguay Round: Competitive Prospects for Intellectual Property Owners in an Integrated World Market' (1993) IV *Fordham Intellectual Property, Media & Entertainment Law Journal* 171; J H Reichman, 'Intellectual Property in International Trade: Opportunities and Risks of a GATT Connection' (1989) 22 *Vanderbilt Journal of Transnational Law* 747; U Uchtenhagen, 'The GATT Negotiations Concerning Copyright and Intellectual Property Protection' (1990) 21 *IIC* 765; E M Seltzer, 'The Future of Section 337 of the Tariff Act of 1930: The Response of the United States Trade Representative to the GATT Panel Report' (1992) *IIC* 352; E Vermulst and B Drierssen, 'An Overview of the WTO Dispute Settlement System and its Relationship with the Uruguay Round Agreement: Nice on Paper but Too Much Stress for the System?' (1995) 29 *Journal of World Trade* 131. Useful documents and comments are also to be found in G Dinwoodie, W Hennessey, and S Perlmutter, *International Intellectual Property Law and Policy* (2001).

[45] Gervais (2003), 3.

existence, in part, it appears, because of US reluctance. From 1948 until the establishment of the WTO on 1 January 1995, the GATT, which had been signed in Geneva in October 1947, was administered on an ad hoc and provisional basis by its own secretariat.[46] The GATT itself was subject to a number of revision rounds (twelve in all) over the succeeding years, dealing principally with trade and tariffs on goods. A number of intellectual property matters, however, were dealt with in the GATT, including limited obligations with respect to marks of origin and geographical indications (article IX) and the protection of patents, trade marks, copyrights, and prevention of deceptive practices (article XX(d)).[47] By the end of the Tokyo Round (1979), concerns about trade in counterfeit goods had begun to be expressed and were highlighted in the report of a group of experts to the GATT Council in 1985.[48] At this stage, there was uncertainty as to whether it was preferable to deal with such matters in the context of GATT or whether they more properly belonged in the forum of WIPO.

These uncertainties had disappeared by the time the next (Uruguay) Round began in 1986, and it seems that US and Japanese pressure was important here in bringing all intellectual property rights, not just trade marks, into consideration. The starting point was the Ministerial Declaration adopted at a conference in Punta del Este (Uruguay) on 20 September 1986 which listed the following matters for inclusion in the round that was about to commence. Insofar as intellectual property rights were concerned, pages 7 to 8 of the Declaration stated:

> In order to reduce the distortions and impediments to international trade, and taking into account the need to promote effective and adequate protection of intellectual property rights, and to ensure that measures and procedures to enforce intellectual property rights do not themselves become barriers to legitimate trade, the negotiations shall aim to clarify GATT provisions and elaborate as appropriate new rules and disciplines.
>
> Negotiations shall aim to develop a multilateral framework of principles, rules and disciplines dealing with international trade in counterfeit goods, taking into account work already undertaken in GATT.
>
> These negotiations shall be without prejudice to other complementary initiatives that may be taken in the World Intellectual Property Organization and elsewhere to deal with these matters.

As Gervais remarks,[49] when this text is compared with the final TRIPs Agreement, there is a considerable gap between the careful language of the Declaration which harks back to pre-existing GATT provisions and the breadth of the

[46] Gervais (2003), 6–8. [47] ibid, 7–8.
[48] The principal points of the report of the group of experts are extracted at ibid, 8.
[49] ibid, 11.

final Agreement that was reached eight years later. The scope of the TRIPs negotiations were steadily expanded to take account of issues of enforcement and dispute settlement as well substantive norms of protection.[50] The various stages of these negotiations are well described in other commentaries, such as those of Gervais, and it is important to note the roles of such countries as the USA and Japan, and the European Community, in bringing certain provisions into the negotiating text, in particular those dealing with enforcement and dispute resolution through the GATT/proposed WTO dispute-resolution machinery. The years 1987 to 1990 witnessed great and continuing negotiating activity, with a rapid move towards the formulation of draft texts. Unlike the traditional WIPO meetings, the negotiations on TRIPs were informal and fast moving. It should also be remembered that they were only part of wider parallel negotiations that were occurring on more intractable issues, such as trade in agriculture, services, and goods. For the purposes of the comparative analysis and treaty interpretation that is contained in the following chapters, it is worth highlighting the following important draft texts that preceded the adoption of the Final Act in Marrakesh on 15 April 1994:

1. The 'Brussels draft': this was presented to the meeting of Ministers in Brussels in December 1990 and represented a nearly complete draft agreement that would have been capable of adoption had other parts of the Uruguay Round negotiations been at the same point. While there were options for various provisions, these were clearly articulated for the negotiating parties, but final agreement was not reached at this stage because of stalemate in the negotiations on trade in agriculture. However, the Brussels draft was very close to the final Act adopted at Marrakesh, with many of the outstanding issues being drafting matters only and generally capable of resolution.[51]
2. The 'Dunkel draft' of December 1991, which now left out options and was also very close in its terms to the final Act. With some exceptions, this represented the culmination of the efforts of the TRIPs negotiators and was now left aside until agreement in other areas, such as agriculture, could be reached. Further changes were negotiated during 1992 and 1993, but essentially this was the text that was finally adopted at Marrakesh in April 1994.[52]

[50] This expansion is well reflected in the brief Ministerial Statement at a mid-term meeting in Montreal, Canada, in Dec 1988 and in Geneva in April of the following year. For the text, see Document MTN/TNC/11 (21 Apr 1989), set out in Gervais (2003), 14.

[51] ibid, 22–3.

[52] See generally ibid, 24–6.

(b) *The principal features of the TRIPs Agreement*

4.34 The TRIPs Agreement works in a simple and efficient way as follows:

1. The protection of intellectual property rights (including copyright and neighbouring rights) is linked to trade through the provision in article 64 that member states may invoke the dispute-settlement procedures of the WTO in the event that another member fails to comply with TRIPs standards in its protection of intellectual property rights belonging to nationals of the complainant country (in the final analysis, this may allow for the imposition of trade sanctions against the offending country, thus providing a real mechanism for achieving compliance that was not provided under the traditional conventions such as Berne).
2. In the case of copyright, the substantive standards of Berne (articles 1–21 and the Appendix) are incorporated directly into the TRIPs Agreement, with some additional obligations and/or clarifications of existing Berne requirements. The fundamental obligation here is contained in article 9(1), which has the effect of requiring countries, whether Berne members or not, to adopt Berne standards if they wish to adhere to the WTO and its agreements.
3. The inclusion in the TRIPs Agreement of specific standards relating to the enforcement of intellectual property rights, noting here that such obligations were, by and large, absent from earlier conventions such as Berne, although they are now part of the WCT and WPPT.

(c) *The requirements of national treatment and most favoured nation treatment*

4.35 As a starting point, the TRIPs Agreement adopts the principle of national treatment, requiring member states to accord to the nationals of other member states no less favourable treatment with respect to the 'protection of intellectual property' than that accorded to their own nationals: article 3(1). In this regard, the term 'protection' receives a wide interpretation as including matters affecting the 'availability, acquisition, scope, maintenance and enforcement of intellectual property rights as well as those matters affecting the use of intellectual property rights specifically addressed in this Agreement'.[53] In the case of copyright, performers and phonogram producers, exceptions allowable within the scope of the Berne Convention are permitted, and exceptions in relation to judicial and administrative procedures are also allowed, so long as these are not inconsistent with the Agreement and are not applied in such a manner to constitute a disguised restriction on trade.

A further obligation in article 4, not present in the Berne Convention but

[53] Note to arts 3 and 4.

common in trade agreements, concerns 'most favoured nation treatment'. This requires that, with regard to the protection of intellectual property, 'any favour, privilege or immunity granted by a Member to the nationals of any other country should be accorded immediately and unconditionally to the nationals of all Members'. This flow-on requirement is intended to prevent special deals being done with other countries (whether members or not) without sharing the benefits with all other members. There are some exceptions to this requirement, the most relevant in relation to copyright and neighbouring rights being with respect to those obligations under the Berne or Rome Conventions that are subject to reciprocity rather than national treatment: article 4(b).

(d) Specific obligations as to substantive norms of protection

While the TRIPs Agreement deals with all intellectual property rights, those concerned specifically with copyright and neighbouring rights are contained in section 1 of Part II ('Standards concerning the availability, scope and use of intellectual property rights'). The most significant additional ('Berne-plus') obligations in this section relate to the protection of computer programs as literary works under Berne (art 10(1)) and compilations of data (art 10(2)), commercial rental rights for computer programs and cinematographic films (subject to certain limitations) (art 11) and enhanced levels of protection and terms of protection for performers, sound recordings (phonograms) and broadcasting organizations (art 14). (The latter, in fact, build upon the framework of obligations contained in the Rome Convention for the Protection of Performers, Producers of Phonograms and Broadcasting Organizations.) Significantly, at the insistence of the USA, the general obligation under article 9(1) for WTO members to comply with articles 1 to 21 of, and the Appendix to, Berne does not include the obligation to protect moral rights under article 6bis of that convention. **4.36**

(e) Obligations with respect to enforcement

Part III of the TRIPs Agreement contains a series of detailed obligations with respect to the enforcement of intellectual property rights. The overall requirement here is that enforcement procedures shall be available so as to permit 'effective action against any act of infringement of intellectual property rights protected by this Agreement' (article 41(1)). There are also obligations to ensure that procedures are 'fair and equitable' and not subject to unreasonable delay (article 41(2)), with decisions made on the merits of a case to be in writing and with reasons (article 41(3)). More specific obligations deal with matters of procedure (article 42), evidence (article 43), remedies to be available, including 'provisional' or interim measures (articles 44–50), border measures (articles 51–60) and criminal procedures (article 61). As noted above, these provisions set the TRIPs Agreement aside from its predecessors such as Berne, which dealt only incidentally with matters of enforcement. **4.37**

(f) Dispute settlement

4.38 The real steel in the spine of the TRIPs Agreement is provided by the dispute-prevention and dispute-settlement provisions in articles 63 and 64. The first of these seeks to ensure 'transparency' of members' laws, regulations, final judicial decisions, and administrative rulings on the protection of intellectual property rights, so that each member can be made aware of laws, decisions, etc that may affect its rights under the Agreement. The second provides that the provisions of articles XXII and XXIII of GATT 1994 as elaborated and applied by the Dispute Settlement Understanding are to apply to consultations and the settlement of disputes arising under the Agreement. The requirement for each member to 'accord sympathetic consideration to, and . . . afford adequate opportunity for consultation regarding, such representations as may be made by another contracting party with respect to any matter affecting the operation of this Agreement' arises under article XXII.1. If consultations do not achieve a resolution, then article XXIII provides for a more formal process of consultation and investigation, with the ultimate application of sanctions against the offending party. In formal terms, these steps can be taken where a party considers that any benefit accruing directly or indirectly under the Agreement is being 'nullified or impaired or that the attainment of any objective of the Agreement is being impeded' by the failure of another contracting party to carry out its obligations under the Agreement, or by the application of any measure by that party that has that effect or by the 'existence of any other situation': article XXIII.1. The detailed procedures under which these matters may be pursued is set out in the Understanding and includes a requirement for the making of representations to, and 'sympathetic consideration' thereof by, the party against whom the complaint is made (article 4); establishment of a Dispute Settlement Body to administer the whole process (article 2); the appointment of panels to hear complaints (articles 6–16); and appellate review by a standing Appellate Body (articles 17–18).[54] Where a panel or the Appellate Body concludes a measure of a member is 'inconsistent with a covered agreement', ie TRIPs, it is to recommend that the member bring the measure into conformity with that agreement, and may suggest ways in which the member concerned can implement the recommendations (article 19). There are time limits and procedures for monitoring implementation of recommendations and rulings (articles 20 and 21), while there are provisions for compensation and the suspension of concessions or other obligations under the agreement in question in the event

[54] An elegant flow diagram setting out the various steps appears in Gervais (2003), 342 and more detailed information as to the operation of the DSB and the steps in the process is to be found on the WTO website: www.wto.org. See also the useful overview by D Palmeter, 'National Sovereignty and the World Trade Organization' (1999) 2 *Journal of World Intellectual Property* 77, 78–81.

that implementation has not occurred within 'a reasonable period of time' (article 22(1)). These are 'temporary measures', the assumption being that members will move to implement recommendations and rulings of a panel or the Appellate Body. However, sanctions in the form of suspension of concessions or other obligations under the Agreement can be applied in a graduated way in the event of non-compliance, and may be applied in 'other sectors' than that covered by the agreement in question (article 22(3)). In other words, it may be possible for concessions to be suspended with respect to a particular member under a different agreement than the actual agreement which that member has been found to contravene, for example, a suspension of a concession with respect to agricultural products might be allowable in case where the member has acted to nullify or impair an obligation under the TRIPs Agreement. There is a subtle calibration of suspensions that is provided for here, subject to the requirements that the level of suspension of concessions or other obligations should be equivalent to the level of nullification or impairment and should not be prohibited by the agreement in question (article 22(4) and (5)).

(g) Institutions and ongoing review

As in the case of services and goods, article IV of the Marrakesh Agreement **4.39** establishing the WTO also establishes a Council for Trade-Related Aspects of Intellectual Property Rights (the 'Council for TRIPs'). This is required to 'oversee the functioning of the Agreement on Trade-Related Aspects of Intellectual Property Rights', and, more specifically under article 68 of the TRIPs Agreement itself is mandated to 'monitor the operation of this Agreement and, in particular, Members' compliance with their obligations hereunder and . . . [to] afford Members the opportunity of consulting on matters relating to trade-related aspects of intellectual property rights'. It has broad powers to carry out these functions and, in particular, to provide assistance with respect to dispute-resolution procedures. An early item on the agenda of the Council was to reach appropriate arrangements for co-operation with WIPO and its bodies (see further para 4.40 below). Another task that the Council and its secretariat have done is to review national laws to identify possible inconsistencies with the TRIPs Agreement. This process was conducted during 1996 and 1997 with respect to the laws of developed countries, and a second stage of reviewing the legislation of developing countries commenced in 2000 (under articles 65 and 66, these countries have longer transitional periods in which to achieve compliance).[55]

---

[55] Gervais (2003), 348–9. See further M Greuze, 'The TRIPS Council and Implementation of the TRIPS Agreement', in H C Jehoram, P Keuchenius, and L M Brownlee (eds), *Trade Related Aspects of Copyright* (1996), 72ff; A Otten, 'Implementation of the TRIPS Agreement and Prospects for its Further Development' (1998) 1 *Journal of International Economic Law* 523.

As with Berne, review and amendment procedures are built into the TRIPs Agreement: despite the far-ranging scope of the Agreement, it is far from comprehensive, and it was recognized that updating and modification would be required, even within the fairly near future. The starting point for the first review to occur was therefore after the completion of the transitional period required for members (other than least-developed countries) to bring their domestic laws into TRIPs compliance: see generally article 71(1). In practical terms, this meant some time after 1 January 2000, and it might have been reasonable to expect that, in the area of copyright and neighbouring rights, this would include modifications to take account of the new norms now embodied in the WCT and WPPT.[56] In fact, the agenda for review appears to have been more focused on implementation issues, with attention also being given to geographical indications, patentable subject matter and the protection of traditional knowledge.[57] Copyright issues appear to have been left aside while these other more controversial topics are pursued.

(h) Relationship with WIPO

4.40 As noted above, there were some early uncertainties about the role of WIPO and the traditional intellectual property conventions in the brave new world of trade-related intellectual property rights. Undoubtedly, there were concerns on the part of WIPO about 'turf' and the possible usurpation of its norm-making role by the brash newcomer (the WTO). On the other hand, as one of the leading TRIPs Agreement negotiators readily concedes, the expertise of WIPO and its officials was needed in the early days of the TRIPs negotiations and it appears that considerable assistance was given to bring the TRIPs negotiations 'up to speed'.[58] The relations between the two international organizations are now embodied in a formal 'agreement of co-operation' dated 22 December 1995,[59] which deals with matters of co-operation at the institutional level (exchange of information, particularly concerning laws and regulations, technical and legal assistance), and can be seen as implicitly recognizing the different

[56] Gervais (2003), 370.

[57] Ministerial Declaration adopted at Doha, Nov 2001, clauses 17–19 (relating to trade-related aspects of intellectual property rights).

[58] See the comments by Lars Anell, chairman of the Negotiating Group on Trade-Related Aspects of Intellectual Property Rights, including Trade in Counterfeit Goods, in the Foreword to the first edition of Gervais (2003), reproduced in ibid, ix. An early example of WIPO assistance to TRIPs negotiators is to be found in a 'communication' from WIPO dated 28 Feb 1990 and corrected 6 Mar 1990, MTN.GNG/NG11/W66 and MTN.GNG/NG11/W66/Corr.1 on the matter of who are beneficiaries of national treatment under WIPO treaties, including Berne, and the exceptions to national treatment allowed by these treaties, also contained in Gervais (2003), Annex 7. In the case of Berne, there is a useful list of exceptions to national treatment where material reciprocity can be required as between members.

[59] For the text of this, see Gervais (2003), 467.

roles played by the two organizations: WIPO as the source of technical expertise and deliberation, with WTO as the forum in which issues of enforcement and compliance can be explored. The TRIPs Agreement itself is open to revision, but, as noted above, to date there have been no substantive changes to its text on the question of copyright and neighbouring rights. However, its dispute-resolution machinery has already been invoked in one instance relating to exceptions concerning the public performance of musical works under US law.[60] More generally, there is a considerable body of decisional law, mostly in the non-intellectual property area, that has already arisen under the WTO dispute-settlement procedures. This has not occurred in a vacuum, as it appears that panels and the Appellate Body will interpret the WTO Agreement and its associated agreements, including the TRIPs Agreement, in accordance with the rules of interpretation found in the Vienna Convention on the Law of Treaties as well as in accordance with the general principles of public international law.[61] On the other hand, it is also possible that the jurisprudence of the WTO panels and the Appellate Body may assume a somewhat incoherent shape over time as it does not appear that panels regard themselves bound by earlier panel or Appellate Body decisions, although clearly such decisions will be influential.[62] As will be seen in Chapter 5 below, TRIPs enforcement proceedings may well, in the future, provide the forums in which issues of interpretation of the Berne Convention, as incorporated in TRIPs, will come up for consideration.

F. Unilateral Trade Measures, Regionalism, and the Return to Bilateralism

While the TRIPs Agreement is an enormously important development in the framework for the international protection of intellectual property rights gener- **4.41**

[60] United States—Section 110(5) of US Copyright Act, Report of the Panel, 15 June 2000, document WT/DS58/AB/R.

[61] See the decision of the Appellate Body in *India-Patent Protection for Pharmaceutical and Agricultural Chemical Products*, document WT/DS50/AB/R (WTO App Body, 19 Dec 1997). It does not appear that WTO panels regard themselves as bound.

[62] This was the view taken by the panel in *EU* v *India*, Panel Report, WT/DS79/R (24 Aug 1998) and some support for this approach might be derived from article 3(2) of the Dispute Settlement Understanding which states: 'Recommendations and rulings of the DSB cannot add to or diminish the rights and obligations provided in the covered agreements'. On the other hand, see Adrian T Chua, 'Precedent and Principles of WTO Panel Jurisprudence' (1998) 2 *Berkeley Journal of International Law* 171 and the author's argument therein that a system of binding precedent would be beneficial in developing state practice in this context. See also the perceptive suggestion in, Dinwoodie, Hennessey, and Perlmutter (n 44 above), 857, that panel and Appellate Body decisions could be argued to be part of 'subsequent practice in the application of the treaty' under article 31(3)(b) of the Vienna Convention and thus part of the 'customary rules of interpretation of public international law' consistently with article 3(2) of the DSU.

ally and copyright in particular, it should also be noted that there were other sources of pressure for enhanced protection of copyright and neighbouring rights that operated in the period under consideration. One of these was the European Union, which began, in the early 1980s, to look at ways to harmonize intellectual and industrial property laws among its member states where these have an effect on the free flow of goods and services between them. In the area of copyright, this has led to the preparation of Directives on such matters as software, topographies of semiconductor chips, databases, rental rights, and the term of protection. These initiatives by the European Union to bring about harmonization of copyright laws have inevitably added to the pressure for change at the broader international level, particularly in the Berne Convention. If new norms of protection, higher than those currently contained in Berne, are set within the EU, this obviously provides an incentive to other Berne states to increase their own levels of protection.

4.42 A further driving force over the past two decades has been the USA, which has engaged in a continuing and vigorous, if not aggressive, campaign to achieve full and effective protection of its intellectual property rights in other countries. This was clearly evident in the GATT and TRIPs negotiations. However, even before the launch of the Uruguay Round the USA had begun to pursue its objectives on a unilateral basis, using the powers of the US Trade Representative under 'Special 301' (of the US Omnibus Trade and Competitiveness Act 1988) to bring pressure to bear upon states that were perceived to be reluctant to rectify or change their domestic intellectual property laws. Countries such as Brazil, Korea, and Singapore have felt the full impact of this pressure, but even countries such as Australia, Germany, and Italy were regarded with some suspicion by US trade officials in areas such as sound recordings, computer programs, and films. At the risk of vast overgeneralization, these activities by the US Government may be seen as part of a concerted effort to shore up US trade interests at a time (the early 1980s) when the US economy was in considerable difficulties, and there appeared to be great threats to these iconic American industries at the hands of unscrupulous persons in other countries, particularly in the developing world. There can be no doubt, however, that pressure from the US played a very considerable part in changing the domestic copyright laws of a number of states, as well as in providing strong momentum for the TRIPs negotiations and the subsequent adoption of the two WIPO treaties in December 1996. By way of conclusion of this chapter, it is therefore worth exploring the role of the USA, both historically and in the future, with respect to the development of the international copyright framework.

(1) The case of the United States of America

Ironies abound in this area, not the least being that, at the very time that US officials were becoming concerned at the threat to US intellectual property rights abroad and the failure of these countries to observe their obligations under the traditional intellectual property conventions such as Berne, the USA itself was not actually a Berne member. It is easy for a cynical European, or even Australian, eye to view this as providing evidence of inconsistency, even hypocrisy, or, at the very least, as reflecting a latter-day conversion to principles and standards that had long been recognized and applied by the more 'advanced' countries of Berne. The historical record, however, is rather more complicated, and is worth considering, before attempting an overview of what the future might hold. As will be seen, one of the principal reasons for the long detachment of the USA from the international copyright system represented by the Berne Convention is to be found in the different copyright tradition in the USA, in particular its commitment to registration systems. **4.43**

(a) The history of US relations with the Berne Union

It has already been seen in Chapters 1 and 2 that US interest in the Berne Convention goes back to its very inception. Indeed, it was the announcement by the US Government that it would attend the 1885 Conference that provided the necessary stimulus for the UK Government to be represented as well.[63] Nonetheless, there was still, at this time, a strong domestic US reluctance to engage in international copyright relations.[64] The US representative, Boyd Winchester, therefore attended both the 1885 and 1886 Conferences only in an observer capacity and was restricted to expressing the general approval of his government for the aims of the proposed Convention.[65] At the first session of the 1886 Conference, he described the attitude of his government as one of 'cautious expectation'.[66] In his report to the US Government, however, he was more forceful in giving his personal views: **4.44**

> . . . the Government of the United States cannot afford to stand before the world as the only important and deeply concerned power persistently refusing to do common justice to foreign authors, and . . . it may be justly anticipated, that the

[63] See para 2.39 above.

[64] See generally T Solberg, 'The International Copyright Union' (1926) 36 *Yale Law Journal* 68; B Ringer, 'The Role of the United States in International Copyright: Past, Present and Future' (1986) 56 *Georgetown Law Journal* 1050; H G Henn, 'The Quest for International Copyright Protection' (1953) 39 *Cornell Law Quarterly* 43; M Kampelman, 'The United States and International Copyright' (1947) 41 *Am Jo Int Law* 406; J J Barnes, *Authors, Publishers and Politicians: The Quest for an Anglo-American Copyright Agreement 1815–1854* (1974).

[65] *Actes* 1885, 60–1 (statement by Winchester to Conference).

[66] *Actes* 1886, 19.

> Copyright Union being formed and acceded to by the more important European countries, it will before long feel it difficult to abstain from being a party to it also, and Congress will proceed to pave the way to adhesion of the United States to the [Berne] Union.[67]

Nonetheless, while the US Government favoured adherence to the Convention and preserved the option of doing so in the future,[68] this was not the predominant view in Congress, and the USA therefore continued to be an observer at both the 1896 and 1908 Revision Conferences. Indeed, the second of these conferences saw the emergence of a deeper gulf than had previously existed between the provisions of US law and the Convention, in particular with respect to the matters of formalities and duration.[69] Despite this, US interest in adhering to the Convention resumed after World War I and a number of Bills to bring US law into line with the Convention were introduced into Congress in the interwar period.[70] The possibility of US adherence also had an effect on the deliberations of the Rome Conference, where US concern over the question of retroactivity led the Conference to extend the time for ratification of the Rome Act so as to allow the USA the possibility of still adhering to the Berlin Act.[71] In the event, the USA did not accede to the Convention, but governmental interest in accession continued during the 1930s and in April 1935 the US Senate actually ratified the Convention.[72] However, no enabling domestic legislation had been prepared, and the ratification was withdrawn two days later.[73] Disagreements on the form of implementing legislation led to the failure of subsequent attempts to secure US adherence prior to World War II.[74]

4.45 Quite apart from the strong domestic sentiment against entering international copyright relations,[75] the incentive to adhere to the Berne Convention was reduced by the possibility of protection for US authors under the Convention by the device of first publication in a Union country (the 'backdoor to Berne', as it was often called).[76] Furthermore, after 1945, the US Government became intimately involved in the preparations for the Universal Copyright Convention

---

[67] Quoted in Solberg (n 64 above), 96.

[68] Thus, the possibility of future accession was mentioned expressly in President Cleveland's annual message to Congress at the end of 1896: Solberg (n 64 above), 97.

[69] See further H Sandison, 'The Berne Convention and the Universal Copyright Convention: The American Experience' (1986) 11 *Columbia-VLA Journal of Law & the Arts* 89, 90ff.

[70] Ringer (n 64 above), 1059; Sandison (n 69 above).

[71] *Actes* 1928, 280–1. See also para 17.10 below. It appeared that the US Government preferred the retroactivity provisions of the Berlin Act to those in the Rome Act.

[72] Ringer (n 64 above), 1059; Kampelman (n 64 above), 421.

[73] ibid. [74] ibid. [75] See n 64 above.

[76] Rome Act, art 6(1). The normal 'backdoor' for American authors was, of course, Canada. See further, *Nimmer on Copyright*, vol 3 (1985), 17–21ff.

('UCC'), of which it became a member in 1955 (this instrument, and its role as a halfway house between Berne and non-Berne members is discussed more fully in Chapter 18 below). This temporarily deflected US attention away from the Berne Union, but it had the significant effect of bringing the USA into fuller participation in international copyright relations. Rather than being a 'bridge convention' between the US (and the other American republics) and the countries of the Berne Union, the UCC could be seen as a stepping stone to Berne, a 'low staircase' which provided a level of protection analogous to that of the Berne Act of 1886.[77] It could therefore be hoped that the USA would draw closer to eventual adherence to the older Convention. This began to occur with the close co-operation that developed through the holding of joint meetings of the Berne Union Permanent Committee and the Intergovernmental Committee of the UCC, and the USA became increasingly concerned with the affairs of the Berne Union. It played a crucial role in resolving the crisis brought about by the claims of developing countries in the years 1967 to 1971 and, with the revision of its own copyright law in 1976, the areas of incompatibility between the provisions of the Berne Convention and those of US domestic law steadily decreased. This was particularly so with respect to the question of duration and the reduction of formalities (notably the abolition of renewal as a condition for securing a second term of twenty-eight years under the previous law and liberalization of the consequences of omission of the copyright notice).[78]

Following the adoption of the new US law, the Director General of WIPO took the initiative of convening a Group of Consultants in 1978 to consider the question of compatibility between the new law and the Berne Convention. After careful consideration, the Group concluded that the 'principal, if not the only, obstacle' to the accession of the USA was the remaining provisions in US law dealing with formalities.[79] This was possibly a generous view of the remaining areas of potential incompatibility, but it enabled the Group to endorse a proposal to summon a diplomatic conference to prepare a protocol to the Convention that would have permitted the USA to apply, for a limited period of time, the provisions on formalities allowed under the UCC.[80] This proposal was ultimately not proceeded with, in the light of declarations by the US Government that it was likely that it would further modify its domestic law so as to make **4.46**

[77] The idea of a 'low staircase' emerged in the third meeting of the Committee of Experts that was examining the basis for the new Convention: Summary Record of Third Meeting of Committee (1949) 2 *Unesco Copyright Bulletin* 186, 188. See further Sandison (n 69 above), 97.

[78] Copyright Act 1976, 17 USC §§ 97, 304(a) (renewal) and 401, 402 (notice).

[79] Report of the Group of Consultants (Geneva, 5–7 June 1978), Doc BE/GC/1: [1979] *Copyright* 95. The sections in question were 17 USC §§ 405(a), 405(b), 408(b), 410(a), 411 (registration); 205(c)(2) and 205(d) (recordation); and 407 and 408 (deposit).

[80] Report (n 79 above). See also the earlier BIRPI study by M B Nimmer: (1967) 19 *Stan L Rev* 499.

it fully compatible with the Convention.[81] Subsequently, US interest in Berne membership increased further as a consequence of that country's growing disenchantment with UNESCO, the international agency responsible for administering the UCC. This culminated with its decision to withdraw from UNESCO at the end of 1984. Although its adherence to the UCC was not affected by this action, it nonetheless diminished US influence over the copyright policies of UNESCO and encouraged the USA to direct its attention to the Berne Convention.[82] Furthermore, as noted above, the USA was now increasingly concerned about the damage to its copyright owners that was occurring in other countries, many of which were Berne members but which appeared to be failing in their Berne obligations. In May 1985, the Senate Judiciary Committee's Subcommittee on Patents, Copyright and Trademarks, chaired by Senator Charles Mathias, heard testimony from a number of important witnesses on the implications of US adherence to the Convention.[83] The State Department also convened an Ad Hoc Working Group of various experts with long experience in the copyright area to examine the technical question of compatibility between the provisions of US law and the Berne Convention.[84] This Group presented a preliminary report at the end of 1985 that was circulated for comment, and in April 1986 further testimony was heard from interested parties by the Mathias subcommittee.[85] In this testimony, the main advantages in favour of US accession were canvassed, but there was also an indication of the kinds of opposition that would be mounted to it.[86] On 18 June 1986, the US President (Ronald Reagan) transmitted a message to the Senate, with the text of the Convention, recommending that the Senate give its consent to US adherence.[87] Following this, a Bill to make the necessary changes to US law to enable accession to occur was introduced and, after careful review by committees in

[81] Bogsch (1986) 298–9. [82] Sandison (n 69 above), 103ff.

[83] These included the Director General of WIPO, the Acting Registrar of Copyright and a former Register (B Ringer), and senior officials from the Department of State, Patent and Trademark Office and US Trade Representative. The hearings were held on 16 May 1985 before the Subcommittee on Patents, Copyrights and Trademarks, Judiciary Committee, US Senate (chairman: Senator C Mathias) (information and statements of witnesses kindly supplied to the author by H Sandison of Washington).

[84] See the Foreword to *Preliminary Report of the Ad Hoc Group on US Adherence to the Berne Convention* (31 Dec 1985), 3 (list of members and affiliations); also reproduced in (1986) 10 *Columbia-VLA Journal of Law & the Arts* 514.

[85] The hearings were held on 15 Apr 1986.

[86] The interested associations presenting submissions included the Association of American Publishers, Inc; the Motion Picture Association of America, Inc; the National Music Publishers' Association; the Computer and Business Equipment Manufacturers' Association; the Information Industry Association; the National School Boards Association; the National Cable Television Association; the American Music Operators' Association; the Authors' League of America, Inc; and the Graphic Artists' Guild.

[87] WIPO Press Release no 58, Geneva, 15 Aug 1986.

both the House and Senate, the Berne Convention Implementation Act was finally passed in 1988, effective 1 March 1989.

(b) The implications of US adherence to Berne

At the time of writing the first edition of the work, US adherence to Berne had not occurred, but the following likely advantages that would flow from this were suggested: the opportunities that US adherence would offer for the more effective enforcement of international copyright protection; the impact it would have on the development of the Convention itself; the effect it would have on other countries still outside the Union; and its ramifications with respect to the general question of implementation of Convention obligations. By and large, the years that have followed US accession have clearly illustrated significant effects in each of these areas. **4.47**

(c) More effective international protection of copyright

It was clear from much of the testimony heard by the Mathias sub-committee in 1985 that clear advantages to US authors and copyright owners were seen to follow from accession to Berne.[88] In the main, this had to do with US initiatives at that time to gain protection for intellectual property rights throughout the world, particularly in countries that were seen as centres of piracy such as Korea, Thailand, Egypt, and Taiwan. The moral standing of the USA in seeking such protection was clearly weakened by the fact that it was not a member of the international convention that embodied the highest level of protection. The subsequent TRIPs negotiations saw the substantive Berne obligations incorporated into that Agreement, with a comprehensive set of new obligations with respect to enforcement and compliance through the GATT dispute-resolution machinery. Likewise, these concerns have been reflected in the new WIPO treaties. In each of these exercises, the contribution of the USA has been seminal, reflecting the oft-quoted statement of the late President Lyndon Johnson to the effect that it is always preferable to be inside the tent looking out rather than outside the tent looking in.[89] **4.48**

(d) The substantive development of the Convention

The impact of US membership on the future development of the Berne Convention itself has already been considerable. In the first edition of this work, it was suggested that this would finally sever the Convention from its European roots and shift its centre of gravity to the common law and English-speaking **4.49**

---

[88] eg those representing publishing, computer and information technology, authors' and artists' organizations: see n 84 above.

[89] The actual quotation is, of course, rather more earthy than the paraphrase in the principal text, but the essential sense of it is still retained!

countries. While this would clearly advance the enforcement of the Convention (see above), it would also bring to the Berne Union and its organs a different intellectual tradition and set of attitudes, and would undoubtedly have far more effect than had a century's membership of the Convention by the UK and Commonwealth countries. While this influence has not yet been felt directly in the text of the Convention itself, there can be no doubt that the USA was instrumental in the development of the digital agenda that led ultimately to the adoption of the two new WIPO treaties of 1996.

(e) Effect on other non-Union countries

4.50 US accession to Berne has clearly been infectious so far as those countries that were still outside the Union at the time of the first centenary of the Convention.[90] As noted above, very few nations now remain outside, and the adoption of Berne standards as the baseline of obligations under TRIPs and the WCT has made Berne the centrepiece of the current multilateral copyright system. In the first edition of this work, it was suggested that US accession would 'encourage' the accession of those countries still outside, and this has, in fact, happened. US pressure on some of these countries, through trade sanctions and otherwise, has also had its effect here, but Berne has provided a useful benchmark for setting the standards of protection. There is nothing new here: at the end of World War I, the Allied Powers that were members of the Berne Union also used their position of strength to require accession to the Berne Union by the various new independent states that had emerged from the dismemberment of former enemy territories.[91]

(f) Implementation of Convention obligations

4.51 US adherence to Berne was instructive in several respects. First, it highlighted the absence, within the Berne Convention itself, of any effective machinery for ensuring compliance on the part of an intending member (and, indeed, of ensuring continuing compliance by existing members).[92] Secondly, it provided a

[90] In the case of China, which was on the brink of accession at the time of the first centenary in 1986, see Gou Shoukang, 'China and the Berne Convention' (1986) 11 *Columbia-VLA Journal of Law & the Arts* 121, 122ff.

[91] Treaty of Peace between the Allied and Associated Powers and Austria of 10 Sept 1919, art 239 in [1920] *DA* 97, 98 (the Treaty of St Germain); Treaty of Peace with Bulgaria of 27 Nov 1919, art 166 in [1922] *DA* 37; Treaty of Peace with Hungary of 4 June 1920 in [1922] *DA* 38.

[92] This point was made by Dr Bogsch, the then Director General of WIPO, in his statement to the Mathias sub-committee on 16 May 1985. Note also that in his testimony, with respect to the US jukebox licence, Dr Bogsch suggested that even if this did provide a theoretically lower level of protection than required by the Convention, this was 'not of sufficient importance from an economic viewpoint' to require any changes in US law in order to permit accession to Berne: referred to in the *Preliminary Report* (n 84 above), ch III, 9–10. As to this, the *Report* states that 'it may be doubted whether the Convention sanctions a lower level of protection based upon the relative economic value of the activity involved'.

striking example of the domestic processes through which the question of compliance was pursued and fundamental questions as to the meaning of particular Berne obligations were canvassed and debated in the US Congress. Given the absence of machinery within the Convention for assessing these questions, it is really left to the good faith and common sense of national legislators and officials to determine these matters for themselves, and, in this regard, the open character of the US Congressional processes is revealing. It is also relevant to note that there was no particular incentive for existing Berne members, who have an interest in obtaining new accessions, to object to apparent failures on the part of an intending member, such as the USA, to make its laws wholly compatible with the Convention. In the case of the USA, the question of compatibility was first carefully analysed by the Ad Hoc Group referred to above.[93] While this found that the areas of incompatibility were significantly reduced under the 1976 Act, it identified a number of inconsistencies that still remained, notably with respect to the compulsory licence for jukeboxes,[94] the requirement of domestic manufacture,[95] the requirement of notice,[96] the requirements of registration,[97] recordation,[98] and deposit,[99] and the public broadcasting licence insofar as it referred to the making of reproductions.[100] On the other hand, it concluded that substantial compliance was to be found in relation to moral rights (under the common law and associated heads of protection),[101] employed authors,[102] and duration.[103] These matters were then debated at length before the respective House and Senate committees of the Congress,[104] before the final implementing legislation was prepared, and particular points of interest, for example, in relation to formalities, moral rights, and retrospectivity, are referred to at the relevant points in the following chapters. In general, it must be said that the US was a conscientious international citizen in its efforts to achieve compliance prior to accession, but the highly visible process that attended its accession highlighted the way in which it is all too possible for new members to obscure particular issues on their accession in order to obtain

[93] *Preliminary Report* (n 84 above). See also Nimmer (n 80 above).
[94] *Preliminary Report* (n 84 above), ch III (17 USC § 116).
[95] ibid, ch IV (17 USC § 601).
[96] ibid, ch VII (17 USC §§ 401 and 402).
[97] ibid, ch IX (17 USC §§ 405(a)(2), 405(b), 408(a), 408(b), 411 and 412).
[98] ibid (17 USC §§ 205(c)(2) and 205(d)).
[99] ibid (17 USC §§ 407 and 408).
[100] ibid, ch VIII (17 USC § 118).
[101] ibid, ch VI.
[102] ibid, ch XIV (17 USC §§ 101 and 201(b)).
[103] ibid, ch X (17 USC §§ 304(a) and 302(c)).
[104] In particular, see the *House Report on the Berne Implementation Act of 1988*, Report No 100–609, 6 May 1988, and the *Senate Report on the Berne Implementation Act of 1988*, Report No 100–352, 20 May 1988, reproduced in Appendices 32 and 35 respectively to D Nimmer and M B Nimmer, *Nimmer on Copyright*, vol 6 (1995).

domestic approval for this step. In the event that real failures in compliance occur at this stage, failure by existing members to object, or even tacit encouragement from them with a view to securing adherence, must be to the ultimate detriment of the Union and the frustration of the Convention's object of achieving as uniform protection as possible. (These matters are explored further at paras 17.80ff.)

(g) The USA, Berne, and beyond

4.52 While US adherence to Berne has been the most pivotal and influential event in the second century of the Convention, a new and disturbing trend must be noted, one that falls largely outside the scope of the present commentary but one, no doubt, that will provide the basis for more reflective and complete discussion in any subsequent edition. This is not a work of political science, but it would be unrealistic for it to proceed without some reference to a world situation that is entirely different from that pertaining at the time of the first edition. In 1987, it was still possible to speak of a world of superpowers: there was a Soviet Union, an arms race and a 'socialist bloc' of nations behind the Iron Curtain. These realities changed dramatically within the space of three years, with the collapse of the Soviet Union, the emergence of democratic regimes in most of Eastern Europe, and the steady emergence of the USA as the only significant world power. Such a development seems unprecedented: even in the time of the Roman Empire, there were counterweights in the east and, of course, the rest of the globe developed relatively unaware of the Pax Romana prevailing within one small area.

4.53 There are obviously many consequences that flow from being a hyperpower, and we have seen many examples of the exercise of this global strength in various spheres, particularly under the current US administration. For those outside the tent, it is frequently difficult to discern the benefit or virtue behind such exercises of strength, but in the area of copyright and neighbouring rights it is relevant to note one development that has profound potential implications for the multilateral system that is represented by Berne, the 1996 WIPO treaties, and the TRIPs Agreement. This is the increasing use of bilateral trade agreements by the USA.

4.54 As noted above, there is nothing in the existing agreements to preclude parties striking better deals as between themselves; in principle, this may even be seen as a desirable development whereby individual states or groups of states can raise the levels of protection between themselves without having to wait for others to catch up. In some areas, the requirements of such agreements may also be relatively non-contentious. Thus, it is possible that the North American Free Trade Agreement between the USA, Canada, and Mexico contains nothing that interferes with or cuts across multilateral obligations that arise in the area of copyright and neighbouring rights. This is not necessarily the case with more recent bilateral free-trade agreements that the USA has negotiated. At the time of writing, there was a steadily growing handful of these, including agreements with Morocco, Jordan, Singapore, Chile, Bahrain, and six Central American republics (agreed 5 August 2004 and covering Costa Rica, Dominican Republic, El Salvador, Guatemala, Honduras, and Nicaragua),[105] while negotiations were being carried on with the Andean Countries (Colombia, Peru, Ecuador, and Bolivia) and Panama.[106] One of the more recent agreements is with Australia, a long-standing Berne member. A significant chapter of this agreement, negotiated in early 2004, dealt with intellectual property rights (others were concerned with matters more dear to Australian hearts, such as access to US markets for beef and other agricultural products), but the provisions with respect to copyright and neighbouring rights were extraordinarily detailed, and sought to reflect in Australian law the detailed requirements of US law, notably with respect to the term of protection, circumvention measures, copyright management information, temporary reproductions, and safe harbours for Internet service providers for copyright infringement. Implementation legislation with respect to just these matters in Australia ran to nearly 100 pages,[107] and further was required by the USA in order to satisfy its trade negotiators.[108] No corresponding change to US domestic laws occurred (or was thought to be necessary for the purposes of the agreement) indicating that the negotiations in relation to copyright and related rights were something of a one-way street, in which Australian legislation was required to conform to US standards, particularly with respect to the provisions of the US Digital Millennium Copyright Act 1998.[109]

---

[105] For the text of these agreements, see www.ustr.gov and go to 'Trade Agreements' and then 'Bilateral Trade Agreements'.

[106] ibid. [107] US Free Trade Agreement Implementation Act 2004.

[108] Copyright Legislation Amendment Act 2004 (Cth). In this regard, the website of the US Trade Representative notes that, 'The United States had raised concerns with Australia that its FTAS implementing legislation, which its Parliament passed in August 2004, did not fully implement a number of the FTS commitments it made on intellectual property': www.ustr.gov/Trade_Agreements/Bilateral/Australia_FTA/Implementation/Section. . .24/02/2005. See further the final 'side letter' from the US Trade Representative to the Australian Government dated 17 Nov 2004, available at www.dfat.gov.au/tarde/negotiations/us_fta/final-text/letters/ip_zoellick_vaile.pdf.

[109] An interesting question, however, may arise as to whether the US itself complies with one of the requirements of the Free Trade Agreement which requires adherence by both countries to the WPPT. Much of the Australian implementing legislation was concerned with giving effect to this requirement with respect to performers and their moral rights, but it is unclear that the US itself actually gives effect to its WPPT obligations in this regard. There are no provisions in the US Copyright Act conferring attribution or integrity rights on performers, and, following a US Supreme Court decision that casts doubt on recourse to the Lanham Federal Trademarks Act to enforce moral rights, it is not clear that performers (or authors) may draw on other provisions of federal law to approximate those rights. See *Dastar* v *Twentieth Century Fox Film Corp*, 539 US 23

4.55 The consequences for multilateralism are significant here, particularly as it appears that the USA is using the Australia Free Trade Agreement format (as developed in earlier agreements such as that with Chile) as a template for its future bilateral trade agreements. There can, of course, be no objection in principle under Berne so long as such agreements do not detract from, or are not inconsistent with, Berne obligations (Berne, article 20). There is, however, a consequence under article 4 of the TRIPs Agreement, namely that Australia (and parties to other bilateral treaties) will have to extend the most favoured nation treatment to be extended to US nationals to nationals of all other TRIPs members.[110] More significantly, the requirements of the US-Australian Free Trade Agreement will require Australia, in any future revision of its domestic law, to have a close eye to whether it complies with this agreement, which now reflects, in a number of important respects, the provisions of US copyright law, rather than the more general requirements and standards contained in the older multilateral agreements. Inevitably, Australian copyright law will come to mirror that of US copyright law—an excellent result, no doubt, for US copyright owners, but possibly to the impoverishment of Australian domestic law-making and policy. More generally, the move towards bilateralism must have implications for the multilateral system as the bilateral agreements come to contain stipulations that reflect the domestic standards of the hyperpower[111]—it is unrealistic to suppose that any subsequent contracting party, with the possible exceptions of China or the European Union, will be able to insist upon

(2003); Jane C Ginsburg, 'The Right to Claim Authorship in US Copyright and Trademarks Law' (2004) 41 *U Houston L Rev* 263 (criticizing *Dastar* and its implications for moral rights). Note, however, the earlier assertion by the US Government to the WIPO Standing Committee on Copyright and Related Rights in July 2003 that its various laws did meet the overall moral rights obligations under article 6*bis* of Berne, and article 5 of the WPPT: 'Addendum to the Annex of the Survey on Implementation Provisions of the WCT and the WPPT (Document SCCR/9/6), submitted by the USA on July 11, 2003' (SCCR/9/6, Add 1) at www.wipo.int/meetings/en/details.jsp?meeting_jd=4823.

[110] This has happened automatically as a result of the operation of regulations made under the Copyright Act 1968: see the Copyright (International) Regulations 1969 (as amended), reg 4. This may not be the case with respect to the extended term of protection, in view of article 7(8) of Berne, but Australia has not availed itself of this facility under its implementing legislation. In this regard, cf the requirement of reciprocity under article 7(1) of the EC Council Directive 93/98, 29 Oct 1993, on the harmonizing of term within the EC.

[111] In this regard, the mechanisms for achieving bilateral free trade agreements that reflect the US view of things are delightfully exposed for all to see at www.ustr.gov. There is an elegant machinery provided for under s 2104(e) the Trade Act of 2002 and s 135(e)(1) of the Trade Act of 1974 for trade advisory committees across all relevant sectors to prepare reports on proposed trade agreements. In the case of the Australia Free Trade Agreement, there were some thirty-one of these advisory committees, and, in the case of intellectual property, the relevant committee (Industrial Property Advisory Committee on Intellectual Property Rights for Trade Policy Matters (IFAC-3)) commended US negotiators for achieving a 'very strong agreement' and 'for a job well done'. In particular, IFAC–3 applauded the negotiators for having incorporated within the agreement the obligations set forth in the WCT and WPPT and 'for convincing Australia to adhere to, and come

incorporation of a norm that reflects its particular view of copyright or neighbouring rights protection.[112]

It is, of course, early days, and the existence of these bilateral agreements scarcely presages the end of the multilateral copyright system and its fragmentation into the kind of complex web of bilateral agreements that prevailed in the pre-Berne period. Indeed, one might say that the multilateral framework which is the subject of the present treatise had not even reached its full maturity until the mid-1990s with the accession of the USA and the other major non-Berne countries such as Russia and China and the negotiation of TRIPs and the 1996 WIPO treaties. The current US tendency to bilateralism could simply be characterized as an overenthusiastic endeavour to elevate standards of protection in advance of the multilateral system which, in time, will catch up. Perspectives differ, according to which end of the spectrum one is placed, and, from the position of smaller and less powerful nations negotiating with a giant, the searching scrutiny of a powerful state such as the USA may appear more fearsome and intrusive than the more familiar collective forums of WIPO and the WTO. In any event, the tendency to bilateralism may simply be a transitory phase, and the epoch of the hyperpower may be all too brief as China and Russia, to say nothing of an expanding European Union, begin to flex their muscles on the international stage. In this regard, it is worth noting the comparative brevity of the international dominance of the British and German Empires in the decades before World War I, when the USA might well have been regarded in the same way as China and Russia are today. Inevitably, things will change and the future will undoubtedly be quite different from what we might predict today. Challenges to the multilateral agreements that are the subject of the present work are also likely to continue to come from other sources, such as digital technologies and networked communications that transcend national and regional boundaries. For the moment, however, we need to deal with the existing framework of agreements, and this is the subject of the rest of this work. 4.56

into full step with, key provisions of those treaties consistent with the manner these were implemented in the US in 1998 in the DMCA'. It is worth noting here that, three years earlier, Australia had reached its own approach to implementation of the WCT, though not all of the WPPT, obligations in the Copyright (Digital Agenda) Amendment Act 2000.

[112] Some provision for recognition or retention of local norms can be made through the provision of side letters of agreement, that then allow the template of the principal agreement to remain unchanged and ready for future use elsewhere! Examples of such side letters are to be found in the case of the Singapore Free Trade Agreement (with respect to anti-circumvention measures).

Part II

PRELIMINARY MATTERS: BERNE AND RELATED AGREEMENTS IN THE FRAMEWORK OF PUBLIC INTERNATIONAL LAW

5

TREATY INTERPRETATION AND THE CONCEPT OF UNION

5.01 This chapter will review the general rules of public international law regarding the interpretation of treaties, and will analyse their application to the Berne Convention. It begins with a consideration of matters of terminology, and then the overall structure of the Berne Convention, before examining specific problems of interpretation and the rules of the Vienna Convention on the Law of Treaties 1969 (the 'Vienna Convention') as applied to the Berne text. The chapter also works through the interplay of the Berne Convention and later texts, specifically the the Agreement on Trade-Related Aspects of Intellectual Property Rights 1994 ('TRIPs Agreement') and the World Intellectual Property Organization ('WIPO') Copyright Treaty ('WCT'). A final section takes up the concept of 'Union'.

I. TERMINOLOGY

5.02 As a matter of terminology, it does not appear that any significance is to be attached to the fact that the Berne Convention is a 'convention' rather than a 'treaty', such as the later WCT, to say nothing of an 'agreement' as in the case of the TRIPs Agreement. Historically, these terms have been used interchangeably, and while the word 'treaty' is often used with reference to bilateral agreements between states and 'convention' or 'agreement' with respect to multilateral agreements, this is by no means invariably the case. Thus, most of the early bilateral copyright agreements were called 'conventions', while the word 'treaty' is used with respect to some very important modern multilateral agreements, such as those establishing the European Economic Community and the North Atlantic Treaty Organization. Both terms refer generally to 'agreements' between states, and in this regard the Berne Convention etc[1] simply take their place in the vast web of international agreements existing between states in the modern world. In current international practice, it seems that the blanket term now used is 'treaty' and that this encompasses all kinds of agreements between states, however called, so long as they are in written form. Thus, the Vienna Convention, which contains a codification of the rules of customary

[1] For convenience, the expression 'Berne Convention etc' will be used henceforth, unless the context indicates otherwise, to refer to the Berne Convention and related agreements, ie the later agreements such as the TRIPs Agreement, the WCT, the Rome Convention for the Protection of Performers, Producers of Phonograms and Broadcasting Organizations 1961 (the 'Rome Convention'), and the WIPO Performances and Phonograms Treaty ('WPPT').

international law relating to treaties, together with some rules that represent 'progressive development', contains the following interpretation:

> 'treaty' means an international agreement concluded between States in written form and governed by international law, whether embodied in a single instrument or in two or more related instruments and whatever its particular designation;

Is it possible, however, to characterize the Berne Convention etc more precisely **5.03** than this? To do so appears possible only at the level of broad generalization. For example, international agreements can be divided into those which are concerned with matters of a 'public' or 'state' nature, and those which are concerned with private rights. This distinction, however, does not take us very far. It is true that some agreements, such as military and political alliances, involve only action at a state level, and do not have any immediate impact on private rights. Most conventions, however, do have such an impact, although many appear on the surface to be concerned principally with the international regulation of matters which are usually handled within each contracting state at a governmental or semi-governmental level, such as the control of maritime pollution, civil aviation, international communications, trade and commerce, public health, and so on. These last-mentioned conventions nonetheless have a profound effect on the way in which individuals within each contracting state conduct their affairs. In the case of the Berne Convention etc, however, the impact on private rights is far more obvious, as these conventions are directly concerned with the protection of the rights of foreign authors and rights holders within each contracting state. Each member state is obliged to accord this protection, irrespective of the level of protection which it accords to its own authors and rights holders. This hardly makes the Berne Convention etc exceptional among international conventions, as there are a large number which have a similar character, not the least important of which is the Paris Convention on Industrial Property. However, one point of difference which can be noted is that, whereas many conventions establish quite elaborate international machinery for the carrying out of their aims, the Berne and Paris Conventions do not. Typical of these first-mentioned conventions are those dealing with posts and telecommunications, the origins of which are older than either the Berne or Paris Convention.[2] While the last two possess their own international organs these are in no way necessary for their successful operation: both conventions depend essentially upon implementation by each contracting state for the fulfilment of their purposes, and, as will be seen below in the case of the Berne

[2] The Universal Postal Convention 1874, and the International Telegraph Convention 1865. See further G A Codding, *The International Telecommunication Union: An Experiment in International Co-operation* (1952), and G A Codding, *The Universal Postal Union: Co-ordination of the International Mails* (1964).

Convention, its institutional or organizational aspects are of limited practical importance only and the same is true of the WCT, WPPT, and the Rome Convention for the Protection of Performers, Producers of Phonograms and Broadcasting Organizations 1961 ('Rome Convention'). This, then, is a distinctive characteristic of the Berne Convention etc, although this by no means makes them unique among international treaties and conventions. In the case of the TRIPs Agreement, a different character again applies as it is linked to membership of an international organization, the World Trade Organization ('WTO'), that has well-developed machinery for its governance and organization (see further paras 4.39ff above).

II. TREATY STRUCTURE: THE DIFFERENT KINDS OF PROVISIONS

5.04 It is useful at this stage to say something briefly about the structure of the Berne Convention, which, to a large extent, is adopted in the other treaties under consideration. For purposes of analysis, the provisions of Berne can be divided into those which deal with substantive matters, such as the classes of persons and works to be protected and the extent of that protection, and those which deal with the administration and operation of the Convention, for example, the functions and finances of the International Office, the issues of review and revision, membership, and the manner in which accessions and ratifications are to be made. The first category is usually called the 'substantive provisions', and the second the 'administrative and final clauses'. In the present Berne text, the substantive provisions are to be found in articles 1 to 21 and the Appendix, while the administrative and final clauses are contained in articles 22 to 38. In this sub-part, we shall be concerned only with the first category (the second is dealt with at length in Chapters 16–18 below). The rules in the first category, in turn, can be further divided into 'conventional rules' (sometimes referred to as the *jure conventionis*) and 'rules of referral'.

5.05 Conventional rules lay down specific requirements or embody specific standards which each signatory state must apply in its protection of authors claiming under the Convention. A good example of such a rule is to be found in article 7 which deals with the general term of protection for works and prescribes a specific term of the life of the author plus fifty years. In a country where treaties are incorporated directly into municipal law, upon ratification, publication, or promulgation, such a provision will probably be regarded as a self-executing norm which is capable of direct application by national courts.

5.06 By contrast, a rule of referral leaves it to each state to deal with the matter in question in its own particular way, although the rule may also stipulate certain limitations within which this discretion is to be exercised. Such rules will almost never be self-executing, as domestic legislation will be required to give effect to them. They are usually adopted in cases where contracting states have been unable to reach unanimity on a uniform approach. In the words of Masouyé, a rule of this kind provides 'no solutions', but simply refers the matter back to each country to resolve as it wishes, 'within such limits as may be laid down'.[3] A good example is to be found in article 9(2), which leaves it to the legislation of each country to permit the reproduction of literary and artistic works in 'certain special cases', provided that this reproduction does 'not conflict with a normal exploitation of the work and does not unreasonably prejudice the legitimate interests of the author'. In this case, it will be seen that the provision places quite strict limitations on the freedom which it allows to contracting states to provide for exceptions to the exclusive reproduction right of the author: see further Chapter 13 below.

As a matter of interpretation, it will be noted that some provisions containing rules of referral state this is to be a 'matter for legislation in the countries of the Union' (for example, articles 9(2), 10(2), and 10*bis*(2)), or for 'national legislation' (for example, article 14*bis*(3)). The word 'legislation', which derives from the French *législation*, may be thought, in English, to be limited to statutory laws, but it was accepted by the drafting committee at the Stockholm Conference in 1967 that it referred to common law as well.[4] As a general rule, it has been seen that, following each successive revision of the Convention, the number of conventional rules has increased, as international consensus on different questions has developed.

The above analysis applies equally to the texts of the WCT, the Rome Convention, and the WPPT. There are differences in relation to the TRIPs Agreement and these are noted at the relevant point in this commentary. **5.07**

III. THE INTERPRETATION OF TREATIES

A. The Obligations Imposed

Our primary purpose in this commentary is the ascertainment of the meaning and import of the provisions of various treaties relating to copyright and neighbouring rights, beginning with the interpretation of the provisions of the **5.08**

[3] C Masouyé, *Guide to the Berne Convention* (1978), 5.

[4] *Records* 1967, vol II, 1134.

present Berne text. It is therefore appropriate at this stage to outline the approach that will be taken to this task. As each treaty is an agreement between states, it imposes certain obligations on each contracting state in relation to the subject matter of the convention, that is, the international protection of authors' rights and neighbouring rights.

5.09 In the case of the Berne Convention, this is expressly provided for in article 36(1) which states that each country which is party to the Convention 'undertakes to adopt, in accordance with its constitution, the measures necessary to ensure the application of this Convention'. Article 36(2) states further it is 'understood' that, at the time that a country ratifies or accedes to the Convention, it will be 'in a position under its domestic law to give effect to the provisions of this Convention'. These provisions, however, are quite neutral as to how contracting states are to fulfil these obligations. This takes account of the varying constitutional requirements of states, and for our present purposes calls for some further explanation.

With respect to the implementation of treaty obligations by states, it is possible to identify two broad categories of national approach. As regards the first, treaties are incorporated into municipal law upon ratification, or upon completion of some other legislative or executive action such as promulgation or publication.[5] This is the situation in many of the civil law countries which are members of the Berne Convention, but a further question which arises with respect to each of these countries is the extent to which the provisions of these treaties thereby become directly applicable to individuals (or are 'self-executing') or require some further domestic measures to give effect to them.[6] This is a matter on which there are many differences of substance and detail between states, but, as a general rule, a treaty provision in a country in this first category will be treated as directly applicable 'when interpretation of its wording, spirit and systematical position permits national courts to apply it to individuals without any further legislative or executive implementation'.[7] There are a number of these provisions in the Berne Convention, in particular article 2(1) which

[5] See generally on these questions, L Wildhaber, *Treaty-Making Power and Constitution: An International and Comparative Study* (1971), ch 7 ('The Municipal Application of Treaties') ('Wildhaber (1971)'). See also the brief comparative survey in the appendix to the study by A E Evans, 'Self-executing Treaties in the USA' (1954) XXX *BYIL* 179, 195–205.

[6] Wildhaber (1971), 195ff. The possibility of direct implementation of the Berne Convention, in particular of its moral rights provisions, was a significant issue for the USA when it acceded to the Convention in 1988; see the Berne Convention Implementation Act of 1988 (Public Law 100–568), s 2, and see further the discussions in the House and Senate Reports on the Act: *The House Report on the Berne Convention Implementation Act of 1988* (Report No 100–609), 28 and following; *The Senate Report on the Berne Convention Implementation Act of 1988* (20 May 1988) (Report 100–352), contained in *Nimmer on Copyright*, vol 6 (1995), Appendices 32 and 35 respectively.

[7] ibid, 231–2.

defines the works protected under the Convention. On the other hand, there is a significant proportion of provisions that clearly require further implementation on the domestic level as they refer expressly to the need for national legislation ('rules of referral', which are discussed above at para 5.06). In these first-category countries, questions of some complexity also arise as to the effect of treaty provisions on inconsistent prior and later domestic laws.[8] As the approach of each state to these matters differs, according to its particular constitutional requirements and juridical traditions, it is not possible in the present text to do anything but to indicate that these differences exist, and that it will be necessary in each case to ascertain exactly what these are in order to understand the relationship between the provisions of the Berne Convention and national legislation in that state. Such an inquiry, however, lies outside the scope of the present work, and readers are advised to consult the relevant laws and texts of the particular state with which they are concerned.

The second category is more straightforward, and does not give rise to the problems referred to above, as treaties affecting private rights in these states will almost invariably require domestic legislation in order to give effect to their requirements. The provisions of the treaty can only be invoked to the extent that has been expressly allowed for in municipal law.[9] No question of relying directly on the provisions of the treaty can therefore arise, as only the stipulations of domestic legislation are relevant. There may, of course, be a question as to whether the latter give effect to the requirements of the treaty, but that is a different matter involving a possible breach of obligations as between states, and will not affect a claim made by an individual who is seeking to protect his or her rights in that state by virtue of the Convention. As a consequence, if the laws of states with this kind of constitutional requirements do not already comply with the provisions of the Convention, they will refrain from ratification or accession until such time as the necessary changes have been made. Most of the common law countries fall into this second category, as well as the Scandinavian states, and it is for this reason that many of these countries have been delayed for considerable periods of time in ratifying the successive texts of the Berne Convention.[10] Implementation and enforcement of Convention obligations, as a **5.10**

[8] See eg W Nordemann, K Vinck, and P W Hertin, *Internationales Urheberrecht und Leistungsschutzrecht der deutschsprachigen Länder unter Berücksichtigung auch der Staaten der Europäischen Gemeinschaft, Kommentar* (1977) ('Nordemann et al (1977)'), 14–16; A Baum, 'Berner Konvention und Landesgesetze' [1928] *GRUR* 648, and same title [1950] *GRUR* 437; A Baum, 'Droit international public: Convention de Berne et lois nationales' [1946] *DA* 85, 101, 114; W Hoffmann, 'Berner Übereinkunft und Landesgesetz' [1928] *GRUR* 897; F Ostertag, 'La Convention de Berne et le droit national' [1941] *DA* 29, 37.

[9] Wildhaber (1971), 190.

[10] eg the UK did not ratify the Brussels Act until 15 Dec 1957, following the enactment of the Copyright Act 1956 ([1957] *DA* 225), and Australia did not do so until 1 June 1969, following

matter between member states of the Berne Union, does not directly concern us at this point, although it is discussed in more detail in Chapter 17 below. However, it should be noted that, as a general matter of international law, states must perform their treaty obligations, and cannot invoke inconsistencies in their municipal laws as an excuse for any failure to do so.[11] Our primary concern in the present work, however, is not with municipal law, but only with the meaning and scope of the international obligations contained in the Berne Convention.

5.11 In the case of the other treaties considered in this commentary, the Rome Convention contains a similar provision (article 26) to article 36 of Berne, and there are corresponding provisions in the WCT (article 14(1)) and WPPT (article 23(1)). However, even in the absence of such provisions, contracting states to treaties are under a general duty in public international law to perform their treaty obligations in good faith (*pacta sunt servanda*, as codified in article 26 of the Vienna Convention). In the case of the TRIPs Agreement, there is express reference in article 1(1) to the obligations on members to 'give effect to the provisions of this Agreement' (which may include more extensive protection, at the member's option). Article 1(1) then goes on to stipulate that: 'Members shall be free to determine the appropriate method of implementing the provisions of this Agreement within their own legal system and practice.'

Finally, it should be noted that, so far as the WCT is concerned, there is a further constraint which arises from article 20 of Berne. The latter provides that Berne members may make 'special agreements' between themselves concerning the protection of authors' rights 'in so far as such agreements grant to authors more extensive rights than those granted by the Convention or contain other provisions not contrary to this Convention . . .'. The WCT is such a 'special agreement' (see WCT, article 1(1)) and accordingly its interpretation will be subject to the restrictions contained in article 20 of Berne (see further para 5.45 below). A similar relationship arises as between the Rome Convention and the WPPT, under which the latter is arguably a 'special agreement' under article 26 of the former instrument (see further para 19.37 below).

---

the enactment of its Copyright Act 1968 ([1969] *Copyright* 94). Note, however, that even in the case of countries where treaties are incorporated directly into municipal law, ratification may still await the passing of domestic legislation. This was the case with the FRG which did not accede to the Brussels Act until 20 Oct 1966, following the enactment of its Law of 1965.

[11] See the authorities referred to in Wildhaber (1971), 184–8.

B. The Interpretation of Treaty Provisions

(1) Languages used

As a general matter, the interpretation of treaties is one of considerable difficulty, particularly as regards the extent to which extrinsic aids may be used in this process. The Berne Convention itself contains no specific rules as to the way in which it is to be interpreted, apart from article 37(1) which deals with the languages of the Convention text. This provides (i) that the authentic (or authoritative) texts of the Convention are to be in French and English ('this Act is to be signed in a single copy in the French and English languages'), and (ii) that in the case of 'differences of opinion' the French text is to prevail. This rule was established under the Brussels Act; prior to this time, the only authentic text of the Convention for the purposes of interpretation was that in French, as this was the language in which the Convention had been signed and ratified from the Berne to Rome Acts. Under the present text, there is also provision for the establishment of 'official texts' in other languages, but in a hierarchical sense these are subordinate to both the French and English versions which are the texts signed by the parties. **5.12**

This still leaves open the question as to what is the meaning of a provision, such as article 37(1), that stipulates that one of several authentic texts in different languages is to prevail in cases of 'differences of opinion'. There are two possible views here, although both will often lead to the same result.[12] The first is to say that one must look at both texts first in order to see to what extent they are in concordance and the correct interpretation of a particular provision will therefore be the one that is consistent with both texts. Using this approach, it will only be in the case of a clear 'difference of opinion' between the two texts that the priority rule in favour of the French version should be applied. On the other hand, this may lead to highly artificial constructions, and it can be said that, as the French text ultimately applies, this might as well be done from the outset and the English text ignored. However, this second approach would put the English text on the same level as the 'official texts' which may be established in other languages, and would make its status as a language of signature meaningless. In addition, the two approaches may lead, in some instances, to different results. Under the first, there may be several possible meanings of which one can be rejected as being incompatible with one or the other of the texts; under the second approach, such a limitation would not apply when one is considering **5.13**

[12] See generally J Hardy, 'The Interpretation of Plurilingual Treaties by International Courts and Tribunals' (1961) XXXVII *BYIL* 73, 123ff.

only one text and where, as a consequence, there is freedom to adopt the interpretation that may have been excluded under the other text.[13] While it seems that the practice of national and international courts is divided as to which of these is the correct approach,[14] the first appears to be the more appropriate one, as the other would deny the English text any effect at all and this is at variance with the provision of article 37 under which it is made an authentic text of the Convention. Thus, one should begin by interpreting the English text, and then compare this with the French text to see if any discrepancies emerge from this comparison. In the event that there is no interpretation that fits readily with both texts, then, and only then, should the French version be applied. As far as the Berne Convention is concerned, however, the above discussion is generally only of theoretical interest, as there are few instances where clear discrepancies arise between the texts. In part, this may be due to the close similarities that are to be found between the French and English languages when applied to the drafting of treaty provisions (unlike, for instance, English and German or French and German); in part, it has also to do with the competence with which these different texts were established at Stockholm and Paris.

5.14 By way of contrast, in the Rome Convention, the WCT, and WPPT, the question of languages is dealt with quite differently. None of these agreements prescribes that a given language is to prevail in the case of conflicting interpretations, and texts are established in several languages—English, French, and Spanish (in the case of Rome), and Arabic, Chinese, English, French, Russian, and Spanish (in the case of WCT and WPPT)—each of which is 'equally authentic'.[15] A similar position applies in relation to the TRIPs Agreement, which as an annexed agreement to the Agreement establishing the WTO was 'done' in the English, French, and Spanish languages, 'each text being equally authentic'. In the event of a difference of meaning arising as between any of these different texts, the appropriate rule to apply would therefore be that contained in article 33(4) of the Vienna Convention. This provides that 'the meaning which best reconciles the texts, having regard to the object and purpose of the treaty, shall be adopted'. This provision will apply to both the WCT and WPPT as these treaties were formulated after the coming into force of the Vienna Convention (see further below), but to Rome only on the basis that article 33(4) of Vienna codifies the previous rule of customary public international law. The TRIPs Agreement will also be covered by the same customary rule, although established after the coming into force of Vienna (see para 5.15 below).

[13] ibid, 126. [14] ibid, 128ff.

[15] Rome, art 33(1); WCT, art 26(1); WPPT, art 32(1).

(2) The rules in the Vienna Convention on the Law of Treaties

In the absence of any other rules of interpretation within the Berne Convention etc, it is therefore necessary to fall back on the general rules of public international law that deal with this matter. Speaking strictly, the rules laid down in the Vienna Convention[16] are inapplicable to Berne and Rome, as Vienna applies only to treaties made after its entry into force and it is required that the parties to those treaties should also be a party to the Vienna Convention.[17] The Berne Convention, even in its latest Act, and Rome are pre-Vienna agreements, although the TRIPs Agreement, the WCT, and WPPT obviously are later in time. In the case of the TRIPs Agreement, however, there is a provision in article 3(2) of the Understanding on Dispute Settlement, to which TRIPs is subject, namely that dispute panels are to construe the TRIPS Agreement 'in accordance with the customary rules of interpretation of public international law'. It appears that the reason for this is that the USA, an important member of the TRIPs Agreement, is not a party to the Vienna Convention.[18] At the same time, it appears that the USA takes the view that the provisions of the Vienna Convention reflect custom,[19] and this seems generally accepted with respect to articles 31 and 32 which deal specifically with the interpretation of treaties.[20] Although the rules contained in these articles are not an exhaustive codification, they are nonetheless of central importance for our present purposes. 5.15

The 'general rule of interpretation' is laid down as follows in article 31:

> 1. A treaty shall be interpreted in good faith in accordance with the ordinary meaning to be given to the terms of the treaty in their context and in the light of its object and purpose.
> 2. The context for the purpose of the interpretation of a treaty shall comprise, in addition to the text, including its preamble and annexes:
>   (a) any agreement relating to the treaty which was made between all the parties in connexion with the conclusion of the treaty;

---

[16] See the *Vienna Convention on the Law of Treaties with Final Act of the Conference, Declarations and Resolutions*, 23 May 1969, Cmnd 4140 (1969). For a more general background on the interpretation of treaties, although principally from a British and Commonwealth perspective, see Lord McNair, *The Law of Treaties* (1961).

[17] Vienna Convention, art 4. As at 6 May 2005, less than two-thirds of Berne members were also parties to the Vienna Convention which had 101 parties as at 28 June 2005 (cf Berne with 159 member states).

[18] See further N W Netanel, 'The Digital Agenda of the World Intellectual Property Organisation: Comment: The Next Round—The Impact of the WIPO Copyright Treaty on TRIPS Dispute Settlement' (1997) 37 *Virginia Journal of International Law* 441, 449.

[19] See further 1 Restatement (Third) of the Foreign Relations Law of the United States 145 (1986)

[20] See generally I Sinclair, *The Vienna Convention on the Law of Treaties*, 2nd edn (1984), 10ff.

(b) any instrument which was made by one or more parties in connexion with the conclusion of the treaty and accepted by the other parties as an instrument related to the treaty.

3. There shall be taken into account together with the context:
   (a) any subsequent agreement between the parties regarding the interpretation of the treaty or the application of its provisions;
   (b) any subsequent practice in the application of the treaty which establishes the agreement of the parties regarding its interpretation;
   (c) any relevant rules of international law applicable in the relations between the parties.
4. A special meaning shall be given to a term if it is established that the parties so intended.

These 'rules' require some further explication.

(a) The search for the 'ordinary meaning'

5.16 Under article 31(1), the primary goal of interpretation is the ascertainment of the 'ordinary meaning' of the terms of the treaty in their 'context' and in the light of 'its object and purpose'. Each of these components requires separate consideration.

5.17 As regards the 'context' of the treaty, the criteria applicable are strictly objective and can be viewed as a series of concentric circles, beginning with (i) the text itself, the preamble, and annexes, (ii) any ancillary agreements and understandings reached by the parties at the time of conclusion of the treaty, (iii) any subsequent agreements made by the parties, (iv) their subsequent practice in relation to their treaty obligations, and (v) such rules of international law as may be applicable to their relations. Each of these matters requires further comment.

(b) The text of the treaty

5.18 It is clear here that one must look at all of the provisions of the treaty, including the preamble and annexes, not just the text of the particular provision one is seeking to interpret. The preamble may be of particular significance here, as it is often in this section that there is a precise attempt to articulate the purpose and object of the convention. At this stage, however, the purpose in looking at this part of the treaty is simply to ensure that the context in which the treaty was formulated is fully appreciated and understood. The specific role of the object and purpose of a treaty in its interpretation is discussed below.

(c) Agreements and understandings between the parties

5.19 These are further described in article 31(2) and may be of various kinds. Thus, article 31(2)(a) refers to 'agreements' that are made at the time of completing the principal treaty. These may take the form of a separate treaty between the parties, but a more typical instance is where the parties adopt an 'agreed statement' at the time of concluding the formal treaty text (this was not the case with the Stockholm or Paris Acts of the Berne Convention but occurred with both the WCT and WPPT in 1996). Article 31(2)(a) of the Vienna Convention requires that such 'agreements' must be between 'all the parties' to the treaty in question—it will not suffice if there is only an agreement between two or a few of them, or if there is simply a unilateral statement of intent by one party as to how it will apply a particular provision of the treaty. However, it does not seem necessary for it to be a written agreement, so long as there is some means of evidencing it, such as a note in the records of the relevant diplomatic conference. Furthermore, it seems that such 'agreements' may include 'uncontested interpretations' given during the course of the diplomatic conference that adopted the final text of the treaty, for example, by the chairman of a drafting committee or plenary session, so long as these are not opposed or dissented from.[21] Agreements of this kind are therefore not part of the 'preparatory work' of the treaty, which may only be used as supplementary means of interpretation pursuant to article 32 (see further below), but will form part of the context of the treaty for the primary task of interpretation under article 31(1). Presumably, it will be necessary for such an interpretation to have been put forward positively, rather than speculatively or in an exploratory way. Such 'agreements' have particular significance in the case of the Stockholm Act, as a number of uncontested statements were made by the chairman of Main Committee I of the Stockholm Conference (the distinguished German scholar, Professor Eugen Ulmer) and therefore need to be taken into account in the interpretation of certain articles, such as article 9(2) (which is concerned with permissible exceptions to the exclusive reproduction right).[22]

While article 31(2)(a) refers to 'agreements', article 31(2)(b) extends this to **5.20**
what might better be described as 'understandings', applying to 'any instrument . . . made by one or more parties in connexion with the conclusion of the treaty and accepted by the other parties as an instrument related to the treaty'. The word 'instrument' implies that this must be in writing, but this could include unilateral statements by a party as well as a statement to which several parties subscribe. For the purposes of the article 31(2)(b), all that is required is that the instrument is 'accepted' by the other parties as 'an instrument related to the treaty'. The term 'accepted' is not entirely clear, as it is used in this context.

[21] Mustafa Kamil Yasseen, 'L'interpretation des traites d'apres la Convention de Vienne sur le Droit des Traites' (1976–III) 151 *Recueil des Cours*, para 20, p 39 and cited with approval by the WTO Panel on *United States: Section 110(5) of the US Copyright Act*, 15 June 2000, p 18, n 56.

[22] Such statements, of course, need to be distinguished from interpretative or explanatory statements that are put forward by members of such committees in the course of deliberations. Such statements, at best, will fall to be considered as part of the preparatory works of the treaty under art 32.

'Acceptance' in the case of a treaty usually requires some formal act of the state concerned, such as signature, an exchange of instruments, ratification, or accession: see article 11 of the Vienna Convention. Article 31(2)(b) appears to contemplate something less formal, and a simple statement, even oral, by a representative of the state concerned should therefore suffice. Presumably, there will need to be 'acceptance' by all parties, but, unlike article 31(2)(a), it might be possible for this to occur after the conclusion of the treaty, as the only temporal reference in article 31(2)(b) is to the making of the instrument. It is also arguable that acceptance might occur through silence or acquiescence, which is a concept recognized in other parts of the Vienna Convention (see article 45). On the other hand, 'dissent' from the instrument on the part of any state would suffice to defeat article 31(2)(b), and could presumably be conveyed in a number of ways by the state concerned, for example, through a verbal statement by the state's representative at the diplomatic conference itself or through some written communication made by the government of that state to other states at the time or afterwards (bearing in mind that this should be done relatively expeditiously so as to avoid any argument of acquiescence).

(d) Any subsequent agreement between the parties

5.21 This refers to agreements made by the parties after the conclusion of the treaty in question—see article 31(3)(a). Presumably, such an agreement will need to be unanimous, but there is no other particular formal requirement. For example, the parties could simply agree on the interpretation and/or application of a particular provision of the treaty, and, so long as this agreement was clearly evidenced and recorded, it would not need to comply with the formal requirements for a treaty, such as those contained elsewhere in the Vienna Convention with respect to such matters as signature, deposit, ratification, etc. In the history of the Berne Convention, there have been no instances of subsequent agreements that would come within the scope of article 32(3)(a). In part, this has been because the requirement of unanimity becomes far more difficult to achieve in the case of a convention such as Berne that provides for the accession of new members. In part, it is also due to the fact that, from its inception, the Berne Convention has provided for its revision through the calling of regular revision conferences that have drafted and adopted entire new texts of the Convention. For the main part, these have attracted signature and ratification by the vast majority of existing members and the consequence has been that, over time, each previous text has been replaced by the new one. The difficulties that arise where member states are bound by differing versions of the Convention are discussed below at relevant parts of the commentary (see paras 17.69ff). It is also worth noting, at this point, that the prospects of another Berne revision must now be remote: as at 19 January 2005, there were 159 members of Berne which must make the possibility of reaching unanimity very remote indeed, as compared with 1886 when there were only nine member states. For this reason, the WCT came into existence in 1996 as a separate agreement.

(e) The subsequent practice of the parties in relation to their treaty obligations

This is referred to in article 31(3)(b) and refers to the possibility that states themselves may change the interpretation and application of a particular provision of a treaty through their own subsequent practice. There is no further guidance, however, on the meaning of the term 'subsequent practice' to be found in the Vienna Convention. Nonetheless, the essence of each of the treaties examined in this treatise is that member states will accord certain rights to foreign claimants who belong to other member states of the treaty in question. Hence, in determining what the practices of member states are with respect to these obligations, it seems reasonable to look for this in the domestic legislative and administrative measures which each member state adopts to give effect to these obligations. Judicial decisions could also be regarded as embodying or representing relevant practice by that state, although much might depend here upon how those decisions are applied and regarded in that state, ie whether they then bind other courts in that state or are simply 'one-off' decisions. **5.22**

Assuming, then, that the 'practice' of member states can be ascertained through an examination of such domestic measures and judicial decisions (where appropriate), the question arises as how this might change the interpretation and application of a particular provision of the treaty in question. For this to occur, it would be necessary to posit that there are two or more sustainable interpretations of such a provision that arise from an appropriate application of the rules of interpretation provided under article 31 of the Vienna Convention (as supplemented by those allowed under article 32 which provides for the use of extrinsic aids in specific circumstances, as to which see paras 5.28ff below). For sake of argument, let us call these 'Interpretation A' and 'Interpretation B' and suppose that it is otherwise unclear which of these is the appropriate one to apply. Member states would therefore be free to adopt either in their domestic implementing legislation and to apply this to claimants for protection from other member states, while still being in compliance with their overall treaty obligations. If, in fact, member states opted for one or the other of these interpretations, and did so in relatively equal numbers, it would then be difficult to draw any conclusions as to their 'practice' in relation to their treaty obligation in this regard, other than to say that, as a whole, it reflected both possible interpretations. **5.23**

In the event, however, that all member states opted for Interpretation A, rather than Interpretation B, it might be possible to conclude that this represented a clear preference for that interpretation to the exclusion of the other. The ultimate conclusion would therefore be that only Interpretation A was the correct one for new member states to adopt in their application because this had now become a binding obligation under the Convention. For this to happen, it seems that the subsequent practice of member states must be unanimous, or at least unopposed—as one distinguished commentator puts it, 'concordant subsequent practice common to all parties'[23] or, as another says, practice that 'clearly established the understanding of all parties regarding its [the relevant treaty term's] interpretation'.[24] In the event, however, that one or more members still positively opted for Interpretation B in their domestic legislation this conclusion would not follow, and it would then remain open to new members to continue to adopt one or other of the interpretations.

Subsequent state practice of the kind described above might also have the effect of clarifying the interpretation and application of a provision of a treaty where it is silent upon a particular matter and where, once again, no solution is to be derived from the application of the rules of interpretation provided by articles 31 and 32 of Vienna. Accordingly, if there is unanimity of practice among member states on this matter, this will form a binding interpretation of the provision that will exclude the possibility of member states, particularly those that are new members, from applying interpretations that might otherwise have been open to them.

5.24 There are not many clear instances of these things happening in the context of the treaties considered in this commentary, although reference will be made to a number of instances of emerging, but still uncrystallized, instances of state practice in the case of the Berne Convention (the most important here relate to computer programs and communication rights with respect to 'pull technologies'). Another interesting example where state practice in relation to Berne may be changing arises in relation to moral rights and is highlighted by reference to the USA which acceded to the Convention in 1988. At this time, the US approach of delegating coverage to other laws, including common law tort claims, was at least consistent with the approaches then adopted in other common law jurisdictions such as the UK and Australia, even if the approach adopted in non-common law member states was to provide such protection through the grant of explicit rights. Since 1988, however, the majority of common law countries, including the UK and Australia, have adopted express legislative regimes for the protection of moral rights, and this may now reflect a changing state practice that applies to both common law and non-common law members of Berne alike. If this had been the case in 1988, it is interesting to speculate whether the US reliance on non-statutory protections would have been consistent

[23] Sinclair (n 20 above), 138.

[24] I Brownlie, *Principles of Public International Law*, 5th edn (1998), 635.

with moral rights obligations under Berne as interpreted through this generalized state practice. As this was not then the case, the US approach in 1988 was Berne-compliant, but may no longer be so.

(f) Any relevant rules of international law applicable in the relations between the parties

This is a more general provision, and essentially means that treaty obligations will need to be interpreted in accordance with any rules of international law that are otherwise applicable to their relations. These might be customary rules, but would obviously include those customary rules as to treaties that are contained in the Vienna Convention. One obvious applicable rule, already referred to above, is that every treaty obligation is binding upon the parties to it and must be performed by them in good faith ('*pacta sunt servanda*').[25] Included here also would be obligations arising under other treaties that might cut across or override obligations under Berne etc: in this regard, however, it should be noted that Berne (and Rome) directly address this possibility in cases where later agreements provide lesser protection than that provided under Berne (or Rome) or are contrary to the provisions of the latter (Berne, article 20 and Rome, article 26). **5.25**

(3) 'Object and purpose'

These may be more difficult to ascertain. However, as one commentator points out, reference to the object and purpose of a treaty is a secondary or ancillary process in the application of the rules of treaty interpretation. The primary search is for the 'ordinary meaning' of the terms of the treaty in their context, and 'it is in the light of the object and purpose of the treaty that the initial and preliminary conclusion must be tested and either confirmed or modified'.[26] At this stage, there may be arguments as to how this second process is to be effected, but the safest and least controversial way of ascertaining the object and purpose of a treaty is clearly to begin with an examination of the text itself (this will already have occurred as part of the primary inquiry into the 'ordinary meaning'). In this regard, if there is a preamble, this will be the most obvious expression of the objects and purposes that the contracting parties wished to achieve in their agreement. In older treaties, unlike their wordier modern successors, preambles were usually quite short and succinct. Indeed, in the case of Berne, there was no preamble until the Paris Act of 1971. Thus, from its inception, the most immediate statement of Berne's object and purpose was to be found in its title ('a Convention concerning the creation of an international union for the protection of literary and artistic works') as supplemented by article 1 which provided: **5.26**

---

[25] Vienna Convention, art 26.

[26] Sinclair (n 20 above), 130.

> The Contracting States are constituted into a Union for the protection of the rights of authors over their literary and artistic works.

The preamble added in the Paris Act now provides:

> The countries of the Union, being equally animated by the desire to protect, in as effective and uniform a manner as possible, the rights of authors in their literary and artistic works . . .

So far as this text is concerned, then, its object and purpose seem quite unambiguous, namely that it is solely concerned with the protection of the rights of authors; there is no reference here to other competing or complementary objects and purposes that might be relevant in this context, such as education and research or the promotion of public access to information. This would suggest that, where a particular provision is open to varying interpretations, the interpretation to be preferred and applied is the one that is more consistent with the protection of authors' rights. Rome, likewise, has a simple and apparently unambiguous statement of purpose in its preamble, which provides:

> The Contracting States, moved by the desire to protect the rights of performers, producers of phonograms and broadcasting organisations,
>
> Have agreed as follows: . . .

5.27 The later treaties, by contrast, are not so straightforward as this. The WCT, for example, has a much more extensive preamble which begins with a reference to the rights of authors, but then proceeds to enunciate a number of other objects that are to be taken into account:

> The Contracting Parties,
>
> Desiring to develop and maintain the protection of the rights of authors in their literary and artistic works in a manner as effective and uniform as possible,
>
> Recognizing the need to introduce new international rules and clarify the interpretation of certain existing rules in order to provide adequate solutions to the questions raised by new economic, social, cultural and technological developments,
>
> Recognizing the profound impact of the development and convergence of information and communication technologies on the creation and use of literary and artistic works,
>
> Emphasizing the outstanding significance of copyright protection as an incentive for literary and artistic creation,
>
> Recognizing the need to maintain a balance between the rights of authors and the larger public interest, particularly education, research and access to information, as reflected in the Berne Convention,
>
> Have agreed as follows:

The last of these objects, with its reference to 'balance between the rights of authors and the larger public interest . . . as reflected in the Berne Convention', is interesting, as it suggests that there is a further dimension to Berne than appears at the first reading of that text, and this issue is explored further below. The preamble to the WPPT follows a similar pattern to that of the WCT, concluding with a reference to the need for 'balance'. 'Balance' is also integral to the text of the TRIPs Agreement. The preamble of this agreement is even more catholic in its statement of objects and purposes than the WCT or WPPT, with trade matters accentuated as well as the interests of developing countries and developmental and technological objectives. There is no specific reference to the importance (or otherwise) of authors and/or creators, although there is a solemn recognition that 'intellectual property rights are private rights'. However, articles 7 and 8 have specific relevance to the matter of object and purpose. Article 7, entitled 'Objectives', addresses the matter of 'balance' explicitly and in the following terms:

> The protection and enforcement of intellectual property rights should contribute to the promotion of technological innovation and to the transfer and dissemination of technology, to the mutual advantage of producers and users of technological knowledge and in a manner conducive to social and economic welfare, and to a balance of rights and obligations.

Article 8 then articulates certain 'principles' that members may take into account in formulating and amending their laws and regulations, allowing them to adopt 'measures necessary to protect public health and nutrition, and to promote the public interest in sectors of vital importance to their socio-economic and technological development' (article 8(1)) as well as adopting 'appropriate measures' to prevent the abuse of intellectual property rights by rights holders (article 8(2)). The TRIPs Agreement is clearly an instrumentalist agreement that views intellectual property rights, including copyright, as means for promoting certain trade, economic, and social purposes: the rights of authors here are only one aspect of the matrix of interests involved.

The different objects and purposes of the above agreements therefore create potential difficulties when seeking to interpret and harmonize their provisions *inter se*, notably with respect to those provisions of Berne that are incorporated in the later agreements, such as the WCT and the TRIPs Agreement. This is particularly so in the case of TRIPs which incorporates the substantive articles of Berne (articles 1–21 and the Appendix), but does so without the preamble and article 6*bis* (which deals with moral rights), suggesting that there may ultimately be an irreconcilable area of difference between the two instruments. (These questions are examined further below at paras 5.44ff.)

(4) Extrinsic aids to interpretation

As to these, or 'supplementary means of interpretation' as they are sometimes **5.28**
called, article 32 contains a fairly restricted regime. This reflects the basic position accepted in customary international law:

> Recourse may be had to supplementary means of interpretation, including the preparatory work of the treaty and the circumstances of its conclusion, in order to confirm the meaning resulting from the application of article 31, or to determine the meaning when the interpretation according to article 31:
>
> (a) leaves the meaning ambiguous or obscure; or
> (b) leads to a result which is manifestly absurd or unreasonable.

Accordingly, supplementary means may only be used by way of confirmation of the interpretation arrived at by the application of the primary rule of interpretation under article 31, or when the circumstances outlined in paragraphs (a) and (b) arise. The supplementary means that may then be employed are not defined exhaustively, but the two principal kinds which are expressly referred to are 'the preparatory work of the treaty' and the 'circumstances of its conclusion'.

(a) 'Preparatory work'

5.29 Although these words are not further defined in the Vienna Convention, it seems reasonable to assume that, in the case of treaties such as Berne Convention etc, they would comprise the documentation usually published as the '*Actes*', '*Documents*', or 'Records' of the diplomatic conferences leading to the treaty's conclusion. This would include the conference programmes and the work of any advisory or expert committee that assisted in its preparation, the proposals and counter-proposals of the different delegations, the minutes of meetings, the reports of any relevant conference committees, and the resolutions or votes taken. Furthermore, although the words 'preparatory work' might, on a strict reading, be taken as referring only to the 'preparatory work' carried out in relation to the latest text that binds the parties, it seems reasonable to interpret them, in the case of Berne, in a broad sense as comprehending all preparatory work done in relation to the Convention at each of its successive conferences. As noted above (at para 5.19), it is possible that, in some instances, statements made in the course of such preparatory work may be elevated to the status of material that is part of the 'context' of the treaty for the purposes of ascertaining the ordinary meaning of the text under article 31(2)(a). The example given above was that of an 'uncontested statement' by a committee chair. In the commentary which follows, extensive reference is made to all these materials in order to provide the background for a clearer understanding of the present provisions of the Convention.

(b) Circumstances of the treaty's conclusion

5.30 This factor allows for consideration of such matters as the historical background against which the treaty was negotiated, and the individual characteristics and attitudes of the contracting parties.[27] These matters may, of course, be quite

[27] Sinclair (n 20 above), 141.

apparent from the preparatory work of the treaty, but may also emerge from a study of the 'other sources' mentioned below. In any event, they only become of relevance for the purposes of interpretation when the conditions of article 32 are satisfied.

(c) Other extrinsic aids to interpretation

As regards the use of other supplementary means, these are not excluded by the terms of article 32, but there will obviously be less certainty about the weight, if any, which is to be attached to them. In this regard, it is possible to adopt the following hierarchy: **5.31**

1. Sources which may be regarded as capable of providing a genuinely 'authentic' interpretation of a treaty, that is, an interpretation which authoritatively confirms one already reached through the ordinary process of interpretation under article 31 or which resolves an ambiguity or absurdity that otherwise arises and which can henceforth be applied by all members of the treaty in question. Under the Berne Convention, these include interpretations that may be given by the International Court of Justice and several of the organs of the Union, namely, its conferences of revision and the Assembly. There are similar provisions in Rome,[28] but the arrangements under the WCT, WPPT, and the TRIPs Agreement are somewhat different and are noted briefly below.
2. Sources which, while not 'authentic' in the sense used in item 1, must nonetheless be regarded as extrinsic aids of considerable persuasive weight. These include the opinions of the Director General of WIPO, the International Office and the various expert advisory committees and working groups of the Union.
3. Other sources which may be accorded less weight as extrinsic aids, including the diplomatic records of the governments which negotiated the original treaty and its successive revisions, the resolutions, reports, and proceedings of various private bodies and congresses concerned with copyright matters, and the writings of learned commentators. A further source is to be found in the decisions of national courts in which the provisions of the Convention have arisen for interpretation.

Each of these 'sources' is considered in more detail below.

[28] Rome Convention, arts 30 and 32.

(d) 'Authentic sources of interpretation'

5.32 **(i) Determinations of the International Court of Justice:** Since the Brussels Act, article 30(1) of Berne has provided that 'any dispute between two or more countries of the Union concerning the interpretation or application of this Convention, not settled by negotiation, may, by any one of the countries concerned, be brought before the International Court of Justice by application in conformity with the Statute of the Court, unless the countries concerned agree on some other method of settlement'. A similar provision is to be found in article 30 of the Rome Convention. Such a determination would be binding as between the countries concerned, but it is unclear whether it would have any more than persuasive weight in the case of other Berne countries, as article 30(1) of Berne (not Rome) goes on to state that 'the country bringing the dispute before the Court shall inform the International Bureau; the International Bureau shall bring the matter to the attention of the other countries of the Union'. Promising, however, as article 30(1) may look as a potential source of conventional jurisprudence, in practice it has never been used for this purpose for either convention. It is necessary for states to bring actions, and given that the impact of breaches of the Convention will usually be felt by private interests, ie authors and owners, it is unlikely that such persons or groups will have the necessary influence to persuade their governments to take such action. More significant, perhaps, is the fact that reservations to article 30 of Berne (not Rome) are allowed, and many states have taken this course, declaring that they will not be parties to or bound by proceedings before the Court. In effect, this makes article 30(1) an 'optional' jurisdiction clause, rather than a mandatory one, with the consequence that it has played no part to date in the interpretation and application of the Berne Convention. The limitations of article 30 are discussed further below (see paras 17.85ff). As noted above, there is no equivalent to article 30 in either the WCT or WPPT.

5.33 **(ii) WTO panels:** Since the adoption of the TRIPs Agreement as an annexe to the WTO, a new interpretative source has been provided by the determinations of panels appointed under the dispute-resolution procedures of the WTO, where a dispute arises between members as to the interpretation of any of the provisions of the Berne Convention (articles 1–21 and the Appendix, except for article 6bis) that are incorporated in the TRIPs Agreement. Strictly, these panel determinations will only bind those states that are party to the dispute and, in strict terms, the dispute concerns the provisions of the TRIPs Agreement rather than those of the treaties such as Berne that are incorporated therein. Moreover, as noted above, the objects and circumstances of an agreement such as TRIPs differ somewhat from those of Berne so it is possible that a panel might arrive at a different interpretation of a TRIPs-Berne provision than might arise in a case where the Berne provision was being considered on its own.

Nonetheless, it will be hard to ignore the weight of any determination, and this is particularly so in the case of article 9(2) of Berne, where there was a decision in 2000 of a WTO panel on the 'homestyle' exemption under US law for the public performance of musical work.[29]

(iii) Conferences of revision: Questions of interpretation may also be dealt with by the periodic conferences that may be convoked for the purposes of revising the treaty in question. In the case of Berne and Rome, there is express machinery provided for the calling of revision conferences,[30] and, as seen above in Chapter 3, Berne went through some seven substantive revision conferences in the period from 1886 to 1971. Issues of interpretation were usually approached here in one of two ways: through adopting changes to the substantive text of the Convention which either confirmed or denied an interpretation of a provision that was previously unsettled or disputed, or through the adoption of a statement as to how a particular provision was to be interpreted. The latter, in turn, usually took one of two forms: a formal interpretative declaration agreed to by all parties represented at the Conference and incorporated into the Convention (as in 1896) and a less formal declaration contained in a resolution of the Conference or in its final report. In each of these cases, as an expression of the unanimous view of the states represented at the Conference, such declarations cannot be regarded as anything other than an 'authentic' or 'authoritative' interpretation of the Convention. As noted above, they also form part of the 'context' of the treaty for the purposes of article 31(2)(a) of the Vienna Convention, rather than matters to be considered as extrinsic aids to interpretation under article 32. **5.34**

In the case of the WCT and WPPT, there is no explicit provision concerned with revision and the calling of revision conferences, but amendment of treaties is always an option open to parties under the general rules of public international law.[31] In the case of the TRIPs Agreement, however, review is built into the system, but in an unusual way that may lead to amendment of the treaty text through a declaration of the Ministerial Conference of the WTO.[32]

(iv) The Assembly of contracting parties: One of the major administrative changes introduced at the Stockholm Revision Conference was the establishment of assemblies of member states in both the Berne and Paris Conventions. In the case of Berne, this body was established under article 22 of the Stockholm Act and consists of all members of the Union that have ratified either that Act or **5.35**

[29] WTO Panel on United States—Section 110(5) of the US Copyright Act, 15 June 2000.
[30] Berne, art 27; Rome, art 29. [31] Vienna Convention, arts 39–41.
[32] TRIPs, art 71(1) and 71(2). See further D Gervais, *The TRIPS Agreement: Drafting History and Analysis*, 2nd edn (2004) ('Gervais (2003)'), 370–1.

the Paris Act. Nothing is expressly said about the interpretative role of this body, but such a power may be implied from paragraph (2)(a) which deals with the functions of the Assembly, and provides, *inter alia*, that the Assembly is to:

> (i) deal with all matters concerning the maintenance and development of the Union and the implementation of this Convention.

In the event of conflicting interpretations arising in relation to a particular provision of the Convention, it may be said that this clause enables the Assembly to make an authoritative ruling on this question, as it can be regarded as integral, not only to the 'maintenance and development of the Union', but also to the 'implementation of this Convention'. In support of this view of the Assembly's role, it can be argued that the Assembly is almost as representative of the members of the Union as any conference of revision, and is therefore the most appropriate body to provide such interpretations. In any event, there can be no doubt that the Assembly possesses such a power in relation to the administrative provisions of the Convention (articles 22–5), as it already has the power to amend these provisions under the special procedure laid down in article 26. As for the substantive provisions of the Convention, no occasion has yet arisen on which the Assembly has sought to provide interpretations, but a precedent for this exists in the case of the Assembly of the Paris Union, which is a similarly constituted body.[33] It is submitted that the Berne Assembly possesses a like capacity, and that this is to be derived from a reading of the above provision. Having said this, it is then relevant to ask whether the normal two-thirds majority which is required for decisions of the Assembly[34] would apply also to the making of such an interpretation or whether this would require a unanimity of votes cast, by analogy with a conference of revision. In view of the fact that this power of interpretation is implied here as part of the Assembly's general function to maintain and develop the Union and implement the Convention, there seems no reason why the normal two-thirds majority rule should not apply to these, as to the other, decisions of the Assembly.[35]

---

[33] This was a 'view' expressed by the seventh ordinary session of the Paris Union Assembly as to the correct interpretation of the Paris Convention in relation to international and regional applications as a basis of priority claims (25 Sept–1 Oct 1985, Geneva: [1985] *Industrial Property* 349). Note, however, as this was only described as a formal expression of the Assembly's 'view' on this matter, it can be said that the Assembly was not taking to itself the power to lay down binding interpretations of the kind discussed in the principal text.

[34] Paris Act, art 22(3)(d).

[35] A contrary argument, however, could be based on the fact that special majorities are required for amendments of the administrative clauses (art 26(2)) and by analogy similar majorities should be present for the expression of a binding interpretation of these provisions, and, by extension, unanimity in the case of interpretations of the other provisions (following the requirements for revision conferences under art 27(3)).

Assemblies are also established under the WCT and WPPT[36] with similar, though not identical, remits that likewise imply a power of interpretation, namely that the 'Assembly shall deal with matters concerning the maintenance and development of this Treaty and the application and operation of this Treaty'. At the time of writing, these Assemblies had only met once (22 September to 1 October 2003),[37] as these treaties came into force only at the beginning of 2002.

Finally, in the case of the TRIPs Agreement, there is the TRIPs Council, which is established under article 69 and which has the role of 'monitoring the operation of this Agreement and, in particular, Members' compliance with their obligations thereunder . . .'. This is part of a broader obligation to assist and consult with member states on matters relating to trade-related intellectual property rights, in particular with respect to disputes arising under the dispute-settlement process. While it is clear that matters of interpretation of the TRIPs Agreement will be an important part of the Council's deliberations, it does not appear directly that it has the power to provide interpretations of disputed provisions: inevitably, this will be done in the dispute-settlement process established under article 64 of the TRIPs Agreement.[38]

(e) 'Sources of considerable persuasive weight'

(i) interpretations offered by the Director General: It has been suggested that possibly the Director General of WIPO, as the chief executive of the Berne Union, can also provide authentic interpretations of that Convention. The basis for this suggestion is to be found in the power of the Assembly under article 22(2)(a)(iii) of Berne to give the Director General 'all necessary instructions concerning matters within the competence of the Union'.[39] Accordingly, if the Assembly possesses the interpretative function outlined in the preceding paragraph, it can be argued that it may instruct the Director General to discharge this function on its behalf. In support of this, it can be said that traditionally the Director General has been a skilled official who usually has the necessary knowledge and expertise to provide such a service, and can, in addition, do so from a position of relative neutrality. Furthermore, in the past, previous directors of the International Office did not hesitate to offer their views as to how particular provisions of the Convention should be applied, although this was usually done **5.36**

[36] WCT, art 15; WPPT, art 24.

[37] See the report of these meetings at www.wipo.int/meetings.

[38] See further Gervais (2003), 337ff.

[39] A Bogsch, 'The First Hundred Years of the Berne Convention for the Protection of Literary and Artistic Works' [1986] *Copyright* 291, 302–3. There is no counterpart provision in either the WCT or WPPT.

anonymously, through the pages of *Le Droit d'Auteur*.[40] Nonetheless, there was no official basis for doing so under earlier Acts of the Convention, and, influential as such opinions often were in the development of the Berne Union (see below), they cannot be relied on as a precedent for the adoption of such a role by the Director General under the present Act. As far as the latter is concerned, it would be difficult to regard any interpretation offered by the Director General on the provisions of the Convention as authentic, and therefore binding on all members of the Union, as ultimately this must remain a matter for those countries themselves acting either through a conference of revision or the Assembly. Accordingly, while the Assembly could instruct the Director General and his staff to prepare an interpretation, the latter would need to be confirmed by the Assembly for it to be regarded as authentic. On the other hand, it should be noted that the opinion of the Director General may still be very influential on particular member states, as was instanced by the testimony of a former Director General, Dr Apard Bogsch, before the US Congress at the time that the US was considering accession to Berne. There can be little doubt that Dr Bogsch's testimony played a considerable role in persuading US congressmen and officials that US law could be made readily to conform with the requirements of the Convention and gave an international imprimatur to Congress's preferred 'minimalist' approach to modification of US law to permit Berne adherence.[41]

5.37 (ii) **The Executive Committee:** An Executive Committee is constituted under article 23 of Berne and consists of a limited number of member states, possessing certain restricted powers which it exercises between sessions of the Assembly.[42] There is nothing in this article from which an interpretative role can be imputed to this body. This is in keeping with the fact that its functions are of a limited nature, and that the more representative Assembly meets at least every two years. Nevertheless, in the past, the annual meetings of the Executive Committee are usually attended by a large number of Union countries, whether or not members of the Committee, and the minutes of the Committee have sometimes recorded the 'general opinion' or view of delegates on particular matters concerning the Convention.[43] This was also done from time to time by

[40] See eg the theory of 'minimum recognition' advanced by the International Office (and presumably by the Director or with his knowledge) in relation to the question of reciprocity under the Convention: [1926] *DA* 49, 52 and see further para 5.66 below.

[41] See *Senate Report on the Berne Convention Implementation Act of 1988* (n 6 above), 15 (referring to the question of US compliance with Berne formalities): *Nimmer* (n 6 above), App 35–15. Dr Bogsch's opinions on moral-rights compliance by the US in a letter to Irwin Karp, dated 16 June 1987, were also quoted in the House Report 100–609 at p 37 (*Nimmer* (n 6 above), App 32–37).

[42] Paris Act, art 23(6).

[43] See eg the views expressed in relation to the question of the protection of videographic works at the sixth extraordinary session of the Executive Committee, 24–31 Oct 1979, Paris: [1979] *Copyright* 294, 296–7.

its predecessor, the Permanent Committee.[44] There has been no claim made that these views represent, in any way, the concluded view of the whole Committee or that they possess any binding force. Nonetheless, in view of the wide spectrum of Union membership that is usually represented at these meetings, such opinions, particularly where they have been uncontested, must be accorded considerable weight as an important extrinsic aid to interpretation. As will be seen in Chapter 16 below, however, the Executive Committee no longer has any 'useful function', in view of other organizational changes that have occurred within the governing bodies of WIPO, and in view of recent changes that have adopted a system of annual Assembly meetings (see further para 16.28 below).

There is no executive committee of members established under either the WCT or WPPT, but under article 32 of Rome an intergovernmental committee is established. This has a similar role to that of the Executive Committee in the Berne Convention (see further para 19.18 below).

(iii) The opinions of the International Bureau: In a similar way, opinions **5.38** expressed by the secretariats of the various conventions (this role is carried out by the International Bureau of WIPO[45]) except in the case of the TRIPs Agreement where the relevant body is the WTO may be a useful extrinsic aid, because of the specialized expertise possessed by members of those secretariats. It is unlikely that unsolicited interpretations of provisions of the Convention will be offered by the International Bureau, although suggested interpretations are often put forward for consideration by the various expert advisory committees and working groups that meet under the auspices of the Berne Union or WIPO.[46] In the first eighty or so years of the Berne Convention, however, the International Office established under the 1886 Act showed no reluctance in commenting upon, and suggesting interpretations of, provisions of that Convention. This was usually done through the pages of *Le Droit d'Auteur*, and played an important role in the development of the Union, particularly during the long periods that elapsed between the meetings of revision conferences.[47] There may have been greater readiness to publish such views at this time, as the

[44] See eg the views expressed by delegates at the thirteenth session of the BUPC concerning the interpretation of art 5 of the Stockholm Protocol, 12–15 Dec 1967, Geneva: [1968] *Copyright* 23, 24.

[45] Berne Convention, art 24; WCT, art 16; WPPT, art 25.

[46] See eg the Guidelines for Translation and Reproduction Licences for Developing Countries under the Copyright Conventions that were formulated by a joint WIPO/UNESCO working group in 1982: [1983] *Copyright* 123. It is made clear in the Advisory Note prepared by the group that these guidelines do not constitute an 'official interpretation' of these provisions: ibid, 126.

[47] See eg the commentaries written after the conclusion of the Paris and Berlin Conferences, and published in *Le Droit d'Auteur* between the years 1898–1904 and 1909–10 respectively. These were probably written by Ernst Rothlisberger, a long-standing official of the International Bureau of the Berne Union and later the Director: see further para 16.33 below.

International Office was the only permanent organ of the Berne Union between conferences of revision. Nonetheless, there was no suggestion that these could form binding interpretations, although such commentaries are obviously another important source of guidance when considering the meaning of provisions of the Convention that are unclear or uncertain, particularly in earlier Acts. More recently, the International Office, acting under the name of the Director General, has provided suggested interpretations of particular provisions, for example on the question of retrospectivity, when asked by member governments.[48]

5.39 (iv) **The opinions of expert committees and working groups:** The various organs of the Berne Union, as well as WIPO, have the power to appoint expert committees and working groups to advise on particular matters concerning the treaties for which they are responsible and to formulate proposals for change. The membership and terms of reference of these bodies vary considerably, but from time to time they may make suggestions, both expressly or by implication, as to the interpretation of provisions of the various treaties.[49] Once again, it has never been suggested that these could be authentic interpretations of these texts, but, in the light of their international character and their Union or WIPO sponsorship, the views of such bodies should also be given careful consideration.

(f) 'Other sources'

5.40 Varying weights are to be attached to these, as each, to some extent, can be regarded as 'tainted' or biased. This is particularly so in the case of governmental records, which will usually represent only the particular view of that government (which may have been in a minority at the various conferences) and not those of the contracting parties at large.[50] The decisions of national courts would also be entitled to some respect, particularly in countries where provisions of treaties may be self-executing, and the court is therefore interpreting the actual treaty provision, rather than some intermediate national legislative provision which purports to give effect to the treaty provision. Nevertheless, such decisions cannot be accorded the same authority as would attach to the decision of an

[48] 'WIPO Views of Article 18', a letter from Dr Arpad Bogsch, Director General of WIPO, to Mr Bruce Lehman, Assistant Secretary of Commerce and Commissioner of Patents and Trademarks, published in [1995] *Journal of the Copyright Society of the USA* 181–96.

[49] See eg in the late 1970s, the work of the Subcommittees of the Executive Committee of the Berne Union and the IGC of the UCC on Legal Problems arising from the Use of Videocassettes and Audiovisual Discs (Paris, 13, 14, and 19 Sept 1978): [1978] *Copyright* 406. More recently, in the post-1996 period, note the role of the Standing Committee on Copyright and Neighbouring Rights: see paras 19.83ff below.

[50] The only diplomatic records referred to by the present authors are those of the UK Government, contained in the officially published Parliamentary Papers and in the archives of the Public Record Office.

internationally constituted tribunal. As for the records of authors' societies and the like, and the writings of learned commentators, in a hierarchical sense these must obviously be placed last, although more weight might be attached to the views of commentators on the basis that these should be less influenced by partisan or national prejudices. However, there is another sense in which all the foregoing materials may be of considerable importance in the process of interpretation, both under articles 31 and 32. In the case of article 31, they may provide evidence of state practice in relation to the way in which particular terms of a treaty have been interpreted and applied. This might be particularly so as regards the decisions of national courts and governmental records. As for article 32, all the above material could clearly perform a similar function in relation to establishing what were the circumstances of the conclusion of the provision of the convention which is in doubt. This might be particularly so in the case of the proceedings and resolutions of authors' societies and other interested groups.[51]

(g) Interpretative declarations by states

Final reference must be made to the effect to be ascribed to unilateral declarations made by states as to the way in which they intend to interpret a particular provision of the convention. Such declarations may be made at different times, but are usually given during a conference of revision (and recorded either in the minutes or in the general report of the conference) or are made more formally upon ratification of, or accession to, the new text.[52] The legal status of such declarations is far from certain. If a declaration purports to modify or exclude the effect of a provision of the convention so far as that state's compliance with the convention is concerned,[53] it will constitute a reservation and its validity will depend upon whether a reservation of that kind is permitted under the convention (the scope for these is now severely restricted under the Berne Convention and there is no provision for reservations under the TRIPs Agreement, the WCT, and WPPT, although there is considerable scope in this regard under Rome: see further para 19.17 below).[54] If, on the other hand, the declaration **5.41**

[51] The importance attached to these can be seen by a perusal of the *Actes* of the revision conferences from Paris (1896) to Brussels (1948): each contains a section containing selections of relevant resolutions from these organizations.

[52] A significant example of a declaration which was made by a number of states on accession to the Brussels Act related to their power to take anti-monopoly measures to control possible abuses of collecting societies under art 11. See further para 13.91 below.

[53] See further the definition of 'reservation' in art 2(1)(d) of the Vienna Convention.

[54] See generally D M McCrae, 'The Legal Effect of Interpretative Declarations' (1978) XLIV *BYIL* 154, 161ff. The scope for making reservations is not entirely ruled out, however, under the rules of customary international law as embodied in the Vienna Convention. Thus, under art 19(c) of that instrument, where the treaty in question does not prohibit the making of reservations it is possible for a state to do so unless the reservation 'is incompatible with the object and purpose of the treaty'.

merely seeks to indicate which, of several possible interpretations, the state in question prefers and will provisionally adopt, this can be seen as a conditional statement of position that the state will abandon in the event that one of the other interpretations comes to be accepted as the authentic one, for example, through express amendment of the provision in question at a subsequent revision or through the emergence of a subsequent state practice among other states which the declarant state then accepts.[55]

(h) Other rules of interpretation

5.42 In the preceding paragraphs, we have referred to the rules of customary international law relating to the interpretation of treaties that are to be found in the Vienna Convention on Treaties. However, it was noted that this was not an exhaustive codification, and that other rules may also be applicable. In this regard, it is clear that the maxim *lex specialis legi generali derogat*—special texts are applicable, in their restricted domain, to the exclusion of texts that are universal in scope—is to be applied to the interpretation of the Stockholm text of the Berne Convention. This was stated as their unanimous approach to the drafting of this text by the drafting committee of the Stockholm Conference,[56] and is clearly revealed by a consideration of the text itself: in cases where the maxim is not applicable, this is expressly declared to be so.

(i) Relationships between different texts of the Berne Convention and between the Berne Convention and later treaties

5.43 Both these topics raise issues of considerable complexity. The first is dealt with in more detail in Chapter 17 below, which is concerned with the final clauses of the Berne Convention etc. However, it is appropriate at this point to deal with the second, as this raises some difficult issues of treaty interpretation.

(5) The relationship of the Berne Convention to later treaties

5.44 None of the treaties dealt with in this commentary falls to be interpreted in isolation from the others.[57] Thus, both the WCT and the TRIPs Agreement build on the foundation of Berne through the incorporation of its substantive provisions as part of each agreement, and then add to these their own substantive ('Berne-plus') obligations (although the TRIPs Agreement, by excluding article 6*bis*, is also 'Berne-minus'): see para 4.36 above. Neither the TRIPs Agreement nor the WPPT builds on Rome in the same way, but both refer to Rome in different respects.

[55] McCrae (n 54 above), 161ff. [56] *Records* 1967, vol II, 1134.

[57] The material which follows in this section is largely derived from S Ricketson, 'The Berne Convention: The Continued Relevance of an Ancient Text', in D Vaver and L Bently (eds), *Intellectual Property in the New Millennium: Essays in Honour of William R Cornish* (2004), 217–33.

The question then arising in relation to each of these later texts is what is to occur when provisions of each come into apparent conflict with those of the earlier (Berne or Rome) or where it becomes necessary to determine the relationship of a later provision to an earlier one, for example, is it intended to cover a gap in the earlier one or to supersede it altogether? A further, and more complicated, question arises in relation to incorporated provisions and is as follows: are these provisions required to be interpreted in the same way as under the earlier instrument? This can become of particular importance in relation to areas where members are allowed a certain latitude in which to act, such as in the case of exceptions and limitations, where the boundaries of what is permissible are set by criteria that require careful interpretation (the 'three-step' test incorporated in article 10 of the WCT and article 13 of the TRIPs Agreement is a good example here). As the objectives of the earlier and later texts appear to differ (see paras 5.26 and 5.27 above), it is possible that diverging interpretations may then arise in relation to the same provision. Thus, where there is a choice of interpretations of a particular provision that might favour authors, in one instance, or some other interest, such as education, research, public health, or development, in another, the first might be preferred under Berne with the second being preferred under the WCT or the TRIPs Agreement, as the case may be.

These possible divergences fall to be resolved in two ways. The first is to be found in express provisions of the later texts; the second is by revisiting the overall text and history of the earlier instruments and reassessing their objects and purposes. These matters are considered in turn below.

(a) Express provisions of the later text

In the case of the WCT, article 1 tackles the problem directly by providing as follows: **5.45**

> Relation to the Berne Convention
>
> (1) This treaty is a special agreement within the meaning of article 20 of the Berne Convention for the Protection of Literary and Artistic Works, as regards Contracting Parties that are countries of the Union established by that Convention. This Treaty shall not have any connection with treaties other than the Berne Convention, nor shall it prejudice any rights and obligations under any other treaties.
> (2) Nothing in this Treaty shall derogate from existing obligations that Contracting Parties have to each other under the Berne Convention for the Protection of Literary and Artistic Works.
>
> . . .
>
> (4) Contracting Parties shall comply with Articles 1 to 21 and the Appendix of the Berne Convention.

These provisions apply immediate constraints on the interpretation of the

WCT's provisions, including those that are incorporated from Berne. Thus, a 'special agreement' under article 20 of Berne can grant to authors more extensive rights than those granted by the Convention, but cannot contain other provisions contrary to this Convention (see further para 6.128 below). More specifically, the non-derogation provision in article 1(2) of the WCT must entail the consequence that no interpretation of a WCT provision should be adopted that would be inconsistent with the interpretation and application of an existing obligation that Berne members that are also WCT members have between themselves. Finally, article 1(4), the incorporation provision, requires compliance with the substantive obligations of Berne, regardless of whether the states concerned are members of Berne or not.

5.46 Article 1 of the WCT therefore 'ties back' WCT obligations to those of Berne in two ways: as a special agreement, it cannot be in conflict with the earlier instrument (article 1(1)) and, in the case of Berne members that are members of the WCT, it cannot derogate from the obligations that those members have towards each other under Berne (article 1(2)). In the case of incorporated Berne provisions, this must mean that it is the Berne interpretation that should be applied to these provisions, even though they are strictly obligations under the WCT. This leaves unanswered the question of what is the position of a non-Berne WCT member—could such a country apply a different non-Berne interpretation to an incorporated Berne provision, on the basis that this will not be in breach of article 1(2), as the country in question is not a Berne member and has no Berne obligations towards any other country that it can breach? But such a possibility may be of theoretical interest only, given the complete overlap to date between Berne and WCT membership.

5.47 A similar position applies under the TRIPs Agreement: there is an identical non-derogation provision in article 2(2), under which nothing in Parts I to IV of the TRIPs Agreement is to derogate from existing obligations that members have towards each other under Berne. While this clearly indicates the primacy of Berne interpretations of incorporated Berne obligations, this may have a more wide-ranging impact than in the case of the WCT. The latter, after all, is a special agreement under Berne. The TRIPs Agreement, by contrast, seeks to achieve other and quite different purposes, and the impact of article 2(2) must therefore be to pare back the TRIPs Agreement to the extent that it is not consistent with Berne. There is an oddity that should be noted here: under article 9(1) of the TRIPs Agreement, it is provided that the obligations of members to comply with articles 1 to 21 of Berne and the Appendix do not extend to rights or obligations arising under article 6*bis*. Accordingly, there can be no requirement under TRIPs to protect moral rights as such. In particular, this is reflected in the formulation of the three-step test that is adopted in article 13, the third step of which refers to the 'legitimate interests of the right holder' as distinct from the 'legitimate interests of the author' under article 9(2) of Berne. This indicates that an exception under article 13 of the TRIPs Agreement to an incorporated Berne right, such as reproduction or public performance, could entail a consequence that was unreasonably prejudicial to the legitimate interests of authors, so long as it did not have this effect on rights holders (who might be quite different persons or entities). An example might be an omission to acknowledge authorship or a licence to make changes to a work without the permission of the author. However, even if such an exception could be justified in terms of article 13, it could, in the case of Berne members, cut across their obligations under article 6bis of that Convention, and therefore be in breach of article 2(2) of the TRIPs Agreement (the non-derogation provision). Accordingly, while the TRIPs Agreement does not require the protection of moral rights by way of incorporation of Berne, it will not be possible for any provision of the TRIPs Agreement to authorize the doing of something that is contrary to moral rights obligations that members have directly under Berne.

The position with respect to neighbouring rights agreements is similar but has **5.48** a broader operation. Thus, under article 1(1) of the WPPT, there is a non-derogation provisions with respect to existing obligations of members under Rome (article 1(1)) and, more generally, in relation to the copyright in literary and artistic works (article 1(2) provides that nothing in Rome is to be interpreted as prejudicing such protection and a similar provision appears in article 1 of Rome). There is no derogation provision with respect to Rome in the TRIPs Agreement, but (as will be seen at paras 19.27ff below), the relation of the TRIPs Agreement to Rome is quite different than in the case of Berne, as there is no incorporation of Rome provisions in the TRIPs Agreement.

(b) The provisions of the earlier text

While articles 1(2) of the WCT and 2(2) of the TRIPs Agreement peg back the **5.49** requirements of that instrument to Berne interpretations, which, as we have seen, appear to favour authors and rights holders, it is also possible that the objects and purposes of the earlier text itself, on a closer reading, travel some way toward the more balanced approach that is embodied in both these later instruments. Thus, as noted above, the WCT preamble refers to 'the need to maintain a balance between the rights of authors and the larger public interest, particularly education, research and access to information, as reflected in the Berne Convention'. This reference may be special pleading—after all, a provision in a later text cannot on its own make the Berne Convention what it is not, namely a convention concerned with balancing the rights of authors against those of the wider public—but it does prompt a further inquiry into what is meant by the expression 'object and purpose' as they appear in article 31(1) of the Vienna Convention. In this regard, it is useful to look beyond the words of the Berne preamble to determine what more may be said about the 'object and purpose' of the Convention. Titles and preambles do not necessarily contain the sum total here, particularly in the case of older agreements formulated before the present fashion of lengthy preambles and recitals. In the case of Berne, it is possible to make the following observations.

5.50 The preamble of the present Paris text only dates from that text (1971): prior to this, there was no preamble at all. There is no explanation for this insertion, other than a statement in the report of the 1971 Revision Conference that it was desired to recognize the work of the previous Stockholm Conference (which was done in the next recital after that quoted above).[58] It will be recalled that the Paris Revision Conference was something of a 'repair job', intended to resolve the divergences that had emerged at the Stockholm Conference four years earlier with respect to developed and developing countries.[59] The object of delegates therefore was to ensure the continuity of what had gone before, but at the same time the overall thrust of the Convention was significantly altered with the adoption of the Appendix and the express recognition therein of the concerns of developing countries. This suggests that the apparently stark pro-author objective in the preamble needs to be interpreted in this light.

5.51 Furthermore, the Berne Convention, viewed overall, has never been limited to just the single objective of protecting authors' rights. An examination of the original and successive texts shows that other interests have long been recognized, albeit somewhat demurely, in its provisions, as the following list of examples shows:

- In the 1886 Berne Act, translation rights were limited to ten years (article 4) and a further article (6), while recognizing the protection of 'lawful translations' as 'original works', acknowledged that once the translation right of a work had fallen into the public domain, the translator could not 'oppose the translation of the same work by other writers'. The interests of user countries in having ready access to translations of foreign texts were clearly recognized in these provisions.
- The Berne Act also contained exceptions in relation to newspaper articles of 'political discussion' and 'news of the day' and 'miscellaneous information' (article 7), while educational and scientific uses were stated 'not to be affected by the present Convention' (article 8).
- The Berne Act also contained (as have all subsequent texts) a 'public order' override for sovereign states (article 13).

[58] General Report of the Diplomatic Conference for the Revision of the Berne Convention (Paris, 5–24 July 1971), para 20.

[59] See further Chapter 14 below.

- The Berlin Act retained and refined the exceptions and limitations of the original text, while expressly acknowledging the interests of the emerging sound-recording industry in the compulsory mechanical reproduction licence that was included in new article 13.
- The Rome Act, while recognizing new exclusive rights in relation to broadcasting and public communication of works, also acknowledged in article 11*bis*(2) the public-interest aspect of these new rights by leaving the regulation of their exercise to national legislation, thus enabling member states to impose compulsory licences.
- The Brussels text continued prior exceptions and limitations and added a specific provision with respect to the reporting of current events (article 10*bis*) and introduced a mandatory quotation right (see now article 10(1)), while the 'minor reservations' doctrine was enunciated in the General Report of Marcel Plaisant as a set of implied exceptions to public performance and communication rights (as to which, see further paras 13.78ff below).
- The limitations with respect to developing countries contained in the Stockholm and Paris texts have already been referred to above (and see further Chapter 14 below).

These matters are examined in more detail at the relevant points of this commentary (see, for example, Chapters 13 and 14 below), but for our present purposes they suffice to illustrate that the reference to 'balance' and the Berne Convention in the WCT preamble is far from meaningless, and points to the need to interpret Berne provisions in a qualified way. As Numa Droz, the Swiss president of the Berne drafting conferences of 1884 to 1886, stated in his closing address to the first conference in 1884, the aim of the drafters was far from absolute: **5.52**

> Whereas, for one thing, certain delegations might have wished for more extensive and more uniform protection of authors' rights, due account did also have to be taken of the fact that the ideal principles whose triumph we are working towards can only progress gradually on the so-varied countries that we wish to see joining the Union. Consideration also has to be given to the fact that limitations on absolute protection are dictated, rightly in my opinion, by the public interest. The ever-growing need for mass instruction could never be met if there were no reproduction facilities which at the same time, should not generate into abuses. These were the various viewpoints and interests which we have sought to reconcile in the draft convention . . . Our work is therefore the result of mutual concessions, and it is with that in mind that it is recommended to all governments for approval.[60]

In this way, it can be said that the approaches to interpretation under Berne and

[60] Minutes of the Sixth Meeting of the Conference for the Protection of Authors' Rights, 18 Sept 1884 in WIPO, *1886–Berne Convention Centenary–1986* (1986), 105.

later instruments such as the WCT and the TRIPs Agreement are not necessarily as far apart as might at first appear. WCT and the TRIPs Agreement members cannot be required to interpret their Berne obligations in any way other than as required by that Convention; on the other hand, the latter should be interpreted in accordance with the modified objects and purposes outlined above. Without doing too much injustice to both, it may be that a halfway house interpretation may properly be adopted in cases where divergences otherwise appear too sharp.

(c) Later 'clarifications' of earlier texts: the constitutive/declarative debate

5.53 A further issue of interpretation concerning the relationship between earlier and later texts is the effect of provisions in a later text, such as the WCT or the TRIPs Agreement, that seek to indicate what is covered, or intended to be covered, by an earlier agreement, such as Berne. For present purposes, the WCT is of more immediate interest, as it contains a number of such 'clarifications', each of which is framed in a different way, for example:

1. *Computer programs*: Article 4 of the WCT provides that these are protected 'as literary works within the meaning of article 2 of the Berne Convention'. It is further provided that such protection applies to 'computer programs, whatever may be the mode or form of their expression'. An 'agreed statement' then provides that the 'scope of protection for computer programs under Article 4 of this Treaty, read with Article 2, is consistent with Article 2 of the Berne Convention and on a par with the relevant provisions of the TRIPS Agreement'.
2. *Exceptions and limitations*: Article 10(2) provides that contracting parties shall, 'when applying the Berne Convention, confine any limitations of or exceptions to rights provided for therein' in accordance with the three-step test. There is an elaborate agreed statement to this provision that seeks to 'clarify' its effect vis-à-vis the Berne Convention.
3. *The right of making available to the public*: While the provisions of the Paris Act of Berne cover the right of communication to the public through a series of provisions (articles 11, 11bis (1), and 11ter), the coverage here seems incomplete, particularly as the scope of protection is dependent upon the nature of the work involved and each of the provisions was formulated in the pre-Internet era (see further Chapter 12 below). Article 8 of the WCT establishes a more comprehensive coverage of the communication right for all protected works, and also introduces a new designation more apt to communications over the Internet, namely the 'right of making available to the public' in such a way that users may 'access these works from a place and at a time individually chosen by them'. A crude dichotomy may be drawn here between 'push technologies', ie those requiring an act of

initiation by the copyright owner, and 'pull technologies', ie those enabling users to access and retrieve the work for themselves. The question which then arises is whether the 'making available right' under article 8 is actually a new and different right, not previously in Berne, or whether it is simply a reaffirmation or confirmation of the scope of rights for which protection was already required, albeit by implication or *sub silentio*, under Berne. Unlike examples 1 and 2, the WCT text does not indicate what the purpose of article 8 is vis-à-vis Berne. However, there is an agreed statement that does purport expressly to address a specific matter of Berne interpretation by stating that the mere provision of physical facilities for enabling or making a communication does not constitute a communication within the Berne Convention.[61]

4. *Application in the digital environment*: There is no provision in the WCT that expressly addresses the scope of the reproduction right under article 9 of Berne, but there is the following agreed statement to article 1(4):

> The reproduction right, as set out in Article 9 of the Berne Convention, and the exceptions permitted thereunder, fully apply in the digital environment, in particular the use of works in digital form. It is understood that the storage of a protected work in digital form in an electronic medium constitutes a reproduction within the meaning of Article 9 of the Berne Convention.

Each of these examples involves an analysis of the relationships between different texts, as well as a consideration of the status of the various accompanying 'agreed statements'. They are dealt with in detail at appropriate points in the following text, but it is useful at this stage to highlight the issue of interpretation that arises. This is most conveniently done using the example of computer programs.

(i) The case of computer programs: At first sight, article 2 of the WCT attempts to resolve an issue that was previously unclear under Berne, namely whether computer programs fell within the scope of the expression 'literary and artistic works' which is defined in article 2(1) of that agreement. As will be seen in Chapter 8 below, the latter provides inclusively that 'the expression "literary and artistic works" shall include every production in the literary, scientific and artistic domain, whatever may be the mode or form of its expression. . .'. A list of examples then follows, but these do not include computer programs, understandably, perhaps, since article 2(1) was last revised in 1967 (at Stockholm), and the importance of computer programs was only dimly perceived at this **5.54**

[61] See further the discussion in Chapter 12 below, and see further J C Ginsburg, 'The (New?) Right of Making Available to the Public', in D Vaver and L Bently (eds), *Intellectual Property in the New Millennium: Essays in Honour of William R Cornish* (2004), 234–47.

stage. Indeed, for some time after 1967, it was unclear whether these were more appropriately protected under patent law or whether some intermediate *sui generis* solution was desirable.[62] It was only by the mid-1980s that it was clear that a number of countries were adopting a copyright approach, protecting computer programs as original literary works.[63] Writing in 1986 on the centenary of the Berne Convention, Dr Arpad Bogsch, the former Director General of WIPO, noted that, although many member countries were now protecting computer programs under copyright, there were still wide differences as to the scope and form of this protection, while some countries had some doubts about this, as this would 'erode the system of protecting traditional forms of authors' works'. Dr Bogsch went on to note that at some stage the importance of this subject matter would be such that:

> . . . complete clarity will be indispensable about the question whether every country to the Berne Convention is obliged—because of its being party to that Convention—to grant protection (with the norms of that Convention) to computer programs and, if so, is obliged to grant such protection to computer programs created or first (or simultaneously) published in any other country member of the Berne Union.[64]

At this stage, therefore, Dr Bogsch was clearly of the view that Berne itself would need amendment, in order to ensure that computer programs were included as literary works. Ten years later, this development had certainly become more pronounced at the national and regional levels, with the 1991 EU Software Directive. Indeed, protection of computer programs as literary works under Berne had become a mandatory requirement under the TRIPs Agreement in 1994.[65] Insertion of a similar requirement under article 4 of the WCT was therefore a logical next step.

5.55 But do these 'collateral obligations' under the WCT and the TRIPs Agreement mean that the protection of computer programs is now mandated under article 2(1) of Berne itself, in the absence of any direct amendment to that provision? There can be no doubt that such an obligation binds members of the TRIPs Agreement and the WCT as part of their wider obligations under *those* agreements, but can it have any effect on those Berne countries that are neither WCT nor TRIPs members? Such a question may be of diminishing practical importance, given the rapidly increasing and overlapping membership of Berne,

[62] After a study by a WIPO Advisory Group of Non-Governmental Experts on the Protection of Computer Programs, model provisions for the protection of computer programs were proposed by WIPO, but were not taken up by any WIPO member: [1977] *Industrial Property* 265.

[63] A notable first was the USA, then not a Berne member, that did so in 1980; Australia followed in 1984; France in 1985; the European Union in 1991.

[64] WIPO, *1886–Berne Convention Centenary–1986* (1986), 69.

[65] TRIPs Agreement, Art 10(1).

the TRIPs Agreement, and the WCT, but it still lacks a ready answer. The dilemma is this—is article 4 simply declarative of what was already the case under Berne, as a consequence of a proper interpretation of the inclusive definition of 'literary and artistic works' in article 2(1)? Or is it constitutive, in the sense of embodying a new norm that is binding on all Berne members? In the case of the first, it may be asked, why have such a provision in the first place, as this will already have been the position and to embody it in an express provision in another convention will create uncertainty where previously there was none. In the case of the second, there is the obvious limitation referred to above, namely that it can only bind those Berne members that are also WCT and/or TRIPs members and cannot create a new norm binding on Berne members generally.

The relevant rules of treaty interpretation are only of limited assistance here. **5.56** Thus, article 31(3)(a) of the Vienna Convention, which refers to subsequent agreements between the parties would allow Berne members to agree with respect to the interpretation of a particular provision, such as article 2(1) of Berne. Such an agreement could be effective in either a declaratory or constitutive sense—declaring an interpretation acceptable to all members or, alternatively, in effectively amending article 2(1) so as to include computer programs in the list of examples of literary and artistic works that appears there. In either case, a country that became a member of Berne after such a subsequent agreement would be bound to protect computer programs as literary works by virtue of its newly assumed obligations under Berne. The obvious hurdle here is that it seems clear that the subsequent agreement would have to be between all *current* Berne members before it could have either effect—and this clearly was not the case with respect to the WCT, either at the time it was signed at the diplomatic conference in December 1996 or subsequently, as only a fraction of Berne members have yet become members of the WCT.[66] In the case of the TRIPs Agreement, the overlap may now be much closer in that it is possible that there will soon be an almost completely common membership between Berne and TRIPs, with the consequence that it will be possible to regard article 10(1) of the TRIPs Agreement as representing a subsequent agreement between Berne members.

The other possibility is provided by article 31(3)(b) of Vienna, namely that **5.57** article 4 of the WCT and article 10(1) of the TRIPs Agreement are simply declarative of the position now applying with respect to the status of computer programs as a matter of the subsequent practice of Berne members. 'State practice' may not require express unanimity as between member states on the issue in question, but it would seem necessary at least that there be no dissent to the

[66] At the time of writing, 159 nations were members of Berne, while the WCT had fifty-two. See www.wipo.int/treaties.

practice in question in the sense of one or more states explicitly adopting a different approach to this question in their treatment of claimants under the Convention. If such unanimity exists, then it may be that the interpretation and application of the treaty provision in question can be changed as a result of this practice, with the further consequence that this interpretation and application will become binding on new members of the Convention as well as upon those that may not previously have adopted it in express terms but have not previously opposed it by adopting a different approach. If this is the case with the protection of computer software, then article 4 of the WCT and article 10(1) of the TRIPs Agreement can have no more than a declarative effect vis-à-vis what has now happened to Berne as a matter of crystallized subsequent state practice.

5.58 **(ii) A note concerning temporal issues:** A final possibility to be considered here is that, under the 'ordinary meaning' to be given to article 2(1) of Berne (following article 31(1) of Vienna), computer software is already covered within that provision. Viewed from the perspective of 2004 and later, it may now seem unexceptionable to regard computer software as being within the inclusive expression of 'every production in the literary, scientific and artistic domain (as per article 2(1))', but, as noted above, it is far from clear that such matters were in contemplation at the time these words were adopted in the Stockholm and Paris Acts in 1967 and 1971. Under article 31(1) of Vienna, the inquiry into the ordinary meaning seems to be fixed at a particular time, namely the date of conclusion of the treaty text, while provision for later changes and extensions in meaning is provided for specifically in article 31(3). Accordingly, unless it can be convincingly shown that, as at 1967 to 1971, computer software fell within the 'ordinary meaning' of a literary and artistic work, the only way in which this ordinary meaning can be changed will be through the kinds of developments outlined in article 31(3).

IV. THE CONCEPT OF 'UNION'

5.59 The following section deals with an issue that is particular to the Berne Convention, namely the meaning and significance of the expression 'Union' which is constituted under article 1. This expression is not used in any of the other treaties under consideration in this commentary. Thus, the WCT, the Rome Convention, and the WPPT begin simply with a recital of objects and the statement that the parties 'have agreed as follows. . .'. None of them, however, involves the creation of a separate entity that is constituted by their agreement. The TRIPs Agreement is similarly worded ('Members . . . Hereby agree as follows . . .'), although it is an annexed agreement to the new international organization, the WTO, that was established at the conclusion of the Uruguay

Round. The expression 'Union', however, is special to the Berne Convention, and accordingly it is necessary to consider its meaning and significance within this context.

A. International Unions in General

(1) Introduction

Article 1 of the Convention provides that: 5.60

> The countries to which this Convention applies constitute a Union for the protection of the rights of authors in their literary and artistic works.

This article has remained unchanged since 1886, except that the 1886 text began with the words 'The Contracting States . . .' instead of 'The countries to which this Convention applies . . .' (the latter were adopted in the Rome Revision of 1928). What is the meaning of 'Union', as used in this article? This is a question of some interest, as the term recurs throughout the Convention, in particular in the phrase 'country [or countries] of the Union', and the abbreviated expression 'Berne Union' is in common use in national and international copyright circles. It will be recalled that the original ALAI resolution of 1882 had called for the establishment of an international copyright union along the lines of the unions already established under the telegraph and postal conventions.[67] Unlike bilateral conventions, these last-mentioned multilateral agreements had an independent existence. They did not fall to the ground with the departure of one or more of the signatory states, and it seemed correct to describe them as creating a new kind of international entity. The postal and telegraph unions were not the first 'unions' by any means, as similar associations of states had been organized on a regional basis for specific purposes from the middle part of the nineteenth century onwards. The best example of such a union was the Union of the Danube, which was established by a treaty of 1856. This comprised eight continental European states, together with Russia and Turkey, and had the purpose of assuring and facilitating the free navigation of the River Danube.[68] Over the next three decades, other unions of a more truly international character were formed, both at a governmental and non-governmental level. Of the 'private' unions, the International Committee of the Red Cross (1863), the International Law Association (1873), the Inter-Parliamentary Union (1889) and ALAI itself (1878) were perhaps the

[67] See para 2.09 above.

[68] For a description of the functions of this union, see L Poinsard, *Les Unions et Ententes Internationales*, 2nd edn (1901), 6–7.

most prominent examples.[69] As regards the 'public' unions, one commentator writing in 1901 listed some thirty-five of these (including several regional unions), ranging from the International Geodisic Association (1864) to the International Union of Weights and Measures (1875), the International Telegraph Union (1865), the Universal Postal Union (1874), and the Anti-Slavery Union (1890).[70] Most of these unions had some kind of permanent international office, and many of these were located in Switzerland, then, as now, the leading neutral state. Of these, the most notable were the Telegraph and Postal Unions, both of which had a wide range of state membership, together with highly expert and influential international offices.

(2) Characteristics of international unions

5.61 With the steady growth of these international unions there also developed a considerable body of academic writing on their nature and attributes. From this literature, a growing recognition that a new kind of international entity had come into existence is to be seen, although there was little agreement among the writers as to its juridical character.[71] Up to this time, the main actors on the international stage had been states, and for a long time there was difficulty in reaching consensus as to how these new entities were to be regarded. Were they separate subjects of international law, possessing the same attributes and powers as sovereign states? Or were they something less, and, if so, how did they differ from states? There were many conflicts among the writers on these matters. Some denied that such bodies could possess any separate international legal personality, while others argued for it, though with many individual differences as to its precise meaning.[72] In the twentieth century, the answers to these questions became clearer, with the proliferation, particularly after World War II, of powerful international organizations such as the United Nations and its specialized agencies, which have been recognized as proper subjects of international law.[73]

5.62 The question of international legal personality, and how this relates to the Berne

---

[69] D W Bowett, *The Law of International Institutions*, 4th edn (1982) ('Bowett (1982)'), 4.

[70] Poinsard (n 68 above), 6ff.

[71] See Poinsard (n 68 above), and an earlier work by the same author entitled, *Études de Droit International Conventionnel* (1894). For an extensive review of the early writings, see F Ruffini, *De la protection internationale des droits sur les oeuvres littéraires et artistiques* (1927), ch IV, and for a succinct bibliography see C W Jenks, 'The Legal Personality of International Organizations' (1945) 22 *BYIL* 267, note 1.

[72] See generally Ruffini (n 71 above).

[73] See in particular the decision of the International Court of Justice in the 'Reparation for Injuries suffered in the service of the United Nations' Case [1949] *ICJ* 174. See further Bowett (1982), ch 11, and H G Schermers, *International Institutional Law* (1980), ch 11.

Union, is taken up below in more detail, but for the moment it suffices to describe briefly the chief characteristics that were generally found in public international unions at the time the Berne Union came into existence.[74] In the first place, they were associations of states, established by some kind of multilateral agreement, and were not simply private associations. Secondly, they invariably had some kind of limited and specific international purpose, for example, the facilitation of international communications or the establishment of uniform regimes on maritime safety. Thirdly, they usually possessed a permanent organ or secretariat which was responsible for the carrying out of certain of the objects of the convention, as distinct from other collective agreements which depended totally upon individual action by each state. Fourthly, they had some element of universality, in that they were open to membership by any state (although obviously this was not true in the case of the more limited regional unions, and in the late nineteenth century the number of states was far less than today). Finally, and most important, the unions were autonomous and continuing associations, in that they did not come to an end when one state left or denounced the convention under which they were established. They therefore had an existence separate from the individual states which constituted them, although it was always open to those states collectively to decide to bring the association to an end.

(3) The Berne Union

Each of the characteristics outlined in the preceding two paragraphs was to be found in the case of the Berne Union. A continuing association of states came into being when the Convention of 1886 entered into force, and this association remained unaffected by the departure or addition of new contracting states.[75] Moreover, it was open to membership by any state that sought admission.[76] Thus, universality and autonomy were fundamental to its existence. Furthermore, from its inception the Berne Union possessed organs—its periodic conferences of revision and the International Office—as well as a budget. It also had a clear purpose, to be derived from its title and article 1: the international protection of the rights of authors in their literary and artistic works. Nevertheless, there is little else concerning the attributes of the Union to be gleaned from the provisions of the Convention; nor, indeed, is much to be found in the preparatory work of the Convention as to why the constitution of such an entity **5.63**

[74] See Ruffini (n 71 above), 94–5. See also H Ballreich, 'Die Interdependenz internationaler Organisationen' (1981) 19 *Archiv des Völkerrechts* 121.

[75] Articles 18 and 20 of the 1886 Act.

[76] Berne Act, art 18 ('Countries which have not become parties to the present Convention, and which make provision by the domestic law for the protection of the rights forming the object of the present Convention, shall be admitted to accede thereto on request to that effect.').

was thought necessary in the context of an international convention on authors' rights. The last is not an idle remark, when a comparison is made with the telegraph and postal unions which were both cited as the appropriate models for the Berne Union. In both these instances, the international organs established by their respective conventions had a more critical role than was the case with the Berne Union. Thus, the Office of the Universal Postal Union played an important part in the collection and receipt of monies owed by and owing to Union countries, as well as in the preparation and interpretation of international postal regulations.[77] Similar functions were fulfilled by the Office of the International Telegraph Union.[78] By contrast, the functions of the Berne Office have always been more limited, and it has no direct part to play in the administration of the international regime established by the Convention (this being left to each member state to implement in its own way). This is not to denigrate the International Office, as its functions in promoting and co-ordinating the international flow of information concerning copyright and related matters have always been extremely important, as has the work which it has performed in the preparations for conferences of revision. Nonetheless, the Berne Convention would continue to operate and to secure its benefits to foreign authors in the event that the Office did not exist; in the same way, the existence of the Berne Union itself would be unaffected, in the sense that there would still be a continuing association of states open to all to join.

(a) Other meanings of 'union'

5.64 Such is the flexibility of language that there are several other senses in which the term 'union' can be used in the context of an international convention on authors' rights, as distinct from meaning an international entity of the kind described above. First, it could have a territorial connotation, indicating the area over which a particular international regime is in operation. This was true in the case of the postal and telegraph unions, where the term 'union' could be used aptly to describe the combined territories of the states and colonies which were party to these conventions and over which the conventions were in operation. Secondly, the term 'union' was apt to describe the legal regime established by such a convention, particularly when this was close to being an international codification of the subject matter in question. This was substantially so, again, in the case of the postal and telegraph conventions, although not in the case of the Berne Convention. In this second, and wider usage, the term 'union' also had a territorial connotation, as it referred to a given territory in which a common set of rules were in operation. Within this territory, therefore, national

[77] See Codding, *The Universal Postal Union* (n 2 above), ch 3.

[78] Codding, *The International Telecommunication Union* (n 2 above), 48ff.

boundaries were irrelevant, as the same law applied everywhere: in this sense, 'union' meant simply 'union of laws'.

(b) History of usage of 'union' in relation to the Berne Union

What further light, if any, is thrown on the meaning of the term 'union' by the discussions in the various conferences which drafted and established the Berne Convention? Such discussions appear to have occurred on two occasions only. The first was during the 1885 Berne Conference where the German delegate requested the deletion of the term because he had difficulty in understanding the notion of a union composed of countries with widely differing legislative regimes on the protection of authors' rights. With the examples of the telegraph and postal unions clearly in mind, he said that he thought that the term would only be appropriate when a universal codification had been achieved.[79] This argument was resisted by the French delegates on two principal grounds. The first, which was not fully spelt out, was clearly based on the basic notion of the Union as an association of states, and, as such, worth retaining, because its deletion would weaken the bonds which should exist between the contracting states.[80] More fundamentally, however, it seems that the French delegates saw the term as fulfilling a vital symbolic function, namely that it embodied the ideal of universal codification, the ultimate end of the Convention. Thus, in 'abandoning this expression, one would appear to be abandoning the very idea itself'.[81] Secondly, on a more practical level, the French delegate also thought that this would make it difficult to know how to designate the proposed International Office.[82] It is hard to see how this last objection could, in reality, be maintained, as the matter of its designation would not have affected the operation of the Office, given that its constitution and functions were clearly outlined in the Closing Protocol of the proposed convention. The force of the symbolic argument, however, is harder to deny. In the event, the 1885 Conference did not dispute either of the French arguments, and the term 'union' was retained in the Convention text. 5.65

The second occasion on which the use of the term 'union' came under challenge was in a British proposal for the Rome Revision Conference. Among other things, the UK Government proposed, in effect, the deletion of 'Union' wherever it occurred throughout the text of the Convention on the ground that it seemed hardly logical to speak of a 'Union' now that a number of limited unions existed, following the reservations system allowed under the Berlin Act.[83] This brought forward an unprecedented and sharp response from the International Office in an article published in *Le Droit d'Auteur* some months before the 5.66

[79] *Actes* 1885, 20 (Reichardt). [80] ibid (Renault and Lavollée). [81] ibid.
[82] ibid. [83] *Actes* 1928, 91ff (for the text of the British proposals).

actual Conference.[84] The Office clearly saw its very existence threatened by the British proposal, and it emphasized and elaborated upon the manifold range of activities that it carried on in the name of the Union. It seems unlikely that the British intended to set the cat among the pigeons quite like this, and their delegate at the Rome Conference stated that there had been no intention to contest the 'juridical personality' of the Union.[85] Accordingly, the proposal was withdrawn, and in its report to the Conference the drafting committee spoke unanimously of its recognition of the 'legal personality of the Union of the contracting States, of which the international office is the organ'.[86] Nothing further was said about the nature and attributes of this 'legal personality', but the report was accepted without demur by the Conference in its plenary session, and the text of the Convention remained unchanged. Since this time, the term 'Union' has continued to occupy its central place in the terminology of the Convention, and in the 1967 Revision Conference at Stockholm two further organs were added to it. These were the Assembly and the Executive Committee.[87]

(c) The literature

5.67 As for the literature on the Berne Convention, this has not usually dealt in depth with the concept of the Union.[88] Where this is the case (chiefly in German writings), considerable differences of opinion are to be seen. Some commentators have seen it simply as an indication of the contractual relationship that exists between the states that are signatory to the Convention.[89] Others have seen it as referring to a community of states with its own peculiar legal personality,[90] and it has also been described, more metaphysically, as a confederation of states on copyright.[91] The meaning and scope of each of these characterizations of the 'Union' is not always easy to identify, particularly in the last case. In consequence, Nordemann et al, appear to doubt that any real significance is to be attached to the concept, noting that 'there are no certain criteria for drawing the line between a union under international law and simple multilateral treaties among state' and pointing to the fact that it is not to be found in the Universal Copyright Convention, which is also a multilateral convention on copyright which states may join and leave without endangering its continuing existence, and has a number of features similar to the Berne

[84] [1927] *DA* 116. [85] *Actes* 1928, 223. [86] ibid.

[87] Stockholm Act, arts 22 and 23.

[88] See eg S P Ladas, *The International Protection of Literary and Artistic Property* (1938), 108–9, where this matter is dealt with only briefly.

[89] See the references in Nordemann et al (1990), 37. [90] ibid.

[91] A Baum at [1950] *GRUR* 437, 478.

Convention, including standing organs.[92] Nonetheless, in one particular instance, these authors concede that the constitution of a Union under the Berne Convention may be of significance: this concerns the relationship between states that are bound by different Acts of the Convention, and is discussed further below.

B. The Meaning of 'Union' under the Present Text of the Berne Convention

In the light of the above, it remains to examine the meaning that the term 'Union' now bears under the present text of the Convention. **5.68**

(1) As an international legal person

In the last fifty years, the general learning on the question of international organizations and their legal personality has developed considerably, and it is now clear that international organizations can be separate subjects of international law.[93] However, this is not to say that they are necessarily the same, or that they possess the same attributes, as sovereign states. Furthermore, the possession of international legal personality does not mean that each organization has the same powers and capabilities. In the words of the International Court of Justice in the *Reparations* case,[94] which was concerned with the juridical status of the United Nations and in particular its right to bring international claims for compensation: **5.69**

> Whereas a State possesses the totality of international rights and duties recognized by international law, the rights and duties of an entity such as the Organization [the United Nations] must depend upon its purposes and functions as specified or implied in its constituent documents and developed in practice.[95]

In the case of international organizations such as the United Nations and its specialized agencies, the content of this international legal personality is obviously highly developed, and comprises many of the powers and privileges possessed by sovereign states, for example, the ability to make treaties and the enjoyment of diplomatic immunity by their officials. However, as the above passage from the judgment of the International Court indicates, the number and kind of these powers and immunities depends upon the 'purposes and functions [of the international organization] as specified or implied in its

[92] Nordemann et al (1977), 27–8; English translation (1990), 37–8.
[93] See generally Bowett (1982), ch 11; Jenks (n 71 above); Schermers (n 73 above), ch 11.
[94] [1949] *ICJ* 174. [95] ibid, 178–9.

constituent documents and developed in practice'. In the case of the Berne Union this analysis does not take us very far. While the bare fact of its legal personality may be acknowledged (as was done by the drafting committee at the Rome Conference of Revision and, to differing degrees, by most of the commentators on the Convention), there is very little concerning the attributes of this personality to be found expressly or impliedly in the provisions of the Convention.

5.70 Thus, article 1 establishes the Union, and the articles dealing with accessions and denunciations confirm its autonomy and continuity. The organs of the Union are established under articles 22 to 26, but their functions and powers are quite restricted. The Union and its organs do not perform any specific administrative function in relation to the protection of authors' rights on an international level. Unlike other international organizations, it does not carry out large-scale projects on its own initiative, process applications or accounts, provide an international registry service, or the like. Likewise, there is no need for the Union to enter agreements with other international legal persons, or to have many of the powers that are necessary in the case of the United Nations and its agencies, for example, the power to bring international claims, to maintain its own armed forces, and so on.

5.71 On the other hand, two of its organs—the conference of revision and the Assembly—do fulfil both a legislative role, in amending the Convention, as well as, potentially, a kind of quasi-judicial function in interpreting its provisions. However, the functions of the International Office itself are best described as educational, informational, secretarial, and co-ordinational, rather than executive and initiatory. Any powers that the Office may have exercised historically with respect to such matters as the ownership of property, employment of staff, the making of contracts, and the like, were conferred under Swiss, rather than international law.[96] Thus, the claims made by the International Office in 1927 that its functions and powers were somehow inextricably bound up with the juridical or legal personality of the Union seem beside the point.

5.72 So far as the Berne Union is concerned, therefore, the essence of its possession of international legal personality seems to mean only that it is a continuing and autonomous association of states constituted for the purpose of according international protection to the rights of authors. This purpose does not necessitate the Union having any of the other usual powers or privileges that are associated with international legal personality, and no such powers or privileges are

[96] Thus, originally the International Office was placed under the supervision of the Swiss Department of Foreign Affairs, and its powers and functions were regulated by an ordinance of the Swiss Federal Council of 11 Nov 1892: see text in *Actes* 1896, 206–7. See further paras 16.28ff below.

expressly conferred on the Union under the Convention or are to be implied as a matter of necessity. Furthermore, since 1970 the limited nature of this international legal personality has become even more abstract in character, following the assumption of the administrative functions of the International Office by WIPO (which possesses a high degree of international legal personality in its own right[97]). Finally, the apparent anomaly referred to by the UK Government in 1927 still remains, namely that a number of states, albeit now very small, are bound only by earlier Acts of the Convention, with the result that it can be said that there is more than one Union in existence, and this thus leaves the term devoid of any practical significance.

It is submitted, however, that this view is mistaken, and points, in fact, to the **5.73** most significant characteristic of the legal personality of the Union. While there are different texts of the Convention still in force between various states, there is only one Union and the relations of all these states towards each other is based on their common membership of the Union, even though there may be no single text to which all states are party and there may be states that are not formally bound by treaty relations with each other, although both are members of the Union. (This important point is discussed further in relation to article 32, which deals with the different texts of the Berne Convention, at paras 17.69ff below.)

(2) As a territorial concept

It will be apparent that the existence of a Union of states in the sense outlined **5.74** above does not necessitate or imply that there is a single Union territory (comprising the territories of all its member states) in which the rights of authors are uniformly protected. While it is not misleading to talk of the 'territory of the Union', as opposed to the rest of the world (which has reduced rapidly since the first edition of this commentary), it should not be forgotten that there are still, within the Union, a wide range of different legislative regimes in force in each member state. All that is provided is a minimum of protection for the rights of authors throughout this territory, and there is only a single Union territory for this limited purpose. Matters are further complicated, of course, by the fact that a few states remain bound by different texts of the Convention, and, as between these and other Union states, differing minimum levels of protection will apply.

(3) As a symbol for future development

The symbolic function of the word 'Union', however, should not be **5.75** underestimated. It can be seen as embodying the ultimate ideal of universal

[97] See generally the Convention Establishing the World Intellectual Property Organization ('WIPO') 1967.

codification—an international regime under which authors are protected uniformly everywhere throughout the territory of the Union. If this ideal now seems obsolete, or even dangerously out of touch with modern realities, it should be recalled that the protection of the Berne Convention has been steadily enhanced over the first century of its existence, and that it does presently embody a limited international codification of the law relating to authors' rights. In this regard, it is worth noting the view of Masouyé that the formation of a Union meant that it would be open to the world at large, and that there would be no discrimination against any particular state wishing to join.[98] In the terms of the provisions of the Convention, this is true, and as a matter of principle the statement may be applauded. However, it would be wrong to assume that universality in this particular sense is a necessary consequence of the concept of 'union', as there are other public international unions in which membership is limited, or subject to satisfying certain conditions.[99]

(4) 'The countries to which the Convention applies . . .'

5.76 As noted above, these words were added to the Convention text in the Rome revision of 1928. Previously, the English translation of article 1 had referred to the 'Contracting States', and this expression had been used throughout the rest of the text.[100] However, this seems an inadequate translation of the term '*les pays contractants*' which is used in the original (and authoritative) French text, particularly when it is realized that these words had been inserted in the 1884 draft in place of the wording used in the earlier draft of the Swiss Federal Council, which was '*les États contractants*'.[101] 'Contracting countries' (which seems the correct translation of '*les pays contractants*') was preferred by the 1884 Conference, in view of the diversity which existed in the internal constitutions of the contracting parties.[102] This last point was certainly true, when account is taken of the fact that, of the original nine signatories of the Convention, six were monarchies of widely differing kinds, and the remainder, including one confederation (Switzerland), were republics. In addition, at least one of the countries represented at the 1884 to 1886 Conferences was not entirely autonomous: this was Tunisia which was a French protectorate. On the other hand, the adjective 'contracting' still implied that the country in question was capable of entering into international agreements, and this was not true, at this time, of a number of British possessions which were largely self-governing (for example, Canada, New Zealand, the Australian colonies, and India), and on behalf of

---

[98] Masouyé (n 3 above), 9.

[99] See generally, Schermers (n 73 above), ch 2.

[100] See the English translations of the 1886 and 1908 Acts, published in the collection of texts compiled by WIPO.

[101] *Actes* 1884, 11 (text of Federal Council draft of art 1).

[102] ibid, 41.

which the UK Government acceded to each of the Acts of 1886, 1896, and 1908.[103] While 'countries' was certainly an apt designation for these last-mentioned territories, 'contracting' did not seem so appropriate, as the UK had 'contracted' on their behalf. On the other hand, they did not really fall within the category of 'colonies and foreign possessions', for which separate provision was made under the 1886 text.[104]

In the 1928 Revision, the UK Government proposed the present wording, which overcame the anomaly referred to above, and this was accepted by the Conference.[105] 'The countries to which the Convention applies' clearly has a wider effect than either of the expressions 'contracting states' or 'contracting countries', as it removes any implication that these territories have become bound by the Convention as sovereign states fully capable of entering into international relations. On the other hand, the Convention applied to them, and they formed part of the Union constituted under the Convention. Furthermore, the adoption of this expression did not derogate from the concept of 'Union', at least insofar as this had been previously developed in areas other than the Berne Union. Thus, the Universal Postal Union comprised many members that were not sovereign states, such as individual colonies or protected territories of metropolitan powers or groups of such colonies or territories;[106] likewise, the membership of other Unions comprised entities that were not sovereign states, but rather were departments or instrumentalities of those states.[107] However, in the Berne context, the British amendment was largely obsolete by the time it was made, as each of the self-governing British Dominions (except for India) had become fully autonomous by 1931,[108] and had acceded successively to the Berlin and Rome Acts as sovereign states.[109] **5.77**

Moreover, while the Convention continued to apply to colonial and other possessions after 1928, the vast majority of these had become fully independent by the time of the Stockholm revision in 1967, and had either elected to join the Union in their own right or to denounce it as no longer relevant to their needs **5.78**

[103] [1888] *DA* 8 (accession on 5 Dec 1887 on behalf of all these countries to the 1886 Act); [1897] *DA* 109 (accession on 9 Dec 1897 on behalf of all these countries to the Paris Additional Act); the accessions to the Berlin Act, however, were made at differing times from that of the UK itself: Australia, 1 July 1912 (same date as the UK, but noted separately in [1913] *DA* 165); Canada, 1 Jan 1924: [1924] *DA* 13; India, 30 Oct 1912: [1914] *DA* 33; New Zealand, 1 Apr 1914: [1914] *DA* 46; South Africa, 1 May 1920: [1920] *DA* 49.

[104] Art 19.

[105] *Actes* 1928, 91.

[106] Codding (n 2 above), 35ff.

[107] Schermers (n 73 above), 41ff.

[108] Following the adoption of the Statute of Westminster in 1931: Statute of Westminster 1931 (22 & 23 Geo 5, c 4).

[109] Australia, 14 Apr 1928: [1928] *DA* 57; Canada, 10 Apr 1928: [1928] *DA* 57; India, 1 Apr 1928: [1928] *DA* 58; New Zealand, 24 Apr 1928: [1928] *DA* 78; South Africa, 3 Oct 1928: [1928] *DA* 133. Note also that the Irish Free State, which was briefly a self-governing Dominion, acceded in its own right on 5 Oct 1927: [1927] *DA* 125.

(see further Chapter 17 below). Accordingly, the historical circumstances which lay behind the adoption of the expression 'the countries to which the Convention applies' have now disappeared, and, in practice, the word 'country' as applied to signatories to the Convention means the same as 'state', in the sense that this is used in modern international law. On the other hand, it should be noted that the Paris and Stockholm Conferences left the wording of the Convention unchanged in this respect, although 'state' was used in the new WIPO Convention which was adopted at Stockholm.[110] Nevertheless, the retention of the word 'country' could still be of use in particular cases that may arise in the future with respect to purported accessions by territories that are not regarded or recognized as 'states' in the conventional sense. It might also cover any territory that was placed under international administration, and possibly defined territories that are subject to the *de facto* administration of a liberation movement or rebel regime. (These matters are discussed further in the context of accessions to the Convention and the membership of the Union in Chapter 17 below.)

(5) 'A Union for the protection of the rights of authors in their literary and artistic works'

5.79 The title of the Convention is 'The Berne Convention for the protection of literary and artistic works'. However, as a statement of the purpose of the Convention, this is now amplified by the preamble (added in the Paris Revision) and article 1. The first states that the countries of the Union,

> being equally animated by the desire to protect, in as effective and uniform a manner as possible, the rights of authors in their literary and artistic works, . . . have agreed as follows,

while the second states that the countries to which the Convention applies have agreed to constitute 'a Union for the protection of the rights of authors in their literary and artistic works'. 'Rights of authors' is a literal translation of the expression '*des droits des auteurs*' which is used in the French text. The latter was inserted by the 1885 Conference, in place of the expression used in the earlier drafts, '*des droits d'auteur*', which in French had the simple connotation of a monetary royalty due to the author[111] (in English, there would appear to be no material difference between the expressions 'the rights of authors' and 'the rights of the author'). Does the expression 'the rights of authors' as it appears in the present text presuppose any particular juridical conception of the nature of authors' rights? This question arose in the 1885 Conference in relation to the title of the Convention, where the French delegates proposed that this be

[110] Convention establishing the World Intellectual Property Organization 1967, Art 5(1).
[111] *Actes* 1885, 40.

entitled 'Draft Convention concerning the creation of a general union for the protection of literary and artistic property'. The reason for this proposal arose out of their dislike of the term '*des droits d'auteur*' which was used in the 1884 text, and which had, in French, the restricted meaning explained above.[112] However, the German delegation, in turn, took objection to the term 'literary and artistic property' on the ground that this was a different juridical conception from that of '*Urheberrecht*' as it had been developed in German law, and that its adoption in the proposed convention would therefore put German participation in doubt.[113] As a result, the Swiss delegation proposed the neutral expression 'protection of literary and artistic works',[114] which had already been used in a number of other bilateral conventions,[115] and this was accepted by the commission in its final report to the Conference.[116] The commission also went on to state that, in adopting this expression in the title, it

> . . . had no desire whatsoever to pronounce in favour of one or other of the current theories as to the juridical nature of the rights which belong to authors in their literary and artistic works. It follows that, in the opinion of the Commission, the title of the Convention is equivalent to the words 'literary and artistic property' and should be translated in each country by the usual expression which is used to designate these rights, for example *Urheberrecht*, copyright, etc.[117]

This passage deserves careful consideration. If the second sentence is considered in isolation, it can only appear nonsensical. In a substantive sense, there was not in 1885 (nor is there now) any exact equivalence between the terms '*la propriété littéraire et artistique*', '*das Urheberrecht*', and 'copyright', to say nothing of the terms used in other jurisdictions.[118] However, the first sentence makes it clear that this reference to equivalence is really only for the purpose of indicating to each state the general domain of the Convention in terms of its own domestic law. The subject matter of the Convention is the protection of literary and artistic works, and more precisely, the rights of authors in their literary and artistic works, however these rights are described (see the preamble and article 1). The Convention itself embodies no particular juridical conception of the nature of these rights. The implication of this statement is that, while each contracting state is obliged, as a matter of its international obligations under the Convention, to protect the rights referred to in that instrument, this does not require it to accept any particular juridical theory that may be thought to underlie or underpin these rights. As noted previously, the Convention only embodies a 'minimum of protection', and plenty of scope is therefore left for each state to give full rein to its conception of authors' rights, provided that they apply the minimum standards required by the Convention. The phrase 'the **5.80**

[112] ibid. [113] ibid. [114] ibid. [115] ibid. [116] ibid. [117] ibid.

[118] See further A Dietz, *Copyright Law in the European Community* (1978), 2ff (on legislation within the EEC).

rights of authors', then, is neutral and value-free, allowing any state to adhere to the Convention, irrespective of doctrine.

5.81 While the foregoing seems correct as an explanation of the passage quoted above from the 1885 final commission report, it nevertheless requires some qualification. A commitment to the protection and enhancement of authors' rights, in itself, involves certain judgements about the basis and nature of those rights. This fact was clearly not lost upon those who, in the early years of the Convention, sought to have it made into a universal codification of the law pertaining to authors' rights.[119] Although this aim was not accepted by the early conferences, and the original text of 1886 therefore left considerable leeway for contracting states to accommodate their obligations under the Convention with their own juridical conception of authors' rights, successive revisions have defined the rights to be protected with increasing particularity and this room for manoeuvre has been correspondingly reduced.

5.82 While it would be wrong to say that the present text embodies any particular national conception of the basis for the protection of authors' rights, it nonetheless embodies elements that are alien to the laws of some Union countries. One prominent example is in the area of moral rights, which historically had no juridical recognition in common law systems. As a consequence, it is not true today to say, as did the commission in 1885, that the word 'copyright' is the equivalent to 'the rights of authors' insofar as the former term did not, until quite recently, comprise, in the majority of common law countries, the moral rights which are required to be protected under article 6*bis* of the Convention. It was for this reason that a proposal by the Swedish Government and BIRPI at the Stockholm Revision to replace the words 'the rights of the author over' by the words 'the authors' copyright in' in the English translation of article 1 was rejected: it was felt that there might be 'some doubt' as to whether 'copyright' included moral rights.[120] It has therefore become more difficult for a country adhering to the Berne Convention to maintain intact its own particular conception of authors' rights, unless this happens to coincide with the conception embodied in the Convention. The latter now represents a hybrid view of authors' rights which is peculiar to itself and is the result of many influences. At this point, it would be superfluous to identify these influences: some of them have already been referred to in the course of Chapters 3 and 4, and others will become apparent as this study progresses.

---

119 See generally Chapter 2 above.

120 *Records* 1967, vol II, 1150 (report of Main Committee I).

Part III

THE BERNE CONVENTION AND BEYOND

6

FUNDAMENTALS OF PROTECTION (ARTICLES 3–6 AND 18–20)

A. Introduction

Articles 3 to 6 lay down the basic structure for protection under the Convention, specifying who is protected and the level of protection to which they are entitled. These articles were extensively reformulated in the 1967 revision, and now embody a reasonably coherent set of rules on these matters, although recent developments in digital communications have put some of the rules under stress. Persons protected are authors who are nationals of or resident in, or who first publish in, a country of the Union. They are entitled, in other Union countries in respect of their literary and artistic works protected under the Convention, to national treatment together with the rights specially granted under the Convention. The subject matter falling within the scope of the expression 'literary and artistic works' is enumerated in articles 2 and 2*bis* and is discussed in Chapter 8 below, while the 'rights specially granted' are dealt with in articles 6*bis*, 8, 9, 11, 11*bis*, 11*ter*, 12, 13, 14, 14*bis*, and 14*ter* and are discussed in Chapters 9 to 12 below. Whereas articles 3 to 6 concern the 'front end' issues of admission to, and the regime of, protection, articles 18 to 20 address what one might call the 'back end' of the Convention: its retroactive application, its effect **6.01** upon national legislation, and its relation to other agreements, whether existing or future, between member countries.

6.02 This chapter will examine the development and current norms of the Convention regarding admission to protection and the regime of protection under the Berne Convention, before turning to the impact of subsequent agreements involving Union countries, including the Agreement on Trade-Related Aspects of Intellectual Property Rights 1994 ('the TRIPs Agreement') and the World Intellectual Property Organization ('WIPO') Copyright Treaty ('WCT'). With regard to admission to protection, the chapter will address points of attachment and country of origin. Analysis of the regime of protection will focus on the rule of national treatment, substantive minima of protection, and retroactive application of the Convention in the case of new accessions.

I. ADMISSION TO PROTECTION UNDER THE CONVENTION

6.03 The provisions of the Berne Convention which are the subject of the present chapter are concerned with two fundamental issues: the categories of foreign authors who are entitled to protection in Union countries apart from their own nationals (articles 3, 4, and 6), and the laws that are to be applied to these foreign authors (article 5). (For analysis of who is an 'author' within the meaning of the Berne Convention, see further Chapter 7 below.) Conceptually, these matters are distinct. The first can be described as a question of the law relating to the condition or status of foreigners, and the second as a matter relating to the law of conflicts. Our present concern is with the first of these questions, and the starting point is article 3(1) which provides as follows:

> (1) The protection of this Convention shall apply to:
> (a) authors who are nationals of one of the countries of the Union for their works whether published or not;
> (b) authors who are not nationals of one of the countries of the Union for their works first published in one of those countries, or simultaneously in a country outside the Union and in a country of the Union.

Article 3(2) assimilates authors who are not nationals of a Union country, but who are habitually resident in a Union country to nationals of that country.

This compressed provision now deals with both Union and non-Union authors; prior to 1967, however, the rights of the latter were contained in a separate article. Under the present formulation, different criteria for protection are applied: in the case of Union authors, their nationality suffices for all purposes, but in the case of non-Union authors the relevant criterion is the place of first publication. Each of these criteria requires further consideration.

A. Points of Attachment for Application of the Convention

(1) Nationality or habitual residence of the author

(a) Union authors

Authors furnish the first point of attachment: the Convention covers all the works of authors who are 'nationals of one of the countries of the Union'. The French expression for this is '*les auteurs ressortissant à l'un des pays de l'Union*', and this has appeared in the French text since the first draft text of 1884.[1] In English, the literal translation of '*ressortissant à*' is 'under the jurisdiction of' or 'subject to', but 'national of' also appears a reasonably approximate translation. The wording originally used in the draft of the Swiss Federal Council which was submitted to the 1884 Diplomatic Conference was '*les sujets ou citoyens de chacun des États contractants*' ('the subjects or citizens of each of the Contracting States'), but the present wording was adopted by the drafting commission following objections from the German delegates that '*sujets ou citoyens*' did not correspond exactly with the expressions employed by the laws of the different contracting states.[2] In the words of the commission, the term '*ressortissant*' was preferable as it indicated clearly that the Convention was intended to protect 'all authors who were native to one of the countries of the Union'.[3] As far as the unofficial English translations of the Acts of the Convention were concerned, the German objections were not taken into account, and the expression 'subjects or citizens' was used until the Rome Act, when the term 'nationals' was adopted.[4] The latter seems more in keeping with the French wording, although it should be noted that it will still be a matter for the law of each Union country to determine precisely what is meant by the terms '*ressortissant*' and 'national'. 6.04

---

[1] 1884 draft text, art 2(1): *Actes* 1884, 77. [2] *Actes* 1884, 41.

[3] ibid. See also *Actes* 1885, 41–2. As for successors in title, it seems clear that their nationality is irrelevant for the purposes of Conventional protection: *Actes* 1885, 42.

[4] This is the wording adopted in the translations of the Berne Convention published by BIRPI, but compare the wording used in the translations published by the UK Government in *Switzerland No 3 (1886), Further Correspondence Respecting the Formation of an International Copyright Union*, Papers presented to Parliament in Sept 1886 ('*Correspondence No 3* (1886)'), 15. In the latter, art 2 was translated as 'Authors of any of the countries of the countries of the Union . . .'.

(b) 'Habitual residence'

6.05 On one point, however, the Convention does contain a clear direction as to one category of persons which is to be included within the scope of the expression 'nationals'. Under article 3(2), authors who are not nationals of a Union country but have their 'habitual residence' in one of them are, for the purposes of the Convention, assimilated to nationals of that country. This was inserted in the Convention only in 1967, but it will be recalled that in the original Federal Council draft of 1884 there was a proposal for the assimilation of non-Union authors who were 'domiciled' in a Union country.[5] This gained strong support from the French delegates, who cited the case of Rossini, an Italian composer living in France, as an instance of the hardships that might be created by the lack of such a provision in the event that Italy did not become a party to the proposed Convention.[6] However, it was opposed by the German delegates on the ground that it would discourage non-Union countries from adhering to the Union.[7] As the Federal Council draft also related to the works of non-resident and non-Union authors published in Union countries, it may have been that the German objection was directed more to this question than to the assimilation of domiciled non-Union authors. However, the proposed draft was not adopted by the Conference, and the position of these authors was not raised in successive conferences of revision, with the exception of a Polish proposal for the redrafting of articles 4 to 6 of the Berlin text which was made at the Rome Conference of 1928. Among other things, this proposal assimilated to nationals non-Union authors who were 'effectively domiciled' in a Union country, but the overall draft met with opposition and was not proceeded with.[8]

6.06 The assimilation of this category of authors therefore waited until the 1967 Conference, when the Swedish/BIRPI programme proposed the assimilation of non-Union authors who were 'domiciled' in a Union country.[9] Coupled with this was a proposal for an additional protocol to the Convention which would enable countries which so desired to assimilate 'stateless persons or refugees having their habitual residence' in those countries (these persons not being usually regarded as 'domiciled' within most national laws).[10] The concept of 'domicile' had been used in the Universal Copyright Convention ('UCC'),[11] and to this extent it was proposed to bring the two conventions into alignment. However, the proposal gave rise to considerable discussion among the delegates, and it appeared from this that the legal concept of 'domicile' varied from one

---

[5] *Actes* 1884, 11 (Federal Council draft of art 3). [6] ibid, 44 (Lavollée).
[7] ibid, 43. [8] *Actes* 1928, 117, 233. [9] *Records* 1967, vol I, 91–2.
[10] ibid, 75. [11] Universal Copyright Convention, art II(3).

country of the Union to another.[12] As this would have led to widely differing interpretations by national courts in countries where protection was claimed, other formulations were put forward, for example, 'effectively domiciled',[13] 'effectively domiciled (habitual residence)',[14] 'domicile or effective residence',[15] and 'principal habitual residence'.[16] Finally, the expression 'habitual residence' was agreed upon, as embodying a factual, rather than a legal, criterion.[17] It also obviated any need for the proposed protocol, as refugees and stateless persons were clearly comprehended.

(c) Time at which the habitual residence criterion becomes applicable

The adoption of this criterion still leaves certain questions to be resolved. The first concerns the point at which habitual residence should become the criterion for protection, as authors may change their place of habitual residence from time to time. The same is also true of nationality, although this may not occur with quite as much frequency. The Convention does not contain any specific guidance on this point, and it is therefore a matter for determination by the law of the country where protection is claimed, or by the courts of that country if the national law is also silent on the point. It is important here to distinguish between published and unpublished works. In the case of the first, three possibilities present themselves: the time of publication of the work, the time when protection is claimed, and habitual residence (or nationality) at both points of time. As the adjective 'published' can be used to refer to both the historic act of initial publication (see further the definition of 'published works' discussed in para 6.22 below) or to a continuing status (a work, once published, remains so), any of these possibilities is tenable. Nonetheless, there is authority to be found in the *Records* of the 1967 Conference that the appropriate time is the time of publication. This was the view of Professor Ulmer, the chairman of Main Committee I,[18] and himself a distinguished commentator, and this was accepted without demur by the delegates present at the meeting of the Committee at **6.07**

[12] *Records* 1967, vol II, 839–41 (minutes of Main Committee I).

[13] Document S/26 (France): *Records* 1967, vol I, 682.

[14] Congo (Brazzaville): *Records* 1967, vol II, 840 (minutes of Main Committee I).

[15] FRG: ibid, 840. [16] Senegal: ibid.

[17] The chairman of Main Committee I invited delegates here to express their opinions, without prejudice to the formula that might be put forward by the drafting committee. The criterion of 'habitual residence' was accepted by twenty votes to sixteen, with five abstentions: ibid. 'Habitual residence' has become a generally referenced point of attachment in international private law instruments. See eg Hague Convention on the Law Applicable to Traffic Accidents, arts 4, 6 (4 May 1971); Hague Convention on the Law Applicable to Contracts for the International Sale of Goods, art 14(2) (22 Dec 1986); Hague Convention on International Access to Justice, arts 1, 5, 14, 18, 19, 20, 28 (25 Oct 1980).

[18] *Records* 1967, vol II, 841.

which he stated this.[19] The implication of this approach is that such a work would remain protected, even if the author subsequently changed his or her place of habitual residence (or nationality). On the other hand, as 'habitual residence' is a state of fact, the works of authors published before or after a period of habitual residence in a Union country would not gain protection unless they were entitled to this under article 3(1)(a) (that is, by virtue of first publication in a Union country). This would obviously not be the case with persons who are 'real nationals', as this capacity is usually maintained quite irrespective of residence in the country of nationality.

6.08 With regard to unpublished works, similar problems arise, and here again there are three possibilities: the date on which the work was created, the date on which, without being published, it 'became available' to members of the public, and the date on which protection is claimed. Again, the Convention leaves this as a question for national law, but it may be remarked that the first would raise the greatest evidential problems, as it is always difficult to prove the precise time at which a work was created. This point was made in the discussions of Main Committee I by the Greek delegate, who suggested that it would therefore be necessary 'to take into account the time when protection was requested'.[20] However, in its final report (prepared by the *rapporteur* Svante Bergström of Sweden), Main Committee I expressed its preference for the second approach suggested above.[21] After stating that this was a question for national courts to determine, it went on to say:

> It is probable, however, that the decisive date will be the date when the work, without having been published, was first made available to the public. If at that date the author has his habitual residence in a country of the Union, he is protected in respect of his work under the Convention. If the work was first made available to the public by an unauthorized person, the author can claim protection against that unauthorized person, if he has his habitual residence in a country of the Union at that date.[22]

By the phrase 'first made available to the public', it is presumed that the Committee meant not only unauthorized publication, but also such acts as public performance and public exhibition (in the case of an artistic work), broadcasting, and cable diffusion, these being acts which are excluded from the concept of publication under article 3(3) (see para 6.43 below), but which may nonetheless result in a work being communicated to the public. However, this interpretation

[19] Note, however, that Mr Bodenhausen, the Director of BIRPI who was present at the same meeting, refused to express an opinion on this point, saying that this was a matter for the countries of the Union and their courts to determine for themselves: ibid.

[20] ibid. [21] ibid, 1136–7. [22] ibid.

involves certain difficulties of a definitional and practical nature. The concept of 'first made available to the public' will not always be easy to apply, as it is close to, without being the same as, the concept of publication. Furthermore, proof of whether and when a work has been 'first made available to the public' may be nearly as difficult as proving the time of its creation (although the problems here should not be overestimated: see para 6.45 below). Accordingly, the commentators Desbois, Françon, and Kéréver urge the adoption of the third approach, which looks at the author's place of habitual residence or nationality at the time protection is claimed for the work.[23] This has considerable appeal, but it should be noted that the interpretation offered in the report of Main Committee I has to be given some weight in interpreting the provisions of article 4(1) and (2), as it was, after all, the view of the Committee, not simply that of the *rapporteur* (as Desbois et al suggest).[24] It is therefore an authentic supplementary means of interpretation to be applied in the interpretation of a provision of a treaty which is unclear (see paras 5.28 and 5.31 above).

(d) Several places of habitual residence

Another problem not dealt with in article 3(2) concerns the position of a person who habitually resides in more than one place. This was raised by several delegates in the meetings of Main Committee I, and several drafts embodying formulations such as 'principal habitual residence' were discussed.[25] No guidance, however, is to be found in the text which was finally adopted, and no unanimous interpretation was agreed by the delegates in Committee I.[26] This therefore remains a question for the courts in the country where protection is claimed. Nevertheless, it is possible to conclude from the fact that the adjective 'principal' was not adopted that this indicates that it may be possible to have more than one habitual residence. This may be of crucial importance to an author in the (now) very limited circumstances in which she has places of residence in both a Union country (say, the UK, Australia, or the Democratic Peoples' Republic of Korea) and a non-Union country (say, Ethiopia, Vanuatu, Myanmar, or Nepal). In cases where she has places of residence in several countries of the Union, there will be no difficulty about whether she is protected under the Convention (except in the unlikely event that the court in question decides that her peripatetic state is such that she cannot be regarded as having an habitual residence anywhere). On the other hand, questions of a great delicacy may arise as to which Union country is the country of origin of such an author, as this has implications in relation to the level and length of protection offered **6.09**

[23] H Desbois, A Françon, and A Kéréver, *Les Conventions internationales du droit d'auteur et des droits voisins* (1976) ('Desbois et al (1976)') 138–9.
[24] ibid, 139. [25] *Records* 1967, vol II, 840–1. [26] ibid.

under the Convention. This problem also arises in relation to persons possessing dual nationality, but it seems more appropriate to defer consideration of these issues to the section below dealing with 'country of origin' (see para 6.68 below).

(e) Works protected

6.10 Authors who are nationals of Union countries (and who are assimilated to nationals) are protected under the Convention in respect of both their published and unpublished works. This provision, making nationality the sole criterion for protection, was introduced in the Stockholm Act. Prior to this (and, indeed, from the time of the Berne Act), the criterion of nationality applied with respect to the unpublished works of Union authors; after these works were published, protection was only available if this had taken place first in a Union country. This second, territorial criterion was in fact the same as that applied to non-Union authors after the Additional Act of 1896.[27] However, the application of these 'mixed' criteria to Union authors in the period before 1967 gave rise to a serious anomaly, in the sense that these authors, having received protection under the Convention in all countries of the Union with respect to their unpublished works, could lose this protection in relation to any of these works which were published for the first time in a non-Union country.

(f) Historical background

6.11 As a matter of history, there had been little controversy about protecting the unpublished works of authors under the Berne Convention on the basis of the author's nationality. Nevertheless, there had been considerable dispute about the appropriate criterion to apply in the case of published works. This question was first hotly debated at the ALAI Conference of 1883, where Clunet and Pouillet were the respective champions of the nationality and territoriality approaches.[28] Distinct philosophical differences underlie each approach. Thus, nationality is more readily related to the conception of a work as the expression of an author's personality, linked to him for all time and in all places.[29] By contrast, the territorial criterion is not so much concerned with the regulation of a personal right (which should apply regardless of place of publication), as with a right of commercial exploitation that depends solely upon the place of first publication.[30] There are practical advantages, as well as disadvantages, associated with each approach. The most obvious advantage of the nationality approach is that it dispenses with any need to inquire into the place of first publication.

[27] Additional Act 1896, art 1(2). [28] See paras 2.12ff above.

[29] See generally '*Commentaire des articles 4, 5 et 6 . . .*' [1910] *DA* 59, 61–2; A Françon, 'A propos d'une éventuelle modification de l'article 4 alinéa (3) de la Convention de Berne sur le pays d'origine de l'oeuvre publiée' [1963] *DA* 32, 33–4.

[30] ibid.

On the other hand, there may be difficulties in determining the question of nationality, and particular problems may be caused by the possession of dual nationality (see para 6.68 below). It may also be thought that the criterion is ultimately inconsistent with the basic Conventional principle of national treatment, under which the author is protected, in other countries of the Union, by the laws of those countries rather than his own. The disadvantages of the territoriality criterion are quite the opposite: whilst the ascertainment of the place of first publication is essentially a factual inquiry, there are difficulties in the meaning and scope of the term 'publication' (see paras 6.22ff below). Furthermore, where protection under the Convention depends upon first publication within a Union country, this may impose unreasonable restrictions upon Union authors wishing to obtain protection in a non-Union country. This was the case for many years with regard to the USA, where first publication (and typesetting) within that country was necessary to obtain copyright protection for British authors.[31] This created difficulties for those authors who wished to obtain protection for their works in the large English-speaking American market, as first publication within the USA deprived them of their protection under the Berne Convention.

In the ALAI draft convention of 1883, it was not entirely clear whether the **6.12** criterion of nationality was applicable in the case of unpublished works.[32] However, so far as published works were concerned, the Pouillet approach triumphed, and protection was accorded, in the same terms as in a number of the earlier bilateral conventions, to 'the authors of literary and artistic works appearing or performed in one of the contracting states'.[33] Oddly enough, however, in the revised draft of the Federal Council which was submitted to the 1884 Diplomatic Conference, no distinction was drawn between unpublished and published works, and the nationality criterion was made generally applicable. Thus, protection was accorded to the subjects and citizens of contracting states 'as far as concerns the protection of the rights of authors in their literary and artistic works'.[34] During the Conference, this was modified so as to apply to the works of Union authors published in a Union country (as explained in paras 6.23 and 6.24 below, the acts of 'performance' no longer remained relevant). This change stemmed from a German proposal, and was accepted by the commission without any clear reason for this being given. However, it was linked to another concept that was beginning to assume importance in the evolving Convention text, the concept of a work's 'country of origin'. This is discussed

[31] Copyright Act 1909 (USA), s 16. The 'manufacturing clause' was initially carried over into the 1976 Copyright Act, 17 USC § 601, but was allowed to expire on 1 July 1986.

[32] See ALAI draft text, art 3: *Actes* 1884, 8.

[33] Article 1: ibid, 7.

[34] Federal Council programme, art 2: ibid, 11.

further at paras 6.53ff below, but for the moment it suffices to say that it was of importance in relation to two particular matters: duration of protection and fulfilment of formalities, with regard to which the principle of national treatment was modified so as to require reference to the law of the country of origin of the work. In the case of unpublished works, this was the country of the author's nationality, and in the case of published works it was the place of first publication of the work. In each instance, however, it was required that these countries be members of the Union. In the case of published works, therefore, it seems logical to conclude that the unspoken assumption was that it would be more difficult, as a practical matter, to apply the law of a non-Union country (in relation to the issues of duration and formalities) than it would be where the law of a fellow Union member was concerned. These 'mixed' criteria of eligibility were left unchanged by the subsequent Conference of 1885, and remained the basis of protection under the Berne Convention until the Stockholm Act. One change was made in the Paris Additional Act of 1896, but this was for purposes of clarification only: the 1886 Act did not refer expressly to the need for publication in a Union country to be for the first time. That this must have been intended can be derived from a reading of that Act. However, the commission at the 1896 Conference, while thinking this to be 'perhaps not very necessary', thought nonetheless that the insertion of these words would clarify the situation.[35]

(2) Non-Union authors: country of first publication

6.13 The second point of attachment for application of the Convention is the country in which a non-Union author first publishes the work. Non-Union authors are only protected under the Convention in relation to their published works, and this is subject to the requirement that these works have been either first published in a country of the Union or simultaneously in a country outside the Union and in a country of the Union (for the meanings of 'published' and 'simultaneously', see paras 6.31–6.42 below). The position of non-Union authors has remained unchanged since the 1896 Paris Additional Act.[36] However, the question of whether these authors should be protected, and to what extent, has always raised questions of principle and strategy: of principle, as regards the nature of authors' rights, and of strategy, as regards whether or not the protection of these authors will encourage the adherence of non-Union states to the Union.[37] In the first edition of this work, the treatment of non-

[35] *Actes* 1884, 41.

[36] *Actes* 1896, 160 (report of the commission, presented by Louis Renault). See also Additional Act 1896, art I(1).

[37] See generally paras 6.14ff below.

Union authors was a matter of considerable importance, given the number of significant countries, such as the USA, China, and the then Soviet Union, that were not then Berne members. With the rapid expansion of Berne membership since this time (1987), this has become a marginal question only, although the policy and strategic considerations involved retain their interest and may still have relevance in other contexts.

(a) History of the protection of non-Union authors based on the country of first publication

In the ALAI draft of 1883, this question was not directly addressed, although the text specifically restricted translation rights to Union authors, and it was a reasonable inference that only Union authors were to be covered by the draft convention.[38] However, the Federal Council programme for the 1884 Conference was quite explicit in this regard, as it assimilated to 'subjects and citizens of contracting states' not only subjects and citizens of non-contracting states who were domiciled in a contracting state, but also any who had published their works in a contracting state.[39] This received strong criticism from the German delegation, which took the view that this would not encourage non-contracting states to join the Union.[40] However, the commission adopted a compromise solution under which protection was conferred on the publishers of literary and artistic works published in one of the countries of the Union, and of which the author was a non-Union national.[41] This was an anomalous provision for a Convention dealing with authors' rights, but it was the best accommodation that could be reached between those, such as the French and Swiss, who saw no reason to restrict the protection of the Convention in this way, and those, such as the Germans, who were opposed to the protection of non-Union nationals altogether.[42] In seconding this compromise amendment to the 1884 text, Lavollée (the French delegate) expressed his opinion that the word 'publisher' ('*l'éditeur*') was to be taken in the widest possible sense so as to apply, for example, to the producer of a dramatic performance[43] (this was not necessarily the view of the commission). The 1884 compromise was retained by the 1885 Conference: while the French delegates again sought to widen the scope of the provision, they withdrew their proposal after satisfying themselves that the Convention did not deprive states of the power to apply more generous principles of protection to foreign authors.[44] However, the anomaly of protecting publishers rather than authors was underlined by an interpretation offered by the 1885 commission to the effect that under this provision the nationality 6.14

38 See ALAI draft text, art 5: *Actes* 1884, 8.
39 See Federal Council programme, art 3: ibid, 11.
40 ibid, 43. 41 ibid. 42 ibid. 43 ibid, 44. 44 *Actes* 1885, 42.

of the publisher was a matter of indifference, provided that the latter had a 'permanent and durable establishment in the Union'.[45] Thus, while domicile sufficed in the case of non-Union publishers, it did not in the case of non-Union authors.

(b) The development of the present position

6.15 The question of protecting non-Union authors arose again at the 1896 Conference, and it was here that the present position was worked out. There were a number of draft proposals which allowed protection to such authors on a quite generous basis,[46] as well as a French proposal to add the promoters of dramatic performances to the existing provision (embodying the interpretation put forward by Lavollée at the 1885 Conference).[47] In the meantime, there had also been a change of position by the German Government, which now favoured the protection of works of non-Union authors where these were published in Union countries.[48] It was agreed by the Conference that the criterion of protection for these authors should be the same as for Union authors, that is, first publication in a Union country, and this was duly included in the Additional Act.[49] The term 'publication' also received interpretation for the first time. In essence, this was confined to the issue of a printed edition, thereby excluding other, more transient, forms of communication such as public performance, which the French proposal had sought to include.[50] The result was that non-Union authors could now claim protection within countries of the Union, but this was more limited than that accorded to Union authors. The former did not receive protection for their unpublished works, which, under the new interpretation of 'publication', included works which had been publicly performed in a Union country. This has remained the position under successive texts of the Convention, and the only changes made have been of a drafting nature. Thus, article 1(II) of the Paris Additional Act was made a separate article in the Berlin Act (article 6), and it remained in this position in the Rome and Brussels Acts until it was incorporated in article 3(1)(a) of the Stockholm, Paris Acts. Again, in the Rome Act, the substance of the Berne Protocol of 1914 allowing for retaliatory measures against non-Union countries which offer insufficient protection to Union authors was added to article 6, and this was retained in that article in the Stockholm, Paris Acts: see para 6.19 below. The scope of protection accorded to non-Union authors is also discussed at paras 6.48 and 6.56 below.

---

[45] *Actes* 1885, 42. It is, of course, possible to see the continuing role of publishers here as a relic of earlier national laws where publishers were the most important beneficiaries of protection.

[46] *Actes* 1896, 112 (proposals by the Swiss and Belgian Governments).

[47] ibid, 37–8.

[48] ibid, 113.

[49] Additional Act, art I(2).

[50] See *Actes* 1896, 37–8.

(3) Supplemental criteria of attachment for cinematographic and architectural works whose authors are not Union nationals or residents

(a) Cinematographic works

Article 4 of the 1971 Paris Act also contains supplementary criteria of entitlement which are applicable to the cinematographic works of non-Union authors. The additional criterion of eligibility for protection was proposed in the programme for the Stockholm Revision to take account of those situations where the author(s) of a cinematographic work was not a Union national and the work was unpublished, or had been first published in a country outside the Union.[51] In such cases, it was proposed that a cinematographic work should be protected if its maker had his domicile or headquarters in a country of the Union. This was an extension of the umbrella of the Convention to non-Union authors, and for this reason was opposed by France.[52] On the other hand, it was of benefit to the film copyright countries which only gave copyright protection to the maker of the film, and, to complement this, the UK proposed the addition of a sentence to the effect that countries of the Union should be free to treat the maker of a cinematographic work as its author.[53] After some discussion, Main Committee I approved the principle of the programme amendment, and the matter of its wording was referred to the working group on cinematographic works.[54] The latter proposed the adoption of the wording in the programme, with the substitution of the words 'habitual residence' for 'domicile', in line with the terminology used in the other provisions of the revised text dealing with criteria of eligibility and determination of country of origin.[55] The UK amendment was also rejected, 'as it was generally admitted that the Convention has always been interpreted in the sense suggested in that proposal, and as the situation would be clarified in the proposed new Article 14*bis*'.[56] These proposals were adopted by Main Committee I, and the resultant text was embodied in article 4 of the new Act as follows: **6.16**

> 4. The protection of this Convention shall apply, even if the conditions of Article 3 are not fulfilled, to:
>   (a) authors of cinematographic works the maker of which has his headquarters or habitual residence in one of the countries of the Union; . . .

It will be seen that this provision only comes into play when the basic criteria for eligibility under article 3 have not been met, that is, the author(s) of the cinematographic work is not a national or habitual resident of a Union country, and

[51] Document S/1, *Records* 1967, 95. [52] Document S/28: ibid, 682.
[53] Document S/42: ibid, 687. [54] ibid, 872–4. [55] Document S/190: ibid, 709.
[56] ibid, 1179 (report of Main Committee I).

the work has not been first published in a country of the Union.[57] It is noteworthy that the Berne revisers selected a means that would increase the possibility of the work's inclusion in the Berne system, but at the price of making the producer, rather than the author, the point of attachment for coverage. Although no reference is made here to the case of joint makers, where one of these is situated in a Union country, the report contains the following statement on this situation:

> The wish was expressed that the Report should state that a cinematographic work which is the result of joint making is protected in the Union if one of the joint makers has his headquarters or his habitual residence in a country of the Union.[58]

As noted above in relation to non-Berne authors and first publication in Berne countries, the significance of article 4(a) in relation to cinematographic works must now be very marginal in view of the expansion of Berne membership since the publication of the first edition of this work in 1987.

(b) Architectural works

6.17 The Paris Act also establishes special points of attachment for architectural works. Article 4 provides that, even if the conditions of article 3 are not fulfilled, the provisions of the Convention will apply to authors of works of architecture erected in a country of the Union (article 4(b)). This takes account of the fixed nature of these kinds of work, as well as of the fact that under the definition of 'published works' (see para 6.45 below) the erection of an architectural work does not constitute publication of that work. Thus, in the absence of a provision such as article 4(b), an architect who is not a national of a Union country but who designs a building that is erected permanently in such a country will not be protected under the Convention unless he fulfils the criterion of article 3(1)(b), that is, by first publication of his work within a country of the Union. The latter, in turn, would involve the making available of copies of the work so as to comply with the definition of 'published works' under article 3(4). In the view of the 1963 Study Group, the very fact of construction should be a sufficient link between the work and the country for the work to enjoy the right to protection under the Convention.[59] This view was approved by the successive groups of experts,[60] and finally by the delegates at the Stockholm Conference.[61] The result is that the unpublished architectural works of non-Union authors are now entitled to protection under the Convention. More controversial, however,

---

[57] *Records* 1967, 1179. This provision might be of considerable practical importance, eg in the case of film crews making documentaries in remote (and non-Union countries) or, as in a recently reported instance, of an Italian director making a film in the Peoples' Republic of China with a Chinese crew and actors.

[58] ibid, 1179–80.

[59] 1963 SG 34–5. See also *Records* 1967, vol I, 102.

[60] ibid.

[61] ibid, vol II, 1138 (report of Main Committee I).

was the proposal of the 1963 Study Group that this should also apply to non-Union authors of graphic and three-dimensional works which were affixed to land or to a building situated in a country of the Union.[62] The argument of 'linkage' was the same as for architectural works, but during the discussions in Main Committee I some delegates expressed concern that the degree of permanence of these works might not be the same as for architectural works, and that the advantage of Convention protection might be gained by works which were only temporarily 'affixed' and then later moved.[63] The final wording which was adopted to take account of this objection was 'other artistic works incorporated in a building or other structure located in a country of the Union'. As with cinematographic works under article 4(a), the provision in article 4(b) with respect to architectural works must now be of very marginal significance.

(c) Successors in title

Although the protection conferred by the Convention now applies only to authors (with the deletion of publishers in the Paris Additional Act), it is clear that, once an author is eligible for protection under the Convention, this protection may also be claimed by successors in title such as assignees, beneficiaries and so on. If this were not so, it would make no sense of article 7 which stipulates that the basic term of protection for works under the Convention should be the life of the author plus fifty years. It is also made explicit in article 2(6), which provides that the protection conferred on the works enumerated in that article shall 'operate for the benefit of the author and his successors in title'. This provision has only been in the Convention since the Brussels Revision,[64] when it was added at British insistence.[65] Prior to this, reference had been made to successors in title ('*les ayants cause*') in article 2 of the original Berne Act.[66] This was deleted at the time of the Berlin Revision on the basis that it was clear that the author's right was not an exclusively personal right, but might be disposed of to third parties. Accordingly, any reference to successors in title was superfluous.[67] This was accepted by the Berlin Conference, but apparently the UK Government had doubts about this, as is witnessed by its successful proposal at the Brussels Revision to reinsert a similar provision and to place the matter beyond doubt. It should be noted that no special requirements as to the 6.18

[62] 1963 SG 34–5. See also *Records* 1967, vol I, 102.

[63] *Records* 1967, vol II (objections raised by the Australian and British delegates).

[64] Brussels Act, art 2(4). [65] *Documents 1948* (1951), 164.

[66] In earlier drafts of the Convention, reference had also been made to the personal representatives of authors ('*les mandataires légaux*'): see 1884 draft text, art 5: *Actes* 1884, 78; ALAI draft of 1883, art 4; and Federal Council programme of 1884, art 6: *Actes* 1884, 8 and 11. At the 1885 Conference, however, the commission deleted this term on the basis that a personal representative stood simply in the shoes of his principal (the author): *Actes* 1885, 42 (report of the commission).

[67] *Actes* 1908, 236 (report of the commission).

nationality of the successor in title apply: once the initial entitlement to protection arises under the Convention, the nationality or residence of the person who succeeds to those rights is irrelevant.

(4) **Restriction of protection for non-Union authors**

6.19 Article 6 of the Stockholm, Paris Acts deals with the retaliatory measures which may be taken by countries of the Union against the works of non-Union authors whose countries fail to protect the works of Union authors in 'an adequate manner'.[68] These provisions first appeared in the Berne Additional Protocol of 1914, the background to which is described in para 3.21 above. In the Rome Act the substance of the Protocol was incorporated in article 6 which dealt also with the entitlement to protection of the works of non-Union authors, and it has been retained in essentially the same form in subsequent revisions. The main difference between article 6 of the present Act and article 6 of the Rome and Brussels Acts is that the former deals with the question of retaliation only, while the entitlement of non-Union authors now falls under article 3 (article 3(1)(b)).

(a) Precondition for retaliation

6.20 The precondition for a Union country to take retaliatory measures under article 6(1) is that the non-Union country in question fails to protect the works of the nationals of the Union country 'in an adequate manner'. Although the article does not specify further what is meant by the expression 'in an adequate manner', it is reasonable to conclude that this imports a condition of reciprocity into the Convention as regards authors from non-Union countries (reciprocity being generally rejected as a condition of protection as between Union countries: see para 6.88 below). Under articles 3(1)(b) and 5(1), non-Union authors are accorded national treatment in respect of works which they first publish in a country of the Union, while in all other countries of the Union they receive both national treatment and the benefit of the rights 'specially granted by the Convention in respect of those same works' (see paras 6.74ff below). The effect of article 6(1), however, is that this protection may be restricted if reciprocity is not accorded to the works of Union authors in the country to which the non-Union author belongs. This is not a general kind of reciprocity between non-Union countries and the countries of the union as a whole: it is a far more specific reciprocity applicable between the country of the Union where the non-Union author first publishes his work, and the country of which that

[68] Article 6(1). For further background on this provision, see 'Le nouveau Protocole additionnel, la Convention de Berne Revisée de 1908' [1914] *DA* 79, 93; S P Ladas, *The International Protection of Literary and Artistic Property* (1938) ('Ladas (1938)'), 282ff; H A Howell, 'International Copyright Relations of the United States' (1917) 27 *Yale Law Journal* 348.

author is a national. To take a hypothetical example, it would not have been open to France (a Union country) to take retaliatory measures against the works of American authors before the USA joined the Berne Convention in 1989 on the ground that the USA did not accord adequate protection to the works of nationals of another Union country, such as Canada, where the works of these American authors were first published. The retaliatory measure must, in the first instance, be taken by Canada which is the Union country whose works would not have received reciprocal treatment under US law. This, in turn, suggests that if Canadian works did receive reciprocal treatment under US law, then France would have had no recourse, even if French works did not enjoy the same protection in the USA as Canadian works. However, once Canada has taken such action, the second sentence of article 6(1) leaves it open to other countries of the Union to impose similar restrictions in respect of these works. This provides that:

> If the country of first publication avails itself of this right, the other countries of the Union shall not be required to grant to works thus subjected to special treatment a wider protection than that granted to them in the country of first publication.

This provision was added at the time of the Brussels Revision to avoid the possibility of a non-Union work continuing to receive the full protection of the Convention in other countries of the Union, after its protection in its country of first publication had been restricted.[69] Nonetheless, it is not mandatory for these other Union countries to take such consequential measures. It also appears from the use of the expression 'country of first publication' that the works in relation to which retaliatory action may be taken are limited to those first published in that country. Accordingly, it would not have been open to Canada, in the example given above, to apply restrictions in relation to the works of American authors which were first published in a country of the Union other than Canada, but which still enjoyed Convention protection in Canada by virtue of articles 3(1)(b) and 5(1).[70]

---

69 *Documents 1948* (1951), 180ff.

70 Article 6(1) does not permit retaliation to take the form of a complete denial of protection, but only that this protection may be 'restricted'. The scope of these 'restrictions' is left for the country adopting the measures to judge for itself, but this still leaves a wide discretion. For example, there would be nothing to prevent a requirement being imposed that works from the non-Union country in question should be subjected to particular formalities (perhaps even to a 'manufacturing' requirement, as under the previous US law). Again, the rights accorded to these works could be limited in duration, or even specific rights denied altogether, such as a broadcasting or diffusion right where none is accorded under the law of the non-Union country. However, there are further limitations in art 6(1) with respect to the persons against whom these restrictions may be applied. They can only be invoked in relation to the works of authors of the non-Union country who, at the date of first publication, are (a) nationals of that country, and (b) not habitually resident in one of the countries of the Union. To refer again to the example given above, Canada could not have restricted the protection given to a French author who first

(b) Appraisal of article 6

6.21 Article 6 provides a means for countries of the Union to prevent any abuse of the protection which they are bound to give to authors from non-Union countries under the Berne Convention. While the Convention does not in general require material reciprocity between member countries of the Union, the implicit requirement of reciprocity in the case of non-Union countries provides a disciplinary procedure which can be brought to bear in the worst cases. In fact, this appears to have happened only once since the adoption of the Additional Protocol, and this involved Canadian restrictions in relation to American works adopting retaliatory measures.[71] This may reflect general acceptance of the view that the carrot is better than the stick, and that non-Union countries are more likely to accord similar treatment to the works of Union authors if their own authors are treated generously rather than harshly within the Union. As to

published his work in Canada, and later became an American national. Likewise, Canada could not have restricted the protection given to the works of an American author first published in Canada where the latter was habitually resident at the time in Canada or in another Union country. These limitations derive from the original Protocol of 1914, although the term used in that instrument, and in the subsequent Rome and Brussels Acts, was 'effectively domiciled'. The adoption of the qualifying adjective 'effectively' was clearly adopted so as to avoid claims for exemption on the part of non-Union authors who were only transiently, or fictitiously, in residence in a country of the Union, as in the case of many American authors who would cross the border into Canada for a few days while their book was published there. See [1914] *DA* 79, 81. The expression 'habitually resident' was adopted by the Stockholm Revision Conference, and is consistent with art 3(2) (see para 6.05 above).

Retaliatory measures taken under art 6(1) cannot have a retroactive effect. Thus, art 6(2) provides that such restrictions are not to 'affect the rights which an author may have acquired in respect of a work published in a country of the Union before such restrictions were put into force'. This is only fair, but it will be noted that only rights already acquired are protected: this would not prevent restrictions being imposed in relation to rights which a non-Union author might otherwise acquire subsequently, eg any additional rights 'specially granted' under a later revision of the Convention or additional rights granted under the domestic law of the country of first publication: ibid, 94.

Article 6(3) contains certain procedural requirements as to the notice that a Union country should give of the fact that it has imposed restrictions in accordance with art 6(1). This must be communicated by written declaration to the Director General of WIPO, and the declaration is to specify (a) the countries in regard to which protection is restricted, and (b) the restrictions to which rights of authors who are nationals of those countries are subjected. The Director General is then required to communicate this declaration to all countries of the Union. The giving of the declaration by the country adopting restrictions can hardly be regarded as mandatory for the purposes of the validity of these restrictions. It is not required that the country or the Director General give notice of these restrictions to the country or countries affected. The only purpose of the requirements in art 6(3) is to bring the fact that these restrictions have been made to the notice of other Union countries so that they may consider their own position, and whether or not they also will apply these restrictions.

[71] Canada imposed restrictions on the rights of American authors under ss 13, 14, 15, and 27 of its Copyright Act 1921 in accordance with the Protocol upon its accession to the Protocol of 7 Jan 1924: [1924] *DA* 13. Note also that the UK Copyright Act 1911, ss 23 and 29, allowed for the making of Orders in Council imposing such restrictions (these predated the Protocol).

whether it is permissible for one country of the Union to adopt retaliatory measures against the authors of another country of the Union where the latter does not provide the same level of protection as the first, this is not a live issue under the Convention in the absence of any requirement of material reciprocity between member countries of the Union (see para 6.88 below and the general discussion of the principles of national treatment and independence of protection). On the other hand, the lower level of protection accorded by one country of the Union to the works of other Union countries may constitute a violation of its obligations under the Convention, for which trade sanctions may now be imposed by virtue of the TRIPs Agreement.

B. The Meaning of 'Published Works'

The expression 'published works' is crucial to the operation of article 3(1), and is defined in article 3(3) as follows: **6.22**

> (3) The expression 'published works' means works published with the consent of their authors, whatever may be the means of manufacture of the copies, provided that the availability of such copies has been such as to satisfy the reasonable requirements of the public, having regard to the nature of the work. The performance of a dramatic, dramatico-musical, cinematographic or musical work, the public recitation of a literary work, the communication by wire or the broadcasting of literary or artistic works, the exhibition of a work of art and the construction of a work of architecture shall not constitute publication.

This identification contains both a positive and negative aspect: positive, in the sense that the first sentence defines what is meant by 'published works' and negative, in that the second sentence specifies certain acts that will not constitute publication. It is a definition which has evolved steadily from the time of its introduction into the Interpretative Declaration of 1896. It is also of general application to the Convention as a whole, but its significance, for our present purposes, relates to the eligibility of works of non-Union authors for protection (following the Brussels Revision, it is no longer of any relevance as regards the works of Union authors). More generally, it is of central importance in ascertaining the country of origin of a work, this being the determinant of the kind of protection applicable to a work under the Convention (see para 6.54 below).

(1) History of the definition

(a) The Berne Conferences

Neither the Berne Act nor any of its predecessors contained any definition of the expression 'published works'. Indeed, the ALAI draft of 1883 did not use the **6.23** expression, conforming instead to the wording used in a number of the earlier bilateral conventions.[72] This distinguished between works 'appearing, represented or executed' ('*oeuvres . . . parues, représentées ou exécutées*'), on the one hand, and 'manuscript or unpublished works' ('*les oeuvres manuscrits ou inédites*'), on the other[73] (in English, 'unpublished' seems the most accurate translation of '*inédites*'). In the Federal Council draft, however, only the second category was expressly referred to.[74] In article 2 of the text settled by the 1884 Diplomatic Conference, the word 'published' was used for the first time in relation to Union authors in the composite expression 'their works, whether manuscript or unpublished, or published' ('*leurs oeuvres, soit manuscrits ou inédites, soit publiées*').[75] This was based on a German proposal, and, in relation to the word 'publish' ('*publier*'), the commission commented that this was to be taken in the sense which had hitherto been attached to it in national legislation and jurisprudence.[76] This did not mean that a uniform approach to the meaning of 'publish' and 'published' was to be found in national laws—this, indeed, was not the case[77]—but no attempt was made at this stage to introduce an international definition into the Convention. At the 1885 Conference, however, a French amendment led to the insertion, in article 2 of the final text, of the more elegant wording 'their works, whether published . . . or unpublished' ('*leurs oeuvres, soit publiées . . . ou soit non publiées*').

(b) The Paris Revision

6.24 At the 1896 Conference, the question of defining 'published works' was discussed extensively, as most delegates now thought that some kind of international solution was warranted, in view of the different approaches taken by many national laws.[78] Particular concern was expressed over the problem of dramatic or musical works which might be publicly performed, without actual copies of the work being made available to the public.[79] 'Performance' was an ephemeral or transient method of communicating a work to the world, but under some laws, such as those of the UK,[80] this was considered to be the

---

[72] See eg the Belgian-Sardinian Convention of 24 Nov 1859; the Franco-Belgian Convention of 1 May 1861; the Franco-Netherlands Convention of 29 Mar 1855; the Franco-Russian Convention of 6 Apr 1861; the Franco-Prussian Convention of 2 Aug 1862. See generally J Delalain, *Recueil des Conventions conclues par la France pour la Reconnaissance de la Properiété Littéraire et Artistique* (1866).

[73] ALAI draft text, arts 1 and 3: *Actes* 1884, 7–8.

[74] Federal Council programme, art 5: *Actes* 1884, 11.

[75] 1884 draft text, art 2: *Actes* 1884, 77.

[76] *Actes* 1884, 41.

[77] See 'Etudes générales: La Convention de Berne et la Revision de Paris. IX. Definition du terme "publication", Part II' [1900] *DA* 50.

[78] *Actes* 1896, 161ff (report of the commission).

[79] ibid, 162.

[80] See *Boucciault* v *Delafield* (1863) Hem and Miller 597 and *Boucciault* v *Chatterton* (1876) 8 Ch D 267 (representation in public constituted publication of dramatic works). According to

equivalent of publication. If such an approach were adopted generally under the Convention, this would mean the loss of protection for the works of Union authors first performed in a country outside the Union, even if no copies of the work were issued there, or the issuing took place subsequently within a Union country. It would also give rise to the converse problem with regard to authors from non-Union countries who were given protection for their published works for the first time under the 1896 Revision. The view of the majority of the commission was that ephemeral acts such as performance should be excluded from the scope of the expression 'published works', and that the concept should be restricted to the act of issuing copies, as this was an act which could be more readily and more objectively determined.[81] The commission also took the view that the exhibition of an artistic work should be equated with performance, and accordingly both performance and exhibition were excluded from the scope of publication in the definition which was finally adopted.[82] This read as follows:

> By *published* works [*oeuvres publiées*] must be understood works of which copies have been issued to the public [*oeuvres éditées*] in one of the countries of the Union. Consequently, representation of a dramatic or dramatico-musical work, the performance of a musical work, or the exhibition of a work of art shall not constitute *publication* within the meaning of the above-mentioned Instruments.

This was inserted in paragraph 2 of the Interpretative Declaration, which was open for signature separately from the Additional Act.[83] This therefore left countries such as the UK free to continue to apply their own interpretation of 'publication' to works claiming protection under the Convention.[84] With respect to countries which adhered to the Declaration, these were now obliged to apply the definition in relation to Convention works, although they naturally remained free to apply a different standard to their own national authors, if they wished.

(c) The Berlin and Paris Revisions

The definition adopted by the 1896 Conference was, in substance, retained in the Berlin Revision, except that it was now incorporated in the main text of the Convention as article 4(4), and the definition was extended so as to include the construction of a work of architecture in the list of acts not constituting **6.25**

W Briggs, *The Law of International Copyright* (1906) ('Briggs (1906)'), 314, the same rule would apply, by analogy to musical works, whilst it had also been held that the exhibition of artistic works in public could amount to publication: *Blanchet* v *Ingram* (1887) 3 TLR 687 and *Blank* v *Footman* (1884) 39 Ch D 678.

81 *Actes* 1896, 163.
82 ibid.

83 Interpretative Declaration, para 2: English translation taken from *Correspondence No 3* (1886), 23.

84 See further Briggs (1906), 313–17.

publication. At the 1928 Conference, there was a Polish proposal to delete the definition, and to refer instead, where relevant, to '*oeuvres non éditées*' and '*oeuvres éditées*'—expressions which can be accurately, if clumsily, translated into English as 'works, copies of which have not been issued to the public' and 'works, copies of which have been issued to the public'.[85] This had the advantage of simplicity, as it clearly excluded, by inference, any ephemeral means of public communication from the scope of publication. However, although there was considerable support for this change among the delegates, the commission decided not to adopt it, but to retain unchanged the existing definition which 'had not to the present time given rise to difficulties of application'.[86]

(d) The Brussels Revision

6.26 This introduced a number of refinements to the definition, although its basic structure, with its positive and negative aspects, remained the same.[87] First, its sphere of application was restricted to articles 4, 5, and 6 (those articles of the 1948 Act dealing with persons protected, and the criteria of protection). Secondly, it was required that the copies which had been issued to the public should have been 'made available in sufficient quantities'. Thirdly, it was stated that these copies might be manufactured in any way ('whatever may be the means of manufacture of the copies'). Finally, public recitation of a literary work and the transmission or broadcast of literary or artistic works were added to the list of acts not constituting publication. As each of these changes bears on the present wording of the definition in article 3(3) of the Stockholm text, they are considered in more detail below where apposite.

(2) The elements of the present definition of 'published works'

(a) Its scope of application

6.27 As noted above, the Brussels Act limited the application of the definition to articles 3, 4, and 5, rather than to the Convention as a whole. The reason for this restriction seems to have been that the Conference wished to allow for the application of wider concepts of publication under national law under the other provisions of the Convention.[88] This was not unusual in national law, for example, in the FRG, where words denoting publication in both a narrow and a wide sense were used ('*Erscheinen*' and '*Veröffentlichung*').[89] Under the Convention, however, the need for a wider meaning of 'publication' was really only of practical significance in relation to article 7(4) of the Brussels Act, where the

[85] *Actes* 1928, 233. [86] ibid, 235. [87] *Documents 1948* (1951), 171ff.

[88] ibid, 170. See also *Records* 1967, vol I, 96 (BIRPI/Swedish Government programme).

[89] See generally ibid, 179–83 (Professor Ulmer).

term of protection ran, in the case of pseudonymous and anonymous works, from the date of the work's publication. In the light of this, the 1963 Study Group thought that it was unsatisfactory for an expression used in the Convention to have two different possible meanings, according to which part of the Convention it appeared in. The Group therefore recommended that the definition be made applicable again to the Convention as a whole, together with an appropriate modification of the wording of article 7(4).[90] This was done simply by the deletion of the words 'for purposes of articles 4, 5 and 6', and this amendment was approved, without demur, by the successive committees of experts, and finally by Main Committee I of the Conference itself.[91]

(b) The need for the author's consent

The requirement for works to be published with the consent of their authors was inserted in the definition in the 1967 Revision, although it seems clear that this had been implicit in its earlier versions. The amendment arose out of the work of the 1963 Study Group which considered that, in view of the differing ways in which a work might be made available to the public (particularly in light of new technological developments), it should be made explicit that this should be done with the author's consent.[92] The wording proposed by the Study Group, however, was that the work should be 'lawfully published', and this met with an objection from the UK Government that it would cover cases where a work was made available to the public without the author's consent, for example, where this happened under a compulsory licence.[93] Accordingly, the UK Government proposed that the word 'lawfully' be replaced with the words 'with the consent of the author'.[94] The main reason for the British proposal appeared to be concern that the Study Group proposal might limit the duration of protection for certain kinds of works under article 7, where the term of protection for such works was calculated from their date of publication (or the date on which they were 'lawfully made available to the public').[95] However, as the only kinds of works affected by this were anonymous and pseudonymous works, the problem was not as great as first appeared. Moreover, there was a possible adverse effect that might flow from the adoption of the British formulation, with respect to non-Union authors whose interest was to have publication within a Union country at the earliest possible time. These authors, therefore, were not likely to be overly concerned by the fact that their works might be **6.28**

90 1963 SG 26–7. See also *Records* 1967, vol I, 170.
91 *Records* 1967, vol I, 97; vol II, 1138–9 (report of Main Committee I).
92 1963 SG 28–9. See also *Records* 1967, vol I, 97.
93 *Records* 1967, vol II, 842 (minutes of Main Committee I).
94 ibid, 687 (Document S/42).
95 ibid, 842 (comments of W Wallace, the British delegate in Main Committee I).

published without their consent in a Union country (say under a compulsory licence), as this unauthorized publication would nonetheless secure them protection under the Convention.[96] In the event, the British amendment was approved by a majority of Main Committee I, and was duly inserted in the definition.[97] One matter, however, on which the definition remains silent is whether the consent of the author needs to be express, or whether it may be implied from the circumstances. This remains a matter for national legislation, but as a general rule it seems reasonable to say that, as the aim of the Convention is the protection of the rights of authors in their literary and artistic works, the interpretation most favourable to the interests of the author in each particular case should be adopted.

(c) Copies

6.29 In the earlier versions of the definition (Paris to Rome Acts), it seems clear that the words 'copies . . . issued to the public' referred principally to printed or graphic reproductions of works. This was confirmed by the exclusion, from the concept of publication, of more ephemeral or transient embodiments of works. However, it will also be clear that, even as early as 1896, there were other permanent forms in which work could be fixed, for example, piano rolls and phonographic recordings (in the case of musical works), and cinematographic films (in the case of dramatic and literary works). As a result, there was uncertainty as to whether publication could occur where copies of these other kinds of fixations were issued to the public. As the Convention provided no specific guidance on this point, it was left to national law, and different national solutions were to be found. Thus, in Belgium, the issue of phonographic cylinders and discs were held not to be an '*édition*', on the ground that these embodiments of works could not be comprehended by human understanding as in the case of a printed sheet of music.[98] In the UK, the issue of phonographic recordings to the public was expressly excluded from the scope of publication under the Copyright Act 1911.[99] On the other hand, a contrary position was adopted by the French courts,[100] and this created a situation of considerable uncertainty.[101] The question was of particular importance in relation to non-Union authors whose works might first become available in a Union country in one of these forms, such as a phonographic record.

[96] ibid (comments of G Straschnov, the delegate for Monaco).

[97] ibid (twenty-two votes to twelve, with two abstentions).

[98] Court of Cassation, Decision of 7 May 1907, noted in [1907] *DA* 76.

[99] Copyright Act 1911, s 1(3).

[100] Court of Appeals, Paris, in *Enoch et Cie* c *Société des phonographs*, 1 Feb 1905, noted in [1905] *DA* 35.

[101] Ladas (1938), 299–300. See also [1901] *DA* 53–4.

In the Brussels Revision, therefore, an attempt was made to introduce a uniform approach on this matter, and the programme, proceeding on the basis that there was no reason to differentiate between these methods of fixation, proposed the addition of the words, 'regardless of the mode or form of issuing to the public (printing, discs, films, etc)'.[102] There was strong support for this approach from a number of delegations, particularly the French,[103] but equally strong opposition came from the British delegation.[104] The reason for the British objections arose from the fact that, in the UK, the copying or reproduction right had always been regarded as distinct from the performing right.[105] A logical consequence of this approach was that a sound recording or film could only be regarded as the fixation of a performance of a work, not as a copy of that work. Thus, the British were opposed to the inclusion of any list, such as that in the proposal of the programme which specifically included sound recordings or films. After the matter was further considered by a sub-committee,[106] a differently worded draft, which omitted the list, was approved by the Conference.[107] This inserted, at the end of the first sentence, the words 'whatever may be the means of manufacture of the copies' ('*quel que soit la mode de fabrication des exemplaires*'). It will be noted that the word 'copies' ('*exemplaires*') was used for the first time in the French text, although this word had always been used in the English translation of the phrase '*les oeuvres éditées*' ('works copies of which . . .'). No real significance, however, could be attached to the use of this word in the French text, as the omission of any list still left to national legislation the task of specifying what were and were not 'copies' for the purposes of the revised definition. Thus, it was open to French law to continue to regard sound recordings and films of works as 'copies' of those works,[108] and for British law to continue to regard them as 'fixations' (a point of some importance in relation to the acquisition of copyright protection under British law), but not as 'copies'. The latter continued to exclude the issuing of records from the scope of publication until the 1988 revision of the copyright law,[109] and this had also been the case with a number of other Union countries which had derived their copyright laws from the UK.[110] The inequity of this approach as regards non-Union **6.30**

[102] *Documents 1948* (1951), 170. [103] ibid, 174. [104] ibid.

[105] See generally Laddie, Prescott, and Vitoria, *The Modern Law of Copyright*, 2nd edn (2000), 56, para 3.8.

[106] *Documents 1948* (1951), 124–5 (there were in fact two successive sub-committees that considered the question).

[107] ibid, 96–7 (report of the *rapporteur général*, Marcel Plaisant).

[108] See further S Durrande, 'The Concept of Publication in the International Conventions' (1981) 111 *RIDA* 72, 86ff.

[109] Copyright Act 1956, s 49(2)(a). Under the UK Copyright, Designs and Patents Act 1988, s 175(4), this is no longer the case.

[110] See eg New Zealand, Copyright Act 1962, s 3(2)(d)(i); New Zealand subsequently adopted the approach of the UK Copyright, Designs and Patents Act 1988, see NZ Copyright Act 1994.

authors of musical works that were brought to the attention of the public in Union countries only in the form of phonograph records will be readily apparent, insofar as these authors would have obtained protection in many Union countries but not in the UK. This may lead to an even more curious situation where the issuing of sound recordings actually took place first within the UK: while the work in question would thereupon gain protection in these other countries of the Union, it would have received none in the UK, but the latter would still have been its country of origin for the purposes of the Convention. Despite these problems, no attempt to reach a uniform international solution on this point was made in the Stockholm Revision, and the Brussels wording continues unchanged in the present text.[111]

(d) Meaning of 'publication' ('edition'*)*

6.31 This is perhaps one of the most difficult questions, not the least because, for English speakers, there are problems of translation from the original French text. As noted above, the original English translation of the French words '*les oeuvres éditées*' was 'works copies of which have been issued to the public'. This left a number of matters unclear. First, what acts constituted an 'issuing' or '*édition*' of a work? Secondly, what quantum was necessary for a work to be considered as 'issued' or '*éditées*'? Thirdly, was it necessary that the making of the copies take place within the same country as the 'issuing' or '*édition*'? Fourthly, should the *locus* for the 'issuing' or '*édition*' be within the country in question, and need there be one central place for this? Fifthly, what was meant by 'the public'? Sixthly, need the 'issuing' or '*édition*' be a conscious act on the part of the author, or was this simply a state of fact to be objectively determined? Finally, at what time was publication to be regarded as having occurred? Some of these questions have been resolved, at least partially, in the subsequent revisions which have been made to the definition; others remain unanswered. While all these issues are closely interrelated, they are considered here separately for ease of exposition.[112]

(e) Acts constituting an 'edition'

6.32 This was not directly addressed in the 1896 Revision, but the commission stated that it understood the term as meaning that the work had been placed 'directly on view or on sale by someone who takes charge and responsibility for the publication'.[113] This was quite a restrictive interpretation, as it is quite possible

[111] See Stockholm, Paris Acts, art 3(4). Cf the UCC, art VI, which defines 'publication' as meaning 'the reproduction and distribution to the public of copies of a work from which it can be read or otherwise visually perceived'. This clearly excludes sound recordings.

[112] See further Ladas (1938), 294ff; Durrande (n 108 above); A Tournier, 'The Out-of-date Notion of Publication in the Berne Convention' (1963) 39 *RIDA* 3; G A Koumantos, 'The Notion of Publication in the Berne Convention' (1964) 40 *RIDA* 4.

[113] *Actes* 1896, 162.

to conceive of ways, other than by sale or exposure to sale, in which a work can be 'issued' or '*éditées*', for example, by free distribution or by loan. Again, if the view is taken that publication can occur where a work is embodied in a cinematographic film, sales to the public do not take place on the same scale as with a printed book, although it might be reasonable to say that a film has been made available to the public when it is released for general exhibition in cinemas, or when video recordings of it become available for hire in video shops. Accordingly, a number of Union countries took more liberal views as to the kinds of acts which could constitute an 'issuing' or '*édition*' of a work.[114] These questions, however, were not considered further by either the Berlin or Rome Conferences, but they were taken up by the UK Government in its proposals for the planned Brussels Conference of 1935. The British suggestion was that the act of publication should be understood as having taken place when copies of a work had been 'placed at the disposal of the public' ('*mis à la disposition du public*').[115] A similar proposal was repeated at the Brussels Revision Conference, and after consideration by the special sub-committee on article 4(4), the words 'made available . . . to the public' were added to the definition.[116] Although there was a change in this wording by the Stockholm and Paris Conferences (see further para 6.35 below), the concept of 'making available' was still retained.[117] This more general formula clearly embraces more than the acts of sale or offering for sale, although its width remains ultimately a matter for national law. It seems clear though that the acts of hiring and free distribution should be included. In addition, it appears (and confirmation for this is to be found in the discussions of Main Committee I at the Stockholm Conference[118]) that a work may become available to the public without the latter being placed in actual physical possession of copies of that work. This could occur through the action of an intermediary who has possession of the copy which he then causes to be communicated to members of the public, as in the case of the manager of a concert hall or the proprietor of a cinema who are responsible for the public performance or exhibition of a large scale orchestral work or cinematographic film. In such circumstances, the works in question are 'made available' to the public, although the physical copies of the work are only received by the concert hall manager or cinema proprietor. These matters are considered further in the following paragraphs.

[114] See Ladas (1938), 295ff.

[115] See the commentary on these proposals by the International Office, published in [1936] *DA* 50, 51.

[116] *Documents 1948* (1951), 174.

[117] ibid, 124–5.

[118] *Records* 1967, vol I, 845ff.

(f) 'Quantum necessary'

6.33 It is clear from the preceding paragraph that the form of the copy of a work affects the way in which it is 'made available' to the public. In this regard, the differences that arise in relation to cinematographic films and orchestral works have already been noted. As a result, it is difficult to lay down any general rule as to the number of copies of a work which should be made available in order to constitute a publication. At one extreme, could the issuing of a single copy suffice (as in the case of a cinematographic or musical work)? At the other extreme, will there be publication where a work is circulated in considerable quantities, but surreptitiously, as was the case of '*samizdat*' editions in certain countries in the former Eastern European communist countries? Furthermore, just as there can be 'colourable' imitations of works for the purposes of infringement, can there also be 'colourable' publications undertaken, for example, by a non-Union author wishing to gain 'back-door access' to the benefits of the Convention, and who does so by making available only a small number of copies?[119]

6.34 The question of quantum was not considered at the Berlin or Rome Revision, although the commission at the Berlin Conference expressed the view that publication should be 'serious and not fictitious'.[120] Another of the changes to the definition of 'published works' suggested by the UK Government in its proposals for the 1936 Conference was directed to this problem, and referred to the need for 'a certain number of copies' to have been placed at the disposal of the public for publication to have taken place.[121] In the 1948 Conference, the sub-committee appointed to consider article 4(4) recommended the insertion of the word 'effectively' before the words 'made available to the public' ('*mis effectivement à la disposition du public*').[122] After further discussions, however, a Belgian and French proposal to add the words 'in sufficient quantities' ('*en quantité suffisante*') was accepted by the Conference,[123] and these were duly incorporated within the final Brussels text. At the very least, this qualification to the definition could be seen as providing some protection against purely colourable or fictitious publications.

[119] Given the large number of member states, authors today may face a different problem. Choice of place of first publication may be motivated not as much by desire to ensure the work's Berne coverage, as by a choice of country of origin. As the further discussion of art 5(4) at paras 6.53ff below reveals, authors are not entitled to the substantive protections of the Berne Convention in their countries of origin. As a result, if the domestic law of one potential country of origin were less author-favourable than in another, the author might seek to publish first in the latter state.

[120] *Actes* 1908, 241.

[121] [1936] *DA* 50, 51.

[122] *Documents 1948* (1951), 124–5.

[123] ibid, 96–7 (report of Plaisant).

Was this formulation also adequate to cover the multiplicity of ways in which different kinds of work might be made available to the public? The 1963 Study Group thought so. In its view, what was a sufficient quantity should depend upon the circumstances of each case, bearing in mind the different conditions under which various works were made available to the public. Thus, the Study Group suggested that in the case of some works, such as the scores of serious musical works, the making available to the public, on a hiring basis, of one or a small number of copies should suffice for publication. This interpretation would also apply to cinematographic works, which at that time usually only became available to the public when they were hired or sold to intermediaries, that is, to cinema proprietors.[124] However, a number of Union countries were not satisfied with this interpretation, and took the position that further clarification was required in the definition, particularly with regard to cinematographic works. A number of proposals were therefore put forward for consideration by the Stockholm Conference, when it met in June 1967. These included the following: '. . . made available in such a manner as to make the work accessible to the public' (the Netherlands),[125] '. . . the availability of such copies is sufficient to render the work accessible to the public' (South Africa),[126] and 'provided that the availability of such copies has been sufficient to satisfy the requirements of the public' (FRG, Luxembourg, South Africa, and Monaco—the 'joint proposal').[127] A French proposal went further, and proposed a separate provision to govern cinematographic works, namely that these were to be considered as published 'as from the date on which one or more copies of the work were distributed with a view to public performance, on condition that such performance effectively took place'.[128] Each of these proposals came in for criticism during the discussions of Main Committee I, but it emerged from these that the majority of delegates favoured a general definition that would encompass cinematographic works, while continuing to exclude fictitious publications.[129] Finally, the joint proposal was adopted by a majority of the Committee,[130] and was then sent for refinement to the drafting committee (chaired by William Wallace of the UK). This committee made three further modifications: for reasons of style, the word 'sufficient' was replaced by the words 'such as'; the word 'reasonable' was inserted before the word 'requirements'; and the notion of 'reasonable requirements' was qualified by the addition of the words 'having regard to the nature of the work' to the end of the sentence, so as to show that it was envisaged that publication could occur in different ways in 6.35

124 *Records* 1967, vol I, 96–7.
125 ibid, 688 (Document S/49).
126 ibid (Document S/53).
127 ibid, 689 (Document S/60).
128 ibid, 682 (Document S/27).
129 ibid, vol II, 845ff.
130 ibid, 847 (twenty-six votes to six, with nine abstentions).

different circumstances.[131] These modifications were unanimously adopted by Main Committee I, and the words finally inserted in the Stockholm text were as follows: '. . . provided that the availability of such copies has been such as to satisfy the reasonable requirements of the public, having regard to the nature of the work'.[132]

(g) 'Reasonable requirements of the public'

6.36 One point, however, that remains unclear in the above wording is whether the copies in question must actually have been communicated to the public for publication to occur, or whether it is sufficient if they are available for this purpose. The obvious case in point here is where a work is available for communication to the public, but there is no demand for it from that public, for example, where the copy of a work is a book and nobody asks for it, or a cinematographic work where nobody goes to a cinema to see it. In such circumstances, is publication deferred until such time as a demand for copies has arisen, and the 'reasonable requirements of the public' have, at that point of time, been satisfied? The wording of the definition indicates that it is the availability of copies that constitutes publication. Thus, if there is no public demand for copies, this should be irrelevant—the copies are available to meet any demand that may reasonably be expected to exist, and the author's Berne coverage should not be prejudiced by the fact that there is none at all. What the reasonable requirements of the public are may differ widely according to the nature of the work, but the final words of the definition expressly take account of this fact. Thus, in the case of certain academic treatises, the demands of the public may be expected to be very small, and it may be perfectly reasonable for the publisher to make available only a small number of copies. Having done this, the status of 'published work' should not be denied the work, simply because no one chooses to buy the book. The same may be true of the first novel of an unknown author. On the other hand, if only a limited quantity of copies of a new novel by a well-known author were to be made available, this might be completely inadequate to satisfy the reasonable requirements of the public, and in such a case publication would not have occurred. The standard of 'reasonableness' seems a fair one to apply in all these cases, and is not a matter that can be made the subject of numerous qualifications in a general conventional definition. In particular cases, these will be matters for decision under national legislation, but there is nothing in the Convention definition which denies the status of 'published work' to a book that no one wants (at least at the start), or, at the other extreme, a work which suddenly becomes an unexpected success, and the initial stocks of which are quickly exhausted.

[131] *Records*, 1967, 855.   [132] ibid.

Nevertheless a particular problem has been identified in the case of works that require the services of an intermediary to effect publication, such as cinematographic works or serious musical works. Is it sufficient that copies of these works have been offered to ('made available to') the intermediary for publication to take place, or must the latter have actually taken steps to communicate the work to the public, for example, by projecting the film in a cinema, or arranging for a public performance of the musical work in a concert hall? Is it possible to talk of satisfying the reasonable requirements of the public if there has been no opportunity to assess whether any demand from the public exists for the work? In the case of books, phonograms, or videograms this is easy—once copies are offered for sale, hire or the like, the public is free to decide for itself. This freedom, however, is non-existent where a work's first public exposure occurs through public performance or exhibition, and an intermediary, such as a cinema proprietor, determines not to exhibit the work in the first place. Differing interpretations of the way in which the Convention definition of 'published works' should be applied in these circumstances are possible. The French commentators Desbois, Françon, and Kéréver argue that publication requires that the requirements of the public have in fact been satisfied, that is, that the film has been projected.[133] An alternative view, put forward by Durrande, asserts that all that is required by the definition in the Stockholm text is that the availability of copies be such as to satisfy the reasonable requirements of the public, without there being in fact any need for communication of the work.[134] According to this view, which is based on a literal reading of the definition, if a work is brought to the notice of the public indirectly, through the services of an intermediary who alone possesses physical copies of the work, the requirement of the definition in article 3(3) is to be interpreted as follows: 'for a cinematographic film to be deemed to have been published, the availability of copies to distributors must have been such as to satisfy the requirements of the public (ie if the distributors decide to programme the film in the cinemas under their control)'.[135] With respect, this second interpretation appears wrong: the purpose of publication is the making available of copies of a work to the public, and while this may be done through intermediaries without the actual copies of the work passing into the physical possession of members of the public ('having regard to the nature of the work'), the simple act of making copies available to the intermediary cannot suffice. The latter are not the 'public' (as to the meaning of this, see para 6.39 below), and it cannot be argued that the requirements of the definition have **6.37**

[133] Desbois et al (1976), 134–5. These authors also suggest an intermediate solution to the effect that if a sufficient number of copies of the film to satisfy the reasonable requirements of the public have been distributed, the work should be considered as published; but that if there is proof that a real exploitation of the work has not occurred; it should not be considered as published.

[134] Durrande (n 108 above), 106–7.

[135] ibid, 108. Cf 17 USC § 101 (definition of publication includes offering the work to a group of persons for public performance).

been satisfied if this is all that has happened. For publication to occur, there must have been some public showing of the work for the reasonable requirements of the public to be met: if there are no such requirements, then a limited number of showings, or perhaps only one, may be all that is necessary for publication to occur. The reverse problem arises in the case of the *samizdat* editions of works mentioned above, where quite large numbers of a work may have circulated illegally among certain groups in a country. This was a phenomenon of cultural life in the former USSR and other former Soviet bloc countries. Again, a similar answer, denying these the status of 'published works', may be given, on the ground that the availability of these copies to a restricted public cannot satisfy the 'reasonable requirements of the public' within the meaning of the definition.[136] As a result, these works could subsequently obtain Berne Convention coverage by being later published in a Union country. While the works remained unpublished, and their authors were not nationals of Union countries, however, the works would not have been protected within the Union.[137]

(h) Place of manufacture of copies and place of publication

6.38 As these questions are closely related, they are considered together. Conceptually, the manufacture of copies and their publication are distinct acts, so no problem should arise if they are made in one country and then brought into another country where they are then made available to satisfy the reasonable requirements of the public in that country. This may, of course, be a common occurrence where non-Union authors are concerned. There is nothing in the definition of 'published works' which requires any contrary conclusion, and this indeed was the view of the commission at the 1896 Conference,[138] and has been the approach which has long been adopted in the laws of many Union countries.[139] More problems, however, arise in relation to the place of publication. Must the making available occur wholly within the country in question, or will it suffice for publication in country A if the requirements of the public in that country are satisfied from suppliers situated in country B, for example, through mail orders? In other words, does distribution or circulation of copies of a work within a country suffice for the purposes of publication within that country? Ladas argues against this conclusion, pointing to the fact that words indicating

[136] On this point, see the decision of the Bundesgerichtshof in the '*August Fourteenth*' case in the FRG: noted in [1976] *IIC* 134 and [1975] *GRUR Int* 361, and commented on by A Dietz, 'Letter from the FRG' [1980] *Copyright* 85, 144. See further Durrande (n 108 above), 150ff. See also *Bodley Head Ltd* v *Flegon* [1972] 1 WLR 680 (the same case in the UK).

[137] With respect to works that would have been deemed published in non-Union Soviet bloc countries, they would not have qualified for protection on publication, but would nonetheless have subsequently obtained protection when their countries of origin later joined the Berne Convention. See further the discussion of art 18 at para 6.117.

[138] *Actes* 1896, 162.

[139] See, the review of national case law by Ladas (1938), 294–7, and the commentary by the International Office in [1936] *DA* 51.

this explicitly would have been included in the definition if this had been intended ('*placées en circulation*' rather than '*éditées*').[140] Thus, there must be an actual making available of copies within the country in question, which implies, in turn, the existence of some centre (or centres) for distribution within that country. This question has not elicited comment in the preparatory materials of the successive revision conferences which have considered the matter of publication. However, support for the Ladas interpretation is to be found in the commentary of the International Office which was prepared in relation to the proposals and counter-proposals which were submitted by Union countries for the postponed 1936 Conference.[141] Furthermore, this seems to be a reasonable interpretation of the wording of the definition, in light of the principal function which the concept of 'published works' now plays in the framework of the Convention with regard to non-Union authors: if the purpose of the definition was to prevent back-door entry to the benefits of Convention protection, it is unlikely that it was intended that publication could occur through mail order. However, a different result may follow in the case of works where the issuing of only a few copies will suffice for the purposes of publication ('having regard to the nature of the work'). Thus, in the case of a cinematographic work, the sending of a limited number of copies from one country to another may suffice for publication in the second country.[142]

(i) The meaning of 'the public'

These words have appeared in each of the successive texts of the definition of 'published works'. Giving them their ordinary meaning, there is no warrant for interpreting them as referring to any restricted group of persons or 'sub-publics', even though, as we have seen, the 'public' for any particular work may be very small, or even non-existent, at the time of publication. The essential requirement is that there is no limitation placed on the persons to whom the work is made available, as is the case when an edition of a book is limited to a special class of persons, such as members of a professional organization or a closed group of subscribers, or when a film is exhibited to a limited audience, as at a film festival. This was the understanding of many delegates who participated in the discussions of Main Committee I at the Stockholm Conference[143] and accords with the position taken in many national laws.[144] **6.39**

[140] Ladas (1938), 297. [141] [1936] *DA* 51.

[142] See here the decision of the Bundesgerichtshof in the FRG in the '*Gold Rush*' case, 19 May 1972, noted in [1973] 4 *IIC* 245. Cf the earlier decision of the Reichsgericht in the '*Zola translation*' case, 20 Sept 1930, noted in [1931] *GRUR* 283.

[143] *Records* 1967, vol II, 846–7.

[144] See eg in the UK the *'Oscar' Trade Mark* case [1980] *FSR* 429 and the '*August Fourteenth*' decision referred to in n 136 above. Cf the discussion of the 'public' in 'communication to the public' at para 12.02 below.

(j) Need for intention

6.40 The definition does not say explicitly whether the act of publication must be an intentional one, or whether it is simply an objective fact to be determined independently of the author's state of mind. Ladas, writing in 1938, favoured the second alternative, after a survey of national case law which had largely held to this effect.[145] A consideration of the wording of the present definition leads to a similar result. It is essentially concerned with a state of facts, namely whether the availability of copies is such as to satisfy the reasonable requirements of the public, having regard to the nature of the work. If this is established, then the author's intentions can have no relevance. In other words, there seems to be no basis, in the definition, for arguing that an author may change the character of a situation where his work is freely available to all from one of 'publication' to one of 'non-publication' by the blunt assertion that he did not intend publication to occur. The only situation where this would not be so is where the author has made it clear that he only wishes his work to be circulated on a limited basis, for example, for criticism or evaluation by friends or colleagues, and it is then made generally available without his consent. The latter situation is, of course, excluded from the scope of publication by the definition: nonetheless, the ascertainment of all these facts, including the author's intentions, is still a wholly objective process.

(k) Time of publication

6.41 The making available of copies may be a continuing process, as copies may become available at different places within a country at successive points of time. At what point of time does publication occur—at the beginning or end of this process? The definition offers no guidance on this matter, and it is therefore a matter to be determined by national legislation. Nonetheless, it is submitted that the question is a purely factual one, necessitating an inquiry as to the point of time at which copies of the work become available so as to satisfy the reasonable requirements of the public. The answer to this will depend very much on the nature of the work, and should be left as a matter for national tribunals to determine for themselves.

(l) 'Simultaneous publication'

6.42 Article 3(4) defines the concept of 'simultaneous publication'. It often happens that a work is published at the same time, or 'simultaneously', in two or more countries. In the case of a non-Union author who publishes his work simultaneously in both a Union and non-Union country, does this suffice to gain him protection under the Convention? Again, where a work is published

[145] Ladas (1938), 297–8.

simultaneously in several countries of the Union, which is to be regarded as the country of origin of the work? The answers to these questions are dealt with in more detail in para 6.56 below, but for the moment it suffices to note that article 3(4) defines 'simultaneous publication' for the purposes of the Convention as meaning the publication of a work in two or more countries within thirty days of its first publication. The notion of 'simultaneous publication' has been in the Convention since the Berne Act,[146] but it was not defined until the Brussels Revision, when a Finnish proposal for the thirty-day period of grace was adopted.[147] Prior to this, the question had been considered at length by the Rome Conference, but it had been impossible to reach agreement on the length of the period.[148]

(3) Acts not constituting publication: the negative aspect of the definition

Under the Stockholm Act, the acts excluded from publication are: the performance of a dramatic, dramatico-musical, cinematographic or musical work, the public recitation of a literary work, the communication by wire or the broadcasting of literary or artistic works, the exhibition of a work of art, and the construction of a work of architecture. The first three can be regarded as ephemeral or transient modes of communication to the public, involving no making available of 'copies' of the work communicated. The last two involve different considerations, and are best considered separately. **6.43**

(a) Performance, recitation, communication by wire and broadcasting

The essence of each of these modes of communication is that no 'copy' of the work communicated is actually made available, either directly or indirectly (as occurs where a cinematographic work is exhibited, or an orchestral work is performed). They are ephemeral or transient events which, by their very nature, are more difficult to prove than the making available of copies. In this regard, it is important to distinguish between these modes of communication, and the concept of 'indirect availability' which is now embraced by the Stockholm definition. Although the public in the latter circumstances receives its knowledge of the work in question through an exhibition or performance, it is not the exhibition or performance itself that constitutes the publication; it is the making available of copies which are then communicated to the public through the subsequent exhibition or performance. The exclusion of ephemeral modes of communication from the scope of publication has been an integral part of the Convention definition since the Interpretative Declaration of 1896: the acts of recitation, communication by wire and broadcasting were added, by way of **6.44**

---

[146] Berne Act, art 2(3).
[147] *Documents 1948* (1951), 174.
[148] *Actes* 1928, 234–5.

analogy, in the Brussels Revision, so as to exclude these 'fugitive' forms of utilization by virtue of which non-Union authors might otherwise be able to claim the protection of the Convention.[149] On the face of it, there is an imbalance in the exclusion of communications by wire and broadcasting as these apply only to literary or artistic works. Does this mean that the communication or broadcasting of musical, dramatic, or cinematographic works will therefore constitute publication of these works, although this would not be the case if they were performed? While the drafting of these exclusions could be clearer, it seems correct to say that this is not the correct construction of this part of the definition of 'published works'. As regards each of the other forms of communication which are excluded from the concept of publication, the indefinite singular article is used to indicate the particular category of work in question, for instance the performance of 'a dramatic, dramatico-musical, cinematographic or musical work', the recitation of a 'literary work', and so on. Furthermore, each of these acts is closely related to the nature of the work with which it is coupled. On the other hand, as regards communication by wire and broadcasting, the use of the plural indicates that what is intended here is the entire category of subject matter covered by the Convention, namely 'literary and artistic works', an expression which is defined in very wide terms in article 2 and embraces, among other things, musical, dramatic, and cinematographic works. This interpretation is confirmed by the fact that in all the preparatory works of the Convention, it is made clear that one of the principal objects of restricting the scope of the definition of 'published works' was to prevent too ready access to the benefits of Berne Union protection by non-Union authors.[150] We will consider later (at para 6.52 below) the effect of communication to the public by digital media on the concept of publication. Digital communications share some of the qualities of broadcasting and other 'fugitive' forms of utilization, but they also allow the members of the public receiving the transmission to make a copy or copies of the work thus communicated.

(b) Exhibition of works of art and construction of works of architecture

6.45 The first of these exclusions was inserted in the original definition of 1896. In recommending its adoption, the commission argued that the exhibition of a work of art was analogous to the performance of a musical or dramatic work, and, if the latter did not constitute publication of those works, neither should the former.[151] The logic behind this is difficult to discern, if regard is had to the

[149] *Documents 1948* (1951), 170 (comments of International Office on programme for Conference).

[150] See eg *Actes* 1896, 165–6 (report of the commission); *Records* 1967, vol II, 846–7 (minutes of Main Committee I).

[151] *Actes* 1896, 163.

reasoning adduced by the commission in support of excluding performances from the concept of publication, namely that their ephemeral nature made them more difficult to prove than the fact of '*édition*'. What could be more easy to prove than the exhibition of a solid object, such as a painting or sculpture? The timing and place of such an event can be as readily recorded and confirmed as in the case of the sale or hire of copies of a book or sound recording (so, too, can the timing and place of a performance or broadcast, a point which is considered below). On the other hand, the exclusion is consistent with the fundamental requirement of the definition that publication consists in the making available of copies of a work to the public. In the case of artistic works, the material object in which the work is embodied is usually of far greater value than are the objects in which other kinds of works are embodied. Thus, the real interest of the public where an artistic work is concerned is to view the original work itself, whether this be a painting, drawing, sculpture, etc, while in the case of other works this interest is usually directed at obtaining copies of the work. This is not to deny that the making available of copies of an artistic work can be an important means of exploiting the rights of the author in that work; nor is it to say that the original manuscript, or even an intact first edition copy of a book or musical composition may not be of great intrinsic value. However, it does point to a general difference between the ways in which artistic and other kinds of work become available to the public. In accordance with the definition of 'published works', when an artistic work is exhibited, there is no making available of copies to satisfy the reasonable requirements of the public, and therefore publication of the artistic work does not occur. The latter will only become a 'published work' when copies of it are made available to the public with the consent of the author. This might occur, for example, when postcards of a sculpture which is exhibited in a public place are put on sale. Strictly speaking, then, the exclusion in the definition in respect of artistic works is superfluous. The same reasoning is applicable to the construction of works of architecture. This exception was added in the Berlin Revision,[152] which was the time when these works were first added to the list protected under the Convention. Architectural works will therefore only be published, when copies, such as photographs or prints, are made available to the public. This solution, however, does give rise to an anomaly: photographs or prints depicting works of painting, sculpture, or architecture are not technically copies, they are derivative works, because they present the work in a different form. Under the 'without prejudice' proviso, the publication of a derivative work should not publish the underlying work. On the other hand, if publication of the derivative work did not 'publish' the underlying work, a painting, sculpture, or work of architecture might never be 'published'.

[152] *Actes* 1908, 241 (report of the commission).

(4) Defects in the definition of 'published works'

6.46 The principal criticism that can be made of the present definition of 'published works' relates to the list of acts excluded from the concept of publication. The usual meaning of 'publication' in both English and French is to make generally known or accessible. Obviously, this result can be achieved as readily through the performance, broadcasting, or exhibition of a work, as through the making available of copies. Thus, Koumantos notes that it can be argued that the definition contains a 'terminological error', in that it reduces the genus of 'publication' to one of its species, namely, '*édition*' or the making available of copies.[153] Moreover, this 'terminological error' has become increasingly apparent as new means of disseminating works come into existence. As we will see (at para 6.52 below) it may be anomalous to deny digital dissemination the status of 'publication'. On the other hand, if digital dissemination does effect a 'publication', then its potential ubiquity creates further anomalies with respect to designating a work's 'country of origin'.

6.47 The existence of the 'terminological error' outlined above cannot be denied, but it would be of only theoretical import if the restricted meaning given to publication in the definition could be justified on other grounds. Historically, evidentiary reasons were advanced for the exclusion of ephemeral modes of communication from the concept of publication.[154] However, as argued in para 6.45 above, this reasoning is hardly applicable in the cases of exhibiting an artistic work or constructing a work of architecture. Both these acts can be easily proved, although they do not entail the making available of copies. Furthermore, it was suggested above that the acts of performance, communication by wire and broadcasting may also be readily proved: in each instance, these transient communications can be easily fixed in some material form, such as a sound or video recording, and the date and place of their occurrence proved in much the same way as the ordinary making available of copies. Evidentiary reasons therefore no longer seem to provide adequate justification for continuing to exclude these kinds of acts from the concept of publication. However, it is worth considering whether these restrictions may be warranted in view of the role which the definition of 'published works' plays in the overall operation of the Convention.

6.48 As regards article 3(1), the definition provides the hinge on which the protection of non-Union authors under the Convention hangs. These authors are protected only in respect of their published works, and the latter must be first published in one of the countries of the Union. It can therefore be argued that,

[153] Koumantos (n 112 above), 6.
[154] See *Actes* 1896, 163 (report of the commission).

as a matter of strategy, this protection should not be too readily available, as would be the case if publication could occur through the simple act of performing, broadcasting, etc, a work within a Union country. If protection is made too easy, this provides no incentive for the countries to which these authors belong to join the Berne Union in order to gain the fuller privileges of Union membership, that is, in respect of the unpublished works of their authors and those works which have been first published outside the Union. The strength of this argument is hard to assess, but it may be compared with the experience of France in 1852 when she unilaterally extended the protection of its laws to works published abroad.[155] Whether or not this was a direct consequence, it is certainly true that in the years immediately after its decree the French Government was able to enter international copyright relations with a large number of foreign governments who had previously resisted such overtures. Thus, it is at least arguable that a policy of altruism is as effective in encouraging non-Union countries to join the Union as is a policy of restricted protection. The former approach is also consistent with that view of authors' rights which sees them as natural rights of property existing above and beyond all artificial restraints of place and time. In the authors' view, one can only decide between these two arguments—and determine their significance as regards the scope of the Convention definition of 'published works'—on the basis of intuition, as there is no real factual data to support one against the other. The experience of France after 1852 may have been due to other factors than its opening up of protection to foreign authors. On the other hand, while the membership of the Berne Union has steadily increased since its formation, it has not been shown that this has been because it has restricted the protection accorded to non-Union authors. The arguments on both sides can be rehearsed with vigour, but there is no real evidence for either. In any event, now that the vast majority of countries are members of the Berne Union[156]—a situation that did not exist even at the time of publication of the first edition of this work—a policy of excluding non-Union authors in order to entice non-member states into joining the Union can no longer furnish a meaningful reason to maintain the publication/transmission distinction.

A third justification for the distinction returns to the 'fugitive' character of the communications excluded from publication status. In this case, the justification inheres not in evidentiary concerns (effectively rebutted above), but in the author's ability to exercise control over copies of the communicated work. **6.49**

[155] Note, however, that France adopted a different policy towards the protection of foreign authors in her Law No 64-689 of 8 July 1964.

[156] As at 6 May 2005, 159 nations had ratified the Berne Convention; see WIPO website: www.wipo.int.

Before modern, mass consumer recording devices and digital media, the public might visually or aurally experience a work, for example, through a performance or a display, but would not be able to make copies. Similarly, distribution of copies to a small number of persons for a limited purpose does not meet the article 3(3) standard of 'reasonable requirements of the public' because the author continues to exercise control over the fate of the copies.[157] Arguably, once the author disseminates the work in a way which no longer permits her to prevent the making of copies, she has entrusted herself to the copyright protection of the jurisdiction(s) in which the work is circulating. In this light, it seems appropriate to peg admission to Conventional protection to the country of first publication. Where the author still retains control over the making of copies, by contrast, she might not be said to have made herself dependent on the coverage of the laws of the countries in which she permits the public to apprehend the work.

6.50 Whatever the merits of this analysis, it breaks down once the author can no longer elect a means of dissemination that enables her to prevent copying.[158] Once the ability of the public to experience a work is no longer ephemeral, because, for example, the public utilizes recording devices that capture the performance, or because the public receives the work through a digital transmission which can be downloaded and preserved, then, from the point of view of right-holder control, there may be no practical difference between a 'publication' by distribution of copies, and a non-'publication' by wired or wireless communication of the work. Moreover, in the case of digital dissemination, the author may in fact authorize the public to make copies from the transmission; the author may seek to make the work available in a way that allows the public to generate copies, for example, because this means of dissemination may allow the author to get copies into the hands of her public directly, without the intervention of a publisher or other intermediary. There seems no justification at all for rejecting the 'published' status of works thus disseminated.

6.51 The other major role played by the definition of 'published works' is in the determination of a work's 'country of origin'. This is discussed in detail later (see paras 6.53ff below), but for the moment it suffices to say that the

[157] Distribution of a limited number of copies to designated persons for a limited purpose corresponds to the former US copyright law concept of 'limited publication', which was deemed not a publication at all. See eg *Estate of Martin Luther King, Jr, Inc* v *CBS, Inc*, 194 F 3d 1211 (11th Cir 1999) (explaining 1909 Act concepts of 'general' and 'limited' publication).

[158] If a justification for the publication/transmission distinction relies on the author's relinquishment of control over distributed copies, the advent of technological protection measures may complicate the analysis. In theory, it is possible for the author to distribute copies equipped with controls that will disable further copying. Would a work be 'published', if all disseminated copies were thus protected?

determination of this matter decides the kind of protection applicable to a work under the Convention in different countries of the Union. The general rule in relation to published works is that their country of origin is the country of the Union where the work is first published.[159] Thus, the question whether a work has been published, and where this has taken place, is one of great general importance, but the only significant reasons that can be advanced for defining 'published works' in a restricted manner can all be effectively rebutted. It is therefore submitted that there is no longer any rationale for retaining the 'terminological error' contained in the present definition of 'published works'. Unfortunately, future revision of the Convention is not likely, and subsequent multilateral instruments (the TRIPs Agreement, WCT) have not addressed the concept of publication. As a result, the 'terminological error' will remain with us, unless another basis for rethinking the publication/transmission distinction is offered and accepted. To that rethinking we now turn.

(a) Digital communications as 'publication'

While the text of article 3(3) distinguishes publication from transmission, digital transmissions might nonetheless in some circumstances meet the terms set out for a 'publication'. Because there is no persuasive policy justification for excluding digital transmissions from the universe of 'publications' (see paras 6.49ff above), it would be desirable if the text of article 3(3) lent itself to a more progressive interpretation. The key feature of 'published' works under that provision is the 'availability of such copies [made with the author's consent] . . . such as to satisfy the reasonable requirements of the public . . .'. Although it uses the expression 'manufacture', article 3(3) is indifferent to the 'means of manufacture of the copies'. It seems that so long as copies are materialized in some format, they come within the scope of article 3(3).[160] Accordingly, the computer of each member of the public to whom the work is made available may be the means of making a digital copy of the work, whether or not that copy is followed up by a printed copy. Arguably, the term 'manufacture', as used in the English version of article 3(3) suggests some more industrial, less individualized, process of creating copies, but in the French text the word 'fabrication' can be understood as simply meaning 'making', and is therefore more neutral as to the **6.52**

[159] Stockholm, Paris Acts, art 5(4)(a).

[160] There may be some question as to whether a RAM copy, stored in a computer's temporary memory but not converted to a more permanent file, should also be considered a 'copy' for purposes of art 3(3). Its ephemeral presence may liken it to the communications excluded by art 3(3). On the other hand, RAM copies can be converted to permanent copies, and some RAM copies may be less ephemeral than others, depending on how long the computer's temporary memory is left active.

means of production.[161] By virtue of article 37(1)(c), this is the interpretation that should prevail. Under this analysis, then, 'publication' does not turn on who makes the copies, but rather on whether enough of them can be made (with authorization) to meet public demand. If the author makes the work available to the public to make copies, for example, by offering it as a download from a publicly accessible website, then the work should be deemed 'published'. By contrast, if the author sends her work to one person, for example, by e-mail, she doubtless intends the recipient to make at least one digital copy, but, unless she has conveyed the contrary intent, she is not authorizing the recipient to make further copies for receipt (and materialization) by the public at large. Accordingly, that communication would not result in a 'publication'.

C. Attributing Nationality to a Work: Country of Origin

(1) Consequences of determining a work's country of origin under article 5(4)

6.53 Article 5(4) gives pride of place to the country of first publication. The country of origin designation applies whether or not the work's point of attachment for admission to protection was the author's nationality or residence, or the country of first publication. Country of origin thus is a concept independent of the criteria for Treaty coverage. As we shall see (at paras 6.74ff below), in most cases, the country of origin does not set the level of protection a Convention-covered work receives. Under the rule of national treatment, that is the task of the country where protection is sought. Rather, the country of origin plays a more limited role. It determines the duration of protection when its term is shorter than that in the country of protection; see article 7(8). It also serves as the reference point for material reciprocity in determining availability in other countries of protection for applied art and the *droit de suite.* Most importantly, under the principle of independence of protection (discussed further at paras 6.83ff below), a Berne Convention work is not entitled to Berne minimum protections in its country of origin. Under article 5(1) and (3), so long as a member state affords the minimum Berne protections to authors whose countries of origin are in *other* Union states, it can provide far less to authors whose works originate in that state. It is unusual for a state to treat its own authors less well than foreign authors, but examples of this kind of discrimination

[161] See eg Claude Masouyé, *Guide de la Convention de Berne* (1978), 30–1 ('il faut en quelque sorte une matérialisation, quel que soit . . . le mode de fabrication des exemplaires.'); the emphasis is on materialization, not on the means by which the materialization is achieved.

exist.[162] As a result, determining the country of origin can affect the practical level of protection a work receives.

(2) Identifying the country of origin

The rules governing this were very largely codified by the Stockholm Revision, and can be summarized as follows: **6.54**

1. For works first published in a country of the Union, their country of origin ('CO') is that country (article 5(4)(a)).
2. For works first published simultaneously in several countries of the Union which grant different terms of protection, the CO is the country whose legislation grants the shorter term of protection (article 5(4)(a)).
3. For works first published simultaneously in a country outside the Union and in a country of the Union, the latter is the CO (article 5(4)(b)).
4. For unpublished works of Union nationals, the CO is the country of the Union of which the author is a national (article 5(4)(c)).
5. For works of Union nationals first published in a country outside the Union, without simultaneous publication in a country of the Union, the CO is the country of which the author is a national (article 5(4)(c)).
6. Special rules in the case of cinematographic works:
    - where these are first published, or published simultaneously, in a Union country, the ordinary rules under 1, 2, and 3 apply;
    - where these are unpublished or first published in a non-Union country, but the maker has his headquarters or habitual residence in a country of the Union, the CO is that country (article 5(4)(c)(ii)) (this provision takes account of the fact that there may be a number of co-authors of a cinematographic work, each with different nationalities or residence).
7. Similar rules apply in the case of works of architecture or other artistic works incorporated in a building or other structure:
    - where these are first published, or published simultaneously, in a Union country, the ordinary rules under 1, 2, and 3 apply;
    - where these are unpublished or first published in a non-Union country, but are erected or located in a country of the Union, the CO is that country (article 5(4)(c)(ii)).

While it is possible to take delight in the elaborate matrix of rules set out above, is it really necessary that they should be so complicated? The CO of a work is a concept which is linked directly to the criterion of territoriality ('the place of **6.55**

[162] See eg 17 USC § 411 (requiring that US works be registered as a prerequisite to suit); 104A (implementing Berne Convention, art 18, restoring copyright protection to certain non-US public domain works).

first publication') as the criterion for entitlement to protection under the Convention. This is no longer relevant to Union authors who are now protected for both their unpublished and published works on the basis of nationality or residence alone. As a point of attachment for admission to Treaty coverage, the criterion of territoriality therefore remains applicable only in the case of the published works of non-Union authors, while special provision is made in article 4 in respect of the unpublished cinematographic and architectural works of non-Union authors. It can therefore be argued that this role for the 'country of origin' is really necessary only in the case of non-Union authors. With respect to the other roles played by the 'country of origin'—in determining duration, regime of protection for applied art, availability of the *droit de suite*, and identification of the country in which the author may claim only local protection without Berne substantive rights—the application of the above rules may add unneeded complexity, because it often means that the CO of a published work will be different from the country of which the author is a national. In such cases, it may be more logical that the CO of a work should be the country of which the author is a national or resident.[163] This would also mean that a Union author would have the same country of origin for all his works, unlike the present situation where he may have different countries of origin in respect of his published works, depending upon where they are published. On the other hand, linking CO to nationality may not always simplify matters. First, authors may change nationality, or, more often, residence. Second, it would be necessary to devise criteria for identifying the CO of a multiple-authored work whose authors are nationals or residents of more than one country.

At the Stockholm Conference, some delegates were in favour of eliminating the concept of CO entirely from the Convention, on the ground that this would considerably simplify its operation.[164] However, discussion centred principally on a more modest Swiss proposal to make the country of the Union of which the author was a national the CO for his published and unpublished works.[165] This had significant implications in relation to questions of duration. For example, in the case of a Swiss author who first published his work in the FRG this would have meant that the term of protection after his death would have been only fifty years under Swiss law,[166] instead of seventy years according to German law[167] (the latter being the applicable law under the provisions of the Brussels Act; see further para 6.56 below). This proposal drew forth considerable opposition from many delegations. Practical difficulties were envisaged in

[163] This point is discussed further in para 6.11 above.
[164] *Records* 1967, vol II, 841 (comments by British delegate in Main Committee I).
[165] ibid, 841–2 and 847ff (Document S/63: for text, see vol I, 690).
[166] Law of 7 Dec 1922, art 36.
[167] Law of 9 Sept 1965, art 64(1).

cases of joint works where authors were of different nationalities, or in cases where the author of a work had dual nationality or subsequently changed nationality.[168] It was also argued that the author ought to have the freedom to decide the country of origin of his work for himself, so that he could choose the country with the longer term of protection for first publication.[169] In addition, it was said that it was easier to determine the place of first publication than the nationality of the author, and that, in any case, the former would still have to be retained as regards works of non-Union authors.[170] After lengthy discussion, the Swiss delegation withdrew its proposal, thereby 'setting an example of international cooperation' (in the chairman's words),[171] and the present provisions were retained in their entirety.

(a) Operation of rules concerning country of origin

The operation of these elaborate rules concerning the CO of a work, and the kind of protection to which it is entitled under the Convention are best demonstrated by the use of a number of examples, taking first the case of a hypothetical Indian author (India being a Union country). In each case, the CO of the work is indicated in square brackets. **6.56**

1. For her unpublished works, an Indian author receives in India the protection of Indian law, but none of the rights 'specially granted' by the Convention. She will receive the latter rights only if Indian law has expressly extended these to Indian writers, as distinct from authors entitled to claim protection in other Union countries under the Convention. As a matter of fact, this is the case,[172] and is likely to be so in every other Union country,[173] but there is no requirement under the Convention for Union countries to secure these advantages to their own nationals [CO in this case is India].
2. For her unpublished works in other Union countries, an Indian author will receive the protection accorded to national authors under their respective laws, together with the rights 'specially granted by the Convention' [CO here is still India].
3. For a work first published in France, another Union country, an Indian author will receive, in France, only those rights accorded to national authors by French law, but not those rights 'specially granted' by the Convention. For the same work, she will receive in other Union countries, including India,[174] the country of which she is a national, both the rights

[168] *Records* 1967, vol II, 842 (Swedish delegate, Main Committee I).
[169] ibid, 848 (FRG and French delegates, Main Committee I).
[170] ibid (FRG delegate, Main Committee I).
[171] ibid, 849 (Professor Ulmer).
[172] See generally, Copyright Act 1968.
[173] But see para 6.53 above (US 'two-tier' approach).
[174] See further para 6.89 below.

accorded to national authors under their respective laws and the rights 'specially granted' by the Convention [CO in these cases is France].[175]

4. For a work first published in a country outside the Union (an unlikely scenario today, but one might envisage here a first publication in the nearby country of Myanmar, which is not a Union country), an Indian author will receive in India only the rights accorded by Indian law, and in all other Union countries the rights accorded by their respective laws, together with those rights 'specially granted' by the Convention [CO in these cases being India].
5. For a work first published simultaneously in India and the FRG, an Indian author will receive the protection of Indian law alone in India, and in other Union countries the protection of their respective laws, together with the rights 'specially granted' by the Convention [CO here being India, the country with the shorter term of protection].[176] If, in this example, the Indian author had first published her work simultaneously in New Zealand and the FRG she would receive only the protection of New Zealand law in New Zealand, and in other Union countries, including India, the rights accorded by their national laws, together with the rights 'specially granted' by the Convention [CO here being NZ, because its term is shorter than India's].[177]
6. For a work first published simultaneously in India and a non-Union country, such as Ethiopia or Myanmar, an Indian author will receive in India the protection of Indian law and nothing more, and in other Union countries the rights accorded by their respective laws, together with the rights 'specially granted' by the Convention [CO here being India]. Again, if first publication had occurred simultaneously in both NZ and India, she would receive only the protection of New Zealand law in NZ, and in other Union countries, including India, the rights accorded by their respective laws, together with those rights 'specially granted' by the Convention [CO here being NZ, because its term is shorter than India's].

In the case of an Ethiopian author, being one of the few instances where there will now be an author from a non-Union country, his position under the Convention is illustrated in the following examples:

---

[175] As a result, an author seeking better protection than that afforded local authors under her national law might seek to publish her work first in another country, and wait thirty days before publishing in her own country. For example, if the author's home country imposes formalities on local works, the author could avoid those obligations by publishing first in a country which does not impose formalities. Because the CO will then be a country other than that of the author's nationality or residence, the latter country could not impose formalities on its own author's works.

[176] FRG Law of 9 Sept 1965, art 64(1) (life of the author plus seventy years); Indian Copyright Act 1957, s 22 (sixty years from the beginning of the calendar year next following the year in which the author dies).

[177] See NZ Copyright Act 1994 s 22 (duration of copyright is 50 years pma).

7. For his unpublished works, there is no protection in any Union country under the Convention (there might, of course, be protection in one or more of these countries pursuant to separate bilateral arrangements, or as a matter of that country's domestic law,[178] but this is another matter).
8. For his works first published in another non-Union country, there is no protection in any Union country under the Convention (leaving aside any bilateral arrangements that may exist).
9. For a work first published in France, he will enjoy the protection of French law alone in that country, and in other Union countries the protection accorded under their respective laws, together with the rights 'specially granted' under the Convention [CO here being France]. In the cases of simultaneous publication outlined in examples 5 and 6, the non-Union author will be in the same position as a Union author, as his CO in each instance would be a Union country.
10. For an architectural work which has been erected in, say, Australia but has not been published, the non-Union author will nonetheless be protected under Australian law, and in other countries of the Union will be accorded the rights given by their respective laws, together with the rights 'specially granted' by the Convention [CO here being Australia]. This would also apply if the work in question was an artistic work incorporated in a building or other structure located in a country of the Union. On the other hand, if copies of the architectural work or artistic work were made available in sufficient quantities to constitute publication in the UK, another Union country, the latter would then be the CO, with the consequences that this entails. Again, if the work was erected or incorporated in a structure erected in a non-Union country, but was first published in Australia, the latter would be the CO, with the consequences that this entails.

(b) Situations not covered by the rules concerning the country of origin of works

Certain situations are not directly covered by the above rules. These may be summarized as follows. **6.57**

(i) The case of Union authors where the CO of their published works is a different country from that of which they are a national: This will happen where an author who is a national of a Union country first publishes his work in another country of the Union. It has been argued that in such cases he should not only receive national treatment in his CO under the Convention (the country of

[178] See, eg, 17 USC § 104(a) (according national treatment to all unpublished works, 'without regard to the nationality or domicile of the author').

first publication), but also in his home country or country of nationality.[179] This is not stated as such in the Convention, but the basis of the suggestion is the assumption that the Berne Convention is not to be interpreted as breaking the bonds between Union countries and their citizens, as it is only concerned with the relations of Union countries to foreign authors. (As will be shown below, however, that assumption is open to question.) The effect of this interpretation is to give such a work two COs: a CO under the Convention with respect to all countries of the Union other than the country of the author's nationality, and a CO that applies only in the case of the latter. This might have significant implications with respect to duration of protection. Thus a German author who first published his work in Canada will have that country as the CO of the work under article 5(4)(a). With respect to duration of protection in, say NZ, he will only be entitled to claim a period of fifty years *post mortem auctoris*, as this is the period applicable in the CO of the work (being Canada). Had the CO been Germany, or indeed any other EU country, this period would have been seventy years, as this is the period applicable in those countries. However, under the interpretation suggested above he will only receive that period in Germany itself, on the basis that he should be entitled to full national treatment in that country as one of its nationals. In this case, the rights which accrue to him under the Convention by virtue of first publication in Canada will be deferred to the fuller rights he possesses under German law as a German national.

On the other hand, the proposal to have two CO's can have other, less author-favourable implications (that the proposal's proponents probably did not anticipate): suppose the author first published in another country in order to avoid her own country's imposition of sub-Berne treatment on its own authors. Under the two-CO approach, the author would continue to receive a standard of protection in her country of nationality that falls below Berne norms. The assumption that the Berne Convention did not intend to divorce the author from her home country may in this light seem less justified, for the Convention also strives to assure as uniform a standard of protection as possible, albeit without directly intervening in domestic law. The author's ability to achieve Berne-level protection despite her home country's recalcitrance toward its own authors might therefore be seen as desirable: if a member state cannot effectively confine its authors within sub-Berne limits, it may feel greater pressure to adapt its domestic law to international norms. The practical implications of this analysis extend to domestic law imposition of formalities, as well as to exceptions or compulsory licences that exceed Berne-permissible bounds.

[179] A Baum, 'Völkerrecht, Berner Konvention und Landesgesetze' [1950] *GRUR* 437, 451 (also in [1946] *DA* 85, 101); W Nordemann, K Vinck, P W Hertin, and G Meyer, *International Copyright and Neighbouring Rights Law* (1990) ('Nordemann et al (1990)'), 75.

(ii) Simultaneous publication in several countries of the Union with the same period of protection: This situation is not provided for in article 5(4)(a), but the possibility of it occurring must be considerable (for example, simultaneous publication in Canada and the Peoples' Republic of China, or in Germany and Austria). It has been suggested by Bergström that in such a case the CO is the country where publication in fact first occurred.[180] Thus, if a work was published on 1 August in Austria and on 10 August in Germany, Austria would be the CO of the work although it would be within the scope of simultaneous publication under article 3(4) of the Convention.

Such a gloss, however, appears inconsistent with the wording of article 3(4) under which it is clear that publication in two or more countries within a period of thirty days means that these works are to be regarded as having been published simultaneously, that is, at the same point of time. It would also fail to resolve the situation where publication occurred on the same day: would this necessitate an inquiry into the precise hour or minute that publication occurred in both countries? This would be an onerous task, given that publication may not be an event that can be readily tied down to a particular point of time. Moreover, if publication is effected by means of digital communications, such as over the Internet, publication may be truly simultaneous, within seconds. Under these circumstances, the argument for designating the country of the author's nationality the CO makes sense, and should not have deleterious consequences for the author, if she enjoys the same terms of protection in her home country as in most of the countries of simultaneous publication. Alternatively, in cases of multiple simultaneous publication the CO might be deemed the country with the most author-favourable domestic legislation. This could give the author an advantage in other cases where a rule of reciprocity under the Convention requires reference to the law of a work's CO, for example, with respect to the *droit de suite* under article 14*ter* or the protection of works of applied art under article 2(7).

(iii) Works with several co-authors from different Union countries: This case also is not expressly provided for in the Convention, but problems will only arise where the works remain unpublished or are first published in a non-Union country (where first publication occurs in a Union country, this will clearly be the CO under article 5(4)(a)). Two alternative situations need to be considered here. Where the countries of the different co-authors have identical terms of protection, the solution suggested in (ii) above seems appropriate: there will be as many COs as there are authors (although this solution could prove

[180] S Bergström, 'Schutzprinzipien der Berner Übereinkunft nach der Stockhom-Pariser Fassung' [1973] *GRUR Int* 238, 240.

problematic if the domestic legislation of any of these countries is in other respects sub-Berne). Where the countries have differing terms, however, article 5(4)(a) suggests that the CO should be the country with the shorter or shortest period of protection.[181]

(c) Country of origin and habitual residence

6.58 The rules governing the determination of the CO of a work do not refer to non-Union authors who have their habitual residence in a Union country. This seems an omission, when it is recalled that these authors are assimilated to national authors under article 3(2). However, as the assimilation under the latter provision is expressed to apply 'for the purposes of the Convention', it is logical to assume that the CO of a work by a non-Union author who habitually resides in a Union country is that country. This will, of course, only be relevant in the case of her unpublished works and works first published in a non-Union country. In the case of a work first published in another Union country, this will be the CO of the work; but this will be so regardless of whether or not she is habitually resident in a Union country. It goes without saying that no assimilation occurs in the case of a national of a Union country who habitually resides in another Union country, such as an Australian author living in the UK: in this case, the CO of that author's unpublished works and works published first in a non-Union country remains Australia, as there is no need for him to be assimilated to British authors under article 3(2).

(3) Problem cases: digital publication and country of origin; changes in the country of origin of a work

6.59 The earlier discussion has pointed out some defects in the treaty's designation of the CO. These become particularly apparent in light of new technology, as the following discussion of digital dissemination indicates. But the problems are not limited to new means of communication. Changes in authors' nationality or residence, and changes in member state accessions cause additional difficulties.

Digital communications bring to the fore the problem of a multiplicity of possible COs. Under the article 3(3) definition of 'published works', a work will be considered 'published' if copies are made available to the public in a manner that satisfies the public's reasonable requirements (see the earlier discussion at paras 6.22ff above). If one interprets 'copies' to include reproductions in RAM (a computer's temporary memory), then posting a work on a website makes 'copies' available to anyone who accesses the website. If one rejects the RAM copying theory, on the ground that a more permanent embodiment is required,

[181] Bergström (n 180 above).

one might contest the characterization of the posting as a 'publication', on the ground that the website is simply making the material available as a communication to the public. As discussed earlier (para 6.44 above), this is not a 'publication' under article 3(3). But, as also discussed earlier at para 6.52 above, any website that permits downloading (as opposed to streaming-only), would effect a publication because the downloading public can store the work to a more permanent format, such as hard disk, CD ROM, floppy disk, or printout.

6.60 Are these copies 'made available to the public in a manner that satisfies its reasonable requirements'? The Internet embodies a change from a model of communication of works to a public of passive recipients of a distribution or performance to a model where networks offer interactive consultation of works at the initiative of that very same public. Public access now can be immediate, individual and instantaneous. These copies are made available 'on demand'. Where there is a demand, and the appropriate digital equipment, there will be copies. As a result, the posting of a work on a website can fulfil the reasonable requirements standard for publication, and thus effect publication in any country in which a sufficient portion of the public is computer-equipped. This, in turn, would mean that copies are simultaneously made available in every country of the world in which there is adequate Internet access at least for downloading. Currently, one hundred and fifty nine countries are Berne Union members. Most, if not all, will have sufficient computing resources to qualify as places of publication.

6.61 If a work initially disclosed over the Internet is simultaneously 'published' in over 150 countries, does that mean that every one of those countries is the 'country of origin' for the purposes of the Berne Convention? The consequences of such a conclusion are bizarre indeed. Recall that article 5(1) explicitly excuses Union members from according Berne-level protection to its members' *domestic* works of authorship. A Union member meets its Berne obligations if it accords protection consonant with Convention minima to *foreign* Berne-Union works. If, however, with simultaneous universal publication via the Internet, every work of authorship could be considered a *domestic* work in each country of the Berne Union, then, ironically, Berne Convention minimum standards of protection might *never* apply, because there will be no foreign works.

6.62 To avoid this preposterous result, one might apply article 5(4) of the Convention to conclude that, when there are multiple countries of first publication, the 'country of origin' is the country whose term of protection is the shortest. This too, however, creates problems. The problems arise from the article 7(8) 'rule of the shorter term' (discussed further at para 9.55 below). According to this rule, if the term in the CO is shorter than that of the country where protection is sought, then the CO's term applies, rather than the term of the country of protection. But if, in the case of multiple countries of first publication, the 'country of origin' is the country whose term is the shortest, then all Internet-published works will be localized in the country with the shortest term.[182]

6.63 These anomalies suggest that the notion of Internet 'publication' for purposes of determining the CO should be limited to a single Berne-Union country: but which one? One might designate as the country of first publication the country from which the author communicated the work, but this characterization has some disadvantages. First, that country may have little relationship to the work, as the author may upload the work from an appropriately equipped computer anywhere in the world (including from countries through which the author is merely travelling). Second, if the public accesses the work from a website, the work is not yet available to the public until the work arrives at its place of residence on that website. This in turn suggests that the country of first publication is the one from which the work first becomes available to the public; that is, the country in which it is possible to localize the website through which members of the public (wherever located) access the work.

6.64 This choice, however, is not problem-free, either. If the author operates her own website, the website may be localized at the author's habitual residence. But if the author is making the work available through a third-party site, localization may prove more uncertain. Unlike countries of traditional, physical first publication, in which authors or publishers consciously organize the locus of economic centre of the exploitation of their work, the country in which the server that hosts the website is located may be completely indifferent, or even unknown, to the author. Similarly, the location of the effective business establishment of the website operator may be insignificant to an author's selection of that site to disseminate the work. For example, if the conditions of publication are the same whatever the geographic location of the website operator's business establishment, then that country's relationship to the publication would seem purely fortuitous. Moreover, the downloading Web-user may not even be aware of the location of the website operator or its host server. In these circumstances, it becomes clear that there are significant difficulties with making 'publication' a criterion for determining the 'country of origin'. When there is a surplus of places of publication, perhaps the simplest solution would be to adopt the approach linking the CO to that of the author's

[182] As discussed at para 9.55 below, if the country of origin's domestic law provides a shorter term of protection than life plus fifty years, other Berne countries would nonetheless accord that work the Berne minimum term. But that is a different matter than the one discussed here, in which one would fix the CO in the country with the shortest term; to avoid anomalies, it is necessary to conclude that art 5(4)(a) implies the shortest *Berne-compatible* term.

nationality or residence, at least where that country's domestic law conforms to Berne minima.

(a) Changes in the country of origin of a work

The possibility of changes occurring in the CO of a work have already been referred to above. For a start, it will be apparent that the rejection of the Swiss proposal at the Stockholm Revision means that the works of a Union author may each have different countries of origin, depending upon whether they are published or not, and, if published, where this first occurred. Moreover, the same work may possess two different COs in succession, where it is published in another country of the Union from that of which the author is a national. The possibilities of these changes occurring flow from the operation of the provisions discussed above. Are there other circumstances in which the country of origin of a work may change? **6.65**

(b) Changes in the author's nationality

There are two possibilities to be considered here: (i) adoption of the nationality of another country of the Union, and (ii) adoption of the nationality of a country which is not a member of the Union (something that will only now occur in very limited circumstances). In the first instance, the author is still a national of a Union country, and there will be no change in the CO of any works which he first publishes in a country of the Union. The rule here under article 5(4)(a) and (b) seems quite clear: the CO of such works is the country of first publication, which is an historic fact unaffected by changes in the author's nationality. Such a view is supported by the records of the Stockholm Revision[183] and by a number of commentators (see para 6.07 above).[184] However, does the CO of his unpublished works now change, as well as the CO of any works which he has first published outside the Union? The author remains a national of a Union country throughout, but at what point of time should his nationality be considered in relation to the determination of the CO of these last two categories of works? No guidance is to be found in article 5(4), but as regards works first published in a country outside the Union it seems logical to look at the country of the author's nationality at the time this occurred (this being consistent with the approach taken in relation to works first published in a Union country). Accordingly, in the case of an Australian author adopting British nationality, the CO of a work first published in a non-Union country would depend upon whether he had already adopted his new nationality at the time of publication, in which case it would be the UK. In relation to **6.66**

[183] *Records* 1967, vol II, 841 (remarks by Professor Ulmer, chairman of Main Committee I).
[184] See eg Desbois et al (1976), 138.

unpublished works, the answer here should obviously be consistent with that given above in relation to entitlement to protection under article 3(1) (see para 6.08 above). It was suggested there that in the case of unpublished works there were three times to be considered: the time of creation of the work, the time at which it became available to the public without actually being published, and the time at which protection under the Convention was sought in relation to that work. The view of Main Committee I was that the second of these was to be preferred,[185] but some commentators (Desbois, Françon, and Kéréver)[186] have argued for the third approach. There are advantages, and corresponding disadvantages, in both approaches. The second ensures that the CO of the work remains the same, until such time as it is published in another country, but there may be problems in proving when the work first became available, particularly when this is some time in the past. The third approach will be easier for the author to establish, but will entail the consequence that the CO of his works may change one or more times before they are published. As a matter of interpretation of the Convention, it was suggested above that the view of Main Committee I should prevail as this is an authentic supplementary aid to interpretation under the general rules of international law relating to the interpretation of treaties.[187] However, in the face of these conflicting interpretations in relation to a matter on which the Convention provides no clear guidance, the final decision remains one for national legislation.

6.67 The interpretation preferred in the preceding paragraph also seems more equitable when the (now unlikely) case of a Union author changing his nationality to that of a non-Union country is considered. Any work first published in a Union country will, of course, continue to receive protection by virtue of its place of publication. However, as regards works which were first published outside the Union at a time when the author was still a Union national, these would lose protection under the Desbois approach, because the author would be unable to show that he had this nationality at the time when he instituted proceedings to protect his work. The same would apply to his unpublished works, which would therefore enter into the public domain throughout the Union once he had changed his nationality. These consequences make the interpretation of Main Committee I more attractive, and this approach is also more in keeping with the object of the Convention, that is, the protection of the rights of authors.

(c) Dual nationality

6.68 Under the domestic laws of some countries, it is possible for a person to possess dual nationality. What implications does this have for the determination of the

[185] *Records* 1967, 1136 (report of Main Committee I). [186] Desbois et al (1976), 139.

[187] Vienna Convention on the Law of Treaties 1969 (the 'Vienna Convention'), art 32.

CO of a work under the Convention? Where an author is a national of both a Union and a non-Union country, there does not appear to be any difficulty: she is a national of a Union country, and this is all that is relevant for the application of the rules in article 5(4)(c). On the other hand, which is the CO where an author is a national of two Union countries? No direct guidance on this point is to be found in the Convention, so this will be a question to be determined under the national legislation of the country where protection is claimed. However, the most sensible solution would be to adopt the approach taken in article 5(4)(a) and in relation to works which are simultaneously published. Thus, where an author is a national of two (or more) Union countries, the CO of her unpublished works and works first published outside the Union should be the country which offers the shorter (or shortest) term of protection. This is also consistent with the solution suggested above for works by co-authors from different countries of the Union.

(d) Publication in a non-Union country which later accedes to the Union

A further situation when the CO of a work will change is where a Union author first publishes a work in a non-Union country, which subsequently joins the Union. As the Convention applies to all works not in the public domain at the time that a country accedes to it (article 18(1)), if such a work is still protected under the law of that country, its CO will thereupon change from that of the author's nationality to that of the country where publication took place (article 5(4)(a)). A possible problem may arise where the term of protection in the new CO is shorter than that in the old CO: is the author of the work to be prejudiced by this change? This raises questions relating to the retroactive effect of the Convention, which are considered below at paras 6.112ff. **6.69**

(e) Position of author whose country of nationality leaves the Union

The reverse of the situation referred to in the preceding paragraph is where the country of which an author is a national leaves the Union. With respect to any works which he creates subsequent to this date there is no problem: he no longer possesses the nationality of a Union country, and his works will only be protected in the Union if he first publishes them in a Union country, which will then be the CO of those works. As regards his works first published within the Union prior to this date he should continue to receive Convention protection by reason of the historic fact of first publication within a Union country. In relation to his other works created before this date—those still unpublished or first published in a non-Union country—if the interpretation preferred by Main Committee I is applied, these should continue to receive Convention protection. However, this would not be so if the Desbois approach were adopted. Reasons of equity therefore favour the first approach in this case as well, but **6.70** again this will remain a matter to be determined by national legislation in the country where protection is claimed.[188]

II. REGIME OF PROTECTION

A. General Considerations

6.71 Thus far, we have considered both the categories of persons and the classes of works entitled to protection under the Convention. It now remains to examine the kind of protection which Union countries are required to apply to these works under the Convention. This involves a more detailed discussion of the principles of national treatment, independence of protection, and absence of formalities, as well as the concept of 'country of origin'.

[188] A particular problem, identified by W Nordemann, 'Determining the Country of Origin According to the Berne Convention' (1984) 121 *RIDA* 2 may arise as a result of the definition of 'simultaneously published' which was inserted in the Brussels text. Prior to this, the meaning of the expression was left undefined, and, in the absence of definition under national legislation could only be interpreted as meaning 'published on the same day'. Thus, if a work was published before this time on the same day in two countries of the Union, one of which (country A) had a shorter term than the other (country B), the CO was country A (Berne, Berlin, and Rome Acts, art 4(3)). On the other hand, if publication in country B had occurred ten days before country A, then the CO was country B. Under the extended definition of 'published simultaneously' in art 4(3) of the Brussels Act, if publication occurred at this interval of time in both countries, the CO would again be country A, as this would be the country with the shorter term. However, in the event that publication in these circumstances had occurred prior to the coming into force of the Brussels Act and the work was still protected under the law of country B, would this effect a change in the CO to country A? If both countries A and B had become parties to the Brussels Act, the answer should be in the affirmative as art 27(1) of that Act provided that this was to replace all other instruments previously in force. Furthermore, art 18(1) of that Act provided that the Convention applied to all works which at the moment of its coming into force had not yet fallen into the public domain through the expiry of the term of protection. These provisions remain, in substance, the same under the Stockholm, Paris Acts. Thus, if at the time countries A and B became bound by the Brussels Act, the work in question was still protected in country B, the CO should then change to country A (the country with the shorter term of protection). If this term had, by this time, expired in country A, the author would thereupon have lost his protection in other countries of the Union. In the same way, if the work was still entitled to protection in country A, the author would nonetheless have lost the benefit of the longer period of protection which he would otherwise have received had country B remained the CO of his work. Nonetheless, these potential losses were only one side of the picture, as there was also the possibility of gain: if the term of protection in country A was extended prior to the work falling into the public domain, the author would be entitled to this additional period under the principle of national treatment provided for in art 4(1) (art 5(1) of the Stockholm, Paris Acts). This, in fact, was the situation in the *Tosca* case discussed by Nordemann, although the court here reached a contrary conclusion, holding that there has been no change in the CO. Nonetheless, the interpretation suggested above appears to be supported by the provisions of both the Brussels and Stockholm, Paris Acts. In any event, following the adoption of the mandatory fifty years *post mortem auctoris* in the Brussels Act, the question will only arise in exceptional cases.

(1) A question of choice of laws

There are three principal ways in which works from country A may be protected in country B pursuant to an international convention. These have already been referred to in Chapters 1 to 3 above, but it is useful to summarize them again at this point in our discussion. In essence, each embodies a fundamental choice in the area of private international law concerning the law to be applied in the protection of the works in question. **6.72**

1. Country B could apply the law of country A (the law of the CO of the work, or the *lex originis*, as this is often called in private international law). Under this approach the CO of the work might be defined by reference to the nationality of the author of the work, or, in the case of a published work, by reference to the place in which publication first took place. In the graphic words of Stewart, '[L]ike the person the work would then, so to speak, have a passport and take its nationality with it wherever it goes.'[189]
2. Country B could treat the work in the same way as it treats the works of its own authors, that is, it could simply apply its national legislation to the foreign work (the law of the country where protection is claimed). This is often referred to as 'assimilation', or the application of the principle of national treatment. Strictly speaking, this approach is not concerned with the question of choice of laws, as it simply removes any differences between national and foreign authors, providing that both are to be treated in the same way under national law. Arguably, it would not be inconsistent with the principle of national treatment, therefore for national legislation to apply a uniform conflict of laws rule to provide that the content and extent of copyright protection for both nationals and foreigners is to be governed by the law of the country or origin.[190] This, however, is problematic, for application of the country of protection's *conflicts* rule to locals and to foreigners could result in different *substantive* protection if the conflicts rule leads to applying the domestic law of the CO to the foreign work, and the scope of coverage differs in the CO and the country of protection. In that event, one could contend that foreigners are not in fact assimilated to nationals, because the outcome of the foreign author's claim may differ from the outcome of the same claim brought by a local author and adjudicated under the domestic law of the country of protection. This would be inconsistent with the indication in article 5(1) and its predecessors that foreigners and nationals should receive the same substantive protections. In

[189] Stephen Stewart, *International Copyright and Neighbouring Rights*, 2nd edn (1989), 38.

[190] See M Walter, 'Contractual Freedom in the Field of Copyright and Conflicts of Laws' (1976) 44 *RIDA* 87, 88.

practice, however, one may anticipate that this will not usually occur, and national treatment will involve only the application of the domestic law of the country where protection is claimed. At the same time, a need arises to define the scope or extent of national treatment or assimilation, as this is usually incomplete and there will still remain matters in relation to which conflict of law questions will arise.

3. Country B could protect the foreign work in accordance with specific rules or standards contained in the international convention itself. In other words, the convention could embody a common code to be applied by each signatory state in the protection of works emanating from any of the other signatory states.

6.73 There are advantages and disadvantages in each approach. The first ensures that the work will receive the same treatment in each country which has signed the convention. On the other hand, it can create considerable difficulties for the national courts of those countries as they have to apply laws which are foreign to them. For this reason, the second has clear practical advantages, as it means that national courts have only to apply their own laws. This, of course, means that works will receive differing treatment in each convention country, and that in some cases works from country A will be more favourably treated in country B than are the works of country B in country A. Such imbalances can be corrected by requiring material reciprocity of protection, but this in turn involves the same difficulty as identified above in relation to the first approach, that is, the need to refer to the law of the CO of a work to ensure that there is equivalence of protection. By contrast, the third approach is simpler in that there is a common set of rules that is applied by each country which is party to the convention. However, it is unlikely that these rules will be all-embracing, and the filling of these gaps will therefore involve decisions as to the law to be applied (perhaps either the *lex originis* or the law of the country where protection is claimed). All three approaches are to be found in the Berne Convention, although the first only applies in specific instances, such as duration of protection and the recognition of the *droit de suite*, and the treatment of works of applied art. Furthermore, while at the start of its life the principle of national treatment was the fundamental mainstay of the Convention, successive revisions of the Convention have now greatly augmented the substantive set of 'rights specially granted by the Convention', making the Conventional rules of far greater importance than at first.

B. Basic Rule: National Treatment

(1) The development of the principle of national treatment

This was the basic approach of the majority of early bilateral copyright conventions, and was adopted by ALAI in its draft of 1883. Article 1 proposed: **6.74**

> Whatever their nationality, authors of literary and artistic works which appear or are performed in one of the contracting states, provided only that the formalities required by the law of that country are complied with, shall enjoy the same rights of protection of their works in all the other states of the Union as nationals.[191]

It will be seen that this formulation still involved some reference to the law of a work's CO, that is, the requirement that the formalities of that country (which had to be a contracting state) be satisfied in relation to the work. In other respects, the protection of the work was a matter for the law of the country where protection was claimed and there was no requirement of material reciprocity. However, one matter which was left unclear was whether the application of the principle of national treatment included any future changes that might be made to the law of the country where protection was claimed. This last point was expressly referred to by the Federal Council in the programme which it submitted to the Diplomatic Conference of 1884. This proposed:

> As far as the protection of the rights of authors in their literary and artistic works is concerned, the subjects or citizens of each of the contracting States shall enjoy, in all the other States of the Union, the advantages which their respective laws currently accord or may subsequently accord to nationals.[192]

The Federal Council programme also added a corollary which may be thought to have been strictly unnecessary, but was a useful amplification of the scope of the principle of national treatment:

> Consequently, they will have the same protection as the latter [nationals of the state where protection is sought] and the same recourse to law against infringements of their rights, provided that they [the subjects or citizens of the other contracting state] have complied with the formalities and conditions prescribed by the legislation of the country of origin of the work.[193]

Both drafts, however, left open the question of how to determine the CO of a work for which protection was claimed under the Convention. This point was of particular importance with respect to the matter of formalities, as both drafts stipulated compliance with the law of the CO in this regard. More generally, it was of importance in relation to the question of whether the work for which

[191] *Actes* 1884, 7. [192] ibid, 11. [193] ibid.

protection was sought originated from a country of the Union. A further pressing question raised by the German delegation in the questionnaire which it prepared for the Conference was that of duration of protection: was this to be determined by the application of the principle of national treatment (national treatment 'pure and simple'), by referral to the law of the CO, or by the specification of some uniform term in the Convention itself?[194] The second solution had been adopted in most bilateral conventions to that date,[195] and the Germans argued in favour of this alternative, in the event that agreement on a uniform term could not be reached.[196] The French and Swiss, however, were opposed to this, urging in support the practical advantages of the application of national treatment in these cases, and citing in aid the general principle of international law that where foreigners are assimilated to nationals they should receive the same advantages and disadvantages, and not be prejudiced thereby.[197] The matter was finally referred to the commission for consideration. The latter, while recognizing the benefit of the adoption of a uniform term, took the view that, in view of the diversity of national legislation on this question, it was not yet worth discussing.[198] It therefore considered the viable options to be national treatment 'pure and simple', and national treatment only as long as protection continued to subsist in the CO (the original German proposal). Opinion was at first equally divided over this second option, but it was finally accepted by a majority of the commission on the ground that the application of national treatment 'pure and simple' would lead to unavoidable inconvenience when a work fell into the public domain in one country while still being protected in another.[199] The draft proposed by the commission (and ultimately adopted by the Conference) therefore made the application of the principle of national treatment subject to the law of the CO in relation to both the matters of duration and formalities. It also modified the language proposed by the Federal Council to take account of changes in the description of persons protected by the Convention (see para 6.04 above), and read as follows:

> Authors belonging to one of the contracting countries shall enjoy, in all of the other countries of the Union, for their works, whether in manuscript or unpublished, or published in one of these countries, the advantages which their respective laws accord presently or may accord subsequently to nationals.
>
> Nevertheless these advantages will only be reciprocally assured during the existence of their rights in their country of origin.

[194] *Actes* 1884, 25 (question 5).

[195] See eg the Franco-Belgian Convention of 31 Oct 1881, art 1; the Franco-Italian Convention of 9 July 1884, art 1.

[196] *Actes* 1884, 30. [197] ibid. [198] ibid, 42.

[199] ibid (of particular weight in this regard appear to have been objections from the Swedish delegate at being required to protect works which had fallen into the public domain: ibid, 43).

This enjoyment is subordinated to the accomplishment of the formalities and the conditions prescribed by the legislation of the country of origin of the work or, when the work is in manuscript or unpublished, by the legislation of the country to which the author belongs.[200]

This draft was still deficient in that it did not specify what was the CO for published works, although as far as unpublished works were concerned it indicated that this was the country of the author's nationality. Furthermore, while adopting the solution favoured by the majority of bilateral conventions on the question of duration, it had refined the formula usually adopted in those conventions by deletion of the requirement that the duration of their enjoyment in the other country should not exceed that granted to their nationals by the country where protection was claimed. This was done on the ground that this wording was superfluous.[201]

At the Diplomatic Conference of 1885, the 1884 draft was revised further by the commission. The latter took the view that the words 'during the existence of their rights in their country of origin' ('*pendant l'existence de leurs droits dans leur pays d'origine*') were too absolute, in that it might be possible to conclude that they obliged national tribunals to apply the law of the CO, in matters other than duration of protection, where this law was less favourable than that of the country where protection was claimed.[202] This interpretation was explicitly rejected by the commission which proposed the following wording to avoid it: 'it [the enjoyment of these rights] shall not exceed, in the other countries, the length of protection accorded to them in their country of origin'.[203] The expression 'country of origin' was also specified in relation to published works. The options here were the country of the author's nationality, and the country where the work was published. The second was advocated by the British delegation (being in accordance with its national legislation),[204] and was accepted by the commission, which nonetheless saw problems arising where simultaneous publication occurred. To overcome this problem, it proposed that, where a work was simultaneously published in several countries of the Union, its term of protection should not exceed that of the country where the work fell first into the public domain.[205] No provision, however, was made for the equally common situation where a work was simultaneously published in a country of the Union and a country outside the Union (a particular problem for publishers in the UK and the USA). In relation to unpublished works, the commission adhered to the criterion of the author's nationality which had been adopted in the 1884 draft. The effect of these provisions therefore was that the CO of the work of a Union author could change when the work was published. For example, the CO of the **6.75**

[200] ibid, 42. [201] ibid. [202] *Actes* 1885, 41. [203] ibid, 41 and 74.
[204] ibid, 41. [205] ibid, 41 and 74.

unpublished work of a Belgian author (Belgium being a Union country) was Belgium, but if the work was first published in the UK, its CO would then be the UK. Thus, the 'nationality' of a work for the purposes of Convention protection might be different from the nationality of the author, even though the latter was a native of a Union country. The text adopted by the Conference, and ultimately incorporated in article 2 of the final text of the Convention, was as follows:

> Authors who are subjects or citizens of any of the countries of the Union, or their lawful representatives, shall enjoy in the other countries for their works, whether published in one of those countries or unpublished, the rights which the respective laws do now or may hereafter grant to natives.
>
> The enjoyment of these rights shall be subject to the accomplishment of the conditions and formalities prescribed by law in the country of origin of the work, and must not exceed in the other countries the term of protection granted in the said country of origin.
>
> The country of origin of the work shall be considered to be that in which the work is first published, or if such publication takes place simultaneously in several countries of the Union, that one of them the laws of which grant the shortest term of protection.
>
> For unpublished works the country to which the author belongs shall be considered to be the country of origin of the work.[206]

(a) *The Paris and Berlin Revisions*

6.76 The system embodied in these provisions was left basically untouched by the Paris Revision, although an amendment was made to clarify the fact that 'published' meant 'published for the first time' (see para 6.12 above), and a further point of clarification in relation to the accomplishment of formalities and conditions was inserted in the Interpretative Declaration (see para 6.103 below). In the Berlin Revision, however, more substantive changes were made. The provisions concerning national treatment and the determination of a work's CO were now to be found in article 4. It was also made clear that protection under the Convention in countries other than the CO comprised two separate elements: national treatment and 'the rights specially granted by the present Convention'.[207] This was an explicit acknowledgement of the fact that the Convention now also contained mandatory provisions to be applied in the protection of works in countries other than their CO, for instance, in relation to translation rights. In addition, it overcame the possibility that where there was a conflict or difference between a provision of national law and one of the mandatory provisions of the Convention that it could be argued that the second prevailed: the present wording made it clear that both were to be applied equally.[208] No

206 *Actes* 1885, 74. 207 Berlin Act, art 4(1). 208 *Actes* 1908, 236–7.

mention was made of the protection applicable to works in their COs, but the only possible conclusion was that there was no obligation under the Convention for these countries to accord their authors any of the rights 'specially granted' by the Convention. This was confirmed by the addition of a new article (article 5) which stated that natives of a Union country who published their works for the first time in another Union country were to have, in the latter country, the 'same rights as native authors'.

(b) Simultaneous publication under the Berlin Act

Another amendment made in the Berlin Revision dealt with the gap left by the 1886 text in relation to simultaneous publication in a Union and non-Union country. This provided that the latter was to be considered exclusively as the CO of the work.[209] In the absence of any Conventional guidance as to the meaning of 'simultaneously published', it could only be assumed that this meant publication on the same day.[210] However, there was nothing to stop national legislation adopting its own definition of the term, and this might, in consequence, vary from country to country. Under the UK Copyright Act 1911, for example, a period of fourteen days was allowed;[211] as a result, a work of a non-Union national published within fourteen days in both the UK and a non-Union country, such as the USA, would not be entitled to protection in other Union countries which did not define the meaning of 'simultaneously published' in their national laws, or which specified a shorter period.[212] To be sure of securing protection throughout the Union by means of simultaneous publication in both the UK and the USA, an American author would therefore need to ensure that publication in both countries took place on the same day. **6.77**

(c) The later revisions

No further changes were made to these provisions in the Rome Revision, although there was quite extensive discussion at that Conference of the question of simultaneous publication, and a number of alternative proposals were **6.78**

[209] Berlin Act, art 4(3).

[210] This was the view of the commission at the Berlin Conference: *Actes* 1908, 241. It was also assumed to be the case by the International Office and Italian Government in their joint programme for the Rome Conference: *Actes* 1928, 67.

[211] Copyright Act 1911, s 35(3).

[212] Note, however, that the International Office in 1927 took the view that an American work published in the UK in these circumstances was to be treated as a British work, and therefore entitled to protection throughout the Union: [1927] *DA* 37. To avoid doubt on this point, it proposed the following amendment to art 4(3) at the Rome Conference: '. . . a work published fourteen days previously is considered as simultaneously published in a country of the Union, if the law of this country admits the "simultaneity"'. See *Actes* 1928, 67, and see also Ladas (1938) 308–10.

considered.[213] However, it was not until the Brussels Revision that the period of thirty days for the purposes of simultaneous publication was finally adopted.[214] At the same time, special provision was made for the determination of the CO in the case of works of architecture and graphic or plastic works forming part of a building: this was the country where the works had been built or incorporated in a building. This was coupled with the previous provision governing the CO of unpublished works, and the two now appeared in a new paragraph (article 4(5)). This combination was correct as a matter of drafting, as it will be recalled that under the definition of 'published works' the construction of a work of architecture or the exhibition of a work of art did not constitute publication of those works. Apart from these changes, the Brussels Act retained the system established by the Berlin Revision.

(d) Implications of the lack of material reciprocity

6.79 Prior to the Brussels Revision, the lack of material reciprocity inherent in the principle of national treatment led to difficulty in two particular respects: the *droit de suite* and the right of public recitation. The first was recognized in only a few Union countries, notably France,[215] Belgium,[216] and Czechoslovakia.[217] Was it possible, therefore, for artists from other Union countries to claim the benefit of it in these three countries, while French, Belgian, and Czech artists were denied any reciprocal protection elsewhere in the Union? In the case of the second, the reverse was true, and the right of public recitation was recognized in all but a few Union countries (namely Austria and Germany).[218] Were Austrian and German authors, therefore, entitled to this right in other Union countries, while authors from those countries were denied such protection in Austria and Germany? The principle of national treatment indicated an affirmative answer to these questions, but the International Office argued for a contrary conclusion. In a commentary published in *Le Droit d'Auteur* in 1926,[219] it put forward a theory limiting the application of the principle of national treatment in the following terms:

> The different rights comprised in literary and artistic property are only operative in contracting states if they are allowed a 'minimum of recognition' in the country of origin. If this minimum is attained, the general principles of the Convention require complete assimilation of unionist and national, as long as the *lex fori* and *lex soli* each provide for the right envisaged. But if that right is not recognised at all in the country of origin, it is not to be recognised in the rest of the territory of the Union.[220]

[213] *Actes* 1928, 234–5. These included a French proposal for a period of a year.
[214] *Documents 1948* (1951), 178.
[215] Law of 20 May 1920 and Decree of 17 Dec 1920.
[216] Law of 25 June 1921 and 23 Sept 1921.
[217] Law of 1 Mar 1927, art 35.
[218] See Ladas (1938), 267.
[219] [1926] *DA* 49.
[220] ibid, 52–3.

There is no basis for this novel theory of 'minimum of recognition' to be found in the provisions of the Convention. Its adoption would reintroduce the notion of reciprocity into the Convention by the back door, as the principle of national treatment under article 5(1) (formerly article 4(1)) is expressed in clear terms, without any qualification or limitation at all. Also, as Ladas notes, it is a 'dangerous theory', as it is capable of indefinite and uncertain extension.[221] Thus, if it applied to the 'rights' granted by domestic law, it might also be applied to the extent of those rights and their means of enforcement. Furthermore, by making it necessary to refer to the law of the CO, it would undermine the clear objective of the Berlin Revision which was to make protection under the Convention entirely independent of the law of the CO. Nevertheless, while the International Office seemed subsequently to resile from its theory of 'minimum of protection', the reasons for its concern are understandable: why, as a matter of fairness, should an artist from a country which does not recognize the *droit de suite* gain the benefit of it in a country which does recognize it? The solution, however, does not lie in constructing a highly artificial gloss to the provisions of the Convention which is both unwarranted in the light of their clear wording and subverts the basic principles of the Convention. The most obvious solution to the problem is to amend the Convention so as to make it a right specifically granted by the Convention to authors claiming protection under it. This, indeed, was the course adopted at the Brussels Revision Conference: the *droit de suite* was added to the rights protected by the Convention, but its availability was made subject to the requirement of reciprocity (see further paras 11.53ff below).[222] The right of public recitation was also added to the rights protected under the Convention at the time of the Brussels Revision, but without any requirement of reciprocity.[223] Accordingly, each country of the Union is now obliged to accord this right to authors claiming protection under the Convention.

(2) Development of the corresponding principle of minimum protection

Reference has been made at various points in the text to the principle that the Convention embodies a minimum standard of protection that Union countries are to apply to works claiming under the Convention. In other words, these countries are free to apply higher levels of protection to works claiming under the Convention, if they so desire. This seems a natural consequence of the principle of national treatment. However, while this has long been regarded as **6.80**

[221] Ladas (1938), 268.

[222] Brussels Act, art 14*ter*; see also *Documents 1948* (1951), 104 (report of Plaisant, *rapporteur général*).

[223] Brussels Act, art 11*ter*.

axiomatic, it took some time before it was fully and correctly expressed in the Convention.

(a) The early Acts

6.81 The principle of minimum protection was clearly understood to underlie the original Berne Act, and was clearly enunciated in the closing speech of Numa Droz to the 1885 Conference.[224] Nevertheless, express reference to it in the Convention was only made with respect to the bilateral treaties currently in force between the contracting states (article 15 of the Berne Act), and no reference was made to the availability of wider protection under national laws. This omission led to some misunderstanding in the case of what might be called 'union treatment *strictu sensu*', that is, those rights specially granted by the Convention which each country was obliged to accord to Union authors. If a Union country was required under the Convention to accord a particular level of protection in relation, say, to translation rights, did this preclude a Union author from claiming the benefit of a more generous stipulation in this regard than might be otherwise available to foreigners? As a matter of general principle, it can be said that the applicable rule in such a case should be national treatment, and the Union author should therefore be accorded this wider protection as a matter of course. However, in the absence of any express positive duty to do this, all that could be said was that there was only a tacit or implied obligation in this regard.[225] Prior to the Berlin Conference, this gave rise to disputes in the Belgian courts in the case of translation rights.[226] Under the 1896 Act, the exclusive translation right was lost after ten years if no authorized translation in the relevant language had been published.[227] Under Belgian law, however, there was no such loss of rights, as there was complete assimilation of translation rights in that country.[228] This assimilation applied equally to foreigners, and did so independently of any treaty or requirement of reciprocity.[229] If a Union author could only claim the more limited translation right accorded under the 1896 Act, this placed him in a worse position than another foreign non-Union author who could claim the full assimilated right. The result was that a British or French author would enjoy less protection for his translation rights in Belgium than a Dutch or Russian author (both the Netherlands and Russia being neither members of the Berne Union nor party to any bilateral convention

---

[224] *Actes* 1885, 65.

[225] See generally A Baum, 'Droit international public: Convention de Berne et lois nationales' [1946] *DA* 85, 101 and 114, at 105–6, and the study of art 19 in [1909] *DA* 45.

[226] See the decisions discussed in 'Lettre de Belgique' [1898] *DA* 103–4. See further the decisions noted in [1904] *DA* 93, [1906] *DA* 45 and [1907] *DA* 76.

[227] Paris Additional Act, art 1(II).

[228] Belgian Law of 22 Mar 1886, arts 1 and 38.

[229] See further the *mémoire* submitted by the Belgian Government to the Berlin Conference: *Actes* 1908, 197, 199.

with Belgium).[230] The anomaly of this situation was outlined in a memorandum submitted by the Belgian delegation to the Berlin Conference,[231] and it was agreed that it should be clarified in the Convention.[232] The result was the adoption of article 19, which read as follows:

> The provisions of the present Convention shall not prevent claims being made for the application of any wider provision which may be made in favour of foreigners in general.

(b) The later Acts

This provision, however, was far from satisfactory, as the words 'in favour of foreigners in general' gave rise to a further problem. What was the position if the national law of a Union country contained a more generous provision than was applicable in favour of foreigners, but only to certain categories of foreigners, for example, to those from certain countries, or those whose countries granted reciprocity? Such a provision was not a provision 'in favour of foreigners in general', and the result was that a Union author would not be able to claim the benefit of it.[233] Such a result, however, was clearly at variance with the views that had been expressed by Droz at the 1885 Conference and with those stated by the Belgian delegation in its memorandum of 1908. Their aim had been to make the additional protection which Union authors might claim as generous as possible, and not to limit it in this way.[234] It was also inconsistent with the basic principle of national treatment, under which Union authors should always be treated on the same basis as national authors (the only exception to this being in relation to the duration of protection where the rule of comparison of terms applied). In the light of these reasons, it is unclear from the records of the Berlin Conference why the words 'in favour of foreigners in general' were inserted. Nonetheless, their effect was to give the new provision little scope for its operation, as the only Union countries which accorded wider protection in favour of foreigners generally were Luxembourg[235] and Morocco.[236] The remaining states of the Union extended such protection on condition either of reciprocity or through specific treaties.[237] An example of the operation of article 19 can be seen in the provisions of the UK Copyright Act 1911 which related to the mechanical **6.82**

[230] ibid, 269 (report of Renault).

[231] See the *mémoire* submitted by the Belgian Government to the Berlin Conference: *Actes* 1908, 197, 199.

[232] *Actes* 1908, 270. See further Ladas (1938), 189–90.

[233] See further [1909] *DA* 45.

[234] ibid, 46.

[235] Law of 10 May 1898.

[236] Law of 23 June 1916. See further the programme for the Brussels Conference in *Documents 1948* (1951), 379. Note, however, that in a study published by the International Office in 1929, France, Portugal, Syria, and Lebanon were added to this group: [1929] *DA* 64. In the case of France, however, foreigners were not allowed to enjoy broader rights than they had in their own country: see further Ladas (1938), 195.

[237] See the survey of national laws in [1929] *DA* 62, 64 and Ladas (1938), 195–7.

reproduction of musical works.[238] These were applied retroactively to all musical works published before the entry into force of that Act, but there was no obligation to accord such protection under article 13 of the Berlin Act.[239] Accordingly, this was a case where the provisions of UK law were more favourable to authors than those of the Convention. Nevertheless, the UK Government limited the application of the provisions of the 1911 Act to nationals and to foreigners in respect of whom an Order in Council had been made.[240] This led to complaints from French music publishers that the UK was failing to apply the principle of national treatment,[241] but the UK Government replied that it was entitled to restrict the provision in this way as it was not a provision in favour of foreigners in general.[242] Although this meant that states were entirely free to determine whether the benefit of additional protection should be applied to all or only some Union foreigners, the British response was well justified on the basis of article 19. At the Rome Conference, therefore, the Italian Government and International Office argued for the rectification of this situation, and proposed the deletion of the offending words in their programme.[243] In defending this proposal, the Director of the Office, Fritz Ostertag, stated:

> National legislation should not be free to accord more favourable treatment to certain categories only of unionist foreigners, and, in particular, it should not have the capacity to limit this more favourable protection to those unionists whose country of origin accords reciprocity of protection.[244]

There was support for this proposal from Germany and Norway,[245] but a number of important states, including France, Poland, and Italy, were against it.[246] Their reasons for this opposition are not easy to understand, but appear to have been based on the fear that any change in the wording might give rise to further doubts.[247] In consequence, the proposal was rejected, and the Berlin text was retained in the Rome Act. It was not revived in the draft programme that was circulated by the International Office in 1934 in preparation for the Brussels Conference,[248] but it did reappear in the second programme that was distributed in 1947.[249] On this occasion, it was more favourably received,[250] and was

238 UK Copyright Act 1911, s 19. 239 Berlin Act, art 13(3).

240 Order in Council of 24 June 1912. See further [1929] *DA* 67.

241 Ladas (1938), 192. 242 ibid. 243 *Actes* 1928, 84.

244 ibid, 272. 245 ibid. 246 ibid, 273 247 ibid. See also [1929] *DA* 64.

248 Published in [1933] *DA* 73, 90, 97, 112, 121 and [1934] *DA* 7 and 13.

249 *Documents 1948* (1951), 380. In this regard, it is of interest to note the contrary proposal that had been made by Dr F Ostertag, the former Director of the International Office, to the effect that Union countries should be free to determine the conditions under which more favourable conditions applicable under national law should be applied to its foreign authors: F Ostertag, 'La Convention de Berne et le droit national' [1941] *DA* 29, 37, 40. This would have meant the introduction of factual reciprocity into the Convention: A Baum, *The Brussels Conference for the Revision of the Berne Convention* (1949) ('Baum (1949)'), 71.

250 *Documents 1948* (1951), 380–1.

duly adopted by the Conference when it met in the following year.[251] In the opinion of one distinguished commentator, the deletion of the words 'in favour of foreigners in general' was probably the most important achievement of the Brussels Conference,[252] and the impact of this small change should not be underestimated. There was no longer any inconsistency between the principle of national treatment in article 4 and the application of wider protection under national laws to Union authors under article 19. The principle of minimum protection was now embodied in unmistakable terms in the Convention, and this has remained the case under the Stockholm and Paris Acts.[253]

(3) Development of principles of independence of protection and absence of formalities

It was seen above that the principle of national treatment was not completely **6.83** adopted in the Berne Act. In relation to both the questions of compliance with formalities and duration of protection, reference to the law of the CO of a work remained necessary. The second of these matters is discussed in detail in Chapter 9 below, and will not be dealt with here. As regards the first, however, the deletion of any need to refer to the law of a work's CO was one of the principal achievements of the Berlin Revision. It was a major augmentation of the principle of national treatment, and remains one of the most fundamental features of the present text.

(a) The Berne Act

Under article 2(2) of this Act, national treatment was available only when the **6.84** author had accomplished the conditions and formalities prescribed by the law of the CO of the work. As many Union countries at this time required compliance with some kind of formality as a condition of protection under their domestic laws, this provision was of considerable importance. Thus, an English author who sought protection for his work in France under the Convention would need to show that he had complied with whatever formalities were required by English law. However, as he was then assimilated to French natives by article 2(2), was he then obliged to comply with whatever formalities were required under French law for the obtaining of protection? This had been necessary under some of the earlier bilateral conventions,[254] with the result that gaining protection under those conventions was often a cumbersome two-stage process. Nevertheless, the wording of article 2(2) was against such an

[251] ibid, 381. [252] Baum (1949), 70. [253] Stockholm, Paris Acts, art 19.

[254] See eg the Franco-Portuguese Convention of 12 Apr 1851; the Anglo-French Convention of 3 Nov 1851; and the Franco-Spanish Convention of 15 Nov 1853.

interpretation: as it subordinated the enjoyment of the rights of native authors to the accomplishment of the conditions and formalities of the CO of the work, and said nothing about any corresponding need to observe the conditions and formalities of the country where protection was claimed, it was reasonable to conclude that compliance with the former was all that was required (*expressio unius est exclusio alterius*). This interpretation was also consistent with the object of the Convention in securing the ready protection of Union works in other countries of the Union, and was endorsed by the early commentators on the Convention. Thus, Soldan said:

> Instead of requiring that the formalities be complied with in each state in which protection is claimed, it [the Convention] provides that it is sufficient for the author to comply with the legislation of the country of origin of his work. The author therefore no longer has to be concerned with the legislation of a dozen different states; if he has conformed with the law of one only, which is that of the country where the work was published for the first time, he will enjoy, in all the countries of the Union, the rights stipulated by the Convention.[255]

(b) The Paris Declaration

6.85 Nevertheless, in the years immediately after the Convention came into force, some national tribunals took the view that works published in other Union countries were required, in the country where protection was claimed, to comply with the same conditions and formalities as were required for native works. This was on the basis that the Convention had only dispensed with compliance with those formalities which might be imposed upon foreign authors (above and beyond those imposed on native authors).[256] To overcome this interpretation, at the 1896 Conference the French Government and International Office proposed the following modification to article 2(2):

> The enjoyment of these rights is assured to authors without any other conditions or formalities than those prescribed by the legislation of the country of origin of the work.[257]

The UK Government, however, opposed this amendment: although the British courts had recently adopted an approach in line with that of the French amendment,[258] it thought that difficulties with certain British colonies made it undesirable for Her Majesty's Government to support the express alteration of

[255] C Soldan, *L'Union internationale pour la protection des oeuvres littéraires et artistiques: Commentaire de la Convention de Berne du 9 Septembre 1886* (1888), 407.

[256] *Actes* 1896, 161 (report of the commission). See also Briggs (1906), 311–13. The main culprit in this regard appeared to be the UK.

[257] *Actes* 1896, 36–7. [258] ibid, 161.

the Convention on this particular point.[259] As a result, the amendment was included in the Interpretative Declaration, which gave it the character of an 'authentic interpretation rather than a new disposition'.[260] It read as follows:

> In accordance with the provisions of Article 2, paragraph 2 of the Convention, the protection granted . . . shall depend solely on the accomplishment of the conditions and formalities in the country of origin of the work which may be required by the legislation of that country.[261]

This made it clear that authors claiming under the Convention could not be required to comply with any of the formalities of the law of the country where they claimed protection. It was, of course, open to any state to refuse to sign the Declaration, and to apply a more restrictive interpretation of article 2(2) to Convention works.

(c) Evidentiary presumptions

The requirement of compliance with the conditions and formalities of the CO still created difficulties for the courts of those countries where protection was claimed. How could they be sure that this precondition for protection had been fulfilled? The Berne Act contained certain evidentiary presumptions to assist here. Article 11 provided that: **6.86**

> In order that the authors of works protected by the present Convention shall, in the absence of proof to the contrary, be considered as such, and be consequently admitted to institute proceedings against pirates before the courts of the various countries of the Union, it will be sufficient that their names be indicated on the work in the accustomed manner.

The onus was therefore on the infringer to show that the work in question was not entitled to protection under the Convention because of failure to comply with the formalities of the country CO. In the case of anonymous or pseudonymous authors, a similar presumption applied in favour of the publisher whose name appeared on the work to be regarded as the lawful representative of the anonymous or pseudonymous author. However, a final proviso to article 11 provided that the courts of the country where protection was claimed might:

> . . . if necessary, require the production of a certificate from the competent authority to the effect that the formalities prescribed by law in the country of origin have been accomplished, as contemplated in Article 2.

---

[259] ibid, 172–3 (declaration by British delegate). The reason for this declaration appeared to be related to the efforts by the Canadian Government at that time to impose stringent conditions on the protection of non-Canadian works, eg, requirements as to printing and publishing in Canada within a given period after publication elsewhere: see Briggs (1906), 313, n 2.

[260] *Actes* 1896, 161 (report of the commission).

[261] Interpretative Declaration, para 1.

It was not made clear what the effect of the production of such a certificate would be: whether it was to be regarded as conclusive evidence of the facts stated therein, or whether it could still be rebutted by evidence brought by the defendant. These were matters for national legislation to determine, although it is reasonable to think that the interpretation more favourable to the interests of the author in securing protection for his work under the Convention was the one to be adopted.

(d) The Berlin Revision

6.87 Despite these evidentiary provisions, the requirements of article 2(2) still created considerable difficulties for authors and courts alike. In 1910, the International Office estimated that, of some 100 cases involving the Berne Convention, at least one-seventh of these had been concerned with the question of formalities.[262] As Ladas points out, it was possible for an author to lose protection under the Convention by reason of a trivial omission, such as failure to deposit the requisite number of copies of his work in its CO.[263] Accordingly, the logic of abolishing formalities altogether became more and more compelling, and this objective was achieved, with reasonable unanimity (including the assent of the UK Government), at the Berlin Revision Conference.[264] This change was coupled with a more radical proposal made by the German Government under which protection in each Union country was to be entirely independent of the existence of protection in the CO of the work.[265] This second proposal embodied the application of national treatment in its most absolute form, although a precedent for it was to be found in the Paris Convention where independence of protection in the case of patents and other industrial property rights protected under the Convention was clearly established.[266] Complete independence of protection also led to the consequence that there would no longer be any need to refer to the law of the CO in relation to the matter of duration. Thus, in the case of a German work claiming protection in France, it would receive the full period of protection accorded to French works (life plus fifty years),[267] and not the lesser period of protection then accorded under German law (life plus thirty years),[268] which was the applicable period under the Berne Act. However, this conclusion was resisted by the French delegation:

262 [1910] *DA* 5.

263 Ladas (1938), 270. See further E Röthlisberger, *Die Berner-Uebereinkunft zum Schutze von Werken der Literatur und Kunst und die Zusatzabkommen: Geschichtlich und rechtlich beleuchtet und kommentiert* (1906), 60ff and 100ff.

264 *Actes* 1908, 37–9, 185 (proposals of German Government and International Office), 237 (report of the commission).

265 ibid, 37–9, 85.

266 Paris Convention, art $4^{bis}(1)$.

267 French Law of 14 July 1866, art 1. See further Desbois et al (1976), 417.

268 German Law of 19 June 1901, art 29.

while the latter accepted the principle of independence of protection, it argued that this could not be separated from the need for a uniform term of protection (a matter on which the French had very strong views).[269] Ultimately, a compromise solution was adopted by the Conference under which the principle of independence of protection (coupled with that of absence of formalities) was embodied in a new article 4(2), and a commitment to a uniform term of protection of the life of the author plus fifty years was enshrined in article 7, but subject to a requirement of reciprocity until such time as this uniform term was achieved. A second sentence added to article 4(2) amplified the principle of independence of protection by making it clear that this also applied to the enforcement of their rights by authors under the Convention:

> Consequently, apart from the express stipulations of the present Convention, the extent of protection as well as the means of redress secured to the author to safeguard his rights, shall be governed exclusively by the laws of the country where protection is claimed.

These provisions dealing with absence of formalities and independence of protection were not changed in the later revisions. By contrast, significant amendments to the provisions on national treatment were made at the Stockholm Conference.

(4) National treatment under the Stockholm, Paris Acts

(a) In general

In the Stockholm Revision, the articles dealing with the classes of authors protected under the Convention, and the application of the principle of national treatment were completely restructured. This was based on a series of proposals formulated by Professor Ulmer, the chairman of Main Committee I.[270] Articles 4 to 6 of the Brussels Act, which had remained substantially unchanged since the Berlin Revision, now became articles 3 to 5 of the Stockholm, Paris Acts. In this revised text, the questions of eligibility for protection, and the level of protection accorded, are dealt with in separate articles. Article 3 specifies the persons entitled to protection under the Convention (article 3(1) and (2); see para 6.04 above) and contains definitions of the expressions 'published works' (article 3(2); see para 6.22 above) and 'published simultaneously' (article 3(4), see para 6.42 above). It is supplemented by article 4, which deals with the protection of non-Union nationals in the special cases of cinematographic and architectural works (see paras 6.16 and 6.17 above, respectively). Finally, article 5 deals with the level of protection to be accorded to persons entitled to protection under articles 3 and 4. It therefore embodies **6.88**

[269] *Actes* 1908, 239ff.

[270] *Records* 1967, vol I, 687 (Document S/44).

the basic principles of national treatment, independence of protection, and absence of formalities, as well as the rules concerning the determination of the CO of a work. These last provisions remain basically the same as under the earlier texts, but some additions and amplifications were made to them.

(b) The application of the principle of national treatment

6.89 This is the same as under the Berlin, Rome, and Brussels Acts, except that article 3(1) now deals separately with the persons entitled to protection under the Convention (formerly articles 4(1) and 6 of the Brussels Act). Under article 5(1), authors entitled to protection under the Convention enjoy, in respect of their works, in countries of the Union other than the CO of the work, the following rights: (i) 'the rights which their respective laws do now or may hereafter grant to their nationals', and (ii) 'the rights specially granted by this Convention'.

As far as protection of works in their CO is concerned, article 5(3) makes explicit what was previously understood to be the case, namely that this is governed by domestic law, with no requirement that the 'rights specially granted' by the Convention also be accorded to these works. This is supplemented by the provision contained in the previous article 5 of the Berlin, Rome, and Brussels Acts that authors who are not nationals of the CO of the work which is protected under the Convention enjoy in that country 'the same rights as national authors'. Thus, Union nationals who publish their works in another Union country are assimilated to the nationals of that country, and will only enjoy the same protection for their works as that enjoyed by national authors, with no entitlement to any of the 'rights specially granted' by the Convention.

(c) The relationship between national treatment and 'rights specially granted'

6.90 These are the twin pillars on which protection under the Convention rests. While theoretically distinct, however, they are closely interrelated, and cover much the same ground. In principle, national treatment does not entail any requirement of material reciprocity on the part of the member states of the Union. This means that there may be an imbalance between the levels of protection available in different states, with the consequence that authors from a state with a lower level will be advantaged in a state with a higher level, and there will be a corresponding detriment to authors from the second state when they seek protection in the first. However, this imbalance will rarely be as great as might be supposed, because of the further obligation that article 5(1) lays on Union states to accord to foreign authors 'those rights specially granted' by the Convention. Although the latter expression is not further defined, it can only refer to those positive measures which Union members are required to take with respect to the protection of works claiming protection under the Convention. Among other things, these include the substantive rights referred to in articles 6*bis*, 8, 9, 11, 11*bis*, 11*ter*, 12, 13, 14, and 14*ter*, as well as the other mandatory provisions concerning absence of formalities (article 5(2)) and duration (article 7). These provisions comprise a basic corpus of authors' rights, and have the consequence that there is a minimum level of protection that is uniformly available to authors in all countries of the Union other than the CO of their works. In practice, however, these rights will almost always overlap with the protection already accorded through the application of national treatment. This is because each Union country will usually accord the same rights to its own nationals, and will therefore usually grant identical protection both to its own authors and to Union authors. The 'rights specially granted' by the Convention will therefore usually not apply separately to Union authors, but will have the effect of defining the central content or core of the protection which the latter will receive under the principle of national treatment. Accordingly, it will only be in the marginal area beyond this 'central core' that differences in the level of protection accorded to Union authors will arise. Nevertheless, even here the differences will be within a relatively small compass, because of the need to place some limitations on the scope of application of the principle of national treatment. (The question is discussed further at paras 6.93ff below.)

(5) Independence of protection and absence of formalities under the Stockholm, Paris Acts

The position here remains the same as when the principle of independence of **6.91**
protection was first adopted in the Berlin Act. After providing that the enjoyment and exercise of rights is to be free of any formality, article 5(2) of the Stockholm, Paris Acts goes on to stipulate:

> . . . such enjoyment and such exercise shall be independent of the existence of protection in the country of origin of the work. Consequently, apart from the provisions of this Convention, the extent of protection, as well as the means of redress afforded to the author to protect his rights, shall be governed exclusively by the laws of the country where protection is claimed.

The implications of the principle of independence of protection have already been discussed (see para 6.87 above). Its purpose is to remove the need for reference to the laws of a work's CO when protection for it is sought under the Convention. Furthermore, the second sentence contains a basic rule in relation to the laws applicable to authors claiming protection under the Convention: the extent of this protection, as well as the means of redress available to enforce it, are to be governed exclusively by the laws of the country where protection is claimed. (Exceptions to this rule will be addressed at paras 6.98ff.)

(a) Formalities

6.92 The position in relation to formalities has not changed since the Berlin Act. The rule is now contained in article 5(2), but its wording remains identical to that adopted in the Berlin Act: 'The enjoyment and exercise of these rights shall not be subject to any formality; . . .'. The effect of this provision is that where an author claims protection for his work in a country of the Union other than the CO of the work, this protection is not to be made subject to any formality. This does not prevent the law of that country imposing such requirements as regards authors of works for which that country is the CO: these authors are usually local authors, and there are no Conventional obligations in respect of them.[271] As a matter of practice, however, the position in relation to these, usually native, authors will usually be the same as for foreign authors first publishing elsewhere and claiming protection under the Convention, as the provisions of the Convention invariably have a strong influence on the content of the domestic laws of its members.[272]

C. The Scope of the Principle of National Treatment

(1) Breadth of coverage of the rule of national treatment

6.93 Article 5(1) refers not only to the rights accorded currently to nationals by the law of the country where protection is claimed (that is, at the time when the Convention comes into force with respect to that country) in works for which authors are protected under the Convention, but also to the rights which may be accorded subsequently. Regarding the subject matter of protection, articles 2 and 2*bis* leave considerable discretion to Union countries to determine what shall be protected under the head of literary and artistic works. As a result, this may be an area where the details of national treatment differ significantly from country to country. (The subject matter required to be protected is discussed further in Chapter 8 below.) Regarding rights which member states may subsequently accord, this means that Union authors claiming under the Convention are entitled to the benefit of any new right which may be later added to the rights

[271] This is stating the obvious, as the Convention deals only with the protection of the rights of authors in countries other than the CO (which usually, albeit not always, is the country of the author's nationality or residence). Thus it was that art 6 of the French Law of 19 July 1793 requiring the deposit of copies as a precondition for the bringing of infringement proceedings continued to apply to French nationals, although under the Convention authors of other Union countries were relieved of this obligation: see *Magalhaes et Moniz c Muroz Escamoz* (Trib de comm de la Seine, 13 Nov 1913, noted in [1914] *DA* 38, 39). See also *Actes* 1908, 237.

[272] But see eg 17 USC § 411 (registration remains a prerequisite to institution of a suit for copyright infringement of a US work; registration not required of non-US Berne works).

accorded to native authors. (See the earlier discussion at paras 6.80ff above on the development of the principle of minimum protection.) However, what meaning is to be attached to article 5(1)'s reference to the 'rights which [the] respective laws' of the countries of the Union grant to their nationals? Does this mean any law applying to literary and artistic works, or, more generally, any law applying to authors? Or is it to be interpreted more restrictively? Is it limited to rights of a kind covered by the Convention, or does it extend to broader rights as well? It surely cannot be the case that national treatment is owed only with respect to those rights whose protection the treaty specifically mandates. First, if the treaty mandates that protection, then member states must provide it, whether or not local authors were entitled to that protection. In that event, a national treatment obligation adds nothing, because if local protections do not meet Berne standards, national treatment may not be enough. Second, the absence of a right from the list of Berne minima does not mean that the right is extraneous to copyright and thus eludes the national treatment requirement. After all, the reproduction right was not explicitly included among the minima until 1967, but it seems clear that from the beginning member states would have been bound to accord foreign Union authors local reproduction rights, that right being at the core of authors' rights. At the very least, then, the right must be of a kind covered by the Convention,[273] or general concepts of copyright law, but what the phrase 'of a kind' means will require further exploration.

These questions are of some practical significance, as, in a number of countries, such rights as the *droit de suite* and public lending right, and, in some countries, remuneration for private copying, are embodied in special laws which are distinct from the general copyright laws of those countries.[274] Thus, if only rights conferred by laws relating to literary and artistic works strictly speaking are covered by article 5(1), it can be argued that these other rights need not be accorded to authors claiming under the Convention. Similarly, if the rights afforded are different in kind from the rights Berne requires to be protected, one might argue that these exceed the mandatory scope of national treatment. This point was apparently taken in the pre-Brussels Revision period in France and Belgium in relation to the *droit de suite* which was governed by separate legislation, and which, it was argued, was an entirely separate right from copyright.[275] **6.94**

[273] Accord, David Vaver, 'The National Treatment Requirements of the Berne and Universal Copyright Conventions (Part Two)' (1986) 17 *IIC* 715, 717 (right under national law should be '*in pari materia*' with Berne rights).

[274] *Droit de suite* was formerly the subject of separate laws in France and Belgium, while in the UK public lending right is dealt with in the Public Lending Right Act 1979, rather than in the Copyright, Designs and Patents Act 1988. See also the Public Lending Right Act 1985 (Australia). On private-copying remuneration regimes, see eg Gillian Davies and Michèle E Hung, *Music and Video Private Copying: An International Survey of the Problem and the Law* (1993), 218–21.

[275] Ladas (1938), 268.

Ladas argues that this was too restrictive an interpretation of the Convention, and that the laws referred to in article 5(1) (then article 4(1)) meant the laws relating to 'authors', who were the persons entitled to protection under that provision.[276] This interpretation, in its turn, seems too wide, as it could potentially include other laws applicable to authors which have only indirect connection with the subject matter of authors' rights, for example, laws relating to the taxation of royalties, or laws which subsidize artistic endeavour through the grant of monetary and other assistance. Later scholars have offered other definitions of the scope of the rule of national treatment in the Berne Convention. For example, in Elizabeth Steup's somewhat narrower statement, '[c]opyright protection includes as essential elements [all three of] the following—that a right is granted to (1) a person in his capacity as author (2) of a determined work, and, (3) the right being related to the utilization of that work'.[277] This formulation avoids the overbreadth that would sweep in local social programmes benefiting authors, but the term 'utilization' is rather vague. David Vaver offers more precision: 'As used in the R[evised] B[erne] C[onvention], an author's right tracks the primary meaning common to most national copyright laws: an author has in relation to his/her work a right to exclude others from reproducing or using the work in some way. The RBC extends this primary meaning to include a right to receive remuneration from the user of the work, even where the author is unable to prevent the use.'[278] Refining the formulations still further, Paul Goldstein proposes: 'Characterized at the highest useful level of abstraction, an economic right subject to national treatment under the 1971 Berne Paris Act consists of three elements: it is effective against the world at large; it enables the author to control, or benefit from, the use of a literary or artistic work; and it values the use of the work, however roughly, proportionate to the work's success or prospective success in the marketplace.' If any one of these elements is present, national treatment may be required; if all are present, it must be extended.[279]

6.95 There is clearly a need to define the field of application for the principle of national treatment, and this is best done by a consideration of the text of the Convention. This suggests the following conclusions. From the preamble and article 1, the object of the Convention is clearly indicated as being the protection of the 'rights of authors in their literary and artistic works'. This object, however, requires further clarification, as an examination of the substantive provisions of the Convention reveals that it is far from comprehensive in the

[276] Ladas (1938), 268.

[277] Elizabeth Steup, 'The Rule of National Treatment for Foreigners and its Application to New Benefits for Authors' (1977) 25 *Bulletin of the Copyright Society of the USA* 279, 284.

[278] See Vaver (n 273 above), 717.

[279] Paul Goldstein, *International Copyright: Principles, Law, and Practice* (2001) 81–2.

protection which it accords. In essence, there are the following elements to this protection:

- the identification of the persons who are eligible to claim this protection (namely, Union authors, and non-Union authors in particular circumstances);
- the subject matter protected (namely, literary and artistic works);
- the substantive rights protected;
- the duration of this protection;
- the exceptions to this protection;
- the remedies afforded.

Each of these elements assists in defining and delimiting the field of application of the principle of national treatment, and has the effect of ensuring that it does not have an open-ended and indeterminate operation. Thus, an author claiming protection under the Convention should have the benefit of whatever are the provisions of national law concerning these matters, insofar as they go beyond what is required by a specific Conventional rule. These matters can be briefly described as relating to the rights and subject matter to be protected, the scope of this protection, and its duration or termination.[280] This is confirmed by article 19 which embodies the basic principle that the Convention only establishes the minimum of protection which is to be accorded to Union authors, and that the latter may claim whatever additional protection is provided to nationals (see paras 6.80ff above).[281] However, where a provision of national law lies entirely outside these matters, it cannot be the subject of any requirement to accord national treatment: there can be no automatic entitlement to the benefits of the law of the country where protection is claimed. For example, if a national law protects subject matter that is not a '[work] for which [authors] are protected under this Convention', ie subject matter that is not a 'literary and artistic work', such as an author's commercial interest in controlling the marketing of her image, a foreign author would not, by virtue of the Berne Convention, be entitled to claim protection for her 'publicity rights' in that jurisdiction.[282]

---

[280] See generally, E Ulmer, *Intellectual Property Rights and the Conflict of Laws* (1978), 1–3, 28–35.

[281] The scope of art 19 may be broader still: if it did no more than reaffirm member states' obligations under art 5(1) to grant to foreign authors the same scope of copyright protection, including protections broader than Berne's minima, that they grant local authors, then art 19 would add nothing to those duties. For art 19 to have independent meaning, perhaps it should apply as well to those protections that a member state accords to certain foreign authors but does not accord to its nationals. This reading would turn art 19 into a kind of 'most favoured nation' clause. That, however, is problematic, in light of art 20, which permits member states to make separate agreements to provide greater protection. See further the discussion at paras 6.126ff below.

[282] See eg David Vaver, 'The National Treatment Requirements of the Berne and Universal Copyright Conventions (Part One)' (1986) 17 *IIC* 577, 591: 'The general rule [is] that the

(This, of course, leaves open the question whether the author would enjoy that protection by virtue of that country's general private international law rules regarding the treatment of foreigners.)

6.96 The above analysis does not necessarily resolve the question of whether rights not presently included in the Convention are to be protected under the principle of national treatment. Although the status of the *droit de suite* and public recitation right are now settled under the Convention, the status of certain other rights remains to be resolved. These include public lending rights and commercial rental rights, which are protected in some national laws, but are not the subject of any Berne Convention rule, although the latter now are partially covered by the TRIPs Agreement and the WCT. Whether the requirement to accord national treatment applies to these rights may depend upon how these rights can be characterized: are they of the same kind as those presently protected under the Convention? Arguably, because these rights attach to physical copies rather than to incorporeal works, they fall outside the normal ambit of copyright (the scope of Berne minimum rights pertaining to physical copies is discussed in Chapter 11 below), even though their exploitation may be economically significant. Under the guidelines evoked earlier, however, commercial rental at least would be a strong claimant for national treatment, as a 'utilization' of particular works of particular authors, which could be remunerated in a manner 'roughly, proportionate to the work's success or prospective success in the marketplace'.[283] Moreover, with respect to moral rights, the incorporeal rights/physical copies dichotomy seems particularly unpersuasive. Member states already are obliged, under article 6*bis*, to protect works against deleterious alterations; these would include mutilations of physical copies of works of visual art. It is generally agreed, however, that article 6*bis* does not reach the destruction of artworks (see the discussion at para 10.26 below). If a member state nonetheless in its national law grants artists the right to prevent the destruction of their works, or compensates them for unjustified destructions,[284] there is a strong argument that all Berne Union artists whose works are threatened with destruction in that member state should receive the benefit of that state's more extensive scope of protection of the right of integrity. Put another way, the determination whether the national law affords rights 'of a kind' with Berne

concept of those works for which national treatment is demanded, is defined by the Convention', quoting Eugen Ulmer, 'The "Droit de Suite" in International Copyright Law' (1975) 6 *IIC* 12, 21. Vaver continues, 'A state that defines works more broadly than required under the RBC is neither obliged nor entitled by the RBC to extend national treatment for these works, nor is it obliged or entitled to claim national treatment for them in another RBC state.'

[283] See Steup (above n 277); Goldstein (above n 279).

[284] See eg 17 USC § 106A (a)(3)(B) (right to prevent destruction of a 'work of recognized stature').

rights, may not turn on formal distinctions, but rather on an analysis of the purpose and implementation of the national law.

(a) Comparison of the scope of minimum rights with the scope of national treatment

Thus, to a great extent, the scope of the rule of national treatment will depend upon the way in which national law articulates and regulates the right at issue. A similar inquiry applies to determining whether the Berne minima oblige the member state to extend the benefits of its legislation to foreign authors, regardless of the rule of national treatment. The problem of remuneration for private copying illustrates the considerations applicable to both questions. Responding to the prejudice to authors arising from uncompensated private copying facilitated by new technologies such as the audio tape recorder and the video recorder, many countries, primarily in Europe, devised levy schemes imposing a surcharge on copying equipment and/or blank recording media, and distributing the revenues among authors, producers, and performers in shares intended to correspond to the extent of copying of the works.[285] Does the Berne Convention require that foreign Union authors share in these proceeds, either as a matter of minimum rights, or as a matter of national treatment?[286] **6.97**

Consider first the nature of the right, remuneration for private copying. This is a compulsory licence for the exercise of the reproduction right. The reproduction right under article 9(1) of Berne is broad in scope, containing no categorical exception for private copying. Thus, member states are obliged to protect that right independently of any obligation of national treatment. Does the nature of the right's implementation, as a remuneration right rather than as an exclusive right, take it out of the Convention's direct reach? It would be perverse were a member state to elude Berne minima simply by recasting exclusive rights as remuneration rights. Moreover, with respect to the reproduction right, article 9(2) of Berne limits the extent to which a member state may impose compulsory licences in lieu of enforcing exclusive rights (see further Chapter 13 below). (For present purposes, we need not explore how private 'private copying' must be to qualify for any exception or limitation on exclusive rights.) For those compulsory licences that do meet the 'three-step test' article 9(2) sets out, it would still be perverse were a member state to limit the licences' proceeds to local authors. Article 9(2) allows the member state in appropriate circumstances to subject the foreign Berne work to a compulsory licence; it follows that the foreign author must reap whatever benefits the licence confers. So far, then, the question is resolved by direct application of Berne minimum standards.

[285] See generally Davies and Hung (above n 274).

[286] For a detailed analysis regarding the German private-copying levy, see Peter F Burger, 'The New Photocopy Remuneration Provisions in the Federal Republic of Germany and their Application to Foreign Authors under International Copyright Law' (1988) 19 *IIC* 488.

Does the analysis change if the member state, instead of distributing the proceeds of the licence to any authors, devotes it to the promotion of general, local, cultural causes? If the member state must compensate Berne authors for the exercise of the reproduction right, it should not matter to foreign Union authors that local authors are not benefiting from the levy. One role, after all, of minimum rights is to ensure that however badly a state treats its own authors, it must afford foreign Berne authors a certain level of protection.

But what if the member state were not obliged to enforce Berne authors' reproduction rights with respect to private copying at all? Suppose that application of the article 9(2) 'three-step test' entitled a member state to exempt some kinds of private copying altogether. (As to whether this outcome is likely or permissible, see further Chapter 13 below.) In that case, the member state would no longer incur an obligation to foreign authors flowing directly from the Berne minima. But suppose further that the same state instituted a private-copying scheme compensating local authors; would the rule of national treatment oblige that state to include foreign Union authors? Put another way, even if Berne did not require a member state to extend exclusive rights or remuneration rights to the private copying at issue, once a member state does so for its own authors, must it do so for foreign Berne authors? This appears to fall well within the scope of national treatment under any of the tests suggested here, and so the answer should be 'yes'.[287]

Finally, still assuming that Berne does not oblige member states to extend exclusive or remuneration rights to at least some kinds of private copying, would it now make a difference if the member state devotes the proceeds of a levy to the promotion of general, local, cultural causes, rather than giving them to local authors? In this instance, participation in the fruits of the levy would not be one of the 'rights which [a member state's] laws do now or may hereafter grant to their nationals'. Although she may benefit indirectly from the cultural programmes the levy subsidizes, a national author does not have a personal claim to a share of the proceeds; to employ Professor Goldstein's formulation, this variation on the levy scheme does not '[enable] the author to control, or benefit from, the use of a literary or artistic work'. Similarly, unlike levies whose proceeds are allocated to authors in shares intended to reflect the extent to which each work is copied, the cultural programmes scheme does not '[value] the use of the work, however roughly, proportionate to the work's success or prospective success in the marketplace'.[288]

---

[287] For a working-through of these tests as applied to private copying, see Goldstein (above n 279), 82; Burger (above n 286).

[288] Accord, Vaver (n 273 above), 717–18.

(2) Exceptions to the rule of national treatment

The effect of the rule of national treatment, as set out in article 5(2), is generally to make the law of the country where protection is sought applicable to determine whether the work at issue is protected by copyright in that country, whether it has been infringed, and what remedies are available.[289] But there are certain modifications of and exceptions to this basic rule. First, the Convention's substantive minima inform the protection local law affords; if local law does not otherwise provide a level of protection consistent with Berne minima, it must nonetheless adhere to these supranational norms when non-local Berne works are at issue. By the same token (as will be discussed further in greater detail at para 6.110 below) the Conventional exclusions from coverage may constitute supranational *maxima* of protection: member states may not extend protection to foreign Berne works or provide rights that fall into these limited categories, even though local works may enjoy those benefits. **6.98**

Second, article 5(2) recognizes expressly that, despite the general rule of national treatment, the provisions of the Convention may provide otherwise ('apart from the provisions of this Convention'). Those provisions all assign a role to the law of the work's CO. Two examples of this are to be found in article 7(8) under which reference to the law of the CO of a work may become relevant as regards questions of duration, and article 14*ter* where reciprocity is required for the recognition of the *droit de suite*. A third example is works of applied art under article 2(7), which refers to the CO to determine whether the work will be protected under a specific local designs and models (design patent) regime, or as an artistic work under the Berne Convention.

Finally, the expressions 'extent of protection' and 'means of redress to protect his rights' appear to limit the application of the rule of national treatment to actual infringement proceedings which are brought to enforce the rights protected under the Convention. This means that other matters concerned with these rights need not be exclusively governed by the laws of the country where protection is claimed as they do not relate to the extent of this protection.

(a) Matters other than existence and scope of protection and remedies

Thus, in the case of an assignment or licensing of his rights by an author it can be said that these transactions are not usually concerned with the protection, or extent of protection, of rights under the Convention, but with the way in which **6.99**

[289] Although art 5(2) is not formally a conflict of laws rule (see further the discussion at para 6.100 and in more detail in Chapter 20 below), in practice, art 5(2) generally leads to application of the principle of territoriality, under which the law of each country where the infringement allegedly occurred determines protectability, scope, and relief.

these rights are exploited (which presupposes, of course, that they are protected in the first place). If this is so, then it should be open to the parties to provide that disputes in relation to the terms of these agreements, for example, as regards such matters as the quantum or method of remuneration, are to be settled in accordance with a law of their choice, which need not necessarily be that of the country where protection is claimed. In such a case, it would then be open to the court in question to apply that law in accordance with the rules of private international law adopted in that jurisdiction. Such a course would be equally open in relation to a wide range of other matters concerned with authors' rights, for example, disputes between joint authors, entitlement under a testamentary disposition, and so on. This interpretation of article 5(2) is quite consistent with its wording, and has the support of a number of commentators.[290] It is also consistent with the interpretation of the scope of the principle of national treatment (suggested in para 6.93 above). By the same token, matters of initial ownership are not clearly covered by article 5(2) (these questions will be addressed in more detail in Chapters 7 and 20 below).

(b) Disjunction between the country where *protection is claimed, and the country* for which *protection is claimed*

6.100 A further situation to be considered in relation to article 5(2) is the less usual one where an author brings infringement proceedings in a country other than the country in which the infringement was committed. This might happen where the defendant has assets in the first country (but not in the second) which will be able to satisfy any monetary award granted to the plaintiff. It might also happen if the plaintiff is bringing in a single forum claims alleging infringements transpiring in more than one country. In these situations, does article 5(2) require the court to apply its own law, or may it apply another, for example, that of the country (or countries) where the infringement is alleged to have occurred (the '*lex loci delicti*')? Desbois et al argue that it would be illogical to insist on the first, as it is the law of the country where the infringing act occurred which should be taken into account.[291]

Is this consistent with the basic rule under article 5(2)? This requires the application of the 'laws of the country where protection is claimed'. Professor Ulmer has argued that, despite the formulation, this does not logically imply a reference to the law of the forum (although in most cases, this country will be the same as the country where the infringing act occurred).[292] Article 5(2) would

[290] See further Desbois et al (1976), 152ff; Walter (n 190 above); Mireille van Eechoud, *Choice of Law in Copyright and Related Rights: Alternatives to the Lex Protectionis* (2003), 109; J Ginsburg, 'The Private International Law of Copyright in an Era of Technological Change' (1999) *Recueil des Cours* 273, 354–5.

[291] Desbois et al (1976), 153.

[292] Ulmer (n 280 above), 10.

have more clearly designated application of the law of the place of the infringement had it provided for application of the 'laws of the country *for which* protection is claimed' (or, even more clearly, laws of *each* country for which protection is claimed).[293] Both the French and the English texts clearly state 'where' ('*où*'), however, which suggests that it may simply have been assumed that suit would be brought in the country in which the infringement allegedly occurred. Professor Ulmer also remarks that, from the point of view of general principles of private international law, it would be consistent for a complete rule of conflict of laws to provide that the protection of intellectual property rights should be governed by the law of the country in whose territory the infringement took place.[294] The ambiguity of the Convention's drafting, however, may make this a matter for national laws to determine for themselves. In most instances, it seems that these national choice of law rules will apply the principle of territoriality, and will therefore restrict the application of local substantive law to infringements committed within their jurisdiction. By the same token, the forum (if it finds the foreign infringement claims justiciable) would apply the laws of the foreign territories concerned to infringements committed abroad.[295] (Conflict of laws issues will be analysed in greater depth in Chapter 20 below.)

D. Substantive Minima

(1) Absence of formalities

(a) Policy underlying the prohibition

In addition to outlining the contours of the rule of national treatment, article 5(2) sets out one of the treaty's foundational substantive minimum rules: protection must be formality-free. After summarizing the policy underlying the prohibition, this section addresses, first, what is meant by 'formality', and then the scope of the prohibition. Finally, this section considers means by which member states may achieve the public benefits of formalities without violating article 5(2). **6.101**

As we have seen at paras 6.83–6.87 above, the Convention has steadily evolved

[293] Several commentators have contended that art 5(2) should be read as meaning 'country for which protection is claimed'. See eg André Lucas, *Private International Law Aspects of the Protection of Works and Objects of Related Rights Transmitted Through Digital Networks 12* (1998), available at www.wipo.int/documents; Silvia Plenter, 'Choice of Law Rules for Copyright Infringements in the Global Information Infrastructure: A Never-Ending Story' [2003] 23 *EIPR* 313, 317 (stating proposition and citing more sources); Desbois et al (1976), paras 135–9; Stefania Bariatti, 'Internet e il diritto internazionale privato: aspetti relativi all a disciplina del diritto d'autore' (1996) V *AIDA* 59, 70.

[294] Ulmer (n 280 above), 10. [295] ibid, 10–11.

away from requiring any compliance with formalities as a condition of a Union work's protection in other Union countries. Because formalities tended to encumber, and even forfeit, the author's enjoyment or exercise of rights,[296] it is understandable that an international instrument whose goal was to strengthen authors' rights would seek progressively to mute the role of preconditions constitutive of or necessary to the enforcement of copyright. To some extent, Berne's twin principles of independence of protection and absence of formalities mirror national law developments away from a conception of copyright as a grant which the state, as grantor, would freight with a variety of declaratory obligations (such as registration of the work with a public authority), toward an understanding of copyright as justified by the act of creation, rather than by an act of public recordation.[297] If formalities do not give rise to national copyright, there is even less reason for them to precondition the existence of international protection, particularly as the latter springs automatically from the creation of a work by a Union national or resident (or by publication by any means of production of copies in a Union country). Indeed, the principle of independence of protection means that a work is no longer 'anchored' in its CO: the work might be without protection as a matter of domestic law, yet still be entitled to protection in other Union countries. Moreover, to the extent formalities serve the notice-giving role of alerting members of the public not to copy or communicate works they might otherwise freely exploit, the presence or absence of some kind of public claim of rights in the CO may do little to inform members of the public in different countries. Logically, the notice-giving function would best be met through national treatment, effectively requiring the work to comply with formalities in each Union country. This, however, would have risked restoring the complicated, often inconsistent and even draconian conditions the Convention sought to remove from the international scene (see further the discussion of the pre-1886 national laws in Chapter 1 above). Similarly, simplification of formalities, through the procedure of certifying the author's compliance with her home country's requirements, proved unwieldy in practice (see the discussion at para 6.100 above). In addition, even had that measure worked better in fact, it would not have performed a reliable notice-giving function, because not all Union countries required the same formalities. As a result, the disuniformity of information emanating from each CO would have undercut its utility.

---

296 See further para 1.19 above.

297 See eg Jane C Ginsburg, 'A Tale of Two Copyrights: Literary Property in Revolutionary France and America', in Brad Sherman and Alain Strowel (eds), *Of Authors and Origins: Essays on Copyright Law* (1994), 131–58 (discussing role of formalities in early US and French copyright regimes).

(b) Meaning of 'formality'

For guidance on this question, it is necessary to refer to the discussions which preceded the formation of the Union. In the ALAI text of 1883, it was provided that protection in a country of the Union other than the CO of the work was to be subject to compliance with the 'formalities required by the law in the country of origin of the work'.[298] In the programme which it submitted to the Diplomatic Conference of 1884, the Swiss Federal Council substituted the composite phrase 'conditions and formalities' for 'formalities'.[299] This was adopted by the commission of the Conference in preference to a German proposal to use the expression 'formal and material conditions', on the basis that the Federal Council draft appeared to it 'to encompass all the conditions and requirements required in the country of origin to constitute an author's rights'.[300] This wording was, in turn, adopted by the Conference,[301] but during the discussion one of the German delegates (Dr Meyer) put forward the following interpretation which was reproduced verbatim in the Conference records: **6.102**

> It is only a matter of noting that the draft proposed by the German delegation: 'formal and material conditions', has been replaced by the words: 'formalities and conditions', and that the word 'formalities' has been taken as synonymous with the term 'formal conditions', comprising, for example, registrations, deposit, etc.; while the expression 'conditions', synonymous in our view with the words 'material conditions', comprises, for example, the making of a translation within the prescribed time. Now the words 'formalities and conditions' comprise everything which must be complied with in order to ensure that the rights of the author with regard to his work may come into existence (in German: '*Voraussetzungen*'), while the effects and consequences of protection (in German: '*Wirkungen*'), in particular the extent of that protection, should remain subordinated to the principle of treatment equal with nationals.[302]

In response to this statement, the president of the Conference (Numa Droz) noted that the Conference was in accord with Meyer as to the significance of the words 'formalities and conditions'.[303] These words were retained, without comment, by the 1885 Conference, except that in the draft finally approved by that Conference they were reversed (without any reason for this being given) so as to read 'conditions and formalities'.[304] It was in this order that they were included in the final Act of 1886.[305] There was no further discussion directly on the question of formalities at the 1885 Conference, but there was an interesting exchange which casts some light on the scope and significance of the expression 'conditions and formalities'. This arose in relation to article 12 which contained

[298] ALAI draft text, art 1: *Actes* 1884, 7.
[299] Federal Council programme, art 2: *Actes* 1884, 11.
[300] ibid, 42. [301] ibid, 43. [302] ibid. [303] ibid. [304] *Actes* 1885, 42.
[305] Berne Act, art 2(2).

certain presumptions as to authorship which might be relied upon in proceedings to enforce rights under the Convention (see now article 15, which remains substantially the same, and see also para 7.16 below). This article provided that if the author's name appeared on his work in the accustomed manner, this would suffice, in the absence of proof to the contrary, for the purpose of bringing proceedings. During the discussion on this provision, it was remarked by the Italian delegate (Rosmini) that this was not in harmony with article 2 which made protection subject to compliance with the formalities of the CO, and therefore some link should be made between the two articles.[306] As to this, the German delegate (Reichardt) said that there was no connection between the provisions, as they dealt with entirely different matters: article 2 was concerned with the 'material conditions' required for the rights of the author to become effective, whereas article 12 was only concerned with a question of procedure, namely the presumption to be applied (in the absence of proof to the contrary) where the author's name was indicated on his work.[307] This distinction was accepted by the commission in its report, but the latter proposed the addition of another paragraph to article 12 (or article 11 as it became) to clarify the relationship between the two articles and to facilitate proceedings by authors seeking to enforce their rights under the Convention. This provided that courts in the country where protection was claimed could require the production of a certificate from the competent authority in the CO stating that the formalities prescribed by its law had been fulfilled.[308] (The effect of this provision has already been discussed at 6.86 above.)

6.103 The question of formalities was not discussed at the Paris Conference of 1896, except in relation to the question of compliance with the formalities of the country where protection was claimed[309] (see paragraph 1 of the Interpretative Declaration). However, at the Berlin Revision the need to comply with formalities was abolished, and the present provision was adopted, together with the principle of independence of protection (article 4(2), now article 5(2)). As a corollary to this, the provision in article 11 of the 1886 Act concerning the production of a certificate from a competent authority in the CO of a work was also deleted. It will be noted that the new provision in article 4(2) of the Berlin Act referred only to 'any formality', rather than 'conditions and formalities'. Was any significance to be attached to this change? For instance, did it mean that authors claiming protection under the Convention might still be required to comply with 'conditions' as distinct from 'formalities' as a precondition for protection? The draft wordings proposed by the German and French delegations at the Berlin Conference appeared to envisage the existence of such a

[306] *Actes* 1885, 34. [307] ibid, 34–5. [308] ibid, 50.
[309] *Actes* 1896, 61 (report of the commission).

distinction, as the first referred to 'any formality or extrinsic condition'[310] and the second more simply to 'any formality or condition'.[311] In its report to the Conference, however, the commission said that the word 'formality' was to be understood as covering both the 'conditions and formalities' referred to in the 1886 Act.[312] This interpretation has not been subsequently disputed, and therefore it can be said that the term 'formality' in the Stockholm, Paris Acts bears the same meaning as did the expression 'conditions and formalities' under the Berne Act. This, in turn, means that it is to be construed in accordance with the view expressed by the German delegate (Meyer) at the 1884 Conference, namely that it refers to 'everything which must be complied with in order to ensure that the rights of the author with regard to his work may come into existence'. These would include such requirements as registration, the deposit or filing of copies, the payment of fees, or the making of declarations. Instances of such requirements, and combinations thereof, were to be found in the laws of the majority of Union countries in 1886, and even as late as 1908.[313] Another example would be a requirement that each copy of a work carry on it a notice claiming copyright (such as the © sign which is required under the UCC).

(c) Formalities as to the exercise of rights

Another amendment made at the time of the Berlin Revision further illuminates the meaning of 'any formality'. The discussion to this point has concerned state-imposed preconditions on the coming into being of the author's rights. But that is only half the problem. An author may be *vested* with copyright, but unable to *enforce* her rights unless she complies with a variety of prerequisites to suit. Hence the addition by the Berlin Act of the word 'exercise', so that article 4(2) now read: 'The enjoyment and exercise of these rights shall not be subject to any formality. . .'. This appeared to cover any provision that, as distinct from making the recognition of an author's rights contingent upon compliance with some formality, made the bringing of proceedings to enforce these rights subject to a formality (perhaps even the same one). An example of this was to be found in the requirement in the French decree of 1793 that copies of a work were to be deposited in the *Bibliothèque Nationale* as a precondition for the bringing of an infringement proceeding.[314] It was held, however, by a French court in 1914 that this did not apply to authors claiming protection under the Convention (although it did apply to French authors), as it was inconsistent with the Convention provision that the 'exercise' of these rights be free of the need to comply with any formality.[315] A similar argument was made by the International Office **6.104**

[310] *Actes* 1908, 284. [311] ibid. [312] ibid, 237.
[313] See generally Ladas (1938), 271ff, for a review of the formalities applied under national laws as late as the mid-1930s.
[314] See n 271 above. [315] ibid.

in 1932 in relation to a provision in a Canadian statute which required collecting societies to make regular deposits of the repertoire of works they controlled.[316] Another 'formality' which would fall foul of this prohibition would be a requirement that authors claiming under the Convention should provide some special security before they are entitled to institute proceedings to protect their rights (the '*caution judicatum solvi*').[317] More recently, the obligation the US Copyright Act imposed on authors to register their works with the Copyright Office as a prerequisite to initiating an infringement action was deemed inconsistent with the article 5(2) prohibition on subjecting the exercise of rights to compliance with formalities.[318] The provision in the UK Copyright, Designs and Patents Act 1988 requiring public 'assertion' of moral rights as a prerequisite to their invocation[319] results from a rather perverse reading of article 6*bis*, that turns the Berne mandate that authors 'shall have the *right* to claim authorship', into an *obligation* to claim authorship in order to make the right enforceable. This hardly seems compatible with article 5(2).

(d) Requirements outside the scope of prohibited formalities

6.105 Not every record-keeping or even litigation-related obligation a state imposes should be considered a Berne-banned 'formality'. For example, Berne does not require the suspension of local rules of evidence or procedure applicable to all judicial proceedings; it targets only copyright-specific measures.[320] Thus, a foreign copyright holder cannot assert that article 5(2) dispenses her from paying court fees that attach to the filing of any kind of claim; but she may object to payment of a fee imposed only on the bringing of a copyright action. It is also necessary to distinguish between local rules that condition the validity or scope of a grant of rights on the formalization of the agreement, and rules that limit

[316] [1932] *DA* 5. The offending provision was in the Canadian Law of 11 June 1931, s 10.

[317] This was a constant grievance on the part of authors in the early days of the Convention: see the resolutions against it made by various ALAI congresses in the early 1890s (*Actes* 1896, 70). See further Briggs (1906), 427–8.

[318] See *Report of the Ad Hoc Working Group on US Adherence to the Berne Convention*, reprinted in (1986) 10 *Columbia-VLA Journal of Law & the Arts* 513, 569–74. The 1988 Berne Convention Implementation Act accordingly lifted the requirement for non-US Berne works, but retained it for US works. See Jane C Ginsburg and John M Kernochan, '102 Years Later: The US Joins the Berne Convention' (1988) 13 *Columbia-VLA Journal of Law & the Arts* 1, 13.

[319] See the UK Copyright, Designs and Patents Act 1988, s 77(1) ('[T]he right is not infringed unless it has been asserted in accordance with section 78.'). The Act contains 'elaborate provisions on the making of effective assertions and the extent to which other persons are bound by them.' Lionel Bently and William R Cornish, 'United Kingdom', in Melville B Nimmer and Paul Edward Geller, *International Copyright Law and Practice* (2003).

[320] See eg Masouyé (n 161 above), para 5.5; 'US Adherence to the Berne Convention' (statement of Donald C Curran, the Associate Librarian of Congress and Acting Register of Copyrights, Copyright Office, at the Hearings Before the Subcommittee on Patents, Copyrights, and Trademarks of the Senate Committee on the Judiciary, 99th Congress 72 (1987)).

the exercise of those rights independently of their ownership. The first class of rules, which may include such requirements as that the transfer be in writing, that it be signed by the author, and that the scope of the grant be clearly articulated,[321] are generally designed to protect authors from ignorant or improvident transfers. The rationale and the effect of this kind of author-protective formalism are profoundly different from public-protective formalities, such as notice or registration, or copyright-specific litigation hurdles, which seek to shield the public from authors' claims. In the former instance, the formal rules tell us *who* is entitled to enforce a copyright whose existence the rules do not call into question. In the latter instance, the formalities limit *any* claimant's enforcement, and may destroy the copyright altogether.[322]

One additional point to be made about this part of article 5(2) is that it would **6.106** be illogical to interpret it as meaning that an author cannot be made subject to any formality that can be imposed in accordance with the provisions of the Convention. The general principle of interpretation, '*lex specialis legi generali derogat*', is obviously applicable here. For example, the criteria of eligibility for protection under articles 3(1) and 4 cannot be incompatible with article 5(2), although they are obviously conditions which have to be satisfied before rights come into existence under the Convention and protection is claimed. Again, it is open to member states, under article 2(2), to stipulate that protection will not be accorded unless the work in question is fixed in some material form. Another example was to be found in article 9(2) which was contained in the Convention until the Stockholm Revision. Under this, certain categories of newspaper articles could be freely reproduced by the press unless such reproduction had been

[321] See eg 17 USC § 204(a) (transfers of exclusive rights require a writing signed by the grantor); France, Code de la propriété intellectuelle, art L 131–2 ('The performance, publishing and audiovisual production contracts defined in this Title shall be in writing.'), art L 131–3 ('Transfer of authors' rights shall be subject to each of the assigned rights being separately mentioned in the instrument of assignment and the field of exploitation of the assigned rights being defined as to its scope and purpose, as to place and as to duration.').

[322] For the same reasons, national law requirements that copyright licensing be carried out exclusively by a collecting society (with little freedom for the author to resist this) should not be deemed to conflict with article 5(2) of the Convention. Accord, Nordemann et al (1990), 5BC, n 7, p 78. For examples of provisions conferring licensing authority on collecting societies, see the German Law of 1965 (as amended in 1988), arts 26(5) (collection of the *droit de suite*), 27(3) (remuneration for video or audio renting and for the public lending right) and 54h (claims such as remuneration from manufacturers of recording and photocopying equipment must be brought through collecting societies). See also the writings referred to by F Schönherr, 'On the Interpretation of Article 5(2) of the Berne Convention: Taking as an Example the Greek Antipiracy Law of July 15, 1980' [1981] *Copyright* 294, 295. Moreover, even were author-protective contract formalism inconsistent with the prohibition on formalities, Schönherr further points out that, as objection has not been made to the imposition of these requirements by any member state in the competent bodies of the Union, this is a 'subsequent practice' of the states that are signatories to the Berne Convention which establishes the agreement of the parties as to the way in which this provision of the Convention is to be interpreted; ibid, 297.

expressly prohibited in advance by the author. Nonetheless, it was clear that this was not a 'formality' for the purposes of article 5(2).[323]

(e) Reconciling the prohibition on formalities with the goals of public notification and identification of right holders

6.107 We have seen that the encumbering or confiscatory effect of mandatory formalities has led successive Berne Conferences to diminish and then eliminate their role in the international scheme (see the discussion at paras 6.83–6.87 above). But formalities have beneficial effects as well. A notice of copyright that bears the date of publication will indicate if the work is still under copyright, either because the work is of a kind whose term of protection runs from publication, or, for those works whose term is calculated from the life of the author, because the publication date will allow the user roughly to judge whether the author is likely to have been dead for over fifty years. A copyright notice which required disclosure of the birthdate (and, where applicable, death date) of the author would be even more helpful. A publicly accessible registry recording not only initial claims to copyright, but the names of subsequent transferees and the scope of rights transferred in each work greatly assists in identifying the right holders with whom a would-be exploiter of the work must deal. But the Berne Convention does not declare that member states may not *institute* a system of formalities; it prohibits making enjoyment and exercise of copyright in non-domestic works *subject to* them. Thus, article 5(2) does not prohibit member states from maintaining public registries or other notice-giving devices; it merely bars making compliance mandatory for non-domestic works. Authors and right holders are free, and indeed should be encouraged, to facilitate both would-be exploiters' clearance of rights, and general knowledge of when a work will fall into the public domain; failure to affix notice, register works, and record transfers, however, should not result in loss of protection or preclusion of an action. The question then becomes: how may a member state achieve the benefits of formalities without punishing authors who fail to fulfil them?

6.108 One approach would be to substitute carrots for sticks. Authors who do comply with registration or other requirements might enjoy evidentiary advantages or qualify for additional remedies.[324] So long as the basic copyright remedies of

[323] *Actes* 1908, 240 (report of the commission).

[324] See eg 17 USC §§ 410(c) (certificate of registration serves as *prima facie* proof of information there recorded, if registration is effected within five years of publication), 412 (statutory damages and attorneys fees available only if work registered before infringement occurred). See [1993] *Copyright* 142, 154, paras 73–6 (permissibility of laws giving registration information the effect of a rebuttable presumption of the correctness of the information). Reinbothe and von Lewinski indicate that measures to 'facilitate proof of authorship' are not prohibited formalities. See Jörg Reinbothe and Silke von Lewinski, *The WIPO Treaties 1996* (2002), 62, para 27.

injunctive relief and actual damages remain available without regard to formalities, one may argue that remedial enhancements remain within the 'means of redress afforded to the author to protect his rights', which article 5(2) leaves to the country of protection's design.[325] Admittedly, the difference between a permissible conditioning of an *enhanced* remedy and an impermissible conditioning of an *effective* remedy may not always be apparent,[326] thus making the distinction a delicate one in practice.

Another approach would be to diversify the means of giving notice, so that members of the public might consult not only government-maintained records, but also registries of collecting societies, and information gathered and maintained by private individuals or associations. Rights management information embedded in digital copies of works also facilitates acquiring information necessary to authorized uses; laws protecting copyright management information do not run afoul of article 5(2)—indeed, the WIPO copyright treaties require member states to protect this information against tampering, but will be addressed in detail in Chapter 15 below. For present purposes, it suffices to underscore the compatibility with the Berne scheme of national laws that encourage voluntary provision of information that facilitates lawful use and licensing of works.

Finally, just as member states may promote the development of multiple sources of information about copyright status and ownership, so may they devise alternative outcomes to an author's failure to provide that information. Depriving the author of her copyright is not an option under Berne, but neither does Berne require that the public interest in making lawful use of the work be frustrated. Imaginative middle paths are possible. For example, an 'orphan work' regime, such as that in force in Canada, is compatible with article 5(2). Under Canadian law, a would-be user who demonstrates to the Copyright Board that she has searched diligently, but has been unable to locate the right holder, may pay a statutory fee for a non-exclusive licence to use the work in Canada;[327] the Copyright Board's annual report publishes the licences granted; if the copyright owner makes a claim within five years, the Board will pay the sum over to the claimant.[328]

---

325 See Ad Hoc Working Group report (n 318 above), 572–4

326 See Ginsburg and Kernochan (n 318 above), 12–15.

327 See Copyright Act 1985 (Canada), s 77(1)(2); Copyright Board of Canada, Unlocatable Copyright Owners, www.cb-cda.gc.ca. The term 'orphan works' does not appear in the Canadian law, but is used in the recent inquiry initiated by the US Copyright Office into possible measures to enable lawful use of works whose copyright owners cannot be found. See US Copyright Office, Notice of Inquiry concerning 'Orphan works', 70 Fed. Reg. 3739–43 (January 26, 2005).

328 Copyright Act 1985 (Canada), s 77(3).

(2) Other substantive minima

6.109 Conventional requirements as to the works that member states must protect will be analysed in Chapter 8 below. The minimum period of duration is taken up in Chapter 9 below. The rights that member states must afford Union works are considered in Chapters 10–12 below. The scope of permissible exceptions will be the subject of Chapter 13 below.

(3) Limitations or restrictions on protection under the Convention: a principle of 'maximum protection'?

6.110 Neither article 5(1) nor article 19 say anything about whether Union members are entitled to accord protection in cases where the Convention specifically limits or excludes protection altogether. Such cases are very few under the present text, and are consequently of minor practical importance. Nevertheless, they raise important questions of principle, as it can be argued that an exclusion or limitation of protection is to be treated as an imperative provision of the Convention which has the purpose of protecting the interests of the public, rather than those of the author.[329] In such a case, it can be said that it will be contrary to the Convention for national legislation to provide protection in a case where this has been specifically prohibited.[330] In the same way that there is a principle of minimum protection that operates under article 19 in favour of Union authors (see the earlier discussion at paras 6.80ff above), so (it can be argued) there is a corresponding principle of maximum protection to be implied in those few cases where the Convention limits or excludes protection.

This question has only once been raised in a revision conference. This was done at Rome by the Austrian delegate who referred specifically to the rights of the public which were involved in such a case.[331] However, the question was taken no further at this time, and was left aside for the next conference of revision.[332] In the event, it was not discussed at Brussels,[333] but it did lead to considerable discussion in the literature. Baum and Hoffmann,[334] for example, argued in favour of the principle, saying that there was no point in inserting restrictive provisions into the Convention if national laws were free to annul them by a contrary stipulation. They therefore urged that the matter should be clarified,

[329] Baum (1949), 71–2. See also A Baum, 'Droit international public: Convention de Berne et lois nationales' (Part III) [1946] *DA* 114, 115.

[330] ibid. [331] *Actes* 1928, 273. [332] ibid. [333] Baum (1949), 71.

[334] A Baum and W Hoffmann [1927] *GRUR* 186, [1928] *GRUR* 684, 897. See also A Baum [1930] *UFITA* 400; B Marwitz [1933] *Il Diritto di Autore* 457; W Hoffmann, *Die Berner Uebereinkunft zum Schutze von Werken der Literatur und Kuns twom 9.September 1886 revidiert in Berlin am 13 November 1908 und in rom am 2 June 1928* (1935), 21ff; Ostertag (n 249 above), 37; Baum (n 329 above), 116ff.

one way or the other, in the Convention. Ladas,[335] on the other hand, objected to the notion that the Convention could contain imperative provisions protecting the rights of the public, arguing that this introduced ideas from domestic legislation that were alien to an international agreement entered into by states. More convincingly, he also argued that the restrictive provisions referred to by Hoffmann and Baum were not imperative in any sense, but simply set the limits beyond which the Convention was not required to apply. There was nothing, therefore, to prevent national legislation from stepping beyond those perimeters.[336] In relation to this last point, it is perhaps worth making the obvious point that in a case where the Convention simply says nothing it cannot be argued that this prohibits national law from regulating the matter, for example, as regards the protection of a particular right or category of work. In such cases, the principle of minimum protection clearly applies, and national legislators are free to accord such additional protection to Union authors as they think fit.

There are nonetheless instances in the present Convention text where protection is either limited or excluded. In the majority of cases where restrictions are imposed, these are left to national legislation to regulate, often subject to strict conditions, with the consequence that member states may determine to make no exception at all. It is therefore possible to identify only two clear imperative restrictions of significance under the present text.[337] These are: **6.111**

- the exclusion of 'news of the day' and 'miscellaneous facts having the character of mere items of press information' under article 2(8); and
- the making of quotations under article 10(1).

The scope of these exclusions are discussed further (see paras 8.104 and 13.39ff below). For present purposes, we are concerned with the policy underlying the exclusions. A concern to maintain the free international flow of basic elements of information appears to animate and unite these exceptions. These are two of the provisions (examined earlier at paras 5.49ff above), that reveal the Convention's solicitude for the broader public interest, notwithstanding the Convention's overall goal to protect the rights of authors. The Convention

335 Ladas (1938), 192ff. 336 ibid.

337 There is also the limited transitional provision in relation to the making of recordings of musical works under the Rome and Brussels Acts prior to the entry into force of the present text. Stockholm, Paris Acts, art 13(2). Prior to the Berlin Act, there was another restriction of far greater importance, namely that which stipulated that the manufacture and sale of instruments for the mechanical reproduction of musical works was not to be regarded as an infringing act. Berne Act, Closing Protocol, para 3. This gave rise to the question of whether those Union countries where national law recognised mechanical reproduction as a form of infringement were entitled to accord such protection to Union authors, but the issue was resolved by the adoption of article 13(1) in the Berlin Act.

cannot prevent a member state from locally privatizing information its own authors generate—that is the consequence of article 5(3)—but it can require that member states preserve the freedom of these excluded elements when the works that contain them traverse borders. Thus, if national legislation purports to grant protection to Union authors in such cases this must be contrary to the Convention. Given the existence of article 19, it would be desirable if these instances of 'maximum protection' were also given express recognition in the Convention, but the absence of such recognition should not affect this conclusion.[338]

E. Retroactive Application of the Convention upon New Member State Accessions

(1) The problem

6.112 When a country enters into copyright relations with another country, there can be no difficulty about the grant of protection to works having the other country as their CO where these are created or published after the date the agreement enters into force. However, a problem may arise in the case of existing works which were previously entitled to protection only in one country but not in the other. That may be the case for a variety of reasons. For example, works may be in one country's public domain because that country previously had no copyright relations with the other, and all works from that country will automatically have gone into the public domain in the other country. Or the term of protection may have expired in one country. Or, if one country imposed formalities as a condition of the existence or persistence of protection, works from the other country may have failed to comply with those conditions and therefore would have lost protection or never acquired it in the first place. One of the main objects of the new agreement will usually have been the gaining or restoring of protection for those works in the second country, but difficulties may occur with respect to the position of persons in that country who have been exploiting the works in the absence of any legal protection. These users have acted in good faith in reliance on a given state of affairs, namely that these works were in the public domain and could be used freely. In pursuance of this reliance, they may also have invested capital and labour in the furtherance of these activities, for instance, in the preparation of a new edition for printing, the making of a

[338] Note here the argument made by Ladas (1938) (and strongly criticized by Baum (1949)) that, had the Austro-Bulgarian proposal at the Rome Conference for a conventional compulsory licence under art 13 been accepted (see *Actes* 1928, 265), this would have required the making of an express exception to art 19: Ladas (1938), 194, and Baum (n 329 above), 117.

translation or other adaptation, or the production and public presentation of the works in question. Are these people suddenly to find themselves in the position of infringers and dealers in infringing copies if the new Convention applies to these works, as well as to works that are created or published after its entry into force? While they may have been capitalizing on the previously inadequate protection their country afforded foreign works, they may also have made substantial outlays in the carrying out of these activities; it would be unfair for the fruits of these undertakings to be forfeited to the foreign copyright owner. In addition, if the new Convention is made completely retroactive, this may have a drastic effect on any local industry which has been built up in the previous legal vacuum. On the other hand, to exclude retroactivity altogether will work harshly against the foreign author, and deprive the new Convention of much of its *raison d'être*. Accordingly, it is necessary to strike some balance between these 'acquired rights' or 'reliance interests' and the newly recognized rights of the foreign author. By definition, such provisions should only be temporary in nature, as all that is needed is sufficient time to allow the prior user to recoup his investment, following which time the foreign author's rights should be entitled to full protection in accordance with the terms of the new Convention. In implementing the transition, member states may be inclined to distinguish between two types of 'reliance parties': those who merely reissue, and those who create derivative works based on work formerly in the public domain. Were the latter subject to the foreign author's 'full protection', the author might demand their suppression. This outcome seems as undesirable as the one which disregards the restored author's rights. In this circumstance, it may be permissible for the member state to impose some kind of licensing requirement that would allow continued exploitation of the derivative work, yet would compensate the restored author.[339] This solution has the merit of accommodating both parties, but is troublesome to the extent that the measure may not be sufficiently 'transitional' as it does not appear to contemplate a phasing out of the licence. The general problem, of course, is not one that is peculiar to international copyright agreements: it arises also in many areas of domestic law where a new regulation is made that renders unlawful activities previously carried on without restriction. However, while there may be agreement in principle on the need for some kind of transitional arrangement in these cases, there are various ways in which this may be done and there is room for argument over which is the most equitable and efficacious.

[339] See eg 17 USC § 104A(d)(3) (authorizing imposition of judicial compulsory licence if restored copyright owner and reliance party owner of derivative works copyright fail to come to a licensing agreement).

(2) Development of Berne Convention retroactivity rules

(a) Retroactivity under early bilateral copyright agreements

6.113 Diverging approaches to the question of retroactivity were to be found in the early bilateral conventions. Some excluded it completely,[340] others were mute on the point, leaving this to be determined by the municipal courts,[341] and others applied the principle, subject to particular exceptions and limitations.[342] Typical provisions of conventions in this last category permitted the completion and sale of copies that were in the process of being made at the time of the convention's entry into force,[343] sometimes subject to strict time limits.[344] Others were more generous, particularly in the case of performing rights, where a work had been already publicly performed.[345] These differences in approach to the question of retroactivity were likewise reflected in national laws in relation to the protection of domestic works at the time of the entry into operation of these laws.[346]

(b) Retroactivity under the Berne Convention: the Berne Act

6.114 At the ALAI Conference in Berne in 1883, this was debated at some length, and the feeling of the participants was that the proposed multilateral convention should be fully retroactive.[347] The following clause was proposed:

> The present Convention applies to all works not yet fallen into the public domain, in the country of origin of the work, at the moment the said Convention enters into force.[348]

This clause was adopted, in turn, in the Federal Council programme for the 1884 Conference,[349] but that conference made a number of changes which had

---

[340] See eg the Convention between Germany (Prussia) and the UK of 13 May 1846; Convention between the UK and Belgium of 12 Aug 1854; Convention between Germany and Switzerland of 13 May 1869, confirmed 23 May 1881 (applied only to dramatic and musical works published or performed after its entry into force). See further [1888] *DA* 119.

[341] See further [1888] *DA* 117.

[342] See eg the Convention between Germany and France of 19 Apr 1883, art 15 and Protocol; the Convention between France and Italy of 20 June 1884, art 13 and Protocol. See further [1888] *DA* 118.

[343] Convention between Germany and France (n 342 above).

[344] ibid (a period of four years).

[345] See eg the Convention between Germany and Italy of 20 June 1884 (in general, musical works were protected retroactively if they had been published prior to the convention's entry into force, but not if they had been performed in public in one of the countries). See also the Convention between Germany and Switzerland of 13 May 1869, confirmed 23 May 1881. See further the commentary in [1888] *DA* 118–19.

[346] See generally 'Étude des dispositions de l'article 14 de la Convention du 9 septembre 1886 et du chiffre 4 du protocole de clôture qui s'y rattache. (Retroactivité)' [1888] *DA* 64, 73, 88, 105, 117.

[347] See the extracts of the debates in [1888] *DA* 61ff.

[348] Draft convention, art 8: *Actes* 1884, 8.

[349] Federal Council programme, art 11: *Actes* 1884, 12.

the effect of modifying its implementation. Thus, it was provided that this should be done 'subject to the reserves and conditions to be determined by common agreement'.[350] It was further provided that this 'common agreement' should take effect according to the relevant stipulations contained in any special conventions concluded to that effect, or, in the absence of such agreements, according to the domestic legislation of the respective countries.[351] These provisions were intended to be transitional only, with the aim that full retroactivity would be ultimately established. This approach was approved in the 1885 Conference, where a number of countries made it clear that they could only accept the principle of retroactivity subject to these kinds of provisions.[352] These delegates were given the following assurances by the German delegate (Reichardt) and by the president of the Conference (Numa Droz):

> Mr Reichardt explained that the draft convention did not recognise retrospectivity properly speaking and did not injure the interests of anyone. In effect, reproductions made or commenced lawfully before the entry into force of the Convention did not fall under the prohibitive dispositions of the latter.
>
> The president joined Mr Reichardt in declaring that the transitional provisions of the Convention contained absolutely nothing which should prevent any government from adhering.[353]

This assurance was confirmed by the commission in its report, although this also reaffirmed the ultimate application of the principle of retroactivity (in the second sentence in the passage quoted below).

> . . . in the closing protocol, the carrying into effect of this article is left to each country of the Union which is to determine the conditions of retroactivity according to its own laws or specific conventions. *However, this reservation being made, it should be understood that the question is to be regulated in each country in the sense of article 15* [the number of the article in the 1884 draft].[354]

The final provision which was approved, and found its place as article 14 in the Berne Act, read as follows:

> 14 Under the reserves and conditions to be determined by common agreement, the present Convention shall apply to all works which at the moment of its coming into force have not yet fallen into the public domain in the country of origin.

As to the establishment of the 'common agreement' referred to in paragraph 4 of article 14 of the Closing Protocol provided:

[350] *Actes* 1884, 59.

[351] ibid, 85. See further N Droz [1884] *Journal du Droit international privé* 454 and [1888] *DA* 63–4.

[352] *Actes* 1885, 36.

[353] ibid.

[354] ibid, 52 (emphasis added). See further [1888] *DA* 64.

> . . . The application of the Convention to works which have not fallen into the public domain at the time when it comes into force shall take effect according to the relevant stipulations contained in special Conventions existing, or to be concluded, to that effect. In the absence of such stipulations between any countries of the Union, the respective countries shall regulate, each in so far as it is concerned, by its domestic legislation, the manner in which the principle contained in Article 14 is to be applied.

(c) The Paris Revision

6.115 Following the entry into force of the Berne Act, authors' organizations began to advocate the deletion of these transitional provisions so as to make retroactivity absolute. These views found particular expression in a series of resolutions passed by successive congresses of ALAI.[355] As a matter of logic, they made complete sense, as the need for transitional provisions must surely diminish with the passage of time, although they might still be required for new members of the Union. It was clearly with this in mind that the French Government, in its programme for the Paris Revision provided for the deletion of any reference to reserves and conditions in article 14, and for a limited capacity only to adopt transitional measures on the part of new accessions under paragraph 4 of the Closing Protocol.[356] It also proposed that a cut-off date should apply where a country had not adopted such measures within a year of its accession: in such a case, it should be regarded as having renounced them in favour of the 'pure and simple application of article 14'.[357] While these proposals attracted considerable support in the Conference,[358] they met opposition from the German and British delegates on the ground that, despite the lapse in time, absolute retroactivity might still injure 'legitimate interests'.[359] Accordingly, the status quo under article 14 was maintained, but a number of other changes were made to the Closing Protocol. These amplified the application of paragraph 4 as follows:

1. The phrase 'in their country of origin' was inserted in the first sentence to make it clear that the work must have fallen into the public domain in that country. This had, in fact, been included in the 1884 and 1885 draft texts,[360] but had been omitted inadvertently.[361] This had allowed the argument to be made that the work must not have fallen into the public domain in the country where protection was claimed, an 'inadmissible proposition',[362] which severely limited the application of the general principle of

[355] The ALAI Congresses at Berne (1889), London (1890), Neuchâtel (1891), Milan (1892): for the text of the resolutions, see *Actes* 1896, 64–5.

[356] ibid, 45–6.

[357] ibid, 46 (proposed change to Closing Protocol).

[358] ibid, 174 (notably France and Belgium).

[359] ibid. See further [1905] *DA* 81, 83.

[360] *Actes* 1884, 59; *Actes* 1885, 52.

[361] *Actes* 1896, 174 (report to Renault).

[362] ibid.

retroactivity as it required that the work in question had already been protected under domestic law or a pre-existing bilateral convention.

2. Article 14 and paragraph 4 were also applied to the exclusive right of translation established by the 1896 Act.[363] Under this Act, if a translation of a protected work was published within ten years of its first publication, the translation right relating to that language was assimilated to the other rights of the author and protected for the same period.[364] Consequently, this extended right was to be protected retroactively, in the event that the ten-year period had not expired at the time the Paris Act came into force. As with the other rights of the author, this was subject to the application of the same kinds of transitional measures.[365]
3. It was finally provided that the 'above-mentioned temporary stipulations' were to apply in the case of new accessions to the Union.[366] The need for such a provision had become obvious since the Berne Act, as there had been several new accessions to the Convention since this date.[367]

(d) The later revisions

The above provisions still left considerable latitude to both old and new Union members as to the way in which they implemented the retroactivity requirement under article 14. In particular, the British provisions governing this[368] attracted strong criticism from ALAI which, after 1896, continued its campaign for full and unqualified retroactivity.[369] These views had little ultimate effect on the provision that was settled at the Berlin Conference, but article 14 and paragraph 4 were nonetheless substantially revised and consolidated in a new article (article 18).[370] Under this, the faculty to adopt transitional measures by both old and new Union members was retained, but several further changes were adopted (see below). Although some additional changes were proposed at the Rome Conference, article 18 was only slightly altered at this time,[371] and it remained **6.116**

[363] ibid. [364] Paris Additional Act, art 1(III).

[365] Paris Additional Act, art 2 (amending para 4 of the Closing Protocol of the Berne Act).

[366] ibid.

[367] These were Luxembourg, 20 June 1888: [1888] *DA* 64; Monaco, 1 July 1889: [1889] *DA* 94; Montenegro, 1 July 1893: [1893] *DA* 33; Norway, 13 Apr 1896: [1896] *DA* 65. See further *Actes* 1896, 175 (Renault).

[368] UK International Copyright Act 1886, s 6 and Order in Council of 28 Nov 1887. See further Briggs (1906), 267–72; I F Iselin, 'L'effet rétroactif de la Convention de Berne en Angleterre' [1905] *DA* 96–8.

[369] In particular, see the resolutions of the ALAI Congresses of Turin (1898) and Heidelberg (1899) which were particularly critical of the British provisions: *Actes* 1908, 90.

[370] ibid, 268 (report of Renault). See further [1909] *DA* 1, 15 and 'De la rétroactivité prévue par l'article 18 de la Convention d'Union' [1926] *DA* 114–19. See also Ladas (1938), 348–52.

[371] *Actes* 1928, 81–2 (programme proposals) and 213–14 (report of Caselli). The change here was to art 18(4), so as to make the provisions of the article applicable also to cases where reservations were abandoned.

essentially unchanged in the successive revision conferences. The provision now provides as follows:

> 18(1) This Convention shall apply to all works which, at the moment of its coming into force, have not yet fallen into the public domain in the country of origin through the expiry of the term of protection.
>
> (2) If, however, through the expiry of the term of protection which was previously granted, a work has fallen into the public domain of the country where protection is claimed, that work shall not be protected anew.
>
> (3) The application of this principle shall be subject to any provisions contained in special conventions to that effect existing or to be concluded between countries of the Union. In the absence of such provisions, the respective countries shall determine, each in so far as it is concerned, the conditions of application of this principle.
>
> (4) The preceding provision shall also apply in the case of new accessions to the Union and to cases in which protection is extended by the application of article 7 or by the abandonment of reservations.

For the sake of completeness, it should also be noted that article 13 also contains a special provision in paragraph (2) relating to the retroactive effect of that article. (The history and present operation of this are discussed in detail at paras 13.59–13.64 below.)

(3) The interpretation of the present article 18

(a) The general principle (paragraph (1)): beneficiaries of protection

6.117 When a new member state accedes to the Union, it must accord copyright protection to works from other Union members if those works remain under copyright in their COs. This applies to foreign Berne works which never enjoyed copyright protection in the new member state, for example, because the new member previously had no copyright relations with other Union members, or because the new member had imposed formalities with which works from other Union members had not complied. The obligation to protect other Union works also extends to works which the new member had once protected but which now are in the public domain because the new member's prior term of copyright protection was shorter than the Berne minimum term. Equally importantly, the obligation to provide or restore copyright protection applies to previous Berne members with respect to works from the newly acceding state. Thus, if the newly acceding state had no prior copyright relations with a longer-standing member state, not only must the new member extend copyright protection to works from the old member, but the old member must now provide coverage to works from the new member. Similarly, if works from the new member fell afoul of formalities that the old member imposed on works from non-Union states (as a Berne member it would have been prohibited from requiring Union works to comply with such conditions), the old member must now restore copyright in those works as well.

(b) Works excepted from the obligation to extend or restore copyright

New members need not extend or restore copyright to Union works which have 'fallen into the public domain in the country of origin through the expiry of the term of protection.' By the same token, other Union members need not restore copyright to works whose protection at home in the newly acceding state already expired (so long as the new member's copyright term was Berne-compatible; see further the discussion at para 9.55 below[372]). The general principle remains the same as in the original Berne Act but it is now made clear that not every reason for the work being in the public domain in its CO permits another member state to withhold copyright protection. The only permissible reason is through the expiry of its term of protection. This addition was made at the Berlin Conference, and clearly excludes other cases where a work might have fallen into the public domain in its CO, for example, because of failure to comply with the formalities required under the law of the CO,[373] or because the CO did not protect the category of work concerned. Thus, even if a work is no longer, or was never, protected in its CO for such a reason, it is still possible to claim protection for it in other countries of the Union under the Convention.[374] **6.118**

It will be noted that the general principle under paragraph (1) applies to both unpublished works and works first published before the Act comes into force: all that is relevant is that these works have not fallen into the public domain in their CO through the expiry of their respective terms of protection. This also means that these works, now they are protected under the Convention, are entitled to any increase in protection that may be subsequently accorded to them by the laws of their CO or any other Union country. The latter is a result of the principle of national treatment, and will include any extension of the term of protection in those countries (subject to the application of article 7(8)). On the other hand, if the laws of such countries refused to apply these benefits retrospectively to national authors, Union authors could not object if they were treated in the same way: this would, after all, be simply an application of the principle of national treatment. **6.119**

The meaning of the phrase 'at the moment of its coming into force' gives rise to some uncertainty, and in this regard it must be noted that paragraph (1) now **6.120**

---

372 But see Reinbothe and von Lewinski (n 324 above), 163–4 (stating that domestic works whose sub-Berne term expired in a newly acceding country are not entitled to Berne minimum term of protection in other Union countries).

373 *Actes* 1908, 268 (report of Renault) and Ladas (1938), 349.

374 On the other hand, the 'comparison of terms' rule under article 7(8) will mean that if the term of protection in the country of origin is longer than that in the country in which protection is claimed, the work will only be entitled to the shorter term of protection applied in that country; see further the comments in [1926] *DA* 114, 115–16 (the latter will, in any event, be at least life plus fifty years under article 7(1)).

deals with a situation that is quite different from that which obtained when the Convention was originally formulated. At that stage, the purpose of the provision was to provide for the retroactive application of the Convention among those states which formed the Union at the time when the Convention originally entered into force. It was contemplated that other countries would later accede to the Union, and provision was duly made for this situation at the time of the Paris Revision. However, it was also envisaged that the Convention would be subjected to regular revision, and that new Acts would come into force.[375] This has, of course, happened, and there have been a succession of Acts, each of which has contained separate provisions specifying when that Act (invariably referred to as 'the present Convention') is to enter into force.[376] The general rule has been that the new Act comes into force at a specified period following its ratification, and a time or condition for the happening of this event is invariably designated.[377] In consequence, article 18(1), which has been repeated in substance in each of these Acts can only *prima facie* apply to those countries which have ratified the new Act and become bound by it at that time: it can only have 'come into force' with respect to those states. The need for retroactive application of the Convention in these cases is clear: it is necessary to provide for the continued protection under the new Act of works that were protected under the previous Act that was in force between those countries. This leaves a potential gap as regards 'old' Union members that do not ratify the new Act, but accede to it at a later time. They are not 'new accessions to the Union', so do not fall within paragraph (4): are they then free from any requirement to apply retroactive protection of works claiming under the Convention? It is unlikely that they would seek to do so, but it is submitted that in any case they are prevented from doing this under paragraph (1). Although the point is far from clear, the words 'at the moment of its coming into force' must be given a wider application than suggested above: although the new Act 'comes into force' in a general sense after its ratification, it only 'comes into force' with respect to an 'old' Union member country that accedes after this time at the time of its accession. Any other result would be absurd, meaning that countries in this category would be free to deny retroactive application of the Convention to the works of other Union members although they had previously accorded such protection, while countries which ratified the new Act and new accessions to the Union would be obliged to accord such protection under paragraphs (1) and (4) respectively.

---

375 See Berne Act, art 17 (concerning conferences of revision).

376 Berne Act, art 20; Paris Additional Act, art 4; Berlin Act, art 29; Rome Act, art 28; Brussels Act, art 28; Stockholm Act, art 28; Paris Act, art 28.

377 See eg Paris Act, art 28(2) (arts 1–21 and Appendix to enter into force three months after (a) at least five countries have ratified or accorded to the Act without making a declaration under the Appendix, and (b) France, Spain, the UK, and the USA have become bound by the UCC).

(c) No renewal of protection (paragraph (2))

This provision operates to bar any claim for renewal of protection under the Convention where the term previously granted in the country where protection is claimed has already expired. It is expressed in the form of a proviso to paragraph (1) (the use of the word 'however'), so it is to be presumed that it applies at the time of the Convention's coming into force. A typical situation, therefore, would be where country A has been a member of the Union with a shorter term of protection than life plus fifty years (as was permitted under the Berlin and Rome Acts). It then adopts the term of life plus fifty years on its ratification or accession to one of the later Acts. If, in such a case, a work from another Union country (country B) had been entitled to protection for the shorter period, say life plus twenty years, and this period has expired at the time the new term is adopted (on the coming into force of the new Act), there can be no claim to a revival of protection for whatever time might remain of the new term of protection (unless that country revived copyrights in domestic works). This notional loss of protection concerned a number of countries at the Rome Conference,[378] and, in the programme, the Italian Government proposed the reversal of this rule so as to provide that: **6.121**

> The present Convention applies to all works for which the term of protection established in accordance with Article 7 has not yet expired at the moment of its entry into force, even if the period of protection previously accorded has already expired at this time. Nevertheless, rights legitimately acquired by third parties under the previous Convention shall be respected.[379]

The rationale for this proposal was that, so long as the rights acquired by third parties in the period after the previous term had expired were protected, there was no reason not to revive the protection enjoyed by these works.[380] This argument has strong logical appeal, as the question of a revival of protection does not appear to raise as difficult issues of principle as does the matter of retroactivity generally. In the latter case, protection is accorded where it formerly did not exist at all; in the former, it has at least existed previously for a time. On the other hand, it can be argued that where protection has been accorded, third parties are more at risk when they act in reliance on the fact that the work will enter the public domain at a specific point in time: they have respected the copyright owners' rights for the time these have been protected, and have made their plans and investments for the period after these rights expire through the effluxion of time. Revival of protection in cases such as these will therefore cause much uncertainty. This was clearly the view taken by the German and

[378] *Actes* 1928, 271–2. See also ibid, 101 (proposals by French delegation).
[379] ibid, 83. [380] ibid, 81–2.

British delegations at the Rome Conference, and they strongly opposed the Italian proposal.[381] Accordingly, it was withdrawn, and the status quo, was maintained.[382]

(d) The application of the principle (paragraph (3))

6.122 This retains the same provision for transitional measures as was contained in the original Berne Act. Thus, the 'application of the principle' of retroactivity may be regulated in one of two ways:

1. By 'provisions contained in special conventions to that effect existing or to be concluded between countries of the Union'. It is contemplated here that individual countries may enter bilateral arrangements in which the conditions and limits of the application of retroactivity as between themselves are agreed. In the case of a new accession to the Union in 2005, this would involve over 150 separate agreements, and is clearly unrealistic.
2. In the event that no bilateral agreements are adopted, it is left to the respective countries to 'determine, each in so far as it is concerned, the conditions of application of this principle'. This, in fact, will be the usual way in which this matter is handled by Union countries, and it is made clear such provisions will only affect the country concerned (although it hardly seems necessary to state this).

6.123 These provisions leave considerable latitude to countries as to how they will implement the principle of retroactivity,[383] enabling them to safeguard any rights which have been acquired in the previous situation where no legal protection applied. It would obviously have been better if the Convention itself had contained the appropriate provisions to be applied, but the difficulties involved here clearly deterred any effort in this direction at the original Berne Conferences, and there have been no later proposals made in this regard. In consequence, wide differences are to be seen in the provisions adopted by member countries. While a study of these differences lies outside the scope of the present work,[384] the following general points should be noted:

---

381 *Actes* 1928, 271.

382 ibid, 272 and 212 (report of Caselli). By contrast, when the European Union harmonized the term of copyright to life plus seventy years, it also provided that so long as the copyright was still in force in any of the EU countries, copyright would be reinstated to the full term of life plus seventy years in all the others. See Council Directive (EEC) No 93/98 of 29 Oct 1993 harmonizing the term of protection of copyright and certain related rights, art 10(2).

383 'Article 18 of the Berne Convention: Correspondence Between WIPO Director General Arpad Bogsch and Assistant Secretary of Commerce and Commissioner of Patents & Trademarks Bruce Lehman' (1995) 43 *Journal of the Copyright Society of the USA* 181.

384 See further the surveys of national laws in Ladas (1938), 353–9; [1926] *DA* 114, 118–19; [1931] *DA* 44, 54 (on German law); [1944] *DA* 122–4.

1. There is no basis on which the principle of retroactivity can be completely denied. The conditions and reservations can only be imposed on the 'application of the principle', that is, its carrying into effect: they cannot be imposed on the principle itself. Thus, it would not be permitted to deny retroactivity altogether in relation to a particular class or classes of works.
2. The provisions should also be of limited duration: although the word is not used, they are transitional in nature,[385] and their essential purpose should be to ensure that third parties who have previously acted in the absence of legal restraint should not be penalized once these restraints have come into operation. On the other hand, this does not authorize these persons to continue their usage indefinitely: a situation must eventually be reached when the work is protected in relation to all persons.
3. There is no time specified as to when these conditions may be imposed. In the normal case, this will be done at the time of ratification or accession. On the other hand, it should be noted that several proposals laying down time limits in this regard were rejected at the early revision conferences,[386] and it is therefore open to a country to impose these conditions at its own convenience. Thus, for example, the acceding country may allow reliance parties a reasonable grace period before the owners may enforce restored copyrights against them.
4. Transitional provisions may require the restored copyright owner to compensate the reliance party whose business will be prejudiced, or terminated, by the enforcement of the restored copyright, but the compensation should not be set so high as to vitiate or undermine the restoration.
5. Where reliance parties have created derivative works based on the restored work, transitional provisions may require the restored copyright owner to grant a licence to the creator of the derivative work. This proposition, however, may run afoul of the principle that transitional measures are not to continue indefinitely.

(e) New accessions and other cases (paragraph (4))

The provision for new accessions has already been referred to and needs little further explanation. It is only logical that the general principle under paragraph (1) should apply to these countries, as well as the provision for transitional measures under paragraph (3). The application of paragraph (2) may look more problematic, as these countries have not been bound by the Convention. However, it is possible that the works referred to in that paragraph may have **6.124**

[385] See again the comments made in the 1885 Berne Conference: nn 353, 354 above.

[386] See eg the proposal of the French Government and International Office at the Paris Conference of 1896: *Actes* 1896, 45–6.

previously received protection under the terms of that country's domestic law, a bilateral convention or perhaps a multilateral convention such as the UCC. In any event, under paragraph (2) there is no requirement for the revival of such protection.

6.125 The other two cases referred to in paragraph (4) are instances where the protection of the Convention may be extended, other than at the time of ratification or accession. The first of these, however, seems no longer to be of any application.

(i) **Cases where protection is extended by the application of article** 7: Article 18(4) filled a necessary gap in these cases when it was inserted at the time of the Berlin Revision. Under article 7 of that Act, the life-plus-fifty-years term of protection was not mandatory so long as it was not uniformly adopted by all countries of the Union. If a country which had not previously adopted the life-plus-fifty-years term did so after it had ratified or acceded to the Berlin Act (or the Rome Act, for that matter), it was extending its protection 'by the application of article 7'. In such a case, the effect of article 18(4) was to require the retroactive application of this extended term to works from Union countries. Such works, however, would have presently to be entitled to protection, as the effect of article 18(2) was that the term of protection of these works could not be revived if it had already expired. Once again, article 18(3) provided that the conditions under which this retroactive protection was to be applied could be regulated under the domestic law of the country concerned or through special bilateral agreements. So long as the life-plus-fifty-years term remained optional under article 7(1) of the Berlin and Rome Acts, the special provision under article 18(4) was necessary: Union countries could extend their term of protection at any time, quite separately from their ratification or accession to those Acts. However, since the Brussels Act, the life-plus-fifty-years term has been mandatory, and this term must be accorded to Union authors by any country which ratifies or accedes to this or any later Act. Accordingly, it is no longer possible for a Union country to extend its protection 'by the application of Article 7'. As the remaining provisions of article 7 either lay down minimum terms to be adopted in respect of particular categories of works or leave such matters to be determined by national legislation, there is no other respect in which protection can be extended 'by the application of Article 7' and to this extent article 18(4) is now otiose.[387]

(ii) Cases in which protection is extended . . . by the abandonment of reservations: A reservation to a treaty is a unilateral declaration made by a state at the

[387] See further Chapter 9 below.

time of its ratification of, or accession to, a treaty. Its effect is to exclude or modify the legal effect of one or more of the provisions of that treaty with respect to that state.[388] The capacity to make reservations under the Berne Convention is now restricted, although there was greater scope for this under the earlier Acts (see further paras 17.22ff below). However, reservations may also be withdrawn by the country which has made them,[389] meaning, in the case of the Berne Convention, that the protection accorded by that country to Union authors will usually be increased. The effect of article 18(4) therefore is that such increases are to be subject to the preceding provisions of article 18: in particular, they may be applied retroactively in accordance with whatever transitional measures the country in question may adopt for the protection of the rights of third parties under paragraph (3). This provision was added at the time of the Rome Revision, and was clearly intended to accommodate the withdrawal of prior reservations that had been promised at that Conference[390] (including reservations made by the UK and Norway with respect to the application of article 18 itself).[391] The principal reservations that will now be caught by this provision are those made in respect of translation rights under article 30(2)(b); those made by a developing country under article II or III of the Appendix; and the miscellaneous reservations which have been maintained by countries from earlier Acts. (The range and kind of reservation now possible under the Paris Act are discussed further at para 17.27 below.)

III. SUBSEQUENT AGREEMENTS BETWEEN UNION COUNTRIES

A. Background

One of the reasons for the formation of the Berne Convention was the desire of states to move away from the complexity and confusion that attended their existing bilateral copyright arrangements.[392] Nonetheless, entering the new Union did not bring an automatic end to those bilateral agreements that had previously existed between member states, and there was no intention by the **6.126**

[388] Vienna Convention, art 2(1)(d) (definition of 'reservation'). See further paras 17.22ff below.

[389] See now Paris Act, art 30(2)(c).

[390] See eg the declaration by Norway at the opening session of the Rome Conference: *Actes* 1928, 167.

[391] See further on the scope and effect of such reservations [1926] *DA* 114, 117–18 and Ladas (1938), 352–63.

[392] See generally Chapters 1 and 2 above.

parties that this should be so. Many continued in force, and often provided greater protection in their bilateral relations than was accorded under the new multilateral instrument. The Berne Act contained two distinct provisions in this regard. The first, the Additional Article, dealt with existing agreements:

> The Convention concluded this day shall in no way affect the maintenance of existing Conventions between the Contracting States, provided always that such Conventions confer on authors, or their lawful representatives, rights more extended than those secured by the Union, or contain other stipulations which are not contrary to this Convention.

Future agreements were dealt with in article 15 as follows:

> It is understood that the Governments of the countries of the Union reserve to themselves the right to enter into special arrangements between each other, provided always that such arrangements confer upon authors or their lawful representatives more extended rights than those granted by the Union, or embody other stipulations not contrary to the present Convention.

The formula adopted in both articles was the same, namely that the agreements in question should confer more extended rights than were granted under the Berne Act, or that they should contain other stipulations not contrary to that Act. These were a clear application of the principle of minimum protection (see above), and this was reflected in a change that was made to the original text proposed in the Federal Council programme.[393] This had stated that bilateral agreements should be maintained 'in so far as these arrangements did not contravene the provisions of the present Convention'.[394] This formulation was criticized as not sufficiently expressing the principle of minimum protection, and the above wording was therefore adopted.[395]

(a) The effect on existing bilateral agreements

6.127 The effect of the Additional Article was to exclude the operation of those provisions of existing agreements that accorded lesser protection than the Berne Act. In addition, a number of these agreements came to an end through denunciation or the passing of time.[396] By the time of the Paris Conference in

---

393 *Actes* 1884, 12. 394 Federal Council programme, art 12.

395 *Actes* 1884, 59.

396 The vast majority of bilateral conventions were entered into for a fixed period of time, and thereafter remained in force from year to year unless denounced (generally the giving of a year's notice was required). See further para 1.41 above. Consequently, these conventions remained in force unless denounced (or terminated for some other reason), even if they were no longer applicable in the light of the provisions of the Berne Convention. However, it does not appear that desuetude, on its own, is sufficient to revoke a convention: see generally, F Majoris, *Les Arrangements bilatéraux en matière de droit d'auteur* (1971), Introduction.

1896, eight bilateral conventions,[397] mainly those of the UK, Belgium, and Switzerland, had been mutually denounced, with the result that the relations of these countries were now governed wholly by the terms of the Berne Act. At the Paris Conference, a resolution was passed, at the request of the German delegation, requesting member countries to examine their existing bilateral agreements with a view to determining whether their provisions were to be regarded as still being in force.[398] This led, in turn, to the denunciation of a further five conventions by the time of the Berlin Conference,[399] as well as to the publication of a comprehensive collection of national laws and current treaties by the International Office in 1904.[400] The Berlin Conference also saw the transfer of the Additional Article to a new article 20 which now dealt with both existing and future bilateral conventions. The conditions for the validity of these agreements remained the same, and the article read as follows:

> The Governments of the countries of the Union reserve to themselves the right to enter into special arrangements between each other, provided always that such arrangements confer upon authors more extended rights than those granted by the Union or embody other stipulations not contrary to the present Convention. The provisions of existing arrangements which satisfy the above-mentioned conditions shall remain applicable.

This provision has been retained in essentially the same form under successive Acts, with only minor drafting changes. Thus, at the Brussels Conference, at the proposal of the French delegation, the phrase 'granted by the Convention' was substituted for the rather strange phrase 'granted by the Union';[401] in the Stockholm Revision the word 'agreements' was substituted for 'arrangements'.[402]

---

397 With effect from 6 Dec 1887, the UK denounced the following conventions: the Anglo-Belgian Convention of 12 Aug 1854, the Anglo-Spanish Convention of 11 Aug 1880, the Anglo-French Convention of 3 Nov 1851, and the Anglo-Italian Convention of 30 Nov 1860: Ladas (1938), 152. Belgium denounced her Convention of 24 Nov 1859 with Italy as of 4 July 1889: [1889] *DA* 113; her Convention of 25 Apr 1867 with Switzerland as of 7 May 1890: [1890] *DA* 66; and her Convention of 31 Oct 1881 with France as of 1 Feb 1892: [1891] *DA* 33. Switzerland denounced her Convention of 23 Feb 1882 with France as of 1 Feb 1892: [1891] *DA* 14.

398 *Actes* 1896, 229.

399 These were the following: the eleven Conventions between the UK and the Confederated German States and the German Empire were suppressed by an exchange of notes of 23 Mar and 18 Apr 1898 ([1898] *DA* 77); the Convention between Germany and Switzerland of 13 May 1869, revised 23 May 1881: denounced as of 18 Nov 1899 ([1899] *DA* 25, 144); the Convention between Switzerland and Italy of 22 July 1868: denounced as of 18 Nov 1899 ([1899] *DA* 25, 144); the Convention between France and Luxembourg of 4 July 1856 and 16 Dec 1865: denounced as of 9 Sept 1899 ([1899] *DA* 113). See further [1911] *DA* 131.

400 International Copyright Office, *Recueil des conventions et traités concernant la propriété littéraire et artistique, publiés en français et dans les langues des pays contractants avec une introduction et des notices* (1904).

401 *Documents 1948* (1951), 382.

402 *Records* 1967, 1299.

B. Interpretation of the Present Article 20

6.128 The applicability of existing and future agreements between Union members under the present text therefore depends upon one of two conditions being satisfied: (i) that the agreement in question confers upon authors more extensive rights than those granted under the Convention, or (ii) that it embodies other stipulations not contrary to the Convention. Both these criteria require further examination.

(1) 'More extensive rights'

It seems reasonable to interpret this phrase as meaning 'more extensive rights in works already protected under the Convention'. The essence of this category therefore is that the agreement amplifies or extends upon matters already covered by the Convention. In consequence, it will not apply to agreements which protect new classes of works or which grant wholly new rights that are not expressly or implicitly referred to in the Convention: such provisions more appropriately fall under the second category of 'other stipulations'. A good example of an agreement within this first category would be one whereby two or more Union member countries undertook to protect the works of each other's authors for a period in excess of the conventional term of life-plus-fifty-years.[403]

(2) Agreements containing 'other stipulations'

As suggested above, these must refer to matters not presently covered by the Convention, in which case the capacity to make, or maintain, such agreements

[403] The recently concluded US-Australia Free Trade Agreement (signed 18 May 2004), art 17.4(4) (agreeing to life plus seventy years) is one such example. A number of such agreements have existed over the years. See eg the exchange of notes between France and Italy (1951 and 1957), Norway (1956 and 1964), Spain (1957), Austria (1956 and 1976), and the FRG (1974). Some have provided for extensions of term on the ground of war loss, see eg the exchange of notes between France and Italy (1951 and 1957), Norway (1956 and 1964), Spain (1957), Austria (1956 and 1976), and the FRG (1974), while others have been between Union members which have both extended their terms of protection, see eg the exchange of notes between Austria and Norway (1956), Spain (1959), France (1964 and 1976), Brazil (1965), the FRG (1967), and Italy (1969). In the early days of the Convention, the French Government also maintained many of its existing bilateral agreements on the ground that they dealt more generously with such matters as translation rights, eg the Conventions with Spain (1880), Norway (1881), and Italy (1884). In 1907, Germany also entered into several new conventions with Belgium, France, and Italy, thereby replacing earlier agreements that had been made prior to 1886. The former provided fuller protection in relation to such matters as translation and performing rights, and the complete abolition of formalities, see eg Germany and Belgium, 16 Oct 1907 [1908] *DA* 81; Germany and France, 8 Apr 1907: [1907] *DA* 93; Germany and Italy, 9 Nov 1907: [1908] *DA* 41. In substance, these conventions were superseded by the provisions of the Berlin Act, except for their respective most favoured nation clauses.

depends upon whether or not they are 'contrary to the Convention'. An example would be an agreement protecting a new kind of subject matter not covered by the Convention, such as sound recordings, television broadcasts, or performers' rights.[404] Other agreements might deal with matters that are ancillary to authors' rights, but nonetheless closely related, such as the licensing and ownership of rights, taxation, and collection of royalties,[405] the administration of collecting societies, provisions for cultural advancement and so on. Article 20 provides no inhibition on the making and maintenance of such agreements, but simply provides that they should not be inconsistent with the provisions of the Convention. A hypothetical instance where an agreement would be contrary to the stipulations of the Berne Convention under this head would be where a treaty on performers' rights required that the mechanical reproduction right of the author of a musical work should not apply in particular circumstances.

C. Agreements Inconsistent with Article 20

The effect of article 20 upon agreements that fail to satisfy the conditions **6.129**
contained in that article appears to be quite limited. So far as existing agreements are concerned, they are not revoked: all that article 20 provides, by implication, is that they shall not be applicable to the extent of their inconsistency. In other respects, they continue in force until revoked by the parties or terminated for one of the general causes recognized in international law.[406] As regards future agreements, more difficulties arise, as there appear to be no readily applicable rules to resolve conflicts that arise between competing treaty obligations. An inconsistent future agreement will clearly constitute a breach of article 20, as this imposes an obligation on Union members not to make such agreements. But that article does not purport to stipulate what the status of those agreements shall be, for example, whether they are to be regarded as void or suspended. The Vienna Convention does not provide any clear guidance on this particular point,[407] although a number of possible solutions have been suggested by various writers, including the application of the maxim *lex posterior generalis non derogi priori speciali*.[408] However, the true position seems to be that stated by Lord McNair:

---

[404] eg the Rome Convention 1961 and the Phonograms Convention 1971, and the WIPO Performers and Phonograms Treaty (1996).

[405] See eg the Madrid Convention for the Avoidance of the Double Taxation of Copyright Royalties 1979: [1980] *Copyright* 12.

[406] See generally Majoris (n 396 above), 39ff; I Sinclair, *The Vienna Convention on the Law of Treaties*, 2nd edn (1984), 93ff; Lord McNair, *The Law of Treaties* (1961), 213ff.

[407] Vienna Convention, art 30.

[408] See further Sinclair (n 406 above), 94ff; McNair (n 406 above), 221ff.

> Where the parties to the two treaties said to be in conflict are the same, an allegation of conflict raises a question of interpretation rather than a question of a rule of law; the parties are masters of the situation and they are free to modify one treaty by a later one.[409]

It is therefore impossible to lay down any general rule as to the status of future agreements between two or more Union members that fail to comply with the conditions stipulated in article 20. Each will need to be considered on its own merits.

(1) Agreements to modify or suspend provisions of the Convention

6.130 It will be clear from the preceding paragraph that the purpose of article 20 is to act as a barrier to any lowering of protection between member states. This was a matter that was considered at some length in the early discussions on the concessions to be made to developing countries at the time of the Stockholm Revision.[410] A number of different formulations were considered, such as regional arrangements between groups of developing countries and developed countries, under which the latter would consent to the lowering of the level of protection accorded to the works of their authors.[411] However, these proposals were rejected on the basis that they were potentially open-ended, and might lead to the complete abolition of protection.[412] As a result, article 20 continues to oblige states not to enter into agreements which modify, rather than extend, protection. The status of such agreements has already been discussed in para 6.129 above. However, it goes without saying that this prevents parties to the Convention agreeing to suspend, even temporarily, the operation of the Convention as between themselves. This is an important point, as the general rule of international law appears to be that parties to a multilateral treaty may do this, unless such a suspension is prohibited by that treaty.[413] Article 20 is clearly such a prohibition, which article 9(1) of the TRIPs Agreement now makes enforceable (see further the discussion at para 6.136 below).

(a) The effect of the UCC

6.131 A large number of Berne Union countries are signatories to the UCC, which generally permits a lower level of protection.[414] Potentially, this could lead to a conflict with the obligations which these states owe to each other under the Berne Convention. As article 20 applies only to agreements between Union members, it cannot, of course, have any effect with respect to the relations

[409] McNair (n 406 above), 219. [410] See Chapter 14 below.
[411] *Records* 1967, 143 (Document S/1). [412] ibid.
[413] See generally Vienna Convention, art 58 and see also Sinclair (n 406 above), 185.
[414] See further Chapter 18 below.

between Union members and non-Union members under the UCC. With respect to relations between Union members, its effect is much less certain (see para 6.129 above). However, this matter is expressly dealt with in the UCC itself, article XVII(1) of which provides:

> This Convention shall not in any way affect the provisions of the Berne Convention for the Protection of Literary and Artistic Works or membership in the Union created by that Convention.

(This provision is discussed further at para 18.27 below.)

D. The Relationship Between Articles 19 and 20

The relationship between these two articles requires some explanation. While the second provides for the application of agreements which grant extended protection, the first will often have the effect of extending these benefits to the authors of other Union countries. Thus, article 19 provides that nothing in the Convention is to be taken as precluding 'the making of a claim to the benefit of any greater protection which may be granted by legislation in a country of the Union'. In a more positive sense, under article 5(1) each Union member undertakes to accord national treatment to works whose CO is another Union member. Accordingly, if Union countries A and B enter an agreement to grant each other's authors greater protection, this will usually presuppose that each country already grants that level of protection to its own authors. Under the principle of national treatment, therefore, countries A and B should also accord this treatment to authors from other Union countries. In consequence, countries A and B will not be able to restrict the benefits of these agreements to their own authors, and the result will be that there will be little, if any, point in individual member countries entering into agreements between themselves for the extension of protection under the Convention. However, there are obvious cases where such agreements will be necessary: **6.132**

1. *Where the agreement relates to matters under the Convention which can only be dealt with on the basis of reciprocity.* The main instances where this can be done are (i) applied works of art,[415] (ii) extensions of the term of protection beyond the mandatory term of life plus fifty years,[416] and (iii) the *droit de suite*.[417] The making of an agreement is not necessary to achieve such reciprocal protection, but will certainly be a common way for Union members to facilitate this. Thus, if countries A and B make an agreement with respect to, say, the extension of the term of protection, countries C and D will only be

[415] Paris Act, art 2(7). [416] ibid, art 7(8). [417] ibid, art 14*ter*(2).

able to claim the benefit of this extended term for their own authors if they also grant the same term or become parties to the same agreement.

2. *Where the agreement benefits only non-local authors.* This situation may not be likely to arise in practice, but it is included for completeness of the analysis. If state A agreed to afford greater protection to state B's authors without benefiting its own authors, and state B did the same, there would be no national treatment basis for authors whose COs are not party to that agreement to demand the greater protection, because local authors would not be receiving that protection either.
3. *Where the agreement contains a most favoured nation clause in favour of non-Union countries.* In general, these clauses will be mostly found in bilateral treaties between Union and non-Union countries, or treaties which were made before both parties became members of the Union[418]—scenarios that are increasingly unlikely today in view of the near-universal character of Union membership. Once both countries are Union members, however, it is difficult to see how such a clause can operate between them, so far as relations with other Union countries are concerned: except in cases where reciprocity is required by the Berne Convention (see item 1 above), any increase in the protection offered by country A to country C under a later treaty will automatically flow to country B under the principle of national treatment and without any need to rely on the most favoured nation clause in the treaty between A and B. However, the clause will continue to have effect where country C is a non-Union member: subject to the conditions of the clause (and these may vary widely),[419] country B should be able to claim the benefit of any additional protection which is accorded by A to C. It goes without saying, of course, that such protection will need to be more extensive than under the Berne Convention.
4. *Where the agreement falls under the second limb of article 20.* These agreements concern matters not covered by the Convention, although it is to be presumed that they will be of a closely related nature. There will be no entitlement for the authors of other Union countries to be admitted to the benefits of these agreements as, by definition, these are not matters in respect of which national treatment can be demanded.

6.133 Might article 19 nonetheless permit Berne authors to claim greater protection in Union countries party to article 20 special agreements that pertain to rights not subject to national treatment? Although the development of article 19 may have anticipated that local legislation would most often benefit local authors (see the

[418] See eg the Convention of 9 July 1884 between France and Italy, art 10.

[419] See here the discussion in Ladas (1938), 173–7 and the study in [1908] *DA* 2.

discussion earlier at para 6.82 above), the text of article 19 would cover situations, such as in item 2 of the list in the preceding paragraph, in which the subjects of the local legislative grant of greater protection are limited to foreign authors. Unlike article 5(1), article 19 is not limited to protections that local legislation grants local authors. If, indeed, 'the provisions of this Convention shall not preclude the making of a claim to the benefit of any greater protection which may be granted by legislation in a country of the Union', then article 19 could even be read to override those provisions that make protection subject to reciprocity. But a purpose of article 20 is to permit limiting 'special agreements' to their parties, subject to the obligation of national treatment. Without article 20, article 19 could be read as a kind of 'most favoured nation' clause, entitling non-party states to the increased protection any Union country's legislation may provide, without regard to whether the protection is provided to local authors or to foreign authors, and without regard to whether the protection is otherwise subject to the rule of reciprocity. The interplay of articles 19 and 20, however, would suggest that authors whose COs are not party to a special agreement are not entitled to any of that agreement's benefits if the contracting state does not extend them to its own authors.

E. Beyond the Berne Convention: Interplay of New TRIPs Agreement and WCT Protections and Berne Convention, articles 5(1), 19, and 20

The TRIPs Agreement and the WIPO Copyright Treaty ('WCT') incorporate **6.134** articles 3 and 5 of Berne, and therefore make no changes in the basic Berne structure regarding admission to protection, the rule of national treatment, and the prohibition of mandatory formalities.[420] The TRIPs Agreement contains a 'most favoured nation' clause requiring member states to extend to all other members any privileges which one member may grant to another, but this provision exempts separately negotiated privileges that the Berne Convention does not make subject to the rule of national treatment.[421] Hence the TRIPs Agreement does not change outcomes, for example, with respect to agreements among a subset of Berne member states to grant each other's works a term of protection longer than life plus fifty years. Each treaty creates new rights or expands on Berne's substantive minimum subject matter and rights, but these aspects will be considered in Chapters 8 to 13 below.

The principal structural issue that the treaties raise concerns the application of **6.135**

[420] See TRIPs Agreement, art 9; WCT art 1.

[421] See TRIPs Agreement, art 4(b).

the rule of national treatment by a member state of the TRIPs Agreement or the WCT to a Berne member state that has not acceded to the TRIPs Agreement or to the WCT.[422] To the extent that the TRIPs Agreement or the WCT mandate protection of rights not explicitly covered by the Berne Convention, such as rental and distribution rights,[423] does article 5(1) require that the TRIPs Agreement or WCT member state extend those protections to a Berne member state that has acceded to either treaty? The earlier discussion (at para 6.132 above), indicates that the answer is 'yes'. The TRIPs Agreement and WCT provisions establish rights which the member state's laws 'hereafter may grant to their nationals', and therefore come within the scope of article 5(1) of Berne, as well as of article 19. One might object that these rights are qualitatively different from the Berne minimum rights, and therefore are excluded from the scope of national treatment. (See the earlier discussion at para 6.97 above.) But distribution of copies is as ancient a right as reproduction; indeed, the two generally go hand in hand. Moreover, the Berne Convention includes or implies some distribution rights, and these will be examined in Chapter 11 below. Rental rights are newer to international treaties, but have long been present in national laws. Moreover, their inclusion in recent multilateral instruments permits an argument that these rights are now recognized as being at the core of copyright.

(1) Consistency of the TRIPs Agreement with Berne Convention, article 20

6.136 Is the TRIPs Agreement an agreement consistent with article 20 of Berne? The TRIPs Agreement requires its signatories to 'comply with Articles 1 through 21 of the Berne Convention (1971)', but it explicitly excludes moral rights from the ambit of the obligations this provision imposes.[424] Does the removal of 'the rights conferred under Article 6*bis* . . . or of the rights derived therefrom' mean that the TRIPs Agreement violates article 20 of the Berne Convention? Put another way, is the excision of article 6*bis* 'contrary to this Convention'? The TRIPs Agreement does not relieve Berne member states of their Berne-incurred obligations to apply article 6*bis*, indeed, the TRIPs Agreement declares that 'nothing in . . . this Agreement shall derogate from the

[422] The universe of Berne member states who are not also WTO members is very small and is shrinking further. As of Jan 2005, Algeria, Andorra, Azerbaijan, Bahamas, Belarus, Bosnia and Herzegovina, Cape Verde, Equatorial Guinea, Holy See (Vatican), Kazakhstan, Lebanon, Libya, Russian Federation, Saudi Arabia, Serbia and Montenegro, Sudan, Tajikistan, Tonga, Ukraine, and Viet Nam were signatories of Berne and observer members of the WTO but not yet actual members. The Democratic People's Republic of Korea, Liberia, Federated States of Micronesia, Monaco, and Syrian Arab Republic are neither WTO members nor observer governments. See www.wipo.int/treaties. By contrast, while, as of September 2005, 159 states were Berne members, only 54 were WCT members.

[423] See TRIPs Agreement, art 11 (rental); WCT, arts 6 (distribution), 7 (rental).

[424] ibid, art 9(1).

existing obligations that Members may have to each other under. . . the Berne Convention . . .'.[425] As a result, it has been contended that 'while certain obligations are not in TRIPs, they continue to apply and no argument under TRIPs could sustain a derogation. This is the case of the moral right, protected under Article 6bis of Berne, which was neither incorporated into TRIPs, nor derogated to by the Agreement.'[426]

But excluding article 6bis has one very important practical consequence: if a WTO member state does not respect its Berne obligations under article 6bis, there is no recourse to the WTO dispute-settlement and trade sanctions that would attend a member state's violation of any other provisions of the Berne Convention.[427] Because the WTO proceedings constitute, as a practical matter, the only effective supranational enforcement of Berne norms, the elimination of article 6bis from the TRIPs Agreement means that moral rights norms are effectively unenforceable. In that light, the TRIPs Agreement might indeed seem 'contrary to the Convention'. On the other hand, the TRIPs Agreement does not leave moral rights claimants any worse off than they were before, because before TRIPs, there was no practical means to compel Berne member states to enforce article 6bis either.[428] **6.137**

(2) Transitional provisions: TRIPs Agreement, article 65; WCT, article 13

For developed countries, obligations under the TRIPs Agreement, including those of compliance with the Berne Convention, went into effect a year from entry into force of the WTO Agreement (a year from 1 January 1995[429]); developing countries, and countries in transition from centrally planned to market economies were accorded an additional four years, and least developed countries, ten years.[430] The TRIPs Agreement does not incorporate more **6.138**

425 ibid, art 2(2).

426 Daniel Gervais, *The TRIPS Agreement: Drafting History and Analysis*, 2nd edn (2003), para 2.33.

427 See discussion in paras 10.40ff below.

428 If one were nonetheless to conclude that the TRIPs Agreement is inconsistent with Berne, art 20, a curious impasse would result. As discussed earlier at para 6.129 above, a subsequent agreement that is inconsistent with the Berne Convention should not be applicable 'to the extent of its inconsistency'. It would follow that the TRIPs exclusion of art 6bis should be without force, and that therefore WTO member states should incur the same obligations, and the same sanctions, with respect to art 6bis as to the rest of arts 1–21. Moreover, while non-compliance with art 20 by a Berne member state before the TRIPs Agreement had no practical consequences, TRIPs makes art 20 enforceable. This would mean that a WTO member (who is also a Berne member) could face trade sanctions for failure to enforce art 6bis, because that non-enforcement would violate art 20.

429 See WTO Agreement, Final Act Embodying the Results of the Uruguay Round of Multilateral Trade Negotiations, art 3 (see www.wto.org).

430 TRIPs Agreement, arts 65 (1)(2)(3), 66(1).

specific transitional provisions, but, by virtue of the article 9(1) compliance clause, a newly acceding member to the TRIPs Agreement would be obliged to grant protection to foreign works in accordance with Berne, article 18. Thus, for example, if a TRIPs member state had not accorded the Berne minimum term of life plus fifty years to Union and WTO works, and had not, upon accession, restored the prematurely defunct copyrights in works still protected in their Union or WTO COs, that member state would be in violation of its TRIPs obligations (as well as of article 18 of the Berne Convention), and could be subject to a dispute-settlement procedure.[431] The WCT, although it also includes a general Berne compliance clause, in article 1(4), explicitly directs its contracting parties in article 13 to 'apply the provisions of Article 18 of the Berne Convention to all protection provided for in this Treaty'. Thus, in addition to according works from other Union and WCT member states the protections required by article 18 of the Berne Convention with regard to Berne minimum rights, article 18 also applies *mutatis mutandis* to the additional (or clarified) protections established by the WCT.[432]

---

[431] See eg *Luck's Music Library, Inc* v *Gonzales*, 407 F 3d 1262 (DCCir 2005) (US restoration of foreign copyrights pursuant to 'Uruguay Rounds Amendments Act of 1994' implementing TRIPs Agreement obligations, including Berne Convention, art 18).

[432] On *mutatis mutandis* application of art 18, see generally Reinbothe and von Lewinski (n 324 above), 162–3.

7

AUTHORSHIP AND OWNERSHIP

A. Introduction

7.01 This chapter addresses issues of signal importance to the international protection of works of authorship, but concerning which the Berne Convention for the Protection of Literary and Artistic Works is at best enigmatic. More often it is silent. The Convention declares that its 'protection shall operate for the benefit of the author and his successors in title',[1] but the Convention neither

[1] Article 2(6).

designates who is an 'author', nor establishes general rules concerning the transfer of title. As a result, it generally leaves the determination of authorship, ownership, and transfer of rights to national law. Because these often diverge, however, the absence of a substantive treaty rule will confront claimants with varying outcomes depending on which domestic rule a court finds competent to resolve a conflict of authorship or ownership. This chapter will first expose the lacunae in the Conventional treatment of individual authors and joint works, although the choice of law aspects will be explored in greater detail in Chapter 20 below. This chapter will next address the special treatment the Convention reserves for the 'makers' of cinematographic works. It will consider the extent to which, despite the lack of explicit provisions on authorship, some definition of authorship may be inferred from the provisions on cinematographic works and from the treaty as a whole. Finally, this chapter will review questions of ownership and transfer of copyright, with particular attention to the elaborate rules set out for cinematographic works.

B. Who is an 'Author'?

(1) The meaning of 'author'

7.02 As we have seen in Chapter 6 above, authorship supplies a key point of attachment for application of the Convention: a work will be entitled to the Conventional minima of protection and to national treatment in Union countries if its author is a national or resident of a Union country. Authors pervade the Convention, starting with article 1, in which the Union countries affirm their desire to protect the 'rights of authors in their literary and artistic works'. The Conventional minimum rights benefit authors; authors furnish the reference point for the duration of copyright in literary and artistic works. However, while the rights protected are now defined with considerable precision, as is the subject matter falling within the expression 'literary and artistic works', nowhere does the Convention actually define who an author is.[2] Perhaps this was originally due to the existence, at the outset, of a fairly general consensus among the nations represented at the early conferences on the question of who was an author.[3]

---

[2] See eg Pascal Kamina, *Film Copyright in the European Union* (2002), 131 ('the Berne Convention appears to leave a total freedom to signatory States. There is no definition of the term "author" in the Convention, and its usual meaning is still the subject of controversy'). The Berne Convention does, however, establish a presumption of authorship; see art 15, discussed further at para 7.16 below.

[3] See Adolf Dietz, 'The Concept of Author Under the Berne Convention' (1993) 155 *RIDA* 2, 10–18 (discussing the understanding of 'author' at the time of the original Berne Convention). See also David Vaver, 'The National Treatment Requirements of the Berne and Universal Copyright Conventions (Part One)' (1986) 17 *IIC* 577, 593 ('From the BC's inception, "author" has meant a natural person, not a juristic person such as a corporation.').

7.03 Further guidance as to what constitutes 'authorship' is to be derived from a consideration of the expression 'literary and artistic works' in articles 2 and 2*bis*. Although this question is discussed in detail in Chapter 8 below, for our present purposes it can be said that the essential requirement for a literary or artistic work, under these provisions, is that it constitute an intellectual creation, regardless of the form in which it may be embodied. Furthermore, novelty or inventiveness, in the sense in which these terms are used in patent law, is not required. Thus, an 'author' need not be especially gifted; any person who has made an intellectual creation qualifies. But because Berne does not set the requisite quantum of creativity, it does not tell us how to identify an individual author, or for that matter, the authors of a work with multiple creative participants. In the latter case, are all the participants 'authors', or are some more authorial than others?

Moreover, Berne does not explicitly tell us whether the person who has made an intellectual creation may be a juridical person, such as the human creator's corporate employer. More broadly, Berne does not expressly speak to the question whether national laws may deem as an 'author' the human or juridical entity at whose behest and expense a work is created. Most Union countries, explicitly or implicitly, confine the authorship designation to human creators of original works.[4] but there are important exceptions, particularly among the common law countries.[5]

7.04 The Convention's failure clearly to designate who is an 'author' may be due to the divergences between national laws on other aspects of authorship that have become more pronounced since the Convention's initial promulgation. One particular point of difference concerns the actual degree of intellectual creation

[4] See eg France, Code de la propriété intellectuelle, art L 111–1(3) (employment contract does not derogate from author's enjoyment of economic and moral rights); Cass, 1re Civ, decision of 17 Mar 1982, JCP 1983 II 20054, note Plaisant (a juridical person cannot be recognized as an 'author'); Germany, Copyright Law of 1965, art 7 ('The author is the creator of the work'), the 'creator' in question does not include juridical persons; see eg Loewenheim, 'Dritter Abschnitt: Der UrheberLoewenheim', in G Schricker, *Urheberrecht*, 2nd edn (1999), § 7 and n 2 with further references; Adolf Dietz, 'Germany', in Melville B Nimmer and Paul Edward Geller, *International Copyright Law and Practice* (2003), § 4[1].

[5] See eg Netherlands Copyright Act 1912, arts 6–8; 17 USC § 201(b) (employer or hiring party is 'considered the author'); US Copyright Act, 17 USC §§ 101, 201(b) (work for hire: 'employer or other person for whom the work was prepared is considered the author for purposes of this title'); Australia Copyright Act 1968, ss 97–9 (stipulating that the 'maker' of a sound recording, cinematographic film, or television or sound broadcast is the initial copyright owner; the sections do not specifically define these people as the 'authors' only the 'owner of any copyright subsisting in the recording/film/broadcast'; however, s 22(4)(b) defines the 'maker' of a film as 'the person by whom the arrangements necessary for the making of the film were undertaken'); UK Copyright, Designs and Patents Act 1988, s 9(2)(a) (defining the author of a sound recording or film as 'the person by whom the arrangements necessary for the making of the recording or film are undertaken'; this person may be a juridical person).

required: common law courts have tended to lay more emphasis on the degree of labour and skill involved,[6] a criterion which might be more appropriate in the context of an investment-protection regime of unfair competition. By contrast, courts in civil law countries, such as Germany, will seek first to reach a judgement on the level of creativity involved in the production of the alleged work before granting protection.[7] Thus national standards of originality may set a higher or lower threshold of creativity requisite to a country's designation of who is an 'author'. This divergence may also account at least in part for the differences in national laws concerning the question whether it is necessary for an author to be a natural person, or whether this status can be enjoyed by juridical persons. In many jurisdictions, the former is required, as it is integral to their whole conception of authors' rights as rights pertaining to the person.[8] In other jurisdictions, particularly those derived from British law, this is not so, and it is possible for other legal entities to be authors (or 'makers') of certain kinds of works protected under the Berne Convention, most notably cinematographic works.[9] In addition, under many national laws, the personal role of the author is diminished by provisions that enable corporate entities to be the first owner—albeit not the 'author'—of copyright in works in particular circumstances (usually those of employment or contracts of commission).[10] This approach is even

[6] See eg *Walter* v *Lane* [1900] AC 539; *G A Cramp & Sons Ltd* v *F Smythson Ltd* [1944] AC 329; *Ladbroke (Football) Ltd* v *William Hill (Football) Ltd* [1964] 1 All ER 465; *Desktop Marketing Systems Pty Ltd* v *Telstra Corporation Ltd* (2001) 51 IPR 257 (Full Federal Court, Australia); *Law Society of Upper Canada* v *CCH Canadian Ltd* (2004) 60 IPR 650 (Supreme Court of Canada).

[7] See the review of German case law on the protection of 'small change' ('*kleine Münze*') in A Dietz, 'Letter from the Federal Republic of Germany: Report on the Development of Copyright Between 1972 and 1979' [1980] *Copyright* 85, 88–92; and on varying standards of originality across a variety of works, including 'small change', see A Dietz, 'News from Germany' (1998) 175 *RIDA* 176.

[8] See eg the German Law of 1965, art 2(2) ('works' include only 'personal intellectual creations'); France, Code de la propriété intellectuelle, art L 111–3 ('These rights shall subsist *in the person* of the author or of his successors in title . . .' (emphasis added)); art 113–7 ('Authorship of an audiovisual work shall belong to the *natural person or persons* who have carried out the intellectual creation of the work.' (emphasis added)); art 113–8 'Authorship of a radio work shall belong to the *natural person or persons* who carried out the intellectual creation of the work.' (emphasis added)).

[9] UK Copyright, Designs and Patents Act 1988, s 9(2)(a) (defining the author of copyright in a sound recording or film as 'the person by whom the arrangements necessary for the making of the recording or film are undertaken'—this includes juridical persons).

[10] See eg UK Copyright, Designs and Patents Act 1988, s 11(2); Italian Law of 1941, arts 11, 38; 12*bis*, 12*ter*, 88; Japanese Law of 1970, art 15; the Netherlands Law of 1912, arts 7, 8. Contrast here the French Code de la propriété intellectuelle, art L 111–1(3), which provides that the existence of or conclusion of a contract to make a work or an employment contract implies no exception to the author's enjoyment of the first rights in his work. See further on this general question, and on the danger of authors' rights developing into a kind of industrial property where

accommodated in the Berne Convention, in article $14^{bis}(2)$, concerning the ownership of copyright in cinematographic works (discussed further at paras 7.30ff below).

Given these divergences in national law, it is not surprising that, whatever the consensus at Berne's founding, attempts to insert a definition of authorship in later versions of the Convention and related documents have been resisted.[11] The most recent such attempt foundered in the 1990s, in the context of 'Model Provisions for Legislation in the Field of Copyright', undertaken by the World Intellectual Property Organization ('WIPO').[12] The Draft Model Law aspired 'to make the protection of [copyright] more effective throughout the world'.[13] The drafters endeavoured to include provisions that would implement the recognition that the common law approach to copyright had by 1990 become more widespread than in the Convention's early years. Although 'the nature of the Berne Convention has not changed during its various revisions, in the sense that it has not ceased to reflect the dominance of the "continental" copyright thinking, the history of the Convention clearly indicates that the "common law" type copyright laws, first in one state, and later in several states, were recognized and accepted by the other states party to the Berne Convention as laws being compatible with the Convention', the drafters proclaimed.[14] Accordingly, the drafters sought to devise provisions that would 'also reflect the agreement expressed at various revision conferences concerning the acceptability of certain specific elements of the copyright legislation of countries with "common law" traditions, and, thus . . . can be applied both in countries with "continental" traditions and in countries with "common law" traditions . . .'.[15] With **7.05**

ownership rights are vested in their employers and other corporate entities, the review by Dietz of then-recent proposed changes to the Swiss Copyright Law: A Dietz, 'Entwickelt sich das Urheberrecht zu einem gewerblichem Schutzrecht?', in W Barfuss, H Torggler, C Hauer, L Wiltschek, and G Kuckso (eds), *Wirtschaftrecht in Theorie und Praxis: Gedenkschrift für Fritz Schönherr*, 111, 114ff. See also Sam Ricketson, 'People or Machines: The Berne Convention and the Changing Concept of Authorship' (1991) 16 *Colum-VLA J L & the Arts* 1.

[11] A proposal to this effect was made by the Austrian delegation at the Brussels Conference, but was rejected: *Documents de la Conférence réunie à Bruxelles du 5 au 26 juin 1948* (1951) ('*Documents 1948* (1951)'), 164–5. The 1976 Tunis Model Law on Copyright for Developing Countries, WIPO Document 812(E) (1976) lacks a definition of authorship. The provisions on ownership, however, appear to assume that the author is a human creator; see s 11(1)(2). Section 11(3) nonetheless allows for vesting of copyright in the 'maker of the work'.

[12] See Committee of Experts on Model Provisions in the Field of Copyright, third session, Geneva, 2–13 July 1990, preparatory document and summary of meeting at [1990] *Copyright* 241, 246–7, 251–3, 290–1. See generally discussion in Dietz (n 3 above), 2–10.

[13] See Committee of Experts (n 12 above) citing WIPO's programme and budget for 1988–9, item PRG.04, 'Setting of Norms in the Field of Intellectual Property Particularly Under the Paris and Berne Conventions', WIPO Document AB/XVIII/2, Annex A.

[14] Committee of Experts (n 12 above), 246, para 34.

[15] ibid, para 36.

respect to authorship, this meant language that would, rather incoherently, have defined 'author' both ways:

> 'Author' is the physical person who has created the work. Reference to 'author' also means the successors in title of the author as well as the original owner of rights other than the author, where applicable.[16]

In other words, the human creator is the author except where the creator is not the initial titleholder, in which case the first owner is the 'author'. Not surprisingly, this excited considerable controversy among the participants in the WIPO meetings.[17] The report of the Committee of Experts suggested that because article 14*bis*(1) of the Berne Convention equates the rights of an author and those of the copyright owner, 'one can ask whether there is really any substantive difference if such an original owner of copyright . . . is simply called "author." It seems that it is not incompatible with the Berne Convention if a legislature gives the answer to that question that there is no substantive difference, and—e.g., as a matter of "drafting economy"—qualifies also such a legal entity as "author"'.[18] This possibly cynical deference to 'drafting economy' was bound to thrust red flags at delegates bullish about human authorship. Perhaps as a result, the report also conceded, nonetheless, that 'it corresponds better to the spirit of the Berne Convention if only physical persons are recognized as "authors"'.[19] The report then asserted that the way could be smoothed were it clearer that the author designation, as applied to an original right holder, does not mean that the right holder *is* the author, but merely that the right holder stands in the shoes of the author, just as does the successor in title.[20] Thus, the next version of the definition proposed:

> 'Author' is the physical person who has created the work. Reference to 'author' includes, in addition to the author, where applicable, also the successors in title of the author and where the original owner of the rights in the work is a person other than the author, such a person.[21]

Of course, this attempt to satisfy everyone pleased no one. Some delegates continued to urge deletion of everything after the first sentence, while others sought more explicit recognition that 'juridical entities could also be recognized or considered as authors'.[22] The language drew particular outrage from ALAI, which passed a resolution 'reminding' the world that 'the Berne Convention has consistently, in both letter and spirit, limited its recognition of the status of author exclusively to the physical person who has created the work'. ALAI

[16] Committee of Experts (n 12 above), 251, para 74.
[17] See ibid, 252, para 75 ('there was a fairly animated discussion about this item').
[18] ibid, para 84. [19] ibid, 253, para 86.
[20] ibid, para 87–8. [21] ibid, para 89.
[22] ibid, 290, paras 52–6.

chided the WIPO Draft Model Law for creating a 'regrettable confusion between the distinct concepts of author and right holder, a confusion which should be denounced and not perpetuated'.[23] Further efforts to create a Draft Model Law ceased, as WIPO turned its attention to developing a Possible Protocol to the Berne Convention;[24] this effort ultimately produced the 1996 WIPO Copyright Treaty ('WCT'). At no stage in the evolution of the Protocol or the WCT did the text include a definition of authorship.[25]

(2) Works by multiple authors

Berne's failure to define authorship, or to articulate the level of creativity requisite to a work's denomination as an 'intellectual creation', has further repercussions. The Convention's silence on these points leaves member states without guidance in determining who among a multiplicity of alleged contributors to a work should be considered its 'author' or 'authors'. Each contribution should perhaps meet a test of originality, but the calibration is left to national law. Moreover, Berne does not specify whether a work which combines the creative efforts of several contributors should be considered a work of co-authorship whose authors jointly control the work's exploitation and share in its profits, or whether it should be deemed a composite work consisting of separately exploitable components, with no contributor controlling the whole (absent contractual agreement). In fact, different member states characterize joint works differently, some limiting this class of works to those melding inseparable contributions, such as a co-written novel,[26] while others also include works composed of separable contributions, such as music and lyrics, that were created to form a single whole.[27] The consequences of these different national characterizations of joint **7.06**

[23] See Resolution of the Executive Committee of ALAI, taken at Helsinki, 30 May 1990: (1990) 146 *RIDA* 345.

[24] This was presaged in the report on the Draft Model law; see [1990] *Copyright* at 246, paras 27–8. At that time, however, the two efforts were expected to be distinct.

[25] See the reports of the Committee of Experts on a Possible Protocol to the Berne Convention, [1992] *Copyright* at 30–53, 66–82, 93–110; [1993] *Copyright* at 72–4, 84–104, 179–96; [1994] *Copyright* at 214–30; [1995] *Industrial Property and Copyright* at 107–10, 299–331, 427–8; [1996] *Industrial Property and Copyright* at 118–19, 235–7; WIPO, *Records of the Diplomatic Conference on Certain Copyright and Neighboring Rights Questions, Geneva 1996* (1999).

[26] See eg Italy, Copyright Act 1941, art 10 (indistinguishable and inseparable contributions); UK Copyright, Designs and Patents Act 1988, s 10(1) (contributions of authors not distinct from each other); Germany, Copyright Act of 1965, art 8(1) (joint authors if 'their respective contributions cannot be separately exploited'); Canada, Copyright Act 1985, s 2 (as amended through 1994) (contributions of authors not distinct from each other); Belize, Copyright Act Chapter 252, revised through 2000, art 3(1) (contributions not separate from one another); Ireland, Copyright and Related Rights Act 2000, s 22(1) (contributions 'not distinct').

[27] See eg 17 USC § 101 (defining joint works as composed of contributions that are intended to be either 'inseparable or interdependent parts of a unitary whole'); France, Code de la propriété intellectuelle, art L 113–2(1) (work of 'collaboration'; inseparability not required); L 113–3(3)

works and joint authorship for the cross-border exploitation of works will be explored in Chapter 20 below.

(3) Multiple creators: the special case of cinematographic works

7.07 Cinematographic works present an exaggerated example of the problem of joint works. In the case of cinematographic works, the difficulties are multiplied because of the large number of contributors. Here, the problem may not be that there is too little creativity, but rather that there is too much of it, or, more precisely, that there are too many creators—which of these are to be regarded as 'authors'? There is the camera operator, the lighting and sound engineer, the film editor, and other technical persons whose contribution is vital for the production of the final film. There is also usually a scriptwriter, the composer of any musical accompaniment which is used, the designer of background sets and costumes, the actors or presenter, and above all the director who welds all these elements into a creative whole. All these individuals may be involved in the making of a cinematographic production. Finally, there is the producer or entrepreneur who undertakes the financing and organization of the making of the film. While it may be argued that he makes no creative contribution to the production of the final film, it cannot be denied that in the vast majority of cases his role is nonetheless crucial. The Berlin Act, which first included cinematographic works in article 2 (and its successors), provided no guidance as to which of these persons were to be regarded as authors. It also left open the question of what element, or elements, of authorship were protected: did protection extend to the technical skills involved in the actual making of the film, in addition to, or instead of, the more explicitly literary and artistic contributions made by such persons as the director, scriptwriter, designer, and composer of the musical soundtrack? The basic requirement for a literary or artistic work under article 2(1) of the Brussels Act, still retained in the Stockholm, Paris Acts, was that the subject matter in question should be a 'production in the literary, scientific and artistic domain'. In the absence of any conventional definition of 'author', the question of who is the creator of a

explicitly contemplates that contributions may 'be of different genres' and thus separable; Spain, Consolidated Text of the Law on Intellectual Property, regularizing, clarifying, and harmonizing the applicable statutory provisions approved by Royal Legislative Decree 1/1996 of 12 Apr 1996, and amended by Law 5/1998 of 6 Mar 1998, incorporating Directive 96/9/EC of the European Parliament and of the Council of 11 Mar 1996 on the Legal Protection of Databases, s 7(1) (defining a work of joint authorship as 'a work that is the unitary result of the collaboration of two or more authors'); Portugal, Code of Copyright and Related Rights (No 45/85 of 17 Sept 1985, as last amended by Law No 114/91 of 3 Sept 1991), art 16(1) (a work is a work of joint authorship if 'it has been disclosed or published in the names of all or some of the co-authors, whether or not it is possible to distinguish their individual contributions').

cinematographic work therefore remained, and remains, in the final analysis, a matter for national legislation.

Different approaches to this question have been taken in member countries. The real problem is that, unlike other works, it is difficult to point to a single person who is the author of a cinematographic work. In some countries, therefore, all the persons who make the necessary literary and artistic contributions to the making of the film are regarded as its co-authors. For example, in the French Code de la propriété intellectuelle, the following persons are presumed, in the absence of proof to the contrary, to be the co-authors of a cinematographic work: the author of the script; the author of the adaptation; the author of the dialogue; the author of the musical composition, with or without words, especially composed for the work; and the director (‘*réalisateur*’).[28] In addition, where a cinematographic work is adapted from a pre-existing work or script which is still protected, the author of the original work is assimilated to the authors of the new work.[29] This approach is followed, with variations in a number of other countries, some of which also make provision for other persons involved in the creation of the film, such as the actors, cameramen, editors, and the like.[30] In the European Union, ‘the principal director of a cinematographic or audiovisual work [is] considered as its author or one of its authors. Member States [are] to designate other co-authors.’[31] Moreover, whether or not a member state designates as co-authors ‘the principal director, the author of the screenplay, the author of the dialogue and the composer of music specifically created for use in the cinematographic or audiovisual work’, the term of protection is calculated from the death of the last survivor of this group.[32] **7.08**

By contrast, in some common law countries, generally those of the Commonwealth, protection in respect of cinematographic films is conferred on the ‘maker’ of the film, who is defined as the person by whom the arrangements necessary for the production of the first copy of the film were undertaken.[33] In **7.09**

[28] France, Code de la propriété intellectuelle, art L 113–7.

[29] ibid.

[30] In a number of countries, this was left to the case law. See the survey of national laws in [1961] *DA* 62, 86.

[31] Council Directive 93/98/EEC of 29 Oct 1993 harmonizing the term of protection of copyright and certain related rights, art 2(1), *Official Journal* L 290, 24/11/1993 P 0009–0013; Council Directive 92/100/EEC of 19 Nov 1992 on rental right and lending right and on certain rights related to copyright in the field of intellectual property, *Official Journal* L 346, 27/11/1992 P 0061–0066, art 2(2).

[32] Term Directive, art 2(2). On the authorship of cinematographic works in the EU, see generally Kamina (n 2 above), 130–60.

[33] See eg the Australian Copyright Act 1968, s 22(4)(a); Indian Copyright Act 1957, s 2(uu) (the author of a film is the ‘producer’ or the person who takes the initiative and responsibility for making the film; see further ‘India’, in Nimmer and Geller (n 4 above), vol 2.

other words, this is the producer who may be either a corporate entity or natural person.[34] As a consequence, the emphasis in these jurisdictions is on the protection of the investment made in the film as an industrial product, and not with the individual creative contributions that have gone into its realization.[35] On the other hand, a number of these contributors, such as the scriptwriter, composer of the music, and set designer, receive protection in respect of their individual contributions insofar as these constitute literary or artistic works in their own right.[36] These laws, however, omit the director from the category of persons protected, as well as a number of other important contributors, such as the camera operators, editors, actors, and so on.[37] The laws of the Commonwealth countries do not, in fact, usually refer to 'cinematographic works' at all: the expression 'cinematographic film' is used, and protection is given under a separate category apart from literary and artistic works (although this is still done by the grant of a 'copyright').[38] In consequence, it seems clear that all kinds of cinematographic film are protected under these laws, and that these may include films that would not be 'productions in the literary, scientific and artistic domain' under article 2(1) of the Convention. There can be no objection to this, as the basis of the Convention is that it only stipulates the minimum of protection that member countries are to accord to each other's works

[34] See eg the now repealed UK Copyright Act 1956, ss 1(5) and 13. (The current provisions, Copyright, Designs and Patents Act 1988, ss 9(2)(a) and 178, do not preclude the possibility that the producer may be a juridical person, and a number of cases have treated corporations as producers, and thus statutory 'authors' of films: *Century Communications* v *Mayfair Entertainment UK Ltd* [1993] EMLR 335 (holding Era Communications Ltd to be author of the film *Raise the Red Lantern*); *Beggars Banquet Records* v *Carlton Television* [1993] EMLR 349 (interim decision intimating that two corporations would probably be joint authors of film of rave).) To similar effect, Australia, Copyright Act 1968, s 84 ('qualified person' with respect to 'makers' of 'subject matter other than works', such as sound recordings and cinematograph films, includes 'body corporate').

[35] Professors Bently and Sherman refer to this type of production as 'entrepreneurial works'; see Lionel Bently and Brad Sherman, *Intellectual Property Law*, 2nd edn (2004), 118.

[36] UK Copyright, Designs and Patents Act 1988, ss 1, 3, and 4. For an example where costumes were protected as artistic works, see *Shelley Features* v *Rex Films* [1994] EMLR 134; for limitations on the protection of set designs, see *Creation Records* v *News Group* [1997] EMLR 444 (collection of objects arranged for photoshoot held not to be work of artistic craftsmanship). Note that the Court of Appeal of England and Wales has taken the view that an original cinematographic work may gain protection not just as a 'film' but also as a 'dramatic work': *Norowzian* v *Arks (No 2)* [2000] EMLR 67.

[37] The laws of the UK and Republic of Ireland now treat 'principal directors' as co-authors of 'films', as regards films made on or after 1 July 1994, in order to meet their obligations under art 2(1) of the EC Term Directive: Copyright, Designs and Patents Act 1988, s 9(2)(ab); Irish Copyright and Related Rights Act 2000, s 21.

[38] See eg UK Copyright, Designs and Patents Act 1988, s 1(b) ('film'); see further the Australian Copyright Act 1968, s 90 ('cinematograph film'); Indian Copyright Act 1957, s 13(1)(b) ('cinematograph film'). But note also the influence of the concept of 'cinematographic work' on Buxton LJ's interpretation of the concept of 'dramatic work' under the UK's Copyright, Designs and Patents Act 1988 in *Norowzian* v *Arks (No 2)* [2000] EMLR 67.

(see paras 6.80ff above). Nor, in the absence of a conventional definition of the author of a cinematographic work, can it be argued that these countries offend against the Convention by protecting the producer, as the maker of the film, rather than any of the possible putative authors.[39] In any case, as will be seen below (at para 7.30), article 14*bis* of the Convention, which was added in the 1967 Stockholm Revision, now accords express recognition to the 'film copyright' system embodied in the legislation of many of the common law countries.

(4) The phenomenon of 'deemed authorship'

7.10 But if film copyright systems are in general consistent with the Convention, this prompts the broader question whether other national laws which deem someone other than the actual creator the 'author', 'maker', or initial owner of copyright, are also compatible with the Convention. This brings us to the phenomenon of 'deemed authorship'—the device of conferring the status of author on persons who are not the actual intellectual creator. The US 'works made for hire' doctrine[40] is one example.[41] This is distinct from according rights of *ownership* on a person other than the actual creator, as is the case with works created under contracts of employment or commission in a number of Union countries.[42] Under such laws, however, the real creator still retains her status as *author*, even though problems may arise, particularly with respect to moral rights protection. By contrast, if someone else is deemed to be the 'author' of her work, the true creator is, in effect, disenfranchised and deprived potentially of her moral rights as well. In certain instances, there may be sound practical reasons in favour of such a divestment, however theoretically unpalatable it may seem: for example, the work may have been created as part of a collective enterprise which makes it cumbersome to identify individual contributors. In such a case, therefore, it may make sense to regard the person or entity in whose name the work is disclosed to the public as the author of the collective whole, at least, in the

[39] The EU Directives (n 31 above) allow for member states to designate 'others' as 'authors' in addition to the principal director. The term 'others', rather than 'other creators' or 'other persons' leaves room for member states to grant authorship status to juridical persons, such as producers.

[40] 17 USC §§ 101, 201(b) ('author' of a work made for hire is the employer, or in certain cases, the commissioning party).

[41] Others include the Netherlands Law of 1912, arts 6 and 7; Turkish Law of 1951, art 8. See further H Cohen Jehoram, 'The Author's Place in Society' [1978] *Copyright* 385; Jacqueline Siegnette, *Challenges to the Creator Doctrine: Authorship, Copyright Ownership and the Exploitation of Creative Works in The Netherlands, Germany, and the United States* (1994), 99–100 and nn 13, 19–22. See generally Ghislain Roussel, 'The Copyright of Salaried and Employed Authors: A Comparative Study of National Laws' [1990] *Copyright* 221–3 (national laws as of Nov 1989).

[42] See eg UK Copyright, Designs and Patents Act 1988, s 11(2); Ireland, Copyright and Related Rights Act 2000, s 23(1)(a) (employer is 'first owner' of copyright in employee works made in the course of employment); Australia, Copyright Act 1968, s 35(6).

absence of the contrary being shown.[43] Similar problems arise in the case of cinematographic works and it has been seen that in this area Union countries take differing views as to which persons are to be regarded as the authors of these works, with the consequence that recognition of these differences is now enshrined in article 14*bis*. Nevertheless, this last case might be thought to constitute a special exception which indicates that, as a general matter, Union countries should not extend the status of 'author' to persons or entities who are clearly not the real creators of works.

7.11 Since the Stockholm–Paris Revisions, however, these special exceptions have proliferated in other multilateral instruments. For example, the 1991 European Union Software Directive provides:

> The author of a computer program shall be the natural person or group of natural persons who has created the program or, where the legislation of the Member State permits, the legal person designated as the rightholder by that legislation. Where collective works are recognized by the legislation of a Member State, the person considered by the legislation of the Member State to have created the work shall be deemed to be its author.[44]

Similarly, the 1996 Database Directive allows:

> The author of a database shall be the natural person or group of natural persons who created the base or, where the legislation of the Member States so permits, the legal person designated as the rightholder by that legislation.[45]

Arguably, computer programs and databases are works of marginal authorship, more entrepreneurial than creative,[46] for which producer-favourable derogations therefore are appropriate. Moreover, given the borderline status of these works, a special regime of author designation should not infect more truly creative works, for which human authorship remains the norm. This somewhat aestheticized

43 See eg France, Code de la propriété intellectuelle, art L 113–5, which gives copyright in a collective work to 'the natural or legal person under whose name it has been disclosed' and specifically calls this person the 'author'; Italian Law of 1941, art 45; Japanese Law of 1970, art 15. See further R Plaisant, 'The Employee: Author and Literary and Artistic Property' [1977] *Copyright* 274; V de Santis's chapter on Italy in S Stewart (ed), *International Copyright and Neighbouring Rights*, 2nd edn (1989), 450–1.

44 Council Directive 91/250/EEC of 14 May 1991 on the legal protection of computer programs, art 2(1), *Official Journal* L 122, 17/05/1991 P 0042–0046.

45 Directive 96/9/EC of the European Parliament and of the Council of 11 Mar 1996 on the legal protection of databases, art 4(1), *Official Journal* L 077, 27/03/1996 P 0020–0028. The Database Directive, however, seems to want to treat the authorship of original databases both ways, because its recital 28 also declares: 'Whereas the moral rights of the natural person who created the database belong to the author and should be exercised according to the legislation of the Member States and the provisions of the Berne Convention for the Protection of Literary and Artistic Works; whereas such moral rights remain outside the scope of this Directive.'

46 See eg Ricketson (n 10 above), 24–7 (questioning the inclusion of these works within the universe of works of authorship).

view, however, is difficult to reconcile with the EU Directives, whose threshold of creativity, requiring that the work constitute the 'author's own intellectual creation',[47] denotes a level of originality surpassing that traditionally required in common law countries for any kind of copyrighted work.[48] Of course, the EU does not *instruct* member states to recognize entrepreneurial authorship; it merely allows those states who do so to retain the equation of producers and authors. Nonetheless, the expansion of permissible categories of works whose 'authors' may be persons or entities other than their actual creators challenges the premise that, by Berne's lights, an 'author' must be the work's human creator(s).

(5) Consistency of 'deemed authorship' with the Berne Convention

With respect to national laws vesting authorship itself in the employer, who may be either a corporate entity or natural person, the question therefore arises whether such provisions are compatible with the Convention. Despite Berne's failure explicitly to define 'author', a reading of its provisions indicates that the Convention's drafters and revisers implicitly took for granted that 'author' refers to natural persons: **7.12**

1. The preamble and article 1 refer to the need to protect the 'rights of authors in their literary and artistic works'. This seems to be a clear reference to personal, rather than corporate, rights.
2. The general term of protection is made dependent upon the life of the author (life plus fifty years), which again is inappropriate in the case of corporate entities which may have an indeterminate existence.
3. Article 14bis, which deals with the exploitation of rights in cinematographic works, makes specific allowance for those legal systems where the author (or 'maker') of a cinematographic work may be a corporate person. It can be argued that the inclusion of this provision confirms the existence of the general rule that only natural persons can be authors for the purposes of the Convention.
4. Further evidence for the existence of this general rule is to be seen in several other conventions which have been established in the past forty years or so to deal with the protection of other kinds of subject matter whose 'makers' are not regarded as authors and need not be natural persons.[49] The

[47] This is the EU standard for computer programs, databases, and photographs; see Software Directive, art 1(3); Database Directive, art 3(1); Council Directive 93/98/EEC of 29 Oct 1993 harmonizing the term of protection of copyright and certain related rights, art 6, *Official Journal* L 290, 24/11/1993 P 0009–0013.

[48] See eg Simon Chalton, 'The Copyright and Rights in Databases Regulations 1997: Some Outstanding Issues on Implementation of the Database Directive' (1998) 20 *EIPR* 178.

[49] In particular, the International Convention for the Protection of Performers, Producers of Phonograms and Broadcasting Organisations 1961 (the 'Rome Convention') and the Convention

relationship between these conventions on 'neighbouring rights' and the Berne Convention is discussed in Chapter 19 below.

7.13 The personal nature of the traditional Berne conception of authorship warrants emphasis.[50] Each of the exclusive rights now enshrined in the Berne Convention stems from, and is moulded by, the personal conception of authorship outlined above. This is obviously true in the case of moral rights, but is equally correct in the case of the economic rights guaranteed by the Convention. The latter are essentially concerned with the ability of the author to control and regulate the dissemination of her work in both material form (through the making of copies and adaptations) and non-material form (through public performance, broadcasting, cable diffusion, and so on). The last century has seen the expansion of these basic economic rights to take account of the effect of technological developments that now make possible new modes of exploitation of works. Undoubtedly, these rights will continue to expand, as is shown by the incorporation of a distribution right into the Agreement on Trade-Related Aspects of Intellectual Property Rights 1994 (the 'TRIPs Agreement') and the WCT, and the distinct statement of a 'making available' right in the latter.

The justifications for according authors such extensive protection are various, including natural-rights theories, arguments of fairness and individual justice, as well as arguments based on incentive and promotion of the public interest. Ultimately, these justifications rest upon the notion of authorship as a human activity, reflected in the lengthy protection accorded to these rights. The human-centred notion of authorship presently enshrined in the Berne Convention embodies a fundamental human right, namely that of the creator over the work he or she creates. There are sound philosophical foundations for this right, and it has been enunciated in article 1 of the Convention from the very start: a Union of states is constituted for the 'protection of the rights of authors over their literary and artistic works'. It also receives more recent and specific endorsement in the International Covenant on Economic, Social and Cultural Rights[51] and was reaffirmed, in grandiloquent terms, by the Assembly of the Berne Union at the time of the Convention's centenary in 1986.[52] However

for the Protection of Producers of Phonograms against Unauthorized Duplication of their Phonograms 1971 (the 'Phonograms Convention').

[50] See also Vaver (n 3 above), 594 (' "Author" in the RBC implies a person who applies his/her personal creativity to produce a literary or artistic work.').

[51] Article 15(1) of which provides: '(1) The States Parties to the present Covenant recognize the rights of everyone: . . . (c) To benefit from the protection of the moral and material interests resulting from any scientific, literary or artistic production of which he is the author.'

[52] See [1986] *Copyright* 373 for the full text of the 'solemn declaration' made by member states at this time. See also the Resolution of the ALAI (n 23 above) (reaffirming that authorship status in the Berne Convention is limited to human creators).

approximately this goal is achieved, the specific prescriptions of the Berne Convention nonetheless derive from this fundamental conception of authorship as a human activity and a human right. It therefore distorts this conception to vest rights initially vested in a person who may well not be a human being. One consequence of this distortion will be the diminution of moral justifications for copyright.[53] Another will be a—justifiable—call for reconsideration of the scope of copyright protection. If copyright simply becomes another investment-incentive scheme, uprooted from its foundation in human creativity, then competing values, including those of anti-trust or competition law, and consumer protection, should play a greater role in setting the contours of the right.[54] Thus, the recognition of a class of deemed authors can only have the effect of diminishing the status of authorship in general: instead of being a recognition of the claims of literary and artistic creativity to protection, it will transmute authors' rights into a form of protection for commercial or industrial investment. This will certainly have an adverse effect, in the long term, on those authors who are not in employment relationships, just as it will in the case of employed authors.[55]

That said, it is necessary to meet a strong counter-argument to the effect that **7.14** this personal conception of authorship, however appealing it may be in theory, and however compelling the policies underlying it, has been overtaken by developments that have already occurred within the framework of the Convention with respect to cinematographic works. The case of films is a clear instance where denial of human authorship can be justified on the following grounds: (i) it is difficult to identify such a person or persons in a meaningful way because of the collective or corporate character of the undertaking, and/or (ii) the nature of that undertaking has more of an industrial character than a literary or artistic one. The first of these explanations is clearly the one adopted by film copyright countries to justify their position. The second is more appropriate to other kinds of productions not covered by the Berne Convention, that achieve protection under a neighbouring rights or *sui generis* regime, such as sound recordings, broadcasts, and the like. Neither provides a sufficient justification for those

[53] See eg William R Cornish, 'The Author as Risk-Sharer' (2002) 26 *Colum J Law & the Arts* 1, 12: '[We should] seek to ensure that copyright laws are not mere pretexts for protecting the investment and entrepreneurial initiative of [authors'] exploiting partners. Why after all do we continue to have copyright laws which derive their legal and moral force from the act of creativity? Why not just have producers' investment laws?'.

[54] See eg Jane C Ginsburg, 'The Concept of Authorship in Comparative Copyright Law' (2003) 52 *de Paul L Rev* 1063, 1092 ('If we no longer value [human] creativity, then we shall require another basis for recognizing exclusive rights in works, be they works of authorship or other productions. More importantly, the scope of the rights we then install would have to be rethought and probably drastically reduced.').

[55] See further Dietz (n 10 above), 111, 114ff.

provisions in national laws which generally deem an employer or commissioning party to be the 'author' of a work rather than its actual creator. As closer examination of Berne's provisions on film copyright (see further paras 7.24–7.41 below) will show, moreover, the compromise struck between film copyright countries and traditional authorship countries is so unwieldy as to resist generalization to other kinds of works, including those produced by multiple authors. The uncertain 'fit' of those provisions within the Convention as a whole in turn highlights the centrality of Berne's premise of human authorship.

7.15 This defence of human authorship may nonetheless ring hollow if, as a practical matter, Berne does not impede the total transfer of the human author's rights to her employer, commissioning party, or any other grantee. Transfers of ownership will be addressed later on (at para 7.22 below). For present purposes, however, it is appropriate to point out that a creator whose authorship status is recognized will at least enjoy moral rights, whereas a creator not deemed to be an 'author' has no claim to those protections. And while Berne does not explicitly prohibit the transfer of moral rights, it does make clear that an author who alienates economic rights does not thereby give up her moral rights (see the further discussion at para 10.17 below).

(6) Proving authorship: presumptions

(a) Presumptions as to authorship in infringement proceedings

7.16 The Berne Convention does not define authorship, but it does set out presumptions to assist in identification of the author. These arise in the context of infringement proceedings, rather than that, explored above, of initial allocation of rights between putative co-authors, or between an employee or hired creator and her employer or hiring party. The basic presumptions here remain the same under the Stockholm, Paris Acts, as in the original Berne Act (see para 6.102 above). The first of these, contained in article 15(1), provides that, in order for the author of a work protected by the Convention to be entitled to institute infringement proceedings in the countries of the Union, it is sufficient for his name to appear on the work 'in the usual manner'. This presumption applies 'in the absence of proof to the contrary'. It is therefore what would be referred to in English law as a 'rebuttable presumption' that places the onus of rebuttal on the person disputing the author's right, that is, the infringer. Since the Brussels Revision, as the result of a French proposal,[56] this presumption has also applied in the case of names which are pseudonyms, where the pseudonym adopted by the author leaves no doubt as to his identity. In the case of other anonymous or pseudonymous works, the second presumption of the 1886 Act applies (see now

[56] *Documents 1948* (1951), 369.

article 15(3)): in the absence of proof to the contrary, the publisher whose name appears on the work is to be deemed to represent the author, and in this capacity to be entitled to protect and enforce the author's rights. This presumption ceases to apply when the author 'reveals his identity and establishes his claim to authorship of the work'. In this last case, it would not seem permissible for the newly revealed author to rely upon the presumption contained in article 15(1), as the reference in article 15(3) to establishing his claim to authorship clearly indicates that he must prove his entitlement. The evidential onus which he bears in this regard will then be a matter for national legislation. It should be noted that both the presumptions under article 15(1) and (3) are limited to infringement proceedings. Again, it will be a matter for national legislation to determine whether they, or any other kind of presumption, should be applicable in other actions before national courts which involve authors' rights protected under the Convention.

In the Stockholm, Paris Acts, several other presumptions were added to article 15. These relate to the makers of cinematographic works (article 15(2)), and the authorship of unpublished works where the identity of the author is unknown but there is every ground to assume that he is a national of a country of the Union (as in the case of works of folklore) (article 15(4)). These are dealt with in turn below.

(b) Presumptions as to the maker of a cinematographic work

The programme for the Stockholm Conference also proposed the insertion in article 4 of the following definition of the maker of a cinematographic work: 'the person or body corporate who has taken the initiative in, and responsibility for, the making of the work'.[57] This was similar to the definition that was used in French law,[58] and had the advantage of defining a term that had not previously been used in the Convention. However, the question arose as to whether it was desirable that the Convention should contain such a definition, in the absence of any corresponding definition of an author or a publisher.[59] Furthermore, the programme proposal was criticized as being insufficiently precise, and several amendments to it were proposed.[60] After further debate there was a majority against the adoption of this, or any other, definition.[61] However, following an **7.17**

[57] Document S/1, *Records* 1967, 97–9.
[58] French Law of 1957, art 17.
[59] *Records* 1967, 871–2.
[60] ibid, 872 (comments by the Czech and Tunisian delegates). See also the various proposed amendments to the definition that were made by the UK (Document S/42: ibid, 687), India (Document S/73: ibid, 690), and the proposals for deletion of the programme proposal made by the French (Document S/27: ibid, 682) and Hungary and Poland (Document S/43: ibid, 687).
[61] ibid, 872.

Italian proposal to this effect,[62] an addition to article 15 was made in relation to the evidentiary presumption that was to be adopted in infringement proceedings in relation to cinematographic works. This read as follows:

> (2) The person or body corporate whose name appears on a cinematographic work in the usual manner shall, in the absence of proof to the contrary, be presumed to be maker of the said work.

The effect of the presumptions contained in article 15(1) has already been discussed (in para 7.16 above). For our present purposes, it suffices to note that paragraph (2) acknowledges that the maker of a cinematographic work may be a body corporate. This is the case in many national laws, irrespective of whether they adopt the system of film copyright. Nevertheless, it is a further indication that film copyright systems, in general, are consistent with the Convention.

(c) Presumption as to the creator of a work of folklore

7.18 Main Committee I at the Stockholm Conference appointed a working group under the chairmanship of Czechoslovakia for the purpose of studying the protection of folklore.[63] The latter took as its starting point the principle that a work of folklore was, by definition, the work of an unknown author, and proposed an amendment to article 15 which treated them as a special category of anonymous work within the meaning of that article.[64] This provided that, where a work was unpublished, the author was unknown and there was 'every ground to presume that the author is a national of a country of the Union', the legislation of that country might designate a competent authority to represent the author, and that this authority was entitled 'to protect the rights of the author in all the countries of the Union'.[65] A further paragraph provided that where such an authority was designated, the country in question was to notify WIPO, giving full information concerning the new authority, and that WIPO, in turn, was to communicate this information to all other Union countries.[66] The term 'folklore' was not used in the proposal, as the working group considered this to be extremely difficult to define.[67] However, while the provision applied to all works fulfilling the three conditions set out above, it was clear that its main field of application would be to 'those productions which are usually described as folklore'.[68] The provision was adopted without change by Main Committee I and became article 15(4) in the Stockholm Act.[69]

[62] Document S/168: ibid, 703. [63] ibid.

[64] ibid, 917 (verbal report of the working group to Main Committee I). See further ibid, vol I, 721, for text of the working group's proposal (Document S/240).

[65] ibid. [66] ibid.

[67] ibid, 1173 (report of Main Committee I). [68] ibid.

[69] ibid, 918.

(7) Proving authorship and ownership: applicable law

(a) How authorship and ownership are to be determined in particular cases

A final matter concerns the determination of who is an author or an owner. The Convention embodies or assumes the broad guidelines for authorship listed above (at para 7.12) in propositions 1 through 4, and enunciates a presumption of authorship in article 15. But, even assuming the Convention requires the 'author' to be the work's human creator(s), how is the question of who is an author or an owner to be determined in a particular case? For example, in the case of a joint work with authors from different Union countries, which country's law determines whether each of the alleged contributors' participation in the work's creation was sufficiently substantial to qualify her as an 'author'? The Convention is not concerned with the protection of authors in their country of origin, but only in countries of the Union other than their country of origin.[70] Absent any specific provision of the Convention dealing with the point, the determination of authorship in such cases would be a matter for the law of the country where protection is claimed. This state of affairs would inevitably involve consideration of the given country's choice of law rules applicable to cases involving a foreign litigant. **7.19**

The Convention does in fact have a specific provision dealing with the determination of ownership, but this clause is limited to cinematographic works, where the ownership of rights is a matter for the law of the country where protection is sought.[71] (This can lead to some incoherence, if the substantive rules in the countries of protection differ.) Arguably, article 14*bis*(2)(a)'s specific reference to one category of work means that cinematographic works are an exceptional case; accordingly, a different approach would apply to all other categories of works. As a result, the determination of the ownership of rights in all other works might be governed by the choice of law rules, rather than by the substantive rules, of the country where protection is claimed. (This does not necessarily avoid inconsistent results, however, because the conflict rules of the countries of protection might designate different applicable laws.) Another option is that ownership would be governed by the substantive rules of the country of the work's origin (this would have the merit of ensuring that the determination of ownership is the same for any given work—other than a cinematographic work—whatever the country of its exploitation). On the other hand, it is also possible to argue that the rule for cinematographic works simply exemplifies a general rule that is implicit in the Convention for all other works. **7.20**

---

[70] See Paris Act 1971, art 5. Under article 5(3), protection in the country of origin is governed by the domestic law of that country.

[71] ibid, art 14*bis*(2).

That conclusion, however, would prove very problematic in practice because it could mean, for example, with respect to joint works, that different persons would be adjudged 'authors' of the same work in different countries, depending on each country's standard for demonstrating co-authorship.[72]

7.21 It can be said that this rather cumbersome conclusion nonetheless follows as a logical consequence of the principle of independence of protection, contained in article 5(2). Pursuant to this provision, exclusive reference is to be made to the law of the country where protection is claimed when dealing with the 'extent of protection, as well as the means of redress offered to the author to protect his rights'.[73] If these matters are determined by that law, it is at least arguable that the same law should govern questions of authorship and entitlement. Traditional conflicts analysis, however, might lead to another conclusion, for example, that the law of the work's country of origin should govern, in the absence of any countervailing public policy of the forum nation. These are issues of considerable importance, which will be explored further in Chapter 20 below.

C. Ownership of Rights

(1) Ownership and exploitation of rights

7.22 Apart from the special provisions on cinematographic works, the Convention does not deal at all with these matters. Most notable here are the problems of employee authors and the contracts of assignment or licensing between authors and the publishers or other disseminators of their works (for example, broadcasters, film-makers, producers and so on). These are matters that are commonly dealt with under municipal laws relating to contracts and proprietary rights, although a number of Union countries have laws that relate specifically to authors.[74] However, they are not matters which are covered by article 5(2)'s principle of national treatment (see paras 6.99 above) and, as far as authors claiming under the Convention are concerned, they are subject to the rules of

[72] Moreover, in one country a work, such as a song, might be deemed the 'joint' production of two authors, and in another the same work would be considered two solo-authored independent works, music and lyrics.

[73] ibid, art 5(2). See to the same effect, the views of Professor Spoendlin in his general report to the Centenary Congress of ALAI in Berne in Sept 1986. Kaspar Spoendlin, 'International Protection of the Author', in *Report on the 56th ALAI Congress under the Patronage of the Swiss Government, Berne, 8–12 September 1986* (ALAI, 1987), 47, 48.

[74] eg the 2002 amendments to the German copyright law contain extensive provisions on authors' contracts, see German Law of 1965, as amended by the Mar 2002 Law on Strengthening the Contractual Position of Authors and Performers, discussed in Cornish (n 53 above), 8–11 and Wilhelm Nordemann, 'New Imperative Contract Rules Implemented Into the German Copyright Law', in *Mélanges Victor Nabhan* (2004), 309. The French Code de la propriété intellectuelle includes detailed provisions both in general, see arts L 131-1–131-5, and on a variety of different contracts, see arts L 132-1–132-17 (publishing contracts); L 132-18–132-22

private international law applied in the protecting country. In some instances, these may be to their advantage; in others, they may not. If authors' ownership interests are to be effectively protected under the Convention, therefore, these are matters which will need to be addressed in the future, either by the adoption of substantive minimum protections, or by agreement as to the applicable national law. Experience to date, however, prompts scepticism as to either approach's likely success. (See also para 7.41 below.)

(a) Effective protection under the Convention: minimum requirements

There have been only two serious attempts in the history of the Convention to adopt, in the Convention itself, provisions that lay down minimum requirements with respect to such matters as the employment relationship, publishing contracts and other agreements for exploitation of rights. There have only been two serious attempts to do this in the history of the Convention. The first, with respect to cinematographic works, was essentially a failure (see paras 7.24ff below) and indicates the difficulties that arise where it is sought to achieve agreement on a detailed set of provisions of this kind. This second is to be found in the Appendix to the Paris Act which deals with the compulsory licences that may be granted by developing countries. The circumstances in which these provisions were arrived at were special (see generally Chapter 14 below), and despite their detail a number of gaps in the regime they established still remain (see paras 14.12 and 14.49ff below). In consequence, it may be said that it is almost impossible, in the context of an international convention, to gain consensus on the rules governing dealings with ownership of private rights and that any attempt to do so, in the Convention itself, will most likely meet with failure. This is as much a problem of uniformity of protection as of effectiveness, but a less ambitious means of promoting both goals would be through the adoption of non-binding model provisions or statements of principle that could provide general guidance for Union countries in formulating their own legislation.[75]

(b) Effective protection under the Convention: adoption of common rules of applicable law

A more fruitful approach might be the adoption of common rules dealing with the conflict of laws issues that arise in these circumstances. Significant progress in this regard has already occurred in other areas of private law, and the work of

(performance-right contracts); L 132–23–132–30 (audiovisual production contracts); L 132–31–132–33 (contracts commissioning works for advertising). See also the Portuguese Code of Copyright and Related Rights, 17 Sept 1985, ch III(1).

75 See eg the alternative sets of model provisions proposed by the Committee of Governmental Experts on Model Provisions for National Laws on Employed Authors (Geneva, 27–31 Jan 1986): [1986] *Copyright* 72.

Professor Ulmer with respect to intellectual property rights in the European Union provides a model for application under the Berne Convention.[76] In theory, it should be easier to reach agreement on adjectival rules of this kind than on detailed rules of a substantive nature. This, in turn, would bring about a greater degree of certainty in the protection of authors' rights and, from this, a greater measure of effectiveness would flow. On the other hand, choice of law agreements may not suffice to mask national differences where the substantive divergences are great, and as much energy may be expended (and lost) addressing applicable law as confronting the substantive disagreements.[77]

(2) Transfers of ownership: 'successors in title'

7.23 Although, with the deletion of publishers in the 1896 Paris Additional Act, the protection conferred by the Convention now applies only to authors, it is clear that, once an author is eligible for protection under the Convention, this protection may also be claimed by successors in title such as assignees, beneficiaries, and so on. If this were not so, it would make no sense of article 7 which stipulates that the basic term of protection for works under the Convention should be the life of the author plus fifty years. It is also made explicit in article 2(6), which provides that the protection conferred on the works enumerated in that article shall 'operate for the benefit of the author and his successors in title'. This provision has been in the Convention only since the Brussels Revision,[78] when it was added at British insistence.[79] Prior to this, reference had been made to successors in title ('*les ayants cause*') in article 2 of the original Berne Act.[80] This was deleted at the time of the Berlin Revision on the basis that it was clear that the author's right was not an exclusively personal right, but might be disposed of to third parties. Accordingly, any reference to successors in title was superfluous.[81] This was accepted by the Berlin Conference, but apparently the UK Government had doubts about this, as is witnessed by its successful proposal at the Brussels Revision to reinsert a similar provision and to place the matter beyond doubt. It should be noted that no special requirements as to

[76] E Ulmer, *Intellectual Property Rights and the Conflict of Laws* (1978).

[77] See Jane C Ginsburg and André Lucas, *Study on Transfer of Rights of Performers to Producers of Audiovisual Fixations*, General Appreciation, AVP/IM/03/4Add (2004) (www.wipo.int/documents) ('Our analysis leads us to some skepticism regarding the effectiveness of any choice of law rule, even if one could be agreed upon . . . It would be easier to resolve questions of applicable law if the process of substantive harmonization were more advanced.').

[78] Brussels Act, art 2(4).

[79] *Documents 1948* (1951), 164.

[80] In earlier drafts of the Convention, reference had also been made to the personal representatives of authors ('*les mandataires légaux*'): see 1884 draft text, art 5: *Actes* 1884, 78; ALAI draft of 1883, art 4; and Federal Council programme of 1884, art 6: *Actes* 1884, 8 and 11. At the 1885 Conference, however, the commission deleted this term on the basis that a personal representative stood simply in the shoes of his principal (the author): *Actes* 1885, 42 (report of the commission).

[81] *Actes* 1908, 236 (report of the commission).

the nationality of the successor in title apply: once the initial entitlement to protection arises under the Convention, the identity of the person who succeeds to those rights is irrelevant.

(3) Ownership of rights in cinematographic works

(a) Background to the problem

Following the Brussels Revision, the exploitation of these rights on an international level began to cause great concern to authors and film-makers, and became the subject of a series of studies carried out by BIRPI.[82] The problems stemmed from the different approaches that had been adopted in national laws. There were two extremes here: the film copyright system which was to be found mainly in the common law countries, and those systems (the rest) which accorded copyright protection to the authors or intellectual creators of the cinematographic work. The first of these systems gave rise to no particular problems in relation to the exploitation of cinematographic works: all the rights in such works were granted to one person, the producer, and, subject to his agreements with the owners of the copyright in any pre-existing works used in the making of the film (the script, the musical accompaniment, and so on), he was free to exploit the cinematographic work as he wished.[83] With the second system, however, difficulties arose as there were usually a series of persons who had made contributions to the creation of the cinematographic work and who were entitled to be regarded as its co-authors. This therefore meant that there had to be agreement between the co-authors in relation to the exploitation of the work. In practice, this difficulty was often overcome by vesting the rights of exploitation belonging to each co-author in a single person, usually the producer. This was done either through the device of a legal assignment of these rights that was 7.24

[82] In brief, these are: E Ulmer, 'Consultation sur le cinématographie et le droit d'auteur' [1953] *DA* 97 (see also the observations on this by H Desbois [1954] *DA* 32); G Lyon-Caen, 'Le cinéma dans la Convention de Berne' [1959] *DA* 217 (presented to the seventh session of the Permanent Committee of the Berne Union, Geneva, 18–23 Aug 1959); Summary of replies to Prof Lyon-Caen's report at [1959] *DA* 225, [1960] *DA* 6, 28, 58; G Lyon-Caen, 'Nouvelles observations au sujet de la protection internationale des oeuvres cinématographiques' [1962] *DA* 153; BIRPI Study, 'The Protection of Cinematographic Works' [1961] *DA* 19, 62, 86; 'Rapport, Groupe d'étude pour la protection internationale des oeuvres cinématographiques' (Geneva, 20–3 June and Madrid 26–9 Sept 1961): [1962] *DA* 38 (Committee of Film Experts). See also the survey of national laws in [1950] *DA* 76, 85, 121, [1952] *DA* 16, 38, 96, 129, [1953] *DA* 5, 63, 74, 88; D Reimer, 'Filmrechtliche Fragen in Rahmen der Berner Union' [1959] *GRUR* 639; R Castelain, 'Cinéma et révision de la Convention de Berne' (1962) 36 *RIDA* 53; A Tournier, 'La Conférence de révision de Stockholm: Cinéma et télévision' (1963) 45 *RIDA* 5.

[83] See eg UK Copyright Act 1956, s 13. In its 1961 survey of national laws, BIRPI gave the following list of countries which adopted the film copyright system (the 'Theory of the Film as a Single Unit'): Australia, Bulgaria, Canada, Ceylon, India, Ireland, Israel, Japan, Lebanon, Norway, New Zealand, Pakistan, Poland, Portugal, Syria, Thailand, Turkey, South Africa, and the UK: [1962] *DA* 101.

deemed to have been made by the co-authors, or through the application of a presumption that such an assignment had been made, in the absence of any contrary stipulation, as part of the initial agreement between the co-authors and the producer. The first of these approaches was to be found in the Italian and Austrian laws;[84] an example of the second was contained in the French Law of 1957.[85] The first (often known as the 'legal assignment' system) had the same effect as the film copyright system, although its starting point was that rights of ownership of copyright could only vest in the natural persons who were the co-authors of the cinematographic work. The 'presumption of assignment' system also shared the same starting point, but led potentially to greater difficulties in exploitation, as individual co-authors might stipulate that the presumption was not to apply. In addition, under the French law, the author of any musical composition used in the film was excluded from the operation of the presumption;[86] on the other hand, the presumption applied to the authors of pre-existing works used in the film, as these persons were also regarded as co-authors of the cinematographic work.[87] Under both approaches, the mandatory or presumed assignment was usually limited to what was necessary for the effective exploitation of the cinematographic work.[88]

(b) The early investigations

7.25 On an international level, these differing systems clearly led to trouble in the exploitation of cinematographic works. For example, in the UK, the director of a French film was not recognized as having any entitlement to protection, whereas in France he was regarded as a co-author and might resist any presumed assignment of his rights to the producer. On the other hand, while in Italy he was treated as a co-author, his rights were subject to a compulsory assignment to the producer. In the absence of any rules in the Convention governing such matters, these differing consequences followed as a natural consequence of the application of the principle of national treatment. The international exploitation of cinematographic works was therefore subject to considerable potential

[84] Italian Law of 1941, art 45; Austrian Law of 9 Apr 1936 (as amended), art 38. Other countries with a similar system ('States that grant Exclusive Rights to a Single Person whilst maintaining the Theory of the Film as a Collective Work') which were identified by the BIRPI survey were: Czechoslovakia, Hungary, Iceland, the Netherlands, Romania, and Yugoslavia [1962] *DA* 101–2. See also the later FRG Law of 1965, arts 88 (grant of exclusive licence by author of pre-existing work in respect of the exploitation of cinematographic adaptations or reproductions of that work) and 89 (grant of exclusive rights by participants in production of cinematographic work).

[85] French Law of 1957, art 17. [86] ibid. [87] ibid, art 14.

[88] eg under art 17 of the French Law the presumption applied to 'the exclusive right of cinematographic exploitation' and under art 46 of the Italian Law the object of the exercise of the rights belonging to the producer was 'the cinematographic exploitation of the work produced'.

restriction, and these problems became particularly marked with the development of television works. Within Europe, the latter question was dealt with in a special Agreement concerning the Programme Exchanges by means of Television Films which was concluded in December 1958 under the auspices of the Council of Europe.[89] This Agreement basically applied the presumption of assignment system to the case of television films made by broadcasting organizations of countries which were party to the Agreement. Subject to any contrary stipulation and to certain other qualifications, an organization in one country was free to authorize the exploitation in other countries of television films of which it was the producer.[90] In the framework of the Berne Convention, considerable work was also undertaken at the same time to develop a similar set of rules that might apply generally to cinematographic works. Beginning with investigations that were carried out by eminent experts such as Professors Ulmer[91] and Lyon-Caen,[92] the most important work was done by a Committee of Film Experts that reported in 1961.[93] This Committee concluded that, while all the existing national systems were compatible with the Convention, it would be impossible to gain agreement on the adoption of one system by all member countries in preference to the others.[94] It therefore suggested that these differences might be reconciled if a system of presumption of assignment, similar to that in the European Television Film Agreement, was adopted (this was preferred to the mandatory legal assignment system of the Italian and Austrian Laws).[95] In making such a proposal, the Committee was proposing that the Convention should deal with agreements, something outside its usual scope, although a precedent in this regard had been already set by the adoption of article 11*bis*(3) of the Brussels Act. This was to be the focus of recurring criticism throughout the debates that followed. Nevertheless, a majority of the Committee recommended the introduction of a system of presumptions into the Convention which could be excluded by specific agreement by the contracting parties.[96]

(c) The preparations for the Stockholm Revision

7.26 In the main, the Film Experts' proposals attracted a favourable response from the various non-governmental organizations which commented on them.[97] They were, in turn, adopted by the 1963 Study Group which thought that:

> . . . it was likely to satisfy the interest which authors have in the maintenance of private autonomy in this field and that, at the same time, it would guarantee

[89] For the text of this, see [1959] *DA* 37 and the commentary on this by G Straschnov at 40.
[90] Agreement, art 1. [91] See n 82 above. [92] ibid. [93] ibid.
[94] [1962] *DA* 38, 39ff. See also comments in Document S/1: *Records* 1967, 129.
[95] ibid. [96] ibid. [97] [1960] *DA* 6 and 28.

security in business affairs by establishing a fixed point of departure capable of serving as a guide to the interpretation of these agreements.[98]

The following series of rules were therefore proposed as paragraphs (5) to (7) of article 14. These went considerably further than those contained in the European Agreement:

(5) In the absence of agreement to the contrary, the authorization to make a cinematographic adaptation and reproduction of a literary, scientific or artistic work shall imply authorization for the maker to reproduce, to distribute, to present or to perform in public, to transmit to the public, to broadcast and to translate the work thus adapted or reproduced.

(6) In the absence of agreement to the contrary, literary or artistic contributions to the making of a cinematographic work shall imply authorization, for the maker of that work, to reproduce, to distribute, to present or to perform in public, to transmit to the public, to broadcast and to transmit the cinematographic work.

(7) Unless national legislation provides otherwise, the provisions of the preceding paragraphs (5) and (6) shall not apply to the rights of public presentation and performance, transmission to the public and radiodiffusion of musical works with or without words, used in the cinematographic work.[99]

It will be seen that the first of these presumptions applied to pre-existing works, and would therefore have required changes in the law of many Union countries, including those with the systems of film copyright or legal assignment (the latter did not usually apply to pre-existing works).[100] With respect to the second presumption, this would not have affected the film copyright and legal assignment systems, as long as they permitted their provisions to be overridden by contrary agreement between the parties. Both presumptions applied only to the exploitation of the cinematographic work itself, and did not therefore affect the independent exploitation of any pre-existing work or literary or artistic contribution. Furthermore, unlike the European Agreement on Television Films, the rights affected by the presumptions were listed rather than referred to in a general formula.[101] Finally, the exclusion of musical works reflected the position adopted in a number of national laws towards this category of works.[102]

7.27 These proposals were reviewed by the 1963 Committee of Experts and the Study Group in its report of 1964, where they were criticized as being too broad on a number of fronts.[103] Thus, it was objected that the presumptions should

[98] Document S/1: *Records* 1967, 129. [99] ibid, 129–30.
[100] See eg the UK Copyright Act 1956, s 13.
[101] Cf the Agreement, art 1. [102] eg the French Law of 1957, art 17.
[103] Document S/1: *Records* 1967, 130.

not apply in respect of unfixed televisual works, that pre-existing works should be also excluded, and that provision should be made for agreements whereby authors reserved to themselves a proportional share of the proceeds from the exploitation of the cinematographic work.[104] After reviewing a number of possible solutions, the Study Group proposed two alternative provisions. The first (Alternative A) retained the two presumptions of the 1963 proposal (paragraphs (4) and (5)), but added two further paragraphs (paragraphs (6) and (7)). The first of these reserved to national legislation the power of determining whether the authors referred to in those paragraphs should be entitled to 'a participation in the receipts resulting from the exploitation of . . . [the cinematographic] work'.[105] The second excluded both musical works and unfixed works or contributions, that is, unfixed televisual works, from the scope of the presumptions, unless national legislation provided to the contrary.[106] By contrast, Alternative B deleted any presumption relating to pre-existing works, and was modelled closely on the provisions of the European Agreement on Television Films, providing as follows:

> (4) The agreement between the maker of a cinematographic work and persons who undertake to bring literary or artistic contributions to the making of that work shall imply, in the absence of any contrary or special stipulation, authorization for the maker to exploit the work. By 'contrary or special stipulation' is meant any restrictive condition agreed between the maker and the persons mentioned above.
>
> (5) Unless national legislation provides otherwise, the provisions contained in paragraph (4) shall not affect
> (a) the works which are not fixed on some material support with the consent of their authors,
> (b) the rights of the authors of literary, scientific or artistic works from which the cinematographic work is derived, and of musical works, with or without words, used in the cinematographic work.[107]

The rules provided for under both alternatives were to be compulsory in order to establish a uniform system throughout the Union, although it was then stated that 'for practical reasons' countries with film copyright or legal assignment systems should be allowed to retain them.[108]

These proposals gave rise to considerable discussion at the 1965 Committee of Governmental Experts, where there was general support for the introduction into the Convention of the system of 'presumption of assignment'.[109] Nevertheless, there were considerable differences as to how this should be done, while several delegates were of the view that provisions of this kind did not belong in the Convention at all.[110] As a result, an intermediate solution was developed, **7.28**

[104] ibid. [105] ibid. [106] ibid. [107] ibid, 130–1.
[108] ibid, 131. [109] ibid. [110] ibid.

according to which the concept of a presumption of assignment was replaced by a 'rule of interpretation'. It was agreed, though not without opposition, that this should apply to both pre-existing works and literary and artistic contributions, and a new paragraph (4) was formulated in the following terms:

> (4) However, and on condition that an agreement exists between the maker and the author authorizing the adaptation and reproduction of the pre-existing work or undertaking to bring literary or artistic contributions to the making of the cinematographic work in accordance with the legislation of the country of origin, such authors may not, in the absence of any contrary or special stipulation, oppose the use by reproduction, distribution, transmission by wire, radiodiffusion, presentation, communication to the public, subtitling and dubbing of the texts, of the cinematographic work.[111]

Along with this, paragraph (6) of Alternative A relating to the authors' participation in the receipts of the maker from the exploitation of the cinematographic work was approved in principle, together with paragraph (7) of Alternative B.[112] In the programme for the Conference, these proposals were developed further, and the following amendments were made:

1. For ease of drafting, the restriction of the rule of interpretation to works fixed on some material support was now contained in paragraph (4).[113]
2. To take account of the particular requirements in certain Union countries, it was proposed that countries might provide that the authorization or undertaking by authors was to be by way of a 'written agreement or an equivalent act'.[114]
3. The exclusion of musical works from the rule of interpretation was preserved.[115]
4. The adoption of these rules of interpretation was to be compulsory for each Union country, but no detailed provision for the way in which this was to be done was proposed. In this regard, the programme assumed that the film copyright and legal assignment systems were to be regarded as compatible with the proposed system

> . . . because, from the practical angle, they lead essentially to the same results in so far as the proposed system is compulsory (i.e. with respect to works which are not included under the heading of pre-existing works).[116]

Nevertheless, a concession in favour of countries with these systems was made by the insertion of a provision allowing them to declare that they would not apply the rules of interpretation to pre-existing works (this facility was, in fact, open to all countries).[117]

[111] *Records* 1967, 132. [112] ibid. [113] ibid, 133.
[114] ibid. [115] ibid. [116] ibid, 134. [117] ibid.

(d) *The final proposals for Stockholm*

These therefore read as follows: 7.29

> (4) Authors who have authorized, in the manner prescribed by the legislation of the country of origin of the cinematographic work, the cinematographic adaptation and reproduction of their works or undertaken, in such a manner, to bring literary or artistic contributions to the making of the cinematographic work fixed in some material form, may not, in the absence of any contrary or special stipulation, object to the reproduction, distribution, public performance, communication to the public by wire, broadcasting, any other communication to the public, subtitling and dubbing of the texts, of the cinematographic work.
>
> The countries of the Union may provide that the authorization or undertaking referred to above shall be given by a written agreement or something having the same force.
>
> By 'contrary or special stipulation' is meant any restrictive condition agreed between the maker and the persons mentioned above.
>
> (5) The countries of the Union may provide, for the benefit of the authors of works referred to in paragraph (4) above, a participation in the receipts resulting from the exploitation of the cinematographic work.
>
> (6) Unless national legislation provides otherwise, the provisions of paragraph (4) above shall not apply to the rights of public performance, communication to the public by wire, broadcasting, any other communication to the public, of musical works, with or without words, used in the cinematographic work.
>
> (7) Any country of the Union, upon becoming party to this Convention, may, at any time, in a notification deposited with the . . ., declare that it will not apply the provisions of paragraph (4) above to the literary, scientific or artistic works from which the cinematographic work is derived.
>
> Any country which has deposited such a notification may withdraw it by a further notification deposited with the . . .[118]

These proposals called forth a large number of amendments from various Union countries. Some proposed their complete deletion and the retention of the Brussels Act,[119] while several others proposed that the film copyright and legal assignment countries should be expressly excluded from the operation of the rules of interpretation.[120] The remaining amendments were directed at the various provisions of the programme proposal, and included the following: that pre-existing works be deleted;[121] that the authorization or undertaking referred to in paragraph (4) be in the form of a written contract,[122] and conversely that it

---

118 ibid. 119 Yugoslavia: Document S/107: ibid, 696.
120 UK: Document S/101: ibid, 696; Monaco: Document S/115: ibid, 697.
121 Japan: Document S/111: ibid, 696; Belgium: Document S/144: ibid, 699.
122 FRG: Document S/92: ibid, 694; France: Document S/130: ibid, 698.

should not;[123] that the text should refer only to 'exploitation' generally, instead of listing the specific actions to which authors might object;[124] that musical works be included within the scope of the rule of interpretation;[125] that participation in the maker's receipts be made compulsory, and again that it should not;[126] and that a new paragraph should be added to the effect that authors should not, subject to article 6*bis* and in the absence of any contrary stipulation, be able to object to alterations that 'might become indispensable for the exploitation of the cinematographic work'.[127] Finally, several important non-governmental organizations that were invited to express their opinions at the Conference stated that they were opposed to the insertion of detailed rules of interpretation of this kind in the Convention, and that article 14 of the Brussels Act should be retained unchanged.[128]

(e) The discussions at Stockholm

7.30 A working group was duly set up to consider these diverging amendments, and this eventually formulated a new set of provisions containing a 'more modest regulation than that of the Programme'.[129] Under these, article 14 was now concerned exclusively with pre-existing works, which were excluded from the interpretation rule.[130] A new article 14*bis* then dealt entirely with all matters concerning cinematographic works and their exploitation. Thus, the previous article 14(2) became paragraph (1) of the new article 14*bis*, and the remaining paragraphs dealt with the interpretation rule. These contained the following modification of the programme proposals:

1. The question of who was the owner of copyright in a cinematographic work was left as a matter for determination by the legislation of the country where protection was claimed.[131]
2. The interpretation rule (called 'the presumption of legitimation') was only to apply in countries which regarded authors of contributions as the owners of copyright in a cinematographic work, with the consequence that the film copyright and legal assignment countries were now clearly excluded from its scope.[132]

---

[123] Japan: Document S/111: *Records* 1967, 696.

[124] Monaco: Document S/115: ibid, 697.

[125] ibid. Monaco: Document S/115: ibid.

[126] Hungary in favour: Document S/139: ibid, 699; Monaco for complete deletion: Document S/115: ibid, 697.

[127] Monaco: Document S/115: ibid, 697.

[128] In particular, the International Writers' Guild and CISAC: ibid, 866–7. Note also that the International Federation of Film Producers' Associations spoke in favour of retaining the Brussels text: ibid, 867.

[129] ibid, 1184 (report of Main Committee I). For the text of the working group's proposals, see Document S/195: ibid, 710.

[130] ibid. [131] ibid (proposed art 14*bis*(2)(a)). [132] ibid (proposed art 14*bis*(2)(b)).

3. The presumption of legitimation was not only excluded in the case of musical works created for the making of the cinematographic work, but also for the authors of scenarios and dialogues, unless national legislation provided to the contrary.[133]
4. For the presumption to apply, the authors of contributions should have done so pursuant to an undertaking to do so, the form of which was to be determined by the legislation of the country where the maker had his headquarters or habitual residence (for example, it might be required that this be in writing).[134]

Even this 'modest regulation' gave rise to prolonged debate in Main Committee I, where opposition was expressed by a number of delegations.[135] Finally, a compromise was reached with the acceptance of two further amendments.[136] The first of these included the director in the list of persons who were excluded from the scope of the presumption, unless national legislation provided to the contrary.[137] This satisfied the objections of a number of countries, such as France and Yugoslavia, which regarded the director as one of the most important intellectual creators of the work.[138] The second amendment, again the result of French pressure,[139] led to a curiously convoluted provision concerning the applicable law to govern the form of the undertaking required for the operation of the presumption. The resultant provisions, which were adopted as article 14bis(2) and (3), read as follows:

> (2) (a) Ownership of copyright in a cinematographic work shall be a matter for legislation in the country where protection is claimed.
> (b) However, in the countries of the Union which, by legislation, include among the owners of copyright in a cinematographic work authors who have brought contributions to the making of the work, such authors, if they have undertaken to bring such contributions, may not, in the absence of any contrary or special stipulation, object to the reproduction, distribution, public performance, communication to the public by wire, broadcasting or any other communication to the public, or to the subtitling or dubbing of texts, of the work.
> (c) The question whether or not the form of the undertaking referred to above should, for the application of the preceding subparagraph (b), be in a written agreement or a written act of the same effect shall be a matter for the legislation of the country where the maker of a cinematographic work has his headquarters or habitual residence. However, it shall be a matter for the legislation of the country of the Union

133 ibid (proposed art 14bis(3)). 134 ibid (proposed art 14bis(2)(c)).
135 ibid, 887ff (in particular the delegates of France and Yugoslavia).
136 ibid, 891. See further Document S/290: ibid, 758 (new drafts of paras (2)(c) and (3) of art 14bis prepared by the drafting committee).
137 ibid (proposed para (3)). 138 ibid, 932–3. 139 ibid, 870, 933ff.

where protection is claimed to provide that the said undertaking shall be in a written agreement or a written act of the same effect. The countries whose legislation so provides shall notify the Director General by means of a written declaration, which will be immediately communicated by him to all the other countries of the Union.

(d) By 'contrary or special stipulation' is meant any restrictive condition which is relevant to the aforesaid undertaking.

(3) Unless the national legislation provides to the contrary, the provisions of paragraph (2)(b) above shall not be applicable to authors of scenarios, dialogues and musical works created for the making of the cinematographic work, nor to the principal director thereof. However, those countries of the Union whose legislation does not contain rules providing for the application of the said paragraph (2)(b) to such director shall notify the Director General by means of a written declaration, which will be immediately communicated by him to all the other countries of the Union.

(f) Interpretation and critique of article 14bis(2) and (3)

7.31 These provisions have been aptly described as 'devoid of practically any real substance',[140] and this must surely be correct: a vast amount of time was spent prior to, and during, the Stockholm Conference to secure a very meagre advance. The stated purpose of the exercise was the production of a uniform international code to regulate the exploitation of cinematographic works so as to promote the free circulation of films.[141] This objective was hardly achieved, and the provisions adopted are the most obscure and least useful in the whole Convention.

7.32 **(i) Ownership of copyright in a cinematographic work:** Paragraph 2(a) confirms the previously accepted position that the ownership of copyright in a cinematographic work is a matter for legislation in the country of the Union where protection is claimed. This leaves each country free to maintain whichever system it prefers: that of film copyright under which the maker of the film is the owner, that of legal assignment under which the rights of the various contributors are assigned to the maker, or that under which the various contributors

[140] R Fernay, 'Oeuvres cinématographiques et télévisuelles' (1967–8) 54–5 *RIDA* 319, 359. For other critical studies of arts 14 and 14*bis*, see D Gaudel-Gruyer, 'The Assimilation of Televisual Works to Cinematographic Works and the Régime of Cinematographic Works in the Stockholm Act of the Berne Convention' [1968] *Copyright* 205; M Ferrara-Santamaria, 'Régime juridique des oeuvres cinématographiques après le révision de Stockholm' (1968) 56 *RIDA* 83; H Desbois, 'Les oeuvres cinématographiques dans le cadre de la Convention de Berne revisée à Stockholm en 1967' (1968) 95 *Journal du droit international* 616; G Koumantos, 'Remarques sur l'application de l'article 14*bis* de la Convention de Berne (Stockholm)' (1969) 60 *RIDA* 27; C Masouyé, 'Nouveau régime international des oeuvres cinématographiques et télévisuelles dans la Convention de Berne (Paris, du 5 au 24 juillet 1971)' (1972) 65 *AUFT* 11.

[141] See Document S/1: *Records* 1967, 129.

are considered as the co-owners of the copyright. Paragraph (2)(a) makes it clear that the ownership of the copyright of any imported film is to be determined by the law of the country of importation. Thus, if protection for a French film is claimed in the UK it is British law which applies, and conversely it is French law which will govern a claim for protection of a British film in France.[142]

(ii) Scope of the presumption: Three points should be noted here. First, the presumption of legitimation does not apply to either film copyright or legal assignment countries. For the others, however, it is mandatory. Thus, it is not possible for any country of the Union which 'regards authors of contributions as owners of copyright in the cinematographic work to maintain or introduce legislation that does not include a presumption of legitimation in accordance with article 14*bis*(2)'.[143] **7.33**

Second, not only is the presumption excluded in the case of pre-existing works, but, unless national legislation provides to the contrary, it does not apply to 'the authors of scenarios, dialogues and musical works created for the making of the cinematographic work, nor to the principal director thereof'. As this covers most of the principal persons who are regarded as authors of contributions under many national laws, only a residual category of authors will be covered by the presumption—for instance, the actors, the designers, the cameramen—insofar as these persons are regarded as co-authors by those laws. It has also been suggested that the words 'scenarios' and 'dialogues' are limited to dramatic kinds of cinematographic work, and that, in consequence, the authors of other kinds of literary contributions will still be subject to the presumption.[144] Examples of such contributions would be the commentaries made for documentary films and news reports, and the texts of filmed lectures or talks—strictly none of these can be regarded as 'scenarios' or 'dialogues'. As for 'scenarios', 'dialogues', and 'musical works', paragraph (2)(b) leaves it to national legislation to determine, in a positive sense, whether the authors of these contributions are to be subject to the presumption. The reason for the exclusion of these works appears to be an extension of the argument that justifies the exclusion of accompanying musical works in some national laws: such contributions are capable of an existence independent of the film and may be exploited separately, as well as enjoying copyright protection in their own right in the same way as do pre-existing works. Nevertheless, the exemption of these contributors substantially negates the attempt by the Stockholm Conference to achieve a uniform international regime on this matter. It also discriminates

[142] ibid, 1185 (report of Main Committee I). [143] ibid, 1187.
[144] Gaudel-Gruyer (n 140 above), 206.

against the authors of other literary contributions such as commentaries and lectures. Finally, it seems hardly necessary, in view of the fact that the presumption applies only in respect of the exploitation of these contributions in the form of the cinematographic work.

The third point to note is that, there was some debate in Main Committee I over the inclusion of the 'principal director' in the list of authors of contributions given in paragraph (3).[145] The adjective 'principal' clearly excludes associate or assistant directors who may be eligible for the status of co-author under some national laws, and therefore remain subject to the presumption.[146] It should also be remembered that a number of countries (chiefly those with the film copyright system) do not regard the director as one of the authors of a cinematographic work, and the purpose of the second sentence of paragraph (3) therefore is to ensure that film-makers from these countries are aware of the position concerning directors in those countries of the Union which do accord such recognition. Thus, if a country in the latter category does not make directors subject to the presumption of legitimation, it must notify the Director General of WIPO of this fact by appropriate written declaration for communication to all other countries.[147]

7.34 **(iii) The form of the undertaking:** The presumption under paragraph (2)(b) applies only where the authors of the contributions have 'undertaken to bring such contributions' to the making of the cinematographic work. 'Undertaking' here refers to the engagement between the author of the contribution and the maker of the film. At the time this provision was discussed at the Stockholm Conference, those countries whose national laws provided for a presumption of assignment or legitimation took differing views as to the form that such an undertaking should take in order for the presumption to have effect. In some, a written agreement was necessary;[148] in others, oral undertakings sufficed.[149] As a consequence, considerable time was spent in Main Committee I on the question of which national law should govern the form of the undertaking. The working group proposed that this should be the country where the film-maker had his headquarters or habitual residence,[150] but this was strongly resisted by France,

[145] *Records* 1967, 932–3.

[146] ibid, 933 (comments of Kéréver, French delegate).

[147] As of Dec 2004, the only country to have made such a declaration was India (6 May 1984): www.wipo.int/treaties.

[148] eg the French Law of 1957, art 17 (see now Law No 92–597 of 1 July 1992, art L 131–2). See also comments by Rohmer of France to Main Committee I in *Records* 1967, 870.

[149] This appeared to be the case in the Netherlands: see the comments of Gerbrandy of the Netherlands at ibid, 935 (exchange of views with the French delegate).

[150] Document S/195: *Records* 1967, 710.

whose law required a written agreement and who objected to applying the presumption in the case of a cinematographic work coming from a country where no written agreement was needed.[151] By way of compromise, the present cumbersome provision was arrived at. The basic position is that the legislation of the country where the maker of the cinematographic work has his headquarters or habitual residence may require that the undertaking be in 'a written agreement or a written act of the same effect'. As to the meaning of the second of these terms, the report of Main Committee I provides the following explanation:

> . . . by 'written act of the same effect' is meant a legal instrument in writing defining sufficiently adequately the conditions of the engagement of persons bringing contributions to the making of the cinematographic work. This notion applies, for example, to a collective employment contract or to a general settlement to which those persons have agreed.[152]

Such collective contracts or settlements would, for instance, be common where persons are engaged or employed by large organizations such as broadcasting organizations or film studios.

This basic requirement under paragraph (2)(c), however, is supplemented by a **7.35** second requirement under which it remains open to the law of the country where protection is claimed to provide that the undertaking should be 'in a written agreement or a written act to the same effect'. Thus, countries such as France are free to continue to impose such a requirement, even where there is no equivalent obligation under the law of the country where the maker of the film has his headquarters or habitual residence. The imposition of such a requirement clearly affects cinematographic works whose makers are situated in countries with either the film copyright or legal assignment systems. Accordingly, the third sentence of paragraph (2)(c) provides that countries that do require a written undertaking should notify the Director General of WIPO of this by means of a written declaration which should then be notified by him to all other countries of the Union.[153] The cumulative effect of the requirements of paragraph (2)(c) can be seen in the following examples:

1. An Australian film-maker will require no written undertaking to claim protection in Australia, as the law of that country confers on him the ownership of any 'cinematographic film' which he makes.[154] In France,

[151] ibid, 888 (Boutet of France).
[152] ibid, 1187.
[153] As of Dec 2004, the only country to have made such a declaration to the Director General was Portugal on 5 Nov 1986: www.wipo.int.
[154] Copyright Act 1968, s 98(2).

however, this will not be so, and, if he wishes to take advantage of the presumption of legitimation provided by paragraph (2)(b), he will need to show some written undertaking from the contributors.[155]

2. A French film-maker will require no written undertaking in Austria in order to take advantage of the system of legal assignment that applies in that country.[156] However, if she claims protection in France, she will still need to satisfy the requirements of French law as to a written undertaking from her contributors.

From the above it will be clear that paragraph (2)(c) suffers from all the defects of a compromise provision: it is so framed as to enable national laws to keep on doing what they were doing before, and it is difficult to see how it promotes the stated objective of facilitating the free circulation and readier exploitation of cinematographic films. It should also be noted that the question which is addressed in this provision concerns only the form of the undertaking as regards the basis of the presumption of legitimation; it has nothing to do with the question of form as a condition of the validity of the undertaking.[157]

7.36 (iv) **'Contrary or special stipulation'**: The presumption under paragraph (2)(b) can be excluded by 'any contrary or special stipulation'. This term is defined in paragraph (2)(d) as meaning 'any restrictive condition which is relevant to the aforesaid undertaking'. This definition is not particularly enlightening, although it implies that the restrictive condition need not be contained in the undertaking itself: it might, for instance, be found in another document which was incorporated in the undertaking or even be in the form of an oral statement. The onus of proving the existence of such a restrictive condition, however, must lie on the author, as he is thereby seeking to exclude the basic presumption of legitimation.[158] Which is the applicable law to determine these questions? No clear guidance to this is provided by paragraph (2)(b), but it is logical to say that this should be the same law which determines the form of the undertaking under paragraph (2)(c). This, ultimately, is that of the country where protection is claimed. As to the difference between a 'contrary stipulation' and a 'special stipulation', the following interpretation has been suggested: a 'contrary stipulation' is one that rebuts the presumption completely, while a 'special stipulation' limits the application of the presumption, for instance, in relation to some only of the rights listed in paragraph (2)(b).[159]

[155] See now Law No 92–597 of 1 July 1992, arts L 131–2 and L 132–24.

[156] Federal Law on Copyright in Works of Literature and Art and on Related Rights (BGB1 No 111/1936, as last amended (BGB1 I No 25/1998)), art 38.

[157] *Records* 1967, 1187.

[158] See Fernay (n 140 above), 357.

[159] Gaudel-Gruyer (n 140 above), 295.

(v) The rights covered by the presumption: Rather than adopting a general formula to refer to the exploitation of the cinematographic work (as in some national laws),[160] paragraph (2)(b) lists the specific rights covered by the presumption. While this runs the risk of omitting some important act or an act that might become important in the future, the list is nonetheless extensive. The express mention of subtitling and dubbing of texts covers an important area of concern to the international film market, although the word 'texts' is a little unclear: does this extend to the dubbing of recorded dialogues or commentaries? **7.37**

(vi) Right to remuneration: There is nothing in the provisions of article 14*bis* which affects the rights of authors to participate in the proceeds from the exploitation of the cinematographic work by the maker. The report of Main Committee I states in this regard: **7.38**

> The countries of the Union are therefore free to introduce any system of remuneration they wish: for example, to provide for the benefit of the author a participation in the receipts resulting from the exploitation of the cinematographic work.[161]

(vii) Application of article 14*bis* to televisual works: It has been suggested that this article has no application to 'televisual works' that are assimilated to cinematographic works because they are 'expressed by a process analogous to cinematography'.[162] The basis for this argument is to be found in the changes to the original programme proposals concerning televisual works that were made at the Stockholm Revision. Originally, it had been proposed that a new paragraph should be added to article 2, providing that: **7.39**

> (2) For the purposes of this Convention, works expressed by a process producing visual effects analogous to those of cinematography and fixed in some material form shall be considered as cinematographic works . . .[163]

This was clearly sufficient to obtain the desired inclusion of televisual works, albeit ones fixed in a material form, in the Convention. However, in the final text, a number of changes were made: the proposed paragraph was deleted. Works 'expressed by a process analogous to cinematography' were assimilated to cinematographic works under the general definition of literary and artistic

[160] Scc cg the Italian Law of 1941, arts 45–6 ('the rights of economic exploitation of a cinematographic work'); French Law No 92–597 of 1 July 1992, article L 132–24. ('exclusive exploitation rights in the audiovisual work').

[161] *Records* 1967, 1187. For discussion of examples of such provisions in national laws, see Cornish (n 53 above).

[162] H Desbois, A Françon, and A Kéréver, *Les Conventions internationales du droit d'auteur et des droits voisins* (1976) ('Desbois et al (1976)'), 221ff. This argument was first raised by Desbois (n 140 above), 646, 670ff.

[163] Document S/1: *Records* 1967, 87–8.

works in article 2(1), and a new paragraph (2) provided generally that Union members could determine for themselves whether fixation in a material form was necessary protection for any or all works listed in paragraph (1). It was noted above that these changes make the status of televisual works under the Convention less clear than would have been the case under the programme proposals (see para 8.39 below), but that probably no substantive difference was intended. Nonetheless, it has been argued that the omission of the proposed paragraph (2), in particular the words 'For the purposes of this Convention', does lead to a more restrictive result, namely that

> . . . the assimilation of televisual works to cinematographic productions should not be absolute; it might very well concern only the structure of authors' rights (para (1) of art 2), except for the interpretative rule on the scope of contracts which is an innovation in the Stockholm Convention, and calls for a restrictive interpretation: televisual works not being named in article 14bis, the assimilation implicitly allowed by article 2(1) does not necessarily extend to the rule of interpretation affecting contracts of engagement.[164]

7.40 This argument, while attractive, cannot be maintained. For a start, the task of interpretation requires the reader to ascertain the ordinary meaning of the words used in the Convention before recourse can be had to supplementary aids, such as the preparatory work for the conference of revision which drafted the text in question. On their face, the words 'to which are assimilated works expressed by a process analogous to cinematography' seem straightforward: these works are to be regarded as cinematographic works throughout the Convention. To argue that they are nonetheless excluded from the scope of cinematographic works for the purposes of article 14bis would require some express indication to this effect in that provision. Furthermore, if the point is still thought to be uncertain, reference to the totality of preparatory work done for the Stockholm Revision, and during that Conference, reveals no intention on the part of delegates to exclude televisual works from the scope of the proposed presumption of legitimation.[165] Indeed, the history of the provision indicates that the concern about this question arose largely out of the rapid expansion in the making of televisual films that occurred in the 1950s, leading to the signing of the special European Agreement dealing with these films.[166]

7.41 **(viii) Other criticisms of article 14bis(2) and (3):** The presumption of legitimation in article 14bis(2) and (3) is open to criticism on several other grounds. As stated above, it is applicable only in a limited number of cases and within a limited number of Union countries. It therefore does very little to achieve the uniform system for the exploitation of cinematographic works that was desired

164 Desbois et al (1976), 223. 165 See paras 8.39ff below. 166 ibid.

by its originators. In practice, it leaves the position that applied under the Brussels Act substantially unchanged: the different national systems of copyright ownership in cinematographic works remain intact, and there is no effective harmonization achieved between them. A more fundamental criticism, however, is that provisions which seek to regulate agreements as to the exploitation of rights lie outside the scope of the Convention which is essentially concerned with the recognition and protection of substantive rights. Private agreements therefore remain a matter for national legislation, and the attempt to introduce an international regulation on this question was therefore misconceived from the outset.

D. Beyond the Berne Convention

There are no provisions in either the TRIPs Agreement or the WCT that directly address the questions either of authorship or of ownership. But both treaties require compliance with Berne obligations (minus article 6*bis* in the case of TRIPs), and the TRIPs Agreement makes violation of articles 1 to 21 (minus 6*bis*) actionable by intergovernmental dispute-resolution proceedings before WTO panels. This prompts the questions: if Berne Convention text and policy implicitly confine to human creators the conferral of authorship status, then are WTO member states whose copyright laws establish 'works made for hire', or similar regimes vesting authorship in employers and juridical persons, violating the Convention? Are they therefore subject to trade sanctions (at least with respect to works other than cinematographic works)? **7.42**

This outcome seems improbable, and not just for the *realpolitik* reason that countries with 'work for hire' or similar regimes were significant proponents of making Berne norms enforceable through the WTO, something they probably would not have urged, had they thought their own laws incompatible with those norms.[167] Arguably, the persistence in Berne countries of juridical person authorship beyond the realm of cinematographic works points to a kind of state practice tolerant of a more ecumenical concept of authorship.[168] The growth of international copyright protection for computer programs and databases may illustrate this shift. Chapter 8 addresses this development in more **7.43**

---

[167] There is another pragmatic cause for scepticism: it is unlikely any member state would initiate a WTO dispute-resolution proceeding against another member state on this account.

[168] See eg Jeremy Phillips, 'The Concept of "Author" in Copyright Law: Some Reflections on the Basis of Copyright in the UK' [1990] *Copyright* 26, 29–30: 'It can be seen that, for good or ill, the common law perspective of economic practicalities has, perhaps, been absorbed subconsciously into the collective copyright psyche of Brussels and that national laws of traditionally "author-oriented" states are no longer being founded upon their philosophical bases.'

detail (see paras 8.120ff below). For present purposes, it suffices to point out that European Union Berne members had acknowledged the possibility of juridical person authorship of computer programs at least since the 1991 Software Directive, and of database authorship at least as of the 1996 Database Directive. The Software Directive declares that computer programs are to be protected 'as literary works within the meaning of the Berne Convention for the Protection of Literary and Artistic Works'.[169] But it also allows for employer and juridical person authorship (see the earlier discussion at para 7.11 above). The EU Commission and member states presumably were not purporting to depart from a Berne norm limiting the conferral of authorship status on human creators.[170] Indeed, under article 20, EU members, all of whom were members of a version of the Convention (albeit some were latecomers to the 1971 Paris text[171]), would have undertaken not to enter into agreements granting fewer rights to authors (see the discussion at paras 6.126ff above). An agreement to deprive certain authors of authorship status would seem quite inconsistent with article 20, had that deprivation not already been countenanced within the Berne Convention.[172] When, three years later, the TRIPs Agreement also required member states to protect computer programs 'as literary works under the Berne Convention',[173] that Agreement also arguably incorporated a broader approach to determining who is the author of a literary work under the Berne Convention. A reading of the Berne Convention that prohibited member states from including non-humans and non-creators within the 'author' category would have placed the TRIPs Agreement at odds not only with the US and some other common law countries, but with all EU members who, whether or not they established 'work for hire' regimes in their domestic law, had all adopted a document which permitted them to set up such a regime for computer programs.

7.44 A similar analysis applies to databases, which, in a clear reference to article 2 of the Berne Convention, the TRIPs Agreement declares to be 'intellectual creations'[174] (see the further discussion at paras 8.128ff below). The EU Directive had not yet been enacted, though it existed in draft form by the time of the

[169] Software Directive, art 1(1).

[170] That the Directive's drafters thought their text in conformity with the Berne Convention is further evidenced by art 6(3), which states, 'In accordance with the provisions of the Berne Convention for the protection of Literary and Artistic Works, the provisions of this article may not be interpreted in such a way as to allow its application to be used in a manner which unreasonably prejudices the right holder's legitimate interests or conflicts with a normal exploitation of the computer program.'

[171] The UK joined in 1990, and Ireland in 2005; see www.wipo.int/treaties.

[172] A similar analysis applies to the WCT, whose article 4 requires member states to protect computer programs as literary works under the Berne Convention.

[173] TRIPs Agreement, art 10(1).

[174] ibid, art 10(2). See also WCT, art 5.

TRIPs Agreement's promulgation.[175] Moreover, Berne and EU member states had long had in place special derogations for 'collective works' vesting initial title in the enterprise that undertook the organization and expense of creating the compilation.[176] If databases are Berne works, they have Berne authors; if member states understand Berne authors to include more than the actual human creator, they either are mistaken and therefore are subject to trade sanctions for violating WTO-enforceable Berne norms, or their collective understanding attests to a permissible interpretation of the Convention.

The TRIPs Agreement suggests another reason to reject a reading that requires human authorship, although, perhaps perversely, this reading would partly reaffirm the role of human authorship in the Berne Convention. TRIPs makes articles 1 to 21 of Berne enforceable, but excludes art 6*bis* and 'the rights derived therefrom'.[177] Article 6*bis* is Berne's provision on moral rights, granting 'the author . . . the right to claim authorship of the work' and to object to violations of the work's integrity that prejudice her honour or reputation. Although article 6*bis* may not be inexorably incompatible with juridical person authorship—entrepreneurial 'authors' may want to receive name credit, and to protect the integrity or authenticity of the work, too[178]—the grounding of article 6*bis* in authors' non-economic interests strongly suggests that 'the author' it contemplates is the human creator. Thus, the right to *claim* authorship implies that the right to *be* an author within the meaning of the Convention is accordingly limited to human creators. But if 6*bis* is the locus of human authorship in Berne, one might contend that the exclusive-to-humans right to be a Berne author is one 'derived' from article 6*bis*. In that case, the right would not be enforceable through a WTO dispute proceeding, even if it were a Berne norm. 7.45

Be the reasons pragmatic or textually driven, it seems unlikely that conferral of authorship status on persons or entities other than the work's human creators 7.46

[175] The first draft of the Database Directive issued in May 1992; see Mark J Davison, *The Legal Protection of Databases* (2003), 53.

[176] See eg France Code de la propriété intellectuelle, arts L 113–2, 113–5 (vesting copyright for collective works initially in 'the natural or legal person under whose name it has been disclosed'); Czech Republic, Law No 35 of 25 Mar 1965, on Literary, Scientific and Artistic Works (Copyright Law) (as last amended by Law No 86 of 14 Mar 1996), art 4(2) ('Copyright to a collected work as a whole shall belong to the person having arranged it'); Estonia, Copyright Act of 11 Nov 1992 (as last amended by the Act of 15 Feb 2000), art 31(2) ('Copyright in a collective work shall belong to the person on whose initiative and under whose management the work was created and under whose name it was published unless otherwise prescribed by contract.'); Italy, Copyright Act of 1941, art 7 ('In the case of a collective work, the person who organizes and directs its creation shall be deemed the author.').

[177] TRIPs Agreement, art 9(1).

[178] See eg *Dastar Corp* v *Twentieth Century Fox Film Corp*, 539 US 23, 123 S Ct 2041 (2003) (motion picture studio brought action alleging failure to attribute producer's name on copies of videograms made from television programme).

would today be deemed in sufficient violation of the Berne Convention as to call forth international trade sanctions under the TRIPs Agreement. The conclusion that Berne contemplates human authors may be the most theoretically compelling, but it relies more on the 'spirit of Berne' than on the flesh of its actual words. The fleshly fares better than the ethereal in the arena of international enforcement. This is regrettable, for the reasons articulated earlier (see para 7.13 above). Without belittling the role of entrepreneurship in Berne countries, the moral centre, the *raison d'être*, of copyright regimes, be they common law or civil law, remains human creativity. To open Berne up to a *droit d'auteur sans auteur*[179] risks undermining the legitimacy of the protections it mandates.

[179] Phillips (n 168 above), 30, attributes the coining of this phrase to Professor Stig Stromholm at the 1988 ALAI Helsinki Conference.

8

WORKS PROTECTED BY THE CONVENTION (BERNE CONVENTION, ARTICLES 2 AND 2BIS; TRIPs AGREEMENT, ARTICLE 10; WCT, ARTICLES 4 AND 5)

A. Introduction

(1) The meaning of 'literary and artistic works': the general definition

8.01 We now come to consider the subject matter protected by the Berne Convention, that is, the meaning of the expression 'literary and artistic works'. Understanding the reach of 'literary and artistic works' is crucial to treaty interpretation, because that characterization marks the threshold to national treatment and minimum rights. Member states incur no obligation to grant national treatment if the domestically protected work is not an 'intellectual creation' in the sense of article 2. Similarly, no minimum rights attach to works falling outside the scope of 'literary and artistic works' within the meaning of the Convention. This is dealt with in articles 2 and 2bis. The basic provision is to be found in article 2(1) which falls into two parts. The first consists of a general definition which reads as follows:

> (1) The expression 'literary and artistic works' shall include every production in the literary, scientific and artistic domain, whatever may be the mode or form of its expression, such as . . .

The words 'such as' then introduce the second part of the provision which comprises a list of examples, intended to be illustrative of the kind of subject matter falling within the general definition. These are:

> . . . books, pamphlets and other writings; lectures, addresses, sermons and other works of the same nature; dramatic or dramatico-musical works; choreographic works and entertainments in dumb show; musical compositions with or without words; cinematographic works to which are assimilated works expressed by a process analogous to cinematography; works of drawing, painting, architecture, sculpture, engraving and lithography; photographic works to which are assimilated works expressed by a process analogous to photography; works of applied art; illustrations, maps, plans, sketches and three-dimensional works relative to geography, topography, architecture or science.

Qualifications, as well as extensions, of the scope of the expression 'literary and artistic works', are to be found in the remaining paragraphs of article 2, and those of article 2bis. These matters are discussed in more detail below, but for the moment our concern is with the general definition itself. It will be seen that this has two principal aspects, the first of which is restrictive, and the second liberating, in its effect. Thus, for a work to be a 'literary or artistic work', it must be a 'production in the literary, scientific and artistic domain'. Once this is established, however, the 'mode or form of its expression' are quite irrelevant for the purposes of protection under the Convention. Both these aspects require further examination.

(2) 'Every production in the literary, scientific and artistic domain'

This phrase can be traced back, with little change, to the definition of 'literary work' which was adopted in the original Act of 1886,[1] and before this to the draft text of 1884.[2] Its antecedents, however, are older than this, and are to be found in the definitions adopted in several of the important earlier bilateral conventions.[3] There was, indeed, no discussion of the meaning of the expression **8.02**

[1] Berne Act, art 4 ('every production whatsoever in the literary, scientific or artistic domain').

[2] *Actes* 1884, 78.

[3] See eg the Franco-German Convention of 19 Apr 1883, art 1 (C Lyon-Caen and P Delalain, *Lois françaises et étrangères sur la Propriété littéraire et artistique* . . . (1889) ('LCD (1889)'), 251) and the Franco-Italian Convention of 9 July 1884, art 1 (LCD (1889), 305).

at any of the drafting conferences of 1884 to 1886, and Briggs suggests that the delegates were content simply to allow themselves to be guided by the experiences of former negotiators and not to undertake the task of framing a new definition for themselves.[4] The principal difference between the definition in the 1886 Act and that of the Stockholm, Paris Acts is that in the former the expression 'every production in the literary, scientific and artistic domain' came after the enumeration of different kinds of works. This inevitably gave rise to debate, in the period immediately after 1886, as to the scope that was to be given to it.[5] This was resolved at the Berlin Revision in 1908, when the definition was placed at the beginning of the provision, so as to make it clear that the list of works which followed was included simply by way of illustration or guidance as to what constituted a 'production in the literary, scientific and artistic domain'.[6] What, then, is meant by this expression?

(3) 'Production'

8.03 In its ordinary meaning, the word 'production' implies the presence of some element of creativity. Thus, a 'production' is the result of some creative activity, which, for the purposes of the Convention, must have taken place in the 'literary, scientific and artistic domain'. However, despite this delimitation (which is discussed below), there is an apparent imprecision about the word 'production'. For example, it is not clear whether the required creative element should be of any particular standard or level. Nor is it clear whether this element must derive from a human agency, or whether the 'production' must assume any particular shape or form. Some guidance on these matters is to be derived from a number of sources, including other provisions of the Convention and the *travaux préparatoires* for the Brussels Revision Conference where proposals to explain the scope of the word 'production' were made by a number of delegations. As to the first, a clear indication that 'intellectual creation' is implicit in the conception of a literary or artistic work is to be found in article 2(5). This paragraph deals with collections of literary and artistic works, such as encyclopaedias and anthologies, and provides that these are to be protected as original works where,

---

[4] W Briggs, *The Law of International Copyright* (1906) ('Briggs (1906)'), 339.

[5] See the general discussion of the different sides in this debate by Briggs (1906), 342ff. See also the report of L Renault at the Berlin Conference: *Actes* 1908, 230ff. See further A D'Orelli, [1889] *DA* 2 and [1891] *DA* 15; A Darras, *Du Droit des auteurs et des artistes dans les rapports internationaux* (1887) ('Darras (1887)'), 535–6; J Kohler, *Die Immaterialgüter im internationalen Recht* (1896), 350, cited in [199] *DA* 132; the International Office [1899] 132, and [1900] *DA* 35; International Copyright Office, *Recueil des conventions et traités concernant la propriété littéraire et artistique, publiés en français et dans les langues des pays contractants avec une introduction et des notices* (1904) ('*Recueil* (1904)'), 7, n 1.

[6] *Actes* 1908, 230 (Renault).

by reason of the selection and arrangement of their contents, they constitute 'intellectual creations' (see further para 8.86 below). The inference from this is that, while such a stipulation is necessary in the case of these kinds of borderline works, it hardly needs to be stated in relation to the 'mainline' works covered by article 2(1).

This is confirmed by a consideration of the *travaux préparatoires* for the Brussels Revision Conference, where an Austrian amendment proposed the insertion of the words 'which have the character of a personal creation' after the words 'literary, scientific and artistic domain'.[7] An alternative Norwegian proposal added the words 'which constitute an intellectual creation, . . . irrespective of merit or purpose'[8] in the same place. There was also a Czech proposal which was similar in effect to the Norwegian one, except that it proposed directly to replace the word 'production' by the word 'creation'.[9] These formulations were discussed at length by the Conference, but were ultimately rejected. The reason for this appeared to be the view that the basis of the Conventional definition of the works to be protected was not to be found in the expression 'productions', but in the expression 'literary and artistic works' itself, which implied basically all the notions referred to in the various proposals, that is, 'intellectual creation', as well as 'personal creation' and 'creation'. Thus, the word 'productions' was only used here as a complementary term to that of 'literary and artistic works', and was to be understood simply in its etymological sense to indicate the necessity for these works to be brought into existence before they merited protection. As a consequence, the introduction of new terms, such as 'creation', 'intellectual creation', or 'personal creation', into the definition would lead to complications and might diminish the protection of authors' rights if they led courts, where these matters were in doubt, to conclude that additional criteria were to be satisfied before a literary or artistic work could be protected under the Convention.[10] In other words while the expression 'literary and artistic works' itself meant 'personal creation or . . . intellectual creation within the sphere of letters and the arts', the word 'production' simply indicated that a work that satisfied this description would be protected once it was realized or brought into existence.[11]

(4) Merit and purpose of work

As a consequence, the quality or standard of this element of intellectual creation is quite irrelevant for the purposes of protection under the Convention. This **8.04**

[7] *Documents de la Conférence réunie à Bruxelles du 5 au 26 juin 1948* (1951) ('*Documents 1948* (1951)'), 147.

[8] ibid, 149. [9] ibid, 150. [10] ibid, 154–5.

[11] ibid, 95 (report of Marcel Plaisant, *rapporteur* for the Conference).

was confirmed by the Conference's rejection of the second part of the Norwegian and Czech proposals concerning the merit or purpose of a work. Again, it was thought that this was implicit in the present definition, and to introduce it at this point might lead to jurisprudential and doctrinal difficulties if it were assumed (mistakenly) that this effected a substantive change in the definition.[12] This approach accords with that taken in the vast majority of national copyright laws: questions of merit are disregarded, and courts are therefore relieved of any obligation to make aesthetic judgements about the works they are asked to protect.[13] The requirement of creativity or 'originality' (as it is referred to in many jurisdictions)[14] is therefore concerned with the way in which a work comes into existence—the act of intellectual creation—and has nothing to do with the aesthetic quality of this act. In the same way, it is generally assumed in most national laws that the purpose for which a work is created is irrelevant,[15] although it will be seen below that the question of 'purpose' has led to problems in relation to the protection under the Berne Convention of artistic works which have been applied industrially (see paras 8.59ff below) and of computer programs (see paras 8.92ff below).

(5) **Originality**

8.05 On the other hand, differences still remain between national laws as to what constitutes intellectual creation or originality, with the Commonwealth countries traditionally taking a more relaxed view on this question.[16] Article 2(1) of

---

[12] *Documents 1948* (1951), 155.

[13] In some countries, such as France, this is specifically stated in their statutory copyright law: Code de la propriété intellectuelle, art L 112–1 ('The provisions of this Code shall protect the rights of authors in all works of the mind, whatever their kind, form of expression, merit or purpose'). See also A Lucas and H-J Lucas, *Traité de la propriété littéraire et artistique,* 2nd edn (2001), paras 70–72; Caroline Carreau, *Mérite et droit d'auteur* (1981); in common law countries, this is to be found in the case law: see generally J A L Sterling and M C L Carpenter, *Copyright Law in the United Kingdom and the Rights of Performers, Authors and Composers in Europe* (1986), 44ff; Robert A Gorman, 'Copyright Courts and Merit Judgments: Abuse or Necessity' (2002) 25 *Colum J L & the Arts* 1.

[14] See eg UK Copyright, Designs and Patents Act 1988, s 1(a); Copyright Act 1985 (Canada), s 5(1); Copyright Act 1968 (Australia), s 31; Code of Intellectual Property Law Act, No 52 of 1979 (Sri Lanka), s 7.

[15] See eg France, Code de la propriété intellectuelle, art L 112–1; Sterling and Carpenter (n 13 above), 214ff.

[16] See eg *G A Cramp & Sons Ltd* v *F Smythson Ltd* [1944] AC 329 and *Ladbroke (Football) Ltd* v *William Hill (Football) Ltd* [1964] 1 All ER 465; *Telstra Corporation Ltd* v *Desktop Marketing Systems Pty Ltd* [2002] FCAFC 112 (Aus Full Federal Court); *CCH Canadian Ltd* v *Law Society of Upper Canada* [2004] 1 SCR 339 (Supreme Court of Canada): 'What is required to attract copyright protection in the expression of an idea is an exercise of skill and judgment. By skill, I mean the use of one's knowledge, developed aptitude or practised ability in producing the work. By judgment, I mean the use of one's capacity for discernment or ability to form an opinion or evaluation by comparing different possible options in producing the work. This exercise of skill and judgment will necessarily involve intellectual effort.' By contrast, other laws express the

the Berne Convention merely lists a series of works that each Union country is to protect; it does not indicate any guidelines there as to how the requirement of intellectual creation is to be applied in each case. But article 2(5) gives some clues: collections of works 'which, by reason of the selection and arrangement of their contents, constitute intellectual creations shall be protected . . .'. This suggests that originality may inhere in the way in which a work is composed, independently of the originality of its components. It does not, however, indicate how substantial the quantum (as opposed to the aesthetic quality) of creativity should be. This therefore allows Union countries to adopt differing interpretations of the minimum of intellectual creation that is required for works already listed in article 2(1). Article 2(1) thus gives rise to two distinct issues: (i) whether a category of work is listed at all; and (ii) if the category is listed, member states must protect works of that class, but not all such works are automatically protected: it becomes necessary, in the absence of a Conventional definition of originality, to determine whether a particular example of a work in the listed category meets the originality standard imposed by national law. The national standard must not be so high as effectively to exclude the category altogether, but can a state raise the bar high enough to disqualify some significant subset within the listed category? Although the Convention does not specify the threshold, allowing member states free rein to define the level of originality may risk conflict with other Conventional principles. For example, while photographs are listed, individual countries may have different thresholds of protection; as a result, some may protect a broader or narrower range of photographs than others (see the further discussion at para 8.57 below). To the extent that aesthetic concerns dictate the boundaries of the narrower range, as was formerly the case under French law respecting photographs,[17] the heightened originality standard may become a suspect proxy for a merit criterion.[18] Similarly, a heightened originality standard may fill in for an illegitimate limitation

requirement for intellectual creation in more specific terms, and this appears to be more strictly interpreted: see eg the German Act dealing with copyright and related rights (Copyright Act) of 9 Sept 1965, art 2(2) (the 'FRG Law of 1965') which provides that the term 'works' includes only 'personal intellectual creations', and see further the chapter on German copyright by E Ulmer in S Stewart, *International Copyright and Neighbouring Rights*, 2nd edn (1989) ('Stewart (1989)', 417. See also the Italian Law for the protection of copyright and other rights connected with the exercise thereof, No 633 of 22 Apr 1941, art 1 which refers to 'intellectual works having a creative character'.

[17] The 1957 Copyright Law, art 3, limited protection of photographs to those having an 'artistic or documentary character.' Given the 1957 law's general pronouncement that copyright subsisted regardless of a work's 'merit or destination', the rule for photographs led to considerable incoherence in the case law. See eg H Desbois, *Le droit d'auteur en France*, 3rd edn (1978), 3ff ('Desbois (1978)'), paras 80–5. The 1985 copyright law eliminated the artistic or documentary requirement.

[18] See Carreau (n 13 above), 359–413.

based on the useful character of a work.[19] Thus, although the Berne Convention leaves the precise contours of originality to national determination, it also implies some limitations on member states' freedom to define those bounds.

(a) 'Literary, scientific and artistic'

8.06 The limitation to 'productions in the literary, scientific and artistic domain' also needs some explanation. The adjectives 'literary, scientific and artistic' derive from the early bilateral conventions,[20] but are not to be taken at their face value. First, 'scientific production' does not refer to such things as scientific discoveries, as the basic principle that copyright does not protect ideas but only the form in which they are expressed applies as much to the Berne Convention as it does to national laws. This is not stated expressly in the Convention, but is an underlying assumption which is discussed further below. As a result, the adjective 'scientific' in the context of 'literary and artistic works' seems unnecessary, as works concerned with scientific matters will invariably be either literary productions (a written description of an experiment, process, device, or the like) or artistic productions (diagrams, drawings, illustrations). Secondly, it must be acknowledged that the expression 'literary and artistic productions' is, on its face, a literally inaccurate description of many of the productions which the Convention expressly contemplates as falling within its scope. This can be seen from a consideration of the list of works which follows the general definition in article 2(1). These include dramatic or dramatico-musical works, choreographic works, and entertainments in dumb show, musical compositions with or without words, and cinematographic works. All these are works that are intended to be represented or performed, rather than read or viewed, as is the case with the usual kind of literary or artistic production. On the other hand, it is still possible to fit them into either category, as such works will usually be presented in some form of notation or as a visual image. However, such a classification exercise hardly seems necessary, given that the enumeration in article 2(1) makes it clear that they are to be regarded, in any event, as productions within the 'literary, scientific and artistic domain'. It is also worth noting that the terms 'literary' and 'artistic' are themselves very vague, and their lack of definition in the Convention is perhaps not without significance. In its ordinary sense, 'literary' may be the more limited concept, referring to written or printed compositions. On the other hand, while 'artistic' may simply refer to works of the visual arts, it can also be used in the wider sense of pertaining to the arts in general, including here music, drama, and literature, as well as the fine arts. Accordingly, the scope

[19] See eg German Federal Republic, BGH decision of 9 May 1985, [1985] *GRUR* 1041 *Inkassoprogram* (requiring a higher level of originality for computer programs).

[20] See eg the Franco-Italian Convention of 9 July 1884, art 1 (LCD (1889) 251).

of the composite expression 'literary and artistic works' can be very widely drawn indeed.

(b) 'Whatever may be the mode or form of its expression'

The wording used in article 4 of the 1886 Act was 'published by any mode of impression or reproduction'. This again had its antecedents in a number of the earlier bilateral conventions.[21] The current wording was adopted in the Berlin Act, except that the word 'reproduction' was used instead of 'expression'. As 'reproduction' refers to a copy of a work, rather than the work itself, this gave rise to some discussion at the Rome Revision Conference, where both the terms 'manifestation' and 'expression' were proposed as alternatives.[22] The Conference finally adopted the latter, and since that time this part of article 2(1) has remained unchanged. The significance of the term 'expression' should not be overlooked. This underscores the point made above (para 8.06) that the protection offered by the Convention to literary and artistic works does not extend to the ideas embodied in those works, but only to the form in which those ideas are expressed. The same is true of factual information and subjects (in the case of artistic works): no writer or artist can have a monopoly over these things, which can be freely used in their works by other authors. Although the Berne Convention does not contain any explicit statement that ideas, facts, and 'subjects' are beyond its scope, this is clearly implied in this part of the definition of 'literary and artistic works', and the general principle has not been doubted.[23] Further confirmation of this basic principle is to be found in article 2(8) which excludes 'news of the day' and 'press information' from the scope of the Convention (see further para 8.104 below). In addition, the definition indicates that the mode or form in which the work is expressed is irrelevant. This clearly accords with the technological developments that have occurred over the past century, and now mean that a work may be embodied in a wide range of forms. By contrast, the **8.07**

[21] See eg the Franco-Spanish Convention of 16 June 1880, art 1 ('any production in the literary, scientific or artistic domain capable of publication by any system of printing or reproduction of present or hereafter known') (UNESCO, *Copyright Laws and Treaties of the World*, France, item 23).

[22] *Actes* 1928, 196 (report of the commission), 223–4 (summary of discussions and proposals).

[23] See eg C Masouyé, *Guide to the Berne Convention for the Protection of Literary and Artistic Works* (1978) ('Masouyé (1978)'), 12; Desbois (1978), 22ff; Lucas and Lucas (n 13 above), para 26; S P Ladas, *The International Protection of Literary and Artistic Property* (1938) ('Ladas (1938)'), 209. By contrast, both art 9(2) of the Agreement on Trade-Related Aspects of Intellectual Property Rights 1994 (the 'TRIPs Agreement') and the World Intellectual Property Organization ('WIPO') Copyright Treaty ('WCT'), art 2, expressly exclude ideas, methods, procedures, etc. This does not, however, justify an anachronistic negative inference that the Berne Convention does protect ideas. See also the earlier discussion at paras 5.49–5.52 above (explicit enunciation in the TRIPs Agreement and WCT of a goal to 'balance' authors' and users' rights, and the absence of such language in 1971 Berne text, do not mean that Berne's focus is solely on authors' rights; closer examination of the Berne text and context reveals a similar 'balancing' norm).

wording of article 4 of the 1886 Act was clearly influenced by the fact that, at that time, writing, printing and similar processes were the chief means of expression for works.[24] It should also be noted that under the present wording there is no necessity that the form or mode of expression of the work should be a material or tangible one. Oral works, for instance, which only exist transiently at the moment of their performance still have a form of expression within the meaning of the general definition in article 2(1). This is confirmed by the express inclusion of such works within the list of works contained in the second part of article 2(1) (see para 8.13 below).

B. The Enumeration in Article 2(1) and its Effect

8.08 The list of works which follows the general definition in article 2(1) is extensive and comprises the principal categories of works historically recognized under the vast majority of national copyright laws. Prior to the Berlin Act, there were different views expressed about the effect of this enumeration.[25] The first was that contracting countries were obliged to protect all the works listed, and to modify their domestic laws accordingly if this was not the case.[26] The second view was quite the opposite, and was that contracting countries were not bound to protect a work simply because it appeared in the enumeration if it was not also accorded the status of a literary or artistic work under its domestic law. According to this interpretation, contracting countries were obliged to protect enumerated works only to the extent permitted by their laws; if this was not the case, there was no onus on them to change their laws to enable this to happen.[27] While there were good reasons for preferring the first of these views, the Berlin Revision put this beyond doubt by adding this paragraph to article 2:

> The contracting countries shall be bound to make provisions for the protection of the above-mentioned works.

In the Brussels Revision, the wording of this provision was changed as follows, and this wording was retained as article 2(6) in the Stockholm, Paris Acts:

> The works mentioned in this Article shall enjoy protection in all countries of the Union.[28]

It is thus clear that the works in question are to be protected under the Convention in each contracting country. This includes all the works enumerated in article 2(1), as well as those dealt with in the other paragraphs of article 2

[24] *Actes* 1884, 41–2. [25] See n 5 above.

[26] See *Actes* 1908, 230 (report of L Renault), and 198 (*mémoire* submitted by the Belgian delegation).

[27] ibid, 230. [28] Brussels Act, art 2(4).

(see below). The mandatory nature of this requirement has always been strongly maintained, and not disputed by any Union member.[29]

The words 'such as', which precede the enumeration, indicate that it is not an exhaustive list: the works enumerated are only instances of the subject matter that fall within the ambit of the expression 'literary and artistic works'. Accordingly, there may be other kinds of work, not enumerated, which are still eligible for protection under the Convention. Certainly, this conclusion follows from the literal, and apparently broadly encompassing opening clause of article 2(1) ('every production . . . whatever may be the mode or form of its expression'), as well as from the clearly illustrative ('such as') designation of the specific kinds of works. The plain meaning of the text would exclude a limitative characterization of the list. Nevertheless, the history of the various revisions of the Berne Convention indicates that this proposition has to be treated with considerable caution. It is of critical importance for a work to be included in the list in article 2(1) because article 2(6) (see above) puts it beyond doubt that such works are then to be protected under the Convention. Although not exhaustive, this list covers the principal categories of works that historically have been recognized in the great majority of national copyright laws. Furthermore, it is a list that has steadily grown from the initial enumeration given in article 4 of the Berne Act, with the insertion of new categories of work at each successive revision. Thus, choreographic and architectural works were added at the Berlin Revision, oral works at Rome, and cinematographic works and works of applied art at Brussels. **8.09**

The history of each of these additions throws an interesting light on the significance and effect of enumeration. Starting from the basic list of the 1886 Act (over which there was surprisingly little debate), there has usually been a prolonged struggle which has preceded the admission of a new category of work to the list. Often this has meant that some kind of conditional or lesser level of Conventional protection has been first accorded before 'list' status has been achieved at a later revision. Even then, this status has sometimes been subject to conditions or qualifications, as in the case of works of applied art. **8.10**

The lesson to be derived from these examples, therefore, is that an unlisted work's potential status in theory as a 'literary or artistic work' for the purposes of article 2(1) has meant very little, if anything, in practice. In the absence of **8.11**

[29] With the exception of a curious proposal which was made by the German Government during the preparations for the 1936 Brussels Conference. The essence of the German proposal was that art 2 be amended so as to provide that member countries had the right to determine the extent to which works referred to in that article should be protected. This received a predictably withering reply from the International Office, and after the War was not proceeded with: see [1936] *DA* 38–9.

enumeration, if Union country A decides that a new category of work is a literary or artistic work entitled to protection under its own law, it is bound to accord the same protection to authors from other Union countries under the principle of national treatment, with all the consequences that this entails with respect to such matters as duration and scope of rights. However, this can only be a unilateral national judgement, and there is no onus on other Union countries to adopt a similar position. The only mechanism provided by the Convention to achieve uniformity among Union members on such a matter is by a revision conference which amends article 2 so as to include the work in question,[30] or by subsequent multilateral agreements, such as those envisioned by article 20 (see further para 6.128 above). Thus, even though article 2(1)'s broad language reaches 'every production . . . whatever may be the mode or form of its expression', and even though the ensuing list is illustrative, not limitative, 'enumeration' remains the only sure guarantee of protection under the Convention. A study of each of the additions that have been made to article 2(1) in successive revisions (see below) confirms this conclusion. Clearly, in the view of those nations and interested groups which have promoted the inclusion of each new category of work, 'enumeration' was a prerequisite to protection. This is why subsequent multilateral copyright agreements building on the Berne Convention have explicitly provided for the coverage of the 'new' categories of computer software and databases (see further paras 8.121ff below).[31]

8.12 It should also be noted that enumeration of a work in article 2(1) does not

[30] Stockholm, Paris Acts, art 27.

[31] It is possible to argue that it may become mandatory for contracting states to protect a new category of work even before enumeration occurs. This is something of a 'bootstraps' argument, and runs as follows. If a sufficient number of Union countries recognize and protect the new work as a literary or artistic work, this might enable one to say this is evidence of a subsequent practice of states party to the Berne Convention which indicates that, in their Conventional relations, the expression 'literary and artistic work' in art 2(1) is to be interpreted as including this new kind of work. Of course, for a 'subsequent practice' to be established for the purposes of treaty interpretation, it would need to be shown that an appropriate number of states had adopted this interpretation, and that the remainder assented to this. But the argument is difficult to maintain, and, to be successful, unanimity among the contracting states would seem to be required, at least in the sense that there was no opposition to the interpretation in question. Accordingly, if there was opposition from one or two states, the fact that the rest thought otherwise would not suffice. This might result in the creation of a limited *de facto* Union in which those states which adopted the particular interpretation applied it in their dealings with each other. However, it would be impossible to argue from this that a subsequent state practice had now been established which would require the recalcitrant states to adopt the same interpretation. The 'bootstraps' element of the argument is that states will only become bound by the interpretation in question when they decide voluntarily to become bound, and the fact that there is dissent simply indicates that the alleged 'practice' has not yet come into existence. The way out of this impasse, then, is for a Revision Conference or a new multilateral agreement to settle the status of the works in question only, and this is what has occurred with each of the new categories of works which has been added to art 2(1) or to new treaties since the Berlin Revision.

conclude matters. None of the terms included in the enumeration is defined, so the meaning and scope to be accorded to such terms as 'books', 'drawings', 'sculptures', and the like, are left to be determined by national laws. As most of the terms used in the enumeration are themselves quite general, this allows national laws to adopt the widest and most liberal interpretations possible. This clearly gives rise to the risk that member states will adopt differing interpretations in relation to particular categories of works, and the cumulative effect of the application of the principles of national treatment and independence of protection will be to create inequalities in the protection accorded to authors in different countries of the Union. The precise measurement of these comparative differences is beyond the scope of the present work, but a general comment may be made. Significant variations will be the exception and will usually only occur at the margin. In the great bulk of cases there will be a reasonable unanimity between national laws as to what constitutes a 'book', a 'drawing', etc, and it will be unlikely that greatly divergent results will obtain from one country to another. The reason for this is simple: states usually enter international arrangements only if they share a common set of assumptions about the goals that they wish to achieve together with their treaty partners. If there are real differences between the parties as to these goals, they will usually not proceed with their agreement, or they will modify its terms explicitly to take account of these differences. At the risk of appearing superficial, this statement is true of the Berne Convention. The detailed evidence in support of it, however, is to be found in the examination which follows of the way in which new kinds of subject matter have been added to the protection of the Convention.

(1) The works specifically addressed by the Convention

This section first will summarize the works whose protection the Convention specifically requires, as well as those whose coverage the Convention either makes optional or precludes altogether. It next will detail the content and development of each category. Also, see the chart at the end of this chapter. **8.13**

(a) The enumeration of protected works

Under the Stockholm, Paris Acts, the works enumerated in article 2(1) fall into a number of distinct categories, which are set out below. For ease of exposition, they will be considered under these heads, together with the other provisions of articles 2 and 2bis where these become relevant. The works which are italicized are those which were in the original enumeration of the 1886 Act.

1. *Books, pamphlets, and other writings.*
2. Lectures, addresses, sermons, and other works of the same nature (oral works).
3. *Dramatic* or *dramatico-musical works.*

4. Choreographic works and entertainments in dumb show.
5. *Musical compositions with or without words.*
6. Cinematographic works to which are assimilated works expressed by a process analogous to cinematography.
7. *Works of drawing, painting,* architecture, *sculpture, engraving,* and *lithography.*
8. Photographic works to which are assimilated works expressed by a process analogous to photography.
9. Works of applied art.
10. *Illustrations,* maps, *plans, sketches,* and three-dimensional works *relative to geography, topography, architecture,* or *science.*

Under several of the remaining paragraphs of article 2, a number of other productions are also protected. These are:

1. Translations, arrangements of music, adaptations, and other alterations of literary and artistic works (article 2(3)).
2. Collections of literary and artistic works (article 2(5)).

(2) **Works excluded or left to national determination**

8.14 By contrast, the Paris Act leaves to member states the option to determine whether or not to protect the following categories of works:

1. Unfixed works (article 2(2)) (1967–71 Stockholm–Paris Revisions).
2. Official texts and their translations (article 2(4)) (1948 Brussels and 1967–71 Stockholm–Paris Revisions).
3. Political speeches and speeches delivered in the course of legal proceedings (article 2bis(1)) (1928 Rome Revision).

The Convention moreover specifically excludes 'news of the day' and facts of press information (article 2(8)). This exclusion dates from the original 1886 Act.

Member states might also determine to extend copyright protection to works whose coverage Berne neither requires nor includes among the works that member states may, but need not, protect. With respect to those unlisted works, and with the exception of news and facts, a member state would be free to grant copyright protection to foreign works in that category. But it would have no obligation to do so. By contrast, if a member state elected to protect a work on the optional list, such as political speeches, it would be obliged to protect the political speeches made by foreign Union authors as well.

C. Specific Categories of Works

(1) Books, pamphlets, and other writings

This was one of the first categories of works protected by the Convention. **8.15** However, its origins are older, as it was referred to in an international agreement as early as the Franco-Portuguese Convention of 11 July 1866,[32] and the terms 'books', 'pamphlets', and 'writings' had long been used in various national copyright laws. Thus, the English Act of Anne in 1709 had referred to 'books and other writings',[33] while the French Law of 1793 had conferred its protection in broad terms upon the authors of 'writings of all kinds'.[34] There was no discussion of the scope of these expressions at any of the Berne Conferences of 1884 to 1886,[35] which suggests that delegates were happy with the way in which these terms had been interpreted in domestic laws, and did not think it necessary to provide any guidelines or restrictions on these matters. On a plain reading, 'books' and 'pamphlets' seem simply to be examples of the wider genus of 'writings', and this indicates that all 'writings', of whatever kind or merit, are to be protected under the Convention. This accords with the general definition of 'literary and artistic work' under which, as we have seen, questions of purpose and merit are excluded from consideration. This goes much further than saying that the works of pulp novelists are to be protected equally with those of Nobel Prize winners. The expression 'writings' comprehends anything in written form, provided that it complies with the basic requirement of 'intellectual creation'. This therefore includes such diverse items as letters, newspaper articles, directories of information, technical and scientific books, catalogues, commercial documents, and advertisements, just as much as works of 'high' literature. This seems to be the approach adopted in the legislation or jurisprudence of all countries of the Union, although there may be individual differences as to whether a particular kind of subject matter constitutes a writing.[36] As to the 'form' of a writing, the Convention offers no guidance, although it seems reasonable to infer that a 'writing' requires some kind of notation. This is one of the 'boundary' questions which the Convention leaves to national copyright laws to determine for themselves, and this may, of course, give rise to different approaches among Union countries. For example, in the USA, the

---

[32] *Recueil* (1904), 301. See also the Franco-German Convention of 19 Apr 1883, art 1 (LCD (1889), vol II, 269), and the Franco-German Convention of 19 Apr 1983, art 1 (LCD (1889), vol II, 251).

[33] Act of Anne 1709, s 1.

[34] Law of 19–24 July 1793, art 1.

[35] See *Actes* 1884, 44–5, and *Actes* 1885, 48.

[36] See further Ladas (1938), 215, and the chapters on national laws in Stewart (1989), chs 13–31.

term 'writings' is used to delimit the scope of the US Congress's constitutional power to legislate on copyright, and as a result over the past 200 years this term has received a very expansive interpretation.[37]

(2) Lectures, addresses, sermons, and other works of the same nature (oral works)

(a) History of their protection

8.16 With most of the categories of work enumerated in article 2(1), the need for existence in some kind of material form seems implicit in the very categories themselves, for example, 'books', 'writings', and so on. However, it was stated above that a work may just as readily be expressed in a spoken, as in a material, form. Although this means that the work has only transient existence, its form is no less complete than when it is fixed in some material medium. This has been the approach taken in many jurisdictions which have accordingly granted protection to oral works.[38] Nevertheless, there are a number of countries, notably those based on British law, where fixation has usually been required as a prerequisite to protection.[39] As a result, oral works were not among those included in the enumeration in article 4 of the 1886 Act, and it does not seem that the question of their protection was raised at any of the Conferences of 1884 to 1888. However, at the ALAI Congress in Dresden in 1895, Ernst Röthlisberger of the International Office and Paul Schmidt of the German Publishers' Association presented a report on 'Divergences Between the dispositions of the Convention of Berne and the Legislation of Countries of the Union'.[40] In this, they recommended that 'oral productions', among other things, should be uniformly protected throughout the Union, and a resolution to this effect was passed by the Congress.[41] After this show of interest, matters appeared to rest for a while. No proposal for the inclusion of oral works was made at the Berlin Revision; nor was any reference made to this question in the model Convention articles which were proposed by the ALAI Congress in Neuchâtel in 1907.[42] It was of course arguable that oral works were, in any event, included under the general definition part of article 4, but this argument was difficult to maintain in light of the

---

[37] See further B Ringer in Stewart (1989), 566.

[38] See eg France, Code de la propriété intellectuelle, art L 112–1; art L 112–2 (protecting lectures, addresses, sermons, pleadings, and other works of such nature); FRG Law of 1965, art 2 ('writings and speeches').

[39] See eg UK Copyright, Designs and Patents Act 1988, s 3(2) ('Copyright does not subsist in a literary, dramatic or musical work unless and until it is recorded, in writing or otherwise; and references in this Part to the time at which such a work is made are to the time at which it is so recorded'); Copyright Act 1968 (Australia), ss 22 and 32. US Copyright Act, 17 USC § 102(a) ('copyright protection subsists . . . in original works of authorship fixed in any tangible medium of expression . . .').

[40] *Bulletin de l'association littéraire et artistique*, 1895, 3ᵉ sér, no 3. Noted in [1895] *DA* 135.

[41] [1895] *DA* 138.

[42] See [1907] *DA* 118; reproduced in *Actes* 1908, 83.

fact that some Union countries quite clearly required the fixation of works. The matter was expressly raised at the Rome Revision with a proposal in the Conference programme that the words 'whatever the mode or form of reproduction' be replaced by the words 'whether this be written, graphic, plastic, or oral'.[43] A number of other proposals on this question were also put forward.[44] Some delegations argued for more direct protection of oral works, with their inclusion in the list in article 2(1), but with reservations leaving it to national laws to determine particular situations in which this protection should not apply, for example, as regards press usage, the reporting of proceedings in public assemblies and the like.[45] It will be seen from the last-mentioned proposals that many delegations, even if they accepted the logic of protecting oral works, still saw that there was a strong countervailing public interest in freedom of information and reporting to be taken into account. A variety of different formulations were proposed by other delegations,[46] and finally a special sub-committee was appointed to consider the matter. In this sub-committee, the polarization between delegates quickly became more apparent. The delegate of the International Institute for Intellectual Cooperation, strongly supported by the French delegation, advocated the protection of all oral works without restriction.[47] On the other hand, the UK, Norway, and Japan, were opposed to such indiscriminate protection,[48] and the US delegate observed that the necessity to protect all oral works would prevent the accession of his country to the Convention.[49] A number of intermediate proposals was considered, and finally a compromise position was adopted under which lectures, addresses, sermons, and other works of the same nature were to be included in the enumeration in article 2(1).[50] This was some way from protecting oral works in general, but apart from Japan, which reserved its position, it secured unanimous support.[51] There then ensued discussion as to the reservations that should be made as regards the reproduction of these works by the press and otherwise. Three propositions were finally adopted, and these were incorporated in a new provision, article 2bis. These were:

1. A Japanese proposal to leave to national legislation the power to exclude, either totally or partially, protection in the case of political speeches or speeches delivered in the course of judicial proceedings.[52] This became article $2^{bis}(1)$.
2. A German proposal which reserved to national legislation the power of specifying the conditions under which lectures, addresses, sermons, and other similar works might be reproduced by the press.[53] This became article $2^{bis}(2)$.

[43] *Actes* 1928, 64. [44] ibid, 223 (summary of proposals and discussions).
[45] See eg the proposals of the Hungarian and Danish delegations: ibid, 224.
[46] Norway, Sweden, UK, Japan, and Germany: ibid, 224–5. [47] ibid, 225.
[48] ibid. [49] ibid. [50] ibid. [51] ibid. [52] ibid, 228. [53] ibid.

3. A Brazilian proposal which reserved the exclusive right of the author of any of these works to make a collection of them.[54] This was included in the second part of the new article 2bis(2).

8.17 These new provisions represented a halfway position between the full recognition of authors' rights in oral works, and the protection of the wider public interest. However, as noted above, the works now included in the article 2(1) enumeration did not embrace oral works as a whole (see further the discussion in para 8.18 below). Nor, on a strict reading, did the wording adopted in article 2(1) preclude the possibility of member countries still requiring that these works should be embodied in some material form before protection was accorded. Nevertheless, the several programmes prepared for the Brussels Revision Conference did not seek to expand this protection. Rather, they were concerned with the scope of the reservations provided for in article 2bis, and proposed that the right of the author to make collections of his works should also apply to the making of collections of political speeches or speeches made in the course of judicial proceedings.[55] The basis for this proposal was that the reasons favouring the exclusion of protection for these kinds of works (which was allowed for in article 2bis(1)) did not apply in the case of the subsequent making of a collection, particularly in light of the fact that the right to make collections was a general right recognized elsewhere in the Convention. The propositions of other delegations went further. Germany and Austria proposed that the words 'laws, decrees, decisions and other similar official acts' be added to article 2bis(1).[56] However, this was misconceived, as any reservation in relation to these kinds of works belonged more properly to article 2, rather than article 2bis which was solely concerned with oral works. More important were successive French proposals which sought, first, to limit the reservation in article 2bis(2) in relation to the press to partial, rather than total, reproductions of lectures, speeches, etc,[57] and, then, to suppress the reservation completely.[58] The French concern was to strengthen the rights of authors in their oral works, and, so far as the public interest was concerned, they pointed to the right of press citation which was already provided for in article 10, as well as to the fact that the possibility of special provisions in relation to political and courtroom speeches was still maintained under article 2bis(1).[59] However, there was strong opposition to the French proposal, particularly from the UK, the Scandinavian countries, Switzerland, and Czechoslovakia.[60] This was based mainly on the public interest, but another relevant consideration was the effect that this might have on likely American

[54] *Actes*, 1928, 228.
[55] See the proposals of the International Office and the Belgian Government in [1933] *DA* 78.
[56] [1936] *DA* 39, and *Documents 1948* (1951), 160.
[57] [1936] *DA* 39, and *Documents 1948* (1951), 161.
[58] *Documents 1948* (1951), 161.
[59] ibid.
[60] ibid, 162–3.

adhesion to the Convention.[61] The French proposition was therefore decisively defeated by six votes to twenty, with five abstentions.[62] Although several other proposals were also considered,[63] the only alteration that was finally made to article 2bis was the addition of a new paragraph which dealt with the right of authors to make collections of their works, including political and courtroom speeches. This was in keeping with the original programme proposal, except that, as the result of a Belgian amendment, it now referred to the right of the author to make collections of 'his works'.[64]

(b) The Paris Act

The Stockholm–Paris Revisions saw a significant addition made to article 2 which finally resolved the vexed question of fixation. This arose in the context of choreographic works, rather than oral works, but was just as relevant for our present purposes. Since the time that choreographic works and entertainments in dumb show had been included in article 2(1) (at the Berlin Revision), this had been subject to the requirement that the 'acting form' of the works be 'fixed in writing or otherwise'.[65] As far as these works were concerned, the requirement of fixation was mainly for evidentiary purposes (see para 8.25 below). However, the requirement of fixation for these works alone gave rise to the implication that, as regards the other works enumerated in article 2(1), Berne Union countries were required to accord protection to them whether or not they were fixed. This question was the subject of considerable discussion in Main Committee I, where the Indian delegation proposed a new paragraph for article 2 under which it would be a matter for legislation in countries of the Union to prescribe that any specified categories of works should be fixed in some material form.[66] This gave express recognition to the fact that many Union countries still required fixation for particular categories of work or even as a general precondition for protection. This proposition was taken up with vigour by the UK delegation,[67] and while there was some opposition to it on the grounds that it might create a new regime of exceptions which would adversely affect the Berne Union and cause difficulties for authors in poorer countries,[68] it was approved by eighteen **8.18**

[61] ibid, 163.

[62] Spain, France, Greece, Morocco, Italy, and Tunisia for; Australia, Belgium, Canada, Denmark, Finland, the UK, Hungary, India, Ireland, Liechtenstein, Norway, New Zealand, Pakistan, the Netherlands, Poland, Portugal, Sweden, Switzerland, Czechoslovakia, and South Africa against; Austria, Bulgaria, Luxembourg, Monaco, and Holy See abstaining: ibid.

[63] ibid. [64] ibid. See Brussels Act, art $2^{bis}(3)$.

[65] Berlin and Rome Acts, art 2(1). See further paras 8.20ff below.

[66] *Records* 1967, vol II, 878–81. For the text of the Indian proposal (Document S/73), see ibid, vol I, 691.

[67] ibid, 878 and 880 (Wallace); a British proposal to similar effect was also proposed (Document S/191): ibid, vol I, 710.

[68] ibid, 880 (Rohmer, France, and Strnad, Czechoslovakia).

votes to nine, with nine abstentions.[69] It was ultimately adopted by the Conference in the following form:

> It shall, however, be a matter for legislation in the countries of the Union to prescribe that works in general or any specified categories of works shall not be protected unless they have been fixed in some material form.[70]

In a sense, this was a retrograde step as regards the level of protection accorded under the Convention. However, it was a necessary recognition of the fact that many national laws were unprepared to take the step of abolishing the requirement of fixation altogether, and that to make this mandatory might drive countries such as the UK out of the Union or discourage possible adherents, such as the USA.[71] The principal reason for retaining the need for fixation is evidentiary: it is hard otherwise to prove the fact of existence of an unfixed work. Likewise, it is difficult to be sure of the scope or content of such a work, and without fixation the protection of such a work may come close to the protection of the 'ideas' or subject of that work. Although in many instances, fixation will be in writing, with the consequence that a lecture or address which is fixed in this way could be just as readily protected under the category of 'books, pamphlets and other writings', fixation may also take other forms, for instance, in a sound recording or a cinematographic film.

8.19 It should also be noted that the Convention obligation to protect these kinds of oral works is limited, and does not extend to oral works in general. While the precise boundaries of the category may be uncertain, the final words 'and other works of the same nature' may indicate that only spoken works of a more formal or considered kind delivered before or to an audience are covered. This would therefore exclude more aleatory or spontaneous forms of oral expression such as the commentary of a broadcaster on the progress of a sporting event or a public occasion, the announcements and incidental 'patter' of a radio or television presenter, the words spoken in a press interview, or the casual dinner conversation of a celebrated person. The distinction between formal and aleatory oral works, however, is troublesome, notably because of the merit criterion it implies. In principle, it is not apparent why sports commentary should be less of an 'intellectual creation' than an unfixed lecture. As to fixed works, the Convention does not require inquiry into whether the work was dashed off or the fruit of mature reflection; it is not clear why, apart from the evidentiary problems, it should do so for unfixed works. In practice, moreover, it may not always be obvious what portions of an oral work are 'considered' and which are

[69] *Records* 1967, vol I, 881. [70] Stockholm, Paris Acts, art 2(2).

[71] See n 57 above, and *Records* 1967, vol I, 879 (comments by Kamminstein, US observer at Main Committee I).

spontaneous; a rule inviting courts to explore this distinction seems ill-advised. With respect to interviews and conversations, by contrast, the phrase 'and other works of the same nature' offers a useful dividing line. The oral works listed in article 2(1) are generally delivered by a single person; their 'nature' thus would be solo authorship. The 'nature' of interviews and conversations, on the other hand, involves at least two interlocutors. The evidentiary problems of attributing authorship of components of the conversation or interview are accordingly considerably more complicated than for individually authored works. Their exclusion from the category of protected oral works thus is justified on principled and practical grounds. While it is open to member countries to extend protection to these kinds of works if they wish,[72] there is nothing under the category of lectures, addresses, etc, in article 2(1) requiring them to do so.

Article 2bis also received consideration and amendment during the Stockholm Revision. Article $2^{bis}(1)$, which dealt with the protection of political speeches and speeches delivered in the course of legal proceedings, was left unchanged. The public-interest arguments in favour of permitting the partial or total exclusion of protection for such works were undisputed by member countries, and no proposition in relation to this paragraph was put forward by any delegation or any of the preparatory groups that drew up the programme for the Conference.[73] It should be noted that the provision imposes no requirement on member countries: it is entirely permissive in form. On the other hand, it places no restriction on the extent to which protection may be denied to these works. This does not only refer to reproduction in printed form, but to all possible forms of exploitation that are comprehended within the rights of authors under the Convention, for example, broadcasting, diffusion over cable networks, and so on. In practice, Union countries have chosen to use the facility provided under this provision in widely differing ways.[74] **8.20**

Article $2^{bis}(2)$ was also revised at the time of the Stockholm Conference but discussion of this is deferred to Chapter 13 which deals generally with restrictions on protection under the Convention (see para 13.56 below). **8.21**

(3) Dramatic or dramatico-musical works

This is another of the original categories of works enumerated in article 4 of the Berne Act, and it was, in turn, adopted, without discussion, from earlier **8.22**

[72] See para 8.18 above. [73] *Records* 1967, vol I, 89.

[74] Compare eg the differences between the French Code de la propriété intellectuelle, art L 122–5(3)(c) (author cannot prohibit dissemination of speeches in any form) and the FRG Law of 1965, art 48 (privilege to reproduce and distribute speeches made in public proceedings, or for purposes of news; but author may prohibit assembly of such speeches into a collection of that author's speeches).

bilateral conventions and national laws.[75] Furthermore, there has been no discussion of these works at any of the successive revision conferences, and this may be taken to indicate that there has always been a fairly general consensus among countries of the Union as to their meaning. In ordinary parlance, 'dramatic' and 'dramatico-musical works' are works which are made to be represented or performed in front of an audience, rather than passively read and enjoyed as a written text by an individual reader (although the latter is usually possible as well). The expression 'dramatic works' clearly includes plays of all kinds, whether these be dramas, tragedies, comedies, farces, short sketches or revues. 'Dramatico-musical works', as their name indicates, have a musical dimension as well as, or perhaps instead of, a spoken dimension, and include all kinds of musical plays, from grand to light opera, musical comedy and musical drama, to simple song and dance routines. However, the precise scope of the expression 'dramatic or dramatico-musical works' is left entirely at large in the Convention. Insofar as these works are reduced to writing, whether this be in the form of dialogue, the words of a song, a description of the plot, or stage directions, they will come under the category of 'writings'. Furthermore, insofar as they consist of a musical accompaniment as in an opera or musical comedy, they will also be protected as 'musical compositions'. On the other hand, article 2(2) makes it clear that member countries may protect such works whether or not they are reduced to writing or some other material form. Thus, even where fixation is required, the words and music of a dramatic or dramatico-musical work may be just as readily recorded in the form of a sound recording or film as in writing.

8.23 It should also be noted that these works, by their very nature, may include more than words or musical accompaniment, for example, such important elements as the gestures and positioning of actors, the way in which incidents are to be physically enacted, the arrangement of sets and props, and background sets and scenery. Some of these may, in turn, be protected under other categories of article 2(1), for example, as works of painting or architecture in the case of background sets. However, the protection of the 'acting' elements, such as gestures, positioning, and other movements, is more uncertain. Inasmuch as the author of the dramatic or dramatico-musical work has included them as an integral part of his work they should be protected, along with the words and music, and it is submitted that the Convention should be interpreted as requiring this. Even if fixation is required as a condition of protection, this should raise no problems, as such elements as movements and gestures can be readily recorded on film. These matters are often as important as the dialogue and music in these kinds of works, and to leave them unprotected would deprive the

[75] See eg the Franco-German Convention of 19 Apr 1883, art 1, and the Franco-Italian Convention of 9 July 1884, art 1. See also LCD (1889), vol I, xliv.

Convention of much of its force in this regard.[76] This is, of course, quite different from protecting the performances of the actors themselves, that is, the particular interpretation which an actor gives to a role. There was an attempt to secure protection for performances at the time of the Rome Revision,[77] but there has been strong reluctance to treat performers as another species of 'authors' and their performances as 'works', so the international solution which has been ultimately adopted has been to deal with this matter in another convention (see Chapter 19 below). It should also be noted that works which consist of action alone do not fall within the category of dramatic or dramatico-musical works. Since 1908, article 2(1) has included choreographic works and entertainments in dumb show as a separate category of works (see para 8.24 below). In addition, cinematographic productions, which at this time meant silent films, were protected by article 14 of the Berlin Revision to the extent that their author had given them a 'personal and original character' by the arrangement of the acting form or combination of incidents represented (see para 8.32 below). The need to include these works separately therefore indicates that prior to this time it was at least doubtful that such works came within the category of dramatic and dramatico-musical works, or indeed the general category of literary and artistic works.

(4) **Choreographic works and entertainments in dumb show**

(a) History of their protection

Works of dance and mime have a long tradition in many countries of the world. **8.24**
Essentially, they are works of movement, in which the actions of the performers are used to convey a story, create an image, or evoke a set of emotions. These may also be accompanied by music, and it is possible that the action may be described in writing or some other form of notation. However, while it was clear that the last two elements were protected under the other categories of article 2(1), it was doubtful that the choreographic or mime elements of such works were protected under the Berne Act. Among the original Berne signatories, Italy was a leading exemplar of the choreographic art, and had protected such works under its domestic law since 1882.[78] Rosmini, the Italian delegate, therefore raised the question of their inclusion as literary and artistic works at the 1885 Conference (Italy did not attend the 1884 Conference). In support of this, he argued that a choreographer 'worthy of the name' was both poet and artist:

[76] Note that the Italian Government and International Office in their programme for the Rome Conference referred to the desirability of protecting 'scenic arrangements', but made no proposal in this regard because of the difficulty they perceived in giving protection where the *mise-en-scène* was not fixed in writing. They also thought that this was not, in any case, a matter of much practical importance. See *Actes* 1928, 65–8.

[77] ibid, 76–7, 229–30.

[78] Italian Law of 18 May 1882, art 1(a).

> . . . he creates the subject; he arranges the scenes, the décor, the costumes, the tableaux, the colours; in addition, the intrigue, the development of the pantomime and dance which express the drama, be it fantastic, mythological or historical. All this constitutes a veritable work of art, and the whole a dramatico-musical work. Because of the composite nature of the work, it is appropriate to protect choreographic action.[79]

This proposal met with opposition from the German delegate, Reichardt, who argued that it was preferable to leave the question of whether such works should be protected to national tribunals.[80] He was also concerned that a satisfactory definition of choreographic work had not yet (to his knowledge) been developed in either national laws or in juridical science. Accordingly, specific enumeration of these works in article 2(1) (then article 4) might mean that a whole range of undeserving subject matter would also have to be protected—did the Conference wish to protect, for example, 'any pantomime, any choreographic scene performed in the circus, the fairground, the barracks, even in the street'?[81] He also pointed out that the musical accompaniment and libretto of a ballet were in any event already protected under other heads.[82] As a result, the commission, by a majority, thought it preferable not to include choreographic works in article 2(1), but to stipulate in the Closing Protocol that those countries whose laws implicitly included these among dramatico-musical works should expressly admit the said works to the benefits of the Convention.[83] This was accepted by the Conference, together with a proviso that any questions which arose as to the application of the clause were to be left to the competence of national tribunals.[84] This was not subject to any requirement of reciprocity, so its effect was that any country which granted such protection to its own nationals (this might be either in its statute law or in its jurisprudence) was bound to protect the choreographic works of authors from other Union countries whose laws did not accord such protection.

8.25 At the Paris Conference in 1896, the Italian Government renewed its efforts to have choreographic works included in article 4,[85] but the German Government maintained its objections and the Commission therefore decided to uphold the status quo.[86] By the end of the century, however, most Union countries, apart from Germany, did accord protection to choreographic works;[87] in addition, they were included in the enumeration of works protected under article 5 of the Convention of Montevideo.[88] By the time of the Berlin Revision, in keeping with these international developments, the German Government had changed

[79] *Actes* 1885, 21. [80] ibid. [81] ibid, 22. [82] ibid. [83] ibid, 43.
[84] Berne Act, Closing Protocol, para 2. [85] *Actes* 1896, 114. [86] ibid, 168.
[87] See the comparative survey by the International Office in [1899] *DA* 13.
[88] The Convention of Montevideo Concerning Literary and Artistic Property, 11 Jan 1889: *Recueil* (1904), 39.

its position,[89] and it included the protection of choreographic works and pantomimes as part of its programme for the Conference.[90] However, it proposed to make this subject to the requirement that the dramatic action of these works should be fixed in writing.[91] The main reason for this was that 'writing' made it easier to prove the existence of the work,[92] but this was opposed by the Italian delegation, which argued that the dramatic action of these works was often fixed in ways other than writing, for example, in a drawing or in other special forms of notation or representation.[93] Finally, a compromise was reached whereby the following words were added to article 2, after the expression 'dramatic or dramatico-musical works': 'choreographic works and entertainments in dumb show, the acting form ["*mise-en-scène*"] of which is fixed in writing or otherwise'. The words 'or otherwise' gave the widest possible latitude so far as modes of fixation were concerned, allowing, for example, the recording of a dance or mime show in a cinematographic film or in a series of photographs.[94]

The status of choreographic works was left untouched by the Rome Revision; nor was it the subject of any of the early proposals made for the Brussels Revision. However, in the proposals submitted before the Conference met in 1948, Austria and Czechoslovakia argued for the deletion of the requirement of fixation altogether, on the basis that there was no reason why choreographic works and pantomimes alone should be subject to this requirement.[95] In support, it was urged that there were many important and remarkable instances of these kinds of works which were not fixed in any medium, and that it was unjust that these should be unprotected. The main opposition to this proposal came principally from France, which maintained that fixation was necessary as a matter of proof, and that this requirement was presently couched in such broad terms that no real hardship was thereby imposed on authors.[96] The French delegation also pointed out that the requirement of fixation was of importance in establishing proof of the existence of the work of an author, rather than that of a performer.[97] The last point was of significance in that the protection of performers under the Berne Convention had been rejected at the time of the Rome Conference,[98] and plans were under way to deal with this question in a separate convention. For these reasons, the Berlin text was retained in the Brussels Revision. **8.26**

[89] See *Actes* 1908, 166 (opening speech to Conference by Osterrieth on behalf of the German Government). See also Ladas (1938), 221, and the commentary of the International Office in [1909] *DA* 78.

[90] *Actes* 1908, 50–1. [91] ibid. [92] ibid, 166 (Osterrieth).

[93] ibid, 231 (report of Renault).

[94] See commentary in [1909] *DA* 78. Note that the German Government changed its legislation in accordance with this article in its amending law of 1910: Law of 22 May 1910, art 1.

[95] *Documents 1948* (1951), 147, 150. [96] ibid. [97] ibid, 155.

[98] *Actes* 1928, 229–30.

(b) The Paris Act

8.27 The fixation issue was finally resolved at the Stockholm Revision. In the preparations for this Conference, opinion among delegates over the question was fairly evenly divided, but the programme for the Conference finally recommended deletion of the requirement.[99] The principal reason for this was the same as had been advanced at the Brussels Revision: the illogicality of requiring fixation for one kind of work, but not for others. Another consideration was the danger that was now facing authors of unfixed choreographic works whose performances were broadcast by television.[100] The opposition to this proposal followed similar lines to that at the Brussels Revision, and there was extended discussion of the question in Main Committee I.[101] Finally, the deletion of the requirement of fixation was agreed to, but this was in consideration of the adoption of a new paragraph which left it to national legislation to determine whether the protection of all or any categories of works should be subject to a requirement of fixation in a material form.[102] This paragraph (article 2(2)) has already been discussed above (see para 8.18 above). As far as choreographic works and pantomimes are concerned, its effect is that national legislation is free to protect these when they are unfixed, but it is equally open to any member state to require fixation as a precondition for protection.

(5) **Musical compositions, with or without words**

(a) History of their protection

8.28 This is another of the original categories of works which was included in the enumeration in article 4 of the Berne Act. Its origins, again, were to be found in national copyright laws and the various bilateral conventions.[103] In the draft ALAI Convention of 1883[104] and the Federal Council programme of the following year,[105] it was coupled with 'arrangements of music'. The latter are often referred to as derivative works, that is, works that are derived from an original musical composition—the basic melody line—but have elaborated this, for example, by the addition of a vocal or instrumental accompaniment. Such a work of arrangement may, in itself, require a very high degree of musical skill and knowledge of such matters as harmony and the character and range of the different instruments or voices for which the work is arranged. There is therefore an excellent case for protecting such arrangements on an equal footing with

[99] *Records* 1967, vol I, 83–5. [100] ibid, 84. [101] ibid, vol II, 880–1.
[102] ibid, 881.
[103] See LCD (1889) vol I, xlv (as to national laws); see also the Franco-Belgian Convention of 31 Oct 1881, art 1 (LCD (1889), vol II, 278), and the Franco-Italian Convention of 9 July 1884 (LCD (1889), vol II, 303).
[104] *Actes* 1884, 7 (art 1). [105] ibid, 11 (art 4).

the original musical compositions themselves, and this was the position under many national laws and bilateral copyright conventions prior to 1888.[106] However, at the 1884 Conference, it was decided to delete 'arrangements of music' from the list of works to be protected under the Convention, and to deal with them under the rubric of infringement.[107] Accordingly, a separate article dealt with 'unauthorized indirect appropriations of works', and these were stated to include musical arrangements.[108] As a result, musical arrangements were not protected directly as literary or artistic works under the Convention, although the making of such arrangements remained the exclusive right of the author of the original musical work. The scope and effect of this article is discussed further below (see paras 8.79 and 11.30), but for the moment it suffices to note that at the Berlin Revision 'arrangements of music', together with other kinds of derivative work, were brought back within the scope of article 2, and accorded protection as original works in a separate paragraph of that article. (This has remained the case since that time, and the protection of these kinds of works is considered further at paras 8.75ff below.)

(b) The Paris Act

Like most other terms used in article 2(1), 'musical composition' receives no further definition. In a broad sense, there can be little doubt that musical compositions fall squarely within the notion of productions in the 'literary, scientific or artistic domain', although they are clearly a distinct genus from books and writings, on the one hand, and works of the visual arts, on the other. Even if they were not specifically enumerated in article 2(1), there would probably be little argument that the notation of a musical work and any words that accompany it would come within the category of 'other writings'. Nonetheless, their specific enumeration in article 2(1) makes it clear that they do come within the scope of the expression 'literary or artistic works', while article 2(2) confirms that the question of whether they must be fixed in any material form is entirely a matter for national legislation. Where fixation is required, this will usually be in the form of musical notation, but it should be noted that a musical composition may be fixed in other ways, for example, in a sound recording, a cassette tape, or digital media. **8.29**

What scope, then, is to be given to the expression 'musical composition'? In 1886, there was probably not a great deal of doubt as to what was meant by 'music', as composers like Richard Strauss, Schoenberg, Berg, and Stravinsky, **8.30**

[106] See eg some of the earlier conventions, such as that between France and Portugal of 11 July 1866 (art 1) (LCD (1889), vol II, 339), and France and Austria-Hungary of 11 Dec 1866, art 1 (LCD (1889), vol II, 269).

[107] *Actes* 1884, 44.

[108] 1884 draft Act, art 10: *Actes* 1884, 55; and ultimately the Berne Act, 1886, art 10.

much less Gershwin or Ellington, had not yet emerged to challenge accepted notions of musical form. A musical composition therefore consisted of an orderly, rhythmic and melodic sequence of sounds. This straightforward conception must be extended today, in the light of developments over the past century which have seen atonal, non-rhythmic and even aleatory or indeterminate creations accepted as musical compositions.[109] It would be hard even for traditionalists to deny persons such as Stockhausen, Berio, and Cage the status of composer. The same is undoubtedly true of many of the popular musical forms that have emerged over the same period, such as jazz, rock'n'roll, reggae, and disco or hip-hop. One inevitably enters here the minefield area of subjective, aesthetic judgements that copyright law has sought generally to avoid. As a consequence, most national copyright laws avoid laying down precise definitions of 'musical composition', and, where such definitions are to be found, they are usually in the older laws and reflect the more settled and confident views of those times.[110] Otherwise, these questions are left to national tribunals to determine for themselves on a case-by-case basis, and in accordance with changing social and cultural tastes. The absence of any definition in the Berne Convention simply confirms that any other approach would be fraught with difficulty.

(6) Cinematographic works to which are assimilated works expressed by a process analogous to cinematography

(a) History of their protection

8.31 This category was added to the enumeration in article 2(1) at the time of the Brussels Revision. Before this, however, the Convention had, since 1908, accorded protection to certain kinds of cinematographic productions. This, in fact, is an instance where the Convention has had an influence on the shaping of domestic laws, rather than vice versa, as cinematographic production had really only come into existence in 1898.[111] Although this new medium of expression grew rapidly over the next decade, the question of its protection had not been really addressed by many Union countries at the time of the Berlin Revision. French courts, however, led the way in holding that a dramatic work might be infringed by its reproduction in a cinematographic film, as well as by the public presentation of that film.[112] Accordingly, the French Government proposed an

[109] See further D P Keziak, 'Copyright Registration for Aleatory and Indeterminate Musical Compositions' (1971) 18 *Bulletin of the Copyright Society of the USA* 311.

[110] See eg the definition of 'musical work' in the old Australian Copyright Act 1905, s 4. For an interpretation of the 1988 UK CDPA, see *Hyperion Records Ltd* v *Sawkins*, [2005] EWCA Civ 565 (holding that scholarly editions of public domain musical compositions are 'original musical works' even though the editor added no 'new notes').

[111] See generally K Brownlow and J Kobal, *Hollywood: The Pioneers* (1979), chs 1–8.

[112] See the account of these decisions in the report of L Renault to the Berlin Conference: *Actes* 1908, 264–5. Similarly, the US Supreme Court shortly thereafter held a novel infringed by a motion picture. See *Kalem Co* v *Harper Bros*, 222 US 55 (1911) (*Ben Hur*).

amendment to this effect at the Berlin Revision.[113] This was duly adopted by the Conference, which incorporated these extended rights of the authors of literary and artistic works in a new article (article 14(1); see further para 11.23 below). At the same time, the Conference recognized that cinematographic films themselves might constitute 'creations' eligible for protection under the Convention.[114] There were two aspects to this, the first relating to the cinematographic film as a particular form of dramatic work, and the second relating to the protection of the film where it was a cinematographic reproduction of a literary, scientific, or artistic work (a 'pre-existing work').

(i) **'Cinematographic productions'**: As to this first category, article 14(2) provided: **8.32**

> (2) Cinematographic productions shall be protected as literary or artistic works, if, by the arrangement of the acting form or the combination of the incidents represented, the author has given the work a personal and original character.

The element protected here was not the subject matter of the film, for example, the life of Mary Stuart, but the way in which this subject was treated—the combination of incidents and the development of plot.[115] This was, perhaps, an unnecessary reiteration of the cardinal rule that the rights of authors should not extend to the ideas or subject of their works, with the consequence in the present case that films of 'natural' or 'ordinary' subjects were not to be protected if they were not the result of any arrangement or ordering by the maker of the film. It seems clear from the wording of this paragraph that protectable 'cinematographic productions' were regarded simply as another species of dramatic work, and little, if any, account was to be taken of the technical skills required to make them—skills that were usually required in equal measure for films of 'unordered' subjects such as landscapes, street scenes, or public events. In other words, under paragraph (2) cinematographic films were not to be protected because they themselves represented 'productions in the literary, scientific and artistic domain', but only insofar as they might embody works that came within this definition by reason of the personal and original character given them by the arrangement of the acting form or combination of incidents. The necessity for a provision limited in this way may be questioned, as such works should already have been protected as dramatic or dramatico-musical works that were simply expressed in a novel form. The requirement that the author should have given the work 'a personal and original character' was also probably unnecessary, as both requirements were implicit in the general definition of a literary or artistic work under article 2(1) (see para 8.02 above).

[113] ibid, 190.
[114] ibid, 268.
[115] ibid, 265 (report of Renault); see also [1909] *DA* 79 and Ladas (1938), 238.

8.33 **(ii) 'Cinematographic reproductions of pre-existing works':** By contrast, article 14(3) went further than article 14(2), providing that:

> Without prejudice to the rights of the author of the original work, the reproduction by cinematography of a literary, scientific or artistic work shall be protected as an original work.

Thus, if the cinematographic film were no more than a reproduction of a pre-existing work, for example, a film of the performance of a play or opera, it was nonetheless protected as an original work in its own right. The analogy that was drawn here by the commission at the Berlin Conference was with the making of a translation which was also protected as an original work under article 2(2) of the Berlin Act.[116] A further analogy can be drawn with the making of a sound recording of a musical work, although in this second case the Convention has, throughout its history, declined to protect sound recordings as original works in their own right.[117] In the eyes of the delegates at the Berlin Conference, it is clear that the filming of a pre-existing work required the application of a level of skill that qualified for the description of 'authorship', although at subsequent conferences it was to be denied that this level of skill was present in the making of a sound recording.[118] The reference to translations, however, indicates that the delegates regarded the process of cinematographic reproduction as being something more than simple copying. Although no further explanation is provided in the records of the Conference, it is clear the making of a film requires a whole series of judgements about the way the pre-existing work is to be filmed; even if the work remains textually unchanged, its fixation on film makes it something quite different. In this respect the word 'adaptation' may be more appropriate to describe both the process of filming and the resultant film, and this word was, in fact, added to article 14(3) at the time of the Rome Revision (as well as being made one of the rights conferred on the authors of pre-existing works under article 14(1)).

8.34 Following the Berlin Revision, the 'makers of cinematographic films' (using this expression in a very general sense) sought an extension of the protection under the Convention for their productions. In September 1910, the first International Congress of Cinematography and its Applications met in Brussels.[119] This comprised representatives of all interests involved with the new industry, and it passed a resolution urging the deletion of the words 'when by the arrangement of the acting form . . . a personal and original character' from article 14(2) so that it should simply read: 'Cinematographic productions are protected as literary and artistic works.'[120] Similar views were also expressed at

116 *Actes* 1908, 268.
117 See paras 8.112ff below.
118 ibid.
119 See the report of this meeting in [1911] *DA* 105.
120 ibid. See also *Actes* 1928, 38.

the ALAI Congress in Copenhagen in 1909,[121] and again at the ALAI Congress in Paris in 1925 where the following resolution was passed:

> Cinematographic works should be protected in the same way as literary and dramatic works, without any restriction; it is appropriate to remove from the Convention of Berne as revised at Berlin the restriction which it contains in this regard.[122]

The use of the word 'work' was significant as it indicated that cinematographic productions were to be regarded as works in their own right. The ALAI resolution was taken up by the French Government in its proposals for the Rome Conference of Revision.[123] These proposals also included a provision to the effect that the copyright in a cinematographic work belonged to the 'intellectual creators of the film' who alone had the right of exploiting the work. No mention was made of cinematographic reproductions under article 14(3), but it was to be presumed that these would fall within the scope of the term 'cinematographic works' insofar as they constituted 'intellectual creations'. The Italian Government and the International Office, however, in their programme for the Conference did not go so far as the French dispositions, and proposed the following 'modest reform': the deletion of the words 'personal and' in article 14(2), and the addition, in the same paragraph, of the qualification that cinematographic works lacking an original character were to be protected as photographs.[124] After considerable discussion, both in the Main Committee of the Conference and in a specially appointed sub-committee, it proved impossible to reach agreement on the French proposals, and the Italian Government and International Office amendments were adopted.[125] Article 14(2) was therefore amended to read as follows:

> Cinematographic productions are protected as literary or artistic works, when the author has given to the work an original character. If this character is missing, the cinematographic production enjoys protection as a photographic work.

This reform was not as 'modest' as might appear at first sight, as it brought the **8.35** requirements for the protection of cinematographic works far closer to those required for other kinds of works. The deletion of the requirement of 'personal character' probably did not change anything, as this was already an implicit requirement of the definition of literary or artistic work (see para 8.02 above). In addition, it is difficult to envisage a cinematographic film in which some personal element is not involved in its making (leaving aside the possibility of films made by computers which were unknown at this time and which raise a different set of problems). As for the retention of the requirement of 'original

[121] [1909] *DA* 99. See also *Actes* 1928, 38.
[122] [1925] *DA* 82. See also *Actes* 1928, 37.
[123] *Actes* 1928, 101.
[124] ibid, 79–80.
[125] ibid, 268–9.

character', this did not add anything, unless it could be argued that this meant something more than was already required under the general definition of literary and artistic work in article 2(1). More important, however, was the omission of any reference to acting form or combination of incident, as this opened the way for the inclusion of other kinds of non-dramatic films which had been outside the previous article 14(2). Nevertheless, the second sentence of the new provision indicated that it was not intended that all cinematographic films were to be within its scope, and that 'unoriginal' films were to be protected as photographs. The last limitation was both unnecessary and uncertain in its scope: unnecessary, in that this was undoubtedly already the case, and uncertain, in that it was left unclear as to what degree of 'unoriginality' was required to deprive a cinematographic film of the status of a literary or artistic work. In the opinion of the International Office, expressed several years after the Rome Revision, 'unoriginal films' were those which did not express any 'creative activity', in the sense that they were simply photographs of objects and phenomena naturally occurring which the cinematographer captured on film without any choice or disposition of the scenes filmed.[126] However, it was clearly arguable that the skill involved in actually making a film—the choice of camera angle, lighting, and so on—was just as worthy of protection as the various skills involved in deciding how the subject matter to be filmed was to be treated. The qualification in the second sentence of article 14(2) therefore highlighted the difficult question of principle as to what was required by way of authorship in the case of cinematographic productions. It further highlighted the difficult question of who was the author of a cinematographic film, a matter on which national laws were developing different responses.

8.36 The Rome Act also retained article 14(3) of the Berlin Act, but with the following changes:

> (3) Without prejudice to the rights of the author of the work reproduced or adapted, a cinematographic work shall be protected as an original work.

The reference to adaptation was in line with article 14(1), where this had also been added to the rights of authors in pre-existing works. Whether its insertion added much to either paragraph is hard to say, given that the Berlin Conference had already treated cinematographic reproduction as a species of transformation akin to translation and therefore worthy of protection. However, it underlined the basic truth that, in most cinematographic treatments of pre-existing works, the very nature of the medium often, if not invariably, required significant changes and modifications that were more aptly described as adaptation rather than reproduction. Article 14(3) of the Rome Act therefore indicated that either

[126] [1934] *DA* 15.

act, however defined, would suffice for the resultant cinematographic film to constitute an original work.

(iii) Note about sound pictures: At the time of the Berlin Revision, the only kinds of cinematographic films that were known were 'silent pictures', in which images alone were embodied. Any spoken or musical accompaniment had to be added separately, for example, with the use of a phonograph player or live players, and such words or music would usually be entitled to separate protection under the Convention as either dramatic or dramatico-musical works or musical compositions. Any written words that actually appeared in the film itself, as either headings or subtitles, were also presumably entitled to protection as dramatic works or as 'other writings'. However, within twenty years of the Berlin Revision 'sound' had been added to cinematographic films, and the cinematographic industry underwent a major revolution.[127] There was nothing in article 14(2) of the Berlin Act to prevent these new 'sound pictures' coming within the scope of the expression 'cinematographic production', as the words 'arrangement of the acting form or the combination of incidents represented' did not necessarily require these matters to be presented only in visual images. The same was also true of article 14(3) which dealt with cinematographic reproductions of literary, scientific, and artistic works. This, indeed, seemed to be the generally accepted view,[128] and no proposal was made at the Rome Revision for the specific inclusion of these new kinds of films. However, the Norwegian Government argued for the contrary interpretation in the submissions which it made for the proposed Brussels Revision of 1938.[129] This suggestion was forcefully criticized by the International Office in a commentary on the submissions, in which it pointed to the fact that the expression 'cinematographic production' was not subject to any qualification in either the Berlin or Rome Act, and accordingly there was no reason to interpret the expression in a restrictive fashion.[130] It also noted that, if sound pictures were not included in article 14(2), this would mean that they were mechanical reproductions under article 13 and would therefore be subject to the possibility of compulsory licensing under that article.[131] This view is undoubtedly correct, and has not been challenged since that time; nor was it thought necessary to make it the subject of any specific amendment at any of the Brussels, Stockholm, or Paris Revisions. Accordingly, the expression 'cinematographic work' covers both the images and sounds embodied in the film. **8.37**

127 See generally, Brownlow and Kobal (n 111 above), chs 6–8.

128 [1936] *DA* (comments by International Office on proposals for Brussels Revision Conference), but note the views of an ALAI sub-committee on the question of whether sound pictures were sound recordings within the meaning of art 13, discussed by the International Office in [1934] *DA* 15.

129 [1936] *DA* 91–2. 130 ibid.

131 ibid, but note the views of ALAI referred to in [1934] *DA* 15.

(b) The Paris Act

8.38 After the Rome Revision, there was no reason why cinematographic films, or at least those possessing an original character, should not be included in the works enumerated in article 2(1), rather than left in article 14 which was more generally concerned with the rights of authors of pre-existing works (see para 11.23 below). A proposal to this effect was made by the International Office in its preparatory work for the Brussels Revision in 1933; it also proposed that the assimilation of unoriginal cinematographic films to photographic works should be retained.[132] The responses to these proposals showed the marked national differences that were emerging on the question of cinematographic works. For example, France was favourable to their inclusion in article 2(1), but subject to the qualification that they were an 'intellectual creation'.[133] On the other hand, the UK argued that all cinematographic films should be protected.[134] In the programme presented for the 1948 Brussels Conference, the Belgian Government and International Office elaborated their 1933 proposals. Arguing that cinematographic works were a *sui generis* kind of work that fell within the general range of literary and artistic works, they proposed that these works be now enumerated in article 2(1).[135] This presumably included the cinematographic reproductions and adaptations of existing works referred to in article 14(3) of the Rome Act (now to be deleted). However, a new article 14(3) was proposed, to the effect that, if a cinematographic work did not have the character of an 'organically constructed creation' ('*une création organiquement constituée*'), it should only receive protection as a photographic work.[136] The phrase 'organically constructed creation' replaced that of 'original character' which had previously appeared in article 14(2) of the Rome Act and, by way of explanation, the Belgian Government and International Office said that they intended this new provision to exclude those cinematographic works which simply consisted of a succession of images taken from nature or society.[137] In other words, such works were no different than photographs, and were therefore to be protected as such. However, as the Brussels Conference saw the promotion of photographic works into the works enumerated in article 2(1), this proposal became meaningless, and was jettisoned.[138] Accordingly, when the Conference approved the inclusion of cinematographic works in article 2(1), it did so without qualification.[139] This still left open the question of what element, or elements, of authorship were thereby protected: did this extend to the technical skills involved in the actual making of the film, in addition to, or instead of, the more explicitly literary and artistic contributions made by such persons as the

[132] [1933] *DA* 74. [133] [1936] *DA* 92. [134] ibid.
[135] *Documents 1948* (1951), 140. [136] ibid, 348. [137] ibid.
[138] Brussels Act, art 2(1). [139] *Documents 1948* (1951), 155.

director, scriptwriter, designer, and composer of the musical soundtrack? The basic requirement for a literary or artistic work under article 2(1) of the Brussels Act, still retained in the Stockholm, Paris Acts, was that the subject matter in question should be a 'production in the literary, scientific and artistic domain'.

(i) Assimilation of 'works expressed by a process analogous to cinematography': Article 2(1) also assimilates to cinematographic works 'works expressed by a process analogous to cinematography'. This was added at the time of the Brussels Revision, although in the latter the word 'produced' was used instead of 'expressed'.[140] Its origins, however, are to be found in article 14 of the Berlin Act, where it was provided that the provisions of that article were also to apply to 'reproduction or production effected by any other process analogous to cinematography'.[141] The reason for this was that the Berlin commission thought, in view of the rapidly developing character of the film industry, that new processes were likely to be invented, and that provision should be made for these to be included under the Convention.[142] A liberal field of protection was therefore envisaged, but apart from the inclusion of sound pictures (see para 8.37 above), the scope of this additional category was not really called into question until the massive development of television after World War II. The techniques used for television were different from those used in cinematography: programmes might be broadcast directly without any intervening fixation in a material form; alternatively, the images and sounds comprising the programme might first be recorded on magnetic tape and then broadcast subsequently.[143] In the second instance, the difference between the two forms of fixation was that in the case of cinematographic films the images were recorded optically.[144] However, there was no practical difference so far as the final product was concerned, when a cinematographic film and a television broadcast (whether pre-recorded or not) were viewed. Both consisted of a combination of visual images and sounds projected onto a screen; in addition, many of the procedures used in the making of a cinematographic work were used in the making of a 'televisual work', for example, the operations of editing, cutting, and montage. Nevertheless, prior to the Stockholm Revision there was considerable doubt as to whether 'televisual works' could be assimilated to cinematographic films, insofar as the former might (i) subsist in an unfixed form, and (ii) where fixed, this was done by a process which was not analogous to cinematography—that is, while the effects produced were analogous, the processes used were not.[145] These questions were subjected to detailed examination by experts during the 1950s,[146] and 8.39

[140] ibid, 158. [141] Berlin Act, art 14(4). [142] *Actes* 1908, 268.
[143] See Document S/1, *Records* 1967, vol I, 85. [144] ibid. [145] ibid.
[146] See the reports of Professor E Ulmer in [1953] *DA* 97, Professor G Lyon-Caen in [1959] *DA* 217, and the Committee of Film Experts in [1962] *DA* 24.

subsequently occupied much of the time of the various bodies which carried out the preparatory work for the Stockholm Revision Conference during the early 1960s.[147] It was generally agreed that televisual works should be considered as cinematographic works, but there were differences of opinion on the question of fixation as countries took diverging views as to the need for this, whether generally or in specific cases.[148] Finally, the Conference programme proposed the following amendments: 'cinematographic works' alone were referred to in the enumeration in article 2(1), and a new article 2(2) was proposed in the following terms:

> (2) For the purposes of this Convention, works expressed by a process producing visual effects analogous to those of cinematography and fixed in some material form shall be considered to be cinematographic works.[149]

This draft assimilated televisual works to cinematographic works by changing the requirement of 'analogous' to the effect produced rather than the process used. Furthermore, while fixation in a material form was required for these works but not for cinematographic works proper, the programme noted that the enumeration in article 2(1) was non-limitative, and that countries were free to protect unfixed works under the general definition of literary and artistic works or even to do so under a different system to that used in the Convention.[150] It is also relevant to note a possible source of confusion that arises here when one speaks of protecting 'televisual works'. By 1967, in some countries, the rights of broadcasting organizations in their television (and radio) broadcasts were protected, sometimes under the rubric of copyright and sometimes under 'neighbouring rights' legislation.[151] These were not in any sense 'authors' rights', but were a form of protection accorded to the enterprises which had undertaken the investment necessary to produce television and sound broadcasts. Apart from the protection of these rights under domestic law, they had also become the subject of a special convention (the Rome Convention for the Protection of Performers, Producers of Phonograms and Broadcasting Organizations (the 'Rome Convention')) which was made in 1961. These rights have therefore to be distinguished from those which were in issue in the present context, that is, the rights of authors in respect of their cinematographic and broadcast works.

8.40 At the Stockholm Conference, there was fairly general agreement that televisual works should be assimilated to cinematographic works.[152] However, there were differences of opinion as to how this should be done. A Bulgarian amendment proposed the specific enumeration of both kinds of works in article 2(1),[153] but

---

147 *Records* 1967, vol I, 85–8. 148 ibid, 88. 149 ibid, 87–8. 150 ibid, 87.
151 See eg UK Copyright Act 1956, s 14.
152 *Records* 1967, vol II, 863–5 (minutes of Main Committee I).
153 Document S/89: ibid, 692.

this received little support.[154] After consideration by a special working group, the following amendment to article 2(1) was proposed: 'cinematographic works to which are assimilated those expressed by a process analogous to cinematography'.[155] This eliminated the need for any special provision governing such works,[156] but it seems clear that it was not intended to have any different effect from the wording proposed in the programme.[157] The latter was more precise, as it referred to the analogy in the results produced, rather than in the processes employed. As a matter of principle, however, such a preoccupation with results was inconsistent with the general concept of a literary and artistic work where the emphasis was on the protection of the creative effort involved in producing the work.[158] Furthermore, it had been accepted during the discussions in Main Committee I that the processes used in making cinematographic and televisual works were analogous, in that the two were often carried on together or interchangeably, and the operations of cutting and montage were common to both.[159] It also seemed to be accepted that where televisual works were fixed in a material form, this was in itself an 'analogous process'.[160] Although there was some uneasiness with this interpretation on the part of delegations from the common law countries,[161] the wording proposed by the working group was unanimously adopted by Main Committee I (with two abstentions)[162] and was duly inserted in the new text. Strangely enough, the foregoing interpretation was not referred to in the report of Main Committee I (an authentic supplementary aid to interpretation), except indirectly in the following statement:

> 122. The Programme suggested a new provision for cinematographic works in the form of a new paragraph (2). The Committee decided to alter the proposed text slightly and to restore it to paragraph (1).[163]

The reference to 'alter . . . slightly' indicates that no substantive change from the programme proposal was intended. On the other hand, there is an interesting interchange noted in the minutes of Main Committee I between the Italian delegate and the Chairman (Professor Ulmer):

> 1138. Mr. CIAMPI (Italy) drew the attention of the Main Committee I to the importance of not giving in the report any interpretation of the assimilation of televisual works to cinematographic works. The responsibility for such interpretations should be left to national legislations.
>
> 1137.1 The CHAIRMAN emphasized that it might be dangerous to leave to the countries of the Union full latitude to interpret assimilation, and that this was

154 ibid, vol II, 863–4. 155 Document S/190: ibid, vol I, 709.
156 Document S/1: ibid, 702. 157 ibid, vol II, 881 (Main Committee I), 1152 (report).
158 See generally paras 8.01ff above.
159 *Records* 1967, vol II, 863–5, 881 (in particular, the comments by Straschnov, Monaco).
160 ibid, 863–4 (comments by Straschnov, Monaco, and Wallace, UK).
161 ibid, 881 (Curtis, Australia). 162 ibid, 891. 163 ibid, 1152.

> not what the Main Committee had voted for, since it had been made clear that there would be assimilation when an analogous procedure was used.[164]

This last statement by Professor Ulmer underlines that the necessary condition for assimilation is the use of an 'analogous process'. However, the 'danger' referred to by him does not seem a very real one, as this formulation defines the categories of works which must be protected by each member country and the non-limitative nature of the enumeration in article 2(1) leaves it open to them to protect other categories of works as literary or artistic works. So far as 'works expressed by a process analogous to cinematography' are concerned, it seems reasonable to interpret these as including works made for diffusion over cable networks as well as works made for broadcasting.

8.41 **(ii) The relationship of 'cinematographic works' to the broader modern category of 'audiovisual works'**: This history suggests that the terms 'cinematographic works' and works 'expressed by an analogous process' should be broad enough to cover 'audiovisual' works, the term generally used today to encompass cinematographic and similar works consisting of a 'series of related images' viewed with the aid of a machine or device.[165] Ironically, if the 'process' element of the protected category once called into question the protectability of audiovisual works whose production entailed different forms of fixation (see para 8.39 above), today, given the many different media and processes used in cinematography,[166] it would seem that there is no longer any meaningful difference between 'cinematographic works', works 'expressed by an analogous process', and audiovisual works in general.

(7) **Various categories of artistic works**

(a) Works of drawing, painting, architecture, sculpture, engraving and lithography

8.42 With the exception of works of architecture, these works were among the original categories of works protected in article 4 of the Berne Act. These are, as Ladas says, 'the artistic works *par excellence*, as distinguished from literary works . . . a different form of expression of the intellect'.[167] They are works which are made to be viewed and appreciated in a visual sense rather than read or performed as in the case of literary or dramatic works or musical compositions. As none of the individual categories receive further definition in the Convention,

---

164 *Records* 1967, vol II, 891.

165 See eg US Copyright Act, 17 USC § 101 (defining audiovisual work). France, Code de la propriété intellectuelle, art L 112–2(6) ('cinematographic works and other works consisting of sequences of moving images, with or without sound, together referred to as audiovisual works').

166 See eg Thomas A Ohanian and Michael E Phillips, *Digital Filmmaking*, 2nd edn (2000), 22.

167 Ladas (1938), 222.

their meaning and scope is left to national legislation to determine. However, as there was no discussion or debate of these matters at either the original Berne Conferences of 1884 to 1886 or at any of the subsequent conferences of revision, it may be deduced that (i) there has generally been consensus on these matters among Union members, and (ii) this has been perceived to be the case by each Union member—otherwise, there would have been proposals to amend the Convention to take account of any differences, or member countries would have made appropriate reservations in their ratification of the various Acts. One situation where conflict has occurred has been where artistic works are applied industrially, and this problem is considered separately (see paras 8.59ff below). Apart from this, the task of defining and fixing the outer limits of these different categories has been left to each country to do for itself, either in its statutory law or in its jurisprudence. For our present purposes, all that can be done is to give some general observations on the nature of artistic works and the different categories enumerated in article 2(1).

(i) **Drawings and paintings:** As a preliminary matter, it should be noted **8.43**
that, although article 2(1) leaves the question of definition to member countries, the opening general definition still presupposes that a wide interpretation will be adopted. As regards the mode of expression adopted to convey the work, the position is quite clear: this is irrelevant. To take the case of a drawing, this may be executed in a wide number of ways, and on a wide variety of surfaces; the same is true of paintings. Furthermore, both may be depicted in any colour or combination of colours, and the choice of subject matter is limitless, from the naturalistic to the highly abstract. Essentially, both are works expressed in two dimensions, but even this is not always the case, as it is possible to have paintings or drawings that are impressed on various raised or uneven surfaces. As with other kinds of work, questions of aesthetic merit should be irrelevant; likewise, the subject matter and purpose of the work should be irrelevant, and no distinction should be made between landscapes and portraits on the one hand, and advertisements and works of caricature, on the other hand. In consequence, it is only at the extreme borders that questions will arise as to whether X is a work of painting or drawing (and even these categories may overlap). These questions are left rightly to national legislation to determine, and the Convention offers neither guidance nor direction, apart from the general guidelines referred to above. It is therefore of little significance, for our present purpose, that one Union country protects as works of painting the coloured lines painted on a pop star's face or the tattoos on an adolescent's belly while another Union country does not.[168] The only clear limitation contained in article 2(1) applies

[168] For an English case in which protection was denied in the first of these examples, see *Merchandising Corporation of America Inc* v *Harpbond Ltd* [1983] FSR 32.

to drawings of a technical or scientific character, such as maps, plans, and sketches. As each of these is specifically listed in the final category of article 2(1), it follows that they do not come under the heading of 'drawings and paintings'. The latter therefore seems restricted to drawings and paintings of the 'artistic', non-utilitarian type. Furthermore, as only plans and sketches pertaining to geography, topography, architecture, or science are referred to in article 2(1), this must mean that other kinds of 'non-artistic' plans and sketches, such as engineering and other technical drawings, are excluded from its scope altogether (see further para 8.73 below). This is an important point, as the laws of some Union countries, particularly those in the Commonwealth, do allow for the protection of such works as artistic works, and this has led to a number of practical problems.[169] However, it seems clear that article 2(1) contains no obligation to protect these works, and that Union countries are therefore free to deny protection in such instances. As far as the question of fixation in material form is concerned, this again is a matter for each country to determine for itself (article 2(2)). However, it should be noted that the factual possibility of unfixed drawings or paintings exists, as in the case of an ephemeral composition on a television screen or visual display unit.

8.44 **(ii) Sculptures:** Similar comments may be made about works of sculpture. These are essentially plastic works of art, that is, works expressed in three dimensions, but the ways in which they may be executed and the media which may be adopted for this purpose have increased enormously over the past century. In its normal usage, 'sculpture' embraces works in relief, in intaglio, and in the round. Casting, moulding, and carving have been the traditional methods of execution, but other methods have become just as acceptable in recent years, and some modern sculptures consist simply of arrangements or combinations of various man-made or natural objects. It goes without saying that size is quite irrelevant, and works of sculpture may range from the monumental, such as the Sphinx, to the minute, such as Meissen figurines and toy soldiers. These illustrations are given only to indicate the scope of the expression 'sculpture'. Once again, article 2(1) leaves it to national legislation to determine these limits. It should therefore be of no consequence that one country protects a borderline instance of sculpture while another does not. Finally, it should be noted that the possibility of unfixed sculptures exists, for example, sandcastles, holograms that are made by laser beams or even *tableaux vivants* that are composed of living figures. As noted above, article 2(2) leaves it entirely within the discretion of Union countries as to whether these kinds of unfixed works are to be protected.

---

[169] See generally Hugh Laddie, Peter Prescott, and Mary Vitoria, *The Modern Law of Copyright and Designs*, 3rd edn (2000) ('Laddie et al (2000)'), para 4.21 and see also *British Leyland Motor Corporation* v *Armstrong Patents Company Ltd* [1986] FSR 281; *Interlego AG* v *Tyco Industries Inc* [1988] RPC 343; *Interlego AG v Croner Trading Pty Ltd* (1993) 25 IPR 65.

(iii) Engravings and lithography: As regards works of engraving and lithography, these stand out as something of an oddity in the list of artistic works given in article 2(1). The reason for this is that both terms refer to the mode of making of the work, rather than the work itself, and are therefore superfluous in the light of the general definition of literary and artistic works which declares that the mode of expression of work is irrelevant. An engraving is an image or impression which is produced from an engraved or impressed plate or block. The engraving or impression may be done by a number of different methods, for example, by engraving a metal plate with acid ('etching'), using the same method to impress a photograph on a metal plate ('photogravure'), engraving on wood or some other soft surface ('woodcut', 'linocut'), and impressing an image onto a silk screen and printing from this ('silk-screen prints'). 'Lithographs' are also a form of engraving, and involve the engraving of an impression on a stone. Although this is not an exhaustive list of all the methods of engraving, the expression 'works of engraving and lithography' in article 2(1) seems unnecessary, as works produced by any of them should already be protected as 'works of drawing or painting', in the case of prints, and as 'works of drawing or sculpture', in the case of the blocks, stones, screens, and plate themselves. The enumeration of these works in article 2(1) can therefore only be explained as a matter of history. These were among the first kinds of artistic work to be protected, and enjoyed an enormous commercial market in the eighteenth and nineteenth centuries. England, for example, was the first country to accord such protection, doing so in 1734 at the behest of Hogarth, a noted engraver and painter of his time.[170] This was nearly 130 years before that country extended a general protection to artistic works.[171] **8.45**

(iv) Works of architecture: The inclusion of these among the works of art specified in article 2(1) requires special mention, as this is a leading instance where pressure from particular nations and interest groups led, relatively rapidly, to their international protection under the Convention, and to their corresponding protection in the domestic laws of all Union members. There was no reference to these works at any of the Berne Conferences of 1884 to 1886, although protection was accorded to 'plans, sketches and plastic works relative to . . . architecture'.[172] This meant that such things as architectural plans, drawings, and models were to be protected by each country. At this time, however, the actual result of the architect's work—the completed building or structure—did not receive specific legislative protection in any Berne Union country, although some accorded protection under the general heading of artistic works **8.46**

[170] Engraving Copyright Act 1735 (8 Geo II, c 13).
[171] Fine Arts Copyright Act 1862 (25 & 26 Vict, c 68).
[172] Berne Act, art 4.

in their jurisprudence.[173] Nevertheless, support for protecting architectural works specifically was to be found among academic authors,[174] and, following the Berne Conferences, international pressure in favour of this began to develop. In an article published in *Le Droit d'Auteur* in 1890, the Belgian writer, Jules Borchgrave, argued that architects were no less worthy of protection than writers, painters, or composers.[175] Starting from the premise that any artistic conception should give birth to an author's right, he urged that:

> works of architecture are obviously only a particular way of manifesting the human intellect in the artistic domain. Architects should therefore be protected in the same way and to the same extent as other artists.[176]

In arguing this, Borchgrave was not suggesting that any 'vulgar or banal' construction should be protected, but only those which, like any other artistic work, displayed an original character and bore the mark of human creativity.[177] His call for protection was soon taken up by ALAI which passed resolutions in favour of including works of architecture in the list of artistic works enumerated in article 4 of the 1886 Act.[178] In a comparative study published prior to the 1896 Paris Conference, the International Office examined the position of architectural works under the laws of different Union members, and recommended that they be accorded specific protection under the Convention as a matter of equity.[179] A proposal to this effect was therefore put to the Conference in the programme prepared by the French Government and International Office.[180] This met with strong opposition by some delegations, particularly the German and British,[181] whose laws did not provide for such protection, and which argued that the protection already accorded to architectural drawings and plans sufficed.[182] However, this regime had gaps so far as architects were concerned, as the construction of a building from plans was not necessarily considered as an infringing reproduction in many Union countries,[183] and in any event some buildings were constructed without pre-existing plans. Accordingly,

[173] See para 1.09 above. See further Darras (1887), 399, and the survey of national laws in [1895] *DA* 91, and [1899] *DA* 1.

[174] eg Darras (1887), 265, and E Pouillet, *Traité théorique et pratique de la propriété littéraire et artistique et du droit de representation* (1908), 85ff.

[175] [1890] *DA* 13. [176] ibid, 14. [177] ibid.

[178] Resolutions were passed at the ALAI Conferences at Neuchâtel in 1891, Milan in 1892 and Anvers in 1894: for the text of these resolutions, see ibid, 55.

[179] [1895] *DA* 91. [180] *Actes* 1896, 38. [181] ibid, 113, 168.

[182] ibid, 113 (Reichardt, German delegate).

[183] This was eg the case in the UK until the passing of the Copyright Act 1911, s 1; see Laddie et al (2000), 329, para 5.119; and in the US until the Architectural Works Copyright Protection Act of 1990, 17 USC §§ 101, 102(a)(8), 120, see *Demetriades* v *Kaufman*, 680 F Supp 658 (SDNY 1988), Jane C Ginsburg, 'Copyright in the 101st Congress: Commentary on the Visual Artists Rights Act and the Architectural Works Copyright Protection Act of 1990' (1990) 14 *Columbia-VLA Journal of Law & the Arts* 477.

the commission at the Paris Conference reached a compromise solution, under which a new paragraph was added to the Closing Protocol.[184] This provided that in countries where protection was accorded not only to architectural plans but also to the architectural works themselves, the latter were to be admitted to the benefits of the Convention as revised in the Paris Additional Act. No obligations, therefore, were laid on countries which did not protect architectural works, but, where this was the case, protection was to be accorded under the Convention. This was to be done without any condition of reciprocity, and the commission expressed the hope that this concession might induce those countries which did not presently accord protection to change their laws accordingly.[185]

It says something for the merits of this approach that within twelve years the attitudes of those governments which had been against protection had changed. In particular, the German Government no longer maintained its previous position, as it had extended protection to architectural works created for an artistic purpose in its new law of 1907.[186] It therefore proposed the protection of these works in the programme which it prepared jointly with the International Office for the 1908 Conference.[187] This took the form of an appropriate amendment to the paragraph of the Closing Protocol which had dealt with such works in the Additional Act of Paris.[188] However, the commission took the view that it was more logical to include them in the list of artistic works already contained in article 4 (now article 2(1)), and this was duly done.[189] Apart from reluctance on the part of the Swedish delegation,[190] the amendment was accepted without opposition, even though a number of countries still did not protect such works under their domestic law. An example of such a country was the UK, whose delegation in its report to the British Foreign Secretary stated that they had been 'convinced by the arguments put by M de Borchgrave, one of the Belgian Delegates, that the protection of works of architecture, as apart from the plans, etc, from which such works are constructed, is perfectly feasible'.[191] The main reason for this 'conversion' on the part of the British delegation was evidence that, in other jurisdictions, only those architectural works which possessed an **8.47**

[184] Berne Act, Closing Protocol, para 1A. See further *Actes* 1896, 166 (report of the commission).

[185] *Actes* 1896, 168.

[186] Law on Artistic and Photographic Works of 9 Jan 1907, art 2. [187] *Actes* 1908, 49.

[188] ibid. This provided: 'The stipulations of the present Conventions shall apply equally to works of architecture.'

[189] ibid, 239–40 (report of the commission). [190] ibid, 240.

[191] *Correspondence Respecting the Revised Convention of Berne for the Protection of Literary and Artistic Works, signed at Berlin, November 13, 1908* ('*Correspondence* (1908)'), 6 (G R Askwith and J de Salis to Sir E Grey).

original character were accorded protection.[192] This point was underlined by the commission in its report which stated:

> Protection will be refused to an ordinary commonplace construction which does not reveal the personality of its author; original artistic works are all that are intended to be protected.[193]

Protection of architectural works in the above sense was soon adopted by those Union countries whose domestic laws required amendment in order to give effect to their obligations under the Berlin Act.[194] The only exception was Norway, which chose to make a reservation upon accession to the new Act, in which it maintained its adherence to article 4 of the 1886 Act.[195] Since the Berlin Revision, architectural works have not received any further consideration in the subsequent revision conferences, except in relation to the issue of points of attachment (see para 6.17 above). Apart from the implicit requirement referred to by the Berlin commission that such works have an 'original character', the meaning of the expression 'work of architecture' remains undefined in the Convention. In its ordinary meaning, it is not confined to buildings, but extends to other kinds of structure which are fixed to the ground, for example, monuments, arches, fountains, steps, and so on. Many of these structures also embody or incorporate other works of art which are added by way of ornamentation or decoration. It seems that these can either be regarded as integral parts of the architectural work or as separate works of sculpture (as in the case of three-dimensional figures or works done in relief). In the absence of any Convention guidance on how these matters are to be treated, they remain for each member country to determine for itself. In this regard, it is of interest to note that in several common law jurisdictions the protection given to architectural works has now been extended even further, so as to cover structures of all kinds regardless of their architectural quality.[196]

(b) Photographic works to which are assimilated works expressed by a process analogous to photography

8.48 **(i) History of their protection**: These have been within the scope of the Convention since its inception, but have only enjoyed the status of enumeration in article 2(1) since the Brussels Revision. At the time of the 1884 to 1886 Conferences, the countries which participated took differing approaches to the

[192] See eg the Belgian case of *Defize* v *Guillemin*, Civil Tribunal, Liege, 7 June 1902, noted in [1902] *DA* 118, and the Danish case of *Christensen* v *Henriksen and Andersen*, Superior Court of Copenhagen, 17 Sept 1906, noted in [1907] *DA* 141.

[193] *Actes* 1908, 232.

[194] See eg Copyright Act 1911 (UK), ss 1(1) and 35(1); the Swedish Law concerning Works of the Figurative Arts, 30 May 1919, art 1.

[195] [1910] *DA* 113.

[196] See eg Copyright Act 1968 (Australia), ss 10(1) and 31.

protection of photographic works. Some, such as France and the UK, protected them along with other artistic works,[197] but others, such as Germany, refused to accord them this status and only granted a lesser level of protection.[198] The reasons for these differences were similar to those that exist in the case of cinematographic works (see paras 8.31ff above). With photographic works, the skill required to produce the final picture may only be the simple manual operation of operating a shutter or pushing a button. On the other hand, there may be considerable elements of skill involved in relation to such matters as choice and arrangement of subject, lighting, perspective, and so on. Whether these skills are those of authors is therefore something on which strong conflicting opinions can be held. These differences came out into the open at both the Conferences of 1884 and 1885, where the French moved for the inclusion of photographic works in article 4[199] and this met with strong German opposition.[200] This led the commission at the 1885 Conference to propose the adoption of an interim solution, whereby the following paragraphs were inserted in the Closing Protocol:

> 1. As regards Article 4, it is agreed that those countries of the Union where the character of artistic works is not refused to photographs engage to admit them to the benefits of the Convention concluded today, from the date of its coming into force. They shall, however, not be bound to protect the authors of such works further than is permitted by their own legislation except in the case of international engagements already existing, or which may hereafter be entered into by them.
>
> It is understood that an authorized photograph of a protected work of art shall enjoy legal protection in all countries of the Union, as contemplated by the said Convention, for the same period as the principal right of reproduction of the work itself subsists, and within the limits of private agreements between those who have legal rights.[201]

It will be seen from the second paragraph that the only photographic works which were to be protected by Union countries were those which were authorized photographs of a 'protected work of art', for example, a photograph of a painting, drawing, or sculpture. This was akin to protecting other kinds of derivative work, such as the translation of a literary work or the adaptation of a novel into a play: in any event, it should be noted that the making of an

[197] Fine Arts Copyright Act 1862 (UK), s 1. Specific statutory protection was also to be found in the Spanish Law of 10 Jan 1879, art 1. In France, this protection was to be found in the jurisprudence: see Darras (1887), para 320, and E Pouillet [1889] *DA* 54. The same was true in Belgium and Italy: see P Wauwermans, *Le droit des auteurs en Belgique* (1894), 144 (for Belgium) and H Rosmini [1889] *DA* 18, 30 (for Italy). For a general survey, see the International Office study in [1895] *DA* 116, 129.

[198] German Law of 10 Jan 1876; see further the commentary on this law in [1895] *DA* 116, 118. To similar effect was the Swiss Law of 23 Apr 1883, art 9.

[199] *Actes* 1884, 44; *Actes* 1885, 43. [200] ibid. [201] *Actes* 1885, 43, 54–5.

unauthorized photograph, translation, or adaptation would have been an infringement of the work photographed, as would the copying of an authorized photograph of the work itself. This provision was also anomalous in that it did not extend to photographs of protected literary works, for example, a photograph of a manuscript.[202] As regards other photographic works, that is, 'original' photographs of such subject matter as persons, animals, landscapes, buildings, and the like, protection under the Convention was limited to the extent to which such works were regarded in a given Union country as artistic works, or the extent to which such works were protected under the terms of a bilateral agreement between the countries concerned. Thus, if country A accorded protection to these photographs as artistic works, as was the case in France and the UK, that country was obliged to protect the photographs of authors claiming under the Convention. As no condition of reciprocity was required, this protection was to be accorded, irrespective of the fact that the countries to which these authors belonged did not protect photographs or accorded protection to them other than as artistic works.[203] This last point was important, because if country B protected photographs under another head, it was not obliged under the principle of national treatment to extend this protection to photographs emanating from another Union country in which artistic copyright protection was given.[204] As to bilateral agreements, there were several of these in operation in 1886 under which photographs were enumerated among the works which each country undertook to protect.[205] These agreements, of course, had no effect so far as other Union countries were concerned (leaving aside the flow-on effect of most favoured nation clauses in other bilateral agreements).

8.49 **(ii) Proposals at the 1896 Paris Conference**: The above compromise was unsatisfactory, as it did not entitle authors from states in which full protection existed to claim whatever protection was available in those countries where non-copyright protection was accorded. This anomaly was rectified by the Paris Revision Conference. Another French proposal for full Conventional protection was made here, but again encountered German opposition.[206] However, the following amendment to the Closing Protocol was proposed by the German delegation[207] and was adopted by the Conference:

> B. Photographic works and works produced by an analogous process shall be admitted to the benefits of these engagements in so far as the domestic laws of each

[202] Ladas (1938), 231–2. [203] [1895] *DA* 116, 118; Ladas (1938), 207–8.
[204] ibid.
[205] See eg the Spanish-Italian Convention of 26 June 1880, art 1, and the Franco-Italian Convention of 9 July 1884, art 1 (LCD (1889), vol II, 303).
[206] *Actes* 1896, 38–9, 113. [207] ibid, 167.

> State may permit, and to the extent of the protection accorded by such laws to similar national works.[208]

The result of this amendment was that each author claiming under the Convention would now be entitled to claim whatever protection was accorded to photographic works by a given Union country. In the words of the commission:

> No country is required to sacrifice its principles in according national treatment to Unionist countries. The essential thing is that protection be assured; the exact nature of this protection is of secondary importance.[209]

As under the Berne Act, no reciprocity was required, but the commission expressed the hope that all Union countries would ultimately protect photographic works,[210] and to this end suggested the following resolution which was adopted by the Conference:

> It is desirable . . . that, in all countries of the Union, the law should protect photographic works and works obtained by an analogous process, and that the length of such protection be at least fifteen years . . .[211]

It was further understood that the protection accorded under this new regime was subject to the provisions of article 2. Thus, the length of protection claimed could not exceed that granted in the country of origin, and no formalities could be required other than those prescribed in the country of origin. This last point as regards formalities was expressly confirmed in the Interpretative Declaration which was adopted by the 1896 Conference.[212] This had the status of an 'authentic' interpretation, and was accepted by all Union members, save one (the UK).[213] The application of article 2 to photographic works, however, gave rise to a practical problem, as it appeared to make it impossible for an author from a country where no protection was accorded to photographs to claim this in a country which did accord it. On the other hand, the Conference had made it quite clear that reciprocity was not required, and that such works were to be protected. The view of the International Office was that this intention was to prevail, and therefore that article 2 did not apply to photographic works which were not protected in their country of origin.[214] This was at least a tenable interpretation, as it could be argued that the Convention left the position of such works unclear, and it was therefore appropriate to have regard to the

---

208 ibid. 209 ibid. 210 ibid. 211 ibid, 229.

212 ibid, 167. This became para 1 of the Interpretative Declaration.

213 [1897] *DA* 104. Although the British delegation was not in disagreement with this interpretation, it felt that it could not sign it because of the difficulties that this might give rise to in relation to certain British colonies: *Correspondence* (1908), 7; see also [1899] *DA* 62, 64. Another reason was that the UK felt unable to accept the paragraph of the Declaration dealing with adaptations: *Actes* 1896, 142.

214 [1899] *DA* 62, 65. See also Ladas (1938), 229, and cf the contrary view expressed by Briggs (1906), 379–80.

expressed intention of the Conference that formulated these changes as a supplementary aid to interpretation. The paradoxical result of this interpretation, however, was that these works would enjoy national treatment without restriction in other Union countries and would therefore receive greater protection than photographic works from a country which accorded a shorter term of protection than that granted in the country where protection was claimed. This interpretation was adopted by at least one national tribunal,[215] and this served to highlight the need for some uniform Conventional provision regulating the protection of photographic works.

8.50 **(iii) Proposals at Berlin:** At the time of the Paris Additional Act, the status of photographic works varied greatly among Union countries. Some accorded protection to such works explicitly as artistic works (for example, the UK),[216] others did so implicitly (for example, France and Belgium),[217] others accorded special protection of a more limited nature (for example, Germany and Norway),[218] while two countries accorded no protection at all (Haiti and Tunis).[219] Over the following decade, however, general agreement between Union members began to emerge on the basic issue of protection, although differences still persisted as to how this should be done (whether as artistic works or otherwise), and over the extent of this protection, in particular, as regards duration. These considerations were reflected in an amendment to the Closing Protocol which was proposed by the German Government and International Office at the Berlin Revision Conference. This was to the effect that the protection of the Convention should apply to photographic works and works obtained by an analogous process, regardless of whether the law of a contracting country protected such works as artistic works or otherwise.[220] This formulation was adopted by the Conference,[221] which placed it in the body of the Convention as article 3. In addition, an express obligation was laid on each Union country to 'assure this protection'.[222] The new provision also omitted the second part of paragraph 1 of the Closing Protocol which dealt with the protection of authorized photographs of protected works of art. This was on the basis that such a provision was superfluous: if a work of art was protected, it was protected against any unauthorized form of reproduction, including photography, while the copying of a photograph of a protected work of art would also be an infringement of the copyright in the original.[223]

---

[215] See *Dobrecourt* v *Laegart*, Civil Tribunal, Brussels, 28 Nov 1906, noted in [1907] *DA* 50.

[216] See n 239 below. [217] See n 238 below.

[218] See n 240 below for Germany; as for Norway, see the Special Law concerning the Protection of Photographic Works of 12 May 1877, art 1.

[219] [1901] *DA* 138. [220] *Actes* 1908, 49–50. [221] ibid, 234–5.

[222] Berlin Act, art 3 (second sentence). [223] *Actes* 1908, 234 (report of the commission).

The Berlin Act represented a considerable advance on the 1896 Act in that each country was now required expressly to protect photographic works claiming under the Convention. The principles of national treatment, independence of protection, and absence of formalities were therefore applicable to these works. On the other hand, nothing was said about the duration of protection which was to be granted, as there was no consensus on this. This meant that widely differing periods of protection might be applied by the various countries of the Union.[224] Furthermore, as photographic works were still not included among literary and artistic works under article 2(1), this meant that they were not covered by those articles of the Convention which applied specifically to literary and artistic works, such as articles 9 and 10 which were concerned with lawful borrowings.[225] Of more fundamental importance was the fact that article 3 now explicitly enshrined the doctrinal differences that existed between Union countries as to the juridical nature of photographic works. In the words of the German Administration: **8.51**

> . . . although opinions as to the intrinsic nature of photographic works still vary greatly, it matters little whether they are considered under national law as works of art or are submitted to any special treatment; the important thing is that their protection be guaranteed in each country of the Union.[226]

This statement was quoted with approval by the commission at the Berlin Conference.[227] However, it should be noted that it contained an internal contradiction: if the Berne Convention was a convention for the protection of the rights of authors in their literary and artistic works, why should it extend protection to a category of subject matter which was not uniformly recognized as having the characteristics of a literary or artistic work by countries of the Union? This, surely, was a derogation from the fundamental object of the Union. On the other hand, from the point of view of those countries which did treat photographs as artistic works, article 3 of the Berlin Act was a satisfactory halfway house, a firm step in the direction of full Conventional recognition which could be attained at a subsequent conference of revision.

(iv) Lack of agreement at Rome: No progress, however, was made at the Rome Conference. This was not because of the absence of proposals—there were a multitude of these[228]—but once again because there was a lack of agreement on how to proceed beyond the basic proposition that some, unspecified form of protection should be accorded. The programme of the Italian Government and International Office included a proposal that the protection of photographic works and works produced by an analogous process should be given **8.52**

[224] ibid, 135. [225] Ladas (1938), 232. [226] *Actes* 1908, 49–50.
[227] ibid, 235. [228] *Actes* 1928, 226, 231.

'regardless of their merit or purpose'.[229] This would have expanded the scope of Conventional protection very considerably, as the Berlin Act had left the definition of what works were to be protected as 'photographic works' as a matter for national legislation. As a consequence, it was open to member countries under article 3 of the Berlin Act to protect all, or only some, categories of photographs. In a number of countries, therefore, only photographs of 'artistic value' were protected, while more banal or 'non-artistic' photographs were accorded a lesser level of protection or not protected at all.[230] The Italian Government/International Office proposal, however, required the protection of all photographs, irrespective of artistic merit. This was accepted by the majority of a special sub-committee which was appointed by the Conference to consider the question of photographic works, but was ultimately rejected by the Conference in its main commission.[231]

8.53 In contrast to the programme proposals, several other propositions at the Rome Conference proposed the inclusion of photographic works in article 2(1) and the deletion of article 3 altogether.[232] On one view, this would have restricted the class of photographs protected under the Convention, as the same element of originality or intellectual creation required for other works under article 2(1) would also have been required for photographic works. This proposal also attracted opposition and was rejected.[233] A more comprehensive amendment submitted by the French delegation proposed inclusion in article 2(1), but the retention of article 3 with new clauses laying down a minimum period of protection (twenty years) as well as compliance with certain formalities (inscription of the date of creation or publication and the name or mark of the author) as a condition of protection.[234] These propositions again gave rise to dissent, and to various counter-proposals.[235] The question of duration was finally dealt with in the context of article 7 where it was left to be determined by national legislation (see further paras 9.28ff below). As to the matter of formalities, this was opposed on the ground that these would be contrary to the basic principles of the Convention.[236] The result of these prolonged discussions was that nothing happened, and article 3 of the Berlin Act was maintained in the Rome Act.

8.54 The debates at Rome were nonetheless of value, as they revealed clearly the marked differences that existed among Union countries over the protection of photographic works. Many countries took the view that these works should be

229 *Actes* 1928, 67.

230 eg in France and Belgium, the courts attempted to protect only 'artistic' photographs, and exclude 'non-artistic' photographs from protection: Ladas (1938), 233.

231 *Actes* 1928, 185 (sub-committee), 290 (general commission).

232 Poland and the UK: ibid, 226 and 231.

233 ibid. 234 ibid, 98, 231. 235 ibid, 232. 236 ibid, 232.

protected as literary or artistic works if they possessed the same degree of originality or personal intellectual creation required for other kinds of works. However, there was considerable difficulty in defining the exact content of this requirement in the case of a photographic work, because of the fear of extending protection to purely banal kinds of photograph such as instantaneous camera pictures of people and events. In France and Belgium, for instance, where this approach was adopted, the courts often found it difficult to draw this distinction.[237] It was also arguable that any photograph, however simple or instantaneous, still required some element of personal creativity in relation to such matters as lighting, choice of perspective, and so on, and in this sense constituted an 'intellectual creation'. As a result, inconsistencies were to be found on these matters in the decisions of the French and Belgian courts, and in several instances protection was accorded to photographs of distant places which were themselves quite 'unartistic' but had great commercial value because of the trouble involved in taking them.[238] By contrast, in the UK, photographs were expressly protected as artistic works, but this protection was extended irrespective of artistic quality:[239] in other words, it was recognized that all photographs were on the same level as other literary and artistic works. In Germany in the 1930s, however, quite the opposite view began to be advanced: photographs of whatever kind were the result of purely mechanical operations involving technical skills, and therefore could not fall within the scope of the expression 'literary or artistic works'.[240] This was not to deny that such productions should be protected, but that this should be on a more limited basis and for a shorter period than in the case of literary or artistic works.[241] On the other hand, the logical result of treating photographic works as literary or artistic works was that they should then be protected to the same extent and for the same period as other kinds of works. This did not mean that non-artistic or unoriginal photographs lacked protection in those countries which sought to distinguish between 'artistic' and 'non-artistic' or unoriginal photographs, but that if such protection was given, it was usually akin to that which the Germans proposed should be given to all photographs under the German model.[242]

[237] Ladas (1938), 233–4.

[238] eg as in the case of photographs taken by Amundsen at the South Pole: *Amundsen* v *Juven*, Civil Tribunal, Seine, 28 Nov 1907, noted in [1909] *DA* 111 affirmed by the Court of Appeal, Paris, 5 Nov 1908, and noted in 'A Letter from France' in [1934] *DA* 105, where a number of later similar cases are also referred to.

[239] Copyright Act 1911, s 35(1): this was by implication, but was made explicit in the Copyright Act 1956, s 3(1).

[240] [1936] *DA* 39–41 (German propositions concerning photographic works for the Brussels Conference).

[241] ibid, 39.

[242] ibid.

8.55 (v) **The views of professional photographers:** Insofar as there was a position on these matters that was adopted by the practitioners of photography, this was to be found in the resolutions of an International Congress on Photographic Law that was held in Brussels in June 1935.[243] These urged that the Berne Convention should protect photographic works as artistic works, and that this protection should be accorded on the same basis as for other works.[244] It was clearly intended that this protection should not extend to 'non-artistic' works. In this respect, the proposals were open to the charge of elitism, in that their adoption would assure a privileged position to the 'art photographer' while leaving the works of ordinary photographers outside their scope. Nevertheless, they were taken as the basis for a French amendment that was submitted for the postponed 1936 Brussels Conference. This proposed that the Convention should protect photographs 'presenting the character of an intellectual creation'.[245] In direct contrast to this was a proposal by the German Government to leave each country free to determine the extent to which it would protect photographs.[246] This was in accord with recent German thinking on the nature of photographs,[247] and would have left each country free to adopt its own regime on the matter without any need to refer to the Convention or to accord protection to authors claiming under it.

8.56 (vi) **The Brussels Revision and the Paris Act treatment of photographs under the Convention:** At the 1948 Brussels Conference, the Belgian Government and International Office made no substantive proposals in relation to article 3, but the German and French proposals were in essence maintained.[248] However, a revised French amendment then proposed the inclusion of photographic works in article 2(1), with the following rewording of article 3:

> The present Convention applies to all photographic works or works realised by an analogous process to photography which constitute intellectual creations, with the exception of ordinary photographic productions.[249]

The inclusion of photographic works in article 2(1) was approved by a special sub-committee of the Conference, but without the addition of any special requirement of intellectual or personal creation.[250] In the view of the sub-committee, not only was the meaning of such a requirement 'inexact', but it was anomalous to apply to one particular category of work 'a criterion which applied to all productions dealt with by the Convention'.[251] This was accepted by the Conference, with the result that article 3 was deleted altogether, and

[243] *Compte-rendu du Congrès International de Droit Photographique, organisé à l'éxposition universelle de Bruxelles du 12 au 16 juin 1935* (1936).
[244] ibid. [245] [1936] *DA* 40. [246] ibid. [247] ibid, 39.
[248] *Documents* 1948 (1951), 167. [249] ibid, 168. [250] ibid, 111–12.
[251] ibid, 111.

photographic works and other works produced by an analogous process were now elevated, without qualification, to article 2(1). This position was left untouched by the Stockholm–Paris Revisions, with the result that photographic works now enjoy full protection as artistic works under the Convention, subject to the special provisions in article 7 concerning the duration of protection of such works (see further paras 9.28ff below).

On one view, the Brussels Revision can be seen as a triumph for the views of the International Congress on Photographic Law and of its sponsor, the French Government. Only 'artistic' photographs were to be protected henceforth under the Convention, and ordinary photographs now lay outside its scope.[252] However, this conclusion is open to doubt, in particular its equation of 'artistic' with 'originality' or 'intellectual creation'. The latter alone is relevant for the purposes of article 2(1), and much therefore depends upon how it is interpreted by the laws of each member country. As noted above, in some jurisdictions this element may be satisfied by the very skill involved in the taking of any photograph. Under this approach, the simple holiday snap is treated as the equal of the high-art photograph, and the skill of the photographer is equated with that of the writer, painter, or composer. Other countries, of course, may interpret the requirement of originality more stringently, and therefore strive to protect only those photographs where some additional artistic element can be seen.[253] However, since the European Union's imposition of a uniform and capacious originality criterion for photographs,[254] in effect in the twenty-five EU member states and in the four candidate states, as well as in other states who aspire to join the EU, there is less room for disparity in Berne Union members' setting of the originality threshold. The main thing to bear in mind is that, whatever the level of originality which one member state selects, that state cannot require the adoption of the same approach by other Union countries in which its own photographic authors seek protection. Thus, if Australia protects all photographs claiming under the Convention as original artistic works, it cannot require the same treatment for Australian authors in other Union countries which interpret the requirement of intellectual creation under article 2(1) more strictly. The room for differing interpretations of this requirement seems greater than is the case with other categories of works, but the debates at Rome and Paris indicate how difficult it is **8.57**

---

[252] See n 243 above.

[253] Under the prior German Law 'simple' photographs were accorded a lesser level of protection, Part II of the Law of 1965, art 72; German copyright law now makes no distinction for simple photographs. Law of 1965, art 72(3), amended by Laws of 24 June 1985 and 23 June 1995. Compare the situation in the UK. Under the UK Copyright, Designs and Patents Act 1988, s 1 protects, among other things, artistic works. Section 4(1)(a) then defines artistic works as including 'a graphic work, photograph, sculpture or collage, irrespective of artistic quality'.

[254] EU Duration Directive, art 6.

to arrive at a uniform view on this matter. A further problem that arises in the case of those countries which require a higher level of originality or intellectual creation is that some of these still accord protection to 'unoriginal' photographs as a species of 'related' or 'neighbouring' right. Such had been the case with the FRG.[255] As a result, the claimant of rights in a photograph that might fail to meet the EU Directive's 'own intellectual creation' standard, for example, an image made in a photomat machine, or one taken by a security surveillance camera, might not have been able to assert protection for his work in Germany by virtue of the Berne Convention, even though the German author of such work was protected under the special provisions of German domestic law. But the protection the domestic law in question affords non-original photographs falls outside the Convention's requirement of national treatment, because Berne does not embrace its subject matter.

8.58 (vii) **Assimilation of works expressed by a process analogous to photography:** The reference to works expressed or produced by 'analogous processes' dates back to the Paris Additional Act.[256] This indicates that, even then, new technical developments in relation to photography were envisaged, and it was intended that there should not be any shortfall in Conventional protection.[257] The Convention and *travaux préparatoires* do not say anything further on the meaning of 'analogous', but it is clear that the expression is intended to have a restrictive effect. This is shown by a comment of the study group which prepared the programme for the Stockholm Conference, when it explained why it did not propose a similar formulation to that which it had proposed for cinematographic works, that is 'works producing visual effects analogous to photography'.[258] 'Analogous effects' in this case would have included other categories of artistic work such as designs, engravings, etc. 'Analogous process', on the other hand, clearly confines this additional category to works produced by the chemical and technical processes characterizing photography.[259] 'Photography' in its ordinary meaning refers to the art or process of producing pictures by means of the chemical action of light on a sensitive film on a basis of paper, metal, glass, etc. Analogous processes therefore would have to involve the use of light in the production of an image, and would include such processes as heliogravure and photogravure (both of which would also fall within the category of engraving).[260] If both light and chemical action are required for the process to be

[255] See n 253 above. [256] Additional Act 1896, art 2.

[257] See the commentary in [1901] *DA* 139–40. A similar disposition was to be found in the German, Japanese, and Swiss Laws: ibid.

[258] *Records* 1967, vol I, 87 (Document S/1). [259] ibid.

[260] See further the views of the early commentators Dambach and D'Orelli referred to in [1901] *DA* 140.

considered 'analogous', then it might be uncertain whether digital photographs would come within the enumerated works. Digital photographs, like analogue photographs, result from the capturing of light, but no chemical action takes place until the image is printed out. If the image remains digitally stored in a computer or a memory card, then arguably, a necessary component of the 'analogous process' would be lacking, even though, in terms of the actual image, there would be no difference between a protected analogue photographic image which has been scanned into a computer, and a digitally generated image that has not yet been printed out. As this outcome seems rather absurd, and it is unlikely that the Stockholm drafters anticipated it when they considered the techniques of photography in the mid-1960s, it might make more sense to tie the concept of 'analogous process' to 'photo'—light—the key component in the term 'photograph'.

(c) Works of applied art

(i) The problem: One of the most vexed issues which has arisen in all national copyright systems had been the extent to which authors' rights in their artistic works should be protected where these works are used for industrial purposes. A closely related issue is the extent to which objects made by ordinary industrial processes for purely utilitarian purposes should be protected as artistic works, insofar as they comprise of artistic elements such as features of design and shape. Instances of the first arise where works of 'pure' art, such as drawings, paintings, or sculptures, are applied to, or incorporated in, utilitarian objects, such as wallpaper or curtains or the base of a lamp. Examples of the second include such everyday objects as furniture, electrical fittings, and motor parts which may still display some 'artistic' element in their general shape or appearance. These are not absolutely opposed situations, although it is true that in the first instance the 'pure' work of art precedes the industrial application, while in the second the artistic element is found in the industrial application itself. Rather, they represent the extreme poles of a vast continuum of articles in which artistic and industrial elements intermingle in differing degrees. This continuum includes such diverse objects as jewellery, glassware, ornamental glass, stained glass windows, clothing, children's toys, household accessories, lace and embroidery, fabric designs, and patterned mass-produced curtains. In each instance, the problem is the same: should the fact that art is applied in the production of objects which also serve a utilitarian purpose deprive the maker of the status of author, and consequently of the legal protection that is otherwise accorded to authors? **8.59**

(ii) National laws before the Berne Convention: Different approaches were adopted to this question by various national systems in the period before the Berne Convention. Many accorded some kind of limited protection to designs which were applied to articles, the earliest examples being found both in the **8.60**

UK[261] and France[262] in relation to textiles and other materials. This protection was usually distinct from copyright, and was closer to according an industrial property right similar to a patent. Novelty and some element of originality were usually required, and the duration of protection was generally for a more limited term.[263] However, it seemed anomalous that many applications of artistic works in the industrial sphere should be denied copyright protection where they quite obviously displayed artistic elements. If the painter of an indifferent landscape or portrait received copyright protection, why should not the artist-craftsman who designed and made an ornate table or dinner service? In France, the view came increasingly to be held during the course of the nineteenth century that the makers of such objects were entitled to copyright protection under the Law of 1793, and likewise that an artist did not lose the protection which he enjoyed in relation to his 'pure' work simply by reason of the fact that he turned it to an industrial use, for instance, by using it as a design for a utilitarian object. In other words, there occurred a total assimilation of all works of art, however they were manifested or applied, to full copyright protection.[264] So far as the separate designs laws were concerned, these continued to exist, but the possibility of cumulative protection under these as well as the copyright law was accepted (the former, of course, was of far less duration).[265] This development did not take place immediately. Indeed, it took nearly a century before French law fully recognized the doctrine that has become known as 'unity of art'.[266] In the course of this development, French courts and legislators experimented with a range of different criteria that would serve to distinguish artistic works from subject matter which was industrial and 'non-artistic' in character. These included the method of reproduction of the work, the purpose behind its creation, the predominant

---

261 The Designing and Printing of Linens Act 1787 (27 Geo 3, c 38); the Designing and Printing of Linens Act 1794 (34 Geo 3, c 23); the Designs Copyright Act 1839 (2 & 3 Vict, c 17).

262 French Law of 1806 (*Bulletin des Lois*, 4th ser, IV, 352, 354). For the background to this law, see G Finniss, 'The Theory of "Unity of Art" and the Protection of Designs and Models in French Law' (1964) 46 *JPOS* 615.

263 See eg the Designs Copyright Act 1839 (UK), s 1, under which it was required that the design be 'new and original', and protection was accorded for only twelve months.

264 See Finniss (n 262 above), 616ff. See further J H Reichman, 'Design Protection in Domestic and Foreign Copyright Law: From the Berne Revision of 1948 to the Copyright Act of 1976' [1983] *Duke Law Journal* 1143, 1153ff; Y Gaubiac, 'La théorie de l'unité de l'art' (1982) 111 *RIDA* 2, 42ff; K M Mott, 'Analysis of the "Unity of Art" Concept in European Legal Systems' (1964) 11 *Bulletin of the Copyright Society of the USA* 242, 243ff. See further S P Ladas, *Patents, Trademarks, and Related Rights: National and International Protection* (1975), 827ff; M A Perot-Morel, *Les Principes de Protection des Dessins et Modèles dans les pays de Marché Commun* (1968), 15ff; Lucas and Lucas (n 13 above), paras 74–6.

265 See nn 262, 263 above.

266 Finniss (n 262 above), 615–18. The chief theorist was Eugène Pouillet: see E Pouillet, *Traité théorique et pratique de la propriété littéraire et artistique et du droit de représentation*, 2nd edn (1894) and *Traité théorique et pratique des dessins et modèles industriels*, 5th edn by A Taillefer and C Claro (1911).

purpose of the work, the status of the creator, and its artistic value.[267] Each was found unsatisfactory, because exceptions could always be envisaged which made the criterion in question unworkable or uncertain. They depended too much on the making of subjective and often arbitrary judgements. For example, utilitarian purposes may exist equally with artistic purposes, or may be mixed together in differing degrees. How are such matters to be ascertained and weighed against each other? On the other hand, a work may be intended to have a purely utilitarian purpose but still have clear artistic value, and vice versa. Again, 'pure' artistic works may still be made by processes that are 'industrial', while manufacturers of commonplace articles may still be artists, and vice versa. It was against this background of uncertainty that French law moved towards the adoption of the doctrine of 'unity of art', which has been explained by one distinguished commentator as follows:

> The theory of 'unity of art' has its basis in the refusal to make any distinction between 'pure art' and 'industrial art'. It extends protection insured by the copyright law to all creations of form, even the most modest, those which, on the 'lower' frontier of applied art, depend on what is called 'industrial aesthetics'. It finds its explanation—and, we think, its justification—in the idea that an adequate distinction is impossible between 'major art' and 'minor art', all criteria to which one may have recourse to this effect being subject to the accusation of subjectivity or being powerless, in other ways, to solve the borderline cases.[268]

In adopting this view, the French were taking the most extreme position. Although its all-embracing nature may be criticized,[269] it is logical and avoids the manifold difficulties that arise when an attempt is made to fix a boundary beyond which works of industrial art will not be protected. This was the case in many other European countries, including Italy and Germany, where their respective laws sought to exclude the more 'industrial' kinds of work from protection.[270] Even more reluctant to protect such works was the UK which maintained a far more rigid separation, and after 1911 denied copyright protection altogether in the case of an artistic work which was 'industrially applied' (defined to mean the multiplication of more than fifty objects to which the work was applied).[271] On the other hand, UK law after that date did accord protection to three-dimensional objects which were entitled 'works of artistic craftsmanship'.[272] The scope of this protection, however, was uncertain, and

[267] Reichman (n 264 above), 1155–6; Gaubiac (n 264 above), 46ff; Mott (n 264 above), 246ff; Finniss (n 262 above), 618ff.

[268] Finniss (n 262 above), 615.

[269] Reichman (n 264 above), 1159ff.

[270] See the commentaries on these laws in [1909] *DA* 114 and 128.

[271] Copyright Act 1911, s 22(1), and Design Rules 1932, r 92. As to the position before the 1911 Act, see the commentary in [1909] *DA* 125ff and Laddie et al (2000), 175ff.

[272] Copyright Act 1911, s 35(1).

gave rise to considerable judicial difficulty in determining the degree of artistic merit that was required for protection to be accorded to such works.[273] This caused particular problems in light of the fact that, as regards other kinds of artistic work, British law expressly excluded any requirement of artistic merit.[274]

8.61 (iii) **The Berlin Revision:** From the foregoing it will be seen that, in the early years of the Berne Convention, there were great differences in the approaches taken by member countries to the question of protection of artistic works in the industrial sphere. The French law at least provided an unambiguous model, while other national laws offered a wide number of alternatives, ranging from those which approximated the French, through those which were increasingly restrictive, to the rigid separatist approach of the UK. Because of this lack of consensus, the question was not discussed at the early conferences of the Berne Convention, and was not raised until the time of the Berlin Revision. At this Conference, the German Administration and the International Office proposed the inclusion of 'works . . . of art applied to industry' ('*oeuvres . . . d'art appliqué à l'industrie*') in the enumeration of works in article 4(1), arguing in support that these works had recently been assimilated to artistic works in some important countries, and that:

> . . . the artificial boundaries established between pure art and art used in everyday life can no longer be maintained, neither from a doctrinal point of view nor from that of practical necessity.[275]

This proposal was supplemented by a French proposition to add the words 'whatever their merit or purpose' immediately after the words 'works . . . of art applied to industry'.[276] This amendment was based on the French Law of 1902 which had introduced a similar provision into French law,[277] and was intended to underline the fact that the protection of a work of art, no more than in the case of a literary work, should not be dependent on the aesthetic opinions of judges or the purpose for which the work may be used. Nevertheless, while there was strong support for these proposals from a number of delegations and they even appeared to command assent from a majority,[278] there was 'irreducible opposition' on the part of certain others, in particular the English and Swiss delegations.[279] The result was that no amendment was made to article 4 (now article 2(1) in the Berlin Act), but works of art applied industrially were dealt

---

273 See further Laddie et al (2000), 195ff.
274 Copyright Act 1911, s 35(1).
275 *Actes* 1908, 42. 276 ibid, 188.
277 Special Law of 11 Mar 1902.
278 *Actes* 1908, 231, 233 (report of Renault, *rapporteur*). See further the commentary in [1909] *DA* 113, 114.
279 ibid, 233.

with in a separate paragraph which followed the precedents already set in relation to choreographic and architectural works by the Paris Additional Act. This paragraph (article 2(4)) provided simply for the application of national treatment, without any requirement of reciprocity, in the following terms:

> Works of art applied to industry are protected to the extent permitted by the internal legislation of each country.

This provision gave rise to grave imbalances, as authors of artistic works from countries of the Union which adopted the 'unity of art' approach would be denied protection in those Union countries which did not take this approach, while authors from the latter countries would receive, in the former, the benefit of protection which they did not enjoy in their own countries of origin. However, it met the objections of the British and Swiss delegations, and so far as the former was concerned left the UK 'free to determine if they [works of art applied industrially] should be protected as works of art or as industrial designs and models'.[280] Furthermore, as an accommodation of two irreconcilable points of view, it commanded fairly general acceptance from Union members: only two countries (France and Tunisia) felt strongly enough about this lack of reciprocity to make reservations in relation to this when ratifying the Berlin Act.[281] The effect of these reservations was that both countries declared, in accordance with article 27 of that Act, that they would continue to apply article 4 of the Berne Act in place of article 2(4) of the Berlin Act so far as works of art applied to industry were concerned. As article 4 had made no mention of these works in the list of literary and artistic works, both France and Tunisia were therefore under no obligation to extend the benefit of their generous 'unity of art' laws to artistic works from other Union countries.

(iv) The fiasco at Rome: The Berlin compromise, however, was only seen as a **8.62**
holding operation by certain countries, notably France, and at the Rome Revision Conference another attempt was made to accord full Conventional protection to works of art industrially applied. In the intervening period, there had been resolutions in favour of this passed by a number of international bodies, including two congresses of ALAI,[282] and it seemed that the national laws of most Union members, including the UK, were moving closer to according full copyright protection to such works, or were no longer excluding them expressly

[280] These were the comments made by the British delegates to the Conference (G R Askwith and J de Salis) in their report to the Foreign Secretary, Sir Edward Grey: see *Correspondence* (1908), 8.

[281] [1910] *DA* 115 (France); [1911] *DA* 29 (Tunisia).

[282] At Copenhagen in 1909 and in Paris in 1925: see *Actes* 1928, 36 and [1925] *DA* 83 for the texts of the respective resolutions.

from protection. This, at least, was the view of the Italian Government and International Office which made the following argument in their programme for the Conference:

> It may therefore be affirmed that the great majority of countries of the Union seem fully in favour of this protection. And this can only be applauded, because it seems inadmissible that a work of art should be deprived of protection because the form in which it is clothed renders it appropriate for a practical use . . . or because the artistic work has been applied subsequently to a practical end . . . or because it has been multiplied industrially. All these applications of the work are foreign to the original creation of the author, which is the only essential element which characterises a protected work.[283]

As to the fact that many countries continued to give special protection by way of laws on designs and models, the programme asserted that this should not prevent the application of copyright laws to those designs and models which resulted from an artistic creation.[284] Accordingly, it was proposed that artistic works applied industrially should be protected without restriction. This involved the deletion of article 2(4), the inclusion of these works in the enumeration in article 2(1), and the amendment of article 2(3) so as to read: 'The above mentioned works enjoy protection in all countries of the Union whatever their merit or purpose.'[285] As another purpose of the programme for the Rome Conference was the reduction of the number of reservations made to the earlier Acts of the Convention,[286] this proposal would have removed the need for the French and Tunisian reservations in relation to these kinds of artistic work. Strong support for it was received from the French, Danish, Polish, Czech, German, Austrian, and Belgian delegations,[287] but there was still opposition expressed by several delegations.[288] The chief of these, oddly enough, was the Italian delegation which had certain reservations about the proposal of which it was co-sponsor. These reservations revealed that a considerable gulf still divided Italy from those countries which accepted the full implications of the 'unity of art' doctrine. Thus, the former still saw the matter of novelty as being relevant to these kinds of work and argued for the need for some form of deposit.[289] It also suggested that it might be difficult to determine the question of duration as the identity of the creator of an industrial model was frequently unknown.[290] Furthermore, one of the Italian delegates argued that the problem would remain of distinguishing 'an artistic work destined for an industrial purpose from a purely industrial product without any artistic character', and insisted therefore on the necessity of

283 *Actes* 1928, 64ff. 284 ibid, 65. 285 ibid, 65, 67.
286 ibid, 62 (comments in the programme).
287 ibid, 227 (summary of proposals and discussions).
288 In particular, the British, Japanese, Hungarian, and Norwegian delegations: ibid, 227–8.
289 ibid, 227. 290 ibid.

leaving to national legislation the power to limit the scope of the original programme proposal[291] (which now became identified with its principal proponents, the French). This ambivalence on the part of the Italian Government introduced an element of confusion into the Conference discussions, but may help explain that Government's later apparent complete *volte-face* on the issue of protection (see below). As for the British Government, its response was more conciliatory: it 'understood' the desire of France to accord such protection and would not deny that account should be taken of it to some extent, but asked that the Convention should leave a certain latitude to contracting states to interpret what was meant by an 'applied work of art'.[292] This view was shared by the Norwegian and Hungarian delegations.[293] Another important industrial nation, Japan, which did not accord copyright protection to these works, also thought that the French proposal went too far, particularly if it applied to works created in a series.[294]

Accordingly, the Conference considered a series of different compromise proposals which sought to take account of these conflicting views, in particular the French objection to the lack of reciprocity under the Berlin provision and the British insistence that, if works of applied art were to be protected, the definition of these works should be left to national legislation.[295] A sub-committee which was appointed to consider the matter failed to reach a firm proposal,[296] and, in the light of the failure of these discussions, the Italian delegation withdrew the proposal which it had made (and only partially supported) in the programme.[297] It therefore proposed that article 2(4) of the Berlin Act should be preserved, and France made it clear that it would maintain its reservation in relation to this provision.[298] After further efforts, a compromise was worked out in negotiations between the French, British, and Norwegian delegations, and the following amendment, to be known as article 2*ter* was proposed: **8.63**

> Works of art applied industrially are to be protected to the extent permitted by the internal legislation of each country. Nevertheless, it is reserved to the legislation of the country where protection is claimed to determine the conditions under which protection is to be accorded to these works. But the countries of the Union are not obliged to accord to these works a longer period of protection than they enjoy in their country of origin. And these works will only be protected by the present article if they are protected without formality by the law of their country of origin.[299]

[291] ibid. [292] ibid. [293] ibid, 228. [294] ibid, 227–8.
[295] See generally ibid, 227–8. [296] ibid, 190. See further Ladas (1938), 249.
[297] ibid, 229. [298] ibid.
[299] For the text of this resolution, see ibid, and for the views of one of the participants in this exercise, see A Raestad, *La Convention de Berne révisée à Rome 1928 . . .* (1931), 140.

It will be seen that this amendment embodied an element of reciprocity, which satisfied French objections: the latter would not be obliged to accord protection under its generous laws to the works of Union authors for any longer than the period for which these works were protected in their country of origin, and would not, in any event, be required to protect works which were only protected in their countries of origin subject to compliance with formalities. This second qualification therefore absolved France from any necessity of protecting works which were only protected under industrial designs and models legislation in countries such as the UK. On the other hand, it meant that, within these limitations, Union authors would now be able to gain protection in France which had previously been denied to them under the reservation made by France in relation to the Berlin Act. At the same time, it left countries free to determine for themselves the scope that was to be accorded to 'works of art applied industrially'. As a result, the UK would be able to maintain its laws under which some applied artistic works were accorded copyright protection, while others were eligible only for registered designs protection. As a compromise formula, article 2ter embodied a fairer solution than that contained in article 2(4) of the Berlin Act, and would possibly have encouraged Union countries to move towards the adoption of uniform approaches to the protection of these kinds of works under their domestic laws. On the other hand, while there were precedents for requiring reciprocity in relation to particular matters under the Convention (see, for example, article 7(3) of the Berlin Act), it was nonetheless contrary to the overall philosophy of the Convention. This was the argument made by the Italian delegation which opposed the compromise,[300] although, as suggested above, another reason for their opposition may have been deep-seated doubts concerning the doctrine of unity of art. The Italian response evoked some anger from the French delegates, who clearly felt frustrated in view of the concessions which they themselves had made in the formulation of the compromise proposal.[301] Certainly, the objection over reciprocity could be viewed as specious: although material reciprocity is not required by the Convention, the fact that it contains a large number of prescriptions on substantive matters ensures that each member country accords a minimum of protection to the works of Union authors and this reduces the effects of imbalances that may arise. In the case of industrially applied artistic works, the requirement of reciprocity could therefore be justified as the Convention contained no substantive

[300] *Actes* 1928, 229, 289 (statement by one of the Italian delegates in the second plenary session of the Conference).

[301] ibid, 227 (speech by G Maillard).

prescriptions in relation to them.[302] Opposition to article 2ter also came from the Japanese, who, unlike the British, would have been required to change their domestic law in order to adhere to this new stipulation, and were clearly unwilling to do so.[303] Accordingly, the article failed to achieve unanimous support from the Conference, with the result that article 2(4) of the Berlin Act was maintained.[304] In the light of this, France declared that it would continue its reservation in respect of this provision, and invited other Union countries to enter into a restricted Union with it on the basis of reciprocity in relation to industrially applied works of art.[305]

The failure of the Rome Revision Conference to achieve anything as regards these kinds of works illustrates something of the strengths and weaknesses of the Berne Convention. As stated above, the proposed article 2ter was an equitable compromise solution which accommodated several widely diverging approaches to the protection of industrial applications of artistic works. Nevertheless, this proposal, which had taken considerable time and effort to arrive at, was defeated by the requirement under article 24 of the Berlin Act that changes to the Convention must receive the unanimous assent of the countries which comprise the Union. Accordingly, it was open to a small minority of member countries (in this instance, two out of twenty-eight)[306] to veto a change which was approved by every other member country. The exercise of the 'veto' on this occasion led to considerable animosity on the part of certain delegations, notably the French,[307] and it is quite possible that this affected other discussions and negotiations that took place during that Conference. Although this is not the place to discuss in full the merits and disadvantages of the principle of unanimity (for this, see para 16.05 below), its application in this instance by the Italians and Japanese can be defended, at least in part, on the ground that the time was not yet ripe for the adoption of the compromise represented by article 2ter. The fact that successive revision conferences have been able to achieve unanimity on a wide number of important substantive issues is in itself remarkable, but an essential precondition has always been that each member country has already adopted the Conventional approach on these matters in its domestic **8.64**

[302] eg a further requirement of material reciprocity was contained in art 7(2) of the Berlin Act in relation to duration of protection. See further the comments of the Belgian Government and International Office in their programme for the Brussels Conference: *Documents 1948* (1951), 143.

[303] *Actes* 1928, 227–8. [304] ibid, 287. [305] ibid, 288–9 (Maillard).

[306] According to the records of the Conference, these countries were Italy and Japan: ibid, 287. However, it appears that Australia was also prepared to apply its veto, but withdrew this after being convinced that the proposed art 2ter did not threaten the established system under Australian law, which was very similar to that of the UK: *International Copyright Conference, Rome, May and June 1928: Report of the Australian Delegate (Sir W Harrison Moore)* (1928).

[307] *Actes* 1928, 288 (Maillard).

copyright law, or has been prepared to see the merit of doing so. Accordingly, a degree of prior consensus has always preceded any advance in the level of protection offered by the Convention. In many instances, this has meant the adoption of transitional provisions which have allowed member countries time to bring their laws into line with the new principle, but even these kinds of provision require readiness on the part of all member countries to move towards this objective. Time and timing are therefore of the utmost importance in making any change to the Convention. So far as works of art industrially applied are concerned, the result of the 1928 Revision should not surprise us. There were still fundamental divisions between member countries as to how these works should be treated, and because of this it was not yet appropriate that the Convention deal with them. Viewed in this light, the Berlin amendment should not have been allowed in the first place, while the final compromise proposed at Rome was simply a repair job aimed at rectifying the damage done by the earlier provision. In truth, the more appropriate (and least painful) course of action at the Rome Revision Conference would have been to remove article 2(4) from the Convention until such time as greater international consensus on the protection of these kinds of works had emerged.

8.65 (v) **The Brussels solution**: The Brussels Revision witnessed the achievement of the regime which continues in substance today under the Stockholm, Paris Acts. Following the debacle of the Rome Conference, the International Office did not include any proposal concerning works of art applied to industry in the preliminary programme which it distributed to member countries in the preparations for the 1936 Conference. Furthermore, no specific proposals were submitted by member countries at this time. In an article published in *Le Droit d'Auteur* in 1938, the International Office suggested that the best way forward might be to establish protection under the Convention for some categories of applied works of art on the basis that some protection was better than none at all.[308] Accordingly, it would be necessary to identify those kinds of works which all member countries agreed merited protection.[309] However, strong support for the grant of full Convention protection to all categories of applied artistic works was expressed at a number of international conferences during the 1930s,[310] and after World War II the International Office, together with the Belgian Government, returned to this position in the revised set of proposals

[308] [1928] *DA* 79, 80. [309] ibid.

[310] See the texts of the resolutions of these conferences in *Documents 1948* (1951), 434ff, in particular that of the ALAI Conference at Montreux in 1935.

they circulated for the 1948 Conference.[311] These rejected the notion of enumerating the kinds of applied works to be protected, arguing that to do so would be a step backwards from the then-current position under the Convention.[312] Accordingly, they repeated the proposals that had been originally put to the Berlin and Rome Conferences: the inclusion of 'works of art applied to industry' in article 2(1), the deletion of article 2(4), and its replacement by a general paragraph providing that the works mentioned in the article should be protected in all countries of the Union 'whatever their merit or purpose'.[313] Once again, this proposal received the predictable support of the French,[314] but as in 1928 it failed to secure unanimous support.[315] In 1941, the Italian Government had enacted a new copyright law under which artistic works were protected even where they were industrially applied.[316] However, this was subject to the condition that the 'artistic value' of the objects thus produced could be distinguished from their 'industrial character'.[317] This last requirement can be readily criticized, but it indicates that under her new law Italy was as far as ever from adopting the doctrine of 'unity of art'. The same was true in the UK and those member countries which derived their copyright laws from the UK.[318] As a result, both countries were only prepared to agree to the inclusion of applied artistic works in article 2(1) if the capacity of national legislation to define the notion of a work of applied art was retained.[319] Both countries also argued that account should be taken of the views of those Union countries which were opposed to the possibility of cumulative protection for works of applied art under copyright and registered designs laws.[320] On the other hand, the French delegation insisted on the need for reciprocity in relation to the conditions, extent, nature, and duration of protection.[321] Following consideration by a special sub-committee, the following amendments were proposed and approved by the general commission of the Conference:[322]

1. 'Works of applied art' were added to the enumeration in article 2(1) after 'photographic works and those produced by process analogous to photography'. The reference to 'industry' was deleted following an objection by

[311] *Documents 1948* (1951), 141–4. [312] ibid, 143. [313] ibid, 146–7.
[314] ibid, 148. [315] ibid, 158.
[316] Italian Law of 22 Apr 1941, art 2(4). See further Reichman (n 264 above), 2000; Ladas (n 264 above) 842, and V de Sanctis, 'Lettre d'Italie' [1956] *DA* 127ff.
[317] ibid.
[318] The Copyright Act 1911 still remained in force, and its provisions concerning industrial applications of artistic works were replicated in many Commonwealth countries, eg in the Australian Copyright Act 1912, which simply adopted the UK Act.
[319] *Documents 1948* (1951), 158.
[320] ibid, see also 122 (report of sub-committee on applied works of art).
[321] ibid, 158–9. [322] ibid, 159.

the British delegation that this was restrictive, as it was possible to envisage the application of artistic works in domains other than industry.[323]

2. Article 2(4) of the Berlin and Rome Acts was replaced by the following paragraph (which now became article 2(5)):

> It shall be a matter for legislation in the countries of the Union to determine the extent of the application of their laws to works of applied art and industrial designs and models, as well as the conditions under which such works, designs and models shall be protected. Works protected in the country of origin solely as designs and models shall be entitled in other countries of the Union only to such protection as shall be accorded to designs and models in such countries.[324]

8.66 These amendments to the Brussels Act represented a more far-reaching compromise solution than that proposed at the Rome Conference. On the one hand, works of applied art had finally attained promotion to article 2(1). On the other hand, it was left to member countries to determine the extent to which such works would be protected under their laws on copyright or their laws on industrial designs and models. This reservation was in turn subject to a condition of reciprocity: where one member country only protected a particular work of applied art as a design or model, the author of that work would only be entitled to receive, in other countries of the Union, the protection that the laws of those countries accorded to designs and models. This removed the principal French objection to article 2(4) of the Berlin and Rome Acts, and enabled that country to withdraw its reservation in relation to that provision. The result of this was that works of applied art of Union authors would now be entitled to full copyright protection in France, as long as their protection in their country of origin was not restricted to that available under laws relating to designs and models. It will be noted that the reciprocity allowed under this paragraph only came into operation where the *sole* protection for a work of applied art in its country of origin was under designs or models legislation. If country A (the country of origin) accorded both copyright and designs protection to such works, country B (the country where protection was claimed) could not restrict the protection available to that work under its laws. In other words, if country B also accorded cumulative protection, it could not limit the foreign work to designs protection, but would have to grant full copyright protection.

8.67 On the other hand, the new provision contained a significant lacuna: no stipulation was made as to what was to happen where a work of applied art was only entitled to designs or model protection in country A, but there was no equivalent protection available in country B. The latter might occur because country B had

[323] ibid, 158. [324] Brussels Act, art 2(5).

no designs legislation (as in the Netherlands),[325] or because the work in question did not qualify for such protection, for example, for such reasons as lack of novelty, failure to register in time, and so on. In these situations, the implication to be drawn from article 2(5) was that these works were not entitled to any protection in country B. Another problem arose where the definition of what was an applied artistic work was not found in national legislation, but was determined on a case-by-case basis by national tribunals. If the jurisprudence of country A took a more restrictive view than the jurisprudence of country B, could courts in country B limit the protection available to works emanating from country A accordingly? In other words, did article 2(5) allow for the application of reciprocity at this level? The answer to this seems to be that a restriction of this kind could not be made for the following reason: member countries were obliged to protect works of applied art under article 2(1), but it was left to each to determine the extent to which their copyright and designs laws applied to such works. However, it was only where copyright protection was excluded in country A by reason of the sole application of designs legislation that copyright protection in country B could be refused. Accordingly, if the only restriction of protection in country A was to be found in the jurisprudence of that country, the courts in country B were not entitled to adopt a corresponding reduction in protection.[326]

(vi) The Paris Act: Article 2(5) of the Brussels Act was left in basically the **8.68**
same form by the Stockholm and Paris Revision Conferences. No real attempt was made in the preparations for these Conferences to move any closer to the concept of 'unity of art', and it may be said that the Brussels 'solution' still represents the most that can be achieved in this regard. The controversy over pure and applied art still continues, but this has shifted to different areas, and is now largely removed from the sphere of the Berne Convention (see para 8.69 below).[327] At the time of the Stockholm Revision, the only proposal in the programme concerning applied works of art related to the duration of their protection (see article 7(4)), and a consequential amendment to article 2(4) made it subject to this provision.[328] A far more radical proposition was made by

[325] The Netherlands had no specific designs legislation until 1975; see generally H Cohen Jehoram, 'Specific Design Protection in Benelux and Dutch Law', in Cohen Jehoram (ed), *Design Protection* (1976), 21; Cohen Jehoram, 'Designs Laws in Continental Europe and their Relation to Copyright' [1981] *EIPR* 235, 237; J H Reichman, 'Designs Protection after the Copyright Act 1976: A Comparative View of the Emerging Interim Models' (1984) 31 *Journal of the Copyright Society of the USA* 267, 289.

[326] See further 'Sur l'interpretation de l'article 2, alinéa 5, de la Convention de Berne revisée à Bruxelles' [1951] *DA* 111, 112–14.

[327] Ladas (n 264 above), 837.

[328] *Records* 1967, vol I, 88 (Document S/1).

Denmark.[329] This proposed the deletion of article 2(5), with the consequence that it would henceforth be obligatory for member states to protect applied works of art without qualification. In support of this, the Danish delegate referred to the experience in his own country where such works were entitled to full copyright protection, which might be cumulative with designs protection in the case of industrial designs.[330] However, the crusading spirit of the earlier conferences was no longer present, and there were no interventions by any of the 'unity of art' countries such as France or Belgium recorded in the minutes. Indeed, the Danish delegate was eager to accommodate the objections of the UK, Australia, Italy, and Japan and proposed a transitional arrangement under which these countries would be able to make reservations concerning their maintenance of industrial designs protection in respect of these kinds of works.[331] This, it seemed, was an acceptable sacrifice to make in order to gain full Convention protection. In the event, the Danish amendment was rejected by thirteen votes to eleven, with eleven more abstentions;[332] a more limited Dutch proposal was also withdrawn.[333] The only change made to article 2(5) (apart from the consequential amendment contained in the programme) came from an Italian proposition which filled the gap (referred to in para 8.67 above) as regards works which enjoyed industrial designs protection only in their country of origin and therefore had no protection in those Union countries which did not have industrial designs laws.[334] Accordingly, the last sentence of article 2(5) (which now became article 2(7)) was reworded as follows:

> Works protected in the country of origin solely as designs and models shall be entitled in another country of the Union only to such special protection as is granted in that country to designs and models; however, if no such protection is granted in that country, such works shall be protected as artistic works.[335]

It will be seen that this appears to permit an imbalance in protection to arise as between different countries of the Union. For example, an artistic work which is registered as an industrial design in a country of the Union which has non-cumulative designs protection will be entitled to full copyright protection in a country of the Union which has no special designs law. However, although there was more likelihood of this situation arising immediately after the Stockholm Revision, this has diminished as the great majority of Union countries now possess some form of designs protection (whether this is exclusive of, or cumulative

[329] *Records* 1967, vol I, 696 (Document S/99).
[330] ibid, vol II, 882 (minutes of Main Committee I).
[331] ibid. [332] ibid, 897. [333] ibid (Document S/140, vol I, 699).
[334] ibid (Document S/161, vol I, 702).
[335] See further ibid, 1152 (report of Main Committee I).

with, artistic copyright protection).[336] The real problem under the Brussels and Stockholm Acts is that it is necessary for the court in the country where protection is claimed to satisfy itself as to the applicable law in the country of origin of the applied artistic work. This is always a difficult process, and one that is avoided where the principle of national treatment is adopted in an unqualified fashion.

(vii) The general relationship between copyright and designs protection: Our discussion of the position of works of applied art under the Berne Convention would be incomplete without some further comments on the general relationship between copyright and designs protection. It will be clear from the above that the Brussels Act really marked the end of international efforts to bring industrial designs and models under the umbrella of artistic copyright. From this time on, more emphasis has come to be placed on the provision of separate, *sui generis* protection for these works, and most Berne Union countries now have their own laws on industrial models and designs.[337] The form of these laws varies, but the distinctive features include the need for registration or deposit,[338], requirements of novelty and originality,[339] and limited terms of protection (for example, article 12 of the 2002 EU Designs Regulation provides for five-year terms, renewable to a maximum of twenty-five years from the date of filing).[340] This national tendency has been reflected in the Paris Convention for the Protection of Industrial Property, under which an express obligation to protect industrial designs has been laid on member countries since the revision of that Convention in Lisbon in 1958.[341] As the membership of the Paris Union **8.69**

[336] See generally Reichman (n 325 above), and Ladas (n 264 above), 844ff.

[337] ibid.

[338] There are two notable exceptions: the UK's unregistered design right, introduced by the Copyright, Designs and Patents Act 1988, which confers automatic protection (against copying) for designs of the shape of three-dimensional articles (whether visually attractive or not) for up to fifteen years; and the EC's unregistered Community Design, introduced by Regulation on the Community Design, 6/2002 of 12 Dec 2001, which gives protection (against copying) to designs which are new and possess individual character for three years from their being 'made available'.

[339] Article 25 of the TRIPs Agreement requires members to protect 'independently created industrial designs that are new or original' but permits members to provide that 'designs are not new or original if they do not significantly differ from known designs or combinations of known design features.' The EU Designs Regulation sets a different threshold: the design must be new and possess 'individual character' (arts 4(1), 6) (in the other four official languages of the Office: 'présente un caractère individuel'; 'carácter singular'; 'un carattere individuale'; 'Eigenart'). The test of individual character is whether 'the overall impression it produces on the informed user differs from the overall impression produced on such a user by any design which has been made available to the public'.

[340] The TRIPs Agreement, art 26(3), imposes a minimum ten-year period of protection for industrial designs.

[341] Lisbon Act (1958), Paris Convention, art 5^{quinquies}. See further G H C Bodenhausen, *Guide to the Application of the Paris Convention for the Protection of Industrial Property* (1991), 88.

largely overlaps with that of the Berne Union, this led a number of 'unity of art' countries, such as Belgium, which previously had no special designs laws, to enact such laws, while in other countries which have always had such laws, these have been retained and, in many cases, have been subjected to scrutiny and revision.[342] At the present time, it is possible to identify three broad national approaches to the protection of works of applied art in Berne Union countries:

1. *Cumulative protection of works of applied art under both artistic copyright and designs laws.* Under this approach, if designs protection is unavailable (for example, because of lack of novelty, prior user, etc) or is not obtained, the artist can fall back on copyright protection. Perhaps the leading example of this approach is to be found in France under the 'unity of art' doctrine.
2. *Partial cumulative protection.* Under this approach, cumulative protection may be accorded, but not for all works of applied art.[343] Thus, some national copyright laws provide that if an industrial design or model is to gain protection it must display some additional quality, for example, it must manifest some 'marked artistic character' (as under the Benelux Law),[344] or fulfil the requirements necessary for an artistic work (as under German Law).[345] There are, of course, significant differences as to what will be admitted to the category of an artistic work under each of these national laws, but the fact that they recognize the possibility of cumulative protection to some degree is an acknowledgement of the 'vagueness of the frontier between designs and works of art'.[346]
3. *Non-cumulative protection.* This approach seeks to distinguish more precisely between artistic works 'properly speaking' and industrial designs, clearly excluding or restricting copyright protection in the case of the latter. The criteria for drawing this distinction vary considerably; for example, in

342 See further Ladas (n 264 above), 836ff; Reichman (n 264 above), 1164ff.

343 This seems to be the minimum required by the EU Designs Regulation. While art 96(2) of the Regulation requires member states to adopt a policy of cumulation of copyright, it leaves it to member states to determine 'the extent to which, and the conditions under which, such protection is conferred, including the level of originality required'.

344 Uniform Benelux Designs Law 1975, art 21(1) and (2). See further Cohen Jehoram (ed), *Design Protection: Reports at an International Symposium Held in Amsterdam, May 20–21* (1975), 21ff.

345 German Law of 1965, art 2(1). On the way in which the German courts approached the issue of copyright protection for such designs, see A Dietz, 'Letter from the Federal Republic of Germany' [1974] *Copyright* 87 and [1980] *Copyright* 85, 90.

346 Ladas (n 264 above), 840. The EU Designs Regulation, art 96(2), allows for cumulative design and copyright protection, and specifies that 'The extent to which, and the conditions under which, such protection is conferred, including the level of originality required, shall be determined by each Member State.' On the Regulation, see eg C-H Massa and A Strowel, 'Community Design: Cinderella Revamped' [2003] *EIPR* 68; M Schlotelburg, 'The Community Design: First Experience with Registrations' [2003] *EIPR* 383.

Australia copyright protection is limited once an artistic work is registered as an industrial design or the work is industrially applied,[347] while in the USA, the design elements of a 'useful article' are protectable by copyright 'only if, and only to the extent that, such design incorporates pictorial, graphic or sculptural features that can be identified separately from, and are capable of existing independently of, the utilitarian aspects of the article'.[348]

There are, of course, a wide range of variations within each approach, but for present purposes it suffices to note that each is compatible with the compromise formula established under the Brussels and Stockholm Acts. As a matter of logic, it might be thought undesirable that works of applied art should fall within the purview of two major international conventions, those of Berne and Paris. However, although considerable work has been carried out on an international level on the content and scope of designs laws, cumulative protection remains a well-established phenomenon, and there have been no significant proposals made to end this situation. Thus, an International Study Group on the Protection of Works of Applied Art and Designs (representing the Berne and Paris Unions and UNESCO) which reported in 1959, agreed that although it might be desirable to make such a distinction this was not easy to do, and that cumulative protection did not really involve any practical difficulties.[349] A similar view is implicit in a resolution adopted by the Congress of AIPPI in 1966,[350] as well as in the WIPO Model Law on Designs which was published in 1970.[351] Accordingly, the current situation under which each member of the Berne Union remains free to determine whether, to what extent, and under what conditions, it will protect works of applied art under separate designs laws appears unlikely to be changed in the foreseeable future.

(d) Illustrations, maps, plans, sketches, and plastic works relative to geography, topography, architecture, or science

(i) History of their protection: This is a miscellaneous category of works which has been included, in substance, in the definition of 'literary and artistic works' since the inception of the Convention. In the draft convention proposed **8.70**

[347] Copyright Act 1968, ss 74–7.

[348] US Copyright Act, 17 USC § 101 (definition of 'pictorial, graphic and sculptural work').

[349] [1959] *DA* 108. See also *UNESCO Copyright Bulletin* [1959], no XII, no 1.

[350] AIPPI *Annuaire* [1966], Part II, Tokyo Congress, 22. For further background to this, see Ladas (n 264 above), 868.

[351] Model Law on Designs for Developing Countries (1970), art 1(2). For further reading on the international protection of industrial designs, see F Hepp, 'La protection internationale des arts appliqués' (1957) 14 *RIDA* 115; J-L Duchemin, 'La protection internationale des oeuvres des arts appliqués' (1956) 12 *RIDA* 85; G Bolla, 'Oeuvres des arts appliqués et dessins ou modèles industriels: vers une solution internationale nouvelle' (1959) 24 *RIDA* 55; R Plaisant, 'La protection des arts appliqués: Besoins nouveaux, ideés nouvelles' [1957] *DA* 160, 192.

by ALAI in 1883, a different formulation was adopted: after the words 'works of drawing, painting, sculpture, engraving, lithography . . .' the words 'geographical charts, plans, scientific sketches . . .' were added.[352] This wording was in turn adopted in the Federal Council programme for the 1884 Diplomatic Conference,[353] but was extended by that Conference to include 'illustrations' and 'plastic [or three-dimensional] works relative to geography, topography, architecture or the natural sciences'.[354] These additions derived from a German proposal,[355] and were accepted by the Conference, which changed the words 'natural sciences' to 'science in general', so as to avoid too restrictive an interpretation.[356] This was left unchanged by the 1885 Conference,[357] and the wording finally adopted in the 1886 Act therefore read as follows:

> . . . lithographs, illustrations, geographical charts; plans, sketches, and plastic works, relative to geography, topography, architecture, or science in general; . . .[358]

The wording has remained substantially the same since this time, except for the following minor changes:

1. 'Lithographs' were coupled with 'engravings' in the Berlin Act, which was a more natural relationship given that they are essentially works of the same kind.[359] In the same Act, the words 'in general' were deleted after 'science': this would not appear to make any substantive difference in meaning.[360]
2. In the English translation of the Rome Act, the semi-colon after 'geographical charts' was deleted, so that the enumeration then read as follows:

   > . . . illustrations, geographical charts, plans, sketches, and plastic works, relative to geography, topography, architecture, or science.[361]

   In the French text, however, the semi-colon between 'geographical charts' and 'plans' was retained in the successive Acts. The significance of this change in punctuation is discussed below.
3. In the Brussels Act, the comma after 'plastic works' was deleted[362] (this comma had never been inserted in the successive English translations of the different Acts).
4. In the Stockholm Act, the English words 'geographical charts' were replaced by the word 'maps'; this, again, did not appear to be a change of any significance, except that 'maps' was a more concise translation of the French expression '*les cartes géographiques*'.[363]

8.71 There is relatively little guidance to be derived from the records of the successive

[352] Article 2, in *Actes* 1884, 7. [353] Article 4, ibid, 11.
[354] ibid, 45 (art 4). [355] ibid, 44. [356] ibid.
[357] *Actes* 1885, 43. [358] Berne Act 1886, art 4. [359] Berlin Act, art 2(1).
[360] Nothing was said directly on this point by the commission in is report: ibid, 229ff.
[361] Rome Act, art 2(1). [362] Brussels Act, art 2(1). [363] Stockholm Art, art 2(1).

revision conferences on the interpretation or scope of any of these terms. As a preliminary point, the difference in punctuation in the English and French texts is of significance, as under the latter it is clear that 'illustrations' and 'maps' are to be treated as a distinct sub-category under article 2(1). Under the English text, however, it might be argued that these works are only to be protected if they are 'relative to geography, topography . . .', etc, and this would therefore exclude categories of illustrations that pertained to other matters. These illustrations might, in any event, be covered under the preceding categories of 'works of painting, drawing, . . . engraving', but it is possible to argue that this should not be so (see para 8.72 below). As for maps, the qualification that these should only be relative to 'geography, topography . . .', etc, is clearly superfluous. As the French text prevails in case of differences of opinion on the interpretation of the various texts,[364] in this instance the French punctuation is to be followed.

(ii) 'Illustrations and maps': What meanings, then, are to be given to these **8.72** terms? In the case of 'illustrations', it might be argued that these are already covered by the categories of drawings, paintings, and engravings. However, it can also be argued that the latter refer to works in their own right, in the sense that a drawing, painting, or engraving stands on its own. 'Illustrations', on the other hand, are intended to accompany other works, usually a literary production such as a book, and the reason for their specific mention in article 2(1) can therefore be seen as a clear indication that such works are not to be excluded from protection under national laws on the basis that they are not 'proper' works of painting, drawing, or engraving. A similar reason can be given for the inclusion of maps, although again these could probably be brought within the same categories. However, 'maps' have a special character, as they generally combine both artistic and literary elements. While they have usually been accorded protection, either explicitly or implicitly, under national legislation,[365] their inclusion in article 2(1) ensures that this will be the case. One matter which article 2(1) leaves to national legislation is whether its protection extends to three-dimensional illustrations and maps. Even in 1886, 'pop-up' illustrations in children's books cannot have been unknown, and in the present age the creation of three-dimensional images by the use of laser beams is a device which has been used in the presentation of illustrations and maps. Furthermore, maps of areas of land may now be shown in a series of changing images thrown onto a visual display screen. While the latter may be eligible for protection as

[364] Stockholm, Paris Acts, art 37(1)(c).
[365] See eg UK Copyright, Designs and Patents Act 1988, s 4(2) (map as graphic work); France, Code de la propriété intellectuelle, art L 112–2; German Law of 1965, art 2(7); Copyright Act 1957 (India), s 2(i).

cinematographic works, there would be no reason why national legislation could not protect them as 'maps'.

8.73 (iii) **'Plans, sketches and plastic works'**: The last category of works—'plans, sketches and plastic works'—is restricted by the requirement that they must pertain to geography, topography, architecture, or science. It seems clear here that a distinction was being drawn by the drafters of the 1886 Act between works that could be protected as paintings, drawings, or engravings, on the one hand, and as plans and sketches, on the other. Likewise, a distinction was intended between sculptures and architectural works, on the one hand, and plastic works, on the other. Nothing is recorded as having been said on these matters in the records of the 1884 to 1886 Conferences, but in the discussions which occurred at the Paris Conference of 1896 in relation to architectural works it seemed to be implicitly accepted that the specific reference in article 2(1) to architectural drawings was necessary to ensure their protection.[366] Writing in 1938, Ladas suggested that the terms 'plans' and 'sketches' were intended to refer to works not in themselves artistic or prepared as studies for artistic works.[367] The same can also be inferred in relation to the term 'plastic works': this must refer to three-dimensional works not in themselves artistic and therefore incapable of constituting sculptures or architectural works. This raises the difficult issue already discussed in relation to works of applied art: how is one to determine whether a work is artistic or not? This remains a matter for national legislation, but the wording of article 2(1) indicates that such a distinction is to be drawn and that the only non-artistic plans, sketches, and plastic works that are required to be protected are those which pertain to geography, topography, architecture, or science. The last four terms will themselves require definition under national legislation, but examples of such works would be sketches of topographical and architectural features and three-dimensional models of landscape, buildings, or scientific experiments. An important consequence follows from this: Union countries are not obliged to protect such works as engineering and technical drawings or models, as these are not 'plans', 'sketches', or 'plastic works' for the purposes of article 2(1).[368] The only way of avoiding this conclusion is to argue that such works pertain to 'science', or alternatively that they are 'artistic', and therefore within the general category of 'drawings'. Both arguments are difficult to maintain, and there is no real point in attempting to do so. As the enumeration in article 2(1) is purely inclusive, it is open to any member country to protect such works as intellectual creations and 'productions in the literary, scientific and artistic domain'. This, in fact, is the case in many Union countries where these works are protected either explicitly or implicitly under

[366] *Actes* 1896, 113 (comments of German delegation).
[367] Ladas (1938), 228. [368] ibid.

national legislation.[369] However, it is equally open to any member country to refuse to accord such protection.

(8) Other categories of works required to be protected under the Convention

Article 2(1) does not list all the categories of works which member countries are obliged to protect under the Convention. Protection is also required to be given to certain other kinds of works under some of the remaining paragraphs of that article. Article 2(3) deals with the position of 'derivative works' such as translations, adaptations, and the like; and article 2(5) relates to collections of literary or artistic works, such as encyclopaedias and anthologies. These are discussed in turn below. This section will conclude with a discussion whether the Convention also requires the protection of two newer categories of works not explicitly enumerated in article 2: databases and computer software. The section that follows will address subject matter excluded from the protection of the Convention. **8.74**

D. Derivative Works: Translations, Adaptations, Musical Arrangements, and Other Transformations of a Literary or Artistic Work

(1) Meaning of 'derivative work'

As a broad generalization, it can be said that the works listed in article 2(1) are original or 'primary' works, in the sense that none of them are derived directly from pre-existing works or subject matter. This last statement requires a little explanation: it should not be taken to mean that these primary works cannot be based on ideas, themes, or subjects that are well known and in the public domain. In most cases, this will be true, but as ideas, themes, and the like are not themselves subject to copyright, this does not prevent works which are based on them from being regarded as primary works. In each instance, the author has given the old idea his or her own particular form of expression, and this entitles his work to be regarded as a 'production in the literary scientific or artistic domain' within the meaning of article 2(1). However, there are a large number of works which derive directly from pre-existing works, in that they use more than the ideas or themes embodied in these earlier works and incorporate **8.75**

[369] eg as in the UK and many Commonwealth countries: see generally Laddie et al (2000), 622ff, and S Ricketson, *The Law of Intellectual Property* (1984), 121–2. Cf the position in the Germany where the extent of such protection appears to be more limited: see A Dietz, 'Letter from the Federal Republic of Germany' [1980] *Copyright* 85, 129 and [1984] *Copyright* 426, 435, and H Davis-Ferid, 'Copyright in Technical Drawings under German Law' [1980] *EIPR* 28.

identifiable parts of the form in which these ideas or themes were expressed. In many instances, these usages or 'borrowings' may be actionable infringements, but it can still be said that the person making the derivative work has expended sufficient skill and labour for the latter to be regarded as an intellectual creation deserving of protection in its own right. In other words, while the person making a derivative work may be an infringer of the rights in another work, he has altered the form of that work in such a way for him to be regarded just as much an author as the author of the primary work. There are many instances of derivative works, but the principal ones which have been recognized historically in both national laws and international conventions have been translations, adaptations, and musical arrangements.[370] In each instance, it is clear that the acts of translation, adaptation, and arrangements go far beyond simple plagiarism; at the same time, the resultant work is parasitic on the work which is translated, adapted, or arranged, and is not a primary work in the sense of the works listed in article 2(1). In the Berne Convention, these matters are dealt with in article 2(3) which provides as follows:

> Translations, adaptations, arrangements of music and other alterations of a literary or artistic work shall be protected as original works without prejudice to the copyright in the original work.

In this formulation, it will be clear from the context that the adjective 'original' is used in two different senses: first, to indicate that translations, adaptations, etc, are to be treated on the same footing as other works protected under the Convention, that is, as intellectual creations and 'productions in the literary, scientific and artistic domain', and, secondly, to distinguish them from the original or primary work from which they are derived, and whose own copyright protection the derivative work does not affect (or 'prejudice').

(a) History of article 2(3)

8.76 In the ALAI draft of 1883, 'arrangements of music' were included in the list of primary works to be protected under article 2 of that text.[371] This was maintained in the Federal Council programme (although now as article 2),[372] but at the Diplomatic Conference of 1884, on the initiative of the German delegation, the words were deleted,[373] and relegated to a separate article in which musical arrangements were treated as a form of infringement of a musical composition (article 10) (see also para 8.28 above). Although the latter article underwent

[370] See eg Laddie et al (2000), 88ff (as to the UK); Desbois (1978), 32ff, 143ff (as to France). For an example of an early bilateral convention which accorded protection to both arrangements of music and translations as original works, see the Franco-Portuguese Convention of 11 July 1866 (LCD (1889), vol II, 339).

[371] *Actes* 1884, 7. [372] ibid, 11. [373] ibid, 30, 44.

considerable revision at the Conference of 1885,[374] the exclusion of musical arrangements from the list of primary works to be protected under article 4 was maintained in the final Act of 1888.[375] As regards 'translations', these were dealt with separately in article 6 of the ALAI text as follows:

> An authorised translation is to be protected in the same way as the original work. In the case of a translation of a work in the public domain, the translator may not object to the translation of that work by other writers.[376]

This became article 8 of the Federal Council programme for the 1884 Diplomatic Conference,[377] which altered the draft so as to apply to translations generally (not simply authorized translations).[378] It also changed the second sentence to take account of the fact that translation rights under the 1884 text were not coterminous with reproduction rights. The new article (now renumbered as article 7) read as follows:

> Translations are expressly assimilated to original works. They shall enjoy the same protection stipulated by articles 2 and 3 as regards their unauthorised reproduction in the countries of the Union. In the case of a work for which the right of translation is in the public domain, the translator may not oppose the translation of that work by other authors.[379]

At the 1885 Conference, the adjective 'lawful' was inserted before 'translations' in the first sentence.[380] No real explanation of this change was given, but it should be noted that 'lawful' is not the same as 'authorised', as something may be lawful in the sense that it is allowed by law even if done without the permission, express or implied, of the author. It may also be said that the question of whether or not a translation is authorized or unauthorized should not be relevant to the question of whether the translation is to be protected as an original work: such recognition does not in any way affect the relations between the author of the original work and the translator. Be this as it may, 'lawful translations' was the wording adopted by the 1885 Conference, and in turn by the final Act of 1886, along with certain other inconsequential drafting changes (including the renumbering of the article as article 6).[381]

It will be recalled that, at the 1884 to 1886 Conferences, one of the principal **8.77** issues that occupied delegates was the extent to which the acts of adaptation, musical arrangement, and the like, should be regarded as illicit reproductions of a literary or artistic work which should be prohibited under the Convention. Particular difficulties were encountered as regards the meaning of these terms, and these matters took up considerable time both at the Berne Conferences[382]

---

374 *Actes* 1885, 48–9. 375 ibid, 43. 376 *Actes* 1884, 8.
377 ibid, 12. 378 ibid, 49–50. 379 ibid, 79. 380 *Actes* 1884, 45.
381 Berne Act 1886, art 8. 382 *Actes* 1884, 34; *Actes* 1885, 48ff.

and at the subsequent Paris Conference of 1898.[383] While these discussions are directly relevant for our present purposes (see below), they did not address the associated issue of whether adaptations and musical arrangements themselves should be protected as original works. However, given that the skills necessary for adaptation and arrangement can be compared to those necessary for translation, it was logical to extend protection to the works resulting from these activities. This was adverted to by the German Association for the Protection of Industrial Property in a resolution which it passed at its congress in Berlin in 1905. This called for the expression 'literary and artistic works' in article 4 of the Berne Act to include 'reproductions or utilisations of a work of all kinds, notably translations, adaptations, dramatisations, reproductions of a drama in prose, abridgements, musical arrangements, . . .'.[384] In turn, the German Government, in the programme which it prepared jointly with the International Office for the Conference, proposed the inclusion of 'adaptations and other transformations of a work' in article 4.[385] It also proposed that article 6 be amended by the deletion of the adjective 'lawful', the addition of the words 'without prejudice to the rights of the author of the original work', and the substitution of the words 'by the present Convention' for the words 'by articles 2 and 3'.[386] In addition, it proposed the deletion of the last sentence of article 6 on the ground that this was superfluous in view of the fact that, if a translator had no rights in the work translated, his only right was to prevent appropriations of his own translation.[387] In the commission, however, it was decided to bring translations within the ambit of article 2, and these were coupled, in a separate paragraph of that article, with 'adaptations, musical arrangements and other reproductions in an altered form of a literary or artistic work'.[388] No mention was made of whether the translation, adaptation, etc, should be authorized or lawful in order to obtain protection. The commission made it clear that these matters were quite irrelevant to the question of whether such works should be protected: there was no justification for allowing the work of the author of an unauthorized translation, adaptation, etc to be 'reproduced with impunity'. If these works had been made without authority, this was solely a matter for the translator or adapter and the author of the original work. To make this clear, the commission proposed the insertion of the words 'without prejudice to the rights of the author of the original work' into the new paragraph.[389] These changes were duly approved by the Conference,[390] and the new provision (now article 2(2) of the Berlin Act) read as follows:

[383] *Actes* 1896, 116–17. [384] *Actes* 1908, 84 (text of resolution). [385] ibid, 42.
[386] ibid, 44. [387] ibid. [388] ibid, 232 (report of Renault).
[389] ibid. [390] ibid, 214.

> Translations, adaptations, arrangements of music and other reproductions in an altered form of a literary or artistic work . . . shall be protected as original works without prejudice to the rights of the author of the original work.

Although there have been other additions and deletions made to this provision, these are not relevant to our present discussion, and the above wording has been retained, in substance, in each successive revision of the Convention (it now appears as article 2(3)). Only drafting changes have been made: at the Brussels Conference, the French word '*ouvrages*' was replaced by '*oeuvres*' (this made no difference to the English word 'works'),[391] and the expression 'reproductions in an altered form' was replaced by the more economical 'alterations'.[392] However, several more substantive attempts at amendment have been made. The first was at the Rome Conference in 1928, where the Polish delegation proposed the deletion of the words 'as original works', on the ground that derivative works could not be completely assimilated to original works as they were always dependent on the existence of the latter.[393] While this is logically correct, as suggested above, the meaning of article 2(2) is plain enough: these works are to be protected in the same way as those listed in article 2(1) (for instance, as to the scope and duration of protection), and this stipulation is not affected by the fact that derivative works are analytically distinct from original or primary works. This was clearly the view taken by the Rome Conference, which was not prepared to make an unnecessary change to the Convention.[394] The second amendment, which arose at the Brussels Conference, originated from an ALAI proposal that the words 'cinematographic adaptations' should be inserted after the words 'translations, adaptations'.[395] This was thought to be unnecessary, because article 2(2) already referred generally to 'adaptations', and a similar attitude was taken to a proposal by CISAC that the words 'of whatever kind' be added after 'adaptations'.[396]

(b) The scope of the present provision: translations

It still remains to consider the meaning and scope of the present article 2(3). As is the case with so many terms used in the Convention, the outer limits of each of the terms in article 2(3) is ultimately a matter for national legislation. So far as translations are concerned, it is quite clear from the records of the early conferences that this term was intended to refer to the product of turning a literary or dramatic work from one language into another. In English, it is possible for 'translation' to bear a more figurative meaning. The *Shorter Oxford English Dictionary* gives the following interpretation: **8.78**

[391] *Documents 1948* (1951), 158. [392] ibid.
[393] *Actes* 1928, 117, 230. [394] ibid, 230.
[395] Referred to in the programme for the Conference in *Documents 1948* (1951), 144.
[396] ibid.

> . . . the expression or rendering of something in another medium, form, or mode of expression. . . . Transformation, alteration, change; changing or adapting to another use.[397]

However, in view of the fact that article 2(3) refers separately to adaptations and alterations, it seems reasonable to restrict translations to changes from one language to another. Even within these limits, there is room for interpretation by national legislation: does translation cover the rendering of spoken work into sign language? Again, does translation cover the changing of a set of written instructions for the programming of a computer into a form which can only be understood by the computer (often referred to as a 'machine-readable' language)? Does it cover revising a computer program written to work on one kind of 'platform' into a program compatible with a different kind of computer? These kinds of questions are left to national legislation to determine, though the increasingly pervasive inclusion of computer software within the subject matter of copyright (see further discussion at paras 8.92ff below) may yield sufficiently similar answers to these questions as a matter of domestic law to constitute a form of 'state practice' affecting interpretation of the Berne Convention.

(c) Arrangements of music and adaptations

8.79 No further guidance is provided by the Convention as to the meaning of these terms. In normal musical usage, an 'arrangement of music' involves the addition of different harmonic and rhythmic parts to a basic melody line, or the rearrangement of a set of parts, as in the case of a pianoforte setting of an orchestral work.[398] 'Arrangement' therefore involves a number of distinct skills, including those of harmonization, transposition, and transcription (the knowledge of how to render a part for one voice or instrument into a part for another). 'Adaptation' is a more generalized concept, and may apply to all kinds of works. The adaptation of a work essentially involves its modification so as to serve another purpose. The most obvious examples to be found in the cultural traditions of most Berne Union members are the following: the transformation of a novel into a play or dramatico-musical work and vice versa, the transformation of a piece in prose to verse and vice versa, the modification of a play or story for cinematographic or choreographic presentation and vice versa; the making of a three-dimensional version of a two-dimensional artistic work and vice versa. Western literary tradition has many celebrated instances of works that have been constantly adapted, including the stories of Romeo and Juliet, Dr Faustus and the Lady of the Camelias (each of which has received dramatic, literary, musical, and cinematographic treatment in succeeding generations).

[397] *Shorter Oxford English Dictionary*, 5th edn, vol II (2002), 3328.
[398] See further, P A Scholes, *The Oxford Companion to Music*, 10th edn (1970), 53ff.

Although little was said at the time of the Berlin Conference as to the precise scope of the term 'adaptations', it seems clear from the later conferences that a wide interpretation was intended. In this regard, the rejection of the proposal to add the qualifying words 'of whatever kind' to article 2(2) at the time of the preparations for the Brussels Conference (see above) is significant: it was assumed that the word 'adaptations' needed no further amplification, and this view was obviously accepted by the Conference (see para 8.80 below).[399]

(d) An historical digression

It is important to note at this point that the sense in which 'adaptation' and 'musical arrangement' were used in article 10 of the Berne Act (which related to the question of illicit reproductions) was much narrower than that accorded it in the present context. Thus, article 10 (which subsequently became article 12 in the Berlin and Rome Acts) provided that: **8.80**

> The following shall be specifically included amongst the illicit reproductions to which the present Convention applies: unauthorized indirect reproductions of a literary or artistic work, of various kinds, such as adaptations, musical arrangements, etc, when they are only the reproduction of a particular work, in the same form, or in another form, without essential alterations, additions, or abridgements, so as not to present the character of a new original work.

It will be apparent that the kinds of adaptations and musical arrangements referred to in this article were those which were not, in themselves, capable of constituting original works. In a sense, the words 'adaptation' and 'musical arrangement' were inappropriate, as the level of adaptation or arrangement in these instances must be minimal for the resultant work not to 'present the character of a new original work'. In reality, the kinds of acts contemplated by article 10 were those which are referred to in Anglo-American copyright law as 'colourable imitations', and nothing more.[400] There was clearly, at this stage, considerable confusion over the scope of these expressions, and article 10 left open the question of whether adaptations and musical arrangements which did constitute original works (and which were surely the bulk of their respective genera) were to be regarded as illicit reproductions if they had been made without the authority of the owner of the copyright in the work adapted or arranged. There were clear differences between member countries on these questions, and considerable time was spent at the Berne and Paris Conferences discussing them.[401] In this regard, the following interpretation which was adopted at the Paris Conference was significant. This provided that:

[399] *Documents 1948* (1951), 144.

[400] See eg Laddie et al (2000), 137ff.

[401] *Actes* 1884, 57–8; *Actes* 1885, 48–50; *Actes* 1896, 172–3.

> Transformation of a novel into a theatrical piece, or of a theatrical piece into a novel shall be governed by the provisions of Article 10.[402]

This was useful inasmuch as it indicated that these were to be regarded as species of adaptations of the 'non-original' (derivative work) kind and hence as illicit reproductions. By parity of reasoning, therefore, in the more usual case where such transformations did constitute original works in their own right they could be regarded as adaptations in the more general sense of that term. However, the status of such works under the Convention was unclear, as the only derivative works specifically protected under the Convention at that time were translations (article 6). When the Berlin Act was adopted further, potential confusion arose. Article 2(2) of that Act now expressly protected 'adaptations', but article 10 (which became article 12) was amended in a strange way. The Interpretative Declaration of Paris was deleted and incorporated in article 12, but rather than treating transformations of novels, etc, as sub-categories of the wider genus of 'adaptations', the former were listed as separated examples of 'unauthorized indirect appropriations of a literary or artistic work'. The relevant part of article 12 therefore read as follows:

> . . . unauthorized indirect appropriations of a literary or artistic work, such as adaptations, musical arrangements, transformations of a novel, tale, or piece of poetry into a dramatic piece and vice versa, etc, . . .

Did this mean that 'adaptations' were not to include transformations of novels, etc, for the purposes of the Convention, with the result that the latter were therefore excluded from the operation of article 2(2)? Although this seemed to be the plain meaning of these provisions, it gave rise to a highly anomalous result. This was not adverted to by any of the delegates at the Berlin Conference and, from the records of that Conference, it is impossible to derive the notion that they intended the term 'adaptation' in article 2(2) to be interpreted in this restricted fashion.[403] The only reasonable conclusion that can be drawn is that 'adaptation' was used with different meanings in both provisions, and that no correlation between them was to be found. Thus, article 2(2) referred to 'original' adaptations, while article 12 dealt only with 'non-original' adaptations. Indeed, as suggested above, the second usage was inappropriate as the subject of article 12 was really 'colourable imitations' involving only minimal amounts of adaptation, arrangement, or transformations which did not in themselves constitute new and original works. Article 12, however, was entirely silent on the question of whether 'original' adaptations and musical arrangements were unlawful indirect reproductions and therefore within the author's power to

[402] Interpretative Declaration, Paris, 1896, para 3.

[403] *Actes* 1908, 257–8.

prevent. These gaps were not corrected until 1948, when they were expressly recognized in the programme for the Brussels Conference,[404] and the following proposal was made to bring articles 2(2) and 12 into line:

> The authors of literary and artistic works enjoy the rights recognised by the present Convention not only for their original works, but also for the transformations of these works which are dealt with in article 2, paragraph 2.[405]

This formulation greatly extended the rights of authors under the Convention, and indicated that, while the authors of derivative works were to be protected as authors of original works, this did not prevent them from being regarded as infringements of the works from which they were derived. Furthermore, 'transformations' was now used as an omnibus term encompassing translations, musical arrangements, adaptations, and other alterations. After some discussion, the proposal was reworded in a more precise and symmetrical fashion, as follows (this remains substantially the same in the Paris, Stockholm Acts):

> Authors of literary, scientific or artistic works shall enjoy the exclusive right of authorizing adaptations, arrangements and other alterations of their works.[406]

This wording explicitly recognizes the rights of authors to adapt, arrange, and alter their works, and complements article 8 which explicitly recognizes the right of authors to make translations of their works. Accordingly, article 2(2) (now article 2(3)) supplements these rights by declaring that the resultant translations, adaptations, etc, are also eligible for protection as original works in their own right, without prejudice to the rights of the author of the work from which they are derived.

(e) Adaptations and other alterations

From the preceding paragraph, it will be seen that the guidance to be obtained **8.81**
from the earlier versions of article 12 on the meaning of 'adaptation' is, to say the least, confusing. However, the view of most commentators has been that the term is to be given a generous interpretation, and that it should include all the permutations that are generally considered to fall within the scope of adaptation in the fields of current literary and artistic endeavour: dramatizations and choreographic or mime adaptations, the making of prose versions of dramatic works, the rendition of a literary or dramatic work into a dramatico-musical form, and so on.[407] While the precise scope of the concept is ultimately a matter for national legislation, there are a number of limitations that can be deduced from the text of the Convention itself.

---

[404] *Documents 1948* (1951), 314–15. [405] ibid, 315.
[406] ibid, 319. For a summary of the discussion, see ibid, 317–18.
[407] See eg Masouyé (1978), 76–7.

(i) **'Cinematographic adaptations'**: In the absence of any other provision, a cinematographic film of a literary or dramatic work would naturally constitute a form of adaptation. However, as cinematographic films are protected as primary works under article 2(1), there is no need to bring them under article 2(3) as adaptations.

(ii) **'Photographic adaptations'**: Prior to their inclusion in article 2(1) of the Brussels Act, it was arguable that photographs of artistic works were adaptations within the meaning of article 2(3).[408] As all photographs are now protected under article 2(1), this argument is no longer of any importance in ensuring their protection. Article 2(3) is still relevant for its reminder that the subsistence of protection in the derivative work is 'without prejudice' to the copyright in the adapted work, that is that the existence of the derivative work cannot decrease (or increase) the protection enjoyed by the underlying work.

(iii) **'Mechanical adaptations'**: A similar argument could be made in relation to sound recordings of musical and literary works, but this seems mistaken for two reasons. First, mechanical adaptation rights are dealt with comprehensively in article 13, and, in the light of the symmetry which now exists between articles 2(3) and 12, it would be anomalous to include this quite distinct form of adaptation within the scope of article 2(3). Secondly, proposals to protect sound recordings as works in their own right under the Convention have been made, and rejected, at a number of revision conferences[409] (see para 8.112 below); these productions are now the subject of a separate convention.[410] It therefore seems clear that the intention of successive conferences has been that these productions should not come within the scope of the Berne Convention, and this intention would be subverted if they fell within the general category of 'adaptations' under article 2(3).

(iv) **'Other alterations'**: The final expression 'other alterations of a literary or artistic work' implies another limitation on the scope of adaptation, although it also has the effect of expanding the scope of article 2(3). It has been suggested above that the very act of adaptation almost invariably involves the application of sufficient independent intellectual endeavour by the adapter for the resultant work to be regarded as a new and original work. Although this view of adaptation was certainly devalued by its use in the earlier versions of article 10 in the context of unlawful indirect reproductions (meaning only colourable imitations

---

[408] See the commentary by the International Office in [1909] *DA* 77, 80.

[409] At the Rome Conference: *Actes* 1928, 263. At the Brussels Conference: *Documents 1948* (1951), 337–8.

[410] The Rome Convention. See also the Convention for the Protection of Producers of Phonograms against Unauthorized Duplication of their Phonograms 1971 (the 'Phonograms Convention').

or alterations of an original work), this confusion was rectified in the Brussels Act. The use of the expression 'other alterations' in article 2(3) also confirms that something more is required than the simple alteration of a work, but leaves open the question of what is meant by 'other alterations'. Unlike the act of adaptation, which it has been suggested is in itself an original act of authorship, a more qualitative judgement appears to be required in the case of 'other alterations'. Colourable imitations or variations of a work cannot be intended here, that is, alterations of a work which simply involve the omission or changing of small sections, or the incorporation of other material, without incremental new authorial contributions. 'Alteration' for the purposes of article 2(3) must imply something further: a change, modification, or transformation of the original work resulting in something which can fairly be regarded as a distinct intellectual creation. This is a matter which therefore remains to be determined by national legislation, most probably by national tribunals on a case-by-case basis.

(2) 'Without prejudice to the copyright in the original work'

It is implicit that a derivative work, to be protected under article 2(3), must manifest some original authorship. The protection attaching to the derivative work covers only the original contribution of the adapter; the copyright in the adaptation does not affect the copyright in the work adapted. Thus, for example, the dramatic adaptation of a novel does not extend, enlarge, or diminish the copyright in the underlying literary work. The duration of the protection for novel will not change by virtue of the novel's later dramatization, nor will the novelist acquire (otherwise than by contract) any rights in the new matter contributed by the adapter, nor will the adapter be entitled to create the derivative work without the accord of the author of the underlying work, when that work is still protected by copyright. Article 14(2) (discussed earlier at para 8.32 above), contains a similar provision: if a cinematographic work based on a prior literary or artistic work is in turn adapted (suppose a motion picture made from a novel is to be adapted into a stage play), the author of the underlying work, as well as of the cinematographic work, must authorize the adaptation. Although the phrase 'without prejudice to the copyright in the original work' might imply that article 2(3) protects only those adaptations made from works still under copyright, this result makes no sense: the basis of the adapter's copyright is her independent intellectual contribution; the in- or out-of-copyright status of the underlying work is irrelevant to assessing the creativity of the adapter's contribution. As a result, the 'without prejudice' phrase should be understood as meaning to 'the copyright, if any, in the original work'. (See further the similar discussion regarding compilations at paras 8.84ff below.) **8.82**

As a general matter, one corollary of the 'without prejudice' proviso is that if the **8.83** copyright in the underlying work impedes the creation of unlicensed derivative works, it would follow that an unlicensed adaptation enjoys no copyright in its own right, regardless of its originality. There may be circumstances, however, in which the 'without prejudice' rule does not apply. These are likely to occur in the context of unlicensed, but lawfully excused adaptations such as parodies and burlesques, and caricatures (in the case of artistic works),[411] each of which has an honoured place in most cultural traditions. In addition, unlike adaptations, these may sometimes not even amount to a reproduction of the original work, insofar as they may rely on a mere suggestion of the idea of the original work as a starting point for their development.

(3) Works of compilation

8.84 Another kind of derivative work which has long received protection under most national laws is the compilation, which consists essentially of the selection and arrangement of works by other authors. Obvious examples are anthologies, encyclopaedias, and biographical directories. In such cases, the element of 'authorship' which is protected is the selection, editing, and arrangement of the different works which have been brought together. The degree of skill involved in each of these processes may be very high, particularly where the subject matter is large and diffuse, and the compiler is pursuing a special theme in his selection and juxtaposition of particular works. Furthermore, while collections of literary works most readily come to mind, the same skills may be equally applied in the making of a compilation of dramatic (for example, Elizabethan plays), musical (for example, Spanish piano works), or artistic (for example, German Expressionist) works. The protection which is accorded to these works of compilation is therefore quite distinct from the protection accorded to the authors of the component parts. As with other derivative works, the author of a compilation will need to ensure that (i) he has the authority of the authors of the individual works to reproduce those works, or (ii) the works used are in the public domain. Under the Berne Convention, compilations are required to be protected under article 2(5), which provides as follows:

> Collections of literary or artistic works such as encyclopaedias and anthologies which, by reason of the selection and arrangement of their contents, constitute intellectual creations shall be protected as such, without prejudice to the copyright in each of the works forming part of such collections.

[411] See eg Laddie et al (2000), para 3.142, and Lucas and Lucas (n 13 above), paras 342–5. The French law, in art L 122-5, says that the author may not prohibit 'parody . . . observing the rules of the genre'. For examples of US decisions upholding parody defences, see eg *Campbell* v *Acuff-Rose Music, Inc*, 510 US 569 (1994); *Suntrust Bank* v *Houghton Mifflin Co*, 268 F 3d 1257 (11th Cir 2001); *Mattel* v *Walking Mt Prods*, 353 F 3d 792 (9th Cir 2003).

(a) History of article 2(5)

Works of compilation have been protected under the Convention since the Berlin Act, where their inclusion stemmed from a German proposal.[412] In this Act, they were referred to simply as 'collections of different works' and were listed, along with other derivative works such as translations, adaptations, etc, under article 2(2). The original German proposal had been to protect 'collections of works of different authors',[413] but this was changed to take account of the fact that many collections consisted only of works of the same author, or that sometimes publishers issued collections in series, each collection comprising selections of the works of one author, for example, a series on 'great poets of the world'.[414] The commission also offered the following explanation of what was intended to be protected under the rubric of 'collections of different works': **8.85**

> . . . it is the work which has been involved in bringing together diverse works following a determined plan, according to a more or less ingenious grouping. As the plan, as the combination, comprises a personal work, the protection given to it is independent of that given to the materials which have been employed. They may be taken from the public domain . . . They may be taken from the private domain, and, therefore, for this to be lawful, the consent of the author or authors may be necessary . . . as . . . for translations and adaptations.[415]

No further proposals concerning collections were made at the Rome Conference, but the International Office and Belgian Government proposed the present wording as a more precise formulation in their programme for both the postponed Brussels Conference of 1936[416] and the actual Conference of 1948.[417] This was duly adopted by the Conference,[418] and became a separate paragraph under the Brussels Act (article 2(4)). No change was proposed or made to this at the Stockholm or Paris Conferences, except that the paragraph was renumbered as article 2(5).

(b) The interpretation of article 2(5)

This is more explicit than article 2(2) of the Berlin and Rome Acts which only mentioned collections 'in passing'. The following points concerning its interpretation can be made. **8.86**

(i) The expression 'collections of literary or artistic works': This expression (or '*les recueils d'oeuvres littéraires et artistiques*') has been retained from the Berlin and Paris Acts. 'Compilations' is another translation of the original

[412] Berlin Act, art 2(2). [413] *Actes* 1908, 42. [414] ibid, 232–3.
[415] ibid. [416] [1933] *DA* 73, 75.
[417] *Documents 1948* (1951), 144–5, 147. [418] ibid, 157, 159.

French word '*recueils*', and was used by Ladas in preference to 'collections' (which appeared in the unofficial English translations of the Berlin and Rome Acts).[419] In English, however, there is a subtle difference between 'compilation' and 'collection', insofar as the former implies that some element of skill has been used in making the compilation, while the latter is more neutral and could include collections which have been made quite indiscriminately without any particular skill. As article 2(5) makes it clear that skill is a prerequisite of protection for these kinds of works, this difference in meaning is not of any significance.

(ii) Distinction from collective works: A further point relating to the term 'collections' concerns a suggestion that was made at the time of the Brussels Revision that the term 'collections' be replaced by 'collective works'.[420] This was rejected on the basis that 'collective works' can also be used to refer to works by several authors, and that its use in the present context would therefore be confusing.[421]

(iii) Collections of works of the same or different authors: It should also be noted that 'collections' is used in a wider sense in article 2(5) than in article 2bis(3), which is concerned with the right of making collections of lectures, addresses, and similar works (see para 11.20 below). So far as the latter is concerned, it is clear from its context that 'collections' refers only to collections of works by the same author. It is clear from the discussions at the Berlin Conference, as well as its context, that this would be an unduly restrictive interpretation of 'collections' as it is used in article 2(5),[422] and that this includes both collections of works by the same author and collections of works of different authors.

(iv) Collections of the same kinds or of different kinds of works: There also seems to be no reason why the expression 'collections of literary or artistic works' should be interpreted to mean collections of one kind of work only. Thus, a collection may consist of a variety of different kinds of works, for example, an anthology of poetry with a selection of relevant artistic works.

(v) Encyclopaedias and anthologies: These are given as examples of 'collections of literary or artistic works'. This does not mean that such works are to be automatically protected: they still remain subject to the overriding requirement that they constitute, 'by reason of the selection and arrangement of their contents,

[419] Ladas (1938), 239ff. [420] *Documents 1948* (1951), 157.

[421] ibid. See eg France, Code de la propriété intellectuelle, art L 113–2 where 'collective work' means a work made by several authors in which the contribution of the individual authors is indistinguishable.

[422] *Actes* 1908, 232–4.

. . . intellectual creations'. Furthermore, as encyclopaedias and anthologies are only given as examples of collections, this means that there is a wide range of other works that should be protected as long as they fulfil the same condition. One instance given above is the biographical directory, such as *Who's Who*, which consists of a large number of biographical entries on various people in a given country or profession (each entry constituting a separate literary work). Other instances are dictionaries, almanacs, and collections of essays ('*Festschriften*'). Another obvious category includes newspapers, magazines, and reviews. There was, indeed, a British proposal at the Brussels Conference to include newspapers and periodicals in article 2(5) as well as encyclopaedias and anthologies.[423]

As stated above, indiscriminate collections involving little or no skill do not fall within the scope of article 2(5). This is one category of work protected by the Convention where the conditions for protection are clearly spelt out: only those collections 'which by reason of the selection and arrangement of their contents, constitute *intellectual creations*' are to be protected. (This concept is explored in greater detail at paras 8.87ff below.)

(vi) 'Without prejudice to the copyright in each of the works forming part of such collections': The phrase is analogous to the provision made in article 2(3) in relation to the original work on which the derivative work is based. In this context, however, certain difficulties arise:

- The phrase is intended to refer only to the rights of the individual author of each component work in his particular work—it is not intended to refer to any other right that such an author may have in the collection as a whole (unless, of course, he is also the person who made the collection).[424] A corollary is that the copyright in the compilation covers only the original matter contributed by the compiler; it does not allow the compiler to reach back to claim any copyright in the compiled components (unless she has obtained the rights by contract).

[423] ibid, 152. In this regard, it is of interest to note the view of the eminent German jurist, Josef Kohler, that the choice and organization of articles in a newspaper was dictated by concern for the interest of readers, and not by any 'preoccupation with giving the journal an intellectual unity expressed as a creative thought': J Kohler, *Gewerblicher Rechtsschutz und Urheberrecht* (1917), 1, referred to by the International Office in [1933] *DA* 72, 75. In any event, this opinion was not shared by the Brussels Conference, which regarded such works as being capable of falling within the scope of the provision if they satisfied its requirements, that is, insofar as they constituted an intellectual creation 'in the way in which their subject matter had been arranged and presented'. *Documents 1948* (1951), 157. Nevertheless, as the general principle of protection was clearly expressed in article 2(5), the Conference refused to add to the two examples which already appeared therein, and the British proposal was not adopted. Ibid, 94 (report of Plaisant), 157.

[424] ibid, 157.

- The phrase implies that the only collections that are covered by article 2(5) are those in which the component parts are still subject to copyright protection. In many instances, such as an anthology of poetry, the works in question may have been wholly or partly in the public domain for a considerable period of time. However, it appears that the correct interpretation of this phrase is '. . . without prejudice to any copyright which subsists in each of the works . . .'. The reason for this view is to be found in the wording of the original proposal in the programme for the Brussels Conference, which was as follows: '. . . without prejudice to the rights of the author existing in each of the works'.[425] This formulation made the inference that non-copyright works were not included in collections for the purposes of article 2(5) even easier to draw. At the Conference, the Danish delegation therefore proposed the following amendment to overcome this apparent gap: '. . . without prejudice to the rights belonging to the authors of the works forming part of these collections'.[426] This wording was not adopted by the Conference, but the word 'existing' was deleted from the proposal of the programme, and in his report the *rapporteur général* indicated that the reason for this change was to take account of the Danish suggestion.[427] Thus, article 2(5) covers collections of works, whether or not these are still under copyright.

(c) 'Intellectual creations'

8.87 Although only article 2(5) specifies the requirement of 'intellectual creation', it may be deduced that 'intellectual creation' is an implicit requirement as regards other works protected under article 2, but that it was only thought necessary to make this explicit in the case of collections, because the authorship inherent in the collection, as opposed to that in the works collected, may not be as readily discernible. The assessment of whether or not the collection itself constitutes an intellectual creation remains, in the final analysis, a matter for national tribunals. Article 2(5) does, however, identify two factors as being relevant to this determination: selection and arrangement. Both expressions have very wide potential meanings. Thus, 'selection' would cover the choice of works for the collection, and should be broad enough to include the important activity of editing, that is, the selection of which particular part or parts of a work are to be included in the collection. 'Arrangement' involves the delicate task of deciding how to present the collection, for example, thematically, by topic groups, or according to some other carefully selected and relevant criterion. The way in which this is done may depend very much on the purpose of the collection, for example, whether it is for teaching purposes, for ready reference or for simple

[425] ibid, 147. [426] ibid, 152. [427] ibid, 95.

pleasure. Hence, it would seem appropriate for national legislation to accord these two expressions a broad interpretation. In this regard, the word 'and' in the phrase 'selection and arrangement' is not to be read conjunctively as meaning that both elements are required. In the original French text, the word '*ou*' is used, and this makes it clear that the collection may constitute an intellectual creation by reason of *either* element being present. While arrangement and selection will almost inevitably be involved in the making of any collection, it is possible to conceive of collections where the only skill applied is that of arrangement, for example, a compilation of every work of a particular author organized in a thematic or chronological fashion. While chronological order may seem too banal a method of organization to qualify as 'original', intellectual endeavour may go into determining the order in which the compiler believes the author in fact wrote the works collected. By the same token, while a compilation of every one of an author's works may by definition eschew 'selection', the compiler may have at first had to judge whether the works attributed to an author were in fact created by her.

(i) Compilations of data or other unprotected subject matter: A final point is that article 2(5), by definition, does not cover collections of subject matter that are not capable of attracting copyright protection, that is, because they are not literary or artistic works in their own right. Instances are the names and addresses in a telephone directory, the brief descriptions of items in a catalogue, and the headings, sub-headings and individual entries in a sporting programme or radio guide. Such collections of non-copyright material may involve selection and arrangement in the same degree as are required for collections of literary or artistic works, but there is no requirement to protect them under article 2(5). In a case where a collection consists of both copyright and non-copyright components, it is submitted that article 2(5) would require them to be protected under the Convention insofar as the selection and arrangement of the literary or artistic works included in the collection constituted an intellectual creation. **8.88**

(ii) Compilations of data and other non-copyrightable subject matter: article 2(1) revisited: Although article 2(5) does not mandate the protection of collections of data, they may nonetheless be protectable as 'literary and artistic works' under the general mandate of article 2(1). As indicated earlier (para 8.87 above) the concept of 'intellectual creation', though made explicit only in article 2(5), applies to all Berne-protectable works; moreover, the elements which make a collection of works an 'intellectual creation'—selection or arrangement—should also serve to make a collection of data an 'intellectual creation'. Because it is clear, by virtue of the 'without prejudice' rule, that the copyright in the collection is independent of the copyright, if any, in the collected material, it should not matter to the assessment of the creativity of the collection whether **8.89**

the collected material is copyrightable or not. This is equally true whether the collected material consists of works still under copyright, works no longer under copyright, subject matter not qualified for copyright, or some combination of any or all of the above. In principle, then, article 2(1) would require member states to protect original compilations of data and other non-copyrightable material.

8.90 It is nonetheless necessary to confront two arguments against that conclusion. First, that the limitation of article 2(5) to collections of 'works' gives rise to a negative inference that collections of non-works are not required to be protected. Second, that regardless of the capacious character of the opening phrase of article 2(1), in practice, any work not actually enumerated does not come within the Berne Convention's mandatory coverage (see earlier discussion at paras 8.08ff above). With respect to the first argument, the 'without prejudice' clause militates against a negative inference that might more readily have been drawn in the absence of the clause. Without the clause, there would be little reason for the separate specification of collections of works, and one therefore might conclude that if collections of works require separate enumeration, that must be because collections of non-works are excluded. But the 'without prejudice' clause justifies the separate statement of coverage for collections of works, because the clause serves as a reminder of the distinction between the copyright in the collection and the copyright in the works collected, just as it does in article 2(3) with respect to the distinction between adaptations and underlying works adapted. The second argument is more troublesome. The pattern of practice under the Convention suggests that, despite the plain meaning of article 2(1), absent enumeration, a given work is not guaranteed protection. In that event, protection of databases and collections of non-works becomes a matter for national legislation, and in many, indeed by now, most, Berne Union countries such collections are protected equally with other literary and artistic works.[428] Even where this is not so, the law of unfair competition may provide protection for those persons whose compilations of non-copyright material are appropriated by a third party.

8.91 **(iii) Subsequent state practice:** If the inclusion of original compilations of non-works (original databases) was ambiguous under the 1971 Paris text, subsequent developments support a conclusion that these works now come within article 2. As will be explored further (see paras 8.128ff below), article 10(2) of the TRIPs Agreement, and article 5 of the WCT, both declare original compilations of data to be 'intellectual creations', and require them to be 'protected as such'.

[428] See eg Copyright Designs and Patents Act 1988 (UK), s 3(1); FRG Law of 1965, art 4; Copyright Act 1957 (India), s 2(o) (as amended 1999); Japanese Law of 1970, arts 12, 12bis.

If 'intellectual creation' is synonymous with 'literary and artistic work' (see para 8.03 above) or with 'production in the literary, scientific and artistic domain', and if most Berne members are also World Trade Organization ('WTO') or WCT members whose laws comply with those instruments' norms, then one may contend that this constitutes 'state practice' that effectively amends the Convention (on 'state practice', see paras 5.23–5.24, 5.40–5.41, 5.57 above). Article 2, accordingly, would require these compilations to be protected. The 'intellectual creation' formulation in the TRIPs Agreement and the WCT nonetheless might provoke some doubt regarding the later instruments' effect on the interpretation of article 2 of the Berne Convention. The doubt springs from comparing article 10(2) of the TRIPs Agreement with article 10(1), and article 5 of the WCT with article 4. Article 10(1) of the TRIPs Agreement and article 4 of the WCT pronounce the protection of computer programs 'as literary works within the meaning of Article 2 of the Berne Convention'. (Regarding computer programs, see further paras 8.92ff below.) If original compilations of data are to be considered works within the meaning of article 2, then why did the later instruments not say so? On the other hand, the WCT's preparatory documents suggest that the Committee of Experts concluded that original compilations already were protected as literary or artistic works under article 2(1).[429]

(iv) Computer software: Does this fall within the meaning of a literary and artistic work under article 2(1)? The protection of software was a contentious issue in a number of Union countries for many years and raised important policy issues, not only in relation to copyright, but to the principles of intellectual property protection in general. The nature of the subject matter involved is complex, but the essential object of a software maker is the production of a **8.92**

[429] See CRNR/DC/4 (30 Aug 1996), 'Basic Proposal for the Substantive Provisions of the Treaty on Certain Questions Concerning the Protection of Literary and Artistic Works to be Considered by the Diplomatic Conference, Memorandum Prepared by the Chairman of the Committees of Experts, Notes on Article 5', para 5.02: 'This provision is of a declaratory nature. It confirms what already is covered by the Berne Convention.' See also Daniel Gervais, *The TRIPs Agreement: Drafting History and Analysis*, 2nd edn (2003), para 2.107 ('one could draw the conclusion that all (original) collections were protected under the Berne Convention'); Mihály Ficsor, *The Law of Copyright and the Internet: The 1996 WIPO Treaties, Their Interpretation and Implementation* (2003), para C5.01.

The WCT's agreed statement concerning art 5 states that 'the scope of protection for compilations of data (databases) under art 5 of this Treaty . . . is consistent with Article 2 of the Berne Convention'. Although the phrase 'consistent with' might suggest something external to and compatible with, but not integral to, the Berne Convention, the agreed statement addresses the extent, not the existence, of coverage under the Berne Convention. The relevant portion of art 2 for purposes of the agreed statement is the art 2(5) 'without prejudice' principle which limits the scope of protection of a compilation to its selection or arrangement, thus excluding the compiled elements. Cf Jörg Reinbothe and Silke von Lewinski, *The WIPO Treaties 1996* (2002), 73 (developing countries sought confirmation of the Berne art 2(5) scope of protection and would have been opposed to broader scope for databases under TRIPs than under the Berne Convention).

program that will direct a computer to perform certain functions.[430] This is usually done in a number of stages, beginning with the drawing of flow charts and other graphical material to the preparation of source code in a special notation or language and the final transformation of this code into machine code that causes the computer to carry out the desired function or achieve a particular result.[431] Considerable skill and intellectual application is required in the making of a successful program and, from the beginning, their makers were keen to obtain protection for the fruits of their work.

8.93 (v) **The WIPO model provisions:** The first area of protection explored at a national level was the law of patents, but it was generally found that this was only of limited value to software makers.[432] At an international level, WIPO, on behalf of the Paris Union rather than the Berne Union, began investigating the possibility of creating a *sui generis* protection, and in 1977 formulated a set of 'Model Provisions for the Protection of Computer Software'.[433] These defined 'computer software' as comprising three components: computer programs, program descriptions, and supporting material. These terms, in turn, were defined as follows:

> '[C]omputer program' means a set of instructions capable, when incorporated in a machine-readable medium, of causing a machine having information-processing capabilities to indicate, perform or achieve a particular function, task or result;
>
> 'program description' means a complete procedural representation in verbal, schematic or other form, in sufficient detail to determine a set of instructions constituting a corresponding computer program;
>
> 'supporting material' means any material, other than a computer program or a program description, created for aiding the understanding or application of a computer program, for example problem descriptions and user instructions.[434]

It was further provided, as a condition for protection, that computer software must be 'original in the sense that it is the result of the creator's own intellectual

[430] See generally H Brett and L Perry, *The Legal Protection of Software* (1981), 1–13; Laddie et al (2000), ch 34, 1609ff; C J Millard, *Legal Protection of Computer Programs and Data* (1985), ch 1.

[431] ibid.

[432] M S Keplinger, 'Authorship in the Information Age: Protection for Computer Programmers under the Berne and Universal Copyright Convention' [1985] *Copyright* 119; G Kolle, 'Computer Software Production: Present Situation and Future Prospects' [1977] *Copyright* 70; D Llewellyn, 'Computers, Software and International Protection' (1986) 11 *Columbia-VLA Journal of Law & the Arts* 183. See also E Ulmer, 'Copyright Protection of Scientific Works with Special Reference to Computer Programs' (1971) 2 *IIC* 56.

[433] [1977] *Industrial Property* 265 and see also the commentary on the provisions at 259ff. See also the reports of the work of the WIPO Group of Non-Governmental Experts on the Protection of Computer Software in [1974] *Copyright* 163 and [1977] *Industrial Property* 259.

[434] Model Provisions, s 1. See further L Perry, 'The Legal Protection of Computer Software: The WIPO Model Provisions' [1979] *EIPR* 34.

effort'.[435] Protection was to be accorded against the disclosure, copying, sale, and use of the software,[436] and a term of protection for twenty years from the date of first use, sale, lease, or licensing but no longer than twenty-five years from the date of creation was allowed.[437] The *sui generis* form of the protection chosen indicates that, at this stage, WIPO was of the view that copyright protection was inappropriate to computer software. In the years following the formulation of the Model Provisions, however, it became clear that national laws were moving towards a copyright solution for this new kind of subject matter. In some cases, this result was achieved by court decisions that computer software fell already within the description of a literary or artistic work and was to be protected as such.[438] In others, this was expressly provided for in national legislation.[439] In consequence, a number of important Union members chose to protect software under copyright.[440] The reasons for this change are not readily identifiable, but the following factors appear to have been relevant: (i) there was strong pressure for protection—any protection—that was brought to bear by software makers; (ii) despite the useful model provisions provided by WIPO, difficulties were seen in the construction of a new *sui generis* kind of protection; and (iii) copyright protection provided a ready pigeon-hole into which software could be slotted with a minimum of trouble. The trend first discerned in the early 1980s has now overtaken most domestic copyright laws, either as a matter of local economic interest, or by virtue of later multilateral instruments mandating the treatment of computer software as 'literary or artistic works under the Berne Convention'.[441] (These international developments are discussed further at paras 8.95 and 8.121ff below.)

It is, of course, open to a Union member to call any category of subject matter a literary or artistic work under its own law and to accord it copyright protection. However, this does not mean that the subject matter thereby automatically becomes a literary or artistic work within the meaning of article 2(1) of the **8.94**

[435] Model Provisions, s 3. [436] ibid, s 5. [437] ibid, s 7.

[438] See eg *La société d'Informatique RDG Inc* v *Dynabec Ltée* [1984] CS 1189, affd, 6 CPR (3d) 322 (Canada); *Computer Edge Pty Ltd* v *Apple Computer Inc* (1986) 6 IPR 1 (Australia).

[439] See eg FRG Amending Law of 23 May 1985, art 1 ('programs for data processing'); French Law No 85-600 of 3 July 1985, art 1(v) ('software'); UK Copyright (Computer Software) Amendment Act 1985. Note also the protection accorded to programs under the US Copyright Act: 17 USC § 101. See also L Bietten, 'Copyright Protection of Computer Programs in the FRG' [1986] *Copyright* 352.

[440] See further Llewellyn (n 432 above); P Grytyanjy, 'Software as a New Subject Matter of Copyright Law?' (1982) 113 *RIDA* 71; 'Copyright Protection of Computer Programs' (1983) 30 *Copyright Law Symposium (ASCAP)* 1; P B Maggs, 'Computer Programs as the Object of Intellectual Property in the United States of America' (1982) 30 *Am Jo of Comp Law* 251; E Ulmer and G Kolle, 'Copyright Protection of Computer Programs' (1983) 14 *IIC* 159.

[441] TRIPs Agreement, art 10(1).

Convention which must be protected by all Union members.[442] On the other hand, as discussed earlier (see paras 5.55–5.58, and with respect to databases, para 8.91 above), the vast number of countries now protecting computer programs as 'works' under the Berne Convention may by now constitute 'state practice' sufficient to bring this subject matter within the scope of mandatory coverage,[443] even though their embrace within article 2(1) may have been doubtful in the period from 1967 to 1971.

8.95 If 'state practice' has *de facto* amended article 2(1), then the question whether, as a matter of first principles, computer software can be regarded as an intellectual creation in the literary and artistic domain becomes moot. In addition, WIPO's position on the copyright coverage of computer software evolved between the 1978 Model Law and the early 1990s, when its International Bureau revisited the matter, raising the question whether the Berne Convention required the protection of computer programs as a category of literary or artistic works.[444] The Bureau's memorandum considered the objections usually raised against assimilation of computer programs to other copyrighted works (see further para 8.99 below), and replied that programs nonetheless come within the scope of article 2(1), primarily because they are a form of writing, and the devising of a computer program leaves room for creativity.

8.96 Nonetheless, to the extent that doubts may remain concerning the effect on the Berne Convention of WIPO's change in position, and of the widespread national incorporation of computer programs into the subject matter of copyright, it is worth inquiring whether, as a matter of first principles, computer programs properly come within the Conventional concept of 'intellectual creations'.

8.97 A formidable argument in favour of the characterization of computer software as an intellectual creation can be mounted. Thus, a clear literary or artistic element is to be seen in some aspects of software creation, for example, in the case of the supporting material and program descriptions.[445] These are readily perceived and understood by humans and there can be little doubt about the

---

[442] See David Vaver, 'The National Treatment Requirements of the Berne and Universal Copyright Conventions (Part One)' (1986) 17 *IIC* 577, 595 and 602–3. See also G Karnell, 'Copyright in Computer Programs: An International Survey' [1985] *EIPR* 126, 128.

[443] Accord, Daniel Gervais, *La notion d'oeuvre dans la Convention de Berne et en droit comparé* (1998), 120 ('Given the fact that States from all parts of the world, with different legal systems and at all levels of economic development, have already recognized this protection [of computer programs as literary works] and affirmed it at the time of the international negotiations at WIPO and the GATT, one may believe that a rule of customary law has emerged in this domain, which the study of national laws tends to confirm.') (translation ours).

[444] BCP/CE/I/2 (18 July 1991).

[445] Vaver (n 442 above), 603.

element of intellectual creation which they require. With programs, however, difficulties arguably begin to arise: source code may be likened to a literary creation in the form of code, but machine code is usually incapable of being understood by anyone and may be embodied in a number of different forms, including disks, tapes, or integrated circuits in semiconductor chip products.[446] But this argument elevates the medium over the message. If the code, when written in a human-intelligible form, is an intellectual creation by virtue of the creative thought it embodies, it should not cease to be an intellectual creation simply because it is expressed in a form destined for machine-reading. As a general principle, the purpose to which a work is put should not detract from its characterization as an 'intellectual creation'.

It can readily be argued that to exclude software in general from article 2(1) **8.98** would embody an unduly restrictive interpretation of that provision based on a nineteenth-century conception of literary and artistic creation that fails to take account of the development of new technology.[447] A more probative, less anachronistic, objection might be advanced based on the utilitarian character of most software. As we have seen above, protection has been refused to subject matter which was of a mechanical or industrial nature. Even in the case of works of applied art, the logic of the French theory of unity of art has not led to acceptance that these should be fully protected as literary or artistic works under the Convention. Some further internal support for the exclusion of software can be gained from the fact that article 2(1) does not expressly require the protection of technical or engineering drawings (see paras 8.43ff, 8.73 above). In the same way, software might be more appropriately described as a production in the technological or scientific sphere, rather than in the literary or artistic domain. This objection nonetheless encounters problems. Applied art notwithstanding, the Berne Convention does not comport a general exclusion of useful works, particularly useful literary works. Thus, how-to books, problem-solving manuals, instructional works, legal treatises (including this one) all come within the scope of article 2(1). Something more is required to demonstrate that this useful literary work falls outside the realm of 'intellectual creations'.

An initially persuasive reason may concern the lack of 'fit' between computer **8.99** software and the scheme of protection applicable to most other copyrighted works. While many, if not all, of the rights presently accorded under copyright may be appropriate, these could equally well be accorded under a separate *sui*

---

[446] ibid, 604.

[447] A persuasive and magisterial early presentation of these arguments is to be found in Ulmer and Kolle (n 440 above), 159. See also the extensive list of references to the FRG literature dealing with these arguments in n 12 at p 163 of their article. See further the earlier article by Ulmer (n 432 above), and the literature referred to therein.

generis system of protection. In addition, such rights could be formulated in a way that was more suited to the particular circumstances of software creation and the needs of its makers.[448] More importantly, protection under the Convention would require an absence of any formalities and a term of protection of the life of the author (the programmer) plus fifty years. With the vast majority of software, which is rapidly superseded, such a term would hardly be necessary. The period of life plus fifty years was worked out in relation to creators of literary or artistic creations whose returns from their works had often to be stretched out over a lengthy period of time and whose works had a continuing significance beyond the end of their lives. In the case of most software, it ceases to be of any value after a much shorter period of time. The fact that this may also be true of other categories of works presently protected would not provide a justification for adding to these categories: rather, it should strengthen the inference that computer software, by its very nature, would not fall within the scope of literary and artistic works under article 2(1). It would, of course, be possible to make provision for a shorter term of protection, by analogy with works of applied art, but the making of such an exception might suggest that computer software should not have been included in the Convention in the first place.

8.100 On the other hand, applied art is not the only subject matter receiving the short end of the duration stick. As discussed in greater detail (see paras 9.28–9.29 below), the Berne Convention allows member states to provide shorter terms for photographs. In this case, the discrimination does not rely on any utilitarian character of the works, but rather on a general suspicion of their machine-tainted unworthiness. Computer software does arguably share a machine-related taint; in this case the work is created for use in a machine, whereas photographs are created by the use of a machine. The passage of time, and corresponding appreciation of photography as a form of art and communication, have dispelled qualms about the originality of all but the most automatic of photographs. By the same token, as the writing of computer programs becomes more familiar to more people, the intellectual creativity of the task may become more widely perceived (although, for some, the conceptual difficulty remains that the program is written to direct the machine to perform a particular function rather than being directed to a human reader).

8.101 This observation does not, however, confront the special concerns spawned by the utilitarian character of computer programs. While one response might have been to create a third exception to duration, this would have put further pressure

[448] For an extensively developed proposal for a *sui generis* law, see Pamela Samuelson et al, 'A Manifesto Concerning the Legal Protection of Computer Programs' (1994) 94 *Colum L Rev* 2308. But see Jane C Ginsburg, 'Four Reasons and a Paradox: The Manifest Superiority of Copyright over Sui Generis Protection of Computer Software' (1994) 94 *Colum L Rev* 2559.

on the unity of treatment of copyrighted works within the Convention. That is, the Berne Convention's substantive minima arguably should establish a one-size-fits-all baseline for copyright; by and large, all kinds of works should receive the same level of protection. Breaking out a particular subject matter for different treatment risks undermining the coherence of the Convention. Instead of one general set of rules, we will have a collection of special rules for special categories.

The problem with this objection is its premise. As should become clear from review not only of Berne's subject-matter categories, but also from the scope of rights guaranteed (and exceptions thereto), as well as copyright ownership (see further, Chapters 7 above and 10–13 below), Berne already *is* a collection of rules establishing disparate regimes depending on a work's subject matter.[449] Most of the general rules apply most of the time, but the details can diverge in ways that are significant. It does not suffice, therefore, in objecting to the inclusion of computer software in article 2(1), to lament the proliferation of specific rules that are designed to accommodate the peculiarities of the subject matter at issue. **8.102**

On the contrary, the principal objections to the inclusion of computer software go not to its creativity, but to the appropriate scope of protection. Only the former should be relevant to the characterization of a work as 'literary or artistic works' under article 2(1). To the extent computer programs give pause because they implement ideas or processes directed to the functioning of a machine, the basic principles underlying the Berne Convention (as well as the later treaties) already foreclose coverage of the underlying idea or method (see the earlier discussion at paras 5.49ff above). To the extent computer programs spark concern because of the potential breadth of exclusive rights, this may justify the application of exceptions or limitations on a case-by-case basis; it does not support excision of an entire category of creative endeavour. **8.103**

E. Exclusions from the Protection of the Convention

(1) Mandatory exclusion: news of the day and miscellaneous facts

Article 2(8) contains an exclusion to the protection offered by the Convention, in the following terms: **8.104**

> The protection of this Convention shall not apply to news of the day or to miscellaneous facts having the character of mere items of press information.

[449] This point was also made by the WIPO International Bureau; see also Gervais (n 443 above), 119, n 92.

The purpose of this provision is uncertain, and its scope is difficult to define. It has only been part of article 2 since the Stockholm Revision. Prior to this, it appeared in that part of the Convention which dealt with restrictions in relation to the reproduction of articles in newspapers and periodicals (article 7 of the Berne Act and article 9(3) of the Berlin, Rome, and Brussels Acts). However, the expression 'news of the day' ('*nouvelles du jour*') can be traced back to the Berne Act.[450] The same is true of the expression 'miscellaneous information' ('*faits divers*'), but this was qualified by the addition of the words 'having the character of mere items of press information' ('*qui ont le caractère des simples informations de presse*') at the time of the Berlin Revision.[451] At the Stockholm Revision, article 9 was extensively amended with the express recognition for the first time in the Convention of the author's exclusive right to reproduction.[452] As article 9(3) dealt more with works protected than restrictions on the reproduction right, it was thought more appropriate for it to be included in article 2 rather than article 9, and it therefore became article 2(8) of the Stockholm, Paris Acts.[453]

8.105 The wording of article 2(8) makes it difficult to discern its purpose. The latter is important, as it has a significant effect on the interpretation to be given to the terms 'news of the day' and 'miscellaneous information . . .'. Is article 2(8) a public-policy exception to the Convention in the sense that it excludes news items from the scope of the Convention in the interests of freedom of information? Alternatively, does it embody a juridical conception of the nature of authors' rights, which excludes these items from protection on the basis that they are incapable of constituting literary or artistic works? If the latter is the correct view, it could then be said that such an exclusion is strictly unnecessary as these items are not, in any event, covered by the Convention, as they fall within the category of facts and items of information which cannot be the subject of copyright protection. The expressions 'news of the day' and 'miscellaneous information . . .' do not in themselves indicate which view is correct, and the following problems of interpretation therefore arise:

1. If article 2(8) is a public-policy exception, it could operate to exclude accounts or reports of daily news that would otherwise be capable of being regarded as literary works within the meaning of article 2(1). This might, in turn, be something of a slippery slope, because news reports differ greatly in their form, from bald 'telegraphic' dispatches to sophisticated analyses of the events reported. Would article 2(8) therefore require that protection be denied in the case of this second kind of article? If it did not, where and

[450] Berne Act, art 7. [451] Berlin Act, art 9(3). See further *Actes* 1908, 249ff.
[452] Stockholm, Paris Acts, art 9(1). [453] *Records* 1967, vol II, 1155.

how would the line between protectable and non-protectable items be drawn?

2. If the second interpretation is to be preferred, this would not cause as much difficulty, as it simply embodies the basic principle that copyright protection does not extend to facts and information per se, but only to the form in which those facts are presented. Even if such a statement is strictly unnecessary, its inclusion in the Convention could then be defended on two grounds:
   - As the basic principle is not expressly stated elsewhere in the Convention, its inclusion in article 2(8) provides a useful confirmation of the fact that the principle is generally applicable under the Convention.
   - If a member country of the Union does, in fact, accord copyright protection to bare items of news and press information, the authors of such items have no right to claim equivalent protection under the Convention in other Union countries. Unlike the other paragraphs of article 2 which lay down the bare minimum of what each country must protect as literary or artistic works, article 2(8) provides a definite exception to this. On the other hand, it only excludes protection under 'this Convention', and this clearly does not prevent member countries from according protection to foreign authors under other heads, for example, their laws of unfair competition, or even their copyright laws. However, because the Berne Convention excludes this subject matter, its obligation of national treatment does not apply. As a result, in the latter case, a Union country which accords such protection to its own authors would be under no obligation to extend this to authors from other Union countries.

It should be noted that public policy, in any event, underpins the second 'juridical' interpretation in that the basic principle that copyright protects only the form in which works are expressed is clearly intended to leave ideas, facts, and information in the public domain for all to use. However, this is a more limited application of public policy than that suggested under the first interpretation above.

In the face of these conflicting views, it is permissible to have regard to supplementary aids to interpretation. Little guidance is to be found in the records of the Berne and Paris Conferences, but at the Berlin Conference the commission implicitly indicated its preference for the second view.[454] This was not to say that the commission thought that the effort and investment involved in the collection of news items should not be protected from acts of unfair competition, **8.106**

[454] *Actes* 1908, 251ff.

as, for example, where a competitor saved himself the trouble of collection and presented such items as his own.[455] The commission, in fact, spent considerable time discussing the form of the protection which should be accorded in such cases, but was unable to agree how this should be done.[456] It finally agreed that the Convention should simply state that these items were not the subject of copyright protection, but that this was not to be taken as precluding member countries from according them other forms of protection.[457] From the context of the commission's remarks, it seems clear that by the expressions 'news of the day' and 'miscellaneous items . . .', it meant only the facts constituting those items, and did not intend to exclude from protection as literary works the articles or reports in which these facts were contained. There are no relevant observations to be found in the records of either the Rome or Brussels Conferences, but the issue was directly addressed in the preparations which were undertaken for the Stockholm Conference by the Swedish Government and BIRPI.[458] In the view of the 1963 Study Group, the immediate object of article 9(3) (as it then was) was:

> . . . to recall the general principle whereby the title to protection of articles of this kind, as in the case of other intellectual works, pre-supposes the quality of literary or artistic works within the meaning of the Convention. At the same time, the provision also permits the conclusion that if the articles are protected by virtue of other legal provisions—for example, by legislation against unfair competition—such protection is outside the field of the Convention. There are grounds, therefore, for drawing, *inter alia*, a second conclusion: the right to assimilation to national authors established by the Convention does not extend to the protection claimed by virtue of these other rules.[459]

The Study Group went on to say that, while this provision could be viewed as superfluous from a systematic perspective, it had formed part of the Convention for a long time and was 'a good expression of a principle from which legislation and jurisprudence . . . [could] take their lead, as well as a reminder of the freedom of information'.[460] It was therefore useful as it recognized the 'practical importance of fixing . . . the line of demarcation between copyright and other means of protection'.[461] The Group recommended the retention of the article without any change, but with some discussion of its interpretation in the documents of the Conference.[462] In keeping with this proposal, the following interpretation of article 9(3) (which was to become article 2(8) in the Stockholm Act) was proposed in the programme for the Stockholm Conference,[463] and was adopted in turn by Main Committee I in its report to the Conference:

---

455 *Actes* 1908, 251ff. 456 ibid. 457 ibid.
458 *Records* 1967, vol I, 115. 459 ibid. 460 ibid.
461 ibid. 462 ibid. 463 ibid, 115–18.

> . . . the Convention does not protect mere items of information on news of the day or miscellaneous facts, because such material does not possess the attributes needed to constitute a work. That implies *a fortiori* that news items or the facts themselves are not protected. The articles of journalists or other 'journalistic' works reporting news items are, on the other hand, protected to the extent that they are literary or artistic works. It did not seem essential to clarify the text of the Convention on this point.[464]

The above paragraph therefore embodies an authentic interpretation of article 2(8) which can be followed in national legislation. Its importance in relation to the more general question of the subject matter of copyright protection has already been referred to (see para 8.07 above).

(2) Optional exclusions: official texts

Most national laws exclude protection in the case of laws, court orders, and other kinds of official documents.[465] There are good public-policy grounds for doing so—such documents should be available to all, and should not be subject to private proprietary restrictions—and this need is recognized in article 2(4), which provides as follows: **8.107**

> It shall be a matter of legislation in the countries of the Union to determine the protection to be granted to official texts of a legislative, administrative and legal nature, and to official translations of such texts.

This provision has only been in the Convention since the Stockholm Revision, although there was a more qualified provision in article 2(2) of the Brussels Act which applied only to translations of official texts. In the programme for the Brussels Conference, this provision had been proposed as an additional paragraph to article 8 which dealt with translation rights.[466] The reason why it was limited to translations of official texts was that, up to the time of the Stockholm Act, the protection of translation rights was expressly required under the Convention, but the protection of reproduction rights was not required (see further para 11.03 below).[467] Accordingly, it was open to member countries to regulate the protection of official texts as they saw fit under their national laws, but an express reservation was required in the case of translations of official texts.[468] This was accepted by the Conference, but for drafting reasons was added to article 2(2) on the basis that this paragraph dealt generally with derivative

[464] ibid, vol II, 1155.
[465] See eg the FRG Law of 1965, art 5; the Italian Law of 1941, art 5; the Japanese Copyright Law, No 48 of 6 May 1970, art 13; the Mexican Federal Law of Copyright of 1996, art 14(VIII).
[466] *Documents 1948* (1951), 223.
[467] See the discussion of this in *Records* 1967, vol I, 111 (Document S/1); see further *Documents 1948* (1951), 157, 226, 237ff.
[468] *Documents 1948* (1951), 22.

works.[469] At the request of the British delegation, it was made clear that there was nothing in this provision which required member countries to deny protection to such translations.[470] In this regard, it should be noted that British law, and many of the laws derived from that law, have differed from other national laws in their reluctance to exclude protection for these kinds of documents.[471]

8.108 At the Stockholm Revision, the exclusive right of reproduction was protected expressly for the first time under the Convention.[472] Although no recommendations concerning article 2(2) were made in the programme for the Conference, a German amendment proposed the extension of the reservation under article 2(2) to apply to the protection of the texts themselves.[473] This was adopted unanimously by Main Committee I,[474] and was put into a separate paragraph, as article 2(4) of the Stockholm Act, by the drafting committee. The effect of this provision is that it is left to national legislation to determine (i) whether such works are to be protected at all, and (ii) if so, to what extent. This permits a high degree of flexibility, enabling member countries to give effect to their differing views of the public interest. As a consequence, countries are free to leave such texts entirely in the public domain, to accord them complete protection as literary or artistic works, or to grant qualified protection subject to generous rights of use on the part of the public. The third course may, in fact, be the most prudent, as a government may wish to retain control over the reproduction of its official texts (so as to guarantee their accuracy), while satisfying the public interest in having ready and immediate access to these documents by the grant of a general licence to members of the public to make private copies. The following points of interpretation concerning article 2(4) also arise:

(a) The meaning of 'official texts of a legislative, administrative and legal nature'

In the original proposal concerning translations which was made in the programme for the Brussels Conference, a more specific list was used: 'laws, decrees, judgments and other similar official instruments' ('*lois, décrets, arrêts et autres actes officiels semblables*').[475] The present, and more general, formulation stems from a French amendment,[476] and seems broad enough to cover all public governmental documents, not only statutory material and court decisions. Given the volume of material generated by most governments in contemporary

[469] *Documents 1948* (1951), 157. [470] ibid, 94 (report of M Plaisant) and 157.

[471] Under UK law, therefore, public access to these documents is regulated through the general fair-use provisions of the Copyright, Designs and Patents Act 1988, ss 163–6, while other common law jurisdictions have provisions concerned specifically with such uses: see eg the Australian Copyright Act 1968, s 182A.

[472] Stockholm, Paris Acts, art 9(1). [473] *Records* 1967, vol I, 694 (Document S/92).

[474] ibid, vol II, 882. [475] *Documents 1948* (1951), 223. [476] ibid, 225.

society, this wording allows a large potential addition to the public domain. From the point of view of an international convention concerned with the rights of authors, this potential override of state ownership of public documents (for example, 'Crown copyright') is not especially troublesome. From the point of view of the creators of public documents, this gap in protection may be in tension with the Convention's author-orientation, as much of the material produced for government (including here local government) may be by individual and identifiable authors. From the point of view of those governed by these documents, their free accessibility would seem crucial to civil and political responsibility. That argument, however, is most pertinent to domestic protection, something the Berne Convention does not purport to regulate. It is less clear why these works should be freely available to users in other countries, who are not bound by the domestic obligations these works may dictate or support. Another theory supporting the public-domain status (domestically and internationally) of official texts emphasizes the absence of a copyright-furnished incentive to create these works. Because these works are created under the aegis of the state, they would have been created whether or not their authors enjoyed a copyright. Where the prospect of exclusive rights does not propel creativity, the argument goes, vesting copyright in the creators of works which would have been created anyway is a windfall wasteful of the public's funds. While this argument may have some intuitive appeal, to the extent it endorses inquiry into the motivations of the author, it may prove troublesome if not pernicious.

The foregoing does not, however, help us determine what *is* an official text. Works created by a state employee in furtherance of her employment constitute a fairly clear category. But what of privately generated texts that are subsequently adopted or incorporated into statutes, regulations, or other government documents? The phenomenon is not unusual: code-writing organizations, preparers of model laws, public-policy groups, reports done for governments by private consultants, commissions of inquiry, etc all may propose texts which a local or national government might take up. Before adoption, these texts are clearly protectable; after adoption does the same text lose its coverage? There does not seem to be anything in the Berne Convention itself to help resolve this definitional issue, so the matter would be left to member state law.[477]

[477] See eg *Veeck* v *Southern Blg Code Cong Int'l Inc*, 293 F 3d 791 (5th Cir 2002) (en banc) (holding that privately generated model building code subsequently adopted by Texas municipalities lost its copyright protection because no one may claim exclusive rights in the texts of 'the law'). Another example is submissions to parliamentary/congressional committees, evidence given to such bodies, and to commissions of inquiry. The Australian copyright law vests copyright in such works in the Crown when they are 'first published' by the Crown, eg in official reports, etc. See Copyright Act 1968 (Aus), s 177.

In any event, article 2(4) permits not only the abrogation of the economic rights of these authors (which may in any case be non-existent in view of their government employment), but their moral rights as well. The position of these authors will therefore depend upon the scope which national legislation accords to the expressions 'official', 'legislative', 'administrative', and 'legal'.

There is, however, evidence in the records of the Stockholm Conference to indicate that a more restricted interpretation than the one suggested above is to be given to the word 'administrative'. In Main Committee I, the British delegate, Mr Wallace, expressed concern about this,[478] and at his request the following statement was inserted in the final report of the Committee:

> 138. In accordance with the desire expressed by the United Kingdom it must be clearly stipulated in this Report that the reference made in the Convention to texts of an administrative nature does not permit countries to refuse protection to all Government publications, for instance, textbooks.[479]

Appearing as this does in the *travaux préparatoires* of the Conference, it must be regarded as an authentic supplementary aid to the interpretation of a term in the Convention that is otherwise uncertain. The authority of this source is also reinforced by the fact that there is no evidence in the records of the Conference that there was any disagreement with it by any delegation which participated in the Conference.[480]

(b) Official translations

The reservation in article 2(4) is limited to 'official translations' of these texts. National legislation is therefore not allowed to exclude or restrict the protection to be granted to translations that are made by 'non-official' persons, for example, a translation of a statute or court decision that is prepared by a private publisher.

F. Other Works not Expressly Mentioned in the Convention

8.109 The non-exhaustive character of the enumeration in article 2(1) has already been commented upon.[481] As a consequence, it is open to any member country to protect, as literary or artistic works, works other than those listed in article 2(1) or the other paragraphs of article 2. There is a significant practical difference between this subject matter and subject matter mandatorily excluded from the Convention, to which the principle of national treatment does not apply:

478 *Records* 1967, 882. 479 ibid, 1154. 480 ibid, 882.
481 See paras 8.07ff above.

Under the principle of national treatment, authors claiming under the Convention will gain protection for these works in that country. On the other hand, such protection will not be available in those countries of the Union which do not treat these as literary or artistic works, as express mention in the Convention is necessary if a particular category of work is to be protected uniformly in each country of the Union.[482] As we have seen, the categories of works protected under the Convention have been steadily enlarged and added to in successive revisions. It is, therefore, useful to conclude this part of the chapter with a brief consideration of unsuccessful proposals that have been made in the past for the inclusion of particular kinds of works, as this casts further light on the present scope and outer limits of the expression 'literary and artistic works' in article 2(1).

(1) Broadcasts, sound recordings, and the interpretations of performing artists

It has been seen above that the inclusions of photographic works and works of applied art in article 2(1) provoked considerable opposition at the time they were first proposed, and it was some time before this was achieved in each case. The same was also true of cinematographic works. This opposition was based mainly on the view that these works did not involve the same degree of authorship that was required for other kinds of works, or that the real object of these claims for protection was the manufacturer's skill and investment. Nevertheless, in each instance admission to the category of 'literary and artistic works' was finally allowed, and the scope of that expression correspondingly enlarged. Other kinds of subject matter, however, remained outside, and have continued to do so, the most prominent examples being sound and television broadcasts, sound recordings, and the interpretations of performing artists. These have received protection in many Berne Union countries under separate 'neighbouring rights' legislation, and, more confusingly, in many common law jurisdictions under the umbrella of copyright. Yet their exclusion from the Berne Convention has been explicit, and in recent years has been confirmed by the formation of two separate multilateral conventions concerned specifically with their protection.[483] While these developments, in turn, make the continued protection of cinematographic and photographic works under the Berne Convention appear more anomalous, the explanation or justification for this is probably better expressed in terms of history than any argument based on the relative merits of the skills required for each kind of production: **8.110**

[482] ibid.

[483] The Rome Convention 1961 and the Phonograms Convention 1970: see para 8.81 and n 410 above.

cinematographic and photographic works gained their Conventional status some time before the notion according *sui generis* protection under a separate international agreement had fully developed. For our present purposes, all that is necessary is to recount briefly the history of the various proposals which have been made to include broadcasts, sound recordings, and the interpretations of performers under the Berne Convention, and the reasons for their rejection. The relationship between the Berne Convention and the later conventions on neighbouring rights is treated separately in Chapter 19 below.

(a) Sound and television broadcasts

8.111 By the time of the Rome Conference, the potential of radio broadcasting in relation to the diffusion of literary, dramatic, and musical works was fully recognized. One of the positive achievements of that Conference was the adoption of article 11bis(1) under which the authors of literary and artistic works were given the exclusive right of authorizing the communication of their works to the public by means of radiodiffusion. Television broadcasting was not yet a reality, although it was comprehended within article 11bis from the start. Revolutionary as it appeared, this article was purely an adjustment which was made to the system of protection established under the Convention to assure the protection of existing categories of works in the face of rapid technological change. However, a proposal made by France at the Rome Conference went much further. This envisaged the protection of radio broadcasts as works in their own right under article 2(1). Originally described in the French proposal as 'radiophonic works' ('*oeuvres radiophoniques*'),[484] the French delegation subsequently modified its proposal in response to objections that radiophonic works did not constitute a separate category, calling them 'works specially created for the purpose of radiodiffusion' ('*oeuvres spécialement créées en vue de la radiodiffusion*').[485] The purpose of this proposal, it was stated, was to cover 'those works *sui generis* which are neither written, nor oral, and the diffusion of which is only possible over radio (for example, the contemporaneous reporting of a football match . . .)'.[486] This objection was withdrawn by France after the Conference had adopted article 11bis, and did not therefore proceed to a vote. While it was open to member countries to protect these kinds of broadcast works under the general definition of 'literary and artistic works' in article 2(1), in the absence of any specific reference to radiophonic works, the persons who really stood to gain from the protection of broadcasts were not the persons who made the broadcasts, but the organizations which owned and operated the transmitters and employed these persons. Both at Rome and in the two decades following, however, these organizations were less interested in obtaining copyright protection

[484] *Actes* 1928, 98. [485] ibid, 226–7. [486] ibid, 227.

for their broadcasts than in gaining rights in relation to the use of material that was already subject to copyright.[487] They were successful in this second object at Rome,[488] and no further proposal was made for a copyright in broadcast works at Brussels. However, the Brussels Conference passed a resolution expressing the wish that the governments of Union countries should consider the best means of assuring the protection of broadcasts, without prejudice to the rights of authors.[489] After this time, no further move for protection under the Berne Convention was made, and the broadcasting organizations became actively involved in the lengthy preparations that were directed to the establishment of a separate international convention concerned with the protection of neighbouring rights (the Rome Convention) (see further Chapter 19 below).[490]

(b) Sound recordings

Following the invention of the phonograph by Edison in the late nineteenth century, a large industry concerned with the manufacture of sound recordings and similar devices had come into existence by the time of the Berlin Conference. At this Conference, authors of musical works were given exclusive rights with respect to mechanical reproductions of their works (article 13(1)), but allowance for the grant of compulsory licences to record manufacturers was also made (article 13(2)). During the Conference, however, the British delegates raised the question of whether it would be desirable to include in the Convention a provision specifically giving international copyright protection, in suitable cases, to the actual instruments on which the musical works were recorded—the gramophone discs, piano rolls, and the like.[491] Against this, it was maintained that these objects were on the borderline between 'industrial property' and copyright, and might conceivably be held to belong more properly to the former category.[492] The British Government repeated its suggestion at the Rome Conference, proposing the inclusion of the following paragraph to article 13: **8.112**

> Without prejudice to the rights of the authors of an original work, recordings, perforated rolls and other instruments by means of which sounds may be mechanically reproduced, shall be protected as original works.[493]

487 See generally Stewart (1989), 220, 222.
488 Rome Act, art $11^{bis}(2)$. See also Brussels Act, art 10bis.
489 *Documents 1948* (1951), 587.
490 Stewart (1989), 222ff.
491 *Correspondence* (1908), 14 (report of British delegates to the Foreign Secretary, Sir Edward Grey).
492 ibid. 493 *Actes* 1928, 94.

In making this proposal, it seems clear that the British Government was concerned with the protection of its own (extensive) recording industry.[494] Once again, it received considerable criticism on the ground that it was concerned with the protection of manufacturing, rather than authors', interests.[495] There were also attacks on the consistency of the UK Government's position, as it had, at the same Conference, opposed analogous proposals for the protection of performers.[496] The result was that no agreement was reached on the proposal, and it lapsed.[497] Although there was considerable discussion of mechanical reproduction rights and the rights of record manufacturers at the Brussels Conference,[498] no further proposal for the protection of recordings in their own right was made. However, the Conference passed a resolution, expressing the wish that countries of the Union should consider the best means of assuring the protection of recordings of musical works, without prejudice to the rights of authors.[499] As with broadcasts, this led record manufacturers to shift their attention from the Berne Convention to the possibility of securing international protection for their products under separate conventions, first, the Rome Convention of 1961, then the Phonograms Convention of 1971, and most recently, the WIPO Performers and Phonograms Treaty ('WPPT').[500] (As to whether sound recordings are, in any event, protected under the Convention as 'adaptations', see para 8.81 above.)

(c) Interpretations of performers

8.113 The claims of performers for protection under the Berne Convention differ somewhat from those of broadcasters and record manufacturers. While the activities of the latter involve considerable skill, it is arguably of a more mechanical or industrial kind, which is not readily akin to the more personalized and intellectual skills required for the authorship of a literary or artistic production. The position of a performer differs again: he seeks protection in respect of the particular interpretation or rendition which he has given to a pre-existing literary or artistic work. Obviously, no problem arises if the performer is also the author of the work which he performs, and the same is potentially the case where he

[494] See eg the submission by the Mechanical Music Industry of Great Britain made to the UK Government prior to the Rome Conference: G S Wood, *Preliminary Observations upon, and Arguments against, the Amendments to the Berne Convention of 1886 . . . proposed by the Italian Government in conjunction with the Office of the International Union for the Protection of Literary and Artistic Works, with General Suggestions for Revision of that Convention along Different Lines* (1927).

[495] *Actes* 1928, 263 (comments by the French delegation).

[496] ibid. [497] ibid, 264.

[498] *Documents 1948* (1951), 320ff. [499] ibid, 587.

[500] See also Stewart (1989), 223ff.

spontaneously creates an oral work in the course of his performance (in jurisdictions where fixation in some material form is not required). However, in the more usual situation where he performs a pre-existing work in which he has no rights, the only basis for a claim of protection under the Berne Convention is that his actual performance constitutes a literary or artistic work in its own right. Most Berne Union countries now accept that performers are entitled to some form of protection, particularly in the situation where their performances are fixed in some material form by a third party without permission and that fixation is then disseminated to the public. However, there has been greater uncertainty over whether this protection should be accorded at the same level as under the Berne Convention. As with oral works, difficulties of proof arise where it is sought to protect an unfixed performance. Another problem is that there may be a large number of performers involved in a particular performance, as in the case of a symphony orchestra. But of more fundamental importance is the question whether a performer, however skilled or individual his performance, can be regarded as an author, given that his performance is essentially parasitic on the work performed and does not usually involve the same kind of adaptations or modifications that are made in the case of other derivative works.

These matters were discussed in some detail at the Rome Conference, where the **8.114** Italian Government and International Office proposed that performers should be protected against unauthorized broadcasts and recordings of their performances,[501] and there were several supplementary proposals to include performances expressly in article 2.[502] While delegates were generally agreed that some kind of protection was warranted, there was no consensus on any of these proposals. It was, of course, open for a Union country to take the view that performances were, in any event, included under the general rubric of 'productions in the literary, scientific and artistic domain', but there was no general acceptance of this among the delegates. In particular, the French delegation made clear its view that performers were not authors,[503] and that performances were therefore not works within the Convention. Finally, a resolution was passed which requested Union countries to consider what measures they could take to protect the interests of performers, and the matter was left there.[504] In the period following the Rome Conference, opposition to protecting performers as authors continued to be expressed by various authors' organizations.[505] With this in mind, the programme for the Brussels Conference included a compromise

[501] *Actes* 1928, 78. [502] ibid, 229, 260. [503] ibid, 256, 260. [504] ibid, 350.
[505] See the texts of the various hostile resolutions collected in *Documents 1948* (1951), 455–7 and 493–4.

proposal for the protection of performances, which left it to each Union country to determine the conditions under which this protection was to be accorded.[506] A more specific British amendment proposed that unauthorized recordings of performances of dramatic or musical works should be prevented.[507] Once again, there was fairly general sympathy with the object of these proposals, but neither was accepted, as the commission now, more clearly than before, took the view that the protection of performers belonged outside the Convention.[508] Following the Brussels Conference, therefore, the path of separate protection was pursued, and eventually performers' rights were dealt with under the Rome Convention, and later the WPPT.[509]

(2) Other categories of works not protected

(a) Titles, slogans, and other insubstantial works

8.115 No mention is made in article 2 of titles, slogans, and other similar short works. These may often be of the greatest commercial value, for example, a catchy title for a book or film, or an arresting slogan for an advertising campaign. The laws of Union countries differ considerably on the extent to which, if at all, copyright protection may be claimed for these kinds of 'insubstantial' work,[510] although other heads of protection may also be available, for instance, laws on unfair competition.[511] As the Convention does not refer to these works specifically, there is no Conventional obligation to protect them unless they constitute 'writings' or 'literary . . . productions' in the more general use. This will therefore be a matter for national legislation to determine.

(b) Proposals to protect titles at the Brussels Conference

8.116 It is of interest to note that, prior to the Brussels Revision, some Union countries were in favour of according some measure of protection to the titles of works under the Berne Convention. This concern was also shared by authors' organizations, such as ALAI.[512] Accordingly, the International Office included a proposal to this effect in the tentative programme which it drew up for the Brussels Conference in 1934.[513] This did not propose that titles should be

[506] *Documents 1948* (1951), 308 (new art 11^{quater}). [507] ibid, 310–11. [508] ibid, 313.

[509] See further Stewart (1989), 221ff.

[510] See Ladas (1938), 242ff; Laddie et al (2000), 87ff; E Ulmer, *Urheber- und Verlagsrecht*, 3rd edn (1980), 173ff; Lucas and Lucas (n 13 above), para 108.

[511] Laddie et al (2000), 87ff; see also Lucas and Lucas (n 13 above), para 108, and Desbois (1978), para 193 (both suggesting that rationale for protection of titles corresponds more to trade marks than to copyright law).

[512] See [1934] *DA* 13, 18. But note that ALAI had some criticisms of the approach suggested by the International Office: see also the resolution to this effect passed by the meeting at Montreux in Jan 1935, reproduced in *Documents 1948* (1951), 465.

[513] [1935] *DA* 13, 18.

protected as 'works', but that they should be protected on the basis of unfair competition principles. This was received favourably by Union countries,[514] and was therefore retained in the programme which was drawn up for the Conference when it finally met in 1948. Designated as article 15*bis*, it read as follows:

> A title of a literary or artistic work, which presents a distinctive character, may not be utilised by a third party to designate another work, if this designation is of such a nature as to cause confusion between the two works.[515]

It will be seen from this that damage to the commercial interests of the 'owner' of the title was not a condition of protection: all that was required was confusion.[516] Prior to the Conference, a number of amendments to the proposal were made. These included a French proposal to stipulate expressly that the protection of titles was to be assured in all countries of the Union, and a British proposal to replace the requirement of distinctiveness by the more rigorous standard of notoriety.[517] However, when these proposals were discussed at the Conference itself, significant opposition to their adoption emerged. In part, this seems to have been reluctance to include a non-copyright type of measure in an international convention concerned with the protection of authors' rights.[518] There were also practical considerations raised by the British delegation: how would authors in one country know, in the absence of some kind of registration system, whether they were using a title which had already been employed in another country?[519] As a consequence, article 15*bis* lapsed, and it was decided that the Convention should not contain any provision concerned with the protection of titles.

(c) Works of folklore[520]

The vast majority of developed and developing countries possess a corpus of works of folklore. This may take widely differing forms, including unwritten songs and melodies, legends and tales, dances and mimes, paintings and carvings, **8.117**

---

[514] See [1936] *DA* 93, 94.

[515] *Documents 1948* (1951), 372 (for further background to the proposal, see ibid, 371).

[516] ibid, 371–2. [517] ibid, 372.

[518] A Baum, *The Brussels Conference for the Revision of the Berne Convention* (1949), 68ff.

[519] *Documents 1948* (1951), 373.

[520] See generally on the question of folklore: Barbara Friedman Klarman, 'Copyright and Folk Music: A Perplexing Problem' (1965) 12 *Bulletin of the Copyright Society of the USA* 277; M Niedzielska, 'Intellectual Property Aspects of Folklore Protection' [1980] *Copyright* 339; C Masouyé, 'Protection des expressions du folklore' (1983) 115 *RIDA* 2; E P Garilov, 'The Legal Protection of Works of Folklore' [1984] *Copyright* 76; A Dietz, *Urheberrecht und Entwicklungsländer* (1981); Gervais (n 443 above), 132–6; Agnès Lucas-Schloetter, 'Folklore', in Silke von Lewinski (ed), *Indigenous Heritage and Intellectual Property: Genetic Resources, Traditional Knowledge and Folklore* (2003), 259–378; WIPO, 'Consolidated Analysis of the Legal Protection of Traditional Cultural Expressions/Folklore', Background Paper No 1 (2003) (www.wipo.int).

and other artefacts. A great deal is often very old, but still in constant use. While this material is, in standard copyright terms, in the public domain, for many peoples there is still a strong spiritual and emotional importance attached to it that is 'proprietary' in character. In addition, there are many works of folklore that are new, either in the sense that they have been recently created as part of a continuing cultural tradition or in the sense that they are adaptations or modifications of older material. While copyright protection under the usual categories is potentially available in these last two instances, this may not be so for several reasons: (i) because of the lack of material fixation in the case of spoken or performed works (in those countries where fixation is a condition of protection), or (ii) the difficulty, and frequently the impossibility, of identifying the author or authors. Many works of folklore are the result of collective effort, and are often not thought of as the creations of individuals, but of a family, tribal, or other social grouping. As a consequence, there are significant gaps in the system of international protection offered by the Berne Convention as far as these kinds of work are concerned. Furthermore, the protection of these works raises issues that go beyond the usual concerns of the Berne Convention, involving important questions of a social, cultural, and religious kind.[521]

8.118 The inadequacy of the Berne Convention in this regard was not recognized until the Stockholm Revision Conference, when the issue was raised by the Indian delegation which proposed the inclusion of works of folklore in the enumeration of literary and artistic works in article 2(1).[522] However, while there was broad sympathy for this proposal among delegates,[523] it became clear that the Indian proposal left many problems unsolved, including the definition of 'folklore' and the way in which these works were to be protected in the absence of an identifiable author or authors. There were also differences between some delegates as to the extent to which works of folklore should be regarded as being in the public domain and therefore open to all to draw upon.[524] Nevertheless, Main Committee I decided to consider the question of folklore further, and appointed a working group under the chairmanship of Czechoslovakia for this purpose.[525] The latter took as its starting point the principle that a work of folklore was, by definition, the work of an unknown author, and proposed an amendment to article 15 which treated them as a special category of anonymous

[521] As is the case eg for the works of folklore of Australian Aborigines: see Australian Copyright Council, Bulletin No 44 (31 May 1983), 'The Protection of Aboriginal Folklore: Report of the Working Party'.

[522] *Records* 1967, vol I, 690–1 (Document S/73).

[523] ibid, vol II, 876–8 (minutes of Main Committee I).

[524] ibid, 878 (comments of the Canadian delegate).

[525] ibid.

work within the meaning of that article.[526] This provided that where a work was unpublished, the author was unknown, and there was 'every ground to presume that the author is a national of a country of the Union', the legislation of that country might designate a competent authority to represent the author, and this authority was entitled 'to protect the rights of the author in all the countries of the Union'.[527] A further paragraph provided that where such an authority was designated, the country in question was to notify WIPO, giving full information concerning the new authority, and that WIPO, in turn, was to communicate this information to all other Union countries.[528] The term 'folklore' was not used in the proposal, as the Working Group considered this to be extremely difficult to define.[529] However, while the provision applied to all works fulfilling the three conditions set out above, it was clear that its main field of application would be to 'those productions which are usually described as folklore'.[530] The provision was adopted without change by Main Committee I and became article 15(4) in the Stockholm Act.[531]

The above amendments were probably all that the Stockholm Conference could hope to achieve in relation to works of folklore, given its crowded agenda and limited time. The notion of a 'designated authority' was useful, as it allowed for the recognition of a special juridical person to represent and enforce the rights of a group of authors who were otherwise disenfranchised from the benefits of the Berne Convention. On the other hand, there is no necessity for member countries to appoint such authorities, and, in the event that they do so, article 15(4) contains no information as to how these bodies are to discharge their functions and responsibilities, for example, as regards the distribution and application of royalties. These matters remain to be determined by national legislation; and it is probably as well that the Convention seeks to go no further than this, as the issues involved in folklore protection go beyond those of a purely legal kind.[532] Article 15(4) contains a number of other limitations which should be noted. As stated above, it treats folklore ('the works of an unknown author') as a special category of anonymous works.[533] This means that the term of protection of anonymous works prescribed under article 7 applies to them; further, if the author of such a work reveals his identity, he may establish his claim to authorship in accordance with the last sentence in article 15(3).[534] However, article 15(4) also ceases to apply in the event that a work is published: the designated **8.119**

[526] ibid, 917 (verbal report of the Working Group to Main Committee I). See further ibid, vol I, 721, for text of the Working Group's proposal (Document S/240).

[527] ibid. [528] ibid. [529] ibid, 1173 (report of Main Committee I).

[530] ibid. [531] ibid, 918. [532] See Niedzielska (n 520 above).

[533] *Records* 1967, vol II, 1173 (report of Main Committee I).

[534] ibid: this sentence provides that the provisions of art 15(3) cease to apply when 'the author reveals his identity and establishes his claim to authorship of the work'.

authority (if one is appointed) will no longer have any jurisdiction for the purposes of the Convention. If the name of the publisher appears on the work published, the publisher will then be entitled to protect the unknown author (under article 15(3)), but this will be of little value if the author of the work is, in any event, unknown. Further regulation is therefore required here, if the interests of authors of folklore are to be protected adequately, as the greatest part of these works are already published. In addition, there is still a need for some kind of protection (not necessarily copyright) in the case of works of folklore that are in the public domain. Issues of a wider cultural and social importance are raised here, and a solution that goes beyond the province of the Berne Convention is required. Some significant international work has been done in this area in recent years,[535] but a consideration of this lies outside the scope of the present study.

G. Beyond the Berne Convention

8.120 The 1994 TRIPs Agreement, and the 1996 WCT, the two principal multilateral instruments to enter into force subsequent to the 1971 Paris text, address the subject matter of copyright in two ways. First, both treaties—article 2(1) of the TRIPs Agreement, and article 1(4) of the WCT—require member states to comply with articles 1 to 21 of the Berne Convention (although the TRIPs Agreement excludes article 6bis: see the further discussion at paras 10.38–10.47 below); article 3 of the WCT also, perhaps redundantly,[536] instructs contracting parties 'to apply *mutatis mutandis* the provisions of [article] 2 . . . of the Berne Convention in respect of the protection provided for in this Treaty'. As a result, those treaties fully incorporate all literary and artistic works covered by the earlier treaty. They also import the same exclusions of subject matter protection, and the same options to protect certain other subject matter.

The TRIPs Agreement and the WCT go further, however, in also mandating member state protection of computer programs and original compilations of data or other material. As we have seen (at paras 8.88–8.103 above), Berne's coverage of those works, though within the literal text of article 2(1) (to the extent those works were original), remained open to debate. The TRIPs

[535] See eg the Tunis Model Law on Copyright for Developing Countries, art 6, drawn up by WIPO in 1978. Note also the work of WIPO and UNESCO in drawing up detailed model provisions: Working Group on the Intellectual Property Aspects of Folklore Protection: [1981] *Copyright* 111–17; Regional Committee of Experts on Means of Implementation in Asia of Model Provisions on Intellectual Property Aspects of Protection of Expressions of Folklore: [1983] *Copyright* 195–200. See further Garilov (n 520 above) and Masouyé (n 520 above). WIPO is again in the process of revisiting the issue, see 'Consolidated Analysis' (n 520 above).

[536] See Ficsor (n 429 above), paras C3.05–3.06.

Agreement and the WCT purport to resolve ambiguities regarding the subject matter of computer programs, for they pronounce computer programs' inclusion within the Berne rubric 'literary works'. Both treaties also denominate original databases 'intellectual creations', and mandate that they be 'protected as such'.

(1) Computer programs

(a) The TRIPs Agreement and computer programs

Article 10 of the TRIPs Agreement provides: 8.121

> (1) Computer programs, whether in source or in object code, shall be protected as literary works under the Berne Convention (1971).
>
> (2) Compilations of data or other material, whether in machine readable or other form, which by reason of the selection and arrangement of their contents constitute intellectual creations shall be protected as such. Such protection, which shall not extend to the data or material itself, shall be without prejudice to any copyright subsisting in the data or material itself.

By the time the TRIPs Agreement was concluded in 1994, many member states of the General Agreement on Tariffs and Trade ('GATT') had already amended or interpreted their laws to protect computer programs. For example, the 1991 EU Software Directive already declared that 'Member States shall protect computer programs, by copyright, as literary works within the meaning of the Berne Convention . . .'.[537] US courts had interpreted the US Copyright Act, amended in 1980 expressly to include computer programs, to protect programs regardless of their form, whether in source or object code, and regardless of whether they were designed to interact with humans or merely to instruct the machine to perform certain functions.[538] Australia also protected computer software from 1984,[539] while Japan had done so by the end of the late 1980s.[540] Thus, at least in Berne member industrialized countries, copyright protection of computer

---

537 Council Directive of 14 May 1991 on the legal protection of computer programs, art 1, 91/250/EEC.

538 See eg *Apple Computer Inc* v *Franklin Computer Corp*, 714 F 2d 1240 (3d Cir 1983).

539 Copyright Amendment Act 1984.

540 See Japanese Law of 1970 (as last amended by Law No 72 of 19 June 2002), art 10(1)(ix), which specifically protects 'program works', although this is limited by art 10(3), which states 'The protection granted by this Law to works mentioned in paragraph (1), item (ix) shall not extend to any programming language, rule or algorithm used for making such works. In this case, the following terms shall have the meaning hereby assigned to them respectively: (i) "programming language" means letters and other symbols as well as their systems for use as means of expressing a program; (ii) "rule" means a special rule on how to use in a particular program a programming language mentioned in the preceding item; (iii) "algorithm" means methods of combining, in a program, instructions given to a computer.'

programs was something of a *fait accompli*.[541] This did not make software's inclusion in the TRIPs Agreement anticlimactic, however. Even if, as a matter of interpretation of the Berne Convention, many countries would have protected computer programs anyway, confirmation of that reading by the TRIPs Agreement, together with its overall Berne-compliance directive, and its requirement that member states implement effective enforcement mechanisms,[542] meant that effective sanctions could now be imposed against member states who had not so interpreted the Berne Convention (or who, regardless of any formal recognition of copyright in computer programs, were not enforcing their laws against infringers of computer programs).

8.122 (i) **Prior versions of article 10(1) of the TRIPs Agreement:** The final version of the computer program provision did not differ substantially from the core provision of preceding drafts. Both the Chairman's Report to the Group of Negotiation on Goods of 23 July 1990,[543] and the 3 December 1990 'Brussels draft'[544] categorized computer programs 'as literary works'. The earlier versions included the proviso that protection did not extend to ideas, procedures, etc, but that proviso was separated out and extended to all works of authorship in article 9(2) of the final version of the TRIPs Agreement.[545] The earlier versions also allowed member states leeway on enforcement of protection (July 1990 draft), and on imposition of formalities and exploitation-facilitating 'adjustments' to rights of reproduction, adaptation, and moral rights (December 1990 Brussels draft). These versions thus reflected some of the uncertainty that persisted throughout the 1980s regarding how to tailor copyright to computer programs. By the time of the final version, however, domestic and regional legislation or case law had largely resolved those doubts in favour of application of traditional copyright standards.

8.123 (ii) **Interpretation of article 10(1) 'whether in source or object code':** This specification is arguably redundant, given the declaration in article 2(1) of the Berne Convention that literary and artistic works are protected 'whatever may be the mode or form of [their] expression'. In context, however, the insistence on explicit repetition is understandable; during the 1980s, courts in different countries had differently resolved the question whether computer programs in

[541] See eg Gervais (n 429 above), 133, n 50 (by 1992 the copyright laws of fifty-four countries had been amended or judicially interpreted to cover computer programs).

[542] TRIPs Agreement, arts 41–61.

[543] Document MTN.GNG/NG11/W/76 (23 July 1990).

[544] Document MTN, TNC/W/35/Rev.1 (3 Dec 1990).

[545] On the history of the evolution of the proviso from art 10 to art 9, see Gervais (n 429 above), paras 2.98–2.99.

object code could be considered works of authorship when their machine-readable form—in 1s and 0s—was incomprehensible to humans.[546]

(iii) **Programs versus methods:** The specification also implies that a computer program is not to be considered per se functional or a 'method of operation' simply because it instructs a machine to carry out various functions. Thus, the prohibition in article 9(2) of the TRIPs Agreement of copyright protection for 'ideas, procedures, methods of operation or mathematical concepts as such', should be understood as distinguishing the method 'as such' from any particular implementation in machine-readable form. The combination of articles 9(2) and 10(1) of the TRIPs Agreement therefore directs member states on the one hand, to maintain the principle of protectability, but on the other to examine assertions of copyright in computer programs closely to ensure that protection of the program does not result in monopolization of the functions the program executes. For example, copyright properly protects a word-processing program as a whole, but the specific code for particular modules of the program may be necessary to carry out particular tasks; in the latter event, article 9(2) reminds member states that copyright in the program as a whole shall not 'extend' to that portion of the code 'as such'. **8.124**

(iv) **Interpretation of article 10(1) 'literary works':** The concept of 'literary works' comprehends works expressed in numbers as well as in words, and therefore applies to computer programs expressed in object code, as well as to computer programs expressed in a higher-level (more verbal) language. In addition, the denomination 'literary works' rather than 'literary and artistic works' clarifies that computer programs are not to be treated as 'applied art', with all of the limitations the Berne Convention permits as to those works.[547] But the categorization of computer programs as 'literary' does not relieve member state courts from inquiring into the extent to which the expression of a computer program, or of portions of it, is necessary to carry out the particular function the program is designed to execute. **8.125**

(b) WIPO Copyright Treaty and computer programs

Article 4 provides: **8.126**

> Computer programs are protected as literary works within the meaning of Article 2 of the Berne Convention. Such protection applies to computer programs whatever may be the mode or form of their expression.

---

[546] cf *Apple Computer Inc* v *Franklin Computer Corp*, 714 F 2d 1240 (3d Cir 1983) (holding US Copyright Act does not distinguish between source and object code) with *Inkassoprogram*, German Federal Republic, BGH Decision of 9 May 1985, [1985] *GRUR* 1041 (object code held unprotectable).

[547] See Gervais (n 429 above), para 2.106. Cf Reinbothe and von Lewinski (n 429 above), 67 (making the same observation regarding the 'literary works' formulation in WCT, art 4).

The WCT provision is essentially identical to article 10(1) of the TRIPs Agreement. The resemblance was intentional. The 'Basic Proposal for the Substantive Provisions of the Treaty on Certain Questions Concerning the Protection of Literary and Artistic Works to be Considered by the Diplomatic Conference: Memorandum Prepared by the Chairman of the Committees of Experts' states: 'Article 4 embodies the essential contents of the provisions of Article 10.1 of the TRIPs Agreement.'[548] The Memorandum, acknowledging the post-TRIPs Agreement (if not, indeed, pre-TRIPs Agreement) *fait accompli*, remarks, 'The provision is of a declaratory nature, and it explicitly codifies the established interpretation.'[549]

There are two differences in the wording of the TRIPs Agreement and the WCT texts. First, where article 10(1) of the TRIPs Agreement mandates that computer programs '*shall be* protected as literary works under the Berne Convention', article 4 of the WCT states that computer programs '*are* protected as literary works within the meaning of Article 2 of the Berne Convention'. The WCT's formulation is slightly more precise (signalling article 2 rather than the entire Berne Convention), and is consistent with the Memorandum's characterization of the WCT text as 'declaratory'. This suggests that if at the TRIPs' Agreement's enactment in 1994, some member states still had to be rallied round to the principle of copyright protection for computer programs, by 1996 this goal had been achieved.

Second, regarding a program's form of expression, where article 10(1) of the TRIPs Agreement states 'whether in source or object code', article 4 of the WCT declares 'whatever may be the mode or form of their expression'. The WCT formulation echoes article 2(1) of the Berne Convention, and has a further merit: it does not specify particular forms of expression. As a result, the WCT text will apply more comfortably than will the TRIPs Agreement in the event that some form or denomination of computer code other than 'source code' or 'object code' is later devised.

8.127 **(i) Interpretation of article 4 of the WCT:** Given the WCT text's deliberate tracking of the TRIPs Agreement, the interpretation given article 10(1) of TRIPs would apply equally to article 4 of the WCT. Moreover, article 2 of the WCT adopts almost verbatim the exclusion of ideas from the scope of copyright protection in article 9(2) of the TRIPs Agreement: 'Copyright protection

[548] Document CRNR/DC/4 (n 429 above), n 4.03.

[549] For more detailed discussion of the drafting history of WCT, art 4, see Reinbothe and von Lewinski (n 429 above), 64–6. For WCT drafting history and earlier developments in national and international copyright protection of computer programs, see Ficsor (n 429 above), para C4.01–4.17.

extends to expressions and not to ideas, procedures, methods of operation or mathematical concepts as such.' Thus, the observations offered earlier (see para 8.124 above), concerning the distinction between computer programs and the functions they execute, pertain to the WCT as well. The agreed statement concerning article 4 of the WCT reinforces this conclusion:

> The scope of protection for computer programs under Article 4 of this Treaty, read with Article 2, is consistent with Article 2 of the Berne Convention and on a par with the relevant provisions of the TRIPS Agreement.

One may note the arguable redundancy of the agreed statement's pronouncement that the Treaty's endorsement of the idea/expression distinction is 'consistent with Article 2 of the Berne Convention'. The WCT is a 'special agreement within the meaning of article 20 of the Berne Convention', as WCT article 1(1) establishes. This means that the WCT 'grant[s] to authors more extensive rights than those granted by the Convention, or contain[s] other provisions not contrary to the Convention'.[550] In other words, article 4 of the WCT, read with article 2 thereof, must not be *in*consistent with article 2 of the Berne Convention. This feature of the agreed statement may simply afford politically desirable surplus reassurance. A less jaundiced view might add that the assertion of the consistency of article 2 of Berne and the combination of articles 2 and 4 of the WCT serve to remind us that the idea/expression distinction is inherent in the Berne Convention as well. (See the earlier discussion at paras 5.49ff above.)

(2) Databases

(a) The TRIPs Agreement and databases

Article 10(2) of the TRIPs Agreement provides: **8.128**

> Compilations of data or other material, whether in machine readable or other form, which by reason of the selection or arrangement of their contents constitute intellectual creations shall be protected as such. Such protection, which shall not extend to the data or material itself, shall be without prejudice to any copyright subsisting in the data or material itself.

Article 10(2), whose text remained unchanged from the 1990 Brussels draft, largely tracks article 2(5) of the Berne Convention, substituting the phrase 'Compilations of data or other material, whether in machine readable or other form . . .' for article 2(5)'s 'Collections of literary or artistic works such as encyclopaedias and anthologies . . .'. The other departures of the text of the TRIPs Agreement from article 2(5) incorporate the clarifications discussed

[550] Berne Convention, art 20.

earlier in connection with the English-language version of the Berne text (see para 8.87 above): consistent with the authoritative French text, the TRIPs Agreement states 'selection *or* arrangement' in lieu of 'selection *and* arrangement'. The TRIPs Agreement also frames the 'without prejudice' clause by reference to '*any* copyright subsisting in the data . . .' instead of article 2(5) of Berne's '*the* copyright in each of the works forming part of such collections'. As discussed earlier (para 8.82 above), if read literally, article 2(5)'s 'without prejudice' proviso would apply only to works still under copyright; this could lead to the undesirable result that selection and/or arrangement of works in the public domain into a collection might accordingly rejuvenate the expired copyrights in the collected works and confer them on the collector. The TRIPs Agreement further avoids this outcome with respect to data and other copyrighted or non-copyrighted material by specifying that the protection attaching to the compilation 'shall not extend to the data or material itself'.

8.129 **(i) Background: protection of databases in domestic and regional law:** By the conclusion of the TRIPs Agreement, database protection may not have been as much of a *fait accompli* in national copyright laws as was protection for computer programs, but it was certainly a *fait en voie d'accomplissement.* Many national laws protected compilations of information under general standards of originality (in some cases, under somewhat relaxed standards of originality);[551] some, particularly in the Commonwealth, applied a more generous 'skill and labour' standard protecting the effort and expense of gathering information, even in the absence of original selection or organization.[552] The European Database Directive,[553] reaffirming the copyright protection of original databases, and harmonizing the standard of originality, was not enacted until 1996, but prior versions had been circulating since 1988.[554] The general principle of copyright protection for original compilations thus was well established, even if different countries may have articulated somewhat different thresholds of creativity.

---

[551] See eg Neeta Thakur, 'Database Protection in the European Union and the United States: The European Database Directive as an Optimum Global Model?' (2001) 1 *Intellectual Property Quarterly* 100, 112 (discussing database protection in Europe before the Directive, noting that Anglo-Irish systems had lower thresholds of originality than continental author's rights-centred systems).

[552] The UK Copyright, Designs and Patents Act 1988, as originally enacted, protected compilations under the same 'skill and labour' standard as other literary works, in s 3(1)(a).

[553] Directive 96/9/EC of the European Parliament and of the Council of 11 Mar 1996 on the legal protection of databases, OJ L 77/20 of 27 Mar 1996.

[554] See Green Paper on Copyright and the Challenge of Technology—Copyright Issues Requiring Immediate Action, Communication from the Commission, COM (88) 172 final of 7 June 1988, ch 6 on database protection; Working Programme of the Commission in the Field of Copyright and Neighbouring Rights, COM (90) 584 final of 17 Jan 1991, ch 6 on databases.

(ii) Interpretation of article 10(2) of the TRIPs Agreement 'intellectual creation': The text is clear that the form of a database's expression, whether digital or analogue, is irrelevant to its protectability. Rather, protection turns on whether the compilation is an 'intellectual creation'. As with article 5(2) of the Berne Convention, the elements of intellectual creativity—originality—are selection and arrangement, and the analysis offered with respect to the originality of collections of works (see para 8.87 above) would apply here as well. While member states retain some leeway to determine how creative the selection or arrangement must be for the work to qualify as an 'intellectual creation' (see para 8.87 above), the deliberate parallelism of article 10(2) of the TRIPs Agreement and article 5(2) of the Berne Convention suggests that the threshold of creativity a member state imposes on selection or arrangement should be the same for collections of works as for compilations of data or other material. Thus, for example, if chronological arrangement is deemed too banal to make a collection of poetry original, the same principle should apply to a collection of meteorological readings. On the other hand, if, in a given member state, the determination of when undated poems were in fact written is deemed to require sufficient intellectual endeavour to make their chronological collection an intellectual creation, then the same principle should apply to the organization of undated weather reports into a chronological compilation. **8.130**

(iii) Protection shall not extend to the data or material itself: This phrase affirms the independence of protection for the compilation from the existence, if any, of protection in the compiled material. It is a corollary of the 'without prejudice' proviso discussed in connection with article 2(5) of Berne (see para 8.90 above). Just as the copyright in a collection of works does not affect the protection, if any, in the collected works, so the compilation copyright cannot enlarge, prolong, or bestow any protection on the compiled components. **8.131**

(b) WIPO Copyright Treaty and databases

Article 5 of the WCT provides: **8.132**

> Compilations of data or other material, in any form, which by reason of the selection or arrangement of their contents constitute intellectual creations, are protected as such. This protection does not extend to the data or material itself and is without prejudice to any copyright subsisting in the data or material contained in the compilation.

This text is, intentionally, almost identical to article 10(2) of the TRIPs Agreement.[555] The Memorandum prepared by the Chairman of the Committees of

[555] The principal difference: WCT employs the phrase 'in any form' in lieu of 'whether in machine readable or other form' (TRIPs Agreement, art 10(2)). There appears to be no substantive difference between the formulations, though the WCT's is somewhat closer to art 2(1) of the Berne Convention.

Experts recognizes that the text 'follows closely' article 10(2) of the TRIPs Agreement.[556] As with the WCT provision on computer programs (see para 8.126 above), the Memorandum asserts that the provision on databases 'is of a declaratory nature. It confirms what is already covered by the Berne Convention.'[557] As we have seen, logically (despite the somewhat more ambiguous history of article 2(1): see paras 8.08ff above), if selection and arrangement are the hallmarks of 'intellectual creation', then original collections of data should come within the Berne Convention to the same extent as do original collections of works. Moreover, many national laws did protect original compilations of data, as well as original collections of works (see paras 8.91, 8.129 above), and by the time of the WCT, the EU Database Directive had been promulgated. Hence, the affirmative statement that compilations of data 'are protected'. As a result, if any WCT contracting party had not previously protected original compilations of non-works, it would, on joining the WCT, henceforth be obliged to do so. (That same state, if a WTO member, would already have assumed a duty to protect original databases per article 10(2) of the TRIPs Agreement, a duty which under this now-dominant reading of the Berne Convention, that state, were it a member of the Berne Union, would already have incurred.)

8.133 (i) **Interpretation of article 5 of the WCT:** The observations offered earlier (see para 8.130 above) concerning 'intellectual creation' and the non-extension of protection to the compiled material in the context of article 10(2) of the TRIPs Agreement apply equally to article 5 of the WCT. In addition, there is an agreed statement to article 5 of the WCT:

> The scope of protection for compilations of data (databases) under Article 5 of this Treaty, read with Article 2, is consistent with Article 2 of the Berne Convention and on a par with the relevant provisions of the TRIPs Agreement.

The observations made with respect to the almost identical agreed statement to article 4 of the WCT apply generally here as well, although it is even less clear what the agreed statement adds to the understanding of the scope of protection for databases. This is because, where the idea/expression distinction that limits the protection of computer programs appears in article 2 of the WCT rather than article 4,[558] the analogous fact/expression distinction limiting the scope of protection for compilations is integral to article 5 of the WCT. It is therefore not apparent what a further cross-reference to the idea/expression distinction contributes to our understanding of (as opposed to our comfort with) the reach of database protection.

[556] Document CRNR/DC/4 (n 429 above), 184.

[557] ibid. For more detailed discussion of the drafting history of WCT, art 5, see Reinbothe and von Lewinski (n 429 above), 70–1, Ficsor (n 429 above), C5.01–5.05.

[558] And in TRIPs Agreement, art 9(2) rather than 10(1).

H. Comparative Table of Works Protected

8.134

	Berne Convention	Gaps left to national law and ambiguities	TRIPS Agreement (beyond article 9(1) compliance clause)	WCT (beyond article 1(4) compliance clause)	Gaps and ambiguities
WORK PROTECTED—					
literary and artistic works	article 2(1)	In theory, none: article 2(1) embraces 'every production in the literary, scientific and artistic domain, whatever may be the mode or form of its expression'. But ambiguities persist regarding what constitutes such a 'production' and what is the required level of originality. Moreover, in practice member states have been reluctant to protect works not specifically enumerated in article 2(1) with resulting uncertainty and disuniformity regarding, notably, computer programs and databases (see below).			
illustrative list of literary and artistic works	article 2(1)	Level of originality required for the protectability of each class of these works			

Continued overleaf

	Berne Convention	Gaps left to national law and ambiguities	TRIPS Agreement (beyond article 9(1) compliance clause)	WCT (beyond article 1(4) compliance clause)	Gaps and ambiguities
derivative works (translations, adaptations, arrangements of music, other alterations of literary or artistic work)	article 2(3)	These works are 'protected as original works' but originality standard not enunciated; 'original' here may mean 'works in their own right' without prejudice to copyright in underlying work.			
compilations of works or of data	article 2(5): collections of literary or artistic works constituting 'intellectual creations' by virtue of selection or arrangement of their contents	Article 2(5) limited to collections of 'works'; collections of *data* covered, if at all, under general art 2(1) rubric of 'literary and artistic works'; standard of originality for 'intellectual creations'	article 10(2) (compilations of data constituting 'intellectual creations' by virtue of selection or arrangement of their contents)	article 5 (compilations of data; same as TRIPs Agreement article 10(2))	standard of originality for 'intellectual creations'
computer programs	article 2(1) coverage of 'whatever may be the mode or form of . . . expression' of literary or artistic work should be broad enough to cover computer programs whether in source or object code, but computer programs not enumerated in article 2(1)	Whether a computer program is a literary or artistic work; standard of originality	article 10(1) (computer programs, whether in source or object code, protected as 'literary works')	article 4 (computer programs protected as literary works, whatever may be the mode or form of their expression) Agreed Statement recalling TRIPs Agreement, article 9(2) and WCT, article 2 exclusion of ideas, procedures, methods of operation or mathematical concepts	

EXCLUSIONS—					
news of the day; miscellaneous facts having character of press information	article 2(8) mandatory exclusion	'Authentic interpretation' resolves ambiguity regarding what constitutes 'news of the day': understood to mean information, not the journalistic account (which may qualify as a literary work)			
ideas, procedures, methods of operation or mathematical concepts	arguably implicit in article 2(8), and in article 2(1) concept of 'expression' and in article 2(5) concept of 'intellectual creation'		article 9(2) mandatory exclusion	article 2 mandatory exclusion	distinction between these items and their protected 'expression'
official legislative, administrative, and legal texts and their official translations	article 2*bis*(1) allows member states to determine protection to be granted (implicitly: allows member states to exclude protection)	What constitutes an 'official' text			
unfixed works	article 2(2) allows member states to exclude	What is 'fixed'; difference between 'fixed' and 'ephemeral'			
works of applied art	article 2(7) allows member states to exclude by limiting protection to non copyright regime of designs and models protection				

9

DURATION OF PROTECTION (BERNE CONVENTION, ARTICLES 7 AND 7BIS; TRIPs AGREEMENT, ARTICLE 12; WCT, ARTICLE 9)

A. Introduction

This is an area where the prescriptions of the Berne Convention are quite specific, and leave relatively little room for interpretation in their application by national legislation. This has happened within a comparatively short period: the first permissive rule concerning duration of protection appeared in the Berlin Act (article 7(1)), and was made absolute and binding in the Brussels Act. It was accompanied by a number of supplementary rules relating to the term of protection in specific cases. Duration is one of the most important issues in international copyright relations, and in this respect the Convention's achievements have been impressive. It is also a striking instance where the Convention has played an educative role in bringing about changes in the domestic laws of a number of Union countries, rather than reflecting changes that had already occurred in those laws. But where the Convention had once set the prevailing (and generous) minimum term, more recently, many of the Union's most significant member states, including the countries of the European Union and the USA, have adopted yet longer terms. The resulting disharmony has prompted bilateral negotiations as Union countries who have implemented longer terms seek to persuade those who have yet to exceed the Conventional minimum.[1] **9.01**

B. General Considerations

(1) Reasons for limiting duration of copyright protection

Placing a temporal restriction on copyright protection is, in one sense, paradoxical. In the great bulk of countries, including those with common law systems, copyright is treated as a property right. Why, then, should it not be perpetual like other rights of property? Neither land nor chattels fall into the public domain after the passing of a particular period of time: why should this happen in the case of authors' rights with respect to their literary and artistic works? The fact remains, however, that in the vast majority of countries copyright protection is of limited duration, usually for the life of the author and a fixed period of years. Within the Berne Union itself, there has been only one country, Portugal, which has allowed protection in perpetuity, and this is no longer the case.[2] What, then, are the justifications for limiting protection in this way? **9.02**

[1] See eg United States-Singapore Free Trade Agreement, art 16.4(4) (signed 6 May 2003) (www.mti.gov.sg); United States-Chile Free Trade Agreement, art 17.5(4) (signed 6 June 2003) (www.ustr.gov/assets).

[2] Law of 27 May 1927, arts 15(1) and 36; see now Code of Copyright and Related Rights (No 45/85 of 17 Sept 1985), arts 31–9.

9.03 Reasons of practicality and convenience can be advanced for doing this. As time passes, it becomes more difficult to trace and identify the person or persons entitled to an author's rights. The latter may have become fragmented, and there may be a multitude of persons with claims to different rights, or to shares in those rights. It therefore saves considerable time and trouble to declare that, after a certain period, these rights will cease to exist, and the works in question will pass into the public domain for anyone to use. It is for these reasons that the common law systems frequently impose strict limitations on the duration of intangible property rights, including copyright.[3] Similar reasons were expressly referred to in the explanatory memorandum ('*Begründung*') to the German Copyright Law of 1965:

> . . . because after only a few hereditary successions owing to the often complex laws of succession and increasing legal fragmentation, the certain determination of the legal owners which is necessary for legal transactions would no longer be at all possible or only with great difficulty.[4]

Such arguments are not altogether convincing, as it is possible that these difficulties could be overcome by measures such as a system of registration or deposit, akin to those most countries have adopted for tracking title in land. While these systems have proven cumbersome in the past, the use of computer databases would now make them far easier to administer.

9.04 However, there are further reasons for placing limitations on the duration of copyright. These go to the nature of the 'property' at issue. While the author's intellectual labour affords one basis for arguing that the fruits of that labour should belong to the author, the analogy drawn from natural-rights justifications for property in land and its fruits is not fully persuasive. Literary property differs from land and chattels in significant ways, most notably in the 'non-rivalrous' manner of its consumption. That is, the supply does not diminish with use: because the work is independent of the physical copy in which it may be incorporated, any number of people may read, listen to, or view the work, without depriving another person of the same enjoyment. Because the work is infinitely replicable, a reader in Australia takes nothing from a simultaneous reader of the same work in the USA; with other kinds of goods by contrast, two persons could not consume the same item without encroaching on the other's allotment.

This also has meant that traditional self-help measures to safeguard property, such as fences and locks, were typically unavailing; once a work was published or publicly disclosed, the author could not physically prevent others from further

[3] See eg the Limitations of Actions Acts in many common law countries preventing the recovery of debts and other property after a period of time.

[4] Law of 9 Sept 1965 (translation taken from A Dietz, *Copyright Law in the European Community* (1978), 161) ('Dietz (1978)').

publishing or performing the work (at least, not before the advent of certain digital technologies). State intervention, generally through judicial process, was therefore required to vindicate the author's rights. The necessary resort to state enforcement tends to mute the absolutism of authors' claims; rather, it prompts characterizations of copyright as a quid pro quo—state assistance in return for something back to society. Literary and artistic works perform other functions than providing remuneration for authors and vehicles for them to disseminate their views and ideas and to enhance their reputations. They inform, entertain, provoke, educate, inspire, and elevate. They therefore have important social, cultural, and economic roles, and there is a clear public interest in ensuring that they continue to do so. The expiration of exclusive rights (as well as the delimitation of their contours; see further Chapter 13 below) can be seen as an essential part of the social bargain.

Reasons inherent to authorship also urge a limited term. The individual author **9.05** should be encouraged to create, and to continue creating, her works. But few works are created whole from the void; many, if not most, authors draw from their predecessors. The copyright term limits the extent of these borrowings; while exclusive rights are still in force they constrain later authors' appropriations. With the passing of time, particularly after the author dies, a work should become 'common property', a part of the general resources for other authors, as well as of a nation and the world at large. At this stage, they should be free for anyone to use in whatever way he or she may choose. Education and general cultural life will be enhanced as a result, and a useful basis is provided for further derivative creative endeavours. This transmutation from the private to the public realm occurs in relation to even the most banal kinds of work: at the very least, the latter come to represent valuable cultural and social records of the past upon which future generations of authors and users may wish to draw.

If private rights in a work are retained beyond a reasonable period, they will **9.06** become oppressive and anti-social. Not only can an excessive term disable later authors, it may not significantly advantage the first author, as the copyright will by then be controlled by someone far removed from the first author. So far as the authors themselves are concerned, they will long since have died, and, if the period of protection after their deaths is carefully determined, there will be no prejudice to the welfare of their immediate successors. For these reasons, it can be said that it is inappropriate for literary and artistic works to be protected in perpetuity.

(2) Length of protection

Deciding that the protection of literary and artistic works should be limited in **9.07** time is one thing; determining how long that period should be is quite another.

What criterion should guide this decision? A study of the development of modern copyright laws shows that the period of protection has steadily increased in most countries. It has long been accepted that the basic term should be the life of the author plus a fixed period of years. The fundamental assumption here seems to be that the author and his or her immediate family should have the prospect of earning some return for the work. Even if the author receives little or no direct remuneration during his or her lifetime, his or her spouse and children may receive some benefit subsequently if the work has delayed success. The increasingly lengthy term of copyright in part reflects the growing life expectancy of the author's heirs. Keying the term of protection to the life of the author also is in keeping with the humanistic characterization—particularly prevalent in civil law countries—of copyright as an emanation of the author's personality.

9.08 But the determination of a particular period of years *post mortem auctoris* is ultimately an arbitrary matter, and does not take account of several important facts. First, the real beneficiary of the copyright may not be the author, it may be an assignee or an employer. In such a case, the new copyright owner may be a publisher, film producer, promoter, or the like, and the copyright therefore represents a protection for the investment that these persons undertake in the publication or presentation of the work in question. In other words, it is a safeguard against the potential unfair competition of other parties who might seek to 'reap where they have not sown'. Unless the author continues to receive royalties from her grantee, fixing the term of protection by reference to the life of the author plus a term of years has no direct relevance in these cases: the real question is whether the term granted is sufficient to allow the investor time to recover its investment and to earn a reasonable return on that investment.

Second, once the work's creator no longer serves as the point of reference, it is very difficult to estimate what an appropriate term for investment recoupment should be, as individual works enjoy varying levels of popularity, and may reach the point of profitability at different times. Furthermore, there are works which never reach this point at all, or only do so after many years with changing fashions. There is always a large element of risk involved: many publishers, for instance, work on the basis that their less successful ventures will be subsidized or offset by their more profitable ones. Determining the appropriate period of protection is therefore a complex matter, and there are few relevant statistics to show, on average, what term of protection would be the minimum required to enable a publisher or promoter to garner a return on its investment that would permit both cross-subsidization of new works and a reasonable profit on the old ones, without placing excessive restrictions on the public. These commercial considerations, however, seem far removed from authors and their immediate concerns, except insofar as the pecuniary interests of the latter continue to be involved with the interests of those who undertake the exploitation of their works. When authors retain no such interest, to talk of the natural or imprescriptible rights of authors is artificial, and theory becomes sharply divorced from reality.

The Berne Convention has not escaped this confusion. While its prescriptions as to duration are quite precise, there has never been any real effort made by the Convention's drafters and revisers to justify why, or to explain how, these terms have come to be adopted. The absence of justification seems particularly jarring in light of the frequent alienation of authors from the exploitation of their works, as discussed above. The reason for this, in part, is to be found in the strong influence which continental European legal doctrine has had on the development of the Convention. This has always emphasized the property rights of authors in their creations, with the consequence that little objection has been made to lengthy terms of protection. In addition, continental authors may retain greater ties to their works than may authors in common law countries. Many continental copyright laws provide for the author's continuing economic return; they require that grantees confer a remuneration proportional to each form of exploitation.[5] As a result, even if the author no longer controls the choice and manner of exploitations, she will continue to be paid for them. The author's retention of an economic interest may justify making the life of the author, and some reasonable period benefiting her heirs, the focal point for the calculation of term. Moreover, collective licensing societies, controlled by authors' representatives, have historically wielded considerable economic power on the continent, and constitute an important counterforce to grantees whose considerable bargaining power authors' collectives can thus offset.[6] Accordingly, many have urged that only the longest possible term which is politically feasible should be accepted.[7] **9.09**

In the common law countries, quite a different approach can be seen. Although **9.10**

[5] See eg William R Cornish, 'The Author as Risk-Sharer' (2002) 26 *Colum J L & the Arts* 1, 7–11.

[6] For examples of EU Commission and other actions against collective licensing societies, alleging abuses of a dominant position, see eg *Lucazeau* v *Société des Auteurs, Compositeurs et Éditeurs de Musique (SACEM)*, Joined Cases 110, 241, and 242/88, [1989] ECR 2811, [1991] 4 CMLR 248; *Ministère Public* v *Tournier & Verney*, Joined Cases 395/87, 110/88, 241–2/88, [1989] ECR 2521, [1991] 4 CMLR 248; *Greenwich Films* v *SACEM*, Judgment of 25 Oct 1979, Case 22/79 [1979] ECR 3275; *Basset* v *SACEM*, Judgment of 9 Apr 1987, Case 402/85 [1987] ECR 1747.

[7] On the debates over the question of perpetuity at the Literary Congress of 1858, see para 2.05 above. See further on the general question of extension of protection, A Ciampi, *La durée du droit d'auteur dans le cadre de l'intégration européenne: La durata del diritto d'autore nel quadro dell'integrazione europea*, 2nd edn (1974). But see Victor Hugo's argument for terminating exclusive rights at the author's death but then establishing a *domaine public payant, Address to Congrès littéraire international de Paris 1878* (1879), 216–18.

copyright in these countries is treated as a property right, it is also viewed in functional terms which place more emphasis on the social and economic effects of protection. Under this approach, the property concept is a legal device which is adopted to achieve certain desirable policy ends—to promote creative endeavour, on the one hand, and to ensure maximum public access to the benefits of these endeavours, on the other. In common law countries, the natural-rights justification for copyright, though present,[8] is often muted, particularly in the Commonwealth; the analogy is instead often drawn with industrial property rights, such as patents and industrial designs, and the emphasis therefore is on shorter, rather than longer, terms. The debates in the UK during the nineteenth century illustrate this way of thinking quite vividly. In the parliamentary debates over the Literary Copyright Act of 1842, Macaulay posited that the principle of copyright, establishing a monopoly, was 'exceedingly bad', and could be justified only because there was no better way to achieve the socially desirable goal of generating 'a supply of good books'. It followed, however, that copyright was tolerable only for so long as it was achieving its object of encouraging authors to write by providing them with the possibility of some reward for their activities. To allow the monopoly to extend beyond the time needed to stimulate creativity would harm the public by keeping the prices of books high in the absence of competition. Accordingly, Macaulay was successful in limiting the original term of sixty years which had been proposed by Serjeant Talfourd to a more modest forty-two years.[9] Similar arguments were made before the 1878 Royal Commission on Copyright by the Board of Trade, which was strongly influenced by free trade ideas. Its secretary, J H Farrer, made a concerted plea for limiting the duration of copyright protection, or even abolishing it altogether, in the interests of 'cheaper books' and increased public literacy.[10] These arguments were not successful, and eventually the UK came to adopt terms in line with those of her continental neighbours. However, the nineteenth-century functionalist approach of the English free-traders has continued to find supporters in the twentieth century, particularly in the USA.[11]

[8] Jane C Ginsburg, 'A Tale of Two Copyrights: Literary Property in Revolutionary France and America', in Brad Sherman and Alain Strowel (eds), *Of Authors And Origins: Essays On Copyright* (1994), 131, 137–9 (reviewing natural-rights bases for US copyright law).

[9] See T Macaulay, *Speeches on Copyright*, ed C Gaston (1914). See further T N Talfourd, *Three Speeches Delivered in the House of Commons in Favour of a Measure for an Extension of Copyright* (1840). The forty-two years did, however, represent a longer term than the one previously in force; Macaulay did not object to term extension per se (in fact he supported the forty-two-year term), but rather to terms not demonstrably tied to the incentive to create.

[10] Copyright Commission, *The Royal Commissions and the Report of the Commissioners*, C-2036 (1878). See also the review of the evidence before the Commission in the *Edinburgh Review*, Oct 1878, No 304.

[11] See eg Sir Arnold Plant, 'The Economic Aspects of Copyright in Books', *Economica*, May 1934; S Breyer, 'The Uneasy Case for Copyright: A Study of Copyright Books, Photocopies and

Asking what is the desirable length of copyright protection inevitably implicates the premises justifying that protection. These include, on the one hand, the 'labour-deserts' and the 'personality of the author' theories, founding a natural-property right in the fruits of the author's creativity or in the authorial presence with which the work is vested, and, on the other, the incentive rationale. The incentive rationale, albeit most often evoking incentives to create, can also apply to incentives to invest in the work. In this latter guise it invites the cross-subsidization corollary. The 'property and personality rights' approaches, if no longer urging perpetual protection, would at the very least ground protection in the life of the author, perhaps plus the lives of the author's dependants. The incentive rationale would inquire how long protection must be afforded in order to convince the author that her work will generate sufficient returns over time to make its creation worthwhile. In the rationale's corporate guise, the reference point would be return on investment, or, for the cross-subsidization corollary, return on investment sufficient to earn a profit on the first work, and have enough left over to invest in other, potentially less profitable, works. (This last version of the rationale, however, may be dangerously self-serving: one would not expect economically motivated publishers to invest in marginal works simply out of altruism or public relations. Rather, the cross-subsidization rationale may serve to prolong the copyright term on the ground that public taste for the cross-subsidized work requires much maturation that may not ripen during a shorter term. As a result, this rationale could lead to the determination that copyright should be prolonged in both the work whose returns subsidize the marginal work, and in the subsidized work as well.) Each question deriving from an incentive rationale is likely to yield a different answer, depending, for example, on the nature of the work (instant bestseller or 'serious' music whose audience develops very slowly over a long time). Were one to follow this through, a highly fragmented, unpredictable, and probably arbitrary system for calculating copyright term would certainly result. But no variation on the incentive rationale is likely to produce a useful guideline for determining appropriate duration. This is because no reliable empirical evidence exists to prove, or disprove, the effects of increased or decreased copyright term on authorial creativity or corporate investment. Recourse to incentive analyses ultimately masks the normative assumptions that more often underlie the inquiry into how long a term a creator or investor 'needs' in order to stimulate creation or dissemination of works of authorship. In asking 'what duration supplies just enough incentive to keep authors writing (or publishers publishing)—and not one day more', this 9.11

Computer Programs' (1970) 84 *Harv L Rev* 281; B Tyerman, 'The Economic Rationale for Copyright Protection for Published Books: A Reply to Professor Breyer' (1971) 18 *UCLA Law Review* 1100; and Breyer (1972) 20 *UCLA Law Review* 75. See also *Eldred* v *Ashcroft*, 537 US 186, 245–8 (2003) (Breyer, J, dissenting).

approach in fact is positing that copyright owners *should* enjoy exclusive rights only for a determined period. The length of that period will reflect the strength of the exponent's advocacy of a vigorous public domain.

Calculating duration by reference to the life of the author may be more objectively coherent, but is no less normative, for it makes creativity the focal point. In so doing, moreover, it may supply its own limiting principle: other creators await expiration of the copyright term in order to make their own variations on prior works. The longer the term, the longer the wait, with the potential for concomitant frustration of creativity.

9.12 In the absence of clear factual evidence on these matters, one can only raise questions, not provide answers. Nonetheless, doubt must remain over two of the linchpins of the Berne Convention provisions on duration: the tendency towards a uniformly longer term for all works, and the length of that term. As will be seen below (see paras 9.14ff), there has never been any attempt during the life of the Convention to examine these questions. The reason for this has been suggested above: the strong emphasis that has always been placed on the natural-property rights of the author in his or her work. In this respect, one copyright ideology has replaced critical inquiry, and has led to a long period of protection—the life of the author plus fifty years—becoming enshrined as an absolute value that has seldom been challenged, except where there have been moves for its further extension, as have successfully taken place as a matter of domestic law in many Union countries, including the USA and the members of the European Union, where the term has now reached life plus seventy years. Even the common law countries, with their more pragmatic approaches to copyright protection, have acquiesced in this development, and the same has been largely true of the developing countries,[12] which have even more reason to question the need for long terms of protection. In the case of the common law countries, particularly the USA, however, the increasing economic significance of copyright to domestic economies may well suggest a different—albeit ever-pragmatic—calculus, now favouring longer periods of exclusivity. Nonetheless, the emergence of this cast-iron orthodoxy surely owes much to the single-mindedness of the founders of the Convention, and is described below (see paras 9.14ff). Before proceeding to this, however, it is necessary to say

[12] Developing countries that have recently joined the Berne Convention with its longer duration for protection include: Saudi Arabia (11 Mar 2004), Syrian Arab Republic (11 June 2004), United Arab Emirates (11 July 2004), Democratic People's Republic of Korea (North Korea) (28 Apr 2003), Micronesia (7 Oct 2003), Djibouti (13 May 2002), and Tonga (14 June 2001). Some countries have signed bilateral agreements providing for even longer terms of protection. For example, Chile has signed a bilateral treaty with the United States extending terms of copyright protection to lengths beyond those provided for under Berne (see n 1 above).

something about moral rights which need to be taken into account in any consideration of the question of duration of protection.

(a) *The dual aspect of copyright*

Under many legal systems, copyright is conceived as having two distinct aspects. The first are the pecuniary or property rights of the author ('*les droits pécuniaires*' or '*patrimoniaux*'). These are the rights to exploit the work, for example, through reproduction, performance, broadcasting, and so on. The second are the personal rights that are linked indissolubly to the person of the author. These are usually referred to as 'moral rights' ('*les droits moraux*'), and are not directly concerned with the commercial exploitation of the work, but relate essentially to the way in which it is presented to the world. In essence, they comprise the rights to determine when and how the work is divulged, to protect its integrity, and to maintain the author's identification with it.[13] As these rights are personal to the author, it can be argued that they should cease on his death. On the other hand, it can be said that, following his death, his family, and perhaps even society as a whole, have an equal interest in upholding them, and that they should therefore be perpetual. **9.13**

The different approaches taken by countries adopting this twofold view of authors' rights introduce further complexity. Some of these countries adhere to a 'dualist' conception of copyright, while others view copyright through a 'monist' lens. The 'dualist' concept of copyright treats pecuniary rights as independent of moral rights. It is therefore possible for each right to have different legal outcomes in relation to such matters as their duration, alienability, and so on. Thus, even if the need for some temporal limitation on pecuniary rights is acknowledged, the same consequence does not necessarily follow for moral rights. By contrast, the 'monist' concept of authors' rights views the pecuniary and moral interests of the author as interdependent and protected by the one homogeneous copyright (or 'author's right'). Dr Dietz explains the implications of this theory as follows:

> . . . the power to object to the amendment or distortion of the work can correspond to the personal interest of the author in keeping his work unadulterated, and also to his financial interest in preventing the exploitation of his work from being impaired by changes or corruptions. Conversely, successful commercial exploitation that leads to the work and its author becoming widely known through reproductions and performances also serves his personal interests, in spreading his ideas and his personal reputation.[14]

---

[13] See generally Dietz (1978), 66ff.

[14] Dietz (1978), 69. See also André Lucas and Henri-Jacques Lucas, *Traité de la propriété littéraire et artistique*, 2nd edn (2001), para 29.

As a result of this interdependence, the question of duration is the same for each set of rights: if pecuniary rights are limited in time, the same period should apply to moral rights and vice versa. Until recently, these different views as to the nature of moral and pecuniary rights were immaterial as far as most common law countries were concerned, as the copyright laws of these countries did not expressly recognize moral rights. Starting in the 1990s, however, the USA (in 1990, but to a very limited extent), the UK (in 1988), Australia (in 2000), New Zealand (in 1994), and Ireland (in 2000) have introduced statutory moral rights provisions.[15] The US version seems to follow the 'dualist' approach, as the moral rights it confers on visual artists expire on their death.[16] The unease with which these countries had historically greeted their obligations under the Berne Convention is discussed further in Chapter 10 below, and the matter of the duration of these rights under the Berne Convention is also discussed in that chapter. Our main concern for the remainder of this chapter will be with the requirements of the Convention with respect to the duration of pecuniary rights.

C. Historical Background

(1) The general term of protection

9.14 Prior to 1886, there was little uniformity in the length of copyright protection accorded in those countries which subsequently formed the Berne Union (see further para 1.10 above). Only three of these (Belgium,[17] France,[18] and Tunisia[19]) had adopted the present term of life plus fifty years. The remainder had widely differing terms, including a period of forty-two years or life plus seven years (whichever was the longer) in the UK,[20] life plus twenty years in Haiti,[21] life plus thirty years in Germany[22] and Switzerland,[23] differing periods in Italy,[24] and life plus eighty years in Spain.[25] In the light of these differences, no proposal for a uniform term was included in either the ALAI draft of 1883 or the Federal

[15] See United States, 17 USC § 106A; United Kingdom, Copyright, Designs and Patents Act 1988, ss 77–89; Australia, Copyright Amendment (Moral Rights) Act 2000, s 195AF(2); New Zealand, Copyright Act 1994, §§94–110 (of 15 Dec 1994); Ireland, Copyright and Related Rights Act 2000, ss 107–19.

[16] See 17 USC § 106A(d).

[17] Law of 22 Mar 1886, art 2.

[18] Law of 14 July 1866.

[19] Law of 15 June 1889, art 2.

[20] Copyright Act 1842, s 3. The period of protection differed for engravings and sculptures: see para 1.10 above.

[21] Law of 8 Oct 1885, arts 5 and 6. See further [1925] *DA* 124.

[22] Law of 11 June 1870, art 8.

[23] Law of 1883, art 2.

[24] Decree of 19 Sept 1882, art 9.

[25] Law of 1879, art 6; see further para 1.10 above.

Council programme for the 1884 Conference.[26] The result of this omission was that authors claiming under either text would, under the principle of national treatment, enjoy the same period of protection as authors of the country in which they claimed protection. This meant that an author would enjoy differing periods of protection throughout the countries of the Union, and might even enjoy a longer period than he was entitled to in his own country (as would be the case with an English or German author in France or Spain). These imbalances were highlighted by the German delegation in the questionnaire which it put before the Conference during its first session. Question 5 read as follows:

> The duration of protection being limited in very diverse ways by different laws, is it not desirable, and even urgent, to regulate this question uniformly throughout all the projected Union? Or should the principle established in previous literary conventions be maintained under which the protection accorded reciprocally to authors of the two contracting countries will only be assured to them during the existence of their rights in their country of origin, and that the period of their enjoyment in the other country may not exceed that fixed by the law for national authors?[27]

These might be described respectively as the 'Conventional' approach, that is, fixing a term in the Convention for all signatories to adopt, and applying the law of the author's own country (*lex loci originis*). The first is obviously the simplest and fairest: authors would receive the same term everywhere in the Union. However, the difficulties of obtaining agreement on the adoption of such a rule are obvious. As for the second, this could be seen as a justifiable exception to the general principle of national treatment as it avoided the inequalities that could arise where national treatment 'pure and simple' (the *lex loci protectionis*) was applied. At the 1884 Conference, strong preferences for this second approach were expressed by the French and Swiss delegates on the ground that it was the easiest to apply and relieved judges of the task of ascertaining what periods of protection were applicable under the laws of other countries.[28] In the commission, the benefits of a uniform term were recognized, but it was thought that it was not yet time to proceed with such a proposal in view of the existing diversity of national laws in this regard.[29] It then appeared that opinion was divided on whether to apply national treatment 'pure and simple' or the *lex loci originis*. After further discussion the latter was adopted by six votes to three,[30] and was embodied in article 2, paragraph (2) of the 1884 draft. This provided simply that the advantages of national treatment were only to be reciprocally assured to authors belonging to a country of the Union 'during the existence of their rights in their country of origin'.[31]

[26] *Actes* 1884, 7 and 11. [27] ibid, 25. [28] ibid, 30. [29] ibid, 42.
[30] ibid. [31] ibid, 78.

9.15 This system did not avoid the possibility arising that a work might fall into the public domain in one country while still remaining protected in another. All it meant was that a work should not be protected in any country for any longer than it was protected in its country of origin. Thus, a French work would fall into the public domain in the UK long before it did in France, but would only be entitled to protection for life plus fifty years in Spain, whereas Spanish works would receive protection for a further thirty years. However, a resolution of the Conference expressed the view that, under domestic law, the period of protection should be the life of the author together with a 'number of years not less than thirty'.[32] At the 1885 Conference, article 2(2) of the 1884 draft was maintained, except for some drafting changes that made it clear that it was only the matter of duration that was to be governed by the law of a work's country of origin, and that this did not include other matters relating to the scope or extent of protection.[33] With these changes, article 2(2) of the 1884 and 1885 drafts then became article 2(2) of the Berne Act.

9.16 The question of duration was not addressed in the 1896 Paris Revision, but international pressure for the adoption of a uniform term began in the years following the Berne Conferences. Pre-eminent in this regard were the resolutions of successive congresses of ALAI, beginning at Madrid in 1887[34] and culminating with a firm proposal for life plus fifty years in the project of revision which was finally adopted by the Congress of Neuchâtel in 1909.[35] However, the programme for the Berlin Conference took quite a different approach, as it proposed the adoption of the principle of independence of protection without any accompanying proposal for a uniform term.[36] This was, in fact, a reversion to the *lex loci protectionis* approach, which the Germans (the principal architects of the Berlin programme) had strongly criticized at the time of the 1884 Conference.[37] Nonetheless, the Germans now argued that it was the logical approach to adopt, as it did away with any need to refer to the law of a work's country of origin. While they recognized the imbalances that this might give rise to as regards matters of duration, they argued that these would be relatively unimportant in practice and would affect only a few works. Such disadvantages would therefore be outweighed by the benefits of adopting the principle of independence of protection.[38] In this regard, it appears that the German Government had misread the extent to which opinion in Union countries had moved in favour of the adoption of a uniform term. By 1908, nine out of fifteen

[32] *Actes* 1884, 88. [33] *Actes* 1885, 42.
[34] See the texts of these resolutions in *Actes* 1896, 53 and *Actes* 1908, 82; also in Appendix 2.
[35] *Actes* 1908, 82. [36] ibid, 37–8.
[37] *Actes* 1884, 30 (comments of the German delegates Reichardt and Meyer).
[38] *Actes* 1908, 38–9.

of these had terms of life plus fifty years or more.[39] Even the UK, whose laws were probably the least satisfactory on this subject, appeared to recognize the need to change its position. This is revealed by the following passage from the instructions of the British Foreign Secretary (Sir Edward Grey) to the British delegates to the Conference:

> The suggested amendments [those of the German Government] do not include provision making a definite minimum period of protection obligatory in all countries. His Majesty's Government agree that such a provision would probably be inadvisable at present, but, in view of the stress which is laid in many quarters on the importance of a uniform period of protection in all countries, they are prepared to regard with sympathy any steps tending to realize such uniformity.[40]

Accordingly, the German proposal encountered strong opposition, and the lack of material reciprocity that would arise under it was strongly criticized as being intolerable.[41] A French counter-proposal for a uniform term of life plus fifty years was put forward, and was made a condition for French acceptance of the principle of independence of protection.[42] There was considerable support for the French position,[43] but the UK was reluctant to commit itself without time for further consideration, particularly if a uniform term were made obligatory.[44] Finally, a compromise was reached and the following terms were adopted:

> The term of protection granted by the present Convention shall include the life of the author and fifty years after his death.
>
> Nevertheless, in case such term of protection should not be uniformly adopted by all countries of the Union, the term shall be regulated by the law of the country where protection is claimed, and must not exceed the term fixed in the country of origin of the work. Consequently, the contracting countries shall be bound to apply the provisions of the preceding paragraph insofar as such provisions are consistent with their domestic laws.[45]

This provision therefore established the period of life plus fifty years as the **9.17** desirable uniform term, but reserved to any Union country which could not accept this period the right to determine duration by its own law subject to the stipulation that the period of protection claimed in another Union country should not exceed that of a work's country of origin. Until uniformity was achieved, the term of life plus fifty years would only apply between those countries whose laws conformed to this standard; relations with non-conforming countries would, in essence, continue to be governed by the provisions of the

[39] These countries were Belgium, Denmark, France, Luxembourg, Monaco, Norway, Spain, Sweden, and Tunisia: see [1910] *DA* 18, 29, and see also *Correspondence Respecting the Revised Convention of Berne for the Protection of Literary and Artistic Works, signed at Berlin, November 13, 1908* ('*Correspondence* (1908)'), 9 (report of the British delegates to Berlin Conference).

[40] *Correspondence* (1908), 1. [41] *Actes* 1908, 238ff. [42] ibid, 178, 185, 200, 239.

[43] ibid, 239–40. [44] ibid, 243, 214–15. [45] ibid, 243.

Berne Act. This continuing reference to the *lex loci originis* was a very significant exception to the principle of independence of protection which was otherwise firmly established under article 4 of the Berlin Act. It also meant that the Convention was some way from establishing a uniform term: the rule in article 7(1) was in no way binding, and it did not commit Union countries to change their laws in this regard in the future. Nonetheless, the prospects of uniformity being achieved appeared encouraging, as Italy had given its support for the original French proposal[46] and during the Conference the German Government indicated that it would give consideration to extending its term.[47] The UK remained non-committal, but was certainly not opposed to the longer term.[48]

9.18 Following the Berlin Revision, the non-conforming states were slower to change their laws than might have been expected. The Germans did not amend their law,[49] and the Swedes, Japanese, and Swiss also continued to maintain their term of life plus thirty years.[50] Moreover, a number of the new adherents to the Union which joined after World War I had the same term: Austria,[51] Bulgaria,[52] Danzig,[53] and Romania.[54] The UK which had been the most reluctant at the time of the Berlin Conference to approve the term of life plus fifty years, acted more quickly and adopted it (with certain modifications) as part of its new law of 1911.[55] Italy did not change its law in this regard until 1925.[56] The other countries which acceded to the Convention after 1908 also adopted this term: Brazil,[57] Greece,[58] Hungary,[59] Morocco,[60] the Netherlands,[61] Poland,[62] Portugal,[63] Syria and Lebanon.[64] The position as regarded duration of protection in the thirty-seven countries of the Union immediately prior to the Rome Conference was as follows:

[46] *Actes* 1908, 239–40.

[47] *Correspondence* (1908), 9 (report of the British delegate).

[48] ibid, 8ff.

[49] This did not occur until 1934: Law Relating to the Prolongation of the Periods of Protection of Authors' Rights of 13 Dec 1934, art 1. See also S P Ladas, *The International Protection of Literary and Artistic Property* (1938) ('Ladas (1938)'), 1029.

[50] See the studies on duration in the countries of the Union in [1925] *DA* 98, 113, 122 and [1926] *DA* 15, 26, 38.

[51] Law of 13 July 1920, arts 43 and 47(1). See further [1925] *DA* 100.

[52] Law of 11 July 1921, arts 11(1) and 18. See further [1925] *DA* 114.

[53] The German laws applied in this state: [1925] *DA* 115.

[54] Law of 28 June 1923, arts 1 and 4. See further Ladas (1938), 1086.

[55] Copyright Act 1911, s 3.

[56] Law No 1950 of 7 Nov 1925, art 26.

[57] Civil Code 1916/1917, art 649.

[58] Law of 16 July 1920, art 2.

[59] Law of 31 Dec 1921, arts 11 and 19.

[60] Law of 23 June 1916, art 21.

[61] Law of 23 Sept 1912, art 39.

[62] Law of 29 Mar 1926, art 20 (for the position prior to 1926, see [1926] *DA* 26).

[63] Civil Law of 1 July 1867, art 579. Note that this term became perpetual in 1927: Law of 27 May 1927, arts 15(1) and 36.

[64] Decree of 17 Jan 1924, art 143: both countries were, at this time, under French mandate.

1. Twenty-four granted protection for life plus fifty years: Australia,[65] Belgium,[66] Canada,[67] Czechoslovakia,[68] Denmark,[69] Estonia,[70] Finland,[71] France,[72] Greece,[73] Hungary,[74] India,[75] Irish Free State,[76] Italy,[77] Luxembourg,[78] Monaco,[79] Morocco,[80] the Netherlands,[81] New Zealand,[82] Norway,[83] Poland,[84] Syria and Lebanon,[85] South Africa,[86] Tunisia,[87] and the UK.[88]
2. Two had terms in excess of life plus fifty years: Brazil (life plus sixty years)[89] and Spain (life plus eighty years).[90]
3. One had perpetual protection: Portugal.[91]
4. Eight retained life plus thirty years: Austria,[92] Bulgaria,[93] Danzig,[94] Germany,[95] Japan,[96] Romania,[97] Sweden,[98] and Switzerland.[99]
5. Two had even shorter periods: Liberia (life plus twenty years)[100] and Haiti (differing periods).[101]

It will be clear from the above that, by 1928, the majority of nations had adopted the life-plus-fifty-years norm, but a significant minority still fell short of this. This led to strong calls from authors' societies throughout this period for the term of life plus fifty years to be made mandatory for all countries of the Union, and the International Office in a study published in *Le Droit d'Auteur* in 1925 and 1926 urged this course, arguing that states with shorter terms would soon fall into line as they would not wish to put their nationals at a **9.19**

[65] Copyright Act 1912, Sch, s 3 (incorporating the UK Act of 1911).
[66] Law of 22 Mar 1886, art 2. [67] Copyright Act 1921, s 5.
[68] Law of 16 Nov 1926, arts 38 and 39. [69] Law of 1 Apr 1912, art 21.
[70] The Russian Law of 20 Mar 1911 was still in force in Estonia at this time: see art 10. See further [1911] *DA* 86 and Ladas (1938), 1010.
[71] Law of 3 June 1927, art 25. [72] Law of 16 July 1866. [73] See n 58 above.
[74] See n 59 above. [75] The UK Act of 1911 applied here by virtue of s 25 thereof.
[76] The same as for India. [77] Law No 1950 of 7 Nov 1925, art 26.
[78] Law of 10 May 1898, art 2. [79] Ordinance of 1889/1896, art 8(2).
[80] See n 60 above. [81] See n 61 above.
[82] Copyright Act 1911 (UK) was extended here by certificate of the Secretary of State: SR & O 1923/1604, 20 Apr 1916.
[83] Law of 4 July 1893, modified 25 July 1910, art 10. [84] See n 62 above.
[85] See n 64 above.
[86] The UK Copyright Act 1911 was applied here by s 43 of the South African Patents, Designs, Trade Marks and Copyright Act 1916.
[87] Law of 15 June 1889, art 2. [88] Copyright Act 1911, s 3(1).
[89] See n 57 above. [90] Law of 10 Jan 1879, art 6. [91] See n 63 above.
[92] See n 51 above. [93] See n 52 above. [94] See n 53 above.
[95] Law on Literary and Musical Works of 19 June 1901, art 25, and Law on Artistic and Photographic Works of 9 Jan 1907, art 25.
[96] Act on Copyright of 3 Mar 1899, art 3. [97] See n 54 above.
[98] Law on Literary Works of 30 May 1919, art 20; Law on Artistic Works of 30 May 1919, art 13.
[99] Law of 7 Dec 1922, arts 37 and 41. [100] Law of 22 Dec 1911, art 3.
[101] Law of 8 Oct 1885, arts 5 and 6.

disadvantage.[102] Concern was also expressed about two other alleged kinds of curtailments of the term of authors' rights that were to be found in the laws of the UK and Italy. In the case of the first, the Copyright Act 1911 (UK) provided for the grant of compulsory licences following the death of the author at two points of time: immediately after the death of the latter if the successor in title refused to publish a new edition or to allow further performances of the work and therefore failed to meet the requirements of the public,[103] and twenty-five years after the death of the author following payment of a fixed royalty.[104]

9.20 Both these licences posed severe potential limitations on the exercise of the author's rights to control the choice and manner of exploiting the work after death, but, arguably, they did not actually result in a shortening of the copyright term, as payment to the author's heirs for the reproduction or performance of the work was still required. A similar argument could also be propounded about the paying public domain provisions of the Italian law prior to 1925.[105] These were rather differently formulated from the paying public domain provisions that are common today (in which the state imposes and collects the payments), being similar to a compulsory licence. Their effect was that, after the death of the author of a work, or at least forty years after its publication, anyone was free, for a further forty years, to reproduce and sell copies of the work as long as they paid a royalty to the copyright owner. There was no cessation of the copyright right to payment under either of these laws, but a life-plus-fifty-years copyright term subject to these kinds of restrictions on the copyright right to control cannot fairly be called the equivalent of an absolute and unfettered term of life plus fifty years.

9.21 This raised the further, and more fundamental, question of the basis of article 7(1) of the Berlin Act. Was it based on the principle of independence of protection or that of material reciprocity? To give a practical example, was a country such as France required to accord a term of life plus fifty years to British works, or was she entitled to restrict this by the imposition of similar compulsory licences (although not applicable to French works under French law) or to grant a term of only life plus twenty-five years or even less? Under the Berlin Act, it could be argued that such a course of action would be contrary to the basic principles of national treatment and independence of protection embodied in article 4 of that Act. On this view, it would only be if the term of protection in the UK was actually shorter than that accorded in France that such a limitation would be justified, as it would be at this stage only that the

[102] 'L'article 7 de la Convention de Berne revisée et la future Conference de Rome' [1926] *DA* 49.

[103] Copyright Act 1911, s 3. [104] ibid, s 4.

[105] Law of 19 Sept 1882, art 2 (a royalty of 5% on the sale of each copy was payable).

provisions of article 7(2) would come into play. However, a compulsory licence or paying public domain system such as that in the pre-1925 Italian law did not have this effect: while it placed restraints on the exercise of authors' rights, the latter nevertheless continued to subsist. Accordingly, if France imposed compulsory licences on British works, but not upon the works of its own authors, this would then contravene the principles of national treatment and independence of protection.[106] Against this, it could be argued that article 7(1) represented an exception to these principles and that material reciprocity was still required between nations in relation to matters of duration. Prior to the Rome Revision Conference, it was uncertain which was the correct view of article 7(1). The International Office appeared to support the first argument, although with some qualifications,[107] while the second was advocated by a number of states, in particular France.

(a) Rome proposals

The basic proposal of the programme was for the complete unification of the term of protection by the deletion of article 7(2).[108] There was some support for this,[109] and it was supplemented by a Spanish proposal to make it clear that the life-plus-fifty-years term was a minimum and that Union countries were free to exceed this.[110] However, there was still opposition from the life-plus-thirty-years group of nations (Germany, Austria, Japan, and Sweden),[111] as well as from the UK,[112] and the proposal lapsed.[113] The second part of the programme proposal, which gave rise to far more discussion, sought to maintain the status quo of the Berlin Act but with a gloss to article 7(2). The intention behind this amendment was to resolve the national treatment/material reciprocity dispute described in the preceding paragraph. With this in mind, the following addition to article 7(2) was proposed: **9.22**

> A difference between the extent of the protection accorded in the country of origin and that which is established in the country where protection is claimed is no obstacle to the application of this provision.[114]

This was clearly intended to show that the basis of article 7(1) was national treatment and independence of protection, rather than material reciprocity. Predictably, this provoked strong opposition from the French delegation,[115] although there was support for it from several life-plus-thirty-years countries which were considering the introduction of systems of paying public domain as

[106] See generally [1926] *DA* 49, 51ff.
[107] See ibid, 52–3 for the International Office's exposition of its theory of 'minimum of recognition'. See further para 6.79 above.
[108] *Actes* 1928, 69. [109] ibid, 239–40. [110] ibid. [111] ibid, 240.
[112] ibid. [113] ibid. [114] ibid, 70. [115] ibid, 240.

part of an extended term of life plus fifty years.[116] Indeed, there was a Swedish suggestion to the effect that any period during which the whole of the authors' rights were subject to a compulsory licence should be regarded as forming part of the term of protection for the purposes of article 7(1).[117] The programme proposal was soon abandoned, but this left the basis of article 7(1) undecided. A German proposal then sought to modify the article as follows:

> If in a country of the Union the period of protection comprises, after the death of the author, a period where, on condition that a royalty is paid to the person entitled to the copyright, the reproduction of the work for sale is lawful, the other countries of the Union are only required, during this period, to apply to works originating from that country treatment corresponding to that provided in that country. [In any case] the duration of the exclusive right should never be less than 25 years from the death of the author.[118]

9.23 This was, in fact, an express acknowledgement that the basis of the provision was material reciprocity, and in this respect satisfied the objections raised by the French delegation. However, it failed to receive unanimous support. In part, this seems to have been due to irreducible Norwegian opposition to this diminution of the principle of national treatment;[119] in part, it was because of misplaced fears that this might require Union members to introduce compulsory licences.[120] As a consequence, article 7(2) was left unchanged, and the French delegation made a declaration reasserting its belief in the need for each country to adopt the same period of protection, and, in the absence of such uniformity, for the Convention to contain a formula based on reciprocity.[121] Following the failure of the German compromise proposal, the French declaration seemed to imply that bilateral arrangements might become necessary in relation to any portion of the term of protection during which a compulsory licence was applicable in the country of origin of a work claiming protection in France.[122] This still left the interpretation of article 7(1) uncertain. The French view was clearly that it was based on the principle of material reciprocity, and that she was therefore free to limit the term of protection available to works from countries which applied restrictions such as compulsory licences or paying public domain as part of their term of protection. On the other hand, the view of the UK Government was that the applicable principles were those of national treatment and independence of protection, and that their works should not be discriminated against in this way.[123] As noted above, this interpretation had also been

[116] eg Germany, Switzerland, and Austria: *Actes* 1928, 240. [117] ibid, 122.
[118] ibid, 241.
[119] ibid, 241–2. See further A Raestad, *La Convention de Berne révisée à Rome 1928* . . . (1931), 164ff for further details of the debates that occurred on this question.
[120] eg Poland: *Actes* 1928, 242–3. [121] ibid, 292 (declaration by G Maillard).
[122] This was the view of the British delegation, expressed in its report to the Foreign Secretary, 5 Sept 1928: Public Records Office, FO371/13444.
[123] ibid.

shared by the International Office immediately prior to the Rome Conference,[124] and had been the basis of its proposal in the Conference programme. Following that Conference, however, all that can be said is that neither interpretation had been accepted or rejected, and accordingly both could be maintained without violating the Convention. As a practical matter, this dispute touched only the UK, as it was clear that the basis of article 7(2) was one of material reciprocity with respect to countries with shorter terms. On the other hand, it was of potential significance in relation to several life-plus-thirty-years countries which were contemplating the extension of their terms of protection to life plus thirty years by the inclusion of a twenty-year system of paying public domain along the lines of the Italian legislation.[125]

(b) The Brussels Revision

In their proposals on duration for the postponed Brussels Conference of 1935 to 1936, the Belgian Government and the International Office sought to rectify the uncertainty left by the Rome Revision. The proposition for a mandatory uniform term of life plus fifty years was renewed, and the German proposal of 1928 concerning reciprocity in the case of compulsory licences was also resurrected.[126] This second proposition represented a change of position so far as the International Office was concerned (see above), but in support it was argued that this did not really represent a major derogation from the fundamental principle of national treatment, as the matter of duration had always been dealt with under the Convention on the basis of reciprocity. The responses to these proposals indicated that a number of Union countries were changing or were prepared to change their previously stated attitudes. In 1934 and 1936 respectively, Germany and Austria had adopted unconditional terms of life plus fifty years.[127] Two other non-conforming nations, Sweden and Switzerland, raised no objections to the proposed changes.[128] Finally, the UK declared its willingness to abolish its compulsory licences.[129] When the Brussels Conference finally met, the term of life plus fifty years was duly made absolute, with the deletion of article 7(2), and the proposal permitting reciprocal treatment in the case of compulsory licences was withdrawn.[130] However, reciprocity was retained in relation to countries which accorded terms in excess of life plus fifty years: in such cases, the term was to be that of the country where protection was 9.24

124 See nn 106 and 107 above.

125 eg Australia: *Actes* 1928, 241. See further Ladas (1938), 319.

126 [1933] *DA* 73, 91.

127 German Law of 13 Dec 1934, art 1; Austrian Law of 9 Apr 1936, art 60.

128 [1936] *DA* 65.

129 ibid.

130 *Documents de la Conférence réunie à Bruxelles du 5 au 26 juin 1948* (1951) ('*Documents 1948* (1951)'), 213ff.

claimed, but this was not to exceed that fixed in the country of origin of the work.[131]

(c) Under the Stockholm, Paris Acts

9.25 The basic term of protection remains the life-plus-fifty-years period made mandatory in the Brussels Act.[132] Prior to the Stockholm Conference, there was some pressure for an extension of this period, and the question was considered by the Permanent Committee of the Berne Union on several occasions,[133] and was studied by two committees of experts in 1961 and 1962.[134] The work of these bodies is considered below (see para 9.26), but for the moment it suffices to say that they concluded that proposals for extension of the life-plus-fifty-years term would impose undue pressure on a number of countries that had already had to extend their terms to comply with the Brussels Act. The danger therefore was that such countries would feel unable to accede to the new Stockholm Act, and that this would ultimately impede the development of the Union. The view of the experts was that, for the moment, any extension of term should take place within the framework of a special arrangement between the countries interested, but that the Berne text should remain unchanged for the present.[135] As a consequence, the programme for the Stockholm Revision Conference contained no proposals for extension of the normal term of protection.[136]

(d) Proposals for longer terms

9.26 Reference was made above (see para 9.25) to the consideration that was given prior to the Stockholm Conference to the question of extending the life-plus-fifty-years term under article 7(1). At the instigation of the Permanent Committee of the Berne Union, this was examined by a committee of experts which met in 1961 and 1962.[137] The feeling of the experts was that the standard term of protection should be extended, although there is no indication that any factual evidence for this conclusion was sought. This is hardly surprising, given that most of the experts were from civil law systems where the emphasis on the proprietary nature of authors' rights often leads automatically to the conclusion that long terms of protection are a 'good thing'. After some discussion, it was concluded that the best way of achieving an extended term would be through a

---

131 Brussels Act, art 7(2).

132 Stockholm, Paris Acts, art 7(1).

133 See [1959] *DA* 206, 209 (eighth session of the Executive Committee, meeting in Munich); [1960] *DA* 324 (ninth session, London); [1961] *DA* 318 (tenth session, Madrid).

134 See [1961] *DA* 56 and [1962] *DA* 173.

135 [1962] *DA* 173ff.

136 *Records* 1967, vol I, 105.

137 [1961] *DA* 56; [1962] *DA* 173.

special arrangement under article 20 of the Brussels Act, rather than a direct amendment to article 9.[138] This would enable those countries which wished to move forward in this area to do so, but would not disturb the main Convention text. Initially, a term of life plus eighty years was proposed,[139] but this was then reduced to life plus sixty-five years, and a number of transitional measures were also proposed.[140] At the Stockholm Conference, the German delegation sought to carry this proposal further by asking the Conference to adopt the following resolution:

> The Stockholm Conference,
>
> Considering that certain countries have expressed a desire for the term of protection to be extended, that certain countries already grant a general term of protection in excess of 50 years after the death of the author, that, moreover, several countries of the Union have extended the term of protection for reasons resulting from the war, that negotiations have already taken place at the international level with the object of providing for an extension of the term of protection by a Special Arrangement, that, in addition, agreements have already been concluded between certain countries for the reciprocal recognition of an extension of the term of protection for reasons resulting from the war:
>
> Proposes that negotiations should be continued between the countries concerned for the conclusion of a Special Agreement on the extension of the term of protection in countries parties to that Agreement.[141]

This was at first rejected by Main Committee I,[142] but on the motion of the chairman (Professor Ulmer) was resubmitted for consideration, on the ground that, while this imposed no obligation on any state, it would be 'a good thing to show authors that the trend of the Conference was not entirely towards a reduction in the term of protection'.[143] The recommendation was duly adopted, but without any great enthusiasm: there were nine votes for, two against, and twenty-one abstentions.[144] No Special Arrangement has come into existence since this time, and the period of life plus fifty years remains the basic requirement of the Berne Convention until such time as it is changed in a subsequent revision. However, several countries with terms of protection in excess of life plus fifty years subsequently concluded a number of bilateral agreements under which each country undertook to accord longer terms to works from the other country.[145] These have been largely superseded by the European Union Duration Directive of 1993, establishing a term of life plus seventy years for Berne Convention works by European Union authors or first published in the European Union.[146]

138 [1962] *DA* 176. 139 ibid. 140 ibid.

141 *Records* 1967, vol I, 714 (Document S/205).

142 ibid, vol II, 898. 143 ibid, 921. 144 ibid.

145 eg those between France and Italy, Norway, Spain, Austria, and the FRG.

146 See Council Directive 93/98/EEC of 29 Oct 1993 harmonizing the term of protection of copyright and certain related rights, arts 1(1), 7(1).

A further attempt to extend the minimum term beyond life plus fifty years was made in connection with the negotiation of the 1996 World Intellectual Property Organization ('WIPO') Copyright Treaty ('WCT'), discussed further below (see para 9.65).

(2) Special terms of protection

9.27 Despite the general approach of the Convention to focus the copyright term on the life of the author, the calculation of term is not uniformly author-centric. Departures from the author-focus occur in two different kinds of cases. One concerns certain types of works, the other addresses difficulties arising when there is a multiplicity of authors, or where the author is unknown. Where the drafters appeared uncertain about the nature or quality of authorship inherent in certain kinds of works, particularly when those works were mechanically assisted or directed, the drafters allowed for shorter terms, running from the acts of publication, public disclosure, or 'making'. This is the case for photographs, cinematographic works, and works of applied art. Works for which calculating from the life of the author may be impractical or cumbersome include anonymous and pseudonymous works, joint works, and works by corporate persons (including, in some countries, cinematographic works). This part of the chapter will review the treatment of these issues in prior versions of the Convention; the solutions adopted in the current Berne text will be analysed below (see paras 9.44ff).

(a) Photographic works

9.28 The position of these works has always been peculiar under the Convention,[147] and this was reflected in the provisions concerning the term of their protection. No agreement on a uniform term was possible at the Berlin Revision, so article 7(3) of the Berlin Act left this as a matter to be determined by a comparison of terms between the country where protection was claimed and the country of origin. The periods of protection adopted by Union countries differed enormously. A few, which treated photographic works as artistic works, accorded the full term of life plus fifty years.[148] Most others granted protection for terms of ten to fifty years, calculated either from the date of publication or the making of the photograph.[149] This lack of uniformity therefore prevented any change being made at the Rome Revision, although modest proposals for

[147] See generally paras 8.48ff above.

[148] eg France and Belgium: see [1910] *DA* 29, 30.

[149] Denmark, Norway, Sweden, and Switzerland (five years post publication, with slight variations); Germany and Japan (ten years post publication); UK (life plus seven years): see generally [1910] *DA* 30.

minimum terms of ten and twenty years were made at that Conference.[150] In their programme for the Brussels Conference, the Belgian Government and the International Office proposed twenty years from the date of publication or twenty years from the date of creation if the photograph was unpublished.[151] This was supplemented by a French proposal to assimilate photographic works to other works by making their term of protection life plus fifty years,[152] and a more limited British proposal for fifty years' protection from the date of making of the negative.[153] In the event, even agreement on the shorter twenty-year proposal proved impossible,[154] and the Rome (and Berlin) text was therefore retained in the Brussels Act.[155]

It was not until the Stockholm Revision that a minimum term of protection for photographic works was introduced. Although several of the states which had accorded only very limited protection at the time of the Brussels Revision had now changed their laws,[156] there was still a significant number of states with terms of only twenty-five years or less post publication or production.[157] Accordingly, the Swedish Government and BIRPI in their proposal limited themselves to a period of twenty-five years, making it clear that this was only intended as a minimum period for all states to adopt.[158] The UK again proposed a term of fifty years, but withdrew this in the face of opposition from the German delegation.[159] The Swedish Government/BIRPI proposal was therefore adopted unanimously[160] and became article 7(4) of the Stockholm Act, discussed further below (see paras 9.44ff). **9.29**

[150] There was a Polish proposal for a term of ten years after the production of the negative, and a Swedish proposal for twenty years after first publication: *Actes* 1928, 245.

[151] [1933] *DA* 92 and in *Documents 1948* (1951), 202–3.

[152] *Documents 1948* (1951), 206–9.

[153] ibid, 209. [154] ibid, 216. [155] ibid.

[156] eg Czechoslovakia had extended its previous terms of ten years post publication to life plus ten years: Law of 25 Mar 1965, art 34. On the other hand, Poland which had declared its willingness at the time of the Brussels Conference to accept the programme proposal and extend its term of ten years after the taking of the photograph did not do so in its new Law of 10 July 1952 which allowed only for a term of ten years post publication (art 27).

[157] eg Argentina, twenty years from first publication (Law No 11723 on Copyright of 28 Sept 1933, art 34); Denmark, twenty-five years after the production of the photograph (Act No 157 on Rights in Photographic Pictures of 21 Mar 1961, art 15); FRG, twenty-five years post publication and twenty-five years from creation, if unpublished (Law of 9 Sept 1965, art 68); Hungary, fifteen years post publication or life plus fifteen years in the case of posthumous photographs (Law of 31 Dec 1921, art 69); Romania, ten years post publication for series of artistic photographs and five years post publication for separate artistic photographs (Decree relating to Copyright No 321 of 18 June 1956, art 7); Turkey, twenty years after being made public (Law on Artistic and Intellectual Works of 10 Dec 1951, art 29).

[158] *Records* 1967, vol I, 108 (Document S/1).

[159] ibid, 899 (the British proposal was Document S/192: ibid, 710).

[160] ibid.

(d) Cinematographic works

9.30 (i) **The early Acts:** Under the Berlin Act, cinematographic productions were protected as literary or artistic works if 'by the arrangement of the acting form or the combination of incidents represented, the author ha[d] given the work a personal and original character'.[161] If these requirements were satisfied, the cinematographic production was then treated as any other work, and the duration of its protection was covered by article 7(1) or (2) of the Berlin Act. This position was maintained, with some changes, under the Rome Act: 'original' cinematographic productions were protected as literary or artistic works, and 'unoriginal' productions as photographic works.[162] Accordingly, no propositions concerning the length of protection for cinematographic works were made at either the Berlin or Rome Conference. Under national laws, only a few countries had special terms for films;[163] most countries simply followed the Convention in assimilating them to literary or artistic works in general, or treating them as photographic works in the case of 'unoriginal' films. When they were added to the enumeration of works in article 2(1) at the time of the Brussels Revision, the programme for that Conference proposed simply that the term of their protection should be reserved to national legislation, without any obligation to grant any longer term than that accorded in the country of origin (the rule of 'comparison of terms').[164] This proposal attracted criticism from a special ALAI commission as being a derogation from the now mandatory term of life plus fifty years,[165] but was defended as being necessary in light of the existing differences in national laws.[166] In addition, the programme asserted that cinematographic films did not, in general, have long lives, and that a lesser period of protection, such as twenty or thirty years from the date of creation would not cause detriment to cinematographers.[167] However, proposals for longer terms were put forward by two Union countries with important film industries, France and the UK. The first proposed protection for the full term of life plus fifty years,[168] while the second argued for protection from the time of making of the film until it was presented in public and then for a term of fifty years following this date.[169] There were also proposals for far shorter terms,[170] and a special sub-committee of the Conference recommended that the principle of comparison of terms should apply, taking the date of making of the negative of the film as the starting point for calculation of the term.[171] There was predictable disappointment from both the French and British delegations, which abandoned their proposals.[172] The

161 Berlin Act, art 14(2). 162 Rome Act, art 14(2).
163 See eg the Netherlands Law of 23 Sept 1912, art 40. See further [1910] *DA* 29, 30–1.
164 *Documents 1948* (1951), 203–4.
165 See comments in programme at ibid, 203.
166 ibid. 167 ibid. 168 ibid, 212. 169 ibid.
170 eg a Polish proposal for a minimum of ten years from the making of the negative: ibid, 217.
171 ibid, 111. 172 ibid, 217.

final result was that article 7(3) of the Brussels Act treated cinematographic works in the same way as photographic works, and the principle of comparison of terms, with its basis in material reciprocity, was applied.

(ii) **The changes at the Stockholm Revision**: In the preparations leading up to the Stockholm Conference, the different national approaches to the question of cinematographic works raised particularly difficult questions in relation to the matter of duration.[173] So far as the film copyright countries were concerned, it was meaningless to fix a term of protection for cinematographic works that was dependent upon the life of a natural person. On the other hand, a large number of other Union countries took the view that only natural persons could be the authors of cinematographic works,[174] and this second view had considerable support in the various bodies which prepared, and commented upon, the programme for the Stockholm Conference.[175] In consequence, the latter proposed that cinematographic works should be protected for the normal term of life plus fifty years.[176] Nevertheless, to accommodate film copyright countries, the programme proposed that, instead of life plus fifty years, Union countries might provide that the term of protection should expire fifty years after first publication, public performance, or broadcast, or, failing such an event within fifty years of the making of the work, fifty years after this event.[177] At the Conference, a Hungarian counter-proposal for a minimum term of twenty-five years was rejected,[178] as was an imaginative Portuguese amendment to leave the period to be fixed by national law 'in such a way as to allow a fair return on the investment made'.[179] Finally, the Conference adopted the programme proposal, but with the following change suggested by the British delegation: the words 'after the work has been made available to the public with the consent of the author' replaced the words 'after the first publication, public performance or broadcast'.[180] This then became article 7(2) of the Stockholm, Paris Acts, discussed further below (see paras 9.44ff). **9.31**

(c) Works of applied art

The protection of these works was left to the law of each Union country to determine for itself under the Berlin and Rome Acts, so it is hardly surprising that **9.32**

[173] See further C Masouyé, *Guide to the Berne Convention for the Protection of Literary and Artistic Works* (1978), 47.
[174] ibid.
[175] *Records* 1967, vol I, 105–6 (Document S/1).
[176] ibid, 106. [177] ibid.
[178] Document S/91: ibid, 694, 875, 899 (minutes of Main Committee I).
[179] Document S/152: ibid, 700, 874–5, 899 (minutes).
[180] Document S/42: ibid, 687, and 874 (minutes).

neither Act contained any provision concerning the duration of their protection. At the Brussels Conference, a compromise solution concerning their status under the Convention was inserted in article 2(5) of the Brussels Act (see para 8.68 above), and this was accompanied by a proposal in the programme for their duration to be determined by a comparison of terms.[181] A French counter-proposal for a term of life plus fifty years was not proceeded with,[182] and the result was that works of applied art were included in article 7(3) of the Brussels Act, together with cinematographic and photographic works.[183] This was qualified by the words 'insofar as they are protected as artistic works'.[184] The clear implication of this was that, as regards works of applied art which a Union country did not protect as artistic works, for example, industrial designs or models, there was no obligation on that country to observe any minimum term at all for these works. At the Stockholm Conference, the programme proposed a minimum term of twenty-five years for works of applied art from their making.[185] There were a number of counter-proposals for terms of ten or fifteen years only,[186] but the programme proposal was accepted without alteration.[187] This then became article 7(4) of the Stockholm, Paris Acts, discussed further below (see paras 9.44ff).

(d) Anonymous and pseudonymous works

9.33 Under the Berlin Act, the term of protection of these works, like photographic works, was left as a matter for comparison of terms (article 7(3)). There were considerable differences in the way these works were treated under national laws,[188] and no proposal for a minimum uniform term was included in the programmes for the Rome and Brussels Conferences. However, a French amendment at the latter conference proposed a term of protection expiring fifty years from the date of first publication.[189] This was subject to the qualification that where the pseudonym adopted by an author left his identity in no doubt, his work was to be accorded the normal term of life plus fifty years applicable under article 7(1).[190] This was adopted by the Conference, with the addition of a further clause providing that the term under article 7(1) would also become applicable where the author of a pseudonymous or anonymous work

181 *Documents 1948* (1951), 203, 204. 182 ibid, 212, 219. 183 ibid, 219.
184 ibid, 218. 185 *Records* 1967, vol I, 108 (Document S/1).
186 ibid, vol II, 897 (minutes of Main Committee I). 187 ibid, 898 (minutes).
188 There were no legislative provisions in France, the UK, Haiti, Italy, Switzerland, and Tunisia; a term of fifty years *post mortem editoris* was awarded in Belgium, Luxembourg, France (in the jurisprudence) and Monaco, and a term of eighty years in Spain; while a term of thirty years from first publication or performance was accorded in Germany and Japan, and fifty years in Denmark, Norway, and Sweden. See the survey of national laws in [1910] *DA* 29, 31–2.
189 *Documents 1948* (1951), 208. 190 ibid, 209.

disclosed his identity. This then became article 7(4) of the Brussels Act. The changes introduced in the Stockholm revision are discussed further below (see paras 9.44ff)

(e) Works of joint authorship

9.34 These are not defined in the Berne Convention, but member state domestic legislation often identifies joint works as collaborative works in which the contributions of the individual co-authors cannot readily be identified.[191] In this respect, they are to be distinguished from other kinds of collaborative works (often called 'collective works') such as encyclopaedias and anthologies where the individual contributions of authors can be identified.[192] No problems concerning the duration of protection arise in relation to collective works: the contributors each enjoy the normal term of life plus fifty years in respect of their separate contributions, while the compiler or editor enjoys a similar term in respect of the overall compilation.[193] However, more difficulties arise in the case of works of joint authorship: there is no separate derivative copyright here, as the contributors are co-authors of the work as a whole and not of any identifiable part of that work. Thus, if each co-author were to enjoy protection for life plus fifty years, this would lead to an absurd situation where one co-author died before the other or others. The rights of the former would expire before those of his collaborators, but it would be impossible to point to any particular part of the work over which his rights had ceased to operate. This would put potential users of the work at a considerable disadvantage: so far as one co-author was concerned, the work would be in the public domain, but authority to use the work would still be required from the other co-authors (or their assignees) who would nonetheless have title only to a portion of the original rights in the work. The common-sense solution is to have a unified term of protection which ensures that the rights of all co-authors come to an end at the same time. Thus,

---

191 This is the definition in s 10(1) of the Copyright Act 1968 (Aust). To the same effect, see eg the UK Copyright, Designs and Patents Act 1988, s 10(1) which defines a joint work as a collaboration 'in which the contribution of each author is *not distinct* from that of the other author or authors' (emphasis supplied). See also eg Italy, 1941 Copyright Act, art 10 (indistinguishable and inseparable contributions); Germany, Copyright Act of 1965, art 8(1) (joint authors if 'their respective contributions cannot be separately exploited'); Canada, Copyright Act 1985, s 2 (as amended through 1994) (contributions of authors not distinct from each other); Belize, Copyright Act Chapter 252, revised through 2000, art 3(1) (contributions not separate from one another); Ireland, Copyright and Related Rights Act, No 28, 2000, art 22(1) (contributions 'not distinct').

192 Under US copyright law, however, the contributions to a joint work can be either 'inseparable', or 'interdependent' and separately identifiable. See 17 USC § 101. To the same effect, see eg France, Code de la propriété intellectuelle, art L 113–2(1) (work of 'collaboration;' inseparability not required); art L 113–3(3) explicitly contemplates that contributions may 'be of different genres' and thus separable.

193 See paras 8.84ff above.

the UK Copyright Act 1911 provided that protection for these kinds of works continued for fifty years after the life of the author who died first, or for the life of the author who died last, whichever was the longer period.[194] While this achieved the desired result of a unified term, it meant that all co-authors, apart from the first, enjoyed a term of protection which was less than the normal term of life plus fifty years conferred under the UK Act.[195] Other national laws took a more generous approach, calculating the term of protection by reference to the death of the last surviving author: in France, for example, this period was fifty years.[196] The reason that such an approach was not adopted in the UK appears to have been fears that such a provision would be used by older, established authors to gain extended terms of protection for their works by inducing younger writers to join them as co-authors.[197] Nevertheless, a strong preference for the French approach was expressed by the ALAI Congress which was held in Warsaw in 1926,[198] and there were a number of proposals made at the Rome Conference which sought to achieve 'unity of term' with respect to co-authors.[199] These became article 7bis(1) which provided:

> The term of copyright protection belonging in common to joint authors of a work shall be calculated according to the date of the death of the last surviving author.

This was made subject to a minimum requirement in paragraph (3) that in no case should the term of protection expire before the death of the last surviving author. This last provision was significant in light of the fact that article 7 itself did not yet contain any mandatory minimum requirements concerning the duration of protection for either works in general or for any particular category of work. Article 7bis(1) and (3) therefore had the effect of achieving unity of term for co-authors, even if this term might be no longer than the life of the last surviving co-author. In this respect, it accommodated the views of the UK which was unprepared, at this stage, to make any changes to its own rules concerning co-authors.[200]

9.35 Article 7bis of the Rome Act also contained a provision embodying the principle of comparison of terms where countries had differing terms of protection in relation to co-authors. Article 7bis(2) provided:

> Authors who are nationals of the countries which grant a term of protection shorter than that mentioned in paragraph (1) cannot claim a longer term of protection in the other countries of the Union.

[194] Copyright Act 1911, s 16(1). [195] ibid, s 3.
[196] Ladas (1938), 1020. See also the Italian Law of 1925, art 28.
[197] *Actes* 1928, 245 (résumé of discussions at Conference).
[198] [1926] *DA* 126–7; *Actes* 1928, 206 (report of Caselli).
[199] *Actes* 1928, 70 (programme proposal), 99 (French proposal), 118 (Polish proposal).
[200] ibid, 245. See further Ladas (1938), 329.

This provision gave rise to several difficulties of interpretation, which are worth commenting upon briefly as several Union members still remain bound by the Rome Act.[201] First, what was the term of protection 'mentioned in paragraph (1)'? This paragraph only stipulated the method by which the term of life plus fifty years was to be calculated in the case of works of joint authors. Presumably, the reference here was back to the permissive term of life plus fifty years contained in article 7(1), but this was not clearly stated. Secondly, the words 'authors who are nationals of the countries which grant a term of protection . . .' were at variance with article 7(2) which laid down the general rule on comparison of terms. Under the latter, the comparison was to be made between the term of protection in the country where protection was claimed and the term of protection in the country of origin of the work. Article 7*bis*(2), however, made no reference to the work or its country of origin; it did not even indicate whether it was necessary that the author claiming protection should be a national of a Union country.

In the Brussels Revision, these problems became irrelevant as both paragraphs (2) and (3) of the Rome Act were deleted.[202] This was the result of a French proposal to unify the term of protection for co-authors;[203] its adoption was aided by a declaration by the British delegation that it would accept the French proposal as it would contribute to the simplification of the Convention by further diminishing the need to refer to the principle of reciprocity.[204] The effect of this change therefore was that the term of protection of co-authors now fell to be determined by the provisions of article 7, while article 7*bis* stipulated the method by which this term was to be determined, that is, by reference to the death of the last surviving co-author. In the normal case, then, the term of protection for each co-author would be the life of the last surviving co-author plus fifty years. In the Stockholm Revision, this was made clearer by the following rewording of article 7*bis*: **9.36**

> The provisions of the preceding Article [Article 7] shall also apply in the case of a work of joint authorship, provided that the terms measured from the death of the author shall be calculated from the death of the last surviving author.[205]

In this regard, it is of interest to note an Indian amendment that proposed the insertion of the words 'who was a national of the country of the Union' after the

[201] As of Jan 2005, these were Lebanon, Malta, New Zealand, Pakistan, Sri Lanka, and Zimbabwe; see www.wipo.int/treaties. Malta, Sri Lanka, and Zimbabwe have ratified arts 22–38 of the Paris Act only.

[202] *Documents 1948* (1951), 220. Note, however, that the original programme proposals sought to remove the problems referred to in the text: [1933] *DA* 92–3 and *Documents 1948* (1951), 219.

[203] ibid, 220. [204] ibid.

[205] *Records* 1967, vol II, 1163–4 (report of Main Committee I).

words 'last surviving author'.[206] This was not accepted by Main Committee I in view of the rejection of another Indian proposal to make the nationality of the author the general criterion of eligibility for protection and the general criterion of country of origin under the Convention (see para 6.55 above).[207]

(3) Categories of work addressed in earlier texts of the Convention

9.37 There are several other kinds of works in respect of which the Convention formerly contained special provisions as to their term of protection, but does no longer, or in respect of which proposals for such provisions have been made. The most important of these are posthumous works and works of corporate or 'juristic' persons, but for the sake of completeness a number of others are described briefly below.

(a) Posthumous works

9.38 The problem of anonymous or pseudonymous works which are published after an author's death has already been referred to (see para 9.33 above). The same problem arises in relation to works of known authors which are not published or otherwise made known until after their deaths. Should such works be restricted to life plus fifty years, with the result that their protection may run for only a short period of time or may perhaps not run at all? Or should a fresh term be granted to them whenever publication occurs? The implications of the second approach are far-reaching when the author has been dead for a long time, particularly if his immediate descendants are long since dead as well. On the other hand, a publisher or promoter in such a case may take a considerable risk if he publishes or presents the work with little or no guarantee of protection for his investment. Examples of both approaches were to be found in the national laws of Union countries in the early years of the Berne Union,[208] and no attempt to lay down a minimum term was made at the Berlin Conference. The term of protection for such works was left purely as a matter for comparison of terms under article 7(3), and this was maintained in the Rome Act.[209] No proposition

---

[206] Document S/73 (ibid, 690–1). [207] ibid, 1164.

[208] According to a study published in *Le Droit d'Auteur* in 1910 the position seems to have been as follows. Union countries with a term *post mortem auctoris* included Germany (life plus thirty years, but ten years post publication in the case of a work appearing twenty-one years or more after the author's death), Denmark and Norway (life plus fifty years—probably) and Spain (life plus eighty years—probably); countries with a term *post mortem editoris* were France (though there was dispute as to whether this was ten or fifty years) and Haiti (twenty years); countries with a term *post publicationem* included Japan (thirty years from first publication or performance), Switzerland (thirty years), the UK (forty-two years), Belgium and Luxembourg (fifty years from first publication, performance, or exhibition), Monaco and Sweden (fifty years), and Italy (eighty years, but not for certain). See generally [1910] *DA* 29, 31.

[209] Rome Act, art 7(3).

concerning this was included in the programme for the Brussels Conference, but proposals were made by several governments, including one by the French Government for a term of life plus fifty years together with an extension for ten years in the event that the work was published within the course of the last ten years of this term.[210] The French amendment, without its ten-year extension, was adopted by the Conference,[211] and this became article 7(5) of the Brussels Act. The effect of this was that posthumous works enjoyed the normal term of life plus fifty years unless they fell into one of the special categories of works dealt with in paragraph (3) or (4) (cinematographic or photographic works, and anonymous and pseudonymous works). It will be seen from this that paragraph (5) was really superfluous, as without it posthumous works would have been subject to all the provisions of article 7 in the same way as were other works. For this reason, the programme for the Stockholm Revision proposed the deletion of the paragraph.[212] There was some criticism of this proposal from several delegations,[213] but it was approved by the Conference and article 7(5) of the Brussels Act was duly deleted from the Stockholm, Paris Acts.[214]

While the laws of many Union countries follow the general rule in article 7(1) as **9.39** regards posthumous works, it should be noted that this is only a minimum period and that there is nothing which prevents any state applying a longer term (see article 7(6) and (8) and para 9.54 below). The member states of the European Union, for example, accord a twenty-five-year term of protection to 'any person who, after the expiry of copyright protection, for the first time publishes or lawfully communicates to the public an unpublished work'.[215] This provision supersedes domestic provisions regarding posthumous works.[216] Like similar dispositions previously enacted in some of the member states,[217] it is designed not to benefit the author's heirs, but to encourage the publication or public communication of undisclosed copyright-expired works. Hence, the Directive's text makes clear that the term of twenty-five years is not a grant of copyright, but rather constitutes 'a protection equivalent to the economic rights of the author'.

(b) Works of corporate persons

Although the Convention contains no definite prescription on the question of **9.40** who is an 'author', the basic assumption is that this is a natural or physical

[210] *Documents 1948* (1951), 209–10. [211] ibid, 215.
[212] *Records* 1967, vol I, 110.
[213] ibid, vol II, 899 (minutes of Main Committee I). [214] ibid.
[215] EU Duration Directive, art 4. [216] ibid, art 13(1).
[217] See eg France, Law of 11 Mar 1957, art 23 (now substantially modified as Code de la propriété intellectuelle, art L 123–4). The public disclosure policy underlying these kinds of dispositions has venerable roots, eg the French text was first adopted shortly after the French revolution, see Decrees of 1 Germinal, year XIII (22 Mar 1805), and of 8 June 1806, cited in Lucas and Lucas (n 14 above), para 451.

person (see further para 7.02 above). This, of course, does not impinge on the question of the ownership of authors' rights, as there is nothing to stop authors who are natural persons from assigning their rights to a body corporate or for their rights to be vested in such a body in advance, as is often the case with employee authors. Neither of these situations poses problems as regards the duration of these alienated rights: they will simply subsist for the normal term of life plus fifty years or whichever of the special terms that may be applicable in the case of a photographic work, work of applied art, and the like. In the event that the author is unknown, then the provisions governing pseudonymous and anonymous works will be applicable, unless and until the author's identity becomes known. However, in some circumstances it may be difficult or cumbersome to determine the duration of corporately owned works in this way because there are a large number of co-authors, some of whom may be impossible to identify. It is for this reason, among others, that 'film copyright' countries extend the concept of authorship to include bodies corporate in the case of cinematographic works (on authorship and ownership, see further Chapter 7 above). Nevertheless, a similar approach to works produced under the auspices of corporate entities was to be found in the laws of many Union countries in the early years of the Union.[218] Under these, copyright was conferred on such entities as the state, municipalities, public instrumentalities, learned and scientific associations, and private corporations. This was an 'original' copyright, rather than a derivative copyright which was assigned to them, or vested in them, by a physical author. Nevertheless, this apparent departure from the 'natural person' basis of authors' rights could be justified as a matter of practical convenience. Countries which adopted this approach included Austria,[219] Bulgaria,[220] Denmark,[221] France,[222] Germany,[223] Hungary,[224] and Spain.[225] On the other hand, countries such as Belgium, the UK, and Switzerland took the view that corporate persons could not be regarded as authors, and could only be assignees of physical authors.[226] In this second group of countries, the term of protection enjoyed by such works fell to be determined by reference to the life of

[218] See generally [1910] *DA* 29, 32; [1925] *DA* 98, 113, 122; [1926] *DA* 15, 26, 38; and Ladas (1938), 334ff.

[219] Law of 13 July 1920, art 40.

[220] Law of 11 July 1921, art 11(3).

[221] Law of 1 Apr 1912, art 3.

[222] These provisions were to be found in the jurisprudence: see generally [1925] *DA* 117–18.

[223] See here the exposition on the German Law in [1925] *DA* 98, 99–100.

[224] Law of 31 Dec 1921, art 15.

[225] The precise position here under the Law of 10 Jan 1879 was unclear: see [1925] *DA* 113, 116.

[226] For Belgium, see [1925] *DA* 98, 101–2 (but note here than Belgian law made provision for special terms in the case of works where the copyright was owned by the state and public authorities); for the UK, see [1925] *DA* 122, 123 (again with special terms provided in the case of Crown publications); for Switzerland, see [1926] *DA* 38. See further Ladas (1938), 335ff.

the natural person who had produced the work, or, in the event that he was unknown, by the provisions concerning the duration of protection of pseudonymous or anonymous works.[227] In the first group of countries, however, different solutions were to be found. Considerable variations were to be seen in the corporate entities which were considered to be 'authors', and there were further differences in the terms of protection accorded to their works. In France, for instance, the state was accorded perpetual protection, while academies, learned societies, and private corporations were given protection so long as they remained in existence, and then for fifty years following their dissolution or liquidation.[228] In other countries, the term was for a fixed period following publication of the work: this period ranged from fifteen years in the case of Brazil[229] to fifty years in the case of Belgium,[230] Denmark,[231] and Germany.[232]

None of these provisions of national law were in conflict with the permissive provisions governing duration in the Berlin Act. Nevertheless, it will be clear that difficulties would have arisen, in the absence of some special provision, once the term of life plus fifty years was made absolute. The 'life' of the author makes little sense in the case of a corporate person, the life of which may be indefinite. Attempts were therefore made at both the Rome and Brussels Conferences to amend the Convention so as to take account of this problem. At the Rome Conference, the French delegation proposed that 'corporate' works should be treated in the same way as pseudonymous and anonymous works, that is, that their term would be determined by a comparison of terms;[233] a more definite term of fifty years after first publication was proposed by the Polish delegation.[234] In the course of the discussions at the Conference, it was recognized that these proposals were only concerned with the original copyright of corporate bodies, not the copyrights which had been assigned to, or vested in, such bodies.[235] It was also agreed that there was nothing in the proposals that would require Union countries to accord an original copyright to corporate bodies.[236] However, the debates revealed that there were further differences between Union countries as to the entities which should be included within the scope of these amendments,[237] and the drafting committee decided finally not to include corporate bodies in the Rome Act. The term of protection for these bodies was therefore left as a matter for national legislation. Given that 9.41

[227] ibid. [228] See n 222 above.

[229] Civil Code 1916–17, art 662 (for publications of the state, government authorities, and municipalities, but it appeared that the life-plus-sixty-years term applied to works published by other corporate persons: see [1925] *DA* 113).

[230] Law of 22 Mar 1886, art 11. See also n 226 above.

[231] See n 221 above. [232] See n 223 above. [233] *Actes* 1928, 99.

[234] ibid, 118. [235] ibid, 243. [236] ibid. [237] ibid.

the term of life plus fifty years remained permissive under the Rome Act,[238] the failure of the Conference to make any provision with respect to the works of corporate bodies was not of any significance.

9.42 In the programme for the Brussels Conference, there was a proposal to treat 'works published by corporate bodies' in the same way as works of applied art, cinematographic works, anonymous and pseudonymous works, and posthumous works: under this, the duration of their protection would have been determined by a comparison of terms.[239] A more refined proposal was submitted by France, under which a term of fifty years post publication should be accorded to works of 'States and other public instrumentalities, academies and universities, learned societies and other non-profit organizations'.[240] Once again, there were difficulties in obtaining agreement among delegates as to the bodies that should be included, and both proposals were not proceeded with.[241] As article 7(1) of the Brussels Act made the term of life plus fifty years mandatory, the absence of any provision governing works of corporate bodies meant that the life-plus-fifty-years period applied to these works unless they fell into one of the special categories contained in the other paragraphs of article 9. This left states which recognized corporate copyright with the following options. They could abolish this concept altogether and determine the duration of the protection of these works by reference to the life of the natural person who was the author of the work in question, applying the provisions governing pseudonymous and anonymous works where it was impossible to identify such a person. Alternatively, they could take the view that nothing in the Convention expressly required the author of a work to be a natural person, and adopt the solution followed in the old French law under which the term of protection lasted for the 'life' of the corporation plus fifty years. In the event, it seems that the nations affected by this problem have generally chosen to abolish the concept of corporate authorship, and have adopted the first approach. Several states still recognize the possibility of corporate authorship, but this is as an equivalent to pseudonymous or anonymous authorship, with the result that, if the identity of the natural author becomes known, the term of protection then becomes life plus fifty years.[242] No further proposal concerning corporate authorship was considered at the Stockholm Conference. It can therefore be assumed that, for the purposes of the present Convention, it is no longer a live issue, apart from the

[238] Rome Act, art 7(1). [239] *Documents 1948* (1951), 204. See also [1933] *DA* 92.
[240] *Documents 1948* (1951), 210–11. [241] ibid, 215.
[242] See eg Japanese Law of 6 May 1970, art 53(1). Note also that, in France, Code de la propriété intellectuelle, art L 113–2 (as last amended by Law No 97–283 of 27 Mar 1997) recognizes that there can be corporate ownership of authors' rights in the case of a collective work where the contributions of individual authors cannot be identified.

case of cinematographic works, discussed earlier (see further paras 9.30 above and 9.47 below).[243]

(c) Other special terms

9.43 Under many national copyright laws in the early years of the Berne Convention special terms of protection were applied in circumstances other than those described above. In the UK, for example, until the Copyright Act 1911 the performing right and the 'copyright' were treated legislatively as two separate rights, although after 1842 both enjoyed the same term of protection.[244] In other national laws, different terms were often accorded to translation rights, and these were maintained well into this century. Often the term granted to these rights was shorter,[245] but sometimes it was the full period of the normal copyright provided that some condition, such as publication of an authorized translation within a prescribed time, was fulfilled.[246] Other instances of special terms were to be found in Hungarian law as regarded the right to reproduce speeches in volume form[247] and in Norway in relation to the right of recitation.[248] In other countries, special terms were provided for particular categories of works, such as newspapers, private letters and manuscripts, and collections of folklore.[249] In this regard, the special term of protection provided in the UK and certain other countries in respect of sound recordings should also be noted,[250] although this ceased to be of any relevance to the Berne Convention

---

[243] The US copyright law does, in certain circumstances, vest copyright ownership in corporate entities, pursuant to the 'works made for hire' doctrine. See 17 USC §§ 101, 201(b). The term of protection for a work for hire is the same as for anonymous or pseudonymous works, ibid, sec 302(c). As a result, no special issue of term is posed by the domestic law of the US, whose entry into the Berne Union substantially postdates the Paris Revision.

[244] The performing right was first granted under the Dramatic Copyright Act 1833, s 1 (28 years after publication or the life of the author, whichever was the longer) and this was made the same as for the 'copyright' under the Literary Copyright Act 1842, s 3 (life-plus-seventy-years or forty-two years after publication, whichever was the longer). Note also that Sweden, under its Law of 29 Apr 1904, art 14, had a shorter term of life-plus-thirty-years for performing rights.

[245] See eg the Bulgarian Law of 11 July 1921, arts 33 and 34 (translation right protected for ten years from publication of original, provided that author reserved his right expressly and an authorized translation appeared within five years). To similar effect was the Estonian law, which applied the Law of 20 Mar 1911 of the former Russian Empire (arts 33 and 34). See also the Greek Law No 2387 of 3–16 July 1920, art 6 (ten-year term for translation rights following publication).

[246] See eg the Japanese Law of 3 Mar 1899, art 7 (authorized translation to appear within ten years of publication of original work); the Netherlands Law of 23 Sept 1912, art 39 (ten years).

[247] Law of 31 Dec 1921, arts 12(1) and 14 (life plus ten years for these works unless published during author's lifetime).

[248] See Ladas (1938), 339.

[249] See eg Bulgaria and Estonia, where the former Russian Law of 1911 applied: see n 245 above and Ladas (1938), 337–8.

[250] Copyright Act 1911, ss 19(1) and 21.

when it became accepted that recordings should be treated under the rubric of neighbouring rights rather than as literary or artistic works.

D. The Present Position

(1) In general

9.44 The general term of protection granted by article 7(1) of the Paris text of the Convention is the life of the author and fifty years after his death. This is supplemented by a series of provisions dealing with duration in specific instances, such as cinematographic and photographic works, works of applied art, anonymous and pseudonymous works, and works of joint authorship (articles 7(2), (3), and (4), and 7bis). Other provisions deal with certain consequential matters, such as grants of term longer than the Conventional minimum, and comparison of member state terms (article 7(5), (6), (7), and (8)).

9.45 So far as the Stockholm, Paris Acts are concerned, there is little scope left now for the adoption of special terms of protection in cases other than those outlined in article 7(2)–(4). Article 7(1) refers simply to the 'term of protection granted by this Convention'. This can only mean national treatment and the rights specially granted by the Convention: accordingly, there is no warrant for a member country to provide for special terms in relation to particular rights, for example, broadcasting or diffusion rights. All rights granted by the Convention must therefore endure for at least life plus fifty years. The only exceptions to this rule are to be found in the provisions of paragraphs (2)–(4), and even here the authority to grant lesser terms of protection applies only to certain categories of works and not to particular rights. There is also no basis for granting shorter terms in respect of categories of works other than those listed in paragraphs (2)–(4), as the wording of these paragraphs makes it clear that these are the only exceptions that are allowed. Where any Union member retains shorter periods of protection for any category of right or work, otherwise than in accordance with these paragraphs, this can only be because it comes within the exemption provided in paragraph (7) (see para 9.53 below), or, being a developing country, it has availed itself of the facilities available to it under the Paris Appendix (article V). The position as regards countries which grant longer terms of protection, whether generally or in particular cases, is dealt with further below (see para 9.54). Finally, it should be borne in mind that the reference to 'rights' in this context excludes moral rights, which are dealt with separately under article $6^{bis}(2)$ and are discussed at Chapter 10 below.

(2) Special classes of works under article 7(2), (3), and (4)

(a) Photographic works

Article 7(4) reads as follows: 9.46

> It shall be a matter for legislation in the countries of the Union to determine the term of protection of photographic works . . .; however, this term shall last at least until the end of a period of twenty-five years from the making of such a work.

It will be seen that this allows Union countries complete freedom to protect photographic works for as long as they like, subject to the minimum requirement that this should be for at least twenty-five years from the making of such a work. It also gives them liberty to calculate the term of protection in whichever way they wish, for example, from the date of publication or from any other event subsequent to the making of the photograph because, in such cases, the term of protection would, in any event, be longer than the stipulated minimum. While, in the past, there was considerable inconsistency among member states respecting the term of protection of photographs,[251] and the Berne Convention has itself done little to bring about uniformity in this area, article 9 of the WCT prohibits parties to that treaty from applying article 7(4) of the Berne Convention, thus making a life-plus-fifty-years term the minimum for WCT members. (See the further discussion at para 9.64 below.) Moreover, the European Union Duration Directive has imposed a uniform term of life plus seventy years on all photographs meeting minimum originality standards.[252] As a result, in a significant number of Berne countries, the term of protection will now exceed the minimum set out at article 7(4). This, in turn, may bring into greater play the application of article 7(8) with respect to the term of protection that photographs from non-European Union countries receive in the EU or in other countries that afford protection longer than twenty-five years from the making of the photographs. (See the further discussion at para 9.55 below.)

(b) Cinematographic works

The term of protection for these is dealt with in article 7(2), which allows Union countries to adopt one of two minimum periods: life plus fifty years or fifty years after the work has been 'made available to the public with the consent of the author', or if this does not happen within fifty years from the making of the cinematographic work, fifty years after its making. The countries of the Union now adopt one or other of these ways of calculating terms,[253] although many 9.47

[251] See the first edition of this book, Sam Ricketson, *The Berne Convention 1886–1986* (1987), para 7.19.

[252] EU Duration Directive, art 6.

[253] Some of the countries which continue to be bound by earlier Acts of the Convention had shorter terms, but all now appear to apply a term of at least fifty years from publication.

now provide even longer terms. For example, the European Union member states now calculate the term of protection as seventy years from the death of the last survivor among the cinematographic or audiovisual work's director, screenwriter, author of the dialogue, and author of music composed specifically for the work.[254] As regards the relations between countries which adopt different terms, material reciprocity continues to be the rule and a comparison of terms will need to be made (see article 7(8)), discussed further below (see para 9.55).

(c) The disjunction between 'made available to the public' and the definition of 'published works'

9.48 A slight anomaly exists between the provisions of article 7(2) and the definition of 'published works' in article 3(3) insofar as it affects cinematographic works. It goes without saying that, for the purposes of article 7(2) a cinematographic work will often be made available to the public when it has not been published within the meaning of article 3(3), namely where it is broadcast or presented in public. On the other hand, there will be some instances where it is published, but has not been made available to the public, and this is not a situation that will usually arise with other kinds of works. This possibility arises in the following way. It will be recalled that the definition of 'published works' under article 3(3) is concerned with the making available of copies of the works in question (see para 6.29 above). It will also be recalled that, during the discussions at the Stockholm Conference, difficulties were seen in this regard with respect to cinematographic works where the copies are not usually made available to the public.[255] Except in the case of videograms, the distribution of such copies is generally confined to cinema proprietors who may, or may not, then show the film to the public. However, it seemed agreed that, given the nature of these works, there was a sufficient 'making available' to the public to satisfy the definition in article 3(3), even where the film was shown to an empty cinema.[256] Does this suffice for the purposes of article 7(2)? The latter refers to making available the work to the public, but without the qualifications that appear in article 3(3) ('reasonable requirements', and 'having regard to the nature of the work'). Accordingly, it is arguable that even where a cinematographic work is 'published' within the peculiar definition of article 3(3), it will not be made available to the public within the terms of article 7(2) until exactly that has happened—the work is shown to the public or broadcast. If this is correct, and neither of these events occurs within fifty years of the making of the work, the

[254] EU Duration Directive, art 2(2).

[255] See paras 6.33ff above. Note here the distinction made in German law between '*Veröffentlichung*' and '*Erscheinen*': see further E Ulmer, *Urheber- und Verlagsrecht*, 3rd edn (1980), 179ff.

[256] ibid.

minimum period of protection for that work within a film copyright country should be fifty years after its making.

(d) Works of applied art

Article 7(4) provides, in relevant part: **9.49**

> It shall be a matter for legislation in the countries of the Union to determine the term of protection of . . . works of applied art in so far as they are protected as artistic works; however, this term shall last at least until the end of a period of twenty-five years from the making of such a work.

As with photographic works, which article 7(4) also covers (see para 9.46 above), this provision gives Union countries complete freedom to protect works of applied art for as long as they like, subject to the minimum requirement that the term should be for at least twenty-five years from the making of such a work. It also allows them to calculate the minimum twenty-five-year term of protection from either the dates of creation or publication (or from any other event subsequent to the making of the photograph). One significant difference in the two subject matters covered by article 7(4), as discussed in greater detail in Chapter 8 above, is that member states must protect photographs (so long as they are original works of authorship, or 'literary and artistic works' within the meaning of article 2), but are not required to protect works of applied art as 'artistic works'. If the member state does not deem the work of applied art an 'artistic work', then the twenty-five-year minimum does not apply (even though another member state might consider that the same design does meet domestic criteria for 'artistic works'.) Thus, for countries such as the USA which exclude certain categories of works of applied art from the scope of copyright, this provision offers no difficulties: under US law, these works are not protected as artistic works,[257] and the absence of protection which is accorded to them does not contravene article 7(4). On the other hand, those works of applied art which are protected as artistic (or 'pictorial, graphic and sculptural') works under US law enjoy the full US copyright term of life plus seventy years,[258] which is far in excess of the minimum stipulated under article 7(4). In the majority of Union countries, the term of life plus fifty (or seventy) years is also the norm for works of applied art that domestic law deems 'artistic works', but there are a small number of states in which shorter terms are accorded.[259]

---

[257] 17 USC § 101 (definition of 'pictorial, graphic or sculptural work'). Designs meeting the statutory requirements of novelty and non-obviousness may be registered for design patents; these enjoy fourteen years of protection 35 USC § 173 (2004). See also the Australian Copyright Act 1968, ss 74–9.

[258] 17 USC § 302(a).

[259] See eg Sri Lanka, Code of Intellectual Property Act, § 19(5) (twenty-five years); Senegal, Copyright Act of 1973, as amended through 24 Jan 1986, art 41(b) (twenty-five years).

(e) Anonymous and pseudonymous works

9.50 Article 7(3) provides:

> In the case of anonymous or pseudonymous works, the term of protection granted by this Convention shall expire fifty years after the work has been lawfully made available to the public. However, when the pseudonym adopted by the author leaves no doubt as to his identity, the term of protection shall be that provided in paragraph (1). If the author of an anonymous or pseudonymous work discloses his identity during the above-mentioned period, the term of protection applicable shall be that provided in paragraph (1). The countries of the Union shall not be required to protect anonymous or pseudonymous works in respect of which it is reasonable to presume that their author has been dead for fifty years.

A number of changes based on the recommendations of the 1963 Study Group were made to this paragraph in the Stockholm Revision, where it became article 7(3) of the Stockholm, Paris Acts. First, the period of fifty years after publication was changed to fifty years 'after the work has been lawfully made available to the public'.[260] As with cinematographic works, discussed earlier (see para 9.47 above), it seems clear that this expression has a wider meaning than that given to 'publication' in article 3(3), and relates to 'every means by which the work is lawfully made accessible to the public'.[261] Thus, it will suffice if the work is broadcast or performed in public although neither act constitutes 'publication' within the meaning of article 3(3). Secondly, article 7(3) makes it clear that the term of protection of pseudonymous and anonymous works expires fifty years after this event. This avoids the impression given by article 7(4) of the Brussels Act that this protection was only granted as from this time and that the work was unprotected prior to publication.[262] Thirdly, a further sentence was added which provides that Union countries are not obliged to protect anonymous and pseudonymous works where it is reasonable to presume that their author has been dead for fifty years. This was inserted to avoid the possibility of such works obtaining larger periods of protection than provided under the principal rule in article 7(1) where they were published after the author's death.[263] An additional consideration here was that, unless some special provision was made in this regard, the publication of certain anonymous or pseudonymous manuscripts might be hampered.[264] It is therefore left to national laws to determine for how long they will protect such works.

(f) Works of folklore

9.51 Special provision for unpublished works of folklore was made in article 15(4) of the Stockholm, Paris Acts. As these are a species of anonymous works, their term

---

260 *Records* 1967, vol I, 107 (Document S/1). 261 ibid.
262 ibid. 263 ibid. 264 ibid.

of protection is also governed by article 7(3). It is also because of this that article 7(3) refers to works having been 'lawfully made available' rather than 'made available with the consent of the author'. A work of folklore might be lawfully made available by an authority designated under article 15(4), but this would not necessarily be with the consent of the author in the strict sense.[265] In the case of works of folklore, moreover, it may be difficult to determine who is the 'author' of a work that may be of communal expression, and may be substantially based on ancient elements.[266]

(g) *Works of joint authorship*

Article 7*bis* provides that the term of protection for works of joint authorship is to be calculated from the death of the last surviving author. Where a joint work is first published in a Union country, its term of protection will be calculated from the death of the last surviving author whether or not she is a national of a Union country. On the other hand, nationality will be relevant where a work is unpublished or is first published in a country outside the Union: in such a case, the dates of death of authors who are not nationals of a Union country will not affect the calculation of the terms of protection of those co-authors who are nationals of a Union country.[267] Thus, the term of protection of such works will be calculated from the death of the last surviving co-author who is a Union national. This could mean that if the first to die is the only Union national joint author, the minimum term in the work will expire before fifty years have run from the deaths of the other co-authors (indeed, under this scenario, the non-Unionist co-authors could conceivably still be alive when the minimum Berne term expires). **9.52**

(3) Calculation of term when some member states' terms are shorter or longer than others

(a) *Accommodation of countries with shorter terms*

At the time of the Stockholm Conference, there was still a small minority of Union countries that had not acceded to the Brussels Act, principally, it appears, because of the mandatory requirement of protection for life plus fifty years. **9.53**

---

265 ibid, vol II, 1161 (report of Main Committee I).

266 See eg Agnès Lucas-Schloetter, 'Folklore', in Silke von Lewinski (ed), *Indigenous Heritage and Intellectual Property: Genetic Resources, Traditional Knowledge and Folklore* (2003), 259, 294–7.

267 *Records* 1967, vol. II, 1164 (report of Main Committee I). Note that, in the case of countries that do not adopt the film copyright system, the question of co-authors may give rise to problems in particular cases: cf France, Code de la propriété intellectuelle, art L 113–7 (as last amended by Law No 97–283 of 27 Mar 1997), defining the owner of an audiovisual work; German Law of 1965, art 89.

These included Poland[268] and Romania,[269] although there were several other countries bound by the Rome Act, such as Czechoslovakia,[270] and Bulgaria,[271] which did accord protection for the full term of life plus fifty years. A Bulgarian and Polish proposal therefore sought some kind of transitional arrangement which would allow these countries to accede to the Stockholm Act, while giving them the right to maintain their shorter terms of protection.[272] This was a clear derogation from the system established by the Brussels Act, and attracted strong criticism from a number of other countries.[273] However, as only a few countries were affected, the question was whether such an accommodation which enabled them to accede to the rest of the new Act was preferable to the greater divergences that would appear if these countries continued to be bound by the Rome Act only.[274] Finally, the following compromise (which became article 7(7)) was adopted:

> Those countries of the Union bound by the Rome Act of this Convention which grant, in their national legislation in force at the time of signature of the present Act, shorter terms of protection than those provided for in the preceding paragraphs shall have the right to maintain such terms after ratifying or acceding to the present Act.[275]

This provision also applies in relation to the other special terms of protection that are provided for under the other paragraphs of article 7 (see paras 9.46ff above). However, its current irrelevance so far as the basic term of life plus fifty years is concerned is shown by the fact that, of the present Berne membership, the last Rome Act country eligible to invoke it, Romania, adhered in 1998 to the Paris Act.[276] Union countries now have normal terms of at least life plus fifty years, and the European Union member states and the US now have terms of life plus seventy years. As a result, the remaining differences in term are now more likely to be between Union members who apply the minimum term, and those whose term exceeds that required by article 7(1). Article 7(8) preserves the principle of comparison of terms, under which reciprocity of protection applies

---

[268] Law No 234 on Copyright of 10 July 1952, art 26. Note that the term of protection under the previous Law of 1926 was life plus fifty years.

[269] Decree relating to Copyright, No 321 of 18 June 1956, art 6 (life plus fifty years for spouse and descendants, life plus fifteen years for other heirs).

[270] Copyright Law concerning Literary, Scientific and Artistic Works, No 35 of 25 Mar 1965, art 33.

[271] Law on Copyright of 16 Nov 1951, art 18.

[272] Document S/50: *Records* 1967, vol I, 688.

[273] *Records* 1967, vol II, 900 (France, FRG, and Italy).

[274] ibid, 901 (remarks of the Czech delegate).

[275] ibid, 1162–3 (report of Main Committee I).

[276] See n 269 above. Poland and Malta had been eligible under art 7(7), but their subsequent membership in the European Union requires them to protect works of authorship for the term of life plus seventy years imposed by the 1993 Duration Directive.

rather than national treatment. (This provision is discussed further at para 9.55 below.)

(4) Countries with longer terms of protection

On its face, article 7(1) appears absolute in its requirement that the term of **9.54**
protection under the Convention is to be life plus fifty years, nothing more and nothing less. Does this prevent those Union countries which accord longer terms under their national laws from extending similar protection to works claiming under the Convention? The general answer is that it does not: under article 19 it is expressly provided that nothing in the Convention prevents the making of a claim to the benefit of any greater protection which may be granted by the law of any Union country. This is the principle of minimum protection which is discussed more generally in Chapter 6 above. However, article 7(6) also puts it beyond doubt that Union countries are free to grant any term in excess of those provided for under that article. This not only applies to the normal term of life plus fifty years, but also to the special terms provided by paragraphs (2) to (4). Of these last-mentioned paragraphs, only paragraph (3) is worded in the same way as paragraph (1); the wording of paragraphs (2) and (4) clearly implies that the terms stipulated in those paragraphs are minimum terms only. Nevertheless, as we have seen above, many Union countries accord longer terms under their national laws in respect of these particular categories of works. Strictly, paragraph (6) is superfluous in view of the general principle contained in article 19, but it was added at the time of the Stockholm Revision as a matter of caution. This was because article 7(2) of the Brussels Act, which embodied the principle of comparison of terms, began with the words 'However, where one or more countries of the Union grant a term of protection in excess of that provided by paragraph (1) . . .'. Article 7(6) was therefore inserted in the Stockholm Act to avoid any adverse inference that might otherwise arise if it were deleted.[277] Furthermore, it was inserted in its present position so as to make it applicable to all terms of protection dealt with under article 7, rather than just the term of life plus fifty years in article 7(1) which was the case under the Brussels Act.

(5) Comparison of terms

This principle, with its basis of material reciprocity, is still retained in article 7(8) **9.55**
of the Stockholm, Paris Acts. This provides:

> In any case, the term shall be governed by the legislation of the country where protection is claimed; however, unless the legislation of that country otherwise

[277] *Records* 1967, vol I, 108 (Document S/1) and 1162–3 (report of Main Committee I).

provides, the term shall not exceed the term fixed in the country of origin of the work.

There are a few circumstances in which this provision will be applicable. First, in the relations between countries of the Union which adopt the minimum terms provided in paragraphs (1) to (4) and those countries of the Union which adopt longer terms. Second, in the relations between countries of the Union which have terms in excess of those provided in paragraphs (1) to (4), but terms which differ in their extent.[278] Finally, a further complication is presented by countries who accede to the Berne Convention, and who extend the minimum term to works from other Berne states, but do not accord that minimum to domestic works. Article 5(3) allows member states to provide less protection to their own works, and while this outcome seems improbable, it does in fact occur, notably in the USA.[279] For purposes of comparison of term under article 7(8), how should the Berne country where protection is sought calculate the term of a work whose country of origin applies a sub-minimum term to its own works? Should the protecting country compare the sub-minimum term to its Berne-consistent term, thus applying the sub-minimum term? This may be literally consonant with article 7(8), but it leads to absurd results: Were the country of protection to apply the domestic term of the country of origin, it would deny a foreign Berne work the minimum term of protection required under the Convention. With the exception of works covered by article 7(7), it must be assumed that the terms to be compared under article 7(8) shall be at least as long as the minimum term set out in the Paris text. Indeed, article 7(7) arguably prompts the negative inference that, in the absence of specific derogation, such as that afforded by article 7(7), Union countries applying the comparison of terms under article 7(8) are to apply the article 7 minima as the baseline.[280] This would mean that if the work received a life-plus-twenty-years term in its country of origin, it would still be entitled to the life-plus-fifty-years term in other Berne countries. By contrast, if the country of origin applied a life-plus-fifty-years term, and the country of protection's domestic law provided for life plus seventy years, article 7(8) would enable the country of protection to deny the last twenty years of local coverage to the foreign work.

---

[278] See eg Colombia, Law on Copyright (No 23 of 28 Jan 1982), art 21 (life plus eighty years); Mexico, Federal Law on Copyright, art 29(I) (life plus seventy-five years for economic rights); Venezuela, Law on Copyright of 14 Aug 1993, art 25 (life plus sixty years).

[279] See 17 USC § 104(A) (restoring copyrights in non-US works expiring before Berne minimum term due to non-compliance with formalities; no restoration of copyright in works for which the USA is the country of origin).

[280] Accord, Daniel Gervais, *The TRIPS Agreement: Drafting History and Analysis*, 2nd edn (2003), para 2.54 ('the two terms are compared and the shorter may be applied, provided it is at least equal to the minimum provided in the Convention.') citing Lucas and Lucas (n 14 above), 898.

In the above situations, the principle of comparison of terms applies rather than the general Conventional principle of national treatment. However, it will be noted that article 7(8) leaves it open to countries to apply national treatment if they desire to do so. At the Stockholm Conference, there was a Swiss proposal to reverse the formula used in the last part of paragraph (8), so as to make national treatment the principal rule rather than the comparison of terms.[281] This attempt to perfect the principle of assimilation was rejected by Main Committee I,[282] and the present formula was unanimously adopted.

(a) Date for computation of term

Article 7(5) contains a useful rule for determining the point of time from which the terms provided in paragraphs (1) to (4) are to be calculated. This stipulates: **9.56**

> The term of protection subsequent to the death of the author and the terms provided by paragraph (2), (3) and (4) shall run from the date of death or of the event referred to in those paragraphs, but such terms shall always be deemed to begin on the first of January of the year following the death or such event.

This provision was first inserted at the time of the Brussels Revision, and stemmed from a French proposal[283] which, in turn, was inspired by the work of ALAI.[284] The effect of it is that an author receives a slightly longer period of protection than he otherwise would if the term were calculated from the precise date of his death or other event. Thus, if an author dies on 2 January 1986, his term of protection will expire on 1 January 2037, rather than 1 January 2036. The rule avoids disputes that might otherwise arise: while it is usually easy to ascertain the year in which a particular event occurred, problems might arise if it was necessary to identify a particular date in that year.

(6) Paying public domain

Reference has already been made to the '*domaine public payant*' provisions of the pre-1925 Italian Law (see para 9.20 above). Under these, a royalty was payable on the use of works which had fallen into the public domain. This royalty was payable to the author for a further forty years after the end of his term of protection.[285] In the Law of 25 November 1925, this system was changed quite considerably: the general term of protection was now life plus fifty years, and after this time a royalty of 5 per cent of gross receipts was payable to the state for each public performance of a musical work.[286] This was, in reality, a form of tax **9.57**

[281] *Records* 1967, vol I, 690 (Document S/69).
[282] ibid, vol II, 900 (minutes of Main Committee I); ibid, 1163 (report).
[283] *Documents 1948* (1951), 212.
[284] ibid.
[285] Decree of 19 Sept 1882, art 9.
[286] Decree-Law of 7 Nov 1925, art 34.

on the public performance of musical works, and did not derogate from the private rights of exploitation of the author and his successors which were enjoyed absolutely throughout the period of life plus fifty years.[287] In return, the Italian Government undertook to make a certain sum payable each year for the general promotion of the performing arts in Italy, particularly in relation to works of cultural and commercial importance.[288] In this Law, there was no immediate nexus between the 5 per cent royalty and the Government subsidy which was thus provided; nonetheless, the latter made it clear that the Government accepted a clear financial obligation to assist in the development of Italian performing arts. In the revised Italian Law of 22 April 1941, this system was extended again, being made applicable to broadcasts of musical works.[289] In addition, a fee became payable on the sale of each copy of a literary, scientific, didactic, or musical work in the public domain.[290] This was an amount based on the price per copy and was payable to the Assistance and Insurance Fund of Authors, Writers and Musicians.[291] This system has since been repealed in Italy,[292] but it formed a model for other national legislative schemes of 'paying public domain'.

9.58 The essence of these schemes is that some kind of fee or charge is payable on works that have entered the public domain, and that the monies thus received are channelled back, directly or indirectly, into the general promotion of cultural activities. The ways in which this is done vary considerably: from the provision of specific pecuniary assistance to authors and their families[293] to wider schemes for the development of national literary and artistic creativity.[294] The bodies charged with administering the funds received and carrying out these functions may also vary: from the state itself or some relevant government agency[295] to an authors' society or similar professional organization.[296]

[287] 'Le nouveau Dècret-Loi italien sur le droit d'auteur du 7 novembre 1925' [1926] *DA* 109 (Part III), 110–11.

[288] ibid, art 35.

[289] Law of 22 Apr 1941, art 175. See also the Copyright Regulations for the Application of the Law of 22 Apr 1941, 18 May 1942, arts 49–51 (on the implementation of these provisions).

[290] Law of 1941, art 179. See also Regulations (n 289 above), 52–6.

[291] ibid. [292] ibid.

[293] See eg the Ivory Coast Law of 28 July 1978, art 3 (application of royalties paid on the use of foreign works in the public domain).

[294] See eg the Burkina Faso Ordinance Affording Protection to Copyright of 29 Sept 1983, art 87 (fees paid to the 'national cultural promotion fund'); see also the Uruguayan Law of 15–17 Dec 1937, art 62, as amended 17 Dec 2003 (proceeds to be devoted to the services of art and culture).

[295] See eg the Mexican Law of 4 Nov 1963, arts 1, 118(iii) (now repealed).

[296] See the provisions for this under the Italian system: Law of 1941, art 179 and Regulations, art 56 (now repealed). See further the imaginative proposals of Dietz for the establishment of a twenty-year period of paying public domain after the expiry of the period of life plus fifty years, with these payments being collected by collecting societies and paid to living authors: A Dietz, 'À

At the present, several Berne Union countries have such provisions in their national laws.[297] The majority of these are developing countries, and the fees payable represent a useful supplementary way of promoting national cultural development. There is no provision in the Berne Convention for paying public domain, and, apart from the discussion of the rather different form in which it existed in the pre-1925 Italian Law which occurred at the time of the Rome and Brussels Revisions (see para 9.20 above), there have been no serious proposals for its inclusion. Nonetheless, provision for it was made in the Tunis Model Law on Copyright which was prepared under the auspices of UNESCO and WIPO in 1976.[298] As a means of raising revenue for general cultural activities, it has obvious attractions, but it should be noted that it is only one among a range of financial measures that may be adopted for this purpose. None of these, including paying public domain, are necessarily linked to legislation on authors' rights and may be implemented in a wide variety of ways, including administrative action and the general revenue laws.[299] A related question concerns the continued protection of the moral or personal interests of authors after their economic rights have fallen into the public domain: this is discussed at Chapter 10 below. 9.59

E. Beyond the Berne Convention

Two treaties concluded subsequent to the 1971 Paris Act, the Agreement on Trade-Related Aspects of Intellectual Property Rights 1994 ('the TRIPs Agreement') (articles 4(b) and 12) and the 1996 WCT (article 9), contain provisions which have a modest impact on the substantive minima set out at article 7 of the Berne Convention. While these provisions do not effect major changes, they do contribute somewhat toward greater harmonization of copyright terms. The TRIPs Agreement contains a general provision on duration of copyright protection, as well as a disposition preserving the material reciprocity permitted by the 9.60

propos de l'harmonisation des législations nationales dans les pays de la C.E.A.' (1983) 117 *RIDA* 48 (this article was subtitled 'Vers une nouveau concept du domain public payant' but this did not appear in the printed text in *RIDA*).

[297] See eg Benin, Brazil, Congo, Guinea, Ivory Coast, Mali, Poland, Rwanda, Senegal.

[298] Tunis Model Law, s 19.

[299] See eg the French Finance Law of 1976 (No 75–1278), art 22 which imposed a levy on book sales (whether in or out of copyright); see further Dietz (1978), 172–3. Note that prior to this, Decree No 56–1215 of 29 Nov 1956 instituted a kind of paying public domain system by granting an extension of fifteen years' protection for literary works in favour of the National Literary Fund (see also arts 5(1) and 6 of the Law of 11 Oct 1946 as amended by the Law of 25 Feb 1956). This system came to an end in 1976: see further Dietz (n 296 above), 70ff. See also the discussion by WIPO and UNESCO Committee of Non-Governmental Experts on the 'Domaine Public Payant' (Geneva, 26–9 Apr 1982): [1982] *Copyright* 179.

Berne Convention. The WCT specifically addresses, and increases, the term of protection for photographs.

(1) The TRIPs Agreement: article 4

9.61 Article 4 of the TRIPs Agreement imposes a 'most favoured nation' requirement, under which

> With regard to the protection of intellectual property, any advantage, favor, privilege or immunity granted by a Member to the nationals of any other country shall be accorded immediately and unconditionally to the nationals of all other Members.

As discussed in para 6.134 above, 'MFN' clauses resemble, but go further than, national treatment. If a state bound by an MFN clause accords national treatment to the authors of any other states party to the same agreement, then it must accord national treatment to all. In addition, going beyond national treatment, if a member state grants the authors of another member state rights over and above the rights it affords its own authors, it must extend those rights to the authors of all other member states. It would follow that a Berne member state that did not apply the article 7(8) comparison of terms to works originating in some states would be obliged to forgo the comparison with respect to works originating in all members of the TRIPs Agreement. By the same token, any special agreements concluded between Union members under article 20 respecting duration in excess of the article 7 minima would also benefit all other TRIPs members. In fact, however, this is not the case, for two reasons.

First, article 4(b) of the TRIPs Agreement exempts from the MFN requirement 'any advantage, favor, privilege or immunity accorded by a Member'

> granted in accordance with the provisions of the Berne Convention (1971) . . . authorizing that the treatment accorded be a function not of national treatment but of the treatment accorded in another country.

This clearly preserves the system established in Berne Convention article 7(8).[300] Second, article 4(d) of the TRIPs Agreement further exempts privileges, etc

> deriving from international agreements relating to the protection of intellectual property which entered into force prior to the entry into force of the WTO Agreements, provided that such agreements are notified to the Council for TRIPs and do not constitute an arbitrary or unjustifiable discrimination against nationals of other Members.

This 'grandfather clause' allows member states who had previously entered into bilateral agreements regarding copyright term to limit the benefits of those

[300] See Gervais (n 280 above), 106–7.

agreements to the signatories, rather than being obliged to extend them to all members of the TRIPs Agreement.

(2) The TRIPs Agreement: article 12

The TRIPs Agreement contains a general disposition on term of protection: **9.62**

> Whenever the term of protection of a work, other than a photographic work or a work of applied art, is calculated on a basis other than the life of a natural person, such term shall be no less than fifty years from the end of the calendar year of authorized publication, or, failing such authorized publication within fifty years of making of the work, fifty years from the end of the calendar year of making.

This text closely recalls article 7 of the Berne Convention, particularly in its furnishing of a point of reference other than the life of a natural person. Nonetheless, the latter remains the default position; even if the TRIPs Agreement is less humanistically oriented than Berne (see the earlier discussion at Chapter 5 above), it does not purport to supplant the basic *post mortem auctoris* calculus. With respect to cinematographic works, the departure points the treaties offer for counting the fifty-year term differ slightly. Both texts refer to the 'making' of the work. But where article 7(2) of the Berne Convention also counts from the 'making [the work] available to the public', article 12 of the TRIPs Agreement counts from 'authorized publication'. As discussed earlier (see para 9.48 above), these two activities may not always be the same; this could, at least in theory, yield different terms. Because the TRIPs Agreement does not, unlike Berne, define publication, however, it may be possible to interpret 'authorized publication' under the TRIPs Agreement in a manner consistent with 'making available to the public' under Berne.[301]

But article 12 of the TRIPs Agreement covers more than cinematographic works; it reaches all works for which the basis of calculus is not *post mortem auctoris*. In other words, this provision appears to cover the issues of corporate authorship left unresolved in the 1971 Paris text. (See the earlier discussion at paras 9.40–9.42 above.) In effect, the TRIPs Agreement directs that such works have a minimum duration equivalent to anonymous and pseudonymous works under article 7(3) of the Berne Convention. The TRIPs Agreement does not, however, expand the categories of works whose term is 'calculated on a basis other than the life of a natural person'; it is left to domestic law to determine whether, for example, a work created by an employee, is a corporate work

[301] But see, Gervais (n 280 above), 142 (suggesting that 'Since TRIPs only mentions publication and not the other forms of making available to the public, TRIPs may in certain cases provide for a longer term of protection, following from a later starting date to the term of protection'), and authorities cited at n 81 therein.

whose term is to be calculated not on the basis of the employee-creator's life, but by some other measure (the 'life' of the corporate entity not being a workable reference point). A comparison of article 12 with an earlier draft of the Agreement makes clear that the TRIPs Agreement does not itself establish a category of corporate works. The draft of 23 July 1990 proposed:

> The term of protection of a work whose author is a legal entity shall be no less than 50 years from the end of the year of authorised publication . . .[302]

This draft would, then, have come much closer to endorsing the authorship status of legal entities, although, arguably, determination of authorship would have remained a matter of domestic law. The draft had the strong support of the US film industry,[303] whose 'employer for hire' status in the USA made them the statutory 'authors' of audiovisual works. A provision such as the draft's could have been interpreted as giving international recognition to the characterization of film producers as 'authors'. This is a result generally resisted by continental lawmakers, and therefore may explain the adoption of a more neutral text. Under article 12 of the TRIPs Agreement as finally adopted, once the member state has, as a matter of its domestic law, determined whether or not the work is one whose term is not calculated *post mortem auctoris*, the TRIPs Agreement dictates that the copyright endure for at least fifty years from the 'authorized publication' or 'making' of the work.

9.63 Article 12 of the TRIPs Agreement leaves untouched the treatment of the duration of photographic works and works of applied art in article 7(4) of the Berne Convention. It appears that the drafters did not intend to alter the discrimination against these works; neither of the prior drafts of article 12 propose any changes in the Berne article 7(4) regime in that respect.

(3) WIPO Copyright Treaty and the duration of photographs

9.64 Change in the minimum duration of photographs awaited the WCT whose article 9 provides:

> In respect of photographic works, the Contracting Parties shall not apply the provisions of Article 7(4) of the Berne Convention.

The preclusion of article 7(4) makes article 7(1) the default position, thus entitling photographs to a minimum term of life plus fifty years, although the term of anonymous and pseudonymous photographs would be governed by article 7(3). Other relevant provisions of article 7, including the date for

[302] 'Chairman's Report to the Group of Negotiation on Goods', document MTN.GNG/NG11/W/76.

[303] See Gervais (n 280 above), 141, n 75, and authorities cited therein.

calculation (article 7(5)), the reminder that Union countries are free to apply longer terms (article 7(6)), the preservation of Rome Act shorter terms (article 7(7)), and the comparison of terms (article 7(8)) apply as well. Article 9 of the WCT thus ends the durational discrimination against photographs; one may infer from this a broader reception of photographs as full citizens of the world of 'literary and artistic works'. (The WCT makes no changes in the duration of works of applied art.) An earlier draft of article 9 (then article 11) would have made explicit reference to articles 7(3) and 7(5) to 7(8) of Berne, but that was deemed unnecessary.[304]

(4) Proposals for a longer term in general

The International Bureau of WIPO had initially proposed to extend the basic minimum term in the WCT from life plus fifty years to life plus seventy years.[305] This proposal coincided with developments in the European Union that produced the 1993 Duration Directive and its term of life plus seventy years. Nonetheless, the proposal received inadequate support,[306] and the drafters limited their efforts to equalizing the term of the protection of photographs to the term of literary and artistic works in general.[307] **9.65**

304 See Jörg Reinbothe & Silke von Lewinski, *The WIPO Treaties 1996* (2002), 115.
305 See [1992] *Copyright*, 66, 80 et seq, paras 159–61.
306 ibid, 93, 107, paras 147–60
307 See Reinbothe and von Lewinski (n 304 above), 114.

9A

GENERAL INTRODUCTION TO CHAPTERS 10–12: RIGHTS PROTECTED

9A.01 The laws of most Berne Union members conceive of the author's copyright as comprising two aspects: pecuniary or economic interests and moral or personal interests. These interests are, in turn, protected by the grant of specific, exclusive rights to the author. There are different views as to the nature of this division, with some jurisdictions taking the position that both sets of interests are quite independent of each other (the 'dualist' approach), and other jurisdictions treating them as inextricably connected (the 'monist' approach). For the moment, this debate does not directly concern us, as its implications relate chiefly to the duration and alienability of the rights that are granted to secure these interests. The object of our discussion in the following Chapters (10–12) is the rights themselves, and the extent to which the Berne Convention and later instruments contain positive prescriptions as to which of these are to be protected.

A. Background: The Articulation of Rights in National Legislation

9A.02 In national legislation, there are considerable differences in the way in which this task of prescription is carried out. Some laws confer a general right on the author, and then define the content of this right in more detail, while others define each right with considerable specificity. At the risk of oversimplifying, one can state that the civil law countries tend toward broadly worded syntheses of the protected rights, while Commonwealth countries follow a more 'pointillist' approach, with the United States incorporating aspects of both legislative techniques.

For example, article L 111-1 of the French Code de la propriété intellectuelle begins with the following general declaration: **9A.03**

> *Article 1.* The author of an intellectual work shall, by the mere fact of its creation, enjoy an exclusive incorporeal property right in the work, effective against all persons.
>
> This right includes attributes of an intellectual and moral nature as well as attributes of an economic nature, as determined by this law . . .

It also includes, in article L 123-1, al 1, the following overarching description of the author's economic rights:

> The author shall enjoy . . . the exclusive right to exploit his work under any form whatever and to take an economic profit therefrom.

While this is a very general formula which entitles the author to benefit from any exploitation of his work, the Code also affords more specific but still generously worded guidance as to what falls within the scope of this entitlement. For example, the reproduction right is described in very general terms as consisting of the 'material fixation of the work by all methods that permit of indirect communication to the public' (L 122-3, al 1). This seems sufficient to cover the making of any kind of copy of a work, whether in analogue or digital form, including the fixation of a musical work in the form of a sound recording or of a dramatic work in an audiovisual work, as well as the making of a translation or adaptation.

By contrast, the copyright laws of Commonwealth countries do not define the economic rights of the author in this general way. The Commonwealth approach has been to define the rights of the author in a specific and exhaustive fashion, with the consequence that nothing is included that is not expressly stated to be so. A good example of this is to be found in the Australian Copyright Act 1968, where section 31(1)(a) provides that, 'for this Act' the 'copyright in relation to work' consists of the following exclusive rights: **9A.04**

> (a) in the case of a literary, dramatic or musical work, to do all or any of the following acts:
> (i) to reproduce the work in a material form;
> (ii) to publish the work;
> (iii) to perform the work in public;
> (iv) to communicate the work to the public;

(v) to make an adaptation of the work;
(vi) to do, in relation to a work that is an adaptation of the first-mentioned work, any of the acts specified in relation to the first-mentioned work in sub-paragraphs (i) to (iv) inclusive; and

(b) in the case of an artistic work, to do all or any of the following acts:
(i) to reproduce the work in a material form;
(ii) to publish the work;
(iii) to communicate the work to the public; and

(c) in the case of a literary work (other than a computer program) or a musical or dramatic work, to enter into a commercial rental arrangement in respect of the work reproduced in a sound recording; and

(d) in the case of a computer program, to enter into a commercial rental arrangement in respect of the program.

The above formulation was closely based upon that adopted in section 1(1) of the UK Copyright Act 1956, but a similar 'listing' approach is to be found in section 16(1) of the UK Copyright, Designs and Patents Act 1988. Similar formulations are to be found in the copyright laws of other Commonwealth countries which are members of the Berne Union.[1] The approach taken by the United States 1976 Copyright Act is something of a hybrid: it does not announce an overall exploitation right, but synthesizes rights into several broad categories, such as the right 'to reproduce the copyrighted work in copies or phonorecords'.[2]

9A.05 While the above divergences may be explained by the different juridical theories of the nature of authors' rights that underlie each law, the rights accorded to authors in Berne Union countries still correspond to a very considerable degree. Leaving aside moral rights, the basic economic rights protected in each country have traditionally fallen into two main categories: reproduction of the work in a material form, and public dissemination of the work in a non-material form. In the terminology of the French Law, the first corresponds to the *droit de reproduction* or right of indirect communication to the public, while the second would be the *droit de représentation* or right of direct communication to the public. While most other national laws lack this neat bipartite classification, they nonetheless contain an aggregation of specific exclusive rights that provide broadly similar protection to authors. (One might note that the neatness

[1] See eg the Copyright Act 1994 (NZ), which is closely based on the 1988 UK Act (this is also the case, though to a lesser extent, in Ireland: Copyright and Related Rights Act 2000); Copyright Act 1985, RSC 1985, c C-42 (Canada), s 3(1); Copyright Act 1957 (India), s 14. For further commentary on the national copyright laws of Comonwealth countries, such as Australia, Canada, and India, and former 'Commonealth' countries, such as Israel and Hong Kong, that have applied UK law, see the national commentaries in M B Nimmer and P E Geller, *International Copyright Law and Practice* (2002).

[2] 17 USC § 106(1).

of the classification has lately proved misleading, as digital media challenge traditional distinctions between dissemination in material and non-material form.) The main difference is that where rights are formulated in more general terms, it is easier to argue that they should be interpreted broadly so as to comprehend novel forms of utilization of a work. Where rights are listed in a more restrictive way, as in the Commonwealth countries, specific legislative action is usually required to cover such situations, and this, of course, will inevitably take more time and effort. As will be seen below, the latter has been true of the Berne Convention. As a result, subsequent multilateral instruments have been adopted to clarify or to enlarge the scope of the Berne Convention rights.

B. The Articulation of Rights under the Berne Convention

During its lifetime, the Berne Convention has sought to embody the minimum statement of rights that each country could agree upon as constituting the central core of rights to be accorded to authors claiming under the Convention (the 'rights specially granted by this Convention'). For this reason, the Stockholm, Paris Acts contain a list of specific exclusive rights rather than a general formulation of the kind to be found in the French law. These rights have been added to the Convention text in a piecemeal way, usually in response to particular contemporary needs and pressures, and without any attempt at systematic organization. Each successive revision of the Convention has therefore seen the addition of a new right or rights. The original Berne Act contained exclusive rights only in relation to the making and public performance of translations of works. Rights in relation to cinematographic adaptations and the mechanical reproduction of musical works were added at the time of the Berlin Revision, broadcasting and moral rights at Rome, public performance and recitation and adaptation, together with the *droit de suite*, at Brussels, and reproduction at Stockholm. The present Act now contains provisions for the protection of both moral and pecuniary rights, the latter comprising the following exclusive rights: **9A.06**

(1) Reproduction rights

- making a collection of speeches, addresses and other similar works (article 2bis(3));
- reproduction in any manner or form (article 9(1)); and
- reproduction of cinematographic works (articles 14(1)(i), 14bis(1)).

(2) Adaptation rights

- translation (article 8);
- adaptation, arrangement, and other alterations (article 12);
- cinematographic adaptation (articles 14(1)(i), 14(2)).

(3) Rights pertaining to physical copies

- distribution of cinematographic works, including cinematographic adaptations and reproductions of literary and artistic works (articles 14(1)(i), 14bis(1));
- the *droit de suite* in original works of art and original manuscripts of writers and composers (article 14ter);
- importation of copies (seizure of infringing copies) (article 16).

(4) Rights of communication to the public

Rights of public performance (to the public present at the performance):

- public performance of dramatic, dramatico-musical and musical works, and of translations of dramatic or dramatico-musical works, by any means or process (articles 11(1)(i), 11(2));
- public recitation of literary works and of translations of literary works (articles 11ter(1)(i), 11ter(2));
- public performance of cinematographic adaptations and reproductions of literary and artistic works (article 14(1)(ii));
- public performance of cinematographic works (article 14bis(1)).

Rights of communication to the public by means of transmissions:

- communication to the public of performances of dramatic, dramatico-musical and musical works, and of translations of dramatic or dramatico-musical works (articles 11(1)(ii), 11(2));
- broadcasting and any communication to the public of literary and artistic works by any means of wireless diffusion of signs, sounds, or images (article 11bis (1)(i));
- communication of literary and artistic works to the public by wire of broadcasts and rebroadcasts (article 11bis(i),(ii));
- public communication of broadcasts of literary and artistic works by loudspeakers or other analogous instruments (article 11bis(iii));
- public communication of recitations of literary works and of translations of literary works (articles 11ter(1)(ii), 11ter(2));
- communication to the public by wire of cinematographic adaptations and reproductions of literary and artistic works (article 14(1)(ii));

- communication to the public by wire of cinematographic works (article $14^{bis}(1)$).

C. The Articulation of Rights under Later Instruments

While this list is extensive, it does not in fact cover the full range of transmissions to the public. Among the kinds of exploitations *not* covered by the disparate Berne Convention provisions on the right of communication to the public are wired transmissions (as opposed to retransmissions) of the text of literary and dramatic works, as well as of still photographic images (and other visual works that are not 'cinematographic works'). This omission becomes particularly significant in light of digital communications. Other gaps or ambiguities in coverage of the communication right will be discussed more fully in Chapter 12 below. **9A.07**

In addition to filling in some of the Berne Convention gaps, later multilateral instruments have also endeavoured to address the challenges of digital communications. While these additions will be treated extensively in Chapters 11 and 12 below, some of the innovations merit mention here. **9A.08**

(1) Rights pertaining to physical copies

Where the Berne Convention included no general provision on distribution or rental rights, the World Intellectual Property Organization ('WIPO') Copyright Treaty ('WCT') provides explicitly for an exclusive right of distribution of physical copies of literary and artistic works (article 6), as does the WIPO Performers and Phonograms Treaty ('WPPT') with respect to phonograms (articles 8, 12). Both the TRIPS Agreement (articles 11, 14(4)) and the WCT (article 7) set out rights with respect to rental of physical copies of computer programs, works embodied in phonograms, and cinematographic works. The WPPT provides rental rights in phonograms (articles 9, 13).

(2) Rights of Communication to the public

The WCT extends the general right of communication to the public, by wire or wireless means, to all literary and artistic works (article 8). The WCT (article 8) and WPPT (articles 10, 14) also articulate a specific subset of the communication right, the 'right of making available to the public', designed to cover on-demand transmissions. **9A.09**

With two exceptions (*droit moral*, particularly in the United States and *droit de suite* in most countries outside the European Union), the Berne Convention and the TRIPs Agreement rights are protected, in one form or another, in the laws of all Union countries. (The rights under the WIPO copyright treaties are supposed to be in force in all member states to those conventions, but the number of Berne Convention member states currently significantly exceeds that of WIPO treaties' members.[3]) Nonetheless, as might be expected in view of the disparities between national approaches to copyright protection, they represent only the lowest common denominator which exists between these laws. For the purposes of the ensuing discussion, we shall examine these rights under the headings of 'moral rights' and 'economic rights,' rather than doing this chronologically in the order in which they were adopted into the Convention. Chapter 10 addresses moral rights in the Berne Convention, and their treatment in later multilateral instruments. Chapter 11 then deals with rights of reproduction, adaptation, and distribution, while Chapter 12 addresses the spectrum of rights comprised within the concepts of 'public performance' and 'communication to the public'. In each instance, analysis of the development of these rights under the TRIPs Agreement and WIPO treaties will follow the examination of the various Berne Convention texts. Permissible limitations and derogations from these rights under the Convention and later instruments are then dealt with in Chapter 13. A chart at the conclusion of each of Chapters 10–12 will summarize and synthesize the rights set out in the Berne Convention and its successors.

[3] Currently (as of 19 Jan 2005), the Berne convention has 159 member states while (as of 28 July 2005) the WCT has fifty-four and (as of 2 September 2005) the WPPT has fifty-three; see www.wipo.int/treaties.

10

THE RIGHTS PROTECTED BY THE CONVENTION: MORAL RIGHTS (ARTICLE 6BIS)

Moral rights have been recognized in the Berne Convention since the Rome Act. They are now protected, in the following terms, under article 6bis of the Paris Act: **10.01**

> (1) Independently of the author's economic rights, and even after the transfer of the said rights, the author shall have the right to claim authorship of the work, and to object to any distortion, mutilation or other modification,

or other derogatory action in relation to, the said work, which would be prejudicial to his honor or reputation.

(2) The rights granted to the author in accordance with the preceding paragraph shall, after his death, be maintained, at least until the expiry of the economic rights, and shall be exercisable by the persons or institutions authorized by the legislation of the country where protection is claimed. However, those countries whose legislation, at the moment of their ratification or accession to this Act, does not provide for the protection after the death of the author of all the rights set out in the preceding paragraph may provide that some of these rights may, after his death, cease to be maintained.

(3) The means of redress for safeguarding the rights granted by this Article shall be governed by the legislation of the country where protection is claimed.

A. History of Moral Rights and the Berne Convention

10.02 Authors' rights have long been recognized as having a non-economic dimension. It is beyond the scope of the present study to examine, in detail, the history and juridical basis for this assertion,[1] but it is, in essence, concerned with the

[1] The studies dealing with this question are legion, but some of the most accessible are as follows: S Strömholm, *Le droit moral de l'auteur en droit allemand, français et scandinave* (1966–71) (published in three parts), in particular Part I ('L'évolution historique et le mouvement international'); A Dietz, *Copyright Law in the European Community* (1978), ch V ('Dietz (1978)'); 'Le droit moral dans les pays de l'Union' [1929] *DA* 110, 123, [1931] *DA* 98, 114, 122, [1932] *DA* 112; M A Roeder, 'The Doctrine of Moral Right: A Study in the Law of Artists, Authors and Creators' (1940) 53 *Harv L Rev* 554; W Strauss, 'The Moral Right of the Author' (1955) 4 *Am Jo of Comp Law* 506; W Strauss, 'Le droit moral et le protection des droits personnels de l'auteur' [1955] *DA* 173, 185, [1956] *DA* 6, 32; P Garson, 'L'arrêt Bonnard et la propriété artistique' (1957) 15 *RIDA* 37; M Rousselet, 'Droit moral de l'auteur' (1962) 35 *RIDA* 3; Z Radojokovic, 'Legal Character of "Moral Right" ' [1965] *Copyright* 203; Z Radojokovic, 'The Historical Development of "Moral Right" ' [1966] *Copyright* 168; R Sarraute, 'Current Theory on the Moral Right of Authors and Artists under French Law' (1968) 16 *Am Jo of Comp Law* 487; R J Da Silva, 'Droit Moral and the Amoral Copyright' (1981) 28 *Bull Cop Soc USA* 1; G Dworkin, 'The Moral Right and English Copyright Law' (1981) 12 *IIC* 476; S Strömholm, 'Droit Moral: The International and Comparative Scene from a Scandinavian Viewpoint' (1983) 14 *IIC* 1; D Vaver, 'Authors' Moral Rights in Canada' (1983) 14 *IIC* 329. See also J A Baumgarten, 'On the Case Against Moral Rights', in P Anderson and D Saunders (eds), *Moral Rights Protection in a Copyright System* (Institute for Cultural Policy Studies, Griffith University, 1992); J A Baumgarten, R Gorman, and C A Meyer, 'Preserving the Genius of the System: A Critical Examination of the Introduction of Moral Rights into US Law' (1990) 8 *Copyright Reporter* 1 (among other things, a response to opponents of the colourization of old black-and-white films); L A Beyer, 'Intentionalism, Art and the Suppression of Innovation: Film Colorization and the Philosophy of Moral Rights' (1988) 82 *Northwestern University Law Review* 1011; A Dietz, 'Legal Principles of Moral Rights in Civil Law Countries' (1993) 11(5) *Copyright Reporter* 1; J Ginsburg, 'Moral Rights in a Common Law System' (1990) 4 *Entertainment Law Review* 121; G Dworkin, 'Moral Rights and the Common Law Tradition' (1994) 5 *Australian Intellectual Property Journal* 5; D Tan,

relationship of authors to their works. The latter can be seen as an emanation or manifestation of the author's personality, as her 'spiritual child'.[2] Any author, whether she writes, paints, or composes, embodies some part of herself—her thoughts, ideas, sentiments, and feelings—in her work, and this gives rise to an interest as deserving of protection as any of the other personal interests protected by the institutions of positive law, such as reputation, bodily integrity, and confidences. The interest in question here relates to the way in which authors present their works to the world, and the way in which their identification with the work is maintained. Historically, three basic rights have evolved to protect this interest: the right of authors to disclose or divulge their work to the world, the right to have their authorship of works acknowledged (sometimes called, in less enlightened times, the 'right of paternity' but more accurately the 'right of attribution'), and the right to prevent unauthorized alterations and changes to works (the 'right of integrity'). In European legal doctrine, the interest protected has usually been called the author's 'moral interest' and the rights which protect this interest are referred to as the author's 'moral rights'. The adjective 'moral' has no precise English equivalent, although 'spiritual', 'non-economic', and 'personal' convey something of the intended meaning. Even in France, the home of moral rights, the adjective 'moral' was not used until some time after these rights had come to be recognized. However, 'moral rights' is now fairly universally used, and for want of a more exact English expression is used in the discussion which follows.

The first country to protect moral rights in a practical way was France, where **10.03**
courts began to do so in a loose and piecemeal fashion from the early nineteenth century onwards.[3] It came to be recognized in the case law that authors retained some control over the use of their works, even after the transfer of all the economic rights to another party. In this respect, the eminent Swedish scholar

'Seeing Red over Stravinsky's Firebird' (1996) 7 *Australian Intellectual Property Journal* 63; Elizabeth Adeney, 'Moral Rights and Substantiality: Some Questions of Integration' (2002) 13 *Australian Intellectual Property Journal* 5; Patricia Loughlan, 'The Right of Integrity: What is in that Word Honour? What is in that Word Reputation?' (2001) 12 *Australian Intellectual Property Journal* 189; Warwick A Rothnie, 'Moral Rights: Consents and Waivers' (2002) 20 *Copyright Reporter* 145; Henry Hansmann and Marina Santilli, 'Authors' and Artists' Moral Rights: A Comparative Legal and Economic Analysis' (1997) 26 *J Legal Stud* 95 (1997) *26 J Legal Stud* 95; Burton Ong, 'Why Moral Rights Matter: Recognizing the Intrinsic Value of Integrity Rights' (2003) 26 *Colum J Law & the Arts* 297; Jane C Ginsburg, 'Have Moral Rights Come of (Digital) Age in the U.S.?', in 'Symposium: The Art and Cultural Property Wars' (2001) 19 *Cardozo Arts & Ent L J* 9.

[2] See generally Radojokovic (1965) (n 1 above); Dietz (1978), 66ff.

[3] Strömholm (1983) (n 1 above), 10ff. See also Strömholm (1966–71) (n 1 above), ch 2 and Radojokovic (1966) (n 1 above), 168.

Strömholm quotes the following passage from Pardessus's celebrated *Cours de droit commercial* published in 1814:

> The selling of a manuscript without reservation does not have the same effect as the transfer of ordinary property. It does not give the purchaser a right to dispose of the manuscript in the most unrestricted manner, e.g. by changing it, making additions or reductions to it. Nor may he destroy the work or omit to print or publish it: in fact he is only a *usufructary* (*usufrutier*), who is entitled to enjoy the fruits of the object but must preserve its substance.[4]

In the decades which followed, the French courts built up a substantial body of case law which accorded protection to the integrity of the author's works. In part, this was based on a wide interpretation of the revolutionary decrees of 1791 and 1793, but reliance also was had to the general rule of liability for torts under article 1382 of the *Code Civil*.[5] By the late nineteenth century, as Strömholm says, 'the legal institute that we know as "moral rights" had emerged, but it was an institute without a generally accepted name and without coherent principles'.[6] By contrast, in Germany a more comprehensive conception of moral rights, drawing on the ideas of the philosopher Kant, had been developed in legal writing, but there was little, if any, legislative or judicial support for it.[7] There were differences between writers as to the juridical basis for moral rights—whether they were simply another aspect of the author's economic or patrimonial rights, or whether they were quite distinct from each other, or yet again part of a curiously 'mixed right'—but there was general agreement on the need for such rights, and limited protection for them was accorded under the German Laws of 1870 and 1876[8] and of 1901 and 1907.[9] At the same time, French writers began to draw on German theory, and to formulate a theoretical basis for their own law. Nevertheless, it was not until the early part of this century, according to Strömholm, that the French courts began to speak of a *droit moral* or moral right.[10]

10.04 By the mid-1920s, a number of Berne Union countries had extended protection to moral rights or were considering doing so.[11] The extent to which such rights were recognized differed, but the main rights protected were those of

[4] Strömholm (1983) (n 1 above), 10. [5] ibid. [6] ibid, 11.

[7] ibid, See also Strömholm (1966–71) (n 1 above), ch 3.

[8] For details of these provisions, see Strömholm (1966–71) (n 1 above), 228ff.

[9] Law of 10 June 1901, art 9, and Law of 9 Jan 1907, art 13.

[10] Strömholm (1983) (n 1 above), 12.

[11] eg the Romanian Law of 28 June 1923, art 13 (right of integrity); Bulgarian Law of 15 Feb 1922, art 20 (right of integrity); Swiss Law of 7 Dec 1922, art 43 (right of paternity); Polish Law of 26 Mar 1926, arts 28–30 (right of respect); Finnish Law of 3 June 1927, arts 29–34 (rights of integrity and paternity); Italian Law of 7 Nov 1925, art 16; Czech Law of 24 Nov 1926, art 16 (rights of paternity and respect).

attribution, integrity, and disclosure, while the French courts, ever innovative, were exploring the possibility of according authors the right to withdraw their works from circulation (in the event of a change of opinion or attitude, but subject to an obligation to indemnify the work's distributors) and, more controversially, the right to prevent excessive criticism of their works.[12] These rights were generally treated as inalienable, remaining exercisable by authors after they had parted with their economic rights, but there were marked differences as to their duration and exercise after death.

These last matters depended very much upon which of the two major approaches to the nature of moral rights was taken—the monist or the dualist approach.[13] The former saw moral and economic rights as inextricably linked and interdependent, and this led to the conclusion that their duration should be the same. By contrast, the dualist approach viewed both sets of rights as distinct and separate, with the consequence that economic rights might be limited in time whilst moral rights were protected in perpetuity. The monist approach tended to prevail in German and Austrian law, but the dualist theory seemed more consistent with the philosophy of French law and those legal systems influenced by France.[14] Of the legislative provisions adopted in national laws at this time, those in the Italian Law of 7 November 1925 were typical. Article 16 of this Law provided as follows: **10.05**

> Independently of the patrimonial rights recognized by virtue of the preceding articles, the author has, at all times, the right to bring an action to prevent the paternity of his work from being unrecognized, or the work being modified or mutilated in such a way as to cause serious and unjust prejudice to his moral rights.

Furthermore, it appeared from other provisions of the Law that the author retained the power to determine when his or her work should be divulged or disclosed to the public, as well as to withdraw it from circulation.[15]

By contrast, throughout this period there was no direct protection for moral rights in the common law countries, as this was a concept that was quite alien to the functional view of authors' rights adopted in these countries. This is not to say that moral rights were entirely unprotected in common law jurisdictions. The common law right of first publication and the case law protecting **10.06**

[12] See Da Silva (n 1 above), 23–6, 32. Note also that the Italian Law of 1925, art 15 conferred a right of repentance.

[13] See further Dietz (1978), 66–9.

[14] ibid. See further [1929] *DA* 110, 123, [1931] *DA* 98, 114, 122, [1932] *DA* 112.

[15] Italian Law of 7 Nov 1925, arts 14 and 15.

unpublished letters and manuscripts[16] covered the author's 'divulgation' interests, at least to some extent. Moreover, the Fine Arts Copyright Act 1862 in the UK had accorded a limited form of protection in respect of unauthorized changes and alterations of artistic works,[17] and the common law actions of defamation and passing off also provided some protection for the rights of integrity and paternity.[18] Nevertheless, these forms of protection were piecemeal in their operation, and, apart from the right of first publication, were quite separate from the general protection accorded to authors under the copyright laws. The essential problem was that it was difficult to accommodate the conception of the moral interests of authors with the strong economic orientation of the common law systems to the nature of authors' rights. Even today, over seventy-five years after the obligation to protect moral rights entered the Convention, the way in which many of the common law countries have fulfilled this requirement raises real questions with respect to the matter of Treaty implementation (see further paras 17.80ff below).

(1) Proposals at the Rome Conference

10.07 It will be clear from the above that it was not until the 1920s that some kind of coherent body of principles concerning the protection of moral rights had emerged in national legislation. This was undoubtedly the reason why no formal proposals to protect moral rights under the Berne Convention had been made at any of the earlier revision conferences. However, by the time of the Rome Conference, clear models were provided by the provisions adopted in such laws as the Italian Law quoted above. Various expert bodies in different countries had also studied the question and produced recommendations for international protection: these included ALAI[19] and the International Institute for Intellectual Cooperation.[20] The Italian Government programme for the Rome Conference did not initially contain any proposal for the protection of moral rights, but the French Government submitted a resolution urging that all countries of the Union should do this.[21] A more specific Polish amendment,

---

[16] *Pope* v *Curl* (1741) 2 Atk 341; 26 ER 608; *Duke of Queensberry* v *Shebbeare* (1758) 2 Eden 329; 28 ER 924 (manuscript); *Macklin* v *Richardson* (1770) Amb 694; 27 ER 451 (play); *Prince Albert* v *Strange* (1849) 1 H & Tw 1; 47 ER 1302. See also *Gee* v *Pritchard* (1818) 2 Swans 402; 36 ER 670; *Moore* v *Edwardes* [1901–4] MacG Cop Cas 44; *Fraser* v *Edwardes* [1905–10] Mac G Cop Cas 10 (KB).

[17] Fine Arts Copyright Act 1862, s 7.

[18] See generally Dworkin (1981) (n 1 above).

[19] See the reports of the ALAI Congress at Warsaw in 1926 [1926] *DA* 119ff; and Lugano [1927] *DA* 72, 73.

[20] International Institute of Intellectual Cooperation, report of sub-committee on the intellectual rights of authors and their extensions, 'Droit moral ou droit au respect' (session of July 1927), in *La Protection internationale du droit d'auteur* (1928), 35ff.

[21] *Actes* 1928, 103.

based upon a draft provision prepared by the International Institute for Intellectual Cooperation, proposed a new article 15 which would protect the author 'against any harm to his character as an author as well as any transformation or mutilation whatsoever which distorted the way in which he wanted to present his work to the public'.[22] In response to these proposals, the Italian Government then drafted a more comprehensive amendment (to be article 6*bis*), which read as follows:

> Independently of the protection of patrimonial rights regulated by the following articles, and notwithstanding any alienation thereof, the author has at all times:
>
> (a) the right to claim paternity of the work;
> (b) the right to decide if the work should appear;
> (c) the right to oppose any modification of the work which would be prejudicial to his moral interests.
>
> It is reserved to the national legislation of the contracting states to establish the dispositions regulating the abovesaid rights, and notably to accommodate the exclusive right of publication with the requirements of the public interest as well as the reconciliation of the power mentioned in paragraph (c) with the right of property in the material copy of the work.
>
> After the death of the author these rights will be exercised by the persons or organs designated by the legislation of the country of origin of the work. The means of recourse for safeguarding these rights will be regulated by the legislation of the country where protection is claimed.[23]

In support of this, the Italian Government circulated a memorandum in which it argued that the time was now appropriate for the recognition of moral rights in the Convention.[24] It pointed here to the implicit recognition that was already accorded, in a limited sense, to these rights, for example, in article 9 where it was required that the source be indicated in the case of articles reproduced from newspapers.[25] Again, Louis Renault, in his report to the Berlin Revision Conference, had used a moral rights argument to justify the complete assimilation of translation rights, namely the need to secure accuracy in translations.[26] While there were clearly doctrinal differences as to the juridical basis for moral rights, the Italian Government argued that their content was now sufficiently settled in national legislation for them to be enshrined internationally in the Berne Convention. It also argued that the need to protect such rights was more pressing in the light of the growing popularity of systems of paying public domain and compulsory licences under national laws, as these posed grave threats to the exercise of their personal rights by authors.[27] On the other hand, it will be seen that the Italian proposal recognized the potential conflict that might arise between moral rights and the general public interest in its provision that the

[22] ibid, 119. [23] ibid, 173. [24] ibid. [25] ibid.
[26] ibid, 174. See here *Actes* 1908, 246–7. [27] *Actes* 1928, 175ff.

regulation of this relationship would be a matter for national legislation. An obvious point of difficulty here, referred to expressly in the proposal, was the property right of the purchaser of a copy; another, which was to become of pressing concern with the development of the cinematographic industry, was the rights of makers of authorized adaptations to change the original work.

10.08 While the Italian proposal formed the basis of discussion in the general commission of the Conference, a number of amendments on moral rights were presented by other delegations, including those of Romania,[28] Belgium,[29] and the International Institute for Intellectual Cooperation.[30] These were finally referred to a special sub-committee chaired by Jules Destrée, a member of the Belgian delegation.[31] In the sub-committee it became clear that there was a general consensus on the desirability of protecting moral rights, but, as might be expected, a problem emerged with respect to the position of the common law countries.[32] However, as stated above, these countries did already provide, under other heads of legal liability, some limited protection for moral rights, and this formed the basis for the compromise that was finally adopted by the sub-committee (based on a further Italian draft). This read as follows:

> (1) Independently of the author's copyright [the literal translation of the French text was 'the patrimonial rights of the author'], and even after the transfer of the said copyright, the author shall have the right to claim authorship of the work, as well as the right to object to any distortion, mutilation or other modification of the said work which would be prejudicial to his honor or reputation.
>
> (2) The determination of the conditions under which these rights shall be exercised is reserved for the national legislation of the countries of the Union. The means of redress for safeguarding these rights shall be regulated by the legislation of the country where protection is claimed.[33]

This was coupled with a non-binding resolution which proposed to member states the desirability of protecting these rights after the death of the author.[34]

10.09 This new formulation embodied a clear Conventional recognition of moral rights. At the same time, it met the principal objections of the common law countries, in particular those of the UK and Australia.[35] Thus, the words 'moral interests' were replaced by the words 'honor or reputation' because the British

---

[28] *Actes* 1908, 237 (records of discussions in general commission). See also ibid, 200 (report of general commission).

[29] ibid. [30] ibid. [31] ibid, 181. [32] ibid, 237–8. [33] ibid, 182.

[34] ibid.

[35] ibid, 201 and 238. See further the report of the British delegates to the Rome Conference to the Board of Trade, 5 Sept 1928: Public Records Office, FO371/13444, 16ff. See also the *Report of the Australian Delegate (Sir W Harrison Moore)*, presented to the Parliament of the Commonwealth of Australia and printed by command 31 Aug 1928, No 255, 6ff.

delegation found the former expression too vague and incapable of conveying any clear meaning in British law.[36] 'Honor' and 'reputation', on the other hand, bore a close resemblance to the kind of personal interests already protected by the common law under the heads of defamation and passing off. Secondly, reference to the right of disclosure was deleted, on the ground that this was difficult to harmonize, as yet, with the rights of licensees and assignees with respect to first and successive publications of works (this was not only a problem with the common law systems). Thirdly, there was nothing in the draft which required that these rights should be protected as part of a country's copyright laws: this therefore left the way open for countries such as the UK to accord protection under heads other than copyright. Fourthly, no mention was made of the protection of these rights after the death of the author: this again accommodated the position of the common law countries where the right to take defamation proceedings died with the author. On the other hand, the draft did make it clear that moral rights were distinct from the economic or patrimonial rights. As Pierre Casselli, the *rapporteur général*, expressed it, this was an acknowledgement that not only was a work of the intellect of economic value, but also that it was an act of the creative mind, having 'a character representative of the personality of the author'.[37] Thus, the phrase that an author 'lives in his work' was not an imaginary notion, as every work presented to the public reflected an author's personality, intelligence, beliefs, and opinions.[38]

Following the Rome Conference, diverging views on the content and extent of moral rights continued to be expressed.[39] The first major point of difference concerned the changes and alterations that might be made to works after the author had licensed or assigned his or her rights. This was of particular importance to the burgeoning cinematographic industry which depended largely upon the adaptation of works to the screen. Sharply conflicting views on these matters were to be found in the debates which took place in ALAI in the early 1930s. On one side, the Italian group opposed any changes to the existing article 6bis under which changes might be made that were not prejudicial to the author's honour or reputation.[40] On the other, a special sub-committee of ALAI, which was strongly influenced by French views, took the attitude that authors should be able to control any modifications that were prejudicial to their 'moral interests'.[41] The latter was a wider and more subjective concept which would cover changes that were in no way damaging to an author's reputation, and might even enhance it. Nevertheless, it was argued they should remain within the 10.10

[36] *Actes* 1928, 210. [37] ibid, 202. [38] ibid.
[39] See the survey of national laws in [1929] *DA* 110, 123, [1931] *DA* 98, 114, 122, [1932] *DA* 112, and the preliminary documents for the Brussels Conference of 1935–6 in [1933] *DA* 90–1.
[40] [1933] *DA* 90. [41] ibid.

scope of the author's moral rights insofar as they impinged upon the work as an expression of his creative self. The difficulty with this last approach was that the problem still remained of maintaining some sensible balance between the spiritual or moral interest of the authors and the legitimate commercial expectations of licensees and assignees. Thus, certain national laws which adopted this wider view still made it subject to qualification, for example, that the proposed modifications would 'seriously compromise his [the author's] spiritual interests'[42] or that 'the personal or artistic interests [of the author] . . . [would be] . . . essentially injured'.[43] A second point of difference concerned the duration of these rights *post mortem auctoris*. Were these tied to the economic rights, subsisting for the same period? Alternatively, did they continue indefinitely? In the latter case, the problem which arose was the identity of the person or institution that should exercise the moral rights in a work after it had fallen into the public domain with respect to its economic rights (the same problem arose, though with less urgency, in relation to the *post mortem auctoris* period).[44]

(2) The Brussels Revision

10.11 The Belgian Government and the International Office addressed both issues in their programme for the Brussels Conference, and proposed the following changes to article $6^{bis}(1)$:

1. In paragraph (1), that the words 'or other modification' be replaced by the words 'any utilization', and the words 'to his honor or reputation' by the words 'to his spiritual interests'.[45]
2. In paragraph (2), after the first sentence, to add the words 'and their protection after the death of the author and after the extinction of the copyright' (referred to here as the 'patrimonial').[46]
3. To add a new paragraph (3) concerning works fallen into the public domain:

> The countries of the Union undertake to accord the right of respect to works fallen into the public domain, and particularly to important works generally admired, irrespective of the period of time to which they belong or their country of origin. Literary, theatrical, musical, plastic, cinematographic or other adaptations of the said works are only permitted on condition that they do not travesty or falsify them in their spirit by distortions, mutilations, changes, cuts or additions capable of falsifying them and seriously injuring the beauty of the work and consequently the moral right of the author and his

[42] Austrian Law of 9 Apr 1936, art 21. [43] Norwegian Law of 6 June 1930, art 13.
[44] See further *Documents 1948* (1951), 185ff (programme for Brussels Conference).
[45] ibid, 186. [46] ibid.

> reputation. Parodies which are presented as such without causing possible confusion with the original work are nonetheless authorized.[47]

There was support for the adoption of the expression 'spiritual interests'[48] in paragraph (1) from several delegations, including those of France and Austria, but more restricted formulations were also proposed, such as 'his [the author's] literary or artistic reputation' (Norway),[49] 'his just spiritual interests' (Poland),[50] and 'his personal interests in the work' (Switzerland).[51] In the Conference, the debates soon revealed that a number of delegations, notably those of the common law countries, were opposed to most of these proposed changes. The initial British position was that the UK would only be able to accept article 6*bis* if it were retained in its present form, and that any additions to it should be embodied in an additional protocol which could be signed separately.[52] Another possibility suggested by the Belgian delegation was that the UK should be able to make an appropriate reservation with respect to whatever changes were included in the new article 6*bis*.[53] However, this course of action was not practicable in view of the fact that the Rome Act had limited the right to make reservations to the case of translation rights.[54] Finally, the various proposals were sent to a special sub-committee chaired by Pilotti of Italy, and comprising representatives of France, the UK, Norway, the Netherlands, Poland, Portugal, Switzerland, and Czechoslovakia.[55] This sub-committee adopted a cautious approach judging it opportune

> to deviate as little as possible from the text of the Convention in force . . . in giving satisfaction to the desire expressed by the French delegation and several others to permit national legislation to develop the protection accorded to the interests of authors in the domain of moral rights.[56]

With this consideration in mind, the sub-committee recommended the following changes to the last part of paragraph (1): '. . . to object to any distortion, mutilation or other alteration to the said work *or to any other action in relation to the said work*, prejudicial to the honor, reputation *or interests* of the author'[57] (emphasis added).

The first of these changes was included because it was thought that the proposal in the programme to include 'utilisations of the work capable of having prejudicial effects' was too wide.[58] Nonetheless, it was far from clear what the difference was

[47] ibid. [48] ibid, 186–7. [49] ibid, 188. [50] ibid, 189.
[51] ibid. [52] ibid, 195. [53] ibid.
[54] Rome Act, art 27(2). This permitted only Union countries to maintain reservations that they had previously made under previous Acts. See also the comments by the Director of the International Office in *Documents 1948* (1951), 195–6.
[55] ibid, 126. [56] ibid. [57] ibid, 127. [58] ibid, 126.

between a 'utilisation' of a work that was prejudicial and an 'action' having the same effect. As to the second change, this was based on a French proposal which had been made to counter objections to the expressions 'spiritual, moral, or personal interests': the first, because it was likely to be misunderstood as having a religious signification, and the other two because they were too vague and lacking in precision.[59] As for the difficult question of duration of protection, it became clear in the sub-committee that certain delegations, in particular that of the UK, were unable to accept a prolongation of moral rights after the death of the author.[60] The sub-committee therefore proposed the addition of the words 'during his life' to paragraph (1) to make it clear that these rights were to receive at least lifetime protection. As to protection after this time, it proposed the following amendment to paragraph (2):

> To the extent that national legislation permits it, the rights accorded to the author by virtue of the preceding paragraph are, after his death, to be safeguarded at least until the expiry of the copyright and exercised by the persons or institutions authorized in this regard by the said legislation.[61]

This formulation established the desirability of *post mortem auctoris* protection of moral rights, but without making this mandatory for Union members. These modifications, with one exception, were accepted by the general commission, and were incorporated into article 6bis of the Brussels Act.[62] The exception was the expression 'the interests of the author', which was deleted out of deference to the wishes of the British delegation.[63] The third paragraph of the programme proposal was also deleted, as it was clear that the continued protection of moral rights after the expiry of the economic rights would hardly be acceptable to those countries, such as the UK, which were opposed to any *post mortem auctoris* protection.[64] In addition, there were objections from several other states that such an extension of protection was inappropriate for a convention dealing with private rights: such protection belonged rather to the sphere of public law, as it raised general questions of cultural and heritage policy.[65] Finally, a Polish proposal for a new article 6ter which proposed that protection should be extended to the moral rights of all authors, whether or not entitled to protection for their economic rights under the Convention, was not proceeded with.[66]

(3) The Stockholm Revision

10.12 Although the original programme proposals at the Brussels Conference were severely cut back, article 6bis of the Brussels Act nonetheless contained some significant advances on the original Rome text: the right of integrity had been

[59] *Documents 1948* (1951), 126. [60] ibid, 127 and 196. [61] ibid, 127.
[62] ibid, 198. [63] ibid, 197. [64] ibid, 198.
[65] eg France at ibid, 192. [66] ibid, 199.

extended (see further below), and it was now clear that moral rights were to be protected for a minimum of the author's life while the desirability of extending this term *post mortem auctoris* to that accorded to economic rights was clearly established in paragraph (2).[67] The programme for the Stockholm Conference proposed that this term should now be made compulsory.[68] This led to considerable debate among the delegates: several argued that moral rights should now be protected perpetually,[69] while others maintained that it should be tied to the term accorded to economic rights.[70] Once again, however, there was opposition to both proposals from the common law countries: *post mortem auctoris* protection of any kind would require changes to their laws, as actions for defamation did not survive the author.[71] Another important consideration was that any requirement to protect moral rights after the death of the author would provide a further barrier to accession by the USA.[72] Finally, the proposal for perpetuity was rejected by fourteen votes to eleven with five abstentions,[73] and attempts were then made to devise a compromise formulation that would accommodate the position of the common law countries. In this respect, the British delegate, William Wallace, laid down the basis for such a compromise by stating that the most that he thought his government would be able to do was to extend the right to claim authorship for a *post mortem auctoris* period of fifty years.[74] After further negotiations, the formulation which was finally arrived at required the maintenance of moral rights for at least the term of the author's life, but subject to the following qualification: those countries whose legislation, at the moment of their ratification or accession to the new Act, did not provide for *post mortem auctoris* protection of all the rights set out in paragraph (1) might provide that some of these rights might cease to be maintained after the author's death.[75] This provided a clear escape clause for the common law countries, and was duly adopted as article 6*bis*(2) of the Stockholm Act.[76]

(4) Moral rights and cinematographic works at the Stockholm revision

Moral rights have been a constant source of concern to film-makers, in relation **10.13**
to the authors of both pre-existing works and contributions to the making of a

[67] See further A Baum, *The Brussels Conference for the Revision of the Berne Convention* (1949), 23.
[68] *Records* 1967, vol I, 104.
[69] See eg the proposal of Bulgaria (Documents S/89 and 197): ibid, 692 and 710; and the joint proposal of Greece and Portugal (Document S/1510): ibid, 700.
[70] eg Denmark and Germany: ibid, 894 (minutes of Main Committee I).
[71] Comments of the British and Irish delegates: ibid, 893 and 894.
[72] ibid, 893 (comments of British delegate and US observer).
[73] ibid, 918. [74] ibid, 919.
[75] Document S/247: ibid, 726 (joint proposal of Australia, Austria, Denmark, the FRG, Finland, Sweden, and the UK).
[76] ibid, 920 (adopted unanimously with two abstentions).

cinematographic work.[77] Considerable changes and modifications to these works or contributions are often necessary for the successful realization of the film, and this clearly has implications for the moral rights of their authors. Furthermore, it may be necessary to make other changes once the film is completed for the purposes of public exhibition, for example, because of censorship requirements or to take account of public taste.[78] To what extent do the authors' moral rights affect the making of these changes? A number of national laws contain specific provisions on these matters, often allowing such changes as are indispensable for the completion of the cinematographic work,[79] but laying down clear obligations as regards recognition of the authors' contributions to the work. These matters also received extended consideration in the preparatory work for the Stockholm Conference. The Committee of Film Experts concluded that the issues involved were too detailed to be treated in an international convention, and proposed simply that they be left to national legislation.[80] In 1963 the Study Group took a similar approach, proposing that it be reserved to national legislation to

> . . . take all suitable measures for the equitable solution of conflicts of interest which might arise in connection with cinematographic works between authors and makers regarding the exercise of the right provided for in Article 6bis of the Convention.[81]

10.14 This proposal was approved by the 1963 Committee of Experts and remained unchanged in the Study Group's report of 1964.[82] However, in the 1965 Committee of Governmental Experts several proposals were made which sought to establish a conventional rule on the question. One proposed that, in the context of cinematographic films, an author might only exercise his rights under article 6bis(1) 'to an extent that takes equitable account of the interests of the other authors and those of the maker of the film'.[83] Another proposed that the author might not, 'subject to the application of Article 6bis, oppose the modifications which are absolutely indispensable to the exploitation of the cinematographic work',[84] while another advocated a deeming provision under which authors would be deemed to have authorized the maker to make any modifications necessary for the making of the cinematographic work.[85] However, it was finally felt that none of these proposals were acceptable, and that the question could not be settled within the framework of the Convention.[86] Consequently, no proposal concerning cinematographic works and moral rights was contained in

---

[77] See para 10.10 above.

[78] See comments in the programme for the Stockholm Revision: *Records* 1967, 135.

[79] See eg the Italian Law of 1941, art 47 ('such modifications . . . as are necessary for their cinematographic adaptation').

[80] Report [1962] *Copyright* 38, 41.

[81] Document S/1: *Records* 1967, 135.

[82] ibid. [83] ibid. [84] ibid. [85] ibid. [86] ibid, 136.

the programme. The matter was not taken any further at the ensuing Conference, and the position under the Convention therefore is that the makers of cinematographic works receive no special dispensation in relation to the moral rights of authors that are protected under article $6^{bis}(1)$.

B. Interpretation of the Present Article 6bis

The need to strike some compromise with the common law countries still means that article 6bis is far from being a full-blooded provision on moral rights. Certainly, at the Stockholm Conference, the common law countries managed to retain, in considerable degree, their freedom of action with respect to the way in which moral rights were to be protected. The obligations imposed under article 6bis are as follows. **10.15**

(1) Independence of moral rights

The moral rights enumerated in paragraph (1) are independent of the author's economic rights in a particular work. This notion of independence is, of course, basic to the whole concept of moral rights. **10.16**

(2) Exercise after transmission of economic rights

Moral rights may be exercised even after authors have parted with their economic rights. This does not appear to be quite the same thing as providing that the former are inalienable: the present wording of paragraph (1) simply confirms the independent and separate existence of moral rights. By contrast, some national laws provide expressly that moral rights are both inalienable and imprescriptible.[87] Accordingly, there is nothing in paragraph (1) which explicitly prohibits national laws from allowing authors to assign or to waive their moral rights either temporarily or permanently. Nonetheless, a boilerplate waiver or assignment of all moral rights together with a grant of economic rights seems in tension with the declaration of the independence of moral from economic rights in article 6bis. One might infer from the language 'independently of the author's economic rights, and even after the transfer of the said rights . . .' that a simultaneous transfer or waiver of economic and moral rights, while perhaps permissible, should require a specific expression or enumeration of which moral rights are granted or waived. Otherwise, the independence of moral and economic **10.17**

[87] Particularly those of France and countries whose legislation has been influenced by that of France, Code de la propriété intellectuelle, art L 121–1; the Senegalese Law of 4 Dec 1973, art 3(a); the Beninese Law of 15 Mar 1984, art 3(a); Central African Republic Law of 5 Jan 1985, art 2(a).

rights risks becoming purely formal, reducing in fact or practice to their independent statement in separate catch-all clauses of the same contract.

(3) Transfer of moral rights

10.18 One might further contend that, even if the Berne Convention tolerates waivers of moral rights, assignability is another matter. While article 6bis does not specifically rule out transfers of moral rights, their assignment would arguably be inconsistent with the very nature of these rights, which are inherently personal to the author. Moreover, it might seem absurd to accommodate the transfer of 'mutilation rights', for example. But, in the language of the Convention, the author would not be transferring an affirmative right to mutilate, she would be conveying certain rights of action: to *claim* authorship; to *object to* any distortion, etc. Thus, the Berne Convention would allow the author to assign these rights to an authors' society or similar association which would then have standing to enforce her moral rights on her behalf. For authors lacking the resources to litigate on their own, this view of transferability appears advantageous. A less benign consequence of this reading would uphold 'ghostwriter' agreements, as the actual author would be transferring to the named (celebrity) author the right to proclaim himself to be the author. It should be recalled, however, that article 6bis sets a floor, not a ceiling, on the scope of protection: member states are entitled to grant greater protections; they thus may make such transfers revocable, or prohibit them altogether.[88]

(4) The right to claim authorship

10.19 This is the first of the moral rights protected under article $6^{bis}(1)$; in essence, it means that the author has the right to have his or her authorship of works recognized in clear and unambiguous fashion, and is fundamental to the way in which the author's work is presented to the public. Paragraph (1) does not specify how this identification is to be achieved, but common sense suggests that the easiest way of doing this is for each copy of an author's work to carry his or her name or pseudonym in an obvious place, for example, on the title page or at the head of the work, in the case of a written work, or at the bottom, in the case of an artistic work. Further analysis indicates that there are three major situations in which the author of a work should be able to invoke this right:

[88] See eg Cass 1st civil chamber, decision of 28 Jan 2003, (2004) 35 *IIC* 464, note Metzger (holding songwriters' blanket waiver of integrity right violated the 'ordre public' character of the French copyright law's provision for inalienability of moral rights set out in Code de la propriété intellectuelle, art L 121-1). Cf Germany, Copyright Law, s 29(1), which has been interpreted to allow specifically defined waivers, see Munich Court of Appeals, *Unendliche Geschichte* [1986] *GRUR* 460. See also A Lucas and H-J Lucas, *Traité de la propriété littéraire et artistique*, 2nd edn (2001), 332–3 (citing lower-court decisions upholding waivers of the attribution right).

1. Where a licensee, assignee, or other party does not make any reference at all to the author on copies of the latter's work (these copies could be authorized or unauthorized).
2. Where a licensee, etc, puts the name of another person on copies of the work so as to imply that that person is the author of the work.
3. Where the name of the true author appears on copies of the work, but this is done in such a way as to be hard to see.

In each of these cases, authors should have the positive right to insist that their identification with their works is maintained. However, it is unclear whether this positive right extends to the negative right of permitting authors to prevent their names from being attached to works of which they are not the authors. In English law, this situation was traditionally dealt with under the heading of 'passing off', and in other common law jurisdictions under the more general heading of unfair competition. More recently, moral rights legislation in common law jurisdictions has joined to the right to claim authorship the corresponding right to disclaim authorship of a work in fact created by another person (sometimes referred to as 'false attribution').[89] Where the author is seeking to deny, rather than to establish, her authorship, one might contend that the right in $6^{bis}(1)$ is not implicated, for that right is described as 'the right to claim authorship', not the right to disclaim it. But in other provisions the Berne Convention recognizes that authors may disclaim authorship, at least where the author presents the work anonymously or pseudonymously. Article 7(3) of the Berne Convention establishes special rules regarding the duration of anonymous and pseudonymous works whose authors do not disclose their identities; it follows that the Convention anticipates that such authors shall not be obliged to reveal themselves under their own names. Nonetheless, there is another reason that the disclaimer rights that common law jurisdictions have incorporated into their moral rights legislation are analytically distinct from moral rights in the sense of the Berne Convention, even though those countries' rights also protect the author's 'honor or reputation'. The author's moral rights pertain to a work of her own creation (whether or not she chooses to present it under her own name); the common law jurisdictions' disclaimer rights here examined concern works the author did *not* create. The essential link between the author and her own work therefore is absent in the case of 'passing off' another's work as the author's. As a result, although providing a right of action against this conduct would give authors important coverage, article 6bis does not appear to require member states to grant such a right.

[89] See eg UK, Copyright, Designs and Patents Act 1988, s 84(5)–(6); Australia, Copyright Amendment (Moral Rights) Act 2000, s 195AC. See also, for the limited context of 'works of visual art', 17 USC § 106A(a)(1)(B).

(5) The right to protect the integrity of the work

10.20 This is the second moral right recognized under paragraph (1), which establishes a two-part inquiry: authors' rights attach against (i) 'any distortion, mutilation or other modification of, or other derogatory action in relation to, the said work', which (ii) 'would be prejudicial to his honor or reputation'. Several matters here require further consideration.

(a) 'Any distortion, mutilation or other modification of, or other derogatory action in relation to . . .'

10.21 The words 'distortion, mutilation or other modification' appear wide enough to cover any change that is made to the actual work. On their own, the first two words could lead to problems, as the concepts of 'distortion' and 'mutilation' appear highly subjective. However, the expression 'other modification' is more objective, and must therefore cover any objectionable change to the work that does not fall within the scope of a 'distortion' or 'mutilation', but that still would be considered 'derogatory', the phrase 'or any *other* derogatory action . . .' (emphasis added) suggesting that all the kinds of alterations listed must have some kind of negative impact on the work. Moreover, a further limitation on the scope of the composite expression 'distortion, mutilation or other modification' is imposed by the objective requirement that these changes must be prejudicial to the honour or reputation of the author (see paras 10.27ff below).

10.22 What kinds of change will fall typically within the expression 'Any distortion, mutilation or other modification'? Obvious examples are typographical mistakes and imperfections in reproduction techniques (including poor or wrong colours in the case of artistic works). More substantive changes would include deletions or additions to the text of a written work; paraphrases and abridgements would also be included, and any 'rewriting' in the case of a literary or dramatic work, for instance, for the purposes of a parody (on parody, however, see para 10.29 below). Musical and artistic works are also susceptible to these kinds of changes: examples would include the rearrangement of a musical work to a different style (such as a 'techno' version of a piece of classical music[90]) and the caricature of a work of art. It will be noted that the above examples relate to changes that are

[90] cf *Schott Musik International GmbH and Co* v *Colossal Records of Australia Pty Ltd* (1996) 36 IPR 267 (Tamberlin J) [1997] AIPC 91–342 (Full Federal Court) (this concerned a 'techno' version of Orff's *Carmina Burana*, but was not actually brought pursuant to moral rights provisions: it was a proceeding concerned with the conditions under which musical works might be recorded pursuant to the statutory recording licence under Australian legislation, where s 55(2) (now repealed) provided that the licence did not apply 'in relation to a record of an adaptation of a musical work if the adaptation debases the work'. See also 17 USC sec 115(a) (2) (compulsory licence to make phonogram includes privilege of making a musical arrangement of the recorded composition 'but the arrangement shall not change the basic melody or fundamental character of the work').

made in the course of reproducing or adapting a work. It is equally possible that a work may be distorted, mutilated, or otherwise modified in the path of its performance or communication to the public, through the particular interpretation that is given to it by the performers or in the way it is presented. Thus, a competent actor may readily transform a tragedy into farce, and vice versa, without changing a word of the written text, and a theatrical or cinematographic director may entirely change the significance of a dramatic or operatic work by altering the location, period, or 'atmosphere' of the piece.[91] It is true that changes of these kinds invariably involve the application of considerable independent creativity on the part of the performers, directors, or producers. Nonetheless, article 6*bis* makes no distinction between this category of wilful alterations and those made in the course of incompetently reproducing or adapting a work, and it is to be assumed that the paragraph applies equally to both (assuming the alterations had not been made under a licence from the author). However, it is also to be expected that different considerations might apply to each when the question of prejudice to the author comes to be considered, and this is discussed further below (see paras 10.29–10.31).

Finally, what is meant by the concluding words '. . . other derogatory action in relation to, . . . the said work'? Once again, the adjective 'derogatory' seems to imply a subjective standard, but this is then made subject to the more objective criterion of prejudice to honour or reputation (see further below). As for the word 'action', this refers to something other than an actual change or interference with the work itself: the latter are covered by the composite expression 'distortion, mutilation or other modification'. What is in question here, therefore, is an action 'in relation to' the work. It will be recalled that these words were added at the Brussels Revision Conference, where they replaced a proposal in the programme to add the words 'utilisations of the work having prejudicial effects'.[92] The latter were thought to be too wide, but they did at least have the virtue of being explicit: what was intended to be covered were uses of the work that were prejudicial to the author. This would clearly cover situations where a work was reproduced in its original form, but this was done in such a manner as to cause the author harm. It also would have been apt to cover situations where a work intended for public communication was performed or interpreted in a way which injured the author (although it has been suggested above that these kinds of acts are already within the scope of 'distortions, mutilations or other modifications'). Examples would therefore include such acts as the publication of a book with an offensive cover, the production of a serious play in a manner which derides the author or his views, and the reproduction of an artistic work **10.23**

[91] See further F van Isacker, 'Letter from Belgium' [1967] *Copyright* 135.
[92] *Documents 1948* (1951), 186.

in juxtaposition with pornographic material.[93] 'Action' does not, in fact, appear to be a more limited term than 'utilisation' or 'use', and would certainly cover the examples given in the preceding sentence.

10.24 Further questions arise concerning the meaning of 'action in relation to, the said work'. First, does the 'action' in question have to be carried out as part of the actions that fall within the author's economic rights, that is, is the derogatory action prohibited only if it occurs in the course of a reproduction, performance, etc, of the work in question? Or does 'action' extend to any derogatory action in relation to the author's work? The second is the preferable interpretation, as article 6bis makes it clear that the rights granted under paragraph (1) are independent of the author's economic rights. Therefore, although the Berne Convention does not recognize a right of exhibition in relation to artistic works, there is no reason why an artist should not be able to complain of a derogatory action in relation to his work where it is exhibited in an inappropriate place, for example, where a 'site-specific' work is uprooted from its surroundings and exhibited elsewhere.

10.25 Second, does the 'action in relation to, the said work' also concern damage inflicted on the original copy of a work, such as the physical mutilation of a painting or a manuscript? Does it include damage done to copies of a work, when the original remains intact? The traditional distinction between the incorporeal 'work' and its physical embodiment in copies—a distinction inherent in the article 2(1) coverage of 'literary and artistic works' 'whatever may be the mode or form of [their] expression'—suggests that article 6bis does not cover harm to individual physical copies. Thus (putting aside all questions of the duration of moral rights), if Marcel Duchamp were to purchase a postcard of the *Mona Lisa*, and draw a moustache on the image, he would not have taken a 'derogatory action in relation to' Leonardo's 'work'. On the other hand, were he to reproduce the altered image, then he would have engaged in an act of 'distortion, mutilation, or other modification, or other derogatory action in relation to [that] work'. With respect to the original copies of literary and artistic works, arguably their alteration does affect the 'work', because it may not be possible to make further accurate reproductions or communications of the work once the original has been mutilated. But this argument resembles those made in connection with the destruction of original copies. As we shall see immediately below, those arguments have not prevailed in the interpretation of the scope of the article 6bis right of integrity.

[93] In the programme for the Brussels Conference, the following examples were given '. . . a literary work . . . published in conjunction with numerous advertisements; an artistic work reproduced together with articles not enjoying a good reputation; a musical composition, profoundly serious and religious in tone, adopted as a part of a filmed operetta': ibid, 185.

(b) Destruction of the work

There has been uncertainty in some national laws as to whether destruction of a work violates the author's right of integrity.[94] This is of particular importance for original works of art and original manuscripts. Quite apart from the personal loss that the author may feel at such an act, it also has consequences to the general public as it becomes impossible to determine the accuracy of any copies of the work that remain. However, in the case of an original work that is sold to a collector, this becomes her personal property, and she should be entitled to deal with this as she wishes. This clearly includes the ability to destroy it, as long as she does not commit some other infringement of the law in doing so (such as provisions in laws relating to the preservation of important works of art, and so on). The question was explicitly raised at the Brussels Revision Conference where the Hungarian delegation proposed that destruction should be included in the list of acts prejudicial to the author's honour or reputation.[95] This was not adopted because some delegates thought that this did not relate to the author's moral interests.[96] However, the matter was referred to in one of the *voeux* adopted at the end of the Conference. This read as follows: **10.26**

> Notwithstanding that article 6bis of the Convention, while it allows the author to object to any distortion, mutilation or other modification of his work, or to any other derogatory action in relation to the same work which is prejudicial to his honor or reputation, does not forbid in express terms the destruction of works, the Conference expresses the view that the countries of the Union should introduce, in their domestic legislation, some dispositions prohibiting the destruction of literary and artistic works.[97]

This was a clear acknowledgement that article $6^{bis}(1)$ did not require Union members to prohibit the destruction of works as part of the protection to be given to moral rights. No proposal to amend article $6^{bis}(1)$ further in this regard was made at the Stockholm Conference, and accordingly destruction still remains outside the scope of the article.

---

94 See Da Silva (n 1 above), 33: Dietz (1978), 77. More recently, cf Trib Civ Namur (Belgium) decision of 31 Mar 2000, *Auteurs & Médias* 200/4 p 427, aff'd, Court of Appeals of Liège, decision of 4 Dec 2000, *Auteurs & Médias* 2001/3 p 363, note Gotzen (destruction of murals on a public building violates the author's right of integrity, but was justified by the unreasonable cost of conserving a heavily damaged work), with *Jelles* v *Gemeente Zwolle*, Netherlands Supreme Court, 6 Feb 2004 (destruction of a unique work of architecture does not violate moral rights, but may constitute the civil law tort of 'abuse of right' if the building owner does not give the architect an opportunity to document the building before its destruction). The Swiss Copyright Law, art 15, requires the owner of a unique copy of a work to give the author an opportunity to recover the work in order to preserve it; with respect to works of architecture, the author's rights are limited to the right to photograph the work and obtain copies of the blueprints. See also, 17 USC § 106A(a)(3)(B) (right to prevent destruction of a work of visual art of 'recognized stature'; this right does not apply to works of architecture, see ibid, § 120(b)).

95 *Documents 1948* (1951), 188. 96 ibid, 197. 97 ibid, 427.

(c) Prejudice to the honour or reputation of the author

10.27 Enough has been said above to show that consideration for the position of the common law countries led the Brussels Revision Conference to avoid reference to any wider concept, such as the 'moral or spiritual interests of the author'. 'Honor' and 'reputation' are more objective concepts, being analogous to the kind of personal interests which are protected by actions for defamation. Prejudice to the author's 'moral or spiritual interests' would raise more subjective issues, as the author himself will inevitably be the best judge of what affects him in relation to his work—matters that may be very real to him, although not in the eyes of an outsider. Nonetheless, there are still problems in determining what is the scope of the expression 'honor or reputation'. This was raised by several delegates at the Brussels Conference: did they refer only to the honour or reputation of the author as an author, or did they refer more generally to his honour or reputation as a man (or presumably, as a woman)?[98] The consensus among delegates was that the wider meaning was intended, and that, while this did not need clarification in the text of article 6bis, it should be referred to in the report of the *rapporteur général*.[99] This was done by Marcel Plaisant in the following passage in his report:

> The author will have the right to take proceedings against any action prejudicial to his honor and reputation and it generally emerged from the debate that the author should be protected as a writer just as much as in his capacity as a personality on the literary scene. This is why you have added that he may object to any other action, implying by this any action likely to be prejudicial to the man, as a result of the distortion of his work.[100]

10.28 The practical operation of this wider interpretation can be illustrated by the following example. Suppose a licensee or assignee of the copyright in a textbook prepares an edition with numerous typographical errors and mistakes in the footnotes: this would clearly be injurious to the reputation of the author as an author, in that it would indicate that his research and academic judgement were at fault. On the other hand, suppose the licensee or assignee changed particular parts of the author's work so as to represent him as possessing certain opinions or views which in fact he did not hold. These changes might in no way affect his reputation as a writer, but might severely affect his general reputation, for example, if he were to be depicted as holding a particular extreme view or supporting a theory which has been shown to be fallacious. In this regard, however, the expression 'honor or reputation' does impose certain limitations, leaving a considerable scope for interpretation by national legislation. Faulty reproductions, and the like will almost always be damaging to an author's

[98] ibid, 197 (Switzerland and France). [99] ibid. [100] ibid, 97–8.

reputation, but changes which misrepresent an author's opinions and beliefs may not necessarily have this effect. In some circumstances, it is possible to conceive that such changes may even (falsely) enhance an author's standing, not only among his peers but also among the general public, for example, a new edition of the classic American silent film *Birth of a Nation*, from which the racist depictions of former slaves and the exaltation of the Ku Klux Klan have been excised. D W Griffith's heirs, and film history aficionados, may find the cuts distressing, but the sanitized version removes the taint of white supremacism and arguably casts the director in a better light by modern standards. In such instances, the criterion of prejudice to honour or reputation is of little assistance; on the other hand, this might not be the case if the criterion was prejudice to the author's moral interests.

Whether the alleged prejudice goes to the author's honour or reputation as a writer or as a person, in either event, the standard of assessment of prejudice is an objective one, akin to the evaluation of defamation.[101] This is an important safeguard against overreaching by oversensitive authors, particularly in the context of licensed, or lawfully permitted, adaptations. It is not enough that the author does not like what was done to her work; the action taken must also reflect badly on her in the public eye. That is the difference between harm to the author's 'moral' or 'spiritual interests' in the work, and harm to 'honor or reputation'. The failure at the Rome and Brussels revision conferences to adopt the former standard over the UK delegation's continuing and strenuous objections (discussed earlier at paras 10.09, 10.11 above), confirms the relatively weak nature of the integrity right protected under article 6bis. For example, it was suggested above (in para 10.22) that a parody of a work might be deemed a 'distortion, mutilation or other modification' within the meaning of article 6bis. But that does not mean that a distortion of this kind is also prejudicial to the parodied author's honour or reputation. Presumably, the audience for the parody would recognize the nature of the 'action' taken in relation to the work, and would not conclude that the author herself created the ridiculed version. That version therefore would not reflect badly on the author either as a creator of that version, or as an espouser of whatever absurd opinions the parody communicates. Arguably, the critique conveyed through the parody could be deleterious to the author's honour or reputation, for example, by portraying an orotund author as a pompous windbag. But it is important to maintain the distinction between prejudicial impingements on the integrity of a work, and acerbic, even hostile, literary and artistic commentary. The 'honor or reputation' standard should enable national courts (whose legislatures have not adopted a 'moral **10.29**

[101] See paras 10.09, 10.11 above.

prejudice' standard) to repel claims that in fact object to the critic's message, rather than to her alleged mutilation of the work.

10.30 The 'honor or reputation' standard may nonetheless allow room for claims of violation of the integrity right even in contexts in which the public is not initially likely to believe that the author created or endorsed the alteration to her work. Suppose, for example, that a wholesome children's song were made part of the soundtrack of an erotic film. The incorporation, made for ironic effect, casts the song in a light unsought by the composer. (We will assume that the composer no longer controls the adaptation rights, and that the song was incorporated under licence from the right holder.) The incorporation may constitute a derogatory action taken in respect to the song, but is the composer's reputation also harmed? One might argue that, unless the film's public believes the composer authorized the use of the song, the composer's reputation remains unaffected. On the other hand, the intermingling of the song and the images could produce an enduring association that will taint the song, and in turn its author, in the minds of those members of the public who saw the film. It remains for national courts to determine whether that public is sufficiently substantial to meet an objective standard of prejudice to honour or reputation.

10.31 Is the requirement of prejudice to be differently interpreted when considering modifications made in the course of performing or communicating a work to the public?[102] This question has already been referred to, and arises from the fact that the performance and production of works for performance are themselves intensely personal and creative acts, which may involve the performer or director in making considerable alterations that may be quite different from the author's original intentions. In a sense, performers and the like are intermediaries between author and her public, and a difficult question arises as to the extent to which these intermediaries are required to behave as mouthpieces for, or may instead independently interpret, the author's work. This is a matter which can hardly be legislated for in advance, as the interests involved are complex and each is deserving of consideration.[103] It is therefore addressed in different ways in various Union countries.[104] Article 6bis does not provide much, if any, assistance in this regard. The criterion remains that of prejudice to the honour or reputation of the author, and this is not necessarily appropriate to a situation where an author feels that her artistic intentions have been betrayed by a

[102] The potentially unfixed nature of the performance does not furnish a reason to distinguish performances from other alterations; the Berne Convention does not make fixation a criterion of protection, it would follow that fixation is also not an element of infringement. Moreover, even where fixation is a criterion of protectability, it need not be one for infringement. For example, moral rights in the UK may be infringed by a public performance that deleteriously alters the work. See 1988 CDPA s 80(3)(a).

[103] See van Isacker (n 91 above), and Dietz (1978), 76–7.

[104] For European countries, see Dietz (1978), 76–7.

particular performance or production of her work, but the latter, albeit imposing the performer's or producer's own artistic vision of the work, cannot be said to harm the author's good name. It is nonetheless important to recognize that some interpretations may reflect the interpreter's artistic judgements, yet still distort the work in a manner potentially harmful to the author's reputation. For example, consider the children's song incorporated in the erotic movie, as discussed above, or the use of the light-hearted anthem 'Singin' in the Rain' to accompany acts of extreme and gratuitous violence in the film *Clockwork Orange.* If the criterion were damage or prejudice to the author's moral or spiritual interests, the conflict might be easier to resolve in the author's favour. As it is, national tribunals will clearly adopt differing views as to whether a particular performance or production is prejudicial to an author's honour or reputation, and it is highly likely that common law courts will take a more restrictive approach here than their counterparts in civil law countries.

A question of some importance which has been raised in relation to the **10.32** requirement of prejudice is whether this applies to each of the different acts listed in the first part of paragraph (1), or only to one or some of these. In the English translation, the first interpretation seems to be the ordinary grammatical meaning of the provision, but it has been argued that, in the original text of article 6bis(1), the intention of the Rome Conference was to make the requirement of prejudice applicable only in the case of 'other modifications'.[105] In other words, any distortion or mutilation was, of itself, sufficient to violate the right of integrity because prejudice was presumed to flow from those acts, and it was only when other modifications were in question that the court had to satisfy itself on the question of prejudice. There was some support for this view in the writings of the distinguished French commentator Desbois, who argued that otherwise the question of whether a brutal mutilation was an infringement would be left 'to the tyranny of public opinion'.[106] But there is little, if any, express support for this view to be found in the records of the Rome Conference, and it seems unlikely that such a distinction could have been intended in view of the main objective of pro-moral rights delegates at that Conference to arrive at a formulation that would be acceptable to the common law countries.[107] At Brussels, the words 'or other derogatory action' were added, but it was stated that there was no intention to make significant changes to the Rome text which 'had stood the test of time'.[108] Furthermore, in the original French version of the Brussels provision the plural form of the adjective 'prejudicial' was

[105] van Isacker (n 91 above).

[106] The reference here was to the first edition of Professor Desbois' treatise on copyright: H Desbois, *Le droit d'auteur*, 1st edn (1950), nos 571 and 572.

[107] See para 10.09 above.

[108] Report of sub-committee on moral rights: *Documents 1948* (1951), 126.

used, so as to indicate that this applied to all the acts listed in paragraph (1).[109] As article 6bis embodies only a minimum standard of protection of moral rights, it is open to national legislation to modify the requirement of prejudice in the way contended for, or even to delete it altogether. Under the standard set out in article 6bis, however, no violation of the right of integrity is established unless the author can show prejudice to her honour or reputation.

(6) Duration of moral rights

10.33 The basic principle established under paragraph (2) is that this is to be for at least the duration of the author's economic rights. Accordingly, the Convention adopts a neutral line on the juridical basis of moral rights, that is, whether these are intimately linked with the economic rights and should therefore expire when the latter do, or whether moral rights exist quite independently of economic rights. A number of Berne Union members adopt the second view, and therefore protect moral rights in perpetuity.[110] Paragraph (2) also allows flexibility in the way in which these rights are to be protected *post mortem auctoris*: national legislation in the country where protection is claimed may stipulate the persons or institutions who are to exercise these rights in that country. In many cases, these persons will be the heirs of the author, but national legislation is left with complete flexibility in this regard. Thus, the protection of moral rights *post morten auctoris* might be entrusted to an authors' society or to a government or public agency concerned with the promotion of national culture or to some other appropriate body. As any heirs of the author would by this time be far removed in time from him or her, this course of action after the economic rights in the work had expired might place allegations of integrity violations in the hands of those better situated to undertake their assessment. Paragraph (2) lays down no stipulations in this regard, but it is worth noting that at both the Brussels and Stockholm Conferences, where proposals for protection of moral

[109] While van Isacker argues that this plural form was simply a typographical error made by the drafting committee at Brussels, there is no reason to suppose that this was the case or to suppose that his interpretation of the proceedings of the Rome Conference is the correct one. See further P Recht, 'Article 6bis of the Berne Convention (Moral rights)' [1968] *Copyright* 15. In this regard, it is of interest to note that a superior Belgian court has taken the view, in interpreting article 6bis, that the requirement of prejudice has to be shown in respect of each of the acts listed in para (1). See 'The Merry Widow': decision of Brussels Court of 29 Sept 1965, discussed at length by van Isacker (n 91 above).

[110] See eg France, Code de la propriété intellectuelle, art L 121–1; Portugal, art 56(2) of the Code of Copyright and Related Rights of 1985 (last amended 1991); Cameroon, art 14(4) of the Law No 2000/011 of 19 Dec 2000; on Copyright and Neighbouring Rights; Paraguay, art 17 of the Law No 1328/98 on Copyright and Related Rights; Peru, art 21 of the Copyright Law (Legislative Decree No 822) of 1996.

rights in the period after expiry of the economic rights were made,[111] a number of delegations expressed the opinion that this was no longer a matter for regulation by law pertaining to private rights and now fell within the sphere of public law and policy.[112]

Article 6*bis*(2) also provides a carefully constructed let-out clause for the common law countries which enables them to adhere to it without having to carry out extensive changes to their domestic laws. Thus, a country whose legislation, at the time of its ratification of, or accession to the Paris Act, does not provide *post mortem auctoris* protection for 'all the rights set out in the preceding paragraph may provide that some of these rights may, after his death, cease to be maintained'. The references to 'some' and 'all' really need to be read as 'one' and 'both', as paragraph (1) only requires the protection of two species of moral right. However, it is not only common law countries that benefit from this concession: any country that prior to the Stockholm Act provided *post mortem auctoris* protection for only one of these rights would be entitled to take advantage of it and continue to deny such protection in respect of the other right. There is an apparent gap in the formulation of this clause, as it might be taken to imply that a country which did not provide for the *post mortem auctoris* protection of either of the moral rights referred to in paragraph (1) would be obliged to protect both rights *post mortem auctoris* once it accedes to or ratifies the Paris Act. This is on the basis that the precondition that 'all [both] the rights set out in the preceding paragraph' are not protected *post mortem auctoris* means that nonetheless 'some [one]' of them must be protected in this period. This would be a problem for a country such as Australia which, prior to 1967, did not accord *post mortem auctoris* protection to either of the rights set out in **10.34**

[111] *Documents 1948* (1951), 186 (proposal in Conference programme), 192 (Austria), 193 (Hungary), 194 (Czechoslovakia). As for the proposals at the Stockholm Conference, see para 10.12 above.

[112] *Documents 1948* (1951), 192 (France); *Records* 1967, vol II, 893–4 (Germany, Denmark, and Austria). In passing, it is also interesting to note a proposal that was made to the Stockholm Conference by Austria at the behest of the International Federation of Musicians for the deposit in national libraries or archives of a country in which a literary, musical, or dramatico-musical work is published of 'a facsimile copy of the earliest and most authentic available text or score of the work in the form and version finished and approved by the author'. Document S/147: *Records* 1967, vol II, 700 (inspired, it seems, by the International Federation of Musicians: ibid, 895). This was framed in such a way as to avoid the Conventional prohibition on formalities, but a number of delegations felt that the implications of the proposal, both practical and theoretical, required further investigation. Ibid, 896 (Monaco, Portugal, Italy, and Australia). It was therefore withdrawn by the Austrian delegation without a vote being taken, and Main Committee I included a recommendation in its report that the International Office should 'undertake a study of the question in order that consideration may be given to the possibility of including provisions relating thereto in a future revision of the Convention'. Ibid, 1189. It does not appear that any further action has been taken on this recommendation.

paragraph (1).[113] However, the records of the Stockholm Conference indicate that this would be too restrictive an interpretation, as Australia was a co-sponsor of the amendment which embodied the present wording,[114] and it seems clear from the discussion in Main Committee I that its purpose was to accommodate the position of those countries which did not at that time provide *post mortem auctoris* protection for any moral rights.[115] On the other hand, this formulation now imposes a specific obligation on these countries to protect 'some [one]' of these rights after the author's death, and this is a significant advance on the position under the Rome and Brussels Acts.

The article 6bis right that common law countries were more likely to protect *post mortem auctoris* would have been the right of attribution, as its common law analogue, claims against passing off, is not tied to the author's person. By contrast, by linking the right of integrity to common law defamation claims, common law countries virtually ensured that the integrity right would not survive the author's death, as defamation claims terminate with the life of the author.[116] In any event, with the adoption of moral rights statutes by most of the major common law jurisdictions,[117] the question has become largely moot.

(a) Duration of moral rights in cinematographic and photographic works and works of applied art

10.35 The general structure and content of article 6bis(2) assume that moral rights will endure at least throughout the life of the author. Because the minimum term of economic rights is generally fifty years *post mortem auctoris*, pegging the duration of moral rights to that of economic rights will usually ensure that moral rights do not predecease the author. But in some instances, the term of economic rights is not calculated on the basis of the life of the author, but rather from the making of the work, or from its being made available to the public.

[113] Prior to this time, Australia applied the Copyright Act 1911 (UK) which did not contain any provision for post-mortem protection of moral rights. In the UK, this Act ceased to apply after the adoption of the Copyright Act 1956.

[114] Document S/247: *Records* 1967, vol I, 726.

[115] ibid, 918–19.

[116] See eg Robert D Sack, *Sack on Defamation: Libel, Slander, and Related Problems*, 3rd edn (release no 3 (Apr 2002)), 2.138–2.139 ('The dead have no cause of action for defamation under the common law, and neither do their survivors, unless the words independently reflect upon and defame the survivors.')

[117] See UK, Copyright, Designs and Patents Act 1988, s 86; New Zealand, Copyright Act 1994, Part 4, art 106; Australia, Copyright Amendment (Moral Rights) Act 2000, s 195AM (Australia does not protect integrity rights in films after the death of the author, but gives full protection otherwise for the *post mortem auctoris* period in all other cases); Canada, Copyright Act 1985, s 14.2(1). See also, for the limited context of 'works of visual art', US 17 USC §§ 106A(d) (federal rights of attribution and integrity in works of visual art endure for the life of the author); 301(f)(2)(C) (preserving state law claims against *post mortem auctoris* violations of integrity and attribution rights).

This is the case for anonymous and pseudonymous works (article 7(3): fifty years from lawful making available), cinematographic works (article 7(2): fifty years from making available or making), and photographic works and works of applied art (article 7(4): twenty-five years from making). A duration problem is not likely to arise in the context of anonymous or pseudonymous works, because any claim to attribution or integrity will result in identification of the author, in which case, the term of fifty years *post mortem auctoris* will apply (see article 7(3)). By contrast, it is conceivable that a co-author of a cinematographic work could outlast the fifty years that follow the film's disclosure, and it is quite likely that a photographer or designer of a work of applied art would survive more than twenty-five years following the making of one of those works. As a result, it is possible that the moral rights tied to the economic rights in these kinds of works would expire before the author does. (Whether this is likely in fact turns on the extent to which national laws provide no more than the Berne minimum term of economic rights for these works.) This would produce an inconsistency between the literal text of the Convention, and its apparent intention to ensure that moral rights last at least as long as the life of the author. To resolve this difficulty, it would be desirable to interpret article 6bis(2) as requiring that all authors' moral rights last at least until their deaths. (A similar problem exists with respect to the duration of performers' rights under article 5(2) of the WIPO ('World Intellectual Property Organization') Performances and Phonograms Treaty ('WPPT'); see the further discussion in Chapter 19 below.)

(7) Mode of protection of moral rights

Although article 6bis does not contain any specific reference to it, it has been **10.36** accepted from the start that Union countries are not obliged to protect moral rights within the framework of copyright. This is confirmed in the general report of Main Committee I of the Stockholm Conference,[118] and leaves countries free to adopt other heads of protection for the rights specified in paragraph (1), for example, through the action of defamation in common law jurisdictions. So long as the member state achieves effective substantive protection of the attribution and integrity rights, the Convention is indifferent to the legal labels under which the state accomplishes that goal. This pragmatic approach, endorsed by then Director General of WIPO, Arpad Bogsch, made it possible for the United States to ratify the Berne Convention in 1988 without amending its law to provide specific moral rights coverage. The USA took the position, and the Director General agreed, that a 'patchwork' of common law actions and other federal statutory claims together afforded the rough equivalent of formal

[118] Document S/247: *Records* 1967, vol I, 1159.

moral rights provisions.[119] Paragraph (3) also makes it clear that 'the means of redress for the safeguarding of these rights' is a matter for the legislation of the country in which protection is claimed. This is the same as for the economic rights protected by the Convention (see article 5(2)), and means that the remedies available in each country may differ considerably. That said, it is at least implicit in article 6bis(1) that member states should protect the author's integrity right not only when harm to honour or reputation has already occurred, but also preventively, when the distortion, etc '*would be* prejudicial' to the author's honour or reputation (emphasis added). Thus, for example, Berne would require member states to make it possible for the injured author to enjoin the broadcasting of a deleteriously altered version of an audiovisual work before the broadcast takes place, rather than merely redressing reputational harm that might follow from a disseminated broadcast.

(8) Right of disclosure

10.37 One of the traditional components of moral rights protected in national laws is the right of disclosure ('*droit de divulgation*').[120] There is no reference to this in article 6bis, but it is possible to argue that such a right is required to be protected, by implication, under the Convention. The basis for this argument is to be found in the provisions dealing with exceptions to protection, notably articles 10 and 10bis. Essentially, these are concerned with uses of works that are publicly disclosed, and the implication can be drawn that corresponding exceptions should not be allowed in the case of unpublished works.[121] The effect of this interpretation would be to grant, impliedly, protection to the right of the author to control the disclosure of his work to the world. The scope of the exceptions allowed by articles 10 and 10bis is discussed in detail in Chapter 13 below.

---

[119] See HR Rep No 100-609 at 37 (1988) (stressing that the Director General of WIPO endorsed the view that US law already met the art 6bis standard). The *Final Report of the Ad Hoc Working Group on US Adherence to the Berne Convention*, a group formed at State Department behest whose report was submitted to Congress, also concluded that US law afforded 'substantial protection for the real equivalent of [the] moral rights [of attribution and integrity]', particularly by recourse to the Lanham Federal Trademarks Act, see *Final Report* at 35, 39–42, reprinted at (1986) 10 *Colum-VLA J L & Arts* 513, 547, 551–4. The claim of functional equivalence has, however, been greeted with some scepticism, see eg Adolf Dietz, 'The United States and Moral Rights: Idiosyncrasy or Approximation? Observations on a Problematical Relationship Underlying United States Adherence to the Berne Convention' (1989) 142 *RIDA* 222. See also Jane C Ginsburg, 'The Right to Claim Authorship in US Copyright and Trademarks Law' (2004) 41 *U Houston L Rev* 263.

[120] Such a right is also to be found expressly protected in many of the common law jurisdictions, eg the UK and Australia: UK, Copyright, Designs and Patents Act 1988, s 16(1)(b), and Copyright Act 1968 (Aust), s 31(1)(a)(ii).

[121] See further C Masouyé, *Guide to the Berne Convention for the Protection of Literary and Artistic Works* (1978), 58.

C. Beyond the Berne Convention

Subsequent multilateral instruments do not add to, or purport to alter, the coverage of moral rights afforded to authors by the Berne Convention. Indeed, specific moral rights provisions are altogether absent from the Agreement on Trade-Related Aspects of Intellectual Property Rights 1994 (the 'TRIPs Agreement') and the WIPO Copyright Treaty ('WCT'). In the case of the TRIPs Agreement, moreover, moral rights not only are absent, they are explicitly excluded from that Agreement's scope. By contrast, with respect to performers, the WPPT sets out their moral rights in aural performances, in a way that is both inspired by, yet departs to some extent from, article 6bis of the Berne Convention. **10.38**

(1) The TRIPs Agreement

This section will analyse the relevant text in light of the exclusion of moral rights from the TRIPs Agreement, and will then examine its implications for the interpretation and application of the Berne Convention's moral rights guarantees. Article 9(1) of the TRIPs Agreement provides: **10.39**

> Members shall comply with articles 1 through 21 of the Berne Convention (1971) and the Appendix thereto. However, Members shall not have rights or obligations under this Agreement in respect of the rights conferred under Article 6bis of that Convention or of the rights derived therefrom.

(a) Genesis of the exclusion of moral rights from TRIPs Agreement, article 9(1)

Neither of the two principal drafts leading up to the TRIPs Agreement would have included moral rights within the scope of Berne Convention protections that WTO members would have been obligated to protect, under threat of trade sanctions. The Chairman's Report to the Group of Negotiation on Goods of 23 July 1990[122] stated: **10.40**

> Parties shall grant to authors and their successors in title the [economic] rights provided in the Berne Convention (1971) . . .

The 3 December 1990 'Brussels Draft'[123] stated:

> Parties shall comply with the substantive provisions [on economic rights] of the Berne Convention (1971). [However, Parties shall not have rights or obligations under this Agreement in respect of the rights conferred under article 6bis of that Convention or of the rights derived therefrom.]

[122] Document MTN.GNG/NG11/W/76 (23 July 1990).

[123] Document MTN, TNC/W/35/Rev.1 (3 Dec 1990).

The bracketed language indicates provisions regarding which agreement had yet to be reached.[124] Although a group of Latin American countries proposed an amendment to eliminate the exclusion of moral rights,[125] the Second 'Draft Final Act Embodying the Results of the Uruguay Round of Multilateral Trade Negotiations' maintained the exclusion.[126] As far as moral rights are concerned, no further changes ensued during the negotiation and drafting processes, apart from the substitution of the reference to articles 1 to 21 of the Berne Convention, in lieu of 'substantive provisions on economic rights'. Without this substitution, member states might have disagreed over whether certain of articles 1 to 21, for example, article 17 (allowing for member state censorship) or article 20 (allowing for separate agreements among member states providing greater protection) in fact were 'substantive provisions on economic rights'.[127]

(b) Justification for the exclusion of moral rights

10.41 The exclusion of moral rights could be said to follow logically from the nature of the TRIPs Agreement. Because TRIPs is an accord on international trade, non-economic rights arguably have no place in its universe. Even under the subjective standard articulated in article 6bis, evaluation of moral rights violations, and, correspondingly, of a member state's adequate and effective protection of moral rights, could prove far more elusive to the participants in dispute-settlement panels than assessment of violations of the rights of reproduction or communication or other economic rights. Further complications would arise with respect to member states that apply a more author-favourable 'moral prejudice' standard, and that would be obliged, under the article 5(1) principle of national treatment, and under article 19, to grant foreign Union authors the benefit of that standard. But there may be additional, less disinterested, explanations. As indicated earlier (see para 10.36 n 119 above), the USA's claim to implementation of its article 6bis obligations has not gone unquestioned. For example, there is no general right of attribution in US copyright or other law; at best, authors had obtained through interpretation of trademarks and unfair competition law a right to challenge misattributions of authorship. But no court had held that authors had a right to compel name recognition in the absence of a contract or of a

[124] See Daniel Gervais, *The TRIPS Agreement: Drafting History and Analysis*, 2nd edn (2003) ('Gervais (2003)'), para 1.21.

[125] Document MTN.GNG/TRIPS/W/2 (16 Oct 1991) (submitted by Colombia on behalf of itself and Bolivia, Peru, and Venezuela).

[126] Document MTN.TNC/W/FA (20 Dec 1991).

[127] See also Gervais (2003), para 2.89 (suggesting that the incorporation of art 21, linking to the Appendix setting forth 'special provisions regarding developing countries', avoided potential conflict between TRIPs norms and the Appendix's allowance for certain compulsory licenses).

miscrediting of authorship.[128] As a result, had moral rights been included among the enforceable Berne guarantees, the USA might have been vulnerable to trade sanctions. Given the importance of the US role in the TRIPs Agreement negotiations, it is not surprising that such a potentially troublesome provision would have been set aside.

(c) Analysis of article 9

10.42 The text seems somewhat self-contradictory. On the one hand, the TRIPs Agreement directs its members to comply with articles 1 to 21 of the Berne Convention: these include article 6*bis*, as well as article 19, entitling authors to greater protections under member state domestic law, including greater moral rights protections, for example, in jurisdictions applying a 'moral prejudice' rather than an 'honor or reputation' standard. On the other hand, despite commanding compliance, the TRIPs Agreement also relieves member states of any obligations under the TRIPs Agreement to comply in fact with article 6*bis*. Had the member state an 'obligation under this Agreement', that obligation would have been enforceable through the TRIPs dispute-settlement procedures, with imposition of trade sanctions as an enforcement measure.[129] In effect, the TRIPs Agreement declares a moral obligation of compliance, but makes that duty completely toothless, for the non-compliant member state incurs no risk of economic retorsion.

(d) '[R]ights conferred under article 6bis of that Convention or of the rights derived therefrom'

10.43 The attribution and integrity rights set out in article 6*bis* are clearly removed from TRIPs enforcement actions. But are all moral rights equally amputated? For example, the right of disclosure or divulgation is not comprehended within article 6*bis*; if it finds a basis elsewhere in the Berne Convention, it would appear that a TRIPs Agreement member state's failure to apply that right could give rise to a dispute settlement. As discussed earlier (see para 10.37 above), this right is arguably implicit in articles 10 and 10*bis*, and therefore should survive the excision of article 6*bis*. Article 10(3) also conditions the quotation privilege on attribution of the name of the author, and the article 10*bis*(1) privilege for news coverage similarly requires attribution of the 'source', which could include the name of

[128] See eg Ginsburg (n 119 above); Roberta Rosenthal Kwall, 'The Attribution Right in the United States: Caught in the Crossfire Between Copyright and Section 43(a)' (2002) 77 *Wash L Rev* 985.

[129] For provisions of the TRIPs Agreement on ensuring compliance with the rulings of the Dispute Settlement Body, see Agreement Establishing the World Trade Organization, Annex 2, Understanding on Rules and Procedures Governing the Settlement of Disputes, arts 21, 22. See also *Implications of the TRIPs Agreement on Treaties Administered by WIPO*, paras 26 et seq, WIPO Document WO/GA/XV/1 (1996).

the author. Thus, these two articles establish some attribution rights independently of article 6bis. Finally, article $11^{bis}(2)$, allowing member states to impose compulsory licences for certain secondary transmissions, contains the limitation that the licences 'shall not in any circumstances be prejudicial to the moral rights of the author'. Thus, there would appear to be a subset of moral rights existing outside article 6bis. Unfortunately for authors, article 9 of the TRIPs Agreement also excludes 'rights derived from' article 6bis. If these extra-6bis rights can be deemed to have 'derived from' 6bis, then they are equally excluded from the universe of rights enforceable under the TRIPs Agreement.

10.44 There is a strong argument that the divulgation right does not 'derive from' article 6bis. That article covers only attribution and integrity. The divulgation right rather derives, or is inferred, from the condition that articles 10 and 10bis place on the quotation privilege, that the work has already 'been lawfully made available to the public'. It may be that an exception (undisclosed works) to an exception (quotation privilege) is a slim reed on which to perch the divulgation right, but at least that reed shares no stalks with the 6bis rights. Moreover, the TRIPs Agreement itself indicates that it is not hostile to the divulgation right. Article 14(1) recognizes the rights of performers to 'have the possibility of preventing' unauthorized fixations and reproductions of unfixed performances, as well as the broadcasting and communication to the public of their live performances.[130] All of these rights may entail divulgation, as the 'live' performances whose fixation, reproduction, and public communication article 14 entitles the performers to control can have taken place in a studio or other place not open to the public; they need not have been made before an audience, and therefore will not necessarily already have been publicly disclosed before their reproduction or communication to the public.

10.45 Establishing the independence of the article 10bis attribution rights may be more difficult, for these rights are of the same kind as those protected by 6bis. The text of article 9 of the TRIPs Agreement, however, does not say 'of the same kind'; it says 'derived therefrom'. In that respect, the final text seems more narrow than the two earlier drafts of article 9, which both included bracketed language limiting TRIPs-enforceable rights to 'economic rights' in the Berne Convention.[131] Arguably, any attribution rights that predate the 1928 Rome Revision (which, it will be recalled, gave rise to article 6bis) cannot be said to be 'derived

[130] But cf WPPT, art 6 (labelling these rights as 'Economic Rights of Performers in their Unfixed Performances'); this may be evidence that then the divulgation right, albeit pertinent to authors' moral interests, is not a 'moral' right in the sense of the TRIPs Agreement.

[131] See 'Chairman's Report to the Group of Negotiation on Goods' (n 122 above); Brussels Draft, Document MTN, TNC/W/35/Rev.1 (3 Dec 1990). The relevant text of both drafts is reproduced at Gervais (2003), 123.

therefrom'. However, although quotation privileges of some kind go back to the original 1886 text (see further Chapter 13 below), articles 10 and 10bis both postdate the Rome Revision; the article 10(3) limitation was introduced in the 1948 Brussels Revision and the 10bis(1) obligation to credit the source came in with the 1967 Stockholm Revision. The article 11bis(2) reminder of the author's moral rights was inserted at the Rome Revision. Thus, the 'derived from' characterization cannot be rejected on the sole basis of a time line.

In the case of the article 11bis(2) moral rights, it may be necessary to concede **10.46**
their derivation from article 6bis, to which they appear to refer, and with which they are contemporaneous. As for articles 10(3) and 10bis(1), however, it may be contended that they are distinct, rather than derivative, for the same reasons for which their inclusion in 1948 and 1967 was deemed not to be superfluous in light of the pre-existing article 6bis. (See further Chapter 13 below.) That is, it is not clear that the article 6bis moral rights otherwise applied to lawful quotations, and the conference records indicate considerable disinclination to recognize the integrity right in the context, notably, of edited versions of text for use in schools.[132] If lawful quotations otherwise fell outside the control of article 6bis, the delegates nonetheless agreed that the author's name should be recognized. Article 6bis having been sidelined, they therefore established an independent basis for the attribution right. If 'derived from' implies 'dependent on', then this history suggests that the distinct basis for articles 10 and 10bis rights of attribution justifies their preservation in the Berne Convention articles that the TRIPs Agreement makes enforceable.

(2) Moral Rights in the WIPO Treaties

The WCT requires compliance with the Berne Convention, including article 6bis. **10.47**
It specifies no additional protections. The WPPT does provide in article 5 for performers' rights of attribution and integrity in live and recorded aural performances. This provision will be examined in Chapter 19 (see paras 19.52–19.53).

[132] See para 13.46 below.

D. Comparative Table of Moral Rights Provisions

10.48

Exclusive right protected	Berne Convention	Gaps left to national law and ambiguities	TRIPs Agreement	WCT (beyond article 1(4) compliance clause)	Gaps and ambiguities
MORAL RIGHTS— to claim authorship	article $6^{bis}(1)$; article 10(3) requires mention of author's name; $10^{bis}(1)$ requires mention of the 'source' of quoted works	alienability of 6bis rights left to member state law	6bis rights excluded by article 9(1)		Whether article 10(3) and $10^{bis}(1)$ requirements 'derive from' art 6bis Whether a member state quotation privilege which did not require acknowledging author's name would afford a basis for a dispute resolution proceeding against that state
to object to derogatory actions, etc (integrity)	article $6^{bis}(1)$	alienability of rights, standard for 'prejudice' to honour or reputation, left to member state law	excluded by article 9(1)		
to divulge the work	May be implicit in articles 10 and 10bis		Not excluded by article 9(1) because does not 'derive from' article 6bis		

11

THE RIGHTS OF REPRODUCTION, ADAPTATION, AND DISTRIBUTION (BERNE CONVENTION, ARTICLES 8, 9, 12, 14, 14^BIS(1), 14TER, AND 16; TRIPs AGREEMENT, ARTICLES 11 AND 14(4); WCT, ARTICLES 6 AND 7)

A. The Exclusive Right of Reproduction and its Derivatives

(1) Introduction

11.01 The reproduction right is one of the most basic, and earliest-recognized,[1] rights in copyright. Yet, curiously, it was a relatively late arrival into the Berne Convention, perhaps because its protection was generally assured through national treatment, for member states' domestic laws in one way or another would have prohibited unauthorized copying. The author's reproduction rights under Berne are not limited, however, to the exclusive right to copy the work in its original form. They also extend to complete or partial reproductions of the work into other forms, and thus encompass the broad realm of adaptations. The Berne Convention sets out a variety of specific adaptation rights—mechanical (indirectly), cinematographic, and translations—although it classifies these as instances of the reproduction right. Berne also establishes a general principle covering 'adaptations, arrangements, and other alterations of [the work]'.[2] Although reproduction and adaptation rights concern the incorporeal work of authorship, Berne also provides for certain rights pertaining to the physical copies. These tend to be specific to certain categories of works, distribution of cinematographic works (articles 14(1), 14bis(1)), resale right (*droit de suite*) in works of art and manuscripts (article 14ter), but article 16 provides for a general right to seize infringing copies imported into Union countries. Article 11 of the Agreement on Trade-Related Aspects of Intellectual Property Rights 1994 ('TRIPs Agreement'), and article 7 of the World Intellectual Property Organization ('WIPO') Copyright Treaty ('WCT'), broaden the rights in physical copies to cover certain rentals, and article 6 of the WCT also sets out a general right of distribution of physical copies.

[1] eg the first copyright statutes in England 8 Anne, c 19 (1710) and the US Act of 31 May 1790, 1 Stat 124 (1790) granted authors exclusive rights of reproduction; rights of public performance came later, UK 1833 Act, 3 & 4 Will 4, c 15 (dramatic works); UK 1842 Act 5 & 6 Vict, c 45, s 20 (musical works). US Act of 18 Aug 1856, 34th Cong, 1st Sess, 11 stat 138 (public performance right; dramatic works); US Act of 6 Jan 1897, 44th Cong, 2nd Sess, 29 stat 694 (musical compositions).

[2] See Berne Convention, arts 8, 12, 14(1) (specific adaptation rights); 12, 14(2), 14bis(1) (general adaptation rights).

This chapter will address the development of the reproduction, adaptation, and distribution rights in the Berne Convention through to the 1971 Paris Revision. The current scope of each right will also be examined. The chapter will conclude with an analysis of the impact of later treaties, the TRIPs Agreement, and the WCT, on the reproduction and distribution rights. **11.02**

B. Reproduction

(1) Development of the right in the Berne Convention

(a) The basic right

Article 9(1) provides that: **11.03**

> (1) Authors of literary and artistic works protected by this Convention shall have the exclusive right of authorizing the reproduction of these works in any manner or form.

In amplification of this, paragraph (3) provides that 'any sound or visual recording shall be considered as a reproduction for the purposes of this Convention' (paragraph (2) which deals with exceptions which may be made to the right of reproduction under national legislation is discussed in paras 13.10ff below). Prior to the Stockholm, Paris Acts, the Convention did not contain any express stipulation as to the right of reproduction, although this is undoubtedly the most fundamental right which has been accorded historically to authors under national legislation. Nevertheless, it was arguable that the Convention implicitly required member countries to protect this right. This was to be deduced from a consideration of several provisions of the Convention which referred incidentally to reproductions. The first was article 7 of the original Berne Act which provided for the lawful reproduction of articles from newspapers or periodicals in certain circumstances (see further para 13.48 below). The second was article 10 of the same Act which listed specific examples of 'illicit reproductions to which the present Convention applies', including adaptations, musical arrangements, and the like (see further para 11.29 below). Thirdly, article 12 of the same Act provided for the seizure of 'pirated works' where these were imported into countries of the Union where the original work enjoyed protection (see further para 11.46 below). From these provisions it was therefore possible to deduce that there was a general right of reproduction that was deemed to be accorded by each Union country. If this were not so, the reference to what might be lawfully reproduced under article 7 would have been unnecessary. The same would also have been true in relation to 'illicit reproductions' under article 12, while the phrase 'pirated works' would have lost much of its force if it did not apply to works which had been unlawfully reproduced. An alternative view was that, even if there was no implicit requirement in the

Convention that Union countries would protect reproduction rights, this would inevitably be the case in practice. This was because each state granted such protection under its domestic laws, and would therefore accord similar protection to works claiming under the Convention, by virtue of the principle of national treatment.

11.04 However, while it is true to say that in 1886 each country which was to join the projected Union accorded protection to the reproduction right, it cannot be said that there was agreement between these states as to the scope and content of this right. This is undoubtedly the reason why no attempt was made at this stage to insert a general reproduction right in the Convention. Historically, the first reproduction right protected in national copyright laws was the right to make printed copies, but with technological progress during the nineteenth century more expansive interpretations of the scope of this right came to be adopted. It became clear that works could be reproduced and embodied in a wide number of forms: for example, two-dimensional artistic works could be reproduced in three-dimensional form, and vice versa in the case of three-dimensional artistic works, and musical works could be embodied in articles such as pianola rolls and gramophone records from which they could be performed. Moreover, literary and dramatic works could be translated into other languages, providing a different outer 'clothing' for a work which remained internally unchanged. Adaptations and other transformations of works were also increasingly recognized as actionable infringements of authors' rights, although there were some juridical disputes, particularly in Germany, as to whether these were to be seen as illicit reproductions or 'copies', or as the subject of a separate right.[3] There were also differences in national laws over whether reproduction rights extended (or should extend) to rights in relation to the distribution and circulation of the copies that were made.[4] These, and other variations, made agreement on a Conventional right of reproduction difficult, if not impossible. Attention at the Berne Conference of 1884 to 1886 was therefore focused on two specific forms of reproduction on which agreement seemed possible. These were translations and adaptations. As will be seen below (para 11.15), some progress was made as regards the first, and this was perfected in later revisions of the Convention. As regards adaptations, there were more difficulties, as delegates could not agree on a clear definition of what was an actionable adaptation. Article 10 of the Berne Act was finally adopted, but this avoided the question of definition and left the scope of the right quite unclear. It was not until the Brussels Revision that the right of authorizing adaptations and other transformations of a work was to be

[3] See J H Spoor, W R Cornish, and P F Nolan, *Copies in Copyright* (1980) ('Spoor et al (1980)'), 10–26.

[4] See generally Spoor et al (1980), Part II.

dealt with satisfactorily under the Convention as a separate right (see further para 11.33 below). However, the Berlin Conference made more progress with respect to two specific techniques of reproduction that were brought clearly within the scope of rights conferred by the Convention: the mechanical reproduction of musical works which was dealt with in article 13 (see further para 11.08 below) and the cinematographic reproduction of literary, scientific and artistic works which was dealt with in article 14 (see further para 11.14 below).

(i) The Brussels Revision: It was not until the Brussels Revision that an attempt was made to introduce a general right of reproduction. This was to be found in similar proposals that were submitted by the French and Austrian delegations.[5] In their proposal, the French argued that it was now time to fill this gap in the Convention, particularly in view of the fact that the rights provided for in articles 8 (translation), 13 (mechanical reproduction), and 14 (cinematographic reproduction) were 'rights derived from the fundamental right of reproduction'.[6] The French also proposed that reproductions of articles in newspapers and periodicals, which were previously permitted, subject to certain conditions, under article 9, should be brought within the scope of the new general right, and that this should embrace the right of putting works and reproductions into circulation.[7] The following draft was therefore proposed to replace the existing article 9(1) of the text: **11.05**

> (1) The authors of literary, scientific and artistic work shall enjoy the exclusive right to authorise:
>
> 1 The reproduction of their works by any mode of impression, including newspapers and periodicals;
> 2 The putting into circulation of the said works and reproductions thereof.[8]

The Austrian proposal was similar in effect, and also included the right of putting into circulation.[9] At this stage, however, there was little support for either proposal, and they were both withdrawn.[10] As regards the French proposal, which was put in the context of newspaper and periodical reproductions, it appears that some of the opposition to it came from countries which were concerned about the possible threat that such a general provision might pose to freedom of information and press usage.[11]

[5] *Documents de la Conférence réunie à Bruxelles du 5 au 26 juin 1948* (1951) (*Documents 1948* (1951)), 230–1 (Austrian proposal), 231–3 (French proposal).
[6] ibid, 232. [7] ibid, 233 (this was, in fact, a revised proposal).
[8] ibid, 233. [9] ibid, 230. [10] ibid, 234–5.
[11] See A Baum, *The Brussels Conference for the Revision of the Berne Convention* (1949), 26 ('Baum (1949)').

11.06 (ii) **Protection of reproduction rights under earlier texts of the Convention:** It may still be relevant to know what is required with respect to reproduction rights under the pre-Stockholm Acts of the Convention as these texts continue to apply to the relations between a small number of Berne Union members that have not acceded to the Paris Act: article 32(1) (and see further paras 17.69ff below). If a country is bound only, for example, by the Brussels Act,[12] may it refuse to grant reproduction rights to Union authors claiming under the Convention if it also refrains from granting these rights to its own authors? On the other hand, are its authors entitled, pursuant to the principle of national treatment, to claim such protection in other Union countries which recognize such rights? It was stated above that there were grounds for arguing that, prior to the Stockholm Act, Union members were still required to protect reproduction rights as this was to be 'implied' from various provisions of the Convention. There are good reasons for rejecting this view, as will be seen below in the context of mechanical reproduction rights. For the moment, it is sufficient to note that the study group which prepared the programme for the Stockholm Revision proceeded on the view that there was no general right of reproduction imposed under the earlier Acts, and this was the basis of the programme proposal for a new article 9(1).[13] It therefore follows that if a Union country which is not bound by the Paris Acts does not accord to its own authors a general right of reproduction, the principle of national treatment will not require the grant of such protection to Union authors claiming under the Convention. On the other hand, authors from that country will be able to claim protection for reproduction rights in another Union country which does accord this protection to its own authors. (This question is discussed further in para 11.10 below.)

(b) Reproduction in other forms: mechanical, cinematographic, and translations

11.07 (i) **Mechanical reproduction rights:** As noted above, the Convention contained provisions relating to these rights long before the recognition of the general reproduction right. However, prior to the Berlin Revision, this form of reproduction was specifically excluded from the scope of the Convention in paragraph 3 of the Closing Protocol of the Berne Act:

> 3. It is understood that the manufacture and sale of instruments for the mechanical reproduction of musical airs in which copyright subsists shall not be considered as constituting an infringement of musical copyright.

[12] As at Dec 2004, this would have been the case with the Bahamas, Chad, Fiji, Madagascar, and South Africa: see the list of Berne signatories at www.wipo.int. There remained bound by Rome as at this date: Lebanon, Malta, New Zealand, Pakistan, Sri Lanka and Zimbabwe.

[13] *Records* 1967, 111–13 (Document S/1).

Similar provisions were also to be found in a number of national laws,[14] and the reasons for this appear to be: first, the modes by which such reproductions could be effected in 1886 were relatively unimportant in that they were only capable of reproducing a few works, for example, musical boxes and clocks, Barbary organs and the like.[15] Second, the early Union members were prepared to make an exception to protect the interests of Switzerland which was then a leading manufacturer of such devices.[16]

The years following the formation of the Union saw the rapid development of a new range of devices which could reproduce musical works far more effectively, in particular the pianola roll and the phonographic record, and the owners of musical copyright began to appreciate the threat which was posed to the exploitation of their works. ALAI became concerned at an early stage, and passed a number of resolutions urging that these newer forms of fixation should not be included within the exclusion in paragraph (3).[17] At the Paris Revision the French Government sought to give effect to these views by proposing that a distinction was to be drawn between those contrivances in which the means for reproducing the musical air were inseparably incorporated, and those contrivances to which something additional, such as a roll or tape, had to be added in order for this to occur. It was argued that the first kind of fixation was of little significance to authors, but that the second posed far graver threats as the tapes or rolls were analogous to printed copies of the works in question.[18] The following addition to paragraph (3) was therefore proposed:

> The benefit of this provision does not apply to instruments which may only reproduce airs by the addition of tapes or perforated rolls or other independent systems of devices, sold separately and comprising musical editions in a particular notation.[19]

This proposal caused sharp divisions among the delegates. Support for it came from Belgium, Italy and Monaco, but it was opposed by Germany, the UK, Spain, Norway, and Switzerland.[20] In the main, these objections were practical. A number of Union countries now had well-established industries based on the free mechanical reproduction of musical works, and it was argued that the effect

[14] See eg Law of 10 Mar 1866 (France); Law of 1883, art 11 (Switzerland).

[15] Remarks of British delegates to the Berlin Conference in their report to the UK Government: *Correspondence Respecting the Revised Convention of Berne for the Protection of Literary and Artistic Works, signed at Berlin, November 13, 1908*, 13. See generally W Briggs, *The Law of International Copyright* (1906) ('Briggs (1906)'), 401–27. See also *Actes* 1896, 46–7 (French programme for Paris Revision), and 'La question des instruments de musique mécaniques' [1895] *DA* 54.

[16] See [1895] *DA* 54, 55.

[17] At Berne 1889, London 1890, Neuchâtel 1891, and Milan 1892: texts of resolutions in *Actes* 1896, 65–6.

[18] ibid, 46–7. [19] ibid, 47. [20] ibid, 175 (report of general commission).

of the proposed restriction would be to encourage the development of these industries outside the Union.[21] It was also said that the proposed distinction would be difficult to make, in view of the range of devices available: for example, would interchangeable cylinders embodying a number of musical airs fall within or without the exclusion in paragraph (3)?[22] There were differences in attitudes of national courts to these matters as well.[23] It was finally concluded that the matter was not yet ripe for international solution, and paragraph (3) was left unchanged.[24]

11.08 The failure of the French amendment at the Paris Conference left the scope of paragraph (3) of the Closing Protocol unclear: did it apply only to those means of mechanical reproduction that had been known in 1886 or did it extend to those which had become known after that date? This led to considerable controversy during the period from 1896 to 1908 as the gramophone industry became firmly established.[25] National responses to the claims of musical copyright owners varied, but the courts of some countries began to accord protection to copyright owners.[26] At the same time, sentiment in favour of a compulsory licensing solution to accommodate the interests of manufacturers began to grow.[27] Thus, Germany proposed the adoption of such a system into the Berne Convention at the Berlin Revision Conference.[28] There was general agreement among the delegates on the need to recognize mechanical reproduction rights, except for the Swiss who wished to retain paragraph (3) unchanged.[29] However, the latter finally consented to a new provision, article 13(1), which declared:

> (1) The authors of musical works shall have the exclusive right of authorising (1) the adaptation of these works to instruments which can reproduce them mechanically . . .[30]

The use of the word 'adaptation' may appear out of place here, at least in the light of the meaning that came to be attached to it in later versions of the Convention. 'Adaptation' in this later sense refers to the making of a derivative work which, without affecting the rights subsisting in the original work itself, constitutes a new work in its own right. In consequence, this was an inappropriate word to use in relation to a reproduction of a work which occurred through a

[21] *Actes* 1896, 176. [22] ibid.

[23] For a succinct summary of these national differences, see Briggs (1906), 407–13. See also [1895] *DA* 5.

[24] *Actes* 1896, 176.

[25] See generally 'État actuel de la question des instruments de musique mécaniques' [1908] *DA* 107.

[26] Notably in France and Belgium: see ibid, 108ff.

[27] See Briggs (1906), 420–1. See also [1899] *DA* 128 (suggested scheme for payment of obligatory royalties which was proposed in Germany).

[28] *Actes* 1908, 54. [29] ibid, 259 (report of general commission). [30] ibid, 260.

particular technical process without resulting in the creation of a derivative work that was then entitled to protection under the Convention. The reason for this misuse of the term 'adaptation' was that, at the time of the Berlin Revision, its meaning had not been properly settled, and the confusion was not eliminated until the Brussels Revision (see para 11.33 below).

The new right recognized in article 13(1) of the Berlin Act was also subject to limitations which reflected the strong vested interests that had rapidly emerged in the preceding decade or so.[31] Paragraph (2) permitted reservations and conditions relative to it to be imposed under national legislation, while paragraph (3) stipulated that it was not retroactive and was inapplicable in any Union country to works which had been lawfully adapted in that country prior to its coming into force. The effect of these provisions is discussed below (see paras 13.59ff), but it will be seen that they represented concessions which were made to the user interests that had developed under the 'free' legal regime that had previously prevailed. In particular, they permitted the adoption of compulsory licensing schemes under which record manufacturers might continue to make their recordings of musical works, subject to the payment to the author of suitable royalties. A final provision (paragraph (4)) dealt with the seizure of lawfully made 'adaptations' which were imported into countries where they would not be lawful (this is also discussed further at para 11.33 below). **11.09**

(ii) **Recording of literary works:** It will be noted that article 13(1) of the Berlin Act spoke only of musical works. However, it was obvious from the start that words could be as equally well reproduced mechanically as music, whether on their own or together with a musical work. At the Berlin Revision, the *rapporteur*, Louis Renault, referred expressly to this point in presenting the report of the general commission. Renault stated at length his view (and presumably that of the commission) that the new article applied only to musical works.[32] This was because it replaced paragraph (3) of the Closing Protocol of the Berne Act which, in turn, had dealt only with 'musical airs'. Renault's opinion was that this had not included the recording of accompanying words or words alone, and that this continued to be the case under the new provision.[33] His deduction from this, however, was more contentious. This was that the reservations permitted under article 13(1) in relation to musical works were, in effect, a concession that had been made to accommodate a particular interest (that of record manufacturers) and that this left the recording of literary works to be dealt with under the general principles of the Convention. Thus, any Union country which sought to apply to such works reservations or conditions **11.10**

[31] ibid, 260–2. [32] ibid, 263–4. [33] ibid.

of the kind permitted under article 13 would be violating the Convention. In other words, he assumed that the Convention implicitly required Union members to protect reproduction rights generally and that this included mechanical reproduction rights in relation to literary works which were not subject to the provisions of article 13.[34] There is logical force in this argument (see para 11.03 above), but it can also be argued that general reproduction rights were only protected under the Convention to the extent allowed under national laws through the application of the principle of national treatment. If this were so, then Union members were free to deal with mechanical reproduction rights in relation to literary works as they wished: they could recognize or deny them altogether or could make them subject to any restriction without contravening the Convention.[35] In the face of these conflicting interpretations, it is permissible to refer to the preparatory work for the Berlin Act for guidance as to which is the correct view and, in this regard, the opinion of Renault (and the commission) is clearly of considerable persuasive force. However, another influential guide is state practice, and in the years following the Berlin Revision a number of states indicated their preference for the second view by imposing reservations and restrictions on the exercise of mechanical reproduction rights in relation to literary works (the words of songs) as well as musical works.[36] This must therefore override the 'Renault view': as one commentator notes, it cannot be assumed that Union members would systematically breach the Convention.[37] Nevertheless, conflicting views on the matter were held by Union members (see below), and the need for the Convention to contain a clear provision dealing with it was clear.

11.11 **(iii) Changes made at Rome and Brussels:** Article 13(1) was left unchanged in the Rome Revision, although there was a French amendment which proposed its extension to all works protected by the Convention.[38] This would have overcome the problem described in the preceding paragraph, but the French delegation did not press its proposal.[39] The same thing also happened with a Norwegian proposal to replace the word 'adaptation' by 'making' ('*confection*').[40] This was resurrected in a slightly altered form by the International Office in its programme for the Brussels Revision, and the word 'recording' ('*l'enregistrement*') was proposed. Article 13(1) therefore now provided that authors of musical works should have the exclusive right of authorizing 'the

34 *Actes* 1908, 263–4. 35 See here Baum (1949), 56ff.

36 See eg Law of 22 May 1910, amending Law of 1901, art 22 (Germany); Copyright Act 1911 (UK), s 19; Law of 7 Dec 1922, art 18 (Switzerland). See further [1927] *DA* 137, 138.

37 Baum (1949), 57. 38 *Actes* 1928, 262.

39 Report of the British delegates to the Rome Conference: Public Record Office, FO371/13444.

40 *Actes* 1928, 261.

recording of such works by instruments capable of reproducing them mechanically'.[41] There was also a supplementary proposal by the Belgian Government which took the view that in some instances it was still necessary to 'adapt' musical works for the purposes of recording—in the sense of creating an independent derivative work—and that reference to this should be included in article 13(1).[42] The addition of the words 'or any adaptation of such works to these instruments' to the programme amendment was therefore proposed.[43] However, the latter phrase hardly seemed necessary: if such adaptations were entitled to protection in their own right, they would be entitled also to mechanical reproduction rights under article 13(1), but this would not affect the rights of the owner of the original work in relation to that adaptation. To use 'adaptation' in the sense suggested by the Belgian Government might therefore cause unnecessary confusion. This was the view taken by a sub-committee of the Conference on radiodiffusion and mechanical rights, and the Belgian wording was therefore deleted from the final draft adopted by the Conference.[44]

(iv) The renewed debate over words: The more important issue considered by the Conference in relation to article 13(1) was whether this should also extend to words that were recorded mechanically. Two main amendments were proposed here. The first was a British proposal for a new paragraph to be added to article 13 which would provide 'that for the purposes of this article a musical work shall be considered as including any work which combines music and text in such a manner that the two elements together form the work'.[45] This was in accordance with the then British law, as well as the laws of several other Union countries.[46] In stark contrast to this was the proposal of the International Office for a new article 13*bis* as follows: **11.12**

> Authors of literary works have the same exclusive rights as those accorded by paragraph 1 of the preceding Article to authors of musical works. The provisions of paragraphs 3 and 4 of the preceding article are applicable to literary works which have been recorded on instruments serving to reproduce them mechanically.[47]

This excluded literary works from the operation of article 13(2), meaning that national legislation would be unable to apply any reservations and conditions that were applicable in the case of musical works. This seemed unrealistic, as a great part of the musical works recorded were combined with literary works in

[41] *Documents 1948* (1951), 322. See also the preliminary proposals for the Brussels Conference in [1934] *DA* 7, 8.

[42] *Documents 1948* (1951), 320. Cf the view expressed in [1934] *DA* 8.

[43] *Documents 1948* (1951), 322.

[44] ibid, 117, 338. See also Baum (1949), 44.

[45] *Documents 1948* (1951), 323.

[46] See n 36 above.

[47] *Documents 1948* (1951), 339–40. See also [1934] *DA* 13–14 (preliminary proposals).

the form of words. Their exclusion therefore would have led, in the words of one commentator, to 'catastrophic consequences' for the recording industry, as the latter might be forced to pay extortionately high fees for permission to use the words of a particular song.[48] This view was shared by a number of delegations which sought to make article 13(2) applicable to the recording of literary works, at least in the situation where they were combined or 'mixed' with a musical work.[49] This was the effect of the British amendment set out above, and was also reflected in a proposal by the International Federation of the Phonographic Industry which suggested that article 13*bis* should only apply to literary works which were not connected with musical works.[50] This view prevailed in the sub-committee on radiodiffusion and mechanical reproduction rights, which, by a large majority (twelve to two), proposed the following redraft of article 13*bis*:

> (1) The authors of literary works have the same exclusive rights as those accorded by the first paragraph of the preceding article to the authors of musical works.
> (2) Nevertheless when a work consists of words and music which are an inseparable unit, paragraph 2 of the preceding article is also applicable to the literary work.[51]

The phrase 'inseparable unit' in paragraph (2) was not a happy choice as it deprived the exception provided for in that paragraph of any practical force: it is always possible to separate the words of a song from their musical accompaniment and vice versa, and it therefore becomes meaningless to speak of them as an 'inseparable unit'. However, the clear intention of the sub-committee had been to bring these kinds of 'mixed works' within the scope of paragraph (2), and, at the suggestion of the British and Swiss delegations, a more suitable form of wording was adopted by the general commission of the Conference:

> Nevertheless, when a work consists of words and music, paragraph 2 of the preceding article is applicable also to the words.[52]

This phrase met with implacable opposition from the French delegation, and the ensuing discussions showed clearly the fundamental differences between the delegations on the existence of general reproduction rights under the Convention. The French view was based squarely on that expressed by Renault for the general commission at the Berlin Conference.[53] It was therefore argued that, if the proposed article 13*bis* was adopted, it would permit the imposition of compulsory licences in relation to the recording of literary works where these were

[48] Baum (1949), 54.

[49] See eg the proposal by Germany: *Documents 1948* (1951), 324; Austria: ibid, 340; and Switzerland: ibid, 341.

[50] Referred to by Baum (1949), 55.

[51] *Documents 1948* (1951), 120.

[52] ibid, 343.

[53] ibid, 343–4.

combined with musical works and that this would be a derogation from rights which had already been unconditionally recognized (albeit by implication) under the Convention.[54] The opposite view was taken by the majority of delegations, in particular the British.[55] According to this view, article 13*bis* was a positive advance because it gave recognition for the first time to mechanical reproduction rights in relation to literary works. The scope for compulsory licences in relation to 'mixed works' was therefore not a derogation from previously accorded rights, but was an improvement on the prior position under which national laws had been free to place whatever restrictions they thought fit in relation to mechanical reproduction or to deny protection altogether to such rights.

In the general commission an attempt at reconciling these conflicting views was made by the Director of the International Office (Bénigne Mentha). While acknowledging the authority of Renault's report, he said that it needed to be recognized that, despite its authenticity, this interpretation had not been allowed by a certain number of states. He therefore asked whether, in these circumstances, 'it would not be better to consent to a certain move backwards in protection to be on the safe side, and suggested to the French delegation that it should consider this aspect of the question'.[56] This was unacceptable to the latter which refused to abandon what it regarded as the 'authentic interpretation' of the Convention.[57] As a result, article 13*bis* was rejected, and the Brussels Act contained no reference to the mechanical reproduction of literary works. Union countries therefore remained free, despite the French insistence on the authenticity of their interpretation, to apply the contrary interpretation and adopt whatever regime they desired in relation to this matter. In consequence, authors of literary works were left more at risk than they would have been had article 13*bis* been adopted. **11.13**

(v) **Cinematographic reproduction**: The cinematographic film did not become commercially feasible until almost a decade after the coming into force of the original Berne Act.[58] Nevertheless, once this happened the potential for the cinematographic reproduction of literary and dramatic works soon became apparent. Although films were at this time 'silent', they could still depict, with considerable precision, the events and characters contained in a novel or play. This new threat to the interests of authors was soon acknowledged by the French tribunals which were prepared to hold such films to be infringements of **11.14**

[54] ibid. [55] ibid; see further the account of the debate in Baum (1949), 54–8.
[56] *Documents 1948* (1951), 344. [57] ibid.
[58] See generally K Brownlow and J Kobal, *Hollywood: The Pioneers* (1979), chs 1–5.

the author's right under the Law of 19 to 24 July 1793.[59] Accordingly, at the Berlin Revision Conference the French delegation proposed the insertion of a similar provision in the Convention itself.[60] This was accepted by the other delegations, and a separate article (article 14(1)) was adopted which conferred on authors of literary, scientific, and artistic works the exclusive rights of authorizing the reproduction and public presentation of their works by means of cinematography. An alternative way of proceeding would have been to include cinematographic reproductions in the list of indirect unlawful reproductions in article 12, but it was thought that a separate article was justified because of the importance of those reproductions and that this would 'be more convenient for the persons concerned who have not necessarily penetrated the depths of our subject'.[61] In recognition of the fact that this was an area where further technological advance was inevitable, it was also stipulated that this provision should apply equally to 'reproduction . . . effected by any other process analogous to cinematography'[62] (as to the interpretation of this, see para 8.39 above).

11.15 (vi) **Translation**: This was the first right recognized in the Berne Convention, and was probably the most important factor which drew states into international copyright agreements in the late nineteenth century.[63] It was '*la question internationale par excellence*', as translation was really the only international means of reproduction in the case of books.[64] It was clearly conceived of as a form of reproduction, but was recognized only in a limited form in the Berne Act. Under article 5 of that Act, an exclusive right of making or authorizing translations of their works by authors entitled to protection under the Convention was granted for a period of ten years from publication of the original in one of the countries of the Union. In the case of works published in incomplete parts ('*livraisons*'), this period commenced from the date of publication of the last part, but works composed of several volumes published at intervals and the bulletins or collections published by literary or scientific societies or by private persons were considered as separate works with regard to this period. This provision was the result of compromises that were made between strongly conflicting views: those delegations, such as France, which favoured the complete assimilation of the translation right to reproduction rights in general,[65] and those with less developed literary and artistic traditions of their own, such as Norway, which wanted to have ready access to foreign works and therefore wished to limit its duration.[66] A particular argument that was urged in favour of

[59] Tribunal civil de la Seine (première chambre), 7 July 1908, noted in [1908] *DA* 118, and discussed by Renault in his report to the Berlin Conference in *Actes* 1908, 264–5.
[60] *Actes* 1908, 190, 292. [61] ibid, 265 (report of Renault).
[62] ibid, 266. [63] See generally Chapter 1 above.
[64] *Actes* 1896, 168 (report of Renault). [65] *Actes* 1884, 47–8; *Actes* 1885, 26ff.
[66] ibid, see further [1893] *DA* 103, 135, and 148; and [1895] *DA* 70.

protecting translation rights was that this would allow authors to ensure the accuracy and quality of translations, and that there was no guarantee of this where translations of foreign works might be made by anyone.[67] Article 5 was also a transitional provision, as was made clear by a resolution of the Conference which supported complete assimilation in the future.[68] This was not achieved at the Paris Conference, as there was still opposition from several member states,[69] but article 5 was significantly modified. Translation rights were now accorded to authors for the entire term of their rights over the original work, but this was subject to the condition that, within ten years of the publication of the original work, an authorized translation in the language for which protection was claimed was published.[70] The effect of this was that, for a period of ten years from first publication of the original work, authors were protected in respect of translations that might be made of their work; after this time, protection only applied in respect of translations into those languages in which an authorized translation had been published in that ten-year period. Once again, this provision was envisaged as being of a transitional character—in fact, it was drafted in such a way that the condition relating to publication within ten years could be readily severed at a subsequent revision so as to leave intact a completely assimilated right.[71] However, it was possibly more difficult to apply in practice than article 5 of the Berne Act. Under the latter, any work could be freely translated after ten years of its original publication; under the Paris Additional Act, a would-be translator had first to ascertain if an authorized translation had been published within this period, because, if this had happened, the author had protection for that translation throughout the whole term of his copyright. By 1903, seven Union countries granted translation rights on a more generous basis than that provided for in the Paris Additional Act.[72] Most of these countries in fact assimilated translation rights completely to reproduction rights, and the question which then arose was whether foreign authors were to be accorded similar treatment by virtue of the principle of national treatment or whether they were only entitled to claim the rights guaranteed under the Paris Additional Act.[73] In the other countries of the Union, national laws either accorded protection on the same basis as provided under the Paris Act[74] or did so at a lesser level,[75] with the result that authors claiming under the Convention in such countries were entitled to a higher level of protection than were the national authors of those countries.

[67] ibid, 48 (comments of Lavollée of France). [68] ibid, 89.
[69] *Actes* 1896, 168–9 (report of Renault). [70] ibid, 169. [71] ibid.
[72] These were Germany, Spain, Belgium, France, Haiti, Monaco, and Tunisia: see the national survey of translation rights in [1903] *DA* 18ff.
[73] ibid. [74] These were the UK, Japan, and Luxembourg: ibid.
[75] These were Italy and Switzerland: ibid.

11.16 Complete assimilation occurred at the Berlin Revision in 1908. There was now general support among all Union members except Japan (see below), and this included 'user' countries such as Norway which had been reluctant to accept assimilation at the earlier conferences.[76] The new right was now contained in article 8 of the Berlin Act which provided:

> The authors of unpublished works, being subjects of one of the countries of the Union, and the authors of works first published in one of those countries, shall enjoy, in the other countries of the Union, during the whole term of the right in the original work, the exclusive right of making or authorizing a translation of their works.

It will be seen that the categories of persons entitled to protection under this provision were the same as the principal categories of persons entitled generally to claim protection under the Convention: see articles 4 to 6. However, there was an omission as regards authors of works which were published simultaneously in both a Union and a non-Union country: these were covered by article 4, but there was no reference to this category of authors in the new article 8. It will also be noted that article 8 referred to 'the whole of the term of the right in the original work', without specifying what was meant by the term 'right'. This would seem to be a reference to the general reproduction right in the original work, but it will be recalled that this was not yet expressly recognized in the Convention. However, if 'right' was taken as meaning the sum of authors' rights granted expressly under the Convention, under the Berlin Act, these included only mechanical reproduction and cinematographic rights. The effect of article 8 therefore was that the duration of the translation right would be the same as for these other rights.

11.17 Although accepted almost unanimously, hesitations concerning the new article were sounded by two important countries which were observers at the Berlin Conference: the Netherlands and Russia.[77] These countries indicated that too strict a rule with respect to translations might delay their accession to the Union.[78] In the event, the Dutch joined the Union four years later, but with a reservation concerning translation rights,[79] and the Russians did not join at all.[80] Opposition to the proposed change came also from an existing member, Japan,

---

[76] *Actes* 1908, 245ff (report of Renault). See further the commentary in [1912] *DA* 45, 63.

[77] Fifty years earlier at the first congress of ALAI (under the presidency of Victor Hugo), the Russian author Turgenev had expressed similar ambivalence about translation rights, arguing for periods only of ten years for books and four years for dramatic works: Societé des gens de letters de France, *Congrès littéraire internationale de Paris 1878, Comptes rendus in extenso et docuuments* (1879), 330–1.

[78] *Actes* 1908, 247. [79] 1 Nov 1912: [1912] *DA* 146.

[80] It was not until 1995 that the Russian Federation, the successor in part of the previous Russian Empire and Soviet Union, joined the Berne Convention: www.wipo.int.

which sought the following amendment to take account of their country's particular needs in relation to readily available translations of European works: 'The translation in Japanese of a work written in a European language and reciprocally is completely free.'[81] In support, it was urged that this was necessary as a means of opening up communications between Europe and Japan with their different modes of thought and different perspectives, and that this would be of ultimate value to the nations of Europe as translations of Japanese works became increasingly available.[82] This proposal was politely, but firmly, rejected by the general commission, which, in its report, spoke of the need to ensure the accuracy of translations, asserting that this could only be achieved when full translation rights were accorded to authors.[83] The result was that Japan, like the Netherlands, made a reservation with respect to article 8 when it ratified the new Act.[84] A number of other states made similar reservations when ratifying or acceding to the new Act. By the time of the Rome Conference, five countries had declared that they would adopt or maintain (as the case may be) the provisions of article 5 of the Berne Act, as modified by the Paris Act: Estonia, Ireland, Italy, Japan, and the Netherlands.[85] A sixth country, Greece, had declared itself bound by article 5 of the Berne Act alone.[86] It will be recalled that one of the principal aims of the Rome Revision was to suppress, or at least limit, the reservations system.[87] Nevertheless, it was recognized, with respect to translations, that the ability to make free translations was of considerable value to less developed countries.[88] Indeed, there was a proposal from the Irish delegation that article 8 should be amended so as to permit national legislation to provide for compulsory licences for translations where an author unreasonably permitted a translation to be made of a work which was in circulation in its country of origin.[89] Safeguards were proposed for the protection of moral rights, but the amendment was forty years ahead of its time (see Chapter 10 above) and was not proceeded with.[90] As for the reservations system itself, this was only partially suppressed at the Rome Revision: Union members were allowed to retain the benefit of reservations already made,[91] and new members were permitted to substitute, 'provisionally at least', for article 8 the provisions of article 5 of the Berne Act revised at Paris 'on the understanding that those provisions shall apply only to translations into the language or languages of that country'.[92] Two

[81] [1912] *DA* 146.
[82] See the Japanese memorandum in support of their proposal: ibid, 201–3.
[83] ibid, 247–8. [84] 9 Sept 1910: [1910] *DA* 86.
[85] See the summaries in *Actes* 1928, 11–12. [86] ibid.
[87] See here the opening comments of the Italian Government and the International Office in the official programme: ibid, 62–3.
[88] ibid, 246 (résumé of propositions and discussions). [89] ibid. [90] ibid.
[91] Rome Act, art 27(2). See further *Actes* 1928, 277–8.
[92] Rome Act 1928, art 25(3). See further *Actes* 1928, 275–6.

nations made reservations pursuant to this provision when they acceded to the Rome Act: Iceland[93] and Yugoslavia.[94] Another nation, Thailand, which acceded to the Convention after 1928, was able, because of time limits, to sign the Berlin Act and to make a wider reservation in accordance with that Act.[95] However, an attempt by Turkey in 1931 to accede to the Rome Act with a reservation in relation to translation rights which was wider than that permitted under the Act was ultimately ineffective,[96] and Turkey remained outside the Union for another twenty years.[97] Finally, Italy and the Netherlands, which had previously maintained reservations under the Berlin Act, abandoned these upon ratification of the Rome Act.[98]

11.18 In the Brussels Revision, the only changes made to article 8 were in relation to the gap referred to above, that is, to bring within its scope authors of works simultaneously published in a Union and a non-Union country. This was done by beginning the article with the more general opening words: 'The authors who are accorded the benefit of protection accorded by the present Convention have the exclusive right . . .'.[99] A proposal to add a new paragraph allowing national laws to make exceptions in relation to translations of laws, decrees, and other official documents was rejected as being superfluous in view of the provisions of article 2(2).[100] Finally, there was a Hungarian amendment embodying a requirement that where a work was translated the title of the work in its original language should be displayed in some prominent place on the translation. It was also proposed that a similar requirement should be observed where a translation of a work was performed or presented by means of cinematography.[101] It appears that the Hungarian delegation saw this proposal as a means of better protecting the moral interests of authors.[102] However, the Conference took the view that this amendment was inappropriate to the subject matter of article 8 and should either be dealt with contractually or in the context of article 6*bis*. Accordingly, the Hungarian delegation withdrew its proposal.[103]

---

[93] 7 Sept 1947: [1947] *DA* 85 ('. . . in respect of the exclusive right of translation into the Icelandic language').

[94] 1 Aug 1931: [1930] *DA* 85 ('. . . in respect of the exclusive right of translation into the national languages of Yugoslavia').

[95] 17 July 1931: [1931] *DA* 85 (under art 28(3) countries were entitled to accede to either the Berlin or Rome Acts up to 1 Aug 1931, but thereafter could only accede to the Rome Act).

[96] See [1931] *DA* 74 for Turkey's purported accession to the Berlin Act. This is discussed further at para 17.18 below.

[97] Turkey adhered to the Brussels Act on 1 Jan 1952: [1951] *DA* 133 (with a permitted reservation 'with respect to the translations into the Turkish language').

[98] Both countries acceded on 1 Aug 1931: [1931] *DA* 73 and 96.

[99] *Documents 1948* (1951), 227. [100] ibid, 223, 226.

[101] ibid, 225–6. [102] ibid, 226.

[103] ibid, 227 (comments by British delegation).

(2) The 1967–71 Stockholm, Paris Acts

(a) The basic right

(i) The Stockholm Revision: In the preparations for this Conference, the Study Group felt initially that the chances of success of a renewed proposal for a general right of reproduction were doubtful.[104] However, after further consideration the Group felt that it was anomalous that the Convention did not recognize this 'fundamental prerogative',[105] and accordingly it proposed the following provision (to be article 9(1)): **11.19**

> (1) Authors of literary and artistic works protected by this Convention shall have the exclusive right of authorizing the reproduction of their works, in any manner or form.

The real problem with this proposal lay not with the proposition that there should be a general right of reproduction, but with the formulation of the exceptions that should be made to it. This occasioned considerable debate among the experts that assisted in the preparations of the Conference programme as well as at the Conference itself.[106] Some delegates saw the proposed amendment as unnecessary, arguing that the adoption of a necessarily general definition of reproduction might weaken the protection accorded under the Brussels text.[107] Other delegates stressed the care that would be required in the drafting of exceptions, so as to avoid undermining the new right.[108] However, there was general agreement that it should be included,[109] and several proposals were made as to the way in which this should be done. An Austrian amendment proposed that the new provision should define reproduction as 'the material fixation of the work by all methods that permit of indirect communication to the public', and that this should be supplemented by a list of examples of the ways in which it could be accomplished:

> . . . in particular, by printing, drawing, engraving, photographing, carting [*sic*], and all processes of the graphic and plastic arts, and by mechanical, cinematographic, or magnetic recording. In the case of architectural works, reproduction shall also consist in the repeated execution of a plan or standard draft.[110]

---

104 *Records* 1967, vol I, 111 (Document S/1). 105 ibid, 113.

106 ibid, 111–13 (Document S/1), vol II, 851ff (minutes of Main Committee I).

107 See eg the comments of the Portuguese and Brazilian delegates: ibid, 851–2. To similar effect, see P Recht, 'Should the Berne Convention Include a Definition of the Right of Reproduction?' [1965] *Copyright* 82.

108 See eg the comments of Kéréver of France: *Records* 1967, vol II, 852.

109 The proposal for adoption of the right of reproduction in the text of the Convention was approved by thirty-two votes to five, with three abstentions: ibid.

110 Document S/38: ibid, 683.

There were two main reasons adduced in support of this amendment: first, to make it clear that the notion of reproduction did not include performances of a work, and secondly to remove any doubt that reproduction by means of recorded sounds and images were included within the scope of the general right.[111] There was agreement in Main Committee I on the first of these points, but there was a reluctance to define the new right too closely and it was left to the report to state clearly that reproduction was distinct from performance.[112] As to the second, it was thought that a list of examples would also be inappropriate for inclusion in the Convention, but that it should be expressly stated that sound and image recording was a form of reproduction.[113] This was done in a new paragraph which became article 9(3) (see above). The adoption of this new provision had the effect that it was no longer necessary for article 13(1) to refer to the author's exclusive right of sound recording. Accordingly, this was deleted, and article 13 henceforth dealt only with the limitations that could be imposed on this right (see 13.62 below).[114] Although it would have been logical to make similar changes in relation to translations, adaptations, and cinematographic reproductions (articles 8, 12, and 13), these provisions were left unchanged. There was also a significant amendment proposed by the UK, which casts further light on the application of the new article 9(1), as well as the other provisions of the Convention which contain the exclusive rights of authors. This was a proposal to add the words 'or any substantial part thereof' to article 9(1).[115] This was consistent with the formulation of rights under British law,[116] but was later withdrawn by the UK delegation for two reasons of relevance to the interpretation of the Convention. The first was that the rights recognized by the Convention applied, by definition, to the whole of a work, or to its various parts, and therefore that the proposed amendment was unnecessary.[117] While this may appear to be a statement of the obvious, there is no reference in the Convention to parts of works, and the opinion of Main Committee I on this point, as expressed in its report, is therefore of great weight as an authentic interpretation of article 9 and the other provisions of the Convention under which rights are conferred on authors. The second reason for not adopting the British proposal was the more immediate one that, as none of the relevant articles referred to a substantial part, to mention it solely with respect to the right of reproduction might give rise to an argument *a contrario* with respect to other rights.[118] As a result, the Conference finally adopted article 9(1)

[111] Document S/38: *Records* 1967, vol II, 851 (Dittrich, Austrian delegate).

[112] ibid, 852–3 (minutes of Main Committee I), 1144 (report of Main Committee I).

[113] ibid, 852–3.

[114] ibid, 1169–70 (report of Main Committee I).

[115] Document S/42: *Records* 1967, 687.

[116] Copyright Act 1956 (UK), s 49(1).

[117] *Records* 1967, vol II, 852 (comments of Professor Ulmer, chairman of Main Committee I), 1144 (report of Main Committee I).

[118] ibid, 852 (Professor Ulmer).

in the same form as proposed in the programme, together with the new paragraph (3).

(ii) Right to make collections of speeches, addresses, etc: This right has been in the Convention since the Rome Act (see para 8.16 above), although it seems strictly incorrect to describe it as a separate exclusive right of the author. Rather, it acts as a limitation on the discretion that is left to national legislation to limit the rights of authors in their speeches, addresses, etc, under article 2*bis*(1) and (2) (see also paras 13.55ff below). The rights which may be abridged under these provisions are, in fact, the author's reproduction rights. In consequence, the 'collection' right now contained in article 2*bis*(3) of the Paris Act is a reservation, to the author, of his right of reproduction in relation to those kinds of works where he wishes to reproduce them in the form of a collection. **11.20**

(b) Reproduction in other forms: mechanical, cinematographic, and translations

(i) Mechanical rights: The conflicting views described above (see paras 11.07ff above), finally became irrelevant with the recognition of a general right of reproduction in article 9(1) of the Stockholm Act. Article 13(1) no longer referred to the right of mechanical reproduction or recording, but only to the reservations and conditions, such as compulsory licences, that might be made to this right. Mechanical reproduction rights were now comprehended within the general right of reproduction (see article 9(3)), and this included the recording of literary as well as musical works. Thus, article 13(1) was amended at the same time to allow compulsory licensing in relation to words as well as music; such a provision would have been unnecessary if it had not been clear that the recording of literary works was now expressly covered by the Convention.[119] (The scope and effect of the compulsory licences that may be imposed by national laws under article 13(1) are discussed further at para 13.63 below.) **11.21**

(ii) Scope of the mechanical recording right under the Paris Act: There is no longer any reference to the concept of 'mechanical reproduction' in the Paris Act, and this is probably just as well. It is a term which was appropriate in 1886 when the principal kinds of devices in which musical works could be fixed were of a mechanical nature: music boxes and clocks, Barbary organs, and the like. But it soon became unsuited to the more sophisticated modes of fixation that came into existence with the development of the gramophone industry. In this respect, the words 'sound recording' in article 9(3) are more appropriate, and are able to cover any mode of recording of the sounds of a musical or literary work, including discs, tapes, laser readable records, digital files, and so on. **11.22**

[119] ibid, 1169–70.

11.23 (iii) **Recording of pre-existing works into cinematographic format (cinematic reproduction)**: The right of cinematographic reproduction has been retained in succeeding versions of the Convention, with the following changes. At the Stockholm Revision, the adjective 'scientific' was deleted, on the ground that it was unnecessary in view of the general definition of literary and artistic works in article 2(1) as including 'every production in the literary, scientific and artistic domain'.[120] Further rights have also been added to article 14(1): the right of adaptation in the Rome Revision[121] and that of distribution of the works adapted or reproduced at the Brussels Revision.[122] On the other hand, no attempt was made at Stockholm to amend article 14(1) in the same way as article 13(1), so as to bring cinematographic reproductions squarely within the scope of the new general reproduction right. Nonetheless, article 9(3) states that 'visual recordings' are to be regarded as reproductions for the purposes of the Convention. A 'visual recording' must be the same as a 'reproduction by means of cinematography' under article 14(1): it is hard to imagine anything that might fall within the scope of the second that did not also come within the scope of the first, particularly as it is clear that cinematography, for the purposes of the Paris Act, includes newer means of fixation of images such as videotaping.[123] In the absence of any contrary provision, it could be readily argued that a cinematographic film which incorporated sounds could also be regarded as a sound recording, and therefore subject to the reservations and conditions permitted in relation to these under article 13(2). This result, however, is avoided by article 14(3). The general conclusion to be drawn, then, is that article 14(1), insofar as it refers to reproduction by means of cinematography is strictly unnecessary, but that it serves a useful purpose in making the existence of this right more explicit. A further question remains as to the meaning and scope of the right of cinematographic adaptation that has been in the Convention since the Rome Revision, and how this differs, if at all, from the right of cinematographic reproduction. This matter is discussed below under the general heading of 'adaptations' (see paras 11.28ff below), as is the further matter of distribution rights (see paras 11.40ff below).

11.24 (iv) **Adaptations of pre-existing works into cinematographic works; adaptations of cinematographic works into other kinds of works**: Under article 14(1), these are distinguished from reproduction by means of cinematography (and analogous processes) and are made the subject of a separate right. As noted above, these adaptations also enjoy performance and diffusion rights. This distinction was first made in the Rome Act, but without any clear explanation as to

[120] *Records* 1967, vol II, 865 (decision of Main Committee I).

[121] *Actes* 1928, 212.

[122] *Documents 1948* (1951), 361.

[123] See para 8.40. See further *Documents* 1967, vol II, 926 (minutes of Main Committee I).

why this was being done. However, the broad division between cinematographic reproductions and cinematographic adaptations would seem to be as follows: the first would be the fixation in film of a play, ballet or dramatico-musical work as it is actually performed, while the second would be the fixation of a work that has been specifically changed for the purpose of being embodied in film. It should also be noted that article 14(2) confers on the authors of original works a further adaptation right in relation to adaptations that are made from cinematographic productions that have been made from their works:

> (2) The adaptation into any other artistic form of a cinematographic production derived from literary or artistic works shall, without prejudice to the authorization of the author of the cinematographic production, remain subject to the authorization of the authors of the original works.

This was added, with slightly different wording, at the Brussels Revision, and was based on a French proposal.[124] Its effect is that if a person wishes to make a further adaptation of a cinematographic production, he must seek the approval of both the authors of the cinematographic work and the original work on which it is based. The words 'any other artistic form' do not seem to merit a restrictive interpretation, for example, a limitation to visual or purely 'artistic' forms of adaptation. This appears from the arguments of the French delegation which were put forward in support of their proposal.[125] Thus, the kinds of further adaptation that might be covered by the provision would include such acts as the making of another cinematographic work, the making of a stage play, and the writing of a novel. It should also be noted that a cinematographic work will usually be derived from several kinds of work, and that permission for a further adaptation will need to be sought from the authors of each of these, for example, the author of the dramatic work that constitutes the film script, the author of the musical work that constitutes the soundtrack, and the author of artistic works that may have been used in the sets for the film.

(v) **The present position with respect to translation rights**: No amendment to article 8(1) was proposed in the programme for the Stockholm Revision, and no change was made to it at that Conference. However, translation rights were the subject of serious discussion in relation to the needs of developing countries, and a special regime in relation to this was adopted and subsequently modified at the Paris Revision four years later. (These provisions are examined further in Chapter 14 below and no more will be said about them here.) Another matter **11.25**

[124] *Documents 1948* (1951), 352–4.

[125] ibid, 53 and 60. See also C Masouyé, *Guide to the Berne Convention for the Protection of Literary and Artistic Works* (1978) ('Masouyé (1978)'), 84. Note the view of Baum, however, that the amendment was not really necessary: Baum (1949), 63.

which concerned the Stockholm Conference in relation to translation rights was the exceptions that might be made to them under national legislation. (Again, this is dealt with in detail in para 13.83 below and will not concern us further here.)

(c) The scope of the present reproduction right

11.26 A fundamental question on which both article 9(1) and (3) fail to offer clear guidance is the actual meaning of the term 'reproduction'. In this regard, the Austrian amendment at the Stockholm Conference was of some assistance when it referred to 'all methods that permit of indirect communication [of the work] to the public'. But, as Professor Ulmer, the chairman of Main Committee I observed, this would not take account of such processes as photocopying for industrial purposes, that is, the making of fixations which did not result in the work being communicated to the public at all.[126] More generally, it is unclear how far the concept of reproduction extends into the area of plagiarism and borrowings that are far from literal copies of works. Some jurisdictions, for example, treat translations and adaptations separately from reproductions,[127] and this, indeed, is the case under the Convention itself.[128] Nevertheless, whether one treats adaptations and translations as forms of reproduction or not, the question still remains of the extent of authors' rights and, ultimately, what elements of their works are to be protected. Put another way, Berne does not dictate the standard for finding infringement. It does not instruct member states as to whether there is a threshold of substantiality that the defendant's copying must cross before it can be held liable. Nor does it indicate, if a member state imposes such a threshold, whether any substantiality standard encompasses qualitative as well as quantitative substantiality. Nor does it tell member states whether 'non-literal similarities', such as the close tracking of a play's plot without copying its dialogue, also come within the concept of reproduction. On the other hand, as discussed earlier (see paras 5.49ff above), the Berne Convention does implicitly incorporate the idea/expression dichotomy. As a result, a member state has no obligation to protect a foreign Berne author who complains that a local defendant has copied the ideas her work discloses.

11.27 With the exception of sound and visual recordings, another key aspect of the scope of the reproduction right under article 9(1) is not completely settled. This

[126] *Records* 1967, vol I, 852.

[127] See eg US Copyright Act, 17 USC § 106(1) (reproduction), (2) (derivative works); FRG Law of 1965, arts 3 and 23; Australia, Copyright Act 1968, s 31(1)(a)(i) and (vi); UK, Copyright, Designs and Patents Act 1988, ss 16(1)(a) (copying), 16(1)(e) (adaptation), 21(3)(a)(i) (an adaptation includes a translation); Congolese Law on Copyright and Neighbouring Rights of 7 July 1982, art 28.

[128] Paris Act, arts 8 (translations) and 12 (adaptations).

concerns the physical nature of the reproduction. It is clear from the minutes of Main Committee I and its report that fixation in some material form is required, so as to distinguish it from performances (see above), and the paragraph itself provides that this may be done in 'any manner or form'. The latter phrase is important, as it indicates how far we have come since the time that handmade or printed copies were the only feasible modes of reproduction. Any manner of fixing the work is now covered, although specific reference is made only to sound and visual records in paragraph (3). The need for the fixation to be in a material form, however, may give rise to different views where the form is invisible, as, for example, where the work is stored in a computer database. Some forms of storage such as CDs are similar to phonograph recordings, but others consist simply of a series of invisible electrical impulses. Accordingly, some national laws have expressly provided that the storage of works in these kinds of invisible forms are nonetheless to be regarded as material form.[129] It is open to debate whether the Berne Convention also requires member states to interpret 'any manner or form' to extend to transient digital fixations. (This is discussed in further detail at paras 11.69ff below in connection with the debate over the scope of the reproduction right in the 1996 WCT.)

C. Adaptations

(1) The development of a general principle of adaptation rights

There are differences in national laws as to whether adaptations and other transformations of works are to be regarded as forms of reproduction, or whether they are the subject of a separate right. For example, the first approach is to be found in French law,[130] whereas the second is to be found in US,[131] **11.28**

[129] See eg Copyright Act 1968 (Australia), s 10(1) (added by the Copyright Amendment Act 1984, s 3(g)). Under this, 'material form' is defined as including 'any form (whether visible or not) of storage from which the work or adaptation . . . can be reproduced'. See also the opinion of Professor E Ulmer, to this effect in a report presented to the Executive Committee of the Berne Union: E Ulmer, 'Copyright Problems Arising from the Computer Storage and Retrieval of Protected Works' [1972] *Copyright* 37, 53; approved by the Executive Committee at its meeting of 3–5 Nov 1921: [1972] *Copyright* 14, 15.

[130] France, Code de la propriété intellectuelle, art L 122-1 states the author's rights cover the rights of reproduction and of performance. Article L 122-3's general definition of reproduction is broad enough to cover adaptation, but does not specifically mention it; art L 122-4, however, specifies that any adaptation requires the author's consent; art L 112-3 provides for separate copyright in adaptations and translations). On the predecessor provision to L 122-1, Law of 1957, arts 26, 28, see further H Desbois, *Le droit d'auteur en France*, 3rd edn (1978) ('Desbois (1978)'), 292ff and 738ff.

[131] 17 USC § 106(2) (exclusive right 'to prepare derivative works based on the copyrighted work').

British,[132] and German law.[133] The second view also seems to prevail under the Paris Act, where adaptation is dealt with as a distinct right under article 12. However, this has not always been the case, and up to the Brussels Revision adaptations were dealt with as a species of reproduction. This raises the question of whether there is any practical difference between the two approaches, or whether they have the same effect. This necessitates an examination of the stages by which the present article 12 has been achieved (see also para 8.80 above).

(a) Background to article 12

11.29 Prior to the Berne Convention, several bilateral copyright conventions had prohibited adaptations, often under the more general heading of 'unauthorized indirect appropriations'. A good example was to be found in article 5 of the Franco-Italian Convention of 9 July 1884, which provided the following list of examples:

> . . . adaptations, imitations made in good faith, transcriptions or arrangements of musical, dramatico-musical or choreographic works, and generally all borrowings whatever from literary, dramatic, scientific or artistic works made without the consent of the author.[134]

Both the draft ALAI convention of 1883[135] and the Federal Council programme of 1884[136] also saw adaptation as a form of infringement which should be prevented under the new convention. However, neither document sought to define the term, and this led to extended discussions at the Conferences of 1884 and 1885. While delegates were generally agreed as to the need to protect authors against unauthorized adaptations of their works, there was a basic division of opinion between those who thought that the term should be defined in the Convention itself and those who thought that this was a matter which was better left for national courts to determine on a case-by-case basis.[137] The leading exponents of the first view were the French, who, at the 1884 Conference, proposed a general provision in the same terms as article 5 of the Franco-Italian Convention (see above), together with the following definition of 'adaptation':

> Adaptation is the disguising of a work, either by subtractions or changes in the text or its intention, or by developments that the original author had not foreseen, with the sole aim of appropriating the work, without appearing to translate or infringe.[138]

[132] See the Copyright, Designs and Patents Act 1988, s 16(1)(a) (copying), 16(1)(e) (adaptation).

[133] FRG Law of 1965, art 23, amended by Law of 22 July 1997.

[134] Convention between France and Italy, 9 July 1884: LCD, vol II, 303ff.

[135] ALAI draft convention, art 7: *Actes* 1884, 8.

[136] Federal Council programme, art 10: ibid, 12. [137] ibid, 57. [138] ibid.

However, after further discussion, the general commission concluded that it was impossible to lay down a definitive rule on this matter.[139] Only one specific form of adaptation was dealt with in the 1884 text: this was the right to make arrangements of musical works, but the application of this provision was left to national law.[140] Other kinds of adaptation were referred to more circumspectly in the Closing Protocol as follows:

> 3. The attention of the Plenipotentiaries has been drawn by several among them to the question whether some steps ought not to be taken to expressly prohibit certain categories of indirect unauthorized appropriation, and especially those that several Conventions in force designate by the name 'adaptation'.
>
> The Plenipotentiaries are agreed in recognizing that piracy comprises all kinds of illegal attempts against authors' rights, but they are of opinion that in place of enumerating and defining them it is preferable to leave to the responsible Tribunals the duty to determine in each special case, the prejudice resulting from any particular form of piracy.[141]

This statement hardly took matters much further—what, for instance, was meant by the statement that 'piracy comprises all kinds of illegal attempts against authors' rights'? Accordingly, at the 1885 Conference, the French delegation returned to its previous proposal that the Convention should contain a list of prohibited acts.[142] Once again this view was rejected by the commission, partly because of the difficulties perceived in arriving at a satisfactory definition of 'adaptation' and partly because of fears that the final part of the French proposal—'generally any borrowing from literary, dramatic, artistic or musical works without the consent of the author'—went too far, and would cut across the proposed right of citation in article 8.[143] However, an attempt was made to accommodate the French view by the adoption of a new article 10 which replaced both article 10 of the 1884 draft and paragraph 3 of the Closing Protocol. This was based on a Swedish proposal which made it clear that adaptations and associated acts were to be regarded as forms of illicit reproduction, but which refrained from any further definition of these terms:

> Specifically included amongst the illicit reproductions to which the present Convention applies are unauthorized indirect appropriations of a literary or artistic work, of various kinds known as *adaptations, arrangements of music*, &c., when they are only the reproduction of a particular work, in the same form, or in another form, with non-essential alterations, additions, or abridgements, without presenting the character of a new original work.

[139] ibid, 58. [140] ibid. [141] ibid, 63. [142] *Actes* 1885, 48.

[143] ibid, 49. The French proposal was supported by Haiti, Honduras, and Tunisia, besides France; those against it were Belgium, Spain, UK, Italy, Sweden, Norway, and Switzerland.

> It is agreed that, in the application of the present Article, the courts of the various countries of the Union will, if it be necessary, take account of the provisions of their respective laws.[144]

11.30 This was hardly satisfactory, particularly in view of the second paragraph which, in effect, allowed national legislation to impose any restriction or limitation that it wished. The concept of a 'musical arrangement' was, perhaps, tolerably clear—the arrangement of a musical work for performance by different instruments or voices. However, the concept 'adaptation' remained uncertain, apart from the words 'in the same form, or in another form'. In general usage, 'adaptation' infers the changing of a work so as to enable it to fulfil another purpose than that for which it was originally created. Obvious examples, 'in another form', are the transformations that are necessary to make a literary work suitable for dramatic presentation (a dramatization). On the other hand, an adaptation may equally occur 'in the same form' where a work is changed to meet the requirements of a different audience, for instance, the shortening of a novel for presentation in serial form in a magazine. The only specific guidance on these matters that is to be derived from the records of the 1885 Conference was that it was envisaged that article 10 should apply to 'dramatisations'.[145] This was a particular matter of concern to the French Government which thought that this 'informal' expression of opinion should be embodied in an 'authentic' interpretation appended to the new Convention. At the final Conference of 1886, it therefore proposed the adoption of a declaration, paragraph (4) of which provided as follows:

> Particularly included among the unauthorized indirect appropriations to which article 10 applies as illicit reproductions are dramatisations, that is the transformation of a novel into a theatrical piece, or vice versa.[146]

This proposal met opposition at the Conference, in particular from the Italian delegation who thought that paragraph (4) implied a modification to the text settled at the 1885 Conference to which it could not adhere.[147] In consequence, the French withdrew their proposal, and article 10 remained a provision of limited and uncertain scope—in the sense that one Union member, at least, did not interpret it as extending to dramatizations and novelizations. Italy, in fact, was not alone here, as the UK also adopted a similar view with respect to dramatizations (though not with respect to novelizations).[148] Article 10 was also

---

[144] *Actes* 1885, 49 (emphasis added). [145] ibid, 50. [146] *Actes* 1886, 16.

[147] ibid, there was also opposition from the British delegation, which explained that it had already had to make changes to its domestic law in order to adhere to the Convention and that the declaration in respect of dramatizations, albeit meritorious, would create further problems for it: ibid, 16–17 (H G Bergne).

[148] See n 147.

severely limited in another way, as it excluded from its scope those adaptations and other transformations of a work which resulted in the creation of a new and original work (a 'derivative work'). In truth, the words 'with non-essential alterations, additions, or abridgements' seemed to limit it to those reproductions which common law legal systems regard as 'colourable imitations'.[149]

Following the adoption of the Berne Act, the uncertainties regarding the treatment of dramatizations and novelizations under national laws became a particular point of concern to ALAI, and was the subject of resolutions passed by successive congresses of that organization.[150] The matter was again taken up by the French Government in its programme for the Paris Revision Conference in 1896. This contained a proposal to add the words 'transformations of a piece of theatre into a novel and *vice versa*' after the word 'adaptation' in article 10, together with the deletion of the second paragraph of that article.[151] This gained almost general support among the delegates,[152] and the view was expressed that this was simply a clarification of the existing position under the Convention, rather than an innovation.[153] This was not strictly correct, as it had been clear immediately prior to the Conference that at least one Union member, the UK, did not wholly share this view.[154] At the Conference itself, the British delegate opposed the French amendment, stating that this did not accord with British law, and that it did not feel able at this stage to adhere to this suggested change.[155] The French amendment was therefore relegated to the general Interpretative Declaration which was adopted by the Conference[156] and which was signed by all member states except for the UK.[157] Although not embodied in the Convention itself, this still represented an authentic interpretation of article 10, which had the further effect that British authors would be able to claim, in other Union countries, protection against unauthorized dramatizations of their novels, even though authors from these other countries might not be able to do the same in the UK. **11.31**

By the time of the Berlin Revision, the British opposition concerning dramatizations had disappeared; with some minor additions, these were now included in **11.32**

[149] See generally *Copinger and Skone James on Copyright*, 12th edn (1980), 185ff.

[150] See, in particular, the resolutions of the ALAI congresses at Berne 1899, London 1890, Neuchâtel 1891, and Milan 1892: *Actes* 1896, 62–3. See further the useful article on adaptations by H Rosmini in [1895] *DA* 21.

[151] [1895] *DA*, 43–4. [152] ibid, 117.

[153] The view of the German delegation: ibid, 172–3.

[154] See *Warne* v *Seebohm* (1888) 39 Ch D 73. See further Briggs (1906) 392–3.

[155] *Actes* 1896, 173 (report of general commission). On the other hand, it appeared that British law did grant protection against the transformation of a play into a novel: ibid, but cf Briggs (1906) 393.

[156] *Actes* 1896, 180.

[157] ibid, 233. See further on the application of the Interpretative Declaration: [1903] *DA* 62 and 74.

the list of unauthorized indirect reproductions appearing in article 10. Paragraph (2) was also deleted, on the ground that it was dangerous: even if a judge thought that a piece was taken from a novel or vice versa, national laws might still require him to hold to the contrary.[158] The new article, which became article 12 of the Berlin Act, read as follows:

> The following shall be especially included among the unlawful reproductions to which the present Convention applies: unauthorized indirect appropriations of a literary or artistic work, such as adaptations, musical arrangements, transformations of a novel, tale, or piece of poetry into a dramatic piece and *vice versa*, etc., when they are only the reproduction of that work, in the same form or in another form without essential alterations, additions, or abridgements, and do not present the character of a new original work.[159]

It will be seen that this provision still remained curiously divorced from the wide range of adaptations and other transformations that resulted in the creation of a new derivative work. The latter were now protected 'without prejudice to the rights of the author of the original work' under article 2(2) of the Berlin Act (see further para 8.87 above), but nothing in article 12 brought these kinds of adaptations, etc, within the scope of unlawful reproductions protected by the Convention. The reason for this lack of coherence may have been the conceptual confusion over the nature of adaptation rights that was to be found in national legislation. This confusion, in turn, was reflected in the list in article 12, where adaptations were enumerated separately from dramatizations and novelizations, although the latter were usually regarded as species of adaptation. This formulation left the meaning of 'adaptation' far from clear: it was a general term, whereas the other kinds of transformation appearing in the list were quite specific. As a result, the only firm requirements imposed under article 12 on Union countries related to the protection of musical arrangements, dramatizations, and novelizations. As far as adaptations were concerned, the content to be attached to this expression was left ultimately to national legislation to determine, and in this respect the deletion of paragraph (2) made no difference.

11.33 No attempt to correct these disparities was made at the Rome Revision, and article 12 was therefore retained unchanged in the Rome Act. However, the programme for the Brussels Revision contained a proposal for the addition of a new paragraph (to be article 12(1)) that was linked directly to article 2(2):

> (1) The authors of literary and artistic works enjoy the rights recognised by virtue of the present Convention not only for their original works but also for the transformation of those works dealt with in article 2(2).[160]

---

[158] *Actes* 1908, 258 (report of general commission). [159] ibid.
[160] *Documents 1948* (1951), 315.

This was a considerable extension to the scope of the existing article 12, as it now clearly comprehended the right to authorize the making of adaptations, etc, that were derivative works in their own right. As for 'non-original' adaptations and the like, these would be covered by the existing article 12 which was now to become article 12(2).[161] There was general support among delegates for this extension of the author's rights,[162] but the wording of the programme proposal gave rise to an important question that had not previously been relevant. This concerned the relationship between the rights of the author of the original work, and the rights of the author of the adaptation. The effect of the proposed article 12(1) appeared to be that the former would enjoy the same rights in relation to both the original work and the adaptation. Did this mean that the author of the original work was to succeed to all the rights that were conferred on the adapter of his work under article 2(2)? Alternatively, did it mean that two sets of rights were henceforth to be recognized in respect of an adaptation: those of the original author and those of the adapter? The consequence of this second view was that a third party wishing to utilize the adaptation by way of reproduction, performance, etc, would need to seek two permissions for that use. The wording of the programme proposal made the first interpretation at least arguable and, for this reason, the general commission adopted a different formulation which remains essentially the same in the present Act.[163] This was based on a British amendment and provided as follows:

> 12. The authors of literary, scientific or artistic works have the exclusive right of authorising adaptations, arrangements and other transformations of their works.[164]

This also replaced the previous article 12, which the programme had proposed to retain as article 12(2), but which the general commission decided to delete as being superfluous.[165] However, although considerably simplified, the new article 12 contained (and still contains) ambiguities. On its face, it only conferred on authors the right of adapting, arranging, or altering their works: it did not accord rights with respect to the further exploitation of those adaptations, arrangements, or alterations. Nevertheless, it is clear from the Conference records that a number of delegates at the Brussels Conference took the view that these further rights were conferred under this wording and were to be exercised concurrently with those of the author of the adaptation (see the second interpretation outlined above).[166]

[161] ibid. [162] ibid, 316ff. See also Baum (1949), 42.

[163] *Documents 1948* (1951), 318 (observations of British delegate). See also Baum (1949) 43.

[164] *Documents 1948* (1951), 319. [165] ibid.

[166] ibid, 318 (comments of French delegate) and 103 (report of general commission); see also Baum (1949) 43. Cf Desbois (1978) 740–1.

(2) The general right of adaptation in the Stockholm, Paris Acts

(a) Scope of the present article 12

11.34 The terms used in this provision are now the same as those used in article 2(3), and are more general than those which previously appeared in article 12: 'adaptations, arrangements and other alterations'. Each of these terms represents different ways in which an original work may be changed. While they overlap to a considerable degree, the following comments can be made about their scope. First, 'adaptation' refers to the rewriting or remodelling of a work into another form. The most prominent examples are dramatizations and novelizations. While these are no longer mentioned specifically in article 12, there is no reason to think that they are not still covered under the general heading of 'adaptations'. Other instances are the writing of a prose work in verse and vice versa, and the telling of a story in pictorial or cartoon form, and a number of national laws refer to these acts specifically.[167] Another kind of adaptation is the execution of an artistic work in another medium or dimension, but some national laws which distinguish between reproductions and adaptations treat this as a reproduction rather than an adaptation.[168]

Second, 'arrangements': under the previous texts, this word was qualified by the adjective 'musical'. Musical arrangements obviously continue to be covered by the more general term, but there is no reason why it should not cover the arrangements that are made of other works, for example, where a play is arranged for broadcast over radio or television. As the word 'adapted' can also be used to describe these kinds of alterations, both 'arrangement' and 'adaptation' overlap here.

Third, 'other alterations' is a residual category which catches all those other changes to a work that do not fit neatly into the preceding two categories. As suggested above (see para 8.81), this would include abridgements, parodies, burlesques, and caricatures. More generally, it would cover what are known in the journalistic and entertainment spheres as 'rewrites'. This is where an original work is rewritten or edited, with cuts, additions, and other modifications, but without any intention to adapt the work into another form or to suit another purpose.

All the above acts are comprehended within the scope of the composite expression 'adaptations, arrangements and other alterations'. However, it remains to

---

[167] See eg UK Copyright, Designs and Patents Act 1988, s 21(3)(a)(iii); Copyright Act 1978 (South Africa), s 1(1)(1)(iv).

[168] UK Copyright, Designs and Patents Act 1988, s 17(3) (copying in relation to artistic work includes making three-dimensional copies of two-dimensional works and vice versa); Copyright Act 1968 (Australia), s 21(3).

national legislation to determine the precise extent to which each will be covered. At the same time, it should be noted that there are two kinds of alteration that are not included within article 12. The first are translations, which are covered by article 8 and have been dealt with above (see para 11.15). The second are cinematographic adaptations (which were considered separately in para 11.24 above).

(b) Ambiguities concerning the respective scope of the reproduction and adaptation rights

11.35 As between the adapter and the author of the underlying work, what is the proper allocation of rights? Does the author of the underlying work succeed to any copyright interest flowing from the adaptation? Or does the author of the adaptation enjoy her own copyright in any adaptation which constitutes an original work of authorship? Even if she does, is not the exploitation of her copyright dependent on permission from the author of the underlying work, because the protection for the adaptation must be 'without prejudice' to the underlying work (see article 2(3) of the Berne Convention)? The answer must depend ultimately upon whether an adaptation is to be regarded as a form of reproduction. If this is so, then as a matter of logic, the author of an original work will always be able to prevent the exploitation of an adapted version of his work, for example, by reproduction or performance, because this will simply be an exploitation of the original work in its reproduced form. There seems no doubt that this is the case under some national laws, with the result that authors in these countries clearly enjoy, with respect to adaptations of their works, rights that are concurrent with those of the adapter.[169] On the other hand, if an adaptation is treated as something distinct from a reproduction, this result does not necessarily follow, unless power to control the further exploitation of the adaptation of his work is conferred, either expressly or implicitly, upon the author of the original work. This, in fact, is the case in British and US copyright laws, where separate rights in respect of adaptations of their works are accorded to authors;[170] the same is also true of the law of Germany.[171] If these different views are to be found in national legislation, are both still consistent with article 12 and the Convention in general, or is one 'wrong' and the other 'right'?

11.36 No clear guidance to this question is to be found in article 12 itself. Unlike the

---

[169] For France, see eg André Lucas and Henri-Jacques Lucas, *Traité de la propriété littéraire et artistique*, 2nd edn (2001), para 216 (the author of the underlying work and that of the derivative work exercise 'concurrent rights').

[170] UK Copyright, Designs and Patents Act 1988, s 16(1)(a) and (e); 17 USA § 106(1) (reproduction) (2) (derivative works). To the same effect, see Copyright Act 1968 (Australia), s 31(1)(vii).

[171] Law of 1965, art 23.

Brussels programme proposal (discussed earlier at para 11.33 above), it makes no reference to article 2(3) (formerly article 2(2)). It also replaces the former article 12, the retention of which had been proposed in the Brussels programme. It is logical to assume therefore that the present article 12 covers both 'original' adaptations, etc, that are protected as derivative works under article 2(3), as well as the 'unoriginal' adaptations that were previously covered by article 12 and treated in that provision as forms of illicit reproduction. On the other hand, since the Rome Act, article 14(1) has drawn a distinction between reproduction and adaptation by means of cinematography. It also confers separate rights in relation to the performance and diffusion to the public by wire of the cinematographic adaptations thus made (this also applies in the case of cinematographic reproductions, but this seems superfluous given that these are still uses of the original work—see para 11.33 above). A similar position also applies with respect to translations: although these were treated historically as reproductions of works, under the present Convention the author of an original work enjoys similar rights with respect to translations of the work.[172] This also accords with some national laws under which translations are treated as adaptations, and separate rights are granted with respect to them to the author of the work which is translated.[173] These provisions therefore highlight a whole series of unresolved issues that underlie not only article 12, but also articles 8, 9, 13, and 14 and lead to the following series of apparently inconsistent propositions.[174] First, if it were thought necessary to confer separate rights in relation to the exploitation of cinematographic adaptations, the failure to do so in relation to adaptations in general under article 12 must mean that the right of the author in the original work is limited to that of authorizing the making of the adaptation and nothing else. For the sake of completeness, this must mean that: (i) translations should now be regarded also as a species of adaptation, and (ii) that the conferring of separate exploitation rights in respect of cinematographic reproductions is superfluous. If these last two assertions are not accepted, then the failure of article 9 to confer further rights of exploitation in respect of reproductions in general would lead to the absurd conclusion that the rights of authors to exploit their works in the ways provided under other provisions of the Convention, for example, by public performance or broadcasting, would be limited to the original work itself and not to reproductions of the work. In this regard, it is significant that article 13(1) which used to confer separate rights in respect of the public performance of sound recordings of musical works does not do so

172 Articles 11(2), 11*ter*(2).

173 See eg Copyright, Designs and Patents Act 1988, s 21(1), (3)(a)(i), and Copyright Act 1968 (Australia), ss 10(1)(c)(i) and 31(1)(a)(vii).

174 See further Desbois (1978), 740–1.

under the Paris Act.[175] In other words, this grant of separate rights was unnecessary, in view of the fact that the rights of authors over the exploitation of their works extended also to the exploitation of reproductions of those works, including sound recordings.

Second, the anomaly remains that, if original adaptations are to be distinguished from reproductions, article 12 still covers some adaptations that are reproductions, that is, those 'non-original' adaptations, arrangements, and other alterations that fell within the scope of the previous article 12. If this were not so, the effect of the Brussels Revision of article 12 would have been that the Convention no longer contained any express provision requiring the protection of authors against those kinds of reproduction. Accordingly, article 12 is now a 'mixed' right that comprises, on the one hand, the making of a particular species of reproduction, and, on the other hand, the making of 'true adaptations' that are not reproductions. The result of this seems to be that the author of the original work enjoys further rights in relation to the exploitation of the first category of adaptation (because they are only another form of reproduction), but not in relation to the second category.

Third, following the adoption of the Paris Act, it is now possible to avoid this last conclusion by the following argument. Article 9 of that Act now confers a general right of reproduction. This is widely framed, and is capable of including reproductions of the non-original kind that historically were covered by article 12. These 'colourable imitations' can therefore be excluded from the scope of the present article 12 which can be interpreted simply as conferring the right to make derivative works of the kind referred to in article 2(3).

The above propositions indicate clearly the lack of conceptual consistency that **11.37**
underlies these provisions of the Convention. Perhaps this is inevitable, in view of the different legal philosophies of Union members and the difficulty in arriving at provisions that are acceptable to all. However, the interpretation suggested in the third proposition provides a symmetry between articles 2(3) and 12, and leads to the conclusion that article 12 only requires Union members to protect adaptation rights as such, with no additional requirements concerning rights of exploitation in those adaptations once made. Accordingly, it is a matter for national legislation to determine what rights are to be conferred on the author of the underlying work in this regard. In effect, this allows Union countries to adopt whatever view they wish of the nature of adaptations. It should also be noted that these rights will, in any case, only be relevant as regards the position of the author of the original work vis-à-vis third parties who

[175] Brussels Act, art 13(1)(ii).

make unauthorized use of the adaptation. As regards the relationship of the author to the adapter of his work, this will almost invariably be covered by some form of agreement between the parties as the adapter would otherwise infringe the author's undisputed right of adaptation.

D. Rights Pertaining to Physical Copies

11.38 Copyright is generally considered an incorporeal right, regulating, *inter alia*, the creation of copies, but not the fate of the physical copies themselves. The latter belong to the realm of chattels, and generally come under the law pertaining to personal property. But there are significant points of intersection. First, the author may need to access a physical copy in order to exercise her reproduction right. If the reproduction right does not imply a right of access, then the owner of the physical copy may enjoy a *de facto* right to frustrate the author's right of reproduction, at least where that copy is the only one in which the work is fixed. Second, the right to distribute the copies has historically accompanied the right to make copies. Hence, the provision in some early copyright statutes entitling the right holder to 'print, reprint, publish or vend' copies of the copyrighted work.[176] Third, the burgeoning markets for rental of copies may deleteriously affect sales of copies; many member states accordingly provide for some control over rental as well as initial sale of copies.[177] Fourth, unauthorized importation of copies furnishes another problem; while the Berne Convention does not mandate a general right to control the circulation of copies, it does require member states to provide for the seizure of copies traversing borders without the author's consent. Finally, some member states have enacted a more persistent form of control over the circulation of copies, by providing for a resale right (*droit de suite*) in manuscripts and original copies of artworks. Berne incorporates the *droit de suite*, but subjects it to a regime of reciprocity.

(1) Author's right of access to a physical copy

11.39 A 'right' which might be thought to relate to the basic right of reproduction is the right of the author to have access to the original of his work after he has parted with the property rights therein. This might be of the greatest value to the visual artist who wishes to exploit the right to make reproductions of his work after he has sold it; the same may apply in the case of a writer or composer

176 See eg US Act of 31 May 1790, ch 15, § 1, 1 Stat 124, 124.

177 See eg Council Directive 92/100/EEC of 19 Nov 1992 on rental right and lending right and on certain rights related to copyright in the field of intellectual property, *Official Journal* L 346, 27/11/1992 P 0061–0066 ('EU Rental Rights Directive').

when it is desired to produce an 'authentic' edition of his works based on the original manuscripts in which those works are embodied. Such a provision is to be found in article 25 of the German Law of 1965, and article 14(7) of the 1987 Spanish Law, but has not generally been regarded as part of the author's rights under national legislation. In the same way, there is no provision for such access in the Berne Convention, but it is of interest to note an Austrian proposal which was made at the Stockholm Revision Conference for the deposit of facsimile copies of musical compositions.[178] This was made in the context of article 6*bis*, and seemed to be more concerned with the securing of authentic texts after the composer's death and, indeed, after the expiry of his economic rights. There was no opposition to the proposal, although questions were raised in relation to the matter of formalities.[179] It was finally made the object of a resolution of the Conference, the desire being expressed that it should receive further examination and discussion.[180] In the interim, no further multilateral accord has emerged, but technology may help make the problem moot. That is, the ease of making and storing digital records of text or images now puts within many creators' reach an archive of their work, whether or not they have alienated the physical originals.

(2) Rights of distribution and subsequent disposal

The laws of many Union countries also confer on authors rights in relation to the distribution and subsequent disposal of their works and reproductions of those works.[181] These rights are distinct from the contractual obligations which an author may impose with respect to such matters in a publishing agreement, in the sense that the former are enforceable against third parties. In some countries, such as the USA and the member states of the European Union, a distinct right of distribution or putting into circulation is granted. Thus, article 4(1) of the 2001 EU Information Society Directive[182] provides that: **11.40**

[178] Document S/147 in *Records* 1967, vol II, 700.

[179] ibid, 896 (minutes of Main Committee I).

[180] ibid, 1189 (report of Main Committee I).

[181] See eg 17 USC § 106(3) (right to distribute copies); Austrian Law of 9 Apr 1936, art 16(1); FRG Law of 1965, art 17(1); Italian Law of 1941, art 17; Swedish Law of 30 Dec 1960, art 2(3); Turkish Law of 10 Dec 1951, art 23. For two interesting studies on distribution rights, see S Strömholm, 'The "Right of Putting into Circulation" in Relation to Copyright: A Study of Comparative Law' [1967] *Copyright* 266, and D Reimer, 'The Right of Distribution with Special Reference to the Hiring and Lending of Books and Records' [1973] *Copyright* 56. See also Spoor et al (1980), 57ff.

[182] Directive 2001/29/EC of the European Parliament and of the Council of 22 May 2001 on the harmonisation of certain aspects of copyright and related rights in the information society, *Official Journal* L 167, 22/06/2001 P 0010–0019.

> Member States shall provide for authors, in respect of the original of their works or of copies thereof, the exclusive right to authorise or prohibit any form of distribution to the public by sale or otherwise.

Section 106(3) of the US Copyright Act grants the author the exclusive right:

> to distribute copies or phonorecords of the copyrighted work to the public by sale or other transfer of ownership, or by rental, lease or lending

In both the USA and the European Union, however, the distribution right generally stops after the first sale of the copy. The principle of 'exhaustion of rights'[183] (or, in US terminology, the 'first sale doctrine'[184]) generally limits the scope of the distribution right to the first putting into circulation of physical copies of works.[185] In some common law countries that originally derive their copyright laws from the UK, there is no general provision relating to the distribution of copies, but there are still certain limited rights in this regard. Thus, under Australian law, a separate right of 'publication' gives the copyright owner the sole prerogative of determining when the first issue of copies of his work to the public shall take place,[186] and there are further provisions dealing with copies that have been unlawfully made, dealt with commercially, or imported by third parties.[187]

11.41 There are two other principal respects in which national laws provide for controls by authors over the subsequent disposal of their works or reproductions thereof. The first are lending rights which protect the interests of authors after their works have been distributed by means of sale. In part, at least, this is a recognition that an author may lose revenue from the exploitation of his reproduction rights if third parties can gain access to his work through the borrowing or hire of a copy rather than through an outright purchase (with the accompanying payment of a royalty that ends up ultimately in the hands of the author or

---

183 See Directive 2001/29/EC (n 182 above), art 4(2) ('The distribution right shall not be exhausted within the Community in respect of the original or copies of the work, except where the first sale or other transfer of ownership in the Community of that object is made by the right holder or with his consent.').

184 This common law doctrine is codified at 17 USC § 109(a).

185 By contrast, rights are not exhausted when the work is communicated by transmission rather than by distribution of physical copies. See Information Society Directive, art 3(3) ('The rights referred to in paragraphs 1 and 2 [communication to the public] shall not be exhausted by any act of communication to the public or making available to the public as set out in this Article.'); recital (29): 'The question of exhaustion does not arise in the case of services and on-line services in particular. This also applies with regard to a material copy of a work or other subject-matter made by a user of such a service with the consent of the right holder. Therefore, the same applies to rental and lending of the original and copies of works or other subject-matter which are services by nature. Unlike CD-ROM or CD-I, where the intellectual property is incorporated in a material medium, namely an item of goods, every on-line service is in fact an act which should be subject to authorisation where the copyright or related right so provides.'

186 Copyright Act 1968 (Australia), s 31(1)(a)(i) and (b)(ii).

187 ibid, ss 37–8. See also 17 USC § 602 (importation right to keep out copies made abroad).

his successor in title). Lending rights are by no means universally protected in Berne Union countries, and the terms and conditions under which such rights may be exercised vary between those countries which do recognize them, although they have been harmonized in the European Union.[188] Accordingly, some protect them as part of copyright,[189] while others do so under separate laws[190] or simply by administrative arrangements.[191]

The second right, which is recognized by only a minority of Berne Union members, although it is now in the process of implementation throughout the European Union,[192] is the right of subsequent disposal or the '*droit de suite*'. This entitles the author to a share in the proceeds of further sales of his work, and is typically confined to works which are of significant value in their original form, for example, works of art and original manuscripts. Once again, there are considerable variations among the countries which do protect this right as to how this is to be done, although the right is being harmonized in the countries of the European Union.[193]

11.42 From the above thumbnail sketch it can be said that most national laws provide, in some measure, for control by authors over the way in which their works or reproductions of those works are distributed to, and subsequently dealt with by, the public. However, the extent of this control differs considerably from country to country, and it is impossible to make any generalization that is applicable across the whole range of Union membership. Thus, Berne contains no general recognition of a right of putting into circulation as there is in the case of the basic right of reproduction. (The WCT does, however, include a general right of initial distribution of copies, discussed further at paras 11.88ff below) Likewise, lending rights and the *droit de suite* are protected in only a relatively small number of states. In consequence, the protection accorded by the Berne Convention in relation to the distribution of works and their copies is patchy, to say the least.

11.43 The lack of coherence in relation to these matters under both national legislation and the Convention may also be explained by the fact that the protection of rights of distribution raises fundamental questions which have implications

188 See the EU Rental Rights Directive (n 177 above).

189 As eg under the FRG Law of 1965, art 27; see further A Dietz, 'The Public Lending Right in the Federal Republic of Germany: Evolution and Regulation' [1976] 7 *IIC* 220 and W Nordemann, 'Public Lending Right in Federal Germany' (1976) 90 *RIDA* 61.

190 See eg the Public Lending Right Act 1979 (UK), s 1; Danish Law of 26 June 1975.

191 As in Australia: S Ricketson, *The Law of Intellectual Property* (1984), 436–7.

192 See Directive 2001/84/EC of the European Parliament and of the Council of 27 Sept 2001 on the resale right for the benefit of the author of an original work of art, *Official Journal* L 272, 13/10/2001 P. 0032–0036.

193 See further paras 11.53ff below.

going far beyond the simple safeguarding of the interests of authors. The first of these concerns the juridical nature of authors' rights. These are usually conceived as incorporeal or intangible rights that have a separate existence from the property rights in the objects in which the work is embodied or reproduced. To extend the author's rights so as to encompass the ways in which these objects are distributed and subsequently dealt with brings these intangible rights into direct conflict with the rights of property that the owner of a copy enjoys once he has purchased it. It can therefore be said that this goes beyond what is reasonably necessary to ensure to the author the enjoyment of the fruits of the exploitation of his intellectual creation which are secured by the present undisputed rights of reproduction, adaptation and public communication in a non-material form. Against this, it may be argued that, for the better and more effective enjoyment of these rights, additional rights over the work in its physical embodiment are necessary. This reasoning has particular force in the case of the lending and hiring of copies, where the reproduction right may be significantly damaged as a result of these activities, and has—partly—carried the day in later multilateral accords, which do provide for limited rental rights (see further paras 11.81–11.87 below, discussing provisions in the TRIPs Agreement and the WCT on rental rights in computer programs, phonograms, and videograms). Nevertheless, doubts over the correctness of this argument may explain, at least in part, the reluctance of some countries, and the failure of those later accords, to adopt fully developed rights in relation to the initial and subsequent distribution of works and copies of works.

11.44 A second matter also needs to be considered. Authors' rights have to be seen in their wider economic and social context. Their exercise can have quasi-monopolistic and anti-competitive effects, and these effects may be accentuated if rights in relation to distribution and other dealings are granted. For example, they may be used to divide up markets territorially and to secure exclusive chains of distribution that enable prices of copies to be artificially maintained while keeping other sellers of copies out of those markets. For this reason, many national copyright laws have to operate in the wider context of trade practices and competition controls; the exhaustion doctrine, discussed earlier (see para 11.40 above), plays an important role in the context. These considerations therefore help to explain the limited protection given to rights of distribution under the Berne Convention. The extent of that protection is addressed below.

(3) Distribution rights under the Berne Convention

11.45 The protection given to these rights is to be found in three provisions: article 14(1), which confers a separate right of distribution with respect to cinematographic adaptations and reproductions; article 14ter, which contains an optional provision concerning the *droit de suite* in respect of original works of art and manuscripts of written works; and article 16 which provides for the seizure of infringing copies of works. (See also article 13(3): phonograms made under compulsory licence in one country but imported without permission 'into a country where they are treated as infringing recordings shall be liable to seizure'.) In chronological terms, article 16 came first, being embodied in the original Berne Act; the remaining two articles were added at the time of the Brussels Revision. Proposals to add a general right of distribution to the Convention have been unsuccessful, despite extensive discussion of the merits and basis for such a right at the Stockholm Revision Conference. A general right of distribution was, however, included at article 6 of the 1996 WCT (discussed further at paras 11.88ff below).

(a) Right of seizure

Article 16(1) provides that: **11.46**

> (1) Infringing copies of a work shall be liable to seizure in any country of the Union where the work enjoys protection.

This provision also applies to reproductions coming from a country where the work is not protected or has ceased to be protected (article 16(2)), and it is left to national legislation to determine how seizure shall take place (article 16(3)). In its original form in article 12 of the Berne Act, provision was only made for the seizure of infringing copies (or 'pirated works') on importation, but at the Paris Conference of 1896 the reference to importation was deleted.[194] This had the effect that seizure could take place in the interior of a country, not only at its borders; it was also to be presumed that it was no longer necessary for the pirated works to have been imported in the first place. However, one remaining point of uncertainty was whether it was possible to seize imported copies that had been lawfully made in another country. This situation could very readily arise as long as Union countries had different terms of protection, or made protection dependent upon compliance with some condition or formality. This was addressed in the Berlin Revision, when the following paragraph was added at the request of the Italian delegation:

> In such a country [meaning a country of the Union where the work enjoyed protection] the seizure may also apply to reproductions imported from a country where the work is not protected, or has ceased to be protected.[195]

This provision remains substantially unchanged in article 16(2) of the current Act. It will be seen that it is irrelevant whether the country from which the imported copies originate is a member of the Union. However, the provision does not cover imported copies of works that still enjoy protection in their

[194] Paris Act, art 1(V).

[195] Berlin Act, art 16(1). See *Actes* 1908, 268.

country of origin but which have been lawfully made in that country, for instance, with the authorization of the person entitled to protection in that country. It seems fair to conclude that this category of imported copies lies outside the scope of article 16, but it should be noted that many additional laws still provide for seizure in such cases, on the basis that these copies would have been unlawful if made in the country of importation.[196]

(b) Method of seizure

11.47 Article 16(3) leaves the method of seizure to be determined by national legislation. Under the Berlin Act, this was qualified by the requirement that the seizure was to be effected by the 'competent authorities' of the country concerned, but this requirement was deleted in the Stockholm, Paris Acts.[197] The words 'competent authorities' indicated that the seizure was to be carried out by the state or one of its instrumentalities. In many countries, this is done by the customs service or police acting at the request of the copyright owner, but the deletion of these words now gives national legislation complete freedom to determine who will effect a seizure. For example, this could be left to the copyright owner himself or his agents, perhaps acting pursuant to a court order or under judicial supervision. A further point to be noted is that, where seizure is carried out by a state authority, article 16 does not require this in the absence of a request by the copyright owner. The word 'shall' was substituted for the word 'may' in the English translation of article 16(1) at the request of the UK delegation at the Stockholm Revision Conference.[198] However, the French text, which says '*peut être saisie*', has remained unchanged since the original Berne Act, and it was agreed at the Stockholm Conference that this did not require the state to take the initiative in effecting a seizure, but that it was required to do this when so requested.[199] A final point to be noted is that article 16 makes no provision as to what is to be done with the copies seized. Options would include confiscation to the owner of the copyright or to the state or destruction, but this remains a matter to be determined by national legislation.

(c) Importation right with respect to mechanical reproductions

11.48 The article 16 seizure right is not a full importation right because it excludes only infringing copies. A full importation right would permit the author to

[196] See (UK) Copyright, Designs and Patents Act 1988, s 22 (secondary infringement: importing infringing copy). See also 17 USC § 602(a) (unauthorized importation violates distribution right, independently of whether the copies were infringing in the country in which they were made; sec 602(b) addresses the latter situation).

[197] *Records* 1967, vol II, 929 (minutes of Main Committee I): there is no record of any discussion on this deletion which was merely a drafting change, according to the report of Main Committee I: ibid, 1173. Nevertheless, the change appears to be more than just a drafting one.

[198] ibid, vol I, 714 (Document S/211) and vol II, 907 (minutes of Main Committee I).

[199] ibid, 907 (minutes of Main Committee I).

prevent entry of any copies to whose distribution in a particular country the author did not consent.[200] Article 16 does expand the class of infringing copies to cover those imported from a country where they were lawfully made because the work is not, or is no longer, protected there. Article 16 does not, however, reach those copies lawfully made under licence in one country, but imported without authorization into another country. By contrast, the article 13(1)(2) compulsory licence regime for mechanical reproductions does limit the effect of the licence to the territory that imposes it, and thus prohibits export of compulsorily licensed phonograms into another Berne country. This has remained essentially unchanged since the Berlin Act. Thus, a recording of a musical work and words which is lawfully made pursuant to a compulsory licence in country A will not carry its 'lawful character' with it when it is exported to other countries of the Union without the consent of the person entitled to the copyright in those works in those countries. In such circumstances, country B is entitled to regard such a recording as an infringing recording, and its lawful production in country A is of no effect. The same applies to recordings which have been made in country A under conditions specified in paragraph (2). It will be noted that paragraph (3) does not require country B to treat these recordings as infringing copies: that is a matter left to the law of that country. However, if they are treated as infringing copies, there is no prescription as to how their seizure is to be carried out, or by whom. The words 'shall be liable to seizure' imply only that the machinery should be there, and the way in which this is done is left to national legislation (see further para 11.47 above).

(d) Distribution right with respect to cinematographic adaptations and reproductions

This was added to article 14(1) at the time of the Brussels Revision. It came from a proposal in the programme,[201] and although it initially attracted opposition from some delegations,[202] it was finally accepted by the general commission.[203] This, in fact, was rather surprising, as a corresponding proposal for a distribution right in respect of musical works embodied in sound recordings under article 13(1) was rejected at the same time.[204] A possible explanation for this may be that a distribution right in the case of cinematographic productions **11.49**

---

200 See eg 17 USC § 602 (right to exclude foreign-made copies, whether or not lawfully made in the country of production). The relationship of the US importation right to the first-sale doctrine is not entirely clear. See *Quality King Distributors, Inc* v *L'anza Research Inst*, 523 US 135 (1998), applying first-sale doctrine to reimportation of works produced in the USA and sold abroad, then resold to the USA. Had the goods been produced abroad under licence it is not clear whether the court would have held that the first-sale doctrine compelled their importation.

201 *Documents 1948* (1951), 350.

202 ibid, 354 (proposal by the UK for its deletion).

203 ibid, 361.

204 ibid, 332–4.

was not considered to be of very great practical importance, as film producers usually make their contracts for distribution with a limited number of distributors and are generally in a strong enough commercial position to impose contractually whatever conditions they desire with respect to the distribution of their films. Having said this, it can then be asked whether the grant of such an 'unimportant' right was necessary. One commentator suggests that this was a potent reason militating against the adoption of a distribution right with respect to sound recordings.[205] These are distributed to a far wider audience than films, and apparently there was a strong fear by certain delegations that this would put too much power in the hands of music publishers, to the prejudice of record manufacturers and broadcasting organizations.[206] There was also opposition from delegations, such as the British, who took the view that any limits on the distribution of copies should be dealt with contractually at the time the copy was sold; otherwise, the purchaser of a lawfully made copy should have the right to dispose of it as he wished.[207] Although the British delegate did not press this argument in the case of cinematographic films, his successor at the Stockholm Conference was to display similar caution in the context of proposals for a general right of distribution.[208] As for sound recordings, the general commission at the Brussels Conference asked the *rapporteur général* (Marcel Plaisant) to make specific reference to the right of authors to make contractual stipulations with respect to distribution in his report.[209] This was done in the following comment:

> The distribution of discs or apparatus was not taken into consideration by the Conference, but it did entrust its Rapporteur-General with mentioning that the authors could specify by contract that the distribution of apparatus or recorded discs was liable to generate liability to payment of a royalty or compliance with a formality. This is an attribute of copyright that should be highlighted here as a source of revenue specific to the author.[210]

This passage has no effect on the interpretation of the Convention, as it deals with matters which the Brussels Conference had decided to exclude from its scope. As a matter of general law, copyright owners are free to impose whatever conditions they wish in relation to the distribution of copies in contracts in which they license or assign their rights. This power is not so much an 'attribute' of copyright, as a normal incident of the laws dealing with contractual obligations. On the other hand, rights against third parties who are not in contractual relations with the author would require the latter to be possessed of

[205] Baum (1949), 60. [206] ibid. [207] *Documents 1948* (1951), 332.
[208] *Records* 1967, vol II, 853 (minutes of Main Committee I).
[209] *Documents 1948* (1951), 334.
[210] ibid, 103. See Baum (1949), 46, for the English translation.

a relevant right as part of his copyright, that is, of the very right of distribution which the Brussels Conference had refused to accord in the case of sound recordings. This did not prevent national laws from recognizing such a right, but there was no obligation under the Convention to do so. This has remained the case under the Stockholm, Paris Acts.

What is the scope of the distribution right now accorded in respect of cinemato- **11.50**
graphic adaptations and reproductions under article 14(1)? 'Distribution' in English is ambiguous, as it may mean 'first distribution' only, or distribution generally, including any subsequent act of distribution of the copy that may occur. Reference to the original French text is of assistance here. This uses the expression '*la mise en circulation des oeuvres ainsi adaptées ou reproduites*', which would be better translated in English as 'the putting into circulation of the works thus adapted or reproduced'. This more clearly indicates that what is intended to be covered is first distribution, that is, the putting into circulation of something that was previously under the control of the copyright owner, with the result that after this has occurred the right of the latter is exhausted. This appears to have been the view of most delegates at the Brussels Conference,[211] but no authentic interpretation supporting this is to be found in the general report. What is required for a 'putting into circulation'? Again, no clear guidance is to be derived from the Conference records, but it would seem reasonable to require that the copyright owner has parted with his proprietary rights in the adaptations or reproductions. This would exclude such acts as lease or hire, where the copies remain ultimately under the control of the copyright owner. It will also be noted that article 14(1) couples the right of distribution with those of adaptation and reproduction, rather than listing it as a separate right (as in the case of performance rights). This is in accordance with French doctrine, where the right of distribution is seen as a component of the wider right of reproduction,[212] but there would seem to be nothing in article 14(1) that would prevent a copyright owner from dealing with reproduction and distribution separately: authorizing one person to make an adaptation or reproduction of his work by means of cinematography and another to distribute the adaptations or copies thus made. Finally, it goes without saying that the interpretation of article 14(1) suggested above is only a statement of the minimum obligations imposed on Union members with respect to cinematographic adaptations and reproductions. They are free, if they desire, to extend the rights of copyright owners to cover subsequent acts of distribution.

---

[211] ibid, 332ff (discussions on right of distribution in relation to phonographic recordings).

[212] See eg Frédéric Pollaud-Dulian, *Le droit de destination: le sort des exemplaires en droit d'auteur* (1989).

(e) Proposals for a general right of distribution

11.51 Proposals to add a general right of distribution to the Convention have been unsuccessful. At the Brussels Revision, a proposal for the recognition of a 'right of putting into circulation' was made by the French Government,[213] and a more extensive proposal covering both circulation and distribution (presumably meaning here subsequent distribution) was put forward by the Austrian Government.[214] Little enthusiasm for these was shown by the other delegates, and both proposals quietly lapsed.[215] At the Stockholm Conference, two further attempts were made to introduce a general distribution right into the Convention. The first was a proposal by Austria, Italy, and Morocco to add the words 'and circulation' after 'reproduction' in article 9(1).[216] This met with opposition from a number of different sides. The British, Australian, and Finnish delegates felt unable to support such a proposal without further consideration (it had not been included in the preparatory documents for the Conference).[217] Their argument was essentially one of caution, although it is likely that these delegations also shared the fear of the Dutch delegate who, while appreciating the value of such a right to authors, felt that there were risks involved in the adoption of a blanket right of circulation.[218] In addition, there was the question of what exceptions to the new right would be necessary.[219] Finally, the Monégasque delegate referred to the severe consequences that the recognition of a distribution right would have for the recording and broadcasting industries which would have to ask for two separate approvals in respect of both reproduction and distribution (three, in fact, in the case of broadcasters, as they would also need permission to broadcast the work).[220] It was argued in vain by those delegations which favoured the proposal that it would provide a more certain protection to authors than was presently provided through contractual arrangements, and that abuses of the new right could be curbed by providing for its exhaustion once the copies had been put into circulation with the consent of the copyright owner.[221] The amendment was finally rejected by seventeen votes to seven with eight abstentions.[222] However, there were intimations by several of the delegations which had opposed it that, with appropriate time for detailed consideration, this should be a matter for a subsequent revision conference.[223] There has not been a revision conference since Stockholm–Paris, but a general

[213] ibid, 233. [214] ibid, 237ff. [215] ibid, 235, 238.
[216] Document S/72: *Records* 1967, vol I, 691.
[217] ibid, 853–4 (minutes of Main Committee I).
[218] ibid, 854 (Mr Gerbrandy).
[219] ibid, 853 (observation of Professor Ulmer, chairman of Main Committee I).
[220] ibid, 854 (Mr Straschnov). [221] ibid (observations of German and Italian delegates).
[222] ibid, 856. [223] eg the delegate of Australia: ibid.

distribution right was finally adopted in a side agreement to the Berne Convention, as article 6 of the 1996 WCT (see the further discussion at paras 11.88ff below).

The second proposal concerning the protection of circulation rights was put forward by the French delegation. It achieved this in an indirect fashion by proposing the addition of the words 'and for any purpose' after the words 'reproduction . . . in any manner or form' in article 9(1).[224] This initially received a favourable response from the British delegation which viewed this simply as a further clarification of the newly recognized reproduction right.[225] However, the proposal went further than first appeared, as it could be interpreted as enabling authors to control the distribution of copies of their works when this was being done by third parties, for example, a wholesaler who had purchased the copies directly from the publisher and then proposed to distribute them to retailers or directly to the public. Although the French delegation denied that it was proposing something that was tantamount to a separate right of circulation,[226] it cannot be denied that in French jurisprudence reproduction rights had come to be interpreted in such a way as to allow authors wide powers in relation to the circulation of their copies.[227] Several delegations therefore took the view that the French proposal could be interpreted in a similar way, and therefore would have the effect of achieving what had already been rejected by Main Committee I. This critical view was neatly encapsulated in the comments of the Monégasque delegate, Georges Straschnov, who argued that the proposal was either superfluous or went beyond what the Committee had already agreed upon. Thus, if it meant merely that an author could limit or determine, in a contract dealing with reproduction rights, the purposes to which his work might be put, this was unnecessary, as an author could attach whatever conditions he liked when negotiating an agreement. On the other hand, if it went further than this, it would result in something comparable in every respect to a right of circulation, and was therefore to be opposed.[228] Finally, the French amendment was rejected by seventeen votes to four with fourteen abstentions,[229] and the **11.52**

224 Document S/70: *Records* 1967, vol I, 690.

225 ibid, 853 (Mr Wallace, British delegate).

226 ibid, 856 (Mr Kéréver, French delegate). See also the comments by Spoor et al (1980), 124–5.

227 See generally Lucas and Lucas (n 169 above), paras 246–55 (overview and criticism of the '*droit de destination*').

228 *Records* 1967, vol II, 856.

229 ibid. Note, however, the strong opinions in favour of the recognition of distribution and lending rights (particularly as regards phonograms and videograms) that were expressed in subsequent international meetings, such as that of the WIPO and UNESCO Group of Experts on the Rental of Phonograms and Videograms that met in Paris, 26–30 Nov 1984: [1985] *Copyright* 16–21. Furthermore, in a questionnaire prepared for the Committee of Governmental Experts on

present Act therefore contains no general provision dealing with the distribution or circulation of copies.

This does not, of course, prevent Union members from providing for such rights, whether in the form of a separate right or as part of a wider reproduction right. In any case, authors remain free to impose restrictions in relation to these matters in contracts dealing with their reproduction rights. With regard to this last alternative, it should be noted that the author's right to impose contractual restrictions, in many instances, may be ephemeral, as the author will be in a far inferior position to a wealthy and established publisher, and it may be argued that his or her position in such negotiations would not be greatly assisted by the grant of a separate right of circulation. On the other hand, if the publisher became entitled to exercise such a right as an assignee of the author, it might become a very potent weapon to use against other distributors and the interests of the public might be adversely affected by higher prices and reduced availability of copies. While the author might benefit indirectly from such a situation, a more effective remedy might be to change the law governing his relations with his publisher so as to strengthen his hand in negotiating agreements. This, in fact, is the case under a number of national laws, where publishing agreements are made the subject of extensive regulation.[230] It is also possible to conceive of situations where a separate distribution right might still be of benefit to an author if the latter is able to preserve such a right to him- or herself or to use it prudently in negotiations with publishers and other third parties. One instance might be where an author transfers rights to record music onto a motion picture soundtrack, and to exhibit the film publicly, but refrains from granting rights in relation to the distribution of copies to the public: in such a case, separate authorizations to distribute copies in the form of video cassettes or DVDs will still be required. Another example arises in those common law countries, such as

Audiovisual Works and Phonograms by the WIPO and UNESCO secretariats (Document UNESCO/WIPO/CGE/AWP/3), dated 26 Mar 1986, a progressive interpretation of art 9(1) was argued for at 16, pursuant to which it is said the right of distribution flows from the right of reproduction recognized under that article. This was only an expression of opinion by the secretariats, and in the light of the discussions at the Stockholm Conference can hardly be regarded as an authentic interpretation of that article. At the subsequent meeting of Governmental Experts, it did not appear that there was unanimous acceptance by the participants of the secretariats' view, although it seems that it was agreed that rental rights fell within the principle of national treatment: [1986] *Copyright* 218, 229–30. For later international developments, see paras 11.70ff.

[230] See eg the German Publishing Rights Law of 19 June 1901, as amended; the Italian Law of 1941, arts 118–35; France, Code de la propriété intellectuelle, arts L 131-4, L 132-1–132-17. See generally, William R Cornish, 'The Author as Risk-Sharer' (2002) 26 *Colum J Law & the Arts* 1 (examining and comparing French and German author-protective legislation).

Australia, that retain the '*Moçambique*' rule refusing jurisdiction in cases involving infringements of foreign copyrights.[231] Assume copies of a work are made in country A but are distributed in country B. Courts of the latter country apply the *Moçambique* rule and will therefore not assume jurisdiction in relation to the infringing acts of copying that have occurred in country A. However, the infringing act of distribution will have taken place within the forum country (country B) and will therefore be actionable there as a local infringement.[232]

(4) The *droit de suite*

In normal usage, this refers to the author's right to a share in the proceeds of subsequent sales of his original work—'original' meaning here the original form (physical copy) in which the work is embodied.[233] Although the expression is French, it has come to be used in many non-French speaking countries. Its literal meaning is 'the right of follow-up' or the 'right of following on', and it was drawn from the French law of real property (although the analogy here does not bear very close examination).[234] Some countries have adopted their own translation of the term, such as 'arts proceeds right' in the USA, '*Folgerecht*' in **11.53**

[231] See *British South Africa Co* v *Companhia de Moçambique* [1893] AC 602, HL. The rule, announced in the context of claims to land situated abroad, has been extended to intellectual property, see eg for the UK, *Tyburn Prods Ltd* v *Conan Doyle* [1991] Ch 75; [1990] RPC 185; *Potter* v *Broken Hill Proprietary Co* (1906) 3 CLR 479, 492 (Australia) (courts do not have jurisdiction over claims requiring application of a foreign copyright law). The rule has, however, been criticized in the UK, see eg *Griggs Group Ltd* v *Evans (No 2)* [2004] FSR 48 (Prescott, QC, deputy judge), appeal (on other grounds) dismissed [2005] EWCA Civ 11.

[232] See eg *Psihoyos* v *Liberation Inc*, 42 USPQ 2d 1947 (SDNY 1997) (unauthorized reproductions of photographs made in Austria and published in magazine there; copies of magazine sold in USA; violation of US distribution right found).

[233] The literature on *droit de suite* is extensive. For our present purposes, see generally, 'Du droit à la plus-value des oeuvres artistiques' [1914] *DA* 34, 57; J-L Duchemin, *Le Droit de Suite des Artistes* (1948) ('Duchemin (1948)'); F Hepp, 'Royalties from Works of the Fine Arts: Origin of the Concept of *droit de suite* in Copyright Law' (1959) 6 *Bull Cop Soc USA* 91; R E Hauser, 'French *droit de suite*: The Problem of Protection for the Underprivileged Artist under the Copyright Law' (1959) 6 *Bull Cop Soc USA* 94; J-L Duchemin, 'Droit de suite' (1967–8) 54–5 *RIDA* 369; R Plaisant, 'Droit de suite' [1969] *Copyright* 157; J-L Duchemin, 'Le droit de suite aux artistes' (1969) 62 *RIDA* 78; P Katzenberger, *Das Folgerecht im deutschen und ausländischen Urheberrecht* (1970); P Katzenberger, 'The Droit de Suite in Copyright Law' (1973) 4 *IIC* 361; W Duchemin, 'Le droit de suite' (1974) 80 *RIDA* 4; W Nordemann 'The 1972 Amendment of the German Copyright Law' (1973) 4 *IIC* 179; E Ulmer, 'Le droit de suite et sa réglementation dans la convention de Berne', in *Hommage à Henri Desbois, études de propriété intellectuelle* (1974), 89; E Ulmer, 'The "Droit de Suite" in International Copyright Law' (1975) 6 *IIC* 12; W Nordemann, 'The "Droit de Suite" in Art 14*ter* of the Berne Convention and in the Copyright Law of the Federal Republic of Germany' [1977] *Copyright* 337. US Copyright Office, *Droit de Suite: The Artist's Resale Royalty* (1992 report), summarized at 16 *Columbia-VLA Journal of Law & the Arts* 318 (1992); Shira Perlmutter, 'Resale Royalties for Artists: An Analysis of the Register of Copyrights' Report' (1992) 16 *Columbia-VLA Journal of Law & the Arts* 157.

[234] See Hauser (n 233 above), 97.

German and '*diretto de sequencia*' in Italian, but more usually the original French expression is preferred.[235]

(a) The provenance of the droit de suite

11.54 The origin of the *droit de suite* is to be found, as the name suggests, in France, and was based on the realization that visual artists lacked the same opportunities to exploit their works as were possessed by writers and composers.[236] Thus, an original artistic work might be sold for a low price by an artist when he was young and unknown, and then be resold years later by the astute purchaser for a much greater sum when the artist had become famous and his works generally commanded far higher prices. In such a case, it seemed inequitable that the artist should not have a share in the good fortune of the purchaser, and it was easy to portray the latter declining into the poverty of his squalid garret surrounded by his starving family while the rapacious art collector became ever wealthier through prudent resales of the artist's early works. The pathos of the situation was intensified when the artist was dead and his wife and children were reduced to begging in the gutter, and this pathos could be turned into outrage when names of particular artists who had suffered in this way—Millet, Dégas, and Bollin among them—were invoked.[237] The concept of a *droit de suite* for visual artists was introduced by Albert Vaunois in an article in the *Chronique de Paris* in 1893,[238] and after this a campaign for its recognition began in France, culminating in special legislation in 1920.[239] This law allowed artists to claim a percentage of the gross sales price on each public sale of their original works. 'Original' here appeared to be used in contradistinction to 'reproduction', thereby excluding such works as lithographs, engravings, and the like where the original plate or block is seldom sold on its own. The exclusion of private sales also meant that the scope of the new right was subject to a severe potential restriction, but this made collection far easier if it were carried out by a collecting society that entered into arrangements with galleries and auction rooms.[240] Furthermore, while limited to visual artists, there was no reason, in principle, why the *droit de suite* should not be extended to other valuable 'originals' of works, for example, the manuscripts of literary or dramatic works or musical compositions. However, there was uncertainty whether the new right was to be seen as part of copyright or whether it was an entirely separate right, and this

[235] Katzenberger (n 233 above), 364.

[236] See generally Duchemin (1948) 17ff.

[237] Katzenberger (n 233 above), 364ff; Duchemin (1948), 17ff.

[238] *Chronique de Paris*, 25 Feb 1893; see also Hauser (n 233 above), 96ff and Duchemin (1948), 35ff.

[239] Law of 20 May 1920; for the course of events leading up to its enactment, see Duchemin (1948), 36ff.

[240] See Hauser (n 233 above), 99–101.

was to become an important question when it was adopted into the Berne Convention (see paras 11.59ff below). Despite this, the French example was soon followed by several other Berne members: Belgium in 1921,[241] Czechoslovakia in 1926,[242] Poland in 1935,[243] and Italy in 1941.[244] Uruguay, at this time a non-member, adopted such legislation in 1937,[245] and after World War II the number of states which recognized *droit de suite* increased steadily. With the adoption of the European Union's *droit de suite* Directive in 2001, the number of countries implementing the artist's resale rights will increase even more.[246]

(b) Justifications for the droit de suite

Is *droit de suite* to be justified simply in terms of a humanitarian concern for the plight of the poor starving artist, as a means of securing him some form of social security in his declining years? This image, potent as it is, may not necessarily be true. There are certainly many artists who do live long enough to reap a handsome financial reward from their later works, even if they received very little for the sales of their earlier works. Equally, there are many artists whose works increase very little in value, or even decrease, both during and after their lifetime. More facts are needed before it can be stated positively that the picture of the starving artist, much beloved of the earlier propagandists of the *droit de suite*, is a true one. If it is, then the *droit de suite* may not, in any case, be the most effective remedy: better regulation of artists' agreements with galleries might be more appropriate, or perhaps even the grant of state subsidies or pensions. Justifying *droit de suite* as a humanitarian gesture may therefore be nothing more than sentimentalism.[247] **11.55**

---

241 Law of 25 June 1921. 242 Law of 24 Nov 1926, art 35.

243 Law of 22 Mar 1935, modifying that of 29 Mar 1926.

244 Law of 22 Apr 1941, arts 144–55. 245 Law of 17 Dec 1937, art 9.

246 Directive 2001/84/EC (n 192 above). National laws currently implementing the *droit de suite* include: Denmark, s 38 of the Copyright Act 1995; Estonia, s 15 of Copyright Act (of 11 Nov 1992, as last amended by the Act of 15 Feb 2000); Finland, art 26i of the Copyright Act (Law No 404 of 8 July 1961, as last amended by Law No 365 of 25 Apr 1997); Greece, art 5 of Copyright, Related Rights and Cultural Matters (Law No 2121/1993, as last amended by Law No 2435 of 2 Aug 1996); Latvia, art 17 of Copyright Act of 6 Apr 2000; Lithuania, art 17 of Law on Copyright and Related Rights (No VIII-1185 of 18 May 1999, as amended by Law No VIII-1886, of 20 July 2000); Poland, has resale right for 'original of a three-dimensional work or of the manuscript of a literary or musical work' (oddly this would seem to exclude paintings), Law of 4 Feb 1994 on Copyright and Neighboring Rights, art 19; Spain, art 24 of Consolidated Text of the Law on Intellectual Property, regularizing, clarifying, and harmonizing the applicable statutory provisions (approved by Royal Legislative Decree 1/1996 of 12 Apr 1996, and amended by Law 5/1998 of 6 Mar 1998, incorporating Directive 96/9/EC of the European Parliament and of the Council of 11 Mar 1996 on the Legal Protection of Databases); Sweden, art 26j of Act on Copyright in Literary and Artistic Works (Act 1960: 729, of 30 Dec 1960, as amended up to 1 Apr 2000). Provision is also made for the *droit de suite* in the Tunis Model Law, art 4*bis*.

247 See eg M E Price, 'Government Policy and Economic Security for Artists: The Case of the droit de suite' (1968) 77 *Yale LJ* 1333.

11.56 However, there are more reasoned arguments which can be advanced in favour of it.[248] The first looks at the increase in value of the original work (where this occurs), and argues that this is, at least in part, due to the subsequent work and fame of the artist, and that he should therefore be entitled to a share in this increased value. In such a case, the purchaser of the work has done little himself to bring about this increase, although his astuteness in purchasing that particular artist's work and other external factors should not be overlooked. Nevertheless, he is in the position of a speculator reaping windfall profits on resale, and therefore some part of these profits should be returned to the artist whose efforts have helped bring about this state of affairs. This has been the approach adopted in some national laws on *droit de suite*,[249] with the consequence that the artist receives nothing if his work is resold at the same or a lesser price. (One practical difficulty with this approach: sellers who wish to avoid paying the royalty, or to avoid paying tax on the increased value, may be tempted to commit accounting fraud in order to disguise the profit.)

11.57 The second argument is quite different, and proceeds on the basis that the artist, by reason of the peculiar nature of his work, is disadvantaged in his exploitation of it by comparison to other categories of author. Thus, the reproduction right may not be of as great value as in the case of a writer or composer (although this may not always be true), and the artist also lacks the same opportunities of exploitation through such forms of public communication as performance and broadcasting. His main source of income derives from his sale of the initial work, and in the absence of a *droit de suite* he is unable to share in the further exploitation of the work which occurs when it is resold. Under this approach, the question of whether the resale occurs at a profit is irrelevant, as the artist is receiving a 'royalty' on the resale of his work in the same way as the writer receives a royalty on the sale of a further copy of his work. The purpose of the *droit de suite* then is to make more effective the artist's exploitation of his work, and to redress the imbalance that otherwise exists as regards other kinds of work.[250] The 'exploitation' approach is to be found in the greater number of national laws on *droit de suite*, and these usually treat this right as part of the author's general copyright.[251]

---

[248] See generally Duchemin (1948), 19ff; Katzenberger (n 233 above), 364ff; Hauser (n 233 above), 103ff.

[249] See eg the Italian Law of 1941, art 152 (2–10% of the increase in value); Brazil, Law No 9610 of 19 Feb 1998, on Copyright and Neighboring Rights, art 38 ('The author has the irrevocable and inalienable right to collect a minimum of five per cent of any gain in value that may be achieved in each resale of an original work of art or manuscript that he has disposed of.').

[250] See Katzenberger (n 233 above), 367–8; Hauser (n 233 above), 106–7.

[251] Namely all those listed in n 246 above, with the exception of those referred to in n 249.

The EU Resale Right Directive takes a similar tack: 'The resale right is intended to ensure that authors of graphic and plastic works of art share in the economic success of their original works of art. It helps to redress the balance between the economic situation of authors of graphic and plastic works of art and that of other creators who benefit from successive exploitations of their works.'[252] By contrast, under the 'increase in value' approach, the *droit de suite* has more of the character of a tax or levy that is imposed on resales of artistic works, and accordingly is more removed from the traditional conception of author's rights. **11.58**

(c) Droit de suite *under the Berne Convention*

Following its adoption into French law in 1920, efforts soon began to bring about the protection of *droit de suite* on an international level. By the time of the Rome Revision in 1928, only two other nations—Belgium and Czechoslovakia—had legislated for it. However, ALAI had long taken an interest in the question, and this interest intensified in the mid-1920s with a series of reports and resolutions urging the adoption of such protection in national laws.[253] The matter was also taken up by the International Institute for Intellectual Cooperation (the 'IIIC'), which advocated action on both a national and international level.[254] At the Rome Conference, the French Government proposed the following '*voeu*' which was based directly on the wording of a resolution passed by ALAI at its Paris Congress in 1925: **11.59**

> It is desirable that the inalienable droit de suite, established in France by the law of 20 May 1920 and in Belgium by that of 25 June 1921, to the profit of artists, in their original works which are publicly sold, should be the object of similar legislative dispositions in other countries, on condition of reciprocity, in each of them, between their nationals and those of countries which have already adopted this measure.[255]

This was supported by the Belgian and Czech delegates,[256] as well as by the IIIC (which was present at the Conference as an observer),[257] but doubts were expressed by the British and Norwegian delegations as to the connection between this and copyright protection in general.[258] A modified text was finally adopted as follows, but a number of delegations, including those of the UK, Hungary, the Netherlands, Norway, and Switzerland, abstained from voting on it:

---

[252] Resale Right Directive (n 192 above), Recital 3.

[253] See Duchemin (1948), 241–5 for an account of ALAI's involvement in the study and promotion of *droit de suite*. See also the resolutions of ALAI passed at Paris in 1912 and 1925, and Warsaw in 1936: *Actes* 1928, 48.

[254] IIIC, *La Protection internationale du droit d'auteur* (1928): includes the report of the IIIC sub-committee on *droit de suite*. For a commentary on the report, see Duchemin (1948), 245–9.

[255] *Actes* 1928, 103. [256] ibid, 283. [257] ibid. [258] ibid.

> The Conference expresses the desire that those countries of the Union which have not yet adopted legislative provisions guaranteeing to the benefit of artists an inalienable right to a share in the proceeds of successive public sales of their original works should take into account the possibility of considering such provisions.[259]

11.60 Following the Rome Conference, both ALAI and the IIIC continued to study the implementation of *droit de suite* on both a national and international scale.[260] The matter was also considered by a number of other international bodies, including the prestigious International Institute of Rome for the Unification of Private Law.[261] More particularly, the Belgian Government and International Office made it the subject of a specific proposal which they included in their preliminary programme for the Brussels Revision in 1934. This proposed a new article 14*bis* which provided for Conventional recognition of the *droit de suite*, applicable not only to artistic works but to original manuscripts as well:

> As far as original works of art and the original manuscripts of writers and composers are concerned, the protection accorded by the present Convention includes equally for the author of the work and his heirs an inalienable right to an interest in any public sale of which the said work is the object after the first sale thereof has been made by the author.
>
> The method and amount of this collection are to be determined by national legislation.[262]

This received a wide range of responses from member nations. Some were hostile to the notion of an obligatory right,[263] while others objected to particular aspects of the programme proposal, such as its inclusion of manuscripts and its apparent inclusion of architectural works and works of applied art, its limitation to heirs, and the failure to link its duration to that of copyright generally.[264] Nonetheless, *droit de suite* continued to receive attention in the preparatory work for the Brussels Revision that continued after the planned conference in 1936 was postponed. Of particular importance was the work of a committee of experts convened by the International Institute for the Unification of Private Law in Rome in April 1935.[265] This committee proposed that certain matters which were not generally regarded as part of copyright but were nevertheless closely related should be dealt with in a convention or arrangement annexed to the Berne Convention which member countries could accede to separately if they wished (but without any obligation to do so). These related or 'neighbouring' matters included the rights of performing artists and rights in broadcasts

---

259 *Actes* 1928, 283.
260 Duchemin (1948), 243ff.
261 ibid, 252ff.
262 ibid, 301 (for text of proposition) and 250ff (for further background).
263 See [1936] *DA* 93.
264 ibid. See also *Documents 1948* (1951), 362–3.
265 Duchemin (1948), 252ff.

and sound recordings, and the committee recommended that *droit de suite* should be added to these.[266] This proposal was elaborated upon in a draft convention that was drawn up by the Director of the International Office, Fritz Ostertag,[267] and was considered by a further committee of experts that met at Samaden in July 1939.[268] This draft made provision, originally, for six categories of neighbouring rights, and *droit de suite* was included as a seventh. Under the regime proposed here,[269] each contracting state undertook to accord the authors of original artistic works 'realized in the domain of painting, sculpture, engraving and drawing "a *droit de suite*" in the price of resale of their works'.[270] This was to be a personal and inalienable right of the author which would belong to his heirs after his death.[271] Certain matters, however, were left to national legislation to determine, including the duration of protection, the method of collection and the amount, and the means of safeguarding the new right.[272] Finally, the proposed convention was open to signature only by present and future Berne Union members.[273]

The Samaden project was aborted by the advent of World War II, although elements of it were to be drawn upon in the post-war negotiations that led ultimately to the creation of a separate convention on neighbouring rights in 1961. As for the proposals concerning *droit de suite*, these were quietly abandoned, and in its renewed programme for the 1948 Conference the Belgian Government returned to its original proposal of 1934 for the addition of a new article 14*bis* to the Berne Convention.[274] In doing so, its clear purpose was to gain acceptance for the *droit de suite* as part of copyright, rather than as something separate—a point of some importance in relation to the application of the Convention today (see para 11.63 below). Nevertheless, since the Rome Conference only two other Berne members had accorded legislative recognition to the *droit de suite*—Italy and Poland[275]—and there were still considerable reservations about the proposal on the part of other members.[276] An Austrian amendment (later withdrawn) proposed that those countries of the Union which had adopted *droit de suite* in their legislation should not be obliged to grant to authors of another member state more extensive protection than that granted in their country of origin.[277] Norway and Finland, however, did not see the need for such a right for their own artists,[278] and the British, without actively opposing the concept, argued that the time was not yet ripe for its adoption into 11.61

266 ibid, 255. 267 ibid, see further [1939] *DA* 62 and [1940] *DA* 109, 121 and 133.

268 Duchemin (1948), 255ff.

269 For the text of the draft relating to *droit de suite*, see Duchemin (1948), 299–301 (the 'draft text'); also in [1940] *DA* 138.

270 Draft text, art 1. 271 ibid, art 5. 272 ibid, arts 6 and 7. 273 ibid, art 9.

274 *Documents 1948* (1951), 364. 275 See nn 243 and 244 above.

276 *Documents 1948* (1951), 363. 277 ibid, 364–5. 278 ibid, 365 and 366.

UK law.[279] A more fundamental objection came from the Dutch delegation which did not see the proposed right as belonging to the realm of copyright and was therefore opposed to it being brought within the framework of the Berne Convention.[280] For these reasons, a further paragraph was added to the Belgian proposal providing that the *droit de suite* should only be claimed in those countries whose legislation provided for it and that this should be on the basis of reciprocity.[281] No objection was raised to this, and the final provision adopted by the Conference as article 14*bis* read as follows:

> (1) The author, or after his death, the persons or institutions authorized by national legislation, shall, in respect of original works of art and original manuscripts of writers and composers, enjoy the inalienable right to an interest in any sale of the work subsequent to the first disposal of the work by the author.
>
> (2) The protection provided by the preceding paragraph may be claimed in a country of the Union only if legislation in the country to which the author belongs so permits, and to the degree permitted by the country where this protection is claimed.
>
> (3) The procedure for collection and the amounts shall be a matter for determination by national legislation.

No proposals for change to this provision were made at the time of the Stockholm Revision, either in the programme or in the proposals submitted by member nations. The text therefore remains the same in the Stockholm, Paris Acts, except for the following minor changes of a drafting kind: (i) the article is now renumbered as article 14*ter*, and (ii) the word 'transfer' was substituted for 'disposal' in paragraph (1) and 'extent' for 'degree' in paragraph (2).

*(d) Interpretation of article 14*ter

11.62 The basic arrangement of this article is as follows. The concept of *droit de suite* (although it is not referred to by this name) is defined in paragraph (1). However, paragraph (2) then makes it clear that there is no obligation on member states to accord this protection, and that it may only be claimed on condition of reciprocity. Finally, paragraph (3) leaves it to national legislation to determine how the collection of the *droit de suite* is to be done, as well as the amount of it.

11.63 The right accorded under paragraph (1) is an 'inalienable' right which immediately distinguishes it from the other pecuniary rights of the author protected under the Convention. In this respect, it is akin to moral rights under article 6*bis*, but any further analogy is misleading. The *droit de suite*, whether or not it is regarded as part of the author's copyright, is a right that entitles the author to an 'interest' in subsequent sales of his work, and it is clear from the preparatory

[279] *Documents 1948* (1951), 367. [280] ibid, 366. [281] ibid, 368.

work for the Brussels Conference that this was considered to be a 'pecuniary interest'.[282] It will be seen that the first sale of his work is excluded, as the artist will usually (but not always) be the person who makes this sale. Only subsequent sales are covered by paragraph (1) but, unlike some national laws[283] and the original proposal of the Belgian Government,[284] this makes no distinction between public and private sales. As to the basis on which the *droit de suite* is to be accorded—whether on all sales or only on those which are made at an increased price—the word 'interest' would seem to indicate that there is an entitlement to a share in the proceeds of sale in any event and that there is no room for the application of the principle of 'increased value'. However, it will be seen below that the wording of paragraph (2) qualifies paragraph (1) in this respect, and would allow for the latter basis to be applied in certain cases to works claiming *droit de suite* under the Convention. Similar latitude is allowed in relation to the works to which the *droit de suite* applies. While paragraph (1) makes the widest possible provision in this respect—to 'original works of art and original manuscripts of writers and composers'—paragraph (2) does permit restrictions of these categories in certain instances (see further para 11.64 below). Paragraph (1) also provides that the 'inalienable right' accorded under that paragraph passes after the death of the author to 'the persons or institutions authorized by national legislation'. These may very well be the persons or bodies that would be entitled to succeed to the other rights of the author in the ordinary course of events, but the provision leaves it open to national legislation to determine otherwise. For instance, it would be possible to provide that this right should be exercised by some public agency after the author's death and for the proceeds to be distributed to authors generally. Finally, no reference to the duration of the *droit de suite* is made under paragraph (1). On the basis that this is regarded as part of the author's copyright, this would then fall to be regulated under articles 7 and 7*bis*. Once again, however, paragraph (2) may allow for the imposition of a different term (see further para 11.64 below).

Having defined the scope of the right to be accorded under paragraph (1), paragraph (2) then stipulates that this may be claimed only on the basis of reciprocity. It will be recognized immediately that this is an exception to the general principle of national treatment, but that exceptions of this kind have been made throughout the life of the Convention in order to secure limited recognition of rights and subject matter that would otherwise remain outside the scope of the Convention. Other leading examples are works of applied art and the comparison of terms in the case of duration. However, the way in which **11.64**

282 ibid, 362ff.
283 eg France, Code de la propriété intellectuelle, art L 122–8 (conferring right to royalty).
284 *Documents 1948* (1951), 364.

the requirement of reciprocity is formulated under article $14^{ter}(2)$ is far from satisfactory, and leaves several matters unsettled. Under this paragraph, protection for the *droit de suite* may only be claimed (i) 'if the legislation in the country to which the author belongs so permits', and (ii) then only 'to the extent permitted by the country where this protection is claimed'. It has been argued that this is not the same as factual reciprocity: if this had been intended, paragraph (2) would simply have provided that authors could claim in a Union country only those rights accorded to authors in their own country, or alternatively that authors could not claim more extensive protection than was accorded in their country of origin.[285] However, the present wording appears to have a different effect, giving on the one hand and taking away with the other. According to this interpretation, even if the country to which the author belongs[286] accords protection to the *droit de suite*, the words 'to the extent permitted by the country where this protection is claimed' permit this second country to restrict this protection in whichever way it wishes.[287] In other words, the second country may accord a different level of protection to that which it accords to its nationals, or even deny it altogether.

11.65 If that conclusion were correct, this would be an absurd situation, as article 14ter would then represent no advance on the pre-Brussels position, where states always had the discretion whether or not to recognize *droit de suite* in the case of foreigners and to regulate the extent to which this protection was to be accorded to foreigners as distinct from nationals. Such a provision would be superfluous, and there is no reason to suppose that an international conference of the authority and weight of that which met at Brussels in 1948 would have undertaken such a pointless exercise.[288] If this view were correct, it would also be an unusual form of drafting to provide for protection, and then to stipulate that the country where protection was claimed might impose whatever other conditions it wished. While the *Documents* of the Brussels Conference are not very helpful on this point, there is no indication in them that the delegates intended anything other than the application of material reciprocity between member countries as regards the *droit de suite.* Professor Nordemann also remarks that:

> . . . to leave member countries free to deny foreigners the rights due to nationals would be a renunciation of the national treatment principle in a fashion hitherto unknown in the history of the Berne Convention. This would amount to a complete reversal in the international protection of authors. One cannot, of course,

[285] See Baum (1949), 67ff and the other German authors referred to by Nordemann (n 233 above) at 339.

[286] This must mean the same as the country of origin of the work: see art 5(3).

[287] See para 11.61 above. [288] See Nordemann (n 233 above), 339.

> rule out the possibility of such a thing occurring; yet I feel that I can safely assume that it would have been expressly mentioned during the Brussels Conference, whereupon there would have been strong protest from the traditional cultural countries . . . I am instead convinced that, in that case, the inclusion of the *droit de suite* in the Brussels Act of the Berne Convention would have been vetoed by more than one country.[289]

Although the wording of article 14*ter*(2) is far from clear, the above considerations indicate that the cumulative conditions listed in paragraph (2) are to be interpreted as making material reciprocity the sole condition for claiming protection of the *droit de suite.*[290] This means that the words 'to the extent permitted by the country where this protection is claimed' are not to be read as conferring on countries a separate discretion whether or not to protect authors belonging to countries which accord the *droit de suite*, but simply as a reference to the nature and extent of the national treatment which is to be accorded to foreigners and nationals alike. In other words, foreign authors are to be protected to the same extent as national authors under the principle of national treatment. If material reciprocity exists between the two countries, the country in which protection is claimed may not impose any further requirement in relation to the author from the other country.[291]

What is required for material reciprocity under paragraph (2)? There are considerable differences in the way that *droit de suite* is protected in those countries which recognize it, although the 2001 Resale Right Directive will have a harmonizing effect in the twenty-five member states of the European Union, as well as in other states who adopt EU norms. Some, for example, do not extend it to original manuscripts[292] or to particular categories of artistic work, such as architectural works or works of applied art.[293] Others accord protection only in respect of increases in value when the work is resold rather than on all sales.[294] Does material reciprocity require that there should be a close equivalence of protection between the countries in question? Or is it enough that the principle **11.66**

---

289 ibid. 290 See also to the same effect Ulmer (n 233 above), 27ff.

291 Moreover, the European Union constrains reciprocity further still, see *droit de suite* Directive (n 192 above), recital 6: 'It follows from the case-law of the Court of Justice of the European Communities on the application of the principle of non-discrimination laid down in Article 12 of the Treaty, as shown in the judgment of 20 October 1993 in Joined Cases C-92/92 and C-326/92 *Phil Collins and Others*, that domestic provisions containing reciprocity clauses cannot be relied upon in order to deny nationals of other member states rights conferred on national authors. The application of such clauses in the Community context runs counter to the principle of equal treatment resulting from the prohibition of any discrimination on grounds of nationality.'

292 See eg France, Code de la propriété intellectuelle, art L 122-8; the FRG Law of 1965, art 26.

293 See eg the FRG Law (n 292 above).

294 As eg in the Italian, Czech, and Brazilian laws: see n 249 above.

of *droit de suite* is recognized and enforced in the country to which the author claiming protection belongs even if there are significant differences in the extent of this protection? In this respect, the wording of paragraph (2) is far from helpful. The words 'to the extent permitted by . . .' establish that the country where protection is claimed is not required to accord any more protection than that which is already available to its nationals. Thus, an author from a country which accords the *droit de suite* in respect of original manuscripts will not be able to claim this in a country which does not extend the *droit de suite* in this way. What should happen in the opposite case? Some writers argue that there must be a 'substantial equivalence' in the sense that the subject matter protected in both countries should be broadly the same, even if there are differences in the details of this protection.[295] This interpretation would certainly be sustainable if paragraph (2) had adopted one of the more usual formulas for material reciprocity, for example, that the author claiming protection should not be accorded greater protection than that accorded him in his country of origin. This, in fact, was the wording of the Austrian amendment which was before the drafting committee at the Brussels Conference.[296] The present wording, however, was preferred by the committee,[297] and we must therefore ask if it is to be interpreted as meaning the same thing. The answer must be that it does, but in a roundabout way. Paragraph (2) requires that the protection provided by paragraph (1) may be claimed by an author only if 'legislation in the country to which he belongs so permits'. It would be possible to interpret this to mean that all the protection provided by paragraph (1) must be accorded, in which case paragraph (2) would become largely ineffective as very few Union members protect *droit de suite* in this extended fashion. Alternatively, it can mean that the particular protection claimed in a country of the Union (being a part of the general protection provided for under paragraph (1)) must also be provided by the legislation of the country to which the author belongs—in other words, there must be substantial equivalence on this matter between the laws of the two countries. This seems the more reasonable interpretation, with the result than an author from a country whose law does not accord the *droit de suite* in respect of a particular category of work cannot claim protection for this in another country which does. The latter, of course, is quite free, as a matter of international comity, to accord such protection in any event.[298]

11.67 Article 14*ter*(3) is really superfluous in view of the words 'to the extent permitted by the country where this protection is claimed' which appear in paragraph (2).

[295] See Nordemann (n 233 above), 339–40 and Ulmer (n 233 above), 26–7.
[296] *Documents 1948* (1951), 364. [297] ibid, 367–8.
[298] See also Ulmer (n 233 above), 27.

As explained above, these words require the foreign author to submit to whatever conditions and restrictions are placed on national authors. These must include such matters as the procedure for determining the amount due to the author, as well as the way in which this is to be collected. These are details which it would be inappropriate to include in a general convention such as this. The words 'to the extent to which . . .' also have a wider operation, in that they permit the protecting country to modify or vary the protection referred to under paragraph (1). For example, it was suggested above that the latter excludes the application of the principle of increased value while requiring the *droit de suite* to be accorded to a wide range of original works. If these were mandatory requirements under the Convention, the laws of many, if not all, Union countries on *droit de suite* would be in conflict with paragraph (1). These words of paragraph (2) therefore permit these countries to maintain their national laws, without any obligation to accord to authors claiming under the Convention the full rights provided for in paragraph (1). These words also have a more far-reaching effect which should be stated, for the sake of completeness. They mean that there is no obligation on Union countries to have legislation on *droit de suite* in the first place: 'to the extent to which . . .' clearly means that there is a sliding scale, the top of which is represented by the full protection defined in paragraph (1) and the bottom of which is no protection at all. If this were not so, it is clear from the *Documents* of the Brussels Conference that the proposal for article 14*bis* would not have been acceptable to many Union members.[299] Paragraph (1), therefore, is like article 7(1) of the Berlin Act with respect to duration of protection: it embodies an ideal standard of protection to which, it is hoped, all member countries will move in time. That this is far slower in happening than in the case of article 7 is indicated by the fact that, although, at the time of the Stockholm and Paris Revisions, twenty-six Union members protected *droit de suite*, this was slightly less than a third of the total membership, and no further changes to article 14*bis* (now 14*ter*) were then proposed.

E. Beyond the Berne Convention

Multilateral agreements entered into since the Stockholm–Paris Revision have focused on two of the more elusive features of the minimum rights established by the Berne Convention. The WCT endeavoured to articulate the scope of the reproduction right in a way that would clarify its application to digital media and communications. As we will see, however, this attempt proved so hotly contested that the proposed provision was dropped, and replaced with an 'agreed statement' **11.68**

[299] *Documents 1948* (1951), 365ff.

whose import resists confident characterization. Whatever was agreed did not result in a very clear statement. Second, regarding rights in physical copies, the TRIPs Agreement requires member states to implement remedial measures to prevent infringing importations. Both the TRIPs Agreement and the WCT also expand the author's rights in physical copies by setting out a limited right to control rentals of copies of certain kinds of works. Finally, the WCT adopted a general provision on distribution rights. Both the TRIPs Agreement and WCT leave the question of exhaustion of rights to national legislation.

(1) The scope of the reproduction right in the WCT

11.69 We have seen that, although the 1971 Paris text's new article 9 set forth a general expression of the right to reproduce a literary or artistic work, it did not define what a 'reproduction' was (see the earlier discussion at paras 11.26–11.27 above). In 1971, the answer to that question may have seemed clear, as the copies most copyright commentators would have envisaged would have been analogue media hard copies. Copies made in a computer's random access memory (RAM) and other temporary digital copies thus most likely did not receive foremost consideration,[300] though the text of article 9, extending the right to reproduction 'in any manner or form', may have been broad enough to cover them.[301] In 1987, the first edition of this treatise acknowledged that the question of whether the right reached storage of works in the form of invisible electrical impulses was 'one respect in which the Berne Convention would benefit from clarification'.[302] By the time of the Diplomatic Conference that would produce the WCT in 1996, when digital copies made not only for permanent retention, but also for temporary viewing or listening, accounted for a good deal of the exploitation of copyrighted works, this 'clarification' seemed all the more urgent.

11.70 Throughout the 1980s and early 1990s, Reports of the WIPO Committee of Experts addressed the need for such clarification,[303] ultimately supporting the

[300] But see Eugen Ulmer, 'Report of the Executive Committee of the Inernational Union for the Protection of Literary and Artstic Works (Berne Union)' [1972] *Copyright* 15, para 18 ('The provisions of the Berne Convention (Stockholm and Paris Acts), in that they clearly protected works at the input stage, appeared . . . to provide a suitable basis for the regulation at international level of problems arising from computer storage and retrieval of protected works.') It is not clear, however, whether Ulmer was anticipating transient as well as more stable storage.

[301] See eg Masouyé (1978), para 9.2 (right covers all methods of reproduction, including those yet to be discovered).

[302] *The Berne Convention 1886–1986* (1987), para 8.10.

[303] See eg report of the Second WIPO/UNESCO Committee of Governmental Experts on Copyright Problems Arising from the Use of Computers for Access to or the Creation of Works: [1982] *Copyright* 239ff, 245ff (acknowledging that computer storage and retrieval of works may implicate the reproduction right protected by the Berne and Universal Copyright Conventions).

European Union and its member states' proposal in their submission for the seventh session of the Committee of Experts that, rather than attempting to modify the existing language of article 9(1) of the Berne Convention, contracting parties to the proposed WCT should confirm in the records of the Diplomatic Conference or in the General Report that permanent or temporary storage of a protected work in any electronic medium comes within the meaning of reproduction in article 9(1).[304] Whether the application of the reproduction right not only to temporary but also to transient computer retention of digital files was a matter merely to be 'confirmed' or 'clarified' in this way, or instead represented an extension of the scope of the right, was widely discussed in commentaries, and proved to be a highly contentious issue in the drafting of the 1996 WCT.

Many international copyright experts, especially in Europe, considered that the article 9(1) text was sufficiently abstract as already to have covered all forms of entry into a computer.[305] As two authors representative of this point of view, Jörg Reinbothe and Silke von Lewinski, have contended, the Paris text formulation is 'future-proof',[306] because it covers 'any manner or form' of reproduction including those unknown at the time of the Treaty's drafting. For these authors, the Berne Convention already incorporated a 'wide concept of reproduction' based on the concept of 'fixation'; a fixation need not be permanent, so long as it can be 'perceived, reproduced or otherwise communicated'.[307] Consequently, article 9(1) would cover temporary copies, including those made in RAM, as **11.71**

[304] WIPO Report on the Second Session of the Committee of Experts on a Possible Protocol to the Berne Convention: [1992] *Copyright* 93, paras 48–57.

[305] See eg Jörg Reinbothe and Silke von Lewinski, *The WIPO Treaties 1996* (2002) ('Reinbothe and von Lewinski (2002)'), 42–3; Mihàly Ficsor, *The Law of Copyright and the Internet* (2003), 96–102; Mihaly Ficsor, 'Copyright for the Digital Era: The WIPO "Internet Treaties" '(Manges Lecture)' (1997) 21 *Columbia-VLA Journal of Law & the Arts* 197, 204 (commenting that '[t]he fact that the storage of works in electronic memories is an act of reproduction has been recognized—and has never been questioned—for a long time'); Pierre Sirinelli, *LAMY Droit des medias et de la communication* (2002), paras 121–4 (reviewing French case law and asserting that 'French decisions have long recognized . . . the exclusive right to reproduce the work directly or indirectly, permanently or provisionally, by any means and in any form' and that 'the fleeting character of the reproduction [in a computer's temporary memory] does not matter'). See also the Information Society Directive (n 182 above), art 5(1), (imposing mandatory exception from reproduction right for certain transient and incidental acts of temporary reproduction; if these acts were not otherwise understood to come within the scope of the reproduction right, no exception would have been needed); 17 USC § 117 (providing exceptions for certain temporary copies made while computer is in operation; were RAM copies not otherwise actionable reproductions, these exceptions would not be needed); Copyright Office report, www.loc.gov/copyright/reports/ (29 Aug 2001), reviewing the text of the US Copyright Act and the case law, and concluding that reproductions in RAM are 'copies for copyright purposes'.

[306] Reinbothe and von Lewinski (2002), 44.

[307] Reinbothe and von Lewinski (2002), 42–3. Cf 17 USC § 101 (defining fixation in closely similar terms).

well as in the course of communicating a work over a digital network.[308] Other commentators, primarily in the USA, expressed concern about the implications of a RAM-copying doctrine, fearing that it would lead to excessive copyright owner control. Accordingly, they argued that the matter was not free from doubt,[309] and that 'the better view of the law is that the act of reading a work into a computer's random access memory is too transitory to create a reproduction within the meaning of [the reproduction right]'.[310]

11.72 The drafters of the WCT initially followed the copyright 'traditionalists'. The Explanatory Notes to article 7(1) of the Basic Proposal for the future WCT insisted that the wording 'in any manner or form' as used in article 9(1) of the Berne Convention 'could not be more expansive in scope. It clearly includes the storage of a work in any electronic medium . . .'.[311] On the other hand, the Notes also acknowledged that 'Some countries may consider that temporary reproduction, at least some acts of reproduction the results of which live only a very short time, does not fall under the right of reproduction, whereas other countries may take a contrary interpretation.'[312] The Notes again adverted to this disagreement in concluding that 'The only way to harmonize effectively the interpretation of the scope of the right of reproduction is to confirm that temporary reproduction falls within the scope of the right.'[313] Although the Notes employ the term 'confirm', implicit in the call for effective harmonization

[308] Drs Reinbothe and von Lewinski hasten to add that exceptions and limitations to the scope of the right may be appropriate and desirable, especially in the digital environment, but the starting point remains that, unless exempted, RAM and transient copies are 'reproductions'; ibid.

[309] See eg P Samuelson, 'The U.S. Digital Agenda at WIPO' (1997) 37 *U Va J IL* 369, 392 ('The most honest thing that can be said about the temporary copying of works in computer memory is that there is no international consensus on this subject.'); ibid at 380–92, and sources cited at 382, n 75. See also, Mark A Lemley, 'Dealing with Overlapping Copyrights On the Internet' (1997) 22 *U Dayton L Rev* 547, 551 (addressing RAM copying in US law, and criticizing both the Ninth Circuit decision in *MAI Systems Corp* v *Peak Computer, Inc*, 991 F 2d 511 (9th Cir 1993) and the National Information Infrastructure task force White Paper for failing adequately to recognize that 'the legislative history accompanying the "fixation" language in the 1976 Copyright Act strongly suggests that Congress did not consider such [RAM] copies to be "fixed" ').

[310] Jessica Litman, 'The Exclusive Right to Read' (1994) 13 *Cardozo Arts & Ent LJ* 29, 42 (discussing scope of US reproduction right); see also Jaap H Spoor, 'The Copyright Approach to Copying on the Internet: (Over)stretching the Reproduction Right', in P Bernt Hugenholtz (ed), *The Future of Copyright in a Digital Environment* (1996), 67.

[311] 'Basic Proposal for the Substantive Provisions of the Treaty on Certain Questions Concerning The Protection of Literary and Artistic Works to be Considered by the Diplomatic Conference', CRNR/DC/4 (30 Aug 1996) ('Basic Proposal'), Explanatory Note 7.01, reprinted in WIPO, *Records of the Diplomatic Conference on Certain Copyright and Neighboring Rights Questions, Geneva 1996* (1999) ('Records'), at 188.

[312] Basic Proposal (n 311 above), Explanatory Note 7.14, Records (n 311 above) at 190.

[313] Basic Proposal (n 311 above), Explanatory Note 7.16, Records (n 311 above) at 192.

may be a recognition that the scope of the application of the reproduction right to digital media was not completely 'obvious'.[314]

Article 7(1) of the Basic Proposal therefore provided:

> The exclusive right accorded to authors of literary and artistic works in article 9(1) of the Berne Convention of authorizing the reproduction of their works shall include direct and indirect reproduction of their works, whether permanent or temporary, in any manner or form.

This sweeping language would certainly have covered RAM copying. The full import of the phrase 'direct and indirect reproduction of their works,[315] whether permanent or temporary', emerged from comparing the affirmative clause with its counterpart in article 7(2), setting out exceptions to the restated reproduction right. It stated: **11.73**

> Subject to the provisions of Article 9(2) of the Berne Convention, it shall be a matter for legislation in Contracting Parties to limit the right of reproduction in cases where a temporary reproduction has the sole purpose of making the work perceptible or where the reproduction is of a transient or incidental nature, provided that such reproduction takes place in the course of use of the work that is authorized by the author or permitted by law.

In other words, absent provisions in the law of a member state exempting transient and incidental reproductions, these would be covered by the reproduction right. This text prompted the interpretation that the temporary digital copies under which the proposed article 7(1) declared the reproduction right covered would include any transient copies made in the course of transmitting the work over the Internet, when the transmission enjoyed neither the author's permission nor a legal privilege.[316] This would have made Internet Service Providers vulnerable to infringement claims. The proposal pleased few and outraged many. Some delegations believed the provision unnecessary in light of the Basic Proposal's general provision on exceptions and limitations to all exclusive rights. Presumably, if the temporary reproduction met the criteria set out in proposed article 7(2), it would also pass the 'three-step test' of proposed

314 By contrast, Mihàly Ficsor, who at the time of the WCT Diplomatic Conference was Assistant Director General of WIPO, unambiguously asserts that it was already 'obvious' that the right of reproduction under Berne, art 9(1) reached entry of a work into a computer's temporary memory. See Ficsor (2003) (n 305 above), 445, para C1.50. See also Ficsor (1997) (n 305 above), 206.

315 The term 'direct and indirect' was borrowed from art 10 of the Rome Convention; the Basic Proposal described 'indirect' reproduction as remote copying, such as copying a work from a broadcast, Basic Proposal (n 311 above), Explanatory Note 7.04, Records (n 311 above) at 188.

316 See Reinbothe and von Lewinski (2002) at 13, attributing some of the controversy over art 7 'to its interface with the more general and also highly controversial question of the liability for online service providers'.

article 12.[317] Others, less sanguine, contended the exception should be mandatory, and still others urged deleting all of proposed article 7.[318]

11.74 Ultimately, the delegates deleted proposed article 7, and substituted an 'agreed statement' on the scope of the reproduction right carried over from article 9(1) of the 1971 Paris Act of the Berne Convention. The agreed statement provides:

> The reproduction right as set out in Article 9 of the Berne Convention, and the exceptions permitted thereunder, fully apply in the digital environment, in particular to the use of works in digital form. It is understood that the storage of a protected work in digital form in an electronic medium constitutes a reproduction within the meaning of Article 9 of the Berne Convention.

Whether or not the Berne Convention already embraced all kinds of reproductions, including the temporary and the transient, the significant contribution of the first sentence of the agreed statement appears to be its emphasis on exceptions to the reproduction right, rather than its, possibly meaningless, announcement that the reproduction right 'fully appl[ies]' in the digital environment. This explicit confirmation of the availability of exceptions to the reproduction right in the digital environment may be designed to prompt member states to re-evaluate existing limitations and exceptions, and to permit them to devise new ones.[319] Unlike proposed article 7(2), which seemed very narrowly to confine the realm of new exceptions to transient reproductions only,[320] the structure of the first sentence of the agreed statement gives the exceptions as much weight as the affirmation of the right.

11.75 Does this affirmation resolve the question of temporary or transient entry into computer memory? Arguably, the 'full application' of the reproduction right in the digital environment should entail all forms of reproduction, however short-lived. But the second sentence of the agreed statement muddies the waters. In providing that 'It is understood that the storage of a protected work in digital form in an electronic medium constitutes a reproduction within the meaning of

[317] The 'three-step test', derived from the Berne Convention 1971 text's art 9.2, and echoed in article 13 of the TRIPs Agreement, limits member states' entitlement to derogate from exclusive rights to 'certain special cases, that do not conflict with a normal exploitation of the work, and do not unreasonably prejudice the legitimate interests of the author'. See the further discussion at para 13.10ff below. Basic Proposal (n 311 above), art 12 was adopted almost verbatim as WCT, art 10.

[318] See Summary Minutes of Main Committee I, 4th Meeting, Mon 9 Dec 1996, Records (n 311 above) at 667–75.

[319] See Reinbothe and von Lewinski (2002) at 44.

[320] The qualifier 'seemed' is appropriate here, because proposed art 7(2) incorporated by reference Berne Convention, art 9(2), which sets out the general, 'three-step test' for exceptions to the reproduction right. The creation of a special exception for volatile copies made in transmission need not invite a negative inference as to the availability of other exceptions to the reproduction right.

Article 9 of the Berne Convention', the text scrupulously avoids detailing the meaning of 'storage'. If 'storage' means retention for some more than transitory period of time, then it might add nothing to 'any manner or form', because 'form' could imply a manifestation more concrete than a transient communication.[321] If, however, the term 'storage' was meant also to cover fleeting passage through a digital network, then one may wonder at the selection of a term whose ordinary meaning implies more lingering than just passing through. Moreover, if the term is to be understood in its ordinary meaning, then one might question whether it also justifies a negative inference: if the copy of the work is not 'stored' because it is transient, can it still be a reproduction? In other words, the scope of the reproduction right that emerges from the agreed statement remains open to highly variable interpretation.[322]

(2) Rights pertaining to physical copies

Both the TRIPs Agreement and the WCT require member states to respect the Berne–Paris text *acquis*.[323] Thus, any minima that Berne establishes with respect to the author's rights over the disposition of copies, such as distribution rights in cinematographic works,[324] are preserved, and in the case of the TRIPs Agreement, rendered enforceable through WTO dispute-resolution proceedings. Both texts also amplify the author's rights in relation to physical copies. Although neither the TRIPs Agreement nor the WCT address these rights comprehensively, both contain provisions granting some control over subsequent disposition of copies through rental,[325] and the WCT introduces a general right of initial distribution of physical copies.[326] The TRIPs Agreement also requires member states to implement enforcement measures against the importation of infringing copies of works.[327] Neither text reaches the *droit* **11.76**

[321] See eg *Lewis Galoob Toys* v *Nintendo of Am* (9th Cir 1992) (interpreting the definition of a derivative work in 17 USC § 101, 'any other *form* in which the work may be recast, transformed or adapted' (emphasis added), to exclude unfixed, or extremely transient, alterations to a video game).

Indeed, the term could be viewed as constraining the art 9(1) formulation, because, arguably, art 9(1) did not compel the conclusion that 'form' excluded evanescent fixations, but 'storage' lends itself much more to that reading. That, however, would mean that the WCT narrows the scope of the 9(1) reproduction right, but this would not be permissible under art 20 of the Berne Convention, see para 6.136.

[322] See eg J Sheinblatt, 'The WIPO Copyright Treaty' (1998) 13 *Berkeley Tech LJ* 535, 550 (both copyright 'maximalists' and copyright 'minimalists' claimed to have been the victors in the WIPO Treaty process).

[323] TRIPs Agreement, arts 2(2), 9(1); WCT, art 1.

[324] Arts 14(1)(i), 14*bis*(1), discussed at para 11.49 above.

[325] TRIPs Agreement, arts 11, 14(4); WCT, art 7.

[326] WCT, art 6.

[327] TRIPs Agreement, arts 41(1) (injunction preventing entry of infringing imported goods); 50(1)(a) (provisional remedies regarding the same); 51 (application to customs authorities to block entry of 'pirated copyrighted goods').

de suite. Both leave the issue of exhaustion for determination by member states.[328]

(a) Importation rights in the TRIPs Agreement

11.77 **(i) Pertinent dispositions of the TRIPs Agreement:** The TRIPs Agreement imposes a variety of obligations regarding the enforcement of intellectual property rights against unauthorized entry of infringing copies into a member state.[329] Among these, article 44(1), on injunctive relief, provides in relevant part:

> The judicial authorities shall have the authority . . . to prevent the entry into the channels of commerce in their jurisdiction of imported goods that involve the infringement of an intellectual property right, immediately after customs clearance of such goods. Members are not obliged to accord such authority in respect of protected subject matter acquired or ordered by a person prior to knowing or having reasonable grounds to know that dealing in such subject matter would entail the infringement of an intellectual property right.

Similarly, article 50(1)(a), on provisional measures, requires judicial authorities to have power

> in particular, to prevent the entry into the channels of commerce in their jurisdiction of goods, including imported goods immediately after customs clearance.

Finally, the 'special requirements related to border measures' include an article, 51, titled 'suspension of release by customs authorities', which directs member states to

> adopt procedures to enable a right holder, who has valid grounds for suspecting that the importation of . . . pirated copyrighted goods may take place, to lodge an application in writing with competent authorities, administrative or judicial, for the suspension by the customs authorities of the release into free circulation of such goods.

However,

> It is understood that there shall be no obligation to apply such procedures to imports of goods put on the market in another country by or with the consent of the right holder or to goods in transit.[330]

'Pirated copyright goods' are defined as

> any goods which are copies made without the consent of the right holder or person duly authorized by the right holder in the country of production and

[328] TRIPs Agreement, art 6; WCT, art 6(2). See Paul Katzenberger, 'TRIPS and Copyright Law', in Freidrich-Karl Beier and Gerhard Schricker (eds), *From GATT to TRIPS, The Agreement on Trade Related Aspects of Intellectual Property* (1996), 59.

[329] TRIPs Agreement, arts 41–61.

[330] Note (b) to ibid, art 51.

which are made directly or indirectly from an article where the making of that copy would have constituted an infringement of a copyright or related right under the law of the country of importation.[331]

Together, these provisions accord a right to prevent importation either after the goods enter the country and clear customs, but have not yet been disseminated, or, in the case of 'pirated copyright goods', to obtain the co-operation of customs officials in blocking the entry of the goods. Each form of border control, however, imposes conditions. **11.78**

With respect to injunctive relief, the copyright owner cannot obtain a court order blocking dissemination if the importer did not have reasonable grounds to know that it was infringing an intellectual property right. Two questions arise. First, what intellectual property rights would the importer infringe? Second, what constitute reasonable grounds to know? Regarding the first question, the most relevant right is likely to be the reproduction right: for the restriction on entry to apply, the importer should have reason to know that the copies were produced without authorization in the country from which they were exported. Suppose, however, the goods were lawfully made, with or without authorization, in the latter case because in the country of exportation there was no copyright protection, or because a compulsory licence applied; the importer would not be infringing a reproduction right. It might be infringing a distribution right, but that would depend on the scope of the distribution right under the law of the country of importation. If, for example, that country's exhaustion rules permitted entry of goods lawfully made in another country, then the importer would not be infringing. Recall that article 6 of the TRIPs Agreement leaves the question of exhaustion to member states. **11.79**

As for the basis of the importer's actual or imputed knowledge, it may not always be apparent that the goods are infringing; knowledge, then, would most likely be acquired by receipt of a cease and desist or similar notice from the right holder before initiation of suit.[332]

With respect to pirated goods, the right holder may obtain the intervention of customs officials to block entry altogether; the right holder may request this intervention even before the goods arrive. But, to be considered 'pirated', the goods have to meet a standard reminiscent of the old English 'double actionability' rule for choice of law in tort claims:[333] the goods must be infringing both in the country of production and in the country of importation. If the goods **11.80**

[331] Note (c)(i) to ibid, art 51.

[332] See Daniel Gervais, *The TRIPs Agreement: Drafting History and Analysis*, 2nd edn (2003), para 2.395.

[333] See eg *Phillips* v *Eyre* (1870) LR 6 QB 1.

were unlawfully made in the country of production, but would not infringe in the country of importation, for example, because of expiry of term, the TRIPs Agreement does not mandate border closure. If the goods were lawfully made, for example, under licence, in the country of production, but would infringe in the country of importation, there is no claim under article 51 of the TRIPs Agreement either. The definition of 'pirated goods' thus would seem to make superfluous the other Note to article 51, that 'there shall be no obligation to apply such procedures to imports of goods put on the market in another country by or with the consent of the right holder or to goods in transit'. But the Note has a wider ambit: it allows countries to permit the 'grey market' in more than pirated copyright goods, so the Note is not superfluous as to the other subject matter. More importantly, the Note also relieves member states of any obligation to block goods that are merely in transit and not destined for the member state's market, even if they are counterfeit. This would seem to be a significant gap in the enforcement structure.[334]

(b) Rental rights in the TRIPs Agreement and the WCT

11.81 Articles 11 of the TRIPS Agreement introduced, for the first time in a general multilateral instrument, exclusive rental rights for authors. The right applies only to certain categories of works, agreement having failed on a general right of rental.[335] These categories are computer programs, and if certain conditions are met, cinematographic works. Article 14 also accords rental rights to producers of phonograms; this is addressed at para 19.31 below.

11.82 **(i) Computer Programs (TRIPs, article 11):** Article 11 of the TRIPS Agreement states:

> In respect of at least computer programs and cinematographic works, Members shall provide authors and their successors in title with the right to authorize or prohibit the commercial rental to the public of originals or copies of their copyright works. . . . In respect of computer programs, this obligation does not apply to rentals where the program itself is not the essential object of the rental.

The rental right in relation to cinematographic works is subject to an important condition, which will be examined hereafter (see para 11.84 below). With respect to computer programs, prior to the TRIPS Agreement, the commercial rental of computer programs had resulted in a proliferation of copying, facilitated by the ease with which they could be copied on to the hard drives of computers.[336] The rental right thus serves the primary purpose of securing the

[334] Although the WCT does not address importation rights, the Basic Proposal (n 311 above) for the WCT had offered two alternative versions of the provision that ultimately became the art 6 distribution right (discussed further at para 11.88 below).

[335] See Gervais (n 332 above), para 2.113.

[336] See ibid and sources cited at n 73.

reproduction right; although the TRIPs Agreement creates rights over subsequent distribution through rental, copyright owners who fear that the rental market is in fact a market for unremunerated reproductions have little incentive to exploit those rights affirmatively, rather than negatively, through prohibiting rentals.[337] The description of the right as 'commercial rental' would mean that lending of programs by non-profit libraries remains outside the copyright owner's control.

Article 11 further limits its scope to rentals in which the computer program is the 'essential object' of the rental. The purpose was to ensure that the copyright owners of programs contained in a variety of rented or leased products, such as automobiles, washing machines, and office equipment, should not be able to leverage control over the rental of the program into control over rental of the object containing the program.[338] The meaning of 'essential object', however, may not always be so clear. Consider video games; these are audiovisual works contained in and generated by computer programs. Is the 'essential object of the rental' the audiovisual work, the computer program, both?[339] Or CD-ROMs or other hardcopy media containing databases with computer-driven search programs: is the 'essential object' the compiled information, the program for accessing the information, both? If 'essential' implies 'primary' or 'principal' object, not just one of two or more equally important components or objects, then the content should predominate over the software-driven means of accessing it, and a rental right would not apply. **11.83**

(ii) Cinematographic works: Under the TRIPs Agreement, a national obligation to provide a rental right in copies of cinematographic works is not triggered **11.84**

[337] The rental right under the TRIPs Agreement thus recalls the US Computer Software Rental Amendments Act of 1990, and its predecessor Record Rental Amendments Act of 1984, both at 17 USC § 109(b), whose purpose was not to foster a rental market, but to protect the reproduction right when it was shown that rentals frequently yielded uncompensated copies, see S Rep No 98-162, 98th Congress 1st sess 2 (1983) ('a record rental and a blank tape purchase is now an alternative way of obtaining a record without having to buy one. The rental is a direct displacement of a sale.').

[338] The 1990 US Computer Software Rental Amendments Act anticipated this problem as well, see §109(b)(1)(B). That some copyright owners might endeavour to leverage copyright protection into inappropriate consumer product protection is not a frivolous concern, cf *Lexmark v Static Controls*, 387 F 3d 522 (6th Cir 2004) (rejecting attempt to invoke anti-circumvention provisions of US Copyright Act against a competitor's production of a compatible printer cartridge; the competitor circumvented the access protection on the computer program that allowed the cartridge to function in the printer).

[339] Cf 17 USC § 109(b)(1)(B)(ii) (exempting from rental right 'a computer program embodied in or used in conjunction with a limited purpose computer that is designed for playing videogames and may be designed for other purposes'); this excludes programs contained in the video game-playing computer; the exclusion does not appear to reach the video game.

unless such rental has led to widespread copying of such works which is materially impairing the exclusive right of reproduction conferred in that Member on authors and their successors in title.

The limitation of the rental right to such circumstances demonstrates that the rationale for the right is not to foster a market for rentals, but to protect the reproduction right (see the discussion earlier at para 11.82 above, regarding the computer program rental right in the TRIPs Agreement). Unlike software, for which a legitimate rental market appears not to have emerged, there was a substantial genuine rental market for videograms, in which the principal purpose of the transaction was to view the motion picture, not to copy it.[340] But the formulation lifting the exemption if the copying that results from videogram rentals 'is materially impairing the exclusive right of reproduction' is potentially troublesome. The terms are inconsistent with the general standard for exceptions articulated in article 13 of the TRIPs Agreement. That provision requires member states to 'confine' exceptions to those meeting the 'three-step test' derived from article 9(2) of the Berne Convention (see the discussion at paras 13.97ff below). Step two disqualifies uses which 'conflict with a normal exploitation of the work'. Is material impairment synonymous with conflicting exploitation? Is it a more stringent standard, so that some uses which conflict with a normal exploitation do not materially impair the reproduction right?[341] But the formulation in article 11 may not be as anomalous as first appears. Article 13 sets the boundaries for exceptions to exclusive rights, both those mandated by the TRIPs Agreement and those required by Berne (article 13 generalizes the test in article 9(2) of the Berne Convention from the reproduction right to all exclusive rights; see paras 13.103ff below). But there is no exclusive right of cinematographic rental in the first place unless the material impairment threshold is crossed. It is not inconsistent to set a higher standard of harm to trigger the right than to create exceptions to the right once recognized.

11.85 **(iii) Rental rights in the WCT, article 7:** Article 7(1) provides:

Authors of

(i) computer programs,
(ii) cinematographic works, and
(iii) works embodied in phonograms as determined in the national law of the Contracting Parties,

[340] This explains the reluctance to provide a domestic rental right for copies of audiovisual works in the US, which in turn underlies the TRIPs carve-out of cinematographic works; see Gervais (n 332 above), para 2.113.

[341] See criticisms raised by Daniel Gervais (n 332 above), paras 2.114–2.115.

shall enjoy the exclusive right of authorizing commercial rental to the public of the originals or copies of their works.

(iv) **Background to the provision:** In the 1992 WIPO Memorandum for the Second Session of the Committee of Experts on a Possible Protocol to the Berne Convention, an exclusive rental right for authors was proposed for a selection of works[342] premised on the economic importance of the rental of those works. In the WIPO Memorandum for the Third Session, the rental right made its appearance as part of a broader distribution right. Moreover, the 'databases' category included in the Second Session Memorandum had developed into a new category of work, 'any other kind of works stored in electronic (including digital) format'.[343] The WIPO Memorandum for the Fourth Session saw the list of works further modified and conditions and exceptions to the proposed right were added based on those found in articles 11 and 14(4) of the TRIPS Agreement.[344] At the Fifth Session, delegates from the European Commission proposed text for an exclusive rental right that applied indistinctly to all categories of works and that was independent from the act of first distribution.[345] The Basic Proposal did not go as far as positing a rental right of mandatorily general application. While the first paragraph of then-article 9 was phrased in general terms, the second paragraph would have allowed member states to exempt all but three classes of works—computer programs, databases, and musical works embodied in phonograms—so long as uncontrolled rental of these other works had not led to 'widespread copying that materially impairs the exclusive right of reproduction'.[346] **11.86**

In the course of the Diplomatic Conference, however, it became evident that many countries were not ready to accept rental rights that went beyond those enumerated in the TRIPS Agreement only a few years earlier. These views prevailed, and the rental rights in article 7 of the WCT largely mirror those in the TRIPS Agreement. In view of those countries that favoured a broader rental right, Main Committee I emphasized that article 7 is a minimum right, and that it remains open to members, in their national legislation, to provide for a higher level of protection.[347]

342 See [1992] *Copyright* 66, 76, paras 126, 129. The listed works were audiovisual works; works the performances of which are embodied in sound recordings; computer programs; databases; and sheet music.

343 See [1993] *Copyright* 84, 91, para 49(b)(iii) and (iv).

344 See [1994] *Copyright* 214, 223, paras 68–72.

345 See *Industrial Property and Copyright* (1995), 299, 325.

346 Basic Proposal (n 311 above), art 9, Records (n 311 above), 199.

347 See Reinbothe and von Lewinski (2002), 91–3.

11.87 (v) **Scope of the WCT, art 7 rental right:** Article 7(1) of the WCT effectively consolidates articles 11 and 14(4) of the TRIPs Agreement. The provisions of article 11 are found in article 7(1)(i), (ii), and (iii) (relating to computer programs, cinematographic works, and works embodied in phonograms respectively). Regarding computer programs, article 7(2)(i) replicates the 'essential object' qualification found in the TRIPs Agreement; regarding cinematographic works, article 7(2)(ii) echoes the material impairment threshold.[348] An agreed statement clarifies that the rental right 'refer[s] exclusively to fixed copies that can be put into circulation as tangible objects'.[349]

(c) General distribution rights in the WCT

11.88 (i) **Background to WCT, article 6:** The 1993 WIPO Memorandum for the Third Committee of Experts proposed to make explicit that an author enjoys a general right of authorizing and prohibiting distribution, subject to exhaustion after first sale.[350] A positive response from the majority of delegations resulted in a proposal in the 1994 WIPO Memorandum for the Fourth Committee of Experts for a general right of distribution subject to exhaustion after first sale; to this the Committee of Experts proposed to add an importation right.[351] But the consensus on a general right of distribution dissipated in the face of the controversy an importation right posed regarding the exhaustion issue; the Basic Proposal therefore offered two alternative versions of the distribution right, one with and one without importation rights as well. Alternative A would have included a right of importation subject to a much narrower exhaustion exception than the TRIPs Agreement allowed.[352] Alternative B concerned only distribution rights, and left wide leeway to contracting parties to provide for exhaustion.[353] At the Diplomatic Conference, Alternative A was widely opposed, principally because of its constriction of contracting parties' exhaustion policies.[354] The delegates ultimately followed an approach akin to article 6

[348] The TRIPS Agreement was drafted in the early 1990s at a time when the loss of quality involved in analogue copying and the need for two video recorders to facilitate analogue copying meant that pirate copying of rented videotapes was insufficiently widespread to 'materially impair' the reproduction right. Reinbothe and von Lewinski have pointed out that, however, with the advent of digital technology and DVD rentals this position may change and the material impairment test may come to take on greater relevance; Reinbothe and von Lewinski (2002), 98, para 23. On the other hand, if the copy-protection systems used with DVDs are effective, material impairment may yet be forestalled.

[349] WCT agreed statement to art 6 and 7.

[350] See [1993] *Copyright* 84, 85–91, paras 13–49.

[351] See [1994] *Copyright* 214, 219–22, paras 45–63; and 223–6, paras 73–84.

[352] See Basic Proposal (n 311 above), art 8, Alternative A, Records (n 311 above) at 195.

[353] See Basic Proposal (n 311 above), art 8, Alternative B, Records (n 311 above) at 197.

[354] See Reinbothe and von Lewinski (2002), 82–3.

of the TRIPs Agreement, by declining to purport to 'affect the freedom' of signatories to determine their own exhaustion policies.[355]

(ii) Scope of WCT, article 6: Article 6(1) of the WCT provides: 11.89

> Authors of literary and artistic works shall enjoy the exclusive right of authorising the making available to the public of the original and copies of their works through sale or other transfer of ownership.

The reference to 'literary and artistic works' plainly extends the right to all categories of works whose protection Berne requires, not just to cinematographic works and works recorded on phonograms. The copies at issue must be tangible objects, according to the same agreed statement as applicable to the rental right.

Article 6(2) makes clear that the right reaches only the initial sale, for it provides:

> Nothing in this treaty shall affect the freedom of Contracting Parties to determine the conditions, if any, under which the exhaustion of the right in paragraph (1) applies after the first sale or other transfer of ownership of the original or a copy of the work with the authorization of the author.

Despite the 'Nothing in this treaty' language, article 6(2) does limit national delineation of the exhaustion doctrine to some extent. Article 6(2) leaves it to national law to determine the exhaustion of distribution rights in copies to whose initial dissemination the author consented, whether at home or abroad.[356] Thus, the rights in copies distributed without consent are not exhausted. That would mean that the distribution right is exhausted neither in copies made in the exporting country under a compulsory licence, nor in copies lawfully made because of an absence of protection in the exporting country.

The text and the agreed statement give rise to several further questions. First, who is 'the public' to whom copies would be made available? Second, because the text of article 6 covers only transfers of ownership, it does not address the question whether the author may control the disposition of copies made available by rental before, or in lieu of, any sale. Presumably all rentals, whether of sold or unsold copies, then would come within the scope of article 7 of the WCT. Third, if only tangible copies are at issue, what is the relationship of the 11.90

[355] cf WCT, art 6(2) ('Nothing in this Treaty shall affect the freedom of Contracting Parties to determine the conditions, if any, under which the exhaustion of the right in paragraph (1) applies after the first sale . . .') with the TRIPs Agreement, art 6 ('. . . nothing in this Agreement shall be used to address the issue of the exhaustion of intellectual property rights.').

[356] See Reinbothe and von Lewinski (2002), 85 (WCT, art 6 does not distinguish between national, regional, or international exhaustion).

WCT distribution right to the reproduction right, as well as to the WCT right of 'making available' of works by communication to the public?

11.91 (iii) **The public**: With respect to 'the public', in the absence of Treaty definition, the delineation of public and non-public offerings of copies would, at first blush, be left to national law. But it may not fall to member states to determine how many rentals must occur before the rental is considered 'public'. It may suffice that the rental was *offered* to the general public, or to a substantial number of unrelated persons outside of a family and its social acquaintance. In this respect, guidance might be sought from the interpretation of a similar phrase in article 8 of the WCT in the context of the right of communication to the public: the author's rights include 'the making available to the public of their works in such a way that members of the public may access these works from a place and at a time individually chosen by them'. As discussed further below (see para 12.58), the 'public' that actually receives the transmission may be very small; what counts is the general *opportunity* given to the public to receive the communication.

11.92 (iv) **Relationship to the reproduction right**: We have seen that the WCT failed to include a provision (re)stating the scope of the reproduction right, and that the agreed statement that replaced the draft provision on the reproduction right is rather Delphic in that regard as well (see further paras 11.74–11.75 above). As reproduction and distribution are closely linked, further light might be shed on the shape of the reproduction right by considering the reach of the distribution right. The more straightforward agreed statement to article 6 of the WCT unambiguously limits the term 'copies' to 'fixed copies that can be put into circulation as tangible objects'. It is generally acknowledged that a 'reproduction' is a 'fixation'.[357] Must it also be one that can be circulated as a tangible object? Were that the case, a temporary fixation, much less a transient one, might not be a reproduction because its transitional character might disqualify it from being a tangible object. The language of the agreed statement might in this regard be compared with a national law definition of a work 'fixed in a tangible medium of expression' as one whose 'embodiment in a copy . . . is sufficiently permanent or stable to permit it to be perceived, reproduced, or otherwise communicated for a period of more than transitory duration'.[358] The latter definition would encompass fixations that are not themselves circulable as tangible objects, but which could be further concretized into a circulable tangible object. For example, a digital file stored in RAM might not be circulable as such, but it could be downloaded to a disk that could circulate. Under this reasoning, if the object of the distribution right is the same as the object of the

[357] See the discussion at para 11.27 above. [358] See 17 USC § 101.

reproduction right, the WCT's drafters would have indirectly (and perhaps unwittingly) resolved the scope of the reproduction right against temporary copies.

That conclusion, however, suggests the fallacy of the reasoning. If the delegates could not agree to resolve clearly the question of RAM copying in connection with the reproduction right, it is unlikely they agreed to resolve the scope of the reproduction right by reference to the scope of the distribution right. Moreover, the agreed statement on the reproduction right is arguably inconsistent with a reading that equates the objects of the reproduction and distribution rights. That agreed statement acknowledges that it is 'understood' that 'storage' in 'digital form in an electronic medium constitutes a reproduction. . .'. Even without a definition of the lifespan of 'storage', it would appear that a reproduction comprehends media that are not 'circulable as tangible objects'. The same temporary copy can be in RAM for a very long time, assuming no one turns off the computer; it probably meets some standard for 'storage', but the RAM is not a circulable object. It follows, then, that the copies covered by the WCT distribution right are a smaller subset of the 'fixations' that constitute reproductions under article 9(1) of Berne, as interpreted in the WCT. **11.93**

(v) **Relationship to WCT making available right**: The agreed statement limiting the object of the distribution right to tangible copies excludes digital transmissions from the scope of the distribution right. This does not mean that member states may not classify digital transmissions as a form of distribution,[359] but only that the WCT does not require them to do so. Moreover, the distinction between distribution of tangible copies of a work, and communication to the public of digital files containing the same work, seems rather scholastic. This is particularly true when one considers that the non-'distributed' digital file can be downloaded to a tangible object.[360] There is nonetheless a significant legal difference between the copy that circulated in a tangible object, and the one downloaded to a tangible object from a file communicated over a digital network. The distribution right in the former, if sold, may be exhausted, while the distribution right in the copy generated from a communication apparently remains intact. While the user has created a physical copy, the author did not **11.94**

[359] As appears to be the case in the US, see eg *Playboy Ents* v *Webbworld, Inc*, 991 F Supp 543 (ND Tex 1997); *Playboy Ents* v *Russ Hardenburgh, Inc*, 982 F Supp 503 (ND Ohio 1997).

[360] Accord, Ficsor (2003) (n 305 above) at 498–9, para C8.08: '. . . with digital interactive transmissions, some hybrid forms of "making available" emerge which do not respect the pre-established border between copy-related and non-copy related rights; on the one hand, works may be obtained and downloaded also for more permanent, deferred uses as a result of transmissions of electronic signals and, on the other hand, even where the basic intention is to make available a work for online watching and/or listening, without any copy to be, maintained thereafter, this also takes place on the basis of temporary copies made in the receiving computer.'

transfer ownership in that copy because that copy was never owned by the author (or right holder) in the first place. As a result, the purchaser of the copy that was distributed in a tangible object may freely resell it, while the purchaser of a download that she recopies to a circulable medium may not sell that copy without the copyright owner's consent. It is not apparent whether one would know the provenance of the digital copy contained in a tangible object, but, more importantly, it is even less apparent that this distinction makes any sense.

F. Comparative Table of Reproduction, Adaptation, and Distribution Rights

11.95

Exclusive right protected	Berne Convention	Gaps left to national law and ambiguities	TRIPS Agreement (beyond article 9(1) compliance clause)	WCT (beyond article 1(4) compliance clause)	Gaps and ambiguities
REPRODUCTION RIGHTS—					
reproduction	article 9(1)	scope of '*in any manner or form*' may be unclear. Does it cover: (i) digital as well as analogue forms of storage? (ii) temporary as well as permanent fixations?	article 10(1)—covers object code	Agreed Statement to article 1(4)—reproduction right under Berne covers digital form and storage	Whether 'storage' covers transient as well as temporary reproductions
to make a collection of speeches, public addresses, and other similar works	article $2^{bis}(3)$	same as general reproduction right re digital copies	same	same	same
to reproduce cinematographic adaptations of literary and artistic works	article 14(1)(i)	same as general reproduction right re digital copies	same	same	same
reproduction of cinematographic works	article $14^{bis}(1)$	same	same	same	same
ADAPTATION RIGHTS—					
to make and authorize a translation of a literary or artistic work	article 8	whether translation rights apply to conversion of computer programs from one programming language or from one platform to another			

Continued overleaf

Comparative table *continued*

Exclusive right protected	Berne Convention	Gaps left to national law and ambiguities	TRIPS Agreement (beyond article 9(1) compliance clause)	WCT (beyond article 1(4) compliance clause)	Gaps and ambiguities
to authorize the adaptation, arrangement, and other alterations of literary or artistic works	article 12	the terms '*adaptation, arrangement and other alterations*' may be subject to interpretation by member states			
to authorize the cinematographic adaptation or literary and artistic works	articles 14(1)(i), 14(2)	relationship of 'cinematographic adaptation' and 'cinematographic work' to audiovisual works			
to authorize the adaptation of cinematographic works 'into any other artistic form'	$14^{bis}(1)$; art 14(2)				
RIGHTS PERTAINING TO PHYSICAL COPIES—					
distribution	articles 14(1)(i) and $14^{bis}(1)$—apply only to cinemato-graphic adaptations and reproductions thereof	meaning of 'cinematographic work' and 'cinematographic adaptation' left to national laws		article 6(1)—right of distribution of physical copies of literary and artistic works	article 6(2) leaves application of exhaustion doctrine to member states

	article 16(2) seizure of unauthorized imported copies	fate of seized copies left to national law			
rental	none	whether national treatment obligation applies to member state's local rental right	articles 11 and 14(4) (computer programs, phonograms, and cinematographic works; member states may except from the last)	article 7 (physical copies of: works embodied in phonograms, if member state grants authors of embodied works any other rights regarding embodied works; computer programs, if essential object of the rental; cinematographic works if commercial rental materially impairs reproduction right) (WPPT arts 9, 13 re phonograms)	national treatment for rental rights in works not covered by TRIPs Agreement or WCT rental rights; determination of 'essential object' of rental; determination of 'material impairment' of reproduction right
droit de suite in original works of art and original manuscripts of writers and composers	article 14*ter*	member states have discretion as to whether to provide such a right; if they do, they may extend it to foreign artists and authors on the basis of reciprocity rather than national treatment			

12

RIGHTS OF COMMUNICATION TO THE PUBLIC (BERNE CONVENTION, ARTICLES 11, 11BIS, 11TER, 14, 14BIS; WIPO COPYRIGHT TREATY, ARTICLE 8)

I. INTRODUCTION

A. Communication to the Public: Direct (Public Performance) and by Transmission

12.01 The first way in which works were disseminated to the public without the making of a reproduction in a material form was through their representation or performance. Obviously, this means of dissemination or communication was suited to particular kinds of work, such as dramatic and musical works which were essentially made for this purpose. Nonetheless, literary works were equally capable of dissemination in a non-material form where they were recited or read out in public, while artistic works could be communicated to the public through exhibition or display. With the advent of new scientific and technological developments, it became possible to disseminate all works on a far wider scale. Thus, a musical work could be performed in public, in the absence of the performers, by means of a sound recording, and a play could be similarly presented by means of a cinematographic film. New techniques of broadcasting sounds and images extended these opportunities even further, and with the aid of satellites, cable systems, and digital communications it is now possible for performances and representations of works to be diffused to every corner of the planet. This global explosion in the means of disseminating information has brought many social, economic, and political possibilities and problems in its train, but for authors the opportunities and difficulties have been particularly intense. They have regularly found new means of exploitation of their works on the one hand, but traditional means of exploitation of their works have been under attack on the other, and this has necessitated a continual reappraisal of the content and scope of their rights. This process is well illustrated by the changes that have occurred in national laws, in the Berne Convention, and in the motivation for new multilateral agreements such as the 1994 Agreement on Trade-Related Aspects of Intellectual Property Rights ('TRIPs Agreement') and the 1996 World Intellectual Property Organization ('WIPO') Copyright Treaty ('WCT'). For the purposes of our present discussion, these rights shall be considered under two main headings: public performance (including public recitation), in a place where the public is present, and communication to the public by transmission, through such means as broadcasting, and dissemination by wire, including cable and the Internet.

(1) Meaning of 'public'

12.02 An important threshold issue is: who is the 'public' before which the work is performed or to which the work is communicated by transmission? Unfortunately, the text and records of the Convention provide little, if any, express assistance regarding the meaning of the requirement that the author's rights extend only to *public* performances and communications *to the public.* The opposite to 'public' is 'private', and it therefore follows that performances and communications of a private character are excluded from the scope of the Convention. The dividing line between 'public' and 'private' is not always easy to draw, and the Convention contains no specific guidance in this regard. However, the following general principle can be derived from a study of the structure of the Convention. Articles 11, 11*bis*, 11ter, 14, and 14*bis* deal with certain of the author's pecuniary rights, that is, some of the ways in which she can exploit her work. Accordingly, the rights of public performance and of communication to the public must refer to the author's capacity to authorize performances of the work before or communications of the work to a substantial number of unrelated persons. The larger and more disparate the audience, the greater the impact on the author's ability to exploit the work in relation to her 'public', that is, those who are willing to pay for the benefit of hearing or seeing the work performed. This understanding therefore will exclude from 'the public' only the immediate family circle. A somewhat broader formulation that remains consistent with the proposition that the 'non-public' should be economically insignificant might be 'normal circle of family and its social acquaintances'.[1] Most national laws in fact include some kind of 'family circle'

[1] See 17 USC § 101 (defining public performance as including to 'a substantial number of persons outside of a normal circle of family and its social acquaintances').

limitation.[2] In the absence of clear Conventional guidelines, the precise demarcation between 'public' and 'private' remains a matter for determination by national legislation, subject to the implied qualification that this line should not be set in such a way as to prejudice the author's right to exploit his work by means of public performance or communication to the public.

II. THE RIGHT OF PUBLIC PERFORMANCE

A. Relevant Texts

Article 11 of the Berne Convention provides as follows: 12.03

> (1) Authors of dramatic, dramatico-musical works shall enjoy the exclusive right of authorizing:
> (i) the public performance of their works, including such public performance by any means or process; . . .
> (2) Authors of dramatic or dramatico-musical works shall enjoy, during the full term of their rights in the original works, the same rights with respect to translations thereof.

Article 11*ter* provides:

> (1) Authors of literary works shall enjoy the exclusive right of authorising:
> (i) the public recitation of their works, including such public recitation by any means or process; . . .
> (2) Authors of literary works shall enjoy, during the full term of their rights in the original works, the same rights with respect to translations thereof.

Articles 14(1)(ii) and 14*bis*(1) provide in relevant part:

> (1) Authors of literary or artistic works shall enjoy the exclusive right of authorising:
> (ii) The public performance and communication by wire of [cinematographic adaptations of these works]

> (1) . . . The owner of copyright in a cinematographic work shall enjoy the same rights as the owner of an original work, including the rights referred to in the preceding Article.

(1) Meaning of 'performance'

'Performance', in its ordinary English meaning, is the presentation of a work in 12.04
a non-material form, whether this is by some human agent such as an actor or

[2] Many national laws contain further exclusions in respect of performances of a charitable or purely gratuitous character. These exclusions do not, however, characterize the relevant performances as 'not public', rather they focus on the non-profit nature of the public performance. See eg the FRG Law of 1965, art 52; Italian Law of 1941, art 71 (military bands); Japanese Law of 6 May 1970, art 38.

musician or by some mechanical means which enables that presentation to be heard or seen. It is the opposite of reproduction, in the sense that no 'copy' is produced by the performance, although obviously a copy may be necessary in order for it to take place. 'Performance' is a general term that is adequate to cover any form of presentation in a non-material form. Other synonyms are 'representation' and 'execution', but they do not have as wide an import. Thus, the former seems apt to cover dramatic and musico-dramatic presentations, while the latter is more appropriate for the presentation of a musical work. This distinction, in fact, is made in the original French text of the Convention ('*représentation*' and '*exécution*'),[3] and was formerly of some significance as musical works were treated somewhat differently under earlier Acts (see para 12.07 below). Since the Stockholm Act, however, the English translation has simply used the word 'performance' as an equivalent to the terms '*représentation et exécution*' that continue to be used in the French text.[4]

12.05 As used in the Berne Convention, a 'performance' need not be made to a live audience, although, as discussed below (see para 12.06), a '*public* performance' does imply an audience. The text distinguishes between 'public performances of their works' (article 11(1)(i)) and 'any communication to the public of the performance of their works' (article 11(1)(ii)). This means that a work may be performed before no audience, for example, in a radio or television studio, but communicated by broadcast or by wire to viewers or hearers located elsewhere. Nor need the performance be experienced live to be a 'performance' within the meaning of the Berne Convention. A sound recording or a cinematographic work capture performances of musical or dramatic works; playing the recording or showing the film will either be a 'public performance by any means or process' of the captured performance if the playing or showing is made before a live audience, or a communication to the public, if the playing or showing is made by transmission to a remote audience.

12.06 As used in the Berne Convention, the combined term 'public performance' means the presentation of the work to a live audience, as distinguished from the communication of the work by transmission to a remote audience. The separate articulation in articles 11, 11*ter*, and 14 of public performance or recitation 'by any means or process' gives those terms a meaning different from 'any communication of' the performance or recitation to the public. As the term 'communication to the public' is elsewhere paired with words such as 'by wire' (articles 11*bis*(1)(ii), 14(1)(ii)), and 'by loudspeaker or any other analogous instrument transmitting . . .' (article 11*bis*(1)(iii)), it is reasonable to conclude that 'communication to the public' implies a public not present at the place of

[3] Berne Act, art 9. [4] Paris Act, art 11(1).

origin of the communication. By the same token, 'public performance' (or 'public recitation') would mean a communication to an audience present at the place of performance.

B. History

(1) History of article 11

Public performance rights were protected at an early stage in most national laws.[5] The conditions under which this was done varied considerably, and in some countries, such as the UK, they were treated quite autonomously from the reproduction right or the 'copyright'.[6] It may be that it was for this reason that both the ALAI and Federal Council drafts of 1883 to 1884 made no special provision for performing rights.[7] However, the need for some international unanimity on this question was alluded to in the questionnaire presented by the German delegation at the 1884 Conference,[8] and proposals in this regard were made by both the German and French delegations.[9] The provision eventually adopted (article 11) was based substantially on the German amendment,[10] and contained the following stipulations: (i) national treatment for the public representation of dramatic and dramatico-musical works, whether published or not; (ii) in the case of translations, protection for the authors of the works translated against their unauthorized public representation; (iii) national treatment for the public performance ('*exécution*') of unpublished musical works, and of published musical works in which the author had expressly declared on the title or head of the work that he forbade this.[11] This was left unchanged by the 1885 Conference,[12] and was adopted into the Act of 1886 as article 9. It will be seen that it was only in the case of translations of works that a specific right of public representation was conferred by the Convention. Apart from this, the rights of public representation (in respect of dramatic and dramatico-musical works) and public performance (in respect of musical works) were only guaranteed the advantage of national treatment, that is, that Union members would grant to foreign authors claiming under the Convention the same rights they accorded to national authors. Thus, if these rights were in some way restricted, these restrictions would apply equally to foreign authors. It also meant that if a Union country accorded no protection at all in this regard, there was no obligation under the Convention for it to do 12.07

5 See para 1.15 above.
6 Dramatic Copyright Act 1833, s 1; Literary Copyright Act 1842, ss 3 and 20.
7 *Actes* 1884, 7–8 and 11–13.
8 ibid, 26 (questions 8 and 9).
9 ibid, 55–6.
10 ibid, 56.
11 ibid.
12 *Actes* 1885, 48.

so. This, in fact, did not seem to be the case under any of the national laws of early Union members, but many contained quite wide exceptions in relation to such matters as the use of works for public ceremonies, educational purposes, religious services, and so on,[13] while one country (Switzerland) allowed public performance of works on payment of the requisite fee.[14] A further restriction which was expressly recognized in article 9 was the requirement that authors of musical works who wished to prevent their unauthorized public performance had to state this on the actual copies of the musical work itself. The reason for this seemed to be the assumption in some national laws that the public should be free to perform musical works, unless this was clearly forbidden in advance.[15] The result was that many composers lost their right of public performance when a publisher negligently omitted to place the reservation notice on their works. This led to difficulties in the relations between composers and publishers as the latter frequently took the view that public performances of a musical work led to an increased demand for copies of the work.[16] This discrimination against their interests became a particular source of complaint for composers, and was a matter frequently referred to in the resolutions of such bodies as ALAI.[17] In the Paris Conference of 1896, the French delegation sought its removal, but without success.[18] This met with strong opposition from the German and British delegations which claimed that public opinion in their countries would find it difficult to adjust to a situation where they would be prevented from performing musical works which contained no notice of reservation.[19] The Paris Conference therefore limited itself to expressing a *voeu* to the effect that it was desirable that the internal laws of Union countries should fix the limits in which the next conference would be able to adopt the principle that published musical works should be protected against unauthorized execution, without the need for a prior reservation in this respect by the author.[20] By the time of the Berlin Conference, national attitudes had changed, and it was the German delegation that proposed the deletion of the notice of reservation.[21] This also had the agreement of the British delegation, who were

[13] See para 1.15 above.

[14] Swiss Law of 1883, art 7.

[15] In particular, the UK Copyright (Musical Compositions) Act 1882, s 1 and the German Law of 1870, art 50(2). See para 1.15 above, and W Briggs, *The Law of International Copyright* (1906), 299ff. Note also that in the UK, at least, the requirement of notice had been adopted as a means of avoiding unjustified claims of infringement: ibid, 300, and G McFarlane, *Copyright: The Development and Exercise of the Performing Right* (1980).

[16] *Actes* 1896, 43 (observations of the French Government in its programme for the Conference).

[17] Venice 1888, Berne 1889, London 1890, Neuchâtel 1891, Antwerp 1894: for text of resolutions, see *Actes* 1896, 61–2.

[18] ibid, 43, 171–2. [19] ibid, 172. [20] ibid, 172 and 229.

[21] *Actes* 1908, 46.

nonetheless concerned with the position of people who had acted in good faith depending on the previous law.[22] The answer made to this objection by the commission was that countries were free to regulate this question however they wished, for example, by way of differential penalties or the provision of defences for 'innocent users'.[23] Opposition still continued to be expressed by the Swedish and Swiss delegations, but they finally withdrew their objections 'in a spirit of conciliation'.[24] In the new text (which became article 11 of the Berlin Act), the following provision was substituted for the previous provision concerning notices of reservation:

> In order to enjoy the protection of the present Article, authors shall not be bound in publishing their works to forbid the public representation or performance thereof.

This was explained in the report of the general commission on the basis that there was a need for a clear statement in view of the old practice.[25] However, the provision was far from being just declaratory: if it had not been inserted, it would have been possible for national laws still to require notices of reservations as part of the application of national treatment. The new provision prohibited this; in addition, it not only applied to the performance of musical works, but also to the representation of dramatic and dramatico-musical works. Apart from this alteration, the new article 11 remained substantially the same as article 9 of the Berne Act (though with some drafting modifications). One question that was raised during the Berlin Conference was whether there was a need to refer to the rights of translators in relation to the performance of their translations, in addition to the rights already accorded under the article to authors of works which had been translated.[26] The view of the commission here was that, as translations were protected as original works in their own right, they would be treated the same as other original works under the principle of national treatment and that there was no need therefore for any express reference to be made to them.[27]

(2) Recognition of performing rights in the case of cinematographic adaptations and reproductions, and sound recordings

Although the Berlin Conference refrained from adopting a general right of public performance, it nonetheless did so in two specific instances where it had **12.08**

[22] ibid, 255–6 (report of Renault).

[23] ibid. See also ibid, 216 for British statement acknowledging the explanation of Renault on this point.

[24] ibid, 256. [25] ibid, 255. [26] ibid, 256–7.

[27] ibid; see further on the scope and limits of art 11, the commentary in [1922] *DA* 101.

also recognized reproduction rights. Thus, article 13(1) accorded protection in respect of the public performance of musical works by means of instruments which reproduced them mechanically, while article 14(1) conferred analogous protection in the case of cinematographic adaptations and reproductions of literary, artistic, or scientific works (the right of 'public presentation . . . by cinematography'). These rights were seen as a natural corollary of the rights of mechanical and cinematographic reproduction and were adopted with little discussion once the decision to protect the latter rights had been agreed. Both were retained essentially unchanged, until the Stockholm Revision (see further para 12.11 below).

(3) Adoption of a general right of public performance

12.09 It was not until the Brussels Act that article 11 required the protection of the public performance right as one of 'the rights specially granted by this Convention'. In this respect, the history of the recognition of this right is similar to that of the general right of reproduction which was not adopted by the Convention until the Stockholm Revision. As long as these rights were only protected under the Convention by virtue of the principle of national treatment, this left member countries free to determine the conditions under which these rights were to be exercised (although the practice of requiring reservation notices in the case of performances of works was now prohibited).[28] However, one factor which made a number of Union countries reluctant to countenance the express recognition of performing rights was the situation that had emerged with respect to the public performance of musical works. This was the development of well-organized national collecting societies which, acting on behalf of composers and writers, licensed the performance of their works.[29] These societies had come to assume monopolistic or near-monopolistic positions with respect to the licensing of performances of musical works, and there was a widespread feeling that the powers that came with such a position were being used to keep licence fees too high, with subsequent detriment to the public interest. Concern about the monopolistic tendencies of collecting societies led to a number of national legislative proposals during the interwar years to control the activities of these

[28] Note, however, that Japan, when it acceded to the Berlin Act made a reservation with respect to art 11, maintaining art 9(3) of the Berne Act which provided for reservation notices: [1910] *DA* 86.

[29] See generally, M Ficsor, 'Development and Objectives of Collective Administration of Authors' Rights' [1985] *Copyright* 341; G Karnell, 'The Relations between Authors and Organizations Administering their Rights' [1986] *Copyright* 45; J-L Tournier and C Joubert, 'Collective Administration and Competition Law' [1986] *Copyright* 96.

societies.[30] As a result, the countries concerned were reluctant to consider the adoption of a general Conventional right of public performance which might limit their powers to regulate these alleged abuses. This attitude was expressed clearly at the Rome Conference,[31] and there were proposals to amend article 11, so as to allow expressly for the imposition of such controls.[32] On the other hand, there was also a proposal made by the Irish delegation to recognize the rights of representation and performance as rights specially protected by the Convention.[33] There was considerable discussion of these proposals in the Conference, but no agreement could be reached on how to proceed.[34] One fear that was expressed in relation to the proposals relating to anti-monopoly measures was that these might permit the introduction of compulsory licences (although it was arguable that these were already permitted under the present regime of national treatment).[35] No consensus on changes to article 11 was possible, and the provision accordingly remained unchanged in the Rome Act.[36] At the same time, it seemed to be accepted by the delegates that member countries were free to take appropriate anti-monopoly measures against collecting societies under article 17 (the power to adopt measures in relation to *ordre public*; see further paras 13.91–13.92).[37] Such measures were indeed considered and adopted by a number of member countries in the years immediately following the Rome Revision.[38]

The proposal for a Conventional right of public performance in respect of dramatic, dramatico-musical, and musical works was taken up by the Belgian Government and International Office in their preparatory work for the Brussels Conference.[39] In support of this, they maintained that the Convention should recognize these rights unambiguously, in the same way as were rights in respect of translations, mechanical reproduction, and cinematographic adaptation.[40] They argued further that this would not prejudice the question of controls over abuses by collecting societies; nor would it prevent member countries from continuing to apply the same kinds of minor reservations and exceptions which they had done under their previous laws.[41] In addition, they proposed that authors should be given the right to authorize the public transmission of **12.10**

---

[30] In particular, in the UK, France, Germany, Canada, and Australia: see the general account in the preparatory documents for the Brussels Conference: [1933] *DA* 112, 113. See further the expanded account in *Documents de la Conférence réunie à Bruxelles du 5 au 26 juin 1948* (1951) ('*Documents 1948* (1951)'), 252–5.

[31] In particular, by the Netherlands, Australia, and New Zealand: *Actes* 1928, 255.

[32] The UK: ibid, 93; Australia and New Zealand: ibid, 255. [33] ibid, 255.

[34] ibid, 255–6. [35] Italy and Belgium: ibid, 255. [36] ibid, 256.

[37] ibid.

[38] See eg the German Law on Performing Rights of 4 July 1933; Canadian Copyright Amendment Act 1931; Australian Copyright Amendment Act 1933.

[39] *Documents 1948* (1951), 257. [40] ibid, 253ff. [41] ibid.

representations and performances of their works by telephone (meaning here the 'theatrephone', which was then in vogue) or any other analogous means.[42] These proposals gave rise to extensive debate as well as to a number of counter-proposals. There was a strong view expressed by some delegations, notably the French, that the recognition of these rights in the Convention was unnecessary as it was already accorded under the principle of national treatment, and undesirable as it might lead to the insertion in the Convention of restrictive conditions not contained in the Rome Act.[43] The fear here was that, although national laws might contain some restrictions on these rights, it was far more dangerous if these exceptions became embodied in the Convention itself. In contrast with this, other delegations were afraid that recognition would threaten the existing restrictions which had been imposed under their national laws, as well as the application of anti-monopoly controls.[44] These conflicting views were considered by a special sub-committee which recommended the adoption of the new rights with the following changes. First, the proposed right of public transmission was formulated in more general terms by the deletion of any reference to communication by telephone.[45] Secondly, the line of demarcation between these rights and those in respect of broadcasting and mechanical reproduction was made clear by providing the former were not to affect the provisions of either article 11*bis* or 13.[46] The text of the new article 11 which was finally adopted by the Conference was as follows:

> (1) The authors of dramatic, dramatico-musical or musical works shall enjoy the exclusive right of authorizing: (i) the public presentation and public performance of their works; (ii) the public distribution by any means of the presentation and performance of their works. The application of the provisions of Articles 11*bis* and 13 is, however, reserved.

The remaining two articles dealing with performances of translations of dramatic and dramatico-musical works and the prohibition of notices of reservation were retained in essentially the same form. It will be noted that, in the new paragraph

[42] To be art 11(1)(ii). See further ibid, 256–7.

[43] The French attitude does not fully emerge from the Conference documents, but is implicit in the summary of discussion in *Documents 1948* (1951), 263. It is also commented on at length by A Baum, *The Brussels Conference for the Revision of the Berne Convention* (1949), 29–30. This may explain the following observation by Plaisant in his report: 'The right of performance is contained in article 11. In the version adopted at Berlin and confirmed at Rome, there was no doubt that the protection of the right of performance could not, in good faith, be disputed. Nevertheless, it was asserted that this was an essential part of copyright that should be formally recognized in the Convention in the form of an exclusive right to authorize public performance.' *Documents 1948* (1951), 100. At the request of the sub-committee on art 11 (ibid, 128), Plaisant also adopted the following statement: '. . . in essence, the right of performance has not been modified, either in its character or its scope. Henceforth, this is indisputable, and it is in place as a protection against conflicting interpretations.' Ibid, 100.

[44] ibid, 263 (in particular, the British delegation).

[45] ibid, 128.

[46] ibid.

(1), the English translation used the word 'distribution'. It is quite clear from the context that this did not mean 'distribution' in the sense discussed above in relation to the distribution of copies, but it was, perhaps, an unfortunate translation of the original French word '*transmission*'. The latter is more accurately translated in English simply as 'transmission' or 'communication', and in the Stockholm Revision 'communication' was, in fact, substituted for 'distribution' in the official English text.[47]

Article 11(1) of the Brussels Act made no reference to exceptions to the new rights which it recognized, but in the debates on the article it was accepted by the majority of delegates that the recognition of these rights did not change substantially the position that applied under the Rome Act. Thus, it was allowed that there was nothing inconsistent between these rights and 'certain minor exceptions provided by national laws, exceptions already allowed under the regime of Rome, for religious, cultural and patriotic purposes'.[48] (The scope for these 'minor exceptions' is discussed further below; see paras 13.78ff.) As to the question of anti-monopoly controls, this again led to extensive discussions at the Brussels Conference, but, as at Rome in 1928, nothing was added to the Convention as it was accepted that each state had the power to impose such controls within its territory[49] (see further para 12.09 above). The only other amendment concerning public performance was in relation to cinematographic adaptations and reproductions of those, where article 14(1) (see para 12.08 above) was amended to refer to the exclusive right of authors of such works to authorize 'the public presentation and performance of the works thus adapted and reproduced'. **12.11**

(4) Right of public recitation

Public performance rights under article 11 are limited to dramatic, dramatico-musical, and musical works. However, it will be clear that literary works may also be 'performed' in public in the sense of being read aloud or recited. This right was accorded in many national laws prior to the Brussels Revision, and was often simply assimilated to the public performance right in respect of dramatic, dramatico-musical, and musical works.[50] Nonetheless, there were several Union members which did not accord such protection, or only accorded it under certain conditions.[51] This incomplete recognition of recitation **12.12**

[47] *Records* 1967, vol II, 1166 (report of Main Committee I).
[48] *Documents 1948* (1951), 263–4 and 102 (report of Plaisant).
[49] ibid, 264. [50] See eg UK Copyright Act 1911, s 1(2).
[51] Notably Germany and Finland, while limitations on such rights were to be found in Denmark and Poland: see *Documents 1948* (1951), 305.

rights in the countries of the Union led to a number of inconsistencies. For example, authors from a country which did not accord such protection would be entitled to claim it in other countries which did, under the principle of national treatment, while authors from countries in the second category would not be entitled to such protection in any of the countries in the first category. Another inconsistency was that all Union countries were required, under article 14, to protect public performance rights in respect of literary works which were reproduced or adapted by means of cinematography. Why, then, should similar protection be denied where the works were recited or read aloud? Accordingly, the Belgian Government and International Office proposed the recognition of a general right of public recitation for literary works in their programme for the Brussels Revision (to be article 11*ter*).[52] This was discussed by the Conference at the same time as it considered the amendments which the programme proposed in respect of public performance rights under article 11, but no attempt was made to assimilate the two rights, or even to make them consistent with each other.[53] The draft adopted by the Conference as article 11*ter* was the same as in the programme and read as follows: 'Authors of literary works shall enjoy the exclusive right of authorizing the public recitation of their works.'[54] Unlike article 11, this formulation omitted any reference to public communications of recitations of literary works. It is not clear from the Conference documents whether this omission was deliberate or unintentional, but if it was the former this would have had the effect of placing authors of literary works in an inferior position to authors of dramatic works. It has been argued by one experienced commentator (Dr Straschnov), who was present at the Brussels Revision, that this was not the intention of the Conference.[55] Both articles 11 and 11*ter* were discussed together in the general commission, and, according to Straschnov, no intention to distinguish between dramatic and literary works in this regard was evident in these proceedings.[56] Consequently, the failure to refer to public communications in article 11*ter* was in the nature of an oversight, although one that should have been rectified in a later revision. Certainly, the wording of article 11*ter* of the Brussels Act left it open to member states to argue that their obligations under this article were not as extensive as under article 11.

[52] *Documents 1948* (1951), 305. [53] ibid, 306–7. [54] ibid, 307.
[55] G Straschnov, 'L'article 11*ter* de la Convention de Berne révisée à Bruxelles' [1951] *DA* 73, 74.
[56] ibid, 74–5.

C. Present Scope of the Public Performance Rights

(1) Present scope of the public performance rights in article 11

With some minor changes (referred to below), article 11 remained substantially the same in the Stockholm, Paris Acts, and its scope can be stated as follows. It still applies only to dramatic, dramatico-musical, and musical works (though choreographic works are assimilated to these works),[57] and under paragraph (1) the right of public performance is treated in two parts. The first deals with public performance by any means or process, and the second with communications to the public of these performances. We will take up the second in part III of this chapter (see paras 12.17ff below). As to the first of these, it has been noted above that 'performance' means the same as '*représentation et exécution*' in the French text. 'Performance', in its ordinary meaning, seems confined to presentations by human actors or performers, but in the Stockholm Revision its scope was extended by the addition of the words 'including such public performance by any means or process'.[58] This took specific account of the public performance of works by means of sound recordings, tapes, and other devices in which these works may be embodied. In this regard, it should be noted that, from the Berlin to the Brussels Act, the right to authorize this kind of public performance in the case of musical works fell within article 13(1). As a consequence of the deletion of article 13(1) at the time of the Stockholm Revision, the drafting committee recommended that this should now come within the scope of article 11(1), and therefore recommended the addition of the words set out above.[59] It remains necessary, however, to distinguish 'public performance by any means or process' from 'communication to the public of the performance'; as discussed earlier (see para 12.05 above), the means or processes may be electronic, but the audience experiencing the performance must still be at the place where the performance is rendered. For example, a public performance of a recorded musical work occurs in a discothèque. If the discothèque also sends the music by wire to other locations, this additional activity is a 'communication to the public' of the recorded performance. **12.13**

(2) Right of public recitation (article 11*ter*(1), (2))

At the Stockholm Revision Conference both articles 11 and 11*ter* were brought into symmetry by the following changes to article 11*ter* (these also took account **12.14**

[57] It seems clear that this expression comprehends choreographic works and works of pantomine: *Documents 1948* (1951), 128 (report of sub-committee on art 11, giving this as its reason for not adopting a Hungarian proposal to include these works specifically in art 11).

[58] *Records* 1967, vol II, 1166 (report of Main Committee I). [59] ibid.

of the changes that were made at the same time to article 11).[60] First, it was provided that the right of public recitation should include 'such public recitation by any means or process'.[61] Secondly, it was stipulated that authors of literary works should also have the right of authorizing 'any communication to the public of the recitation of their works'.[62] Thirdly, at the recommendation of the drafting committee, a second paragraph was added to article 11*ter*.[63] This corresponded to article 11(2), and provided that authors were to enjoy, during the full term of their rights in the original works, the same rights with respect to translations thereof. As for limitations or exceptions which can be made to article 11*ter*, the same regime applies as under article 11 (the effect of these is discussed further at paras 13.79ff below).

(3) Public performance of cinematographic adaptations and reproductions of works and cinematographic works (articles 14(1)(ii), 14*bis*(1))

12.15 There is another form of public performance of works that does not come within article 11. This is the public performance of cinematographic reproductions and adaptations of literary, scientific, and artistic works, which has been provided for under article 14(1) since the Berlin Act (see further paras 12.08 and 12.11 above).

In the case of cinematographic works themselves, these have been treated in the same way as other original works since article 14(2) of the Berlin Act, and this position is continued under article 14*bis*(1) in the Paris Act. This specifically includes the same rights of public performance that is conferred on the authors of literary and artistic works under article 14(1)(ii).

D. Beyond the Berne Convention

12.16 None of the later multilateral instruments affect the scope of the Berne Convention provisions on public performance. Specifically, article 8 of the WCT limits its focus to communication to a remote public by transmission. One may infer that article 8 does not apply to the Berne Convention articles conferring public performance rights because article 8 specifies that it is 'without prejudice' to the various Berne Convention articles establishing rights in communications to the public by transmissions, but makes no mention of the Berne Convention public performance rights.[64]

---

[60] The changes were made on the basis of an FRG amendment: Document S/92: *Records* 1967, vol I, 694.

[61] ibid, 1168 (report of Main Committee I). [62] ibid. [63] ibid, 1169.

[64] Accord J Reinbothe and S von Lewinski, *The WIPO Treaties 1996* (2002) ('Reinbothe and

III. RIGHTS OF COMMUNICATION TO THE PUBLIC BY TRANSMISSION

A. Relevant Texts of the Berne Convention and Later Instruments

The current Berne Convention texts do not consolidate the right of communication to the public by transmission into a single comprehensive and coherent article. Rather, the right is scattered across a variety of dispositions, leaving several gaps both as to subject matter covered by the right, and as to the exclusive rights conferred. **12.17**

Article 11*bis* reaches the widest subject matter—all Berne-protected works—but does not cover all forms of transmissions:

> (1) Authors of literary and artistic works shall enjoy the exclusive right of authorizing:
> (i) the broadcasting of their works or the communication thereof to the public by any other means of wireless diffusion of signs, sounds or images;
> (ii) any communication to the public by wire or by rebroadcasting of the broadcast of the work, when this communication is made by an organization other than the original one;
> (iii) the public communication by loudspeaker or any other analogous instrument transmitting, by signs, sounds or images, the broadcast of the work.

Notably, as will be discussed further (see para 12.47 below), article 11*bis*(1) does not cover initial communications by wire, as opposed to third-party retransmissions.

Article 11(1)(ii) and (2) give to the authors of musical, dramatic, and dramatico-musical works

> the exclusive right of authorising . . . any communication to the public of the performance of their works . . . [and of] translations thereof.

Article 11*ter*(1)(ii) and (2) give to authors of literary works

> the exclusive right of authorising . . . any communication to the public of the recitation of their works . . . [and of] translations thereof.

---

von Lewinski (2002)') ('. . . the fact that the "without prejudice" clause of Article 8 WCT refers only to those provisions of the Berne Convention that do not include a right of public performance (as opposed to forms of transmission to a remote place) shows that it uses the term "communication to the public" in the same sense as . . . the Berne Convention, namely as excluding forms of public performance').

These texts appear to address all forms of transmission ('*any* communication to the public' (emphasis supplied)); to avoid overlap with article $11^{bis}(1)$, however, as will be discussed further (see para 12.28 below), they have in fact been read to cover those forms of communication left out of $11^{bis}(1)$.

Finally, articles 14(1)(ii) and $14^{bis}(1)$ give to authors of literary and artistic works adapted into cinematographic works, as well as to the owner of copyright in a cinematographic work

> the exclusive right of authorising . . . the communication to the public by wire of the works thus adapted . . . [or of the cinematographic works].

Thus, all Berne-protected works enjoy an exclusive right of wireless communication to the public, and exclusive rights of secondary transmission whether by wire or wireless means, but an exclusive right of primary transmission by wire applies only to:

1. Cinematographic works;
2. Literary and artistic works to the extent they are adapted into cinematographic works;
3. Literary, musical, dramatic, and dramatico-musical works, but only as performed or recited.

As a result, the text of literary works (including computer programs), and musical, dramatic, and dramatico-musical text, as well as still artistic images remain outside the scope of the Berne Convention right of primary communication by wire.

Article 8 of the WCT fills in the Berne Convention blanks with respect both to subject matter and scope of the communication to the public right:

> Without prejudice to the provisions of Articles 11(1)(ii), $11^{bis}(1)$(i) and (ii), $11^{ter}(1)$(ii), 14(1)(ii) and $14^{bis}(1)$ of the Berne Convention, authors of literary and artistic works shall enjoy the exclusive right of authorising any communication to the public of their works, by wire or wireless means, including the making available to the public of their works in such a way that members of the public may access these works from a place and at a time individually chosen by them.

This expression of the communication to the public right draws no distinction between wired and wireless communications, nor among protected subject matter. All transmissions to the public come within the scope of the exclusive right. Article 8 contributes further detail to the communication to the public right, by specifying that it includes the 'right of making available to the public' of all Berne-protected works to any member of the public on an on-demand basis. (The meaning and scope of the 'making available' right will be discussed in paras 12.57ff below.)

Finally, articles 10 and 14 of the WIPO Performers and Phonograms Treaty ('WPPT') extend the 'making available' subset of the communication to the public right to performers and producers of phonograms, that is, to subject matter excluded from the Berne Convention scope of minimum subject matter protected.

B. History

(1) General background

Such has been the enormous expansion of technology in this area since the 1920s, but more particularly since the 1960s, that a brief historical and technical background is required for the purposes of this part of our discussion.[65] The transmission of information by means of radio waves had already become an important feature of international communications by the time of the Berlin Revision, particularly with regard to shipping and defence. However, the potential for the commercial exploitation of authors' works by this means did not become apparent until after World War I, when both private enterprises and state organizations began to establish broadcasting stations for the transmission of news, music, plays, and the like to individual receivers located in private homes and other places.[66] This brought an entirely new dimension into the way that works could be communicated to the public. Thus, a musical composition or dramatic piece could be performed live in the studio and then broadcast to a far wider audience than would ever have been able to see or hear the performance in a theatre or auditorium. It was equally easy to broadcast sound recordings of these performances. By 1930, sound broadcasting had become a reality in many developed countries, and nationwide networks of stations, both privately and state owned, had come into existence. The information and propaganda potential of this new means of communication was not lost on governments, and through the next decade radio came to play a vital role in both totalitarian and democratic systems. At the same time, another form of broadcasting was developing, television, in which images could be transmitted together with sounds. Although this technology was largely perfected by the start of World War II, it was not until after the hostilities that television broadcasting came to play as important a role as sound broadcasting.[67] Just as the latter opened a window to the wider world for many millions of people **12.18**

[65] See generally Asa Briggs, *The BBC: The First Fifty Years* (1985).
[66] ibid, chs 1 and 2.
[67] ibid. See also B Sendall, *Independent Television in Britain*, vol I (1982).

in the 1930s, so television has played a similar role for many more millions from the 1950s on, even in many of the poorer countries of the world. The advent of satellite transmissions in the 1960s and individual reception dishes in the 1980s made the ready reception of sounds and images from around the world in the privacy of one's home a pervasive fact of life, further reinforced by widespread public access to the Internet in the 1990s.

12.19 These massive social and cultural changes have also been accompanied by rapid changes in the technology of broadcasting and other transmissions with and without wires. Indeed, the term 'broadcasting' has been used so far in a very loose sense, without any clear indication of its meaning and scope. Essentially, it refers to the transmission of sounds or images, or both, by electromagnetic waves without any artificial means of guidance or support (such as a wire or cable), for the purpose of enabling reception of the sounds or images which are transmitted by members of the general public.[68] Even before the advent of digital media, there were many ways, apart from broadcasting in its pure sense, in which sounds and images could be transmitted to the final listener or viewer. For example, it has long been possible to do this with the aid of an artificial conductor, such as a wire or cable, and the range of conductors has now expanded enormously, even including such intangible means as laser beams.[69] These methods can also be used in combination with broadcasts, for example, as a means of further diffusion once a broadcast has been received. This might be essential if broadcast programmes are to be received in particular areas where the ordinary broadcast signals are not readily received because of high buildings or mountains, or in the case of large concentrations of people in blocks of apartments and the like where broadcast programmes can be received on a 'community antenna' and then diffused by wire to individual listeners or viewers.[70]

12.20 The advent of satellites has also expanded the scope for broadcasting enormously. There are two broad categories of satellites used for the transmission of programmes: 'fixed service satellites' ('FSS') and 'direct broadcasting satellites' ('DBS'), although technological developments have largely superseded the

[68] This is in keeping with the broad definition adopted in a report on 'Annotated Principles of Protection of Authors, Performers, Producers of Phonograms and Broadcasting Organizations in Connection with Distribution by Cable', by three sub-committees of the Executive Committee of the Berne Union, the Intergovernmental Committee of the Rome Convention: [1984] *Copyright* 131, 145 ('Annotated Principles on Cable').

[69] See further A Kéréver, 'Droit d'auteur et satellites spatiaux' (1984) 121 *RIDA* 26.

[70] See generally F Klaver, 'Current Developments in Wire Television: Copyright and Neighbouring Rights Problems' [1969] *Copyright* 56; M Walter, 'Cable Television in the Austrian Copyright Amendment Law 1980' [1982] *Copyright* 254.

distinction.[71] The first comprises, in turn, two sub-categories: point-to-point satellites and distribution satellites. In the case of point-to-point satellites, transmissions are made, via the satellite, from one earth station to another for further transmission by the second station. In the case of distribution satellites, however, the signals are transmitted to a greater number of earth stations in a smaller geographical area. By contrast, a DBS requires no intermediary earth station, as the signals are distributed from the satellite directly to the general public who receive them with their own antennae or dishes. Satellites have therefore made possible the diffusion of programmes from one continent to another, and even to most of the world at one time, with the result that national boundaries are now of little relevance.

12.21 The border-effacing effects of satellite transmissions may seem modest compared to the subsequent development of digital networks. While a satellite 'footprint' covers multiple countries, a digital transmission over the Internet reaches all countries in which a user is equipped with a computer and Internet access, for example, by means of an ordinary telephone line. The 'global village' has become a reality, and these technological changes have had profound effects on such matters as popular education and entertainment, the conduct of international trade and business, diplomacy, and defence. The impact as regards the protection of authors' rights has been equally profound, as literary and artistic works form a large part of the content transmitted over the new communication networks. The questions for both national laws and the international copyright conventions have ranged from the relatively modest—how to accommodate the traditional view of authors' rights with these new modes of communication—to the radical: do these new modes of communication fundamentally challenge the allocation of power over protected works as between authors and users? If the more radical approach has primarily been confined to the domain of legal theory, the question remains for those who seek to ensure the continuing viability of authors' exclusive rights over new technological modes of exploitation: are new formulations of rights required, or do the old formulations still hold good, necessitating only a flexible interpretation to apply to these changed conditions? As we will see, the more broadly worded the old formulations, the more adaptable they have proved to changed conditions. Nonetheless, the drafters of revisions to the Berne Convention and of later instruments have occasionally opted to devise new formulations, not only to correct earlier rigidities but also to resolve ambiguities in coverage that arose either from the prior texts or from prior practice.

[71] See the secretariats' *Questionnaire* [1986] *Copyright* 230. See further, E Ulmer, 'Protection des auteurs lors de la transmission par satellite des programmes de radiodiffusion' (1977) 93 *RIDA* 4 and Kéréver (n 69 above), 27ff. See also discussion at para 12.30 below.

(2) History of broadcasting and cable distribution rights under the Berne Convention

12.22 As often happens with new technological developments, national laws reacted with varying degrees of swiftness to the sudden burgeoning of public sound broadcasting systems that occurred after World War I. Few laws dealt expressly with the matter, but a number were able to adapt or interpret their existing rules to grant authors protection against the unauthorized exploitation of their works by the new medium.[72] At the international level, authors' societies were quick to realize the potential harm to their interests, and at Paris in 1925 ALAI passed a resolution urging that the 'radio-electric transmission' of a literary, dramatic, or musical work should be subject to the approval of the author, and that where this transmission occurred in a public place it should be treated as a public performance.[73] Three years later, the Berne Convention was at the forefront of legal development, as the recognition of a broadcasting right was made part of the programme for the Rome Revision in 1928.[74] The programme proposal (for a new article 11*bis*(1)) was framed in quite far-reaching terms, as follows:

> Authors of literary or artistic works shall enjoy the exclusive right to authorize the communication of their works to the public by telegraphy or telephony whether by wire or not, or by any other analogous means serving to transmit the sounds or images.[75]

While the words 'telegraphy' and 'telephony' clearly harked back to the forms of 'person-to-person' communication that had been pioneered in the late nineteenth century by Edison and Marconi, the reference to 'the public' and to 'other analogous means' made obvious the new dimension that was intended to be covered. In addition, the inclusion of artistic works and the word 'images' were clear references to the possibilities posed by the imminent advent of television. There was ready acceptance by the delegates of the principle contained in the programme proposal, but there were considerable differences concerning the way in which this new right should be regulated.[76] Some of these objections were similar to those already discussed above in relation to collecting societies and the public performance right (see paras 12.09 and 12.10), and the injury to the public interest that might occur if these bodies were able to assume monopolistic positions with respect to the licensing of broadcasting rights.[77] Related to this were the concerns of broadcasters, who would be the persons to suffer most directly from high licence fees or denials of permission.[78] In many

---

[72] See the background study on 'Droit d'auteur et radiophonie' [1925] *DA* 14.

[73] For text of resolution, see *Actes* 1928, 58.

[74] ibid, 76.

[75] ibid.

[76] ibid, 256–61.

[77] Notably the Australian and New Zealand delegations: ibid, 256–7.

[78] ibid, 258.

instances, these were state organizations, and a new element became apparent here that had not usually been present in the case of other aspects of authors' rights (although an analogy from the early days of the Convention is provided by the case of translation rights). From the inception of public broadcasting in most Berne Union countries, there had been close government involvement and supervision, arising from concern for the public educational, informational, and cultural role of sound broadcasting.[79] In some instances, such as Nazi Germany and Fascist Italy, this concern was to be debased as the governments of those countries sought to use radio as a means of controlling and forming public opinion.[80] Leaving aside these extreme instances, however, there was still a strong 'public interest' aspect to broadcasting that was not so apparent in the case of other kinds of authors' rights. This was to have a significant effect on the development of broadcasting rights under the Convention, and at the Rome Conference it occupied most of the delegates' discussions as they sought to determine the reservations and limitations that should be allowed in respect of the new right.[81] This aspect is considered in more detail at paras 13.67ff below, and will only be noted in passing here.

The wording finally adopted by the Rome Conference dealt with the new right in the following terms (as article 11*bis*(1)): **12.23**

> (1) Authors of literary and artistic works shall enjoy the exclusive right of authorizing the communication of their works to the public by radio-diffusion.[82]

Paragraph (2) then dealt with the conditions that might be imposed on the exercise of this right under national legislation. As for paragraph (1), it will be noted that the term 'radio-diffusion' was more limited in scope than the wording originally proposed in the programme, in that it did not include diffusion of signals over wire. On the other hand, it was clear that the adjective 'radio' did not simply refer to sound broadcasting, as this would have made the reference to artistic works quite meaningless. While queries were raised as to whether it included television broadcasts, this was accepted as being implicit in the very notion of broadcasting.[83] This paragraph received extensive amendment in the Brussels Revision, with protection being given to a number of associated acts besides that of broadcasting.[84] Television was then clearly covered by the final words 'communication . . . to the public by any other means of wireless diffusion of signs, sounds or images', which made clear that the right

---

[79] See generally Briggs (n 65 above)

[80] See generally A Bullock, *Hitler* (1964); E Wiskemann, *Europe of the Dictators 1919–1945* (1966).

[81] *Actes* 1928, 258ff.

[82] ibid, 210 (report of general commission). [83] ibid.

[84] Brussels Act, art 11*bis*(1)(ii) and (iii). See *Documents 1948* (1951), 304.

conferred under article $11^{bis}(1)(i)$ was not to be narrowly interpreted. However, technological developments that could not readily be envisaged in 1948 made it difficult to be as certain about the meaning of broadcasting later in the twentieth century. The most important question that arose here concerned the need for a broadcast to be directly received by the public, rather than mediated by intervening services. In 1948, direct reception seemed self-evident in the light of general international practice, as is shown by the definition of 'broadcasting service' in the Radio Regulations of the International Telecommunications Union ('ITU') which were adopted at a conference at Atlantic City in 1947.[85] These referred to a 'radiocommunications service of transmissions to be received directly by the general public', and it seems likely that delegates at the Brussels Conference saw no need to insert a definition of broadcasting in the Berne Convention because this was the general international understanding of broadcasting at that time.[86]

Other changes implemented at the Brussels Conference included a third paragraph dealing with the making of ephemeral recordings for the purposes of deferred broadcasts.[87] There were lengthy debates about the changes to paragraphs (1) and (3), but the wording adopted in the final Brussels Act was left essentially unchanged in both the Stockholm and Paris Revisions, except that 'broadcasting' was now used in the official English version as the translation of the original French '*radiodiffusion*'.[88]

(3) Cable and other retransmissions

12.24 Developing technology soon brought additional complexity to communications to the public by means of broadcasting, as broadcasters sought to disseminate the programming through multiple acts of diffusion. The technical reasons for such an arrangement were various, but usually had to do with such factors as topography, intervening man-made structures, distance, and differences in time

[85] ITU, Radio Regulations, art 28A. See further BIRPI, 'Final Report of the Working Group on Copyright Problems of Satellite Communications (Geneva, October 14 to 16, 1968)' [1968] *Copyright* 230.

[86] The utility of the ITU Regulations for interpreting the meaning of 'broadcasting' in the Berne Convention subsequently encountered considerable criticism, see WIPO Committee of Experts on Model Provisions for Legislation in the Field of Copyright, July 1990 Working Paper, Document CE/MPC/III/2, 23–4, para 97: 'There is no reason to replace the definition of "broadcasting" offered by the Berne Convention by a definition contained in an international instrument adopted for the purposes of a branch of law other than copyright. An analysis of the situation in the field of fixed-service satellites shows clearly that the application of that definition of telecommunication law in the field of copyright is not only unnecessary but would also run into serious difficulties.'

[87] Brussels Act, art $11^{bis}(3)$; *Documents 1948* (1951), 304

[88] 'Broadcasting' was adopted as the English translation of 'radiodiffusion' in the Paris Act; in the Brussels Act, both the English and French texts used the word 'radiodiffusion'.

zones. Thus, a particular area may have been difficult to reach with the original broadcast because it was situated in a valley or blocked by tall buildings. Alternatively, in large countries such as Australia or Canada, long distances may have required signals to be 'strengthened' by a fresh transmission from an intervening station so as to ensure that far-flung communities would be reached by the original broadcast. In many instances, differences in time, even in the one country, required the broadcast to be recorded by the relay station so that it could be retransmitted at a more convenient time. Considerations of time became even more critical when broadcasts were made from one country to another, or from one continent to another (as in the case of the point-to-point satellites).

The question that arose in each of these instances was whether the subsequent transmission of the original broadcast was to be regarded as a fresh act of broadcasting, or whether it was to be regarded as within the scope of the original broadcast. While it was clear that the making of a recording of the original broadcast for the purposes of a deferred transmission raised the matter of liability for the juridically separate act of reproduction, there was no difference in principle whether the retransmission was made immediately after the original broadcast had been received or at some later stage. In either instance, an audience was reached which would otherwise not have been within the broadcaster's range, or would only have been reached with difficulty. **12.25**

This notion of a 'new audience' suggested that the retransmission should be treated as a fresh act of broadcasting (or 'radio-diffusion') under article 11*bis*(1) as it stood after the 1928 Rome Revision, leading to the result that the originating organization would be liable for two acts of broadcasting, in the event that it controlled the relay station, or, if the latter were controlled by a third party, to the separate liability of that party.[89] This was an easy distinction to make in theory, but it broke down in practice, as it depended upon there being a functional distinction between the original audience for the broadcast and the new audience reached by the retransmission. A geographical criterion might have appeared the easiest to adopt in this regard, but how was this to be determined? Some broadcasting networks operated on a national level, in which case their original audience could be said to be the whole population. But in many cases, **12.26**

[89] See generally 'Retransmission des Emissions' (1963) 41 *RIDA* 101; Klaver (n 70 above); M W Walter, 'Telediffusion and Wired-Distribution Systems: Berne Convention and Copyright Legislation in Europe' [1974] *Copyright* 302; Walter (n 70 above); R Dittrich, 'On the Interpretation of Article 11*bis*(1) and (2) of the Berne Convention' [1982] *Copyright* 294; F Gotzen, 'Cable Television and Copyright in Belgium: A Study of the Belgian Law in Relation to the Berne Convention and the Treaty of Rome' [1982] *Copyright* 307; W Rumphorst, 'Cable Distribution of Broadcasts' [1983] *Copyright* 301; V Hazan, 'The "Body Other than the Original Broadcaster" in Cable Transmission: Article 11*bis*(1)(ii) of the Berne Convention' [1984] *Copyright* 228.

regional time differences made it necessary to service this population by means of relay stations. For example, in a country the size of Australia, powerful transmitters are able to reach all parts of the nation, but this could lead to considerable inconvenience if the same programmes were broadcast simultaneously: in the case of the 7am news this would necessitate the residents of Western Australia arising out of their beds at 4am if they were to receive the national news broadcast from Sydney at the same time as their counterparts in the eastern states. Again, on a smaller scale, topographical factors may require retransmitting in order to reach particular parts of an audience that would be readily reached by the original broadcast in other areas.

12.27 These practical factors therefore made it difficult to draw a clear distinction between the original audience for a broadcast and a new audience, as what would be a new audience in one case may very well be part of the original audience in another. It was for this reason that delegates at the 1948 Brussels Revision Conference were unable to agree to a programme proposal under which liability was imposed under article $11^{bis}(1)$ in respect of 'any new communication to the public . . . of the work broadcast'.[90] In support of this, it was argued that a fresh authorization should be required wherever a retransmission 'procured a fresh circle of listeners'.[91] It does not seem that there was any intention to include simple relays that were made in order to carry an original broadcast, but the problem of distinguishing between these kinds of acts was apparent. While there was considerable sympathy for the programme proposal, many delegates thought that its scope was far from clear.[92] A number of other proposals were considered, including a French amendment that imposed liability where the transmission went beyond that which had been authorized in the contract agreement for the original broadcast.[93] This, in turn, was rejected, and, after lengthy debate, the present formulation which appears in article $11^{bis}(1)(ii)$ was adopted.[94] This confers on authors the right to authorize 'any communication to the public by wire or by rebroadcasting of the broadcast of the work, where this communication is made by an organization other than the original one'. Thus, the right covers all kinds of third-party secondary transmissions, whether by cable or other form of wired communication, as well as by rebroadcasting. Primary transmissions by cable or other form of wired communication, by contrast, do not come within the scope of article $11^{bis}(1)(ii)$.

---

[90] *Documents 1948* (1951), 270. [91] ibid, 266.

[92] ibid, 275 (delegation of Monaco); 279 (Norway and the Netherlands); 289–90 (general discussions in the general commission).

[93] ibid, 290.

[94] ibid, 115–16 (discussions in sub-committee on art 11bis); 290–1 (discussions in general commission).

(4) History of satellite transmission rights under the Berne Convention

The advent of satellite transmissions in the 1960s brought the formulation of the right of communication to the public under close scrutiny and considerable tension. The question was whether this form of communication was 'to the public'. In the case of FSS satellites, the body which transmitted the signals carrying the author's work (sometimes called the 'originating organization')[95] transmitted then to a satellite which then conveyed them back to an earth station (the 'receiving organization'). Unlike a DBS transmission, the signals thus transmitted were generally not then capable of being received directly by receiving devices owned by members of the public, and required some 'decoding' by the earth station, which then transmitted them to the public or distributed them through a wire or cable service.[96] This sequence of events arguably meant that the 'injection' of the original signals into the satellite by the originating organization was a communication not to the public, but to a relay station, and therefore did not constitute a broadcast within the scope of article 11*bis*. Under the traditional view, there would have been no broadcast, as these signals could not be received by the public, but required the intervention of the receiving earth stations in order to achieve this. If anyone was broadcasting, according to this view, it was the latter, as they emit the signals carrying the programme that are actually received by the public. Accordingly, it is to these persons that the author should have recourse.[97] The drawbacks of this view were apparent, however, as earth stations may have been situated in a number of different countries, and the author's entitlement to remuneration would depend upon whether the country in question accorded protection to broadcasting rights under the Convention. Even if no problems arose in this regard, the practical matter of enforcement and collection of royalties would have been far greater than would be the case if a single claim against the originating organization were possible.[98] 12.28

---

[95] See the definition in the Satellites Convention 1974, art 1, and the report of the *rapporteur général*, B Ringer, in [1974] *Copyright* 267, 276.

[96] See the *Questionnaire* (n 71 above), 24. See also Ulmer (n 71 above), 5–7.

[97] See eg BIRPI (n 85 above), 230–1. See also Ulmer (n 71 above), 12ff; C Masouyé, 'The Place of Copyright in the Use of Space Satellites' (1972) 72 *RIDA* 10, 20ff; Kéréver (n 69 above), 34ff. See further A Lokrantz-Bernitz, 'Les télésatellites et le droit d'auteur' (1970) 68 *RIDA* 68; G Straschnov in *WIPO Series of Lectures* (1971); R Plaisant, 'Propriété intellectuelle et communications par satellite' (1971) 70 *RIDA* 79; J von Ungern-Sternberg, 'Transmission d'émissions de radiodiffusion par satellites et le droit d'auteur' (1973) 75 *RIDA* 2; P Gaudrat, 'Protection de l'auteur lors d'une retransmission spatiale de son oeuvre' (1980) 104 *RIDA* 3; I Szilagyi, 'Questions of Broadcasting by Satellite with Special Reference to Authors' Rights' [1981] *Copyright* 222; V Nabhan, 'Satellites and Copyright in Canada' (1984) 120 *RIDA* 2. To the same effect, see also the decision of the Supreme Court of Canada in *Capac* v *CTV Television Network* [1968] SCR 676, discussed by Nahban, op cit, 18ff.

[98] This is one of the principal reasons for the European Union's rejection of this approach, see

12.29 Fortunately, a more flexible interpretation of 'broadcasting' was possible and ultimately prevailed. This proceeded on the basis that the intention of the originating organization in transmitting the signals containing the copyright work to the satellite is, ultimately, to effect a communication to the public. Accordingly, the passage of the signals through one or more intermediaries on their journey to the final consumer should make no difference, even if the initial transmission can only be received by the intermediary who has to modify or decode the signals before they can be finally transmitted to the public.[99] This approach forgoes any requirement that the public receive the signals directly from the transmitting organization; but, whatever the assumptions of the Brussels revisers, no such requirement appears in the text of article 11*bis* in any event. What 11*bis* does require is a 'communication to the public'; to say that the originating transmitting entity communicates to a station rather than to the public is to elevate form over substance. In addition, this approach has the clear advantage of fixing liability for broadcasting on the originating organization, although the further question arises as to whether there is a fresh act of broadcasting carried out by the earth station when it transmits the signals to the public. In other words, are there two acts of broadcasting in respect of which the copyright owner has a claim? This potential liability to make double payments drew predictable criticism from broadcasting interests, as well as from many commentators.[100] Alternative or intermediate solutions were proposed, for example, the recognition of a distinct right of 'injection' of signals to a satellite, which would make the subsequent act of broadcasting by the receiving organization a juridically different act.[101] It was suggested that both originating and receiving organizations should be jointly liable for one composite act of broadcasting, the former on the basis that it 'commenced' the broadcast, even if its transmission was to a satellite which is not the 'public', and the latter on the basis that it 'completed' the broadcast by making it available to the public.[102]

Council Directive 93/83/EEC of 27 Sept 1993 on the coordination of certain rules concerning copyright and rights related to copyright applicable to satellite broadcasting and cable retransmission, art 1(2)(b), *Official Journal* L 248, 06/10/1993 P 0015–0021.

[99] See Kéréver (n 69 above), 40ff; Ulmer (n 71 above), 24ff; Plaisant (n 97 above), 106. See also the *Questionnaire* (n 71 above), 231ff.

[100] See eg Ulmer (n 71 above), 32; Masouyé (n 97 above), 24ff.

[101] Masouyé (n 97 above), 22ff.

[102] Ulmer (n 71 above), 34ff. See also P Gaudrat (n 97 above), 26ff. This also is the view taken in the *Questionnaire* (n 71 above), 22–4, where the following principles are proposed: '*Principle AW15*. In the case of fixed service satellites, the whole process of transmission of program-carrying signals (emission, "up-link", "down-link", transmission from the earth station onwards) should be considered as one broadcasting composed of different phases. *Principle AW16*. Both the broadcasting organization originating the program and the broadcasting organization transmitting it from

While this issue received some attention in the first edition of this book,[103] it seems that subsequent technological developments have rendered it a moot point. First, as the European Convention Relating to Questions on Copyright Law and Neighbouring Rights in the Framework of Transfrontier Broadcasting by Satellite (May 1994) declares in its preamble, 'technical developments . . . have resulted in the blurring of the technical differences between direct broadcasting satellites and fixed service satellites'.[104] Because the FSS/DBS distinction is largely effaced—'nowadays advanced satellite antennas allow users to receive also signals which are transmitted by fixed satellites'[105]—the European Satellite convention states that transmissions of FSS signals that can be received by the general public 'shall be treated as broadcasting'.[106] Secondly, whatever the characterization problems that may persist regarding FSS transmissions, these do not plague DBS communications. Thus, it has generally been recognized from the outset that DBS transmissions constitute 'broadcasts' within the meaning of the Berne Convention.[107] As a result, even if transmissions via satellite were clearly not in the minds of delegates at Brussels in 1948, a progressive interpretation of the broadly worded requirement of a 'communication to the public' accommodates this significant evolution in communications technology. 12.30

receiving earth station onwards are—jointly—responsible towards the owners of copyright in audiovisual works . . . whose rights may be concerned by such broadcasting as far as the final phase of the broadcasting (from the earth station onwards) is concerned. The originating organization alone is responsible towards the owners of rights for the phases preceding the final phase of broadcasting' [1986] *Copyright* 218, 235. Cf the earlier, more hesitant view of the BIRPI Working Group on Satellite Communications in 1968 (n 85 above).

103 Sam Ricketson, *The Berne Convention 1886–1986* (1987), paras 8.80–8.83.

104 European Convention Relating to Questions on Copyright Law and Neighbouring Rights in the Framework of Transfrontier Broadcasting by Satellite (May 1994) ('ESC'), preamble. Accord, *Protection of Broadcasting Organizations* for the Standing Committee on Copyright and Related Rights (seventh session, 13–17 May 2002) (Document SCCR/7/8, www.wipo.int/documents, prepared by the WIPO Secretariat) at 7, para 29: 'Due to the development of powerful reception equipment, however, signals from fixed service satellites can now also be received directly by consumers and therefore they are in many cases treated as those from direct broadcasting satellites. The distinction which was originally made between fixed service satellites and direct broadcasting satellites is thus not generally applied anymore.'

105 Natalie Helberger, *Neighbouring Rights Protection of Broadcasting Organisations: Current Problems and Possible Lines of Action* (report prepared for the Council of Europe), at 11 (1999), www.ivir.nl/publications.

106 ESC art 1(2). Art 1(1) provides: 'The transmission of works and other contributions by direct broadcasting satellite is broadcasting.'

107 See eg Mihály Ficsor, *The Law of Copyright and the Internet: The 1996 WIPO Treaties, Their Interpretation and Implementation* (2003), para 4.42; Makeen Fouad Makeen, *Copyright in a Global Information Society: The Scope of Copyright Protection Under International, US, UK and French Law* (2000), 186.

C. Present Scope of the Berne Convention Rights of Communication to the Public by Transmission

(1) 'Any communication to the public' under articles 11 and 11ter

12.31 As we have already seen (at paras 12.13–12.15 above), articles 11 and 11ter set out exclusive rights of public performance or public recitation of musical, dramatic, dramatico-musical, and literary works (and translations of these works). The Berne Convention further provides for the exclusive right to authorize 'any communication to the public' of those performances or recitations. Despite the apparent overarching character of the rights accorded, this has also to be read subject to the other provisions of the Convention, notably article 11bis which deals with broadcasting and which is therefore excluded from its scope.[108] (The broadcasting right is addressed further in para 12.34 below.) There are two principal kinds of communications that will fall within the 'any communication' provisions of articles 11(1)(ii) and 11ter(1)(ii). First, relaying a live performance to a larger audience by means of loudspeakers and other amplification systems in the case of sounds, and by closed circuit visual display screens in the case of images; in the case of a broadcast work, this would be covered by article 11bis(1)(iii) (see further para 12.36 below). Second, the transmission of a live or recorded performance by wire to subscribers or other recipients. At its inception, this right may have seemed of marginal significance;[109] today, the economic consequences of the right are ever-expanding. The right covers musical and dramatic programming distributed by cable services when the

[108] The report accompanying the proposal to add the provision that became art 11(1)(ii) at the 1948 Brussels Revision Conference distinguishes transmissions covered by the broadcasting and retransmissions right in 11bis from the wire-originated transmissions newly covered by art 11(1)(ii), Principally, the proponents of the new right sought to ensure that it would not be subject to the compulsory licensing art 11bis entitled member states to impose on broadcasting and on retransmissions of broadcasts. See *Documents de la conférence réunie à Bruxelles*, p. 256. The text of the Brussels version of art 11(1)(ii) also reserved the application of art 11bis. That reservation was dropped from the text of the 1967 Stockholm revision, but there is no indication that the drafters intended to exempt broadcasts and secondary transmissions of performances of musical, dramatic, and dramatico-musical works from the scope of the 11bis allowance for compulsory licensing. The Stockholm records invoke the general interpretive rule of *lex specialis* (see WIPO Records of the Intellectual Property Conference of Stockholm, 11 June to 14 July 1967, volume 2 (1971), 1134 (statement made in connection with relationship of art 9(2) to other reproduction right exceptions). Although it is debatable which rule here should be considered the specific and which the general, it is likely that art 11bis, greater specificity as to rights would control the interpretation of the scope of rights under art 11(1)(ii).

[109] eg the 'theatrephone', was the particular concern of those who prepared the programme for the Brussels Conference; see *Documents 1948* (1951), 255–6. A 'theatre phone' allowed customers to listen to a musical or dramatic performance at home via a telephone line. See Fouad Makeen (n 107 above), 229.

services originate the transmission of, rather than retransmit, the programming. The growth of independently programmed cable services in the last twenty-five years attests to the importance of the right. Moreover, with digital communications, the exclusive right to authorize wired transmissions gives authors of musical or literary works that have been performed or recited and recorded, ie, musical or literary works that have been fixed in phonograms, the right to control the communication of their thus-fixed works over digital networks, for example, by means of webcasting. (Recall that the phonogram is not itself a protected work under the Berne Convention; for communication rights of performers and producers of phonograms under subsequent multilateral instruments, see further Chapter 19.)

(2) Communication to the public by wire of cinematographic works

Articles 11 and 11*ter* overlap to some extent with the exclusive rights set out in **12.32** article 14(1)(ii) 'to authorise the communication to the public by wire' of literary and artistic works adapted into cinematographic works. If the performance of the musical or dramatic work (or the recitation of a literary work) has been fixed in a film or videotape or cassette or digital video medium, transmission of the contents of the videogram by means of wire or cable would fall within article 14(1)(ii). Article 14*bis*(1) extends exclusive rights over wired transmissions to the cinematographic works themselves. Thus, the owner of copyright in a film, video game, or other 'cinematographic work' enjoys the exclusive right to authorize its initial communication over cable or digital networks. If, however, the wired transmission further disseminated a cinematographic or underlying work that had been previously broadcast, this would fall within the scope of article 11*bis*(1)(ii) (see further para 12.36 below).

(3) The scope of the present article 11*bis*

Of the various articles conferring exclusive rights of communication to the **12.33** public, article 11*bis* is the most general, and, as we have seen (see paras 12.22ff above), qualifies the scope of the rights contained in articles 11 and 11*ter*. It is important to ascertain the scope of article 11*bis* vis-à-vis other rights of communication to the public in the Berne Convention and subsequent multilateral instruments because article 11*bis*(2) allows member states to impose compulsory licences on the rights that 11*bis*(1) confers, but not on the other rights of communication to the public. Article 11*bis*(2) will be the object of further discussion in Chapter 13 below.

Article 11*bis*(1) covers four main kinds of transmissions:

1. Broadcasting, including by satellite;
2. Rebroadcasting (in specific circumstances), including by satellite;

3. Wired redissemination of broadcasts (in specific circumstances), including by cable and digital dissemination (for example, by the 'streaming' of radio or television broadcasts);
4. 'Public communication by loudspeaker or any other analogous instrument' of the works broadcast.

These are considered in turn below.

(4) Broadcasting

12.34 The Convention contains no definition of this term. As seen above, the text adopted in the Rome Act was clearer, in that it referred to the 'communication of their works to the public by radio-diffusion'. The present article $11^{bis}(1)(i)$ makes no express reference to the need for the broadcast to involve 'communication ... to the public', although this is referred to separately in that sub-paragraph in a way that implies the extension of that description back to broadcasting. By covering 'communication to the public by any *other* means of wireless diffusion . . .' (emphasis supplied) article $11^{bis}(1)(i)$ appears to assume that broadcasting is one means of wireless communication to the public. Moreover, it seems clear from the records of the Brussels Conference that the substitution of the term 'broadcasting' ('*radiodiffusion*' in French) was not intended to change the meaning of the formulation adopted in the Rome Act, but only to simplify it.[110] No need was felt to define the term any further, as no one really took issue with the view expressed in the programme that '[t]he notion of broadcasting is today known to everyone'.[111] A similar conception is to be found in the definition of broadcasting that was adopted in the Rome Convention for the Protection of Performers, Producers of Phonograms and Broadcasting Organizations in 1961: under article 3(f), this is 'transmission by wireless means for public reception of sounds or images and sounds'.

(5) Satellites

12.35 While the characterization of a wireless communication as 'to the public' may once have been in doubt in the case of FS satellites (see paras 12.28ff above), DBS transmissions (and more recently, many FSS transmissions) are generally accepted as a broadcasting within the traditional meaning of that term, as the signals pass from the originating organization via the satellite to the individual receivers of members of the public.[112] As DB satellites increasingly displace

[110] *Documents 1948* (1951), 265.

[111] ibid, 114–15 (sub-committee on art 11bis) and 286–7 (discussion in the general commission).

[112] See eg ESC, art 1(2). Art 1(1) provides: 'The transmission of works and other contributions by direct broadcasting satellite is broadcasting.'

FS satellites,[113] reservations about the appropriate characterization of satellite communications are likely to recede. Moreover, the 1993 European Union Satellite Directive identifies the act of 'communication to the public' as occurring at the point of uplink from the transmitting entity to a satellite (whether an FS or a DB satellite).[114] It may therefore be possible at this point to assert that a general recognition exists that dissemination of works by satellite transmissions constitutes communication to the public by wireless means, and therefore comes within the scope of article 11*bis*(1)(i).[115]

(6) Rebroadcasting

Article 11*bis*(1)(ii) confers on authors the right to authorize 'any communication to the public . . . by rebroadcasting of the broadcast of the work, where this communication is made by an organization other than the original one'. Mention was made above (see para 12.26) of the relay of a broadcast via some intermediate station by means of which the broadcast may be further diffused to the public. To take the simplest example, a broadcast may be simultaneously received by members of the public as well as by another receiving station which then conveys the signals bearing the programme on to a further section of the public. Article 11*bis*(1)(ii) applies only if the entity that further conveys the signals is different from the original broadcaster. The original broadcaster can retransmit its original broadcast as far and as wide as it desires, but must do this itself through its own relay stations. There is also no restriction on recording the original broadcast, so that retransmission can be made at a later time (in such a case, the broadcaster will, of course, have to ensure that it has authority to make the recording; see further para 13.72 below). However, fresh authorization is required once the retransmission is made by another organization. Under this formulation, a national broadcasting organization will need only the one authorization where it retransmits a broadcast through its local stations, but separate authorizations will be required by these stations if they are independently owned. In any event, even in cases where only the one authorization is required, it will always be open to the copyright owner, in granting that authorization, to limit the scope of that authorization as he wishes. **12.36**

[113] See eg Ficsor (n 107 above), para 4.55, p 181 ('with the ever more spectacular increase of the capacity and power of telecommunication satellites, nearly all such satellites are becoming direct broadcast satellites').

[114] Satellite Directive (n 98 above), art 1(2)(b).

[115] See eg Ficsor (n 107 above), para 4.42, p 172 ('[there] was [not] any doubt about the question of whether [satellite] transmissions by direct broadcasting satellites are covered by the right of broadcasting . . .').

(7) Distribution of broadcasts by cable and other means of wired transmissions

12.37 Article 11bis(1)(ii) also deals with the communication to the public of broadcasts 'by wire', where this is made by an organization other than the original one. The Convention does not provide any definition of this term, but today the term would encompass both cable transmissions and digital transmissions, for example, over telephone lines. The term 'by wire' is usually accorded a very wide scope, being used in the general sense of an artificial device through which signals are conducted from one point to another. In this regard, it is used in contradistinction to 'broadcast' where signals by Hertzian waves are transmitted in space without any artificial guide or conductor. In the absence of a Conventional definition, national legislation is free to define 'wire' or 'cable' for itself, so long as the definition broadly encompasses actual and potential media of transmission, consistent with the text's direction to cover '*any* communication to the public by wire . . .' (emphasis supplied). Useful guidance as to the potential scope of the term is to be derived from the following working definition which was formulated by the secretariats of WIPO, UNESCO, and the ILO as part of a set of annotated principles on the distribution of programmes by cable in 1984:

> cable means a wire, beam or any other conducting device through which electronically generated program-carrying signals are guided over a distance; . . .[116]

12.38 Distribution of programmes by cable has many different advantages, not the least of which is aesthetic, in that it permits large areas to be served without the unsightly overhead antennae or dishes that are required for the reception of broadcasts. It can also allow for distribution in areas that would otherwise be difficult to serve by direct broadcasts, for example, low-lying areas or high-density areas, such as blocks of apartments. In addition, it can allow for distribution of programmes along a wide number of different channels and drawn from two principal sources: the programmes originated by the cable operator itself, and the programmes received from ordinary broadcasting systems. With the advent of satellites, the scope for this second kind of distribution is now vast, and the wealth of programmes available in countries with developed systems of cable distribution is enormous. Article 11bis(1)(ii) deals only with the redistribution of broadcast programmes, and does this under the same condition that applies to rebroadcasting: a separate authorization for this secondary utilization of a broadcast is only required where the 'communication by wire' is done by an organization other than the original one. In the same way, no question as to whether this communication is made to a 'new public' arises, so long as this is a

[116] Annotated Principles on Cable (n 68 above), 145. See further the articles referred to in *Questionnaire* (n 71 above), 232–3.

communication to the public.[117] In the case of the original organization, therefore, it is free to distribute its broadcast programmes by cable without having to seek further permission.

This 'licence' can be viewed in several ways. On the one hand, it enables a broadcasting organization to carry out its broadcasting effectively, particularly in areas where direct reception of programmes is difficult and would involve the broadcasting organization in additional expense if it had to rely on broadcasting alone. In this sense, cable distribution can be assimilated to rebroadcasting. On the other hand, the character of the act, involving as it does distribution through some form of artificial conductor, is qualitatively different from broadcasting, and the question arises as to whether it should be treated as a distinct act of dissemination requiring the authorization of the copyright owner. It is for this reason, that some national laws have treated the acts of broadcasting and cable distribution as distinct acts, even where the cable distribution is of programmes which have been broadcast by the same organization.[118] In this regard, it should be noted that the character of the act of cable distribution itself may vary considerably, ranging from the provision of a simple community antenna receiving and distributing broadcasts to a block of apartments to a highly sophisticated receiving station which distributes broadcast programmes to subscribers over a wide geographical area. In the first of these cases, however, it may be doubted whether there is a true secondary communication to the public, in that the community antenna simply replaces a multitude of individual antennae on the same building or buildings and this is therefore no more than a reception of the primary broadcast. It may also be argued that there is no 'organization' which makes the communication in such a case, apart from the

[117] See eg the two Swiss decisions on this point which are discussed by M Pedrazzini, 'Letter from Switzerland' [1984] *Copyright* 292, 297.

[118] See eg the Australian Copyright Act 1968, s 31(1)(a)(v), repealed in 2000. As enacted, the UK Copyright, Designs and Patents Act 1988, s 20 differentiated between 'broadcasting of the work', broadcasting being defined as 'transmission by wireless telegraphy' and 'its inclusion in a cable programme service' which referred to a service consisting in the sending of information 'by means of a telecommunications system, otherwise than by wireless telegraphy'. However, the UK dropped this differentiation as of 31 Oct 2003, as part of its implementation of the EC Information Society Directive. Section 20, as amended, confers a broad right of 'communication to the public' which includes a right to 'broadcast' a work, and a right to make a work available to the public. In turn, 'broadcast' is defined, in s 6 of the 1988 Act, to cover any 'electronic transmission of visual images, sounds, or other information which: (a) is transmitted for simultaneous reception by members of the public and is capable of being lawfully received by them, or (b) is transmitted at a time determined solely by the person making the transmission for presentation to members of the public'. While a series of provisions exclude from the definition of 'broadcast' certain 'Internet transmissions', the inclusion of copyright material in an 'Internet transmission' will nevertheless violate the amended s 20 insofar as it amounts to a 'making available'. See Lionel Bently and Brad Sherman, *Intellectual Property Law*, 2nd edn (2004), 82–5, 143–6. On the 'making available' right in the WCT, see further paras 12.57–12.61 below.

body representing the owners or tenants of the building in question. It can therefore be concluded that such forms of cable distribution fall outside the scope of article $11^{bis}(1)(ii)$, and this appears to be the view that has been taken at both a national and international level.[119]

Finally, it should be reiterated that article $11^{bis}(1)(ii)$ applies only to the cable distribution of broadcast programmes containing protected works: where an organization distributes programmes directly by cable to the public that do not originate from a broadcast or, if they do originate from a broadcast, are not distributed simultaneously with that broadcast, this will come within the public performing right and will require authorization under article 11(1)(ii). Programmes distributed in this way are sometimes referred to as 'cable-originated programmes', to distinguish them from 'broadcast programmes'. This is an important distinction to bear in mind, as article $11^{bis}(2)$ does not permit the imposition of compulsory licences in the case of cable-originated programmes.

(a) Cable distribution of FSS transmissions

12.39 As noted above (see para 12.30), for some time there was uncertainty concerning the correct characterization of FSS transmissions as distinct from DBS transmissions. If the former, unlike DBS transmissions, were not to be treated as broadcasts, it could be argued that article $11^{bis}(1)(ii)$ would not apply as this would not be the cable distribution of the 'broadcast' of the work in question. Against this, it could be argued that the broadcast had already taken place when the originating organization transmitted the signals with a view to their ultimate distribution by cable, in which event article $11^{bis}(1)(ii)$ should be applicable. In their 1986 *Questionnaire*, the secretariats of WIPO and UNESCO thought that the first of these views was correct, but on a rather different basis, namely that when the work was distributed by cable this was the final stage of the primary broadcast.[120] The result of this was that there was no distribution of a broadcast of the work as the work had not yet been completely broadcast. The WIPO/UNESCO Committee of Governmental Experts on Evaluation and Synthesis of

[119] eg note the decision of the Brussels Court of Appeal, 30 Mar 1979, [1979] *JT* 502, upheld by the Supreme Court of Appeals, 3 Sept 1980, discussed by J Corbet, 'Letter from Belgium' [1980] *Copyright* 193 and J Corbet, 'The Berne Convention and the Belgian Copyright Law' [1986] *Copyright* 260. Note also that a similar principle was agreed in the Annotated Principles on Cable (n 68 above) (Principle 8), where the following exclusion to the right of cable of distribution of broadcast works was suggested: '. . . to individual receiving sets within a limited area consisting of one and the same building or a group of neighbouring buildings, provided that the cable transmission originates in that area and is made without gainful intent'. The US Copyright Act, 17 USC § 111(a)(2) exempts relays of broadcast signals made by the management of a hotel or apartment building to private lodgings of guests or residents, when no charge is made for the relay, and when the relay is not made by a cable service. See also C Masouyé, *Guide to the Berne Convention for the Protection of Literary and Artistic Works* (1978), 65.

[120] *Questionnaire* (n 71 above), 239–40.

Principles of Various Categories of Works subsequently determined that cable distribution of audiovisual works transmitted by FS satellites 'should be considered as a distribution in the framework of a cable originated program . . . '.[121] One way of solving this apparent gap in protection would be to hold the cable distributor jointly responsible with the originating organization for the one composite act of broadcasting, and this was the basic solution suggested by the secretariats and the Committee of Experts.[122] On the other hand, if it is accepted that, with the convergence of technologies that has occurred, FSS transmissions can be treated equally as 'broadcasts' with DBS transmissions, then article 11*bis*(1)(ii) should be applicable in any event. However, even if a member state were to adopt the first interpretation outlined above, determining that there is no distribution of a broadcast of a work in such circumstances, the cable distributor should still be liable under articles 11(1)(ii), 11*ter*(1)(ii), 14(1)(ii) and 14*bis*(1) (at least to the extent of the subject matter covered by those articles).

(b) Webcasting and other digital secondary transmissions

The broad understanding of the expression 'by wire' extends the 11*bis* communication to the public right to wired digital retransmissions as well. (This is equally true for the rights of primary 'communication to the public by wire' in articles 14(1)(ii) and 14*bis*(1), as well as 'any [primary] communication to the public' in articles 11(1)(ii) and 11*ter*(1)(ii).) As a result, a third party's secondary transmissions of broadcasts, for example by webcasting, come within the scope of the 11*bis*(1)(ii) right. A broadcaster who also audio or video streams its own broadcast transmissions, however, is not obliged, under article 11*bis*(1)(ii), to obtain separate authorization for those webcasts. Thus, for example, under the Berne Convention, the BBC is not obliged to obtain additional permission from a foreign author whose work the BBC broadcasts with authorization if the BBC also communicates the broadcast via bbc.co.uk. **12.40**

(c) Other public communications of broadcasts

Since the Brussels Revision, article 11*bis*(1)(iii) has also conferred on the author of a work the exclusive right of authorizing 'the public communication by loudspeaker or any other analogous instrument transmitting, by sign, sounds or images, the broadcast of the work'. The importance of this means of public communication had become apparent in the years immediately prior to 1948, and had received a far from uniform approach under national laws.[123] It was clearly similar to the public performance of a work, except that the size of the **12.41**

[121] Principle AW35 (July 1988): [1988] *Copyright* 372.
[122] *Questionnaire* (n 71 above), 239–40; Principle AW36: [1988] *Copyright* 372.
[123] See comments in programme for Brussels Conference: *Documents 1948* (1951), 266ff.

potential audience was immensely increased. It was for this reason that the programme for the Brussels Conference proposed that the playing of broadcast programmes in public should be brought within the scope of article 11bis(1).[124] There was no significant opposition to this proposal.[125] The practice of retransmitting broadcast programming has become quite widespread, as restaurants and retail establishments relay radio transmissions through on-site sound systems to provide musical ambience, and bars and taverns offer broadcast sports and other programming on television screens.[126] It goes without saying that the receiving of broadcast works in private ('within the family circle') does not fall within the scope of article 11bis(1)(ii). As to what is meant by the 'public' in this case, the programme for the Brussels Revision offers the following guidance: 'above all, where people meet: in the cinema, in restaurants, in tea rooms, railway carriages . . .'.[127] It also appears from the programme that perhaps the most important of these 'public places' were those where people worked and conducted their business, such as factories, shops and offices.[128] A more precise definition as to what is meant by 'public', however, remains a matter for national legislation.[129]

(d) Interpretation of article 11bis

12.42 At the Brussels Revision, the French delegation proposed the addition of a further amendment to article 11bis(1). This was to the effect that the authorization to exploit a work by one of the means stipulated in that paragraph did not imply any authorization to use the work by any of the other means listed in that paragraph.[130] This proposal was rejected by the sub-committee on broadcasting and mechanical instruments on the ground that, as a general matter, the Convention should not contain rules on the interpretation of contracts between authors and their licensees.[131] Nonetheless, there can be little doubt about the

[124] *Documents 1948* (1951), 270.

[125] Although a number of delegations suggested that exceptions should be made in the case of communications in particular kinds of public places, such as schools and hospitals: ibid, 277–8 (Hungary), 278 (Monaco), 280 and 291 (the Netherlands). However, the sub-commission on broadcasting and mechanical instruments pointed out that such a limitation was unnecessary, as para (2) of article 11bis allowed for national laws to regulate the conditions under which the exclusive rights provided for under para (1) were to be exercised: ibid, 115. Article 11bis(2) currently requires that member states provide equitable remuneration for the exercise of the public communication rights.

[126] The United States was recently found to have violated art 11bis(1)(iii) when it exempted, without compensation, the retransmission of radio and television programming through on-site receiving equipment in retail and restaurant establishments. See United States—Section 110(5) of US Copyright Act—Report of the Panel, WT/DS160/R (15 June 2000), Document No 00-2284.

[127] *Documents 1948* (1951), 266. [128] ibid.

[129] ibid, 115 (sub-committee on art 11bis) (report of M Plaisant).

[130] ibid, 277. [131] ibid, 115.

general wisdom of the interpretation suggested by the French delegation, and this was clearly accepted by the sub-commission.[132] Each of the rights listed in paragraph (1) is a distinct right that can be dealt with by the author as she wishes. This clearly includes the power to limit the scope of any authorization that she may grant, but any implications that may be drawn in respect to other matters will depend entirely upon the terms of what the parties have agreed.

D. Gaps and Ambiguities in Coverage

This analysis has revealed a variety of gaps in coverage, with respect both to subject matter and to rights. Because the Berne Convention does not confer a uniform communication right across all protected subject matter, and does not cover sound recordings at all, it is necessary to divide the analysis by type of communication, and by type of work. The broadest right, with respect to subject matter, does not cover all kinds of communications (those communications most implicated by digital transmissions may receive the shortest shrift); the broadest right, with respect to covered communications, does not extend to all types of works. We will first consider neglected subject matter, and then we will turn to incompletely or ambiguously assured rights. **12.43**

(1) Works of visual art (other than cinematographic works)

It has already been seen, in the context of the *droit de suite*, that the opportunities for exploitation of their works by visual artists are generally not as great as in the case of other works. Public performance rights make little sense as far as an artistic work is concerned, but there are still ways in which the work may be communicated to the public in a non-material form. One of these is by inclusion in a television broadcast, and another is by inclusion in a cinematographic film. Both these acts are covered by the relevant provisions of the Berne Convention,[133] but important acts of public communication of artistic works are still omitted. Wired transmission of still images, for example, over the Internet, will not be covered unless the transmissions are third-party retransmissions of a broadcast. Even more significantly, the public exhibition of the work falls outside the Berne Convention rights. For many works of art, however, this is the most important means of exploitation as there is always a strong public interest in viewing the original of a work rather than a copy or a transient televised or cinematographic representation. According visual artists rights in respect of the public exhibition of their works can therefore be seen as a way of enabling them **12.44**

[132] ibid. [133] Articles $11^{bis}(1)$ and 14(1).

to realize more fully their general right of economic exploitation. Like the *droit de suite*, such a right can be seen as a means of correcting the balance between visual artists and other authors who may more readily exploit their works through reproduction and performance. Nevertheless, relatively few countries in the Berne Union have expressly recognized public exhibition rights in their domestic copyright laws,[134] and there have been no proposals to include such a right in the Convention itself.

(2) Rights of public exhibition of artistic works through national treatment

12.45 The question which therefore remains is whether authors from Union countries which do not recognize exhibition rights in respect of artistic works may nonetheless claim such protection in those Union countries where such rights are accorded. The general principle of national treatment indicates an affirmative answer to this, but, as with other rights not expressly recognized in the Convention, the preliminary question arises as to whether public exhibition rights are part of copyright or whether they are distinct and unrelated rights.[135] There is evidence to be found, both within and outside the Convention, to suggest that the first of these views is correct. As to the external evidence, it seems that where national laws protect exhibition rights they do so, either expressly or implicitly, as part of their general copyright laws.[136] As to the internal evidence, the wording of article 17 also indicates that exhibition is within the scope of authors' rights for the purposes of national treatment under the Convention. This article, which deals with the 'police power' of states to place restrictions on the exercise of copyright, reads as follows:

> The provisions of this Convention cannot in any way affect the right of the Government of each country of the Union to permit, to control or to prohibit by legislation or regulation, the circulation, presentation, or exhibition of any work or production in regard to which the competent authority may find it necessary to exercise that right.

While this provision is principally concerned with state censorship powers (see further para 13.90 below), the expression 'circulation, presentation, or exhibition' indicates that these acts fall within the scope of the copyright

[134] FRG Law of 1965, art 18: see further E Ulmer, 'Letter from Germany' [1965] *Copyright* 275, 277–8. See also Denmark, Act on Copyright (1995), art 2(3)(ii); Mexico, Federal Law on Copyright (1996), art 85 (by implication). The US 1976 Copyright Act includes an exclusive right to display a work publicly, 17 USC § 106(5), but it also exempts public displays made by or under the authority of the owner of the physical copy of the work, 'to viewers present at the place where the copy is located', 17 USC § 109(c).

[135] See eg the similar arguments that arise with respect to the *droit de suite* in the pre-Brussels texts of the Convention: see para 11.54 above.

[136] This is the case in each of the laws referred to in n 134 above.

owner's rights, even if they are not exhaustively protected under the Convention. It would be clearer if the provision referred only to those rights expressly accorded under the Convention. However, this would leave a gap where national laws accorded more extensive protection, and would lead to the anomalous situation that states would be able to exercise their police powers in respect of rights 'specially granted' under the Convention but could not apply them in respect of any additional rights as this would infringe the principle of national treatment. 'Circulation, presentation, or exhibition' are therefore deliberately general, and refer to the totality of copyright, whether or not individual rights are protected expressly under the Convention. As far as circulation rights are concerned, there can be little doubt that these are regarded as part of copyright, although not fully recognized in the Convention (see further paras 11.45, 11.50–11.51, and 11.88 above). Likewise, if the word 'exhibition' is to have any operation, it must cover the public exhibition of artistic works. The result is that article 17 is to be read as conferring on member states the capacity to exercise their police powers in respect of authors' rights to control the exhibition of their works insofar as such rights are conferred under national legislation. It follows therefore that where this is the case, an author claiming under the Convention is still entitled to such protection as part of the application of the principle of national treatment, even though there is no equivalent protection in the country of origin of his work.

(3) Text of literary, musical, dramatic, and dramatico-musical works

Although the combination of articles 11, 11*bis*, and 11*ter* gives performed versions of these works exclusive rights over wired and wireless primary and secondary transmissions, these works, like works of visual art, receive almost no protection against primary or secondary communication of the text itself. Given the easy and instantaneous communication over digital networks of digitized text, and especially of computer programs (recall that these also are 'literary works'; see paras 8.92ff above), the limited Berne Convention coverage of these works is a significant lacuna. **12.46**

(4) Communications not clearly covered

Because wire-originated communications are not covered under article 11*bis*(1), only those works protected under arts 11(1)(ii), 11*ter*(1)(ii), 14(1)(ii), and 14*bis*(1) will enjoy rights with respect to original cable or wired webcast transmissions. Even as to those works, a significant ambiguity arises in connection with digital communications. Up to now, we have considered only those digital communications that resemble cable transmissions and broadcasts, that is, which communicate preselected programming to a passive public. These are also known as 'push' communications. A different set of **12.47** questions arises when the transmissions are made on an on-demand (or 'pull') basis. These questions apply whether the transmission is by wire or wireless means (as wireless access to the Internet is likely to become increasingly prevalent). In addition, an intermediate form of on-demand communication should be considered: preprogrammed pay-per-view cable and broadcast services.

(5) On-demand digital transmissions

12.48 To the extent that any of the communication rights may apply, must the 'public' to which the work is communicated receive the work at the same time? While it is implicit in the broadcasting and retransmissions rights that the members of the receiving public may be separated in space, the Berne Convention does not specify whether they may also be separated in time. To discern the application of the Berne Convention transmission rights to the full range of digital communications it is necessary to resolve at least two issues. First, at whose impetus, the sender's or the recipient's, must the transmission occur? Second, what constitutes the 'public'? For example, if only one person initiates an on-demand transmission (even assuming 'pull' transmissions are covered), has there been a 'communication to the public'?

12.49 Although articles 11, 11*bis*, 11*ter*, 14, and 14*bis* address traditional 'push' technologies—broadcast or wired transmissions from an originating (or retransmitting) entity to a passively receiving public—nothing in the concept of 'communication to the public' *excludes* 'pull technologies'.[137] Indeed the term 'communication' is sufficiently open-ended to be neutral as to its initiator. (Whether the communication is 'to the public' will be considered hereafter.) The term '*broad*casting', by contrast, may well imply widely sending a communication simultaneously to many recipients. If that is the case, then only those works covered by the 'any communication to the public' right or by the right of primary communication by wire, will also be protected with respect to on-demand digital transmissions.

(6) On-demand transmissions 'to the public'

12.50 If only one person initiates the on-demand transmission at a time (or ever) is there a 'communication to the public' within the meaning of the Berne Convention? The number of recipients should not in fact matter; what should count is the availability of the communication to 'the public'. For example,

[137] Even though those technologies may not have been contemplated in 1928, when the broadcasting right was first introduced (see para 12.22 above) or even in 1967, when the 'communication to the public' language was added to art 11 (see para 12.10 above).

there is a 'communication to the public by wire' of a cinematographic work (article $14^{bis}(1)$) if a film is transmitted on cable television, even if no viewer in fact selects that channel to watch. What makes the communication 'to the public' is the invitation to any member of the public to turn on the television and view the programme. Even when the cable transmission is restricted, for example, to paying subscribers, it still is 'to the public' because any member of the public is invited to pay the fee. By the same token, one might assert that an on-demand digital communication, for example, from a website, should also be considered 'to the public'. Any member of the public may access the website and respond to its offer to receive a communication (by streaming or downloading) of the work. The same analysis would apply to peer-to-peer file 'sharing': a computer user who has designated files on her hard drive as available for 'sharing' invites any member of the public who has acquired the appropriate file-sharing program to initiate a communication of a copy of the designated file from the offeror's computer to the acquirer's. By contrast, a website whose access was restricted to the operator's family and friends would not be communicating to the public, nor would a file sharer who similarly limited access to her hard drive.

While it may be reasonable to construe the rights under the Berne Conven- **12.51**
tion of communication to the public, with the possible exception of broadcasting, as extending to on-demand digital transmissions, it may also be overly bold to contend that the Berne Convention not only permits this construction, but mandates it. There is sufficient ambiguity regarding the question whether 'the public' may be separated not only in space but also in time, that the scope of 'communication to the public' in this regard may be a matter of interpretation by member states. (On the other hand, as we will see at paras 12.56ff below, the WIPO copyright treaties have eliminated member state discretion on this score, in favour of a much broader right of communication to the public.)

(7) Pay per view

Finally, pay-per-view broadcast and cable services present a half-way point **12.52**
between traditional 'push' transmissions, and the individualized 'pull' transmissions made possible by digital media. These services offer the public the choice of programmes at a variety of times. Although the receiving public is not completely passive, it is still the transmitting entity that selects the programe and the transmission times; as a result, these kinds of communications should be analysed in the same way as more traditional wired or wireless transmissions.

E. Beyond the Berne Convention

(1) The TRIPs Agreement

12.53 No provisions of the TRIPs Agreement directly address the scope of the rights of public performance or communication to the public in Berne Convention-protected works. Article 14(1), however, confers on performers of works fixed on phonograms the 'possibility of preventing' the unauthorized 'broadcasting by wireless means and the communication to the public of their live performance'. We will address this provision in the context of Chapter 19 below, which analyses neighbouring rights agreements.

(2) WIPO Copyright Treaty

12.54 Article 8 of the 1996 WCT sets out a right of communication to the public of general application, and further specifies that this right includes the right of 'making available to the public of their works in such a way that members of the public may access these works from a place and at a time individually chosen by them'. These rights are, however, 'without prejudice to' the various provisions of the Berne Convention on 'communication to the public'. There is also an 'agreed statement' accompanying article 8 regarding the meaning of 'communication' and the application of Berne Convention article $11^{bis}(2)$. In the following paragraphs we will consider the drafting history of article 8 of the WCT; the meaning of 'communication'; the interpretation of the 'making available' right; and the relationship of article 8 of the WCT to the Berne Convention provisions on 'communication to the public'.

(a) Communication to the public

(i) Drafting history: The text proffered by the Basic Proposal for the Copyright Treaty was virtually identical to the final version. Proposed article 10 provided:

> Without prejudice to the rights provided for in Articles 11(1)(ii), $11^{bis}(1)(i)$, $11^{ter}(1)(ii)$, 14(1)(i) and $14^{bis}(1)$ of the Berne Convention, authors of literary and artistic works shall enjoy the exclusive right of authorising any communication to the public of their works, including the making available to the public of their works, by wire or wireless means, in such a way that members of the public may access these works from a place and at a time individually chosen by them.

The changes to the 'without prejudice' clause were essentially clarifications or corrections, as was the transfer of the phrase 'by wire or wireless means' to qualify 'any communication to the public', instead of qualifying 'the making available to the public'. With this change, there could be no doubt that the communication to the public right was technologically neutral and all-encompassing. As the 'making available' right remained syntactically dependent on the communication to the public right,[138] its neutrality as to the means of making available was also preserved. Other proposals to clarify the text of the Basic Proposal were adopted as part of the agreed statement, discussed hereafter.

(ii) The meaning of 'communication' in Article 8: The agreed statement specified: **12.55**

> It is understood that the mere provision of physical facilities for enabling or making a communication does not in itself amount to a communication within the meaning of this Treaty or the Berne Convention . . .

This portion of the agreed statement was adopted in response to concerns raised by telecommunications organizations and Internet Service Providers. They sought to ensure that they would not be held liable for infringing communications to the public originated by others. The text of the agreed statement does not, however, establish a blanket immunity; only exempted is the 'mere provision of physical facilities for enabling or making a communication'. This suggests that providing anything more than physical facilities, for example, providing software for enabling communications, may be considered an act of communication. Similarly, only the 'mere' provision of physical facilities is shielded; provision of physical facilities and something more, such as actual or constructive knowledge of the content of the communication, may 'amount to a communication'.

(iii) Communication to the public: relationship to Berne Convention rights: The WCT specifies that its generalized right of communication to the public is 'without prejudice' to the various provisions of the Berne Convention that include broadcasting and communication rights (articles 11(1)(ii), 11bis(1)(i) and (ii), 11ter(1)(ii), 14(1)(ii), and 14bis(1)). In other words, the WCT fills in the gaps, but does not override the prior rights.[139] Thus, the WCT would mandate a right of primary wired communication of works not covered by articles 11, 11ter, 14 and 14bis; it would not affect transmissions already covered, **12.56**

[138] The Australian delegation offered an amendment to separate the 'making available' right from the 'communication to the public' right, but this was 'widely and sucessfully opposed, because the making available right was considered to be an aspect of the communication right.' Reinbothe and von Lewinski (2002), 103, citing Summary Minutes of Main Committee I in WIPO, *Records of the Diplomatic Conference on Certain Copyright and Neighboring Rights Questions, Geneva 1996* (1999), para. 307.

[139] Nor does it override limitations in the Berne Convention on those rights, as the agreed statement to art 8 makes clear: 'Nothing in Article 8 precludes a Contracting Party from applying article 11bis(2).' See further discussion in para 13.128 below.

for example, by those articles or by the broadcasting right. Article 8 retains the Berne Convention's communication rights floorboards; it also ensures that works no longer fall through those boards' cracks in coverage of subject matter or of communications technology.

One may nonetheless question the application of the 'without prejudice' proviso to the filling in of the Berne Convention's gaps. For example, article 11*bis*(1)(ii) does not extend to retransmissions effected by the original broadcaster (see the earlier discussion at para 12.36 above). Is a retransmission by the same organization of its original wireless transmission now covered by the communication right under article 8 of the WCT?[140] Or does one infer from article 11*bis*(1)(ii) a free pass for the original broadcaster? At first blush, there may seem to be no practical difference, because the original broadcaster would have paid for primary and secondary transmission rights anyway. But if the originating broadcaster's retransmission falls outside article11*bis*, then the author's rights over that retransmission are 'exclusive' rights under article 8 of the WCT, not subject to compulsory licence, even though the original broadcast might have been made pursuant to a compulsory licence.

(b) 'Making available to the public'

12.57 The WCT's principal innovation is its specification that the right of communication to the public includes a right of 'making available to the public of [literary and artistic] works in such a way that members of the public may access those works from a place and at a time individually chosen by them'. This right targets on-demand transmissions (whether by wire or wireless means), for it makes clear that the members of the public may be separated both in space and in time. As we have seen (at paras 12.48ff above), it was possible to interpret the Berne Convention to cover at least wired on-demand transmissions of certain kinds of works, but it was not clear that the Berne Convention *required* member states to extend the communication to the public right to these transmissions. The WCT therefore supplies the missing mandate, and applies it to all Berne-protected works, as well as to subject matter, such as computer programs and databases, whose Berne coverage the WCT has either clarified or added to (see the earlier discussion at paras 8.120ff).

12.58 The WCT does not define the 'public' to whom the works are made available, but it may give greater indication than does the Berne Convention that the relevant 'public' is comprised of 'members', and, accordingly, need not be populous, although the greater the numbers to whom a work is made available, the more apparent the conclusion that the making available was to 'the public'. But

[140] Reinbothe and von Lewinski (2002) at 107, suggest that it is.

simply offering the work on an undiscriminating basis, so that any member of the general public may access the work, should come within the scope of the right. Even more restricted offers, such as to all university students, or to all aficionados of obscure Australian or Estonian poetry, appeal to an audience potentially too large for a 'family circle' or similar exclusion. It is not necessary that the offer be accepted: 'making available' embraces incipient as well as effected communications.

(c) Modes of 'making available'

The technological means of 'making available' are irrelevant; article 8 of the WCT is expressed in technologically neutral terms. Juridically, member states may comply with the right either through local communication rights, or, for those countries who have applied the distribution right to temporary digital copies, through the right to distribute copies, as the United States urged during the drafting period.[141] In adopting what came to be known as the 'umbrella solution', allowing member states to implement the making available right through any exclusive right under domestic law, the drafters opted for an approach of juridical as well as technological neutrality.[142] **12.59**

(d) Direct and indirect 'making available'

The scope of the making available right may be broader still, as it may encompass certain forms of indirect supplying of literary and artistic works. Consider the following scenario: a website aggregates links to other websites from which users can download unauthorized copies of recorded music. Some links are identified by the name of the music file; clicking on these links takes the user directly to another website and automatically downloads the named file from that website to the user's hard drive. Other links are identified by the names of the other websites; clicking on these sends the user to the website, from which she may elect to download a variety of files. The principal site does not directly send digital files of the recorded music to users who access the site. From the user's point of view, the experience of clicking on the first kind of link to acquire the file is the same, whether or not she knows that the file is coming from the site she contacted, or from some other site; either way, she contacts the first site and receives the file without the apparent further intervention of another website operator. In the second case, the user knows she is being taken to another site, from which she may download files of recorded music. In either case, the linked-to websites are making works available to the public in the same **12.60**

[141] See 1996 *Records* at 675, para 301.

[142] For extensive discussion of the 'umbrella solution', by the coiner of the term, see Ficsor (n 107 above) at 204–9, 496–509. See also Reinbothe and von Lewinski (2002) at 102–3 and n 15.

way that a direct-delivery website does. But, in either case, is the first-accessed site, by rerouting to the other sites, also 'making [the files] available' to the members of the public who contact the site?[143]

12.61 The article 8 (and 10 and 14 under the WPPT) 'making available' right gives authors the exclusive right of allowing members of the public to access literary and artistic works (and recorded performances) 'from a place and at a time individually chosen by them'. The 'place' contemplated most likely refers to the place where the member of the public is located (for example, at home, or at an Internet café). But the text might also be read to refer to the networked 'place', for example, website, that the user contacts in order to gain access to the work.[144] Applying that interpretation, in the second case, the connection between accessing the first site and the communication of the work may be too attenuated, because the user knows that the site from which she is receiving the work is no longer the site she first contacted. The other site becomes the place from which the user chooses to access the work. In the first case, by contrast, the place from which the user appears to be accessing the music is the site the user initially contacted, which is the only site she chose. Accordingly, though the source of the communication is ultimately another site, the user's selection would control.[145] If so, then the WCT 'making available' right will reach certain acts of indirect infringement.

(3) Exclusive rights and compulsory licences

12.62 Article 8 of the WCT specifies that the communication and making available rights are 'exclusive'. Therefore, member states should not be permitted to impose compulsory licences. But article 8 also is 'without prejudice' to article 11*bis*(1)(ii) of the Berne Convention, which, under article 11*bis*(2), allows member states to limit broadcasting and retransmission rights, subject to providing remuneration. The agreed statement to article 8 of the WCT specifically preserves the application of article 11*bis*(2).[146] As a result, if a Berne member had

[143] This scenario is inspired by the facts of *Universal Music Australia Pty Ltd* v *Cooper* [2005] FCA 972 (14 July 2005) (holding that the website operator and its host service provider infringed copyright by authorizing the infringements of copyright by the operators of the remote websites or by the internet users who downloaded the music sound recordings).

[144] Nothing in the Records of the Diplomatic Conference on Certain Copyright and Neighboring Rights Questions (WIPO, 1996), indicates that the language 'from a place and at a time individually chosen by them' received special attention, apart from general endorsement of its adaptability to digital communications.

[145] On the other hand, this interpretation might mean that the website from which the content is in fact (despite appearances) obtained is not 'making [the content] available'. Nonetheless, if that website were also offering content directly to users, it would still be 'making available', even though it delivers some of its content to users who are not aware of the source of the content.

[146] See agreed statement to WCT, art 8: 'It is further understood that nothing in Article 8 precludes a Contracting Party from applying article 11bis(2).'

previously treated wireless on-demand communications as coming within the local equivalent of the broadcasting and wireless diffusion rights, then that state would be entitled (but not obliged) under article 11*bis*(2) to subject those transmissions to compulsory licensing. Moreover, upon joining the WIPO treaties, those countries would be permitted to continue to maintain the compulsory licence regime. The regime would apply only to wireless on-demand transmissions; wired on-demand transmissions would not have come under article 11*bis*(1)(ii), and the Berne Convention therefore would not have permitted compulsory licensing with respect to those transmissions. Had the member state deemed the right either outside the Berne Convention altogether, or included only within the 'communication to the public' rights set out in other articles of the Berne Convention, then, upon joining the WCT, that state must treat the making available right as an exclusive right.

F. Comparative Table of Performance and Communication Rights

12.63

Exclusive right protected	Berne Convention	Gaps left to national law and ambiguities	TRIPS Agreement (beyond article 9(1) compliance clause)	WCT (beyond article 1(4) compliance clause)	Gaps and ambiguities
PUBLIC PERFORMANCE—					
Public performance by any means or process of dramatic, dramatico-musical, and musical works and of translations of these works	articles 11(1)(i), 11(2)	Public exhibition not covered. The terms 'public' and 'performance' are not defined, but the combined term may imply that public be present at the place of performance. 'By any means or process' may reach the playing of performances (live or recorded) over loudspeakers or receiving devices located in public places.		Article 8 does not address 'public performance' to public present at performance; see comment following $11^{bis}(1)$(iii)	

public recitation of literary works and translations of literary works	articles 11*bis*(1)(i), 11(2)	The terms 'public' and 'recitation' are not defined, but the combined term may imply that public be present at the place of performance: 'By any means or process' may reach the playing of recitations (live or recorded) of literary works over loudspeakers or receiving devices located in public places.	Same
Public performance of cinematographic adaptations and reproductions	article 14(1)(ii)	The terms 'public,' 'performance' and 'cinematographic adaptation' are not defined.	Same
Public performance in a cinematographic work	article 14*bis*(1)	'Cinematographic work' not defined. Nor are, 'public' and 'performance'.	Same

Continued overleaf

Comparative table *continued*

Exclusive right protected	Berne Convention	Gaps left to national law and ambiguities	TRIPS Agreement (beyond article 9(1) compliance clause)	WCT (beyond article 1(4) compliance clause)	Gaps and ambiguities
COMMUNICATION TO THE PUBLIC BY TRANSMISSION—					
Broadcasting and any communication to the public by any means for wireless diffusion of signs, sounds or images; applies to all literary and artistic works	article $11^{bis}(1)(i)$	The terms 'broadcasting' and 'public' are not defined; not clear if recipient-initiated on-demand transmissions covered. Article $11^{bis}(2)$ permits member states to impose compulsory licences.		Article 8 communication to the public by '. . . wireless means' and 'making available' right	
Communication to the public by wire of broadcasts and rebroadcasts; applies to all literary and artistic works	article $11^{bis}(1)(ii)$: communication to be made by an organization other than the original one	The phrase 'communication to the public' is not defined; 'cable originated' and other initial wired transmissions are not covered. Article $11^{bis}(2)$ permits member states to impose compulsory licences.		Art 8 'communication to the public by wire . . .'	'Communication to the public' remains undefined; right is 'without prejudice' to Berne Convention, article $11^{bis}(1)(ii)$. Agreed statement preserves Berne Convention, article $11^{bis}(2)$ 'Making available' right covers on-demand transmissions

Public communication of broadcasts by loudspeakers or other analogous instruments; applies to all literary and artistic works	Article $11^{bis}(1)(iii)$	The phrase 'public communication' is not defined, but implies something different from 'communication to the public': The latter is to a remote audience, former is a secondary communication to a public place. Article $11^{bis}(2)$ permits member states to impose compulsory licences. The secondary communication to a public place right may overlap with the art 11(1)(i) right, but article 11bis (1)(iii) covers a broader range of subject matter.			Absence of 'without prejudice' to Berne Convention, article $11^{bis}(1)(iii)$ in WCT, article 8 suggests WCT does not affect secondary communications to a public present at the output, ie secondary communications akin to public performances
Communication to the public of performances of musical, dramatic, and dramatico-musical works and translations	article 11(1)(ii), (2)	Includes communications not covered by 11bis, eg initial wired transmission; but because 'communication to the public' not defined, not clear whether on-demand transmissions are covered		article 8	The word 'public' remains undefined; on-demand transmissions covered; right is 'without prejudice' to article 11(1)(ii).

Continued overleaf

Comparative table *continued*

Exclusive right protected	Berne Convention	Gaps left to national law and ambiguities	TRIPS Agreement (beyond article 9(1) compliance clause)	WCT (beyond article 1(4) compliance clause)	Gaps and ambiguities
Communication to the public of recitations of literary works and translations	article $11^{ter}(1)$(ii), (2)	Includes communications not covered by 11bis, eg initial wired transmission; but because 'communication to the public' not defined, not clear whether on-demand transmissions are covered		article 8	The word 'public' remains undefined; on-demand transmissions covered; right is 'without prejudice' to $11^{ter}(1)$(ii).
Communication to the public by wire of cinematographic adaptations and reproductions of literary and artistic works, and of cinematographic works	articles 14(1)(ii), $14^{bis}(1)$	Includes communications not covered by article 11bis, eg initial wired transmission; but because 'communication to the public' not defined, not clear whether on-demand transmissions are covered		article 8	The word 'public' remains undefined; on-demand transmissions covered; right is 'without prejudice' to article 14(1)(ii) and $14^{bis}(1)$.

13

RESTRICTIONS ON THE EXERCISE OF RIGHTS: LIMITATIONS AND EXCEPTIONS

A. Introduction

13.01 Even in those countries where there is the most vigorous commitment to the advancement of authors' rights, it is recognized that there is a need for restrictions or limitations upon these rights in particular cases. This was acknowledged in national laws at an early stage, and, at the outset of the negotiations that led to the Berne Convention, Numa Droz reminded delegates that it should be remembered that 'limits to absolute protection are rightly set by the public interest'.[1] Thus, from the Berne Act on, the Convention has contained a number of provisions granting latitude to member states to limit the rights of authors in certain circumstances. In a general sense, these might be described as instances where it is considered that the 'public interest' should prevail against the private interests of authors. Typical examples are uses of copyright works for educational purposes and for the reporting of news, situations which were recognized from an early stage in Berne. 'Public interest', however, is a shifting concept that requires a careful balancing of competing claims in each case and one that is frequently interpreted in different ways at the national level, depending upon historical, cultural, and social circumstances. This balancing process occurs in all national copyright systems, even in those which proclaim the rights of authors most absolutely, and, as the present chapter will show, the same has been true of the Berne Convention. Nonetheless, although the need for limits on protection is generally recognized, there have been lengthy debates throughout the history of the Convention as to how these are to be set. In 'machinery terms', this can be done in three main ways:

(i) Subject matter limitations: By provisions excluding protection altogether in the case of particular categories of works, for example, news of the day (article 2(8)), or by provisions that do not require protection to be given to particular categories, leaving this as a matter for national legislators to determine for themselves, examples here being official texts of a legislative, administrative,

[1] See *Actes* 1884, 67 (closing speech to the 1884 Conference). See also A Baum, *The Brussels Conference for the Revision of the Berne Convention* (1949) ('Baum (1949)'), 58, and G Koumantos, 'Le droit d'auteur et la rémuneration équitable' [1983] *GRUR Int* 424.

and legal nature (article 2(4)), and speeches delivered in the course of legal proceedings (article 2bis(1)). For the purposes of analysis, these might be described as 'limitations' on protection, in the sense that there is either to be no protection given, or there is no requirement for it to be given, with respect to particular categories of works.

(ii) Use limitations: By provisions according immunity from infringement proceedings for particular kinds of use, for example, for the purposes of news reporting or education, or in specific situations where the usage appears to threaten only a minimum of harm to the author. These can be termed 'permitted uses', and are dealt with in articles 2bis(2), 9(2), 10, and 10bis. There are also parallel exceptions that are to be implied in the case of translations and 'minor reservations' that are permissible in the case of performing, recitation, broadcasting, recording, and cinematographic rights. Analogous exceptions are to be found in article 15 of the Rome Convention, while article 13 of the Agreement on Trade-Related Aspects of Intellectual Property Rights 1994 ('TRIPs Agreement'), article 10 of the World Intellectual Property Organization ('WIPO') Copyright Treaty ('WCT'), and article 16 of the WIPO Performances and Phonograms Treaty ('WPPT') adopt and extend the template of the three conditions in article 9(2) of Berne as the basis for exceptions that are to be applied generally under that agreement (the 'three-step' test, of which more below).

(iii) Use limitations requiring compensation: By provisions allowing a particular use of copyright material, subject to the payment of compensation to the copyright owner. These are usually described as 'compulsory' or 'obligatory licences', and specific dispositions permitting them are found in articles 11bis(2) and 13, as well as in the Appendix containing Special Provisions regarding Developing Countries. It is also possible that such licences may be allowable under other provisions of this and the other conventions dealt with in this study, so long as certain conditions are met.

The juridical basis for each kind of provision is different. The first proceeds on **13.02** the assumption that there are clear reasons of public policy why copyright protection in the works in question might not be required, for example, because it is necessary, in the interests of participatory democracy or the free flow of information, that these works should be readily and widely available. The second represents a more limited concession to the effect that certain kinds of uses of works that are otherwise protected should be allowed because there is a public interest present here that justifies overriding the private rights of authors in these particular circumstances. In the third category of cases, the author's rights continue to be protected but are significantly abridged or even transmuted into something different: public interest may still justify the continuance of the use, regardless of the author's consent, but this should be subject to the payment of appropriate remuneration (the transmutation here being from an exclusive right to a right to remuneration).

The Berne Convention contains instances of all three kinds of provision. For the most part, these are not made mandatory, but are left as matters for the national legislation of member states to determine, although the exercise of this discretion is usually made subject to strict conditions. The first category (of works that may be excluded from protection) has already been discussed (see paras 8.104ff above) and will not be dealt with here again except where this becomes relevant to the others. The present chapter is therefore concerned with the second and third categories of permitted uses and compulsory licences. With the development of new technological means of reproduction and dissemination of works in recent years, these exceptions have become of ever greater importance, and their scope is in need of some clarification. Furthermore, while the above classification may suggest that permitted uses and compulsory licences are the subject of distinct provisions in the Convention, the following analysis will show that both are potentially available under each provision. Accordingly, we shall examine each of the relevant articles in turn, beginning with the most general, which deals with exceptions to the reproduction right (article 9(2)), then with specific exceptions, such as rights of quotation (article 10(1)), uses for teaching purposes (article 10(2)), press usage (articles $10^{bis}(1)$ and (2), and $2^{bis}(2)$), reservations and conditions on the exercise of mechanical reproduction rights under article 13, and conditions for the exercise of broadcasting and other rights under article 11bis. It will also be necessary to discuss a number of situations where exceptions to particular rights, although not expressed in the Convention, are nonetheless to be implied (the so-called 'minor reservations'). This will then set the scene for a consideration of how the question of limitations and exceptions has been taken up and extended in the TRIPs Agreement and the WCT.[2] Because of their scope and complexity, the compulsory licences that may be applied by developing countries under the Appendix to the Berne Convention are dealt with separately in the following chapter (this chapter also chronicles a most significant crisis in the development of the Convention in which the interests and concerns of developed and developing countries came

[2] This chapter also draws upon material appearing in studies written by S Ricketson for WIPO (*WIPO Study on Exceptions and Limitations of Copyright and Related Rights in the Digital Environment*, SCCR/97, 5 Apr 2003 and the Centre for Copyright Studies, Sydney (*The Three-step Test, Deemed Quantities, Libraries and Closed Exceptions* (2002)); see also Ricketson (1999) 1 *Intellectual Property Quarterly* 56–94. For recent, detailed commentary on the three-step test, see MRF Senftleben, *Copyright, limitations and the three-step test: an analysis of the three-step test in international and EC copyright law* (2004) and, with respect to the famous 2000 WTO panel decision, see: J Ginsburg, (2001) 187 *RIDA* 3; J Oliver, (2002) 25 *Columbia Journal of Law & the Arts* 119; M Ficsor, (2002) 192 *RIDA* 111; and P Johnson [2004] 26 *EIPR* 265.

into sharp and near fatal conflict). (Limitations and exceptions with respect to neighbouring rights are also discussed separately at paras 19.11–19.16, 19.33, and 19.69 below.)

B. Permissible Restrictions under the Berne Convention

(1) Development of a general exception concerning reproduction rights (article 9(2))

While this is the most recent exception to be included in the Berne Convention, it is useful to discuss this first, as it has become the centrepiece of the exceptions regimes that have been incorporated in the TRIPs Agreement and the WCT. Prior to the Stockholm and Paris Acts, the Berne Convention contained no general provision recognizing reproduction rights. Although it has been argued that there was an implicit requirement under earlier Acts to provide such protection, the better view is that no such obligation existed.[3] Accordingly, Union members were free to impose whatever restrictions they wished on reproduction rights, or even to deny protection altogether. In practice, reproduction rights were universally recognized under national legislation, but the exceptions to these rights varied considerably from country to country. In some countries, these were quite widely drawn,[4] while others adopted a narrower approach.[5] These differences meant that, in the event that the Convention were to embody a general right of reproduction, care would be required to ensure that this provision did not encroach upon exceptions that were already contained in national legislation.[6] On the other hand, it would also be necessary to ensure that it did not allow for the making of wider exceptions that might have the effect of undermining the new right of reproduction. **13.03**

Until such time as an exclusive general reproduction right was recognized in the Convention, there was no occasion to discuss the permissible restrictions that **13.04**

---

[3] See para 11.06 above.

[4] See eg the Finnish Law of 8 July 1961, arts 11–21; the Maltese Copyright Act 1967, ss 7, 9, and 10; the Indian Copyright Act 1957, s 52.

[5] Cf French Law of 1957, art 41.

[6] The Swedish/BIRPI Study Group noted in its work for the 1967 programme that the 'exceptions most frequently recognized in domestic laws' related to the following methods of use: (i) public speeches, (ii) quotations, (iii) school books and chrestomathies, (iv) newspaper articles, (v) reporting of current events, (vi) ephemeral recording, (vii) private use, (viii) reproduction by photocopying in libraries, (ix) reproduction in special characters for use by the blind, (x) sound recording of works for the blind, (xi) texts of songs, (xii) sculptures on permanent display in public places, (xiii) use of artistic works in film and television as background, and (xiv) reproduction in the interests of public safety. To this list might be added reproductions for judicial and administrative purposes, eg in the course of court proceedings: *Records* 1967, vol I, 112 (Document S/1).

would have to be applied to this right.[7] When a proposal for recognition of a general reproduction right became part of the agenda for those preparing for the Stockholm Revision Conference, it was soon concluded that this would need to deal with the question of exceptions to that right. In the words of the Swedish/BIRPI Study Group in its 1964 report:[8]

> This prerogative was of fundamental importance in the legislation of member countries of the Union; the fact that it is not recognised in the Convention would therefore appear to be an anomaly. However, if a provision on the subject is to be incorporated in the text of the Convention, a satisfactory formula will have to be found for the inevitable exceptions to this right.
>
> On the one hand, it is obvious that all forms of exploiting a work which have, or are likely to acquire, considerable economic or practical importance must in principle be reserved to the authors. Exceptions that might restrict the possibilities open to the authors in these respects are unacceptable. On the other hand, it must not be forgotten that national legislations already contain a series of exceptions in favour of various public and cultural interests and that it would be vain to suppose that States would be ready at this stage to do away with these exceptions to any appreciable extent.

13.05 The same Study Group provided a taxonomy of the 'exceptions most frequently recognized in domestic laws' (these are listed in note 6 to para 13.04 above).[9] The text of the Convention then in force (the Brussels Act) contained exceptions with respect to the first six of the listed exceptions, although under the programme ultimately adopted and approved by the Stockholm Revision Conference, the third of these exceptions was deleted. Leaving aside these 'established' exceptions, however, the balance of those listed by the Study Group were all acceptable limitations so far as national laws were concerned, and would remain so until the principle of an exclusive reproduction right was recognized under the Convention. At that point, and at that point only, would it become necessary for the Convention to contain provisions as to the scope of permissible exceptions and limitations.

13.06 These matters occupied a considerable amount of time in the preparatory work for the Stockholm Revision. After examining a number of possible approaches,[10] the 1964 Study Group suggested that the following proviso to the proposed new right of reproduction in article 9(1) should be made:

---

[7] This was the view of the study group that was set up by the Swedish Government and the *Bureaux internationaux reunis pour la protection de la propriete intellectuelle* ('BIRPI', the predecessor to WIPO), at the time that preparations for the Stockholm Conference began: Swedish/BIRPI Study Group, June 1963, Document DA/20/2, 44: 'If this question [that of whether there should be a reproduction right] is passed by in silence, there would seem to be no occasion to discuss the restrictions which would have to be applied to a general right of reproduction.'

[8] This was a further report of the same Swedish/BIRPI Study Group that reported in 1964 and was adopted by a committee of governmental experts in 1965: Document DA/22/2, 47ff.

[9] ibid, n 23. See n 6 above.

[10] *Records* 1967 vol I, 111–12.

> However, it shall be a matter for legislation in the countries of the Union, having regard to the provisions of this Convention, to limit the recognition and the exercising of that right, for specified purposes, and on the condition that these purposes should not enter into economic competition with these works.[11]

In support of this proposal, the Study Group stressed three points: (i) that it was necessary to have regard to existing exceptions under the Convention (such as articles 10, 10*bis*, 11*bis*(3), and 13(2); (ii) that exceptions were only to be made for clearly specified purposes, such as private use, etc, and that generalized exceptions were not permitted; and (iii) that these exceptions should not compete with the work economically: 'all forms of exploiting a work which have, or are likely to acquire, considerable economic or practical importance, must be reserved to authors. At the same time, the formula chosen opens the way for other exceptions of lesser importance.'[12]

The Group also commented that the proposed formula expressed the 'thought that it is advisable to take special precautions before countenancing exceptions that may be applied without giving authors the right to claim remuneration. If this right is granted, the right to make exceptions widens to some extent.' In this regard, it should be noted that, in an interesting precursor to the modern debates about exceptions to protection, the Group had considered, but rejected, the possibility of adopting an exclusive list of exceptions: **13.07**

> On the one hand, a list of this kind—even if it were to be limited to the main exceptions—would be very long and would considerably restrict the authors' rights. At the present time, most countries only recognise some of the exceptions indicated above—they vary from one country to another—or else they grant a remuneration to the authors for the use permitted by certain of these rules of exception, as in the case of the Nordic countries. There is every reason to fear that the introduction of a list of this kind would encourage the adoption of all the exceptions allowed and abolish the right of remuneration. On the other hand, a list, however long, would be inadequate, because it could never cover all the special cases existing in national legislation.[13]

By contrast, the 1965 Committee of Governmental Experts, which considered the recommendations of the 1964 Study Group, took the view that some specific exceptions should be mentioned in the proposed provision. It opted first, though by the barest of margins, for a French proposal specifying 'private and personal use' and, then, by a larger majority, to the modified wording of 'private use'. Secondly, the Committee unanimously adopted an exception 'for judicial and administrative purposes' and, after considerable debate, agreed to a final residual category of exceptions which could arise 'in certain particular cases where the reproduction is not contrary to the legitimate interests of the author and does not conflict with a normal exploitation of the work'. The final formulation **13.08**

---

[11] ibid, 112. [12] ibid. [13] Documents DA/22/2, 49, n 24.

adopted by the Committee that was then included in the programme for the 1967 Conference[14] provided for a separate paragraph (article 9(2)) as follows:

> It shall be a matter for legislation in the countries of the Union to permit the reproduction of such works
>
> (a) for private use;
> (b) for judicial or administrative purposes;
> (c) in certain particular cases where the reproduction is not contrary to the legitimate interests of the author and does not conflict with a normal exploitation of the work.[15]

13.09 In the Conference, this proposal elicited a wide range of amendments from delegates. A number were aimed at restricting its scope. Thus, France (in line with the formulation in its own law)[16] proposed the substitution of the words 'for individual or family use' for the words 'for private use', so as to avoid the possibility of commercial enterprises claiming that their copying was for private purposes.[17] In the same way, a Dutch amendment proposed qualifying paragraph (b) by making this for 'strictly judicial or administrative purposes', and the following formulation for paragraph (c):

> in certain special cases where this reproduction is not prejudicial to the interests of the author or his successors in title and does not prejudice the normal exploitation of the work, on condition that the legislation of the country where protection is claimed expressly permits this method of reproduction.[18]

A German proposal required a third condition for paragraph (c), namely that reproduction should not conflict with the author's right to obtain equitable remuneration.[19] By contrast, a second group of amendments sought to expand the range of exceptions. In particular, India proposed the addition of a fourth paragraph permitting, in effect, a general compulsory licence, arguing that such a provision was necessary to ensure that monopolistic interests did not hamper the dissemination of works which had been lawfully made available to the public.[20] A similar, but more limited, proposal was made by Romania,[21] but both were rejected decisively by the Conference.[22] These differences perhaps made delegates more ready to consider a proposal advanced by the UK which sought to embrace all possible exceptions within a single generalized exception consisting simply of paragraph (c) of the programme amendment.[23] Although this, in turn, attracted some criticism,[24] it was accepted by Main Committee I

[14] *Records* 1967, vol I, 112–13. [15] ibid, 113. [16] French Law of 1957, art 41.
[17] Document S/70: *Records* 1967, vol I, 690. [18] Document S/81: ibid, 691.
[19] Document S/67: ibid, 690. [20] Document S/86: ibid, 692.
[21] Document S/75: ibid, 691.
[22] ibid, 857 (twenty-eight votes to two, with three abstentions).
[23] Document S/42: ibid, 687.
[24] ibid, 857–8 (eg from the Netherlands and French delegates).

which gave the task of drawing up a suitable draft to a special working group under the chairmanship of Italy.[25] The final form of words suggested by the Working Group, and accepted by Main Committee I[26] as article 9(2), was as follows:

> (2) It shall be a matter for legislation in the countries of the Union to permit the reproduction of such works in certain special cases, provided that such reproduction does not conflict with a normal exploitation of the work and does not unreasonably prejudice the legitimate interests of the author.

(a) Interpretation of article 9(2)

Despite the unanimity that accompanied its adoption at the Stockholm Conference, there is still considerable uncertainty and even ambiguity over its scope. As noted by the 1964 Study Group (see above), some specific exceptions to reproduction rights were, in any event, already covered in other provisions of the Convention, such as articles 10, 10*bis*, and 2*bis*(2) (see further paras 13.38ff below). Although article 9(2) makes no reference to these provisions, it seems clear that their operation is unaffected by it, and that the uses allowed under them are therefore excluded from its scope.[27] Apart from these, article 9(2) stipulates three distinct conditions that must be complied with before an exception can be justified under national law: (i) the reproduction must be for a specific and limited purpose: it is only allowed 'in certain special cases'; (ii) it should 'not conflict with a normal exploitation of the work'; and (iii) it should 'not unreasonably prejudice the legitimate interests of the author'. **13.10**

These conditions are cumulative, and each raises its own problems of interpretation. However, they now possess an importance that transcends article 9(2): as will be seen below, they have been adopted as the template for exceptions generally under the TRIPs Agreement and the WCT (see paras 13.94ff and 13.126ff below). Some assistance in their interpretation, under these later agreements as well as under Berne itself, is provided by the decision of the WTO panel which, in 2000, considered their application in the context of the TRIPs Agreement dealing with the 'homestyle' and business exemptions for public performances of musical works under the US Copyright Act 1976 (see further below). With a faint allusion to ballroom dancing, the three conditions of article 9(2), as now transposed to the WCT and the TRIPs Agreement, have become generally known as the 'three-step test'. Each of these 'steps' is therefore analysed and interpreted in turn below.

---

[25] *Records* 1967, vol I, 858 (minutes of Main Committee I).

[26] Document S/109: ibid, 696.

[27] See the comments by the Monégasque delegate at ibid, 885, and the general comments on interpretation in the report of Main Committee I: ibid, 1134.

13.11 (i) **'Certain special cases'**: These adjectives suggest that there must be limits to any exception to the reproduction right that is made under article 9(2). Thus, after consulting various dictionary definitions of 'certain' ('known and particularized, but not explicitly identified', 'determined, fixed, not variable; definitive, precise, exact'[28]), the WTO panel stated that this meant that:

> . . . an exception or limitation in national law must be clearly defined. However, there is no need to identify explicitly each and every possible situation to which the exception could apply, provided that the scope of the exception is known and particularised. This guarantees a sufficient degree of legal certainty.[29]

As to the meaning of 'special' ('having an individual or limited application or purpose', 'containing details; precise, specific') the WTO panel noted that this means that more is needed

> . . . than a clear definition in order to meet the standard of the first condition. In addition, an exception or limitation must be limited in its field of application or exceptional in its scope. In other words, an exception or limitation should be narrow in quantitative as well as in a qualitative sense. This suggests a narrow scope as well as an exceptional or distinctive objective. To put this aspect of the first condition into the context of the second condition ('no conflict with a normal exploitation'), an exception or limitation should be the opposite of a non-special, i.e. a normal case.[30]

Accordingly, these two adjectives require that a proposed exception ('case') should be both clearly defined and narrow in its scope and reach. This interpretation also seems consistent with the context and object and purpose of the Convention, ie, as a treaty to constitute a Union for 'the protection of the rights of authors in their literary and artistic works'. In any given case, this will involve a consideration of all aspects of a proposed exception, including such matters as the right(s) and works covered, the persons who may take advantage of it, and the purpose of the exception.

13.12 *'Special purpose'*: Does the composite phrase 'certain special cases', however, require that there should be some 'special purpose' or justification underlying the exceptions that are made in a national law? In the first edition of this commentary, it was argued that some such justification is required: not only should the use in question be for 'a quite specific purpose', but that there must also be 'something "special" about this purpose, "special" here meaning that it is justified by some clear reason of public policy or some other exceptional circumstance'.[31] It was then suggested that this would not include exceptional circumstances that were external to the use itself, for

[28] *New Shorter Oxford English Dictionary* (*SOED*), 364.
[29] Report of the Panel, 15 June 2000, document WT/DS/160/R ('WTO Panel'). [30] ibid.
[31] Sam Ricketson, *The Berne Convention 1886–1986* (1987), 482.

example, it would not be open to a country which had a foreign currency crisis to claim that this was a special case justifying it to take advantage of article 9(2) for the purpose of allowing the general reproduction of textbooks from abroad. This has received some support from later commentators on the WCT,[32]but is not a point that is addressed by any of the other main commentators on the Berne Convention itself.[33]

Although the WTO panel on the 'homestyle' exception used the adjectives 'exceptional' and 'distinctive' in this context (see the passage quoted at para 13.11 above), it nonetheless took some pains to indicate that it was not thereby equating the term 'certain special cases' with 'special purpose'. In this context, of course the panel was dealing with the meaning of the phrase 'certain special cases' as it appears in article 13 of the TRIPs Agreement rather than article 9(2) of Berne. The former deals with permissible exceptions and limitations to all the exclusive rights of the copyright owner and not just the reproduction right. Furthermore, the panel was dealing with a provision (article 13 of the TRIPs Agreement) which appears as part of a wider series of WTO obligations and, in this context, it was relevant for the panel to have regard to the interpretations that have been applied by the Appellate Body to other WTO rules, such as the national treatment clauses of the General Agreement on Tariffs and Trade ('GATT') and the GATS, where the latter had rejected interpretative tests based on the subjective aim or objective pursued by national legislation.[34] Accordingly, in the context of article 13 of the TRIPs Agreement, the panel took the view that the first condition should be interpreted without reference to the policy underlying it: **13.13**

> In our view, the first condition of Article 13 requires that a limitation or exception in national legislation should be clearly defined and should be narrow in its scope

[32] See eg M Ficsor, *The Law of Copyright and the Internet* (2001) ('Ficsor (2001)'), 284, takes a similar view; to similar effect, see Jörg Reinbothe and Silke von Lewinski, *The WIPO Treaties 1996* (2002) ('Reinbothe and von Lewinski (2002)'), 124–5.

[33] eg C Masouyé, *Guide to the Berne Convention for the Protection of Literary and Artistic Works* (1978) ('Masouyé (1978)'), 55–6, does not comment on the meaning of the phrase 'certain special cases'; neither do the leading German commentators, W Nordemann, K Vinck, P W Hertin, and G Meyer, *International Copyright and Neighbouring Rights Law* (1990) ('Nordemann et al (1990)'), 108–9, or the leading French commentators, H Desbois, A Françon, and A Kéréver, *Les Conventions internationales du droit d'auteur et des droits voisins* (1976) ('Desbois et al (1976)'), paras 172–3.

[34] In this regard, the panel referred to the Appellate Body Report in *Japan—Alcoholic Beverages*, adopted 1 Nov 1996, document WT/DS8, 10, 11/AB/R, 19–23 (rejection of the so-called 'aims and effects' test in the context of the national treatment clause of art III of GATT 1994) and the Appellate Body Report on *European communities—Regime for the Importation, Sale and Distribution of Bananas*, adopted on 25 Sept 1997, document WT/DS27/AB/R, paras 241, 243, 246 (rejection of the 'aims and effects' test in the context of the national treatment clause of art XVII of GATS).

> and reach. On the other hand, a limitation or exception may be compatible with the first condition even if pursues a special purpose whose underlying legitimacy in a normative sense cannot be discerned. The wording of Article 13's first condition does not imply passing a judgment on the legitimacy of the exceptions in dispute. However, public policy exceptions stated by law-makers when enacting a limitation or exception may be useful from a factual perspective for making inferences about the scope of a limitation or exception or the clarity of its definition.[35]

In taking this view, the panel acknowledged that it was adopting a 'cautious' approach that differed from that stated in the 'teaching of the most highly qualified publicists of the various nations' (referred to as a 'subsidiary source for the determination of law' under article 38(2) of the Statute of the International Court of Justice).[36] The only 'publicist' cited by the panel in this regard was the first edition of this commentary: as noted above, this is not a matter which is specifically considered by other commentators on the Berne Convention itself. But, even apart from the views of the 'publicists', a valid basis for distinguishing the 'cautious' approach taken by the panel is that already given above, namely that the panel was concerned with a broader kind of provision that is applicable to all exclusive rights of copyright owners, not just reproduction rights, and one, moreover, that appears in a trade agreement rather than a treaty purely concerned with intellectual property rights (see further paras 13.94ff below). These factors alone might justify the 'cautious' approach taken by the panel, but it should be noted that the panel's approach has received cogent support from the other co-author of this edition of the commentary.[37] In her view, the phrase 'certain special cases' should not receive a normative interpretation, noting that the purpose behind any given exception will fall to be tested by the second and third steps of the test, ie, whether it conflicts with the normal exploitation of the work and whether it is unreasonably prejudicial to the legitimate interests of the author. She also argues that there is nothing in the drafting history of article 9(2) which indicates that the adjective 'special' is to have such a connotation, noting that (i) it was to be presumed that all existing exceptions under national laws would fall within the category of 'certain special cases', and (ii) not all of these could be regarded as having a clear public-policy justification. Her conclusion is that 'special cases' can include 'unworthy as well as laudable exceptions so long as they are sufficiently narrow. The normative inquiry is deferred to the second two steps.' More colourfully, she comments that the records of the Stockholm and Paris Conferences do not 'clearly preclude pork barrel-type exceptions (if they are sufficiently discrete), and the WTO may be ill-suited to condemn local giveaways of this kind'.

---

[35] WTO panel, 34. [36] ibid, 33, n 114.

[37] J Ginsburg, 'Towards Supranational Copyright Law? The WTO Panel: Decision and the "Three-Step Test" for Copyright Exceptions' (2001) 187 *RIDA* 3.

In strict terms, the panel's finding and the comments of Professor Ginsburg are directed at article 13 of the TRIPs Agreement, not article 9(2) of Berne. Nonetheless, they carry some force with respect to article 9(2), and there seems to be little sensible rationale for maintaining the interpretation in the first edition of this commentary that the expression 'certain special cases' requires also that a given exception in national law should have an underlying justification in public policy. While the object and purposes of the Berne Convention are more confined than those of the TRIPs Agreement, and may therefore support the argument that the expression bears a different meaning in the context of article 9(2), the preparatory work for the Stockholm Revision tends to bear out the Ginsburg approach. First, it should be noted that not all of the exceptions recognized under national laws prior to the adoption of article 9(2) were characterized by a clear public-policy justification. Thus, of the list of exceptions formulated by the 1964 Study Group (see n 6 above), the exceptions for 'private use', 'ephemeral use', and 'texts of songs' do not immediately suggest any rationale for their recognition other than convenience for the user or the fact that they are possibly *de minimis* uses that will not affect the copyright owner. While the other categories of exceptions listed by the Study Group have more obvious justifications, such as the reporting of news and educational and research purposes, it is clear that the intention of the Group and the subsequent Diplomatic Conference was to find a formula that would cover existing exceptions, some of which might be 'worthy' while others might not. On this basis, a more realistic interpretation of the expression 'certain special cases' is that the exceptions in question should be finite and limited in scope. 13.14

Second, it is difficult to escape the logic of the argument that normative questions, ie justifications, for any given exception are more appropriately considered under the second and third steps of the three-step test, to be considered below. For such issues to be tested under each step is to create unnecessary complexity. On the Ginsburg approach, which is fully accepted by the other co-author of the present edition of this commentary, the first step assumes a more coherent role as providing a threshold requirement for consideration of the real normative issues under the second and third steps. Finally, there is no apparent reason why this step should be interpreted differently for article 9(2) of the Berne Convention and article 13 of the TRIPs Agreement: different interpretations would introduce considerable complexity for no good reason.

(ii) 'Conflict with the normal exploitation of the work': Of the second and third steps, there seems little doubt that the second is the more important. In the original UK proposal, the order of these was reversed, but this was deliberately changed by Main Committee I, as the following passage from its report shows: 13.15

> 85. The Committee also adopted a proposal by the Drafting Committee that the second condition should be placed before the first, as this would afford a more logical order for the interpretation of the rule. If it is considered that the reproduction does not conflict with the normal exploitation of the work, the next step would be to consider whether it does not unreasonably prejudice the legitimate interests of the author.[38]

No guidance, however, is given as to the meaning of the expression 'normal exploitation of a work', although the report provides an example of a use that would conflict with this, namely the photocopying of a 'very large number of copies' for a particular purpose.[39] The minutes of Main Committee I, however, furnish no further assistance on this matter.

13.16 Dictionary definitions, again, were relied upon by the WTO panel in its determination on article 13 of the TRIPs Agreement, and these provide a useful starting point for ascertaining the ordinary meanings of the words 'normal' and 'exploitation' in relation to article 9(2). The second of these words is perhaps the most straightforward: 'exploit' and 'exploitation' refer to 'making use of' or 'utilizing for one's own ends',[40] and, in the context of 'works', can be taken as referring to the activity by which copyright owners employ the exclusive rights given to them, including the reproduction right, to 'extract economic value from their rights to those works'.[41] A consequence of this might be that there may be certain acts of reproduction that will not be 'exploitations' of works by a third party because they are not done for any commercial end. Private copying is the most striking of such non-exploiting activities, at least where no further dissemination of the copy occurs (as in peer-to-peer copying over the Internet). Private copying is considered further below (see para 13.33), but, for present purposes, it is enough to say that 'exploitation' under article 9(2) must refer to 'exploitations' by the author, rather than by the third party for whom an exception to liability is sought.[42]

As for the qualifying adjective 'normal' before 'exploitation', this has a dictionary meaning of 'constituting or conforming to a type or standard; regular, usual, typical, conventional . . .'.[43] In the view of the WTO panel, these definitions gave rise to two possible connotations of the phrase 'normal exploitation': the first of an empirical nature, ie what is regular, usual, typical, or ordinary in a factual sense, and the second reflecting a 'somewhat more normative, if not dynamic, approach, ie conforming to a type or standard.'

[38] WTO panel, 1145. [39] ibid, 1146. [40] *SOED*, 888. [41] WTO panel, 44.

[42] Even if such copying would not be 'exploitation' for the purposes of art 9(2) and therefore does not conflict with the second step, it may implicate the third step, thus calling for a compensation scheme: see further para 13.33 below.

[43] *SOED*, 1940.

Under the empirical approach, the question to ask would be whether the exempted use would otherwise fall within the range of activities from which the copyright owner would usually expect to receive compensation. Framing the question in this way, however, involves 'an obvious circularity', as Professor Goldstein has noted: **13.17**

> At least historically, an author will normally exploit a work only in those markets where he is assured of legal rights; by definition, markets for exempted uses fall outside the range of normal exploitation. Consequently, it might be thought that to expand an exemption is to shrink the 'normal market', while to expand the definition of 'normal market' is to shrink the permitted exception.[44]

A preferable way of approaching this question might therefore be to postulate that the owner has the capacity to exercise his or her rights in full, without being inhibited one way or another by the presence of an exemption, and to ask simply whether the particular usage is something that the copyright owner would ordinarily expect or seek to exploit. This would involve looking at what presently is the case, and, while it might take account of markets that might be likely to be developed in the future,[45] would disregard potential modes of exploitation not yet developed or in contemplation. The 'normative' or dynamic approach, on the other hand, would look beyond this purely quantitative assessment and would specifically seek to take into account such matters as future technological and market developments, even though these might not presently be realistic or even imagined. In this regard, it is quite possible that uses presently not controlled by copyright owners might subsequently become so, as the result of technological change—an example might be private copying where the transaction costs involved in monitoring such uses might now be reduced because of the new technologies. On this more qualitative or dynamic approach, 'normal exploitation' will therefore require consideration of potential, as well as current and actual, uses or modes of extracting value from a work.

Differences will clearly arise, depending upon which of these approaches is followed, but the second seems more consistent with the context of the Berne Convention, and with 'its object and purpose' (article 31 of the Vienna Treaty). Accordingly, the phrase 'normal exploitation' should be interpreted as including 'in addition to those forms of exploitation that currently generate significant or tangible revenue, those forms of exploitation which, with a certain degree of likelihood and plausibility, could acquire considerable economic or practical **13.18**

[44] P Goldstein, *International Copyright: Principles, Law, and Practice* (2001), § 5.5.

[45] To quote the formulation used by the US Federal Court in *American Geophysical Union* v *Texaco* 60 F 3d 913 (2d Cir 1994), where the court rejected the defence of fair use, regarding systematic photocopying of scientific journal articles in furtherance of for-profit research, the court looks to the impact on 'traditional, reasonable or likely to be developed markets' in assessing § 107(4) factor of 'effect upon the potential market for or value of the copyrighted work'.

importance'.[46] Exceptions under national law that do not enter into economic competition (present or potential) with non-exempted uses should therefore not be contrary to the second condition of article 9(2). This would clearly include insignificant uses of the kind that traditional English and American jurists would have dismissed in any event, on the basis of *de minimis non curat lex*. Such a principle, no doubt, is readily recognizable in most legal systems.

13.19 What then is to be made of a use that does not enter into economic competition with the interests of the copyright owner but which nonetheless creates an economic benefit for the user? Should this be considered to be a use within the scope of a normal exploitation of that work? In this regard, it must be remembered that article 9(2) was intended to accommodate those exceptions already existing under national laws, some of which could have been regarded as capable of creating an economic benefit to the user.[47] This point was commented upon, albeit indirectly, in the Swedish/BIRPI programme for the Stockholm Conference:

> In this connexion, the [1964] Study Group observed that, on the one hand, it was obvious that all the forms of exploiting a work which had, or were likely to acquire, considerable economic or practical importance must in principle be reserved to the authors; restrictions that might restrict the possibilities open to authors in these respects were unacceptable. On the other hand, it should not be forgotten that domestic laws already contained a series of exceptions in favour of various public and cultural interests and that it would be in vain to suppose that countries would be ready at this stage to abolish these exceptions to any appreciable extent.

The WTO panel, however, did touch upon this point in express terms, saying that:

> . . . in our view, not every use of a work, which, in principle is covered by the scope of exclusive rights and involves commercial gain, necessarily conflicts with a normal exploitation of that work. If this were the case, hardly any exception or limitation could pass the test of the second condition and Article 13 might be left devoid of meaning, because normal exploitation would be equated with full use of exclusive rights.[48]

The panel then went on to say:

> We believe that an exception or limitation to an exclusive right in domestic legislation rises to the level of a conflict with a normal exploitation of the work (i.e., the copyright or rather the whole bundle of exclusive rights conferred by the ownership of the copyright), if uses, that in principle are covered by that right but exempted under the exception or limitation, enter into economic competition

[46] WTO panel, 48, para 6.180.
[47] *Records* 1967, vol I, 112 (Document S/1)
[48] WTO panel, 48, para 6.182.

> with the ways that right holders normally extract economic value from that right to the work (i.e., the copyright) and thereby deprive them of significant or tangible commercial gains.[49]

Non-economic normative considerations: There is another aspect of the adjective 'normal' that is not considered in the passages quoted above, namely the extent to which this term embraces normative considerations of the true type, ie considerations of what the copyright owner's market *should* cover, as well as the more empirical inquiries into what is presently, and may in the future be, the case. On the facts that arose in the WTO 'homestyle' case, there was no real need to consider this, as the 'pork barrel' exception in issue there had none of the significant justifications that often underlie copyright exceptions, such as free speech, scholarship, education, and so on.[50] In other instances, however, this will be an important question, for example, where the exception relates to research and scholarship or to uses by libraries. The question then arising is, whether these are 'markets' that the copyright owner should be able to control in a normative sense? 'Normal' and 'normative' here suggest an inquiry that looks to non-economic as well as economic considerations, and inevitably involves some kind of balancing process. **13.20**

If one has regard only to the object and purposes of the Berne Convention ('. . . a Union . . . to protect, in as effective and uniform manner as possible, the rights of authors in their literary and artistic works'), there is little, if any, support to be found for such a balancing approach. At the same time, even on such an approach it would be necessary to have regard to the situation of second and subsequent authors (those who critique, analyse, and/or build on, their predecessors' works) as these should also be within the Convention's purview. Furthermore, as noted in Chapter 5 above, under both customary international law and the Vienna Convention, treaty interpretation requires that this should be done in the 'context' of the treaty as well as its objects and purposes. This clearly involves consideration of the text of the treaty as a whole and, as noted above, the Berne Convention contains, and has contained for a long time, a series of provisions that acknowledge that limitations and exceptions to authors' rights may be made in certain specified circumstances that are justified by other non-economic 'public policy' considerations: see, for example, articles 2(4), 2*bis*(1), 10(1) and (2), 10*bis*(1) and (2) that (discussed at paras 13.38ff below). Each of these is subject to differing conditions, but is underpinned by some kind of non-author centred and non-economic normative consideration, such as freedom of information and 'participatory democracy' (articles 2(4) (official **13.21**

[49] ibid, para 6.183. [50] ibid.

texts) and article $2^{bis}(1)$ (political speeches; legal proceedings)), criticism and review (article 10(1)), educational purposes (article 10(2)), news reporting (article $10^{bis}(1)$ and (2)) and even competing industry pressure (as in the case of the mechanical reproduction licence under article 13(1)). The only difference between these provisions and article 9(2) is that the former embody, in the text of each provision, the results of the balancing process that has been achieved by the successive revision conferences that have adopted them, whereas article 9(2) is consciously framed as an omnibus or umbrella provision that is both prospectively and retrospectively applicable to all other exceptions to the reproduction right that fall outside these specific provisions. It may well be the case that some of the uses allowed under these exceptions would fail the second step of article 9(2) (the licence allowed under article 13(1) would be such an instance: see paras 13.59ff below), but their presence in the Convention reveals a long tradition of balancing competing interests, with differing 'deals' being struck in relation to each kind of use. Viewed against this background and the wider context of the treaty, it therefore seems logical to conclude that a similar balancing exercise is also implicit in the second step of article 9(2) itself, requiring consideration of non-economic as well as economic normative considerations.

This interpretation is also consistent with what is to be found in the preparatory work for the Stockholm Conference, a legitimate supplementary aid to treaty interpretation. In this regard, it will be recalled that the Conference programme contained the comment, 'that it should not be forgotten that domestic laws already contained a series of exceptions in favour of various public and cultural interests and that it would be in vain to suppose that countries would be ready at this stage to abolish these exceptions to any appreciable extent'.[51] Furthermore, the records of the Conference and the various amendments proposed by delegates indicate that they were seeking to reach some general description of the purposes for which exceptions might be made that would accommodate the existing public-interest exceptions in national laws. Finally, it must be said that if a wholly economic approach is taken to the second step of article 9(2), this leaves little, if any, work to be done by the third step which is concerned specifically with the interests of the author (see further below). Leaving aside uses that are purely *de minimis* in scope or effect, the great bulk of uses that fall within article 9 could be regarded as being within the scope of the normal exploitation of a work, at least potentially, as technology reduces transaction costs. Any free use that is permitted under article 9(2) will therefore have the potential of being in conflict with a normal economic exploitation of the work, leading to the consequence that the third step will never be reached. Bringing non-economic considerations and justifications into play in the second step,

[51] *Records* 1967, vol I, 112 (Document S/1)

however, means that there may well be uses that will not be in conflict with what *should* be within the scope of a normal exploitation of the work (in a truly normative sense), but that may still not satisfy the third step (see further the examples discussed below at paras 13.31ff).

While the foregoing has the semblance of coherence, it nonetheless leaves the application of the second step of article 9(2) somewhat open-ended and uncertain. The words 'normal exploitation' give no guidance as to the kinds of non-economic normative considerations that may be relevant here, and the extent to which they may limit uses that would otherwise be within the scope of exploitation by the copyright owner. Striking this balance is left as a matter for national legislation. Value judgements will need to be made, and these will clearly vary according to the society and culture concerned. In keeping with the first step, however, these non-economic purposes will need to be clearly and specifically articulated, and will need to be set against the stated objective of the Convention, which is the protection of the rights of authors. This indicates that such justifications will need a clear public-interest character that goes beyond the purely individual interests of copyright users.[52] In this regard, it can be said that they should be of analogous significance to those already accepted as appropriate under other provisions of the Berne Convention, such as article 10 and 10*bis*. **13.22**

(iii) 'Does not unreasonably prejudice the legitimate interests of the author': If the normal exploitation of a work, both economic and non-economic, is threatened by a proposed use, this is an end of the matter and no exception is authorized by the terms of article 9(2). If the contrary is true, then the question of unreasonable prejudice to the legitimate interests of the author arises. Again, little guidance on the meaning of this condition is to be found in the records of the Stockholm Conference, apart from the observation in the Conference programme that there was 'the considerable difficulty of finding a formula capable of safeguarding the legitimate interests of the author while having a sufficient margin of freedom to the national legislation to satisfy important social or cultural needs'.[53] The additional comment was offered that the formulation proposed in the programme 'seems likely, however, to offer a **13.23**

[52] There is a further nuance that may fall for consideration in relation to art 13 of the TRIPs Agreement (see further paras 13.97ff below). TRIPs is concerned with governmental actors, ie what member states do with respect to their wider WTO obligations, whereas Berne is concerned specifically with individual authors and copyright owners who are to be protected under national laws in compliance with its provisions. This implies that a broader focus is necessarily to be implied under the TRIPs Agreement, whereas in the case of the Berne Convention a national court may be looking at the relevant exception from the narrower perspective of the particular litigant.

[53] *Records* 1967, vol I, 113 (Document S/1, 43).

guarantee to all the opposing interests concerned'. These remarks indicate that some further balancing of interests is required by the third step of article 9(2), and this is confirmed by a closer consideration of the meanings of the key words used in its formulation.

13.24 Thus, in the present context, the 'interests' in question are those of the 'author', not those of the 'right holder' as in article 13 of the TRIPs Agreement (see further paras 13.97ff below). As the rights of authors that are protected under Berne include both economic and non-economic (moral) rights (under article 6bis), it is clear that 'interests' in article 9(2) covers those of both a pecuniary and non-pecuniary kind.[54] As for the term 'legitimate', this has a dictionary meaning of 'conformable to, sanctioned or authorized by law or principle; lawful; justifiable; proper'.[55] This could mean lawful in a positivist sense, but the WTO panel also noted that this has the connotation of legitimacy from a more normative perspective.[56] It therefore seems reasonable to conclude that, while the phrase 'legitimate interests' covers all the interests (economic and non-economic) of authors that are to be protected under the Stockholm, Paris Acts, this is not an unqualified or absolute conception: there must be some normative justification underpinning these interests. In other words, there is a 'proper' sphere of application for authors' interests, and that the latter are not to be pursued regardless of other considerations. This appears to bring us back again to the kind of balancing process that applies under the second step of article 9(2), although clearly the third step goes further than consideration of just the economic interests of the author.

13.25 However, the fundamental assumption at the Stockholm Conference appears to have been that any exception to the right of reproduction would inevitably prejudice the author's interests, and accordingly, the qualification that this prejudice should be 'unreasonable' was introduced.[57] The translation of this term into French posed some difficulties, and eventually the expression '*ne cause pas un préjudice injustifée*' was used in the French text.[58] There was also criticism of the concept of 'unreasonable prejudice' as being 'too typically British to be easily understood by judges in continental countries'.[59] Be this as it may, it is difficult to think of any other adequate way of restricting the otherwise absolute

[54] Nordemann et al (1990) at 109 make the point that the reference to the 'author' in art 9(2) should always be interpreted to read 'author and his successors in title or other holder of exclusive exploitation rights' and go on to say: 'The balancing of interest undertaken here . . . concerns not only the personal interests of the author but also the economic interests that can be represented by copyright proprietors.' In the case of art 13 of the TRIPs Agreement, however, this would not necessarily be the case as moral rights are expressly excluded from the scope of TRIPs.

[55] *SOED*, 2496. [56] ibid.

[57] *Records* 1967, vol I, 883 (comments by Professor Ulmer in Main Committee I).

[58] ibid, 884–5 (minutes), 1147 (report).

[59] ibid, 858 (remarks of the Netherlands delegate).

requirement of prejudice, and the reference to a flexible standard of reasonableness to be ultimately determined by each national law appears as good a way as any. It also seems clear from the report of Main Committee I that 'unreasonable prejudice to the legitimate interests of the author' may be avoided by the payment of remuneration under a compulsory licence (although this would not, of course, 'cure' a use that conflicted with the normal exploitation of the work—by definition, the receipt of royalties under a compulsory licence could not be regarded as part of the normal exploitation of a work[60]). Thus, in its report, Main Committee I expanded upon the following example given by Professor Ulmer[61] in the course of its discussions:

> . . . a rather large number of copies for use in industrial undertakings . . . may not unreasonably prejudice the legitimate interests of the author, provided that, according to national legislation, an equitable remuneration is paid. If a small number of copies is made, photocopying may be permitted without payment, particularly for individual or scientific use.[62]

This clearly envisages that exceptions under article 9(2) may take the form of either absolute exceptions or compulsory licences, depending essentially on the number of copies made. This provision of a 'halfway house' has been stringently criticized as being an unjustified interpolation to article 9(2), on the ground that the demarcation between the two kinds of provision will be difficult to draw in practice, and the choice should simply be between permission and prohibition.[63] Nonetheless, there was no specific opposition to Professor Ulmer's interpretation in Main Committee I, and it was adopted as part of the Committee's report—an authentic supplementary aid to interpretation. As a matter of language, it also makes sense. The facility under article 9(2) is to permit the reproduction of works in certain special cases, and there is nothing in the wording of the provision which forbids the imposition of conditions on the grant of such permission, such as an obligation to pay for it, or to acknowledge the source of the work reproduced, for that matter (in this regard, compare articles 10(3) and 10*bis*(1) which condition the exceptions for quotation and news reporting on identification of the source; see further paras 13.46 and 13.53 below). It must also be borne in mind that article 9(2) was conceived of as being capable of covering all existing exceptions to reproduction rights under national laws, apart from those already covered by other provisions of the Convention. As some national laws already had compulsory licences for particular

[60] In this regard, however, it is worth noting the temptation that the structure of the three-step test may provide to national legislators and courts alike: when in doubt, they may conclude that there is no conflict, so that they can go on to consider a compensation scheme under the third step.

[61] *Records* 1967, vol I, 883 (minutes).

[62] ibid, 1145–6.

[63] Desbois et al (1976), 207.

kinds of use,[64] it cannot be presumed that it was intended that such licences were to be precluded by the new provision. In this regard, the fact that the Indian proposal which expressly allowed for compulsory licences was rejected by Main Committee I is irrelevant: during the course of that Committee's discussions, it was made clear that compulsory licences were within the scope of article 9(2), so long as they were confined to situations corresponding to the third step.[65] In this regard, it can be assumed that any compulsory licence then existing under the national laws of Berne members would be automatically 'grandfathered' as passing the third step of article 9(2) on the basis that the history of the provision indicates that none of these members would have voted for a text under which that country's existing compulsory licence would have been invalid. It would also follow that, as at that time, the uses for which they were granted passed the first two steps of the three-step test, and, in particular, did not conflict with a normal exploitation of the work.

13.26 As for the remaining terms used in this condition, 'prejudice' connotes 'harm, damage or injury', while 'unreasonable' and 'not unreasonable' connote not being 'proportionate' or 'within the limits of reason, not greatly less or more than might be thought likely or appropriate' or 'of a fair, average or considerable amount or size'.[66] It will obviously be more difficult to show 'unreasonable prejudice' than would be the case if the test were 'prejudice' alone.[67] The words 'not unreasonably prejudice' therefore allow the making of exceptions that may cause prejudice of a significant or substantial kind to the author's legitimate interests, provided that (i) the exception otherwise satisfies the first and second conditions stipulated in article 9(2), and (ii) it is proportionate or within the limits of reason, ie if it is not unreasonable. The requirement of proportionality clearly implies that there may be conditions placed on the usage that will make any prejudice that is caused 'reasonable', for example, where these interests are protected through a requirement that the usage should only occur subject to certain conditions or within certain guidelines, that there should be attribution (where there might otherwise be unreasonable prejudice to an author's moral rights), or especially that payment should be made for the use.[68]

---

[64] See eg the FRG Law of 1965, art 54, and see further E Ulmer, 'Letter from Germany' [1965] *Copyright* 275.

[65] *Records* 1967, 884–5 (exchange between Professor Ulmer and Mr Gae, the Indian delegate, in Main Committee I).

[66] *SOED*, 2496 (meaning of 'reasonable').

[67] *Records* 1967, vol II, 883 (observation of Professor E Ulmer, chairman of Main Committee I). So also to the same effect is the WIPO *Guide*: Masouyé (1978) who states (at 56): '. . . all copying is damaging to some degree: a single photocopy may mean one copy of the journal remaining unsold and if the author had a share in the proceeds of publication he lost it'.

[68] Specific support for this last possibility is contained in the report of Main Committee I which expands upon the following example given by Professor Ulmer, the chair of that

It is therefore clear that exceptions under article 9(2) may take the form of either free uses or compulsory licences, depending essentially on the number of reproductions made.[69] Nonetheless, quantum issues may need to be approached with some care, depending on the kinds of reproductions that are being made, as the number of reproductions taken individually may look quite different when considered cumulatively. In this regard, compare the activities of individual photocopying, with individual home taping, and individual file sharing. The first might well pass all three steps, although maybe not from a cumulative point of view; the second, looked at cumulatively, might pass step two but not step three, leading inevitably to some kind of compulsory licence. The third should not pass step two, because of its open-ended character, and would not therefore arise for consideration under the third step. In this regard, national legislators should not fall into the trap of assuming that any unreasonable prejudice that might otherwise result to authors can always be assuaged through the imposition of a compulsory licence: by definition, there will always be some 'prejudices' that cannot be remedied in this way. While article 9(2) is far from providing a 'bright line' rule that can be readily applied, the individual and cumulative effect of each of the three steps, in particular the third, is to highlight the need for care, moderation, and constraint in constructing any compulsory licensing scheme under national law. **13.27**

(iv) **Unpublished or undisclosed works**: Article 9(2) contains no reference as to whether the work reproduced needs to be published or otherwise lawfully made available to the public (the latter being a broader concept). The desirability that this should be so was adverted to by one delegate in Main Committee I,[70] but no further reference to it was made in the Committee's report. A reading of the Convention as a whole, however, indicates that article 9(2) is applicable to both published and unpublished works. Thus, article 10(1), which deals with the making of lawful quotations, applies only to works that **13.28**

committee, in the course of its discussions: '. . . a rather large number of copies for use in industrial undertakings . . . may not unreasonably prejudice the legitimate interests of the author, provided that, according to national legislation, an equitable remuneration is paid. If a small number of copies is made, photocopying may be permitted without payment, particularly for individual or scientific use.' *Records* 1967, vol II, 1145–6. Professor Uulmer's comments appear at 883.

[69] To similar effect, see Nordemann et al (1990) at 109: 'In general, we consider the interests of the author always to have been unreasonably invaded when he can demonstrate a reasonable interest that this type of exploitation should remain reserved for him or that it should be permitted only upon payment of a suitable royalty.' Contrast the views of Desbois et al (1976), 207: 'A la verite, l'introduction de la licence obligatoire procede d'une interrpolation, car le formule de l'art.9, al.2 n'en fait pas etat. Le choix parait devoir etre restreint a la permission ou a l'interdiction.'

[70] *Records* 1967, 858 (Mr Strnad, Czech delegate).

have been 'lawfully disclosed to the public' (see further paras 13.41ff below), and article $10^{bis}(1)$, which deals with reproduction by the press, applies only to articles in periodicals and newspapers that have been published or broadcast (see further paras 13.53ff below). The absence of any such limitation in article 9(2) therefore must mean that this paragraph applies equally to published and unpublished works (in the strict sense of 'publication' under the Convention) as well as to works that have not been disclosed to the public in any other way. However, this does not lead to the result that the latter works may be reproduced to the same extent as published works, as the following analysis shows.

13.29 Where an unpublished work is reproduced without the author's consent, this may not always be in conflict with the normal exploitation of the work, for example, where the work has not been published within the meaning of article 3(3), but has still been lawfully disclosed to the public through such means as broadcasting or public performance. Nonetheless, where it is essentially undisclosed to the public, the author has had no opportunity to exploit it all, and any claim that the unauthorized use satisfies the second step of article 9(2) would require the most searching scrutiny. Furthermore, it is unlikely that the third step will ever be satisfied, as the prejudice to the author's legitimate interests may be far greater where the work is unpublished as this will be a direct interference with her right to divulge the work. This moral right is implicitly recognized in the Convention (see para 10.37 above), and should therefore be a factor that is highly relevant to the determination of what are her 'legitimate interests'. Accordingly, the question of whether these interests have been 'unreasonably prejudiced' is far more likely to be answered in the affirmative where the work is unpublished, although it would also be relevant to take account of the extent to which the work has already been disclosed where it has been performed, broadcast, etc, without having actually been published within the terms of article 3(3). In this indirect way, then, it can be said that the author's moral right of disclosure is protected, at least partially, under the Convention (see further para 10.37 above).

13.30 (v) **Moral rights considerations:** Does the freedom to make reproductions pursuant to article 9(2) absolve the user from observing those moral rights of the author that are protected under article $6^{bis}(1)$, namely the rights of paternity and respect? The answer to this seems quite straightforward. Article 9(2) only authorizes the making of exceptions to the author's right of reproduction. This does not in any way excuse the user from observing the author's moral rights in the particular use which he makes of the latter's work. The author therefore could object if the reproduction in question distorted or mutilated his work or failed to acknowledge her authorship. As noted above, such matters must inevitably fall for consideration under the third step in any event.

(b) Instances of uses covered by article 9(2)

(i) General formulas versus detailed lists: In adopting the three-step test in article 9(2), the Stockholm Conference took the view that it was unwise to attempt to list all possible exceptions that might be made under national legislation. Lists tend to be arbitrary and can never be comprehensive, with the risk that 'deserving' candidates, both present and future, may be omitted. In the same way, the Conference declined to give particular examples by way of illustration, preferring to adopt a generalized formula contained in the criteria of the three-step test. The advantage of this is that it leaves considerable discretion to national legislators to fashion exceptions with specific reference to their own economic, social, and cultural circumstances; the disadvantage is that there may be concern as to the outer limits of what are permitted by the generalized formula. **13.31**

Nonetheless, there are certain instances that will tend to recur in national legislation, and concerning which it may be possible to draw tentative conclusions about their compatibility or otherwise with the three-step test. Some of the more common of these are considered below.

(ii) Judicial and administrative uses: This was one of the specific exceptions referred to in the programme proposal for article 9(2), and it must therefore be assumed that it continues to fall within the scope of the present general formula. Nevertheless, if this is the case, the exception is more narrowly confined than it was under the programme proposal as there it was not stated to be subject to the twin conditions of absence of conflict with the work's normal exploitation and lack of prejudice to the author's legitimate interests.[71] These two factors still remain relevant when considering the extent to which works may be reproduced for judicial or administrative purposes. **13.32**

(iii) Private use: This, again, was a specific category which was included in the programme proposal, and it is similarly to be assumed that it continues to fall within the scope of article 9(2) although subsequent technological developments may call into question its consistency with the article 9(2) criteria. There is the prior terminological question referred to above (see para 13.16) as to whether private use constitutes 'exploitation' in the first place, and therefore is outside the scope of article 9(2) in any event, but it was suggested there that 'exploitation' for the purposes of article 9(2) is to be considered from the perspective of the author rather than user. As with judicial or administrative uses, private use therefore remains subject to the conditions stated in that **13.33**

[71] *Records* 1967, 113 (Document S/1).

paragraph. Potentially, the scope of this exception will give rise to the most controversy in national legislation, and indeed a number of delegates at the Stockholm Conference made it clear that they thought it should be interpreted as strictly as possible.[72] By its very nature, 'private use' would appear to be confined to the making of single copies, and the basis for it a kind of *de minimis* argument, coupled with an acknowledgement that authors' rights should not impinge upon what is done in the purely private sphere. Nevertheless, at the time private use was being discussed in the preparations for, and the deliberations of, the Stockholm Conference, the techniques for private copying were far more rudimentary than they are today. Essentially, private use exceptions in national laws at that time were predicated upon the basis that these copies were made by hand or with the use of a typewriter, and that the quantity of such copying could scarcely conflict with either the normal exploitation of the work or the legitimate interests of the author.[73] Typical examples of such copying were the copies made by students of their professors' lectures, or the handwritten transcription of parts of works in libraries or public archives. With the development of reprographic reproduction, audio and video recording, and digital copying the scope of what may be copied privately has now expanded beyond recognition. Facsimile and perfect digital copies of whole works may now be reproduced swiftly and cheaply, with the aid of equipment which is readily accessible to the individual. Indeed, personal computers and printers, and digital recording equipment have now becoming standard household goods in most countries.[74] Reproduction by such means will usually lie outside the scope of article 9(2): as the normal way for a copyright owner to exploit his work is by licensing others to make reproductions of it, a conflict must inevitably arise if private individuals are able to make their own copies, at least when the quality of those copies substitutes completely for a licensed copy. In such cases, the copyright owner loses the opportunity of authorizing the individual in question to

[72] *Records* 1967, 857 (Italy and Denmark).

[73] Masouyé (1978)', 56. Although the audio tape recorder was already available to the mass market, and in 1965 the German Supreme Court had decided the *Grundig* case against the manufacturer, and the German legislature had responded with the first private copying levy, see German Copyright Act 1965, art 54 and further E Ulmer and H H von Rauscher, 'Germany' in S Stewart (ed), *International Copyright and Neighbouring Rights*, 2nd edn (1989), 422–3; Peter F Burger, 'The New Photocopy Remuneration Provisions in the Federal Republic of Germany and their Application to Foreign Authors under International Copyright Law' (1988) 19 *IIC* 488; and A Dietz, 'Germany', in Melville B Nimmer and Paul Edward Geller, *International Copyright Law and Practice* (2002), 8[2](f)(i). See also A Dietz, 'Audio and Video Recordings and Reprography for Private Use in the Law and Practice of the Federal Republic of Germany' (1980) 1 *Journal of Media Law and Practice* 237; R Kreile, 'Collection and Distribution of the Statutory Remuneration of Private Copying . . . in Germany' (1992) 23 *IIC* 449.

[74] For a general survey, see G Davies, *Private Copying of Sound and Audio-Visual Recordings* (1984); Gillian Davies and Michèle E Hung, *Music and Video Private Copying: An International Survey of the Problem and the Law* (1993), 218–21.

make a copy (and pay a fee), or of authorizing a third party to make a copy which may then be bought by that individual. In this regard, it is useful to note the careful attempt that has been made in article 5(2)(b) of the EU Information Society Directive to formulate an exception with respect to private use that complies with the three steps under article 9(2). This applies:

> in respect of reproductions on any medium made *by a natural person for private use* and for *ends that are neither directly nor indirectly commercial*, on condition that the rightholders receive fair compensation which takes account of the application or non-application of technological measures referred to in Article 6 to the work or subject-matter concerned;

This limits the provision to individuals and makes it clear that the use must be confined to non-commercial purposes (first step). It then assumes that such uses do not conflict with the normal exploitation of the work (second step), presumably on the basis that it is almost impossible for the author/copyright to regulate this through private licensing arrangements and also because this is a private, as distinct from a public, use of the work, a non-economic normative factor that is to be weighed against the author's economic interests. Finally, so far as unreasonable prejudice to the right holder's interests is concerned (third step), it requires that the right holder receive fair compensation that takes account of the application, if any, of technological protection measures (see further Chapter 15 below).

By contrast, the US fair use provision has left this kind of issue to be worked out by the courts on a case-by-case basis, with results that may be highly contestable in some instances. One early instance was allowing the practice of uncompensated time shifting of free broadcast television programming by home video recording machines;[75] later US courts appear to have been more sceptical about the effects of 'space shifting' arguments and have held the fair use defence did not apply to such uses, notably because they involved retention of copies of works which their copyright owners were offering at a price.[76]

Furthermore, it should be noted that court-ordered solutions in this situation may provide more flexibility than a legislative provision such as that in the EU Directive which may need revisiting as circumstances change. As a starting point, it should be noted that the consistency of private copying with the second step of article 9(2) is not immediately apparent, in that the making of a copy by a private user that substitutes for a paid copy certainly looks like a conflict with a normal exploitation. If this nonetheless passes the second step, as under the present EU provision, this will be because of such matters as the empirical

[75] *Sony Corp of America* v *Universal City Studios, Inc*, 464 US 417 (1984).

[76] See eg *A & M Records, Inc* v *Napster, Inc* 239 F 3d 1004 (9th Cir 2001); *In re Aimster*, 334 F 3d 643 (7th Cir 2003).

consideration of practical enforceability, as well as the non-economic normative consideration of privacy. But if transaction costs can be reduced in the future, for example, through improved technological measures that facilitate private licensing, the non-economic normative consideration of privacy would then become the only operative factor in relation to the second step. Should this continue to govern the question of whether there is compliance with that step? Bear in mind that presently compensation is required under the third step, where the justification is both transaction costs (enforceability) and privacy. But if the primary justification becomes privacy alone, it would then be anomalous for member states to continue to impose compulsory licences, in circumstances where technology now makes market licences possible. In other words, the second step would no longer be satisfied, unless the member states in question were to advance the bold argument that privacy considerations in themselves are sufficient to take such usages outside the scope of normal exploitation.

13.34 (iv) **Research and scientific purposes:** Individual copying for these purposes was clearly contemplated as falling within the scope of article 9(2) by several delegates in Main Committee I. Likewise, multiple copying for use within scientific and research institutes might be allowed, perhaps subject to a compulsory licence, if the conditions laid down in the paragraph are satisfied. Prior to the Stockholm, Paris Acts, such copying was covered by article 10(2), but was deleted in that text for the reason, *inter alia*, that it was already covered by other provisions of the Convention.[77] Article 9(2) is clearly such a provision.

13.35 (v) **Industrial and commercial purposes:** The making of multiple copies of works for internal use in industrial and commercial enterprises was contemplated specifically by Professor Ulmer and Main Committee I in its report as falling within the scope of article 9(2) if an equitable remuneration was paid under a compulsory licence.[78] However, much will clearly depend upon the quantities which are copied in this way, as the question of whether there is a conflict with the normal exploitation of the work in question will always have to be first answered. In many instances, there will be no conflict where only small parts of works are copied for the use of employees, and there will be no unreasonable prejudice to the author if the use is remunerated.

13.36 (vi) **Copying for teaching purposes:** This is already dealt with specifically in article 10(2) (see paras 13.45ff below), so it seems reasonable to assume that copying for this purpose would not fall within the scope of article 9(2). Copying of materials for use by students in the course of instruction, however, might well

[77] *Records* 1967, 885 (De Sanctis, chairman of Working Group on Excerpts from Protected Works).

[78] ibid, 883 (Professor Ulmer); 1146 (report).

be justified within article 9(2), where this is for the purposes of research and private study, is subject to appropriate limitations, and is subject to compensation.[79]

(vii) Other permissible purposes: The decision of the Stockholm Conference to delete any list of permissible purposes leaves a considerable area of discretion to national legislation. While this means that there will be divergences between national laws on these matters, it has the considerable advantage that each country is able to take into account its own particular needs. In each case, of course, the criteria specified in article 9(2) will have to be satisfied, but this seems a preferable approach to an exhaustive list of purposes that, over time, would prove to be inadequate. Examples of exceptions that might be justified under article 9(2), and which are to be found in national laws, include the following: the making of special copies of works, such as Braille versions, or sound recordings, of works for handicapped readers,[80] copying for preservation purposes in libraries and archives,[81] and the inclusion of artistic works in exhibition catalogues.[82] **13.37**

(2) Specific exceptions to reproduction and other rights

(a) Quotation rights

A further basic exception to exclusive rights, including that of reproduction, relates to the making of quotations from works. Quotation is an integral part of many kinds of intellectual activity, ranging from the writing of historical treatises and critical commentaries to the composition of polemical tracts. Accordingly, provision for it is made in most national laws,[83] as well as under the Convention where it is governed by article 10(1). Unlike article 9(2), this is a mandatory requirement of the Convention to which each Union member must give effect in relation to works claiming protection under the Convention. It provides as follows: **13.38**

> (1) It shall be permissible to make quotations from a work which has already been lawfully made available to the public, provided that their making is compatible with fair practice, and their extent does not exceed that justified by the purpose, including quotations from newspaper articles and periodicals in the form of press summaries.

---

[79] See eg the carefully constructed statutory licence schemes under Part VB of the Australian Copyright Act 1968.

[80] See eg the Finnish Law of 8 July 1961, art 18; Australian Copyright Act 1968, Part VB; US Copyright Act 17 USC § 121 (copies 'reproduced or distributed in specialized formats exclusively for use by blind or other persons with disabilities').

[81] UK Copyright, Designs and Patents Act 1988, ss 37ff; Australian Copyright Act 1968, ss 48–52; US Copyright Act 17 USC § 108.

[82] German Law of 1965, art 58; France, Code de la propriété intellectuelle, art L 122–5(3)(d).

[83] See eg the French Law of 1957, art 41; German Law of 1965, art 51; UK Copyright Act 1956, s 9; Beninese Law of 15 Mar 1984, art 13.

13.39 (i) **Origins of article 10(1):** This provision has only been in the Convention since the Brussels Act, but it was agreed by the delegates at the 1885 Conference that the right to make quotations might be dealt with in national legislation as part of the general discretion accorded to Union members under article 8 of the Berne Act to regulate the taking of excerpts of works for educational and scientific publications, and for inclusion in chrestomathies.[84] However, no attempt to incorporate a specific provision permitting the making of quotations was made until the Rome Revision Conference, when a proposal to allow the making of 'analyses or short textual quotations of published literary works for the purposes of criticism, polemical discussion or teaching' was contained in the programme.[85] At this time, it proved impossible to reach agreement on the scope of the proposed exception. Several delegations thought that the range of allowable purposes should be expanded,[86] others proposed that musical and artistic works should be included,[87] while others again were unhappy at the quantitative restrictions proposed, arguing that in some instances quotation of larger sections of a work, or even the whole of it, were required in the interests of fairness.[88] Finally, there were fears on the part of some delegations, in particular the French, that, if too wide a restriction was adopted as part of the Convention, this would be to the detriment of authors.[89] Specific concern was expressed here about artistic works. In the light of these widely diverging views, it was decided not to proceed with the programme amendment.[90] As the Convention did not at this time contain any express obligation to protect reproduction rights (and was not to do so until the time of the Stockholm Act), Union members were therefore entirely free to regulate the conditions under which quotations might be made.

13.40 The Belgian Government and International Office did not revive the proposal for a Conventional rule on quotations in their programme for the Brussels Conference.[91] However, a limited proposition was made by France under which it was to be 'permissible in all countries of the Union to make short quotations from newspaper articles and periodicals, as well as to include them in press summaries'.[92] This was accepted by the delegates,[93] and ultimately incorporated in the Brussels Act as article 10(1), although a number of other detailed French

[84] *Actes* 1885, 47. 'Chrestomathy' is not a term commonly used today, but has a dictionary meaning of a 'collection of choice passages' (*Concise Oxford Dictionary*, 4th edn (1951)). In the present context, this might be rendered as 'educational compilations'.

[85] *Actes* 1928, 74.

[86] ibid, 250–1 (eg Hungary and Switzerland).

[87] ibid (Switzerland, Japan, and Norway).

[88] ibid (Switzerland and Japan).

[89] ibid, 251.

[90] ibid.

[91] The reasons for this seemed to be: (i) that they thought that the earlier Rome proposal was too narrow; and (ii) that a wider formulation would involve dangers for authors: *Documents 1948* (1951), 244.

[92] ibid, 246.

[93] ibid, 248–2413.

proposals relating to further kinds of permitted use were rejected.[94] The new provision was considerably more restricted than the present article 10(1), in that it referred only to quotations from works appearing in newspapers and periodicals.[95] The need for quotations to be 'short' was also a severe limitation, as in many instances an extensive quotation might be necessary for the particular purpose, for example, to substantiate a criticism or to support a line of argument. Finally, the reference to press summaries, although it reflected French legal practice,[96] was not entirely clear (see further para 13.41 below). On the other hand, it will be noted that, unlike the programme proposal of 1928, the new provision was not limited to quotations from literary works: other works, such as artistic works, were included, so long as they were contained in a newspaper or periodical.

(ii) **The present article 10(1) and its interpretation**: The present wording of this provision was proposed in the programme for the Stockholm Conference. Most important were the deletion of the adjective 'short' and the restriction that the work quoted must be contained in a newspaper or periodical. The three conditions to be satisfied before a quotation must be allowable under this provision are as follows. **13.41**

First, the work in question must have been 'lawfully made available to the public'. This is the same as the requirement in relation to anonymous and pseudonymous works under article 7(3) in the matter of duration.[97] On the other hand, it is wider than the concept of a 'published work' under article 3(3) where such acts as broadcasting and public performance are excluded from the scope of 'publication' and it is required that the work be published 'with the consent of the author'. The requirement of 'lawful availability' under article 10(1) is significantly different in that it includes the making available of works by any means, not simply through the making available of copies of the work. Thus, if a dramatic or musical work is performed in public or broadcast, article 10(1) should permit the making of quotations from it by a critic or reviewer who takes down passages verbatim for use in his review. If the opposite had been intended, article 10(1) would have begun as follows: 'It shall be permissible to make quotations from a work copies of which have already been lawfully made available to the public, . . .'. It should also be noted that 'lawful availability' under article 10(1) covers the situation where this has occurred

[94] ibid.

[95] This did, however, provide a nexus with art 9(1) and (2) of the Brussels Act: see further para 13.33 above.

[96] *Documents 1948* (1951), 247.

[97] But compare art 7(2) which deals with cinematographic works 'made available with consent of author'.

under a compulsory licence, although in the case of sound recordings the compulsory licence allowed for under article 13(1) only comes into operation when the author has authorized a first recording, and presumably the making available, of his musical work through the distribution of the recording (many recorded musical works may, however, already have been made available through authorized public performances or broadcasts).[98] Finally, it will be seen that article 10(1) contains no limitation on the kinds of work that may be quoted.

Second, the making of the quotation must be 'compatible with fair practice'. In the programme, this was stated to imply that 'the use in question can only be accepted after an objective appreciation'.[99] Nothing further was said about this requirement in the minutes or report of Main Committee I, as the discussions in this body were principally concerned with the length of the quotations to be allowed. Length is certainly a matter which is relevant to the question of 'fair practice', as is the purpose of the quotation (see further below). 'Fair practice' is a concept that is more familiar to Anglo-American lawyers than their continental European counterparts,[100] and this seems essentially a question for national tribunals to determine in each particular instance. However, the criteria referred to in article 9(2) would appear to be equally applicable here in determining whether a particular quotation is 'fair': does it conflict with a normal exploitation of the work and unreasonably prejudice the legitimate interests of the author?[101] There is no mention in article 10(1) of the possibility of uses taking place pursuant to a compulsory licence, but in principle where a use by way of quotation is remunerated and 'does not exceed that justified by the purpose' (see below), this should more readily satisfy the requirement of compatibility with fair practice than would a free use.

The third condition is that the extent of the quotation must 'not exceed that justified by the purpose'. As noted above, Main Committee I endorsed the programme proposal to delete any list of specified purposes on the ground that such a list could not hope to be exhaustive.[102] Nevertheless, it is clear from the preparatory work for the Conference and the discussions in Main Committee I that quotations for 'scientific, critical, informatory or educational purposes' are within the scope of article 10(1).[103] Other examples are quotations that are made in historical and other scholarly writing by way of illustration or evidence for a particular view or argument. Again, in the 1965 report of the Committee

---

[98] Note that Desbois et al (1976) take the view that a similar limitation applies in respect of compulsory licences under art 13(2): *Documents 1948* (1951), 188. This view is considered at para 13.45 below.

[99] *Records* 1967, 117.

[100] Nordemann et al (1990), 83.

[101] See also ibid, 83–4.

[102] *Records* 1967, 860–1.

[103] ibid, 116–17 (Document S/1), 860–1 (minutes).

of Experts reference was made to quotations for judicial, political, and entertainment purposes.[104] Finally, another instance that was given in both the programme[105] and the discussions in Main Committee I was quotation for 'artistic effect'.[106] This did not only mean the reproduction of 'artistic works' or parts of such works for the purposes of illustrating a text or to provide the basis for discussion, as in the case of a book on artistic styles,[107] but also the quotation of works in general for 'artistic effect' as in some modern works of fiction or poetry.[108] In one respect, however, it will be noted that article 10(1) makes reference to a specific kind of quotation, namely 'quotations from newspaper articles and periodicals in the form of press summaries'. This preserves some of the wording of article 10(1) of the Brussels Act, but not without a change in its meaning, at least so far as the English text is concerned. The Brussels provision referred generally to the making of short quotations, and then provided that this extended to the right to include such quotations in press summaries. The present English wording, however, does not have this meaning and makes little sense: while a summary of a newspaper or periodical article may include a quotation from that article (as envisaged by the Brussels text), the making of the summary is not the same thing as the making of a quotation. It is difficult therefore to know what the present article 10(1) means when it refers to a quotation in the form of a summary.[109] When regard is had to the French text, however, these difficulties disappear. The French expression '*revue de presse*' does not readily translate into 'press summaries' in English. A '*revue de presse*' is not really a summary of an article appearing in a newspaper; rather, it is a collection of quotations from a range of newspapers and periodicals, all concerning a single topic, with the purpose of illustrating how different publications report on, or express opinions about, the same issue. In consequence, the genre of '*revue de presse*' necessarily includes quotations, but there is no ready English language equivalent to this. This is one of the few instances in the Berne Convention where linguistic differences arise as between the French and English texts, and where the interpretation rule contained in article 272(1)(c) needs to be applied (see further paras 5.12ff above).

(iii) Other points relating to the interpretation of article 10(1): Several other points may be made here. **13.42**

[104] ibid, 117. [105] ibid. [106] ibid, 861 (comments by Swedish delegate, Mr Hesser).
[107] ibid. See also Nordemann et al (1990), 83. [108] *Records* 1967, 861 (Hesser).
[109] See here the explanation in the report of Main Committee I, which hardly takes matters much further: 'It was also pointed out that the last phrase, referring to press summaries, gave rise to some ambiguities. It was felt, however, that it would be difficult to get rid of that ambiguity which the courts would be able to decide upon, but that it was not absolutely essential to do so.' *Records* 1967, 1147.

The meaning of 'quotation': Although article 10(1) does not define 'quotation', this usually means the taking of some part of a greater whole—a group of words from a text or a speech, a musical passage or visual image taken from a piece of music or a work of art—where the taking is done by someone other than the originator of the work.[110] There is nothing in the wording of article 10(1) to indicate that this exception is only concerned with reproduction rights: quotations may be made just as easily in the course of a lecture, performance, or broadcast, as in a material form such as a book, article, or visual work of art. Indeed, the '*revue de presse*' category further supports this conclusion, because '*revues de presse*' have been a staple of broadcast news programming for a long time in some Berne countries, such as France and Australia (where broadcast segments of 'what the newspapers say' are a regular feature). Article 10(1) therefore assures the right to make quotations in these instances.

Length of quotation: No limitation is placed on the amount that may be quoted under article 10(1), although as suggested above, 'quotation' may suggest that the thing quoted will always be a part of a greater whole rather than the whole itself. Several delegations at the Stockholm Conference were gravely concerned about the question of length and therefore favoured the retention of the qualifying adjective 'short' before the word 'quotations'.[111] In this sphere, however, quantitative restrictions are notoriously difficult to apply, and Main Committee I preferred to leave this as a matter to be determined in each case, subject to the general criteria of purpose and fair practice.[112] Thus, in some instances it may be both consistent with the purpose for which the quotation is made and compatible with fair practice to make lengthy quotations from a work, in order to ensure that it is presented correctly, as in the case of a critical review or work of scholarship. In other circumstances, dictionary definition notwithstanding, quotation of the whole work may be justifiable, as in the example given by one commentary of a work on the history of twentieth-century art where representative pictures of particular schools of art would be needed by way of illustration.[113] Another might be cartoons or short poems where these are quoted as part of a wider work of commentary or review.

Mandatory character of article 10(1): Finally, it should be noted that article 10(1) is the one Berne exception that comes closest to embodying a 'user

[110] See here the first meaning given in the definition in the *Concise Oxford Dictionary*, 10th edn (2001), 1176.

[111] ibid, 860–1 (Switzerland, France, Hungary, Italy; cf the approach of the FRG and UK). In particular, note the Swiss proposal for the reintroduction of the adjective 'short' and the substitution of the words 'justified by the purpose' by the words 'that they serve as explanation, reference or illustration in the context in which they occur': Document S/68 at *Records* 1967, 690. See also Document S/45 (France) at ibid, 688.

[112] ibid, 1147 (report).

[113] Nordemann et al (1990), 83.

right' to make quotations ('it shall be permissible to make quotations . . .'), in contrast to the other exceptions considered in this chapter which are couched more in the language of privileges or allowable concessions to users, leaving these as matters to be determined by national legislation. Article 10(1) exceptions are matters that *must* rather than *may* appear in national laws.

(b) Utilization for teaching purposes

The ability to allow the reproduction of works for teaching purposes has always been reserved to national legislation under the Convention. The present provision is article 10(2), which provides as follows: **13.43**

> (2) It shall be a matter for legislation in the countries of the Union, and for special agreements existing or to be concluded between them, to permit the utilization, to the extent justified by the purpose, of literary or artistic works by way of illustration in publications, broadcasts or sound or visual recordings for teaching, provided that such utilization is compatible with fair practice.

(i) **Origins of article 10(2):** This provision may be traced back to the Berne Act, where it appeared in a somewhat different form as article 8: **13.44**

> As regards the liberty of extracting portions from literary or artistic works for use in publications destined for educational or scientific purposes, or for chrestomathies, the effect of the legislation of the countries of the Union, and of special arrangements existing or to be concluded between them, is not affected by the present Convention.

This, in turn, was a modification of article 8 of the 1884 draft which had been based on a German amendment. The latter had been more generous to educators in its terms, providing for the reciprocal protection in Union countries of the publication of 'extracts, fragments and entire pieces of a literary or artistic work . . . provided that this publication was specially . . . adapted for teaching or had a scientific character'.[114] It also had a separate provision applying to the inclusion of pieces in chrestomathies.[115] However, this had given rise to lengthy debates at the 1885 Conference, where it proved impossible to retain agreement on the form of a uniform international regulation of these kinds of 'borrowings'.[116] The consequence was that the 1885 draft, which ultimately became the Berne Act, reserved these matters to national legislation and bilateral agreements.[117] It was also agreed that this reservation applied to the making of quotations (see para 13.39 above),[118] and that the term 'teaching' ('*l'enseignement*') comprised elementary as well as advanced teaching, and further that

[114] *Actes* 1884, 50–1. [115] ibid. [116] *Actes* 1885, 46–7. [117] ibid, 47.
[118] ibid (French declaration, with which the other delegates associated themselves).

works intended for self-instruction were covered by the expression 'having a scientific character'.[119] Article 8 of the Berne Act remained essentially unchanged until the Stockholm Revision, apart from its renumbering as article 10 in the Berlin Act. No substantive amendments were proposed at either the Paris or Berlin Revision Conferences, but, at the Rome Conference, France proposed its replacement by a uniform international rule. This included quantitative restrictions on the amount that might be copied for chrestomathies, anthologies, and educational publications (no more than three pages per work and no more than half in the case of a musical work).[120] In this regard, it was similar to some of the more detailed regulations that were being adopted in national laws,[121] but it met with opposition from a number of delegations[122] and was ultimately withdrawn.[123] The result was that the Rome Act retained article 10 in its original form, but the Rome Conference adopted a resolution calling on each member state to define clearly in its legislation the limits for such borrowings.[124]

No proposal to amend article 10 was made in the programme for the Brussels Revision Conference,[125] but again an amendment was proposed by the French delegation.[126] This was less ambitious than its proposal of 1928, and modified the existing provision so as to make it applicable to the

> . . . inclusion of short extracts of literary, scientific or musical works in works and publications destined for educational purposes or having a scientific or documentary character, as well as in works of criticism or discussion.

A separate provision dealing with the use of 'short extracts' in chrestomathies and anthologies was also proposed.[127] Once again, these proposals encountered opposition, in particular the limitation to 'short extracts'.[128] As a result, article 10 was retained in substance (as article 10(2)), but with the added qualification that national legislation should only regulate the use of extracts 'in so far as this inclusion is justified by its purpose'.[129] A further comment about the scope of this exception is to be found in the report of Marcel Plaisant where he contrasted it with the scope of the newly recognized right of quotation in article 10(1) as follows:

[119] *Actes* 1885, 47. (French declaration, with which the other delegates associated themselves).

[120] *Actes* 1928, 100.

[121] eg the detailed regime in the Netherlands Law of 1912, s 6 of ch 1. See further 'Emprunts licities, étude générale de régime de l'Union et des législations intérieures' [1926] *DA* 37, 52, 67, 77, 87.

[122] *Actes* 1928, 251–2 (Japan, Switzerland, Belgium, Romania, and Norway).

[123] ibid, 252.

[124] '*Voeu* II': ibid, 349.

[125] *Documents 1948* (1951), 244–5.

[126] ibid, 246–8 (note that there were two successive French amendments submitted. The first of these did not use the adjective 'short').

[127] ibid, 248.

[128] ibid, 248–9 (Belgium and the UK).

[129] ibid, 249.

> The permission accorded by the second paragraph is larger than the tolerance allowed by the first: it is justified by the purpose of the taking, which is for an educational or scholastic or scientific work or a chrestomathy.[130]

(ii) The present article 10(2) and its interpretation: No changes to this were proposed in the programme for the Stockholm Revision Conference, and there were no other proposals for the adoption of a uniform international rule. However, there were conflicting propositions from the Netherlands delegation for the complete deletion of the provision,[131] and from Bulgaria, Czechoslovakia, Poland, and Romania for its extension to radio and television broadcasts and phonograms.[132] With some modifications made by a working group,[133] this second proposal was adopted, and became article 10(2) of the Stockholm Act. The following nine points about its interpretation should be noted. **13.45**

First, the use of works for teaching purposes still remains a matter for national legislation, or for bilateral agreements between Union members (see also article 20). All that article 10(2) does, therefore, is to set the limits within which such regulation may be carried out.

Second, the word 'excerpts', which was used in the Brussels Act, has been replaced by the word 'utilization'. In the programme for the Stockholm Conference, the word 'borrowings' was proposed as an attempt to bring the English translation closer to the original French word '*emprunts*', but it received considerable criticism from the British delegate in Main Committee I.[134] This was on the basis that it might be taken to mean not only that parts ('excerpts'), but the whole, of a work might be taken. To counter this possibility, the French delegate suggested that a more appropriate wording would be 'the lawful borrowing of extracts'.[135] However, the Working Group proposed a different wording: 'the utilization, to the extent justified by the purpose, . . . by way of illustration . . . for teaching, provided that such utilization is compatible with fair practice'. These references to purpose and fair practice are similar to those in article 10(1), and make the provision more open-ended, implying no necessary quantitative limitations. The words 'by way of illustration' impose some limitation, but would not exclude the use of the whole of a work in appropriate circumstances. For example, in the case of an artistic work or short literary work it might be argued that it is necessary to reproduce the whole work if it is to be properly utilized for teaching purposes. Unfortunately, no further guidance on these matters is to be found in the report of Main Committee I, although this

[130] ibid, 100. [131] Document S/108: *Records* 1967, 696.
[132] Document S/83: ibid, 692.
[133] Document S/185: ibid, 708 and 885–7 (minutes of Main Committee I).
[134] ibid, 862 (Mr Wallace). [135] ibid (Mr Touzery).

was urged by at least one delegate.[136] However, it has been pungently remarked in one leading commentary on the Convention that:

> . . . the reading or televising of an entire work is not necessary to appreciate the genius which has inspired it. The purpose of teaching may be satisfied by efficaciously and wisely chosen extracts.[137]

On the other hand, it is clear that at least one delegate, W Wallace, the British delegate, did not take this view, and that he also thought that this was true of the other delegates. In this regard, it will be recalled that Wallace had originally raised the problem of the meaning of the word 'borrowings'. He is reported to have said to Main Committee I:

> . . . the working party which had revised the English version of the Berne Convention as prepared at Brussels had substituted the word 'borrowings' for 'excerpts' as a translation of the French '*emprunts*' on the ground that the intention behind the paragraph was to provide for the utilization not only of parts of works but also of whole works. If, as he thought, the Main Committee generally took the same view, the Program text of Article 10(2) became extremely ambiguous. it could be read as permitting the grant of compulsory licences to publish for the purposes specified. He did not think that it was to be interpreted in that way, however, and he therefore strongly supported the wording proposed in document S/185 [the Working Group proposal] because the two safeguards it contained removed the ambiguity and succeeded in making the paragraph reflect what he believed was the consensus.[138]

In the light of these comments, it is therefore arguable that the use of an entire work might be allowable within article 10(2), at least in some circumstances.[139]

The third point is that the utilization must be 'by way of illustration' for the purpose of 'teaching'. The scope of the latter expression received considerable attention from the delegates at the Stockholm Conference, and the following exegesis of their views was provided in the Committee's report:

> The wish was expressed that it should be made clear in this Report that the word 'teaching' was to include teaching at all levels—in educational institutions and universities, municipal and State schools, and private schools. Education outside these institutions, for instance general teaching available to the general public but not include in the above categories, should be excluded.[140]

This is a restrictive interpretation,[141] as it clearly excludes the utilization of

[136] Document S/185: ibid, 886 (Mr Godenhielm, Finland).

[137] Desbois et al (1976), 202.

[138] *Records* 1967, 886.

[139] This seems consistent with the suggestion in the preceding text that the reproduction of some works, such as poems, short stories, and pictures might be necessary for the purposes of illustration by teachers.

[140] *Records* 1967, 1148.

[141] Note, that in Main Committee I some delegates thought that this was too limiting: ibid, 886 (Mr Reimer, FRG).

works in adult education courses which are very popular in many countries, although it would seem to be otherwise if such courses were actually offered by the formal educational institutions themselves. In developing countries, it would also exclude adult literacy campaigns, although the latter use may be covered by the provisions of the Appendix to the Paris Act. A final question is whether the word 'teaching' is confined to actual classroom instruction, or whether it also extends to correspondence or (now) Web-based courses where students receive no face-to-face instruction from a teacher. The latter are of importance in many countries, and it is submitted that there is no reason to exclude them from the scope of 'teaching' for the purposes of article 10(2), although this conclusion may make the difference between instruction offered by educational institutions and adult education courses unaffiliated with such institutions seem even more dubious.

Fourth, the requirement that the utilization be 'compatible with fair practice' is the same as that imposed for lawful quotations under article 10(1). This involves an objective appreciation of the situation, and, as suggested above, would require consideration of the criteria referred to in article 9(2).

Fifth, the range of utilizations permitted by article 10(2) is now much wider than under the Brussels Act: not only are publications included, but also broadcasts and sound or visual recordings. This enables educationalists to take full advantage of the new means of dissemination provided by modern technology. In this regard, it should be noted that, even in 1967, 'sound or visual recordings' included tapes and videograms as well as phonograph records and cinematographic films, and there is no reason today to argue that it should not extend to digital fixations of works. However, a particular problem arises with respect to broadcasting, that does not occur in the case of publications and recordings. It is easier to control the destination of the latter so as to ensure that they are used only for teaching purposes. An educational broadcast, however, may be made to a far wider section of the public than those for whom the instruction is intended. This possibility concerned the French delegation at the Stockholm Conference who sought therefore to limit the scope of the exception to educational broadcasts carried out in teaching establishments or in schools.[142] By a vote of nineteen to eight (with six abstentions), Main Committee I decided against the imposition of any restrictions on broadcasting.[143] Accordingly, the inclusion of works in a broadcast for schools and other educational institutions will be permitted by article 10(2), even where the broadcast is receivable by a much larger section of the general population. Furthermore, the exception does not only apply to the making of the broadcast itself, but to the public

[142] ibid, 886. [143] ibid, 887.

performance of that broadcast, for example, in the schoolroom or lecture theatre.[144] More questionable, however, would be whether article 10(2) should be extended to transmissions other than broadcasting, for example, on-demand digital transmissions. Under article 11*bis*(1), broadcasting is treated as a distinct kind of transmission, even if its definition and scope are left to national law. Accordingly, there is no basis for interpreting the reference to 'broadcasting' in article 10(2) as extending to on-demand transmissions.

The sixth point to note is that forms of utilization not referred to in article 10(2) include the distribution of a work either as part of an original programme or as part of a broadcast over a cable system, or a digital on-demand transmission. This is included in other provisions dealing with exceptions to authors' rights (article 10*bis*(1) and (2), as to which see para 13.53 below), so its omission from article 10(2) must be regarded as deliberate. (As to whether this gap is now met by the provisions of the WCT, see further paras 13.125ff below.)

Seventh, article 10(2) no longer contains an exception for works 'having a scientific character' or for inclusion of works in chrestomathies or anthologies. The first was deleted on the recommendation of the Working Group which took the view that it was unnecessary 'in view of the expansion of the field of science and the number of exceptions to the right of reproduction which were already included in the Convention'.[145] This must be correct: the legitimate interests of scientific research are now adequately served by the broader right of quotation allowed under article 10(1) and by the general exception to reproduction rights allowed under article 9(2). In addition, the use of scientific works will continue to be allowed under article 10(2) where this is for the purposes of teaching. As for chrestomathies and anthologies, while it is always possible that some may fall within the scope of article 10(2), it is more likely that they will not, as it will be a distortion of language to describe an anthology of poetry (with the complete texts of the poems) or a 'course pack' consisting of chapters taken from various books about the subject to be covered in the course, as being used 'by way of illustration . . . for teaching'. Such usages are well-developed forms of exploitation in many countries, subject to voluntary licensing arrangements or even compulsory licensing schemes that meet the requirements of article 9(2).[146]

The eighth point is that article 10(2) does not lay down any restriction on the number of copies that may be made in the case of publications and sound or

---

[144] See Masouyé (1978), 60, and art 7(1)(c), Tunis Model Law 1976, and para 47 of the commentary thereon.

[145] *Records* 1967, 885 (comments of Mr de Sanctis, chairman of the Working Group, in introducing the proposals to Main Committee I).

[146] As in Australia, eg under Part VB of the Copyright Act 1968.

visual recordings that are made for teaching purposes. Just as no limitation is imposed in respect of the public which is reached by a broadcast intended for teaching purposes, so there can be no limitation on the number of copies that can be made for the same purpose. The only further qualification applied here is that the making of multiple copies must be compatible with 'fair practice'. Obviously, if this competes with the author's normal exploitation of his work and unreasonably prejudices her legitimate interests, article 10(2) should not apply. In this regard, the amount copied will also be a highly relevant factor, particularly where large numbers of copies are made for individual classroom use by students.

Finally, article 10(2) applies to all works protected by the Convention. The expression 'literary or artistic works' is used, and although different formulations are used in other provisions which deal with exceptions to the rights protected under the Convention, there is no reason to interpret this expression in any other way than that stipulated under article 2(1).

(c) Protection of the right of paternity in respect of lawful quotations and utilizations for teaching purposes

Since the Brussels Act, there has been express protection of the author's right of authorship (or paternity) in respect of both the exceptions allowed under article 10. Thus, paragraph (3) of that article provides that: **13.46**

> (3) Where use is made of works in accordance with the opening paragraphs of this Article, mention shall be made of the source, and of the name of the author if it appears thereon.

This is a mandatory requirement. While it may seem superfluous in the light of article 6*bis*, it was thought appropriate that it should be added to article 10 in order to remove any doubt that the right of paternity was to be respected in the case of quotations and utilizations made under that provision.[147] This may raise a problem as regards the right of respect or integrity: is the application of this requirement under article 6*bis* thereby excluded from the provisions of article 10? A statement in the report of Main Committee I notes that delegates were generally agreed that article 6*bis* applied in respect of exceptions authorized by the Convention, including article 10.[148] However, it is interesting to note that contrary views had been expressed at the Rome Conference.[149] Here, an amendment by the French delegation proposed that 'any borrowing recognized as lawful [under article 10] should conform entirely to the original text . . .'.[150] There was opposition to this from a number of delegations which argued that

[147] *Documents 1948* (1951), 245 (comments in the programme). See also preliminary proposals for the postponed Conference of 1935: [1933] *DA* 99.

[148] *Records* 1967, 1165. [149] *Actes* 1928, 252ff. [150] ibid, 100, 252ff.

there was frequently a need to make alterations when making such borrowings,[151] and a compromise German amendment proposed that these 'should conform to the original work in so far as the purpose of the borrowing did not require a modification'.[152] No agreement, however, could be reached on these amendments, and the general commission therefore decided to retain article 10 in its Berlin Act form.[153] No further argument about the application of article 6bis was made, although its inclusion in the Rome Act had already been agreed. Accordingly, the statement in the report of Main Committee I at Stockholm removes any doubt that might otherwise have arisen as to the need for integrity rights under article 6bis to be respected in the making of exceptions under article 10.[154] As a matter of principle, this is desirable as well: while modifications within reason may be required when works are utilized for teaching purposes, this should not give *carte blanche* to educators to make deleterious, reputation-damaging alterations.

It should also be noted that article 10(3) may fill a gap which is left open by article 6bis. Under the Brussels Act, this provision did not require the protection of the right of paternity after the death of the author, and it is still possible under article 6bis(2) of the Stockholm, Paris Acts for a Union member to deny such protection (see paras 10.33ff above). Where this happens, article 10(3) makes it clear that such a country must still accord this protection in the case of quotations and utilizations falling under article 10.

(d) Exceptions made for the benefit of the press

13.47 From its inception, the Convention has contained exceptions in favour of the press for reasons that may be broadly described as the 'promotion of the free flow of information'. The exclusion of protection under article 2(8) for 'news of the day' and 'miscellaneous facts having the character of mere items of press information' have already been dealt with (see paras 8.104–8.106 above). The other provisions concerned with press usage fall into two broad categories: the use of articles in newspapers and periodicals (article 10bis(1)) and the use of works for the purposes of reporting and informing the public (articles 2bis(2) and 10bis(2)).

13.48 **(i) The use of articles in newspapers and periodicals:** The uses that might be made of articles in newspapers and periodicals were the subject of extensive discussion at both the initial Berne Conferences and the early conferences of revision. Thus, article 7 of the Berne Act provided that such articles published in

[151] *Actes* 1928, 252–3 (Switzerland, Japan, Belgium, Germany, Czechoslovakia, and Egypt).
[152] ibid, 252. [153] ibid, 253.
[154] In this regard, it should be noted that a contrary opinion based on an *expressio unius* argument was expressed in the first edition of this commentary (n 31 above) at para 9.28.

any country of the Union could be reproduced or translated in the other countries of the Union unless this had been expressly forbidden by the authors or publishers of those articles. It provided further that no prohibition was allowable in the case of articles of 'political discussion . . . news of the day or miscellaneous information'. At the Paris Revision Conference, a more complicated, three-tiered provision was adopted.[155] At the first level, serial stories, including 'tales', published in newspapers or periodicals of one of the countries of the Union were protected against reproduction, in the original or in translation, in other countries of the Union. This protection was accorded *de jure conventionis* without qualification. At the second level, protection was extended to other articles in newspapers or periodicals where the authors or editors had expressly prohibited their reproduction in advance: where no prohibition had been made, these articles might be freely reproduced as long as their source was indicated. At the third level, protection was denied altogether in the case of articles of 'political discussion . . . news of the day or miscellaneous information'.

At the Berlin Revision Conference, these provisions were the subject of numerous amendments and debate.[156] The same three-tier structure was retained as in the Paris Additional Act, but with the following changes: **13.49**

1. Complete protection was now extended to 'serial stories, tales and other works, whether literary, scientific or artistic, whatever their object, published in the newspapers or periodicals of one of the countries of the Union': article 9(1).
2. The freedom to reproduce articles unless this had been prohibited in advance was now limited to newspaper articles, with the exception of serial stories and tales: article 9(2). Articles in periodicals were now excluded from this dispensation, gaining absolute protection under article 9(1). In addition, the freedom to reproduce newspaper articles was restricted to other newspapers: it did not apply to individuals. This last restriction owed much to the advocacy of the Belgian Government which, prior to the Conference, had concerned itself with ascertaining the views of journalists and newspaper editors on the legal regime that most readily accommodated their professional activities.[157] The freedom to reproduce articles from newspaper to newspaper, except where this was expressly prohibited, was regarded as essential, particularly where small newspapers, with limited resources, were concerned.[158]

[155] *Actes* 1896, 171 (report of Renault).
[156] *Actes* 1908, 249ff (report of Renault).
[157] Note, in particular, the memorandum presented to the Berlin Conference by the Belgian Government: *Actes* 1908, 203–7.
[158] ibid. See also the resolutions of the International Congress of the Press set out in ibid, 87.

3. Protection was now denied completely only in the case of 'news of the day' and 'miscellaneous information which is simply of the nature of items of news': article 9(3).

Although this formulation was only arrived at after lengthy discussion and compromise,[159] it was hardly satisfactory and was made the subject of reservations by a number of Union members.[160] There was a contradiction between the general protection given to all works appearing in a newspaper under article 9(1) and the restrictive regime which applied under article 9(2) in respect of 'any newspaper article'. There were differing views on the correct interpretation of these provisions, with some commentators arguing that article 9(2) was to be confined to 'newspaper articles properly speaking' and that it did not cover articles of a scientific, technical, or entertaining nature.[161] On the other hand, if the expression 'newspaper articles' was more widely interpreted, this meant that many serial stories and tales of a mediocre nature which appeared in a newspaper would be protected, while more serious articles in the same publication would be subjected to the regime under paragraph (2). Furthermore, if the same articles appeared in a periodical rather than a newspaper, they would then be protected under paragraph (1).

13.50 These inconsistencies led to renewed debate at the Rome Revision Conference, with a proposal in the programme to amend article 9(2) so as to allow the reproduction from one periodical to another of 'articles of economic, political and religious discussion and others of the same kind'.[162] This wider formulation was strongly contested by some delegations, particularly France,[163] and the draft finally adopted read as follows:

> (2) Articles on current economic, political or religious topics may be reproduced by the press unless the reproduction thereof is expressly reserved . . .

The word 'press' here referred to both newspapers and periodicals, and thus overcame one of the difficulties in the Berlin text.[164] However, the formulation to 'articles on current economic, political or religious topics' excluded a large number of other articles, and accorded them complete protection under article 9(1).

---

[159] *Actes* 1908, 249ff and 287ff (table of amendments). See also the declaration by Belgium at ibid, 215.

[160] These were made by Greece: [1920] *DA* 133; Norway: [1910] *DA* 113; Romania: [1926] *DA* 121; Sweden: [1919] *DA* 109.

[161] See comments of the Italian Government in the programme for the Rome Conference: *Actes* 1928, 72ff. See also generally on the Berlin text of art 9: 'La Convention de Berne et le droit de reproduction en matière de journaux et de publications périodiques' [1926] *DA* 73.

[162] *Actes* 1928, 73. [163] ibid, 248 (résumé of discussions).

[164] ibid, 210 (report of Casseli).

No change to these provisions was made at the Brussels Revision, but it is of interest to note that the deletion of paragraph (2) was proposed in the programme, together with the addition of the expression 'articles on current economic, political and religious topics' to paragraph (1).[165] In support of these changes, the Belgian Government and International Office argued that the need to provide exceptions of the kind in paragraph (2) had now disappeared, and that the general desire of journalists was now that their articles should be protected in the same way as other works under the Convention.[166] However, the prevailing mood at the Conference was that the article should be left unchanged in the interest of press freedom.[167] **13.51**

It was not until the Stockholm Conference, therefore, that article 9 was revised. **13.52** This, in fact, occurred in a radical fashion, as paragraph (1) of the Brussels Act was subsumed into the new general right of reproduction that was recognized in paragraph (1) of the new text. As for paragraph (3), this was retained, but was transferred to article 2(8) (see further para 13.47 above). As for paragraph (2), the proposal in the programme was for this to be deleted, on the ground that '[i]n our day, . . . it can hardly be compatible with the moral principles recognized in the press to reproduce an article published in another newspaper without having first obtained the author's permission'.[168] It was argued further that the press was still free to give reports on protected works where this was required without infringing copyright—in the form of summaries—and where literal reproduction was required this was assured by an appropriately drawn right of quotation.[169] This approach also had the support of the International Federation of Journalists, the principal persons who would be affected by this change.[170] In Main Committee I, however, the proposal for deletion encountered strong opposition from the delegations of Czechoslovakia, Hungary, Poland, and Japan which argued that the exception in article 9(2) still played a valuable role in promoting the free flow of information.[171] Thus, it enabled articles in foreign newspapers to be reproduced (in translation) and made available almost immediately to the populations of their countries before they had lost their currency. This was of particular value to isolated communities, and this purpose could not be satisfactorily served by a right of quotation.[172] These delegations also proposed that the exception should be extended to broadcasting.[173] Although there was opposition to these views from a number of delegations,[174] the principle of retaining article 9(2) and widening its scope was adopted by

[165] *Documents 1948* (1951), 230. [166] ibid, 228–9. [167] ibid, 233–4.
[168] *Records* 1967, 114. [169] ibid. [170] ibid. [171] ibid, 859–60.
[172] ibid (see comments of Mr Ascensio, Portuguese delegate).
[173] Document S/51 (Czechoslovakia, Hungary, and Poland): ibid, 688; and Document S/80 (Japan): ibid, 691.
[174] eg France and Denmark: ibid, 859.

twenty-four votes to eight, with seven abstentions.[175] In the new Act, this became article $10^{bis}(1)$, and read as follows:

> (1) It shall be a matter for legislation in the countries of the Union to permit the reproduction by the press, the broadcasting or the communication to the public by wire of articles published in newspapers or periodicals on current economic, political or religious topics, and of broadcast works of the same character, in cases in which the reproduction, broadcasting or such communication thereof is not expressly reserved. Nevertheless, the source must always be clearly indicated; the legal consequences of a breach of this obligation shall be determined by the legislation of the country where protection is claimed.

13.53 *Interpretation of article $10^{bis}(1)$*: This is a compromise provision, in that it contains some advantages to the author that were not present in the Brussels text, but derogates further from her rights in other respects. The following points can be made:

1. Unlike article 9(2) of the Brussels Act, it is no longer an exception that Union members must provide for, as a matter *de jure conventionis*. It is left now purely as a matter for their internal legislation. This formulation met the objection of those countries such as France and Denmark which no longer saw any reason for the exception.[176]
2. The acts which may be allowed are now wider: reproduction, broadcasting, and communication to the public by wire.
3. The subject matter of the exception is also wider: not only are articles published in newspapers and periodicals included, but also 'broadcast works of the same nature' (but not 'works . . . of the same nature' that have been communicated to the public by wire). The balance between reproduction and broadcasting is thus maintained, and it will be noted that it is contemplated here that entire works can be taken. On the other hand, the qualification that these be articles or broadcast works of the same nature 'on current economic, political or religious topics' remains, and therefore excludes a wide range of newspaper and periodical writing, such as literary and artistic reviews, sports reports, articles on scientific and technical matters and so on. The word 'current' should also not be ignored here: the articles in question must be of immediate importance, as the purpose behind the exception was to expedite the free flow of information on current events.[177] Longer articles which review these topics in a longer-term framework should not therefore be included.

[175] Document S/51: ibid, 860. [176] ibid.

[177] Note eg the statement of the Czech delegate which implies that he saw this as being concerned principally with statements by public figures: ibid, 859.

4. An interesting question now arises as to the scope of the exception under article $10^{bis}(1)$ in the online environment, given that many traditional hard-copy newspapers and periodicals are available in electronic formats, as well as a whole stable of new publications that are available only in electronic formats. Given that the terms 'broadcasts' and 'broadcast works of the same nature' refer to a specific form of transmission, these would not, in their terms, cover online publications that are available on demand. Ultimately, it would seem to be a matter for national laws to determine what are 'newspapers and periodicals' and whether these extend to electronic versions that are made available online. However, there is nothing in article $10^{bis}(1)$ that excludes such extensions.

5. The proposal of Czechoslovakia, Poland, and Hungary also referred to the right to reproduce and broadcast articles in translation.[178] This was not thought necessary, as the view was taken that the right of translation under article 8 was implicitly subject to the same exceptions as those of reproduction and broadcasting[179] (see further paras 13.83ff below).

6. As the provision was no longer confined to the reproduction of articles, it was thought more appropriate to place it in article 10bis which already dealt with the reporting of current events by such other means as broadcasting.

7. As with article 10(2), where a work covered by this provision is broadcast or communicated to the public by wire, this must also cover any further dissemination that occurs in the reception of the broadcast or wire service, for example, where it is played in public.[180] In the case of reproduction, there can clearly be no limitation on the number of copies made.

8. As this is now a matter reserved to national legislation, article $10^{bis}(1)$ merely sets the limits within which the rights of authors may be derogated from in the case of articles on current economic, political, and religious topics. Accordingly, national law may impose more rigorous limitations, or allow no derogations whatsoever. The only condition to be complied with, if limitations under the provision are adopted, is that the source of the article must be indicated (see further below). These limitations will obviously only have effect within that particular country. There is also no reason why a country invoking article $10^{bis}(1)$ should not make such uses subject to the payment of a compulsory licence fee: this, after all, would be a lesser derogation than that which the provision allows.[181] In this regard, it should be noted that this provision, unlike other exceptions allowed by the

[178] Document S/51: ibid, 688. [179] ibid, 1149 (report of Main Committee I).
[180] See also to the same effect, Masouyé (1978), 61.
[181] See also to the same effect, Desbois et al (1976), 198–9.

Convention, clearly contemplates that whole works may be used ('articles' and 'broadcast works of the same nature').

9. If national legislation provides exceptions pursuant to article $10^{bis}(1)$, it must require that the source of the article be indicated. This is a recognition of the author's right of attribution, but is differently worded from the requirement which appears in article 10(3). Under the latter provision, compliance with this requirement is necessary if the quotation or utilization in question is to be lawful. Under article $10^{bis}(1)$, however, the legal consequences of the breach of this obligation are left to be determined by the legislation of the country where protection is claimed. Thus, it would be open to national legislation to decree that a breach involves some lesser penalty, such as liability to a sum of damages or a fine, and does not make the use itself unlawful.

13.54 **(ii) Use of works in the reporting of current events:** Following the protection of cinematographic reproduction rights in the Berlin Act and broadcasting rights in the Rome Act, it became apparent that a problem arose where works protected by the Convention were incidentally used in filmed or broadcast reports of current events. Thus, a radio or newsreel report of a public ceremonial occasion might incorporate snatches of a protected musical work that was performed by a military band.[182] Again, parts, or even the whole of a protected artistic work, such as a sculpture, painting, or building, might be captured in a filmed report of the same or some other current event, such as a sporting occasion or an interview with a famous person. By the 1930s, newsreels and radio news programmes had become a common feature of daily life in many Union countries, and the problems of this kind of incidental secondary use became more intense. There was little doubt that these were infringements of the exclusive rights recognized under the Convention and national legislation,[183] but they could be readily justified on the basis that they were often difficult to delete from the report without undue mutilation, and that to gain the advance authorization of the author was usually impracticable, if not impossible. Under national laws, the question first raised itself in the context of cinematographic reports, and the responses differed. For example, court decisions in the UK[184]

---

[182] A famous example in UK law concerned the making of a newsreel of a parade of naval cadets in the presence of the then Prince of Wales (later Edward VIII and the Duke of Windsor), during which the band played 'Colonel Bogey's March': *Hawkes & Son (London) Ltd* v *Paramount Film Service Ltd* [1934] 1 Ch 593 (Court of Appeal).

[183] This was certainly the view of the Belgian Government and International Office in the programme they drew up for the Brussels Conference of 1948: *Documents 1948* (1951), 348–50. On the other hand, it was arguable that such restrictions were justifiable under the heading of 'minor exceptions' which was acknowledged at the Brussels Revision: see paras 13.79ff below.

[184] *Hawkes* case, decision of the Court of Appeal, 26 Apr 1934 (noted in *Documents 1948* (1951)). See further [1937] *DA* 74.

and Germany[185] held that film reports that incorporated protected works were infringing uses, but subsequent legislation in Germany,[186] as well as Austria,[187] granted specific exceptions in favour of them. The scope of the German and Austrian exceptions differed, but the view taken by the International Office was that these were nonetheless in conflict with these countries' obligations under the Convention—or, rather, that such restrictions, whilst applicable to German and Austrian nationals, could not be applied to authors claiming under the Convention.[188] In their programme for the Brussels Revision Conference, the Belgian Government and International Office did not propose any amendment to article 14 to deal with this problem, taking the view that it was not appropriate for the drafters of the Conference programme to 'suggest the introduction into the Convention of a restriction to copyright', and that their obligation was simply to point to the discordance that presently existed between the provisions of the Convention and those of the German and Austrian laws.[189] This reticence, however, was not shared by the Italian delegation at the Conference which proposed that the question of use of works for film reporting should be considered.[190] This was done by the sub-committee which examined the programme proposals concerning article 14(3) (the relationship between cinematographic and photographic works). The sub-committee took the view that this was a wider issue that also concerned broadcasters and photographers, and was more properly dealt with in article 13.[191] Consequently, a new paragraph (4) to that article was proposed:

> It is reserved to national legislation to make provision for the reproduction and public presentation of literary and artistic works included in sounds or images made in the course of a photographic, cinematographic or broadcast report.[192]

This proposition did not receive unanimous support, as certain delegations took the view that it was only concerned with a 'small exception' which was not of any international significance.[193] The sub-committee, however, thought that this view was debatable, particularly in the case of film reports which were very often exported.[194] The question therefore was discussed further in the general commission, and a number of amendments were proposed, including the possibility of a compulsory licence,[195] the restriction of the exception to 'brief extracts' of works,[196] and its extension to broadcast reports.[197] It was finally decided to include the provision in a new article, article 10*bis*, which read as follows:

---

185 Decision of the Berlin Kammergericht, 16 Oct 1934 (ibid).
186 German Law of 30 Apr 1936 (text in [1936] *DA* 61).
187 Austrian Law of 9 Apr 1936 (text in [1936] *DA* 61).
188 *Documents 1948* (1951), 349–50. 189 ibid, 350. See further [1937] *DA* 74, 76.
190 *Documents 1948* (1951), 358. 191 ibid, 129. 192 ibid, 251.
193 ibid, 129 (noted in report of sub-committee on art 14(3)). 194 ibid.
195 ibid, 251 (Italian proposal). 196 ibid (Spanish proposal).
197 ibid (Swiss and Monégasque proposal).

> It shall be a matter for legislation in countries of the Union to determine the conditions under which recording, reproduction, and public communication of short extracts from literary and artistic works may be made for the purpose of reporting current events by means of photography or cinematography or by radiodiffusion.[198]

The limited nature of this exception was underlined in the report by Marcel Plaisant, where he described it as an extension of the right of lawful borrowing and short quotation and as a 'new concession accorded to freedom of information'.[199] He then stated that he was sure that he was interpreting the general sentiment of the Conference correctly in saying that it only applied to 'short extracts whose use appeared indispensable for the giving of a faithful account of current events'.[200]

13.55 **(iii) The present article 10*bis*(2) and its interpretation:** A number of minor changes were proposed and made at the Stockholm Revision Conference,[201] where the following provision was adopted as paragraph (2) of article 10*bis*:

> (2) It shall also be a matter for legislation in the countries of the Union to determine the conditions under which, for the purpose of reporting current events by means of photography, cinematography, broadcasting or communication to the public by wire, literary or artistic works seen or heard in the course of the event may, to the extent justified by the informatory purpose, be reproduced and made available to the public.

The following four comments can be made about this provision. First, it is not framed as a mandatory requirement of the Convention, but is simply left as a matter 'for legislation in the countries of the Union to determine the conditions under which, . . .'. This is differently formulated from article 10*bis*(1) where no reference to 'conditions' is made. It therefore seems clear that, in providing for the uses detailed in article 10*bis*(2), a Union member may make one of these conditions the payment of remuneration under a compulsory licence.[202] It would also be open to a Union member not to provide for any of these uses.

Second, the means of reporting that are covered by the provision are photography, cinematography, broadcasting, and communication to the public by wire. The last was added at the Stockholm Revision Conference to cover an increasingly important means of communication.[203] However, it will be noted that, apart from photographs and cinematographic films, reproduction generally of works in the course of reporting current events is not allowed. One

---

198 *Documents 1948* (1951) (Swiss and Monégasque proposal).

199 ibid, 100.

200 ibid. Cf Baum (1949), 28–9.

201 This seems to have been done with very little debate in Main Committee I: *Records* 1967, 1148–50 (report of Main Committee I).

202 See also Desbois et al (1976), 201.

203 *Records* 1967, 1149.

particular problem that may flow from this is the case of sound recordings of a current event that are made for subsequent broadcast: as the soundtracks of films fall within art $10^{bis}(2)$, the exclusion of sound recordings seems anomalous. Such uses will therefore have to be justified under the right of quotation in article 10(1) or as being within the general exception under article 9(2). Moreover, it should be noted that the making of recordings for subsequent broadcasting is covered under another provision of the Convention (article $11^{bis}(3)$: see further paras 13.72ff below).

Third, the subject of the report must be a 'current event', and the work in question must be 'seen or heard in the course of the event'. This places an important temporal limitation on the provision. It would not be permissible after the report has been made to embellish it by the addition of a picture of a work of art or a musical accompaniment, as neither of these would have been 'seen or heard in the course of the event'.

Finally, a further limitation is added by the requirement that the use of the work must be 'justified by the informatory purpose'. This expression replaced the requirement under the Brussels text that only 'short extracts' might be taken.[204] The latter, however, was inappropriate in the case of particular kinds of works, such as artistic works, where the whole of the work might quite incidentally appear in the filmed or televised report, for example, the report of a public ceremony held in front of a protected building or sculpture. In its initial proposals, the 1963 Study Group sought to take account of this by proposing that such reports be limited to:

(a) short extracts from literary or artistic works,
(b) works of architecture, isolated works of graphic, plastic or applied arts and isolated photographs which may be seen or heard in the course of the event.[205]

However, the 1963 Committee of Experts felt the same objective was more elegantly achieved by a general formula.[206] The expression 'to the extent justified by the informatory purpose' was therefore proposed and adopted in the Conference programme.[207] From this, it will be seen that there is no *carte blanche* for the reproduction of whole works under this provision. This will only be permitted where the nature of the work is such that it would not be possible to make the report without reproducing the whole work: examples would include a report on the dedication of a new public sculpture or building, and a report on a sporting event where the stadium is covered with various works of art.[208] On the other hand, a report on the opening of a new art gallery would not justify the

[204] ibid, 119 (Document S/1). [205] ibid, 118. [206] ibid, 118. [207] ibid, 120.
[208] ibid, 119.

reporter showing all the works of art in the gallery, or broadcasting all the music played at a concert to raise money for the purposes of famine relief: neither of these would be in any way necessary for the adequate reporting of these events.[209]

(e) Reporting of lectures, addresses, and other similar works

13.56 Article $2^{bis}(2)$ also permits member states to regulate the conditions under which these kinds of oral works may be used for the purposes of reporting. The background of this provision has already been dealt with already (see paras 8.16–8.17 above) and the changes made to article $2^{bis}(1)$ at the time of the Stockholm Revision were discussed earlier (see paras 8.18–8.21 above). As for article $2^{bis}(2)$, no proposition in relation to this was made by the Study Group in either of its 1963 or 1964 reports. However, it was arguable that to allow simply for reproduction by the press (assuming this meant only reproduction in printed form) was too narrow, and that provision should also be made for other means by which lectures, sermons, etc, could be disseminated to the public for example, by radiodiffusion and wire diffusion.[210] The 1965 Committee of Governmental Experts, with some dissentients, took this view, and the matter was referred back to the Study Group for its consideration.[211] The latter nonetheless concluded that there was no need for amendment. In reaching this conclusion, it referred to other articles of the Convention which were concerned with exceptions in relation to the broadcasting of news and current events (articles 10 and 10bis), as well as the possibility of introducing compulsory broadcasting licences under article 11bis for the purposes of disseminating information.[212] The Study Group was also concerned at the enormous expansion of the scope of article $2^{bis}(2)$ that might occur if broadcasting were allowed: works of great value, such as scientific speeches, might be disseminated to vast audiences without the consent of the author. By the same token, it was arguable that the present provision which allowed reproduction by the press itself went too far.[213] However, the conclusion of the Study Group was not shared by a number of Union countries, and a range of propositions involving extension of the scope of article $2^{bis}(2)$ was put forward at the Conference. A joint proposal by three then socialist states, Bulgaria, Poland, and Czechoslovakia, suggested the addition of the words 'or broadcast' after the words 'reproduced by the press'.[214] An Indian proposal went further, proposing the words 'reproduced by the press' be replaced by the words 'reproduced in original or in translation by the press or cinematography or broadcasting'.[215] By contrast, a proposal by the FRG advocated a more limited solution, suggesting the addition of the following words

[209] *Records* 1967 (Document S/1), 119. [210] See *Records* 1967, vol I, 89. [211] ibid.
[212] ibid, 90. [213] ibid, 89. [214] Document S/79: ibid, vol I, 691.
[215] Document S/73: ibid, 690, 691.

'and, when they refer to news, may be broadcast by radio or communicated by wire to the public'.[216] Concern was also expressed over the need to include sermons within the provision.[217] Finally, the Netherlands suggested that the best course might be to delete it altogether.[218] The various proposals were duly referred to a working group, which recommended that the press and broadcasting should be placed on an equal footing, but subject to certain qualifications. The first was that sermons should be deleted from the scope of the provision; the second was that the remaining works—'lectures, addresses and other works of the same nature'—must have been given in public; and the third was that the use allowed by the provision was only permitted if justified by its 'informatory purpose'. The Group also proposed that the provision apply to communication to the public by wire as well as the other modes of communication to the public that were envisaged by article 11*bis*(1)[219] (see further para 8.76 above). The wording finally approved by Main Committee I and incorporated in the Stockholm Act was almost identical to that of the Working Group and was as follows:

> It shall also be a matter for legislation in the countries of the Union to determine the conditions under which lectures, addresses and other works of the same nature which are delivered in public may be reproduced by the press, broadcast, communicated to the public by wire and made the subject of public communication as envisaged in Article 11*bis*(1) of this Convention, when such use is justified by the informatory purpose.[220]

While this provision is obviously wider than in the Brussels Act (as regards the means of dissemination embraced), its scope is nevertheless reduced. Lectures, addresses, etc, that are delivered to private groups are clearly excluded. This can be seen as a vindication of authors' rights, as the previous provision which permitted the reproduction in a mass-circulation newspaper of a private lecture or address was potentially a grave infringement of these rights. The latter could also be seen as a serious intrusion into authors' rights of confidentiality and privacy (although these, of course, receive differing levels of protection in many Union countries). The complete exclusion of sermons is also of significance, as these are works which are frequently disseminated by broadcasting organizations, and the possibility of a *carte blanche* under article 2*bis*(1) can be seen as going beyond the general public interest in receiving news and information.[221] Finally, the public-interest rationale of the provision is now made explicit, with the overriding requirement that the uses allowed by it are to be justified by the **13.57**

[216] Document S/92: ibid, 694.

[217] ibid, vol II, 892 (Main Committee I, comments by Straschnov, Monaco, and Ulmer, chairman).

[218] ibid (Gerbrandy).

[219] Document S/239: ibid, vol I, 721. See also ibid, 916–17 (discussion in Main Committee I).

[220] Stockholm, Paris Acts, art 2*bis*(2).

[221] *Records* 1967, vol II, 892 (comments of Straschnov, Monaco, in Main Committee I).

'informatory purpose'. This does not mean that the works reproduced, broadcast, etc, must themselves be 'news'—for example, a major address to representatives of business on exchange rates by a finance minister. This was, in fact, the effect of the proposed West German amendment, but the working group saw the justification of these uses in wider terms.[222] In the report of Main Committee I, it is therefore made clear that the informatory purpose of the use does not apply 'to the subject dealt with in the lecture, address, etc, but to the actual utilization with the object of informing the public'.[223] In other words, if the reproduction, broadcast, etc, is made with the purpose of informing the public—and presumably this is to be taken in the widest sense—this will suffice.

13.58 The following points of comparison with article $10^{bis}(2)$ should be noted. First, as the conditions under which these uses may occur are left to national legislation, it is likewise open to Union members to make them subject to compulsory licences and the payment of remuneration. Second, the provision covers general reproduction, making it permissible to allow the reproduction of lectures, addresses, and the like in newspapers and periodicals (the 'press'), as well as dissemination through broadcasting and wire diffusion. On the other hand, article $2^{bis}(2)$ does not cover the making of a cinematographic film of these works. Finally, the requirement that the use be justified by its 'informatory purpose' is to be differently applied than under article $10^{bis}(2)$: the latter requires that this is for the purposes of reporting 'current events' while under article $2^{bis}(2)$ the reporting of the oral works in question must be for the purposes of informing the public. Thus, the lectures, addresses, etc, need not themselves be 'news': their reporting may be permitted so long as the purpose is to inform the public of their contents.[224] The reporting of a public talk about an historic figure or past event will therefore be justified under this provision. This, in turn, means that the reporting of the whole of the lecture, address, etc, may be permitted, whereas a more restrictive approach is necessary under article $10^{bis}(2)$.

(f) Reservations and conditions with respect of the recording of musical works

13.59 (i) **Background**: If there is some kind of public interest that can be pointed to by way of justification for each of the exceptions discussed above—whether this be the needs of education, research, or freedom of information—the same cannot be said with respect to the reservations which the Convention allows in the case of the recording of musical works. It is, in truth, an instance where the rights of authors have had to be reconciled with the private interests of another

[222] *Records* 1967, vol II, 916 (remarks by Masouyé in presenting recommendations of Working Group).

[223] ibid, 1157. [224] ibid, 1157 (report of Main Committee I).

powerful group, those of record manufacturers. The reason for this is to be found in the way in which the recording industry was allowed to develop in its initial stages. In general, its activities were subject to no copyright restrictions, as the rights of authors to control the mechanical reproduction of their musical works was only slowly established in both national and international law.[225] In this transitional period, the recording industry was able to flourish and by the time that authors' rights in respect of mechanical reproduction were recognized, it had become an important interest group with powerful arguments to deploy in defence of its free copying activities. Not the least of these was the major investment involved in the new industry, with all the implications that this carried for employment and trade balances. Furthermore, in some countries, record manufacturers were able to point to the monopolistic practices that applied in the music publishing industry as an argument against the recognition of mechanical reproduction rights.[226] Accordingly, the notion that there should be some halfway house, which accommodated both the interests of authors and record manufacturers, began to grow. An obvious means of achieving this result was through the recognition of mechanical recording rights, subject to a regime of compulsory licences in favour of the manufacturers. This, in fact, was the solution adopted by the United States in its new Copyright Act of 1909,[227] and was followed by Germany in 1910.[228] Germany also proposed the adoption of such a licence as part of its programme for the Berlin Revision Conference.[229] It was stipulated that this licence should not come into effect until the author had permitted the utilization of his work in this way, and that an equitable remuneration was to be paid. Nevertheless, the significance of this proposal so far as the Berne Convention was concerned should not be underestimated: if a compulsory licence were allowed in favour of a particular interest group such as record manufacturers, it would be easier for other major users of copyright works to press claims for similar consideration on future occasions. In consequence, the German proposal provoked considerable opposition, particularly from the French delegation which saw this as an impermissible derogation from authors' rights.[230] It was impossible to arrive at a clear agreement on how this matter should be regulated. Finally, the following provision, based on a British amendment, was adopted as article 13(2):

[225] See para 6.78 above. See also the national survey of laws in [1907] *DA* 107.

[226] This was particularly so in the USA: see the account of legislative proposals (leading to the Copyright Act 1909) in that country in [1907] *DA* 10 and 60 and [1908] *DA* 86.

[227] US Copyright Act 1909, s 1(e).

[228] German Law of 22 May 1910, amending art 22 of the Law of 1901. See also note in [1910] *DA* 130.

[229] *Actes* 1908, 51–2.

[230] ibid, 261 (report of Renault).

> (2) Reservations and conditions relating to the application of this Article may be determined by the domestic legislation of each country in so far as it is concerned; but the effect of any such reservations and conditions shall be strictly limited to the country which has put them into force.

Two further provisions dealt with the problems of retroactivity and the importation of mechanical adaptations. The first (article 13(3)) provided that the new rights of mechanical reproduction and public performance recognized under article 13(1) were not to apply to adaptations lawfully made in any country of the Union prior to the coming into force of the Berlin Act, or prior to the date of accession to the Union of any new member state. The second (article 13(4)) provided that adaptations that had been lawfully made under either paragraph (2) or (3) were liable to seizure in any country of the Union into which they were imported where they would not be lawful.

13.60 From the point of view of authors, article 13(2) represented a clear derogation from the new rights which had been recognized under paragraph (1).[231] On the other hand, the original German proposal to make a compulsory licence part of the Convention had been rejected, and paragraph (2) simply allowed for the imposition of such licences. Nevertheless, it was the subject of renewed controversy at the Rome Revision Conference. By this time, a number of Union countries, apart from Germany,[232] had adopted compulsory licensing systems for the mechanical reproduction and adaptation of musical works. A number of others, however, had not taken such an approach.[233] As a result, there were conflicting amendments put forward at the Rome Conference:[234] some proposed that the compulsory licence should now be made a requirement under the Convention;[235] others proposed the deletion of the existing paragraph (2) altogether.[236] In the middle was the UK, supported by Norway, which argued for the maintenance of the status quo.[237] Several compromise proposals were also considered, including a German one to limit the reservation under paragraph (2) to reproduction rights alone.[238] Agreement finally proved impossible, and it was decided to leave the paragraph unchanged.[239] The question of retroactivity under article 13(3) also was the subject of lengthy debate. There was particular concern that the Berlin text allowed the continued mechanical

231 See the views of ALAI referred to by the International Office in [1909] *DA* 19, 22. For the texts of the ALAI resolutions disapproving of such licences, see *Actes* 1928, 37ff.

232 The chief countries which had adopted such licences were Austria, Bulgaria, the UK, and Switzerland. See eg the Swiss Law of 7 Dec 1922, arts 17–21; see also [1927] *DA* 137 and 'A propos des droits musico-mécaniques' [1926] *DA* 87.

233 These included Italy, Belgium, and Czechoslovakia: *Actes* 1928, 264.

234 No proposal concerning the paragraph was made in the programme: ibid, 78.

235 In particular, Austria: ibid, 89 (new art 13*bis*), supported by Bulgaria, Germany, and Switzerland (ibid, 265).

236 eg France: ibid, 265.

237 ibid.

238 ibid.

239 ibid, 266.

adaptation of works that had been lawfully adapted prior to the entry into force of the Convention, and the programme proposed that this immunity should only apply to those adaptations which had been made before this date.[240] This was supported by France,[241] but was strongly opposed by Germany and the UK,[242] and was consequently rejected.[243] A further proposal to limit the provision to 'pieces of works' was also rejected,[244] although the application of article 13(3) of the Berlin text had the effect that if part of a musical work, such as an air from an opera, was lawfully adapted prior to the Convention's entry into force, the non-retroactive effect of that provision applied subsequently to the whole of that work. No changes were made to paragraph (4).

At the Brussels Revision Conference, further efforts were made to reduce the scope of article 13(2). The programme proposed that it should not apply to performing rights,[245] and the French delegation again pressed for its complete deletion.[246] As at Rome, the French proposal met with strong opposition from those countries, such as the UK, which had well-entrenched recording industries.[247] However, the latter was prepared to compromise over the question of performing rights (which had no direct relevance to record manufacturers), and proposed further that the making of reservations and conditions under article 13(2) should be made subject to the obligation to pay equitable remuneration.[248] These amendments were considered by the sub-committee on broadcasting and mechanical rights which decided to reject the French proposal as well as the more limited programme proposal,[249] but adopted the British proposal concerning equitable remuneration.[250] A further matter that was considered was the effect of article 13(2) on the protection of moral rights. As to this, the sub-committee took the view that any reservations or conditions made under that paragraph were subject to the protection of moral rights, but that no express mention of this was required in the Convention text.[251] The recommendations of the sub-committee were accepted by the general commission (though not without further debate),[252] and were duly incorporated in article 13(2) of the Brussels Act. The requirement to pay equitable[253] remuneration was a significant innovation in that it excluded the possibility of countries applying paragraph (2) in such a way as to allow for free use in particular cases or to permit use for less than equitable remuneration. In the view of one **13.61**

[240] ibid, 78–9. [241] ibid, 266–7. [242] ibid, 267. [243] ibid.
[244] ibid (Italian proposal). [245] *Documents 1948* (1951), 323. [246] ibid, 329.
[247] ibid, 336–7. [248] ibid, 329.
[249] ibid, 116–17. Even though, as Baum reports, there was agreement to this by the International Federation of the Phonographic Industry: Baum (1949), 47.
[250] *Documents 1948* (1951), 119–20. [251] ibid, 118. [252] ibid, 336, 338.
[253] In one English translation promulgated by WIPO, the word 'just' is used rather than 'equitable', but it must be doubted whether there is any difference in meaning between the two words.

commentator, Baum, this meant that the laws of several countries were now in conflict with the new provision and would require amendment.[254] Paragraph (3) was also left unchanged in the new Act, although there was another attempt by France to limit its effect.[255] There was renewed opposition to this from the UK which resisted any change that would affect acquired rights.[256] Paragraph (4) also remained unchanged, except for the substitution of the word 'recordings' for the word 'adaptations'.

13.62 **(ii) Background to the present article 13:** Some significant changes were made to article 13 at the Stockholm Revision Conference, although these occupied relatively little time in comparison with that which had been spent on this subject at the earlier conferences. Article 13(1) was deleted with the recognition of a general right of reproduction under article 9(1), as well as the inclusion of performing rights for mechanical reproductions in article 11(1).[257] As for the remaining paragraphs, the 1963 Study Group decided at an early stage that, although authors continued to be opposed to compulsory licences, they were now too well established in a number of Union countries for there to be any chance of arriving at a unanimous decision to abolish them.[258] Accordingly, a modified proposal was advanced under which the reservations and conditions under article 13(2) (now article 13(1)) would be applicable only to mechanical reproduction rights (now called 'recording rights').[259] This was accepted by Main Committee I, as were a number of other amendments.[260] The latter was concerned chiefly with extending the application of article 13(1) to the recording of accompanying words.[261] Prior to the adoption of a general Conventional right of reproduction, member states had been able to regulate for themselves the conditions under which the words of songs, etc, might be recorded (see further paras 13.03–13.04 above). However, the introduction of article 9(1) now made it necessary for the new article 13(1) to take specific account of this if compulsory licences presently existing under some national laws were not to be in conflict with it. There was some opposition to the general principle, particularly from France, which referred to the rejection of a similar proposal at the

[254] These were the Swiss Law of 7 Dec 1922, art 21, which permitted the free public performance of lawfully made recordings; the German Law of 1901 (amended 1910), art 22a to the same effect; the Austrian Law of 1936, art 53. See Baum (1949), 47–8.

[255] *Documents 1948* (1951), 330, 337. [256] ibid, 337.

[257] *Records* 1967, 1142ff (report of Main Committee I). [258] ibid, 124 (Document S/1).

[259] ibid. [260] ibid, 1170–1 (report).

[261] Proposal by the FRG (Document S/92): ibid, 694; proposal by UK (Document S/171): ibid, 704. Note also that there was a Brazilian amendment (Document S/217) to provide expressly that art 9(2) applied to musical works: ibid, 715. This was withdrawn during the discussions of Main Committee I on the ground that it was unnecessary: ibid, 906. In this regard, there is an error in the report of Main Committee I which ascribes to the Brazilian amendment precisely the opposite effect to that which it sought to obtain: ibid, 1170.

time of the Brussels Conference (see further para 13.61 above).[262] It was approved by a narrow majority,[263] but difficulty was still encountered in finding a suitable formulation.[264] Finally, the drafting committee proposed a wording based on the licensing provisions found in British and German law where the starting point was that the compulsory licence only came into operation when the author of the musical work and the author of the words had given their consent for the first recording of their works.[265] Once this was given, the compulsory licence could operate in respect of both works, but the initial decision to exploit their works in this way remained with the authors. This was duly adopted by Main Committee I and incorporated in article 13(1).[266] As for article 13(2) (previously article 13(3)), the programme proposed that this should be severely restricted, and suggested that the period for the lawful making of recordings without the author's consent under this provision should be very short.[267] It was finally agreed that this should expire two years after the date when the country where the recordings were made became bound by the Stockholm Act.[268] Article 13(4), which now became article 13(3), was retained in its previous form with the appropriate consequential changes. In its final form, article 13 now provides:

> (1) Each country of the Union may impose for itself reservations and conditions on the exclusive right granted to the author of a musical work and to the author of any words, the recording of which together with the musical work has already been authorized by the latter, to authorize the sound recording of that musical work, together with such words, if any; but all such reservations and conditions shall apply only in the countries which have imposed them and shall not, in any circumstances, be prejudicial to the rights of the authors to obtain equitable remuneration which, in the absence of agreement, shall be fixed by competent authority.
>
> (2) Recordings of musical works made in a country of the Union in accordance with Article 13(3) of the Conventions signed on June 2, 1928, and at Brussels on June 26, 1948, may be reproduced in that country without the permission of the author of the musical work until a date two years after that country becomes bound by this Act.
>
> (3) Recordings made in accordance with paragraphs (1) and (2) of this Article

262 ibid, 906 (Mr Boutet, France).

263 ibid. The vote was thirteen to five, with twenty abstentions.

264 ibid. See eg an early proposal by the drafting committee (Document S/269: ibid, 734) which referred to the imposition of 'reservations and conditions on the exclusive right granted to the author of a musical work and to the author of any words which, with the consent of the author of those words, are normally performed with that work . . .'. See the criticisms of this draft in Main Committee I: ibid, 928.

265 Document S/290: ibid, 758, and see also ibid, 1170. The relevant national provisions to be found in the Copyright Act 1956, s 8 and the FRG Law of 1965, art 61.

266 *Records* 1967, 931.

267 ibid, 125 (Document S/1).

268 ibid, 1171 (report).

and imported without permission from the parties concerned into a country where they are treated as infringing recordings shall be liable to seizure.

13.63 **(iii) Interpretation of article 13(1):** The following eight comments can be made about this paragraph. First, it still operates as a permissible derogation from the general right of reproduction granted under article 9(1). Accordingly, there is no obligation on any Union member to impose reservations or conditions on the exercise of that right in respect of the recording of musical works and words.

Second, reservations and conditions may only be applied in respect of the sound recording of musical works and words; under the earlier texts, up to the Brussels Act, this was also possible in the case of the public performance of such recordings. It does not appear that the latter facility was much invoked in national legislation, as the principal concern of record manufacturers was with the mechanical reproduction right.

Third, reservations and conditions may only be imposed if the recording of the musical work and words has already been authorized by the author. As stated above, this leaves the author with the prerogative to decide when the first mechanical exploitation of her work shall occur: it is only after this time that reservations and conditions may be imposed. This provision thus preserves, in substance, the author's right of divulgation, one of the basic moral rights that is not expressly recognized under the Convention. It has been noted, however, that there is an apparent problem that arises here with the drafting of paragraph (1).[269] A literal reading suggests that reservations and conditions in relation to both musical works and words can only be imposed where the author of the words has consented to their recording. This is on the basis that the words 'the latter' refer only to the author of the words. It is hard to believe that this was the intention of the delegates at the Stockholm Conference, particularly in view of the fact that the provision had, up until this time, dealt only with the authors of musical works. Why, then, should the provision make a distinction between the respective authors, adopting a more favourable approach to the author of the words? Furthermore, if the literal interpretation is adopted it would have the effect that, in the case of a recording of the musical work alone, a compulsory licence could be imposed before the copyright owner had authorized this to be done. This would clearly be inconsistent with the intention of the Stockholm delegates,[270] and would also be inconsistent with the national legislation on

[269] Desbois et al (1976), 191.

[270] ibid, 928–9 (remarks of Mr Wallace, the chairman of the drafting committee, and Professor Ulmer), and 931 where Professor Ulmer states clearly the consent of both authors is required.

which this amendment was said to be based.[271] The better view, therefore, must be that the prior authorization of both authors is required before the compulsory licence can be imposed.

Fourth, in any event, the reservations and conditions authorized by article 13(1) do not apply to the recording of words alone: these must accompany the musical work, as in the case of a song, opera, oratorio, and so on. While it was feasible to make reservations and conditions in respect of words alone under the earlier Acts, this is no longer possible under the Stockholm, Paris Acts.

The fifth comment to make about article 13(1) is that the reservations and conditions which are applied can only have effect in the country which has imposed them. (This condition is reinforced in article 13(3) which allows member states to treat compulsorily licensed copies imported without permission as infringing copies (see the further discussion at paras 13.64–13.65 below). This might once have seemed a superfluous statement, as it was difficult to envisage circumstances under which restrictions imposed under one national law would have effect in another country of the Union; this position may now change, however, if the compulsory licence extends to digital copies, making it difficult thereafter to confine the availability of those copies to the country imposing the licence. The practical consequence of this is that musical works and accompanying words which are protected under the Convention will be subject to differing legal regimes in each country of the Union.

Sixth, if a country imposes reservations and conditions under article 13(1), this is subject to the condition that they are not 'prejudicial to the rights of these authors to obtain equitable remuneration which, in the absence of agreement, shall be fixed by the competent authority'. This is normally taken to mean that the conditions and reservations which are imposed will take the form of compulsory licences.[272] Its effect is certainly to exclude provisions which enable the free recording of works, or to permit this for less than an equitable remuneration. In this regard, however, reference must be made to the contrary comment made by Marcel Plaisant, the *rapporteur général* at the Brussels Conference, where he said of the introduction of this condition:

> Your reporter thinks that a text of this nature is incompatible with the regime of compulsory licences and that in any case it reinforces the position of the author considerably *vis-à-vis* the publishers of discs in any equitable negotiation of their relative rights.[273]

This statement seems wrong on several counts. First, this part of article 13(1)

---

[271] See eg the UK Copyright Act 1956, s 8 and the German Law of 1965, art 61.
[272] See eg Nordemann et al (1990), 102. [273] *Documents 1948* (1951), 103.

was proposed, and supported, by a number of delegations at the Brussels Conference whose national laws had compulsory recording licences.[274] It is therefore difficult to conceive that they would have consented to the provision if it had required them to abandon these licences. Secondly, as a general matter, the reference to equitable remuneration would be superfluous if the possibility of imposing compulsory licences under article 13(1) was not open, as the author's entitlement to equitable remuneration would be unquestioned in the event that no reservations or conditions to her right of authorizing the recording of his work were allowed. Thirdly, the stipulation that this remuneration is to be fixed, in the absence of agreement, by a competent authority indicates clearly that ultimately the use allowed under article 13(1) may take place under compulsion. In this regard, the words 'shall be fixed' mean that the competent authority is to fix the remuneration to be paid in the last resort, and is not envisaged as an arbitral tribunal to which the parties may have recourse at their convenience.

The seventh comment to make about article 13(1) is that no guidance as to the meaning of the expression 'equitable remuneration' is to be found in the Convention or in the records of the Brussels or Stockholm Revision Conferences that adopted the expression. However, it does not necessarily follow that this can be the market value of the use in question, that is, the equivalent remuneration which the author would have received if she had been free to authorize the use in the absence of a compulsory licensing provision. Although it is left to the parties to negotiate this amount between themselves in the first instance, the existence of such a provision inevitably weakens the bargaining position of the author. For this reason, the role of the competent authority is crucial, as it will have to make a notional judgement as to what amount would have been negotiated in the absence of a compulsory licence. This will ultimately remain a matter for national legislation. In this regard, it is worth recalling that the proposal for equitable remuneration was originally a German proposal made to, but not accepted by, the Berlin Revision Conference. According to the report of the Berlin Conference (by Louis Renault), the German proposal was based on the system of compulsory licences then found in German patent law[275] and it appears that this bears a more nuanced meaning than simple 'market equivalence'. Thus, according to one recent German court decision, this means that the 'licence fee must be set within two boundaries: it should grant the patentee reasonable compensation, but it should also enable the licensee to sustain the operation of his business'.[276] Such a 'halfway house' might therefore be an

[274] eg the UK and Switzerland: ibid, 335–7. [275] *Actes 1908*, 261.

[276] Case No 3 Li 1/90 (EU), 7 June 1991, decision of the German Federal Patent Court noted in (1993) 23 *IIC* 397, 404. See further the discussion in D J Brennan, *Retransmission and US Compliance with TRIPS* (2003), 14–15.

acceptable interpretation of the 'equitable remuneration' requirement in article 13(1), in the absence of any other signpost or guideline in the Convention or the preparatory materials[277] (noting here that a similar requirement also appears in article $11^{bis}(2)$, as to which see para 13.71 below).

Finally, article 13(1) contains no prescriptions relating to the competent authority, so this again remains a matter for national legislation. In some common law countries, this is done by the executive, rather than a judicial or legislative, body.[278]

(iv) Interpretation of article 13(2): Up until the Stockholm, Paris Acts, it was provided that the mechanical reproduction right did not apply to works which had been lawfully adapted to mechanical instruments before the coming into force of the Berlin Act, or, in the case of a country which had acceded subsequently to the Convention, before the date of its accession.[279] The effect of this was that further recordings of these works might continue to be made after those dates; furthermore, there was the possibility that an extended immunity might be conferred on whole works, such as operas, of which parts only had been lawfully recorded prior to these dates (see para 13.59 above). Article 13(2) of the Stockholm, Paris Acts now effectively abolishes this immunity, and operates in the following way. **13.64**

For a country which accedes to the Convention for the first time under the Stockholm, Paris Acts, article 13(1) applies to any recording of a protected musical work and words that is made after the date of that accession, irrespective of whether a recording had been lawfully made before this time. However, in the case of existing Union members, the freedom previously conferred under article 13(3) of the Rome and Brussels Acts to record works lawfully made before the Berlin Act or the date of the country's accession (if this was later) is abridged to a two-year period of grace after the country becomes bound by the Stockholm, Paris Acts. This obviously applies to countries bound by either the Rome or Berlin Act, of which there are still a small number. In the case of a country bound only by the Berlin Act, its right to continue to record works which had been lawfully adapted before that Act came into force disappeared

[277] See further the interesting discussion by Brennan, ibid, 13–15.

[278] eg, at the time of the Stockholm Conference, in the UK this was fixed by the Board of Trade: Copyright Act 1956, s 8; and in Australia by the Governor General after an inquiry had been held by the Copyright Tribunal: Copyright Act 1968, s 58. This has now changed in the case of Australia, where the remuneration is fixed only by the Copyright Tribunal: Copyright Act 1968, s 152A. In the USA, the mechanical compulsory licence rates are set, in the absence of voluntary agreement, by Copyright Arbitration Royalty Panels convened by the Librarian of Congress, see 17 USC § 115(c).

[279] Berlin, Rome, and Brussels Acts, art 13(3).

immediately it ratified the Stockholm, Paris Acts as the two-year grace period did not apply to such a country. Following the accession of Thailand to the substantive provisions of the Paris Act in 1995, there is no longer any member state affected by this.[280]

13.65 (v) **Interpretation of article 13(3):** This has remained essentially unchanged since the Berlin Act. Its effect is that any immunity which pertains to recordings which have been lawfully made under article 13(1) or (2) has only a territorial effect within the country of their making. Thus, a recording of a musical work and words which is lawfully made pursuant to a compulsory licence in country A will not carry its 'lawful character' with it when it is exported to other countries of the Union without the consent of the person entitled to the copyright in those works in those countries. In such circumstances, country B is entitled to regard such a recording as an infringing recording, and the fact that it was lawfully made in country A is of no effect. The same applies to recordings which have been made in country A under conditions specified in paragraph (2). It will be noted that paragraph (3) does not require country B to treat these recordings as infringing copies: that is a matter left to the law of that country. However, if they are treated as infringing copies, there is no prescription as to how their seizure is to be carried out, or by whom. The words 'shall be liable to seizure' imply only that the machinery should be there, and the way in which this is done is left to national legislation (see further paras 11.46ff above).

(g) Contributions to the making of a cinematographic work

13.66 Although this has already been dealt with in Chapter 7 (see paras 7.31ff above), for the sake of completeness in our treatment of exceptions and limitations, reference should be made to article 14bis(2)(b), which has a restricted operation in relation to those Berne member countries whose laws include among the owners of copyright in a cinematographic work 'authors who have brought contributions to the making of the work'. Where this is so, such authors may not 'in the absence of any contrary or special stipulation, object to the reproduction, distribution, public performance, communication to the public by wire, broadcasting or any other communication to the public, or to the subtitling or dubbing of texts, of the work'. The categories of authors who are affected here are potentially very limited, in view of article 14bis(3) which provides that, unless contrary provision is made under the national law in question, these persons do not include authors of scenarios, dialogues and musical works created for the making of the cinematographic film, and the principal director of the film.

[280] See the list of Berne accessions at www.wipo.org. At the time of the first edition of this work, Thailand was bound only by the Berlin Act as to the substantive provisions of the Convention: [1986] *Copyright* 8.

However, in the event that such categories of authors are recognized under a given national law, the exception contained in article 14*bis*(2)(b) must be applied, unless that law makes some contrary provision. The purpose behind article 14*bis*(2)(b) is clear enough: to facilitate the exploitation of the cinematographic work as a whole, and to ensure that this is not restricted or inhibited by objections from co-authors whose contributions to the overall work may be regarded as comparatively minor. It is interesting to note that in a 1996 study by the International Office of WIPO, it was suggested that this was a limitation or exception to protection which, 'if correctly applied', would not conflict with the normal exploitation of the work or unreasonably prejudice the legitimate interests of the right holders.[281] Neither of these criteria, however, are included in article 14*bis*(2)(b) itself, which provides for no conditions or restrictions on the making of this exception.

(h) Conditions on the exercise of broadcasting and other rights

(i) **Background**: The same pressures that arose in the case of the recording of musical works were also evident from the very start of the broadcasting industry.[282] In this instance, it was the broadcasters who wished to have unimpeded access to protected works for the purposes of their broadcasts, and a greater public interest appeared to support their arguments than was the case with record manufacturers. Fears were expressed at the monopolistic practices or tendencies of the various national collecting societies which controlled the performing rights in most musical works, and which might be tempted to abuse these rights in relation to the new medium of broadcasting.[283] Emphasis was also placed on the educational and informatory role of broadcasting, and this was underlined by the fact that in many countries this function was carried out by, or under the close supervision of, governmental or public authorities.[284] Ultimately, the precedent already set in the case of sound recordings made it correspondingly more difficult to resist compulsory licences in respect of broadcasting when this right became the subject of protection under the Convention in the Rome Act. **13.67**

[281] 'The Implications of the TRIPS Agreement on Treaties administered by WIPO', published in [1996] *Industrial Property and Copyright* 164, 171.

[282] For a useful overview of this history, see Brennan (n 276 above), 15–18.

[283] See in particular the comments of the Australian and New Zealand delegates at the Rome Conference: *Actes* 1928, 256–8. These fears also seemed to be shared by the Scandinavian and Netherlands delegates. See further paras 12.22ff above.

[284] eg the British Broadcasting Corporation in the UK, and the various national broadcasting authorities that were established along similar lines in other Commonwealth countries in the late 1920s and early 1930s, such as the Australian Broadcasting Commission, the New Zealand Broadcasting Commission and the Canadian Broadcasting Commission.

13.68 These issues were extensively debated at the Rome Conference where the recognition of the broadcasting right was first proposed.[285] Many delegations favoured restrictions on the exercise of this right, in particular Norway, Australia, and New Zealand.[286] However, the nature of the suggested restrictions varied considerably: from the imposition of a straightforward compulsory licence[287] to limited exceptions for particular uses[288] and more general controls over abuses of the new right, particularly by collecting societies.[289] By contrast, some delegations, led by the French, were opposed to any restrictions at all, arguing that in this new area the Convention should uphold the cause of authors' rights by protecting the new right in absolute terms.[290] These conflicting proposals were sifted by a special sub-committee which sought to effect a compromise.[291] The latter was essentially based on a French amendment which avoided any reference to the recognition of a Conventional compulsory licence, but proposed reserving to national legislation the power to regulate the conditions under which the broadcasting right could be exercised, subject to three conditions:

1. the effect of such restrictions were to be confined to the country which imposed them;
2. they were not to affect the author's moral rights; and
3. they should not prejudice the author's right to an equitable remuneration, fixed by the competent authority.[292]

Although some states would have preferred the formulation of a more generous exception which explicitly recognized the overriding interest of the public,[293] the sub-committee's text was finally adopted by the general commission and duly became article 11*bis*(2) of the Rome Act.[294] In this regard, it is worth noting the view of the sub-committee that a 'country should only avail itself of the possibility of making limitations to copyright, in the case of broadcasting, where the necessity for them had been established by the experience of that country'.[295]

13.69 Article 11*bis*(2) remained essentially unchanged at the Brussels Revision Conference, except that it was extended so as to apply to the additional rights recognized by paragraph (1) of the new text, namely those of retransmission, wire diffusion, and public communication by means of loudspeakers and the like.[296]

---

285 *Actes* 1928, 256–60 (résumé of discussions). 286 ibid.

287 Norway: ibid, 112 and 257. Czechoslovakia: ibid, 257.

288 Denmark ('certain exceptions' to be allowed): ibid, 256; Hungary (similar exceptions as for the press): ibid, 259.

289 Australia, New Zealand, the Netherlands, Sweden, and Norway: ibid, 256–9.

290 ibid, 256ff. France, however, later proposed that exceptions in respect of education and popular instruction might be allowed: ibid, 259.

291 ibid, 259. 292 ibid, 183 (report of sub-committee). 293 eg Sweden: ibid, 259.

294 ibid, 260. 295 ibid, 183 and 260. 296 *Documents 1948* (1951), 304.

Nevertheless, the Conference nearly reached an impasse over these additions to the scope of paragraph (2). Once again, a series of conflicting proposals were put forward. France advocated the deletion of the paragraph altogether,[297] the programme proposed that it be limited only to retransmission and wire diffusion,[298] while the states with large broadcasting interests argued that it should apply to all the additional rights recognized under paragraph (1).[299] The last group carried the day in the sub-committee on broadcasting,[300] but debate was renewed when the recommendation of the sub-committee came back to the general commission.[301] At this stage, the real controversy concerned the possibility of imposing compulsory licences on television broadcasting. The Spanish delegation, supported by France, argued strongly for the exclusion of television from such restrictions.[302] The main reason for this, it seems, was fear of the threat that such licensing might pose to live theatre and other performances.[303] It was only after extended debate, spread over several sessions, that the Spanish delegation withdrew its proposal.[304] Along with several other delegations, it abstained from voting for the sub-committee recommendation which was then accepted by the general commission.[305] In the event, only a small textual amendment to paragraph (2) was required to give effect to this change—the substitution of the words 'the rights provided for in paragraph (1) above' in place of the words 'the right provided for in the preceding paragraph.' In the words of one observer at the Conference, this change did not show 'what efforts had been required to get unanimous approval'.[306]

No changes to article 11*bis*(2) were proposed in the programme for the Stockholm Conference, although the Study Group was aware that authors' groups were in favour of its deletion.[307] Nevertheless, it thought that there was no likelihood of achieving unanimity on this point, and therefore refrained from making any proposal of this kind.[308] During the course of the Conference, however, the scope of paragraph (2) came into question with respect to the broadcasting of cinematographic films. Several delegations took the view that this should not be subject to the possibility of compulsory licensing, or that the scope for such licences should be limited.[309] The latter approach was taken by **13.70**

[297] ibid, 281. In an earlier proposal, the French Government suggested the replacement of the Rome text with specific exceptions relating to newspaper articles.

[298] ibid, 270.

[299] eg Monaco: ibid, 282; Switzerland: ibid, 283; and a slightly modified amendment to this effect by the UK: ibid, 281.

[300] ibid, 119 (report of sub-committee). [301] ibid, 295.

[302] ibid, 295ff. [303] ibid, 296. See further Baum (1949), 35.

[304] *Documents 1948* (1951), 297. [305] ibid. [306] Baum (1949), 35.

[307] *Records* 1967, 122 (Document S/1). [308] ibid.

[309] See eg a proposal by the FRG to exclude the broadcasting, etc, of cinematographic films from art 11*bis* (Document S/92): ibid, 694. See further ibid, 865 (minutes of Main Committee I).

the Working Group on Cinematographic Works, which proposed that the provisions of paragraph (2) should only apply in respect of the cinematographic work or works adapted or reproduced in the cinematographic work itself only insofar as they related to the rights provided in paragraph (b)(ii) and (iii), that is, the rights of rebroadcasting, wire diffusion, and public communication by loudspeaker, but not to the actual right of broadcasting itself.[310] This aroused considerable opposition, particularly as it considerably reduced the scope of compulsory licensing with respect to pre-existing works embodied in cinematographic films, and eventually Main Committee I voted to maintain paragraph (2) unchanged.[311]

13.71 **(ii) The present article 11*bis*(2) and its interpretation:** This provision shares a number of features in common with article 13(1). The following points should be noted. First, as in the case of sound recordings, there is no Conventional obligation for Union members to impose compulsory licences on the exercise of the rights recognized under article 11*bis*(1). This is left as a matter for national legislation to determine.

Second, the formula adopted in article 11*bis*(2) is different from that in article 13(1), in that the former refers only to the determination by national legislation of the 'conditions' under which the rights in paragraph (1) may be exercised. By contrast, article 13(1) refers to the imposition of 'reservations and conditions', which implies that in certain circumstances it might be permissible for national legislation to deny protection altogether. This would not seem possible under article 11*bis*(1), as the power to impose 'conditions' on the exercise of rights does not carry with it the power to deny those rights. However, the difference between the two formulations is semantic rather than real, as both paragraphs contain the requirement that equitable remuneration must be paid, and under article 13(1) this applies in the case of both reservations and conditions. Under the latter provision, therefore, compensation must be paid for the unauthorized exercise of the sound recording right whether or not this right is otherwise protected under national legislation.

Third, the reference to 'conditions' in article 11*bis*(2) is usually taken to refer to the imposition of compulsory licences, but the form of these licences is left to national legislation to determine. For example, these licences could be made applicable only in certain specified situations, leaving the author in sole control of the exercise of his rights in all other instances.

Fourth, compulsory licences may be imposed in respect of all or any of the

[310] Document S/195: ibid, 710. [311] ibid, 903–4 (minutes), 1168 (report).

rights listed in article $11^{bis}(1)$. The attempts which were made to limit their application in earlier revision conferences has already been referred to above, but for the sake of completeness it should be noted that paragraph (2) authorizes the imposition of the following compulsory licences (see further para 12.38 above): (i) broadcasting of sounds and images, including by satellite; (ii) rebroadcasting of broadcasts of works where this is done by an organization other than the original one, including by satellite; (iii) wired rediffusion of broadcasts of works where this is done by an organization other than the original one, including by cable and digital dissemination (for example, by the 'streaming' of radio or television broadcasts); and (iv) public communication by loudspeaker or any other similar instrument of the broadcast of the work.

For sake of clarity, it is also useful to list what article $11^{bis}(2)$ does *not* cover, ie original wired transmissions (Internet) and retransmissions of works originally communicated by wired transmissions (see further paras 12.43ff above).

The fifth point to note is that article $11^{bis}(2)$ applies to all works protected by the Convention, including cinematographic works. Paragraph (1) refers generally to 'literary and artistic works', and in the absence of any contrary indication this expression must be interpreted in accordance with the definition in article 2(1). Furthermore, as noted above, the limitation of compulsory licences in respect of cinematographic works was discussed but rejected at the Stockholm Conference.[312]

Sixth, any compulsory licences imposed pursuant to article $11^{bis}(2)$ can only have application in the country which imposes them. In other words, a broadcaster can only claim the benefits of a compulsory licence within the territorial limits of the member country whose legislation authorizes this; in any other member country which does not contain such provisions in its legislation, he will be required to seek the authorization of the author of the work to make a broadcast in that country. In the light of the differing interpretations of the concept of 'broadcasting' under the Convention, the importance of this limitation will be apparent (see further para 12.35 above). For example, in the case of a satellite transmission, if the act of broadcasting is regarded as being completed in the country from which the transmission is made, the broadcaster will need to consider only the law of that country.[313] If, on the other hand, there are

[312] *Records* 1967 vol II, 1168.

[313] See eg Council Directive 93/83/EEC of 27 Sept 1993 on the coordination of certain rules concerning copyright and rights related to copyright applicable to satellite broadcasting and cable retransmissions, OJ L 248/15, art 2(b). This Directive localizes the act of communication 'solely in the Member State where, under the control and responsibility of the broadcasting organization, the programme-carrying signals are introduced into an uninterrupted chain of communication . . .'.

separate acts of broadcasting in each of the countries in which the transmission is received, the laws of each of these countries will be applicable. In the event that only one or some of these countries provide for compulsory licences, the broadcaster will have to seek separate permission from the person entitled to the copyright in each of the other countries.

Seventh, any compulsory licences imposed under article 11*bis*(2) must not 'in any circumstances be prejudicial to the moral rights of the author'. This stipulation appears superfluous, in view of the generally accepted opinion that this is an implicit limitation that applies in the case of any restriction to authors' rights that is authorized by the Convention (see para 13.46 above).[314] Nevertheless, it was thought appropriate to insert such a requirement in paragraph (2) at the time of its adoption by the Rome Conference and its inclusion has not been questioned since this time. The issue that then arises is the meaning of the expression 'moral rights'. The obvious answer to this is that it refers to the specific moral rights which member countries are required to protect under article 6*bis*(1), that is, those of paternity and respect. However, many national laws protect additional moral rights, in particular, that of disclosure or divulgence.[315] Accordingly, it has been argued that this right is included within the expression 'moral rights' in article 11*bis*(2), with the result that this provision embodies a similar precondition to the exercise of a compulsory licence to that in article 13(1), namely that the author's work must first have been disclosed to the public (see para 13.63 above).[316] This interpretation is consistent with the argument made above (see para 10.35 above) that the moral right of divulgation is implicit in the Convention.

Finally, the obligation that any compulsory licence imposed under article 11*bis*(2) is not to be prejudicial to the right of the author to obtain equitable remuneration is the same as that under article 13(1), and the comments made above in relation to this apply equally here (see further the seventh comment at para 13.63 above).

(i) Ephemeral recordings of broadcast works

13.72 (i) **Background**: Where a protected work is broadcast, it is not always possible or feasible to do this directly, that is, to broadcast the performance or presentation of the work as this actually occurs. Where the work broadcast is already fixed in the form of a sound recording or cinematographic film, no

314 See also the report of Main Committee I on this point: *Records* 1967, 1165.

315 See eg the German Law of 1965, arts 12, 42, and 46; the French Law of 1957, arts 19 and 32.

316 See Desbois et al (1976), 190.

problem will occur so long as the broadcaster has received the authorization to transmit the broadcast from the copyright owner[317] and the copy is lawfully made. However, where the work is performed or presented in the broadcasting studio, difficulties of timing may readily arise. It is often easier for the broadcaster to make a recording of the performance or presentation at a mutually convenient time and then to broadcast it at a later time or date. This is particularly so in large countries where there are significant time differences between the various places at which the broadcast may be received. In such cases, however, the question arises as to whether permission for the making of this recording is also required from the copyright owner. This problem was not addressed in the Rome Act, and the *prima facie* position as regards the making of recordings of works for deferred broadcasts was as follows. Under article 13(1), the author of a musical work was granted the sole right to make mechanical reproductions or adaptations of that work. Accordingly, a broadcaster would require the authorization of the author of a musical work to make a sound recording of that work for the purposes of broadcasting. The only amelioration of this position was the possibility that this might be permitted by national legislation pursuant to a compulsory licence under article 13(2). In the absence of a general Conventional right of reproduction, however, national legislation was free to determine the circumstances under which sound recordings of other works might be made. Finally, in the case of television broadcasting (which only became a realistic commercial possibility after World War II), a broadcaster would require permission for the fixation of a performance of a literary, scientific, or artistic work in the form of a tape for deferred broadcasting, as this would constitute the making of a cinematographic film under article 14(1).

The legal position outlined above was not necessarily accepted by all member countries or by the various groups interested in the question, particularly broadcasting organizations. One school of thought, represented by both France and the UK, took the view that the acts of broadcasting and recording were clearly differentiated, and that authorization to carry out the former did not imply any permission to make a reproduction for the purposes of the broadcast.[318] On the other hand, there was an opposing view that the grant of a permission to make a broadcast carried with it the concomitant right to do whatever else was **13.73**

[317] Note that, in many countries, permission to broadcast from the maker of the sound recording will also be required.

[318] See the responses by the UK and France to the programme proposal at the Brussels Conference: *Documents 1948* (1951), 283. See further 'Les enregistrements éphémères selon l'article 11*bis* de la Convention de Berne révisée à Bruxelles' [1951] *DA* 37.

necessary to enable the broadcast to be made.[319] This second view seemed clearly at variance with articles 11*bis*(1) and 13(1) of the Rome Act.[320] Nevertheless, there was strong pressure from broadcasting interests that some concession for their needs should be made in the Convention,[321] and in any event, from the point of view of authors, there was still a gap as regards the making of recordings of non-musical works. Accordingly, there was a need for the Convention to be clarified on this point, whichever view prevailed. The programme for the Brussels Conference therefore proposed the following amendment to article 11*bis*:

> (3) In the absence of any contrary stipulation, an authorization accorded pursuant to the first paragraph does not carry with it any authorization to record, by means of instruments capable of fixing sounds or images, the work broadcast.[322]

This proposal gave rise to extended debate at the Conference, and secured support from only a few nations, including France and the UK.[323] As for the rest, there were a number of alternative propositions which were submitted, each of which had the aim of assuring some latitude to broadcasters. At one extreme was the proposal of the Monégasque delegate that the recording of sounds or images required for the purposes of broadcasting should not require the authorization of the author under article 13(1) and should not be subject to the payment of any remuneration.[324] The other proposed amendments sought to place more precise limits on the making of recordings by broadcasting organizations. These included a Swiss proposal that such recordings should only be made where, for 'technical and timetabling reasons', it was necessary to defer the making of the broadcast, and that after having been used for that purpose it should be destroyed or otherwise rendered incapable of any new use.[325] Again, there was a broader Dutch proposal that authorization for the making of a recording was unnecessary where this was done by a 'broadcasting organization, and was intended only for subsequent broadcasting'.[326] This last proposal was expanded in a further amendment made by the Benelux countries under which authorization would be unnecessary where the recording was made by 'a broadcasting organization by its own facilities and only for the purposes of broadcasting, when the recording was of a precarious [temporary] nature'.[327] None of these formulations secured unanimous support from the delegates, and

[319] See eg the Italian Law of 1941, art 55 and Regulations, art 5. See also the distinction drawn between recording by a broadcasting organization and recording under art 13(1) by the Netherlands delegation in its submission for the Brussels Conference: *Documents 1948* (1951), 285.

[320] 'Les enregistrements éphémères . . .' (n 318 above), 38.

[321] Baum (1949), 36–7. See also the proposals of Monaco for the Brussels Conference: *Documents 1948* (1951), 284.

[322] *Documents 1948* (1951), 270. [323] ibid, 283. [324] ibid, 284.

[325] ibid, 298. [326] ibid. [327] ibid, 299–300.

the search for a compromise was pursued through informal meetings of delegates and various sub-committees.[328] Finally, after lengthy negotiations, in which the Monégasque delegate fought a valiant rearguard action in support of the interests of broadcasters, the following text was adopted as a new paragraph (3) to article 11*bis*. This refrained from formulating the new exception in terms of a mandatory Conventional rule, and also took account of a Swedish proposal that provision should be made for the retention of recordings for archival purposes.[329]

> (3) In the absence of any contrary stipulation, permission granted in accordance with paragraph (1) of this Article shall not imply permission to record the radio-diffused work by means of instruments recording sounds or images. It shall, however, be a matter for legislation in the countries of the Union to determine the regulations for ephemeral recordings made by a broadcasting organization by means of its own facilities and used for its own broadcasts. The preservation of these recordings in official archives may, on the ground of their exceptional documentary character, be authorized by such legislation.[330]

(ii) The present provision and its interpretation: Article 11*bis*(3) was left unchanged in the Stockholm Revision. No proposal for its amendment was made in the programme, as the Study Group took the view the rules embodied in it 'formed an acceptable compromise between conflicting interests'.[331] However, proposals for change were submitted by the British, Japanese, and Monégasque delegations. Those of the UK and Japan sought essentially to define the scope of the permissible exception with more precision,[332] while that of Monaco sought, predictably, to extend it.[333] However, in the discussions in Main Committee I it became clear that the majority of delegates shared the view of the programme that no change to the paragraph was required, and each amendment was withdrawn. The following points about the interpretation of paragraph (3) should therefore be noted. **13.74**

The first sentence of the paragraph distinguishes clearly between the acts of broadcasting and recording, by providing that permission to do the first does **13.75**

328 ibid, 297ff. See further Baum (1949), 37ff and 'Les enregistrements éphémères . . .' (n 318 above), 38ff.

329 *Documents 1948* (1951), 300.

330 ibid, 302.

331 *Records* 1967, 122 (Document S/1).

332 The British proposal (Document S/171) deleted the requirement that the recordings be made by the broadcasting organization 'by means of its own facilities' and restricted the making of such broadcasts to cases where 'for technical or other reasons, the broadcast cannot be made at the time of performance of the work': ibid, 704; Document S/112. The Japanese proposal (Document S/112) proposed the replacement of the words 'by means of its own facilities and used for its own broadcasts' by the words 'as a mere technical means for the use of broadcasts made with permission': ibid, 696.

333 Document S/77: ibid, 691.

not automatically carry with it permission to do the second. Strictly, this statement is superfluous, as the Stockholm, Paris Acts now clearly differentiate between these acts in articles $11^{bis}(1)$ and 9(1) and (3) (where sound and visual recording is expressly brought within the scope of the general reproduction right). The gap that previously existed under the Brussels Act with respect to recordings of non-musical works has therefore been removed. Nevertheless, the sentence has a clear educative value, in that it underlines the important fact that the conditions under which works may be broadcast and recorded is a matter for broadcasters and copyright owners to agree between themselves. In practice, this is commonly the case, and the making of recordings by broadcasters is covered in blanket agreements entered into with the appropriate authors' organizations.[334] In the absence of such consents, however, no permission to record is to be implied from a bare authorization to broadcast.[335]

13.76 Under the second and third sentences of article $11^{bis}(3)$, member countries retain the power to vary the above position for very specific purposes. Thus, it is a matter for national legislation to 'determine the regulations for *ephemeral recordings made by a broadcasting organization by means of its own facilities and used for its own broadcasts*' (emphasis added). This is far from being a general reservation to national legislation in respect of recordings made by broadcasting organizations. The limits within which such recording may be regulated are set by the italicized phrases.

'Ephemeral recordings': The provision gives no definition of this term, and this is a matter which is therefore left to be determined by national legislation. Express confirmation of this is to be found in the report of the Brussels Conference.[336] In its ordinary meaning, 'ephemeral' means 'transitory' or 'passing', and is used in contrast to 'durable' or 'permanent'. It seems clear from the discussions at the Brussels Conference that this was the distinction that the delegates had in mind.[337] On the other hand, there were considerable differences as to the precise scope of the adjective 'ephemeral', and this must be the reason that this was left to national legislation. Where member countries have chosen to avail themselves of the facility under paragraph (3), the periods adopted have varied considerably from one month to a year.[338] In any event, it will be clear that, with the exception of archival preservation (see below), the making of permanent recordings is not authorized by paragraph (3). The implication is that any recordings which are made under regulations made pursuant to the

334 Document S/77: ibid, 903. 335 Masouyé (1978), 71.

336 *Documents 1948* (1951), 102 (report of Plaisant). 337 ibid, 300ff.

338 eg the German Law of 1965, art 55(1) (recordings to be destroyed after one month); Tunis Model Law, s 8 (six months); Australian Copyright Act 1968, s 47(5) (recordings to be destroyed within twelve months or else delivered to National Library for preservation).

paragraph will have to be destroyed or otherwise rendered unsuitable for further use once the period of 'ephemerality' has passed.[339]

'Made by a broadcasting organization by means of its own facilities': This clearly excludes recordings made by an agent or some other outside body. At the Stockholm Conference, the Monégasque delegation sought to modify paragraph (3) so as to permit the making of recordings 'by or for a broadcasting organization', but this amendment was withdrawn in the course of discussions in Main Committee I.[340]

'Used for its own broadcasts': The recording must only be used for the broadcasts made by the organization which has made it. Once again, the Monégasque delegation sought to liberalize this at the Stockholm Conference by proposing that such recordings might also be used for the broadcasts of 'other organizations under the jurisdiction of the same country', but this was likewise withdrawn.[341] On the other hand, paragraph (3) does not place any limitation on the number of broadcasts in which the recording may be used, as long as they are the broadcasts of the organization in question. Furthermore, it does not contain any stipulation as to when the recording should be made. It may therefore be made in advance for subsequent broadcasting, or recorded contemporaneously with the broadcast and then rebroadcast. These are matters on which the regulations made by national legislation may vary.[342] Nevertheless, the effective limitation will be that the broadcasts will need to be made within the period of the recording's 'ephemerality'.

Unlike article 11*bis*(2), the making of ephemeral recordings is not subject to any requirement of payment of equitable remuneration. This, then, is a matter for national legislation, some of which require remuneration under a compulsory licence while others do not.[343]

(iii) Archival preservation: The final sentence of article 11*bis*(3) provides an exception to the conditions that are generally applicable to the making of ephemeral recordings under the second sentence. National legislation is given the power to authorize the 'preservation of these recordings in official archives . . . on the ground of their exceptional documentary character'. Once again, this exception is strictly limited: the preservation must be done in 'official archives', **13.77**

339 See the examples of national legislation given in n 338 above.
340 *Documents 1948* (1951), 903 (Document S/77: ibid, 691).
341 ibid.
342 Such distinctions do not generally appear to have been made in national legislation: see eg the national laws referred to in n 338. See also Masouyé (1978), 72.
343 eg remuneration is required under the Italian Law of 1941, art 55, but not under the German Law of 1965, art 55; nor US Copyright Act, see 17 USC § 112(a).

which would not normally include the archives of the broadcasting organization itself, and must further be justified on the ground of the 'exceptional documentary character' of the recordings in question. These phrases will require definition in national legislation, and may clearly vary.[344] Nevertheless, no general power to preserve recordings for general archival purposes is to be inferred. In consequence, any broadcasting organization that desires to do this will fall outside the scope of paragraph (3), and will require authorization to this effect from the copyright owner. In practice, this use of ephemeral recordings can be readily covered by a blanket licence granted to the broadcasting organization by the relevant collecting society.

(3) Implied exceptions under the Convention

13.78 In addition to the express exceptions which are contained in the provisions of the Convention discussed in the preceding paragraphs, there are a number of exceptions that are to be implied and which, according to the wishes of successive conferences of revision, will not be in conflict with the Convention if they are embodied in the national legislation of member countries. These fall into two main categories: those in relation to performing, recitation, broadcasting, recording, and cinematographic rights, and those in relation to translations.

(a) 'Minor reservations'

13.79 The question of implied exceptions to the Convention first arose in the case of public performing rights, which were only recognized in the Brussels Act. Prior to this, member nations were free to impose whatever restrictions they wished on the exercise of these rights, or even to deny them altogether. In fact, most national laws contained provisions permitting the unauthorized public performance of works in particular circumstances, and in 1933 the International Office gave the following list of typical instances: 'musical performances made in the course of religious worship, concerts given by military bands, charitable performances, public concerts organized on the occasion of particular festivals or holidays'.[345] Did these minor exceptions remain permissible under the new article 11(1) of the Brussels Act, or did they require express authorization under the Convention? This question was addressed by the Belgian Government and International Office in their preparatory work for the Brussels Conference. They took the view that it would be impossible to list all these exceptions

[344] Some laws eg such as that of Australia, do not attempt to define the character of the recordings so long as they are delivered to the National Library (clearly an 'official archives' within the meaning of art 11*bis*(3)).

[345] [1933] *DA* 112, 114.

exhaustively in the Convention as they were too varied.[346] On the other hand, it would not be feasible to demand their suppression, as most were based on long-standing exceptions which member countries would be loath to renounce.[347] The possibility was then considered of inserting a general provision in the Convention, under which it would be permissible for member nations to retain limitations presently existing in their national laws. However, a proposal of this kind had been unanimously rejected by a congress of CISAC in 1933,[348] and the drafters of the Brussels Act took a similar view: it was feared that the adoption of such a general provision would 'positively incite' those nations which had not, to this time, recognized such exceptions to incorporate them in their laws.[349] For this reason, no provision concerning exceptions to the new right of public performance was proposed in the Brussels programme, although it seems clear that the drafters of the programme did not think that this would lead to conflict in relation to exceptions currently found in national legislation.[350]

By and large, this view prevailed in the Conference. Several amendments were submitted of a general nature allowing states to limit public performing rights 'in certain specific cases',[351] but in the sub-committee on articles 11 and 11*ter* it was recommended that this matter should be dealt with in the general report, rather than the Convention itself, and the following wording in relation to both articles was proposed for this purpose: **13.80**

> The wording as now adopted in Article 11(1) [and article 11*ter*] makes no substantive change to the import of the text as it appears in the Berne Convention according to the Berlin and Rome revisions, given that certain exceptions admitted by some Union countries for clearly defined purposes have no international import.[352]

This recommendation was confirmed by the general commission, but the rapporteur général, Marcel Plaisant, did not adopt the wording proposed by the sub-committee and expressed the declaration in his general report in the following terms:

> Your *rapporteur général* has been entrusted with making an express mention of the possibility available to national legislation to make what are commonly called minor reservations. The Delegates of Norway, Sweden, Denmark and Finland, the Delegate of Switzerland and the Delegate of Hungary, have all mentioned these limited exemptions allowed for religious ceremonies, military bands and the needs of child and adult education. These exceptional measures apply to articles 11*bis*,

346 *Documents 1948* (1951), 255. 347 ibid.
348 Referred to in the programme: ibid. See also [1933] *DA* 112, 114.
349 *Documents 1948* (1951), 255.
350 ibid. 351 eg Germany and Poland: ibid, 260–1. 352 ibid, 128.

> 11ter, 13 and 14. You will understand that these references are just lightly pencilled in here, in order to avoid damaging the principle of the right.[353]

Although there are obvious difficulties in rendering a completely intelligible English translation of this passage from the original French, some additional aid is to be gained from the records of the general commission. These note the following:

> The majority of delegates manifested a concern that the legal situation was not substantially changed by the substitution of an exclusive and conventional right for the provision of the text of Rome under which unionists were assimilated to nationals.
>
> To obtain such a result, it sufficed for the Conference to allow that this exclusive right was not incompatible with certain exceptions provided by national laws, exceptions already allowed under the regime of Rome, for religious, cultural or patriotic purposes. The Conference declared itself in favour of this, in accordance with several governmental propositions. The delegation of Sweden, in particular, expressed the opinion that such exceptions should be extended to articles 11bis, 13 and 14, as well as to articles 11 and 11ter and requested, in the name of the Nordic Governments, that this remark be inserted in the General Report.
>
> On the proposal of the *rapporteur* of the Sub-Committee, M Walkiers, the Conference noted nevertheless that these limitations should have a restricted character and that, in particular, it did not suffice that the performance, representation or recitation was 'without the aim of profit' for it to escape the exclusive right of the author. As to the question of how the text of the Convention should be interpreted, the Conference was of the opinion that a mention of this matter should be inserted in the General Report, taking account of the view expressed, in particular that of the Swedish delegation.[354]

These minutes are of value, in that they provide a clearer context for the more compressed comments of M Plaisant. In particular, they indicate the source of the further reference to articles 11bis, 11ter, 13, and 14. This arose from the concern of the Nordic countries that proposals in their draft laws which were then in the course of preparation should not be in conflict with the Convention if they permitted the free performance or broadcasting of works for such purposes as divine worship or religious education.[355] That such exceptions were permitted in respect of these other articles was clearly endorsed by the Conference.[356] The minutes also amplify the last sentence of M Plaisant's statement, insofar as they underline the insignificant or *de minimis* nature of the use that was to be allowed. These points are taken up further below.

13.81 It is clear that the above interpretation in the Brussels report did not give rise to

[353] *Documents 1948* (1951), 100. This translation has been taken from that prepared by WIPO in their centennial volume of 1986: *The Berne Convention for the Protection of Literary and Artistic Works from 1886 to 1986* (1986), 181.

[354] ibid, 263–4. [355] ibid, 258. [356] ibid, 263–4.

any particular concern among member countries: no reference was made to it in the programme for the Stockholm Conference and no propositions concerning it were submitted by the delegates. However, in one of the last meetings of Main Committee I, the Swedish delegate, speaking on behalf of the Nordic countries, proposed that the *rapporteur* of the Committee should insert in the general report a sentence to the effect that the possibility allowed for in the general report of the Brussels Conference for the making of minor reservations was still valid.[357] This was duly done in the Stockholm report, which endorsed the remarks of M Plaisant, as well as providing a further explanatory gloss:

> 209. In the General Report of the Brussels Conference, the Rapporteur was instructed to refer explicitly, in connection with Article 11, as to the possibility of what had been agreed to call 'the minor reservations' of national legislation. Some delegates had referred to the exceptions permitted in respect of religious ceremonies, performances by military bands and the requirements of education and popularization. The exceptions also apply to Articles 11*bis*, 11*ter*, 13 and 14. The Rapporteur ended by saying that these allusions were given lightly without invalidating the principle of the right (cf. *Documents de la Conference de Bruxelles*, page 100).
>
> 210. It seems that it was not the intention of the Committee to prevent States from maintaining in their national legislation provisions based on the declaration contained in the General Report of the Brussels Conference. It accordingly seems necessary to apply to these 'minor reservations' the principle retained for exceptions to the right of translation, as indicated in connection with Article 8 (see paragraph 205).[358]

The second sentence in paragraph 209 refers to the second category of implied exceptions which apply in the case of uses of translations of works (see further paras 13.83ff below). While the latter involve somewhat different considerations than apply in the case of minor exceptions to article 11, etc, in the present context the relevant principle is that, 'on the level of general principles, . . . a commentary on the discussion [of Main Committee I] could not result in an amendment or extension of the provisions of the Convention . . .'.[359] This last is a statement of an obvious, but sometimes overlooked, truth in relation to the role of supplementary aids in the interpretation of international conventions (see further paras 5.28ff above).

(b) General comments on the scope of 'minor reservations'

If there are difficulties with interpreting the precise meaning of many of the present provisions of the Convention, there is greater difficulty in interpreting general statements of the kind given in the foregoing paragraphs. It would therefore be a mistake to subject the statements of M Plaisant or Main **13.82**

[357] *Records* 1967, 924 (minutes of Main Committee I).
[358] ibid, 1166.
[359] ibid, 1165.

Committee I to the same kind of detailed textual analysis that one would apply to the articles of the Convention itself. These statements are in no way part of the Convention, and their effect can only be to assist in defining the scope of the exclusive rights granted in articles 11, 11*bis*, 11*ter*, 13, and 14. Insofar as they represent the intentions of the delegates at the Brussels and Stockholm Conferences, and are to be found embodied in the preparatory records of those Conferences, they are a legitimate supplementary aid to the interpretation of those provisions. With this in mind, the following general comments can be made:

First, essentially, these statements are based on the *de minimis* principle of interpretation, namely that the law is not concerned with trifles. In the present context, this means that exceptions to the rights granted in the relevant articles of the Convention must be concerned with uses of minimal, or no, significance to the author. This point is emphasized in the last sentence of M Plaisant's statement ('these references are just lightly pencilled in here, in order to avoid damaging the principle of the right'); by the remark in the minutes of the Brussels general commission that these limitations should have a 'restricted character', in particular, that it did not suffice for a particular use to be made 'without the aim of profit'; and finally by the comment in the report of Main Committee I on the role of supplementary aids to interpretation of Convention provisions.

Second, the fact that both Conferences rejected the option of inserting in the Convention a provision expressly reserving the right of national legislation to make such minor exceptions also confirms these exceptions are acceptable only when they are of a *de minimis* kind. If an express provision had been inserted, this would make it far easier for member nations to assert that the Convention recognized their right to make such exceptions and that they were therefore free to go beyond those of a purely *de minimis* kind, for example, because of a particular public interest that might justify the abridgement of the authors' rights in these circumstances.

Third, is it to be presumed that the exceptions which existed in national legislation at the time of accession to either the Brussels or Stockholm Acts fall, as a matter of course, within the scope of these *de minimis* exceptions? This would appear to have been the tacit understanding of the delegates at both revision conferences, but it is submitted that the question of conflict with the requirements of the Convention cannot be answered by reference to an automatic presumption of this kind. In each case, it is the obligation of every state to ensure that its existing exceptions are actually of a *de minimis* kind. Moreover, the characterization of a use as *de minimis* may need to be re-examined in light of evolving practices and technology. Uses which once were of 'no significance' to the author may become more widespread, and thus cumulatively impact the author's exclusive rights.

Finally, the examples of uses given in the records of the Brussels and Stockholm Conferences are in no way an exhaustive list or determinative of which particular exceptions will be justified. In each case, it is possible to envisage circumstances where the use in question may substantially undermine the author's rights, for example, a general provision exempting all military bands from liability for public performances of protected works whatever the place or occasion. As noted above in the second general comment, the particular public interest that might justify the making of a specific exception under the Convention is not relevant to the general principle of construction embodied in the *de minimis* exception.

(c) Implied exceptions with respect to translation rights

The basis for this category of implied exceptions is different to that applying in the case of 'minor reservations' to performing rights and the like. There are also widely varying national interpretations as to the scope of this second category. The problem can be stated as follows. The majority of exceptions provided in the Convention relate to the right of reproduction, for example, articles 9(2), 10, and 10bis, although some of these provisions relate as well to other rights such as broadcasting. However, there are no express limitations provided in relation to the right of translation itself which is contained in article 8. On its face, this omission imposes severe restrictions on persons wishing to use literary and dramatic works protected under the Convention where these works are in other languages. While the Convention makes provision for the reproduction, in particular circumstances and for certain purposes, of such works in their original language, these exceptions are not expressed to be applicable where translations of those works are made in the same situation. This appears illogical, as the making of reproductions of works in their original language will be of little use to populations which do not speak or understand that language. Moreover, because the Conventional minima do not apply to domestic works, the works at issue here will necessarily be foreign. In many countries, that also means that the works at issue will necessarily be in a foreign language. There does not seem to be any good reason for Union members whose domestic language is a world language, such as English, French, Spanish, or Arabic, to be better situated to avail themselves of the articles 9(2), 10, and 10bis exceptions than Union members whose language is more territorially circumscribed, such as Norwegian, Thai, or Tagalog. There are two possible bases on which this result can be avoided, at least so far as exceptions to the reproduction right are concerned. **13.83**

First, it can be argued that translations are a species of reproduction, and are therefore automatically covered by any exception to the reproduction right. In other words, article 8 is merely a particular application of the broader right granted under article 9, and accordingly any exception to the latter must embrace the former. This point has already been discussed above, where it was noted that the provisions of the Convention are inconclusive as to the precise relationship between reproductions and translations (see paras 11.35ff).

Alternatively, it can be argued that, if these are to be treated as two distinct rights, the implication of parallel exceptions in relation to the making of translations is imperative for the effective operation of the Convention. Not to do so would reduce the effect of the exceptions permitted by the Convention in respect of reproduction rights, and would lead to an absurd result that cannot have been intended by the framers of the Convention and its revised Acts. Such a result could also be said to be in conflict with the fundamental nature of the Berne Union, as an international union of states with widely differing linguistic backgrounds.

13.84 These conflicting arguments leave aside the further question of whether corresponding exceptions are to be implied in respect of other uses of translations, such as broadcasts, although the second basis suggested above could just as easily be called in aid here to support such a conclusion. The question of such exceptions, however, was not directly addressed until the Stockholm Conference. No change to article 8 was proposed in the programme,[360] but the report of Main Committee I states that the starting point of the programme seemed to be:

> . . . the idea that it was fairly obvious that exceptions to the other exclusive rights, such as the right of reproduction, implied corresponding exceptions in respect of the right of translation and that the Convention had generally been applied in this way.[361]

In addition, the programme expressly noted that the right to reproduce press articles under article 9(2) of the Brussels Act included the right to reproduce them in the form of translation.[362] At the Conference, no amendments were submitted by delegates in relation to article 8 but a number of proposals concerning translations were made in relation to other articles. Thus, there was a joint proposal by Czechoslovakia, Hungary, and Poland to include the making of translations within the scope of articles 10(1) and 10*bis*(1) (formerly article 9(2)),[363] while an Indian amendment proposed an exception in respect of translations to article 2*bis*(2).[364] During the discussions in Main Committee I, there was general agreement that there was a need for some general statement of principle to be made with respect to translations, to the effect that exceptions to

[360] *Records* 1967, 110 (Document S/1). [361] ibid, 1164.

[362] ibid, 144 (Document S/1: made in relation to the proposed Protocol in Respect of Developing Countries).

[363] Document S/51: ibid, 688. [364] Document S/73: ibid, 691.

the right of reproduction should be equally applicable to the making of translations.[365] However, there were differences of opinion as to whether this should take the form of a specific amendment to article 8 or should be dealt with in the Committee's report as a matter of interpretation.[366] The task of finding a suitable wording, within the framework of article 8, was therefore remitted to the drafting committee.[367] The latter refrained from proposing a specific amendment to article 8, but after discussion advanced the following propositions for the consideration of Main Committee I:

> (1) In relation to the provisions of *Article 2bis, paragraph (2), Article 9, paragraph (3)* (the former paragraph (2) of the Brussels text), *Article 10, paragraph (1),* and *Article 10, paragraph (2),* it seems normal that the exceptions introduced into the provision for the right of reproduction should also apply to the right of translation, that is to say, should also apply to the translated version of the work.
>
> (2) In relation to *Article 9, paragraph (2)* (*new*), the problem presents certain difficulties but it would appear possible to consider that there is likewise extension to the translated version of the work only if the conditions provided in paragraph (2) are also fulfilled for that translated version.
>
> (3) In relation to *Article 10bis, Article 11bis* and *Article 13*, the question remains open, by virtue of the fact that those provisions do not refer solely to the right of reproduction but also to the right of broadcasting.[368]

These provisions gave rise to considerable discussion in Main Committee I.[369] **13.85** There was unanimous approval of the first, and it was decided that it would be sufficient to include this in the Committee's report (although some delegates would still have preferred an express amendment to article 8 in this regard).[370] As to article 9(2), it was resolved that this should be applicable to the making of translations of works so long as the conditions provided in that paragraph were satisfied, although once again there were differences as to whether this should be specified in the article itself or simply left to mention in the report.[371] In the event, the latter course was chosen, both for this provision and for article 10*^bis^*.[372] As for articles 11*^bis^* and 13, however, real divisions appeared among the delegates, and a number took the view that the compulsory licences available under both provisions should not be applicable in respect of translations of works which might be used in their original form under these licences.[373] There was a significant minority against the extension of article 11*^bis^* in this regard,[374] and the

[365] *Records* 1967, 901–2. [366] ibid. [367] ibid, 902.

[368] Document S/248: ibid, 726. [369] ibid, 921–3.

[370] eg Bulgaria, Israel, Monaco, and Tunisia were initially in favour of inclusion in the Convention: ibid, 902; cf the views of the UK and Italy that express mention in the report was enough: ibid, 922.

[371] ibid, 923. [372] ibid. [373] eg France and the UK: ibid, 923.

[374] Twenty to seven, with seven abstentions: ibid.

proposal in respect of article 13 received only the smallest possible majority of votes, with a number of abstentions.[375] This led to some difficulty as to what statements should be made in the final report in respect of both articles.[376] Finally, the following passage, based in substance on a text proposed by the French delegation, was adopted:

> 205. As regards the right of translation in cases where a work may, under the provisions of the Convention, be lawfully used without the consent of the author, a lively discussion took place in the Committee and gave rise to certain statements on the general principles of interpretation. While it was generally agreed that Articles $2^{bis}(2)$, 9(2), 10(1) and (2), and $10^{bis}(1)$ and (2), virtually imply the possibility of using the work not only in the original form but also in translation, subject to the same conditions, in particular that the use is in conformity with fair practice and that here too, as in the case of all uses of the work, the rights granted to the author under Article 6bis (moral rights) are reserved, different opinions were expressed regarding the lawful uses provided for in Articles 11bis and 13. Some delegations considered that those Articles also applied to translated works, provided the above conditions were fulfilled. Other delegations, including those of Belgium, France and Italy, considered that the wording of those Articles in the Stockholm text did not permit of the interpretation that the possibility of using a work without the consent of the author also included, in those cases, the possibility of translating it. In this connection, the said delegations pointed out, on the level of general principles, that a commentary on the discussion could not result in an amendment or extension of the provisions of the Convention (see also paragraph 210 below concerning the so-called 'minor reservations' to Articles 11, 11bis, 11ter, 13 and 14).[377]

13.86 What status does this passage have as an 'authentic interpretation' of the Convention? The following comments can be made. First, as the final sentence emphasizes, this passage cannot have the effect of amending or extending the provisions of the Convention. It can only fulfil the following functions: (i) provide confirmation that the words of a given provision have a particular meaning according to the usual principles of interpretation (the 'confirmatory function'), and (ii) act as a legitimate supplementary aid to interpretation insofar as it points to the context, object and purpose of the Convention where an interpretation arrived at under (i) results in ambiguity or obscurity, or leads to a manifestly absurd or unreasonable result (the 'explanatory function').[378] This passage carries out both functions in respect of the various articles to which it refers.

Second, if the notion that translations are a species of reproduction is accepted

---

[375] Twelve to eleven with thirteen abstentions: ibid.

[376] ibid, 923 and 926. For the text submitted by the drafting committee, see Document S/269: ibid, 735.

[377] ibid, 1165 (report). For the substantially similar French draft, see ibid, 926.

[378] See paras 5.12ff above on the general question of interpretation of treaties.

(itself a question of prior construction of the Convention), the application of the exceptions in articles 9(2) and 10(1) follows as a matter of course, as the user is only reproducing the work in a different way. This can only partially apply to articles 2*bis*(2), 10(2), and 10*bis*(1) and (2), as the latter also apply to broadcasting and cable diffusion.

Third, in the event that the above view of the nature of translations and reproductions is not adopted, the passage from the report can be used as a legitimate extrinsic aid to interpretation. Thus, if it can be said that the exclusion of translations from the exceptions provided in these articles will lead to a manifestly absurd or unreasonable result, it will be legitimate to have regard to the report as an indication of the understanding of the parties to the Convention, and hence of its context, object, and purpose. It can readily be said that this is so, as such an interpretation would render the provisions of the Convention ineffective in many countries of the Union where translation of a work is clearly necessary if full advantage is to be taken of the exceptions in these provisions (whether in respect of reproduction, broadcasting, or cable diffusion).[379] Accordingly, the unanimous view of the delegates recorded here in the report goes to show that this result was not intended, and that these exceptions are applicable in respect of the making of translations. In this regard, it is superfluous, though undoubtedly a useful reminder, to state that these exceptions apply subject to the same conditions that operate in the case of uses of the original version of a work.

Finally, the above argument, however, cannot be made with respect to the compulsory licences allowed under articles 11*bis* and 13. As regards the first, all that can be said is that no assistance is to be derived from the report as an extrinsic aid as it shows only that delegates were divided on the applicability of the provision to broadcasts of translations. In consequence, a country which desires to extend article 11*bis*(2) or (3) in this way will be hard pressed to find other extrinsic aids to justify this interpretation. The same applies to article 13, unless the view is taken that the making of a translation is only a form of reproduction, in which case the recording of a translated version of the words accompanying a musical work would be justified. If such an argument is accepted, the inconclusive views noted in the report could not be prayed in aid, as there would be no occasion to refer to them as an extrinsic aid.

The preceding paragraph shows that the Stockholm Conference may have **13.87**
been wiser to adopt a specific provision or provisions of the Convention to

[379] eg there is nothing in the '*revue de presse*' concept that suggests it is to be confined to comparing the reports or opinions of the foreign press from countries sharing a common language with the country availing itself of the exception.

deal with exceptions to translations. The basis for applying the interpretation given in its report is unclear, and is open to challenge. Thus, the relationship between reproductions and translation may be disputed (see paras 11.35ff above); likewise, the conclusion that a contrary interpretation leads to an absurd or unreasonable result justifying reference to the unanimous view of the delegates expressed in the report may also be doubted, although it may be buttressed by the consideration that the Convention applies only to foreign works, and the absence of a good reason for discriminating against countries whose languages are not 'world languages'. Above all, it may be argued that the second approach does exactly that which the last sentence of the passage of the report warns against, namely amending or extending the Convention so as to apply to translation rights exceptions which, in the Convention, are expressed to apply to other rights, including that of reproduction. These problems of uncertainty would have been avoided by the insertion, in the Convention, of provisions which reflected the intentions of the delegates as revealed both in the minutes and report of Main Committee I. The best way of doing this would have been by a specific amendment to each of the relevant provisions, as follows:

1. The addition of the words 'either in their original language or in a translated version' after the words 'communicated to the public by wire' in article $2^{bis}(2)$.
2. The insertion of an equivalent provision to article 9(2) in article 8.
3. The addition of the words 'either in its original or in a translated version' after the words 'from a work' in article 10(1) (the right of quotation).
4. The addition of the same words after the words 'of literary or artistic works' in article 10(2).
5. The addition of the words 'whether in their original language or in a translated version', after the words 'current economic, political or religious topics', and the word 'translation', before the words 'reproduction, broadcasting or such communication' in article $10^{bis}(1)$.
6. The addition of the words 'or translated' before the words 'and made available to the public' in article $10^{bis}(2)$.

These amendments would have left a gap in the case of articles 11bis and 13, as the absence of any reference to translations in either of these provisions would have clearly indicated that they were inapplicable. However, given the disagreement among the delegates over this question, such a result could scarcely be criticized. It would, after all, have been in accord with the basic aim of the Convention which is concerned with the protection of the rights of authors and not with derogations from those rights. Moreover, articles 11bis and 13 lack the didactic purposes that underlie articles 10 and 10bis, and that make local-language comprehensibility essential to those public goals. Article 9(2) is not explicitly so confined, but the conditions for application of that exception still seem more restrictive than for articles 11*bis* and 13.

(4) Other limitations on authors' rights imposed in the public interest

(a) The police power under article 17

It has long been recognized that, in particular circumstances, sovereign states have the unquestioned power to limit or deny private rights as part of their obligation to maintain 'public order'. In the context of literary and artistic works, the principal power in question here is that of censorship, and the particular circumstances are those of state security and the protection of public morals. These are, of necessity, flexible terms that have been, and are, interpreted with great variations by different states. Nonetheless, the earliest international copyright conventions expressly recognized the capacity of states to impose such controls, even where this meant an abridgement of rights otherwise granted to authors under those instruments,[380] and the Berne Convention has also contained such a provision from its inception. This is to be found in article 17, which has remained unaltered (except for minor drafting changes) since the Berne Act. It provides: **13.88**

> The provisions of this Convention cannot in any way affect the right of the Government of each country of the Union to permit, to control, or to prohibit by legislation or regulation, the circulation, presentation, or exhibition of any work or production in regard to which the competent authority may find it necessary to exercise that right.

This provision gave rise to little comment in any of the revision conferences until that of Stockholm. The question of whether it also reserved to states the right to control the exercise of authors' rights where these resulted in restrictive trade practices was canvassed at the Rome and Brussels Conferences (see paras 13.91ff below), but the general view was that it was concerned principally with matters of 'public order', rather than matters relating generally to the public interest.[381] At the Stockholm Conference, however, there was considerable debate on the provision, in the light of a UK proposal to delete the words 'to permit'.[382] The reason for this was to remove any inference that a member **13.89**

[380] See eg the Franco-Sardinian Convention of 28 Aug 1843, art 9 (J Delalain, *Recueil des Conventions conclues par la France pour la Reconnaissance de la Properiété Littéraire et Artistique* (1866) ('J Delalain (1866)'), 1); the Franco-Portuguese Convention of 12 Apr 1851, art 14 (J Delalain (1866), 13); Franco-Austro-Hungarian Convention of 11 Dec 1866, art 14 (C Lyon-Caen and P Delalain, *Lois françaises et étrangères sur la Propriété littéraire et artistique . . .* (1889), vol II, 269): see further para 1.39 above.

[381] *Actes* 1928, 254–9; *Documents 1948* (1951), 264. See further Masouyé (1978), 99, and para 13.91 below.

[382] Document S/171 in *Records* 1967, 704.

nation might, in the absence of the author's consent, authorize the circulation, presentation, or exhibition of a work or production, or to invoke the article as a justification for the imposition of compulsory licences.[383] This received the support of all delegates, except one. This was the South African delegate, who took the view that, under article 17, Union members, as sovereign states, were 'free to "permit" the dissemination of the work, even against the will of the author, if that were necessary as a matter of public policy in the country'.[384] The reasons for this view are a little hard to understand, but the South African delegate was obdurate, and this led to the defeat of the proposed amendment and the retention of article 17 in its existing form.[385] However, Main Committee I recorded in its report that the 'overwhelming majority' of the Committee interpreted article 17 in another sense, even with the inclusion of the words 'to permit'.

> This Article referred mainly to censorship: the censor had the power to control a work which it was intended to make available to the public with the consent of the author and, on the basis of that control, either to 'permit' or to 'prohibit' dissemination of the work. According to the fundamental principles of the Berne Union, countries of the Union should not be permitted to introduce any kind of compulsory licences on the basis of Article 17. In no case where the consent of the author was necessary for the dissemination of the work, according to the rules of the Convention, should it be possible for countries to permit dissemination without the consent of the author.[386]

As a matter of treaty interpretation, this must be regarded as an authentic interpretation of article 17. The words 'to permit' give rise to two differing interpretations. In such a case of ambiguity, it is therefore appropriate to have regard to extrinsic aids, and the clearly stated view of the overwhelming majority of the Committee, expressed unambiguously in its report, is clearly to be preferred to that maintained by the South African delegate.

13.90 (i) **Other matters concerning article 17:** Four other points concerning the scope of this provision should be noted. First, it was noted above that the power 'to permit, to control, or to prohibit' has been traditionally seen as concerned with state powers of censorship. The latter, however, is itself a wide concept, and may be invoked by a state for a variety of reasons, for example, to prevent obscenity and pornography, to protect national security, particularly in times of war, and as a means of regulating political and social activity. The legitimacy of some of these exercises of censorship powers will be questioned by many people, but there can be no doubt that the various member nations of the Union have

[383] Document S/171 in *Records* 1967, 907 (explanation of Mr Wallace, the British delegate) and ibid, 1174 (report).

[384] ibid, 929 (minutes of Main Committee I) and 806 (minutes of Plenary of Berne Union).

[385] ibid, 806. [386] ibid, 1174.

used them for all these purposes at various times in their history. At the Stockholm Conference, however, there was a suggestion by several delegates that the right of states referred to in article 17 was concerned primarily with matters of obscenity.[387] There is no reason to suppose that this is correct: the article refers in an unqualified way to the right 'to permit, to control, or to prohibit', and the harsh reality is that states of all political hues have frequently invoked their powers to censor literary and artistic works in circumstances quite apart from those involving questions of obscenity and public morality. There is no evidence that, so far as the Berne Convention is concerned, member states have interpreted article 17 as limiting their powers of censorship in this respect, and the same is true of the earlier bilateral conventions that contained similar provisions. At all stages through its history, the Berne Union has contained member states whose governments have exercised wide-ranging censorship powers, and this remains true today. These powers have been reserved in an unqualified way to member states by article 17, and there can be no basis for attempting to limit them on ideological or political grounds because of dislike for the particular use that is made of them by one or more countries. On the other hand, the particular interpretation given to the words 'to permit' in the report of Main Committee I above should be borne in mind: this does not give member states the power to permit the dissemination of works without the consent of the author. The power reserved under article 17 is therefore the negative one of censorship, not a general licence for governments to meet the social or political needs of their peoples at the author's expense.

Second, the words 'legislation or regulation' pose a potential limitation on the way in which the rights reserved under article 17 are to be exercised. However, these words may have different connotations in various countries. 'Legislation' generally means the laws made by the principal national legislative body, while 'regulation' may mean rules that are derived from, or based on, those laws or simply the administrative measures that are taken by governments as part of their general executive function and without any necessary legislative base. The wording used prior to the Brussels Act was even more suggestive in this regard: this referred to 'legislation or police' which indicated clearly that simple administrative decisions by police authorities were included.[388] The possibility that administrative actions were covered caused concern to the Italian delegation at the time of the Stockholm Conference, and it proposed the deletion of the words 'or regulation' on the ground that laws voted by a parliament provided much greater safeguards than regulations which could be adopted by

[387] ibid, 907 (remarks by Mr Wallace in Main Committee I).
[388] Berne, Berlin, and Rome Acts, art 17.

administrative measures.[389] In the event, this change was not made, but it appears from the minutes of Main Committee I that there was general agreement that administrative measures or regulations under article 17 should be based in national legislation.[390]

Third, the words 'circulation, presentation, or exhibition' indicate that the right reserved under article 17 does not entitle member states to cut entirely across the rights of authors. These words show rather that the article is only concerned with measures in relation to the public dissemination of protected works—the essential concern of a censorship power—and therefore only permits controls over the rights of authors insofar as they are exercised to this effect, for example, through the circulation of copies, public performance, broadcasting, and the like. Other substantive rights, such as those of reproduction, adaptation, translation, and recording are not automatically covered as these acts may be carried without any accompanying 'circulation, presentation, or exhibition'. Indeed, as the acts of circulation and exhibition are not expressly recognized by the Convention, it may be said that the reference to them in article 17 is unnecessary.[391]

Finally, the words 'any work or production' have been in the Convention since the Berne Act, but in view of the definition of literary and artistic works in article 2(1) the word 'production' adds nothing to the basic proposition that the article applies to works protected by the Convention.

(b) Limitations in respect of abuses of monopoly

13.91 At the Rome and Brussels Conferences a number of delegates expressed concern over the potential abuse of the positions of monopoly that might be committed by collecting societies in relation to performing and broadcasting rights.[392] This led to extended discussion at both conferences as to the right of states to regulate such practices, and it was generally agreed that the Convention left them free to do so.[393] Although it was suggested that this fell within article 17, there was some objection to this by the French delegation which took the view that such controls were not really related to the matters of public order that were the subject of that article.[394] The better view therefore seemed to be that, as a general principle, a Convention concerned with the protection of private rights did not interfere with the power of sovereign states to regulate matters in the

[389] Document S/226: *Records* 1967, 716; comments by Mr Ciampi, Italian delegate: ibid, 911.

[390] ibid, 911 (remarks by Professor Ulmer).

[391] Except where a member state which recognized these rights refused to accord them to authors claiming under the Convention. Such a denial would be contrary to the principle of national treatment, but would be permitted under art 17 if it were done for purposes of censorship.

[392] See *Actes* 1928, 256ff; *Documents 1948* (1951), 264.

[393] *Actes* 1928, 255–9.

[394] ibid, 256, 259.

public interest. Thus, controls over collecting societies or other abuses of authors' rights did not come into conflict with the provisions of the Convention. However, this question still caused concern to the British delegation at the Brussels Conference, and it made the following declaration in relation to article 11:

> The Government of His Majesty accepts, for the United Kingdom of Great Britain and Northern Ireland, the disposition of article 11, it being understood that the Government of His Majesty remains free to promulgate any legislation that it thinks necessary in the public interest to prevent or remedy any abuse of the exclusive rights belonging to a copyright owner by virtue of the laws of the United Kingdom. I am charged equally to say that New Zealand, whose representative is absent at this moment, has associated itself with the declaration of the United Kingdom.[395]

Apart from the New Zealand delegation, the following delegations also associated themselves with this declaration: South Africa, Switzerland, Canada, Ireland, the Netherlands, Australia, India, Pakistan, and Norway.[396] This was not a reservation to the article, as reservations were not permitted under the Brussels Act except in very limited circumstances.[397] Accordingly, this statement did not operate to limit or deny the operation of article 11,[398] but was simply a declaration of the interpretation which these delegations would apply to the article.[399] In the light of the discussions at the Rome and Brussels Conferences this seemed a perfectly correct approach to this question. Nevertheless, the British Government continued to feel some uncertainty about the effects of its declaration, particularly after the constitution of a Performing Right Tribunal under the UK Copyright Act 1956 for the purpose of regulating the activities of collecting societies in the area of performing rights.[400] Similar concern was also felt by the Australian Government in its preparatory work for a new Copyright Act, as it desired to establish an analogous tribunal with wider-ranging powers of supervision in relation to other rights such as broadcasting.[401] In fact, as regards the latter, there was probably no problem, as article 11*bis*(2) already contemplated the establishment of appropriate tribunals in respect of compulsory broadcasting licences. However, both governments thought that the legitimacy of their anti-monopoly measures should receive express sanction in the Convention, and to this end proposed amendments to article 17 at the Stockholm Revision Conference. That of the UK proposed the addition of a new paragraph leaving countries free to enact such legislation as was necessary 'to prevent or deal with

395 *Documents 1948* (1951), 82. 396 ibid. 397 Brussels Act, art 27.
398 On the effect of such declarations, see generally para 4.19 above. 399 ibid.
400 Copyright Act 1956, ss 23 and 24.
401 See generally the *Report of the Committee appointed by the Attorney-General of the Commonwealth to Consider what Alterations are Desirable to the Copyright Law of the Commonwealth* (1965), para 343.

any abuse, by persons or organisations exercising one or more of the rights in a substantial number of different copyright works, of the monopoly position they enjoy'.[402] The Australian proposal was of more general effect, reserving to each country the right to take such legislative measures as it deemed necessary to prevent abuses which might result from the exercise of the rights conferred by the Convention. However, it was further provided that such measures should not be prejudicial to the moral rights of the author or his right to obtain equitable remuneration.[403]

13.92 There was some support for these proposals, but they also attracted opposition on the basis that their insertion might provide a positive basis for states to allow uses of copyright works without the consent of the author and contrary to the rights protected under the Convention.[404] It was also argued that the amendments were really directed at matters which were not covered by the Convention in any event: nothing in the Convention was in conflict with the right of states to take anti-monopoly measures in the public interest in relation to collecting societies and the like, and the proposals in question were therefore superfluous.[405] As stated above, this had been the understanding of the delegates at both the preceding revision conferences, and, on the basis that this was still the case, the British and Australian delegates agreed to withdraw their amendments.[406] This was referred to in the report of Main Committee I in the following passage:

> 263. The Committee accepted, without opposition, the proposal of its Chairman that mention should be made in this Report of the fact that questions of public policy should always be a matter for domestic legislation and that countries of the Union would therefore be able to take all necessary measures to restrict possible abuses of monopoly. Whereupon, the proposals of Australia and the United Kingdom relating to abuse of monopoly were withdrawn.[407]

This declaration cannot be said to settle matters entirely, as the minutes of Main Committee I indicate that some states adopted different views as to the extent of measures which might be taken to prevent or control monopolistic abuses. Thus, the chairman of Main Committee I appeared to express his disapproval of the possibility that national legislation, considering that authors' royalties were excessive, might choose to treat this as an abuse and introduce compulsory licences as a remedial measure.[408] Nevertheless, in some circumstances, the fixing of excessive royalties might be the clearest possible evidence of the abuse of a position of monopoly, and the imposition of compulsory licences the most effective way of preventing this. Accordingly, the following approach seems to

[402] Document S/171: *Documents 1948* (1951), 704.
[403] Document S/215: ibid, 715.
[404] ibid, 909 (comments of Mr Rohmer, France).
[405] ibid, 910–11 (in particular, the delegates of the Netherlands, Hungary, and Austria).
[406] ibid, 911.
[407] ibid, 1175.
[408] ibid, 910.

be the correct one. Berne Union members are free to take all necessary measures to restrict possible abuses of monopoly, and this will not be in conflict with the Convention so long as this is the purpose of the measures, even if, in some instances, this means that the rights of authors are restricted. All private rights have to be exercised in accordance with the prescriptions of public law, and authors' rights are no exception to this general principle. This, therefore, would not exclude the imposition of such measures as compulsory licences or price controls where this provided the most effective way of controlling the abuse in question. However, as with any exercise of power, this would have to be the genuine purpose behind the measure, and not simply the pretext for abridging rights which states are obliged to protect under the Convention.

(5) Illustrative table of limitations and exceptions under Berne

Table 13.1 summarizes the effect of the different provisions of the Berne Convention concerned with limitations on, and exceptions to, authors' exclusive rights. **13.93**

C. Beyond

(1) Limitations and exceptions under the TRIPs Agreement

(a) TRIPs Agreement provisions referencing the Berne Convention (articles 9(1) and 3(1))

As noted in Chapter 4 above, the TRIPs Agreement is both a concise and efficiently drafted instrument, in that it incorporates a wide number of existing international obligations and treats these as a platform for its own additional requirements. In the case of the Berne Convention, article 9(1) of the TRIPs Agreement requires that members will comply with articles 1 to 21 of Berne, regardless of whether the country in question is a Berne member (this obligation does not extend to moral rights, which are protected under article 6bis of Berne). So far as limitations and exceptions to protection are concerned, the TRIPs Agreement deals with these in several places. **13.94**

(i) **Compliance with article 9(1) of the TRIPs Agreement**: Compliance with this provision obviously means that members can apply the specific limitations and exceptions that are contained in articles 1 to 21 of the Berne Convention. The scope of these provisions has been discussed above, but it is worth recalling that they are of two principal kinds: mandatory and permissive. Accordingly, under article 9(1), it will be obligatory for members to provide for exceptions for quotations under article 10(1), this being the one mandatory exception **13.95**

Table 13.1

Source	Subject matter	Justification	L, E, or CL	M or P	Rights	Conditions
2(4)	Official texts (LW)	Informatory	L	P	All	None
2(8)	News of the day and press information (LW)	Informatory	L	M	All	None
2bis(1)	Political and legal speeches (LW)	Informatory	L	P	All	None
2bis(2)	Public lectures, etc (LW)	Informatory	E	P	R, B	Informatory purpose
9(2)	General (all works)	General	E, CL	P	R	Three-step test
10(1)	Quotation (all works)	Informatory	E, CL	M	All	1. Fair practice 2. Justified by purpose
10(2)	Illustration in teaching (all works)	Educational	E, CL	P	R, B	1. Illustration 2. Fair practice
10bis(1)	Newspaper, etc articles, broadcast works (LW)	Informatory	E	P	R, B	1. No reservation 2. Indication of source
10bis(2)	Reporting current events (all works)	Informatory	E	P	Photos, cine, B	Informatory purpose
11bis(2)	Broadcasting (all works)	Public access	CL	P	B	1. Equitable remuneration 2. Moral rights respected
11bis(3)	Ephemeral recording (music and words)	Convenience, archival preservation	E, CL	P	R	1. Must be 'ephemeral' 2. Exceptional documentary character' (archival)
13(1)	Recording of music and words	New industry	CL	P	R	1. Already recorded 2. Equitable remuneration
14bis(2)(b)	Cine works—co-authors (limited)	Convenience	E	P	R, B, PP	No contrary stipulation

17	Censorship (all works)	State power	L	P	All rights	Must be for censorship reasons, none other
Implied/ancillary agreement between member states	Minor reservations	*De minimis*	E	P	PP, B, PR	*De minimis*
Implied/ancillary agreement between member states	Translations	Necessity	E	P	R, PP, PR, B (not arts 11bis, 13)	Those applicable under arts 2bis, 9(2), 10 and 10bis
Implied/ancillary agreement between member states	Anti-monopoly controls (all works)	State power	L	P	All rights	Must be for anti-trust reasons, none other

Abbreviations
LW = literary works
E = exceptions
L = limitations
CL = compulsory licence
R = reproduction
B = all rights under art $11^{bis}(1)$
PP = public performance
PR = public recitation
P = permissive
M = mandatory

under Berne. With respect to the others, there is no compulsion for any of these limitations or exceptions to be recognized, but, if they are, then the conditions contained in the relevant Berne articles will need to be observed.

13.96 **(ii) As part of the national treatment requirement under article 3(1) of the TRIPs Agreement:** A further reference to 'exceptions' appears in article 3(1) of the TRIPs Agreement which is the national treatment provision of that instrument. Pursuant to this, members must accord to nationals of other members treatment no less favourable than they accord to their own nationals, 'subject to the exceptions already provided in, respectively, . . . the Berne Convention (1971) . . .'. This confirms more explicitly that members can apply those exceptions allowed for under the Berne Convention, so far as foreigners claiming protection under the TRIPs Agreement are concerned.

(b) As a specific TRIPs obligation under article 13 of the TRIPs Agreement

13.97 The above provisions relate back to those of the incorporated instrument (the Berne Convention) and therefore take their colour from that instrument. However, article 13 of the TRIPs Agreement contains a free-standing TRIPs obligation in relation to limitations and exceptions that purports to apply a general formula or template. This adopts the language, slightly modified, of the three-step test in article 9(2) of the Berne Convention and provides as follows:

> Members shall confine limitations and exceptions to exclusive rights to certain special cases which do not conflict with a normal exploitation of the work and do not unreasonably prejudice the legitimate interests of the right holder.

This has to be interpreted as part of the TRIPs Agreement, rather than as part of Berne, and its sphere of operation needs more detailed examination.

13.98 **(i) 'Works' to which article 13 applies:** A starting point here is a consideration of the subject matter to which the article applies. It can be assumed that the reference to the 'work' in article 13 is a reference to any work that is required, by virtue of article 9(1) of the TRIPs Agreement to be protected because it is a work to which articles 1 to 21 of the Berne Convention apply. This raises an interesting question with respect to two categories of subject matter, the status of which under Berne may not have been entirely clear, namely computer programs and compilations. The first of these is not mentioned specifically in the illustrative list of works that appears in article 2(1) of Berne, while article 2(5) appears only to require protection of collections of literary or artistic works 'which, by reason of the selection and arrangement of their contents, constitute intellectual creations' and does not refer to compilations of data or other material which are not literary or artistic works. These subject matter are, of course, the subject of specific obligations under article 10(1) and (2) of the TRIPs Agreement respectively, although the nature of these obligations differs somewhat: in the case of computer programs, article 10(1) requires that these are to be protected as 'literary works under the Berne Convention', while the obligation under article 10(2) is less precise, requiring only that compilations of data and material that constitute intellectual creations are to be protected 'as such'. The effect of article 13 on these categories of subject matter therefore needs to be considered carefully.

(ii) Computer programs: As these are not specifically referred to in article 2(1) of the Berne Convention, there must be some uncertainty as to whether there is an obligation as between Berne members to protect this category, although it is clearly arguable that this is the case as they fall within the general description in article 2(1) of a 'production in the literary, scientific and artistic domain, whatever may be the mode or form of its expression'. Leaving aside this debate for present purposes, there can be no doubt that article 10(1) requires members of the TRIPs Agreement, whether or not they are Berne members, to protect computer programs as literary works within Berne. It must therefore follow that these members are obliged, by virtue of article 9(1) of TRIPs to apply articles 1 to 21 of Berne to this subject matter in the same way as they do to any other subject matter that falls within the description 'literary or artistic work'. However, the non-derogation clause in article 2(2) of Berne will only apply here in cases where Berne members of the TRIPs Agreement do regard themselves as obliged under Berne to protect computer programs. If not, it would be arguable that there will be no limitations on the application of article 13 of the TRIPs Agreement on the basis that any greater exception or limitation that might be permitted under this provision (see above) will not involve any breach of article 2(2) of TRIPs. Such countries (and there may only be a few of them) would therefore be able to apply article 13 and the three-step test without having to concern themselves with whether they were stepping outside the limitations and exceptions contained in articles 1 to 21 of Berne. **13.99**

(iii) Compilations of factual and other material: As noted above, the wording of article 10(2) of the TRIPs Agreement is far less precise than that of article 10(1): the obligation is to protect such compilations 'as such' (as intellectual creations) but there is no specific reference to article 2(5) of Berne or even to Berne in general. To the extent that compilations of this kind fall outside the scope of article 2(5) (and article 2(1)) of the Berne Convention, article 10(2) appears to be a free-standing TRIPs-only obligation. This raises interesting questions to which there is no clear answer: if these compilations are not assimilated to collections under article 2(5) of the Berne Convention, how can there be any obligation to apply articles 1 to 21 of Berne to them? The requirement under article 10(2) to accord protection 'as such' is then quite open-ended and, subject to the requirement to accord national treatment, by virtue of article 3(1) of the TRIPs Agreement, TRIPs members would be free to fix the level of **13.100**

protection for such compilations as they see fit. In this regard, article 13 would have no operation, as the only exclusive right in respect of which that provision could apply would be the rental right under article 11 which does not apply to compilations, in any event.

13.101 (iv) **Exclusive rights to which article 13 applies:** The reference to 'exclusive rights' is somewhat ambiguous: is the provision limited to those rights that must be protected under the TRIPs Agreement itself, or does it also apply to the exclusive rights under articles 1 to 21 of the Berne Convention that TRIPs members are obliged to protect by virtue of article 9(1) of the TRIPs Agreement? Under the first of these interpretations, article 13 would have a very limited sphere of application, as the only non-Berne exclusive right required to be protected under the TRIPs Agreement is the rental right, which applies only in limited cases (computer programs and cinematographic works).[409] However, as article 9(1) of the TRIPs Agreement requires members to comply with articles 1 to 21 of Berne (other than article 6*bis*), the better view must be that article 13 applies to all the exclusive rights listed in Berne, including that of reproduction, as well as the rental right in TRIPs.[410] The question of whether the three-step test in article 13 is compatible with the more specific Berne exceptions and limitations, as well as with the three-step test in article 9(2) of the Berne Convention itself, is considered below (see paras 13.105ff).

13.102 (v) **Relevant factors to the interpretation of article 13:** The interpretations of the three-step test in relation to article 9(2) of Berne are clearly relevant to article 13, if only because of the close identity of language and subject matter. At the same time, there are specific features of the TRIPs Agreement that suggest that the individual components of the three-step test in article 13 should bear a different nuance or emphasis, although ultimately these differences may be more apparent than real. Thus, the following five matters should be noted.

First, the TRIPs Agreement is a trade agreement, and is concerned with removing barriers to trade among member countries, in this case with respect to trade in intellectual property rights (IPRs), including copyright. Thus, the need to have effective protection of IPRs is put squarely at the beginning of the preamble of the Agreement, along with the declaration that 'intellectual property rights are private property rights'. This suggests that, as with the Berne Convention, the TRIPs Agreement is concerned with maximizing the protection of IPRs and that a 'maximalist' pro-rights interpretation should be taken, wherever

[409] See generally, TRIPs Agreement, art 11.

[410] This was the interpretation taken by the WTO panel in relation to the 'homestyle' and business exemption under section 110(5) of the Copyright Act 1976, Report of the Panel, 15 June 2000, document WT/DS/160/R, 30.

necessary (moral rights being the one area where protection is not required under the TRIPs Agreement).

The second matter to note is that the preamble to the TRIPs Agreement, however, is broader than this, and contains other objectives that need to be taken into account. Among other things, these include recognition of 'the underlying public policy objectives of national systems for the protection of intellectual property, including developmental and technological objectives'. More specifically, articles 7 and 8 point to other factors that member states are to take into account in implementing their TRIPs obligations. Thus, article 7 is headed 'Objectives' and provides:

> The protection and enforcement of intellectual property rights should contribute to the promotion of technological innovation and to the transfer and dissemination of technology, to the mutual advantage of producers and users of technological knowledge, and in a manner conducive to social and economic welfare, and to a balance of rights and obligations.

Third, article 8(1) then provides that member states may, in formulating or amending their laws and regulations, adopt 'measures necessary to protect public health and nutrition, and to promote the public interest in sectors of vital importance to their socio-economic and technological development, provided that such measures are consistent with the provisions of this Agreement'. Article 8(2) allows further for 'appropriate measures . . . consistent with the provisions of this Agreement' that may be needed to prevent the abuse of IPRs or 'practices which unreasonably restrain trade or adversely affect the international transfer of technology'. It is clear from these provisions that, when interpreting provisions of the TRIPs Agreement in their context and in the light of its object and purpose,[411] it will be necessary, to adopt a more balanced approach that weighs the interests of rights holders against other competing public interests, such as educational and developmental concerns. In other words, it would be mistaken to adopt the maximalist pro-rights view referred to under the first matter noted above.

The fourth matter to note is that the TRIPs Agreement also has a number of provisions that deal specifically with its relationship to the Berne Convention, and these, in turn, modify the application of the 'balanced' approach outlined under the matter noted above. Thus, article 2(2) of the TRIPs Agreement provides that 'nothing in Parts I to IV of this Agreement shall derogate from existing obligations that Members may have towards each other under . . . the Berne Convention'. Thus, to the extent that article 13 of the TRIPs Agreement

[411] As required under the rules of treaty interpretation at customary international law: TRIPs is not an agreement that is covered by the Vienna Convention.

might permit further limitations or exceptions to the exclusive rights protected under the Berne Convention than are presently allowed under that text, article 2(2) of the TRIPs Agreement would require that article 13 should not be applied in this way, as that would represent a derogation from these rights. This would be so, even though application of article 13 might otherwise permit a more generous range of exceptions because of the balancing process referred to under the third matter noted above. Article 2(2) only operates as between Berne members, but given the near universal membership of Berne this will cover virtually all states that are also parties to the TRIPs Agreement.[412] Support for this limiting approach is also to be found in article 30(2) of the Vienna Convention, which provides that when a treaty specifies that it is 'subject to, or that it is not to be considered as incompatible with', an earlier or later treaty on the same subject matter, the provisions of that other treaty prevail.[413]

Finally, a further limiting factor is to be found in article 20 of the Berne Convention, which is incorporated into TRIPs by virtue of article 9(1) of that Agreement. This provides that Berne members can make 'special agreements among themselves' insofar as such agreements grant to authors 'more extensive rights than those granted by the Convention or contain other provisions not contrary to this Convention'. On the basis that TRIPs is such a 'special agreement', the second limb of article 20 is particularly relevant in the case of limitations and exceptions to exclusive rights other than the reproduction right. As Professor Goldstein has noted, it has the consequence that article 13 of the TRIPs Agreement cannot be regarded as providing Berne members with 'a general charter for imposing such limitations on rights other than the reproduction right' and cannot therefore be used 'to justify derogation of any minimum right established by Berne'.[414] Thus, exceptions to any of the rights protected under Berne (apart from that of reproduction) will need to find a basis under that Convention, rather than in the general language of article 13 of the TRIPs Agreement.

[412] As at 17 Jan 2005, 159 nations had ratified the Berne Convention as at 31 May 2001, as at 16 February 2005 there were 148 members of the WTO: information available from www.wipo.org and www.wto.org. There are some notable absences, however, at present from WTO membership from countries that are Berne members, notably the Russian Federation.

[413] However, as the Vienna Convention does not appear to apply to the TRIPs Agreement (see para 5.15 above), art 30(2) could not itself be directly relied upon for this conclusion. Furthermore, it seems generally that art 30 of the Vienna Convention, unlike arts 31 and 32, is not a codification of the relevant customary rules of international law, but rather is a statement of residuary rules that may be applied by states when faced with competing successive treaty obligations: I Sinclair, *The Vienna Convention on the Law of Treaties*, 2nd edn (1984), 94–8. Given that the language of art 2(2) of the TRIPs Agreement is reasonably clear in its intent, it is unnecessary to consider what the situation would be, in the absence of such a provision.

[414] Goldstein (n 44 above), 295.

(vi) The scope of application for article 13: In the light of article 2(2) of the TRIPs Agreement and article 20 of the Berne Convention, it does not seem possible to argue for any wider application of the three-step test under article 13 of TRIPs than would otherwise be allowed under the Berne Convention. What sphere of operation does article 13 therefore have as a substantive provision of the TRIPs Agreement? It is necessary to examine this question in relation to the different exclusive rights to which article 13 may be applied. **13.103**

(c) The exclusive reproduction right and article 9(2) of Berne

As noted above, the exclusive reproduction right protected under article 9(1) of the Berne Convention must also be protected under TRIPs by virtue of article 9(1) of that Agreement. In this regard, with one qualification discussed below, the three-step test in article 13 of the TRIPs Agreement simply replicates the three-step test in article 9(2) of Berne. To the extent that the differing objectives of TRIPs might allow for a more generous interpretation of the various components of the three-step test, the non-derogation clause in article 2(2) of TRIPs and article 20 of Berne do not allow for this. However, one qualification to this is found in the wording of the last of the three steps outlined in article 13, namely that the exception or limitation in question must 'not unreasonably prejudice the legitimate interests of the right holder'. By contrast, in article 9(2) of Berne, the reference is to the 'author'. While 'authors' and 'right holders' may frequently be the same persons, in many cases this will not be so, and this may therefore lead to a significant difference in the application of the third step. It was suggested above that the 'legitimate interests' of authors include non-monetary (moral) interests as well as monetary ones (see para 13.24 above). On the other hand, right holders who are not authors will not have moral rights concerns to be protected. Accordingly, it would be possible for an exception to the reproduction right that was allowable under article 13 to contravene article 9(2) if, for example, it did not require attribution of authorship or it contravened the right of integrity, and these represented an unreasonable prejudice to the author's legitimate interests. While not a contravention of article 13 *simpliciter*, this would clearly be a derogation from existing obligations under Berne (article 2(2) of TRIPs) and therefore, on the face of it, not allowable. However, article 2(2) would have to be read here subject to a specific provision concerning moral rights that appears in article 9(1) of the TRIPs Agreement. Thus, the latter provides that members do not have rights or obligations under this Agreement with respect to the rights conferred under article 6bis of Berne or of the 'rights derived therefrom'. In such a case there would be a breach of Berne (if the country in question was a member of that Convention), but not of article 13 of TRIPs. This, in turn, would mean that the dispute-resolution procedures under **13.104**

TRIPs would not be available to a country that wished to complain of the breach.[415]

(d) Other exclusive rights and exceptions

13.105 As noted above, article 13 of the TRIPs Agreement applies to other 'exclusive rights' apart from reproduction that are protected under articles 1 to 21 of Berne, namely translation (article 8), public performance (article 11), broadcasting and other communications (article 11*bis*), public recitation (article 11*ter*), and adaptation (article 12). It also applies to rights that are protected expressly under the TRIPs Agreement itself, in this instance the limited rental right under article 11. In addition, it must be read together with the other limitations and exceptions allowed under Berne, some of which apply to reproduction as well as other exclusive rights. Each of these matters requires separate attention.

(e) Rights under the TRIPs Agreement

13.106 In the case of the rental right (and any other exclusive right that may be added to subsequent versions of TRIPs), article 13 will allow the making of exceptions or limitations in accordance with the three-step test, without the need to refer to any qualifications that may arise because of the incorporation of articles 1 to 21 of Berne standards pursuant to article 9(1). As a stand-alone TRIPs provision, it would therefore be open to a national legislature to allow for a more generous range of exceptions to this right on the basis that the TRIPs Agreement, to a greater extent than Berne, allows weight to be given to social goals adverse to the interests of right holders.

(f) Rights and exceptions under Berne (other than article 9(2))

13.107 It is tempting to argue here that article 13 allows member states to enact similar exceptions based on the three-step test alone, but this cannot be done without reference to the non-derogation article 2(2) of the TRIPs Agreement and article 20 of the Berne Convention (see para 13.99 above). Thus, any exceptions or limitations in relation to these rights will need to be consistent with what is already allowed under articles 1 to 21 of Berne. As seen above, there are already established exceptions under these provisions, for example, the specific teaching and news reporting exceptions in articles 10 and 10*bis*, the restrictions on broadcasting and other communication rights that are permitted under article 11*bis*(2), and the 'minor exceptions' or 'minor reservations' that have been

[415] A possible argument against this is to say that such an exception, albeit allowable under art 13, would nonetheless fall foul of art 20 of Berne which is incorporated into TRIPs via art 9(1) of that Agreement. Thus, to the extent that the provision was contrary to art 6*bis* of Berne, this would also represent a breach of art 9(1) of TRIPs. But such a reading of art 20 would seem to run directly against the clear intent of art 9(1), which specifically excludes moral rights from the ambit of TRIPs and cannot be correct.

implied into the text of the Convention with respect to performing, recitation, and broadcasting rights. The proper scope of these exceptions, particularly the implied minor exceptions, is not always clear, as they do not expressly rely on the same kinds of criteria that are contained in article 9(2) of Berne and some, such as article 11*bis*(2), expressly contemplate that the usage in question can take place on the payment of remuneration. In the case of the minor exceptions, it might also be possible to argue that they are not incorporated into the TRIPs Agreement via article 9(1) of that instrument as they are not part of the actual text of articles 1 to 21 of Berne, but come into that text as 'ancillary agreements' by virtue of article 31(2)(a) of the Vienna Convention. In this regard, however, it should be noted that the WTO panel on the US 'homestyle' and business exemptions was called on directly to consider this question, and reached the view that the incorporation in article 9(1) of the TRIPs Agreement also included the applicable interpretations and agreements that had been made under the Berne text by successive revision conferences, that is, the Berne *acquis* rather than just the Berne provisions *simpliciter*. Accepting this to be so, any exception under the national law of a Berne country that is also a member of TRIPs will need to be consistent with the express and implied exceptions provided for in Berne if it is not to fall foul of the non-derogation provision of article 2(2) of TRIPs.[416]

Does article 13, then, add anything further with respect to existing limitations and exceptions that are allowable under articles 1 to 21 of the Berne Convention? In answering this, it is useful to distinguish between two extremes: **13.108**

- *Provisions that extend the scope of existing Berne limitations and exceptions, even though otherwise sustainable under article 13 of TRIPs*: As already noted, it must follow that such provisions will be unacceptable because they will place Berne members in breach of article 2(2) of the TRIPs Agreement. A more general principle of treaty interpretation may be prayed in aid here, namely that of *lex specialis legi geneali derogat*: as both texts were adopted at the same time, it cannot be supposed that the more general (article 13) was intended to replace the more specific (the particular Berne limitation or exception in question).
- *Provisions that restrict the scope of existing Berne limitations and exceptions*: The reason for this might be that, in a given case, the three-step requirement in article 13 of the TRIPs Agreement provides a more rigorous set of criteria. In principle, it might be said that there is nothing wrong with requiring members to comply with both sets of requirements, as restricting

[416] Professor Goldstein also suggests that this would put the country in question in breach of art 20 of Berne: Goldstein (n 44 / n 414 above), 295.

the scope of an exception or limitation under Berne can hardly be in derogation of Berne members' obligations towards each other under article 2(2). Again, as both sets of provisions were adopted at the same time, it can be assumed that the contracting states intended to be bound by both. This, of course, assumes that there is consistency between them, a point which is taken up below.

13.109 Neat as this dichotomy may appear, it is far from easy to apply it to the specific limitations and exceptions that are contained in the Berne Convention and its ancillary or subsequent interpretative agreements (the 'Berne *acquis*'). This is because the language in which these limitations and exceptions is couched is generally different from that of the three-step test in article 13, and it is therefore difficult, if not impossible, to determine whether these differing criteria are, in effect, the same or whether one extends beyond the other or is more restricted. This point needs further examination.

13.110 **(i) Berne provisions that effectively overlap with article 13:** Some of the specific exceptions contained in the Berne Convention appear to meet the three-step criteria in any event. Thus, it has been suggested above that, in the case of article 10(1) and (2), the references to being 'compatible with fair practice' may correspond to the second and third steps of the three-step test, while the limited scope of those provisions undoubtedly brings them within criteria contained in the first step (see further paras 13.41 and 13.45 above). Accordingly, the requirements of both these provisions and article 13 of the TRIPs Agreement will overlap for all practical purposes, and no issue of conflict arises. There is an interesting question, however, that arises with respect to the obligation under article 10(3) of Berne to identify the source and authorship of the work that is used under article 10(1) or (2). Is this a 'right conferred under article $6^{bis}(1)$ of [the Berne] Convention' or a right 'derived therefrom', and therefore excluded from the TRIPs Agreement under article 9(1) thereof? Accordingly, will a failure to identify source and authorship be exempted from the requirements of TRIPs compliance or will it nonetheless be caught? No reference is made to 'moral rights' in article 10(3) (by contrast with article $11^{bis}(2)$; see below), and this appears to stand as a separate requirement, quite apart from article 6bis. Furthermore, the requirement to identify the source of the work is distinct from that of identifying the author. Accordingly, it is submitted that both requirements in article 10(3) need to be complied with for the purposes of the TRIPs Agreement. (See the discussion earlier at paras 10.41 and 10.44 above.)

13.111 **(ii) Berne provisions that are silent on the requirements of article 13:** It is less clear that such equivalences exist in the cases of article $10^{bis}(1)$ and (2), although these provisions contain their own internal conditions for their application, for example, lack of express reservation of rights in the case of paragraph

(1) and 'informatory purpose' in the case of paragraph (2). In either instance, however, it might be possible that a provision of national law that meets these conditions will fail to comply with the three-step criteria in article 13, notably the second and third. These are not instances of inconsistency (see below), but rather instances where the provisions in question simply make no explicit reference to the kind of factors contained in the three-step test. As suggested above, the fact that both provisions were adopted at the same time as part of the TRIPs Agreement indicates that both are to be applied cumulatively, and that an exception that is made under national law will need to comply with both articles (this will only be of relevance for TRIPs compliance, not compliance under Berne).

(iii) Berne provisions that are inconsistent with article 13: It is also possible that the requirements for a Berne exception or limitation are quite different from those in article 13 of the TRIPs Agreement and cannot therefore logically be applied together. An example is article 11*bis*(2) of Berne, which allows the imposition of 'conditions' on the exercise of exclusive rights under article 11*bis*(1), subject to protection of the author's moral rights and the right to receive equitable remuneration. In the 'homestyle' case it was submitted by the EC that compliance with both article 11*bis*(2) and article 13 was required, but the panel disagreed, on the basis that article 11*bis*(2) and article 13 covered 'different situations': **13.112**

> On the one hand, Article 11*bis* (2) authorizes Members to determine the conditions under which the rights conferred by Article 11*bis* (1)(i)–(iii) may be exercised. The imposition of such conditions may completely replace the free exercise of the exclusive right of authorizing the use of the rights embodied in subparagraphs (i)–(iii) provided that equitable remuneration and the author's moral rights are not prejudiced. However, unlike Article 13 of the TRIPS Agreement, Article 11*bis* (2) of the Berne Convention (1971) would not in any case justify use free of charge.[417]

Accordingly, this is an instance where article 13 of the TRIPs Agreement might justify a free-use exception to the rights protected under article 11*bis*(1) of Berne but where it would be necessary to have equitable remuneration by virtue of article 11*bis*(2). This would clearly be a result that would breach article 2(2) of the TRIPs Agreement and cannot have been intended by the drafters of that instrument. In this case, therefore, article 11*bis*(2) should be applied on its own, without reference to article 13, and it would also be possible to pray in aid the maxim *lex specialis legi geneali derogat.* On the other hand, it could not be argued that the obligation about moral rights under article 11*bis*(2) could be required as a TRIPs obligation, in view of article 9(2) of that instrument (see the discussion

[417] WTO Report (n 410 above), para 6.87.

above with respect to article 10(3) of Berne) as the reference to moral rights in article 11bis(2) is quite explicit.

13.113 (iv) **Application of article 13 to Berne *acquis*, in particular the minor reservations doctrine:** As noted above, the WTO panel took the view that the obligations of TRIPs members under article 9(1) extended to what may be called the Berne *acquis*, that is, any agreements made at the time of adoption of the Convention or subsequently on the interpretation of various Berne provisions. One such agreement is clearly the 'minor reservations' doctrine which has been discussed above. This was held to be relevant in the 'homestyle' case, because the panel took the view that article 11bis(2) was inapplicable in the absence of a requirement to pay remuneration under the US provision in dispute. Accordingly, the latter could only be justified, if at all, under the minor reservations doctrine, and, in applying this, the panel concluded that article 13 of the TRIPs Agreement had a very positive role to play in articulating and defining the criteria that should apply in the case of minor exceptions. It was by this route that the panel then came to apply the three-step test to US 'homestyle' and business exemptions to broadcasting and public performance rights, which it found had not been met.[418]

13.114 Without questioning the appropriateness of the panel's ultimate decision in this case, it must be queried whether it was correct to apply the three-step test under article 13 as part of the minor reservations doctrine. As noted above, the contours of this doctrine are far from precise, but central to it is the notion that a minor reservation must be of *de minimis* character. By definition, this will mean something that is clearly defined and limited in scope (step 1), does not conflict with a normal exploitation of the work (step 2), and does not unreasonably prejudice the legitimate interests of the rights holder (step 3). But it is possible to imagine exceptions that are not *de minimis* but that still meet the requirements of the three-step test. For example, as suggested above, there may be non-economic normative considerations that will take a use through the second step on the balancing approach suggested there; there may even be such uses that do not unreasonably prejudice the legitimate interests of the rights holder because remuneration is paid or other conditions are imposed. Indeed, as a general proposition it might be said that the three-step test is concerned with uses that are more than *de minimis* and which therefore require testing for compliance with its requirements: *de minimis* uses are therefore only a subset of what article 13 may allow. In this regard, the WTO panel's decision may go too far: while on any view the disputed US provision failed the three-step test conclusively, the

[418] WTO Report (n 410 above), 29–30.

implication should not be drawn from the decision that any exception that satisfies the three steps is within the minor reservations doctrine and therefore allowable (assuming that it does not otherwise fall under other exceptions allowed by Berne). If the application of the three-step test under article 13 could be used in this way to justify wider exceptions than are permissible under the minor reservations doctrine or any other specific Berne exception, this would represent a derogation from their obligations *inter se* by Berne members who are members of the TRIPs Agreement.

Does a similar problem arise with the other important part of Berne *acquis*, namely the rule implying parallel exceptions in relation to translations of protected works? These operate subject to the same exceptions and conditions that apply to uses of such works in their original languages, and will therefore fall to be tested in the same way as those exceptions: see here the analyses under the preceding three subheadings. **13.115**

(g) Illustrative table of the relationship between article 13 of the TRIPs Agreement and Berne (see Table 13.2 overleaf)

(2) Limitations and exceptions under the WIPO Copyright Treaty

The WCT deals with these in two ways, both of which incorporate and apply the three-step test contained in article 9(2) of the Berne Convention. The first occurs indirectly under article 1(4), while the second is done explicitly under article 10. These provisions need to be considered separately. **13.116**

(a) WCT provisions referencing Berne

(i) Under article 1(4): This provision applies directly to the reproduction right, as it requires contracting parties to comply with articles 1 to 21 and the Appendix of the Berne Convention. Accordingly, if a contracting party is not a member of Berne (now an increasingly unlikely circumstance), it still has to apply the three-step test exceptions to the reproduction right by virtue of article 9(2) of Berne. More problematic, however, is the effect of an 'agreed statement' to article 1(4) of the WCT which was adopted by the 1996 Diplomatic Conference at the time of adopting the text of the WCT itself. This provides for a possible extension of the operation of article 9(1) and (2) through the adoption of the following interpretation: **13.117**

> The reproduction right, as set out in Article 9 of the Berne Convention, and the exceptions permitted thereunder, apply fully in the digital environment, in particular to the use of works in digital form. It is understood that the storage of a protected work in digital form in an electronic medium constitutes a reproduction within the meaning of Article 9 of the Berne Convention.

Table 13.2

Rights under the TRIPs Agreement	**Rights under Berne**	**Berne E & L: coterminous**	**Berne E & L: cumulative**	**Berne E & L: inapplicable**	**Subject matter: compilations of data**	**Application in the digital environment**
Article 11 (rental)	Articles 8, 9, 11, 11bis, 11ter, 13, 14 (not article 6bis)	Article 10	Article 10bis	Articles 11bis, 13, minor reservations	TRIPs, article 10(2)	Not dealt with specifically
*TRIPs three-step test applies *simpliciter*		TRIPs three-step test applies—covers same ground	TRIPs three-step test *plus* specific conditions of article in question	TRIPs three-step test does not apply	TRIPs three-step test alone applies	

Abbreviations
E & L = Exceptions and Limitations
* The reference to TRIPs three-step test means that: (i) moral rights considerations are excluded from the third step, and (ii) a more balanced approach to normative considerations under both the second and third steps may be required.

On its face, this statement appears to remove any doubts that might otherwise exist as to whether the reproduction right under article 9(1) of the Berne Convention, and the exceptions permitted under article 9(2), apply to digital/electronic usages. It is far from clear whether such an interpretation was required in view of wording of article 9(1) in any event, namely as the 'exclusive right of authorizing the reproduction of . . . works, in any manner or form'. However, as article 9(1) was adopted some years before the development of digital technology, it was presumably thought that it was now necessary, or at least useful, to spell out the scope of the reproduction right more clearly. Thus, the Basic Proposal for the WCT had proposed a specific article on reproduction to be included in the WCT.[419] This declared that the exclusive right in article 9(1) of Berne included 'direct and indirect reproduction . . ., whether permanent or temporary, in any manner or form'. There was much debate about the need for this article at the 1996 Diplomatic Conference (in Main Committee I), as well as over a further proposal concerning the possibility of limitations on the reproduction right in the case of temporary reproductions made for the 'sole purpose of making the work perceptible or where the reproduction is of a transient or incidental nature, provided that such reproduction takes place in the course of use of the work that is authorized by the author or permitted by law'.[420] While there seemed to be general support for the first part of this proposed article, delegates had differing views about the meaning and scope of the second part, particularly in the light of their own national laws.[421] It was therefore ultimately decided that it would be preferable to leave these matters to be dealt with under the existing article 9 of Berne, but supplemented or elaborated upon by an 'agreed statement' in the terms set out above. (See also paras 11.69ff above.) The significance of the statement, in terms of international law, needs to be considered in three contexts: first, as a possible agreement between the parties at the Diplomatic Conference with respect to the interpretation and application of a provision of the WCT (article 1(4)); secondly, as a possible subsequent agreement between Berne Convention members as to the interpretation and application of a provision of that Convention (article 9); and thirdly, as a possible subsequent agreement between TRIPs members as to the interpretation and application of an incorporated provision of that Agreement (article 9 of Berne).

(ii) As part of the WCT: As an agreement relating to a provision of the Treaty (article 1(4)) that was made between the parties in connection with the **13.118**

[419] WIPO, *Records of the Diplomatic Conference on Certain Copyright and Neighboring Rights Questions, Geneva 1996* (1999) ('*Records* 1996'), vol I, 189 (this was to be art 7(1) of the WCT).
[420] ibid.
[421] See, in particular, the summary of the first debate on this draft article in Main Committee I by the chairman at *Records* 1996, 674–5.

conclusion of that Treaty, this is part of the 'context' of the Treaty (pursuant to article 31(2)(a) of the Vienna Convention). It can therefore be used as a guide by WCT members in their interpretation and application of their obligation under article 1(4) of the WCT to comply with articles 1 to 21 of the Berne Convention (including article 9). In other words, quite apart from any obligation that such states might have under the Berne Convention itself, membership of the WCT will require the interpretation of article 9 of Berne as incorporated into the WCT, in accordance with terms of the agreed statement.

13.119 The only difficulty with this interpretation of the agreed statement is that article 31(2)(a) of the Vienna Convention requires that such an agreement should be 'be made between all the parties in connexion with the conclusion of the treaty', and this was not the case with the agreed statement to article 1(4). Thus, the *Conference Records* explicitly note that the statement was adopted by majority vote, rather than by consensus (fifty-one votes in favour, five against, and with thirty abstentions[422]). It appears that the minority was concerned by the second sentence of the statement relating to electronic storage. While there was 'consensus' during the discussions of Main Committee I with respect to the first sentence,[423] this was not the case with respect to the second. In the plenary session of the Conference, however, the statement was voted on as a whole, meaning that it cannot therefore be said that either the first or second sentence was agreed to 'between all the parties' within the terms of article 31(2)(a) of the Vienna Convention. This lack of unanimity therefore reduces the significance of both sentences of the agreed statement as an aid to the interpretation of WCT obligations under article 1(4) with respect to article 9(1) and (2) of the Berne Convention.[424] This point was made by several delegates during the discussions in Main Committee,[425] and, while the majority of delegates (led by the USA) pushed for a vote to be taken on the issue, it is unclear what they thought that this would achieve. Article 31(2)(a) of the Vienna Convention is quite definite on the need for unanimity, and it would hardly be open to delegates at a diplomatic conference unilaterally to vary its terms, so as to allow a majority vote to have the same status as one reached by consensus. As a matter of treaty interpretation, the relevance of the agreed statement will have to be under article 32, as a supplementary means of interpretation where an interpretation according to article 31 leaves the meaning ambiguous or obscure or leads to a manifestly absurd or unreasonable result. In this regard, the majority agreed statement

[422] *Records* 1996, 628. [423] ibid, 784–98. [424] ibid, 628–9.
[425] ibid, 789 (delegate of Cote d'Ivoire), 791–2 (delegate of the Philippines)

could clearly be regarded as forming part of 'the circumstances of [the treaty's] conclusion'.[426]

The argument in the preceding paragraph about the correct application of article 31(2)(a) of the Vienna Convention is by no means accepted by all commentators on the WCT or even by the WIPO Secretariat itself. Thus, Dr Ficsor, in his commentary on the Internet Treaties, argues that majority acceptance of an agreed statement should be enough in view of the two-thirds majority rule that applies with respect to the adoption of the text of a treaty under article 9(2) of the Vienna Convention.[427] Dr Ficsor also notes that a similar rule was adopted in rules of procedure for the 1996 Conference (rule 34(2)(iii)), and goes on to state: **13.120**

> It would be an absurd—and, therefore, unacceptable interpretation of the Vienna Convention to consider that a provision of the treaty may be adopted by such a majority but an agreed statement to it would require consensus. Also in the case of an agreed statement, it is obviously sufficient that it is adopted 'between all the parties' (that is, first at the session of the competent Committee, and then at the Plenary), rather than at a separate forum in which not all the parties are present. It is not required that the parties adopt it by consensus; it should simply be adopted according to the majority prescribed by the Rules of Procedure of the diplomatic conference (fixed in harmony with the Vienna Convention).[428]

While there is some force in Dr Ficsor's opinion, the following arguments against it need to be considered. A starting point is his reference to the two-thirds majority rule in rule 34(2)(iii) of the rules of procedure for the 1996 Diplomatic Conference. This states that, in the absence of consensus, the following decisions require a majority of two-thirds of the Member Delegations present and voting: '. . . adoption by the Conference, meeting in Plenary, of the Treaty or Treaties; . . .'. The agreed statement to article 1(4), however, was not the 'Treaty' within the meaning of article 31(2)(a) of the Vienna Convention; rather, it was an 'agreement relating to . . . [that] treaty', and the requirement that this should be an agreement 'between all the parties' seems unambiguous. In this regard, there is nothing inherently absurd and unacceptable in requiring consensus on the interpretation of a provision of a treaty, even if it is possible for the latter to be adopted by a two-thirds majority pursuant to article 9(2) of the Vienna Convention. It should also be noted that the latter provision is quite specific in that it refers to the voting on the 'adoption of a text of a treaty at an international conference'. An agreement on the interpretation of a provision of such a treaty cannot be regarded as the 'text of a treaty'; rather, as article 31(2)(a)

[426] It might be difficult to regard it as part of the 'preparatory work of the treaty', although it clearly arose from the work of the Diplomatic Conference in finalizing and adopting the WCT text.

[427] See generally Ficsor (2001), 446–7.

[428] ibid, 447.

indicates, it is part of the 'context' of that treaty for the purposes of interpreting that treaty.

13.121 The question of whether article 31(2)(a) requires unanimity is not touched on directly by Sinclair, one of the leading commentators on the Vienna Convention, but it is noteworthy that, in his general discussion of article 31(2), the instances of such agreements that he cites were made unanimously.[429] Unanimity is also a requirement of a number of other provisions of the Vienna Convention, for example, article 20(2) with respect to reservations not otherwise authorized by the treaty, article 44 with respect to withdrawal by a party from part of a treaty, article 54(b) with respect to termination or withdrawal by a party from a treaty otherwise than in accordance with its provisions, and article 59(1) as a precondition to the suspension of an earlier treaty where all the parties to it conclude a later treaty. Accordingly, it is submitted that the better view is that the reference to 'all the parties' in article 31(2)(a) means just that: there must be consensus on the interpretation contained in the agreed statement for it to be regarded as part of the 'context' of the treaty for the purposes of its interpretation.

13.122 Accepting, therefore, that there may be different views on the correct characterization of the majority agreed statement to article 1(4) of the WCT, what practical differences flow from this? First, on the Ficsor view, if it falls within the scope of article 31(2)(a) of the Vienna Convention, it will form part of the 'context' of the WCT and will therefore be a matter to be taken into account by member countries and applied in their interpretation of the WCT and, in particular, their application of article 9 of the Berne Convention in their domestic laws. If a member country therefore failed to recognize digital uses, including temporary storage and transient copying, as part of the reproduction right, this would then be a breach of their international obligations under article 1(4) of the WCT.

On the other hand, if it is not an agreement within article 31(2)(a) of the Vienna Convention, its only relevance will be under article 32, and the following consequences will apply. Where country A (a party to the WCT though not necessarily to Berne and therefore bound by article 1(4) to comply with article 9 of Berne) has doubts as to whether the right of reproduction required to be protected under article 9(1) includes digital uses, it would be permissible for that country to refer to the agreed statement as a supplementary aid to inter-

[429] Sinclair, *The Vienna Convention on the Law of Treaties*, 2nd edn (1984), 129. Sinclair cites the Declaration on the prohibition of military, political or economic coercion in the conclusion of treaties adopted by the Diplomatic Conference on the Vienna Convention itself, and suggests that the unanimously adopted Experts' Reports in conventions reached by the Council of Europe would be another.

pretation. This would be on the basis that there is 'ambiguity', or possibly 'obscurity' in relation to the correct interpretation of article 9, which then brings article 32 of the Vienna Convention into play. In such a case, it would then be open to Country A to have regard to the majority interpretation embodied in the agreed statement to article 1(4) and to change its national law accordingly. On the other hand, there would be no obligation on Country A to adopt the majority interpretation (unless, of course, that interpretation had become crystallized in subsequent state practice under article 31(3)(b)). In other words, so far as article 1(4) of the WCT is concerned, it will be up to contracting parties whether or not to give effect to the interpretation contained in the agreed statement.

(iii) As part of the Berne Convention itself: The agreed statement to article 1(4) of the WCT may also be binding on those states that are Berne members as a 'subsequent agreement' between 'the parties' regarding the interpretation of that treaty (Berne) or the application of its provisions (in this case, article 9) pursuant to the rule of interpretation embodied in article 31(3)(a) of the Vienna Convention. Unlike article 31(2)(a), article 31(3)(a) does not refer to the subsequent agreement having to be between 'all parties' to the Berne Convention, and it might therefore be possible to argue that the agreed statement embodies a subsequent agreement on the interpretation of article 9 by all those Berne members that 'agreed' with the statement at the 1996 Diplomatic Conference, plus any new accessions to the WCT who are Berne members and who therefore accept the statement as part of their accession to that treaty. The effect of this would be to create a kind of sub-Union among Berne members on the particular question of interpretation of article 9, obliging these members to apply the interpretation to each other, notwithstanding whatever their obligations on this matter under the WCT might be. This would have no effect on the obligations of non-WCT Berne members towards each other. **13.123**

(iv) As part of the TRIPs Agreement: A final way in which the agreed statement to article 1(4) could operate is in relation to the TRIPs Agreement as a subsequent agreement between the parties for the purposes of article 31(3)(a) of the Vienna Convention. Under article 9(1) of TRIPs (as under the WCT) parties are required to comply with articles 1 to 21 of Berne, and it can therefore be argued that the agreed statement to article 1(4) of WCT operates as a subsequent agreement between those TRIPs parties that are also signatories to the WCT with respect to the way in which article 9 of Berne is to be interpreted as part of TRIPs. However, the agreed statement to article 1(4) refers only to Berne and not to TRIPs, and the better view must be that the agreed statement has no relevance to the TRIPs obligations with respect to article 9. **13.124**

(b) Article 10

13.125 Unlike article 1(4), the three-step test appears directly in the text of article 10, and has a much wider potential application than just to the reproduction right (an obvious model in this regard being article 13 of TRIPs, as to which see paras 13.94ff above). Article 10 provides:

> (1) Contracting Parties may, in their national legislation, provide for limitations of or exceptions to the rights granted to authors of literary and artistic works under this Treaty in certain special cases that do not conflict with a normal exploitation of the work and do not unreasonably prejudice the legitimate interests of the author.
>
> (2) Contracting Parties shall, when applying the Berne Convention, confine any limitations of or exceptions to rights provided therein to certain special cases that do not conflict with a normal exploitation of the work and do not unreasonably prejudice the legitimate interests of the author.

Both paragraphs have a different sphere of operation. The less problematical is article 10(1) which applies only to the rights to be accorded under the WCT, namely the new rights of distribution (article 6), rental (article 7, WCT) and communication to the public (article 8). By using exactly the same language as in article 9(2) of Berne in relation to reproduction rights it seems logical that we can refer to the interpretations that have been developed in relation to that article, although it will also be necessary here to have regard to the terms of an agreed statement that was adopted at the same time by the 1996 Conference (see para 13.128 below).

13.126 Article 10(2), on the other hand, is more problematic in that, like article 13 of TRIPs, it purports to apply to all the rights protected under Berne and does so in far more explicit terms: 'Contracting Parties shall, when applying the Berne Convention, . . .'. What does this mean, so far as existing Berne limitations and exceptions are concerned? On its face, it appears to place another requirement on WCT members in applying their Berne obligations, to make any limitations and exceptions subject to the three-step test, above and beyond the conditions contained in those provisions. This, indeed, was stated in the Basic Proposal for the 1996 Diplomatic Conference, which suggested that article 10(2) (and, by inference, article 13 of TRIPs) may imply greater restrictions on the scope of permissible exceptions than would otherwise apply to these rights. It went on to postulate that this might arise in the case of the indeterminate implied category of 'minor reservations'. Thus, if a minor reservation applied under national law exceeded the limits set by the three-step test, the Basic Proposal indicated that this would no longer be allowable under article 10(2) of the WCT.[430]

---

[430] Given the *de minimis* interpretation of minor reservations suggested above, this must be very unlikely.

> It bears mention that this Article is not intended to prevent Contracting Parties from applying limitations and exceptions traditionally considered acceptable under the Berne Convention. It is, however, clear that not all limitations currently included in national legislations would correspond to the conditions now being proposed. In the digital environment, formally 'minor reservations' may in reality undermine important aspects of protection. Even minor reservations must be considered using sense and reason. The purpose of the protection must be kept in mind.[431]

In the discussions in Main Committee I of the 1996 Diplomatic Conference, it became clear that some delegates viewed the proposed article 10(2) (then article 12(2)) as having a wider effect, namely that it might make a 'straitjacket' for existing exceptions in areas essential for society,[432] and that these limitations should not be curtailed by the change from a physical to a digital format.[433] Quite apart from the 'minor reservations' question, one delegate (from Singapore) pointed to the possibility that article 10(2) might narrow what was already permitted by the following articles of the Berne Convention, namely articles 2(4), 2(8), 2*bis*(1), 10(1), 10*bis*(1), 10*bis*(2) and 11*bis*(2), with the consequence that article 10(2) would be in breach of article 20 of the Berne Convention.[434] Other delegations, however, thought that article 10(2) should not affect existing limitations and exceptions either way, although it should be possible to carry these over into the digital environment.

The final text of the WCT addresses these concerns through express provisions of the treaty itself and through the device of an agreed statement of the kind already discussed above. Thus, under article 1(1), the WCT is declared to be a 'special agreement' within the meaning of article 20 of Berne, which indicates that the WCT is to be interpreted according to the criteria expressed in that provision, ie as only granting authors more extensive rights than those granted in the Convention or as not containing provisions contrary to the Berne Convention. Article 1(2) then follows article 2 of TRIPs in providing that 'nothing in this Treaty shall derogate from existing obligations that Contracting States have to each other under the Berne Convention . . .'. As membership of Berne is not a prerequisite for membership of the WCT, article 1(4) completes the circle by requiring that all Contracting Parties will comply with articles 1 to 21 and the Appendix of Berne (see further above). **13.127**

In addition to the above, there is the following agreed statement to article 10 that was adopted by the 1996 Diplomatic Conference: **13.128**

431 *Records* 1996, 214. 432 ibid, 704 (delegate of Denmark).

433 ibid, 705 (delegate of India)

434 ibid. This seems a misplaced comment, as how would it violate art 20 to cut back on exceptions so that authors gain greater protection?

> It is understood that the provisions of Article 10 permit Contracting Parties to carry forward and appropriately extend into the digital environment limitations and exceptions in their national laws which have been considered acceptable under the Berne Convention. Similarly, these provisions should be understood to permit Contracting Parties to devise new limitations and exceptions that are 'appropriate in the digital environment'.
>
> It is also understood that Article 10(2) neither reduces nor extends the scope of applicability of the limitations and exceptions permitted by the Berne Convention.

Unlike the agreed statement to article 1(4), this statement was adopted by consensus at the 1996 Diplomatic Conference, and can therefore be regarded as part of the context of the WCT for the purposes of article 31(2)(a) of the Vienna Convention. Having said this, it is uncertain that the agreed statement takes us much further along the road to an understanding of the effect of article 10. The following five comments can be made here. First, it does not have any direct application to article 10(1), which is concerned only with the new rights established under the 1996 Treaty. However, it needs to be remembered that the new communication right under the WCT inevitably includes the rights covered under existing article 11*bis*(1) of Berne, which are subject to the imposition of conditions allowable under article 11*bis*(2), as well as the rights of communication to the public that are contained in articles 11(1)(ii) and 11*ter*(1)(ii). A possible conflict may therefore arise between what is permissible by way of exception to article 8 of the WCT (applying the three-step test) and what is permissible under article 11*bis*(2). In this regard, it may be noted that the WTO panel, in the context of article 13 of TRIPs, held that article 13 had no application to article 11*bis*(2). This seems appropriate in the present context as well: WCT signatories are required to apply articles 1 to 21 of Berne and there should be no possibility of article 10(1) of the WCT permitting free uses to the rights specified in article 11*bis*(1) of Berne in cases where equitable remuneration would be required under article 11*bis*(2).

Second, this would leave open the application of free use exceptions to article 8 WCT rights that go beyond those specified in article 11*bis*(2) of Berne. An example would be webcasting, which would not usually be broadcasting (by wireless means) within the meaning of article 11*bis*(1)(i). In the case of webcasting, however, there is still the possibility that, so far as communications of sounds (performances of musical and dramatic works and recitations of literary works) are concerned, these will fall within the scope of either articles 11(1)(ii) and 11*ter*(1)(ii) of Berne[435] and will therefore not be amenable to compulsory licensing. They will, however, be subject to the minor reservations doctrine. If

[435] See further Ficsor (2001), 495.

the latter is treated, as the WTO panel suggested (see para 13.112 above), as coterminous with the three-step test, no problem will arise. On the other hand, if the minor reservations doctrine has a narrower compass than the three-step test, this will provide another limitation on the application of the latter to rights under article 8 of the WCT (this possibility is taken up at para 13.114 above).

Third, with respect to existing Berne exceptions (these would include exceptions to the reproduction right under article 9(2)), article 10(2) of the WCT neither reduces nor extends the scope of their applicability (second paragraph of the agreed statement). It is clear from the discussions in Main Committee I of the 1996 Diplomatic Conference that the intention here was not to alter the status quo under Berne, but it is equally clear that it was accepted that some, at least, of the existing limitations and exceptions under national law might not meet the three-step criteria although they fell within the scope of either other express provisions of Berne or the minor exceptions doctrine. While the views expressed in the Basic Proposal indicate that it was intended to modify these existing exceptions, where necessary, so as to conform with the three-step test, this was not accepted by the delegates, and the wording of the second paragraph of the agreed statement confirms this. Accordingly, WCT members are not required to modify limitations and exceptions that are consistent with the present Berne text, even if these would not pass the three-step test in article 10(2). There will, of course, be room for argument as to whether any of the existing Berne exceptions and limitations, including the minor reservations doctrine, do, in fact, go beyond the limits of the three-step test, but, to the extent that this is so, it seems clear that the three-step test cannot 'trump' these existing limitations and exceptions.

Fourth, the agreed statement also contemplates the extension of existing limitations and exceptions which have been considered 'acceptable' under the Berne Convention into the digital environment, provided that this is done 'appropriately'. But there is an element of question begging here: what is 'acceptable' and what is 'appropriate'? What is 'acceptable' presumably refers to existing limitations and exceptions that meet the present Berne criteria, but what is 'appropriate' so far as digital extensions are concerned is less clear: what if these digital extensions still meet the relevant Berne criteria but would not satisfy the three-step test? Article 10(2) indicates that the three-step test should be applied in these cases, but the second paragraph of the agreed statement may pose a difficulty, as this will clearly lead to a reduction in the scope of a permitted Berne exception which the second paragraph says is not to happen. By contrast, with article 13 of the TRIPs Agreement it is suggested above that it might be possible to impose the three-step test as an additional requirement where the relevant Berne provision is silent on the question, as this would not be a breach of article

2(2) of TRIPs. The second paragraph of the agreed statement, however, appears to preclude this possibility with respect to the WCT.

The final matter contemplated by the agreed statement is the making of *new* limitations and exceptions that are 'appropriate in the digital environment'. By definition, such uses will not be covered by either existing exceptions or limitations or by extensions of the latter into the digital environment, but must be 'new', in the sense of being different, limitations and exceptions that only become relevant because of the advent of the digital environment. But it seems to be stretching article 10(2) too far to suggest that it authorizes the creation of new limitations and exceptions that lie outside the Berne regime. The only possibility is that these might arise under the minor exceptions doctrine, in which case it is unlikely that the three-step test will need to be prayed in aid, on the basis that these should only be *de minimis* exceptions that will be narrower than the requirements of the three-step test. It is therefore difficult to ascribe any operation to this part of the agreed statement. If a distinct regime for new limitations and exceptions is envisaged under the WCT, this would need to be the subject of an express provision of that Treaty.

(c) Illustrative table setting out relationship of article 10 of the WCT to the Berne Convention (see Table 13.3 below)

(3) Technological protection measures and exceptions

13.129 A final matter for consideration is the relationship between the obligations with respect to technological measures that are contained in articles 11 of the WCT and the WPPT (see further Chapter 15 below) and the provisions in the various conventions discussed above concerning limitations and exceptions. To what extent, if any, can measures adopted in furtherance of articles 11 and 18 preclude users from relying upon limitations and exceptions that are otherwise allowable under any of the above provisions?

Article 11 provides as follows (article 18 is to similar effect):

> Contracting Parties shall provide adequate legal protection and effective legal remedies against the circumvention of effective technological measures that are used by authors in connection with the exercise of their rights under this Treaty or the Berne Convention and that restrict acts, in respect of their works, which are not authorized by the authors concerned or permitted by law.

As discussed in more detail in Chapter 15 below, this is an entirely new kind of provision to be included in an international copyright agreement, requiring member states to take certain steps to prevent third parties circumventing technological measures that have been taken by authors to protect the exercise of their substantive rights. These measures could be of various kinds, from devices

Table 13.3

Rights covered	Relevant WCT provision	Test to be applied	Works covered	Application in digital environment	New exceptions outside Berne
New rights under WCT	Article 10(1)	three-step test applies	All Berne works plus computer programs and compilations of data	Yes (as well as in physical environment)	Allowable
Rights under Berne (including moral rights)	Article 10(2)	three-step test applies only where compatible; otherwise does not*	All Berne works plus computer programs and compilations of data	Yes (as well as in physical environment)	Not allowed

* This is the effect of the agreed statement to article 10 where it states that Berne exceptions are not be expanded or reduced in scope.

that prevent access to a work except on certain conditions, or copy-protection or other devices that restrict or prevent various infringing uses. Article 11 is drafted in broad terms and leaves a great deal to the discretion of member states.[436]

13.130 The interrelationship between article 11 (and 18) and limitations and exceptions to protection is a difficult and controversial one from the point of view of copyright policy.[437] On the one hand, users of protected works argue that anti-circumvention measures should not be able to preclude users from doing what they are otherwise free to do under existing limitations and exceptions, for example, in relation to such matters as research, criticism, and review. On the other hand, authors and right holders fear that limitations and exceptions in relation to their anti-circumvention measures may undermine the value of those measures, and that, in any event, the legitimate public interests involved may be adequately provided for in appropriate voluntary licensing arrangements.[438]

13.131 These matters are examined in more detail in Chapter 15 below, in particular the genesis of the present text through the discussions before and during the 1996 Diplomatic Conference. For present purposes, however, the following four comments may be made. First, the central requirement under articles 11 and 18 is that contracting states must provide 'adequate legal protection'[439] against the circumvention of 'effective technological measures'[440] that are used by authors in connection with the exercise of their rights under the WCT or the Berne Convention (or by performers or phonogram producers under the WPPT, as the case may be). It seems clear that the rights referred to here are the exclusive rights provided under the WCT (distribution, rental, and communication to the public) and those rights that are specified in articles 1 to 21 of Berne (both economic and moral rights). In the case of article 18 of the WPPT, these will be the exclusive rights that are granted to performers and phonogram producers under that instrument (see further Chapter 19 below for a discussion of these requirements). There is, however, no obligation for contracting states to require that authors and right holders adopt such measures: the obligations under articles 11 and 18 only come into operation when and where authors and right holders have elected to do so.

---

[436] For detailed discussions of the article, its background and comparative studies of national provisions with respect to such matters, see Ficsor (2001), 544 ff and Reinbothe and von Lewinski (2002), 135.

[437] See further T Foged, 'U.S. v E.U. Anti-Circumvention Legislation: Preserving the Public's Privileges in the Digital Age?' [2003] *EIPR* 525; T Heide, 'Copyright in the E.U. and United States: What "Access Right?" ' [2001] *EIPR* 469; F W Grosheide, 'Copyright Law from a User's Perspective: Access Rights for Users' [2001] *EIPR* 321.

[438] Reinbothe and von Lewinski (2002), 146.

[439] On the meaning of this expression, see further ibid, 143.

[440] See further ibid, 145.

Second, these 'effective technological measures' must restrict 'acts, in respect of their works [performances or phonograms], which are not authorised by the authors concerned [or performers or phonogram producers] or permitted by law'. The 'acts' restricted here will be those of circumvention, which appear to fall into two broad categories: those restricting access to a work, performance, or phonogram, and those which restrict the carrying of certain acts, for example, the making of reproductions, in relation to the work, performance, or phonogram.[441]

Third, the obligations under articles 11 and 18 to provide protection against these acts do not apply where they are authorized by the author (performer or phonogram producer) or are 'permitted by law'. The first of these qualifications should pose no difficulty, although it may be difficult to envisage situations where national laws would still provide protection in cases where the act of circumvention had been authorized by the author, performer, or phonogram producer. The second qualification is also clear, although limited in its effect. The words 'permitted by law' must refer to national laws and therefore indicate that particular circumvention activities may be allowed by the law of the contracting state in question. However, this does not mandate that any particular exceptions or limitations to anti-circumvention protection must be provided for under that law, for instance, that exceptions must be made where access or copying is needed for national security and intelligence-gathering purposes, or for library or educational purposes or, indeed, for any of the situations that are contemplated under the exceptions and limitations allowable under any of the instruments discussed in this chapter. Whether exceptions or limitations are provided under national laws to the protective measures required by articles 11 and 18 is therefore a matter entirely within the contracting state's discretion.[442] Neither the preparatory documents for the 1996 Conference[443] nor the discussions during the Conference itself throw any further light on this matter, although it is clear that some delegates were concerned about the potential of measures applied pursuant to articles 11 and 18 to

[441] See further Ficsor (2001), 548. Ficsor suggests that these articles apply as much in the physical, offline environment as in the digital environment, although obviously their principal application will be in the latter.

[442] This has been dealt with in different ways by various national laws, eg see the elaborate provisions in US law, introduced by the Digital Millennium Copyright Act 1998, now in Copyright Act 1976, s 1201(d) (non-profit libraries, archives, and educational institutions), (e) (law enforcement, intelligence, and other governmental activities), (f) (reverse engineering), (g) (encryption research); EU Information Society Directive, art 6(4); and the Australian Copyright Act 1968, s 116A(2)–(7). See further the discussion in Ficsor (2001), 557 ff.

[443] Thus, the wording in the Basic Proposal (proposed art 13(1)) referred to devices or services 'used for, or in the course of, the exercise of rights provided under this Treaty that is not authorised by the rightholder or the law': *Records* 1996, vol I, 217.

abridge exceptions that might otherwise be available to users of copyright materials.[444]

Finally, with the exception of quotation rights under article 10(1) of the Berne Convention, it is also not possible to spell out any general positive obligations concerning limitations and exceptions from the various provisions of the conventions that we have considered in this chapter. As we have seen above, these limitations and exceptions are of a permissive character, and there is no requirement for contracting states to apply them: it is only where they do so that they must comply with the various conditions and limitations contained in the relevant provision or provisions. Accordingly, there can be no obligation on such states to apply these limitations or exceptions to any anti-circumvention measures they adopt pursuant to articles 11 and 18. They may decide to adopt only some, or even none, of these limitations and exceptions; they are also free, as has happened in many national laws, to devise other kinds of limitations and exceptions that are not contained in these conventions. An interesting formulation is that in article 6(4) of the EC Directive, which requires member states, in the absence of voluntary measures taken by right holders, including agreements between right holders and other parties concerned,

> . . . to take appropriate measures to ensure that rightholders make available to the beneficiary of an exception or limitation provided for in national law in accordance with Article 5(2)(a) [photocopying], 2(c) [libraries, educational establishments, museums, archives], 2(d) [ephemeral recordings made by broadcasting organizations], 3(a) [illustration for purposes of teaching and scientific research], 3(b) [persons with a disability] or 3(e) [public security and reporting of administrative, parliamentary, or judicial proceedings] the means of benefiting from that exception or limitation, to the extent necessary to benefit from that exception and where that beneficiary has legal access to the protected work or subject-matter concerned.

A proviso to this article also allows for member states to take similar measures with respect to exceptions or limitations under article 5(2)(b) (private copying), subject to certain conditions.

(a) The case of quotation rights

13.132 Nonetheless, article 10(1) of the Berne Convention, which deals with the making of quotations from works that have been 'lawfully made available', is of a

[444] See eg the comments of the Korean delegates in Main Committee I in ibid, vol II, 710, para 518. A Korean amendment, not adopted by the Conference, sought to deal with this more specifically as follows: 'It shall, however, be a matter for legislation in the Contracting Parties to lay down conditions on technological measures designed to protect productions which are not original nor protected by law and productions in which the exclusive rights are limited by law, only to the extent permitted by the Berne Convention and this Treaty:' Document CRNR/DC/24 at *Records* 1996, vol I, 408.

mandatory character, and may pose problems so far as article 11 of the WCT is concerned. Under article 1(4) of the WCT, contracting states are obliged to adopt such an exception, whether or not they are Berne members. Accordingly, anti-circumvention measures may cut across this exception, where the effect of such measures is either to deny users access to the works protected for the purpose of making quotations or is to prevent them making the necessary reproduction or dissemination of the quotation. Is it therefore necessary for national laws to allow such an exception to any anti-circumvention measures that they adopt? In this regard, it is worth noting that none of the national and regional laws referred to above do so.

The answer to this question must turn upon the meaning and scope of the words 'a work which has already been lawfully made available' that are used in article 10(1). These were clearly formulated in the pre-digital era when works were only made available in hard-copy formats to users who could then access and use them without the copyright owner being able to impose any physical or technical limitations upon what the user could do. If anything, at this stage, the balance ran in favour of the user, although the formulation of provisions such as article 10(1) sought to place legal limitations upon what the user could do. In the digital environment, however, the balance is potentially shifted sharply the other way, in favour of the copyright owner, if the latter can first apply effective technological measures to deny access completely, except on conditions that the owner specifies. The words 'lawfully made available' in article 10(1) pose a problem here: a work made available in a digital protected format is just as much lawfully made available as a work in a traditional hard-copy format, even if the owner then imposes a veto on what users and other third parties may do with that version.

These considerations lead to the conclusion that the obligation in article 11 of the WCT to provide for anti-circumvention protection is subject to the qualification that the latter should not abridge the exercise of rights of quotation under article 10(1) of Berne. Clearly, if a work has already been made available in hard-copy analogue form, it will be possible for such rights to be exercised, even it cannot be done in relation to a digital version protected by an effective technological protection measure (it can be said that a copyright owner is not required to unlock the back storeroom if there are already copies out on the shelves in the shop). On the other hand, if a work is only available in a digital protected format, with no provision for the making of quotations other than on the terms specified by the right holder, would the effect of this be to deny the exception under article 10(1) altogether? If this were so, it would obviously have far-reaching consequences into the future as more and more works become available in digital protected formats only. Further reflection, however, suggests that such terms of access would usually only cause third-party users inconvenience, rather than deny them the benefit of the exception under article 10(1) altogether, in that, even if it is not possible to make ready digital cuts from the work, it is still usually possible to make transcriptions manually from digital versions or to film or make photographic images. While allowances for digital quotation might well be desirable (and desired by users), there would be no breach of article 10(1) so long as the making of quotations through these more 'traditional means' remained possible.

In light of the above, there are several ways for national legislators to proceed in relation to quotation rights: (i) to bring these rights within the scope of a general provision such as article 6(4) of the EC Directive (such an approach would highlight the continuing relevance of such rights in the case of digital protected formats); or (ii) to provide that the exception *does not or need not* apply to digital protected versions so long as analogue versions are available[445] but that there should be no restrictions placed on the making of quotations, even if only permitted in the form of manual transcriptions, films or photographs, in cases where a work is only available in digital protected formats. In the case of the second alternative, making things more difficult or cumbersome for users does not ultimately impair the utility of the quotation right.

[445] A formulation that is used in the Australian legislation, albeit in different contexts, is that 'a copy (not being a second-hand copy) of the work cannot be obtained within a reasonable time at an ordinary commercial price)': see eg Copyright Act 1968, s 49(5)(b) (in relation to the making of reproductions by libraries and archives).